FROMMER'S

CARIBBEAN

DARWIN PORTER

Assisted by
Danforth Prince
and Margaret Foresman

☐

1990 EDITION

Published by Prentice Hall Trade Division
A Division of Simon & Schuster Inc.
Gulf + Western Building
One Gulf + Western Plaza
New York, NY 10023

ISBN 0-13-332454-0

ISSN 1042-833X

Text design by Levavi & Levavi, Inc.

Manufactured in the United States of America

CONTENTS

MAPS

WHAT THE SYMBOLS MEAN: Travelers to the Caribbean may at first be confused by classifications on rate sheets. I've used these same classifications in this guide. One of the most common rates is **MAP,** meaning Modified American Plan. Simply put, that usually means room, breakfast, and dinner, unless the room rate has been quoted separately, and then it means only breakfast and dinner. **CP** means Continental Plan—that is, room and a light breakfast. **EP** is European Plan, which means room only, and **AP** is American Plan, which is the most expensive rate of all because it includes not only your room but three meals a day.

A DISCLAIMER: Although every effort was made to ensure the accuracy of the prices and travel information appearing in this book, it should be kept in mind that prices do fluctuate in the course of time, and that information does change under the impact of the varied and volatile factors that affect the travel industry. As the guide goes to press, I believe I have obtained the most reliable data possible. Nonetheless, in the lifetime of this edition, the wise traveler will anticipate some price increases.

FROMMER'S CARIBBEAN

□ □ □

One of the world's greatest travel oases, the Caribbean spins its own sunny web of enchantment.

The dream is real enough, and all but the unimaginative can picture themselves part of the lazy life of these striking islands, often called the "Eighth Continent of the World."

In just a few hours by plane from the North America, you're submerged in lands that have absorbed the cultures of other continents, including both Americas, Europe, and Africa.

On a white sandy beach, shaded by a row of palm trees, you've just returned from a swim in gin-clear waters and are lying in the tanning sun, listening to the murmur of the surf, cooled by trade-wind–fed breezes. Your tall rum punch drink arrives—a sundowner before you dine on a West Indian buffet and dance to a steel-drum band as you look out upon a shimmering sea under moonlight.

Although this fantasy comes true often enough for dreamers and lovers, I do not suggest that the complex, often perplexing Caribbean region is just a romantic mirage, without its problems. Few single travel destinations pose such confusion and require such advance, detailed information—data you need to know not just when you get off the plane, but in advance, when you ask the important question, "Which island should I choose?"

Leading you through this maze of emerging nations and colonial outposts is the purpose of this guide.

THE GOALS OF THIS GUIDE: In brief, this is a guidebook giving specific, practical details (including prices) about the hotels, restaurants, sightseeing attractions, and nightlife of the Caribbean. Establishments in *all* price ranges have been documented and described, from the classily elegant Round Hill on a 98-acre peninsula in Montego Bay, Jamaica (where everybody from Coward to Porter to Rodgers used to play the resident piano), to a "Mom and Pop"–run, casual inn in Tortola in the British Virgin Islands.

In all cases, establishments have been judged by the strict yardstick of value. If they "measured up," they were included in this book—regardless of the price classification. The uniqueness of the book, I think, lies in the fact it could be used by everybody from Jacqueline Kennedy Onassis to a free-wheeling, adventure-seeking collegian who seeks a different type of vacation—not wanting just the sand and sea, but wanting to learn something about other people and their lands, the intoxicating power of the Haitian Créole or the mystery of the Rastafarians who consider themselves Africans, not Jamaicans, and worship the late Emperor Haile Selassie I of Ethiopia as the Messiah.

But the major focus of the book is not centered either on the impecunious whose sole resources jingle in their pockets, or the affluent whose gold rests in

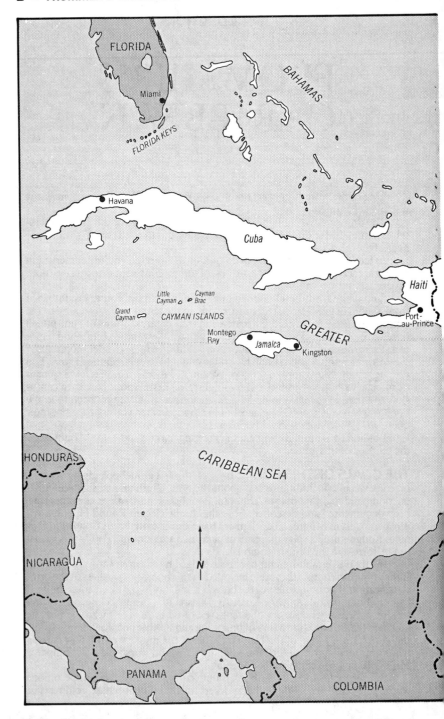

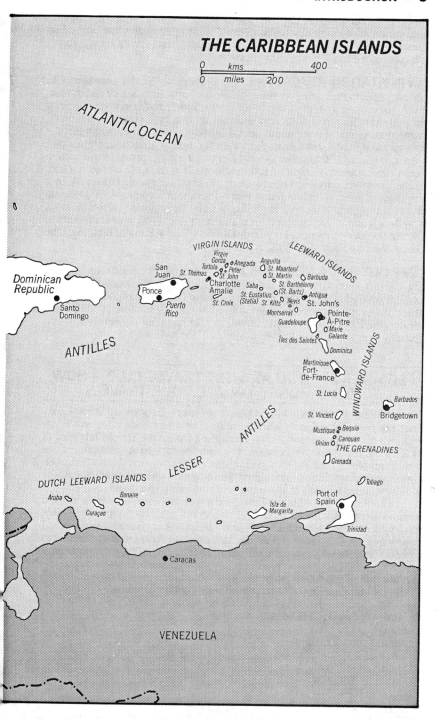

THE CARIBBEAN ISLANDS

```
0        kms          400
0       miles      200
```

ATLANTIC OCEAN

VIRGIN ISLANDS

LEEWARD ISLANDS

Virgin
Gorda
Tortola
St. Thomas
St. John
St. Croix

Anegada
Peter

Anguilla
St. Maarten/
St. Martin
Saba
St. Eustatius
(Statia)
St. Kitts
Montserrat
St. Barthélemy
(St. Barts)
Nevis

Barbuda
Antigua
St. John's

San
Juan
Charlotte
Amalie
Ponce

Puerto
Rico

Dominican
Republic
Santo
Domingo

ANTILLES

Guadeloupe
Marie
Galante
Îles des Saintes
Dominica

Pointe-
À-Pitre

Martinique
Fort-
de-France

St. Lucia

St. Vincent

Mustique
Union
Bequia
Canouan
THE GRENADINES
Grenada

WINDWARD ISLANDS

Barbados
Bridgetown

LESSER

ANTILLES

Tobago

DUTCH LEEWARD ISLANDS

Aruba
Curaçao
Bonaire

Isla de
Margarita

Port of
Spain

Trinidad

Caracas

VENEZUELA

numbered accounts in the Cayman Islands. Rather, my chief concern is the average, middle-income-bracket voyager who'd like to patronize some of the less-documented hotels of the Caribbean, those places travel agents are sometimes reluctant to tell you about because the commission is not high.

AN INVITATION TO READERS: Like all Frommer Guides, *Frommer's Caribbean* hopes to maintain a continuing dialogue between its author and its readers. All of us share a common aim—to travel as widely and as well as possible, at the best value for our money. And in achieving that goal, your comments and suggestions can be of tremendous help. Therefore, if you come across a particularly appealing hotel, restaurant, shop, even sightseeing attraction, please don't keep it to yourself. Remember too, the fact that a listing appears in this edition doesn't give it squatter's rights in future editions. If its services have deteriorated, its chef grown stale, its prices risen unfairly, these failings should be known. Or if you enjoyed every place and found every description accurate—that, too, can cheer many a gray day. Every letter will be read by me personally, although I find it well-nigh impossible to answer each and every one. Send your comments to Darwin Porter, c/o Prentice Hall Trade Division, Gulf + Western Building, One Gulf + Western Plaza, New York, NY 10023.

TIME OUT FOR A COMMERCIAL: Many visitors erroneously consider The Bahamas part of the Caribbean, and may wonder why this world tourist mecca is not covered here. I do not mean to overlook The Bahamas. In fact, the publisher of this guide considers them important enough to create a companion volume, the 1990–1991 edition of *Frommer's Bermuda and The Bahamas,* which you may want to peruse in your search for an island hideaway.

FROMMER'S™ DOLLARWISE® TRAVEL CLUB—HOW TO SAVE MONEY ON ALL YOUR TRAVELS

In this book we'll be looking at how to get your money's worth in the Caribbean, but there is a "device" for saving money and determining value on *all* your trips. It's the popular, international Frommer's Dollarwise Travel Club, now in its 29th successful year of operation. The club was formed at the urging of numerous readers of the $-A-Day and Frommer Guides, who felt that such an organization could provide continuing travel information and a sense of community to value-minded travelers in all parts of the world. And so it does!

In keeping with the budget concept, the annual membership fee is low and is immediately exceeded by the value of your benefits. Upon receipt of $18 (U.S. residents), or $20 U.S. by check drawn on a U.S. bank or via international postal money order in U.S. funds (Canadian, Mexican, and other foreign residents) to cover one year's membership, we will send all new members the following items.

(1) Any *two* of the following books
Please designate in your letter which two you wish to receive:

Frommer ™ $-A-Day® Guides
Europe on $40 a Day
Australia on $30 a Day
Eastern Europe on $25 a Day
England on $50 a Day
Greece on $30 a Day

Hawaii on $60 a Day
India on $25 a Day
Ireland on $35 a Day
Israel on $30 & $35 a Day
Mexico (plus Belize and Guatemala) on $25 a Day
New York on $50 a Day
New Zealand on $40 a Day
Scandinavia on $60 a Day
Scotland and Wales on $40 a Day
South America on $35 a Day
Spain and Morocco (plus the Canary Is.) on $40 a Day
Turkey on $25 a Day
Washington, D.C., & Historic Virginia on $40 a Day
($-A-Day Guides document hundreds of budget accommodations and facilities,
helping you get the most for your travel dollars.)

Frommer Guides
Australia
Austria and Hungary
Belgium, Holland, & Luxembourg
Bermuda and The Bahamas
Brazil
Canada
Caribbean
Egypt
England and Scotland
France
Germany
Italy
Japan and Hong Kong
Portugal, Madeira, and the Azores
South Pacific
Switzerland and Liechtenstein
Alaska
California and Las Vegas
Florida
Mid-Atlantic States
New England
New York State
Northwest
Skiing USA—East
Skiing USA—West
Southeast and New Orleans
Southeast Asia
Southwest
Texas
USA
(Frommer Guides discuss accommodations and facilities in all price ranges, with
emphasis on the medium-priced.)

Frommer ™ Touring Guides
Australia
Egypt

Florence
London
Paris
Scotland
Thailand
Venice

(These new, color illustrated guides include walking tours, cultural and historic sites, and other vital travel information.)

Gault Millau

Chicago
France
Italy
London
Los Angeles
New England
New York
San Francisco
Washington, D.C.

(Irreverent, savvy, and comprehensive, each of these renowned guides candidly reviews over 1,000 restaurants, hotels, shops, nightspots, museums, and sights.)

Serious Shopper's Guides

Italy
London
Los Angeles
Paris

(Practical and comprehensive, each of these handsomely illustrated guides lists hundreds of stores, selling everything from antiques to wine, conveniently organized alphabetically by category.)

A Shopper's Guide to the Caribbean

(Two experienced Caribbean hands guide you through this shopper's paradise, offering witty insights and helpful tips on the wares and emporia of more than 25 islands.)

Beat the High Cost of Travel

(This practical guide details how to save money on absolutely all travel items—accommodations, transportation, dining, sightseeing, shopping, taxes, and more. Includes special budget information for seniors, students, singles, and families.)

Bed & Breakfast—North America

(This guide contains a directory of over 150 organizations that offer bed & breakfast referrals and reservations throughout North America. The scenic attractions, and major schools and universities near the homes of each are also listed.)

California with Kids

(A must for parents traveling in California, providing key information on selecting the best accommodations, restaurants, and sightseeing attractions for the particular needs of the family, whether the kids are toddlers, school-age, pre-teens, or teens.)

Frommer's Belgium
(Arthur Frommer unlocks the treasures of a country overlooked by most travelers to Europe. Discover the medieval charm, modern sophistication, and natural beauty of this quintessentially European country.)

Frommer's Cruises
(This complete guide covers all the basics of cruising—ports of call, costs, fly-cruise package bargains, cabin selection booking, embarkation and debarkation and describes in detail over 60 or so ships cruising the waters of Alaska, the Caribbean, Mexico, Hawaii, Panama, Canada, and the United States.)

Frommer's Skiing Europe
(Describes top ski resorts in Austria, France, Italy, and Switzerland. Illustrated with maps of each resort area. Includes supplement on Argentinian resorts.)

Guide to Honeymoon Destinations
(A special guide for that most romantic trip of your life, with full details on planning and choosing the destination that will be just right in the U.S. [California, New England, Hawaii, Florida, New York, South Carolina, etc.], Canada, Mexico, and the Caribbean.)

Marilyn Wood's Wonderful Weekends
(This very selective guide covers the best mini-vacation destinations within a 200-mile radius of New York City. It describes special country inns and other accommodations, restaurants, picnic spots, sights, and activities—all the information needed for a two- or three-day stay.)

Manhattan's Outdoor Sculpture
(A total guide, fully illustrated with black and white photos, to more than 300 sculptures and monuments that grace Manhattan's plazas, parks, and other public spaces.)

Motorist's Phrase Book
(A practical phrase book in French, German, and Spanish designed specifically for the English-speaking motorist touring abroad.)

Paris Rendez-Vous
(An amusing and *au courant* guide to the best meeting places in Paris, organized for hour-to-hour use: from power breakfasts and fun brunches, through tea at four or cocktails at five, to romantic dinners and dancing 'til dawn.)

Swap and Go—Home Exchanging Made Easy
(Two veteran home exchangers explain in detail all the money-saving benefits of a home exchange, and then describe precisely how to do it. Also includes information on home rentals and many tips on low-cost travel.)

The Candy Apple: New York for Kids
(A spirited guide to the wonders of the Big Apple by a savvy New York grandmother with a kid's-eye view to fun. Indispensable for visitors and residents alike.)

The New World of Travel
(From America's #1 travel expert, Arthur Frommer, an annual sourcebook with

the hottest news and latest trends that's guaranteed to change the way you travel —and save you hundreds of dollars. Jam-packed with alternative new modes of travel that will lead you to vacations that cater to the mind, the spirit, and a sense of thrift.)

Travel Diary and Record Book
(A 96-page diary for personal travel notes plus a section for such vital data as passport and traveler's check numbers, itinerary, postcard list, special people and places to visit, and a reference section with temperature and conversion charts, and world maps with distance zones.)

Where to Stay USA
(By the Council on International Educational Exchange, this extraordinary guide is the first to list accommodations in all 50 states that cost anywhere from $3 to $30 per night.)

(2) Any *one* of the Frommer ™ City Guides
Amsterdam
Athens
Atlantic City and Cape May
Boston
Cancún, Cozumel, and the Yucatán
Chicago
Dublin and Ireland
Hawaii
Las Vegas
Lisbon, Madrid, and Costa del Sol
London
Los Angeles
Mexico City and Acapulco
Minneapolis and St. Paul
Montréal and Québec City
New Orleans
New York
Orlando, Disney World, and EPCOT
Paris
Philadelphia
Rio
Rome
San Francisco
Santa Fe, Taos, and Albuquerque
Sydney
Washington, D.C.

(Pocket-size guides to hotels, restaurants, nightspots, and sightseeing attractions covering all price ranges.)

(3) A one-year subscription to *The Dollarwise® Traveler*
This quarterly eight-page tabloid newspaper keeps you up to date on fastbreaking developments in low-cost travel in all parts of the world bringing you the latest money-saving information—the kind of information you'd have to pay $35 a year to obtain elsewhere. This consumer-conscious publication also features columns of special interest to readers: **Hospitality Exchange** (members all over the world who are willing to provide hospitality to other members as they pass through their home cities); **Share-a-Trip** (offers and requests from members

for travel companions who can share costs and help avoid the burdensome single supplement); and **Readers Ask . . . Readers Reply** (travel questions from members to which other members reply with authentic firsthand information).

(4) Your personal membership card

Membership entitles you to purchase through the club all Frommer publications for a third to a half off their regular retail prices during the term of your membership.

So why not join this hardy band of international budgeteers and participate in its exchange of travel information and hospitality? Simply send your name and address, together with your annual membership fee of $18 (U.S. residents) or $20 U.S. (Canadian, Mexican, and other foreign residents), by check drawn on a U.S. bank or via international postal money order in U.S. funds to: Frommer's Dollarwise Travel Club, Inc., Gulf + Western Building, One Gulf + Western Plaza, New York, NY 10023. And please remember to specify which *two* of the books in section (1) and which *one* in section (2) you wish to receive in your initial package of members' benefits. Or, if you prefer, use the order form at the end of the book and enclose $18 or $20 in U.S. currency.

Once you are a member, there is no obligation to buy additional books. No books will be mailed to you without your specific order.

CHAPTER I

PLANNING A TRIP

◻ ◻ ◻

1. GETTING THERE
2. A TRAVELER'S ADVISORY
3. TRAVELING YEAR ROUND
4. WHERE TO STAY
5. FAMILY VACATIONS
6. ALTERNATIVE AND SPECIAL-INTEREST TRAVEL

Each island of the Caribbean is unique, often reflecting a colonial past, especially British, French, Spanish, or Dutch. Regardless of individual histories, each island country, even the smallest ones, has forged its own personality and identity. Therefore, even though they are about the same part of the world, each chapter in this guide is different, focusing on special food, characteristics, and attractions.

Because all of the islands of the West Indies share similarities of geography, however, I have packed this opening chapter with information you need to know when planning a holiday in the Caribbean. Many questions will come to mind, including temperature, summer versus winter travel, wardrobe, a hotel versus a guesthouse, or traveling with children. Of course this section doesn't pretend to answer all the general questions you may have, so I'll follow with another chapter devoted to more background, including climate, geography, history, food, and drink.

From Miami to Trinidad at the southern tip of the Caribbean is a distance of some 1,800 miles. A lot of islands are strung out between Florida and the coast of South America. Someone once estimated that if you don't count the rocks sticking up in the Caribbean, there are some 7,000 islands. That's a lot of islands. Fortunately for the page count of this guide, most of them are not inhabited, and many of those that are inhabited don't have hotels. At least that simplifies our task a bit.

Nevertheless, the Caribbean is an overwhelming piece of geography, and making a choice of islands is one of the most formidable decisions you'll have to make. After all, none of the islands is really remote anymore. Even the so-called remote ones can usually be reached after a change of planes, unless you live at an inconvenient transportation point.

One of the most serious suggestions of this guide is to recommend that you island-hop as never before, instead of locating in one spot for a week or more and perhaps getting bored after the fourth day. Transportation schedules have never been more convenient, and you can now experience a vastly different culture after perhaps just a 15-minute flight. For example, if you're visiting the island of St. Martin, you might consider flying to Saba, Statia, Anguilla, St. Kitts, Nevis, or St. Barts. Such island-hopping for not a lot more in transportation cost can lend much richness to a Caribbean vacation and can help avoid sterile stopovers.

I'll begin with the first point of consideration—that of getting there in the first place.

1. GETTING THERE

FLYING SOUTH: From North America, it's easy to wing your way south to the Caribbean. In just a matter of hours you can flee the arctic winds and be lying on the beach, sipping your rum punch.

Travel agents who keep up-to-the-minute schedules can inform you about special stopover privileges, since "island-hopping," as mentioned, is becoming an increasingly popular diversion for both a summer or winter holiday.

All the biggest islands have air links to the North American continent, with regularly scheduled service. The smaller islands are tied into this vast network through their own carriers. For example to reach Montserrat, you fly, say, from Chicago to Antigua, where a smaller craft will take you the rest of the short distance.

For a specific description of how to reach each island in this guide by plane, refer to the individual "Getting There" sections.

TOURING BY PLANE: Chances are, you'll spend less than half a day flying from your point of embarkation in North America to your Caribbean island, and unless connecting links are impossible, that includes time lodged in waiting for inter-island flights. Obviously, the less time spent in getting there means more time on the beach. Direct flights from New York and a few other major cities are possible to all major cities or islands of the Caribbean, including Antigua and Puerto Rico.

You face a choice of booking a seat on a regularly scheduled flight or else a charter plane, the latter being cheaper, of course. On a regular flight you can cancel your ticket without penalty. On a charter you do not have such leeway.

Charter Flights

Now open to the general public, charter flights allow you to travel at rates cheaper than on regularly scheduled flights. Many of the major carriers offer charter flights at rates that are sometimes 30% (or more) off the regular air fare.

There are some drawbacks to charter flights that you need to consider. Advance booking, for example, of up to 45 days or more may be required. You could lose most of the money you've advanced if an emergency should force you to cancel a flight. However, it is now possible to take out cancellation insurance against such an eventuality.

Unfortunately, on the charter flight you are forced to depart and return on a scheduled date. It will do no good to call the airline and tell them you're in Trinidad with yellow fever! If you're not on the plane, you can kiss your money goodbye.

Since charter flights are so complicated, it's best to go to a good travel agent and ask him or her to explain to you the problems and advantages. Sometimes charters require ground arrangements, such as the prebooking of hotel rooms.

While there, ask about APEX fares, meaning advance purchase. These individual inclusive fares often include land arrangements along with your excursion fare, and can represent a considerable savings to you.

TOURING BY CRUISE SHIP: If you'd like to sail the Caribbean, having a home with an ocean view, the cruise ship might be for you. It's slow and easy, and it's no longer to be enjoyed only by the idle rich who have months to spend away from home. Most cruises today appeal to the middle-income voyager who probably has no more than one or two weeks to spend cruising the Caribbean. Some 300 passenger ships sail the Caribbean all year, and in January and February that figure may go up another hundred or so. You might want to pick up a copy of *Frommer's Cruises* for more detailed information.

Most cruise-ship operators suggest the concept of a "total vacation." Some promote activities "from sunup to sundown," while others suggest the possibility of "having absolutely nothing to do but lounge." Cruise ships are self-contained resorts, offering everything on board but actual sightseeing once you arrive in a port of call.

If you don't want to spend all your time at sea, some lines offer a fly-and-cruise vacation. Terms vary widely under this arrangement. You spend a week cruising the Caribbean, another week staying at an interesting hotel at reduced prices. These total packages cost less (or should) than if you'd purchased the cruise and air portions separately.

On yet another interpretation of "fly and cruise," you fly to meet the cruise and to leave it. Although multifarious in nature, most plans offer a package deal from the principal airport closest to your residence to the major airport nearest to the cruise departure point. Otherwise, you can purchase your air ticket on your own—say, from Kansas City to Fort Lauderdale—and book your cruise ticket separately as well, but you'll save money by combining the fares in a package deal.

Miami is the "cruise capital of the world," and vessels also leave from San Juan, New York, Port Everglades, Los Angeles, and other points of embarkation as well.

Most of the cruise ships prefer to do their traveling at night, arriving the next morning at the day's port of call, as anybody who has ever had a hotel room overlooking the water in St. Thomas can testify. In port, passengers can go ashore for sightseeing and shopping (it's also possible to have lunch at a restaurant of your choice to sample some of the island specialties and break the monotony of taking every meal aboard ship). Prices vary so widely that I cannot possibly document them. Sometimes the same route, stopping at the identical ports of call, will carry different fares.

TOURING BY CHARTERED BOAT: There is perhaps no more dream-fulfilling way of having a holiday in the Caribbean than from the deck of your own yacht. An impossible dream? Not really. No one said you had to *own* that yacht. You can charter it or go on a prearranged cruise.

Experienced sailors and navigators, with a sea-wise crew, can charter "bareboat," a term meaning a rental with a fully equipped boat but with no captain or crew. You're on your own, and you'll have to prove you can handle it before you're allowed to go on such a craft. Even if you're your own skipper, you may want to take along an experienced yachtsman familiar with local waters—waters that may in some places be tricky. (The company that insures the craft will definitely want to know that the vessel in question is in safe hands.)

Of course, if you can afford it, the ideal way is to charter a boat with a skilled skipper and a fully competent crew. Four to six people, maybe more, often charter yachts varying from 50 to more than 100 feet. Sometimes a dozen people will go out; at other times, a more romantic twosome.

Both the U.S. and British Virgin Islands are good cruising grounds, as are the Leeward and Windward Islands, which stretch from Antigua to Grenada, taking in such jewels of the French West Indies as Martinique and Guadeloupe. St. Vincent and the satellite Grenadines are also beautiful cruising grounds.

Most yachts are rented on a weekly basis, with a fully stocked bar, plus equipment for fishing and water sports. More and more bareboat charters are learning that they can save money and select menus more suited to their tastes by doing their own provisioning, rather than relying on the yacht company that rented them the vessel.

Unless money is no problem to you, the immediate question the average sailor asks is "How much will it cost?" Depending on the type of boat and the facilities offered, one person can count on spending from $90 to $150 a day. That doesn't mean you can't go out for less, and you certainly can sail for a lot more. Perhaps in summer, when business might be slow, you might get some yacht companies to charter you a boat for four or five days instead of a week or longer.

Some of the best-known firms in the charter business include the following:

Stevens Yachts, 252 East Ave., East Norwalk, CT 06855 (tel. 203/866-8989 within Connecticut, or toll free 800/638-7044 elsewhere in the U.S.). This outfit specializes in yacht chartering from its bases in Tortola (the British Virgin Islands) and St. Lucia. Bareboat and crewed yachts between 39 and 56 feet are available from a well-maintained fleet of Sparkman and Stephens–designed sailing craft. Heidi Patty, the charter manager, suggests that four- to six-month advance bookings (which require a 50% deposit) are a good idea for locked-in dates. Clients whose schedules are more flexible need only about a month's reservations in advance. Insurance and full equipment are included in the rates.

Windjammer Barefoot Cruises, Ltd., P.O. Box 120, Miami Beach, FL 33119 (tel. 305/534-5447, or toll free 800/327-2600, 800/432-3364 in Florida), offers trips on large sailing ships through the Caribbean. Its *Flying Cloud* goes through the British Virgin Islands; its *Polynesia* sails the Leeward and Windward Islands; its *Yankee Clipper* sails from Antigua; and *Fantome,* from the Virgin Islands. The newest ship, *Mandalay,* makes 13-day cruises out of Grenada and Antigua. Rates start at $675. Air-sea package deals are offered. S/V *Fantome,* S/V *Polynesia,* and S/V *Yankee Clipper* are registered in the British Virgin Islands, and the *Flying Cloud* is registered in The Bahamas. All ships comply with international safety standards except 1966 fire safety standards.

Nicholson Yacht Charters, 9 Chauncy St., Cambridge, MA 02138 (tel. 617/661-8174, or toll free 800/662-6066), or write P.O. Box 103, St. John's, Antigua, West Indies. This company, one of the best in the business, handles charter yachts for use throughout the Caribbean basin, particularly the route between Dutch-held St. Maarten to Grenada, as well as the routes around the U.S. and British Virgin Islands. Specializing in boats of all sizes, they can arrange rentals of motor or sailing yachts of up to 164 feet long (in this case, a Hanse motor yacht), with a skipper and crew, or smaller boats accommodating anywhere from 2 to 12 people in private single or double cabins. Especially popular are arrangements where two or more yachts, each sleeping eight guests in four equal double cabins, race each other from island to island during the day, anchoring near each other in secluded coves or at berths in Caribbean capitals at night. Nicholson's offers a series of possibilities. The price per day for renting a yacht depends on the number in your party and the size of the vessel. It ranges from $200 to $500 per day. Most yachts are rented on a weekly basis.

It's also possible to cruise in the Caribbean on yachts that have set sailing dates. On this type of craft, depending on its size, of course, there might be anywhere from 6 to 100 passengers. You are in fact a cruise passenger.

PACKAGE TOURS: If you want everything done for you, plus want to save money as well, you might consider traveling the Caribbean on a package tour. General tours appealing to the average voyager are commonly offered, but many of the tours are very specific—tennis packages, golf packages, scuba and snorkeling packages, and, only for those who qualify, honeymooners' specials.

Economy and convenience are the chief advantage of a package tour, in that the cost of transportation (usually an airplane fare), a hotel room, food (sometimes), and sightseeing (sometimes) are combined in one package, neatly tied up with a single price tag.

There are extras, of course, but in general you'll know in advance roughly what the cost of your vacation will be, and can budget accordingly.

If you booked your flight separately, likewise your hotel, you could not come out as cheaply as on a package tour—hence their immense and increasing appeal. There are disadvantages too. You may find yourself in a hotel you dislike immensely, yet you are virtually trapped there, as you've already paid for it.

Everybody from Idaho potato growers to birdwatchers of Alcatraz seemingly offers package tours to the Caribbean. Choosing the right one can be a bit of a problem. Your travel agent may offer one. Certainly all the major airline carriers will. It's best to go to a travel agent, tell him or her what island (or islands) you'd like to visit, and see what's currently offered.

These packages are available because tour operators can mass-book hotels and make volume purchases. You generally have to pay the cost of the total package in advance. Transfers between your hotel and the airport are often included, and this is more of a financial break than it sounds at first, as some airports are situated a $40 or more taxi ride from a resort. Many packages carry several options, including the possibility of low-cost car rentals.

The single traveler, regrettably, usually suffers, as nearly all tour packages are based on double occupancy.

2. A TRAVELER'S ADVISORY

Will I be safe in the Caribbean? This is one of the questions most often asked by the first-time visitor, and it's one of the most difficult to answer. Can a guidebook writer safely recommend traveling to New York or any major American city? Are you, in fact, free from harm in your own home?

The "attitude toward the visitor" takes on a wide range of meaning depending on whose attitude you are talking about. The Caribbean is composed of many nations, some of whom have broken, at least on paper, from colonial powers that dominated their cultures for years; others, such as Montserrat, preferring to retain their safe links with the past. Some islands, such as Guadeloupe and Martinique, are actually part of France, while other Caribbean nations prefer to seek help anywhere else but from their former colonial masters.

That attitude I mentioned might mean friendliness and hospitality, or it could encompass everything from indifferent service in a hotel dining room to theft and perhaps violence.

Many tourist boards are increasingly sensitive to the treatment of visitors, because their fragile economies depend on how many people their islands attract. Rudeness, room burglaries, anything that results in unfavorable publicity can cause damage. As a result, many islands are taking steps to make their own people more aware of the importance of tourism, and to treat their guests as they themselves would want to be treated if traveling in a foreign land.

Of course, many of the problems have come from the tourists themselves. A white person arriving in a predominantly black society may feel threatened—or worse, superior—and that can create difficulties. The people of the Caribbean must be given their respect and dignity. A smile usually wins a smile.

In addition, many of the islanders are deeply religious, and are offended by tourists who wear bikinis on shopping expeditions in town. One West Indian woman who runs a small hotel in Antigua had rented rooms to a film crew making a pirate adventure. When the men on that crew started running drunk and nude on the beach, a sight witnessed by the woman's two teenage daughters, she was deeply shocked. She handled the situation by posting a sign—"Pirates Must Wear Bathing Suits on the Beach."

Don't leave valuables such as cameras and cash-stuffed purses lying unattended on the beach while you go for a swim. Would you be so careless of your possessions in any town or city in Europe or America? Caribbean tourist officials often warn visitors, "If you've got it, don't flaunt it."

Problems do exist, and tomorrow's headlines may carry the story of a Caribbean disaster. Let me point out, however, that trouble in, say, Kingston, Jamaica, doesn't mean trouble in Barbados, no more than a bombing in London means you should cancel your trip to Munich.

Know that most of the people in the West Indies are proud, very proper, and most respectable, and if you treat them as such, they will likely treat you the same way. Others—certainly the minority, but a visible minority—are downright antagonistic. Some, in fact, are skunks. But every country on the globe has its share of that type.

Some islands are more hospitable to tourists than others. Your greeting in Montserrat is likely to be friendlier than it is in more jaded St. Thomas. But, then, Montserrat doesn't have five cruise ships a day docking at its harbor.

3. TRAVELING YEAR ROUND

More and more, the Caribbean is becoming a vacation goal for all seasons. Although they have more rain in the late spring and summer, the West Indies islands have so little variation in temperature that you can enjoy a visit there at any time. Installation of air conditioning in many accommodations, plus the whirling ceiling fans in almost every room you'll see, make for personal comfort everywhere. Sunshine is practically an everyday affair, even between the showers. So come on down!

IN WINTER: The so-called "season" in the Caribbean runs roughly from the middle of December to the middle of April. Hotels in the Caribbean charge their highest prices during the peak winter period when visitors fleeing from the cold north winds crowd into the islands. Winter is generally the dry season in the islands, but there can be heavy rainfall regardless of the season. For example, winter can be a wet time in mountainous areas, and you can expect showers especially in December and January on Martinique, Guadeloupe, Dominica, St. Lucia, on the north coast of the Dominican Republic, and in Jamaica's northeast section.

During the winter months, make reservations two to three months in advance, and if you rely on writing directly to the hotels, know that the mails are unreliable and take a long time. At certain hotels it is almost impossible to secure accommodations at Christmas and in February. One hotel in particular, Caneel Bay Plantation in St. John, books its rooms in February about a year in advance. Instead of writing to reserve your own room, it's better to book through one of the many Stateside representatives all major and many minor hotels use, or else to deal directly through a travel agent. If you don't want to do that, you should telephone the hotel of your choice in the Caribbean, agree on terms, and rush a deposit to hold the room.

Air-conditioned by trade winds, the temperature variations in the Caribbean are surprisingly slight, averaging between 75° and 85° Fahrenheit in both winter and summer, although there can be really chilly days, especially in the early morning and at night. However, the Caribbean winter is usually like a perpetual May.

IS THE SUMMER TOO HOT? For many travelers the islands of the Caribbean simply do not exist except when fearsome winds beat around corners and ice and slush pile up on the sidewalks up north. Regrettably, because everybody wants to visit the islands at these times, "the season" developed. Knowing they had a hot item to sell—warm, sandy beaches when much of North America was hit by blizzards—hotel entrepreneurs charge the maximum for their accommodations in winter, "the maximum" meaning all that the traffic will bear.

When North America warms up, vacationers head for Cape Cod or the Jersey shore or the beaches of California, forgetting the islands in the sun, thinking perhaps that the Caribbean is a caldron. This is not the case. The fabled Caribbean weather is balmy all year, with temperatures varying little more than 5° between winter and summer. The mid-80s prevail throughout most of the region, and trade winds make for comfortable days and nights, even in cheaper places that don't have air conditioning.

Truth is, you're better off in the West Indies most of the time than you are suffering through a roaring August heat wave in Chicago or New York.

Dollar for dollar, you'll save more money by renting a house or self-sufficient unit in the Caribbean than you would on Cape Cod, Fire Island, Laguna Beach, or the coast of Maine. Sailing and water sports are better too, because the West Indies is protected from the Atlantic on its western shores, which border the calm Caribbean Sea.

In essence, because of the trade winds and the various ocean currents, the Caribbean is virtually "seasonless." Even on islands where the noonday sun may raise the temperature to around 90°, cool breezes usually make the morning and late afternoon and evening more comfortable than in many parts of the U.S. mainland.

20% TO 60% REDUCTIONS: The off-season in the Caribbean—roughly from mid-April to mid-December (although this varies from hotel to hotel)—amounts to a summer sale. Except that summer in this context is eight months long, stretched out to include spring and autumn, often ideal times for travel.

In most cases, hotel rates are slashed a startling 20% to 60%, and these rate reductions are emphasized in this guide by being set in *italics*. It's a bonanza for cost-conscious travelers, especially families who like to go on vacations together.

In the chapters ahead, I'll spell out in dollars the specific amounts hotels charge during the off-season.

OTHER OFF-SEASON ADVANTAGES: In addition to price slashes at hotels, there are some other important reasons for visiting the Caribbean in spring, summer, and autumn.

□ After the winter hordes have left, a less hurried way of life prevails. You'll have a better chance to appreciate the food, the culture, and the local customs.

□ Swimming pools and beaches are less crowded—perhaps not crowded at all.

□ Because summer business has grown, year-round resort facilities are offered, often at reduced rates. This is likely to include, among other activities, snorkeling, boating, and scuba-diving.

□ To survive, resort boutiques often feature summer sales, hoping to clear the merchandise they didn't sell in February. They've ordered stock for the coming winter, and must clean their shelves and clear their racks. Duty-free items in free-port shopping are draws all year, too.

□ You can often walk in unannounced at a top restaurant and get a seat for dinner, a seat that would have been denied you in winter unless you'd made reservations far in advance. Also, when the waiters are less hurried, you'll get far better service.

□ The endless waiting game is over in the off-season. No waiting for a rented car (only to be told none is available). No long tee-up for golf. More immediate access to the tennis courts and water sports.

□ The atmosphere is more cosmopolitan in the off-season than it is in winter, mainly because of the influx of Europeans. You'll no longer feel as if you're at a Canadian or American outpost. Also, the Antilleans themselves travel in the off-season, and your holiday becomes more of a people-to-people experience.

□ Some package-tour fares are as much as 20% cheaper, and individual excursion fares are also reduced between 5% and 10%.

□ All accommodations, including airline seats and hotel rooms, are much easier to obtain.

□ Summer is the time for family travel, which is not possible during the winter season. Or else parents can travel while children are away at camp.

□ Finally, the very best of wintertime attractions remain undiminished— sea, sand, and surf, usually with lots of sunshine.

WHAT TO WEAR: In this day when dress is such a personal statement, I can no longer present checklists of what to pack. Many beachcombers arrive in the Caribbean with the jeans they're wearing, a toothbrush, and a bathing suit (perhaps!). Most travelers today are aware of clothing needed in subtropical or tropical climates. You'll want to dress casually to stay cool, and you'll want to select apparel that is easy to clean, of course.

If you're living at deluxe and first-class hotels, women should be prepared for at least an evening cocktail party. Some restaurants and hotels—and admittedly it's a hopeless battle—still require men to wear a jacket and tie in the evening.

Treading the balance between a personal statement in apparel and a concern for others, clothing in the Caribbean ultimately becomes a matter of taste. Some resorts that used to have dress codes—that is, men required to wear jackets after 6 p.m.—have, in despair, posted signs that dress should be "casual but chic." You are allowed to interpret that according to your wishes. I have attempted to give clues in individual writeups when hotels have set particular standards of dress. Obviously, you should take coordinated clothing so that you can travel lightly.

4. WHERE TO STAY

If deciding on the island or islands to visit seems complicated, selecting the place to live once you get there may be even more perplexing. Few travel destinations in the world offer such a wide range of accommodations: a tropical villa in St. Thomas, a millionaire's estate in Jamaica, a 17th-century great house in St. Kitts, a 200-year-old sugar warehouse in St. Vincent, or a beachfront apartel in Puerto Rico. You can even perch in a treehouse by the sea! In this guide, I've surveyed the widest possible range of accommodations, from deluxe citadels to simply-furnished, low-cost cottages near the sea.

HOTELS AND RESORTS: One of the most galling occurrences is to learn that the couple next door is staying in the same hotel that you are, even enjoying an ocean view as opposed to your "mountain view," but is paying some $200 to $300 less per week than you are. That happens more often than you'd imagine.

A lot of it stems from a zeal among Caribbean hoteliers, especially during the slow months, to promote business. There are package deals galore, and though they have many disadvantages, they are always cheaper than rack rates (what an individual pays who literally walks in from the street). Therefore it's always good to go to a reliable travel agent to find out what is available in the way of a land-and-air package before booking into a particular property.

There is no rigid classification of Caribbean hotel properties. The word "deluxe" is often used—or misused—when "first class" might have been a more appropriate term. First class itself often isn't. For that and other reasons, I've presented fairly detailed descriptions of the properties, so that you'll get an idea of what to expect once you're there. However, even in the deluxe and first-class properties, don't expect top-rate service and efficiency. "Things," as they are called in the West Indies, don't seem to work as well in the tropics as they do in certain fancy resorts of California or Europe. Life in the tropics has its disadvantages. When you go to turn on the shower, sometimes you get water and sometimes you don't. You may even experience island power failures. To prepare yourself, read the Herman Wouk novel *Don't Stop the Carnival,* and go to the West Indies already armed with the information that a hotel operation might not work as well as it would back home.

Facilities often determine the choice of a hotel. For example, if golf is your passion, you may want to book into a hotel resort such as Casa de Campo in the Dominican Republic. If scuba-diving is your goal, then head, say, for the Cayman Islands and a "dive resort." Regardless of your particular interest, there is probably a hotel catering to your need.

THE WEST INDIAN GUESTHOUSE: An entirely different type of accommodation is the guesthouse, where most of the Antilleans themselves stay when they travel in the Caribbean. Some of these are surprisingly comfortable, often with swimming pools and private baths with each room. You may or may not have air conditioning. The rooms are sometimes cooled by ceiling fans or trade winds blowing through open windows at night. Of course, don't expect the luxuries of a fabulous resort, but for value the guesthouse can't be topped. Staying in a guesthouse, you can journey over to a big beach resort, using its seaside facilities for only a small charge, perhaps no more than $3.

Although bereft of frills, the guesthouses I've recommended are clean, decent, and safe for families or single women. Many of the cheapest ones are not places you'd like to live in all night and day too, because of their simple, modest furnishings.

However, many of today's new breed of travelers to the Caribbean don't want to spend more than eight hours in their rooms anyway. Otherwise, you'll find them on the beach, snorkeling or going scuba-diving, and at night patronizing the native taverns serving local food and just getting to know people. To this type of traveler a hotel is a mere convenience, to go to for sleep after an activity-filled day and a nightlife-packed evening.

Dressing up for dinner and otherwise practicing a routine familiar at American country clubs may not appeal to many of today's more adventurous travelers, who often arrive in the West Indies with a bathing suit, a T-shirt, and a pair of jeans.

In the Caribbean, the term "guesthouse" can mean anything. Sometimes so-called guesthouses are really like simple motels built around swimming pools. Others are small individual cottages, with their own kitchenettes, constructed around a main building in which you'll often find a bar and a restaurant serving local food.

SELF-CATERING HOLIDAYS: Particularly if you're a family or friendly group, a housekeeping holiday can be one of the least expensive ways of vacationing in the Caribbean. These types of accommodations are now available on nearly all the islands previewed. Sometimes you can rent individual cottages; others are housed in one building. Some are private homes rented when the owners are away. All have small kitchens or kitchenettes where you can do your home-cooking, shopping for groceries, and whenever possible, buying freshly caught fish and some Caribbean lobster.

A housekeeping holiday, however, doesn't always mean you'll have to do maid's work. Most of the self-catering places have maid service included in the rental, and you're given fresh linen as well.

Cooking most of your meals yourself and dining out on occasion, such as when a neighboring big hotel has a beachside barbecue with entertainment, is the surest way of keeping holiday costs at a minimum.

FOR SINGLE TRAVELERS: If you've ever read bargain-travel advertisements, you'll sometimes see an asterisk, indicating below (in fine print) that the tempting deal being presented is based on "double occupancy." If you're a lone wolf or without a traveling companion, you'll often get hit with a painful supplement called a "surcharge" that can be at least 35% and perhaps a lot more. The hotelier in the Caribbean, of course, likes to shelter at least two in a room, and sometimes they crowd in three or four. It's the same room, and two to three persons spend a lot more on drinks, water sports, and food.

In addition to the cruises for singles that have gained mass popularity in the past few years, there is another way to keep costs bone-trimmed and take advantage of some of the package tours, cruises, and cut-rate hotel deals. But it means you may have to join a club.

One of the most successful such groups is **Gramercy's Singleworld,** 401 Theodore Freud Ave., Rye, NY 10580 (tel. 914/967-3334), which for some 30 years has catered to single and unattached persons—the never-married, the separated, divorced, widowed, and those traveling alone. They have no age limits, although most of their club members are under 35. Certain cruise and tour departures are designated for people of all ages or under 35.

Anyone who is single or traveling alone is eligible for membership. The membership fee is $20 (non-refundable). However, it is effective from the date of a departure for one full year. Singleworld emphasizes that they are *not* a lonely-hearts club, *not* a matrimonial bureau, and do *not* guarantee equal numbers of men and women in their groups.

Because Singleworld offers more than 500 departures a year, the prices offered for the cruise and tour departures are competitive. In addition, you can avoid the extra expense of a single-room accommodation by sharing a unit with another member.

5. FAMILY VACATIONS

The islands of the Caribbean contend for top position on the world list of places for vacations for the entire family. The smallest toddlers can spend blissful hours on sandy beaches and in the shallow sea water or pools constructed with them in mind. There's no end to the fascinating pursuits offered for older children too, ranging from boat rides to shell collecting to horseback riding, hiking, even discoing. Perhaps yours are old enough to learn to snorkel and explore the wonderland of the underwater Caribbean.

There are places where such skills are taught as weaving hats of coconut-palm fronds, learning circus performance skills, swimming, windsurfing, and a variety of other activities unique to the islands.

There are important pointers to keep in mind when you're planning a family vacation anywhere in the Caribbean so that your trip is fun for all with a minimum of worries. Most resort hotels will advise you as to what there is in the way of fun for all ages, and many have play directors and supervised activities for the young of various age groups. However, there are some tips for making the trip a success which parents should attend to in advance, so that when the family finds itself in the sunny paradise, nobody will think they've gone the wrong direction.

Take along a "security blanket" for your child. This might be a pacifier, a favorite toy, or books the child likes especially—something to make him or her feel at home. An older offspring might take along a treasure such as a baseball cap, a favorite T-shirt (even though there'll be plenty to buy down there), or some special trinket or good-luck piece.

Take protection from the sun. For tiny tots, this should include a sun umbrella, while the whole family will need sunscreen (a "15" is a good idea) and sunglasses.

Take along anti-insect lotions and sprays. You'll probably need these both to repel such little unwanted island denizens as mosquitoes and sand fleas as well as to ease the itching and possible other after-effects of insect bites.

Arrange ahead for such necessities as a crib, bottle warmer, and car seat (if you're driving anywhere) for the very young, as well as for cots in your room for larger children. Find out if the place you're staying stocks baby food, and if not, take it with you.

Draw up rules for your family to follow during your holiday. These should be flexible, of course—after all, this trip is for fun. But guidelines on bedtime, eating, keeping tidy, being in the sun, even shopping and spending, can help make everybody's vacation more enjoyable.

Babysitters can be found for you by most hotels, but you should insist that yours knows at least rudimentary English in order to avoid traumatic experiences for young children. Talk with the sitter yourself, and introduce him or her to those to be cared for before you leave the hotel room or nursery.

In addition to fundamentals that you should take along whenever you travel with children—such as a thermometer, basic first-aid supplies, and medications your doctor may suggest—don't forget swimsuits, beach and pool toys, waterwings for tiny mites, flip-flops for everybody, and terrycloth robes.

6. ALTERNATIVE AND SPECIAL-INTEREST TRAVEL

Mass tourism of the kind that has transported vast numbers of North Americans to the most obscure corners of the map is well established. It has come about as a by-product of the affluence, technology, and democratization that only the last half of the 20th century was able to produce.

With the advent of the 1990s, and the changes this decade promises to bring, some of America's most respected travel visionaries have perceived a change in the needs of many of the world's most experienced (and sometimes jaded) travelers. There has emerged a demand for specialized travel experiences whose goals and objectives are clearly defined well in advance of an actual departure. There is also an increased demand for organizations that can provide like-minded companions to share and participate in increasingly esoteric travel plans.

Caveat: Under no circumstances is the inclusion of an organization in this section to be interpreted as a guarantee either of its credit-worthiness or its competency. Information about the organizations coming up is presented only as a preliminary preview, to be followed by your own investigation should you be interested.

INTERNATIONAL UNDERSTANDING: About the only thing the following organizations have in common is reflected in that heading. They not only promote trips to increase international understanding, but they also often encourage and advocate what might be called "intelligent travel."

Servas, 11 John St., New York, NY 10038 (tel. 212/267-0252). Servas (translated from the Esperanto, it means "to serve") is a non-profit, non-government, international, interfaith network of travelers and hosts whose goal is to help build world peace, good will, and understanding. They do this by providing opportunities for deeper, more personal contacts among people of diverse cultural and political backgrounds. Servas travelers are invited to share living space in a privately owned home within a community, normally staying without charge for visits lasting a maximum of two days. Visitors pay a $45 annual membership fee, fill out an application, and are interviewed for suitability by one of more than 200 Servas interviewers throughout the country. They then receive a Servas directory listing the names and addresses of Servas hosts who will allow (and encourage) visitors within their homes. In the Caribbean, Servas "hosts" are located in Jamaica, Puerto Rico, Martinique, Guadeloupe, Trinidad, Barbados, and the U.S. Virgin Islands.

International Visitors Information Service, 733 15th St. NW, Suite 300, Washington, DC 20005 (tel. 202/783-6540). For $4.95, this organization will mail anyone a booklet listing opportunities for contact with local residents in foreign countries. The Caribbean is heavily featured, especially Jamaica and Barbados. For example, if you want to find lodgings with a Jamaican family whose members make their living from commerce with Britain, this booklet will tell you how. Checks should be made out to Meridian House IVIS.

Many of the world's travelers hold a concern for the future of less wealthy societies whose borders are invaded annually by floods of big-spending tourists. One highly reputable organization, the **Center for Responsible Tourism,** 2 Kensington Rd., San Anselmo, CA 94960 (tel. 415/258-6594), tries to raise the consciousness of travelers as to the unhappy effects which cultural conflicts can bring to fragile third-world societies. Although it doesn't actually sponsor organized tours into the Caribbean, its newsletter and the schedules of its meetings might be of interest to visitors who are motivated by humanitarian feelings of concern for less-developed societies. The center, in its own words, "exists to change the attitudes and practices of North American travelers and to persuade North Americans to be part of the struggle for justice in tourism in the third world." The organization thrives on contributions and for a small fee will send new members its newsletter and information about upcoming seminars.

SENIOR CITIZEN VACATIONS: One of the most dynamic organizations of post-retirement studies for senior citizens is **Elderhostel,** 80 Boyleston St., Boston, MA 02116 (tel. 617/426-8056), established in 1975. Elderhostel maintains an array of programs throughout Europe as well as several programs in the Caribbean, especially in Jamaica, with new courses being offered frequently. In Jamaica, the focus is on tropical marine biology, with courses taught in cooperation with Hofstra University's marine laboratory in St. Ann's Bay. Most courses last for two to three weeks, representing good value considering that air fare, hotel accommodations in student dormitories or modest inns, all meals, and tuition are included. Courses involve no homework, are ungraded, and center mostly on the liberal arts. In no way is this to be considered a luxury vacation, but rather an academic fulfillment of a type never possible for senior citizens until several years ago. Participants must be more than 60 years of age. However, if two members go as a couple, only one member needs to be over 60. Anyone interested in participating in one of Elderhostel's programs should write for their free newsletter and a list of upcoming courses and destinations.

TRAVEL AND LEARNING: An international series of programs for persons over 50 years of age who are interested in combining travel and learning is offered by **Interhostel,** developed by the University of New Hampshire. Each program lasts two weeks and is escorted by a university faculty or staff member, arranged in conjunction with a host college, university, or cultural institution. Participants can extend a stay beyond two weeks if they wish. Interhostel offers programs that consist of cultural and intellectual activities, with field trips to museums and other centers of interest, especially in Puerto Rico. For information, get in touch with the University of New Hampshire, Division of Continuing Education, 6 Garrison Ave., Durham, NH 03824 (tel. 603/862-1147). It's best to phone between 1:30 and 4 p.m. EST.

TOURS FOR NATURALISTS: Lectures on wildlife and the environment of Puerto Rico are offered by the **Commonwealth of Puerto Rico Department of Natural Resources,** especially for scientists and students. Also, private tours of nature reserves on the island are possible through prior arrangement. The name of the reserve you are interested in visiting should be specified in a request made either to Mildred Rodriguez or to the Forest Service, Resident Biologist, both at the Commonwealth of Puerto Rico Department of Natural Resources, P.O. Box 5887, Puerto de Tierra, PR 00906 (tel. 809/724-8774).

ADVENTURES FOR WOMEN: Run for and by women, New Dawn Adventures offers Caribbean trips in Puerto Rico and sailing voyages around the American and British Virgin Islands. A Caribbean Getaway at New Dawn's Retreat on the little Puerto Rican island of Vieques includes outings to put women in touch with nature, plus activities geared to the interests, needs, abilities, and experiences of all the women participating. Complete facilities are available for food and lodging. A Tropical Tripping expedition includes hiking and camping in the mountains of Puerto Rico's tropical rain forest, El Yunque, and an introduction to all of the island vegetation. A 54-foot ketch, *Sasanoa,* is used for five-day trips from Vieques around the Virgin Islands, with the opportunity for persons taking the cruise to learn something about sailing. Headquarters for **New Dawn Adventures, Inc.,** are at 518 Washington St., Gloucester, MA 10930 (tel. 617/283-8717). You can also get information by writing to New Dawn at P.O. Box 1512, Vieques, PR 00765.

WOMANSHIP: A program for women who are beginning sailors as well as those with experience is offered by **Womanship, Inc.,** 137 Conduit St., Annapolis, MD 21401 (tel. 301/269-0784). Expert sailing instruction and a vacation adventure in the Caribbean, among the British and U.S. Virgin Islands, is offered. Participants can choose between week-long training cruises and a series of shorter sessions on board, to be taken in the evening, during the day, or on weekends. Womanship attracts women from all walks of life, usually ranging in age from 20 to 65. They learn through working as ship's crew, with instruction in the theory, principle, and practice of sailing, leading up to hands-on experience and possible culmination in serving as watch captain and acquisition of the expertise needed to instruct newcomers. On Womanship cruises, all responsibilities are shared among crews and instructors. On completion of a course, participants are presented Certificates of Accomplishment that can possibly be used toward qualifying for bareboat charters of sailing vessels. The Virgin Islands program courses are scheduled for most months of the year. For more information, get in touch with Womanship, Inc., at the address given above.

A TRAVEL COMPANION: A recent American census showed that 77 million Americans more than 15 years of age are single. However, the travel industry is far better geared for double occupancy of hotel rooms. One company that has made heroic efforts to match single travelers with like-minded companions is now the largest and best such company in the United States. Jens Jurgen, the German-born founder, charges $29 to $66 for a six-month listing in his well-publicized records. New applicants desiring a travel companion fill out a form stating their preferences and needs. They then receive a mini-listing of the kinds of potential partners who might be suitable for travel. Companions of the same or opposite sex can be requested. Because of the large number of listings, success is often a reality. For an application and more information, write to Jens Jurgen, **Travel Companion,** Box P-833, Amityville, NY 11701 (tel. 516/454-0880).

CHAPTER II

WHAT IS THE CARIBBEAN?

□ □ □

1. GEOGRAPHY AND CLIMATE
2. BEFORE THE EUROPEANS
3. HISTORY SINCE EUROPEAN CONQUEST
4. THE CARIBBEAN TODAY

The question—What is the Caribbean?—is a legitimate one. The bewildering variety of islands in the sun sowed confusion in its first tourist, Christopher Columbus, back in 1492. To Isabella back home in Spain, he wrote in a rapturous letter, "I saw so many islands that I could hardly decide which to visit first." As far as decisions go, things haven't changed that much for today's southbound, sun-seeking tourist.

As diverse in mood as they are in number, the islands of the Caribbean are each gifted with a distinctive sparkle and style, even when part of the same nation. The short trip from St. Kitts to Nevis, when the plane goes up merely to set down again, has taken you not just to a sister state, but a nostalgic island of decaying, once-flourishing plantations, remarkably unlike the place you left only ten minutes before.

First, some basic orientation. The Caribbean Sea is ringed by the Greater Antilles in the north (Cuba, Jamaica, Hispaniola, and Puerto Rico), the Lesser Antilles on the east, the coasts of Venezuela, Colombia, and Panamá on the south (once referred to as the Spanish Main), and the countries of Central America and the Mexican Yucatán peninsula on the west. Its total area comes to over one million square miles!

For the purposes of this book, I've concentrated on the West Indies, which form the border between the chilly Atlantic and the warm, calm Caribbean Sea. The West Indies begin with Cuba, curving south to Trinidad, lying between the peninsula of Florida and the northern coast of South America. The Dutch Leewards, often called the "ABC Islands," lie off the coast of the Spanish Main or what is today Venezuela.

The question of a specific destination depends largely on who you are and what your vacation goals are—to sunbathe in the buff on the nudist beaches of Guadeloupe; to snorkel and scuba-dive off Bonaire; to scale a volcanic crater in Saba; to sail as Lord Nelson did from English Harbour in Antigua more than 200 years ago; to take a donkey ride in Haiti to the Citadelle (one of the seven man-made wonders of the world); to explore Santo Domingo, the oldest city in the

Americas; or to shop the winding alleys in the merchandise-loaded bazaars of St. Thomas and St. Croix in the U.S. Virgin Islands.

1. GEOGRAPHY AND CLIMATE

The islands of the Caribbean lie around the Caribbean Sea, which is divided into three main parts: the Cayman Sea in the northwest, the Venezuelan Basin in the southeast, and the Columbian Basin in the southwest and center. The amazing variety of form and structure of these islands—which stretch from 10° north of the Equator almost to the Tropic of Cancer—is shown in size, topography, and depths of the sea around them, but all are tropical and fascinating to vacationers, historians, sociologists, geologists, mariners, fishermen, a host of people with all sorts of interests.

The islands and island groups are referred to by different names, which since the time of Columbus has caused confusion. Are you going to the West Indies? the Windward Islands? the Leewards? Hispaniola? or to the Greater or Lesser Antilles? perhaps the Caribbees?

The name "West Indies" has had a number of meanings since Columbus first called his discoveries *Las Indies Occidentales* (the West Indies), thinking he had reached Asia, but the name is now fairly widely taken to include the groups of islands once called the Greater Antilles and the Lesser Antilles. A medieval legend placed an island called Antilia someplace in the Atlantic Ocean, supposed to have been a refuge for Christians fleeing Portugal and Spain when the Moors invaded. (The Azores were once called Antilia.) In the 15th and 16th centuries the name Antilles was given to the tropical islands ringing the Caribbean.

Cuba (once known as the "Pearl of the Antilles," but no longer due to its virtual isolation from the capitalist world), Jamaica, Hispaniola (the island comprising Haiti and the Dominican Republic), Puerto Rico, and the Cayman Islands lie in the Greater Antilles. The title Lesser Antilles was given to the remainder of the chain of islands forming the eastern perimeter of the Caribbean Sea, an arc of islands also widely known as the Caribbees. Included are the Leeward Islands, curving from Anguilla in the north to Dominica in the south, and the Windward Islands, from Martinique to Grenada, but not including Barbados (although it's also a Caribbean island). There is also a little island chain paralleling the South American coast embracing three of the six islands today called the Netherlands Antilles.

Oddly, the Leeward Islands lie more to the windward than do the Windwards. All this had something to do with the accuracy of mariners who originally named the parts of the archipelago, and it can be quite confusing when you realize that three of the Netherlands Antilles islands—Sint Maarten, Sint Eustatius, and Saba—are the Dutch Windwards, but they lie in the Leeward Islands. On the other hand, the other three islands of the Netherlands Antilles—Aruba, Bonaire, and Curaçao—lying off the coast of South America, are called the Dutch Leewards.

However, you needn't let this varied nomenclature be a worry insofar as a visit to the Caribbean is concerned—unless, of course, you're going by your own boat. Whatever they're called, all the Caribbean islands enjoy the warm waters of the sea lapping their shores, the movement of the trade winds and the sea breezes, and almost constant sunshine. A rainy season usually lasts from around May or June through October, but winter is known as the dry season. Such weather conditions as hurricanes, which sometimes come in summer and fall, need not create the fear those seasons once did, because constant watch is kept and warnings issued early enough for safety to be fairly certain. Rather cool weather is likely to visit the highland areas of some of the islands, but the only cold zones are found at altitudes reached by some mountain peaks, such as the 7,402-foot Blue Mountain in Jamaica and a 10,417-foot peak in Haiti. In all the hill sections, you can expect cool nights at most times of year.

2. BEFORE THE EUROPEANS

Many pictures have been painted of the landing of Columbus and later Spanish expeditions on islands of the West Indies, with the unsuspecting Indian inhabitants showing little fear of the strange, overdressed (for the climate) beings from across the big water. The age of self-rule for these islanders came to an abrupt end—and, in the sweep of history, so did their very existence.

The peoples indigenous to the islands of Greater Antilles, The Bahamas, and some of the Lesser Antilles were related, all speaking forms of the Arawak language. They are thought to have come originally from South America's Amazon basin, risking their lives in oar-propelled dugout canoes to find better, safer places to live as fiercer South American Indians disrupted their home territories. Of the various tribes of these people linked through their Arawak-tongue background, one of the strongest was the Taíno. Some traces of this tribe have been found in Cuba and Puerto Rico, while a few artifacts from other tribes have been unearthed in Haiti, the Dominican Republic, and Jamaica. It is believed that the route of the Taíno, which probably took several centuries, was from South America to Puerto Rico and on to Hispaniola and Cuba. There were surely many stops lasting years at a time in islands of the Antilles, and it is known that some tribes even made their way as far north as the southern Bahamas.

Much of the travel of the Arawak indigenous peoples was in flight from the blood-thirsty Caribs, another group from South America, who took control of some of the Lesser Antilles and Hispaniola.

It didn't take the Spaniards long to wipe out the American Indian population throughout the West Indies. The *conquistadores* inflicted unspeakable cruelties on the natives, enslaving the survivors of small battles and using them as tools to dig precious metals from the ground, dive for pearls, and perform constant back-breaking labor for the new masters. The Caribs, being warlike, lasted a little longer than did any of the Arawak tribes, but it was only about a century after Spanish claims were established before the Indians from the Caribbean islands were almost entirely annihilated.

About the only places where traces of Arawak blood may still exist are Cuba and the Dominican Republic, where you sometimes see white people with Indian facial characteristics. The stronger Caribs have left their mark in Dominica and St. Vincent, where there are little groups of people called "black Caribs," of mixed Negro and West Indian blood. Also, on Aruba you'll meet many *mestizos,* whose blood is mixed Indian and white, but their ancestors probably came much later from South America than did the Arawaks and Caribs.

3. HISTORY SINCE EUROPEAN CONQUEST

All the Caribbean islands, which today have a wide variety of governmental structures, belonged to Spain in the late 15th and 16th centuries. Their "discovery" by Columbus and other explorers who claimed the widespread area for Spain was soon followed by seizure of some islands and initial landings by representatives of other European countries. Britain, France, and the Netherlands established Caribbean/West Indian colonies in competition with Spain. Other governments followed suit, and by the 18th century Denmark, Sweden, and the now-defunct German principalities of Brandenburg and Courland once counted Caribbean possessions among their assets.

In the beginning, Spain, hungry for gold and with the support of the Catholic church, laid claim to everything in sight—and to a lot of lands only rumored to be in the area. On his four voyages Columbus explored Cuba, Hispaniola (the whole island then being called Haiti, or "High Land," by the inhabitants), Dominica, Guadeloupe in the Lesser Antilles, Puerto Rico, the Cayman Islands, Jamaica, and Trinidad, as well as Central and South American territories. From the early 16th century the Spaniards' quest for gold and silver led to some colonization of towns at the good natural harbors, but they were not really settlers in these new lands. The harbors served as ports on favorable sea lanes among the islands along which treasures were sent back to Spain. The newcomers spread their religion and their communicable diseases to the indigenous inhabitants, who died off rapidly as they were enslaved and brutalized by the Spaniards.

The treasures of the Antilles proved too tempting for other Europeans to pass up, and by the middle of the 16th century sea-going plunderers from various European nations were preying on the galleons bearing rich cargoes from the New World to fill the coffers of Spain. The Dutch, French, British—called variously corsairs, freebooters, pirates, privateers, filibusters, and buccaneers—prowled the seas, leaving their legacy of blood-spattered romance.

From the middle of the 17th century assorted peoples from Western Europe began to settle in the new lands, which changed flags frequently as first this nation and then that claimed ownership. The British, French, Danes, and Dutch were chief among the claimants as Spain was forced out of the running with its decline as ruler of the waves. The Dutch held Curaçao and the French kept Martinique, although the claims were long disputed. By 1670 Britain had seized Jamaica, its colonial government being recognized by the ousted Spanish. The French government, following in the footsteps of freebooters, took over all of Hispaniola, which was renamed Saint-Domingue.

As colonization took hold, the new landowners established sugar plantations, first in the Lesser Antilles and then on islands of the Greater Antilles. With the plantations came the slave trade—the importation of blacks from Africa as the labor force of the West Indies.

In 1763, after years of conflict (particularly between Britain and France) over the fortune-generating islands, the treaty ending the Seven Years' War in Europe gave Britain the upper hand in many areas of the Caribbean, but it did not end the strife. Everybody wanted a piece of the rich sugar pie. Britain seized Guadeloupe. Major turmoil erupted in Hispaniola: as the 19th century dawned, the long discontent of blacks and mulattoes boiled up in revolt; the sons and daughters of Africa took eastern Hispaniola from Spain, which had regained control from France, but were soon forced to relinquish the prize. However, they threw off their chains of slavery and succeeded also in throwing off the yoke of French sovereignty in the western third of the island, establishing a republic and naming it Haiti.

Following the Napoleonic wars, treaties distributed the Caribbean islands as follows: France had only Martinique and Guadeloupe (and satellite islands) in the Lesser Antilles; the Netherlands finally got a clear claim to Curaçao; Britain held Jamaica, the Cayman Islands, and most of the Lesser Antilles (except for the French colonies and some small island possessions of the Danes and the Dutch); and Spain kept Puerto Rico, Cuba, and eastern Hispaniola, by now called Santo Domingo. The tribulations of Haiti were not over, although it was considered independent of European rule. The new republic kept trying to include eastern Hispaniola under its flag, but by the middle of the 19th century that part of the island had achieved independence from both Spain and Haiti, and the Dominican Republic had been set up. Hispaniola was henceforth an island of two separate republics.

During these years slavery was coming to an end from island to island as the various controlling nations abolished the trade, but by then blacks and persons of mixed blood whose ancestors were imported from Africa were deeply rooted in the West Indies.

The United States became a presence in the Caribbean in 1898, not through colonization but by military and monetary power. Spain lost Cuba and Puerto Rico to the big neighbor to the north in the Spanish-American War. The U.S. occupied Haiti from 1915 to 1934 because of a bloody power struggle in the island republic between blacks and mulattoes, performing the same service for the Dominican Republic from 1916 to 1924, this time to protect U.S. interests. The people of Puerto Rico became U.S. citizens in 1917 and were granted limited self-government. In that same year the Danish Virgin Islands were bought by the United States and became territories of the new owners, known as the U.S. Virgin Islands. The people there are U.S. citizens, but they cannot vote in federal elections. In 1952 the internally self-governing Commonwealth of Puerto Rico was established, and the island may eventually become one of the United States of America.

The 20th century has seen the end of colonialism in most of the Caribbean. The Netherlands Antilles now have internal self-government. Martinique and Guadeloupe were made overseas *départements* of France. Some of the former British colonies now have various forms of their own government. There are constitutional states, independent states, one presidential republic, one independent republic, and one British Associated State, all within the British Commonwealth. The British monarch is still head of state (represented by a governor) for the British Virgin Islands, the Caymans, and Montserrat, which are designated as Crown Colonies.

4. THE CARIBBEAN TODAY

Discoverers, fortune-hunters, pirates, planters, shipwrecked sailors, slaves, and free men have all splashed their colorful personalities across the canvas of the Caribbean. From the day Christopher Columbus dropped anchor at an island he named San Salvador in The Bahamas until today, the mystique of the Caribbean and its exotic islands endures.

THE PEOPLE: After the indigenous population of the West Indies had been virtually annihilated, the population of the numerous bits of land took on a variegated hue. Colonists brought European culture, customs, and languages of several nations, many of which imports still exist, although inevitably they have been influenced by the tropical ambience. As the colonists came, particularly the big planters, they needed a vast labor force, and as mentioned earlier, this need was met by bringing in black slaves from Africa by the hundreds of thousands. These reluctant immigrants, although they were forcibly "converted" to Christianity, retained many beliefs and tribal customs of their native lands. This is seen in the mixture of pagan and Christian religious rites as observed by the *voodoo* followers in Haiti, *santería* in Cuba, and *xango* (shango) in Trinidad. The basic beliefs and rituals from Africa have been fitted in comfortably with Roman Catholic worship forms and figures, and Protestant faiths as followed in predominantly black and mulatto sections are also strongly affected by the African heritage.

Abolition of slavery ended the importation of blacks, but already they were a large part of the population, and today by far the majority of the islanders are descended from those African slaves (of which, more below).

When the white colonials were no longer allowed to augment their possessions by bringing in African blacks, the British and French turned to a system of importing indentured servants from India, and some Chinese and Lebanese also came to the West Indies. These have added to the mixed bloodlines of the Caribbean populace, although some have maintained their ethnic purity, culture, religion, and customs through the years. Blacks predominate in most of the islands, especially where vast numbers were imported to work the sugar plantations, but there are also many mulattoes in these areas whose skin color ranges from very light to dark—an outcome that makes it nearly impossible to fix any certain population breakdown along these lines.

It is estimated that in the former British and French colonies, the colored population (descendants of former slaves, with or without other ancestry) tops 90%. In the islands settled by Spain (Puerto Rico and Cuba), on the other hand, the white ancestry strongly predominates (less strongly in the Dominican Republic, which was affected by being twice made a part of black Haiti). There were fewer blacks in those islands in the colonial period because the plantation system did not develop there in the early days. By the time it did, slavery was no longer permitted, and the labor force for the Spanish-held islands came from the mother country and from the Canary Islands.

As to the East Indian population, it is mainly found in former British and French colonies. On Trinidad and Tobago you'll find that Asians make up some 40% of the count, and they are found in lesser numbers in Barbados, Curaçao, Grenada, Guadeloupe, Martinique, St. Lucia, St. Vincent, St. Kitts, Nevis, and a smattering in Haiti and Jamaica—and probably elsewhere.

Class distinctions throughout the islands were once based on race and color as well as wealth, a system which is undergoing change. Instead of a small, mostly white, rich upper class and a large, poor, largely black, mulatto, or otherwise mixed lower class, today a middle class is developing as a result of industrialization and other economic changes and improved education.

LANGUAGES: With such a mélange of backgrounds, it's not surprising to find a linguistic mixture also. The language of former colonial overlords is the official tongue of each island, even Haiti. There, the form is French, but the common speech is a French Créole. In fact the speech you'll hear when you travel in rural areas of many of the countries is heavily dependent on local dialects and patois, some with many phrases of African origin.

Official languages of the islands are:

English—the Caymans, Jamaica, the U.S. and British Virgin Islands, Antigua, Barbuda, Montserrat, St. Kitts, Nevis, Anguilla, Dominica, St. Lucia, Barbados, Grenada, St. Vincent, The Grenadines, Trinidad, and Tobago.

Spanish—the Dominican Republic and Puerto Rico (where English is a second language), and Cuba.

French—Haiti, St. Martin, St. Barthélemy, Martinique, and Guadeloupe.

Dutch—Sint Maarten, Sint Eustatius, Saba, Aruba, Bonaire, and Curaçao.

CULTURE: The ethnic heritage of the islands has enriched the cultural life of the Caribbean islands. Multinational influences are seen in architecture (places of worship, plantation great houses, villages, and huts), fine arts, and entertainment. Afro-Caribbean music, dancing, and island (especially Haitian) painting are the most widely known of fine-arts aspects of the islands, but there have also been literary efforts and other expressions of cultural interest displayed.

Music and Dancing

Calypso, reggae, the beat of voodoo drums in the faraway mountains—these terms spring to mind when the music of the Caribbean is mentioned. And rightly so, because these are the sounds of the islands which long ago drowned out the tinkling harpsichord notes drifting through the great houses of plantations. The gutsy, aggressive beat and soul of African music was brought in with the cargoes of slave ships, shaped and augmented by the misery and the joys of generations of blacks and mulattoes, fused with the melodies of Spain and certain structures and harmonies from other countries. The result was the music of the Caribbean.

The **calypso** music, which originated with the blacks in Trinidad, is such a mixture—basically African but with Afro-Spanish rhythms, English verses, and traces of French structure. The words to calypso tunes were originally (and sometimes still are) spontaneous improvisations, based on all sorts of subjects—love, sex, politics, whatever. Of more recent origin is **reggae,** which originated in Jamaica and is closely linked with the Rastafarian religious cult (whose messiah is Haile Selassie, the Promised Land being Ethiopia). Reggae, developing out of an old form of folk music in Jamaica, embraces elements of music from Africa most strongly, but also uses ideas from Europe and India, calypso, the rumba, and the limbo. Reggae verses tend to accentuate views on politics, religion, social change, and, unfortunately, anti-white (where white equals imperialism) feelings.

A basic source of Afro-Caribbean music is the percussion instrument, which is seen and heard in several forms, ranging from the tom-toms used in Haitian voodoo rites, African in shape and decoration, to conga, mambo, and the more modern steel drums that originated in Antigua but really came into popularity in Trinidad in the 1940s. Other instruments of African inspiration are marimbas and banjos, while from Spain comes the infusion of guitar and wind instruments. To the conventional brass, woodwinds, and strings, the blacks, mulattoes, and people of the Spanish peasant ancestry have added other sources of sound as they came to hand: gourds, pots and pans, bamboo sticks, garbage cans and lids, cowbells, saws, even the jawbones of asses and horses and the trunks of trees. The making of music on old oil drums has become an art in itself when done by the steel bands of the islands.

African dances, like the music, were mainly brought to the West Indies by slaves who had been born into the cultures of Dahomey and the Ashanti in what is now Ghana, along the Upper Guinea coast, and Nigerian Yoruba. Even today in Africa, especially in Ghana, the same kind of extempore verses are sung to the same rhythms as you'll hear in the calypso of the Caribbean. The **limbo** dance of the islands is a descendant of ancient tribal rites of Africa. Another dance form, seen mainly in Haiti, is the **merengue,** a dance ballad similar to calypso but usually more erotic in nature.

Spanish and Afro-Spanish influences are reflected in such dances as the **rumba, tango,** and **samba,** closely related to the Afro-French **calenda,** a dance whose movements were considered so suggestive by slave-owners in Martinique and Guadeloupe that they had it banned. Outlawing the calenda didn't entirely kill it, however, and it even played a part in development of the **béguine** in those islands.

The best way to see the music and dancing of the Caribbean is at **carnival** time. In islands with strong Roman Catholic ties this is similar to Mardi Gras in New Orleans, with several days and nights of celebration and parades. For some islands, carnival (*carnaval,* where French is the official language) lasts from Epiphany (January 6) to Ash Wednesday, with parades and dancing in the streets especially on each Sunday before Lent. On other islands, festivals, fiestas, and special days, many held in summer, take the place of carnival. For example, Barbados holds a Crop-Over Festival in June/July celebrating the end of the sugarcane harvest.

The carnivals and festivals are marked by flamboyant masqueraders parading and dancing to the pervasive island music, together with feasting on the foods common to the area. People of each island present folklore in song and dance at these events. If you can't be there for carnival, you may still have a chance to enjoy this bright facet of island life, as many hotels and nightclubs present abbreviated versions by folkloric groups as part of the entertainment program.

Art

Other Caribbean islands have followed the lead of Haiti in producing—and selling—the primitive art of the people. The best of this Haitian primitive (or naïve) painting, almost unknown before the 1940s, is highly stylized, done in bold colors and using or centered on Haitian subjects. You can see the work of the top artists, whose paintings command high prices, at galleries on a number of the islands, but you may be able to acquire a good and characteristic painting at a street show or even off the walls of some little café. Keep looking.

Woodcarvings are interesting art objects of the islands. They range from rough animal and human figures to fierce masks to smoothly finished statuary of mahogany and other native woods.

Literature

Much has been written about the West Indies since their conquest, but it was not until this century that what is known as "the literature of negritude" developed in Africa and the West Indies. Missionary priests wrote about various aspects of the Caribbean islands. History, poetry, drama, and a few novels were written by people born in Guadeloupe, Martinique, Puerto Rico, the Dominican Republic, and Haiti during the 17th, 18th, and 19th centuries. This early literary output, whether in English, French, or Spanish, had little originality of thought or form, and in some cases the writers even sought to distance themselves from their island roots by seeking recognition in the capitals of the colonial empire rather than on the home scene. The lack of literary progress among the nonwhite islanders was largely due to the lack of any education even after the abolition of slavery.

During the present century a literature has developed in the Caribbean (and in Africa) in which individuality of expression and originality of subject matter have come to the fore. Because of the African heredity it was natural for the new literature to be written using African expression patterns and to be based on African traditions. This literature of negritude has played an important role in strengthening the racial pride and independence of thought and feeling among the people of African ancestry. That the natural literature of the islands is in its nascency is attested by a statement by George Lamming, novelist from Barbados, in 1960: "The West Indian novel, by which I mean the novel written by the West Indian about the West Indian reality, is hardly 20 years old."

There were a few leaders in the field of the literature of negritude working before and after Lamming's 1940 watershed date. Among them are Jamaican Claude McKay, poet and first professional Caribbean novelist; Jacques Roumain, essayist, poet, and novelist of Haiti; St. Lucia–born Trinidad-dweller Derek Walcott, playwright and poet; John Hearne, Canada-born Jamaican novelist; and Roger Mais, Jamaican short-story writer, poet, and novelist.

Perhaps the spirit of the writers of the West Indies today was best voiced by Aimé Césaire, a poet born in 1913 in Martinique of poor peasants from Africa, one of the three founders of the negritude movement in Paris in 1937. He described his negritude by saying, "I want to rediscover the secret of great speech and of great burning . . . The man who couldn't understand me couldn't understand the roaring of a tiger." At a conference on "Negritude, Ethnicity, and Afro cultures in the Americas," held in 1988 at Florida International University at Miami, Césaire said, "Negritude, to my eyes, is not a philosophy, not metaphysics. It is the transfer of men from one continent to another, the debris of assassinated cultures." He continued that after centuries of "black diaspora," blacks must create a rehabilitation of their values themselves, re-rooting themselves "within a history, within a geography, within a culture."

FOOD AND DRINK: Throughout the Caribbean, hotel chefs prepare a presentable American and continental cuisine, dishes usually familiar to most visitors from Canada and the United States. However, in recent years hotels have placed a greater emphasis on local dishes, everything from curried goat stew to *lambi* (conch meat). Even so, it's still better to order a $15 meal at a local native restaurant than it is to have a $50 dinner in a so-called gourmet restaurant of some deluxe resort.

Many recipes in the West Indies date back to the days of the Arawak and Carib Indians, the original settlers. Since they weren't able to enjoy chateaubriand airlifted from Miami, they relied on what was available locally. Then came the conquerors from Europe and variations began to appear in the cuisine, not only French, but Dutch, English, Spanish, and of course African, the latter because of the slave trade. Even later influences would include Hindu, Chinese, and Indonesian dishes, such as a rijsttafel, or rice table, so popular in Aruba and Curaçao.

The abundance of fruit in the islands is naturally reflected in the cuisine, which you'll see first at breakfast, usually on a platter freshly sliced. Coconut, for example, is used in everything from breads to soups. Naturally, it's most popular as an ingredient in desserts, but can also appear in a main course, perhaps mixed with chicken. Soursop ice cream appears on some menus, and the guava might turn up in anything from juice to cheese. Papaya is called *paw paw,* and it will most often be your melon choice at breakfast. Native cooks also use it in many other ingenious ways, including preparing it as one would squash fritters. Mango is ubiquitous, used in chutney, but also in drinks and desserts. But it's never better than when fresh, ripe, and unadorned. The avocado, most often called "pears," is used in fresh seafood salads and often stuffed with fresh crabmeat.

By now most visitors know that plantain (which is similar to a banana but red in color) is not eaten raw. These are served most often as a cooked side dish, the way we might present french fries. Puerto Ricans eat dried plantains, called *tostones,* from cellophane bags in lieu of potato chips. Plantains can also be served mashed or boiled, and they turn up in many desserts, especially when mixed with coconut and pineapple.

Two staples of the Caribbean islands have always been rice and pigeon peas. Balls of cornmeal, called *fungi,* have also long been a staple of the West Indian diet. They often accompany a salt pork main dish known as *mauffay.* Sometimes these cornmeal concoctions will appear on the menus of native restaurants as *coo coo.* Roast suckling pig is nowhere better than in Puerto Rico and the Dominican Republic. Everything that appears unattractive and less desirable in the pig usually turns up in *souse,* most often the head, tail, and feet. Souse is usually served with black pudding.

One of the most common vegetables in the islands is *christophine* (sometimes called *foo foo*), a chayote which is green and prickly and tastes somewhat like zucchini. Breadfruit, introduced to the islands by Captain Bligh (of *Bounty* fame) is green and ball shaped. It is used by the West Indians much as we use potatoes. Often it's simply boiled and served with salt, pepper, and butter. When a chef gets fancy, he'll concoct something like a breadfruit soufflé or vichyssoise. Potatoes and yams are also local favorites. The leaf-like *callaloo* (regardless of how it's spelled) is one of the best-known vegetables in the West Indies. It's like spinach and is often served with crab, salt pork, and fresh fish with floating fungi as a garnish. You might call it the Caribbean version of bouillabaisse.

Throughout the islands, lobster is the king of the sea and the most sought-after—and most expensive—main course to order. Many readers might take pot luck and order the "catch of the day," which is most likely to be red snapper or grouper but could also be shark or barracuda.

In a truly native restaurant in the Caribbean, you'll see hot peppers placed on the table. Be sparing. A selection of these hot pepper pastes is called *sambal*.

As you travel from island to island, you'll find many variations on Créole cookery. For example, on Dominica and Montserrat, "mountain chicken"— sometimes known as *crapaud*—is a delicacy. It's not chicken at all, but large frog's legs. The national dish of the Dominican Republic is *sancocho,* which is a soupy stew made with seven different kinds of meat.

In Puerto Rico the cuisine even today reflects the former inhabitants, ranging from the peaceful Taíno Indians to the Spanish conquerors. The most popular dish is *sopa de frijoles negros,* or black bean soup. *Arroz con pollo,* or chicken with rice, long ago traveled north of the border. *Asopao* is a thick rice-based soup to which seafood has been added, and *mofongo* is a baseball-sized patty made with plantains, pork rind, and lots of garlic.

Martinique and Guadeloupe are said to have the best food in the Caribbean. Of course, Mother France is the main influence, and all the classic French dishes, such as duck in orange sauce and beef bourguignonne, are served on both islands. Native cooks have created their own unique recipes, however. The most popular dishes include *crabes farcis* (stuffed land crabs), *colombo de poulet* (a spicy chicken curry), and *acrats de morue* (salt codfish fritters).

In some areas, you may be offered iguana or turtle. It would be better to choose another dish. Both the iguana and the turtle are endangered species, and, even though many are still killed and eaten, the consumption of these large reptiles is frowned upon in more enlightened circles. Please do not contribute to the extinction of these increasingly rare animals.

Your best bet when traveling through the islands is to sample what Barbadians call a "cohoblopot," or a medley of "the best of it all."

Drink in the Islands

Since the late 16th century rum has been a legend, involved with slavery, Yankee traders, pirates, and bootlegging. A whole series of rum barons arose, with names that became famous around the world: Bacardí, González, Myers, and Barceló, to name only a few. "Kill-devil," as rum was once called, is of course the established drink of the islands.

Distilled in a not-very-complicated process from sugarcane, rum has played a major role in the history of the West Indies as the greatest naval powers of Europe struggled for supremacy. It can be argued that even slavery existed to service the flourishing sister industries of sugar, molasses, and rum. Today the rusted machinery and tumbledown ruins of distilleries (once an almost certain source of pleasure and prosperity) are considered tourist stopovers on dozens of Caribbean islands. Be sure to note the names of whatever foundry cast the original mechanisms. In the best traditions of the industrial revolution, many of the machines were imported from Glasgow.

The enormous crushing devices were powered, depending on the natural circumstances, by wind, water, or steam. The resulting mash was fermented in open vats and then distilled through long lengths of copper tubing. Conditions were far from sanitary, as everything from bat dung to spiders to crumbled leaves would routinely fall into the bubbling, foul-smelling mash.

Today the rum that adds zest to your piña colada will probably have been made in modern distilleries using methods vastly more sanitary than those adopted by the colonials of a century ago. Each island seems to turn out the type of rum which its inhabitants claim is their particular favorite. However, when masked with the layers of fruit, syrup, and sugar that usually are included in a rum-based drink, it's difficult to tell the difference. Planter's punch in its many variations is the most popular drink in the islands.

The average bar in the Caribbean is likely to offer a bewildering array of rum-based drinks. Available in all the hues of the spectrum, they might contain just about anything. However, should you be concerned with morning-after hang-overs, diabetic overdoses, or high caloric intake, you'd better stick to scotch or vodka.

About beer, don't think that the only brew you'll be able to find will be imported from Milwaukee or Holland. Of course, Heineken is ubiquitous, as is Amstel, especially in the Dutch islands. Many, many islands have their local favorites. Red Stripe from Jamaica is the most famous.

A word of caution: The innocent-looking pastel-colored drinks that taste so yummy and look so pretty can make neophytes lethally drunk on very short notice. Partly because of their elevated sugar content, and partly because of the heat of the Caribbean, be alert to your limits, especially if you're driving on unfamiliar roads.

You can always drink water. Water is generally safe throughout the islands, but many tourists get sick from drinking it. Sometimes that's simply because it's different from the water they're accustomed to. If available, it's better to order bottled water, which will be easier on your stomach.

HEALTH: Anyone planning a trip to the Caribbean should consult his or her doctor about any shots that may be required or advisable for maintaining good health during a journey. Injections or booster shots are wise against hepatitis, polio, typhus, tetanus, cholera, and yellow fever, and whatever precautions your doctor advises against malaria should be taken. It's always good to take with you an international vaccination certificate, which will be of assistance should you fall ill while traveling. You may be in the pink of health, but in certain Caribbean islands, a mosquito bite has the potential of giving you either dengue (or break-bone) fever, a painful though not life-threatening ailment; or yellow fever; or malaria. Many of the islands are free from these illnesses, but it's always best to be aware of the possibilities.

One of the most important health precautions you can take is to be sure that the water you use for drinking, washing, swimming in, or preparing food has come from an unimpeachably pure source or has been treated to kill any contamination. Intestinal parasitic infections, bilharzia, polio, hepatitis A, and other illnesses can be transmitted through contaminated water, either through direct contact or through eating fish and other seafood carrying the infection. Ice is no safer than the water used to make it. The sea is usually safe for swimming, but fresh surface water may carry the unseeable bearers of disease.

In the tropics, it is not wise to eat raw vegetables or cold foods in restaurants or at street vendors' stands.

If you have heart or other problems, ask your doctor about precautions you should take against hazards to your health that might be a result of high humidity and high altitudes you may meet in the tropics.

METRIC MEASURES: In the Caribbean, you will run into the metric system, so become familiar with the equivalents, or follow the formula instructions if you feel the need to convert.

Length
  1 millimeter = 0.04 inches (*or* less than 1/16 in)
  1 centimeter = 0.39 inches (*or* just under 1/2 in)

```
1 meter     = 1.09 yards (or about 39 inches)
1 kilometer = 0.62 mile (or about ⅔ mile)
```

To convert kilometers to miles, take the number of kilometers and multiply by .62 (for example, 25 km × .62 = 15.5 mi).

To convert miles to kilometers, take the number of miles and multiply by 1.61 (for example, 50 mi × 1.61 = 80.5 km).

Capacity
```
1 liter = 33.92 ounces
        = 1.06 quarts
        = 0.26 gallons
```

To convert liters to gallons, take the number of liters and multiply by .26 (for example, 50 l × .26 = 13 gallons).

To convert gallons to liters, take the number of gallons and multiply by 3.79 (for example, 10 gal × 3.79 = 37.9 l).

Weight
```
1 gram     = 0.04 ounces (or about a paperclip's weight)
1 kilogram = 2.2 pounds
```

To convert kilograms to pounds, take the number of kilos and multiply by 2.2 (for example, 75 kg × 2.2 = 165 pounds).

To convert pounds to kilograms, take the number of pounds and multiply by .45 (for example, 90 lb × .45 = 40.5 kg).

Area
```
1 hectare (100m²) = 2.47 acres
```

To convert hectares to acres, take the number of hectares and multiply by 2.47 (for example, 20 ha × 2.47 = 49.4 acres).

To convert acres to hectares, take the number of acres and multiply by .41 (for example, 40 acres × .41 = 16.4 hectare).

Temperature

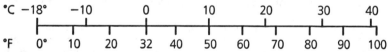

To convert degrees C to degrees F, multiply degrees C by 9, divide by 5, then add 32 (for example 9/5 × 20°C + 32 = 68°F).

To convert degrees F to degrees C, subtract 32 from degrees F, then multiply by 5, and divide by 9 (for example, 85°F − 32 × 5/9 = 29°C).

THE CAYMAN ISLANDS

□ □ □

Columbus first sighted the Cayman Islands in 1503, calling them *Las Tortugas,* or "the turtles." The name *Cayman* comes from an Indian name for a species of lizard. The first colonists consisted of a motley crew—buccaneers, beachcombers, bands of shipwrecked sailors. Rollicking Sir Henry Morgan once lived here, but in time Scottish fishermen arrived to forge a quiet, peaceful, God-fearing settlement that today is an oasis of tranquility at the western edge of the Caribbean.

Don't go to the Cayman Islands expecting the fast-paced excitement of some of the Caribbean islands to the south. The world of the Cayman Islands centers on the sea. Snorkelers find it a paradise, as do beach buffs who are attracted to the powdery sands of West Bay Beach, renamed Seven Mile Beach with the opening of the Holiday Inn.

The Cayman Islands, 480 miles due south of Miami, consist of three islands —the pretentiously named Grand Cayman, Cayman Brac, and Little Cayman. Despite its name, Grand Cayman is only 22 miles long and 8 miles across at its widest point. The other islands are considerably smaller, of course, containing very limited tourist facilities. In contrast, Grand Cayman has become well developed just in the past two decades or so.

These islands were once a dependency of Jamaica. But when that island opted for independence in 1962, the Cayman Islands preferred to remain a British Crown Colony, a land where there is no income tax.

Unlike the rest of the Caribbean, the population of the Cayman Islands is predominantly mixed. Essentially, the islanders are a self-reliant people who for years have enjoyed their unspoiled natural beauty in isolation, but at long last are inviting the world to come and share it with them.

Appointed by Queen Elizabeth II, a governor heads the local government, and English is the official language of the islands, although often spoken like an English slur mixed with the American southern drawl and finished off with a lilting Welsh accent.

George Town on Grand Cayman is the capital, the hub of government, banking, and shopping. Money rests here in more than 400 banks, free from the tax bite.

GETTING THERE: The Cayman Islands are easily accessible by air from the U.S. mainland. The national flag carrier, **Cayman Airways,** which celebrated its 20th anniversary in 1988, operates nonstop scheduled Boeing 727-200 jet service to Grand Cayman from Miami, Houston, Tampa, Atlanta, and Kingston (Jamaica). The most popular flight—Miami to Grand Cayman—takes off 16 times a week, and flying time from Miami is one hour and ten minutes. In addition, Cayman Airways is the only airline servicing the sister islands of Cayman Brac and Little Cayman. The airline offers passengers both first-class and economy seating on their jet service, and they also have their own frequent flyer program. For reservations, call Cayman Airways toll free at 800/422-9626.

During the winter season, special charter service offers more direct flights to the Caymans from such destinations as New York, Boston, Detroit, Chicago, Philadelphia, Baltimore, St. Louis, Atlanta, and Minneapolis.

Passengers arrive at Grand Cayman in a modern terminal building, Owen Roberts International Airport. Air conditioned, it has up-to-date facilities, duty-free shopping, and restaurants.

Wholly owned by the government of the Cayman Islands, Cayman Airways offers a one-day package to Cayman Brac. For only $78 per person, you get a 30-minute morning flight from Grand Cayman to Cayman Brac, a sightseeing tour, lunch, and then a free afternoon before the 4:15 return to Grand Cayman. In addition, Cayman Airways operates a "Shorts" service not only to Cayman Brac but also to Little Cayman, for those seeking an offbeat holiday. The Shorts SD 3-30 is a commuter aircraft operating between Grand Cayman and its "little sisters," daily to Cayman Brac and four times a week to Little Cayman.

Most visitors flying to the Caymans use Miami as their gateway. The routes from airports in the Snow Belt into Miami are some of the most hotly contested in the country. However, I have found that the airline that most efficiently services Miami from dozens of key northern cities is **American Airlines.** From the New York area alone, many flights leave from the area's three major airports, as well as from Long Island's Islip airport every day. American charges competitive prices and operates one of the most modern facilities at Miami International Airport.

Another well-respected contender for the air routes into the Caymans, in addition to Cayman Airways, is **Northwest Airlines,** which makes between five and seven flights into Grand Cayman per week. These flights originate in Memphis, Tennessee, and pick up passengers in Miami. Finally, **Eastern Airlines** also makes daily flights from Miami into Grand Cayman.

Prices for any of these carriers change often, sometimes daily, especially with the season. Call around or use an experienced and reliable travel agent to get the best fare.

GETTING AROUND: All arriving flights are met by **taxis,** and the rates are fixed by the director of civil aviation (tel. 809/947-4491). A typical one-way fare

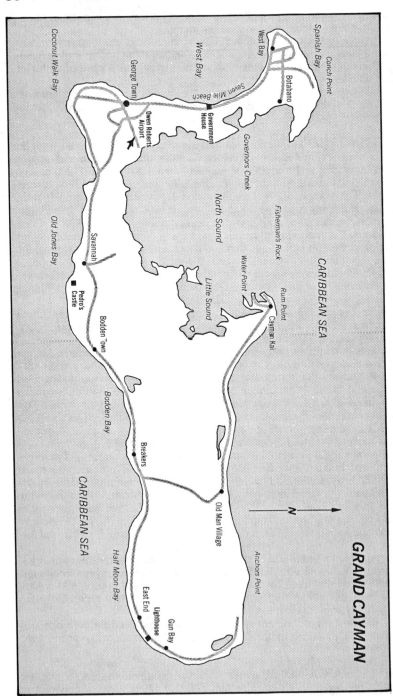

GRAND CAYMAN

from the airport to George Town is $6.25. However, to the Holiday Inn on Seven Mile Beach, the fare is $10. If you've booked a room at Rum Point on the North Shore, the fare is about $35. Taxis also transport visitors on around-the-island tours. Five people can ride in the same cab.

Between George Town and West Bay, there is **bus** service approximately hourly. Many visitors use the much cheaper buses when shopping or dining in George Town, where you can catch buses at Panton Avenue, near the By-Rite Super Market.

Several **car-rental companies** operate on the island, where the competition is keen. These include such familiar U.S.-based contenders as **Avis, Hertz, National,** and **Budget.** Each will issue the mandatory Cayman Island driving permit, priced at $3 U.S. Each requires between 24 and 36 hours' advance reservation to qualify for the most economical rates. In high season cars begin at around $26 per day, coming to slightly less if you rent a vehicle on unlimited mileage for a full week. If possible, ask for a car with air conditioning. For more information or reservations, call each of the companies at their toll-free U.S. numbers: Avis at 800/331-2112 (locally it's 809/949-2468); Hertz at 800/654-3001 (locally, 809/949-7861); National at 800/328-4567 (locally, 809/949-4790); and Budget, which tends to offer slightly cheaper rates, at 800/527-0700 (locally, 809/949-4808). If you're interested in a local contender, try **Coconut Car Rentals** (tel. 809/949-4037).

Remember to *drive on the left* and to reserve your car as early as possible, especially in midwinter. You can return your car to the airport when you leave the island, but because of the local taxi drivers' union, you can't pick it up at the airport. Rather, take a taxi to your hotel and phone for your car.

Another increasingly popular means of transport is a Honda, rented from **Caribbean Motors,** opposite Burger King (tel. 809/949-8878) and opposite Holiday Inn (tel. 809/947-4466), for C.I. $16 ($20) to C.I. $25 ($31.25) per day. These motorcycles can carry two persons. The same outfit also rents mopeds from C.I. $11 ($13.75) per day.

PRACTICAL FACTS: To make your visit to the Caymans more enjoyable, I have gathered a few items of information which you may find helpful. The best time to go is from mid-November to March, as violent rains often lash these islands in summer. Mosquitoes, once the scourge of the islands, are now kept under control through a government program.

Banks: That most important part of Cayman Island life, the bank (or banks) is open from 9 a.m. to 2:30 p.m. Monday to Thursday and from 9 a.m. to 1 p.m. and 2:30 to 4:30 on Friday.

Currency: The legal tender is the Cayman Islands dollar, its value based on the U.S. dollar. At prevailing exchange rates, one Cayman dollar equals about $1.25 in U.S. currency. Or one U.S. dollar brings about C.I. 84¢. Canadian, U.S., and British currencies are readily acceptable throughout the Cayman Islands. Most hotels quote rates in U.S. dollars. However, many restaurants quote prices in Cayman Islands dollars, leading you to think that food is much cheaper. Unless otherwise noted, quotations in this chapter are in U.S. dollars. The cost of living is about 20% higher than in the U.S.

Documents: No passports are required for U.S. or Canadian citizens. However, proof of citizenship is (voter registration card, birth certificate). Your return ticket is also required.

Drugs: The Cayman Islands have very severe laws on the use of marijuana and other drugs. Large fines and prison terms are given out to offenders.

Electricity: It is 110 volts, 60 cycles—therefore American appliances will need no adapters.

Post Office: In Grand Cayman at George Town, the post office is open from 8:30 a.m. to 3:30 p.m. Monday to Friday and 8:30 to 11:30 a.m. on Saturday. It also has a Philatelic Bureau.

Taxes: A government tourist tax of 6% is added to your hotel bill. Also, a departure tax of $7.50 (U.S.) is collected when you leave the island.

Telegraph and Telex: The Cable and Wireless, Anderson Square, George Town (tel. 809/949-7800), handling these is open from 8 a.m. to 5 p.m. Monday to Friday, to 1 p.m. Saturday, and to 11 a.m. Sunday.

Telephone: A modern automatic telephone system links the islands to the world via a submarine coaxial cable. Automatic-switching links in Jamaica enable the Cayman operators to dial numbers worldwide as a 24-hour service. International direct dialing was introduced in 1984. When calling the Caymans from the North American mainland, dial area code 809, then a seven-digit number. In the islands, dial only the last *five* digits of the numbers given in this chapter.

Time: Eastern Standard Time is in effect all year. Daylight Saving Time is not observed. Therefore, when Miami is on Daylight Saving Time and it's noon there, it's still 11 a.m. in the nearby Cayman Islands.

Tipping: Many restaurants add a 10% to 15% charge in lieu of tipping.

1. WHERE TO STAY

The true dollarwise hotel shopper will rent an apartment or condominium (most often shared with friends or families), as in my opinion these units offer the best value. As they're furnished with kitchenettes, you can cut costs considerably by cooking your own breakfast, perhaps preparing a light lunch, then dining out for only one main meal of the day. Divers are often attracted to hotels or small resorts that include a half day's dive in their tariffs. I'll lead off with the most expensive choices—and the best properties—along Seven Mile Beach, then follow with the moderate range and what few bargains there are. After that, I'll preview a selection of the best values in condominium living on Grand Cayman.

HOTELS AND RESORTS: If you're willing to pay the price, Grand Cayman has some of the finest resort living in the Caribbean, as reflected by the recommendations outlined below.

The Upper Bracket

Hyatt Regency Grand Cayman (Britannia Beach Hotel), Seven Mile Beach, Grand Cayman, B.W.I. (tel. 809/949-1234). By anyone's standards, this is the best managed, most stylish, and sophisticated hotel in the Cayman Islands. The hotel, opened in 1987, is a major component in the 90-acre Britannia Resort community, including the Britannia Golf Course. Two acres of the frontage opens onto Seven Mile Beach. In the hotel's design, the best elements of neoclassicism were combined with burgeoning gardens, modern art, and an adaptation of British colonial airiness. Perhaps the most memorable features are the dozens of Doric arcades with pinnacles festooned with flowering vines whose tendrils cascade beneath reflecting pools and comfortable teakwood settees. The hotel incorporates into its elegant grounds the most complete array of water sports in the Caymans (more about this later; also see the notes on golf coming up). Low-rise buildings surround a large landscaped courtyard that contains gardens, waterfalls, and a one-third-acre swimming pool with a whirlpool and swim-up bar.

The Hyatt offers 236 world-class luxury rooms. All accommodations have ceiling fans and air-conditioning, TV, fully stocked servi-bar, and a private veranda. Two buildings and 43 rooms are devoted to the posh Regency Club, with concierge service. Two people in the Regency Club in winter pay $350 a night, *the price lowered to $250 the rest of the year.* Other singles or doubles cost from

$200 to $275 a night in winter, *$130 to $175 in summer.* The hotel also offers one-, two-, and three-bedroom luxury villas along the Britannia golf course or waterway. They have fully equipped kitchens, central air conditioning, ceiling fans, TV, phone, and easy access to the resort's many facilities. Guests in the villas have access to their own private pool, whirlpool, cabaña, and patio area. The villas offer golf course or waterfront views. A one-bedroom villa for two persons costs $300 in winter, *dropping to $200 in spring, summer, or fall.*

For dining, the resort offers several choices, including the Garden Loggia Café, serving breakfast, lunch, and dinner (a buffet champagne brunch on Sunday is a special feature). Its seafood specialty restaurant, Hemingway's, is recommended separately, and you can also patronize the Britannia Golf Club and Grille a few steps away from the first tee, offering lunch daily.

Grand Pavilion Hotel and Transnational Conference Centre, P.O. Box 69, West Bay Rd., Grand Cayman, B.W.I. (tel. 809/947-4666). Just before the completion of one of Grand Cayman's most prestigious office complexes, its developers, Transnational Enterprises, decided to devote about half of the floor space to a luxury hotel. In what almost became a series of private offices are lushly upholstered interiors which duplicate some of the most prestigious hotels of France and England. Near the lobby lies the entrance to a quality restaurant, le Diplomat. Within the glass-covered interior is a splashing Tahiti-style fountain cluster, a small swimming pool, palm and date trees, a thatch-covered bar (where employees of the adjoining companies often enjoy the mid-afternoon music and happy hour), and a sprawling garden restaurant. Each of the well-decorated, air-conditioned bedrooms contains Louis XV–style furniture in bleached or pickled oak, thick carpeting, French fabrics, cable TV, and air conditioning. Furnishings for each unit cost $10,000. Depending on the accommodation, winter prices for singles are $165 to $190, and doubles cost $175 to $205. *Summer prices for two people are $110 to $130, $95 to $115 for singles.* A continental breakfast is included.

Treasure Island Resort, West Bay Rd., P.O. Box 1817, Grand Cayman, B.W.I. (tel. 809/949-7777), is the hotel that country music built. A minority interest in this beachfront property belongs to a consortium of Nashville-based country music stars, including luminaries such as Conway Twitty. The musical acts presented at the hotel's night club are the most outstanding on the island (more about this later). Opened in 1987, it is the largest hotel on the island, including no less than four lagoon-inspired water cascades, a labyrinth of passages leading to the efficiently decorated bedrooms, and a stylish restaurant on the second floor flooded with sunlight from large expanses of glass. On the beach is a water sports kiosk plus a thatch-roof Polynesian-style bar. Because each of the accommodations was originally designed as a time-share unit, each has a wet bar, refrigerator, and (in some of them) a large amount of floor space. Each accommodation also offers a wood-railed balcony, but only a few open onto sea views. Ceiling fans and air conditioning keep things cool. In high season, singles or doubles range from $159 to $249, depending on the accommodation. *In summer, single or double occupancy costs from $120 to $155 daily.* For reservations and information, call toll free 800/251-3052.

Caribbean Club, P.O. Box 504, West Bay Beach, Grand Cayman, B.W.I. (tel. 809/947-4099), is an exclusive compound of 18 luxuriously furnished one- and two-bedroom villas, each with a full-size living room, dining area, patio, and kitchen. When the owners are away these villas are rented to guests who prefer the style, taste, and discrimination of a self-contained retreat. The club is actually a cluster of pink villas, either on or just off the beach. Oceanfront villas are always more expensive, of course. In winter, a one-bedroom villa ranges from $210 as a single to $280 as a double. *In summer, a one-bedroom villa costs $150* *single, $200 double.* All tariffs are on the EP. The winter season requires casually elegant wear in the evening, either in the Green Turtle Lounge or in the dining room. At the core of the colony is the club center, rising two stories with tall, graceful arches and picture windows. On the grounds is an abundance of foliage —many palm trees and flowering shrubbery—and there's a professional tennis court as well.

West Indian Club, P.O. Box 703, West Bay Beach, Grand Cayman, B.W.I. (tel. 809/949-2494), true to its name, is like a small private club, right on the white sands. It offers some of the poshest comfort on the entire island, with nine individually decorated one- and two-bedroom housekeeping apartments. Each apartment, furnished in a tropical decor, has a large living room with patio or balcony overlooking the beach. Best of all, a full-time maid comes with each apartment. She will not only cook, clean, and do your laundry, but she can prepare local foods and is also trained in the standard American cuisine. Her hours are 8:30 a.m. to 3:30 p.m. (never on Sunday). The West Indian Club, an imitation Tara, is reached by an entrance drive lined with palms. Rates in winter are $230 per day for two people in a one-bedroom unit and $300 per day for four in a two-bedroom apartment. *In summer, these tariffs drop to $170 and $215 per day.* There is also an efficiency unit available for two people, costing $140 in winter, *$120 in summer.* An extra person is charged $25 per day. Bedrooms are air-conditioned, and all have ceiling fans and phones. Local calls are free. Children of guests must be age 8 or older, and a stay of at least a week in winter and three days in summer is requested.

Holiday Inn Grand Cayman, P.O. Box 904, Seven Mile Beach, Grand Cayman, B.W.I. (tel. 809/947-4444), is an all-purpose, all-inclusive resort three miles from George Town and five miles from the airport. The location is along a prominent stretch of Seven Mile Beach. This is a modern, 215-room beachfront hotel. Bedrooms have a bright, tropical flair, with floral prints. Most of them have sitting areas, and all have baths with dressing rooms, plus air conditioning. Each unit has a southern-style balcony whose white balustrades overlook a garden courtyard planted with palms and shrubs. Ocean-view and oceanfront rooms are more expensive, of course, than island-view units. Depending on the accommodation, in winter, one or two persons pay $148 to $238 per day. *In summer, tariffs are reduced to $118 to $188 for one or two people.*

Chez Jacques is one of the island's best restaurants. There is a theatrically designed swimming pool, lagoon-like with arched bridges and surrounding areas for sunbathing and entertainment. You can order tall rum punches beside the pool. Bars include the Corsair's Wharf, poolside, and the Wreck of the Ten Sails, for evening entertainment with a live band. At the Corsair's Wharf the bar is set into the shell of a wooden boat and sheltered from the sun with a high roof from which swing symbolic hangman's nooses from a re-created ship's yardarm. There is a fully equipped dive shop on the premises, and sailboats, waterskiing, and deep-sea fishing are available. Tennis is played on the inn's four courts (lit at night).

Moderate to Budget

The Beach Club, West Bay Rd., P.O. Box 903, Grand Cayman, B.W.I. (tel. 809/949-2023), is set across the road from its more glamorous (and more expensive) neighbor, the Hyatt Britannia Beach Hotel. The Beach Club is one of the oldest and best-located hotels on the island. Built in the early 1960s along Seven Mile Beach, it established a scuba-diving center and has since attracted a loyal clientele. Designed like an enlarged version of a colonial pink-walled plantation villa, it has a formal Doric portico, lots of lattices, and a popular bar separating the hotel from the beach. There, calypso music and rum flow freely for a clientele who seem to be dressed in bathing suits throughout most of the day. The divers who opt for week-long scuba packages usually take one of the tile-floored villas clustered amid trees at the edge of the beach. Otherwise, most accommodations are within simple but comfortable bedrooms in the main hotel. Each unit comes with air conditioning, private bath, phone, and a veranda with a range of furniture including everything from Caribbean rattan to reproductions of English Sheraton. In winter, singles or doubles rent for $135 to $215 daily. *Prices are lowered in summer to $85 to $130 daily, either single or double.*

Cayman Diving Lodge, P.O. Box 11, East End, Grand Cayman, B.W.I. (tel. 809/947-7555), 20 miles from George Town and 19 miles from the airport, is primarily for divers. The lodge is a two-story half-timbered building set against a backdrop of tropical trees on a private beachfront. Ocean-view rooms are modern, pleasant, simple, and air-conditioned. In the southeast corner of the island, the lodge is on a coral sand beach with a live coral barrier reef just offshore. Meals are prepared by Caymanian chefs who serve abundant portions. The accent is on fish. In summer or winter the single rate is $124 daily, rising to $198 in a double. This tariff includes not only a room but also one two-tank dive daily, unlimited shore diving, and one night dive on seven-day packages. Diving on the day of arrival and departure is not included. Nondivers deduct $30 per person nightly.

Caribe Inn, P.O. Box 1410, North Side, Grand Cayman, B.W.I. (tel. 409/947-9636), is an isolated 11-room resort about 11 miles from the airport and some 25½ miles from George Town on the relatively undeveloped north shore. Each accommodation is air-conditioned, with big sun-flooded windows and home-like bedrooms filled with cozy touches. With breakfast included, winter prices are $119 to $128 daily in a single, $129 to $138 in a double. *In summer, singles cost $89 to $98 daily, and doubles rent for $99 to $108, depending on the exposure.* An outstanding feature of the place is the ground-floor bar and restaurant, offering such island specialties as cracked conch, ham with pineapple, turtle steak, and house-style lobster. During the day, drinks are served on a terrace close to the surf.

Spanish Cove, P.O. Box 637, Spanish Bay, Grand Cayman, B.W.I. (tel. 809/949-3765), is a resort for divers on a remote, rugged beach on the northern tip of the island, which offers good scuba-diving. A dining room and bar is constructed out of coral rock and natural wood. There are 46 rooms, pleasantly designed with ceramic tile floors and rough wood trim. The restaurant is outstanding on the island. The food is well-prepared, with luncheon served buffet style. The dining room is at beach level with a large outdoor patio and barbecue. The bar and lounge are on the second floor overlooking the water. There is a pool on the premises. All rooms have two queen-size beds, air conditioning, and ceiling fans. Four rooms are suitable for families or small groups. The double rate is $140 in winter, *$105 in summer.* Spanish Cove is a full-service dive resort and that means a NAUI/PADI training facility. Facilities include a sheltered three-boat slipway, two outstanding dive boats, and the latest in rental equipment. To make reservations in the U.S., call toll free 800/458-8690.

Condo Living

Tamarind Bay, P.O. Box 952, Grand Cayman, B.W.I. (tel. 809/949-8098), built in 1980 is one of the most luxurious and pleasant condominium complexes on the island. It occupies a stretch of Seven Mile Beach about 1½ miles west of George Town on West Bay Road. It was designed a bit like an interconnected series of modernized Tuscan villas, with zigzagging paths linking the curved walls of the swimming pool with privacy barriers of crotons, ferns, boxwood, miniature date palms, bougainvillea, and mahogany trees. A pair of feathery casuarinas shade the frond-covered beachside gazebos and surfside hammocks from the sun. Accommodations in the privately owned villas are beautifully furnished, flooded with sunlight, and impeccably maintained. Each contains two bedrooms, two baths, central air conditioning, ceiling fans, cable TV, and a private screened-in patio overlooking the sea, along with a fully equipped kitchen and maid service. For single or double occupancy, units rent for $255 to $295 daily in winter, *$165 to $215 in summer.*

The Colonial Club, P.O. Box 320W, Seven Mile Beach, Grand Cayman, B.W.I. (tel. 809/947-4600), although smaller than the properties flanking it on three sides, occupies a highly desirable stretch of the famous beach. Built in 1985, it is a three-story condominium about five minutes from George Town and some ten minutes from the airport. First-class maintenance, service, and accommodations are provided in the centrally air-conditioned apartments, all with kitchen fans, TV, maid service, and laundry facilities. Usually only 10 of the 24 apartments are available for rent, the rest being privately owned and occupied. You have a choice of units with two bedrooms and three baths or units with three bedrooms and three baths. In winter, prices are from $300 to $340 daily for two people, $340 to $380 for three to four guests, and $380 to $420 for five to a maximum of six occupants. The most expensive rates are for waterfront apartments. *In summer, charges are $160 to $200 daily for two people, $200 to $240 for three to four occupants, and $240 to $280 for five to six guests.* Facilities include tennis courts (lit at night), a heated Jacuzzi, and a freshwater pool. Incidentally, master bedrooms in most apartments are equipped with Jacuzzi spas.

Pan-Cayman House, P.O. Box 440, Seven Mile Beach, Grand Cayman, B.W.I. (tel. 809/947-4002). The Georgian-style beachfront façade of this popular choice was attractively altered to suit its Caribbean setting. There are only ten apartments, but each has its own fully equipped kitchen, air conditioning, a private balcony or patio with an unrestricted view of the sea, and comfortable summer-type furniture. Hotel-type maid service is provided as part of the rental of these two- and three-bedroom apartments. Rates vary with the season and according to the number of people staying in an accommodation. In high season, two-bedroom apartments rent for $175 to $225 daily, while a three-bedroom unit, holding up to six people, costs $285. *In summer, two-bedroom apartments rent for $115 to $135 daily, while three-bedroom accommodations go for $185.* This place tends to be so popular that it's sometimes fully booked long in advance of the winter season.

Villas Pappagallo, P.O. Box 952, Barkers, Grand Cayman, B.W.I. (tel. 809/949-3568, or toll free 800/232-1034 in the continental U.S.). Its Mediterranean-style red tile roofs and white stucco walls are arranged symmetrically around formally landscaped semitropical gardens. One end opens onto a stretch of white sandy beach while the other is exposed to an isolated road about ten miles west of George Town. Nestled between groves of palms and bougainvillea, is a two-tiered swimming pool. On the grounds is a tennis court. Built in 1980, the establishment contains 45 one- or two-bedroom privately owned units, about 15 of which are usually available for rentals. *One-bedroom units for two people cost $165 in summer, and two-bedroom apartments, suitable for up to four people, go for $195 off-season.* In winter, a one-bedroom unit for two costs $205, and a two-bedroom apartment for up to four guests, $255 a day. An extra guest costs another $20.

Villas of the Galleon, P.O. Box 1797, Grand Cayman, B.W.I. (tel. 809/949-6485), is a cluster of stucco villas on a well-landscaped property at the heart of Seven Mile Beach between the main highway from George Town (three miles away) and the water. There are 75 air-conditioned one-, two-, and three-bedroom apartments, each well furnished and equipped with a kitchen, private bath, and wood-railed balcony. In winter, depending on the accommodation, two people are charged $205 to $225 daily. Two-bedroom apartments suitable for up to four people cost $255 to $295, and three-bedroom units, housing up to five guests, rent for $315 to $355. *In summer, tariffs are lowered to $165 to $185 daily for two, $195 to $215 for four, and $230 to $250 for up to five occupants.* Watersports are available through the dive shop next door.

Victoria House, P.O. Box 236, West Bay Beach, Grand Cayman, B.W.I. (tel. 809/947-4233), is an apartment complex standing at the north end of the beach. It's an expanded and modernized version of the colonial plantation style of architecture, with a U-shaped garden encompassing palmettos and palms. The management is among the most helpful on the island. Twenty-five studio, and one- and two-bedroom apartments are rented, each with an open, airy feeling, furnished tastefully, generally in white bamboo with colorful fabrics. Kitchens are not only equipped with dishes and cutlery, but have a stylish appearance, and the dining area is in the living room. In high season, December 1 to April 30, two persons pay $125 to $155 daily in either a studio or one-bedroom apartment; and four persons are charged from $195 to $215 in a two-bedroom unit. *Off-season, for these same units, two people are charged $95 to $120; four people, $145 to $160.* Daily maid service is included, but not tax and service. Between swims, hammocks are strung up between the trees for naps, and a professional tennis court is on the premises.

Silver Sands, P.O. Box 952, Seven Mile Beach, Grand Cayman, B.W.I. (tel. 809/949-3343), is a modern, eight-building complex arranged horseshoe fashion directly on the beach. The air-conditioned apartments are grouped around a rectangular freshwater pool. The eight apartment blocks contain either two-bedroom and two-bath, or three-bedroom and three-bath units. Each apartment has a private sea-view balcony, kitchens are fully equipped, and hotel-type maid service is offered. The resident manager will point out the twin tennis courts and two utility rooms with washer-dryers. In winter, a two-bedroom unit accommodating up to four people rents for $255 daily, a three-bedroom apartment for up to five people costing $315. *Summer rates are $195 daily for the two-bedroom accommodation, $230 for a three-bedroom unit.*

Harbour Heights, P.O. Box 688, West Bay Beach, Grand Cayman, B.W.I. (tel. 809/947-4295), is a beachfront condominium where you can stay in style and comfort by the day, week, or month. You're "on your own" for meals, but there's a good-size recreation area and a large free-form swimming pool with a surrounding tile terrace (filled with white lounge furniture). Apartments are of generous size, each having a living room and dinette, an attractive and complete kitchen, two bedrooms, two baths, and ample closet space. Each apartment has its own balcony or patio; furnishings are all in white tropical designs with decorative fabrics and accent rugs. Daily maid service is included. It's six miles to George Town for shopping or restaurants. In the high season, a two-bedroom and two-bath apartment rents for $225 for one to four persons, with each additional person charged $15 daily. A minimum stay of five days is required year round. *In the off-season, mid-April to mid-December, that same apartment costs $140 for one to four persons.*

2. EATING OUT

American and continental dishes predominate, although there is also a cuisine known as Caymanian, featuring specialties made from turtle (*Note:* environmental groups consider this species to be endangered). Fresh fish is the star, and conch is used in many ways. Native lobster is in season from late summer through January. While most visitors dine at their hotels, many of my recommendations are apartments or villas, which do not always serve meals, allowing you to sample some of the island's many restaurants. Since most dining places have to rely on imported ingredients, prices tend to be high.

THE UPPER BRACKET: A beautiful white mansion, **Chef Tell's Grand Old House,** Petra Plantation, South Church St. (tel. 809/949-2266), is a former plantation house built at the turn of the century by a Bostonian coconut merchant. It lies amid venerable trees about five minute's drive south of George Town. Built on bedrock near the edge of the sea, it stands on 129 ironwood posts supporting the main house and a bevy of gazebo satellites. Converted into a restaurant in 1969, it was purchased in 1986 by the German-born chef, Tell Erhardt, as a showcase for culinary specialties which have been widely publicized throughout Europe and the United States. The Grand Old House is the island's premier caterer, hosting everything from lavish weddings and political functions, to informal family celebrations. The restaurant's oceanfront gazebos are a favored location for glamorous island weddings. Chef Tell specializes in conch fritters, Swedish gravlax, and lobster Chef Brian's way, to name a few. Expect to spend around $40 for dinner including beverage. The dining room is open daily from 6 to 9:15 p.m., and reservations are recommended. Smart casual dress is advised. In winter, lunch is served also, from noon to 2:30 p.m. daily.

Ristorante Pappagallo, West Bay Rd. (tel. 809/949-1119), is one of the most whimsically amusing and memorable restaurants on the island, on the western edge of the island, eight miles from George Town, at the end of a series of winding roads that traverse many of the island's residential neighborhoods. Its designers incorporated both Caymanian and Aztec weaving techniques in its thatched roof, whose soaring heights top leaded-glass doors, black marble, polished brass, mixing a kind of Edwardian opulence into an otherwise Tahitian decor. As you dine, a fountain shoots water skyward from the saltwater pond outside. Owners Cosimo Pisano, chef, and Lodovico Testori, maître d', serve dinner from 6:30 p.m. till midnight every day except Monday in summer. For around C.I. $25 ($31.25) and up, they offer an array of northern Italian dishes which include such specialties as shrimp bisque with cognac, fettuccine in cream sauce with mushrooms and parmesan cheese, carpaccio, and Italian-style veal and chicken dishes. Don't overlook this place as a location for a nightcap, where you'll select from a wide choice of fruited drinks.

Caribbean Club, West Bay Rd. (tel. 809/947-4099), in the middle of Seven Mile Beach, already recommended for its accommodations, is one of the best places for dining on Grand Cayman. Popular for all three meals a day, it offers such hot dishes for breakfast, served from 7 to 10:30 a.m., as thick French toast. For lunch, from noon to 2:30 p.m., you can enjoy Cayman conch fritters and turtle cutlets. (*Note:* this is one of the few places left in the world where turtle meat can be found, due to the fact that the species has been decimated. Even here sea turtles are not exactly abundant.) The Governors Dining Room, totally renovated in 1987, serves evening meals from 6 to 10 p.m. amid elegant decor and candlelight. Specialties include everything from fettuccine to grilled seafood. Try, if featured, dishes such as fish mousse, "lobster sausage," or a red snapper done just right. Gratinated bananas, a slice of one of the chef's freshly baked pies, or chocolate pâté makes a tasty dessert. You can choose that special wine from the club's international wine cellar to accompany your meal. Reservations are requested for dinner. Expect to pay around $4.50 for breakfast, $12 for lunch, and $35 and up for dinner.

Hemingway's, Hyatt Regency Grand Cayman (tel. 809/949-1234), opening directly onto Seven Mile Beach, is a seafood specialty restaurant, considered the finest on the island. It is not only named after the novelist, but is inspired by Key West, former residence of "Papa," in both its decor and cuisine. For example, you might begin with a Key West salad, then follow with scallops Key Largo (named for the old Bogie and Bacall movie). The "treasure" of Hemingway's is fresh fish based on the catch of the day, which might include snapper, swordfish, or tuna, among others, charbroiled or "blackened." Caribbean spiny lobster is regularly featured, and the chef also does a superb Spanish paella. Hours are daily from 11:30 a.m. to 2:30 p.m. and 7 to 10 p.m. Meals are priced from C.I. $25 ($31.25).

Periwinkle Restaurant, West Bay Rd. (tel. 809/949-2927), named after the flowers that flank its concrete foundations, is a pleasantly unpretentious bungalow offering some of the best Italian/Caribbean cuisine in town. You'll find it about three miles from the center of George Town, beside the road that parallels Seven Mile Beach. The establishment offers an al fresco terrace, a cedar-lined bar with some of the best piña coladas on the island, and a pleasantly sun-flooded dining room where full dinners cost around $30. Main dishes are likely to include grilled dolphin in basil butter, baked swordfish New Orleans, and the catch of the day meunière. Dinners, which usually require a reservation, are served daily from 6 to 10 p.m. Lunches, served Monday to Friday only between noon and 2:30 p.m., cost around $15.

Lobster Pot, North Church St. (tel. 809/949-2736), is one of the island's best-known restaurants, overlooking the water from its second-floor perch right outside George Town. True to its name, it offers lobster prepared in many different ways: Cayman style, bisque, salad, or a lobster potpourri with conch, tuna, and shrimp also included. Conch schnitzel and seafood curry are on the menu, together with the increasingly rare turtle steak (rare because the species is endangered). The place is also known for its prime steaks. For lunch, served from 11 a.m. to 2:30 p.m., you might like the English fish and chips or perhaps a seafood basket of fried oysters and shrimp. The midday meal costs around $15. Dinner is served from 5:30 to 10 p.m. in the restaurant, a complete repast costing $25 and up. A pleasant place for a drink is the Lobster Pot's pub, with its oak booths. You may find someone to challenge to a game of darts while you enjoy an English ale. The restaurant lies at the western perimeter of George Town.

MODERATE-TO-BUDGET DINING: On a stony plot of land at the edge of the sea, **Captain Bryan's,** North Church St. (tel. 809/949-6163), a short distance from the heart of George Town, isn't the most glamorous restaurant on the island, yet many visitors quickly adopt it as their preferred hideaway for a candlelit meal. You might enjoy a before-dinner drink or two at the spacious bar where the walls are sheathed with pine planks and fish nets. Afterward, on the outdoor patio or in the air-conditioned, nautically decorated interior, you can select a dimly illuminated table. Full meals cost from C.I. $22 ($27.50). They could include fried plantains, seafood chowder, coconut-flavored grouper, and such "land fare" as curried chicken or grilled steak. Dessert might be a slice of coconut pie or a heady brew of West Indian liqueur with Blue Mountain coffee. Because of its popularity, reservations are suggested. It's open daily for lunch from noon to 2:30 p.m. and for dinner from 5:30 to 10:30 p.m.

The Cracked Conch, Selkirk Plaza, West Bay Rd. (tel. 809/949-5717), invites you to eat as "Caymanians eat." After that, the menu lists what they mean: conch in every known way, ranging from conch burgers to conch fritters, from cream-style conch chowder to Manhattan conch chowder, not to mention marinated conch and cracked conch, as well as conch stewed in coconut milk. If any of that is too exotic for you, order vichyssoise, followed by lobster tails or the fish of the day. The place is open daily from 11:30 a.m. to 4:30 p.m. and 6 to 10:30 p.m. You'll spend $10 to $25 for a meal. Closed Sunday. The location is about a five-minute drive from George Town. The restaurant, staffed by Caymanians, is a family operation.

Tony Roma's, West Bay Rd. (tel. 809/949-8669), the "ribs place," has successfully invaded the Caymans. Near many of the grand island properties, such as the Hyatt, the dining room turns out the famous rib selections, perhaps original baby back ribs, St. Louis–style ribs, or beef ribs. You can also order barbecue, not only ribs but also chicken and shrimp. Added touches are a children's menu, soups, salads, and appetizers such as potato skins. Weekday specials are likely to include stewed conch. Food is served from 11:30 a.m. to 11 p.m. Monday to Thursday, from 11:30 a.m. to midnight Friday, Saturday, and Sunday.

The Cook Rum, North Church St. (tel. 809/949-8670), is one of the best of the local restaurants, serving an authentic Caymanian cuisine. They guarantee that if you taste it, you'll like it. In an old Cayman home across from the Lobster Pot on the western outskirts of George Town, meals are served from 11:30 a.m. to 2:30 p.m. and 6:30 to 10 p.m. Monday to Saturday. They almost always have turtle steak along with such daily specials as red snapper in a Créole sauce. You could begin with a soup of the day, perhaps red bean. You're given a bill of around $25 for dinner.

FAVORITE LOCAL HANGOUTS: An unpretentious restaurant, **Morgan's Harbour,** Batabano, West Bay (tel. 809/949-3948), offers dinner from 5:30 to 10 p.m. every day except Tuesday and during September. The distantly related partners, Eugene and Leonard Ebanks, serve a full array of island specialties, with full meals costing from C.I. $12 ($15). Menu items, always prepared from fresh ingredients, include conch chowder, shrimp Créole, and several lobster dishes. From 9 a.m. to 1 a.m. Monday to Friday, 9 a.m. to midnight Saturday, and 1 p.m. to midnight Sunday, you can rub elbows with the islanders at the plank-sided veranda bar, whose wood frame is supported by a pier stretching out above the water. Service is good, with clients coming from the adjacent marina. If you stop in for lunch, you can order sandwiches, hamburgers, and salads from the nearby snackbar, whose cabaña design occupies an isolated position near the water.

Crow's Nest Restaurant, South Sound (tel. 809/949-6216), on the beach four minutes by car from George Town, with a view of Sand Cay and a lighthouse, is one of those places evoking the Caribbean "the way it used to be." Meals are served from noon to 2:30 p.m. and 6 to 10 p.m. Monday to Saturday. Lunches cost around $10, and dinners go for $15 to $20. There is no pretense or fussiness here. What you get is good, honest Caribbean cookery. Try one of the daily specials or perhaps sweet, tender Caribbean lobster, the most expensive item on the menu. Other dishes might include grilled tuna steak with akee or Jamaican chicken curry with roast coconut. For dessert, treat yourself to Key lime mousse pie, if it's available.

Welly's Cool Spot, North Sound Rd. (tel. 809/949-2541), is the place to go for local dishes. The emphasis is on those old reliable friends, the conch and the turtle. The cook also does lobster superbly, and in fact offers different specials every night. If you give him advance notice, he will do something special— maybe curried goat. Lunch costs C.I. $8 ($10), and dinner goes for C.I. $10($12.50) to C.I. $15 ($18.75). It's open from 7 a.m. to 3 p.m. and 6 to 10 p.m. Monday to Saturday. On Sunday, it is open only for dinner, from 6 to 10 p.m.

3. THE SPORTING LIFE

What they lack in nightlife, the Caymans make up in water sports—fishing, swimming, waterskiing, and diving are among the finest in the Caribbean.

DIVING AND OTHER WATER SPORTS: *Skin Diver* magazine has written that "Grand Cayman has become the largest single island in the Caribbean for dive tourism." There is lots of marine life, a large variety, and many coral formations. There are plenty of boats and scuba facilities. Coral reefs encircle the islands, and these reefs are filled with marine life. However, the government bans scuba-divers from taking any form of marine life. It's easy to dive close to shore —therefore, boats aren't necessary.

But for certain excursions I recommend a trip with a qualified divemaster. For rentals, the island maintains many "dive shops." Hotels also rent in-house facilities as well; however, a dive shop will not rent scuba gear or supply air to a diver unless he or she has a card from one of the national diving schools, such as NAUI or PADI. Hotels arrange snorkeling and scuba-diving trips.

Established in 1957, the best-known dive operation in the Cayman Islands is **Bob Soto's Diving Ltd.,** P.O. Box 1801, Grand Cayman, B.W.I. (tel. 809/ 949-2022). Owned by Ron Kipp, the operation has grown to include full-service dive shops at the Holiday Inn, the Scuba Centre on North Church Street, and Coconut Plaza. A resort course, designed to teach the fundamentals of scuba to beginners who know how to swim, costs $85. This requires a full day with a morning spent in the pool, use of all necessary equipment, and an afternoon one-tank dive from a boat. Nondivers can take advantage of the glass-bottom boat and daily snorkel trips. Besides a wide range of scuba gear, underwater cameras with free film and snorkeling gear can be rented at reasonable rates. At Bob Soto's, people are helpful and highly professional.

FISHING: Grouper and snapper are most plentiful for those who bottom-fish along the reef. Deeper waters turn up barracuda and bonito. The flats on Little Cayman are said to offer the best bonefishing in the world. Sports people from all over the world come to the Caymans for the big ones—tuna, wahoo, marlin. Most hotels can make arrangements for charter boats. Experienced guides are also available.

THE MOST COMPLETE WATER SPORTS: Universally regarded as the most up-to-date and best-equipped water sports facility in the Cayman Islands, **Red Sail Water Sports,** Hyatt Regency Grand Cayman, P.O. Box 1588 (tel. 809/949-8754), maintains headquarters in a gaily painted wooden house beside the beach at the previously recommended deluxe resort. The array of options available here include:

Deep-sea fishing: Excursions over the sea in search of such fish as tuna, marlin, and wahoo are arranged on the Hyatt's custom-built 45-foot Royce-made vessel, the *Ocean Spirit.* One of the most luxurious fishing boats in the Caymans, it is air-conditioned with three overnight cabins and an experienced crew. Tours depart at 7:30 a.m. and 12:30 p.m., lasting half a day and costing $400 (a full day goes for $600). The cost can be split among eight persons.

Scuba diving: Red Sail offers excursions appealing to the least-experienced beginners as well as to long-time aficionados of the deep. A two-tank morning dive includes exploration of two different dive sites at depths ranging from 50 to 100 feet, lasts a full morning, and costs $45. Beginners can take advantage of a resort course offered daily costing $100 per person. A full certification course, requiring a maximum of five days, goes for $350.

Windsurfing: Sailboards rent for $12 to $16 per hour, depending on the quality of the board.

Hobie Cats: The most popular catamarans in the Caribbean rent for $12 to $25 per hour, depending on the time of day.

Sailing: One of the best-designed catamarans in the Caribbean is berthed in a canal a short walk from the water sports center. Some 65 feet in length, with an aluminum mast 75 feet tall, it is both fast, stable, and exhilarating. A sail to "Stingray City," with snorkeling equipment and lunch included in the price of $50 per person, sets out twice daily. A sunset sail from 5 to 7 p.m., with hors d'oeuvres, goes for $27 per person.

Waterskiing: This can be arranged at a cost of $40 to $60 per hour. The price can be divided among several persons.

BEACHES: About the finest in the Caribbean, Grand Cayman's **Seven Mile Beach** has sparkling white sands with Australian pines in the background. In addition, beaches on the east coast and north coast are also fine, as they are protected by an offshore barrier reef. In winter the average water temperature is 80°, rising to 85° in summer.

SUBMERSIBLES: For a once-in-a-lifetime experience, you can take a deep dive in a submarine during your visit to the Cayman Islands, even choosing between a submersible vessel that can go to a depth of 150 feet and others that can plunge downward to as deep as 800 feet below the surface.

One of the island's most popular attractions is the world's first commercial service submarine, *Atlantis I,* a craft 50 feet long, weighing 49 tons, built at a cost of $1.8 million and carrying 28 passengers. Passengers drop 150 feet below the surface on one-hour voyages, either day or night. The cost is $48 during the day and $56 at night. Children four to 12 pay half fare. Passengers can view the briny deep through large viewports two feet in diameter, eight on each side of the vessel, as it cruises along at a speed of 1½ knots. Attractions in this living world of a tropical reef, including a wrecked ship, are explained by a guide. At night, colors not normally visible during the day come to vivid life under probing lights. Nocturnal marine life can also be seen at this time. The vessel makes 12 dives a day, leaving the dock on the hour from 9 a.m. to 8 p.m. For more information, write **Atlantis Submarine,** P.O. Box 1043, Grand Cayman, B.W.I. (or for reservations call 809/949-7700).

Research Submersibles Ltd., P.O. Box 1719, Grand Cayman, B.W.I. (tel. 809/949-8296), operates the *Deep Explorer 3* and the *Deep Explorer 8* research submarines, each carrying a pilot and two passengers on four dives a day, going as deep as 780 to 800 feet. Grand Cayman is the top of an underwater mountain, the side of which is known as the Cayman Wall, which has a 500-foot sheer drop down its side before becoming a steep slope falling away for 6,000 feet to the bottom of the ocean. The *Deep Explorers,* in their 1½-hour trips, allow passengers to see the variety of sea life at different levels of the dive. Weather permitting, each trip goes down to the wreck of the *Kirk Pride,* a cargo ship that sank off George Town Harbour in 1976 and was lodged on a rock ledge of the wall at 780 feet. The submarines are dry and at one atmosphere pressure, so no previous experience is necessary. Each passenger receives a certificate of the dive and a sub crew T-shirt. It's possible to take pictures with 400 ASA film in your camera. The *Deep Explorer* trips cost $245 per passenger, and they're open to everyone over the age of 8. Reservations should be made at least a week in advance.

GOLF: The only golf course on Grand Cayman is the **Britannia** (tel. 809/949-7440), next to the Hyatt Regency on Seven Mile Beach. The course, the first of its kind in the world, was designed by Jack Nicklaus and is unique in that it incorporates three different courses in one: a nine-hole championship layout, an 18-hole executive setup, and a Cayman course. The latter was designed for play with the Cayman ball, which goes about half the distance of a regulation ball. Greens fees for the nine-hole championship course are $30, play on the Cayman course costing $25. Fees for playing the executive course are $35 for nine holes, $50 for 18 holes. A two-hour lesson costs $40. Guests at the Hyatt and Britannia community can book a maximum of 72 hours in advance. Other players are allowed as 24-hour advance booking.

FITNESS CENTER: Just across from the airport, the **Nautilus Fitness Centre,** Crewe Rd. (tel. 809/949-5132), is available for the use of visitors. Activities include aerobics, dance classes, Nautilus machines, free weights, sauna, whirlpool, and shower facilities. Visitors register at the front desk. The center is open from 6:30 a.m. to 8 p.m. Monday, Wednesday, and Friday; 8:30 a.m. to 8:30 p.m. Tuesday and Thursday; 7:30 a.m. to 1 p.m. Saturday; and 6 to 8 p.m. Sunday. Rates are $10 per day, $25 per week.

4. EXPLORING THE ISLAND

The capital, **George Town,** can easily be explored in an afternoon. It is principally a place to visit for its restaurants and shops (or banks!)—not sightseeing. It does offer a clock monument to King George V and the oldest government building in use today, the post office on Edward Street. Stamps sold there are avidly sought by collectors.

The **Cayman Maritime and Treasure Museum,** P.O. Box 904, North Church St. (tel. 809/949-7470), on the waterfront near the heart of George Town, offers a wide assortment of displays ranging from the exploration of the New World by Columbus to the most modern, sophisticated treasure-recovery technique. Admission is $5 (U.S.) for adults, $3 for children. Hours are from 9 a.m. to 5 p.m. Monday to Saturday. Genuine treasure, artifacts, and a variety of souvenirs are available in the museum's gift shop which can be visited free.

Elsewhere on the island, you might go to **Hell!** That's at the north end of West Bay Beach, a jagged piece of rock named Hell by a former commissioner. There the postmistress will stamp Hell, Grand Cayman, on your postcard to send back to the States.

Cayman Turtle Farm, Northwest Point (tel. 809/949-3894), is the only green sea turtle farm of its kind in the world as well as being the most popular land-based tourist attraction in the Caymans, with some 70,000 visitors annually. Once the islands had a multitude of turtles in the surrounding waters. Columbus called the islands "Las Tortugas," but today these creatures are sadly few in number (practically extinct elsewhere in the Caribbean). The turtle farm has a two-fold purpose: to provide the local market with edible turtle meat and to replenish the waters with hatchling and yearling turtles. The sale of decorative shells and jewelry was effectively ended in 1978 when the United States banned importation of such items, the green sea turtle having been designated as an endangered species. *You cannot bring turtle products into the U.S.* Visitors today can look at 100 circular cement tanks in which these sea creatures can be observed in every stage of development, the hope being that one day their population in the sea will regain its former status. Turtles here range in size from six ounces to 600 pounds. At a snackbar and restaurant, you can sample turtle dishes. Hours are daily from 9 a.m. to 5 p.m. Admission is $5 for adults, $2.50 for children six to 12.

At **Botabano,** on the North Sound, fishermen tie up with their catch, much to the delight of photographers. If you've got your own kitchenette, you can buy lobster (in season), fresh fish, even conch, from these fishermen. A large barrier reef protects the sound, which is surrounded on three sides by the island, a mecca for divers and sports fishermen.

If you're driving, you might want to go along **South Sound Road,** lined with pines and, in places, old wooden Caymanian houses. After leaving the houses—old and modern alike—behind, you'll find good spots for a picnic.

Pedro's Castle is reached by going along Old Prospect Road to Bodden Town. A few miles from there, you turn right at the crossroads at Savannah. Originally called St. James Castle, Pedro's is the oldest standing building in the Caymans. Erected by slave labor, today it houses a restaurant.

Also, just outside Savannah, on Spots Bay, is the island's best-known cave, **Bat Cave.** Frankly, I recommend this attraction to cave buffs only. Backtracking from Pedro's Castle, you go just beyond the speed restriction sign, as if heading back to George Town. On your left (the sea side of the road), you'll see a dirt road. Follow it to the end. Once you reach the sea, turn left. Walking along the cliff edge for some 30 yards, you'll reach a sandy beach. After climbing down ten feet, you'll spot the cave's low mouth. The cave is explored on your hands and knees (thankfully, the floor is sandy). The bats will squeak loudly at your entrance but they're harmless.

On the road again, you reach **Bodden Town,** which was once the largest settlement on the island. At Gun Square, two cannons commanded the channel through the reef. They are now stuck muzzle-first into the ground.

On the way to the **East End,** just before Old Isaac Village you'll see the onshore sprays of water shooting up like geysers, their sound like the roar of a lion. These are called "blowholes."

Later, you'll spot the fluke of an anchor sticking up from the ocean floor. As the story goes, this is a relic of the famous "Wreck of the Ten Sails" in 1788. A modern wreck can also be seen—the *Ridgefield,* a 7,500-ton Liberty ship from New England which struck the reef in 1943.

Old Man Bay is reached by a road that opened in 1983. Head back to town along the cross-island road through savannah country, where royal palms sway in the breeze and the appearance is veldt-like. You might even spot the green Cayman parrot. At Old Man Bay, you can travel along the north shore of the island to **Rum Point,** with its good beach, which is as fine a place as any to end the tour.

An annual event, **Cayman Islands Pirates' Week,** is held in late October. It's a national festival with cutlass-bearing pirates and sassy wenches storming George Town, capturing the governor, thronging the streets, and staging a costume parade. The celebration, which is held throughout the islands, pays tribute to the nation's past and its cultural heritage. For information as to the dates of the festival each year, get in touch with Pirates Week Festival Administration, P.O. Box 51, Grand Cayman (tel. 809/949-5078).

5. FREE-PORT SHOPPING

This is not the most compelling reason to take a vacation in Grand Cayman. However, having said that, it should be noted that there is free-port shopping, with merchandise from all over the world available in the stores of George Town. Often you'll find bargains in silver, china, crystal, Irish linen, French perfumes, British woolen goods, and such local crafts as black coral jewelry and thatch-woven baskets. However, you should know the prices prevailing in U.S. stores. I have found them to be the same on many items.

Don't purchase turtle products. They cannot be brought into the U.S.

In George Town, my recommendations follow:

Caribe Island Jewelry, North West Point, West Bay (tel. 809/949-1077), offers locally made jewelry from black coral, caymanite, whelk, and conch. The jewelry is produced in many forms, including necklaces, bracelets, and earrings. The store is on the way to the turtle farm.

Viking Gallery, Harbour Drive on the waterfront (tel. 809/949-4090), offers two floors of handcrafts, as well as hand-painted skirts and tops, a calypso boutique, local bolt material, and Caribbean paintings. They also sell pewter, crystal, black coral, fine jewelry, porcelain, and bank tax-haven books.

Bridget's Fashions and Fragrances, Harbour Drive, Freeport Plaza (tel. 809/949-2699), opposite the cruise-ship passenger landing, offers a selection of fashions from around the world. These include Gottex swimwear from Israel, handcrafted batik from Bangkok, Irish linen, Cayman map wall hangings, special design (woven) turtle ties for men, and Cayman coat-of-arms ties, along with sportswear for men.

Caymandicraft, South Church St. (tel. 809/949-2405), a short distance from the center of George Town, imports 4711 colognes, soap, and powder, cashmere scarves, kilts, mohair stoles, and blankets from Scotland, Irish linen, and a wide range of Liberty of London fabrics.

English Shoppe, Harbour Drive (tel. 809/949-2457), stocks duty-free perfumes, along with a fine collection of watches and other fine jewelry. They also carry Irish crystal and collectors' items. All prices are quoted in U.S. dollars.

The **Jewellery Factory,** Fort St. (tel. 809/949-2719), is one of the most interesting jewelry shops on Grand Cayman. Look for their Spanish gold doubloons and silver pieces of eight, stylishly framed in 14-karat and 18-karat gold. Gold jewelry is mostly sold by weight, and prices vary with the London bullion fix for that day.

Black Coral and . . . , Fort St. (tel. 809/949-4948), is where you can see and purchase some of the fine handcrafted black coral pieces designed by Bernard Passman, the renowned sculptor who introduced the black coral art medium to the world. Some of the sculptures and jewelry in the shop are done with gold and gems. Passman designed and executed the wedding gifts of the Cayman Islands people to Prince Charles and Princess Diana—a 97-piece cutlery set of black coral and silver.

Coral Arts Collections, Old Fort Building, on the waterfront (tel. 809/949-3951), offers rare and ancient coins, conch pearls, and a wide selection of jewelry, much of it designed "by Mitzi" (owner Mitzi Mercedes Callan). She uses many types of coral—black, pink, angelskin, oxblood, apple, gold, tiger, and blue—all crafted in 14-karat and 18-karat gold.

Kirk Freeport Plaza, Cardinal Ave. and Panton St. (tel. 809/949-7477), has a treasure trove of gold jewelry, watches, china, crystal, perfumes, cosmetics, leather goods, and sweaters.

6. CAYMANIAN NIGHTLIFE

PUBS: Because of its links with Britain, nightlife in the Caymans has a decidedly English tilt. Your options might include a sampling of rum-based drinks beneath swaying coconut palms, but you'll probably order it from a paneled bar whose accessories resemble those of a roadside pub. Here's a survey of the action.

Silver's, Treasure Island Resort, West Bay Rd. (tel. 809/251-3052), is the most innovative and musically excellent night club on the island. Contained within a hotel partially financed by a consortium of Nashville-based country music stars, its entrance is connected to the lobby of a previously recommended hotel. Designed with a recording studio on its upper balcony, it uses the same acoustical principles as both the Grand Ole Opry in Nashville and La Scala, the opera house in Milan. The door charge is $5, with beer costing $3. The club offers live music performed from 9 p.m., and hours are nightly except Sunday from

7 p.m. to 1 a.m. It contains Caribbean-inspired colors, two commodious bars, and a dance floor.

Wreck of the Ten Sails Lounge, Holiday Inn (tel. 809/947-4444). In spite of its location in one of Grand Cayman's largest hotels, many residents of the island drop in at regular intervals. There they enjoy the large murals of swashbuckling pirates above smallish tables raised on platforms. The elongated bar with its adjacent floor is usually a good place for a conversation, especially as the evening wears on. Open nightly except Sunday from 8:30 p.m. to 12:45 a.m., it has as its drawing card live music presented by the island's most vivid musical personality, "Barefoot Man" and his band. There's a cover charge of $5 for non-residents of Holiday Inn. Once inside, hard liquor begins at $3 a drink. The barman's specialty is a Cayman Mama, made with coconut, rum, and banana liqueur.

Cayman Islander Nightclub, off West Bay Rd. (tel. 809/949-7603), is a nightlife complex. Hours are from 8 p.m. to 1 a.m. Tuesday to Saturday. The cover charge ranges from free to C.I. $5 ($6.25), depending on the night of the week or what entertainment is offered. Drinks cost C.I. $3 ($3.75). Live music, including island floor shows, have been presented here in the past, but check its current status before going. There's usually plenty of disco action as well. It's closed on Sunday and Monday but open otherwise from 9 p.m. to 1 a.m.

Lord Nelson Pub, Trafalgar Place, West Bay Rd. (tel. 809/947-4595). The Caribbean sunlight streams through leaded-glass windows, but the interior is fashioned after thousands of pubs found in the English countryside. Beneath blackened ceiling beams and polished saddle brasses, you can enjoy pub grub, foamy mugs of English ale, and the animated conversation of some of the island's British expatriates. A pint of ale costs around C.I. $4 ($5) and might be accompanied by steak-and-kidney pie, fish and chips, and meat-stuffed pastries. The establishment is open daily from noon to 3 p.m. Weekdays it reopens from 5 p.m. to 1 a.m. (on weekends 5 p.m. to midnight). Dinner is served nightly from 6 to 10 p.m.

The **Lone Star Bar & Grill,** West Bay Rd. (tel. 809/949-5575), is really just a little corner of the Texas Panhandle transported to gilt-edged real estate in the Caribbean. You can enjoy some of the juiciest hamburgers in the Caymans beneath the heavy trusses of the smoke-filled dining room, unless you prefer to head to the satellite bar in back. There, beneath murals of Lone Star beauties lassoing rattlesnake-entwined bottles of tequila, you can watch replays of some of last season's best football games. The house specialty drink is a banana split (that's right—it's pulverized with rum, banana liqueur, and ice cream). A plate of nachos is C.I. $5.25 ($6.56), and most guests go whole-hog for three kinds of fajitas, or Texas-style cheese steak (hot chili peppers cost extra). Full meals cost from C.I. $12 ($15). The club is open for lunch daily except Monday from noon to 3 p.m. and for dinner from 6 to 10 p.m. It closes a bit later on Monday and Thursday, as those are fajitas nights.

Monkey Business, Cayman Falls Shopping Centre, West Bay Rd. (tel. 809/947-4024), is one of the island's newest and biggest clubs. It offers music nightly, with a $5 (U.S. cover charge). This is a hot spot (usually), attracting a lot of locals and any visitor who happens to find out about it. The club is open nightly from 9 until "the wee hours," closing time depending on business.

THEATER: A varied program of productions by the **Cayman National Theatre Company,** P.O. Box 1684 (tel. 809/949-5477) ranges from Cayman drama to *Macbeth,* as well as West Indian musicals and Broadway revues. Some presentations are at Harquail Cultural Center on West Bay Road. The box office is on

North Church Street, Grand Cayman. The theater season is from October to June.

7. CAYMAN BRAC

The "middle sister" of the three Cayman Islands is Cayman Brac, a piece of limestone and coral-based land 12 miles long and a mile wide, about 89 miles east-northeast of Grand Cayman. It was given the name *Brac* (Gaelic for *bluff*) by 17th-century Scottish fishermen who settled here. The bluff for which the island was named is a towering limestone plateau rising to 140 feet above the sea, covering the eastern half of Cayman Brac. Caymanians refer to the island simply as Brac, and its 1,200 inhabitants are called Brackers, hospitable people, as folk with seafaring backgrounds tend to be.

In earlier years, when Brac was a shipbuilding island (which ended with World War II), extremely hard wood used as the ribs for sailing ships came from the bluff, and there were little vegetable garden plots in pockets of fertile soil there. Today, with the need for home-produced vegetables no longer pressing, the thick vegetation of the bluff is a winter home or stopover for migratory birds. Frangipani, century plants, and oleanders burgeon on the heights.

The big attraction of the bluff today isn't something new. There are more than 170 caves honeycombing its limestone height. In the early 18th century the Caymans were in the hands of pirates, and Edward Teach, the infamous Blackbeard, is supposed to have spent quite a bit of time around Cayman Brac, lurking in protected coves. What could be more natural than for him to have hidden some of his loot in one or more of the bluff's caverns, a lure for treasure-hunters? (They haven't found any yet.) Some of the caves are at the bluff's foot while others can be reached only by climbing over jagged limestone rock. One of the biggest of them is Great Cave, with a number of chambers. Harmless fruit bats cling to the roofs of the caverns.

On the south side of the bluff, you won't see many people, and the only sounds are the sea crashing against the lava-like shore. The island's herons and wild green parrots are seen here.

Now to the inhabited north side of Cayman Brac: Most of the Brackers live here, many in traditional wooden seaside cottages, some built by the island's pioneers.

One of the most popular attractions is the home and gift shop of **Eddie Scott,** Stake Bay Rd. (tel. 809/948-4219), an industrial arts teacher who obviously likes to work with wood. Around his yard you'll see such handmade articles as a sailboat, a weathervane with a turtle logo, a sundial, and inviting love seats. Of special interest is a beautifully carved miniature tanker. The house has intricately worked balconies, and Scott has turned out little wooden trains, planes, and trucks which children love.

The islanders must all have green thumbs, as attested by the variety of flowers, shrubs, and fruit trees in many of the yards. On Cayman Brac you'll see all sorts of vegetation: poinciana trees, bougainvillea, Cayman orchids, croton, hibiscus, aloe, sea grapes, cactus, and of course coconut and cabbage palms. The gardeners grow cassava, pumpkins, breadfruit, yams, and sweet potatoes.

There are no actual towns on the island—only settlements such as **Stake Bay** (the "capital"), **Spot Bay, The Creek, Tibbitt's Turn, The Bight,** and **West End,** where the airport is located.

The **Brack Museum** (tel. 809/948-4222), in the former Government Administration Building, has an interesting collection of Caymanian antiques, including pieces rescued after shipwrecks. The museum is open from 9 a.m. to 4 p.m. Monday to Friday, noon to 5 p.m. Saturday and Sunday. Admission is free.

Of course, the biggest lure to Cayman Brac is the variety of water sports—swimming, fishing, snorkeling, and some of the world's best diving and exploration of coral reefs. There are undersea walls on both the north and south sides of the island, with stunning specimens lining their sides. All the hotels offer the services of Brac Aquatics or Dive Tiara, which provide a variety of diving excursions.

WHERE TO STAY: A favorite resort on the island is **Brac Reef Beach Resort,** P.O. Box 235, Cayman Brac, B.W.I. (tel. 809/948-7323, or toll free 800/327-3835, 800/233-8880 in Florida), occupying a sandy plot of land on the south shore, near some of the best snorkeling in the region. The resort contains 40 motel-like units, each comfortably furnished and outfitted with air conditioning, carpeting, ceiling fans, and modern well-lit baths. Once the location was little more than a maze of sea grapes, a few of whose venerable trunks still rise amid the picnic tables, hammocks, and boardwalks of this well-maintained resort.

You'll pay for your drinks with doubloons, which one of the receptionists will sell to you in a blue velvet bag. A hideaway no guest should miss is the thatch-roofed two-story bar whose stout wooden columns rise from above the surf. Perfect for a moonlit tryst, it has a breeze-filled interior where nightcaps are served to the occupants of boats moored alongside. Laundry, maid service, and meals appear from one of the well-mannered staff members. Lunches are informal affairs accented with sunlight and water, while dinners are most often served buffet style in copious quantities under the stars. On the premises are a pool, a Jacuzzi, a water-sports facility, and the rusted remains of a Russian lighthouse tower which was retrieved several years ago from a Cuban-made trawler. Most guests who stay here opt for one of the all-inclusive packages. Otherwise, year-round prices are $69 daily in a single, $79 double, and $89 triple. MAP can be arranged for another $54 per person daily.

Divi Tiara Beach Resort, P.O. Box 238, Cayman Brac, B.W.I. (tel. 809/948-7553), part of the Divi Divi hotel chain, attracts divers and honeymooners. The location is about two miles from the airport. Many newcomers respond immediately to the landscaping, incorporating retaining walls of porous stone with fences of croton, bougainvillea, and palms. Each of the 58 air-conditioned accommodations is in two-story motel-like outbuildings, many of which offer a view of the surf, the outlying reef, and an array of palm-thatched outbuildings. A square swimming pool is raised above a white sand beach whose boardwalks run beneath groves of palm trees. On piers jutting down into the water is a Tahitian-style thatch-roofed bar where drinkers can gaze out to the sea. Seven of the units are luxury apartments, each with an ocean view, Jacuzzi, king-size beds, color TV, and phone. In winter, doubles cost $120 to $180 daily, *the price dropping to $80 to $100 daily in summer.* Singles pay $5 less per day per room, and MAP can be arranged for $30 per person per day. However, ask about one of their many special package plans, which are the best bargains. On the premises is an excellent Peter Hughes dive operation. There is entertainment at the hotel twice weekly.

A DIVE OPERATION: For information about the island's waters, go to **Brac Aquatics** (tel. 809/948-7429, or toll free 800/327-3835, 800/233-8880 in Florida). The island's authorities on the outlying reefs and underwater features of Cayman Brac are Winston and Denise McDermot. From a position a few steps from the Brac Reef Beach Resort, boats negotiate a narrow channel through the reef into the open sea beyond it. Scuba and snorkeling lessons and equipment are available on a per-day basis. Most seriously dedicated scuba-divers, however, negotiate a combined hotel-meal-dive package with the Morrises, the managers of the hotel. The inclusive deal offers better value.

8. LITTLE CAYMAN

Smallest of the Cayman Islands is Little Cayman, measuring ten miles long by about one mile at its widest point, lying about 75 miles northeast of Grand Cayman, some five miles from Cayman Brac. This cigar-shaped island, which today has only about 30 or so permanent inhabitants, was first colonized in the 17th century by European adventurers. However, they soon became the target of pirate raids and the little island was abandoned. With the stifling of pirate enterprise, settlers from Grand Cayman moved to Little Cayman in 1833, and it has been home to a few people ever since, although economic endeavors, including turtling and coconut growing, were not successful. It is believed that there may still be pirate treasure buried on the island, but it is in the dense interior of what is now the largest bird sanctuary in the Caribbean.

Little Cayman is home to a unique species of lizard that predates the iguana. It is the oldest species of New World reptile, and there are only 50 specimens in the world, two of which live under the generator shed and compressor/dive shop of Pirates Point Resort, recommended below. The entire island is coral and sand. Any rocks here were brought in from elsewhere, probably used as ballast in pirate ships.

The islands of the Caymans are mountaintops of the long-submerged Sierra Maestra Range, which runs north under the sea and into Cuba. The peaks were slowly built on by living corals after the drowning of the mountains, thus forming the islands of today and leaving subsea walls down the mountain precipices on which coral and other marine life grew for centuries, unseen and undisturbed. Little Cayman's Bloody Bay offers one of the walls nearest the surface, a stunning sight for snorkelers and scubadivers.

The island seems to have come into its own now that fishing and diving have been recognized as its main resources. This is a near-perfect place for such pursuits. The waters around the little island were hailed by the late Phillipe Cousteau as one of the three finest diving spots in the world.

Fine bonefishing is available just offshore, and an inland brackish pool can be fished for tarpon. Even if you don't dive or fish, you can row 200 yards off Little Cayman to isolated and uninhabited Owen Island where you can swim from the sandy beach and picnic by a blue lagoon.

Blossom Village, the island's "capital," is on the southwest coast. There are no shops on Little Cayman and only two private phones and one pay phone.

FOOD AND LODGING: For water activities or just relaxing, **Pirates Point Resort, Ltd.,** Little Cayman, Cayman Islands, B.W.I. (tel. 809/948-4210), offers a family environment with gourmet cuisine. The owner and manager, Gladys Howard, is a graduate of Cordon Bleu in Paris, has studied with such stars of the kitchen as Julia Child and James Beard, and has written several cookbooks. She uses fresh vegetables locally grown in her menus.

The place has six remodeled and comfortably furnished rooms with private baths, rented for occupancy by one to four people. Winter rates for full board are $165 daily in a single, $125 per person double, and $115 per person triple or quad, *dropping to $150 single, $110 per person double, and $100 per person in a room for three or four people in low season.* The charge for the resort's package holidays is $200 in a single, $160 per person in a double, and $140 per person in a room occupied by three or four guests. *In summer, package rates are $185 in singles, $145 per person in doubles, and $125 per person in triples or quads.* A package includes the room, three excellent meals per day with appropriate wines, two-tank boat dives daily featuring the Bloody Bay Wall, the Cayman trench, and Jackson Reef, plus unlimited beach diving and a special happy hour with hors d'oeuvres and free spirits daily. Nondiving activities include snorkeling, birdwatching, bonefishing, tarpon fishing, an Owen Island picnic, and exploring.

Southern Cross Club, Little Cayman, Cayman Islands, B.W.I. (tel. 809/ 948-3255, or 317/636-9501 in Indiana), is a 10-unit resort on a natural lagoon one mile from the airport. Bedrooms have ceiling fans. A double with three meals per day costs $110 per person from December through April, *the price dropping to $90 per person from May to the end of November.* You bathe in salt water. Dining is on the premises. Scuba-diving, fly and deep-sea fishing, and snorkeling are among the attractions. This was a millionaire's private fishing club before its conversion to a public resort. It is said to provide deep-sea tarpon and bone-fishing 'like nowhere else on earth," as one commentator put it.

CHAPTER IV

PUERTO RICO

□ □ □

It was on Columbus's second voyage to the New World in 1493 that he sighted the island of San Juan (St. John the Baptist), later renamed Puerto Rico. The island's government has undergone many changes since the days of its first governor, Ponce de León, to its present status as an American Commonwealth.

However, the beauty and charm have remained since the first navigators set foot on Puerto Rican soil. They called it "the island of enchantment."

Even though the island is in the "torrid zone," found between the Tropics of Capricorn and Cancer, it enjoys a lower temperature than that typical of the region. Trade winds blow in from the northeast toward the southwest of the island, acting as a gigantic fan, cooling and protecting the island from excessive heat. The sea, land, and mountain breezes further contribute to maintaining the temperature at a comfortable level.

Puerto Rico's climate, one of the best in the Caribbean, is fairly stable all year, with an average temperature of 76° Fahrenheit. The only variants are found in the mountain regions, where the average temperature fluctuates between 66° and 76° Fahrenheit, and on the north coast, where the temperature goes from 70° to 80°.

It may date from the European discovery of the New World, but Puerto Rico, at least in San Juan, its capital, is as modern as tomorrow. The "bootstrap" island is remaking itself and holding out much promise for a bright future. It is no longer called "the poorhouse of the Caribbean."

Lush, verdant Puerto Rico is only half the size of New Jersey, roughly speaking. Its location is some 1,000 miles southeast of the tip of Florida. As such, it is at the hub of the Caribbean chain of islands, and you'll probably fly in and out of San Juan at least once if you're doing much touring in the area.

After a slump in the mid '70s and early '80s, tourism has greatly improved. Now you'll find some of the best golf and tennis in the Caribbean at such posh resorts as the Hyatt Dorado Beach and Palmas del Mar. Accommodations have also greatly improved at out-on-the-island cities such as Mayagüez with its Hilton. Paradores—government-sponsored inns—are sprinkled across the island for visitors who want a deeper look than that provided by the posh hotels and gambling casinos of San Juan, with their Las Vegas–type shows.

GETTING THERE: From North America, Puerto Rico is the most accessible Caribbean island. It is, in fact, the airline capital of the Caribbean. Even if you're not planning a holiday in Puerto Rico, chances are you'll pass through here if you do much extensive touring in the Caribbean Basin.

In the past few years, **American Airlines** has become "the airline of the Caribbean." In 1987, it spent $40 million on making San Juan its hub of operations for serving the area, and more millions have been earmarked to develop such features as curbside check-in, special transfers, and a separate reservation center.

Daily flights are currently available from 14 U.S. cities, which is double what it was back in 1985. In 1987, American added nonstop daily flights from Chicago, Baltimore, Hartford, Philadelphia, Raleigh-Durham, Toronto, and Montréal to its already existing service from New York, Newark, Boston, Miami, and Dallas–Fort Worth. It also has daily service to San Juan from Washington-Dulles and Orlando-Tampa. The carrier now offers 23 daily nonstop flights—to Puerto Rico from the U.S.

American Airlines in San Juan makes many connecting flights to other Caribbean destinations, with American Eagle, American's commuter airline partner, providing 94 daily flights from San Juan to 36 destinations in Puerto Rico and other Caribbean islands.

Eastern Airlines also runs its Caribbean operations from San Juan, bringing in 28 daily flights from the U.S. mainland. Normal service offers flights from Atlanta, Boston, Baltimore, Newark, New York, Miami, Hartford, Dallas, Washington DC, Raleigh-Durham, Philadelphia, and Pittsburgh, as well as one-stop service from Chicago, Detroit, Cleveland, Los Angeles, Houston, and Orlando. Service to other cities in Puerto Rico and the Caribbean is provided via Eastern Metro Express and Eastern Express LIAT. However, at presstime a strike has curtailed Eastern service, and the future of the airline is uncertain. Its toll-free number is 800/535-6660.

Delta flies between San Juan and Orlando and has two flights a day from Dallas and Los Angeles. The acquisition of Western Airlines by Delta has enabled the carrier to link new gateways in the western U.S. **TWA** has flights from New York and a daily nonstop Miami–San Juan run. It also flies from St. Louis to San Juan. TWA has an agreement with Virgin Island Seaplanes to provide service between San Juan and the U.S. Virgin Islands.

Six airlines—Aero Virgin Islands, American Eagle, Eastern Metro Express, Eastern Express LIAT, Vieques Air Link, and Virgin Island Seaplane Shuttle—offer regional service connecting San Juan with other Puerto Rican cities and surrounding islands.

International carriers also fly into Puerto Rico, including British Airways from London, Lufthansa from Frankfurt, and Iberia from Madrid, as well as Air France from Paris.

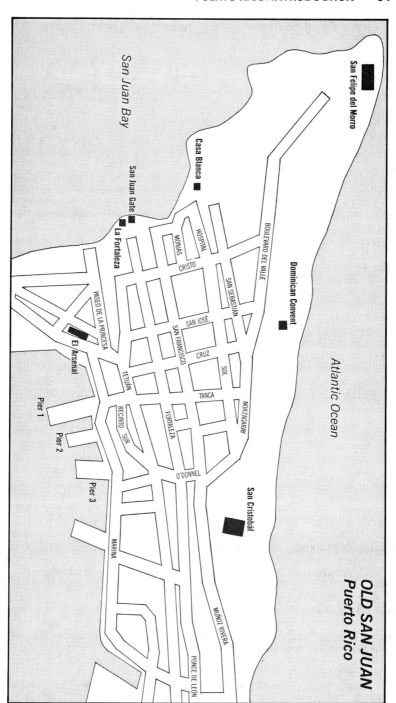

OLD SAN JUAN
Puerto Rico

San Juan Bay

San Felipe del Morro

Casa Blanca

San Juan Gate

La Fortaleza

Dominican Convent

Atlantic Ocean

BOULEVARD DEL VALLE

HOSPITAL

MONJAS

CRISTO

SAN SEBASTIÁN

SAN JOSÉ

SAN FRANCISCO

CRUZ

SOL

TANCA

NORZAGARAY

PASEO DE LA PRINCESA

El Arsenal

TETUAN

FORTALEZA

RECINTO SUR

Pier 1

Pier 2

Pier 3

O'DONNEL

San Cristóbal

MARINA

MUÑOZ RIVERA

PONCE DE LEÓN

GETTING AROUND: After you land at **Luis Muñoz Marín International Airport** in San Juan, your first problem is to get to your hotel. A taxi from the airport to one of the Isla Verde or Condado hotels will cost between $6 and $10, while a taxi to Old San Juan will cost around $12. If an arriving passenger is a guest of one of the island's more luxurious hotels, the hotel or casino might send one of the house limousines to pick her or him up free or for a minimum charge.

Public Transportation

Taxis are metered in San Juan, and the meter handle should be up when you get in, down as the taxi pulls out. Rates begin at 80¢, going up 10¢ for each additional one-eighth of a mile. Each suitcase carries a supplement of 50¢, and tipping is very much allowed. Waiting time costs $8 per hour.

Públicos are cars or minibuses which provide low-cost transportation and are designated with the letters "P" or "PD" following the numbers on their license plates. They run to all the main towns of Puerto Rico. Passengers are either let off or picked up along the way. Rates are set by the Public Service Commission. Públicos usually operate during daylight hours, departing from the main plaza (central square) of a town. For example, a one-way fare between San Juan and Mayagüez is now $10. Information about the públicos is available at **Lineas Sultana,** 898 Esteban Gonzalez (tel. 809/767-5205).

Buses run both day and night and operate on a fixed-fare system. Some are air-conditioned. City terminals are on the Plaza Colón and at Pier One.

Car Rentals

Car rentals are readily available, and some local agencies may tempt you with special slashed prices. But if you're planning to tour out on the island, you won't find any local branches should you run into car trouble. Also, some of the agencies widely advertising low-cost car deals don't take credit cards and want cash paid in advance. If you plan to do much touring, it's better to stick with one of the reliables, including **Avis** (tel. 809/721-8605) and **Hertz** (tel. 809/791-0840).

For my latest trek across Puerto Rico, I tried out the services of **Budget Rent-a-Car** (tel. 809/791-3685), which operates two offices in San Juan and a well-maintained fleet of late-model cars. As soon as visitors pick up their luggage, they can head for the Budget kiosk near the airport's busy taxi stand. An employee will arrange for a mini-van to transport arrivals to the agency's main office at Luis Muñoz Marín International Airport. Another, smaller, office is at La Concha Hotel on Ashford Avenue in the hotel zone of the Condado. An advance reservation, which can be made by calling toll free 800/527-0700 from anywhere in the U.S., usually guarantees a less expensive rate. The agency provides service 24 hours a day. Considered by Budget to be one of their best branches in the Caribbean, its prices are sometimes a bit cheaper than those of its two major competitors.

Added security comes from the antitheft double-locking mechanisms that have been installed on most of the agency's cars. The inventory consists mainly of Japanese-made cars which perform well on the narrow roads. There is also a fleet of American-made cars, such as four-door Ford Tempos.

As an indication of prices, the Tempo with unlimited mileage included costs $48 for a one-day rental, or $235.95 for the week. Most visitors, however, will settle for a less expensive model, a peppy Mitsubishi Mirage with manual transmission. A daily rental costs from $34; a weekly contract, from $215. Unlimited mileage is included.

Renting a car in Puerto Rico is easy. Motorists should remember that distances are often posted in kilometers rather than miles, but speed limits are in miles! Drivers on the island must be at least 21 years old. Drivers who don't purchase collision damage waivers (around $9.95 per day) are responsible for the full damage to their vehicles in case of an accident. I strongly recommend purchasing the extra insurance. I always do.

Sightseeing Tours

Sightseeing bus tours are convenient for people who don't want to drive. **Borinquen Tours, Inc.,** 868 Ashford Ave., Condado (tel. 809/725-4990), operates some of the best tours. You can arrange to be picked up at your hotel for a tour which can usually be booked at the hotel desk.

One of the most popular half-day tours, leaving at 9 a.m. daily (also at 1 p.m. Saturday), lasting four hours and costing $15 per person, goes along the northeastern part of the island to El Yunque rain forest, later making a stop at Luquillo Beach.

A city tour of Old and New San Juan departs at 9 a.m. daily, and at 9 a.m. and 1:30 p.m. on Saturday, Sunday, and holidays. The 2½-hour trip costs $10 per person. Another tour within Old San Juan takes you on a sightseeing jaunt and then to Bacardi's Rum Distillery, where you're treated to a complimentary rum drink. The tour, lasting three hours and costing $12 per person, leaves from hotels at 1:30 p.m. daily except Saturday, Sunday, and holidays. Borinquen has offices at the Caribe Hilton Hotel, Howard Johnson Hotel, and Condado Beach La Concha. It will pick up passengers at all the major hotels.

For a sea excursion, **Capt. Jack Becker** (tel. 809/863-1905) invites you to go out aboard his 40-foot catamaran, *Spread Eagle,* at a cost of $35 per person, including a buffet lunch and snorkel gear. It ties up at the Villa Marina Yacht Harbour in Fajardo, about an hour's drive east from San Juan. Departures for Icacos Island are at 10 a.m. Once there, you can swim, beachcomb, snorkel, or whatever. The *Spread Eagle* sails back at 2:30 p.m., the trip taking about an hour. To make reservations, telephone Captain Jack from 7 a.m. to 10 p.m. Transportation is available from metro San Juan for $10 round trip. Some 60% of the passengers on the *Spread Eagle* are repeats or referrals. For information, write P.O. Box 445, Puerto Real, PR 00740.

PRACTICAL FACTS: As mentioned, Puerto Rico has Commonwealth status with the United States, even though thousands of local citizens want to break away and be an independent nation. However, Puerto Rico is vitally linked financially to the United States, and many other citizens want statehood. The country elects its own governor, who serves a term of four years.

Currency and Banks: The U.S. dollar is the coin of the realm. All major U.S. banks are located in San Juan, and hours are 8:30 a.m. to 2:30 p.m. Monday to Friday. Canadian currency is accepted by some big hotels in San Juan, although reluctantly.

Documents: To get into Puerto Rico, American citizens do not have to have a passport or visa. Canadians, however, should carry some form of identification, such as a birth certificate.

Electricity: The electric current is 110 volts, as it is in continental U.S. and Canada.

Emergency numbers: In an emergency, call the local **police** (tel. 809/343-2020); **fire department** (tel. 809/343-2330); **ambulance** (tel. 809/343-2550); or **medical assistance** (tel. 809/754-3535).

Information: As you arrive at Luis Muñoz Marín International Airport in Isla Verde, you'll find a tourist information center. However, if you're seeking more details, you can visit the head office at 301 San Justo in the old town (tel.

809/721-2400). Out in the island, it's best to go to the local city hall for tourist data. Ask for a copy of *Que Pasa,* the official visitors' guide containing much useful information.

If you need information before leaving North America, there are several Puerto Rican tourist offices to help you. They include: 575 Fifth Ave., New York, NY 10017 (tel. 212/599-6262); 3575 W. Cahuenga Blvd., Los Angeles, CA 90068 (tel. 213/874-5991); 11 E. Adams St., Chicago, IL 60603 (tel. 312/922-9701); 3637 Rialto Way, Grand Prairie, TX 75051 (tel. 214/660-8343); 200 SE 1st St., Miami, FL 33131 (tel. 305/381-8915); and 11 Yorkville Ave., Toronto, Ontario M4W 1L3 (tel. 416/925-5587).

Language: English is understood at the big resorts and in most of San Juan. Out in the island, the language of Spain is still *numero uno.*

Newspaper: The *San Juan Star,* an English-language newspaper, is published daily.

Public holidays: Puerto Rico has many public holidays when stores, offices, and schools are closed. They include New Year's Day, January 6 (Three Kings' Day), Washington's Birthday, Good Friday, Memorial Day, July 4, Labor Day, Thanksgiving, Veterans' Day, and Christmas, plus local holidays such as July 25 (Constitution Day) and November 19 (Discovery Day).

Taxes and Tips: Some hotels add a 10% service charge to your bill in addition to the government tax. If they don't, you are expected to tip for services rendered. Tip as you would in the U.S. There is no airport departure tax.

Telephones: The telephone area code used to dial Puerto Rico from the U.S. is 809. For calls within Puerto Rico, it is not necessary to use the area code.

Time: Puerto Rico operates on Atlantic Standard Time, which is one hour earlier than Eastern Standard Time. However, when the eastern part of the U.S. goes on Daylight Saving Time, Puerto Rico does *not* change its time.

SAN JUAN

The capital of Puerto Rico is today an urban sprawl, one municipality flowing into another to form a great metropolitan area. San Juan introduces you to Puerto Rico, and the look of this old city ranges from decaying ruins that recall the Spanish empire to modern, beachfront hotels that evoke Miami Beach.

The city roughly breaks down into general divisions, including the old walled city on San Juan Island (see "What to See in San Juan"); the city center on San Juan Island containing the Capitol building; Santurce, on a larger peninsula, which is reached by causeway bridges from San Juan Island (the lagoonfront section here is called Miramar); and Condado, the narrow peninsula that stretches from San Juan Island to Santurce.

The Condado strip of beachfront hotels, restaurants, casinos, and nightclubs is separated from Miramar by a lagoon. Isla Verde is in the vicinity of the airport, which is detached from the rest of San Juan by an isthmus.

1. WHERE TO STAY IN SAN JUAN

From a guesthouse directly on the beach to a restored convent in Old San Juan, the choice of accommodations in the Puerto Rican capital is wide ranging, as are the tariff sheets. It's easy to spend $200 a day here, or else get by for $35. There are package deals galore, and you may want to check with a travel agent to see if one fills your needs.

Most of the hotels lie in Condado and Isla Verde, out by the airport. Both these sections border the beach. However, I'll also have other choices for those who prefer to live in sectors such as Ocean Park. I'll start where San Juan started, even though you'll find fewer accommodations in the old town than anywhere else.

Note: All hotel rooms in Puerto Rico are subject to a 6% tax.

IN OLD SAN JUAN: Considered by many as the "Grand Hotel of Puerto Rico," **Ramada El Convento,** 100 Cristo St., San Juan, PR 00901 (tel. 809/723-9020), is an authentically restored, 300-year-old Carmelite convent boasting a solid Spanish brick and limestone structure. It stands directly across the street from a building which was the original city hall in 1521 (during the Spanish colonial period) and a few steps from the cathedral where the remains of Juan Ponce de León are buried. Most of the historical landmarks of the colonial walled city are within walking distance. Some of the 100 rooms, furnished in a Spanish style of heavy wood, have a view of either the old town square (Little Plaza of the Nuns) or of San Juan Bay, where one can spot modern ships and island schooners go past the ancient fortress of El Morro. Because of its location there are no beach facilities, but the pool in the downstairs patio will serve you daily buffets. *In summer, singles range in price from $85 to $115 daily, while doubles go for $95 to $125.* In high season, a single costs $115 to $150 daily; doubles begin at $125, climbing to $175.

PUERTA DE TIERRA: A complete resort, the **Caribe Hilton,** San Jeronimo St., PR 00901 (tel. 809/721-0303), stands near the old Fort San Jeronimo, which has been incorporated into its complex. With Old San Juan at its doorstep and San Juan Bay at its backyard, the Caribe Hilton can be called the gateway to the walled city of San Juan. Near what was once the ultra-exclusive Escambrón Beach Club, it is the only major luxury hotel in the Old San Juan sector. There are times when tourists to the island arrive at the airport, go directly to the Caribe Hilton, and stay within the hotel confines and in Old San Juan for the duration of their vacation. The main reason for this is that the hotel has so much to offer that, according to the less adventurous visitor, there is no need to venture farther inland or anywhere else. Built in 1949, the Caribe Hilton was a new breed of resort, offering total entertainment and luxury. It still offers all that and more. Set in a 17-acre tropical park, the 638-room hotel has a private palm-shaded beach and swimming cove. One can walk to the 16th-century fort or spend the day on a tour of Old San Juan, then come back to either of two freshwater swimming pools, work out at the health club, play a tennis match (day or night), swim at the beach, or simply lie on the white sand under a palm tree.

Some of the rooms are in the 20-story tower added in 1972. The Garden Wing units are decorated in tropical fashion. On the family plan, there is no charge for children regardless of age, if they stay in the same room as their parents. *In summer, singles pay $102 to $192 daily, with doubles going for $122 to $212.* In winter, two people pay $205 to $305, and singles are charged $195 to $285. MAP is an additional $45 per person per day. The Terrace restaurant complex of the hotel features cuisine of the world, with a different menu each night of the week on its Dine-Around Plan. You can take dinner on the Terrace, at El Café, or at El Batey restaurant, and for dessert, go to the Fiesta Club Caribe show in the elegant nightclub. In addition to the special nights, each of the restaurants serves regular menus. Another eating facility at the hotel is La Rôtisserie (see my dining recommendations). The Club Caribe, which features headline entertainment, is previewed in "After Dark in San Juan." One of San Juan's leading discos, Juliana's, is also on the premises.

CONDADO: Once this area was devoted to residences for the very wealthy, but with the construction of the Puerto Rico Convention Center, all that changed.

Private villas were torn down to make way for high-rise hotel blocks, restaurants, and nightclubs. The Condado shopping area, along Ashford and Magdalena avenues, became a high-fashion center, with an extraordinary number of boutiques. There are good bus connections into old San Juan, or you can take taxis that are usually available.

The Leading Hotels

Condado Plaza Hotel & Casino, 999 Ashford Ave., San Juan, PR 00907 (tel. 809/721-1000), is a two-in-one hotel complex, an original oceanfront structure linked by an elevated passageway across Ashford to its Laguna section. In the recently renovated Laguna wing, which has its own lobby with direct access from the street, every room is air-conditioned and has a private terrace. Units have king-size or double beds. The deluxe part of the hotel, the Plaza Club, has 75 units with five remodeled suites occupying two floors, connected by a stairway. This section has a VIP lounge reserved for the use of its guests, and accommodations have cable TV, private check-in/check-out service, and each has a special key. The least expensive rooms offered by the hotel are labeled Ashford, the higher-priced units called either Laguna View or Oceanfront. From December 1 to the end of April, singles range from $205 to $295 daily, doubles costing $220 to $315. *Summer tariffs range from $165 to $225 for singles, $175 to $275 for doubles.*

The Condado Plaza Casino has been expanded, and the hotel has dining choices in several price ranges. The Lotus Flower, a fine Chinese restaurant, is next door to a superb seafood dining room and oyster bar. The Capriccio has northern Italian seafood as well as a collection of classic Italian dishes. La Posada, open 24 hours a day, is known for its prime beef and seafood. For nighttime entertainment, La Fiesta offers live Latin music, and you can dance to the disco beat at Isadora's. If the San Juan temperature becomes unbearable, guests can take a dip in any of the five swimming pools or practice one of the wide variety of watersports offered. At the beach or poolside, chaise longues and towels are provided free. There is a fitness center in the Laguna wing, and the hotel has two lit Laykold tennis courts.

Condado Beach Hotel, 1071 Ashford Ave., San Juan, PR 00907 (tel. 809/721-6090; 800/468-2775 toll free for reservations). The jutting eaves, formal garden, and Spanish colonial design of this hotel evoke the feeling of an archbishop's palace. Built by the Vanderbilts as the first hotel (in 1919) along what is now the heavily congested Condado, its interior has been upgraded and modernized many times.

Many of the almost 250 bedrooms are within a rambling modern wing (invisible from the street) whose red-tile roof mimics the detailing of the original core. During the day many visitors ignore the nearby beach in favor of the wind-sheltered pool area, where a double-tiered waterfall is ringed with miniature palms. On the premises is a handful of relaxing bars, including the Trade Winds. The El Gobernador offers fresh seafood, among other dishes, and courteous service. The oceanfront rooms in the west wing have private balconies. In winter, singles rent for $155 to $215 daily, and doubles go for $165 to $235. *Summer prices are $105 to $170 in singles, $15 to $185 in doubles.* The higher rates are for the exclusive and private Vanderbilt Club "concierge" floor.

Hotel La Concha, Ashford Ave., San Juan, PR 00907 (tel. 809/721-6090). Built in 1956, and named after its gracefully curved roof which resembles a section of a large sea shell, this comfortable hotel was once connected to its more prestigious neighbor, the Condado Beach Hotel. Now independent and thriving because of its proximity to one of the island's large convention centers, the hotel offers 234 renovated bedrooms and a cluster of drinking and dining facilities.

You register in a sun-flooded marble-floored lobby where plaster bas-reliefs cast striking images. On the premises is the popular disco, Club Mykonos, plus a pleasant restaurant, the Ocean Patio Terrace, open to the breezes that sweep in from the adjacent beach to the enclosed swimming pool. Naturally, the exterior of the complex is painted the same rosy coral color as a mature seashell. Most of the accommodations have private balconies facing the sea and cable color TV. In winter, singles cost $135, and doubles rent for $143. *In summer, singles go for $87 and doubles for $95.*

Ramada San Juan Hotel and Casino, 1045 Ashford Ave., San Juan, PR 00907 (tel. 809/724-5657), is an intimate 96-room first-class hotel right on the beach in the heart of the Condado section. The facilities and services anticipate the needs of all their guests whether on vacation or business trips. You can bask in the sun by the pool or on the sandy beach, have lunch or drinks on the sundeck, and dance the night away in the Polo Lounge to live music alternating between Latin rhythms and soft romantic melodies. The intimate Polo Restaurant serves local specialties or continental fare from 6 a.m. to 11 p.m. The hotel's casino is open daily from noon to 4 a.m. In addition, shopping, sights, and island nightlife are within walking distance or only a short ride away. Rooms are classified as standard, superior, and deluxe. In winter, singles rent for $170 to $205 daily, the price depending on the room category. Doubles cost $180 to $215, triples go for $200 to $235, and rooms accommodating four people are priced at $220 to $255. *Summer charges are $90 to $130 daily for singles, $100 to $140 for doubles, $120 to $160 for triples, and $140 to $180 for quads.*

A Budget Hotel at Condado

Condado Lagoon Hotel, 6 Clemenceau St. (P.O. Box 13145), San Juan, PR 00907 (tel. 809/721-0170), in Santurce at the corner of Joffre, boasts of its smallness and the fact that because it is not a gigantic, cavernous hotel, one can get personal service. If you are booking from the States, allow plenty of time (two to three weeks will do) since the lodge has only 49 rooms, which go fast both in and off-season. The suitably furnished rooms all have TV and refrigerators. Singles rent for $85 daily and doubles for $95 in winter, the prices dropping to *$60 in a single and $70 in a double from mid-April to mid-December.* Tariffs include use of the hotel's swimming pool and gym. A mini-market is on the premises, and you can dine at La Fragua Restaurant from 6:30 to 11 p.m. daily. Parking is available at no extra charge. Although it isn't on the beach, the sands are only a short walk away from the hotel, which is a block from the main drag of Condado where entertainment, casinos, and restaurants abound.

Condado Guesthouses

El Canario Inn, 1317 Ashford Ave., San Juan, PR 00907 (tel. 809/722-3861), offers one of the best bed-and-breakfast values in San Juan. You'll recognize the building by its arched veranda and the porte-cochère which covers a side yard filled with plants, a fountain, and a gazebo. Keith and Jude Olson are the accommodating owners. The hotel, completely remodeled in 1988, consists of a main house and two nearby sets of servants' quarters, all linked by a terrace. On the premises are an outdoor breakfast bar and lots of quiet corners for conversation. The 25 bedrooms are air-conditioned and have private baths and phones. *In summer, singles cost $45 daily, and doubles go for $60.* High-season rates are $60 in a single daily, $70 in a double. All prices include a continental breakfast and a morning newspaper. There are rooms with two double beds, with twin beds, and with one double bed. There is a communal kitchen, if you feel like cooking, although many restaurants are nearby. The beach is a short block away, and a tour desk is available in the lobby.

El Canaría by the Lagoon Hotel, 4 Clemenceau St., San Juan, PR 00907 (tel. 809/722-5058), is a 40-room European-style hotel operated by the Olsons in a quiet residential neighborhood just a short block from Condado Beach. The attractive air-conditioned rooms all have their own balconies, cable TV, phones, and private baths. *In summer, singles cost $50 daily, and doubles are priced at $60.* In winter, the rates are $75 daily in singles, $85 in doubles. All prices include a continental breakfast and complimentary morning newspaper. A relaxing informal atmosphere prevails.

Casablanca, 57 Calle Caribe, San Juan, PR 00907 (tel. 809/722-7139). Despite its self-image as an informal guesthouse, it occupies a valuable plot of land just a few paces from the Condado and some of the glitziest hotels in the Caribbean. Originally built as a guesthouse in the 1940s, it was expanded by a former resident of Massachusetts, Alex Leighton, and his wife, Suzanne, formerly a model in New York. You'll find it behind a wrap-around veranda, a wall, and a garden across Ashford Avenue. Inside, a total of seven small and simple rooms usually have a ceiling fan and copies of movie posters from the golden age of Hollywood. An honor bar is open throughout the day, turning the front porch into a social center for guests. You shouldn't expect the Ritz if you select this place, but you'll probably benefit from the cumulative advice that the Leightons have assembled during their sojourn on the Condado. Year-round prices range from $40 to $45 daily in a single, from $50 to $55 in a double. In winter only, a continental breakfast is served on the front veranda and included in the price of the room.

HOTELS IN MIRAMAR: Miramar, a quiet, residential sector, is very much a part of metropolitan San Juan, and a long brisk walk will take you where the action is. The beach, regrettably, is at least half a mile away.

San Juan Clarion Hotel & Casino, 600 Avenida Fernández Juncos, San Juan, PR 00907 (tel. 809/721-4100). Soaring above a commercial and residential district, this glistening 27-story hotel is the tallest skyscraper in the Caribbean. Its lobby and many of its public rooms are sheathed in marble. Near the reception desk a splashing fountain sustains clusters of plants. There's a swimming pool in back and a long cylindrical tunnel leading to a pleasant restaurant. The angled windows of its uppermost story contain an elegant restaurant. Windows of the Caribbean, which evokes something you might encounter in South America. Each of the accommodations of this restored and redecorated hotel offers TV, phone, air conditioning, and a color scheme of stylish cream and pastels. In winter, singles rent for $140 daily, and doubles go for $150. *In summer, singles cost $85 daily; doubles $95.*

Hotel Excelsior, 801 Ponce de León Ave., San Juan, PR 00907 (tel. 809/721-7400), is a 140-room facility which offers handsome accommodations and good service. Built in 1966, the hotel has an elegant lobby graced by four sculptures especially commissioned. The bedrooms have been completely refurbished, with cotton pastel fabrics from Denmark and Holland. Many have fully equipped kitchenettes, and all are air-conditioned and have baths, color TV, hairdryers, two phones (one in the bathroom), and marble vanities. The corridors of the ten guestroom floors have fine woolen carpets. *Summer rates are $72 to $96 daily on singles, $84 to $108 in doubles.* In winter, singles rent for $100 to $127 daily, doubles for $113 to $139. Included in the prices are use of the swimming pool, daily coffee, a newspaper, shoe shines, and transportation to the nearby beach, as well as parking in the underground garage or the adjacent parking lot. Children under age 10 are allowed to share a room with two adults free, and there is no charge for a crib. The Excelsior's Augusto's Cuisine operates El Gazebo, a new pyramid-shaped wooden structure at poolside where guests can order a full American breakfast. A cocktail lounge, gift shop, and beauty shop complete the hotel's facilities. This hotel is known for its excellent maintenance and meticulous housekeeping.

A GUESTHOUSE AT OCEAN PARK: The former private residence of the Spanish consul is now **La Condesa Inn,** 2071 Calle Cacique, San Juan, PR 00911 (tel. 809/727-3698). You're about a five-minute drive from most of the casinos, restaurants, and entertainment centers. Because La Condesa is limited to just 20 accommodations, I recommend that you book and plan accordingly. It is in the residential Ocean Park–Condado area, just 60 yards from San Juan's most spacious beach. All but the upstairs suites have their own private entrances. Some rooms contain complete individual kitchens and dining bars. There is also a pool restaurant. *In the off-season, a single rents for $35 daily and a double goes for $42.* In winter, regular singles cost $50 and doubles are $57.

A GUESTHOUSE AT PUNTA LAS MARIAS: Midway between Isla Verde and Condado, **Tres Palmas Guest House,** 2212 Park Blvd., San Juan, PR 00913 (tel. 809/727-4617), lies ten minutes from the airport, on the ocean between Parque Barbosa and Punta Las Marias. Benjamin Lawlor and Catherine Lawlor Nadeau, owners of the Old Village Inn in Ogunquit, Maine, are the innkeepers who purchased Tres Palmas in 1985. Screened windows and ceiling fans allow tropic breezes to flow through the brightly colored bedrooms, and there are air conditioners if needed. The seven rental units vary in size and amenities, prices in high season ranging from $55 to $80 daily *and in low season from $35 to $60,* tariffs based on double occupancy. A continental breakfast, usually with homemade muffins, which you can enjoy at tile patio tables with umbrellas and benches, is included in the rates. The tropic mini-pool is refreshing after a day at the beach or sunning on the rooftop deck. The living area of the main house became like a private den back home, where guests relax, read, watch HBO, or enjoy just chatting. At night the rooftop deck provides a private gateway to the sunset and stars. This guesthouse is one of the best bargains on the island.

ISLA VERDE: Beach-bordering Isla Verde is closer to the airport than the other sections of San Juan. Hotels here lie farther from the old town than do those considered in Miramar, Condado, and Ocean Park. However, a few of these establishments are among the deluxe showcases of the Caribbean. If you don't mind the isolation and want access to the fairly good beaches, then you might consider one of the following hotels.

Deluxe Living
El San Juan Hotel and Casino, Rt. 187 (P.O. Box 2872), San Juan, PR 00902-2872 (tel. 809/791-1000, or toll free 800/468-2818). For dozens of reasons which involve more than its spectacular physical plant, this is considered the best hotel in Puerto Rico, and some say the best in the entire Caribbean basin. Built in the 1950s, and graced with much handcrafted detailing, it fell into sad neglect. But in 1985, with the infusion of $45 million and the enlightened guidance of a sophisticated manager, Klaus Reincke, the hotel entered a renaissance. It appears from the exterior like one of the dozens of other high-rise towers lining the Isla Verde section of San Juan's sea-coast, but the hotel is surrounded by 350 palms, century-old banyans, and lavish gardens designed by Edward Durrell Stone. The hotel's sandy beach with its almond trees is probably the finest in the San Juan area, visibly wider and less violent than the beaches that flank some of

the older hotels of the Condado. Socially the hotel has sky-rocketed into prominence and is known for its glamorous functions filling its banqueting halls and conference rooms.

The hotel has a lobby that is perhaps the most opulent and memorable in the Caribbean. Entirely sheathed in russet-colored marble and hand-carved mahogany paneling, the public rooms stretch on almost endlessly. The in-house casino is an important attraction, and it's open daily from noon to 4 a.m. Gamblers and gourmets alike work out their energy in the rooftop health club or promenade down a re-creation of a waterfront street in Hong Kong to a Chinese restaurant. La Veranda Restaurant, close to the sands, is open 24 hours. Dar Tiffany, a steak and seafood restaurant, is open nightly, or you might prefer The Crabhouse, serving seafood every night. Good Italian food is served for lunch and dinner at La Piccola dining room.

The opulent accommodations have intriguing touches of hi-tech. Each makes maximum use of irregular spaces to include such amenities as dressing rooms, three different phones, air conditioning, video-linked TV, and ceiling fans. A few feature Jacuzzis. Each benefits from a harmonious color scheme of restful but stimulating Caribbean colors. About 150 of the 400 accommodations are within the outer reaches of the garden. Each is designed as a rustic but comfortable bungalow. Known as *casitas,* they include the accessories that most honeymooners fantasize about, including Roman tubs, atrium showers, and access to the fern-lined paths of a tropical jungle a few steps away. In winter, singles rent for $240 daily, doubles costing $390. *In summer, singles are priced at $200 daily, doubles at $310.* The hotel is near the airport, about a five-minute drive away.

Sands Hotel & Casino, 187 Isla Verde Rd., Isla Verde, PR 00913 (tel. 809/791-6100 or toll free 800/443-2009), is a spectacular 429-room resort, evoking the high-rolling spirit of the Sands at Atlantic City with its casino, the most lavish in the Caribbean. The public rooms are filled with museum-quality art, ranging from a seven-foot lion-headed bird from the royal palace of Singaraja in Indonesia to temple dogs from China. Everywhere you turn are pink and white marble floors, Lalique crystal, and tropical fabrics.

All this provides the setting for 420 deluxe air-conditioned rooms, including 51 luxurious suites, with either mountain or ocean view. Amenities include remote control cable color TV, direct-dial phones, private balconies, and mini-bars. Depending on the room, *singles in summer rent for $110 to $180 daily and doubles for $120 to $190.* In winter, prices range from $189 to $289 daily in a single and from $199 to $299 in a double. MAP is another $60 per person daily. Even more elegant is a wing of the hotel, the Plaza Club, with private garden suites, sometimes called a hotel within a hotel. It has a private entrance, 24-hour concierge service, complimentary food and beverage buffets, and private spa and beach facilities. *In summer, singles or doubles are charged $270 daily.* In winter, tariffs rise to $390 daily, either single or double occupancy.

The resort boasts the Caribbean's largest free-form swimming pool, complete with waterfalls, rockscapes, and a swim-up bar. Its most elegant restaurant is Leonardo's, one of the most elegant dining rooms around, decorated in metallic hues of pewter, copper, and brass, and serving a northern Italian cuisine. The Tucano, open 24 hours a day, is light and breezy, an informal place, with Puerto Rican and international dishes. The hotel also offers Reina del Mar, an excellent seafood restaurant. Its nightclub books some of the island's leading entertainment in winter.

El San Juan Towers, Rt. 187 (P.O. Box S3445), Isla Verde, San Juan, PR 00913 (tel. 809/791-5151, or toll free 800/468-2026), offers the closest thing a vacationer can get to apartment living. About a third of the 451 units are privately owned and occupied year round, while the rest are rented for at least part of the year as hotel accommodations. Each accommodation is completely air-conditioned, with a fully equipped kitchen, cable color TV, and a private balcony. *Off-season rates range from $135 daily in a minimum studio or efficiency for two, rising to $160 in a deluxe. A one-bedroom unit costs from $200 minimum to $270 daily, and two- and three-bedroom accommodations are also available.* In winter, studios and efficiencies for two range from $160 to $260 daily, while one-bedroom units cost anywhere from $270 to $335 daily. While at the hotel, you have access to the well-equipped private health club, with separate facilities for men and women. An outdoor playground and an indoor nursery for children are both supervised. The ground-floor restaurant, the Happy Apple, is open for breakfast and lunch, closing just before dinnertime. In a bar and lounge, the Mano-a-Mano, you can dance to low-key disco music after doing your shopping at the lobbyside mini-market. A car wash and laundry are on the premises.

A First-Class Choice

Carib-Inn Hotel, Rt. 187, P.O. Box 12112 Loiza Street Station, San Juan, PR 00914 (tel. 809/791-3535), is a complete tennis club and casino just eight minutes from the airport. The 225 high-ceilinged bedrooms and the cabanas, many with balconies, have outside views. Most overlook a giant racquet-shaped swimming pool, with a generous sunning and refreshment terrace, plus the Bohio Bar. The rooms are traditionally furnished, most having two double beds. Rooms are graded moderate, superior, and deluxe. *Summer tariffs are $55 to $90 daily in singles, $60 to $95 in doubles.* In winter, the prices are $95 to $135 daily in singles, $100 to $140 in doubles. Meal plans are available for a seven-day stay. Action is lively at night, particularly in the intimate casino. La Tinajita Restaurant serves local and international cuisine, and Cousin Ho's, a Chinese eatery, is one of the best restaurants in town. La Tinajita lobby bar provides live entertainment and dancing until the early hours. Tennis is taken seriously here, with four professional Laykold-surfaced courts and four clay courts, of which four are lit for night games. The largest tennis facility in the San Juan area, the Carib-Inn features a group of tennis professionals at your command to sharpen your game. A ball-throwing machine and a large tennis club membership always ensure an opportunity to play. There's a health center for men and women, including a gym, steam room, and sauna.

On a Budget in Isla Verde

Green Isle Inn and Casa Mathiesen Inn, 36 Calle Uno, San Juan, PR 00913 (tel. 809/726-4330), are twin establishments within a one-minute walk of each other, in the heart of Isla Verde, near El San Juan, Sands, and other luxury hotels, casinos, restaurants, and nightlife. They are ten minutes from the airport and within walking distance of the beach. Some 60% of the guests are repeats or referrals from other satisfied customers of the inns, one of the best bargains in Greater San Juan. Cleanliness and comfort are the main concerns, and rooms have private baths, air conditioning, cable TV, and daily maid service, as well as stocked kitchenettes in some rooms. The charge for two persons is $28 to $69 daily in high season (mid-December to the end of April), *$33 to $50 daily in summer.* Free airport pickup and use of the swimming pools and laundry facilities are among the amenities. The Lobster House, a seafood and steak restaurant, is on the premises of Casa Mathiesen.

La Playa, 6 Amapola St., San Juan, PR 00913 (tel. 809/791-1115), is a bargain. Its situation and atmosphere make it a persuasive choice. It's a two-story, L-shaped hotel, directly on the water, with rooms overlooking a courtyard crowded with lush, semitropical trees and shrubbery. The second-floor bedrooms, with long balconies, are preferred. Across from the front entrance lies the beginning of a two-mile-long beach. Each of the 16 well-furnished bedrooms has a private bath, air conditioning, and a bright ambience. *In summer, doubles cost from $49 to $59 and singles from $39.* Tariffs go up to $59 to $69 in a double in winter, $49 in a single. The hotel's waterfront bar is one of the most popular on the island (see my nighttime suggestions), and its restaurant is open from 8 a.m. to 11 p.m.

The Duffy's Inn, 9 Isla Verde Rd., San Juan, PR 00913 (tel. 809/726-1415). Built as a private home in the 1930s, but converted into a guesthouse in 1946, it resembles a secluded California bungalow compound hidden by flowering trees. There's a parking area where you can leave your car before heading in to meet the Rochester-born owner, Madeline Weihe. Everything is a bit time-worn, but that is perhaps what makes the place so low-key and mellow. Each of the 14 accommodations has air conditioning, a ceiling fan, phone, cable TV, and a view of the vegetation outside. They lie in a motel-like conversion of an older house a few steps away. Winter rates cost $50 daily in a single, $60 in a double. *Summer tariffs are $40 daily in a single, $50 in a double.* Guests congregate and socialize in a rear compound ringed with a wall in an area known as Duffys' Restaurant. Full dinners, costing up to $15 each, include grilled pork chops and chicken Cordon Bleu and are served from 5 p.m. to midnight daily. The bar, open 24 hours a day, serves sandwiches and soup.

Don Pedro Hotel, 4 Rosa St., San Juan, PR 00913 (tel. 809/791-2838), was created in the old Spanish style, with its L-shaped room block overlooking a courtyard, a swimming pool, and an adjoining garden restaurant. It's quite informal. Each of the bedrooms has tile floors, basic furnishings, with good-size closets and a tile bath. The furnishings are hit and miss, with older chests, maybe a vintage rocker, simple beds—in all, good for sleeping, and most important, clean. Each room is air-conditioned, and some have tiny kitchenettes opening onto a bed-sitting room. In winter, a single costs $50 daily, and a double goes for $62.25. *In summer, singles cost only $43.25, with doubles going for $52.25.* Rates include a continental breakfast.

2. DINING OUT IN PUERTO RICO

In recent years San Juan restaurants have returned to a greater appreciation of Puerto Rican cooking. Now many of the leading restaurants, although they still offer Stateside dishes, also feature a selection of local specialties as well. Even big hotels such as the Caribe Hilton are in on the act. Although Puerto Rican cookery has similarities to both Spanish and Mexican cuisine, it has its own unique style. It differs as well from American fare not only in cooking methods but also in seasonings and basic ingredients—coriander, papaya, cacao, nispero, apio, plantains, and yampee all being indigenous to the island.

Cocina Criola (Créole cooking) was initiated by the Arawaks and Taínos, the original inhabitants of the island. Long before Columbus arrived, these peaceful people thrived on diets of corn, tropical fruits, and seafood. When Ponce de León arrived with Columbus in 1493 and began colonizing the island, the Spanish added beef, pork, rice, wheat, and olive oil to the island's foodstuffs. Soon after, the Spanish began planting sugarcane and imported slaves from Africa, replacing the decimated local population, to do the labor involved in its growth. The Africans brought with them okra and taro, known in Puerto Rico as *yauita.* The mingling of flavors and ingredients passed from generation to generation among the different ethnic groups that settled on the island to create the exotic blend of today's Puerto Rican cookery.

Lunch and dinner generally begin with sizzling hot appetizers such as *bacalaitos,* crunchy cod fritters; *surullitos,* sweet, plump cornmeal fingers; and *empanadillas,* crescent-shape turnovers filled with lobster, crab, conch, or beef. Next, a bowl of steaming *asapao,* rice with chicken or shellfish prepared to the consistency of a hearty gumbo soup, may be followed by *lechón asado,* roast suckling pig; *pollo en vino dulce,* succulent chicken in wine; or *bacalao,* dried salted cod mixed with various roots and tubers and fried. No matter the selection, main dishes are served with *tostones,* deep-fried plantains (green bananas) that are salted to taste, and plentiful portions of rice and beans.

The aroma that wafts from kitchens throughout Puerto Rico comes from *adobo* and *sofrito*—blends of herbs and spices that give many of the native foods their distinctive taste and color. Adobo, made by crushing together peppercorns, oregano, garlic, salt, olive oil, and lime juice or vinegar, is rubbed into meats before they are roasted. Sofrito, a potpourri of onions, garlic, and peppers browned in olive oil or lard and colored with *achiote* (annatto seeds) imparts the bright yellow color to the island's rice, soups, and stews.

Dessert is usually a form of *flan* (custard) or perhaps *nisperos de batata,* sweet potato balls made with coconut, cloves, and cinnamon, or guava jelly and *queso blanco* (white cheese).

Visitors to Puerto Rico longing for authentic island cuisine can rely on *mesones gastronomicos* (gastronomic inns). This established dining "network" sanctioned by the Puerto Rico Tourism Co. highlights restaurants recognized for excellence in preparing and serving Puerto Rican specialties at moderate prices.

Mesones gastronomicos are limited to restaurants outside the San Juan urban area that are close to major island attractions. Membership in the program requires that restaurants have attractive surroundings and comply with strict standards of good service. Members must specialize in native foods and offer a sampling of main dishes that start as low as $7.

Of course, out on the island ask for any fresh fish dish and chances are you'll be pleased. Finish your meal with Puerto Rican coffee, which is strong, black, aromatic. Perhaps you'll have only a small cup. Rum is the national drink, and you can buy it in almost any shade. In Puerto Rico it's quite proper to order a cold beer before one even looks at the menu. Popular among the locals is India, brewed in Mayagüez, famous for its pure water.

MEALS IN OLD SAN JUAN: Old Spain is recaptured at **La Zaragozana,** 356 San Francisco (tel. 809/723-5103), with its white adobe walls, rough-hewn beams, slate and terracotta floors, as well as antiques, murals, brass lamps, and wine racks. In the beamed bodega, you can enjoy a before-dinner drink. The restaurant, which specializes in Spanish, Cuban, and Puerto Rican cuisine, is run by the much-awarded Wilberto Alejandro. On my most recent rounds I was served my finest meal in Old San Juan in this restaurant. The top specialty is called "The Chef's," a filet of beef tenderloin stuffed with Spanish ham and cheese in a burgundy wine sauce with mushrooms. The kitchen has long been known for its classic black-bean soup, but other kettles are likely to contain gazpacho, caldo gallego, or fish soup. Other temptations include snails Zaragozana, Valencian paella, a zarzuela of seafood, or perhaps lobster Créole. Puerto Rican dishes include filet of pork Old San Juan, followed by "custard from heaven." Count on parting with $30. The restaurant is open daily from 11:30 a.m. to midnight, and reservations are important.

Los Galanes, 65 San Francisco (tel. 809/722-4008), links Old Seville with Old San Juan. It's a 16th-century setting on a one-way street, an easy walk down from El Convento. As you enter, on your right is a small bar for a before-dinner drink (it's fashionable to order a dry sherry). The maître d' and his staff are courtesy-oriented. The familiar selection of international appetizers is presented on the elaborate scroll of the parchment menu, including gazpacho, homemade pâté, and escargots bourguignonne. The main courses are usually good and sometimes excellent—filet of sole meunière, shrimp in garlic sauce, veal marsala, filet mignon, and chicken Cordon Bleu. Another specialty is paella, prepared for two or more. For dessert, most diners seem to prefer the chocolate cheesecake. For a complete dinner here, expect to spend from $30. The restaurant is open from 7 to 11 p.m. for dinner only, and reservations are imperative. It is closed Sunday and Monday.

Restaurant Amadeus, 106 Calle San Sebastian (tel. 809/722-8635). An abstract watercolor portrait of a young Mozart decorates the wall near the entrance of this restaurant where lovers of music and fine food feel at home. The other paintings, many by emerging Puerto Rican artists, change as rapidly as the menu items which emerge from the kitchen. In the kitchen, Caribbean ingredients are given a nouvelle twist. You might enjoy an appetizer of fried green plantains with caviar and fish mousse, fried dumplings in guava sauce, ceviche, a cassoulet of shrimp with black beans and sausages, marlin, shark in white wine sauce, and rabbit with prunes and red wine sauce. Full meals cost from $18 at dinner, from $12 at lunch. The establishment is open daily except Monday from noon to 2 a.m., although the kitchen closes at 12:30 a.m. The establishment lies in the heart of the old city, across from the side of the Church of San José.

El Patio de Sam, 102 San Sebastian (tel. 809/723-1149), stands across from the San José Church, the oldest building on the island, and faces the statue of Ponce de León, the island's first governor. This popular place is a gathering spot for American expatriates, newspeople, and shopkeepers in the old town. It's known for having the best hamburgers in San Juan. Even though the dining room is not on the outside, it has been transformed into a patio. The illusion is so credible you'll swear you're dining al fresco: every table is strategically placed near a cluster of potted, outdoor plants, and canvas panels and awnings cover the skylight. For a cooling and satisfying lunch, ideal after you've strolled through the streets of the old town, try the black-bean soup, followed by the cold meat platter, and topped with a Key lime tart. Other main dishes include various steaks, barbecued ribs, filet of sole stuffed with crab, and fish and chips. At lunch, expect to pay around $10, the tab rising to $15 and up for dinner. The place is open from 11 a.m. to 2 a.m. Sunday to Thursday, with the kitchen closing at 1:30 a.m. Hours are from 11 a.m. to 4:30 a.m. Friday and Saturday, when the kitchen closes at 3:30 a.m.

La Mallorquina, 207 San Justo (tel. 809/722-3261), is San Juan's oldest restaurant, founded in 1848. A bit of Old Spain transplanted to the New World, the restaurant is in a three-story, glassed-in courtyard with arches and antique wall clocks. Even if you've already eaten and are shopping in the old town, you might want to visit just to perch at the old-fashioned wooden bar which runs the length of the left wall as you enter. The waiters appear as if they've been hired by central casting, and they slip in the back to eat the food too. The chef specializes in the most typical Puerto Rican rice dish—asopao. You can have it with either chicken, shrimp, or lobster and shrimp (if you're feeling extravagant). Arroz con pollo is almost as popular. I suggest you get your dinner rolling by ordering garlic soup. If that frightens you, gazpacho is served also. Among other recommended main dishes are grilled pork chop with fried plantain, and beef tenderloin, Puerto Rican style. The assorted seafood stewed in wine is good. Lunch is busy, and dinners are sometimes quiet. A full dinner should cost between $15 and $25. It's best to go between noon and 2 p.m. and 8 and 10 p.m. It is closed Sunday.

El Meson Vasco, 47 Cristo St., corner of San Sebastián (tel. 809/725-7819), serves savory Basque specialties right in the old town. A corner building, the restaurant opens directly onto the Plaza de San José. Even if you prowl the streets of Seville, you couldn't find a more Spanish restaurant. High arched windows and a beamed ceiling add the right architectural details, and as you sit on raffia-covered chairs you can check out the paintings and woodcarvings. The very leisurely service is from 12:30 p.m. to midnight. The chef's specialties are garlic chicken, Spanish hake in green sauce, trout molinera, and eggs Bilbaina. Every time I'm in San Juan I journey here for an order of the small white beans, Basque style (with sausages), a meal in themselves. Soups are good, especially the *porrusalda* (potato and leek). If you eat here, expect a tab ranging from $18.

La Chaumière, 367 Tetuán (tel. 809/722-3330), is decorated like an inn in provincial France, with heavy ceiling beams, black and white checkerboard floors, large rows of wine racks, and half-timbered walls. Menu items include beef Wellington, a surprise in a French restaurant, rack of lamb for two, chateaubriand for two, pheasant flambéed with Calvados, onion soup, vichyssoise, pâté maison made with pork, chicken, and duck liver, and daily specials, such as fish soup. Full meals range upward from $40. It's open daily except Sunday from 6 p.m. to midnight. Upstairs is La Crêperie, a French pancake house.

Butterfly People Café, 152 Fortaleza (tel. 809/723-2432), has gossamer wings. This butterfly venture (see my shopping recommendations) is the special world of Attenaire Purington, who was a Jordanian translator at the United Nations before opening this second-floor café in a restored mansion in Old San Juan. Next to the world's largest gallery devoted to butterflies, you can dine in the café, opening to a patio. It is mainly a bar, with 15 tables serving drinks and lunch from 11 a.m. to 6 p.m. Monday to Saturday. The café specializes in tropical and light European fare utilizing only the freshest ingredients. You might begin with gazpacho or vichyssoise, follow with quiche or one of the daily specials, and top it all off with chocolate mousse or the tantalizing raspberry chiffon pie with fresh raspberry sauce. A full bar offers tropical specialties featuring piña coladas, fresh-squeezed Puerto Rican orange juice, and Fantasias—a frappé of seven fresh fruits. Wherever you look, framed butterflies will delight you. At times, especially the afternoons when cruise-ship passengers aren't visiting, the place has a private-club atmosphere, where the customers play chess and backgammon.

La Bombonera, 259 San Francisco (tel. 809/722-0658), is a long-enduring favorite. In fact, it was established in 1901 and ever since has been serving its homemade pastries and endless cups of coffee (said to be the best served in Old Town). For decades a rendezvous point for the island's literati, as well as of families, it has never been as popular with tourists as with locals. In fact, it looks shabby and rundown, but the food is authentic and cheap. You can dine well here for $15 daily from 7:30 a.m. to 8:30 p.m. They serve sandwiches, but most patrons prefer one of the main regional dishes, perhaps spaghetti with chicken, rice with squid, roast leg of pork, or a seafood asopao. For dessert you might choose stuffed ripe plantain pie, apple, pineapple, or prune pie, or else one of the many types of flan. Service is polite, if a bit rushed, and the place fills up quickly at lunchtime.

Maria's, 204 Calle Cristo (no phone). Every time I get off the plane in San Juan, I head for this narrow little bar with back tables in the old part of town. There, perched on a stool, you'll be served some of the coolest and most refreshingly original drinks in the capital—a banana frost, a pineapple frost, an orange freeze, a papaya freeze, a chocolate frost, a lime freeze, a mixed fruit frappé. The students, TV personalities, writers, and models who gather here also enjoy Mexican dishes such as chili with cheese, a taco, or an enchilada. If that sounds too heavy on a hot day, then I suggest the fruit salad. Count on spending from $6 up for a drink and a snack. The blender continues to whir from 11 a.m. until 2 a.m. seven days a week.

PUERTA DE TIERRA: One of the most elegant—and best—restaurants in Puerto Rico is **La Rôtisserie,** in the Caribe Hilton (tel. 809/721-0303). The restaurant is tastefully appointed, located on the second floor of the deluxe hotel next to the casino. Reservations are necessary, and in the evening men are requested to wear jackets. Meals usually average around $35 to $40. For that, you are likely to be tempted with roast prime rib of beef, two succulent double lamb chops, perhaps duckling with wild rice. There is always fresh fish, such as red snapper, or else you can order the pescador platter of assorted fresh fish. The Caesar salad is always spectacular, and you might want to conclude with a hot chocolate soufflé. Lunch is served from noon to 3 p.m. Monday to Friday and dinner every day from 7 to 11 p.m.

CONDADO: One of the best restaurants on the island, the **Charthouse,** 1214 Ashford Ave. (tel. 809/728-0110), is also one of the most popular bars in the Caribbean. The lattice-trimmed villa, built in 1910 and once the home of the German consul, attracts on any night literally hundreds of sociable local residents, mostly aged 18 to 40, to its long bar in what used to be a spacious salon. Today the heavy ceiling beams have been exposed, track lighting installed, and paintings added to create a warm ambience. The food here is beautifully prepared. The prime rib dishes may be the best in the entire Caribbean. You can enjoy New England clam chowder, the copious salad that comes with all main courses, blue marlin, fresh broccoli, top sirloin, shrimp teriyaki, one-tail Australian lobster, Hawaiian chicken, and a dessert called "mud pie." Full meals are often less than $30, although if you drink a lot (and that's part of the fun here) you can spend a lot more. The Charthouse is part of a chain of ambience-filled restaurants scattered across the American West, based in California. The bar is open from 5 p.m. to 1 a.m. Meals are served daily: from 6 to 11 p.m. daily except Friday and Saturday when it closes at 12:30 a.m. Reservations are imperative.

    Lotus Flower, 999 Ashford Ave., Laguna Wing of the Condado Plaza Hotel and Casino (tel. 809/721-1000, ext. 1950), on Condado Beach, is one of the finest Chinese restaurants in the Caribbean. Overlooking the Condado Lagoon, the restaurant serves dishes that are a savory medley of flavors. It's open Monday to Friday from noon to 3 p.m. and 6 to 11:30 p.m. On Saturday it is open only from 6 to 11:30 p.m., and on Sunday from 1 to 11:30 p.m. The chef is equally at home in turning out Hunan, Szechuan, or Cantonese cookery. He'll even do a Peking duck if you order it far enough in advance. Specialties include lemon chicken, beef with scallops and shrimp in a hot sauce, and Szechuan Phoenix, made with prime beef and chicken in a hot sauce. Open your meal with the noodles in sesame sauce, a delectable dish. Count on spending around $30.

    Reina de España, 1106 Avenida Magdalena (tel. 809/721-9049), with a refined cuisine, is a touch of old Spain. One of the most distinguished dining places in Puerto Rico, the elegantly decorated restaurant prepares what it terms a *cocina imaginativa*. It's also been called "New Créole" cooking, a style pioneered by the owner and chef, Jesús Ramiro. You might begin with peppers stuffed with a blood sausage mousse, ripe plantain croquettes, or else anchovy pâté. The chef also prepares cream of casave soup. For your main course, any fish or meat can be charcoal grilled for you upon request. Unusual main dishes include the fish of the day prepared with a green sauce and served with clams as well as jumbo shrimp with halibut mousse. You are faced with many homemade desserts, like fresh strawberry sherbet or the chef's fried ice cream. Hours are from noon to 3 p.m. and 6:30 to 11 p.m. Monday to Thursday, noon to 3 p.m. and 6:30 to 11 p.m. Friday, and 6:30 to 11:30 p.m. Saturday. Closed Saturday at lunch and on Sunday.

SANTURCE: One of the finest dining rooms in Puerto Rico, **La Casona,** 609 San Jorge, corner of Fernández Juncos (tel. 809/727-2717), offers the kind of dining usually found in Madrid, complete with a strolling guitarist. Since 1972, the chefs here have dispensed their special bland of Spanish and international dishes in a turn-of-the-century mansion surrounded by gardens. Guests enter among sweet-scented plants past trailing bougainvillea, into a much renovated but still charming and sophisticated gastronomic enclave. The place draws some of the most fashionable diners in Puerto Rico. Paella marinara, prepared for two or more persons, is a specialty, as is a zarzuela de mariscos or seafood medley. You can select such tasty dishes as filet of grouper in Basque sauce or octopus vinaigrette. You might also enjoy the rabbit stew or a rack of lamb prepared in the oven as they do in Segovia. Open daily except Sunday from 11:30 a.m. to 11:30 p.m., La Casona serves complete meals for around $50. It's highly recommended.

Operation of the **Swiss Chalet,** Hotel Pierre, De Diego (tel. 809/721-2233), has continued successfully for more than 30 years. The menu is large, with a host of cheese dishes and other Swiss specialties, including everything from sauerbraten to minced veal in white wine sauce with mushrooms, a favorite in Zurich. Hors d'oeuvres offered are a dozen escargots du Jura maison and soups such as French onion, green pea, and vichyssoise. The main dishes are well prepared, and you can enjoy a Swiss bratwurst with onion sauce or roast rack of lamb provençale. Fish and seafood are good too. Try the Mexican Gulf shrimp sautéed in garlic and herb butter. Among the desserts, I like Bavarois au kirsch with raspberry sauce. Meals average around $25. The management suggests that you dress "elegantly casual." Hours are daily from noon to 10:30 p.m.

MIRAMAR: An interesting choice is **Augusto's,** Hotel Excelsior, 801 Ponce de León Ave. (tel. 809/721-7400) a European enclave of aesthetics and cuisine in the middle of San Juan, although tropical ingredients are used as much as possible as a concession to island tastes. It is operated by one of Puerto Rico's most successful chefs, Austrian-born August Schreiner, who first came to prominence on the island during his long stay at La Rôtisserie at the Caribe Hilton, a tenure during which he won many awards for outstanding international cuisine. The restaurant has a sophisticated decor with light gray walls, masses of fresh flowers, and a sweeping view over the illuminated waters of an outdoor swimming pool. Specialties include escargots baked in Pernod-flavored butter, venison medallions with juniperberry sauce, jumbo shrimp in a provençale sauce, and baked redskin potatoes with sour cream and caviar. You can also order salmon steak baked in filo pastry. Full meals cost from $40, and lunch is served from noon to 3 p.m., dinner from 7 to 10 p.m. Closed Sunday.

Windows on the Caribbean, 600 Avenida Fernández Juncos (tel. 809/721-4100), occupies the 27th floor of the tallest skyscraper in the Caribbean, in the previously recommended Clarion Hotel & Casino. In addition to being one of the city's finest restaurants, it offers a sweeping view over the seacoast and San Juan. The restaurant is on one side, with a popular piano bar on the other. Lunch is served daily from noon to 3 p.m. and dinner from 6 to 11 p.m., except on Friday and Saturday when the kitchen stays open until midnight. The chef specializes in such dishes as breast of chicken stuffed with crabmeat and covered with a lobster sauce, medallions of filet of beef Cordon Rouge stuffed with pâté de foie gras in champagne sauce. The restaurant is also known for creating 13 variations of Valencian paella. Meals cost from $40, and reservations are important.

ISLA VERDE: One of the best choices in San Juan for a taste of the good life, **Dar Tiffany,** in the Hotel El San Juan, Rt. 187 (tel. 809/791-1000), is usually jammed, especially on weekends, with the island's resident literati, glitterati, and beautiful people. On the ground floor of Puerto Rico's most glamorous hotel, it provides considerate service. You dine within a labyrinth of etched glass whose palm-leaf motifs mimic the plants growing outside. A few steps away, just on the other side of the translucent walls, you'll glimpse the whirling ceiling fans of one of the hotel's more popular tropical bars. The wine list is actually more extensive than the food menu, which offers such carefully aged and seasoned specialties as prime rib, filet mignon, veal chops, jumbo lobster, sea scallops, and filet of fresh Norwegian salmon. A Caesar salad and a temptingly caloric dessert might be the appropriate beginning and ending for a meal here. Dinners, served between 6:30 p.m. and midnight seven days a week, cost from $35, and reservations are recommended.

    Back Street Hong Kong, Hotel El San Juan, Rt. 187 (tel. 809/791-1224). To reach it, you promenade down a disconcertingly realistic re-creation of a backwater street in Hong Kong. Disassembled from its original home at the 1964 New York World's Fair, it was purchased and rebuilt, with the exposed electrical meters and lopsided façades of its original design intact. A few steps later, you enter one of the best Chinese restaurants in the Caribbean. Beneath a soaring redwood ceiling, and ringed with teakwood lattices, iron filigree, and formally dressed employees, you can enjoy meals for around $30. The Mandarin/Szechuan/Hunan menu includes pineapple fried rice served in a real pineapple, a superb version of scallops with orange sauce, Szechuan beef with chicken, steamed fish, sizzling three delicacies (beef, shrimp, and scallops), and a dragon and phoenix (lobster mixed with shrimp). Lunch is served only on Sunday from noon to 3 p.m., and dinner lasts from 6 p.m. to midnight seven days a week.

FOOD ON THE ISLAND: In your tour out on the island, you'll find few well-known restaurants, except those in the major hotels. However, there are plenty of roadside places and simple taverns. The most popular restaurant outside of San Juan follows:

IN THE RAIN FOREST: Right in the heart of the island's exotic El Yunque rain forest, **El Yunque Restaurant** (tel. 809/790-4237), has been in business since 1936. You can dine on some of the most authentic Puerto Rican specialties offered on the island. On the narrow ledge of a mountain road, this chalet restaurant is made of wood, with a stone fireplace at each end. The side of the dining room with the best view has an all-glass wall. The atmosphere is rustic, and at some time during your meal it will definitely rain—I can guarantee that! You park your car on the road above, walking down a covered staircase to this seemingly remote spot. The soups, served in pewter bowls, are excellent and home-made, ranging from a regional garlic version to the classic caldo gallego. The specialty is asopao, that soupy Puerto Rican rice dish, prepared here with everything from land crab to squid. The best, I think, is the asopao paella, a really big meal. Also good are land crab prepared native style and a casserole of shrimp and lobster in wine sauce. First-timers might be attracted to the *yuquiyu*. This is half a pineapple shell filled with meat and Spanish sausage, pigeon peas, and crushed fresh pineapple. If you don't want such heavy food for lunch, try a native fruit salad, followed by custard. A full repast will cost from $22 per person. Hours are daily from 9 a.m. to 6 p.m.

3. WHAT TO SEE IN SAN JUAN

The streets are narrow and teeming with traffic, but a walk through Old San Juan—in Spanish, El Viejo San Juan—is like a stroll through five centuries of history. You can do it in less than a day. In a historic landmark seven-square-block area in the westernmost part of the city, you can see on foot many of Puerto Rico's chief historical sightseeing attractions, and when you tire of monuments, you can combine your tour with some shopping along the way. Many of the museums in Old San Juan close at 11:45 a.m. for lunch and don't reopen until 2 p.m.

The Spanish moved to Old San Juan in 1521, and the city founded there was to play an important role as Spain's bastion of defense in the Caribbean. Once the city was called Puerto Rico (Rich Port), as the name San Juan was given to the whole island.

I'll begin our tour at the northeast corner of Old San Juan. On Calle Norzagaray stands the 1783 **Fort San Cristobal**, which was built to defend San Juan against attacks by land, as well as to form backup support for El Morro if that fort were attacked from the sea. Composed of six independent units, the fort is connected to a central structure by means of tunnels and dry moats. You'll get the idea if you look at a scale model on display. On a site of 27 acres, the fort is overseen by the National Park Service. Be sure to see the Garita del Diablo, or the Devil's Sentry Box. The devil himself, it is said, would snatch away soldiers on guard duty at the box. Free guided tours are offered daily at 9:30 and 11 a.m. and at 2 and 3:30 p.m.

The **Tapia Theater,** Avenida Ponce de León, was paid for by taxes on bread and imported liquor. Standing across from the Plaza de Colón, it is one of the oldest theaters in the western hemisphere, built about 1832. In 1976 a restoration returned the theater to its original look. Much of Puerto Rican theater history is connected with Tapia. It's named after the island's first prominent playwright, Alejandro Tapia y Rivera (1826–1882). Adelina Patti (1843–1919), the most popular and highly paid singer of her day, made her operatic debut here when she was barely 14.

Before you leave, pause to look at the **Plaza de Colón.** Once named the Plaza de Santiago, it had its name changed to honor Columbus on November 19, 1893, the 400th anniversary of the island's discovery. In the center of the square is a statue of Columbus, and at its base are plaques tracing incidents in his globe-trotting life.

La Casa del Callejon, Calle San Francisco (tel. 809/725-5250), run by the Institute of Puerto Rican Culture, houses two museums. On the first floor of this 18th-century house, the Museum of Colonial Architecture has scale models of El Morro and La Fortaleza which may give you some perspective before you see the real thing. Exhibits of iron and woodwork, along with ceramic tiles, can also be seen. I find the second-floor Museum of the Puerto Rican Family much more interesting, as it gives you a glimpse into the life of how these island people lived in the 19th century. The rooms are small, and the life, as depicted here, was definitely middle class. Hours are 9 a.m. to noon and 1 to 4:30 p.m. Admission is free. Guided tours are conducted Tuesday through Saturday at 9 a.m. and again at 4:30 p.m. However, it has been temporarily closed, so check its status at the time of your visit.

El Arsenal, La Puntilla (tel. 809/724-5949). The Spaniards used a shallow craft to patrol lagoons and mangroves in and around San Juan. Needing a base for these vessels, they constructed El Arsenal at the turn of the century, and it was at this same base that they, so to speak, staged their last stand, flying the Spanish colors until the final Spaniard was removed in 1898, at the end of the Spanish-American War. Exhibitions are held in the building's three galleries. Part of the arsenal is being renovated for additional gallery space. Hours are from 9 a.m. to noon and 1 to 4 p.m. Wednesday to Sunday.

Cristo Chapel, on Calle Cristo, was built to commemorate what legend says was a miracle. Horse racing down Cristo Street was the highlight of the fiestas on St. John's Day, the patron saint of the city. In 1753 a young rider lost control of his horse and plunged over the precipice. Moved by the accident, a spectator, the secretary of the city, Don Mateo Pratts, invoked Christ to save the youth. He had the chapel built that same year. Today it is a landmark in the old city and one of its best-known historical monuments. The chapel's Campèche paintings and gold and silver altar can be seen through its glass doors.

La Casa de Libro, 255 Calle Cristo (tel. 809/723-0354), is a restored 18th-century house sheltering a library devoted to the arts of printing and bookmaking, with examples of fine printing from the 15th century to the present, as well as some medieval illuminated manuscripts. Special exhibits are usually shown on the first floor, open from 11 a.m. to 4:30 p.m. Monday to Friday.

La Fortaleza, at the west end of Calle Fortaleza overlooking the San Juan Harbor (tel. 809/721-7000, ext. 2211), is the office and residence of the governor of Puerto Rico. The oldest executive mansion in continuous use in the western hemisphere, it has served as the island's seat of government for more than three centuries. Yet its history goes back even further, to 1533, when construction began for a fortress (*fortaleza*) to protect San Juan's settlers during raids by cannibalistic Caribs. The original medieval towers remain, but as the edifice was subsequently enlarged into a palace, other modes of architecture and ornamentation were also incorporated, including baroque, Gothic, neoclassical, and Arabian. La Fortaleza has been designated a National Historic Site by the U.S. government. Tours in English are conducted every hour on weekdays from 9 a.m. until 4 p.m.—but don't show up in your bikini.

San Juan Gate, Calle San Francisco and Calle Recinto Oeste, built around 1635, just north of La Fortaleza, was the main gate and entry point into San Juan —that is, if you came by ship in the 18th century. The gate is the only one remaining of the several entries to the old walled city.

City Hall, Calle San Francisco (tel. 809/724-7171), was ordered built in 1604, but work suffered many delays because of lack of money. Rebuilt twice in the 18th century, it was finally ready to be occupied in 1789. The clock in the tower was installed in 1889. Guided tours are given Monday through Friday, except holidays, from 8 a.m. to 4:15 p.m.

San Juan Cathedral, Calle Cristo and Caleta San Juan, was begun in 1540. Since that time it's had a rough life. Restoration today has been extensive, so it hardly resembles the thatch-roofed structure that had stood there until 1529 when it was wiped out by a hurricane. Hampered by lack of funds, the cathedral slowly added a circular staircase and two adjoining vaulted Gothic chambers. But along came the Earl of Cumberland in 1598 to loot it, and a hurricane in 1615 to blow off its roof. In 1908 the body of Ponce de León was brought here. After he'd died from an arrow wound in Florida, his body had originally been taken to San José Church. The cathedral faces the Plaza de las Monjas (or the Nuns' Square), a tree-shaded old town spot where you can rest and cool off. Open from 6:30 a.m. to 5 p.m. daily.

Plazuela de la Rogativa, Caleta de las Monjas, basks in legend. In 1797 the British across San Juan Bay at Santurce held the old town under siege. However, that same year they mysteriously sailed away. Later, the commander claimed he feared the enemy was well prepared behind those walls, apparently seeing many lights and thinking them to be reinforcements. Some people believe those lights were torches carried by women in a rogativa, or religious procession, as they followed their bishop. A handsome statue of a bishop, trailed by a trio of torch-bearing women, was donated to the city on its 450th anniversary.

Casa Blanca, 1 Calle San Sebastian (tel. 809/724-4102). Ponce de León never lived here, although construction of the house (built in 1523) sometimes is attributed to him. The house was erected two years after the explorer's death, and work was ordered by his son-in-law, Juan Garcia Troche. The parcel of land was given to Ponce de León as a reward for services rendered to the Crown. Descendants of the explorer lived in the house for about 2½ centuries until the Spanish government took it over in 1779 for use as a residence for military commanders. The U.S. government as well used it as a home for army commanders. Today it's a museum, showing how Puerto Ricans lived in the 16th and 17th centuries. Guided tours are Tuesday to Sunday from 9 a.m. to noon and 1 to 4:30 p.m.

Back on Calle Cristo, **San José Church** is centered in San José Plaza, right next to the Dominican monastery. Initial plans were drawn in 1523 and work, supervised by Dominican friars, began in 1532. Before going into the church, look for the statue of Ponce de León on the adjoining plaza. It was made from British cannons captured during Sir Ralph Abercromby's unsuccessful attack on San Juan in 1797.

Both the church and its monastery were closed by decree in 1838, the property confiscated by the royal treasury. Later, the Crown turned the convent into a military barracks. The Jesuits restored the badly damaged church. The church was the place of worship for Ponce de León's descendants, who are buried there under the family's coat-of-arms. The conquistador was interred there until his removal to the cathedral in 1908.

Although badly looted, the church still has some treasures, including *Christ of the Ponces,* a carved crucifix presented to Ponce de León. Packed in a crate, the image survived a terrible shipwreck outside San Juan Harbor. The church has four oils by José Campèche and two large works by Francisco Oller. Many miracles have been attributed to a painting in the Chapel of Belém. It's a 15th-century Flemish work called *Virgin of Bethlehem.* Hours are from 10 a.m. to 4 p.m. Monday to Friday and 11:30 a.m. to 4 p.m. Sunday. Closed Saturday.

Adjacent to the church, at the corner of the square, the **Pablo Casals Museum,** 101 San Sebastián (tel. 809/723-9185) is devoted to the memorabilia left by the artist to the people of Puerto Rico. Born in 1876, Casals of course achieved fame as a cellist, and also won renown as a conductor and composer of symphonies and symphonic poems. Later in Puerto Rico, his "Casals Festivals" drew worldwide interest, attracting some of the greatest performing artists. The festival is still held every June. The maestro's cello is here, along with a library of videotapes, played on request, of some of the festival concerts. This small, 18th-century house also contains manuscripts and photographs of Casals. It is open from 9 a.m. to 5 p.m. Tuesday to Saturday, noon to 5 p.m. Sunday. Closed Monday.

Casa de los Contrafuertes (House of the Buttresses), 101 San Sebastián (tel. 809/724-5949), stands adjacent to the Pablo Casals Museum at Calle San Sebastian. The building with its thick buttresses is believed to be the oldest residence remaining in El Viejo San Juan, and it's open from 9 a.m. to noon and 1 to 4 p.m. Wednesday through Sunday. This is a three-in-one museum, containing a Pharmacy Museum, which existed in the 19th century in the town of Cayey. Even more interesting is its Museo de Santos (saints carved in native woods). Both of these museums are on the ground floor. If you go upstairs, you'll find a Graphic Arts Museum, displaying an exhibition of watercolors, prints, and paintings by local artists.

Dominican Convent, 98 Calle Norzagaray (tel. 809/724-0700), was started by Dominican friars in 1523, shortly after the city itself was founded. It was the first convent in Puerto Rico, and women and children often hid here during Carib Indian attacks. The friars lived here until 1838 when the Crown closed down the monasteries, turning the building into an army barracks. The American army used it as its headquarters until 1966. Today it is the center of the Institute of Puerto Rican Culture. The institute promotes cultural events all over the island. On the ground floor is a permanent display of treasures, featuring a medieval altar piece. Gregorian chants help re-create the long-ago atmosphere. The Chapel Museum is open from 9 a.m. to noon and 1 to 4 p.m. Wednesday to Sunday. The Arts Museum hours are from 9:15 a.m. to 4:15 p.m. Monday to Saturday.

The **City Walls,** Calle Norzagaray, around San Juan were built in 1630 to protect the town against both European invaders and Caribbean pirates. The thickness of the walls averages from 20 feet at the base to 12 feet at the top, with an average height of 40 feet. Between San Cristobal and El Morro, bastions were erected at frequent intervals. You can start seeing the walls from your approach from San Cristobal on your way to El Morro.

The **San Juan Cemetery,** Calle Norzagaray, officially opened in 1814 and has since been the final resting place for many prominent Puerto Rican families. The circular chapel is dedicated to Saint Magdalene of Pazzis and was built in the 1860s. Aficionados of old graveyards can wander among marble monuments, mausoleums, and statues, marvelous examples of Victorian funereal statuary. However, there are no trees or any form of shade in the cemetery, so don't go wandering in the noonday sun.

El Morro, Calle Norzagaray (tel. 809/724-1978), stands on a rocky promontory, dominating San Juan Bay. Called the Castillo San Felipe del Morro, it was ordered built in 1539 and construction started the following year. The original fort was a round tower which can still be seen inside the main bastion of the castle. More walls were added, a line of batteries installed. By 1787 the structure reached its present stage. Sir Francis Drake was turned away in 1595. The fort is run and administered by the U.S. National Park Service. As one of the loftiest points in the old town, it is a labyrinth of dungeons, barracks, outposts, and ramps. Guided tours are offered daily at 9:30 and 11 a.m. and at 2 and 3:30 p.m. Slide shows in English and Spanish are presented. Admission is $1 for adults, free for children.

Museo del Niño is a museum devoted to children and sheltered in an 18th-century powder house, within the grounds of El Morro. It deals with arts and sciences, concentrating on exhibits that can be touched. Displays are devoted to sun, earth, and family. Hours are daily except Monday and Thursday from 9 a.m. to noon and 1 to 4:30 p.m.

Unless you've grown weary of forts, there's one more. **Fort San Jeronimo,** or what's left of it, stands east of the Caribe Hilton at the entrance to Condado Bay. Completed in 1788, it was badly damaged in the English assault of 1797. Reconstructed in the closing year of the 18th century, it has now been taken over by the Institute of Puerto Rican Culture. A museum has been lodged there, with life-size mannequins wearing military uniforms. Ship's models and charts are also displayed. Charging no admission, the museum is open from 9 a.m. to noon and 1 to 4:30 p.m. Wednesday to Sunday.

The **Museum of the University of Puerto Rico,** Recinto de Río Piedras, has good collections of paintings by Puerto Rican artists, including Francisco Oller and José Campèche, the first important artist of the country (18th century). There is also a large collection of pre-Columbian Puerto Rican Indian artifacts from the Ingeri, sub-Taíno, and Taíno civilizations. In the museum's temporary exhibition hall, you can see such attractions as the work of contemporary Puerto Rican artists, retrospectives of important aspects of Puerto Rican art, and exhibits of the work of Puerto Rican and United States artists. Admission to the museum is free. It's open Monday to Friday from 9 a.m. to 9 p.m. and on Saturday and Sunday from 9 a.m. to 3 p.m.

A WALKING TOUR OF OLD SAN JUAN: For a sweeping view of the 200-acre city of Old San Juan, climb to the top of **El Morro,** the formidable fortress rising 140 feet above the ocean. From that lofty spot you can get your bearings and, at the bottom, begin your walking tour of the old city. **Plaza de San José,** a favorite meeting place, is just two short blocks from the fort's exit. Look for the statue of Ponce de León, Puerto Rico's first governor, built from bronze cannons captured from the British. The **San José Church** where the coat-of-arms of the conquistador hangs above the altar is facing the plaza. The church, started by the Dominicans in 1523, is said to be one of the oldest Christian places of worship in the New World. The **Pablo Casals Museum** stands at the corner of the plaza adjacent to the church. Across the street is the **San Juan Museum of Art and History,** built as a marketplace but restored in 1985 to house galleries displaying Puerto Rican art, with a big patio for concerts and cultural events.

Adjacent to the Pablo Casals Museum on the corner of Calle San Sebastian is **Casa de los Contrafuertes** (House of the Buttresses), an 18th-century structure thought to be the oldest civilian building on the island. Between San José Church and Calle Norzagaray is the **Dominican Convent,** built in 1523, which houses the Institute of Puerto Rican culture. Head west on Calle San Sebastian toward San Juan Bay to see **Casa Blanca** (White House), built for Ponce de León by his son-in-law, although the conquistador never lived there. This structure, started in 1521, is supposed to be the oldest continuously inhabited residence site in the New World.

From Calle del Sol, just south of Casa Blanca, past streets that are actually stone stairways, turn right and continue downhill on Calle del Cristo until you reach **San Juan Cathedral.** Recent renovations and restoration have brought the famed house of worship back to its original beauty. As you leave the cathedral, face the square on the right where you'll see an imposing building, **El Convento,** a 17th-century convent with great wooden doors.

From El Convento, you can explore more of Old San Juan's colorful past by following Caleta de las Monjas (Little Street of the Nuns) downhill to the **Plaza de la Rogativa** at the city wall. You'll see a statue of a bishop and three women, commemorating the time in 1797 when British soldiers mistook a religious procession for the arrival of Spanish reinforcements and fled.

Turn left off Calle Recinto Oeste at the west end of Caleta de las Monjas, and walk downhill past San Juan Gate to **La Fortaleza,** the oldest executive mansion in the western hemisphere, home to some 170 governors of Puerto Rico. It was built in 1533 as a fort and enlarged to its present state in 1846. Proceed east along Calle Fortaleza and turn right onto Calle del Cristo. At the end of this street is **Parque de las Palomas,** named for its resident pigeons. The park is a good place to sit and rest while viewing the cluster of ancient buildings, including tiny **Cristo Chapel** with its silver altar visible through glass doors. Along Calle del Cristo is **La Casa del Libro,** a small 18th-century museum dedicated to books, and also the **Museum of Puerto Rican Art,** with collections ranging from pre-Columbian to contemporary, displayed in a beautiful example of 18th-century Spanish architecture.

If you're not worn out yet, follow the wall east one block to **Bastion de las Palmas,** a defense emplacement that is now a park with a magnificent view of San Juan Bay and the mountains beyond. Turn north on Calle San José and walk two blocks to the **Plaza de Armas,** faced on the west by the neoclassic Indendencia, which houses some State Department offices, and on the north by City Hall, where a Tourist Information Center is to be found near the main entrance.

Follow either Calle San Francisco or Calle Fortaleza to **Plaza de Colón,** with its statue of Christopher Columbus, erected in 1893 to commemorate the 400th anniversary of the discovery of Puerto Rico, and the **Tapia Theater,** recently restored to its original 19th-century elegance. Proceed one block west of the plaza on Calle Fortaleza, and you'll come to the **Museum of Colonial Architecture** that features scale models of El Morro, La Fortaleza, and some private houses—a good place to conclude your walking tour of Old San Juan.

4. A SHOPPING TOUR

Puerto Rico has the same tariff barriers as the U.S. mainland. That's why you don't pay duty on items brought back to the United States. That means you don't walk away with great bargains, either. Nevertheless, there are a number of boutiques and specialized stores—especially in the old town—that may tempt you into a purchase.

Native handcrafts can be good buys. Look for "santos," hand-carved wooden religious figures, needlework (women no longer get 3¢ an hour for it!), straw work, ceramics, hammocks, guayabera shirts for men, papier-mâché fruit and vegetables, and paintings and sculptures by Puerto Rican artists.

IN OLD SAN JUAN: You might begin your shopping tour as you emerge from El Convento onto Calle del Cristo.

Galería Botello, 208 Calle del Cristo (tel. 809/723-2879), is a contemporary Latin-American art gallery. It's a living tribute to the success story of the late Angel Botello, considered one of the most outstanding artists working in Puerto Rico. He died in 1986. He was born in a small village in Galicia, Spain, although he fled after the Spanish Civil War to the Dominican Republic. Then there was a 12-year period in the dynamic, art-conscious country of Haiti. His paintings and metal sculpture, while to the knowing eye evocative of his colorful background, were done in a style very much his own. This galería is his former home, and he did the restoration on the colonial mansion himself. Today it's an appropriate setting to display his paintings and sculpture. Most of the salons open onto courtyards. The gallery offers a large collection of Puerto Rican antique santos, which are small, carved wooden figures of saints, and it carries the work of some of Puerto Rico's leading artists. You'll also find colorful posters.

José E. Alegría & Associates, 152-154 Calle del Cristo (tel. 809/721-8091), opposite El Convento Hotel, is housed in an impressive old Spanish building dating from 1523 with rooms opening onto patios and courtyards. It displays antique furniture and paintings, its collection considered the finest in San Juan. It specializes in 18th-century furniture and paintings and also has a collection of French furnishings and Spanish exhibits from the 16th to the 19th century. Intermingled are the paintings of contemporary artists who live in Puerto Rico. Prices are not low, but the quality is very high. There is a wine boutique in the old cellars.

Don Roberto, 205 Calle del Cristo (tel. 809/724-0194), is one of the oldest and most established shops in Old San Juan. It's owned by Tom Catlett, who seems to know everything there is to know about unusual sources for gifts. His taste is excellent, his prices realistic. The collection is eclectic. He offers a superb collection of soft leather items imported from Bogotá, Colombia, at prices sometimes half those of the U.S. Another hard-to-find item is antique santos (saints), and he has a fine collection of ceramics, molas, tapestries, hammocks, and swings. You'll find an intriguing collection of "gold" jewelry (actually pewter, gold plated, and replicas of jewelry) from Bogotá. You may be tempted by the replicas of the coquí, the tree frog that sounds like a bird.

Butterfly People, 152 Fortaleza (809/723-2432), is a museum and café in a handsomely restored building in Old San Juan, where Attenaire Purington, who used to sell her butterflies on the beach at Condado, now presents them, with the aid of her assistants, in artfully arranged boxes. The cost can range from $20 for a single butterfly to as much as $70,000 for a swarm. What began as a decorating scheme for the room of Attenaire's expected child turned into a successful business. The butterfly bodies are preserved by a secret formula, and the color is forever. The dimensional artwork is sold in limited editions, and the gallery ships boxes worldwide. This is the largest privately owned collection of mounted butterflies in the world, second only to the collection at the Smithsonian Institution. Attenaire and her helpers share scientific information with the Smithsonian from time to time. They don't use any endangered species, although butterflies come from virtually every tropical region of the world, with the most beautiful coming from the densest jungles of Borneo and Malaysia. The most expensive item on display is a 9-by-18-foot mural composed totally of hundreds of rare butterflies.

Puerto Rican Art and Crafts, 204 Fortaleza (tel. 809/725-5596), is a series of high-ceilinged brick rooms within a 200-year-old colonial house loaded with handmade products from around the island. Owned and operated by the Amador family, the shop offers vividly painted papier-mâché carnival masks which leer down at visitors with macabre grins. Other items include pottery, textiles, serigraphs and original artworks, batiks, woodcarvings, hand-knotted hammocks, ceramic and brass jewelry, and a colorful series of art.

Olé, 105 Fortaleza (tel. 809/724-2445), is the kind of store where even if you don't buy anything, you can still learn a lot about the crafts displayed. Practically everything here that wasn't made in Puerto Rico came from South America, and all is artistically displayed in a high-ceilinged room decorated clear to the top. If you want a straw hat from Ecuador, hand-beaten Chilean silver, Christmas ornaments, or Puerto Rican santos, this is the place to buy them. Olé is open daily except Sunday.

Hathaway Factory Outlet, 203 Calle del Cristo (tel. 809/723-8946). The selection of dress shirts, known for their "Red H," may vary widely in this factory outlet, but if you happen to be there shortly after stock is replenished, you can stock up at bargain prices on shirts that could easily cost twice as much back home. Most items are top-quality dress and knit shirts from the Hathaway factories in Waterville, Maine, and while you shop, a video will play over and over again a story about how the shirts are sewn. Most items, including articles by Chaps, Ralph Lauren, or Christian Dior, are reduced by 30% to 50%.

Polo Ralph Lauren Factory Store, 201 Calle del Cristo (tel. 809/722-2136), is one of the best places in Old Town if you're looking for sports wear for either men, women, or children. At certain times of the year, discounts of 40% to 50% are offered.

200 Fortaleza, 200 Fortaleza St., corner of Cruz St. (mailing address: P.O. Box 607, San Juan, PR 00904; tel. 809/723-1989), is known as a leading place to buy fine jewelry in Old San Juan. It has famous-name watches, and you can purchase 14- and 18-karat gold chains, which are measured, fitted, and sold by the weight, priced accordingly to the gold market. You can buy your initial in diamonds set in 14-karat white and yellow gold for $90, or even a 14-karat gold ring set with a diamond for $135.

La Plazoleta del Puerto, Marina Street in front of Pier 3 (tel. 809/722-3053), is one of the most important achievements of San Juan's municipal government: the first Puerto Rican crafts market. Once a depressed waterfront building, the structure has been restored by city hall to simulate a typical street of Old San Juan. It attracts local visitors as well as tourists. The artisans' shops are open between 9 a.m. and 6 p.m. daily. Folk art is displayed in various forms, including the work of ceramists, dollmakers, needle-workers, and other craftspeople.

ON THE CONDADO: One of the best-known specialty shops on the island is **Jolie Boutique,** 1015 Ashford Ave. (tel. 809/723-5575). The owner, Mrs. Calderon, offers a large selection of exclusively imported bathing suits, maillots, bikinis, and pareos, as well as high-fashion loungewear and beachwear. The boutique is next door to the Condado Plaza Hotel and the Regency Hotel complex, with ample free parking.

ISLA VERDE: Named after the Warren Beatty movie, **Shampoo,** Cond. Tropicano (tel. 809/791-2211), in the vicinity of El San Juan Hotel & Casino and the Sands, is one of the only hairstyling salons in the Caribbean with a horseshoe-shape bar, a jewelry boutique, a clothing salon, and a real estate office sharing space with a bevy of highly skilled hair stylists. Presiding over this well-choreographed menagerie is entrepreneur Michael Rivera, who, between phone calls, might preside over the party games and humorous conversation around the bar. Haircuts for men cost $14, and those for women go from $20 up. A manicure costs $7, a pedicure $17, plus tip. Appointments are recommended.

PLAZA LAS AMERICAS: The biggest and most up-to-date shopping plaza in the Caribbean Basin is Plaza Las Americas, which lies in the financial district of Hato Rey, right off the Las Americas Expressway. The complex, with its fountains and advanced architecture, has a total of 200 shops, most of them upmarket. Hours are 9:30 a.m. to 6 p.m. Monday to Saturday. Friday is for late-night shopping—that is, until 9:30 p.m.

5. AFTER DARK AROUND THE ISLAND
Puerto Rico has the most varied nightlife of all the Caribbean islands.

CASINOS: These are one of the island's biggest draws. Many visitors come here on package deals, staying at one of the posh hotels at Condado or Isla Verde, with just one intent—to gamble at games ranging from blackjack to baccarat.

One of the splashiest game rooms is at **El Centro,** the government-owned complex that connects the Condado Beach and La Concha Hotels, reviewed earlier. All the other game rooms are in hotels, the plush ones certainly. Therefore you can try your luck at the **Caribe Hilton** (one of the better ones), **El San Juan,** at Isla Verde, and the **Condado Plaza Hotel & Casino.** There are no passports to flash, admissions to pay, or whatever, as there often is in European gambling casinos.

The largest casino on the island is the **Sands Casino** at the previously recommended Sands Hotel & Casino at Isla Verde, on Isla Verde Road. Open from noon to 4 a.m. daily, this 10,000-square-foot gaming facility is an elegant rendezvous. One of its Murano crystal chandeliers is longer than a bowling alley. The casino offers 197 slot machines, 22 blackjack tables, five dice tables, six roulette wheels, two regular baccarat tables, and one mini-baccarat table. Puerto Rican law provides that a percentage of gaming revenues be set aside for education funding.

The best casinos "out in the island" are those at the **Hyatt Regency Cerromar Beach** and **Hyatt Dorado Beach.** In fact, you can easily drive to either of these hotels from San Juan to enjoy their nighttime diversions. There is also a casino at Palmas del Mar and yet another at the Mayagüez Hilton in western Puerto Rico.

Most casinos are open from 1 to 4 p.m. and again from 8 p.m. to 4 a.m. Jackets and ties for men are sometimes requested, as the Commonwealth is trying to keep a "dignified, refined atmosphere."

SHOWS AT HOTELS: For after-dark amusements, the resort hotels have the most beautiful, swank (and expensive) meccas, ranging from Las Vegas–type shows (everybody from Liza Minnelli to Joan Rivers) to discos.

Tropicoro Supper Club, Hotel El San Juan, Isla Verde (tel. 809/791-1000), is the premier nightclub attraction of the premier hotel of Puerto Rico. It engages big stars to entertain, including Rita Moreno, Peter Allen, and Suzanne Somers, alternating with revues. The acts change frequently, so you'd be well advised to call before your arrival, not only to find out who's playing, but to make a reservation and find out what times shows are presented. You sit beneath garlands of tropical vines stretched thickly over a glistening lattice. Two drinks are included in the cover charge of $25 per person when big stars are booked. Featured at the club is a Sunday brunch with unlimited champagne and dance music.

The Caribe Hilton at Puerta de Tierra (tel. 809/721-0303) contains one of the most complete entertainment complexes on the island, drawing thousands of visitors into its nightlife facilities every season. The most prominent is the **Club Caribe,** where the live music from some of the western hemisphere's biggest entertainers—as well as a promising crop of newcomers—sometimes wafts down to the customers at the surrounding bars and restaurants. You can visit just for the show, not dining, for $35 to $42 per person. This includes two free drinks. Music begins around 10 p.m., with closing times varying. The club also contains a popular dining room, the stage being visible from many of the tables. Dinner is served from 6:30 to 10 p.m. daily. A sumptuous buffet is offered Monday, Wednesday, Thursday, and Friday night. Depending on the night, the price ranges from $21 to $30 per person. Otherwise, meals are à la carte, costing around $35 per person. If you eat dinner and remain at your table for the show, you'll pay a nominal cover charge (around $10 per person). Men must wear jackets, but neckties are not required.

Condado Plaza Hotel & Casino, 999 Ashford Ave., Condado (tel. 809/721-1000), offers a wide variety of alternatives for nighttime entertainment. Enjoy dinner and a professional Tango Show at the Copa Room where $25 includes the cover charge and two drinks, or relax at La Fiesta Lobby Lounge with a cool drink while enjoying soft live Latin music. Sing along to oldies and goodies at the Casino Lounge or dance to the disco beat at Isadora (see below).

DISCO FEVER: At the Caribe Hilton in the Puerta de Tierra section is **Juliana's** (tel. 809/721-0303), affiliated with Juliana's of London. It's a private disco club at this deluxe hotel, drawing some of the most sophisticated of San Juaneros along with visitors every night from 9 p.m. till 4 a.m. It's considered "the right sound and the right place." You may prance to every beat from merengue to salsa to a waltz. Because of discreet sound engineering, it's even considered possible to converse. It is built arena style, with bamboo and rattan seating and graceful art nouveau lighting. Singles drink at a bar on the upper ledge. There are two kinds of prices (guests of the hotel are admitted free). Nonguests on Friday and Saturday pay a $20 cover with a two-drink minimum (at $4.75 per drink). On weekdays and Sunday the cover charge is lowered to $14. It opens earlier, but the action doesn't get under way until 10:30 p.m. or later.

Amadeus Disco, El San Juan Hotel, Isla Verde (tel. 809/791-1000). Its conservative art deco interior welcomes a widely divergent collection of the rich and beautiful, the merely rich, and the gaggle of onlookers pretending to be both. It's contained within the most exciting hotel in San Juan (see my hotel recommendation), so a visit here would at least offer the possibility of examining the adjacent casino and the best-decorated lobby in Puerto Rico. The cover charge is $15 Sunday to Thursday, $25 Friday and Saturday, with two drinks included. After paying it, you'll be admitted to a duplex area with one of the best sound systems in the Caribbean. Don't overlook the more sedate piano bar on the upper floor.

Club Mykonos, Hotel La Concha, Ashford Ave. (tel. 809/721-6868). This place dazzles with a decor that might be described as futuristic Pharonaic. It's on the lobby level of La Concha Hotel. Don't come here expecting to be admitted in sloppy clothes, since the owner, Juan Santoni, has set a precedent for relative stylishness. Be sure to notice the frescoes near the entrance and above the bar and the hi-tech versions of Hellenistic columns whose summits flash strobes of multicolored lights. The cover charge is $15 Sunday to Thursday, $20 on Friday and Saturday, although couples are admitted for $25 on Saturday. This entitles you to admission and two free drinks of your choice, after which a libation costs $4.50. The club is open from 10 p.m. to around 5 a.m.

Isadora's, Condado Plaza Hotel & Casino, 999 Ashford Ave. (tel. 809/721-1000), is one of the most elegant discos and after-dark rendezvous points in Puerto Rico. This strobe-lit jungle garden is named after the legendary dancer. Sometimes you get music from the '50s—or what John Lennon's son, Sean, called "the old stuff from the '70s." The interior is in shades of russet and peach, with etched glass, mirrors, and padded corners. The $16 minimum includes the first two drinks, and the club opens daily at 9:30 p.m. and closes at 4 a.m.

FLAMENCO: In La Rada Building in Condado, the **Copacabana,** 1020 Ashford Ave. (tel. 809/723-0691), features flamenco entertainment nightly, with typical Spanish food in the true Spanish fashion and tradition. Main dishes include paella valenciana as well as lobster and beefsteak. You can also order highly seasoned red snapper filet. One of the most reasonably priced flamenco shows in the world, it has a nightly dinner beginning at 7 p.m., with a show starting at 8 p.m. A fixed-price meal at a table with a view of the show costs $10, although drinks are not included in this price. A more expensive meal goes for $13. Scotch and soda costs $2.50.

AN OLD TOWN BAR: A popular spot is **Tiffany's,** 213 Calle del Cristo in Old San Juan (no phone). Many young guests have wandered in here expecting a quick piña colada or daiquiri, only to stay all evening. The drawing card is the video rock concerts and occasional full-length movies which the bartender shows on a big screen behind the hanging Tiffany-style lamps and the dark-wood bar. If you order beer, it will probably be served in the can. Tropical drinks and frappés (chocolate-peanut is a favorite) are also popular. Hard drinks cost from $3.50. The establishment, lying behind a wooden façade and a big window on one of the main streets of Old San Juan, is open from 2 p.m. to 2 a.m. On Friday and Saturday, it closes at 3 a.m. The bar is closed on Sunday.

SUNSET WATCHING: A busy nightspot at **Hotel La Playa,** 6 Amapola St., Isla Verde (tel. 809/791-1115), is built out over the water in back. It's a disco bar, and although no one might actually be dancing, it's still one of the hottest places in town every night during and after happy hour, weeknights from 4 to 7 p.m. The boat-shaped bar is open to the breezes from the ocean, and colored lights hang from the beamed ceiling, illuminating everyone from athletes to artists to bona fide tourists. There's live Latin music Wednesday from 8 to 11 p.m. and Friday from 9 p.m. to midnight. Calypso music begins Sunday at 5 p.m. Free drinks are given to women for a one-hour period on Wednesday and to men for a similar period on Thursday.

An adjoining restaurant, in addition to the bar, serves hamburgers, chili, and roast chicken. Drinks cost from $1.75. The restaurant is open from 8 a.m. to 11 p.m., and the bar from 11 p.m. to 5 a.m., seven days a week.

CULTURAL EVENTS: Built in 1981, the **Performing Arts Center** (tel. 809/724-4747) is in the heart of Santurce, a six-minute taxi jaunt from most of the hotels on Condado Beach. Costing $18 million (relatively modest for such a complex), the center contains 1,883 seats in the Festival Hall, 760 in the Drama Hall, and 210 in the Experimental Theater. Some of the events here will be of interest only to those who speak Spanish, while others attract an international audience. When the Puerto Rico Symphonic Orchestra performs, seats generally sell for around $12 up to $50.

LE LO LAI FESTIVAL: This is a year-round vacation package that has many savings for the visitor who plans to stay in Puerto Rico at least a few days. Le Lo Lai is a name created by the island people to express their love of song and dance and a cultural heritage that comes from Spanish, Indian, and African traditions. The government-sponsored Le Lo Lai Festival welcomes visitors to a complimentary week-long celebration, with the pre-purchase, at several participating San Juan hotels, of a seven-night stay from December 15 to April 14 and a five-night stay from April 15 to December 14.

A 26-page discount booklet offers additional sightseeing suggestions and cents-off coupons to many of the island's boutiques and shops. There are admission tickets to several folkloric shows which will entitle the holder to a free souvenir upon presentation at the event. In 1988, for example, the package included car rental and Paradores Puertorriqueños (country inns) special offers, and museum and theme park admissions, all outside San Juan city limits. The package of tickets is sold in San Juan at authorized travel agencies for those visitors who do not qualify for them on a free basis. The selling price is $8 for adults, $6 for children.

For further information, write to the **Le Lo Lai Festival,** P.O. Box 4195, San Juan, PR 00905, or call 809/723-3135. If in Puerto Rico, you can drop in at the Le Lo Lai Festival office at the street level of the Convention Center in the Condado area.

OUT IN THE ISLAND

The Puerto Rico Company of Tourism (a government agency) has been quite successful in its efforts to have Puerto Rico known as "The Complete Island." Tourism promoters in the island agree with this concept and add that since it is the complete island, why then stay in only one place and say that one has seen Puerto Rico?

After seeing and enjoying San Juan, there is a lot more yet to see, do, and enjoy in the rest of the island. It's amazing how many visitors return home unaware of the many attractions and places they could have visited beyond the San Juan area. There are 79 towns and cities, each having its unique charm and flavor. Puerto Rico has a rich countryside with many panoramas, centuries-old coffee plantations, sugar estates still in use. foreboding caves and enormous boulders with mysterious petroglyphs carved by the Taíno Indians (original settlers of the island), colorful but often narrow and steep roads, and meandering mountain trails leading out to tropical settings.

6. HOTELS OUT IN THE ISLAND

Until recently, this other Puerto Rico was thought of as "too far out" for the fast-moving visitor. Because of the efforts of Paradores Puertorriqueños, a chain of privately owned and operated inns under the auspices and supervision of the Commonwealth Development Company, today everyone can enjoy the Puerto Rican countryside.

THE PARADORES: These hostelries are easily identified by a Taíno grass hut in the signs and the logo of each inn. The *paradores puertorriqueños* are modeled after Spain's parador system. The Puerto Rico Tourism Company established the program in 1973 to encourage tourism across the island. Each of the 17 paradores is situated in a historic place or at a site of exceptional scenic beauty and meets demanding criteria. Varying in size, the paradores are easily affordable, beginning at $35 per night, double occupancy. All have hospitable staffs and share a good standard of service and cleanliness. While some paradores are in the mountains, others are by the sea, and all but one have swimming pools. They are known for their excellent Puerto Rican cuisine, with meals starting at only $6. Many of the paradores are within easy driving distance from San Juan.

For complete data on the paradores and to make reservations, get in touch with **Paradores Puertorriqueños Reservation Office,** Old San Juan Station, San Juan, PR 00905 (tel. 809/721-2884).

My survey of the paradores of Puerto Rico follows. For other paradores, refer to the sections on Mayagüez and San Germán.

Parador Baños de Coamo, P.O. Box 540, Coamo, PR 00640 (tel. 809/825-2186). Legend has it that the hot springs of Baños de Coamo were the fountain of youth sought by Ponce de León. It is believed the Taíno Indians, during pre-Columbian times, held rituals and pilgrimages here as they sought health and well-being. For more than 100 years (1847 to 1958) the site was a center for rest and relaxation where many Puerto Ricans as well as others had enjoyable stays, some on their honeymoon, others in search of the curative powers of the thermal springs, which lie about a five-minute walk from the hotel. The spa is a parador offering hospitality in the Puerto Rican tradition. Even so, the place has a somewhat Mexican atmosphere. Buildings range from a lattice-adorned, two-story motel unit with wooden verandas, to a Spanish colonial pink stucco building housing the restaurant. The cuisine is both Créole and international, and the coffee Baños style is a special treat. All 48 units are air-conditioned and roomy. The decor has been restored to its original 19th-century style. All year the parador charges $55 daily in a double, $45 in a single.

Coamo is inland on the south coast, about two hours from San Juan, and swimming is limited to an angular pool, but one can always drive to a nearby public beach. Horseback riding is unique at Baños de Coamo—here you can ride Paso Fino horses. This beautiful breed of Arabians is the pride of Puerto Rico's equestrian breeders. The Baños lists many notables among its past visitors, including F. D. Roosevelt in 1933, as well as Frank Lloyd Wright. Alexander Graham Bell and Thomas Edison were also visitors.

Parador Hacienda Gripiñas, Rt. 527, km. 2.5 (P.O. Box 387), Jayuya, PR 00664 (tel. 809/824-9790), is a former coffee plantation in the very heart of the Central Mountain Range, reached by a long, narrow, and curvy road. This home-turned-inn is a delightful blend of hacienda of days gone by and the modern conveniences of today. The plantation's ambience is found everywhere—

ceiling fans, splendid gardens, hammocks on a porch gallery, and more than 20 acres of coffee-bearing bushes. You'll taste the home-grown product when you order the inn's aromatic brew. You can swim in the pool (away from the main building), soak up the sun, or go and enjoy the nearby sights such as the Indian Ceremonial Park at Utuado or the Pool of the Petroglyphs. Boating and plenty of fishing are just 30 minutes away at Lake Caonillas. The parador is also near the Rio Camuy Cave Park (see below). The restaurant of the parador, reached from San Juan in about 2½ hours, features a Puerto Rican and international cuisine. Each of the 19 rooms has a private bath, and most come with ceiling fans. Rates are modest: $40 daily in a double and $35 in a single. MAP is an extra $17 per person per day. These prices are in effect year round.

Parador Martorell, 6A Ocean Dr., Luquillo, PR 00673 (tel. 809/889-2710). Back in 1800 the Martorell family came to Puerto Rico from Spain and fell in love with the island. Today their descendants own and manage the Parador Martorell in Luquillo, in the vicinity of the most impressive beach in all of Puerto Rico. When you arrive at the parador, you will enter an open courtyard by a tropical garden. *Off-season rates are $26 in a single and $38 to $40 in a double.* In high season, tariffs are $40 in a single, $50 to $58 in a double.

Meals in the patio of the guesthouse come with fragrant flowers, the elusive hummingbirds, and the occasional music of the coquí, the tiny Puerto Rican tree frog that few people are privileged to see. Breakfast at the Martorell is a surprise. The buffet breakfast always features plenty of freshly picked fruit and baskets full of homemade breads and compotes. While at the parador, try to include the rain forest in your itinerary. At day's end you can come back to the parador, where guests often gather on the patio to swap anecdotes and taste the homemade "Ponche María" as an apéritif. The main reason for staying at the Martorell is Luquillo Beach, with its shady palm groves, crescent beaches, coral reefs for snorkeling and scuba-diving, and the surfing area.

Parador Hacienda Juanita, Rt. 105, km. 23.5 (Apartado 838), Maricao, PR 00706 (tel. 809/834-2550). Right at the foot of the state forest in the mountain region where the Taíno Indians offered their final resistance to the Spanish conquistadores, the Hacienda Juanita has preserved intact the flavor of an old coffee plantation. Every room has a private bath. There is a bar featuring a balcony from which you get a magnificent view of the country greenery surrounding the parador. For relaxation, the swimming pool is always available. There is always a volleyball or basketball game in progress. Near the former plantation house, the new rooms are pleasantly furnished, containing private baths. In all, 21 units are rented out. Despite their modernity, the accommodations still have a traditional feeling. The same rates are charged all year—$35 daily in a single, $40 in a double. Children under 12 are sheltered free, and a third adult in the room pays $6. For MAP (breakfast and dinner), add another $17 per person daily. The hearty cuisine includes many regional dishes, and every single plate served you is enough for two.

From the parador, you can visit the only fish hatchery that supplies the lakes and rivers of Puerto Rico with native fish, tour the town's grotto dedicated to its patron saint, John the Baptist, visit a colonial cemetery, trek through the state forest, and explore the town of Maricao, one of the smallest in the island (pop. 3,000), which still retains many of its colonial traditions. Mayagüez is only 12 miles away.

Parador El Guajataca, Rt. 2, km. 103.8 (P.O. Box 1558), Quebradillas, PR 00742 (tel. 809/895-3070), lies along the north coast 60 miles west of San Juan. Service, hospitality, and the natural beauty surrounding El Guajataca—all this, plus modern conveniences and a family atmosphere, add up to a good visit. The parador is set on a rolling hillside which reaches down to the surf-beaten beach. Each of the 38 air-conditioned rooms is like a private villa with its own entrance and private balcony opening onto the turbulent Atlantic. All year, prices are the same—$52 to $57 daily in a single, $60 to $65 in a double. On the grounds are two swimming pools, one for adults, another for children, and there are two tennis courts free to guests, plus a playground for children. For breakfast, you're served eggs and fresh fruit tasting as if they were brought directly from the farm to your table. Room service is available, but meals are more enjoyable in the glassed-in dining room where all the windows face the sea. Dinner is an experience, with a cuisine that is a mixture of Créole and international specialties. A local musical group plays for dining and dancing on weekend evenings. On Sunday there is a traditional buffet dinner from noon to 3 p.m. The native bar is open daily from 11 a.m. to 10 p.m. (until 1 a.m. on weekends). Friday is Créole night, when the chef pulls out all the stops with an array of Puerto Rican dishes, buffet style. For the shell and fossil collectors, early-morning jaunts along the beach and along the cliffs where the ocean and mountains meet may turn up some interesting finds.

Parador Villa Parguera, 304 Main St., P.O. Box 273, La Parguera, Lajas, PR 00667 (tel. 809/721-2884 in San Juan and 899-3975 in La Parguera). Although the water in the bay alongside this hotel is too polluted for swimming, guests still benefit from a view of the water, a swimming pool, and a pleasantly isolated kind of peacefulness. This parador is known for its seafood dinners, the air-conditioned comfort of most of the rooms, and its location beside the glistening phosphorescent waters of one of the coast's best-known bays. Each of the 50 rooms is air-conditioned and contains a bath and color TV. The price year round is $60 in either a single or double room with air conditioning. The dining room offers daily specials, plus chef's favorites including filet of fish stuffed with lobster and shrimp as well as several other dishes.

Parador Vistamar, P.O. Box T-38, Quebradillas, PR 00742 (tel. 809/859-2065). High atop a mountain, overlooking greenery and a seascape in the Guajataca area, this parador, one of the largest in Puerto Rico, sits like a sentinel surveying the scene. There are gardens and intricate paths carved into the side of the mountain where you can stroll while you take in the fragrance of the tropical flowers that grow in the area. Or you may choose to search for the calcified fossils which abound on the carved mountainside. For a unique experience, visitors can try their hand at freshwater fishing in the only river in Puerto Rico with green waters, just down the hill from the hotel. Flocks of rare tropical birds are frequently seen in the nearby mangroves. Whether you are a seasoned professional photographer or just like to tote an Instamatic about with you, you're sure to get some pictures. A short drive from the hotel will bring you to the popular Punta Borinquen Golf Course. Tennis courts are just down the hill from the inn itself. Sightseeing trips to the nearby Ionospheric Observatory in Arecibo, with the largest radiotelescope in the world, and to Monte Calvario (a replica of Mount Calvary), are side trips available. Another popular visit is to the plaza in the town of Quebradillas, where you can tour the town in a horse-driven coach. Back at the hotel, prepare yourself for a typical Puerto Rican dinner, or choose from the international menu, in the dining room with its view of the ocean. Rates are in effect all year—$43 daily in a single, $43 to $56 in a double. Children under 12 in the same room stay here free (a maximum of two).

Parador La Familia, Rt. 987, km. 4.2, Las Croabas, Fajardo, PR 00648, is a modern building lacking antique charm, but it offers a total of 22 comfortably furnished bedrooms, seven of which have balconies. In the older section, singles rent for $37 daily, with doubles costing $45. In the newer wing, singles go for $45 and doubles for $55, with an additional cot in a room costing $10 per person. On the premises are one swimming pool for adults and another for children.

There is a refrigerator in every bedroom. Facilities include private parking, a cocktail lounge, and a good restaurant serving lunch and dinner from 11 a.m. to 11 p.m. The location is near the beach in this northeast fishing village, a major boating and sailing center. Close by are the coral-bordered offshore islands, the most popular being Icacos, a favorite among snorkelers and divers.

Parador Boquemar, Rt. 101 (P.O. Box 133), Cabo Rojo, PR 00623 (tel. 809/851-2158), lies near Boquerón Beach in the southwest corner of Puerto Rico, between Mayagüez and Ponce. The beach at Boquerón is considered one of the best bathing beaches on the island. The hotel is not right on the beach, but it's just a short walk away. There is also a swimming pool—popular with Puerto Rican families—in back of the hotel. The Boquemar rents 41 rooms, all air-conditioned. Refrigerators are small but serve the purpose. Year-round rates are $45 to $66 daily in a single or double. An à la carte restaurant is on the premises.

Parador Posada Porlamar, Rt. 304 (P.O. Box 405), La Parguera, Lajas, PR 00667 (tel. 809/899-4015), offers life in a simple fishing village where you can enjoy the restful tempo of the Caribbean. That and all the modern conveniences you want in a vacation are what you find at this "Guest House by the Sea," in the Parguera section of Lajas in the southwestern part of the island. The area is famous for its Phosphorescent Bay and good fishing, especially snapper. The guesthouse is near several fishing villages and other points of interest. If you like to collect seashells, you can beachcomb. Other collectors' items found here are fossilized crustacea and marine plants. If you prefer fishing, you can rent boats at the nearby villages, and even bring your catch back to the guesthouse, where you can prepare it in your own kitchenette. The drive to Lajas is several hours from San Juan, but if you prefer, you can fly from San Juan to Mayagüez and then take the much shorter drive to Lajas. Porlamar has only 18 rooms, so early reservations are necessary to ensure a booking. All the rooms are air-conditioned and include kitchen facilities. All year, rates are the same: $36 daily in a single, $45 in a double.

PONCE: A description of the sightseeing possibilities of Ponce is carried in section 9 ("Touring the Island"). However, those not going back to San Juan will find good accommodations in Puerto Rico's second city:

Meliá, 2 Cristina St., Ponce, PR 00731 (tel. 809/842-0260), offers southern hospitality. A city hotel, often attracting business people, it has no connection with other hotels in the world bearing the same name. The location is a few steps away from Our Lady of Guadalupe Cathedral and from the Parque de Bombas (the red-and-black firehouse). The lobby floor and all stairs are covered with Spanish tiles of Moorish design. The desk clerks, oftentimes family members, are well versed in English, and in their courteous way will attend you. Once you have checked in and parked your car in the lot nearby, a pleasant surprise awaits you when you open your room door. The central air conditioning is turned on just right for comfort, every room has a television set, and most have a balcony facing either busy Cristina Street or the old plaza. The rooms are comfortably furnished, pleasant enough. Year-round rates are $55 daily in a single, $65 in a double. Breakfast is served on a rooftop terrace with a good view of Ponce, and the hotel's dining room serves some of the best cuisine in town.

MAYAGÜEZ: Overnighting in Puerto Rico's "third city" has these interesting possibilities:

Hilton International Mayagüez, P.O. Box 3629, Mayagüez, PR 00709 (tel. 809/834-7575), is a country club–style hotel set on 20 acres of lushly planted tropical gardens. Reasonable in price, it is nevertheless the finest hotel to be found in western Puerto Rico. Its grounds have been designated as an adjunct to the nearby Mayagüez Institute of Tropical Agriculture by the U.S. Department of Agriculture. There are no fewer than five species of palm trees, including the royal palm (native to Puerto Rico), eight kinds of bougainvillea, and numerous species of rare flora. If you want to get deep into botany, the Mayagüez Institute of Tropical Agriculture has the largest collection of tropical plants in the western hemisphere. The hotel stands at the edge of the city, and can be reached from San Juan after a scenic 2½-hour drive. Or else it's a half-hour flight aboard either Eastern Metro or American Eagle.

Built in 1964, the hotel has been completely refurbished and in fact is better than ever. Some 141 well-appointed rooms open onto an Olympic-size swimming pool. Many units contain private balconies. Year-round rates in effect depend on whether you take a standard, superior, or a deluxe accommodation. Singles cost $125 to $152, and doubles go for $146 to $173. The hotel is very sports oriented. Not only does it offer three good tennis courts, but there are also physical fitness trails. Deep-sea fishing can also be arranged, as can skindiving, surfing, and scuba-diving. A Jacuzzi under a huge rubber tree near the pool has been added to the hotel's facilities. An 18-hole golf course lies at Borinquen Field, a former SAC airbase, about 30 minutes from the Hilton. Of course, some of the most beautiful beaches on the island can be reached in an easy drive. Boquerón, for example, is a four-mile stretch adorned with palms.

The elegant Rôtisserie Dining Room turns out the best food on the west coast of Puerto Rico. The food is a blend of Puerto Rican and international specialties. There is even a section called flambé fireworks which features "El Pescador," fresh lobster and jumbo shrimp sautéed with local herbs. Freshly caught fish of the day is also a specialty. The chef also prepares international beef recipes featured in sister Hilton hotels around the world. The Hilton is also the entertainment center of the city. On Saturday, a Mexican Night buffet is offered. The cost is only $18 per person. There is a casino established in 1987, which has free entrance and is open daily from noon to 4 a.m. In addition, you can dance to the latest hits at the Baccus Music Club from 9 p.m. to 3 a.m. or later Tuesday to Saturday. Entrance is free for hotel guests, but nonresidents pay from $7.50 to $10, which includes one free drink. You can enjoy your favorite drink on the Vista Terrace overlooking the pool area while you listen to soft music every day from 6 p.m. to 1 a.m. if you're not in a dancing mood.

Parador El Sol, Calle Santiago Riera Palmer, 9 Este, Mayagüez, PR 00708 (tel. 809/834-0303), is a modern cement building with no distinctive charm, yet it provides one of the most reasonable and hospitable accommodations in this part of Puerto Rico. The parador's 40 guest rooms are in a restored hotel in the heart of the west-coast port city. Central to the shopping district and to all western region transportation and highways, the modern seven-floor property offers up-to-date facilities that include cable TV, a restaurant, and a swimming pool. Year round, single rooms range from $31 to $36 per day, with doubles costing from $39 to $45. An additional cot in a room goes for $8.

GUESTHOUSES: That hidden little guesthouse "out in the island" may appeal to a certain type of traveler interested in a more offbeat experience. If so, I have a handful of recommendations:

Caribe Playa Resort, Rt. 3, km. 112, Guardarraya, Patillas, PR 00723 (tel. 809/839-6339), on the southeast coast of the island where the Guardarraya Mountains meet the Caribbean Sea, appeals to nature lovers. The 36-unit efficiency resort is sheltered in tropical greenery on a coconut palm tree farm, just 75 feet from the water's edge on a crescent-shape beach, perfect for snorkeling, surf fishing, or swimming. Walking along the shore in a spot nicknamed "Scrounge Point," you can collect numerous seashells and odd-shaped colored glass and stone formations washed ashore. To get to the Caribe Playa Resort, you must either rent a car (a 1½-hour drive from San Juan) or make arrangements with the management. However you choose to get there, your visit, with some of the most beautiful and interesting scenery on the island, will be well worth the trip.

Accommodations are in three modern two-level breezeway-style concrete buildings. The studios are large and well appointed, each containing a private bath and kitchenette. Up to four persons can be accommodated in each unit, all with outdoor patios or balconies. The studios cost $65 nightly in winter with occupancy by one or two persons. *In summer, the price is $59.* Each additional person is charged $12 extra, with children under ten being permitted to stay free in their parents' room. For reservations, phone the resort directly or write to them at HC764 Buzon 8490, Patillas, PR 00723.

Parador Villa Antonio, Rt. 115, km. 12.3 (P.O. Box 68), Rincón, PR 00743 (tel. 809/823-2645), offers air-conditioned cottages and apartments by the sea with sand at your doorstep, privacy, and tropical beauty around you. On the westernmost point of the island, Rincón has one of the most exotic beaches on the island, drawing surfers from around the world. The most sensible way to get there is by way of Mayagüez airport, just 15 minutes by car from Villa Antonio. Facilities at this guest complex include a children's playground, two tennis courts, and a swimming pool. Surfing and fishing can be done just outside your front door. And you can bring your catch right into your cottage and prepare a fresh seafood dinner in your own kitchenette. All year, the rates charged by the hosts, Ilia and Hector Ruíz, are the same, with two-bedroom units suitable for up to four guests renting for $69 to $80 daily (the latter price for beachfront cottages). A one-bedroom apartment with kitchenette rents for $53 daily for two people. A single with kitchenette costs $43 daily. The beachfront one-bedroom apartments cost $64 for one or two persons and $10 for each additional person.

7. DORADO

The name itself evokes a kind of magic. Along the north shore of Puerto Rico, about a 40-minute drive west of the capital, a world of luxury resorts and villa complexes unfolds. The big properties of the Hyatt Dorado Beach Hotel and Hyatt Regency Cerromar Beach Hotel occupy choice real estate in this section of Puerto Rico, enjoying white sandy beaches.

Many clients book into either of these hotels directly, stopping off in San Juan only to arrive and leave by plane. Others, particularly first-timers, may want to spend a day or so sightseeing and shopping in San Juan before heading for one of these complete resort properties, since, chances are, once there they'll never leave the grounds. The hotels are self-contained, with beach, swimming, golf, tennis, dining, and night-life possibilities.

The site was originally purchased in 1905 by Dr. Alfred T. Livingston, a Jamestown, N.Y., physician, who had it developed as a grapefruit and coconut plantation of 1,000 acres. Previously, the *finca* (farm) had been used as pastureland and as a source of lumber. The grapefruit plantation at one time had as many as 35 to 40 families living in homes furnished by Dr. Livingston. He also provided what amounted to a large free clinic and fostered the first school (named in his honor) in the area about 45 years ago. Dr. Livingston's daughter, Clara, widely known in aviation circles and a friend of the late Amelia Earhart, owned and operated the plantation after her father's death. It was she who built the airstrip here. The building housing Su Casa Restaurant, previewed below, was for many years the plantation home of the Livingstons.

Reservations can be made through travel agents or by calling the Hyatt Worldwide Reservation Center toll free at 800/228-9000 or directly to the hotels.

Hyatt Dorado Beach Hotel, Dorado, PR 00646 (tel. 809/796-1600) sprawls across the plantation, filled with palms, pine trees, and purple bougainvillea, and a two-mile stretch of sandy ocean beach. It's 22 miles west of San Juan. Two side-by-side 18-hole championship golf courses, designed by Robert Trent Jones, are its big draw (see "The Sporting Life," below). Tennis buffs find seven all-weather courts, and there are two swimming pools, as well as a private airfield and a casino. The present hotel, originally a Rockefeller playground, opened in 1958, and many repeat guests, including celebrities, have been going back ever since that time. After several owners, Hyatt Hotels Corporation is in charge and has spent millions on improvements.

The 300 bedrooms all are totally renovated, with marble baths, spacious mirrors, and exceptional lighting. The flooring throughout is terracotta. Rooms are available on the beach or in villas tucked in and around the lushly planted grounds. Casitas, private beach or poolside houses, cost two persons $485 daily in winter, *dropping to $185 in summer.* In winter, standard singles or doubles rent for $290 daily, going up to $395 for deluxe units. *In summer, guests can stay here for $110 to $185 either single or double.* MAP is another $47 per person year round. Breakfast can be taken on your private balcony and lunch on an outdoor ocean terrace. Dinner is served in a three-tiered main dining room where you can watch the surf. Hyatt Dorado chefs have won many awards, and the food at the hotel restaurants and Su Casa Restaurant (not included in the MAP) is considered among the finest in the Caribbean.

The **Hyatt Regency Cerromar Beach Hotel,** Dorado, PR 00646 (tel. 809/796-1010) stands near its elegant sister, the Hyatt Dorado Beach Hotel, although occupying its own sandy crescent beach. Cerromar is a combination of two words—*cerro* (mountain) and *mar* (sea)—and true to its name, you're surrounded by mountains and ocean. Approximately 22 miles west of San Juan, Cerromar shares the 1,000-acre former Livingston estate with the Dorado, enjoying the Robert Trent Jones golf courses. Guests of Cerromar have the use of the facilities at the next-door hotel. A shuttle bus runs back and forth between the two resorts every half hour. Like its sister resort, this hotel was acquired by the Hyatt Hotels Corporation in 1985.

Every room or suite has a sweeping ocean view. The rooms have luxury appointments and are well maintained. Naturally, they are air-conditioned and contain private baths. *In summer, attractive package deals are offered (ask your travel agent). Otherwise, you pay $110 daily in a standard single or double June to the end of September. Shoulder-season tariffs are quoted for April 24 to the end of May and October to December 19: $155 to $220 double or single. MAP is an additional $47 per person daily.* In winter, guests on the EP pay $220 to $295 daily in a single or double. The hotel has a total of 506 rooms, of which 19 are suites. The majority of units have private balconies. Most of the totally renovated and refurnished rooms are spacious, with marble baths, three-way mirrors, and excellent lighting. Floors throughout are tile and furnishings are casual tropical, in soft colors and pastels. All rooms have honor bars and in-room safes.

The outdoor Swan Café is triple level with a dramatic staircase. Some tables are at the edge of a lake, complete with swans and flamingos, paralleling the hotel's swimming pool. The Orchid Pavilion restaurant was named for the profusion of the flowers. The Flamingo bar offers a wide, open-air expanse overlooking a swimming pool water-playground and the sea. The water playground contains the world's longest freshwater swimming pool—a 1,776-foot-long fantasy pool inaugurated in 1986, with a current like a river because of differing heights in five connected free-form pools. It takes 15 minutes to float from one end of the pool to the other. There are 14 waterfalls, tropical landscaping, a subterranean Jacuzzi, water slides, walks, bridges, and a children's pool. A full-service spa and health club provides services for both body and skin care, including Swedish massages and a "Powercise" machine that "talks" to you, coaching you during exercises and reporting your progress to other machines. In addition to 14 tennis courts, there is a children's day camp for guests aged 5 through 13, open from mid-June to Labor Day, at Christmas, and at Easter. While the children are at play, grown-ups can enjoy the beach, bicycle riding, or just plain sunning. Snorkeling and scuba equipment are available for a reasonable rental. Guests from both the Hyatt Regency Cerromar Beach and the Hyatt Dorado Beach hotels may interchange dining and recreation facilities.

Su Casa, in the Hyatt Dorado Beach Hotel (tel. 809/796-1600), the Livingston family plantation home on the resort property, has been extensively renovated by the Hyatt Hotels Corporation to resume a place of eminence as one of the area's most outstanding and inviting restaurants. The Spanish colonial building with tile courtyards has been a favorite dining place for the rich and famous since the Rockefellers entertained guests at their posh Dorado Beach hideaway, and today persons of international prominence still frequent the fine restaurant. Diners sit at candlelit tables and enjoy the serenade of strolling entertainers as they partake of gourmet Puerto Rican and classical European dishes. The chef produces an innovative cuisine, using Puerto Rican fruits and vegetables whenever possible. These include plantain, spinach, eggplant, and other island-grown ingredients.

Don't plan to rush through a meal at Su Casa, but allow yourself time enough to enjoy the quality of your dinner in this relaxed tropical setting. It's best to show up at 8 p.m., and reservations are mandatory. Expect to pay from $40 for a dinner.

Puerto Rico's liveliest club is **El Coquí,** at the Hyatt Regency Cerromar Beach Hotel (tel. 809/796-1010). Because of the effective sound system here, you can actually talk if you don't want to dance. Favored perches are the basket couches. Glass-etched coquís, those singing tree frogs, are lit in the corners. There's action from 9:30 p.m. to 3 a.m. Hotel guests enter free, and nonguests are charged $10 for admission plus $10 per person minimum for drinks. In winter it's closed on Monday and Tuesday; off-season it's likely to be open only on Friday and Saturday.

8. PALMAS DEL MAR

It's called a "new American Riviera" in the making. The resort residential community of Palmas del Mar lies on the island's southeastern shore, 45 miles from San Juan, outside the town of Humacao, about an hour's drive from the San Juan airport. It's also possible to fly in from San Juan.

Once there, you'll find the place so vast you'll need a rental car to reach your friends staying somewhere else on the grounds. Hiking on the resort's grounds is another favorite activity. There is a forest preserve with giant ferns, orchids, and hanging vines.

The resort also has one of the most action-packed sports programs in the Caribbean (refer to "The Sporting Life" section, coming up, for more details).

The New York sales and reservations office for the Puerto Rican resort of Palmas del Mar and its Candelero Hotel and Villas and the Palmas Inn is at 600 Third Ave., 18th Floor, New York, NY 10016 (tel. 212/983-0393 or toll free 800/221-4874).

ACCOMMODATIONS: Lying on 2,700 acres, **Palmas del Mar,** P.O. Box 2020, Humacao, PR 00661 (tel. 809/852-6000), is a former sugar plantation including a stretch of the Caribbean coastline. Guests are housed in villas built around a marina, a tennis complex, and a championship golf course. You have a choice of either rooms or villas, depending on your space needs. Within the same complex are some privately owned condominium homes which the landlords make available to guests when they're not living in them. In addition to the villas, guests can stay at the luxurious Palmas Inn or the Candelero Hotel.

The **Palmas Inn** is a gem, containing only 23 deluxe junior suites, each with a panoramic vista of sea and mountains. The inn also shelters Paolo's Restaurant and La Galería lounge, previewed below. Accommodations are decorated in a Spanish antique style, and baths are designed so that you can sit in the tub while drinking in a view of the Caribbean. Your continental breakfast is left on a service counter in the entrance hall. The inn's decor evokes that of a Mediterranean villa, with a spacious, airy feeling. In winter, rooms are rented as doubles, costing from $240, *dropping to $145 daily for doubles in summer. Singles are accepted in the same suites in summer at $125 per night.* For breakfast and dinner, add $45 per person per day.

At the **Candelero Hotel,** rooms come in a variety of sizes, some with king-size beds. High cathedral ceilings accentuate the roominess which is further extended by patios on the ground floor. In all, there are 102 rooms and mini-suites. Its main dining spot is Las Garzas restaurant, previewed below. Many of the units have private balconies, with views of the sea. The beach and golf course are near at hand. The hotel doesn't have the charm of the Palmas Inn, but many of its units are cheaper. All rates are EP. Depending on the quality of the room, charges are from $180 to $220 daily in winter, either single or double. *In summer, the prices are from $75 to $110 daily in a single, $95 to $130 in a double.* Year round, MAP is an additional $40 per adults, $32 per child under 13.

Candelero Villas, adjacent to the hotel, might be more suitable if you're a group. The management rents out one-, two-, and three-bedroom villas, each handsomely furnished and well equipped. Accommodations are in attached houses, and these villas are privately owned. However, when the owners are away, villas are rented out to transient guests. Villas overlook the beach, the golf course, or else are built on a hillside overlooking the tennis courts. Those called "Harborside," naturally, open onto the waterfront. In winter, a one-bedroom villa for up to two persons costs $260 daily; two bedrooms for up to four people, $380; and three bedrooms, suitable for up to six people, $440. *In summer, a one-bedroom villa costs $150; two bedrooms, $225; and three bedrooms, $290.* All the above prices are EP, quoted per unit. MAP costs an extra $40 per adult per day, $32 per child under 13. However, most guests at Palmas del Mar book in here on a package plan, perhaps taking one of the sports options such as golf. Most packages are for seven days and six nights.

WHERE TO DINE: Moods for dining come in a wide variety, depending on which "village" you're staying in. Paolo's Ristorante Italiano is arguably the best, serving northern Italian food, but the choice is vast. If management continues its policy of a dine-around plan, MAP guests need not be bored. On my most recent visit, MAP guests could select from a choice of six specialty restaurants on the grounds, as well as five restaurants off the property. They could also enjoy five theme nights, including a Western night and a Mexican night.

To reach restaurants below for which I have listed only an extension number, call 809/852-6000, then ask for the individual extension.

Paolo's Ristorante Italiano, at the Palmas del Mar complex at Humacao (ext. 13417), serves northern Italian cuisine at the Palmas Inn. It is a venture for tennis entrepreneur and former Italian Davis Cup star Paolo Bodo. Bodo claims that his is the only Puerto Rico restaurant serving *real* northern Italian food. "The Italian restaurants in San Juan are all southern Italian, overlaid with U.S.–Puerto Rican flavors." The restaurant opens at 6:30 p.m. and stays open until 11 p.m. A complete meal will easily cost from $30, plus your wine. The kitchen makes its own pastas, such as ravioli, tortellini, or spaghetti carbonara. You might follow with such dishes as red snapper, eggplant parmigiana, filet of sole, jumbo shrimp, and veal cutlet Valdostana. The setting is elegant. You dine on blue-and-white tiles, with the sea on your side, in an enclosed courtyard. It's chic and airy.

Adjoining the restaurant (actually a part of it) is **Avo's Piano Bar,** where Avo Uvezian entertains nightly from 8 o'clock.

Las Garzas (ext. 50) is the outstanding restaurant in the Candelero Hotel. Cooled by trade winds, it overlooks a courtyard and swimming pool, and is an ideal choice for either breakfast, lunch, or dinner. Hours are 7 to 11 a.m., noon to 3 p.m., and 6 to 10:30 p.m. Lunches cost $12 and up and are likely to include sandwiches and burgers galore. If you want heartier fare, you can ask for the Puerto Rican specialty of the day, perhaps red snapper in garlic butter, preceded by black-bean soup. Dinner is more elaborate, costing from $25. Perhaps you'll begin with ceviche, following with two center-cut pork chops seasoned with adobo or a nine-ounce churrasco served with the salad bowl and a baked potato. At Friday's Seafood Buffet, you can eat to your appetite's content from an array of giant shrimp, lobster, and smoked salmon. Saturday is Steak and Wine Night when you can feast on steaks and salads.

Chez Daniel, The Marina (ext. 4785). It's French, it's nautical, it's fun, and it's the preferred dining area for the occupants of the yachts that moor at its adjacent pier. You can enjoy a filet of sole stuffed with pulverized crabmeat, a grouper-based bouillabaisse, salmon in green sauce with a tarragon soufflé, asparagus mousseline, shrimp salad with orange vinaigrette, and a changing array of daily specials. Full meals cost from $30 and are served daily from 11 a.m. to 5 p.m. and 6 to 10 p.m. Closed in June and on Tuesday in summer.

Polynesian Restaurant (ext. 2503). Directed by Hong Kong–born Stanley Yau and his wife, Adele, this restaurant serves Chinese food and the kind of frothy mai tais you find in Hawaii. Lunches are relatively simple, but spicy and flavorful, with a limited menu of Oriental-Polynesian dishes costing $10 for a full meal. Dinners are more elaborate, from $12.50 for a fixed-price menu, rising to $25 for a full-fledged luau-style spread. Specialties include shrimp Bora Bora, sizzling Honolulu steak, lobster aloha, and Peking-style duck. Lunch is served daily between 11:30 a.m. and 3:30 p.m., and dinner from 6 to 11 p.m.

The **Café de la Place** evokes Old Spain. It occupies a village square setting in the evening to serve its buffets. Here, families bring their children to enjoy hamburgers, crêpes, and spaghetti, dinners costing from $15. Each night a different Puerto Rican specialty is featured. Lunch is served only in high season, from noon to 3 p.m. daily. Dinner is from 5 to 10 p.m. daily in winter. In summer, no dinner is served Tuesday or Wednesday.

Le Bistroquet (tel. 8474) in Montesol, close to the tennis courts, is done in typical French-bistro style in the atmosphere of the 1930s. Here Martine and Robert Gaffori serve French food in air-conditioned comfort, with dinners costing from $30 per person. You might choose as your main dish coq au vin, entrecôte bordelaise, escargots, or lobster bisque. Only dinner is served, seven days a week from November to the end of April, Tuesday to Saturday the remainder of the year. Hours are 7 to 11 p.m.

This has been only a preview of the dining possibilities. You will discover several more on your own. All the restaurants are open during the winter season; however, in summer, only three or four may be fully functioning.

WELLNESS CENTER: Palmas del Mar has installed a Wellness Center which uses the newest techniques of fitness analysis and exercise. It is equipped with state-of-the-art Hydra-Fitness exercise apparatus with hydraulic action for resistance, providing the ultimate training program for all fitness levels from the novice to the professional athlete. You can have a full workout in about 30 minutes, burning more calories than you would in the same time spent jogging. The center also uses the Medi-Fit Health Assessment System, which provides a choice of the newest and most reliable medically approved computerized evaluations. The nine-category fitness assessment covers areas from blood pressure to muscular endurance, an analysis of body composition with exercise and weight-loss recommendations, and a nutritional evaluation.

A basic exercise program includes classes in aerobics, aqua-aerobics, yoga, and stretching. Free weight-training supervision is also offered. Lifestyle management programs have been designed to help you manage stress, stop smoking, lose weight, and eat right. There are also special activities such as prenatal fitness classes, programs for toddlers and their mothers, and sports programs in tennis, running, cycling, skiing, basketball, and other fields.

The Wellness Center staff is made up of experts in the various program areas, all specialists in their sphere of activity. For information, get in touch with the Palmas del Mar offices in New York (cited above).

AFTER DARK: The most romantic spot in Palmas del Mar is **La Galería,** a lounge bar near the casino where guests can drink and dance to live music five nights a week, Wednesday through Sunday, from 8 p.m. to 2 a.m. The $8 minimum includes your first drink.

The **casino** in the Palmas del Mar complex, near the Palmas Inn, is in the Culebra Room on the second floor of the building that houses La Galería bar. The casino has nine blackjack tables, two roulette wheels, a craps table, and dozens of slot machines. The place is open from 6 p.m. to 2 a.m. daily. However, in summer it closes on Monday and Tuesday. Guests are requested to dress with "casual elegance." Under Puerto Rican law, drinks cannot be served in a casino. You can have a drink in the lounge adjoining the gaming room or in La Galería downstairs.

9. TOURING THE ISLAND

Even though Puerto Rico is an island barely 100 miles long by 35 miles wide, it offers a variety of scenery, from the rain forests and lush mountains of El Yunque to the lime deposits of the north and the arid areas of the south shore, where irrigation is a necessity and the cactus grows wild. In Puerto Rico you will find some of the most complicated geological formations in the world.

While driving on the mountain roads of Puerto Rico, blow your horn before every turn, contrary to urban zone regulations. Commercial road signs are forbidden, so make sure you take along a map and this guide to inform you of restaurants, hotels, and possible points of interest. The kilometer information refers to the roadside markers painted on a white background with black letters telling you the kilometer and hectometer.

Puerto Rico is a subtropical country, yet you can see seasonal changes. In November the sugarcane fields are in bloom, and in January and February the flowering trees along the roads are covered with red and orange blossoms.

When spring comes, the Puerto Rican oak is covered with delicate pink flowers and the African tulip tree is ablaze with its deep-red blossoms. Summer is the glorious flamboyant time when the roadsides seem as if on fire.

A HALF-DAY TRIP AROUND SAN JUAN: I'll suggest a number of itineraries, beginning with a half-day trip around the metropolitan San Juan area up to a rum distillery, Isla de Cobras, Loíza Aldea, and Boca de Cangrejos.

From San Juan, take Rt. 2 up to km. 6.4. To the right you will see a small park containing the ruins of the house erected in 1509 by Juan Ponce de León in Caparra, the first Spanish settlement in Puerto Rico.

Continue on Rt. 2 until you reach Bayamón. Facing the town plaza you have the old church, built in 1877, an excellent example of period architecture.

Afterward, you can then continue on Rte. 167 toward Catano, turning left at km. 5.2. Within a short distance you will find yourself in the **Barrilito Rum Distillery.** To the left you will see a 200-year-old mansion with grand outdoor staircases leading to the second-floor galleries. This is the original mansion of the Santa Ana plantation (which once covered 2,400 acres) and is still occupied by members of the family, owners of the distillery. There's an office on the right, near a tower which was originally a windmill from which the entire valley and bay could be seen. Along the bay is the **Bacardi Rum** plant, where 100,000 gallons of rum are distilled in a day. Guided tours are available.

Back on Rt. 167, drive until you reach Catano, then take Rt. 165 going west and turning left (hugging the shoreline) until you reach **Isla de Cabras.** From this point, you can see the entire bay of San Juan. At the end of the road in Isla de Cabras you will come upon Fort Canuelo, erected in 1610 and reconstructed in 1625 after the Dutch attack on Puerto Rico. Originally built on what was then a tiny islet, the fort seemed to be emerging from the water. Today, however, because of modern landfill techniques it is connected to Isla de Cabras. Picnic facilities are available. Here, the breezes are cool and you have a good view of San Juan Bay and El Morro, built in 1539.

On the way back, drive toward Catano where you can take a short ferry ride to Old San Juan. Boats leave every half hour from 6:15 a.m. to 10 p.m., taking the same time to cross each way. The fare is 20¢ per person, round trip. A more extensive tour of the bay is offered by the Port Authority, leaving from the San Juan Terminal only on Sunday and holidays at 2:30 and 4:30 p.m. The tour takes you near the Coast Guard base, and you have a view of the governor's palace, the San Juan Door (Puerta de San Juan), and El Morro. The trip lasts 1½ hours and the price is $2.50 for adults and $1.25 for children.

From Catano, continue on Rt. 24 until the Caparra intersection on Rt. 20; then take Rt. 20 to Guaynabo until you reach Rt. 21. After going past the psychiatric hospital, the medical center, and the state penitentiary, continue until the Río Piedras intersection, turning left toward Carolina by way of Avenida 65 de Infantería (Rt. 3), from which you can see El Yunque. When you reach km. 18.3, turn onto the bridge and stay to the left to reach **Loiza Aldea.** If you are in Puerto Rico between July 19 and 29, the trip to Loiza Aldea will be quite an experience. This is when the whole town comes out to celebrate the feast day of its patron saint (Santiago Apostol). The festivities are unusual and bizarre, a mixture of pagan Afro-Caribbean and Christian elements forming part of the celebration and carnival.

The Church of San Patricio (St. Patrick), dating from 1645, in Loiza Aldea is in front of the road that leads you to the barge for crossing the Río Grande de Loiza. It's a bit of a thrill to cross this river (with your car) on a barge propelled by a man with ropes. Continue for half an hour on a sandy (but hard) road lined with coconut palms and shady trees until you reach the Nautical Club, then on to Santurce and San Juan.

RAIN FORESTS AND BEACHES: From San Juan, if you have two days to explore, you can take the following itineraries, going on the first day to Trujillo Alto, Gurabo, El Yunque (rain forest), Luquillo Beach, and Fajardo. Perhaps you'll find the makings of a picnic lunch at one of the thatched "kioskos" along the road, eating it at El Yunque (there is also a restaurant in the rain forest—see "Dining Out in Puerto Rico"). On the second day you can explore Fajardo,

Naguabo, Humacao, Yabucoa, Patillas, and Caguas, returning to San Juan in the late afternoon.

Water is considered one of Puerto Rico's most important resources; another is its fertile soil. During the period of a year, 400 billion cubic feet of rain falls on the island. The Spaniards nicknamed the island "The Land of Rivers." To harness this water for public consumption, many dams were built, creating lakes which can be visited.

From San Juan, go to Río Piedras and take Rt. 3 (Avenida 65 de Infantería, named after the Puerto Rican regiment which battled in World War II and in Korea). Turn, heading south on Rt. 181 toward Trujillo Alto, then take Rt. 851 up to Rt. 941. At the end of the valley you can spot the **Lake of Loíza.** Houses can be seen nestled on the surrounding hills. You can even see local farmers (*jíbaros*) riding their horses laden with produce, on the way to and from the marketplace. The lake is surrounded by mountains.

Your next stop is the town of **Gurabo.** This is tobacco country and you'll know you are nearing the town from the sweet aroma enveloping it (tobacco smells sweet before it's harvested). Part of the town of Gurabo is set on the side of a mountain, and the streets are made up of steps. One street has as many as 128 steps.

You will leave the town by way of Rt. 30. Then get on Rt. 185 north, then Rt. 186 south. This road has views of the ocean beyond the valleys. You will at this stage be driving on the lower section of the **Caribe Experimental Forest;** the vegetation is dense and you'll be surrounded by giant ferns. The brooks descending from El Yunque become small waterfalls on both sides of the road. If you have plans to have lunch at El Yunque, turn to go up on Rt. 191.

At about 25 miles east of San Juan, **El Yunque** consists of about 28,000 acres and is the only tropical forest in the U.S. National Forest system. It is said to contain some 240 different tree species native to the area (only half a dozen of these are found on the mainland). In this world of cedars and satinwood (draped in tangles of vines), you'll hear chirping birds, see wild orchids, and perhaps hear the song of the tree frog, the coquí. The entire forest is a bird sanctuary, and may be the last retreat of the rare Puerto Rican parrot.

El Yunque is 3,493 feet high, and the peak of El Toro rises 3,532 feet. You know you'll be showered upon, as more than 100 billion gallons of rain fall here annually. However, the showers are brief, and there are many shelters.

You might go first to the Visitor Center on Rt. 191, at km. 11.6. It's open daily from 9:30 a.m. to 5 p.m., and guides here will give lectures and show slides. Groups, if arranged in advance, can go on guided hikes.

To make your way back, head north along Rt. 191, connecting with Rt. 3. If you drive east for five miles, you will reach **Luquillo Beach,** lying about 30 miles east of San Juan. Edged by a vast coconut grove, this crescent-shaped beach is not only the best in Puerto Rico, it's one of the finest in the Caribbean. You pay to enter with your car, and you're allowed to rent a locker, take a shower, and have a place to change into your bathing suit or bikini. Luquillo gets very crowded on weekends, and if possible go on a weekday when you'll have more sand to yourself. Picnic tables are available as well.

The beach is open from 9 a.m. to 5 p.m. daily. It is closed on Monday, however. If Monday is a holiday, then the beach will shut down on Tuesday that week. Before entering the beach, you may want to stop at one of the roadside thatched huts, selling Puerto Rican snacks, the makings for your picnic.

Continuing east, Rt. 3 leads to **Fajardo,** a fishing port hotly contested in the Spanish-American War. Fishermen and sailors are attracted to its shores and to nearby **Las Croabas,** which has a lot of native fish restaurants. Puerto Ricans are fond of giving nicknames to people and places. For many years the residents of Fajardo have been called *cariduros* ("the hard-faced ones"). However, don't be misled by that. The people here are very friendly.

At Fajardo you can also rent boats or take the ferry ride to the islands of Vieques and Culebra.

On the second day, you can continue south on Rt. 3, following the Caribbean coastline. At **Cayo Lobos,** not far from the Fajardo port, the Atlantic meets the Caribbean. Here, the vivid colors of the Caribbean seem subdued compared to those of the ocean.

Go across the town of Ceiba, near the Roosevelt Navy Base, to reach **Naguabo Beach,** where you can have coffee and "pastelillos de chapin," pastry turnovers used as tax payments in Spanish colonial days. At km. 70.9, briefly detour to Naguabo and enjoy the scented shady laurel trees from India in the town's plaza.

Continue on Rt. 3, going through **Humacao** and its sugarcane fields. When the cane blooms around November and December, the tops of the fields change colors according to the time of day. Humacao is of little interest, but it has a balneario-equipped beach. From here you can detour to the 2,800-acre resort, Palmas del Mar, already described.

After the stopover, you can continue until the town of Yabucoa, nestled among hills. The road suddenly opens up through **Cerro** (mountain) **La Pandura,** giving you some of the most spectacular sights in Puerto Rico. Take note of the giant boulders, beyond which you will see the Caribbean.

After passing the town of Maunabo along Rt. 181 (a tree-lined road which runs next to Lake Patillas), stay on the highway until you reach San Lorenzo, across the mountains. You then take Rt. 183 to reach Caguas, then Rt. 1 back into San Juan.

PINEAPPLES, COFFEE PLANTATIONS, AND CAVES: The trip outlined below takes two days, as you cross an extraordinary limestone region. However, the itinerary can be cut down to one day if you eliminate a stay at the coffee plantation.

The trip takes you across the famous "Karst" district in Puerto Rico, one of the most developed regions of this type in the world. This area was formed by the wearing down of limestone by acids in the water, leaving a maze of deep fissures and mounds. Some of the depressions in the area are 400 feet across and as deep as 160 feet. The radar/radio telescope in nearby Arecibo is built inside one of these craters, the crater being 160 feet deep and 1,300 feet wide (see below). Underground rivers are sometimes formed in this type of geological environment. An example of this is the Tanama River, which emerges and disappears at five different places.

From San Juan, take Rt. 2 heading west toward Manati, after which you will pass the pineapple region. At km. 57.9, turn onto Rt. 140 south to Florida. At km. 25.5 you will find a coffee cooperative where during harvest time the beans are processed, ground, and packed. At km. 30.7, turn right toward Hacienda Rosas. A coffee plantation is interesting at all times, but especially around harvest time (from September to December, sometimes as late as January) when the pickers, gathered in groups, walk under the bushes and pick the crimson beans while other workers process the already-picked yield.

Continuing, take Rt. 141 to Jayuya, where you can stay at the Parador Gripiñas (refer to "Hotels Out in the Island").

After a restful day there, take Rt. 141 north until you are back on Rt. 140. Head west on Rt. 140 until you pass Caonillas Lake. There, turn onto Rt. 111

west, go across the town of Utuado, and continue to km. 12.3. Here you will find the **Taíno Indian Ceremonial Ball Park**. Archeological clues date this site to approximately two centuries before the discovery of the New World. It is believed that Indian Chief Guarionex gathered his subjects on this site to celebrate rituals and practice sports. Set on a 13-acre field surrounded by trees are some 14 vertical monoliths with colorful petroglyphs, all arranged around a central sacrificial stone monument. The ball complex also includes a museum, open from 9 a.m. to 5 p.m., charging no admission. There is also a gallery, Herencia Indígena, where visitors can purchase Indian relics at very reasonable prices, including the sought-after Cemi (Taíno Indian idols) and the famous little frog, the coquí.

Continue next on Rt. 111 up to Rt. 129 north and head toward Arecibo (going across the Karst region) until you reach km. 13.6. Take Rt. 489 south to La Cueva de la Luz (Cave of Light).

Next, follow Rt. 489 until the Barrio Aibonito, Pagan sector. If you have any doubts, ask anyone for **"La Cueva de Pagan Pagan"** (Pagan Pagan's cave). A narrow road will lead you, only to end at a general store where anyone will find Pagan for you. Only the agile and those who like to explore should venture inside the cave. The cave is lit by daylight, but the floor is rough and irregular. (Wearing slacks and possibly sneakers or rubbersoles is a good idea here.) There are no bats in the cave. Inside, a stone vessel contains fresh water which some believe has rejuvenating qualities. Other caves in this area have not been explored fully, but Indian relics have been found. Return by way of Rt. 489 to Rt. 129 north, to Arecibo.

Going Underground

A drive about 2½ hours west of San Juan at Hatillo takes you to the 300-acre **Rio Camuy Cave Park** (Parque de las Cavernas del Rio Camuy), developed and operated by the Puerto Rico Land Administration, to enable visitors to see Empalme Cave as well as seeing the area of canyons, caverns, and sinkholes in a subterranean network. The third largest underground river in the world, Rio Camuy, runs through the network of caves that were cut through the limestone base of the island over the course of millions of years. The caves were known to the Taíno Indians, the pre-Columbian inhabitants of the area, and to Puerto Rican farmers, coming to the attention of speleologists in the 1950s. They were opened to the public in 1987. Gardens in the focal point of the park surround buildings where tickets can be purchased, after which a short film about the caves is shown in a theater. Visitors then descend to where open-air trolleys carry them on the downward journey to the actual caverns. The trip goes through a 200-foot-deep sinkhole, a chasm where tropical trees, ferns, and flowers flourish, to the delight of birds and butterflies. The trolley takes passengers to the entrance of Empalme Cave, one of the 16 in the Camuy Caves network, where they begin a 45-minute cave walk, viewing the majestic series of rooms rich in stalagmites, stalactites, and huge sculptures carved out and built up through the centuries. Other—some larger—caves in the network are being prepared for public viewing.

The caves are open from 8 a.m. to 5 p.m. Wednesday to Sunday, with the last tour starting at 4 p.m. Tickets are $4 for adults, $2.50 for children 2 to 12. For information, phone the park at 809/898-3100 or in San Juan at 809/756-5555. The park complex contains a cafeteria and a souvenir shop. To reach the park, take Rt. 22 from San Juan, the Diego Expressway, paying a 50¢ toll. At the end of the expressway, about 15 miles from San Juan, follow signs to Arecibo for about ¼ mile along Rt. 165, then go 27 miles on Rt. 2 to another section of the expressway, where another 25¢ toll will be collected to the Arecibo bypass. Watch for the exit from the bypass to Lares, the second exit to Rt. 129, and follow the signs for 11 miles to the park entrance on the left. Parking is $1. (Signs on the right are for the privately owned Cueva de Camuy, not for the park you are seeking.)

Arecibo Observatory

The world's largest and most sensitive radar/radio telescope, a 20-acre dish set in an ancient sinkhole, is a two-hour drive west of San Juan, not far from the Rio Camuy Cave Park. The telescope, whose dish or "radio mirror" is 1,000 feet in diameter and 167 feet deep, allows scientists to examine the ionosphere, planets, and moon with powerful radar signals and to monitor natural radio emissions from distant galaxies, pulsars, and quasars. It has been used by scientists as part of the Search for Extraterrestrial Intelligence (SETI), whose basic proposition is that highly advanced technological civilizations throughout the universe might communicate via radio waves. Arecibo is called an "ear to the heavens."

Under the giant dish, vegetation flourishes, with rain and filtered sunlight encouraging a lush growth of ferns, grasses, and other plants, including wild orchids and begonias. Wildlife under the dish includes mongooses, lizards, frogs, dragonflies, and an occasional bird. Suspended above the dish is a 600-ton platform similar in design to a bridge. Hanging in midair on 12 cables, strung four each to reinforced concrete towers, it resembles a space station. In addition to the visual spectacle presented by the huge facility, Arecibo Observatory offers tours in which visitors can learn about the universe from the experts. The tours are given at 2 p.m. Tuesday to Friday. On Sunday, the observatory is open to the public from 1 to 4:30 p.m. It is a 35-minute drive south from the commercial city of Arecibo. Take Rts. 129, 134, 635, and 625.

There is a souvenir shop on the grounds. The observatory is part of the National Astronomy and Ionosphere Center, a national research center operated by Cornell University under contract with the National Science Foundation. For further information, contact the Puerto Rico Tourist Co. in New York (see above).

From Arecibo, you can take Rt. 2 east back to San Juan.

A FOUR-DAY TRIP: More ambitious than the itineraries considered so far, this next trip takes you to the west coast and south on the island:

On the first day, follow Rt. 2 from San Juan west up to **Guajataca**. Just before you reach km. 103.4, you will spot a sign for the Guajataca recreation area. Make a right turn and stay on the road to the parking area.

Go back to Rt. 2 and to the Guajataca Beach. It is so fine a beach you may want to stay there for at least one more day. (The Parador Guajataca is just above the hill from the beach.)

When you decide to continue, take Rt. 2 up to km. 91 and turn toward the south, across the Karst region (see the previous tour) until you reach man-made Guajataca Lake. Follow the lake's shoreline for about 2½ miles and turn left at km. 19 to Rt. 455 until you reach a bridge spanning the Guajataca River, which runs through the lush mountainside.

Return by way of Rt. 119 and continue toward San Sebastián and to Rt. 109 across coffee plantations to Anasco. Turn onto Rt. 2 and head for Mayagüez.

Mayagüez

On your second day you can explore what Puerto Ricans have nicknamed "The Sultan of the West." This busy port city, not architecturally remarkable, is the third largest on the island. Once considered the needlework capital of the island, it still has women who do fine embroidery and drawn-thread work. Some of the older downtown shops sell it, and the clever shopper will seek out some good buys.

Mayagüez dates from the mid-18th century. It was built to control the location of the Mona Passage, a vital trade route for the Spanish empire. Queen Isabel II of Spain recognized its status as a town in 1836. Her son, Alfonso XII, granted it a city charter in 1877.

Mayagüez is the honeymoon capital of Puerto Rico. The tradition dates from the 16th century, when, it is said, local fathers kidnapped young Spanish sailors who stopped for provisions there en route to South America. Because of the scarcity of eligible young men, the farmers needed husbands for their daughters.

The major industry is tuna packing: 60% of tuna consumed in the U.S. is packed here.

The chief sight is the **Tropical Agriculture Research Station.** At the administration office, ask for a free map of the tropical gardens, which contain one of the largest collections of tropical species useful to people, including cacao, fruit trees, spices, timbers, and ornamentals.

The location is on Rt. 65, between Post Street and Rt. 108, adjacent to the University of Puerto Rico at Mayagüez campus and across the street from the **Parque de los Próceres** or patriots' park. The grounds are open Monday to Friday from 7 a.m. to 4 p.m., charging no admission. For more information, call 809/831-3435.

The **Puerto Rico Zoological Garden,** Rt. 108 (tel. 809/834-8110), at Mayagüez, exhibits birds, reptiles, and mammals, plus a South American exhibit, all contained in a lush tropical environment. Hours year round are 9 a.m. to 5 p.m. Tuesday through Sunday, and admission is $1 for adults, 50¢ for children, and $1 for parking.

Mayagüez might also be the jumping-off point for a visit to **Mona Island,** "the Galapagos of the Caribbean," which enjoys many legends of pirate treasure and is known for its white sand beaches and marine life. Accessible only by private boat or plane, the island is virtually uninhabited, except for two policemen and a director of the institute of natural resources. The island attracts hunters seeking pigs and wild goats, along with big-game fishermen. But mostly it is intriguing to anyone who wants to escape civilization. Playa Sardinera on Mona Island was a nesting ground of pirates. On one side of the island, Playa de Pajaros, there are caves where the Taíno Indians left their mysterious hieroglyphs.

Camping is permitted at Sardinera Beach, costing $1 per night per camper.

After touring Mayagüez, you can pick up the tour by taking Rt. 105 up to Rt. 120 as far as **Maricao.** The town is colorful and rather small. On the outskirts look for a sign that reads "Los Viveros" **(The Hatcheries);** then take Rt. 410. Here, the Commonwealth Department of Agriculture hatches as many as 25,000 fish for stocking the Puerto Rican freshwater lakes and streams.

Go back to Maricao to Rt. 120 south up to km. 13.8 until you reach the **Maricao State Forest** picnic area at a height of 2,900 feet above sea level. The observation tower provides a splendid view across the green mountain range up to the coastal plains. Continue on Rt. 120 across the forest to the town of Sabana Grande (Great Plain). Rt. 2 will then take you to San German.

San German

This town is a little museum piece. It was founded in 1512, and destroyed by the French in 1528. Rebuilt in 1570, it was named after Dona Germana de Foix, King Ferdinand of Spain's second wife. Once it rivaled San Juan in importance, although it has now settled into slumber, a living example of Spanish colonization. Gracious Old World buildings line the streets, and flowers brighten the patios as they do in Seville. Also as in a small Spanish town, the population turns out to stroll in the plaza in the early evening.

On a knoll at one end of the town stands the chapel of **Porta Coeli** (Gate of Heaven), dating from the 17th century, oldest in the New World. Restored by the Institute of Puerto Rican Culture, it contains a museum of religious art which is open (admission free) Tuesday to Sunday from 9 a.m. to noon and 2 to 4:30 p.m. The museum has a collection of ancient santos, carved holy figures and saints. Guided tours are offered Wednesday through Sunday. For more information, call 809/892-5845.

It's possible to spend the night in comfort in the town at the **Parador Oasis,** 72 Luna St., San German, PR 00753 (tel. 809/892-1175), housed within a 200-year-old building. Originally this parador was a fashionable private mansion; later it was a winery and a small family-run hotel. Today it offers the same ornate verandas and decorative latticeworks—called *soles truncos*—that it used to, except everything has been considerably restored. Here visitors will see examples of *mediopunto,* a decorative room divider usually made of fine wooded lacework, highly characteristic of architecture in Puerto Rico between 1890 and 1940. Below are underground tunnels once believed used for contraband. All the 50 pleasantly furnished rooms are air-conditioned. Units contain private baths, and some face the inner patio, which is a gathering place for both guests and local patrons. Year round, rates in the old building are $49.70 daily single, $57.12 double. In the new part of the parador, rents are $52.88 daily single, $59.24 double. Up to two children can stay free when accompanied by an adult. Good regional food is served in the 18th-century dining room, known for its frescoes. The Parador has an elegant and contemporary disco, the Club Elite, and a convention center. Ask about their honeymoon package.

From San German, take Rt. 320 to Rt. 101. Then on to Lajas, where Rt. 116 will lead to Rt. 304, which will take you to La Parguera. There you can visit the **Phosphorescent Bay** (best on a moonless night). A boat leaves Villa Parguera pier nightly from 7:30 p.m. to 12:30 a.m., depending on the demand. The experience of seeing fish leave a luminous streak on the surface and watching the boat's wake glimmer in the dark is unique. Phosphorescent Bay is near the fishing village of La Parguera. The phenomenon, incidentally, is caused by a big colony of dinoflagellates, a microscopic form of marine life. They produce these sparks of chemical light when their nesting is disturbed.

On the third day, take Rt. 104 up to Rt. 116 to Ensenada. From there you can continue on Rt. 116 to Guánica Bay. Or you could turn off on Rt. 333 to Cana Gorda Beach, to have a swim or lunch. While there, look for the species of cacti typical of the region. Continue on Rt. 2 to Yauco, then take Rt. 132 and head for—

Ponce

Puerto Rico's second-largest city, Ponce—called "The Pearl of the South" —was named after Ponce de León. Founded in 1692, it is today Puerto Rico's principal shipping port on the Caribbean. The city is well-kept and attractive, as reflected by its many plazas, parks, and public buildings. There is something in its lingering air that suggests a provincial Mediterranean town. Look for the *rejas,* or framed balconies of the handsome colonial mansions.

Any of the Ponceños will direct you to their **Museum of Art,** at Las Americas Ave. (tel. 809/848-0505). This excellent museum was donated to the people of Puerto Rico by Luís A. Ferré, a former governor. The building in which the museum is housed was designed by Edward Durell Stone (the designer of New York's Museum of Modern Art), and it's been called "The Parthenon of the Caribbean." In spite of such a fanciful label, its collection represents principal schools of American and European Art of the past five centuries. Hours are 10 a.m. to noon and 1 to 4 p.m. Monday through Friday, 10 a.m. to 4 p.m. on

Saturday, to 5 p.m. on Sunday and holidays. The museum is closed on Tuesday. Adults pay $2.50; children under 12, $1.50.

All visitors as well head for the **Parque de Bombas,** on the main plaza of Ponce. This old firehouse is fantastic—painted black, red, green, and yellow. It was built for a fair in 1883, and is today the headquarters for the government tourism agency's Ponce Information Office.

Around from the firehouse, the trail will lead to the **Cathedral of Our Lady of Guadalupe.** The church rises between two plazas.

The marketplace at Atocha and Castillo Streets is colorful, the Perla Theater historic, and the Serralles rum distillery is worth a visit. Or perhaps you'll want to just sit at the plaza, watching the Ponceños at their favorite pastime, strolling in the plaza.

The oldest cemetery in the Antilles, excavated in 1975, is on Rt. 503, km. 2.7. The **Tibes Indian Ceremonial Center** (tel. 840-2255) contains some 186 skeletons, dating from A.D. 300, as well as pre-Taíno plazas from A.D. 700. Bordered by the Portugués River, the museum is open daily except Monday from 9 a.m. to 4:30 p.m. Admission is $1 for adults and 50¢ for children. Guided tours in English and Spanish are conducted through the grounds. Shaded by such trees as the calabash, seven rectangular ballcourts and two dance grounds can be viewed. The arrangement of stone points on the dance grounds, in line with the solstices and equinoxes, suggest a pre-Columbian Stonehenge. A re-created Taíno village includes not only the museum but an exhibition hall which shows a documentary about Tibes, a cafeteria where you can find refreshments, and a souvenir shop.

Built in 1833, **Hacienda Buena Vista** preserves an old way of life, with its whirring waterwheels and artifacts of 19th-century farm production. Once it was one of the most successful plantations in Puerto Rico, producing coffee, corn, and citrus. It was a working coffee plantation until the 1950s. Eighty of the original 500 acres are still part of the estate. The rooms of the hacienda have been furnished with authentic pieces from the 1850s. Tours of Hacienda Buena Vista are conducted Friday to Sunday at 8:30 and 10:30 a.m. and at 1:30 and 3:30 p.m. Reservations are required and may be made by getting in touch with the Conservation Trust of Puerto Rico at 809/722-5882. Tours cost $4 for adults, $1 for children. The hacienda lies in the small town of Barrio Magueyes on Rt. 10 from Ponce to Adjuntas.

On the fourth and final day, leave Ponce by Rt. 1. As vast sugarcane fields fade from view, take Rt. 3 to **Guayama,** one of the handsomest towns in Puerto Rico. There, find Rt. 15, going north. If you travel this road in either spring or summer, you'll be surrounded by the brilliant colors of flowering trees.

At km. 17.1, in Jajome, you can see the governor's summer palace, an ancient, now restored and enlarged, roadside inn. Continue on Rt. 15; then get on Rt. 1 which leads directly back to San Juan.

BEACHES ALONG THE ATLANTIC: An interesting scenic trip to the beaches between San Juan and Arecibo follows. Allow at least 5½ hours, not counting beach time.

The ever-changing colors of the Atlantic make this trip a memorable experience. Start at Rt. 2 to the Caparra intersection, where you turn onto Rt. 24 to Catano; then continue west on Rt. 165. El Morro and Old San Juan can be seen across the bay.

After passing a dense coconut grove, you will reach Levittown City (a housing development). The sea turns a blue-green shade at this spot. Continue up to the river and the town of **Dorado** by way of Rt. 690 north. Within a short distance, you will reach **Cerro Gordo Beach.** Watch your time, for you might be mesmerized by the natural beauty of this beach and stay longer than planned.

If you can break away from Cerro Gordo, take Rt. 688 back to Rt. 2 headed toward **Vega Baja** (founded in 1776). The residents of Vega Baja are nicknamed "melao-melao" ("molasses-molasses") because of the large amount of molasses produced in the town.

Route 676 north takes you to a spectacular beach in the west, where the water turns jade green with touches of purple and lots of white foam. Over to the east of this beach the water is less turbulent, held back by a giant rocky barrier where the waves crash thunderously. This beach is dotted with cabins and cabañas belonging to the local residents. Continue on Rt. 686 until you reach Rt. 648, which will take you to **Mar Chiquita,** where the high rocks enclose an oval lagoon perfect for swimming.

Return by way of Rt. 648 to Rt. 685, which will lead you to Rt. 2. Head north on Rt. 2 to Rt. 140 until you get to Barceloneta; then take Rt. 681 up to the Plazuela sugar mill and go through cane fields edged with almond trees.

Continue toward the beach and look for a sign which reads **"La Cueva del Indio"** (The Indian Cave). Many Indian symbols can be seen on the cave walls.

Leave the area by way of Rt. 681 up to where it meets Rt. 2 in Arecibo. Route 2 east will take you back to San Juan through cane fields and perfumed pineapple plantations.

10. THE SPORTING LIFE

Dorado Beach, Cerromar Beach, and Palmas del Mar are the chief centers for those seeking the golf, tennis, and beach life. Hotels on the Condado/Isla Verde coast also have, for the most part, complete water sports.

BEACHES: Beaches in Puerto Rico are open to the public, although you will be charged for parking and for use of balneario facilities, such as lockers and showers. The public beaches on the north shore of San Juan at Ocean Park and Park Barbosa are good, and can be reached by bus. Luquillo, on the north coast, some 30 miles east of San Juan, is discussed separately in the touring section. Also refer to the touring section for more tips on beaches west from San Juan. Public beaches shut down on Monday. If Monday is a holiday, the beaches are open then but close the next day, Tuesday. In winter, beach hours are 9 a.m. to 5 p.m., to 6 p.m. in summer.

Along the coastal roads of Rt. 2, to the north of Mayagüez, lie what are reputed to be the best surfing beaches in the Caribbean. Surfers from as far away as New Zealand are attracted to these beaches. The most outstanding of all, comparable to the finest surfing spots in the world, according to competitors in the 1988 World Surfing Championship held there, is at Punta Higuero, on Rt. 413 near the town of Rincón. In the winter months especially, uninterrupted Atlantic swells with perfectly formed waves averaging five to six feet in height roll shoreward, and rideable swells sometimes reach 15 to 25 feet.

SNORKELING AND SCUBA: The coral reefs and cays around Puerto Rico make it ideal snorkeling country. Most major hotel water-sports offices also offer scuba-diving instructions. All the major hotels have water sports, but one of the most professional outfits is **Caribe Aquatic Adventures** (tel. 809/721-0303, ext. 2447), at the Caribe Hilton on Puerta de Tierra in San Juan. Karen Vega, the president of the resort division, is a NAUI-PADI certified instructor. She's helped by her husband, Tony, a NAUI divemaster. Their shop is a NAUI Pro facility. They offer resort scuba courses and all levels of scuba certification, as well as check-out dives. The best snorkeling and dive sites in San Juan are off the Hilton's beach. The Vegas have snorkel tours and scuba dives four times daily, with occasional night dives. Prices range from $30 to $40, which includes tanks and weights. Icacos Island sailing/diving picnics are also available.

A nearby competitor of the Hilton, **San Juan Watersports,** Condado Plaza Hotel & Casino, 999 Ashford Ave. (tel. 809/721-1000), operates a full dive shop on its premises also. David Gil, a certified PADI instructor, directs scuba facilities. Programs are available for everyone from novices to advanced divers. A half-day program, which includes classroom, pool, and underwater work, costs around $65 for a complete introduction to scuba. Once a beginner has completed this, he or she can qualify for diving off the beach, boat, or during an expedition to a deserted island. PADI courses are required three hours daily for a minimum of five days. Boat dives are available daily from the hotel. All equipment is included in the program. A snorkel trip with lunch to the rich aquatic grounds of Caicos Cay costs $69 for a full day.

Palmas del Mar Aquatics (tel. 809/852-6000, ext. 4701) has been set up by Coral Head Divers, Puerto Rico's largest scuba-diving operation, at the resort's marina. The operation, supervised by Jim Abbott, owner of Coral Head Divers, offers diving, snorkeling, coastal cruising, and wing sailing. It carries a range of equipment for rent, including canoes, kayaks, boogie boards, floats, and fishing rods and reels, as well as underwater photographic equipment. Abbott, a member of NAUI and PADI, and his staff do research and commercial diving work as well as resort diving and diver training at all levels.

DEEP-SEA FISHING: It's top-notch. Allison tuna, white and blue marlin, sailfish, wahoo, dolphin, mackerel, and tarpon are some of the fish that can be caught in Puerto Rican waters where 30 world records have been broken. Charter arrangements can be made through most major hotels and resorts.

It is said in Puerto Rico that **Capt. Mike Benitez** sets the standards by which to judge other captains. He is especially praised by marlin fishermen. You can write him directly at P.O. Box 5141, Puerta de Tierra, San Juan, PR 00906 (call 809/723-2292 daily to 9 p.m.). The captain has chartered out of San Juan for almost 40 years. He takes his clients out on his 45-foot, air-conditioned, deluxe Hatteras, *Sea Born.* Fishing tours cost $325 for a half day, $575 for a full day, and a maximum of six sportsmen.

Some of the best year-round fishing in the Caribbean is found in the waters just off Palmas del Mar, the resort complex on the southeast coast of Puerto Rico (tel. 809/850-7442 after 6 p.m.). There **Capt. Bill Burleson** operates charters out of Palmas's harbor. His 44-foot customized sportsfishing boat *Karolette* is the second-largest charter fishing vessel operating out of Puerto Rico. He has fished the Caribbean for more than 20 years. Burleson prefers to take visiting fishermen to Grappler Banks, 18 nautical miles away. The banks are two sea mounts, rising to about 240 feet below the surface and surrounded by deeps of 6,000 to 8,000 feet. They lie in the migratory paths of wahoo, tuna, and marlin. Reservations can be made at Palmas del Mar's Candelero Hotel, at the guest service desk. The cost is $625 per day; maximum is six persons.

SAILING: In Humacao, the **Palmas del Mar Sailing Center** (tel. 809/852-8114) offers a satisfying collection of wind-related water sports every day from 9 a.m. to 5 p.m. From a kiosk on a flat sandy area of scrub grass, a mini-van ride from the resort's lodging facilities, Capt. Carol Fernandez and Doug Smith, two American-born entrepreneurs, maintain a full and complete sailing school. Spearheads of the Copa de Palmas races, which occur here every Labor Day weekend, they offer for rental (with a captain) sailboats which range from between 27 and 46 feet in length. On a less grand scale, a windsurfer rents for $15 per hour, and a two-hour lesson costs $30. Sunfish and paddleboats cost the same price, while waterskiing is $15 for a 15-minute ride.

WINDSURFING: The place to go if you're interested in windsurfing is **San Juan Watersports,** Condado Plaza Hotel & Casino, 999 Ashford Ave. (tel. 809/721-1000, ext. 1361), that maintains an annex at El San Juan Hotel & Casino. A certification class, including eight hours of instruction, water time, and a test, costs $125. A two-hour resort course goes for $40, with boards renting for $20 per hour or $35 per half day.

GOLF: A golfer's dream, Puerto Rico has some splendid courses, too many for me to document here. The **Hyatt Resorts Puerto Rico** (tel. 809/796-1234), with 72 holes of golf, constitutes the greatest concentration of the sport in the Caribbean. The 18-hole Robert Trent Jones courses at the Hyatt Regency Cerromar and the Hyatt Dorado Beach are rated the finest anywhere.

The **Club de Golf,** at Palmas del Mar in Humacao (tel. 809/852-6000, ext. 2526), is one of the leading courses for golf in Puerto Rico. On Puerto Rico's southeast coast, it has a par-72, 6,690-yard layout designed by Gary Player.

The **Mayagüez Hilton** (tel. 809/834-7575) makes arrangements for guests to play at a nine-hole course at a nearby country club. Punta Borinquen, at Aguadilla, the former Ramey Air Force Base, has an 18-hole public golf course which is open daily.

TENNIS: Again, the sister resorts of Dorado and Cerromar (tel. 809/796-1234) have the monopoly on this game, a total of 21 courts between them. The charge is $12 an hour. Take your racquet and tennis outfit along (attire and equipment are often available in shops, but prices are high, the selection minimal). Lessons are available and cost $50 per hour.

In San Juan, the Caribe Hilton, the Condado Plaza, Carib Inn, and the Condado Beach and La Concha have tennis courts. Also in the San Juan area there's a public court at the old navy base, Isla Grande, Miramar. The entrance is from Fernández Juncos Avenue at Stop 11.

The Tennis Center at Palmas del Mar in Humacao, run by All American Sports, features 20 courts (5 Hartru, 15 Truflex). Court fees are $14 per hour for hotel guests during the day and $18 at night. All American Sports also runs tennis clinics of three to seven days' duration. Special tennis clinic packages are available, including accommodations. Call 809/852-6000, ext. 51, for more information.

HORSE RACING: Great thoroughbreds and outstanding jockeys compete all year at **El Comandante,** Rt. 3, km. 15.3 at Canóvanas (tel. 809/724-6060), a modern track. Races are held Wednesday, Friday, Sunday, and holidays at 2:30 p.m. Admission to the clubhouse is $3, and you pay only $1 for the grandstand. An air-conditioned terrace dining room opens at 12:30 p.m. on each race day. Telephone for luncheon reservations. Most credit cards are accepted.

COCKFIGHTING: Puerto Ricans are tremendously fond of this "sport," as are most Latin Americans. The **Club Gallistico,** Rt. 187, km. 1.5, Isla Verde (tel. 809/791-1557), is air-conditioned, complete with restaurant and cocktail lounge. General admission is $9; ringside admission, $16. Fights are on Saturday from 1 to 7 p.m.

HORSEBACK RIDING: The equestrian center at **Palmas del Mar,** under the direction of Fernando Salgado, a riding instructor of international experience, has 42 horses, including English hunters for jumping, plus a variety of trail rides and instruction on all levels of ability. The land set aside for equestrian pursuits abuts the resort's airstrip and is bounded on one side by a stream. Trail rides skirt this creek, following paths through the coconut plantation and jungle and swinging along the beach.

11. VIEQUES

About six miles east of the big island of Puerto Rico lies Vieques (pronounced Bee-*ay*-kase), an island about twice the size of Manhattan with some 8,000 inhabitants and scores of palm-lined white sand beaches. Since World War II some two-thirds of the 21-mile-long island has belonged to the United States military forces. Much of the government-owned land is now leased for cattle grazing, and when there are no military maneuvers the public can visit the beaches, sometimes restricted. Being allowed use of the land does not, however, totally cover local discontent and protest at the presence of the navy and Marine Corps personnel on the island.

The Spanish conquistadores didn't think much of Vieques. They came here in the 16th century but didn't stay long, reporting that the island and neighboring bits of land held no gold and were therefore "Las Islas Inutiles" (useless islands). The name Vieques comes from an Indian word for small island, *bieques*. Later Spanish occupation is attested to by the main town, **Isabel Segunda,** on the northern shore. The last Spanish fort in the New World was started around 1843 under the reign of the second Queen Isabella, for whom the town was named. The fort was never completed and is not of any special interest. The **Punta Mula lighthouse** north of Isabel Segunda provides panoramic views of the land and sea. The island fishermen and farmers conduct much of their business in Isabel Segunda.

On the south coast, **Esperanza,** once a center for the island's sugarcane industry, now a pretty little fishing village, lies near **Sun Bay** (Sombe) **public beach.** Sun Bay is a government-run, magnificent crescent of sand. The fenced area has picnic tables, a bathhouse, and a parking lot. Admission is $1 per car. A recently built resort and marina, and other facilities, add to the lure of the many scalloped stretches of sandy waterfront along the south coast.

Few of the island's 40-some beaches have even been named, but most have their loyal supporters—loyal, that is, until too many people learn about them, in which case the devotees can always find another good spot. The U.S. Navy named some of the strands, such as **Green Beach,** a beautiful clean stretch at the island's west end. **Red and Blue Beaches,** also with navy nomenclature, are great jumping-off points for snorkelers. Other popular beaches are **Navia, Half Moon, Orchid,** and **Silver,** but if you continue along the water, you may find your own nameless secluded cove with a fine strip of sand. **Mosquito Bay,** which glows with phosphorescence on moonless nights, is a short way east of Esperanza. (This inlet is sometimes called Phosphorescent Bay, probably to discourage ideas of being the target of mosquitoes.) Less well known than the handful of other phosphorescent bays scattered throughout the Caribbean, the one at Vieques is in some ways the most vivid. The luminosity filling its waters is a function of millions of microorganisms—technically known as dinoflagellata—which thrive on the roots of red mangrove trees.

The best way to see this amazing light show is to head for Parador Villa Esperanza for an evening tour offered daily, usually around 7:30 to 9 p.m., depending on the time of year. Tours leave from the parador's dock, cost $10 per person, and usually last 1½ hours. Transportation is on a 32-foot motor launch, owned and operated by the hotel. You stand a better chance of seeing the glowing waters if you phone the hotel in advance (tel. 809/741-8675) to find out any last-minute changes. Those who decide to swim off the side of the boat are amazed at the way the whorls of churning water created by their moving bodies seem to come alive with the glow of an eerie kind of phosphorescence.

GETTING THERE: Small **planes** fly to Vieques from Isla Grande Airport in San Juan, a 15-minute cab ride from San Juan International Airport. After a 30-minute flight, costing about $49 round trip, your plane lands at the airstrip about 15 minutes from Esperanza. For information, call Vieques Airlines (tel. 809/722-3736).

Ferryboats ply the waters between Vieques and the port of Fajardo on the east side of Puerto Rico, making the voyage in about 1½ hours for $2 per trip for adults, $1 for children.

GETTING AROUND: Públicos transport people around the island. Car rentals exist on the island, but most of them seem to be at someone's private home somewhere in Isabel Segunda. On one of my recent trips to Vieques, I had the feeling that I had rented a not-very-well maintained private car of a local family and deprived them of a long-awaited outing. You might be more secure heading for the largest car-rental facility on the island, a member of the Budget Rent-a-Car franchise, at the Parador Villa Esperanza, recommended below. There, owner Ramon Ruíz-Cox will rent you a late-model Nissan or Mitsubishi for around $45 per day from his inventory of 15 rental cars. This will require that you show a valid driver's license and either make a $100 deposit or present a valid credit card. The phone is 809/741-8173.

There is a much smaller Budget Rent-a-Car subsidiary in the center of Isabel Segunda, but its cars are not as well maintained and because of its smaller inventory (around five vehicles), you may not be able to secure one when you arrive. You must take a taxi from the airport to reach either of these branches of Budget Rent-a-Car.

WHERE TO STAY: Established in 1985 on the site of an abandoned sugar plantation, whose sandy boundaries encompass a fine beach and a 900-acre national park, the **Parador Villa Esperanza Beach Club & Marina,** Esperanza, Vieques, PR 00765 (tel. 809/741-8675), is the most interesting and best-managed hotel on the island. You register between the massive brick walls and the soaring ceiling of a 19th-century Spanish warehouse. Scattered amid the outbuildings of the parador's 30 acres are the 19th-century remains of the wood-burning steam-powered locomotives which used to haul sugarcane to the refinery. The 50 simple but stylish accommodations are contained within Caribbean adaptations of alpine chalets which lie scattered over the surrounding lawns. Each contains large windows, private baths, whirling ceiling fans, and lots of sun-flooded space. Some 25 of the units are air-conditioned. In winter, singles rent for $48 to $68 and doubles for $56 to $76.80 daily. *Summer charges are $35 to $8 in singles, $42 to $56 in doubles.* Children under 12 are accommodated free in doubles with their parents.

On the premises is a swimming pool, copses of well-placed mahogany trees, a handful of century-old banyans, two tennis courts, and a 550-foot concrete dock stretching out toward a pair of uninhabited islands known throughout the region for their excellent offshore snorkeling. Some guests spend at least part of their afternoons sipping piña coladas beneath the shade of a thatch-roofed outdoor bar, where comfortable chairs and cooling breezes make the sea even more beautiful. The hotel's fine restaurant, La Marina, is reviewed separately. Mr. Ruíz-Cox, one of the most charming hoteliers in Puerto Rico, grew up in New York where his father was a professor at the Juilliard School of Music. An experienced sailor, he served as the coach for Puerto Rico's Olympic sailing team for many years. He's happy to show guests an adjoining building used in 1962 by a film crew shooting *Lord of the Flies.*

La Casa del Frances, P.O. Box 458, Barrio Esperanza, Vieques, PR 00765 (tel. 809/741-3751). Set in a field near the southern coastline, its columns and imposing façade rise from the lush landscape surrounding it. It was completed in 1905 by a retired French general as the headquarters for his working sugar plantation. In the 1950s it was acquired by W. F. Woolworth, who installed a swimming pool and transformed it into an oasis for the R&R of his executives. In the 1970s a retired optometrist from Boston, Irving Greenblatt, transformed 19 of its high-ceilinged bedrooms into pleasantly old-fashioned hotel accommodations. Each contains a private bath, and many enjoy access to the sweeping two-story verandas ringing the white façade. With MAP included, doubles rent for $110 per night throughout the year. Scattered throughout the dozen acres attached to the main house are century-old tropical trees and a glass-fronted shrine to the Virgin. The estate's architectural highlight is the two-story interior courtyard whose center is lush with bamboo, palms, philodendron, and well-chosen examples of Haitian art. The fixed-price dinners, costing $12 each, are attended by many island residents who enjoy the changing array of Italian, barbecue, or Puerto Rican buffets which the staff presents with flair beneath a 200-year-old mahogany tree. The location is about a 15-minute drive southeast of Isabel Segunda, just north of the center of Esperanza.

Bananas, P.O. Box 1300, Barrio Esperanza, Vieques, PR 00765 (tel. 809/741-8700). During the 1986 making of the film *Heartbreak Ridge,* the actors and crew transformed this establishment's windswept porch into their second home. Located on the beach and best known for its bar and restaurant, this guesthouse also has six simple, clean, and comfortable rooms, some recently renovated. Each has a private bath and ceiling fan, and one is air-conditioned and has its own screened-in porch. *Off-season rates are from $40 to $48 per person daily.* Winter prices are $50 to $55 per person, based on double occupancy. The real heart of the place, however, is in the pleasant veranda restaurant operated by the owners, Lynn and John Jersild. Open daily from 11:30 a.m. to 1 a.m. in high season, the establishment serves meals and potent rum punches to anyone who arrives. You can choose from deli sandwiches, burgers, grilled Caribbean lobster, such local fish as snapper and grouper, fresh prime rib, and filet mignon, plus homemade desserts. Lunches cost $3 to $7.50, and dinners go for $5 to $20. Off-season, the restaurant closes two days a week.

Trade Winds Guesthouse, Barrio Esperanza, Vieques, PR 00765 (tel. 809/741-8666). Along the shore on the south side of the island, in the fishing village of Esperanza, this pleasant guesthouse offers nine bedrooms, three of them air conditioned and with terraces. The others have ceiling fans, and some also have terraces. High-season prices are $50 to $55 daily in a single, $60 to $70 in a double. *In summer, rates are reduced by $10 per night.* A three-night deposit by check or money order is required. The establishment is well known for its open-air restaurant overlooking the ocean and its hospitable atmosphere.

Posada Vistamar, P.O. Box 495, Esperanza, Vieques, PR 00765 (tel. 809/741-8716), is very simple, but its convenience to the beach at Sun Bay is an asset. Each of the half dozen bedrooms is in a low-lying motel-like building adjacent to the establishment's restaurant. Each unit has a private bath with twin beds and a ceiling fan. Year round, single or double rooms rent for $25 per night. Astor Luís Benitez and Olga Ortiz are the kindly owners.

WHERE TO DINE: Designed to look like an Indian shack, **La Campesina** ("The Country Place"), La Hueca (no phone), is an unusual and excellent restaurant built in the forest a few steps from one of the richest archeological deposits of Taíno Indian artifacts in the Caribbean. The location is about six miles southwest of Isabel Segunda in the untrammeled fishing village of La Hueca. Only dinner is served, usually from 7 to 9:30 p.m. every evening from mid-November to early May, but don't count on it. You'll have to inquire locally when you arrive. Full meals cost from $15. Occasionally a potent cocktail is available, perhaps a mulets made with rum and local fruits or a billi made with local quenepa, rum, and cognac.

Restaurant La Marina, Parador Villa Esperanza, Esperanza (tel. 809/741-8675), is contained in an octagonal building which the best hotel on the island uses as a dining room. Most guests select a table on the wrap-around veranda, but there's a pleasant wood-sheathed interior if you prefer to dine indoors. Full dinners cost $15 to $20, and luncheon buffets, held in high season only, go for $12 for all you can eat. Lunch is served from noon to 2:30 p.m. and dinner from 6 to 10 p.m., seven days a week. The meals might include shrimp with garlic, many versions of fresh fish, and thick overstuffed lunchtime sandwiches. The piña coladas are creamy, but after your second or third you may want to switch to a tamaringo (tamarind juice with rum) or a guayacol (guava juice with rum).

The Tradewinds, Barrio Esperanza (tel. 809/741-8368), is an attractively raffish kind of restaurant where you can enjoy a drink on the veranda bar before moving to the upper sundeck for your meal. The club is open only four days a week, even in high season. Only dinner is served, from 6:30 to 9 p.m. Thursday to Sunday. Menu items which might tempt you include surf and turf, several shrimp dishes, and pompano or grouper en papillotte. Full meals cost from $15 each.

Restaurant El Quenepo, P.O. Box 688, Barrio Esperanza, Vieques, PR 00765 (tel. 809/741-8541). Named after a large fruit tree growing between it and the nearby coastal road, this open-air pavilion is the year-round domain of Mario Abreu and his wife, Carmen. You dine beneath a raftered ceiling where revolving fans stir up a bit of the indolent air. Natives of Vieques, the Abreus prepare the specialties for which the island is best known: lobster and conch or an octopus salad, certainly a thick and deliciously spicy lobster soup (asopao), many varieties of locally caught fish, and several kinds of chicken. Full meals cost $10 to $20 each and are served daily except Tuesday from 9 a.m. to 7 p.m. The establishment also has a few rooms to rent, costing $35 to $45 daily for two people.

Richard's Café, Calle Antonio Mellado, Isabel Segunda (tel. 809/741-5242). Its oilcloth decor and low-slung façade might remind you of an unpretentious coffeeshop, but this is actually a substantial restaurant. The location is beside the road near the entrance to town. It's considered one of the most popular and reliable of the inexpensive restaurants on the island. You can order a snail or octopus salad, a T-bone steak, pork chops, and a savory version of asopao made from well-spiced hunks of lobster or shrimp. Full meals cost from $12 each, but one of the sandwiches, averaging around $3, makes an ample repast. The establishment is open daily except Sunday from 11 a.m. to 2:30 p.m. and 6:30 to 11 p.m.

12. CULEBRA

A tranquil little island, Culebra lies in a mini-archipelago of 24 chunks of land, rocks, and cays in the sea, halfway between Puerto Rico and St. Thomas, U.S. Virgin Islands. Seven miles long and three miles wide, with nearly 2,000 residents, the inviting little island is in U.S. territorial waters belonging to Puerto Rico, 18 miles away. This little-known, year-round vacation spot in what was once called the Spanish Virgin Islands was settled as a Spanish colony in 1886, but like Puerto Rico and Vieques, it became part of the U.S. after the Spanish-American War in 1898. In fact Culebra's only town, **Dewey,** was named for Adm. George Dewey, American hero of that war, although the locals call the fishing village **Puebla.**

For a long time, beginning in 1909, Culebra was used by the U.S. Navy as a gunnery range, even becoming a practice bomb site in World War II. In 1975, after years of protest over military abuse of the island's environment, the navy withdrew from Culebra, with the understanding that the island be kept as a nature preserve and habitat for the many rare species of birds, turtles, and fish that abound there. The four tracts of the Culebra Wildlife Refuge, plus 23 other offshore islands, are managed by the U.S. Fish and Wildlife Service. Culebra is one of the most important turtle-nesting sites in the Caribbean. Large seabird colonies, notably terns and boobies, are seen.

Today vacationers and boating people can explore the island's beauties, both on land and in the sea. Culebra's white sand beaches—especially Flamenco Beach—the clear waters, and long coral reefs invite swimmers, snorkelers, and scuba-divers. The landscape ranges from scrub and cactus to poincianas, frangipanis, and coconut palms.

Culebrita, a mile-long coral isle satellite of Culebra, has a hilltop lighthouse and crescent beaches.

GETTING THERE: As with Vieques, you can take a small plane or a ferry to Culebra from Puerto Rico. **Flamenco Airways** (tel. 809/724-7110) flies from Isla Grande Airport in San Juan, about a 30-minute hop, for $46 round trip; and from Fajardo, 12 minutes, for $26 round trip. **Prestige Aviation** (tel. 809/742-3141), another small airline, makes the flight from Isla Grande for $50 per round trip, from San Juan's Isla Verde Airport for $60 round trip, and from Fajardo for $26 round trip.

You can take a ferry from Fajardo, bringing your car for $26.50 per round trip (reservations required). A ferry for passengers lets you make the voyage in air-conditioned comfort taking only one hour between Fajardo and Culebra, costing $4.50 for a round trip. For information on ferry service, phone 809/742-3161.

You can also fly to Culebra from St. Thomas in the U.S. Virgin Islands for around $40.

WATER SPORTS AND SAILING: Increasing numbers of divers have recognized Culebra as a treasure trove of marine zoology. The best and most experienced dive operation there is **CUDA, Culebra Underwater Diving Association** (tel. 809/742-3839). It was created by an Ohio-born entrepreneur, Jim Kneaskern. After escaping from his engineer's job in Cleveland, he adopted as a full-time career his hobby of exploring an underwater world.

Culebra School of Sailing (tel. 809/742-3839) is owned and operated by Hugh and Diane Callum, who hail from Indiana and Québec, respectively. Daily sails cost $25 per hour. At their disposal is a regatta of five sailboats which vary between 27 and 48 feet in length. Currently this is the only sailing school on the island. It operates out of the Callums' home on a 42-foot sailboat moored off Enseñada Honda.

WHERE TO STAY: Across the road from an inlet of the sea, about an eight-minute drive from the center of town, **Club Seabourne,** P.O. Box 357, Culebra, PR 00645 (tel. 809/742-3169), is a pink-and-white clapboard building, off which lie the eight elegantly simple bedrooms. Most of these are found in chalet-style outbuildings for additional privacy. However, the conviviality of the poolside restaurant is never far away. Year-round rates range from $75 to $100 nightly for two persons. This place is within a garden of crotons and palms, lying at the mouth of one of the island's best harbors, Enseñada Honda. The owners are also the managers of a sailboat-chartering business in case you want to rent a boat.

Flamenco Resort and Fishing Club, P.O. Box 241, Culebra, PR 00645 (tel. 809/742-3144), is the only guesthouse or hotel which lies close to the white sands of one of the best beaches in the region, Flamenco Beach. It contains eight rooms, though not all have a private bath. Each unit has access to a communal kitchen. The place would really be ideal for a cluster of friends or an extended family, since the accommodations are arranged around spacious sitting rooms much like those in an informal beach house. Weekly rates year round are $455 per person in a studio, $560 per person in a bedroom villa, and $1,225 per person in a villa with two bedrooms. There is a small store on the premises where guests can stock up on food staples, but most meals are consumed in a breeze-swept oceanside terrace. An array of supplemental diversions includes day trips on a sailboat to one of the nearby islands, snorkeling, and fishing expeditions.

Punta Aloe, P.O. Box 292, Culebra, PR 00645 (tel. 809/742-3167; 207/882-5203 in the U.S.), is a series of waterfront homes on Culebra's beautiful Enseñada Honda (bay). Each villa has a large deck overlooking the bay and/or the sea, two bedrooms (one with a queen-size bed and one with two singles), two baths, a living room/kitchen, and two additional sofas for sitting or sleeping. Kitchens are fully equipped. Rates year round are from $295 per week for a couple in a cottage to $650 per week in winter, $450 in summer for a villa accommodating up to six guests. Free use of a washing machine and of windsurfers and snorkeling gear is provided, and cars and boats are available for rental by guests. Your hosts are Tania and Dick Hayes.

Villa Boheme, Enseñada Honda (P.O. Box 218), Culebra, PR 00645 (tel. 809/742-3508). Trade winds blow through the five bedrooms and three apartments offered for by-the-week rental by former Maine resident Renée Coolman, who maintains what's become almost a mini-marina. The units are arranged in a split-level format, each with its own private entrance, a view of the harbor, a king-size bed, a table or ceiling fan, windows protected by metal louvers, and a private bath. No meals are served, but there are two communal kitchens where guests can prepare their own meals. Also, several restaurants are within walking distance. The apartments include full kitchens and rent for $485 per week year round. The five rooms cost $425 a week in winter, *$325 in summer,* single or double occupancy.

Villa Fulladoza, P.O. Box 162, Culebra, PR 00645 (tel. 809/742-3576). Built as an apartment complex in 1982 by a Culebra-born sailor, Carlos Feliciano. This place is unpretentious, clean, and pleasant. Its small, sandy backyard abuts the harbor, where you can admire the marine activity of the moored boats. Each of the seven units contains its own bathroom, kitchenette, private porch, and ceiling fan. My favorite is on the upper floor, a room which benefits from access to the building's pebble-decorated upper veranda. Weekly rates year round are $210 to $350 for two persons, depending on the apartment chosen. Daily charges for two are $35 to $55 on weekdays, $45 to $65 on weekends. There is an outside grill and waterfront tables for dining, plus bicycles and two windsurfers for the use of guests. The location is about a quarter mile east of town and a five-minute walk from a grocery store. It remains open all year.

WHERE TO EAT: Located behind a low-slung façade near the port, across the street from the Town Hall, **El Pescador Pizzeria,** 14 Pedro Margúez (tel. 809/742-3175), is a good place to go in the evening from 5 to 10. Depending on business, the bar stays open later. Virtually every yachtsman visiting enjoys at least one drink around the copious bar in the anteroom. Meals cost from $6. In winter, El Pescador is closed Tuesday.

Tina's (El Caobo Restaurant), Calle Muñoz Marín, Sector Clark (tel. 809/742-3235). Except for the welcome offered by the owner, this looks to be little more than an open veranda with a tin ceiling, slightly rickety tables, and floor fans. The location is in a poor residential neighborhood within a seven-minute walk north of the center of town. Andres Abreo named his restaurant after his wife, Tina. It opens early every morning, keeping no set hours, as it melds breakfast, lunch, and dinner into one long socializing session. Full dinners cost from $10 and might include lobster, octopus, fish fries, rice with beans, meat pies, and various kinds of beefsteak. Lunchtime sandwiches cost $2 each, and a full breakfast goes for only $1.75. Any of these meals is washed down, local style, with a can of cold beer which everyone on the island seems to fetch for himself from the frost-dappled refrigerator in back.

El Batey, 250 Carretera (tel. 809/742-3828), across from the harbor, is a large, clean place which maintains a full bar as well as an array of deli-style sandwiches, costing $3. Coffee and doughnuts are served every morning. Beer is a popular drink, and the pool tables make the place lively, especially on weekends when many locals throng in. Weekdays, it's much calmer. The owners, Digna Feliciano and Tomás Ayala, are friendly and have many fans on the island. Breezes from the harbor cool the place. Service is from 10 a.m. to 10 p.m. Closed Monday. They also operate a popular disco and have a new pier for tying up dinghies.

CHAPTER V

THE U.S. VIRGIN ISLANDS

□ □ □

1. ST. THOMAS
2. ST. JOHN
3. ST. CROIX

By a quirk of geographical demarcation, the U.S. Virgin Islands lie in two bodies of water: St. John is entirely in the Atlantic Ocean, St. Croix entirely in the Caribbean Sea, and St. Thomas separates the Atlantic and the Caribbean. These islands enjoy one of the most perfect year-round climates in the world. They lie directly in the belt of the subtropical, easterly trade winds. At the eastern end of the Greater Antilles and the northern tip of the Lesser Antilles, the U.S. Virgins are some 40 miles east of Puerto Rico, 1,500 miles southeast of New York City, and 1,100 miles east-southeast of Miami. Some of their sugar-white beaches, experts cite, are among the most beautiful on the globe.

Christopher Columbus (there's that name again) sighted the Virgin Islands on his second voyage to the New World, in 1493. He anchored at Salt River on St. Croix, naming the islands for St. Ursula and her 11,000 virgins claimed to have been martyred by the Huns at Cologne in the Middle Ages.

In 1666 the Danes took formal possession of St. Thomas. According to Issac Dookan in *A History of the Virgin Islands of the United States,* the Danes departed the settlement after 19 months and then made a second attempt to colonize St. Thomas in 1672. That island, whose capital was renamed Charlotte Amalie in 1691, was divided into plantations, and an attempt was also made to colonize the island with convicts and prostitutes.

To help guard the Panama Canal, the United States purchased the islands in 1917 at a cost of $25 million, a price considered scandalously high at the time. Of course, the Americans feared German U-boat flotillas. These American outposts in the Caribbean today have territorial status, governed by an elected 15-member legislature and a governor.

GETTING TO ST. THOMAS AND ST. CROIX: Travelers living in the northeast quadrant of the United States will probably find that **American Airlines** offers the easiest link to and from the two Virgin Islands. Two flights leave within 90 minutes of one another from New York's JFK Airport every morning. Both planes fly nonstop to St. Thomas, where passengers transfer to go to St.

Croix, often on another aircraft. Passengers bound for St. Croix usually choose the second of American's daily flights because the connection in St. Thomas is more efficient. Travelers can arrange to have their luggage routed directly to their final destination. In the afternoon, both flights return to New York, both originating in St. Thomas and then touching down briefly to pick up passengers in St. Croix before continuing on nonstop to New York. American also has good connections to Boston.

Bargain-seeking passengers can always call American and ask to be connected with the tour desk. There, someone can arrange discount air passage if a hotel reservation is made through American at the same time. A wide array of accommodations and flight dates is available, although the options are so varied and complicated that only an airline staff member (or a travel agent) can describe them in detail. Most travelers, however, opt for a cost-conscious APEX ticket, whose simple restrictions don't usually present any hardship. It requires a seven-day advance purchase and a minimum stay of 3 to 30 days before you can use the return half of your ticket. If you change any detail of your passage before departure from North America, American will impose a $50 penalty. Changes in the date, but not in the routing of your return, are permitted without any penalty once you arrive at the farthest point of your itinerary. As with any airline, American's APEX fares vary with the season, and travel in both directions on a weekday usually qualifies a passenger for a slightly reduced fare.

For passengers whose schedules don't permit a seven-day advance purchase and a stopover of 3 to 30 days, it still pays to reserve and pay for a ticket as far in advance as possible. For promotional purposes, American keeps a controlled inventory of coach-class seats on each of its flights which cost less than the regular coach-class fares. If your schedule is flexible and you're looking for one-way passage, ask a reservations clerk for his or her advice about the cheapest way to travel. New York–U.S. Virgin Islands flights usually last around 3½ hours. The flight between St. Thomas and St. Croix takes about 20 minutes.

Hint: A flight to the U.S. Virgin Islands is sometimes less expensive if you request a change of aircraft at American's hub in nearby Puerto Rico. The airline's service from many parts of North America changes aircraft there before being rechanneled to scattered parts of the Caribbean basin on smaller planes. These are usually owned by American's partner, **American Eagle.** This routing, which may or may not have an efficient connection depending on many factors, might save you money over the APEX fare on a nonstop flight from New York. For more information and reservations, call toll free, 800/433-7300.

If you're coming from Miami, you'll find that **Eastern Airlines** has nonstop jet service from Miami to St. Thomas/St. Croix. However, at presstime a strike has curtailed Eastern service, and the future of the airline is uncertain. Its toll-free number is 800/535-6660.

To compare prices and routings, check the **Pan American** daily nonstop service from New York and Miami to St. Thomas. As with American, Pan Am's flights touch down first on St. Thomas before continuing on to St. Croix. Pan Am routes Middle Atlantic and midwestern passengers through Miami. A daily nonstop flight departs Miami every day at 5:40 p.m., leaving plenty of time to hook up with connections from the rest of the country before continuing nonstop to St. Croix. Pan Am's toll-free number is 800/221-1111.

Midway Airlines also features nonstop jet service from Chicago and Miami to the U.S. Virgin Islands. For more information, call toll free at 800/621-5700.

For information on getting to St. John, refer to Section 2 in this chapter.

PRACTICAL FACTS: Since the Stars and Stripes fly over these islands with their old-world Danish towns, you don't have a language barrier and you don't have to exchange the Yankee dollar for some other currency.

Banks: Several major banks are represented in the U.S. Virgins, although hours vary from bank to bank and island to island. However, they are mainly open from 9 a.m. to 2:30 p.m. Monday to Thursday. Friday hours are often different: 9 a.m. to 2 p.m. and 3:30 to 5 p.m.

Customs: The big attraction of these islands, in addition to serving as a winter playpen and an increasing summer destination, is that every U.S. resident can bring home $800 worth of duty-free purchases, including a gallon of alcoholic beverages per adult. In addition, you can mail home an unlimited amount in gifts valued at up to $100 each. (At other spots in the Caribbean, U.S. citizens are limited to $400 worth of merchandise and a single bottle.)

Driving Tip: *Remember to drive on the left.* This comes as a surprise to many visitors who expect that U.S. driving practices will hold here. Some have erroneously attributed the "drive on the left" to Danish rule, which is unlikely, since in Denmark you drive on the right. Of course, obey speed laws, which are 20 mph in town, 35 mph outside.

Electricity: Whatever appliances you use on the mainland (hairdryer, etc.) should work for you here. The electrical current in the Virgin Islands is the same as on the mainland: 120 volts AC, 60 cycles. No adapter or converter is needed.

Holidays: In addition to the standard legal holidays observed in the United States, the islanders also observe the following: January 6 (Three Kings' Day); March 31 (Transfer Day—transfer of the Danish Virgin Islands to the Americans); June 20 (Organic Act Day—in lieu of a constitution, they have an "Organic Act"); July 3 (Emancipation Day, commemorating the freeing of the slaves by the Danes in 1848); July 25 (hurricane supplication day); October 17 (hurricane thanksgiving day); November 1 (Liberty Day); and December 26 (Boxing Day to the British but called Christmas Second Day in the U.S. Virgins). The islands also celebrate two carnival days on the last Friday and Saturday in April: Children's Carnival Parade and Grand Carnival (adults') Parade.

Hospitals: The St. Thomas Community Hospital is the Health Center (tel. 809/776-8311). On St. John, the Morris DeCastro Clinic is in Cruz Bay (tel. 809/776-6252), and there is another clinic at Susannaberg (tel. 809/776-6400). On St. Croix, the primary hospital is the St. Croix Community Hospital (tel. 809/778-5080).

Newspapers: Daily newspapers from the mainland are flown in to St. Thomas and St. Croix every day, and local papers such as the *Virgin Island Daily News* on both islands also carry the latest news. St. Croix has its own daily newspaper, *The St. Croix Avis.*

Postage: Since the Virgin Islands are part of the U.S. Postal System, postage rates are the same as on the mainland.

Radio and TV: St. Thomas receives both cable and commercial TV stations. Radio weather reports can be heard at 7:30 p.m. and 8:30 a.m. on 99.5 FM.

Telephone: For a local call at a telephone booth, place 25¢ into the meter. From many points on the mainland you can dial direct to the Virgin Islands using the area code 809, which is unnecessary once you are there. Cable service is available as well.

Time: When it's 6 a.m. in Charlotte Amalie, it's still 5 a.m. in Miami. The U.S. Virgins are on Atlantic Time, which places the islands an hour ahead of Eastern Standard Time. When the east coast goes on Daylight Saving Time, Virgin Island clocks and those on the mainland record the same time.

Tipping: As a general rule, it is customary to tip 15%. Some hotels add a 10% to 15% surcharge to cover service. When in doubt, ask.

Water: There is ample water for showers and bathing in the Virgin Islands, but you are asked to conserve. Hotels will supply you with all your water for drinking.

Weather: From November through February, temperatures here average about 77° Fahrenheit. The average temperature divergence is 5° to 7°. Sometimes in August, the temperature peaks in the high 80s, but the subtropical breezes keep it comfortably cool in the shade. The temperature in winter may drop to as low as the low 60s, but this happens rarely.

1. ST. THOMAS

The busiest cruise-ship harbor in the West Indies, St. Thomas is the second largest of the U.S. Virgins, lying about 40 miles north of St. Croix, which is larger. St. Thomas, with the U.S. Virgins' capital at **Charlotte Amalie,** is about 12 miles long and 3 miles wide. The capital is also the shopping center of the Caribbean (refer to the section on what to buy).

Hotels on the north side of St. Thomas look out onto the Atlantic, and those on the south side front the calmer Caribbean. It's possible for the sun to shine in the south as the north experiences showers.

Holiday makers discovered St. Thomas right after World War II, and they've been flocking back ever since in increasing numbers. Shopping, sights, and sun prove a potent lure. Tourism has raised the standard of living here until it is one of the highest in the Caribbean. Condominium apartments have grown up over the debris of bulldozed shacks.

St. Thomas is a boon for cruise ship shoppers, who flood Main Street, the shopping center, basically three to four blocks long in the center of town. However, this center which gets very crowded is away from all beaches, major hotels, most restaurants, and entertainment facilities. Also, at a hotel "out on the island," you can still find the seclusion you may be seeking.

If you're visiting in August, make sure you carry along mosquito repellent.

GETTING AROUND: The chief means of transport is the **taxi,** which is unmetered. Therefore it is important to agree with the driver *before* you get into the car. Actually, taxi fares are controlled and are widely posted, perhaps at your hotel desk. In St. Thomas cabs are plentiful. Surcharges, ranging from $1 to $1.50, are added on after midnight. If you rent a taxi and a driver (who just may serve as a guide) for the day, the cost is about $25 for two persons for two hours of sightseeing. Each additional passenger pays another $12.

St. Thomas has an open-air "safari bus." Departures are from Red Hook dock on the hour from 7:15 a.m. to 6:15 p.m. They also depart from the Market Place for Red Hook on the hour from 8:15 a.m. to 5:15 p.m., costing $2 for a one-way ticket.

Manassah Country Bus goes between Charlotte Amalie and Red Hook nearly every hour. Service starts at 6 a.m. from Charlotte Amalie, ending at the last run at 8 p.m. from Red Hook, all for a one-way ticket cost of 75¢. Throughout the day, other buses depart from Rothschild Francis Square in Charlotte Amalie, heading across St. Thomas as far west as Bordeaux, a one-way passage going for 75¢. For information about exact schedules, telephone 809/774-5678.

Of course, if your means of getting around the Virgin Islands is by private boat, then you may want to get a copy of the newest **Yachtsman's Guide to the Virgin Islands,** available at major marine outlets, bookstores, book departments of major yachting publications, or direct from Tropic Isle Publishers, Inc., P.O. Box 610935, North Miami, FL 33161 (tel. 305/893-4277). The guide, revised annually, is supplemented by sketch charts, photographs, and landfall sketches and chartlets showing harbors and harbor entrances, anchorages, channels, and landmarks, plus information on preparations necessary for cruising the islands.

Car Rentals

Partly because of its status as a U.S. territory, St. Thomas has many leading North American car-rental firms prominently represented at the airport. Because of the island's high accident rate (partly a function of the unaccustomed requirement of driving on the left), as well as the island's winding and hilly roads, prices tend to be expensive. Before you go, it pays to compare the rates of the "big four" car-rental companies by dialing their toll-free numbers: **Hertz** at 800/654-3001, **Avis** at 800/331-2112, **National** at 800/328-3876, and **Budget Rent-a-Car** at 800/527-0700.

A comparison of prices shows that for the least expensive category of car, with manual transmission but without air conditioning, Budget offers the least expensive vehicles. High season rates for Budget's four-door Chevy Sprint is $210 per week, with unlimited mileage. Hertz offers a Jeep-like Suzuki Samurai with a removable canvas top for a few dollars more (but without air conditioning).

For visitors who prefer a larger vehicle, Budget offers a highly competitive price for a Mazda 323 hatchback, with automatic transmission and air conditioning, suitable for four passengers. The high season price is $260 weekly. Tariffs go down in summer. To qualify for the prices listed, you must reserve a vehicle at least two business days in advance by calling Budget's toll-free number given above. Vehicles are late models and are well maintained. Uninsured drivers are obligated to pay up to the first $3,000 worth of damage should a mishap occur with a Budget car. At the other big-name companies, uninsured drivers are responsible for up to the full value of the car. All three agencies charge around $10 per day for this insurance. Additional personal accident insurance is available at all agencies for $2.50 per day.

Sightseeing Tours

American Sightseeing International is headquartered at Travel Services, Inc., in the Red Hook Shopping Center, Upper Level (tel. 809/775-9035), and can provide visitors with a private car and limo service. The air-conditioned vans are $35 per hour and can seat 11 to 14 passengers. The tour of the island generally takes two hours, three hours if Coral World is included.

Local Air Services

If you'd like to hop over to St. Croix or perhaps Tortola (the capital of the British Virgin Islands), call on **Virgin Islands Seaplane Shuttle.** For reservations, telephone 809/773-1776 or toll free 800/524-2050. From Puerto Rico, call toll free 800/595-9504. The seaplane also flies to St. John in case you don't want to take the ferryboat.

HOTELS: There are more hotels in the Virgin Islands than anywhere else in the Caribbean. Nearly every beach has its own hostelry. You're faced with a choice of staying in the capital, Charlotte Amalie, or at any of the far points of St. Thomas. Perhaps St. Thomas has more inns of character than anyplace else in the Caribbean. I've included a wide-ranging survey, hoping to find the one place that will meet your needs. Rates are subject to a 7½% government tax.

Luxury Leaders

Stouffer Grand Beach Resort, P.O. Box 8267, Smith Bay Rd., St. Thomas, USVI 00801 (tel. 809/775-1510), seven miles northeast of Charlotte Amalie, is perched on a steep hillside above a 1,000-square-foot white, sandy beach beside the Caribbean. The resort occupies 34 acres on the northeast shore of St. Thomas. Accommodations are in two separate areas, the poolside with 86 units and the hillside with 204 rooms. The 12 two-story townhouse suites and 24 one-bedroom suites have Jacuzzis, and all units are stylishly outfitted in shades of rose and mauve and encircled with a conglomeration of acute angles, fan-shape windows, open balconies, and lighting. Each accommodation is air-conditioned and has color cable TV with HBO, direct-dial phone, mini-bar, and hairdryer. Winter rates, single or double occupancy, are $275 to $360 daily. *Spring and fall prices are $175 to $245, and summer tariffs are $165 to $235, these prices also for single or double occupancy.* MAP can be arranged for an additional $55 per person daily.

You can enjoy beachfront breakfast, lunch, and dinner at BayWinds, featuring continental and authentic Caribbean cuisine. Sumptuous breakfast buffets, mesquite-grilled dishes, and late night desserts are served in Smugglers. Lighter fare is offered at the poolside snackbar. For cocktails, live entertainment, and nightly dancing, there's the Smugglers Lounge. On the premises is one of the most innovative swimming pools on the island, with zigzag edges that provide a hi-tech version of an Aztec ritual bath, plus another pool, a collection of boutiques, and a water sports desk where you can rent sailboats or snorkeling equipment. Guests can also go scuba diving, windsurfing, and deep-sea fishing, and there are six lit tennis courts and an exercise facility. An 18-hole golf course is just ten minutes away. The hotel is undergoing a $15 million overhaul to make it an even grander Grand Beach.

Bluebeard's Castle, P.O. Box 7480, Charlotte Amalie, St. Thomas, USVI 00801 (tel. 809/744-1600, or toll free 800/524-6599), is almost a monument in St. Thomas, a popular, all-around resort lying on one side of the bay overlooking Charlotte Amalie. The history of this spot is long, as it dates from 1665. The U.S. government turned what had been a private home into a hotel in the 1930s, on one occasion attracting Franklin D. Roosevelt. Over the years, Bluebeard's has had many additions and extensions to accommodate the ever-increasing throng of holiday makers. The hotel has a freshwater swimming pool and two whirlpools, but the guests are also provided free transportation to famous Magens Bay Beach. Championship tennis courts are on the premises. Bedchambers come in a wide variety of shapes and sizes—170 units in all, pleasantly decorated and air-conditioned. You may find the best way to stay here is on a package deal (ask your travel agent what is currently offered). Winter rates, single or double, are $190 to $230 daily. *In summer, tariffs are lowered for single or double to $135 to $170 daily.* Additional persons in a room are charged $30 per person per day. MAP costs $45 per person extra. More expensive suites and condos are also available. The Terrace Restaurant commands a breathtaking view and offers many American and Caribbean specialties, open-air brunching, lunching, or late-night dining.

Frenchman's Reef, P.O. Box 7100, Charlotte Amalie, St. Thomas, USVI 00801 (tel. 809/776-8500), has a winning southern position on a projection of land overlooking both the harbor at Charlotte Amalie and the Caribbean. The hotel stands in such a conspicuous position that the traveler with the worst possible sense of direction can't help but find it. Everywhere you look are facilities devoted to the good life—two giant swimming pools, suntanning areas, a poolside bar, tennis courts, every kind of water sports (snorkeling, scuba-diving, sailing, deep-sea fishing). Whatever your holiday needs, chances are you'll find them met at "The Reef." To reach the private beach, you take a glass-enclosed elevator. The bedrooms vary greatly, but in general are furnished in a traditional manner, with various color groups and quite good taste. In winter, except during the Christmas season when prices are increased, singles or doubles range from $240

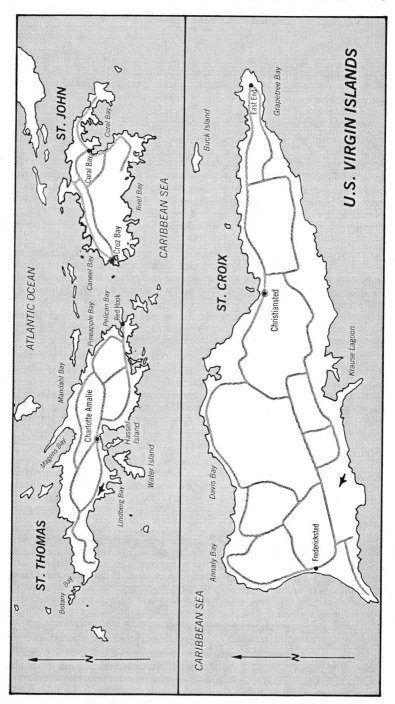

to $375 daily. For breakfast and dinner, add about $44 per person to the room tariffs. *In summer, singles or doubles cost $185 to $275 daily.* Seafood with a continental flair is served in the Waves Restaurant that resembles the inside of a cruise ship and has a view of the harbor. You can also get meals at the Lighthouse Bar, once an actual lighthouse. In the evening, the Top of the Reef, a supper club, offers entertainment, or you can go to La Terraza lounge. The Raw Bar is another possibility. For reservations, call 800/524-2000 toll free.

Morning Star Beach Club, Frenchman's Reef Beach Resort, Charlotte Amalie, St. Thomas, USVI 00802 (tel. 809/776-8500). Both its public areas and its plushly outfitted accommodations are among the most desirable on the island. They were built on the landscaped flatlands near the beach of the well-known Frenchman's Reef Beach Resort, as the elegant twin sister of the older hotel. The resort has five cruciform buildings, each containing between 16 and 24 units. Guests have the amenities and attractions of a large hotel nearby, yet maintain the privacy of an exclusive enclave. Each accommodation has rattan furniture, a color scheme of lilac, plum, and red mahogany, and views of the garden or beach. In winter, singles or doubles cost $300 to $375 per night. *In summer, singles or doubles rent for $275 daily.* MAP costs another $44 per person daily. Swimming can be supplemented with a wide array of water sports. The establishment's restaurant, the Tavern on the Beach, is recommended separately. For reservations, phone 800/524-2000 toll free.

Sapphire Beach Resort & Marina, P.O. Box 8099, St. Thomas, USVI 00801 (tel. 809/775-6100 or toll free 800/524-2090), is a modern luxury resort, one of the finest in the Caribbean, that merits an extended stay rather than a hurried visit. At this secluded retreat in the East End, guests can arrive by yacht to occupy a berth in the 67-slip marina or else take a superb suite or villa.

Casual elegance is seen in the accommodations. The decor of the rooms, opening onto a horseshoe bay, is satisfying, often in unified tones of sapphire, white, and turquoise. Both the one- and two-bedroom suites are fully equipped kitchens with microwaves, bedroom areas, living/dining rooms with queen sofa beds, complete baths, and cable TV, as well as large, fully tiled outdoor galleries with lounge furniture. Villas are on two levels, the main one containing the same amenities as the suites while the upper level includes a second full bath, a bedroom and sitting area with a queen sofa bed, and a sundeck with outdoor furniture. *In summer, two people can occupy a suite for $150 daily or a villa for $200, the charges for three people being $175 and $225, respectively, while four guests pay $300 and $380.* In winter prices go up: Two people can occupy a suite for $250, a villa for $330. Three guests are billed $275 and $355, depending on whether they take a suite or a villa, and four pay $300 and $380, respectively. Some villas are suitable for five or six guests.

Included in the rates are such extras as snorkeling equipment, beach towers, Sunfish sailboats, tennis, and windsurfing boards. Meals are served at the beach bar and grill, and at night you can dine at the Seagrape, stretched along the seashore, one of the island's finest eating places. Sometimes a ten-piece band is brought in so you can dance under the stars.

First Class

Ramada Yacht Haven Hotel & Marina, Long Bay Rd., P.O. Box 7970, St. Thomas, USVI 00801 (tel. 809/774-9700; toll free 800/229-2898), lies behind a shell-pink façade, centrally located near the beaches and the shops. It is adjacent to one of the largest and best equipped private marinas in the Caribbean and to the West Indies cruise-ship dock. Each of the 150 spacious units contain extra-large twin or king-size beds, air-conditioning, baths, radios, color cable TV,

VCRs, and direct-dial phones. Singles or doubles cost $130 to $170 daily in winter, *$85 to $110 daily in summer,* depending on the view. MAP can be arranged for another $30 per person daily. The hotel has a pool with a swim-up bar, a favorite spot for swimming and relaxation or lunch and libations. The Bridge in the marina has a relaxed atmosphere for casual dining, offering a view of the yachts and cruise ships. Pastels, a restaurant and lounge, is in the main hotel complex with a view of the marina. A complimentary cocktail welcomes guests to the hotel.

Pavilions & Pools, Rt. 6, St. Thomas, USVI 00802 (tel. 809/775-6110), is ideal for either a honeymoon or an off-the-record weekend. It seems the ultimate in small-scale luxury—your own air-conditioned villa, with floor-to-ceiling glass doors opening directly onto your own private swimming pool. The resort is a string of condominium units, built and furnished with good taste. After checking in and following a wooden pathway to your attached villa, you don't have to see another soul until you check out, if that is your desire. The fence and gate are high, and your space opens into tropical greenery. Around your own swimming pool is an encircling deck. Inside, a high room divider screens a full, well-equipped kitchen. Each bedroom has its own style, with plenty of closets behind louvered doors. The bath may intrigue you, as it has a garden shower where you can bathe surrounded by greenery, yet are protected from Peeping Toms. Inquire about honeymoon packages if that's what you're on. Otherwise, in winter expect to pay $215 to $240 daily in a double. *Two people in summer pay $165 to $185 daily.* A small bar and barbecue area is set against a wall on the reception terrace, and here rum parties and cookouts are staged. There's also an informal dining room. Occasionally a musician or singer will entertain. There's free use of snorkeling gear, and you also can play on adjacent tennis courts. The resort adjoins Sapphire Bay with its good beach.

Inns of Character

Hotel 1829, Kongens Gade (Danish for Kings Street; P.O. Box 1567), Charlotte Amalie, St. Thomas USVI 00804 (tel. 809/776-1829), is my favorite nest in St. Thomas. After a major renaissance, this once-decaying historical site has become one of the leading small hotels of character in the Caribbean. Right in the heart of town, it stands about three minutes from Government House, built on a hillside with many levels and many steps (no elevator). It is reached by a climb. The 1829 has actually been a hotel since the 19th century, entertaining such celebrated guests as King Carol of Rumania (and his mistress, Madame Lupescu), Suzy Parker, Edna St. Vincent Millay, and Mikhail Baryshnikov.

Amid a cascade of flowering bougainvillea, you can reach the upper rooms which overlook a central courtyard with a miniature swimming pool. The units, some of which are small, are beautifully designed, comfortable, and attractive. All have private baths, air conditioning, mini-bars, and phones, and most of them have cable TV. In the restoration, the old was preserved whenever possible. In high season, the cheapest and smallest double rents for $80 daily, a single for $70. All have baths and air conditioning. However, superior and deluxe doubles range in price from $115 to $170 daily; singles in that category cost $105 to $160. A few special suites cost $230 to $250 for two people. There are only 15 rooms in all, most of which face the sea. A few have antiques such as four-poster beds. *In summer, singles range from $55 to $110 daily, with doubles costing $65 to $120. Two people can rent a suite for $155.* The hotel cannot take children under 12.

Harbor View, Frenchman's Hill (P.O. Box 1975), Charlotte Amalie, St. Thomas, USVI 00801 (tel. 809/774-2651), was a once-scandalous *maison de* *tolerance*, built in the 1700s by French Huguenot political refugees at the western edge of Charlotte Amalie. After a remarkable transformation by two cosmopolitan American women, Arlene Lockwood and Lenore Wolfe, it became not only one of the finest restaurants in St. Thomas (see my dining recommendations) but an inn, often touted as "the most sophisticated small hotel in the West Indies." They brought individuality and chic to the ten air-conditioned bedrooms, which contain many four-poster beds, old chests, dressing tables, mellow paintings, flower prints, and, of course, coordinated fabrics at the windows and on the beds. Guests have access to the garden living room and a swimming pool combined. It's like a classic terraced garden in Portofino; *Harper's Bazaar* called it "very Tennessee Williams." Winter rates, in effect from November 1 to May 1, are $100 in a double and $80 in a single. *In the off-season, lasting from May 1 to Labor Day, prices go down: $70 daily in a double and $50 in a single*. Rates include a continental breakfast, and a full breakfast is available at an extra charge. Lunch is available to house guests, except on Tuesday.

Galleon House, P.O. Box 6577, Charlotte Amali, St. Thomas, USVI 00801 (tel. 809/774-6952, or toll free 800/524-2052). You walk up a long flight of stairs past a neighboring restaurant's veranda to reach the concrete terrace that doubles as this hotel's reception area. The 14 rooms are scattered in several hillside buildings, and each contains a ceiling fan or air conditioning and TV. There's even a small pool on the grounds. The main attraction of this place is its location, set next to the Hotel 1829 on Government Hill about one block from the main shopping section of St. Thomas. Donna and John Slone are the owners of this pleasant little guesthouse, renting rooms in winter for $55 to $90 daily in singles, $60 to $105 in doubles. *Summer charges for singles are $45 to $65 daily, for doubles $50 to $75*. A home-cooked continental breakfast, consisting of fresh baked goods, juice, and coffee, is included, served on the veranda overlooking the harbor. Donna is a Cordon Bleu–trained chef, who prides herself on the breakfast goodies.

Blackbeard's Castle, P.O. Box 6041, Charlotte Amalie, St. Thomas, USVI 00801 (tel. 809/776-1234), required the inspiration of an Illinois businessman to transform what had been a private residence into a genuinely charming 16-room inn. It enjoys one of the finest views of Charlotte Amalie and its harbor, thanks to its perch high on a hillside above town. The owner, Bob Harrington, wasn't alone in his appreciation of this location. In 1679 the Danish governor erected a soaring tower of chiseled stone as a lookout for unfriendly ships. Legend says that Blackbeard himself lived in the tower half a century later. Each of the bedrooms has some kind of semi-secluded lattice-enclosed veranda, a flat-weave Turkish kilim, air conditioning, cable TV, terracotta floors, and consciously simple furniture, along with a private bath and phone. *In summer, singles or doubles cost $90 to $140 daily,* rising in winter to $125 to $175. A continental breakfast is included. Guests enjoy use of a swimming pool whose waters almost lap the edge of the famous tower. The establishment's social center is within the stylish bar and restaurant, which is covered later.

A Three-in-One Resort

Bolongo Bay Resorts, P.O. Box 7337, St. Thomas, USVI 00801 (tel. 809/776-4770 or toll free 800/524-4746), is a unique property on St. Thomas—a resort complex that offers a beachside location where you can choose to stay in the only all-inclusive resort on the island; in a comfortable accommodation with up-to-date amenities and even your own efficiency kitchen; or at an all-suites "pocket of posh." The three facilities are Bolongo Limetree Beach Hotel, Bolongo Bay Beach and Tennis Club, and Bolongo Bay Villas.

Completing the complex is the St. Thomas Diving Club (see Scuba and Snorkeling under The Sporting Life section below).

Bolongo Limetree Beach Hotel is an all-inclusive resort. Opening onto Frenchman's Cove just ten minutes from Charlotte Amalie, three-story villas are set into some two dozen beautifully landscaped acres. You can walk across the "iguana bridge," and pay close attention to the pets of the property, a family of iguanas who will like you even more if you offer them their favorite food, hibiscus blossoms. Accommodations are spacious and comfortable, done with an island motif. Some contain sleeping lofts, and all are air-conditioned with color TV. The hotel quotes double rates only. Bookings are by the week, with a minimum seven-day stay required, or increments of seven days' duration. No eight- or 10-day visits are allowed, for example. *In summer, depending on your room, rates range from $2,091 to $2,231 for two people per week.* Everything but tax is included. Winter prices were not set at press time, but they can be expected to go upward to more than $3,000 per couple for a week. Check with either the hotel on its toll-free number, 800/524-4746, or with a travel agent.

The package includes such items as service, wine with dinner, a PADI scuba course or two free dives, an all-day motor yacht cruise to St. John, a half-day sail on a 50-foot catamaran with snorkeling, one-day Budget car rental for an island tour, admission to Coral World, live entertainment and dancing every night, theme night carnival buffets, and a wide range of sports activities, including two tennis courts and such water sports as Sunfish sailing. Other hotel facilities are a large swimming pool, Jacuzzis, and an exercise and weight room.

Bolongo Bay Beach and Tennis Club occupies some ten beachside acres about six miles east of Charlotte Amalie. It is among the best places to swim on St. Thomas. The 77 well-furnished rooms open onto an 800-foot white sand beach lined with palm trees. All the units have private balconies and air conditioning, and there are also ceiling fans. Other amenities include phones, cable color TV, and efficiency kitchens, ideal for midnight snacks. Some guests like to cook their own dinner sometimes. Depending on the room assignment, in winter, singles cost $180 to $195 daily, with doubles renting for $190 to $205. *Summer charges are $120 to $125 in singles, $135 to $150 in doubles daily.*

On the grounds, areas are set aside for do-it-yourself cookouts and barbecues. Most guests, however, prefer the generously served, good-tasting food at the Sea Shell Restaurant, opening onto the pool area. You can also order food at Coconut Henry's, the beach grill. The hotel emphasizes sports, providing guests with snorkel gear and Sunfish sailboats. Also available to guests are special day and overnight trips to the British Virgin Islands aboard the club's yacht, *Mohawk II*. After only one day here, you'll know why this place is called "Club Everything."

Bolongo Bay Villas, P.O. Box 7337, St. Thomas, USVI 00801 (tel. 809/775-1800 or toll free 800/524-4746), is an all-suites resort, a pocket of posh. The 60 air-conditioned suites have ocean views, cable TV, phones, kitchens, balconies, king-size or double beds, fully stocked snack and beverage bars, electronic safes, and baths. In winter, a mini-suite costs $215 for double or single occupancy. One-bedroom units accommodating one to four persons, go for $185; two bedroom suites also for one to four persons, for $235; and three-bedroom accommodations, housing one to six persons, for $360. *In summer, the charges, respectively, are $160, $185, $235, and $250.* Included in all the rates are a continental breakfast, introductory scuba lesson, tennis, snorkel gear, Sunfish sailboats, and floats. If you stay seven or more nights, you can take a complimentary cruise aboard the club yacht to St. John or Magens Bay. Ask about such specialties as the Honeymoon Plus, Couples with Kids, and Just Friends.

Small, Special Resorts

Secret Harbour Beach Hotel, P.O. Box 7576, St. Thomas, USVI 00801 (tel. 809/775-6550, or toll free 800/524-2250), directly on the beach at Nazareth Bay, is built in a contemporary style on the south coast, about a 15-minute ride from Charlotte Amalie. At first you'll think you've arrived at a South Seas island beach resort, set apart from civilization. Spread out in a setting of tall palm trees is a row of air-conditioned accommodations. Each suite or bedroom has its own private veranda, and the rooms have a distinct charm, as they are decorated to the taste of each individual owner. There are three kinds of accommodations: studio apartments with a bed-sitting room, patio, and bath, as well as a dressing room; one-bedroom suites with a living/dining area, a separate bedroom and bath, plus a sun gallery; and the most luxurious—a two-bedroom suite with two baths. Accommodations have fully equipped kitchens. *In summer, a studio apartment for two persons costs $155 daily, going up to $180 for a one-bedroom apartment and $265 for a two-bedroom unit suitable for four guests.* In winter, a two-person studio apartment costs $195 daily, rising to $255 for a one-bedroom apartment and $380 for a two-bedroom apartment suitable for four guests. The Bird of Paradise restaurant offers meals either indoors or on an outdoor terrace in a setting on the beach. Seated in a peacock chair, you dine by candlelight. Before that, you may want to go to the Beach Bar or Gazebo for drinks. There's a full water-sports center on the beach, and two championship tennis courts.

Magens Point Hotel, Magens Bay Rd., St. Thomas, USVI 00802 (tel. 809/775-5500 or toll free 800/524-2031), has a personality and charm of its own. On the northern shoreline, an eight-minute ride from downtown, it lies on a hillcrest overlooking Magens Bay with its beach that the *National Geographic* called "one of the ten best in the world." Naturally, there's regularly scheduled transportation to and from the beach and the adjacent Mahogany Run Golf Course as well as to the downtown free-port shopping. The hotel is small enough to retain its individuality, yet large enough to provide excellent holiday facilities. The main building is constructed with taste in native stone, with two rows of view balconies and a shingled town-house style of roofing. There's a wide, tree-shaded terrace with in- and outdoor dining. Buffets are often set out on long tables decorated with hibiscus bushes. On a cliff, the swimming pool is set in the midst of rough stones, giving it a rain forest look, with a sunbathing ledge on one side.

Bedrooms are air-conditioned, each with color TV and phone, framed watercolors, and Caribbean furnishings. From every unit there's a generously proportioned veranda. A single in winter, on the EP, rents for $138 to $148 and a double for $148 to $160 daily. *In summer, these same singles cost $90 to $103, doubles going for $103 to $115.* Suites, with small kitchenettes, refrigerators, coffee-makers, toasters, and microwave ovens, rent for $225 single or double, $275 for two, three, or four people in winter. *Summer rates for suites are $155 single or double, $235 for doubles, triples, and quads.* Inquire about special honeymoon packages. For your use are several tennis courts, lit at night, and you can also make arrangements for golf, scuba-diving, deep-sea diving, and sailing. Overlooking the sea is the popular restaurant, the Green Parrot. Unfortunately, a condominium blocks the view of the bay at sunset. Sometimes entertainment is provided. If you don't stay here, call before striking out from Charlotte Amalie or wherever.

Point Pleasant Resort, Estate Smith Bay No. 4, St. Thomas, USVI 00802 (tel. 809/775-7200 or toll free 800/645-2300), is a very private, unique resort on Water Bay, on the far northeastern tip of St. Thomas, remote enough to connect you with the sea and islands. From your living room gallery, you look out on a Virgin collection—Tortola, St. John, and Jost Van Dyke. The hotel complex is set on a bluff with flowering shrubbery, century plants, frangipani trees, secluded nature trails, old rock formations, and lookout points. Hummingbirds cheer your breakfast.

Living arrangements are varied, and all units (except the bedrooms) feature fully equipped kitchens and private galleries facing that view. Guests are always close to the three freshwater swimming pools. In winter, standard rooms (living/sleeping quarters) rent for $210 daily in singles, $215 in doubles. Superior units, with bedrooms closed off by wooden louvered doors, cost $240 single, $245 double. Deluxe suites, with separate bedrooms, go for $315 single or double, $345 triple, and $375 for four occupants. Two-bedroom suites (with two baths) rent for $455 for four persons, $515 for six guests. *In summer, prices drop to $145 daily for singles in standard rooms, with doubles charged $150. Superior units cost $155 single, $160 double. The charge in deluxe accommodations is $200 single or double, $220 triple, and $240 for a quad. In two-bedroom suites, four people pay $300, six occupants being charged $345.* The furnishings are light and airy, mostly with rattan and floral fabrics. Service is included in the rates. Guests at the resort can use the lit tennis courts where rackets are available, snorkeling equipment, windsurfing boards (for the experienced), and Sunfish sailboats. Tennis and windsurfing lessons are offered on the premises. Free use of a car four hours per day is included on a sign-out basis.

The resort's restaurant, Agave Terrace, is one of the finest on the island, and you may want to drive out for a meal even if you aren't staying here. *Agave* is the Latin name for the century plant found throughout the property. (Contrary to legend, it doesn't bloom just once every 100 years but rather every 25 years.) Meals costing from $40 are served daily from 11:30 a.m. to 2 p.m. and 6:30 to 10 p.m. This open-air restaurant, which has won awards, offers a happy blend of nouvelle American dishes with Caribbean specialties. The lobster fettuccine alone is worth the trip here, but you can also order such dishes as New York–strip sirloin and grouper with fresh herbs.

Budget Inns and Guesthouses

West Indies Inn, P.O. Box 4976, St. Thomas, USVI 00803 (tel. 809/774-1376), set on a peninsula in Frenchtown behind a screen of palms, the secluded yet central waterfront location is just a short walk from the town shops, inter-island ferries, and seaplane shuttle. Each of the 13 hillside rooms has air conditioning, a ceiling fan, and a private bath. Winter rates are $97 to $125 daily in singles, $108 to $147 in doubles. *Summer tariffs are $62 to $72 in singles, $70 to $83 in doubles.* Prices include a continental breakfast, and dinner can be ordered at the inn's Chart House Restaurant or enjoyed at any of a dozen nearby Frenchtown restaurants. The freshwater pool, terraced into the slope, has a large sundeck and flowering borders.

Miller Manor, Princess Gade, P.O. Box 1570, St. Thomas, USVI 00801 (tel. 809/774-1535), has been around for a long time, but it wasn't always a guesthouse. This is a 150-year-old Danish town house/villa, built on a bluff up in the residential section on Frenchman's Hill, about five minutes from downtown Charlotte Amalie. The owner-manager, Aida Miller, has lived here since she was seven years old. The house has a heavy collection of antiques, mixed with modern pieces. You enter through wrought-iron gates into a small courtyard with flowering bushes. The two lounges have crystal chandeliers, island antiques, and adjoining is a covered dining terrace with a view of the bay. The bedrooms are on four levels, each with its own style and furnishings. Many have tropical bamboo, ornate headboards, brass chandeliers, and a few have exposed-brick walls. There are 22 rooms in all, each with private bath and some with ceiling fans, others with air conditioning. *In summer, a single costs $35 daily, and a double goes for $38.* In winter, singles go for $45, doubles for $48.

Maison Greaux Guest House, 23 Solberg Rd., P.O. Box 1856, St. Thomas, USVI 00893-1876 (tel. 809/774-0063), is a three-story white building with yellow trim, surrounded by palms, bougainvillea, poinciana (flamboyant) trees, and other tropical vegetation. It's perched on a bluff above Frenchtown. A panoramic view of the harbor from Yacht Haven through Hassel and Water Islands and the submarine base is provided from the upper terrace reached by an outdoor staircase. The terrace is also a favorite place to enjoy cocktails at sunset and on into the night, with the view of the harbor lights. The guesthouse has ten rooms on its three levels, and there's a second-floor terrace for special privacy. Some of the rooms have private baths. Units are air-conditioned or have ceiling fans. *In summer, singles rent for $29 to $39 daily and doubles for $34 to $44.* Winter rates are $35 to $47 in a single, $45 to $61 in a double. Reader Steve Kralick, a writer who makes his home on St. Thomas, says that "most of the repeat clientele at Maison Greaux prefers to idle away the hours at the honor bar on the windswept terrace, where sounds of calypso strains sift softly up the steep mountainside which is a pleasant 5°-plus cooler than below." At the guesthouse you're only minutes from downtown Charlotte Amalie and the many excellent restaurants. It's an easy walk down, Mr. Kralick warns, but "take a cab back up!"

Island View, P.O. Box 1903, St. Thomas, USVI 00803 (tel. 809/774-4270 or toll free for reservations only, 800/524-2023), is a 15-room guesthouse 545 feet up on Crown Mountain overlooking St. Thomas harbor and the town of Charlotte Amalie. You enter onto a large gallery with this breathtaking view. There are four main-floor rooms, two with private baths; poolside rooms and a suite with private baths; and six units in a recent addition, three with kitchens and all with baths and balconies. All the bedrooms are cooled by natural breezes and fans, and the newer addition has optional air-conditioning. In winter, main-floor singles cost $50 daily, poolside singles going for $60 and those in the addition for $80. Doubles pay $55 on the main floor, $65 poolside, and $85 in the newer section, with the suite costing $74 for a double. *In summer, these rates are lowered to $37 daily in a single, $42 in a double.* All prices include a continental breakfast. A self-service, open-air bar on the gallery is run on the honor system. The freshwater pool provides a view of the town and the harbor, and tropical fruits and flowers abound on the premises.

Bunkers' Hill View Guest House, Bunkers' Hill, 9 Commandant Gade, Charlotte Amalie, St. Thomas, USVI 00802 (tel. 809/774-8056), is a clean and centrally situated guest lodge that would be suitable for students and others on an economy budget who don't want to sacrifice comfort and safety. Hubert V. Rawlins, the owner and manager, operates this establishment, renting pleasant rooms, most of which contain air conditioning and TV. Bunkers' Hill View lies right in the heart of town, just a short walk from the Main Street and all the major restaurants of Charlotte Amalie. Daily rates in winter are from $45 in a single, going up to $55 or more in a double. *Summer tariffs are $40 daily in a single, $50 in a double.* Rates include breakfast and limousine service to the airport. A kitchenette is provided if you want to prepare your own meals, and a laundromat stands about 25 yards from the guesthouse.

DINING OUT: The restaurants in St. Thomas have a cuisine that puts them among the top in quality in the entire West Indies. Prices, unfortunately, are high, and many of the best spots can only be reached by taxi. With a few exceptions, the finest and most charming restaurants aren't in Charlotte Amalie but out on the island.

Dining in Charlotte Amalie

Au Bon Vivant, Government Hill (tel. 809/774-2158), is known for its superb view of Charlotte Amalie and the lights in the harbor. It is also known for its classic French cookery, carefully supervised by José Chevrotée, the owner and chef. You may order French champagne by the glass while choosing from an extensive selection of fine dishes. Hot hors d'oeuvres are likely to include an onion tart or escargots de Bourgogne. Soups are imaginative and include cream of watercress and fresh fish flavors. The chef also takes care with his salads, avoiding the iceberg lettuce monotony by using endive, fresh mushrooms, and romaine lettuce, each served with a different dressing. Main-dish specialties include a rack of lamb aux herbes and fish normande. You might also select the Dover sole stuffed with fish mousse, or baby veal sautéed and steamed with plums and flamed with champagne. Dinner, from $35, is served Monday to Saturday from 6:30 to 10 p.m. Reservations are necessary.

Hotel 1829, Government Hill (tel. 809/776-1829), has some of the finest food in St. Thomas. The building is graceful, and historic too (see the previous hotel recommendations). For carefully prepared food and drink, with a distinctive European flavor, guests walk up the hill and climb the stairs of this old structure, heading for the attractive bar for a before-dinner drink. Dining is on a terrace or in the main room whose walls are made from ships' ballast and whose cooling is by ceiling fans. The floor is made of Moroccan tiles, two centuries old. For an appetizer, you might select escargots maître d'hôtel or perhaps one of the velvety-smooth soups such as cold cucumber. Try also the lobster bisque, which is made here fresh daily. Fish and meat dishes are usually excellent along with many grill dishes. The specialty of the house is one of the award-winning soufflés such as chocolate, amaretto, or raspberry. If you plan to dine here, expect to spend from $40 per person. Dinner is from 6 to 10:30 p.m., and reservations are requested. Closed Sunday.

Blackbeard's Castle (tel. 809/776-1234) lies within the previously recommended 16-room hotel. This elegant and ambitious dining room presents seafood and nouvelle American cuisine. Awarded a trio of gold medals for ambience, Caribbean dishes, and overall food in local culinary contests, owners Bob Harrington and Henrique Konzen serve lunch every weekday from 11:30 a.m. to 2:30 p.m., Sunday brunch with *The New York Times* and board games available from 11 a.m. to 3 p.m., and musical dinners nightly from 6:30 to 10:30 p.m. Full dinners, costing from $35, include such frequently changing specials as sautéed duck with pink peppercorn demi-glace, sautéed lobster with grapefruit beurre blanc and caviar, and sole Napoleon with Frangelico beurre blanc. Pastas are available in half portions as appetizers. Lunches are slightly less elaborate and about one-third the price, featuring salads, delicately seasoned platters, and frothy rum-based drinks. Reservations are suggested for dinner. Don't miss the elaborately ornate cast-iron chandelier hanging in the anteroom of the bar. The laughing cherubs decorating its many arms were found in a Danish manor house and installed in their new home overlooking one of the best harbor views on the island.

Yesterdays, 1 Commandant Gade (tel. 809/774-3088), begins where Back Street ends. Cooled by ceiling fans, it's a casual place, a favorite with the locals who gravitate to the relaxed atmosphere. You can select a table outside on the veranda fronting the street, or else one covered with a gingham cloth resting under ceiling fans. Wood floors, a good-size bar (with the coldest beer in town), a dart game, paintings on driftwood for sale—you get the picture. All patrons seem to know each other. Table hopping is commonplace. Sandwiches, a lunch in themselves, are served on pita or french bread. The chef's special is a hamburger seasoned with sweet vermouth. But that's only one of many hamburgers from around the world that are served, ranging from Texas to Japan. You can also order the baby back ribs in the evening, the chef's specialty. You might begin with a banana daiquiri, arguably the best on the island. The typical meal will cost from $10 to $12. One of the oldest bars on the island, Yesterdays is behind Cardow Jewelers. For amusement, you can watch rock concerts on the video screen. Service is until around midnight.

On Frenchman's Hill

Harbor View, Frenchman's Hill (tel. 809/774-2651). Two sophisticated American women, Arlene Lockwood and Lenore Wolfe, have welcomed guests to their gracious 19th-century Danish manor house for some 25 years. When magazines such as *Mademoiselle, Cosmopolitan,* and *Harper's Bazaar* started publishing reports of their imaginative cuisine—true creative cookery—the world came to their doorstep. Countless diners return again and again, and have become friends of the management. The setting alone is dramatic (described in part in the hotel recommendations). One of the staff shows you to a terrace with a view of Charlotte Amalie and the harbor. Later you are shown through a montage of sweeping brick arches to your candlelit table, a polished mahogany set with a pewter service. One of the three dining rooms is in the original kitchen. Forget the expense for one night, and sit back to enjoy fine food, a Mediterranean cuisine, and impeccable service.

Recommended appetizers include mozzarella in carozza marinara and a cassolette of fresh mushrooms prepared with sour cream and herbs. The chef is noted for his classic gazpacho, but one should also inquire about the soup du jour. Main dishes are served with salad greens and a choice of potato soufflé or a side order of pasta. My favorite orders include a delicate dish of sautéed shrimp and cream sauce embellished with grated cheese and dry sherry, or steak pizzaiola (filet mignon cooked to order and prepared with an herbed tomato sauce). Each day the cooks bake tasty pies from their collection of house recipes. Dinner is served nightly, except Tuesday, and reservations are imperative. Count on spending $35 or more for a complete dinner, served from 7 to 10:30 p.m. On certain nights in season it seems that half the denizens of St. Thomas drive up the narrow, wiggly road from the marketplace to this hillside-hugging gastronomic retreat. I suggest you join them. The restaurant is open year round except for a vacation period just after the Labor Day weekend.

At Compass Point

Raffles, Compass Point (tel. 809/775-6004), named after the legendary hotel in Singapore, is an establishment filled with tropical accents more evocative of the South Pacific than of the Caribbean. The furnishings include peacock chairs, lots of wicker, and ceiling fans. Dinner is served daily except Monday from 6:30 to 10:30 p.m. A pianist plays Gershwin and Porter during dinner, and showtime is at 10:30 p.m.—a little risqué, with Noël Coward renditions, but its lots of fun. You can choose from dishes which are organized on the menu into categories, including fresh seafood, beef, veal, lamb, chicken, and live Maine lobster. The fish of the day is freshly caught and well prepared, with various tasty sauces. Full meals range from $25 upward. Raffles nestles beside the lagoon at Compass Point, a few miles east of Charlotte Amalie.

Windjammer Restaurant, Compass Point Seaport (tel. 809/775-6194). Much of the paneling and the smoothly finished bar of this cozy place are crafted from thick slabs of island mahogany, which is illuminated by light streaming in from the open windows looking out onto the nearby marina. Dinner is served from 6:30 to 10 p.m. daily except Tuesday. Of course, no one will mind if you want to join the drinkers at the commodious bar for a round or two before tucking into a few of the house specialties. The selection of house drinks ranges from a "Shiver Me Timbers" to the "Half Hitch" to the "Drunken Sailor." On the menu is a wide selection of seafood, such as queen triggerfish, a Caribbean delicacy, five different shrimp dishes, a Teutonic rahmschnitzel (veal cutlets with spices in a heady cream sauce), a well-prepared Wiener schnitzel, and a fisherman's platter. Full meals cost from $18 up.

For the Birds, Scott Beach, near Compass Point (tel. 809/775-6431). Set in a low-slung bungalow whose green roof matches the growth around it, this pleasant restaurant offers reasonably priced, well-prepared food in gargantuan helpings. A few steps from the restaurant's big windows, the surf and a sandy beach beckon. Service is daily from 11 a.m. to 3 p.m. and 6 to 10:30 p.m. You can eat for $15 and up, selecting from such spicy tempers as a dinner platter smothered with heaps of nachos or an entire loaf of deep-fried onion rings, a plate of the best baby back ribs on the island, filet mignon, and southern fried catfish. There's also a selection of such Mexican specialties as beef or chicken enchiladas, chimichangas and burritos. Margaritas are huge, 46 ounces, and beer comes in mason jars. Entertainment such as live rock 'n' roll is featured.

At Frenchtown

Café Normandie, rue de St. Barthélemy, at Frenchtown (tel. 809/774-1622), is my favorite dining nook in this colorful section of St. Thomas. It also offers one of the best dining values on the island. From 6:30 to 10 p.m. daily except Monday you can order a table d'hôte menu for $16, which might begin with hors d'oeuvres, perhaps made with seafood, plus soup, often French onion. You're served not only a salad and sherbet (to clear your palate), but are allowed to choose from a selection of main-dish specialties ranging from langouste to beef Wellington (an odd name for a French restaurant), or hasenpfeffer (pieces of hare, bacon, and steak in a rich, savory sauce). The dessert special (not featured on the set meal) is their original chocolate fudge pie. All the food writers from such magazines as *Food and Wine* and *Gourmet* have so far been unsuccessful in getting the chef to part with the secret recipe. The restaurant is air-conditioned, and the glow of candlelight makes it quite elegant. It's beautifully run, and the service is excellent. There is a relaxed informality about the dress code, but you shouldn't show up in a bathing suit. Reservations are absolutely mandatory, and if you're dining there from mid-December to May 1 you may need to call several days in advance.

Alexander's, Frenchtown (tel. 809/774-4349), will accommodate you in air-conditioned comfort with picture windows overlooking the harbor. It is named for its Austrian-born owner, Alexander Treml. There are only 12 tables, but on them, Austrian specialties are served with flair. A few seafood dishes are offered, among them a conch schnitzel, but most of the others are strictly Middle European. They include a mouthwatering Wiener schnitzel, Nürnberger röstbraten, goulash, and homemade pâté. For dessert, you might try the homemade strudel, either apple or cheese, or else the richly caloric Schwartzwald torte. A full dinner, from 6:30 to 10 p.m. seven days a week, costs from $25. Lunches, served from noon to 3 p.m., are considerably cheaper, around $12. Midday meals consist of a variety of crêpes, quiches, and a daily chef's special.

Barbary Coast, Frenchtown (tel. 809/774-8354). Chianti bottles hang from the walls of this dimly lit restaurant, which serves some of the best Italian food on the island. The ambience is informal and can be a lot of fun, especially around the large bar in the outer room which many patrons abandon only reluctantly to head inside to dinner. If you want a touch of the Caribbean, you might try the conch parmigiana. Otherwise, you'll have to stick to savory dishes such as veal served either piccata, marsala, or parmigiana, many versions of pasta, and a fresh fish dish of the day. Fresh homemade desserts are a specialty. Wine is sold by the bottle or by the glass. The restaurant is closed for lunch. Dinner is from 6 to 11 p.m. The bar opens daily at 5 p.m., staying open till around 4 a.m. Full meals cost from $25.

Gregerie East, 17 Crown Bay (tel. 809/774-2252). Named after the East Gregerie Channel, at the side of which it sits, this restaurant is a good choice for a quiet afternoon of boat watching. Guests anchor in at the mahogany bar beneath mulberry-colored ceiling beams and swirling fans in a breezy pavilion whose minimum of walls are sheathed in diagonal strips of varnished pine. You can head here for a drink throughout the day (and often late into the night), but meals are served only from 11:30 a.m. to 3 p.m. and 6 to 10 p.m. Sunday brunch lasts from 10:30 a.m. to 3 p.m. Lunch is seven days a week, costing from $8 and likely to include a choice of deli sandwiches, veal piccata, and omelets. Dinner is served nightly except Monday, costing from $15 and featuring such dishes as sautéed snails in an anchovy-and-caper sauce, poached filet of red snapper with mushroom sauce, lamb chops with rosemary and a chutney-curry sauce, and pepper steak.

Red Hook

Piccola Marina Café, at Red Hook (tel. 809/775-6350), a popular eatery, has an open veranda offering a close-up view of the yachts moored at this popular marina. Lunch, costing from $5.50, is served from 11 a.m. to 3 p.m. Monday to Saturday. The menu includes various salads from Caesar to Greek to a fresh antipasto primavera, an assortment of sandwiches, not to mention the charcoal-broiled hamburgers. Sunday brunch offers everything from the traditional eggs Benedict to flaky croissants filled with Canadian bacon. Dinner is served daily from 6:30 to 10 p.m., costing from $12. All the food is homemade using only fresh ingredients. Fresh pasta dishes, such as Alfredo, carbonara, pesto, and others, are on the menu. In addition, the restaurant offers fresh fish, plus lamb, chicken, and shrimp. To end a good meal, homemade desserts include a homemade brownie specialty on Sunday and award-winning cheesecakes.

Scattered Choices

Fiddle Leaf, Watergate Villas (tel. 809/775-2810). Airy, open, and sophisticated, this imaginative restaurant offers some of the most deliciously creative food on the island. Nestled in a well-heeled condo complex, it offers a slick decor, suggesting a tropical Manhattan. Carefully aimed pin lighting, lattices, and ficus trees enhance the Haitian metal sculptures and framed posters. The menu rotates every week, making maximum use of fresh ingredients flown in from the U.S. Note the fettuccine with mushrooms, pesto, and olives, and many other varieties as ingredients come into season. Other specialties are likely to include beef tournedos stuffed with brie, filet mignon with wild mushrooms, kiwi sorbet, and chocolate pâté with raspberry sauce. Dinners cost from $40. The restaurant is open only for dinner, every night (except Monday in low season) from 6:30 to 10 p.m. Reservations are strongly advised.

Tiffany's, Cabrita Point (tel. 809/776-5430), is a fine restaurant highly appreciated by those who seek it out in its hard-to-find location in the East End. At first, you'll think you're entering a well-decorated private home. Head for a table on the terrace in the rear where you can peruse the menu while enjoying a tropical rum punch. The chef, José Chevrotée, creates French cookery that has its own distinctive flair, and he experiments with the school of nouvelle cuisine, as reflected by his ginger scallops with a watercress lime glaze. He also prepares dishes from the classic repertoire equally well. Many diners come here seeking fish, and the kitchen rarely disappoints, offering such dishes as yellowtail almondine. Another specialty is veal medallions Tiffany. The menu undergoes frequent changes based on the season and the availability of fresh produce. Count on spending $40 and up for a topnotch dinner, served only Thursday to Tuesday from 6:30 to 10 p.m. During parts of the off-season, the place may be closed, so always call for a reservation before heading there.

Chart House Restaurant, at the West Indies Inn (see above) in Frenchtown (tel. 809/774-4262), was the site of the Russian consulate in the 19th century. The restaurant is on the same property but is run separately from the hotel. You may want to journey out past Frenchtown Village for dinner in this tranquil spot. The restaurant is in the rebuilt Victorian villa. In the bar area you can listen to divers' "bull sessions." The dining gallery is a large open terrace fronting the sea. Dinner at the Chart House is served Sunday to Thursday from 5 to 10 p.m. and Friday from 5 to 11 p.m. Cocktail service starts at 5 p.m. seven days a week, and the bartender will make you his special drink called a Bailey's colada. The restaurant features the best salad bar on the island, with a choice of 30 to 40 items, which comes with dinner. Dinners begin at $14, going up to $29, and menu choices range from chicken to Alaskan king crab. Of course, this chain is known for serving the finest cut of prime rib anywhere, and here it comes loading down a plate at 22 ounces. For dessert, you can order the famous Chart House "mud pie," which, in spite of its name, is a shockingly calorie-laden ice-cream concoction. You don't make a reservation. Seating is on a first-come, first-served basis, so just arrive and hope you'll get a table. If you get here before sunset, you can watch the seaplanes land directly in front of the restaurant.

Victor's Hide Out, 32A Sub Base, off Rt. 30 (tel. 809/776-9379), is operated by Victor Sydney, who comes from Montserrat. You don't know who is likely to show up here on any given night. Maybe Bill Cosby. Perhaps José Feliciano. It has some of the best seafood and native dishes on the island, but first you must find it, as it's truly a place to hide out. If you're driving, call for directions. Otherwise, a taxi will take you there. From a hilltop perch, it is a large, airy restaurant, serving such dishes as fresh lobster prepared Montserrat style (that is, in a creamy sauce) or else grilled in the shell. You might also ask for a plate of juicy barbecued ribs. Meals cost from $18 unless you order the more expensive lobster. For dessert, try coconut, custard, or apple pie. Lunch is from 11:40 a.m. to 3:30 p.m. Monday to Saturday, with dinner being served from 5:30 to 10 p.m. seven days a week.

Eunice's, 67 Smith Bay (tel. 809/775-3975), is one of the best-known local restaurants that went from a simple shack to a modern building. A hard-fisted collection of Stateside construction workers, West Indian locals, and dozens of tourists from nearby Stouffer's Grand Beach crowd into its confines for savory platters of island food served in generous proportions. A popular concoction called a Queen Mary (a combination of tropical fruits laced with dark rum) is a favorite. The establishment is open from 9 a.m. to 10 p.m. seven days a week. It lies just east of the Coral World turnoff. Dinner specialties include conch fritters, boiled or fried fish, especially dolphin, sweet potato pie, and a number of chalkboard specials which are usually served with fungi, rice, or plantain. Full dinners cost from $20 and lunches from $12. On the lunch menu are fishburgers, sandwiches, and such daily specials as Virgin Islands doved pork or mutton. Key lime pie is a favorite dessert. Reservations are a good idea for dinner.

WHAT TO SEE: The color and charm of a real Caribbean waterfront town vividly come to life in the capital of St. Thomas, Charlotte Amalie, where most visitors begin their sightseeing exploration of the small island. In days of yore seafarers and adventure seekers from all over the world, including the prostitutes who kept them amused, flocked to this old-world Danish town, as have pirates, slaves, and members of the Confederacy using the port during the American Civil War. St. Thomas was the biggest slave market in the world.

The old warehouses, once used for storing pirate goods, still stand, for the most part housing the merchandise I'll preview in the shopping expedition. Cruise-ship passengers have taken the place of Captain Kidd and Blackbeard the pirate, walking the same old streets, called "gade" here in honor of their Danish heritage.

The main streets of town are now a virtual shopping mall, and are usually packed. Sandwiched among these shops are a few historic buildings, most of which can be covered on foot in about two hours.

Before starting your tour, you might stop off in the so-called **Grand Hotel.** Mercifully, it's no longer a hotel, for which its last tenants can be grateful. Along with shops, it also contains a Visitors' Bureau, near tiny **Emancipation Park** where a proclamation freeing African slaves and indentured European servants was read on July 3, 1848. The architectural relic was built in 1841.

West of the park, and across the street, the **Central Post Office** displays WPA-type murals by Stephen Dohanos, who later became famous as a *Saturday Evening Post* cover artist.

Next, you can climb a steep street, Kongens (Danish for "king") Gade, passing the entrance to the historic **Hotel 1829,** which has already been previewed in both the hotel and restaurant sections.

Continue past the hotel until you reach **Government House,** the administrative headquarters for all the Virgin Islands. It's been the center of official life in the islands since it was built around the time of the American Civil War. Visitors are allowed on the first two floors, weekdays from 8 a.m. to noon and from 1 to 5 p.m. Some paintings by former resident Camille Pissarro are on display, plus works by other St. Thomian artists.

Nearby is one of the few remaining streets of the old Danish town. Called the **99 Steps,** it was erected in the early 1700s.

After climbing the stairs, you can see the façade of **Crown House,** built in the mid-18th century, a stately home which was the residence of two of the past governors of the Virgin Islands. Here the rich and privileged lived in the 18th century, surrounded by Chinese wall hangings, a crystal chandelier from Versailles, and carved West Indian furniture. It was once the home of von Scholten, the Danish ruler who issued a proclamation of emancipation in 1848.

Southeast of Emancipation Park stands **Fort Christian,** dating from 1672. Named after the Danish king Christian V, the structure has been everything from a governor's official residence to a jail. Many pirates, it is said, were hanged in the courtyard. In some cells the Virgin Islands Museum has been installed, displaying some minor Indian artifacts. Admission free, it is open Monday to Friday from 8 a.m. to 5 p.m. and on Saturday from 1 to 5 p.m.

The oldest **synagogue** building in continuous use under the American flag still maintains the tradition of sand on the floor, commemorating the exodus from Egypt. It stands on Crystal Gade, and is reached by a steep walk up from Main Street. Not as old as the synagogue in Curaçao, this one was erected in 1833 by Sephardic Jews. The synagogue was built of local stone, along with brick from Denmark and mortar made of molasses and sand. It's open from 9 a.m. to 4 p.m. Monday to Friday for visitors, and conducts its religious school for children on Saturday morning from September through May.

At the point where Main Street intersects Strand Gade, Rothschild Francis

Square (or the Market Place) was the center of a large slave-trading market before the emancipation was proclaimed. Roofed over, it is an open-air fruit and vegetable market today, selling, among other items, genips (you break open the skin and suck the pulp off a pit). The wrought-iron roof came from Europe, and at the turn of the century covered a railway station. It's open every day but Sunday, reaching the peak of its activity on Saturday.

If the genip didn't satisfy you, you can take Strand Gade down to the waterfront. There you can purchase a fresh coconut, getting the vendor to whack off the top with his machete. Then you can drink the sweet milk from its hull.

After finishing your tour in Charlotte Amalie, head west on Main Street. Turn off at the sign to the West Indies Inn to visit **Frenchtown.** The French people who settled here, once known for wearing "cha-chas" or straw hats, are descendants of immigrants from the French islands who spoke an unusual patois. The colorful village, many of whose residents still engage in fishing, contains some interesting restaurants and taverns.

Later, you can strike out for **Mountain Top,** the traditional stopping-off point for a banana daiquiri.

To cap your tour, locate **Drake's Seat** on a good map and head there for the most spectacular view in St. Thomas. According to legend (and not really to be believed), Sir Francis Drake sat there charting the channels and passages of the Virgin Islands. Nevertheless, you have spread at your feet the entire sweep of almost 100 Virgin Islands, both U.S. and British.

One of the most popular attractions on St. Thomas is **Coral World,** Rt. 6 (tel. 809/775-1555), a marine complex that features a three-story underwater observation tower 100 feet offshore. Through windows large and clear you get to see sponges, deep-sea flowers, fish, and coral—underwater life in its natural state. In the Marine Gardens Aquarium, 21 saltwater tanks display everything from seahorses to urchins. Also included in the marine park is a restaurant, Vista View Bar, duty-free shops, and a tropical nature trail. The complex is open seven days a week from 9 a.m. to 6 p.m. Adults pay $10, children $6. Shark and fish feeding is at 11 a.m.

West of the center of Charlotte Amalie, on the campus of the College of the Virgin Islands, the **Reichhold Center** (tel. 809/774-8475) is one of the major cultural centers in the Caribbean. Frequent art exhibits of local artists are staged here at this Japanese-inspired amphitheater set in a natural valley. About 1,200 spectators are accommodated here, and big-time cultural entertainment has arrived in St. Thomas. Ask about possible events during your visit. You might see, perhaps, the Joffrey Ballet. The smell of gardenias will only add to the evening's pleasure.

SHOPPING: The $800 duty-free allowance makes every purchase a double bargain. If you go over the $800 limit, U.S. Virgin Islands purchases are dutiable at a flat rate of 5% up to $1,000 rather than the 10% imposed on goods from other countries. It is also possible to send as many gifts as you want to family or friends —but not more than one per day. Your spending allowance is limited to $100 per day before duty. Such items do not have to be declared on your exemption. Often well-known brand names are presented at savings of up to 60% off Stateside prices. However, that's likely to be an exceptional purchase. I don't want to paint too optimistic a picture. To find true value, you often have to plow through a lot of junk. Many items offered for sale—binoculars, stereos, watches, cameras —can be matched in price at your hometown discount store. Therefore, you need to know the price back home of the item involved to determine if you are in fact making a savings. Having sounded that warning, I'll survey some St. Thom-

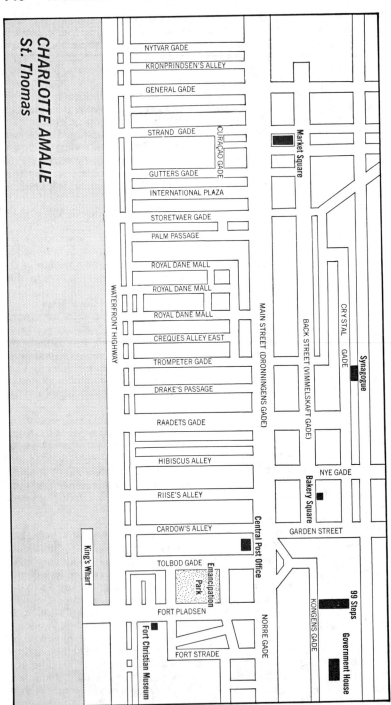

CHARLOTTE AMALIE
St. Thomas

as shops where I have personally found good buys. Know that there are lots more you can discover on your own.

Most of the shops, some of which occupy former pirate warehouses, are open from 9 a.m. to 5 p.m., regular business hours, and some stay open later. Nearly all stores close on Sunday and major holidays—that is, unless a cruise ship is in port. Few shopkeepers can stand the prospect of hundreds of potential customers, their purses full, wandering by their padlocked doors. Therefore those gates are likely to swing open, at least for half a day on Sunday. Friday is the biggest cruise-ship visiting day at Charlotte Amalie (one day I counted eight at one time)—so try to avoid shopping then.

Cardow Jewelers, Emancipation Garden Station (tel. 809/774-1140), often called the Tiffany's of the Caribbean. It boasts the largest selection of fine jewelry shown in the world. This fabulous shop, where there are more than 6,000 rings displayed, offers savings because of its worldwide direct buying, large turnover, and duty-free prices. Unusual and traditional designs are offered in diamonds, emeralds, rubies, sapphires, and Brazilian stones, as well as pearls and coral. Cardow has a whole wall of Italian gold chains. Also featured are antique coin jewelry and Piaget watches. The Treasure Cove has case after case of fine gold jewelry.

A. H. Riise Gifts, 37 Main St. at Riise's Alley (tel. 809/776-2303), offers the customer a memorable shopping experience. Displayed in a restored 18th-century Danish warehouse that extends from Main Street to the waterfront is an unusually wide and fine selection of quality imported merchandise. Special attention is given to the collection of jewelry and watches from Europe's leading craftspeople, including Patek Philippe, the most prestigious watch in the world, Ebel, Concord, Heuer, and many others. Waterford, Lalique, Daum, Baccarat, Wedgwood, Royal Crown Derby, Royal Doulton, Royal Copenhagen, and Lladró are but a few of the internationally known names in the crystal and china departments. The perfume and cosmetics line is one of the largest parfumeries in the Caribbean, all at duty-free prices. Specialties also include Crabtree & Evelyn, Liberty of London, Oriental rugs, Gold Pheil leather goods, Hilda Icelandic woolens, liquor, tobacco, and duty-free art featuring a wide selection of Caribbean prints and note cards. Toll-free shop-by-phone service is available by calling 800/524-2037 from the U.S. Merchandise inquiries and orders are welcomed, or you can call to request a free brochure.

Lion in the Sun, Riise's Alley (tel. 809/776-4203), is one of the most expensive clothing stores on the island, but patrons go here because it has the best collection of designer casual chic apparel in Charlotte Amalie. Whether it's tanks, tees, shorts, pants, or skirts, this store is likely to have what you're looking for, including clothes by such designers as Sonia Rykiel. But because of those prices mentioned previously, it's better to start your shopping first at the sales rack, looking for some discounts. Otherwise, the owner is firm about prices as marked —no bargaining here.

Tropicana Perfume Shoppes, 2 Dronnings Gade (tel. 809/774-0010), stand at the beginning of Main Street near the Emancipation Gardens post office. They are the exclusive agents of Capucci's Yendi and Cappucci de Capucci. The first of the two shops is billed as the largest parfumerie in the world. Behind its rose-colored façade, it offers all the famous names in perfumes and cosmetics, including Poison, Opium, and Chanel for women and men. Men will also find Europe's best colognes and aftershave lotions here. Then you return home, you can mail-order all these same fragrances by taking advantage of Tropicana's toll-free number, 800/233-7948.

Little Switzerland (tel. 809/776-2010), with three stores in downtown Charlotte Amalie and one on the dock at Havensight Mall, sells fine watches, a wide selection of jewelry from Europe and the Orient, and the best in crystal and china. Such names as Rolex, Ebel, Omega, Rado, Baume & Mercier, Heuer, and many more are sold. In chinaware and crystal, Little Switzerland offers Baccarat, Lalique, Waterford, Rosenthal, Royal Doulton, Wedgwood, Villeroy & Boch, and many other well-known makers. They also maintain the official outlets for Hummel, Lladró, and Swarovski figurines. Little Switzerland has branched out elsewhere in the Caribbean, with locations also in St. Croix, St. Martin, St. Barthélemy, Antigua, Aruba, and Curaçao, as well as in The Bahamas.

H. Stern Jewellers (tel. 809/776-1939) offers colorful gem and jewel creations at six locations in St. Thomas—two on Main Street, in Havensight Shopping Mall, and branches at Bluebeard's Castle, Stouffer Grand Beach Resort, and Frenchman's Reef Hotel—as well as in a store at Sint Maarten, Netherlands Antilles. Every shop has the same duty-free prices, a considerable savings for visiting shoppers. Stern gives worldwide guaranteed service, including a one-year exchange privilege.

If you want to combine a little history with shopping, you might go into the courtyard of the old **Pissarro Building,** entered through an archway off Main Street. The celebrated impressionist painter lived here as a child. The old apartments have been turned into a warren of interesting shops.

The Leather Shop, Inc., Main Street and Havensight Mall (tel. 809/776-3995), has a good selection from Italian designers. Many handbags are from chic Italian boutiques: Fendi, Bottega Veneta, Michel Clo, Furla, Prada, and Il Bisonte. You'll find a wide assortment of belts, sized to order with your choice of buckle. There are many styles of wallets, briefcases, and attaché cases, as well as all-leather luggage from Land.

The Straw Factory, 2 A Garden St. (tel. 809/774-4849), a stroll up from Post Office Square, has the island's largest selection of straw hats, from classic Panamas to beachcomber bargains. There is a wide variety of handcrafted items, especially straw baskets of every size and description and handcarved, brightly painted parrots and fish. The factory also has a big selection of handbags in straw and fabric, from huge totes to tiny purses and a wide choice of imprinted sportswear. Check their large assortment of dollar souvenirs. Stop at the counter outside for an ice-cream cone and eat it seated in the shade of the Straw Factory patio.

The aroma of spices will lead you to **Down Island Traders,** at the waterfront (tel. 809/776-4641) and on Back Street (tel. 809/774-4265). These outlets have an attractive array of spices, teas, seasonings, jams, and condiments, most of which are packaged from natural Caribbean products. Look also for candies and jellies. This is an original native market. The owner also carries a line of local cookbooks, as well as silkscreened island designs on T-shirts and bags, Haitian metal sculpture, and children's gifts.

Blue Carib Gems and Rocks (tel. 809/774-8525), the Bakery Shopping Square, is perched behind Little Switzerland on Back Street. For a decade the owners prospected for gemstones in the Caribbean, and these stones have been brought direct from the mine to you. The raw stones are cut and polished and then fashioned into jewelry by the lost-wax process. On one side of the premises you can see the craftspeople at work, and on the other side view their finished products, including such handsomely set stones as larimar, the sea/sky-blue-patterned variety of pectolite found only in the Caribbean. A lifetime guarantee is given on all handcrafted jewelry. Since the items are locally made, they are duty free and not included in the $800 exemption. Incidentally, this establishment also provides emergency eyeglass repair.

Royal Caribbean, 33 Main St. (tel. 809/776-4110), 23 Main St. (tel. 776-5449), and Havensight Mall (tel. 809/776-8890), is the largest camera and electronic store in the Caribbean. Since 1977 it has offered good values in cameras and electronic equipment, including all accessories. The store carries top brands such as Minolta, Nikon, Pentax, Canon, Olympus, Leica, and Ricoh, several of which have special camera packages. Royal Caribbean is the authorized Sony dealer, with a complete selection of Sony products. They also have good buys in Seiko, Movado, Raymond Weil, Gucci, Corum, and Swatch watches, Mikimoto pearls, Dupont and Dunhill lighters, jewelry for both men and women, and gift items.

Sheela's Jewel Palace, 23 Main St. (tel. 809/776-5449), under the same ownership as the Royal Caribbean, carries a complete range of fine jewelry and a full collection of watches from all over the world.

Irmela's Jewel Studio, in the Old Grand Hotel at the beginning of Main Street (tel. 809/774-5875 or toll free 800/524-2047), has made a name for itself in the highly competitive jewelry business in St. Thomas. Here the jewelry is unique, custom designed by Irmela and handmade by her studio or imported from around the world. Irmela has the largest selection of cultured pearls in the Caribbean, including freshwater Biwa and South Sea pearls. Choose from hundreds of clasps and pearl shorteners. Irmela has a large selection of unset stones, such as rubies, sapphires, emeralds, and unusual ones including tanzanite and alexandrite. Diamonds range from pear-shaped to emerald cut, marquis, even heart-shaped, in sizes from tiny two pointers to several carats.

Colombian Emeralds, with shops on Main Street, on the waterfront in Royal Dane Mall, and in the Scandinavian Center (tel. 809/774-3400 for information about all three locations), has a fine selection of Colombian emeralds and emerald jewelry, plus Seiko, Omega, Tissot, Swatch, and Citizen watches. They also offer gold, ruby, sapphire, and diamond jewelry. Colombian Emeralds is the largest distributor of emerald jewelry in the world.

For fine leather goods, you can't beat **Louis Vuitton,** 24 Main St. at Palm Passage (tel. 809/774-3644), where the complete French line by the world-famous designer is available: suitcases, handbags, wallets, and other accessories are carried here, plus DuPont lighters and pens.

The English Shop, Main Street at Market Square (tel. 809/776-5399) and Havensight Mall (tel. 809/776-3776), has a wide selection of china, crystal, and figurines from the world's top makers. Fine Limoges, Royal Doulton, Noritake, Royal Worcester, Spode, Coalport, and Haviland china represent only a small portion of the many brands carried. Crystal includes Stuart, Edinburgh, Gobel, and several Irish-blown pieces, while you can choose figurines from a wide range of makers: Bing & Grondahl, David Winter Cottages, Irish Dresden, Boehm, Nao by Lladró, and Beatrix Potter among them. For information before you go, phone toll free 800/524-2013.

Java Wraps (tel. 809/774-3700), in Palm Passage on the waterfront in Charlotte Amalie, is all white tiles with traditional Javanese matting decorated with exotic Balinese woodcarvings on the walls. Locals and tourists alike buy the hand-batiked resort-wear line specializing in shorts, shirts, sundresses, and children's clothing. Java Wraps is known for its sarong pieces and demonstrates the tying of them in at least 15 different ways.

The **Linen House** is considered one of the best stores for linens in the West Indies. It has two locations, one at 7A Royal Dane Mall (tel. 809/774-8117) and another at Palm Passage (tel. 809/774-8405). You'll find a wide selection of placemats, decorative tablecloths, and many hand-embroidered goods. There are many high-fashion styles.

The Cloth Horse, Bakery Square (tel. 809/774-4761), sells the celebrated Marimekko of Finland fabric as well as the French Oulivado fabric from Provence, both at a 40% saving over Stateside prices. You can also buy ready-made items such as scarves, handbags, and pillow covers. The Caribbean products carried here are natural cotton bedspreads, wall tapestries, placemats, baskets, and mahogany plates from Haiti.

At **Al Cohen's** big warehouse at Havensight, 18A Estate Thomas (tel. 809/774-3690), across from the West Indian Company dock, where cruise-ship passengers come in, you can purchase discount liquor, fragrances, T-shirts, and souvenirs. Your purchases are delivered free to the airport or your ship.

A visit to the art gallery and craft studios of **Jim Tillett,** P.O. Box 7549, Tillett Gardens, Tutu (tel. 809/775-1405), is a sightseeing expedition. The Tillett compound was converted from a Danish farm called "Tutu." The Tillett name conjures up high-fashion silkscreen printing by the famous Tillett brothers, who for years had their exquisite fabrics used by top designers and featured in such magazines as *Vogue* and *Harper's Bazaar.* Jim Tillett settled in St. Thomas, after creating a big splash in Mexico, where his work was featured in *Life* magazine. At his compound you can casually visit the adjoining workshops, where you can see silk-screening in progress. Mr. Tillett and his staff produce about 40,000 yards a year. He's daring in his color consciousness.

Upstairs is an art gallery which has an abundance of maps, paintings, sculpture, and graphics made by local artists. Mr. Tillett created a series of maps on fine cotton canvas which have been bestselling items. *Shopping tip:* Buy a square of florid Tillett fabric and frame it when you return. It can make a vivid wall hanging.

Arts Alive Fairs are held in the Tillett Gardens three times a year—in autumn, spring, and summer. These fairs give local artists a showcase for their work and offer crafts demonstrations and such special features as puppet shows for children; folkloric dancers; other dancing such as tap, ballet, and modern; steel bands; calypso music; and other activities.

THE SPORTING LIFE: Chances are, your hotel will be right on the beach, or very close to one, and this is where you'll anchor for most of your stay, perhaps occasionally going out in a Sailfish or Hobie Cat. All the beaches in the Virgin Islands are public, incidentally.

Beaches

Most of the beaches lie anywhere from two to five miles from Charlotte Amalie. I've already extolled the glory of **Magens Bay,** three miles from the capital, which charges 50¢ for adults and 25¢ for children. Dressing rooms are provided, and snorkeling equipment and small sailboats can be rented. There is also a restaurant.

Others include **Morning Star Beach,** about two miles outside Charlotte Amalie, which also has dressing rooms and a restaurant, charging adults an admission of $2 (children under 12 are admitted free). **Lindberg Beach,** adjacent to the airport, is another favorite, as is **Coki Point** at Coral World (at the latter you can rent snorkeling gear).

Boating

The biggest charter business in the Caribbean is done by Virgin Islanders. In St. Thomas most of the business centers around the Red Hook and Yacht Haven marinas.

Perhaps the easiest way to go out to sea is to charter "your yacht for a day," from **Yacht *Nightwind,*** Red Hook (tel. 775-4110), for only $60 per person. You're granted a full-day sail with a champagne tropical lunch and open bar, aboard the 50-foot yawl *Nightwind*. You're also given free snorkeling equipment and instruction. For reservations, call between 8 a.m. and 9 p.m. daily. Stephen and June Marsh, operators of the service, natives of New Jersey, offer special attractions such as the "Bumperoo" show with the most photographed dog in the Caribbean and a break-dancing finale.

My Way is a 35-foot Pearson sloop which sails to the uninhabited island of Hans Lollick for $60 per person (call 809/776-9547 for reservations). Snorkeling equipment and instruction are provided, and there's an all-day bar. You take lunch on a deserted beach. Everything is included. Sailings leave from the north side of St. Thomas.

True Love is a sleek Malabar schooner, used during the filming of *High Society* starring Bing Crosby and Grace Kelly. It gave its name to the Cole Porter duet they sang. At 54 feet in length, it sails at 9:15 a.m. from Red Hook into Pillsbury Sound. Bill and Sue Beer have sailed it since 1965. You can join one of Bill's snorkeling classes and later enjoy one of Sue's gourmet lunches with champagne. Call 809/775-6547 for reservations. The cost is $60 per person.

Of course, if you want something more elaborate, you can go bareboating. That may suggest nudity, but it means renting a craft where you're the captain. However, you must prove you're able to handle the craft before you're allowed to go out in it alone. If you'd like everything done for you, a fully crewed yacht with a captain at your service is the way to go on a charter plan. This type of charter rental is available through **Avery's Boathouse**, P.O. Box 5248, Veterans Drive Station, Charlotte Amalie, St. Thomas, USVI 00803 (tel. 809/776-0113).

A Side Trip to Water Isle

The fourth largest of the U.S. Virgins, Water Isle is only half a mile long and about a half to one mile wide. At its nearest point, it comes about three-eighths of a mile from St. Thomas. Visitors go there to spend the day on Honeymoon Beach where they swim, snorkel, sail, waterski, or just sunbathe while they relax under the palm-shaded beach, ordering lunch or a drink from the beach bar. The highest elevation is only 300 feet above sea level, and the Arawak Indians were the first to inhabit it. Originally the island had freshwater ponds from which sailing vessels replenished their casks. The army used Fort Segarra as a base in World War I.

It's possible to go on your own. A ferry runs between Water Isle Dock and the Sub Base at St. Thomas, a seven-minute ride costing $3.50 each way. Service is daily from 7 a.m. to midnight. For information, phone 809/774-1207.

Going Under the Sea

A major attraction is the *Atlantis* **submarine,** which takes you on a one-hour voyage to depths of 150 feet, with a world of exotic marine life unfolding. For those who have never gone scuba-diving, this is a unique experience. You can gaze upon coral reefs and sponge gardens through two-foot windows on the air-conditioned 65-foot-long sub, which carries 48 passengers but no children under 4. You board a surface boat at the West Indies Dock, right outside Charlotte Amalie, heading for the submarine, which lies near Buck Island (the St. Thomas version, not the more famous island near St. Croix). Both day and night sub dives are offered, the view of the nocturnal ocean world being especially enchanting. Daytime fare is $48 per person, going up to $56 at night. Children 4 to 12 pay half fare. The *Atlantis* operates seven days a week, and reservations are absolutely necessary. For tickets, go to the Havensight Shopping Mall, Building 4, or else call 809/776-5650.

Another possibility for undersea adventure is to take a voyage on a "yellow submarine," the *Looking Glass,* which is booked through Submarine Tours of St. Thomas, Ramada Yacht Haven (tel. 809/775-0744 for information). A "sub-bus" will take you to the dive site where you board this modern submarine, with six-foot-four-inch headroom. In air-conditioned comfort, seated on an individual cushion seat, you plunge to the depths, taking in the marine sights through a panoramic 30-inch viewing window. A member of the crew describes the sea life you're witnessing. At one point, scuba divers appear, surrounded by colorful marine life. On this 95-ton vessel, 48 passengers are taken aboard at one time. Service is daily beginning at 9 a.m., and you should allow 1½ hours from dock to dock. Adults pay $48. Children under 12 are charged half fare.

Scuba and Snorkeling

With 30 spectacular reefs just off St. Thomas, the U.S. Virgins are rated as one of the "most beautiful areas in the world" by *Skin Diver* magazine.

St. Thomas Diving Club, Bolongo Bay Beach and Tennis Club, P.O. Box 7337, St. Thomas, USVI 00801 (tel. 809/776-2381), is a full-service, PADI five-star center, considered the best on the island. If you're a resident at the previously recommended Bolongo Bay Resorts, you get such extras as a sail on the club's 53-foot catamaran *Ho-Tei* to St. John, if you stay seven or more nights. Also available to guests are special day and overnight trips to the British Virgin Islands aboard the club yacht, *Mohawk II.* But nonresidents can avail themselves of the scuba and snorkeling facilities at St. Thomas. An open-water certification course, including four scuba dives, costs $275. An advanced open-water certification course, including five dives that can be accomplished in two days, costs only $220. Every Thursday, participants are taken on an all-day scuba excursion that includes a dive to the wreck of R.M.S. *Rhone* in the British Virgin Islands. This two-tank dive costs $99. You can also enjoy snorkeling for $20.

Another good bet for dive operations is **Joe Vogel Diving Co.,** 12B Mandahl Rd., Rt. 42, a one-minute drive east of the Mahogany Run Resort. It's run by ex-U.S. Navy frogman and company founder, Joe Vogel, and his wife, Debby Powers-Vogel. Joe still personally conducts all dives and limits each group to six or seven divers for your greater safety and enjoyment. Debby is company manager and an established underwater photographer. Scuba portraits by Debby cost $50 for 36 professional-quality color prints of your dive with them. For details on their NAUI certification-checkout dive service, courses, and other information, write P.O. Box 7322, St. Thomas, VI 00801, or call 809/775-7610 between 9 a.m. and 5 p.m. Monday through Saturday.

Deep-Sea Fishing

It's very good in the U.S. Virgins. Nineteen world records have been set in recent years (eight for blue marlin). Sports fishing is offered on the *Fish Hawk.* Captain Al Petrosky of New Jersey sails from Fish Hawk Marina Lagoon at the East End on his 43-foot diesel-powered craft, which is fully equipped with rods and reels. Telephone 809/775-9058 for information.

Tennis

Many courts are lit for night play, and St. Thomas has a lot of them. Outstanding ones are at the **Bolongo Bay Beach and Tennis Club** (tel. 809/775-2489), which has four courts, two of which are lit until 11 p.m. It caters to members and hotel guests only, except for lessons, which cost $16 per half hour.

At **Frenchman's Reef Tennis Courts** (tel. 809/774-8500, ext. 444), four courts are available and those not hotel guests are charged $8 a half hour per court. Lights stay on until 10 p.m.

At the famous **Bluebeard's Castle** (tel. 809/774-1600), nonguests are charged $3 per hour to play on its two courts.

Golf

On the north shore, **Mahogany Run,** Mahogany Run Golf & Tennis Resort, P.O. Box 1224 (tel. 809/775-5000), is an 18-hole, par 70 course, charging greens fees of $24. A golf cart is required at $12 per person. Bargain tip: After 2 p.m., the cost for 18 holes is only $26, including cart rental. The 6,300-yard course was designed by George and Tom Fazio. *Signature* magazine called it "a miracle of a gold course." The most difficult part of the course is nicknamed "The Devil's Triangle," holes 13 to 15, bordering the Atlantic. The 14th hole, par 3, demands a short drive spanning an Atlantic gorge. This is where many golfers, as would be expected, drop a ball or two into the ocean.

AFTER DARK: There are no casinos, no supper Las Vegas–type shows. However, there's plenty of action occurring, mostly at the—
Frenchman's Reef (tel. 809/776-8500) has the most nightlife, and enjoys a deserved reputation as "the entertainment center of St. Thomas." Occasionally top acts are imported to perform at the stage show at its **Top of the Reef Supper Club,** Monday to Saturday, with dancing offered not only before the show but until the early hours of the morning. Guests go for dinner, at which time they can order the chef's specialties, meals costing from $35. Dinner is from 8 to 10 p.m.
In addition, the hotel also offers **La Terrazza,** where a steel band often plays and a limbo show is staged. Pop music and country and western are sometimes added to the evening's entertainment. Check at the desk for what's on. Dance music by top-flight entertainers is played from 9 p.m. to 2 a.m. except Monday. No minimum is charged, and drinks cost $3.50.
Bluebeard's Castle Hotel (tel. 809/774-1600) is another entertainment center. Call and see what's playing. Overlooking the pool and yacht harbor, the Dungeon Bar offers piano bar entertainment nightly except Thursday. You can dance, too. On Thursday and Friday nights there's a lively steel band. On Saturday night you can dance the night away to the music of one of the island's great combos. There is continuous entertainment until 1 a.m. All drink specialties are named after Bluebeard himself—Bluebeard's wench, cooler, and ghost. Most drinks cost from $2.50, although some specialty drinks are priced from $3. The Dungeon Bar is a popular gathering spot for both residents and visitors.
The **Carib Beach Hotel** (tel. 809/774-2525) is another lively spot. Perhaps you'll journey out here on Friday night for a steel band and limbo show. Currently, on Saturday night, there is a barbecue buffet dinner along with live entertainment, and on Wednesday night, hotel guests are invited to the complimentary manager's cocktail party, where raffles are held and prizes awarded. Count on spending from $25 per person for dinner. Always call for reservations and changes in the entertainment program.
In town, I like the **Greenhouse,** Waterfront (tel. 809/774-7998), which enjoys a harbor view and features live entertainment Tuesday to Sunday from 10 p.m. to 2 a.m. At this restaurant-lounge, the chef offers a full breakfast from 7 to 11 a.m. and a lunch menu with a native special. There are also five kinds of hamburgers. Dinner is served every night, costing from $15. A breezy waterfront oasis, the Greenhouse will answer your questions about specials and entertainment if you give them a ring.
Club Z Ristorante and Disco, Contant Rd., Rt. 33 (tel. 809/776-4655), is one of the most popular late-night spots in St. Thomas, drawing a young crowd. It is reached by taking a drive up a steep hill. Overlooking Crown Bay, it is partic-

ularly dramatic at night, and guests often sit drinking by its swimming pool. Many go early to enjoy the Italian cuisine, with meals costing from $30. Typical dishes are fettuccine with salmon or carpaccio with arugula and parmesan. Dinner is served from 7 to 10:30 p.m. daily except Sunday, and diners aren't charged the $10 cover charge otherwise required to enter the disco section, which is in action from 10 p.m. to 4 a.m. daily except Sunday. In the disco, a hard drink costs from $3. Calypso, reggae, Latin, jazz—the musical repertoire of the club is versatile.

In Charlotte Amalie, a popular nighttime diversion is to patronize one of the local pubs along "Back Street," which is literally in back of the shopping malls fronting the waterfront. However, this street can be extremely dangerous at night—so don't go alone.

Walter's Living Room, Back St. (tel. 809/774-5025), is a popular local disco open from 11 a.m. to 4 a.m. Monday to Saturday, 6:30 p.m. to 4 a.m. Sunday. Walter's is in a restored early 20th-century wooden town house. It has a lively ambience. Drinks cost from $2.50, and on Friday and Saturday, the cover charge is $3.

2. ST. JOHN

About two miles east of St. Thomas, little St. John lies just across Pillsbury Sound. It is about seven miles long and three miles wide, with a total land area of some 20 square miles.

The smallest and least populated of the three main U.S. Virgins, St. John has more than one half of its land mass, as well as its shoreline waters, set aside as the Virgin Islands National Park, dedicated in 1956.

Once it was slated for big development when it was under Danish control, but a slave rebellion and a decline of the sugarcane plantations ended that idea. For that reason and others, St. John has remained truly virginal, unlike some other U.S. Virgins.

GETTING THERE AND AROUND: Among the many methods of reaching the island, the easiest and most frequented is by **ferryboat,** leaving from Red Hook landing on St. Thomas, the trip taking about 20 minutes. Beginning at 6:30 a.m., except weekends and holidays, boats depart every hour. The last ferry back heads out of Cruz Bay at St. John at 11:15 p.m. Because of such frequent departures, even cruise-ship passengers, anchored in Charlotte Amalie for only a short time, can visit St. John for a quickie island tour, perhaps a picnic and a swim at one of its fine sandy beaches, returning in time for dinner. The one-way fare is $2 per adult, $1 for children. Schedules can change without notice, so call 809/778-6111, ext. 220 for more information.

Should you ever get stranded, water-taxi service is available 24 hours a day for about $40 for two persons, but this should be negotiated in advance. Call 809/775-6501.

To reach the ferry, you can take an open-air shuttle which departs from the Market Square in Charlotte Amalie. It will take you on weekdays (not on Sunday) to the ferry dock at Red Hook. The fare is $2 per person each way.

It's also possible to board a boat directly at the Charlotte Amalie waterfront for a cost of $5 one way, the ride taking 45 minutes. The first boat departs St. Thomas at 9 a.m. The last one to leave Cruz Bay heading for Charlotte Amalie is at 5:15 p.m.

Also, a launch service leaves from the dock at Caneel Bay at St. John heading for the National Park Dock at Red Hook on St. Thomas. This one-way fare, however, costs $9 per person, $12 to Charlotte Amalie.

In addition, **Virgin Islands Seaplane Shuttle** will take you from either St.

Thomas or St. Croix on either Tuesday or Thursday. For reservations, telephone 809/773-1776. The Seaplane Shuttle has daily flights from St. Thomas to St. John at 11:30 a.m. Flights from St. Croix to St. John on Monday, Wednesday, and Friday depart at 11:30 a.m. On Tuesday, Thursday, Saturday, and Sunday, there are three St. Croix–St. John flights at 8 and 11:30 a.m. and 4 p.m.

Getting Around

Once on St. John, there are several methods of getting around, the most popular of which is by **surrey-style taxi.** If you just want to go from the ferry landing dock to Trunk Bay, for example, the cost is about $6 for two passengers. Between midnight and 6 a.m., fares are increased by 40%.

The **St. John Taxi Association** (tel. 809/776-6060) also conducts a historical tour of St. John, including swimming at Trunk Bay and a visit to the Caneel Bay resort, at a cost of $18 for one or two persons. Depending on demand, tours depart Cruz Bay seven days a week.

It's also possible to use the **bus** service running from Cruz Bay to Maho Bay, stopping at Caneel and Cinnamon Bays. The one-way bus fare costs $3.50 for adults.

Varlack Ventures, P.O. Box 300, St. John, USVI 00830 (tel. 809/776-6412). Many visitors feel that the real beauty of St. John lies away from Cruz Bay, along some of the relatively inaccessible coastline. Should you wish to reach such places, a Jeep might be the best means of getting there. Rentals of these four-wheel drives cost $50 to $55 per day, with $5 per day for insurance. Renters are required to post a deposit and must be between the ages of 25 and 65. Gas is not provided, although there's usually just enough in the Jeep to get you to one of the two gas stations on the island. It's never a good idea to drive around St. John with an almost-empty tank. Varlack, about a block from the ferryboat pier, also rents a limited number of air-conditioned cars, priced at $45 per day.

Many newcomers to St. John hope to explore at least a part of the island, yet are frustrated because of the poorly marked, sometimes barely passable roads. You can always rent a four-wheel-drive vehicle, but even then you'll lack the guidance of a leader who knows the charming hidden inlets and the most panoramic vistas. Margie Brown-Boynes, who used to work for the mayor's office in Philadelphia, might offer a solution. Her company, **B&B Photo Tours** (tel. 809/776-6979), has created a choice of unusual ways to while away your hours on St. John. Photographers appreciate the dozens of stops which a guide makes for perfect picture-postcard mementos. A tour of the land and waters ringing St. John, in posh circumstances, costs about $30 per person. For more information, get in touch with Ms. Brown-Boynes.

WHERE TO STAY: From a tropical retreat, one of the most spectacular in the Caribbean, to a campsite, the choice of accommodations in St. John is limited, and that's how most people would like to keep it.

Deluxe Living

Caneel Bay, Inc., Virgin Islands National Park, St. John, USVI 00830 (tel. 809/776-6111), grew out of a dream of an idealistic man, Laurance S. Rockefeller, and it's a remarkable achievement. Operated by Rockresorts, it's a luxurious resort on a 170-acre portion of St. John, built on the site of a mid-1700s sugar plantation on the bay, with a choice of seven beaches. The hotel caters to people with full purses who know their needs can be met with style. The main buildings are strung along the bays, with a Caribbean lounge and dining room at its core. Other, separate units—really bedroom villas—stand along the beaches, so all you have to do is step from your private veranda onto the sands. Not all of the

170 rooms, however, are on the beaches. Some are set back on low cliffs or headlands. AP rates in winter range from $330 to $510 daily in a single, from $395 to $575 daily in a double. *In summer, daily AP charges in a single go from $205 to $320 and in a double from $235 to $350. In shoulder season, November 1 to December 19, singles rent for $235 to $365 and doubles for $265 to $395.* But if you're coming down for the summer, you should ask about one of the special packages likely to be offered, everything from honeymoon to boating to one that combines a visit at Caneel Bay with a stay at Little Dix Bay in the British Virgins. The most loyal devotees of Caneel Bay book their favorite room in winter a year in advance, and February is almost always sold out.

The buildings have a quiet understatement in decor, with rich woods, handwoven fabrics, elegant furnishings, and plantation fans. The choice spot at Caneel Bay is the Turtle Bay Estate House, part of the 18th-century Dutch sugar plantation, serving now as one of a trio of dining locations (for the most part, only guests dine here; the other dining facilities are described in the "Where to Eat" section, which follows the hotel recommendations). Surrounding all buildings are skillfully planted gardens filled with sea grape, brilliant-red flamboyant, the geranium tree, the golden shower tree, poinsettias, hibiscus, oleander, the red ixora, and of course plenty of bougainvillea to wash everything with color. When man has intruded architecturally, it is generally with natural elements such as wood and native stone. There are many scheduled activities per week, ranging from a fishing trip to a walk through the ruin of the old sugar mill. Of course, in addition to its beaches, the plantation also opens onto an undersea world, as there are endless inlets and secret reefs to explore. Snorkeling lessons are given free each day, and divers can go on trips to historic shipwrecks. A fleet of boats awaits your command, and there is complimentary use of the resort's sailboards for windsurfers. Perhaps the pursuit of the elusive wahoo will send you on a deepsea fishing trip. In the evening you can listen to calypso music, dance, perhaps enjoy a steel band.

Virgin Grand St. John, Great Cruz Bay, St. John, USVI 00830 (tel. 809/776-7171 or toll free 800/323-7249), is the splashiest and best-designed hotel in St. John. It sits on 34 acres of what used to be scrub forest on the southeast side of the island. Its design is filled with ziggurat-shaped angles, soaring ceilings, large windows, and an overall style that seems inspired by Aztec, Egyptian, or neocolonial models. A total of 13 cedar-roofed buildings contain the 264 bedrooms and the handful of stylish restaurants and bars, including Fronds which has a fine wine list and an exemplary cuisine. Herringbone-patterned brick walkways interconnect the gardens (where 400 palms were imported from Puerto Rico) with the beach and the zigzag borders of the most unusual swimming pool in the Virgin Islands. Tennis courts, a sandy 1,200-foot beach, an array of water sports, and an enthusiastic staff make this place memorable. Each of the stylish accommodations contains fan-shaped windows, curved ceilings, unusual but pleasing dimensions, and a softly vibrant color scheme of rose and mauve. The hotel charges winter rates of $395 to $595 daily in a double, with full board. *Off-season, AP rates are $295 to $495 in a double.* Singles can deduct $60 from the tariffs quoted. Junior suites, one-bedroom suites, and a two-bedroom town house are also available but at far higher charges, of course.

The Virgin Grand Villas is a 96-condominium development that is part of the Virgin Grand St. John. Available for rent are fully furnished villas ranging from studio terrace suites to spacious three-bedroom pool villas, each with its own private pool. Villas have individual architectural features and such details as floors of European marble, tile patios, and Italian lacquer custom furnishings. All contain dishes, linens, washers, dryers, microwave ovens, dishwashers, and

TVs with VCRs. In winter, studio villas rent for $475 daily for two people, the pool villas costing $1,550 and accommodating six guests. Summer rates are $375 to $1,450, depending on the size of the villa. All are EP. Villa guests enjoy the amenities of the Virgin Grand St. John. Guests from North America use the hotel's special waiting lounge at the St. Thomas airport, where connections are made for transportation to St. John.

Campgrounds

Maho Bay, P.O. Box 310, Cruz Bay, St. John, USVI 00830 (tel. 809/776-6240; 800/392-9004 toll free). What I like most about this place is that there is a help-yourself center where groceries, books, and magazines are left by departing campers for new arrivals to take. That sets the tone for this interesting concept in ecology vacationing, where you get about as close to nature as you can, but with considerable comfort. Maho Bay is a deluxe campground set in the heart of the Virgin Islands National Park, seemingly inspired by Fire Island (New York) where the technique of running wooden walkways through vegetation was advanced. Utility lines and pipes are hidden underneath.

You stay in a tent-like cottage made of canvas. Each unit has a choice of a double bed or two movable beds, a couch, electric lamps and outlets, a round dining table, chairs, a propane stove, and an ice chest (cooler). That's not all—you're furnished linen, towels, dinner service, and utensils. There's a store where you can buy (expensive) supplies. You do your own housekeeping and cooking, although you can eat at the camp's outdoor restaurant. Guests share a community bathhouse. Each unit is cantilevered over a thickly wooded area, providing a view of the sea, sky, and beach. *From mid-April to mid-December, no minimum stay is required and cottages (limited to two adults) rent for $45 per day. Children under age 7 pay $7 per night per person; over 7, $10 each.* In season, the minimum stay is seven nights, and the cost is $67 per cottage, occupancy by two persons. Others sharing a cottage pay from $10 per person nightly.

Maho Bay has a community center, housing a restaurant which serves breakfast every morning for $3 to $5. This includes juice, eggs or french toast, and coffee. There is no charge for extra juice or coffee. For dinner, they have asked some of the best cooks on St. John to cater. Menus are posted and people who are interested sign up in advance. Typical meals are fresh fish or chicken, goat stew, whelk stew, conch stew, quiche, and lasagne. Prices range from $7 to $10 for a full dinner. This allows guests to meet the local people who function as entrepreneurs rather than staff, and also to taste local cooking. The islanders, by making the food preparation a family endeavor, can offer a good meal much cheaper than the camp could. Meals are served on a covered patio which overlooks the water. This same patio functions as an amphitheater where they have nature lectures, concerts of folk music, scuba and sailing movies, and lectures by park rangers. The location is an eight-mile drive from Cruz Bay, and there's regularly scheduled bus service. The camp also has the best program of water sports on the island (see below).

Cinnamon Bay Campground, P.O. Box 720, Cruz Bay, USVI 00831-0720 (tel. 809/776-6330), established by the National Park Service in 1964, is the most complete campground in the Caribbean. The site is directly on the beach, and thousands of acres of tropical vegetation surround you, an opportunity to get insect-repellent close to nature. Life is simple here, and you have a choice of three different ways of sleeping—tents, cottages, and bare sites. In winter, a cottage rents for $64 a day for two persons, a tent for $50, and a bare site for $10. *In the off-season, cottages cost $36 to $50 per day for two persons; tents $27 to $40; and bare sites, from $10.* At the bare campsites, nothing is provided except general facilities. Canvas tents are 10 by 14 feet with floor, and a number of facilities are offered, including all cooking equipment. Even your linen is changed weekly. Cottages are 15 by 15 feet, a screened room with two concrete walls and two screen walls. They consist of four twin beds, and two cots can be added. Cooking facilities are also supplied. Lavatories and showers are in separate buildings nearby. Camping is limited to a two-week period in any given year. Near the road is a camp center office, with a grocer and a cafeteria (serving $8 dinners).

Management is handled by Rockresorts, and reservations can be made at 30 Rockefeller Plaza, Room 5400, New York, NY 10112 (tel. 212/586-4459 in New York City, or toll free 800/223-7637, 800/442-8198 in New York state).

Housekeeping Holidays

Gallows Point, P.O. Box 58, St. John, USVI 00830 (tel. 809/776-6434), is a cluster of appealing cottages whose villa-style architecture ensures privacy. Nestled into a carefully cultivated garden, they were patterned after 18th-century Danish manor houses. The clapboards, the latticework, the fan-shaped windows, the panoramic porches, and the louvered French doors are stained a shade of putty. Each villa contains four separate units, the most desirable being on the top floor. These have massive exposed beams of Canadian cedar, yards and yards of planking, sleeping lofts, and comfortable tropical furniture. The ground-floor (garden) units have sunken living rooms, wooden decks facing the water, and bathrooms full of greenery. Each has its own fully equipped kitchenette. In winter, a garden suite costs $225 per night; a loft suite, $250. *In summer, a garden suite rents for $125 and a loft unit for $140.* The management suggests that you call 800/323-7229 for reservations. You'll notice this complex of stylish buildings from the ferryboat as it enters the mouth of Cruz Bay, because of its sentinel position above the yachts bobbing below.

Estate Zootenvaal, Hurricane Hole, St. John, USVI 00830 (tel. 809/776-6321, 216/861-5337 in the U.S.), lies within the boundaries of the U.S. National Park at the edge of a horseshoe-shaped bay. Local mariners know this bay is usually safe from even the most violent hurricane. It's a good choice for escapees from urban areas who want the minimum of interference. Consisting of cement-sided villas and a two-bedroom house, each with exterior walls of driftwood gray with white trim, it sits within earshot of the waves on the grounds of what used to be a private estate called Zootenvaal. The accommodations have been renovated, with designer interiors using fabrics in muted tones. Each has its own color scheme, and all have Danish flatware and Arzberg china. Each has a fully equipped kitchen. A few have housed novelists holing up to complete a manuscript. Maid service can be arranged for an extra cost, on an as-needed basis. In winter, two persons can live here for $140 per day or $800 per week. *The summer daily rate for two persons is $115, the weekly charge quoted at $650.* There is a private beach known for snorkeling.

WHERE TO DINE: Visitors over just for the day generally like to have lunch at the **Sugar Mill Kitchen** on the grounds of Caneel Bay (tel. 809/776-6111). From 11:30 a.m. to 3 p.m., it offers à la carte lunches for $20. A favorite dish is grilled fish of the day. You can order tasty tropical drinks, such as a plantation punch or a peach daiquiri. From the restaurant there is a panoramic view overlooking St. Thomas and its surrounding cays. Diners are seated on a "horse-mill" platform (when the wind was insufficient to turn the mills in the old days, beasts of burden such as one-eyed donkeys were used). Guests come here for sundowners at 6:30 p.m. For $38, you can enjoy a buffet dinner served nightly except Sunday on a reservation-only basis. Featured are a choice of grilled main dishes, a salad bar, and a dessert table. Dining is only from 7 to 8:30 p.m. Dress is informal, but no shorts are permitted in the evening unless worn with knee socks.

Before someone has settled into St. John, he or she has been told about the buffets served overlooking the water at the **Caneel Bay Beach Terrace Dining Room** (tel. 809/776-6111), on the grounds of the Caneel Bay Hotel, right below the Sugar Mill. The $19 buffet luncheon, from 11:30 a.m. to 3 p.m., is one of the best in the Virgin Islands. It is always necessary to make a reservation. After you're assigned an open-air table overlooking the beach and the water, and you've given your drink order, you proceed to the buffet counter. I suggest a visit first to a side counter where freshly cut tropical fruit such as pineapple is spread around a bowl of cold soup (my recent bisque of almond sent me rushing back to the chef for the recipe). After soup and fruit, you can proceed to the tempting array of salads (usually one made of avocado) and cold meats. As an elegant touch, fresh mushrooms are sliced, awaiting your favorite dressing. Corn chutney, smoked oysters, and many other plates await your selection. If, after all that, you still have room for hot dishes, you'll find those followed by a big table of desserts, including such delectable pies as blueberry cheese. Drinks are extra.

In the evening, if you return for dinner from 7 to 8:30, you should make a reservation, and men are required to wear jackets from November to May. At that time you can have a complete dinner for $40 per person. Appetizers might include papaya with prosciutto, followed by excellently prepared soups. Salads are invariably good, including the marinated green bean or the tossed garden greens mimosa. Main dishes are likely to include baked filet of red snapper or roast prime rib of blue-ribbon beef carved to order with natural juices. There are always some calorie-loaded desserts such as strawberry cheesecake or Boston cream pie. Menus are changed nightly. On Sunday the chef offers a sumptuous buffet of West Indian, continental, and American dishes from 7 to 9 p.m.

Ellington's, Gallows Point, Cruz Bay (tel. 809/776-7166), is by far the most stylish and exciting independent restaurant on St. John. Set near the neocolonial villas of Gallows Point, its putty-colored exterior has the same kind of double staircase, fan windows, louvers, and low-slung hip roof found in an 18th-century Danish manor house. Inside is a collection of tropical hardwoods, fashioned into generous sheaths which envelop bar tops, tabletops, stair treads, and the floor. Drop in for a drink on the panoramic upper deck where unfolds a view of Cruz Bay. The establishment is named after a local radio announcer ("The Fat Man"), raconteur, and mystery writer whose real estate developments helped transform St. John into a stylish enclave for the American literati of the 1950s and '60s. Named Richard "Duke" Ellington (not to be confused with the great musician), he entertained his friends, martini in hand, around a frequently photographed table painted with a map of St. John. The tabletop today hangs in the Ellington's dining room.

Breakfast is served daily from 8 to 10 a.m., followed by lunch, costing from $6 and served from 11:30 a.m. to 2:30 p.m. The menu might include crab salad sandwiches, hot Italian steak sandwiches, crisp salads, and New England conch chowder. The most popular Caribbean buffet lunch on the island is served on Sunday, costing $14. Dinners are elegant, elaborate, and lighthearted affairs. Specialties include mushrooms stuffed with crabmeat, coconut-laced chicken, and shrimp with scallops dijonnaise. Costing from $20 each, dinners are served nightly from 6 to 10 p.m.

The **Upper Deck,** Cruz Bay (tel. 809/776-6318), has the best view and the most atmospheric location of any restaurant on St. John, outside of Caneel Bay. Reached by a bumpy Jeep ride, it's a honey. The bar opens at 5 p.m. and I recommend that you go then for your sundowner, enjoying that view while it's still daylight. You don't need a reservation—just arrive, but only Wednesday to Sunday. No luncheons are served, only dinner, anytime from 6:30 to 9 p.m. The decor is casual and rustic, like an overscale mountain cabin. Tables, lit by candlelight, are placed on an open deck. The location is about five minutes from Cruz Bay dock. Your hosts are Clarence and Sis Thomas, both Americans. He worked for an advertising agency in New York, producing TV shows before finding his little oasis on St. John. Sis never went to cooking school, and she has no pretensions in that direction: "At 16 I learned to cook for hungry farmers in Pennsylvania." She offers plain, ordinary cookery, and it's good. Each day she makes a pot of soup, such as New England clam chowder. Many of her dishes come from the charcoal grill, including lamb chops, sirloin steak, and pork chops. From the sea, a nightly fish special with accompaniments is served. Try also her fried scallops followed by one of her homemade desserts. An average repast here is likely to cost from $18 per person.

Mongoose Restaurant, Café, and Bar, Mongoose Junction (tel. 809/776-7586). Some visitors compare its soaring interior design to a large Japanese birdcage because of the strong vertical lines and its 25-foot ceiling. Set among trees and built above a stream, it's a lot like a structure you'd come across in Marin County in northern California. Many guests create a perch for themselves at the bar for a drink and sandwich; other possibilities for seating lie on an adjacent deck where a canopy of trees filters the tropical sunlight. The bar offers more than 20 varieties of frothy island-inspired libations. Lunches, cost from $12 and include well-stuffed sandwiches, salad platters, and main courses such as seafood Créole, island fishcakes, and vegetable stir-fries. Dinners include more of the same but are slightly more expensive, from $18 each. The salad bar is served in an old-fashioned boat. The establishment is open daily, serving breakfast from 8:30 to 11 a.m., lunch from 11 a.m. to 5 p.m., and dinner from 5:30 to 10 p.m. A special four-course dinner is offered on Friday for $14.95, and on Saturday you can eat your fill of barbecued chicken and ribs for $13.50. An especially popular Saturday and Sunday brunch, served from 9 a.m. to 3 p.m., costs $10 per person.

Old Gallery, Cruz Bay (tel. 809/776-7544), a short walk from the ferryboat landing, is on the second floor of an old island building. Much of the nighttime scene passes under the balcony. You'll find no better bargain in Cruz Bay. Cheaper, yes, but when it comes to the quality of the food and the generosity of the servings, Old Gallery is tops. There's always fish, a catch of the day, most often sautéed and served with lime butter. Among other dishes, there may be conch in butter sauce, roast pork, and codfish. Johnnycakes (unleavened fried bread) accompany many dishes. Lunches cost from $8 to $10, with dinners going for $10 to $20. Winston and Alecia Wells, the proprietors, keep the place open from 11 a.m. to 11 p.m. daily except Sunday.

Café Roma, Cruz Bay (tel. 809/776-6443), is an Italian restaurant and pizza parlor. Diners climb a long flight of concrete exterior steps before reaching this rustic domain. Open daily for dinner only, from 5 to 10 p.m., the establishment charges around $20 for a full meal. You might begin with a strawberry colada, then enjoy one of four kinds of spaghetti, lasagne, fettuccine Alfredo, or five different kinds of veal. Italian wines are sold by the bottle or glass, any one of which could be followed by a cup of espresso.

The Lime Inn, Lemon Tree Center, Cruz Bay (tel. 809/776-6425), pleasant and airy, and sheathed with glowing strips of well-finished pine, is the perfect choice for a well-prepared meal and a suitably frothy drink. It's in a labyrinth of boutiques and shops in the center of Cruz Bay, decorated with lattices and plants and crowned by a solidly trussed tin roof. Lunch is served Monday to Friday from 11:30 a.m. to 5:30 p.m. Dinner is daily except Sunday from 5:30 to 10 p.m.

An island event is the all-you-can-eat shrimp dinner, every Wednesday, costing $15 per person. Other nights, the menu items include filet mignon stuffed with bleu cheese and brie, smoked marlin salad, Caribbean lobster, and three kinds of shrimp. Full meals cost from $18 per person.

Shipwreck Landing, Coral Bay (tel. 809/776-8640), eight miles east of Cruz Bay, in an isolated position at the edge of Coral Bay, qualifies as an attractive destination after an island sightseeing tour. You dine near palms and old trees, on a deliberately rustic veranda of a raffish and rakish island house. Open-air tables grace the deck, along with an intimate bar. Open daily for food and drink from 11 a.m. to 4 p.m. and 6 to 10 p.m., the place serves potent cocktails made with four kinds of rum and a deceptively bland fruity base. Menu items include chicken teryaki, blackened ocean perch, and surf and turf, along with shrimp dijonnaise with fettuccine. Meals cost from $15, a good bargain. The landing lies on the road between Cruz Bay and Salt Pond Beach.

Lucy's Restaurant, in the Coral Bay area (tel. 809/776-6804), is almost guaranteed to give you your most authentic native experience. For years, Lucy Smith has been known as the best tour conductor on the island. But at night, this busy islander turns her talents to the stove, offering one of the best native cuisines in the Virgins. Although she is likely to be there only at night, her home is open to visitors from 11 a.m. to 10 p.m. daily, but you should call first before showing up. It's best to make up your own group. Chances are, you'll dine on her porch, enjoying piquant chicken, rice and beans, coconut-fried plantain, and johnnycakes. Of course, her spicy conch is superb. As for dessert, the gods have smiled on you if she decides to make her guava and coconut pie. Meals cost from $20.

Vie's Snack Shack, East End (tel. 809/776-6486), looks like little more than a plywood-sided hut on the island's East End, about 12½ miles from Cruz Bay. Nonetheless, its charming and gregarious owner is known as one of the best local chefs in St. John. Her famous garlic chicken is considered the best on the island. She also serves conch fritters, johnnycakes, and coconut and pineapple tarts. Don't leave without a glass of homemade limeade made from home-grown limes. Full meals cost from $3.50. The place is open most days from 10 a.m. to 5 p.m., but as Vie says, "Some days, we might not be here at all." So you'd better call before heading out.

WHAT TO SEE: I personally like to spend lots of time at Cruz Bay, where the ferry docks. In this West Indian village there are interesting bars, restaurants, boutiques, and pastel-painted houses. It's pretty sleepy, but amusing to some after the fast pace of St. Thomas. The museum at Cruz Bay isn't big, but it does contain some local artifacts and will teach you something about the history of the island. It's at the public library, and can be visited from 9 a.m. to 5 p.m. Monday through Friday.

Most cruise-ship passengers seem to dart through Cruz Bay, heading for the island's biggest attraction, the **Virgin Islands National Park.**

Before going to the park, you may want to stop at the Visitor's Center at Cruz Bay, which is open daily from 8 a.m. to 4:30 p.m. There you'll see some exhibits and learn more about what you'll be viewing. Regular briefings are given.

By 1981 the size of the park totaled 12,624 acres, including submerged lands and waters adjacent to St. John, and since 1956 a trail system of 20 miles has been developed. This is the only national park in the Caribbean area.

In 1952 Laurance S. Rockefeller purchased a small resort here and developed it, eventually donating it to the non-profit Jackson Hole Preserve, an organization founded and supported by the Rockefeller family. Jackson Hole, in turn, after purchasing more than 5,000 acres of St. John, about half the island, donated the land to the U.S. government.

If time is very limited, try a visit to the **Annaberg Ruins,** where the Danes launched sugar-mill plantation life in 1718. On Tuesday, Wednesday, and Friday from 10 a.m. to 1 p.m., St. John islanders show you their own style of native cookery and explain basketweaving.

Trunk Bay is considered by those who know such things as "one of the world's most beautiful beaches," but beware of pickpockets. The beach is also the site of one of the world's first marked underwater trails.

Park rangers conduct **national park tours** of St. John. You can explore a three-mile trail which goes by the petroglyphs, figures (still undeciphered) carved on boulders by mysterious people of the past. You'll also pass by the ruins of sugar mills and a great house. You must make a reservation for all tours by calling 809/776-6201. A bus tour leaves on Monday. To catch up with it, you must be on the 8 a.m. ferry from Red Hook. Once on St. John, you board a special bus for $12 per passenger, leaving from the National Park Visitor's Center at 9 a.m. The tour lasts three hours.

Every Thursday the rangers conduct a Reef Bay hike at 9 a.m. This time, it is necessary to take the 9 a.m. ferry from Red Hook in St. Thomas. The bus ride, costing $2, leaves from the National Park Visitor's Center at 10 a.m. A special boat, costing $5 per passenger, takes you back to Cruz Bay at 3:30 p.m. when you can catch another ferry to St. Thomas. Bring your own food and beverage.

Fort Berg (called Fortsberg) at Coral Bay dates from 1717 and played a disastrous role in history in the 1733 slave revolt that devastated the economy of St. John. The fort may be restored as a historic monument.

THE SPORTING LIFE: Don't visit here expecting to play golf. Rather, anticipate some of the best snorkeling, scuba-diving, swimming, fishing, hiking, sailing, and underwater photography in the Caribbean. The island is known for its coral-sand beaches, winding mountain roads, trails past old, bushcovered sugarcane plantations, and hidden coves.

Water Sports

The most complete line of water sports available on St. John is offered at the **Cinnamon Bay Watersports Center** on Cinnamon Bay Beach (tel. 809/776-6458). Specializing in sailing, the staff will charge you $45 for a full day's outing, ($30 for a half day) aboard the yacht *Gratia*. Snorkeling equipment and stopoffs at secluded reefs and uninhabited islands provide some of the most vivid underwater viewing in the region. Beer, sodas, and snorkeling equipment are covered by the cost of the trip, but you must bring your own picnic lunch.

If you're only interested in snorkeling, you can make trips on the M/V *Cinnamon Bay,* which circumnavigates St. John every Wednesday, leaving at 9 a.m. and stopping frequently for snorkelers to explore little-visited reefs. The cost is $25 per person.

Windsurfing here is some of the best to be found anywhere. You can rent a board for $10 per hour, $25 for half a day. A 90-minute lesson costs around $25.

Swimming

Trunk Bay is the word. It's the biggest attraction on St. John and a beach collector's find. To miss its great white sweep would be like going to Europe and skipping Paris. As mentioned, **Caneel Bay** fronts seven beautiful beaches, and the camps at **Cinnamon** and **Maho Bay** have their own beaches where forest rangers constantly have to remind visitors to put their swimming suits back on, if they have any.

Hiking

It's the big thing here, and a network of trails covers the national park. However, I suggest a tour by Jeep first, just to get your bearings. At the Visitor's Center at Cruz Bay, ask for a free trail map of the park. It's best to set out with someone experienced in the mysteries of the island. Both Maho and Cinnamon Bays conduct nature walks.

Tennis

Caneel Bay (tel. 809/776-6111) has seven courts and a pro shop. However, these courts aren't lit at night, and are likely to be used almost exclusively by guests. There are two public courts at Cruz Bay, however.

Virgin Grand St. John, Great Cruz Bay (tel. 809/776-7171), is in the swing of things, with six tennis courts, all lit at night.

SHOPPING: Compared to St. Thomas, it isn't much, but what there is is interesting. The **Caneel Bay Boutique** is the place to go for island resort wear—no contest. The style here is casual but sophisticated, and the prices are high.

The boutiques and shops of Cruz Bay are individualized and quite special. Most of the shops are clustered at **Mongoose Junction,** in a woodsy area beside the roadway, about a fast five-minute walk from the ferry dock. I've already endorsed dining in this avant-garde complex, and it also contains shops of merit.

Donald Schnell Studio, P.O. Box 349, Mongoose Junction (tel. 809/776-6420) is a working studio and gallery at Mongoose Junction on St. John. Mr. Schnell and his assistants feature one of the finest collections of handmade pottery, sculpture, and blown glass in the Caribbean. They can be seen producing daily and are especially noted for their rough-textured coral work. Water fountains are a specialty item, as are house signs. The coral pottery dinnerware is unique and popular. The studio will mail works all over the world. Go in and discuss any particular design you may have in mind. They enjoy designing to please customers.

The **Canvas Factory,** Cruz Bay (tel. 809/776-6196), produces its own handmade, rugged, and colorful canvas bags in the "factory" in Mongoose Junction. They also specialize in well-made, practical, 100% canvas clothing.

Virgin Canvas and Crafts, Cruz Bay (tel. 809/776-6223), offers canvas bags and fine gifts, consisting of locally made jewelry, baskets, hats, clothes, and hammocks, along with an array of canvas bags and luggage manufactured on the premises. Marine canvas work is a specialty. The establishment is one block west of the Chase Bank.

The **Clothing Studio,** Mongoose Junction (tel. 809/776-6585), is the Caribbean's oldest hand-painted-clothing studio, in operation since 1978. You can watch talented artists create original designs on fine tropical clothing, including swimwear, daytime and evening clothing, and articles for babies, children, men, and women. The shop studio will create custom designs just for you.

Fabric Mill (tel. 809/776-6194), another Mongoose Junction shopping attraction, has some exciting fabrics. Specializing in silkscreened and batik prints from around the world, Fabric Mill also carries locally silkscreened fabric displaying island motifs. Interesting accessories, soft sculptures, and unique gift items are also made in this studio shop.

R and I Patton Goldsmithing, P.O. Box, Cruz Bay (tel. 809/776-6548), by the entrance to Mongoose Junction, has a large selection of island-designed jewelry in sterling, gold, and precious stones.

D. Knight & Company, P.O. Box 376, Cruz Bay (tel. 809/776-7958), is an establishment of interest only to a limited handful of readers who are intrigued by fine cabinetry and tropical hardwoods. In an industrial building on the east side of Cruz Bay on Rt. 104 you'll find one of the finest collections of exotic woods in the Caribbean. Mr. Knight's inventory includes beautifully striated Brazilian angelim, red locust from Dominica, honey-colored samaan, Burmese teak, ebony, black jacaranda, brown heart, green heart, purple heart, and rosewood. Unless you plan to buy massive quantities of the stuff, shipping it home will be a problem, but if you're just looking for a few boards for the top of something you're rebuilding in your workshop, Mr. Knight can arrange shipping through the mail.

Before you set sail for St. Thomas, you'll want to pay a visit to **Wharfside Village,** just a few steps from the ferry departure point on the waterfront, opening onto Cruz Bay. Here in this pastel complex of cool courtyards, alleys and shady patios, you can explore this tropical mall whose shops seem to change with the season. It's a mishmash of all sorts of boutiques, along with some restaurants, fast food joints, and bars.

3. ST. CROIX

The largest of the U.S. Virgin Islands, 84 square miles of real estate, St. Croix was a stop for Columbus on November 14, 1493, but the reception committee of Carib Indians was far from friendly. He anchored his ship off Salt River Point, on the north shore of St. Croix, before the Indians drove him away. However, before leaving he named the island Santa Cruz (Spanish for Holy Cross). Those cannibalistic Indians made later colonizing parties less than eager to settle in St. Croix.

However, the Dutch arrived, as did the English, and for a short time St. Croix was owned by the Knights of Malta, no great pioneers. The Spanish drove the British out, only to be driven out themselves by the French, and so the familiar story of Caribbean colonization went. It wasn't until 1650 that the French laid claim to the island, later abandoning their attempts at colonization.

The Danes purchased St. Croix in 1773, attracted to the island because of its slave labor and sugarcane fields. This marked the golden era for both planters and pirates. However, the sugar boom ended, with eventual slave uprisings, the introduction of the sugar beet in Europe, and the emancipation of 1848. Even though seven different flags have flown over St. Croix, it is the nearly 2½ centuries of Danish influence that still permeates the island and its architecture.

St. Croix has some of the best beaches in the Virgin Islands, and ideal weather. It doesn't have the sophisticated nightlife of St. Thomas, nor would its permanent residents want that.

African tulips are just some of the flowers that add a splash of color to the landscape, and stately towers that once supported grinding mills are but lonely ghosts on moonlit nights.

At the east end of St. Croix, which, incidentally, is the easternmost point of the United States, the terrain is rocky, arid, with cacti growing, evoking parts of Arizona. However, the west end is lusher, with a rain forest of mango and mahogany, tree ferns, and dangling lianas. Rolling hills and upland pastures characterize the area lying between the two extremes.

GETTING THERE: For a description of the air transportation offered by **American, Pan American, Eastern** and **Midway,** refer to the "Getting There" section at the beginning of this chapter.

GETTING AROUND: At the airport you'll find official taxi rates posted. Per-person rates require a minimum of two passengers. One person would be double the fares listed below. Expect to pay about $4 per person from the airport to

Christiansted and about $3.25 per person from the airport to Frederiksted. As the cabs are unmetered, you'll want to agree on the rate before getting in. The **St. Croix Taxicab Association,** offering door-to-door service, can be reached by calling 809/773-5220 or 809/778-1088.

Buses

Fares are cheap, the rates depending on the distance you go. The main route is between the towns of Christiansted and Frederiksted.

Car Rentals

This is a suitable means of exploring for some, but know that if you're going into "bush country," the roads are often disastrous. Sometimes the government smooths them out before the big season begins.

Three of North America's major car-rental companies maintain popular branches at the St. Croix airport. After reviewing the prices of all the "Big Three," I concluded that **Budget Rent-a-Car** (tel. 809/778-9636 locally in St. Croix) maintains the most consistently inexpensive rentals. Any of its fleet can be reserved by calling toll free 800/527-0700 at least two business days in advance. But, as any dollarwise shopper should do, you might also compare up-to-the-minute prices at **Hertz** (tel. toll free 800/654-3131) or at **Avis** (tel. toll free 800/331-1212).

High-season prices at Avis and Budget are about the same. However, more of Budget's cars offer air conditioning than similarly priced vehicles at Avis. On the other hand, tariffs for most of the cars at Hertz were almost always higher than either of its two major competitors. Keep in mind, of course, that Hertz at any time could initiate a series of promotional fares.

On my most recent visit, insurance premiums tended to be slightly cheaper and to buy more coverage at Budget than at either Hertz or Avis, and the number of days of advance booking at Budget is usually less than that required for rentals at Hertz and Avis. All the major car-rental companies usually announce off-season reductions after April 15.

All of Budget's rental vehicles come with automatic transmission as a standard feature. Its least expensive rental is a peppy four-door Mitsubishi capable of holding four passengers in air-conditioned comfort. A similarly priced Isuzu at Avis did not offer air conditioning. Budget's Mitsubishi Mirage rents for $256 a week, with unlimited mileage included. Day-long rentals of this car cost $42 with unlimited mileage included. Budget also offers a wide range of other well-built Japanese cars in ascending price order. If you're looking for a more substantial vehicle, Budget offers a solid Mazda 626 with automatic transmission and air conditioning for $360 a week or $60 a day, including unlimited mileage.

Drivers at Budget's St. Croix subsidiary must be between the ages of 25 and 70. For more information about insurance costs, refer to the section on "Car Rentals" in St. Thomas, since basically the same insurance situation applies to Hertz, Avis, and Budget on both islands.

Taxi Tours

Many prefer to see St. Croix this way, resting at their hotel or shopping for the rest of their stay after a strenuous day's outing which, for a party of two, will cost from $20 for two hours. This fare is to be negotiated and definitely agreed upon in advance.

Scooter Rentals

To rent a two-wheel motor scooter to ride around the island, go to **R. J. Scooter Rentals,** 3 Hospital St., in Christiansted (tel. 809/778-8822). It's about 50 yards from the Old Fort. From 9 a.m. to 5 p.m. daily you can rent a scooter by the half day, day, or week.

Local Air Services

The **Virgin Islands Seaplane Shuttle, Inc.,** Seaplane Ramp (tel. 809/773-1776 or toll free 800/524-2050), offers scheduled downtown-to-downtown flights to St. Thomas, St. Croix, and St. John in the U.S. Virgin Islands, Tortola in the British Virgin Islands, and San Juan, Puerto Rico.

WHERE TO STAY: You can stay at one of the many charming waterfront inns at Christiansted, or at one of the resorts, plantations, or condominium units scattered throughout the island, many at beachside perches. Rates for the most part are steep, and all rooms are subject to a 7½% hotel room tax.

Luxury Leaders

Carambola Beach Resort & Golf Club, P.O. Box 3031, Kingshill, St. Croix, USVI 00850 (tel. 809/778-3800), is a luxurious Caribbean hideaway which was conceived as a West Indies fishing village, with architectural motifs borrowed from Spanish, French, Dutch, and English styles. Opening onto Davis Bay, its major drawing card is its championship golf course designed by Robert Trent Jones (more about this later). A shining sapphire of Rockresorts, the complex is named for the star-shape fruit of the islands. On beautiful and secluded grounds, it offers 157 spacious guestrooms. Bougainvillea, sea grapes, and palms abound, and accommodations are in clusters of six, with their own large sitting areas and screened-in porches. The ambience is one of cool tiles, island woods, tasteful art, ceiling fans, and mahogany furniture. Each room is air-conditioned, other amenities including walk-in closets, oversize tile showers, and double-sink vanities. Winter tariffs, with all meals included, are $410 daily in a single and $475 in a double. *Off-season rates range from $220 to $265 daily in a single, $280 to $325 in a double.*

Drinking and dining facilities include the Saman Room, featuring lunch buffets and four-course dinners served in a bright, airy, tropical ambience, and the Flamboyant Bar, a two-story, open-air cocktail lounge where a steel drum band plays in the evening. The superb club-like dining room, The Mahogany, is recommended separately. The hotel's spacious pool and Jacuzzi overlook the ocean. In addition, the Beach Club gives guests a chance to swim in either a freshwater pool or the sea, and the tennis center offers five HydroCourt clay courts shaded by large saman, mahogany, and palm trees. The resort is the core of a residential community extending over more than 4,000 acres of the north shore of the island, an area evoking the tropical splendor of Hawaii.

The Buccaneer, P.O. Box 218, Christiansted, St. Croix, USVI 00820-0218 (tel. 809/773-2100), is a big, fancy resort. Among other offerings, it opens onto a trio of the island's best beaches. With its hilltop perch and its beachside sites, it is almost two resorts rolled into one. The location is about a four-mile drive from Christiansted, in a sweeping, rolling landscape. Once the Buccaneer was a sugar plantation, and its first estate house, dating from the mid-17th century, stands near the freshwater swimming pool. Pink and patrician, the hotel offers you a choice of rooms in its main building or in one of its beachside properties. The baronially arched main building has a lobby opening toward drinking or viewing terraces, with a sea vista on two sides. The architecture is inspired by the Danish custom of free use of arched colonnades.

The interiors of the suites and rooms effectively use slanted wood ceilings, chalk-white walls, and all-white furniture to create a fresh, uncluttered look. Rooms are categorized as deluxe, sea-view, and standard. *In the off-season, EP* *rates for two range from $130 to $210 daily.* However, in winter double occupancy costs $170 to $300 daily. Prices quoted are on the EP, but there are many choices for meals. Most guests lunch lightly in the sun at the Grotto, tanning as they enjoy juicy hamburgers or hot dogs. Lunch is also served at the Little Mermaid Restaurant, the beach, and in the Terrace Dining Room of the main hotel. Cocktails and dinner are available at the Mermaid and the Terrace. Entertainment nightly, with a variety of music ranging from Jimmy Hamilton's jazz to island steel drums, is a feature at the Terrace. One of the most elegant places to dine is the resort's Brass Parrot Restaurant (see the recommendations to follow).

The resort has the best sports program in St. Croix—eight championship tennis courts, two lit at night, and an 18-hole golf course, as well as horseback riding, sports fishing, scuba-diving, and snorkeling available from its own dock. Excursions are arranged to Buck Island's reef. For reservations, get in touch with Ralph Locke, toll free 800/223-1108.

First-Class Hotels

Cormorant Beach Club, 108 La Grande Princesse, St. Croix, USVI 00820 (tel. 809/778-8920), is set amid a colony of 1,000 king palms, about four miles west of Christiansted on Pelican Cove. Its sumptuous setting strikes a perfect balance between seclusion and accessibility. Long Reef, one of the better-known zoological playgrounds of the Caribbean, lies a few hundred feet from the hotel's sandy beachfront. Its social center revolves around a wood-sheathed and high-ceilinged clubhouse, whose walls were removed for a firsthand taste of the salty air. Radiating out from its central core is a well-stocked library, the largest freshwater pool on St. Croix, and a tastefully airy dining room, where half a dozen large fan-shaped windows encompass a view of the beach.

Accommodations lie in well-maintained outbuildings. Each contains a spacious bath lined with coral blocks, a tastefully stylish and clean decor of pleasing colors, cane and wicker furniture from the Dominican Republic, and bouquets of seasonal flowers. Units are priced on a basis used nowhere else in St. Croix. Dubbed the CBC Plan (Cormorant Beach Club Plan), it includes breakfast, lunch, and all drinks until 5 p.m., tennis, snorkeling, and aerobic classes. In winter, with these features included, singles cost $325 daily, doubles going for $350 and suites for $450. *Off-season, prices are $175 daily in singles, $200 in doubles, and $300 in suites.* Dinners, served à la carte, are elegantly lighthearted affairs, featuring California cuisine, costing about $25 per person and including such island delights as fresh local fish, chicken, and steaks served with interesting Caribbean accompaniment of mango, papaya, coconut, and Cruzan rum sauce. In winter, children under 16 are politely discouraged, a fact many vacationers appreciate.

In the U.S., the representative of Cormorant Beach Club is David B. Mitchell & Co. (tel. 800/372-1323 toll free or 212/696-1323 in New York City).

Divi St. Croix Beach Resort, at Grapetree Beach, P.O. Box 4289, Christiansted, St. Croix, USVI 00820 (tel. 809/773-9700), was built on a fine stretch of sugar-white sand by another hotel group, but in 1987, this three-part hotel complex was acquired by the well-respected Divi Hotels. Set amid a grove of coconut palms between a scrub-covered hill and the sea, it offers 86 first-rate accommodations. Each unit is air-conditioned and pleasantly furnished, with a tropical motif. Depending on the room assignment, singles or doubles rent for $210 to $240 daily in winter, *these rates dropping to $90 to $115 in summer.* On the premises is a rectangular swimming pool with a bar and restaurant open to the sea breezes, where breakfast and lunch are served. Dining is by candlelight in the Spinnaker Restaurant one flight up, overlooking the pool and the sea. The resort has two tennis courts, and Divi is always associated with dive operations. Here they also offer a complete water-sports facility, featuring trips to Buck Island. The resort lies about a 15-minute drive east of Christiansted, and the staff maintains a daytime shuttlebus service to and from the capital.

Hotel on the Cay, Protestant Cay, Christiansted Harbor, P.O. Box 4020, Christiansted, St. Croix, USVI 00822 (tel. 809/773-2035 or toll free 800/524-2035), is an isolated resort set on a sandy island across from Christiansted, whose dockside is just a one-minute ferry ride away. The hotel offers ferry service to its guests and visitors from 6 a.m. to 1:30 a.m. daily. The establishment has the only beach in Christiansted, as well as a clean freshwater pool. For guests who wish to dip more extensively in the world of water sports, a complete program is offered, with on-property experts to teach, guide, and recommend activities for everyone, from the novice to the more experienced. For the tennis lover, the Cay has three fine, well-kept courts. Play is complimentary to guests. Continental and West Indian fare are offered in the hotel's main dining room and tropical terrace, with a less formal beach barbecue Tuesday night. Island entertainment accompanies dinner on most evenings, followed by dancing. The 55 clean, air-conditioned rooms are decorated in good taste. All units have either a sea view or overlook the gardens and waterfalls. *Accommodations are available in summer at $87 daily single occupancy, $97 for two people.* In winter, singles rent for $165 daily and doubles for $177. Breakfast and dinner can be included for an additional $33 per person daily.

The Special Inns of Christiansted

Club Comanche, 1 Strand, Christiansted, St. Croix, USVI 00820 (tel. 809/773-0210), lives up to my idea of what a West Indian inn should really be like. Right on the Christiansted waterfront, it's the domain of innkeepers Dick and Mary Boehm. The main house is old, but has been completely adapted to modern tastes in its remodeling. At every turning, you come upon a charming setting. Take the open iron-cage elevator, where you expect Katharine Hepburn to descend in *Suddenly Last Summer.* Some of the bedrooms have slanted ceilings with handsomely carved four-poster beds, old chests, and mahogany mirrors. Reached by a covered bridge, the newer addition passes over a shopping street to the waterside. Other rooms, more recently constructed, are the poolside and harborfront buildings. A honeymoon suite is a re-creation of an old sugar mill, sitting on the wharf, perhaps the cutest accommodation in town. It boasts a downstairs salon and a king-size bed upstairs. At one side is a waterfront refreshment bar where you can order drinks and watch yachts come into dock. On the EP, four different sets of rates are offered. The highest prices are charged from December 15 to mid-April: doubles for $65 to $145 daily and singles for $60 to $89. *From mid-April to December 14, doubles go for $52 to $92 daily and singles for $42 to $52.* The club is also one of the leading choices for dining in town.

Anchor Inn, 58A King St., Christiansted, St. Croix, USVI 00820 (tel. 809/773-4000 or toll free 800/524-2030), is one of the few hotels lodged directly on the waterfront, in a quiet courtyard close to such historic buildings as Government House and the Old Danish Customs House. Of course, it's right in the heart of the shopping belt as well. The space is so compact and intimate you might not believe it holds 30 units, each with executive refrigerator, radio, phone, cable color TV, bath, and a small porch. Air conditioning is individually controlled. A few suites (without porches) have king- and queen-size beds. In winter, tariffs are $98 to $111 daily in a single, $116 to $129 in a double, and $133 to $146 in a triple. *In off-season, singles rent for $68 to $76 daily, doubles for $85 to $93, and triples for $101 to $109.* All rates are EP. Furnishings for the rooms are warmly conventional, with good color combinations used. (The Anchor Inn restaurant, under separate management, is recommended in the "Where to Dine" section, following.) Directly on the waterfront is a sundeck and small swimming pool, as well as the Anchor Inn's own boardwalk, where catamarans and glass-bottom boats operate daily to Buck Island. There are also deep-sea fishing boats, a scuba-dive shop, and honeymoon and family package tours.

Pink Fancy, 27 Prince St., Christiansted, St. Croix, USVI 00820 (tel. 809/773-8460), was restored and turned into this small, unique private hotel in downtown Christiansted, offering 13 efficiency rooms, with ceiling fans and color TV, in four buildings. All but four units contain air conditioning. In winter, the charge is $130 to $170 daily for either single or double occupancy, *dropping to $65 to $85 daily in summer.* The location is one block from the Annapolis Sailing School and the V.I. Seaplane Shuttle. The oldest part of the four-building complex is a 1780 Danish town house, now one of the historic places of St. Croix. Years ago the building was a private club for wealthy planters. Fame came when Jane Gottlieb, the Ziegfeld Follies star, opened it as a hotel in 1948. In the '50s the hotel became a mecca for writers and artists, attracting among others, Noël Coward. Built on different levels, the units are clustered around the swimming pool. A complimentary continental breakfast is served every morning; otherwise, you're on your own for meals. Units are known by estate names such as "Sweet Bottom." If that's too suggestive a selection for you, ask instead for, say, "Upper Love."

King Christian Hotel, King's Wharf, P.O. Box 3619, Christiansted, USVI 00820 (tel. 809/773-2285), is Betty Sperber's own special place, and she's one of the finest innkeepers on the island. The location is right in the heart of everything, directly on the waterfront. All its front rooms have two double beds, cable color TV, refrigerator, room safe, and private balconies overlooking the harbor. No-frills economy-wing rooms have two single beds or one double but no view or balconies. All units are air-conditioned and have private baths and phones. Winter EP tariffs range from $70 to $100 daily in singles, $80 to $105 in doubles. *Summer prices are $60 to $78 daily in singles, $65 to $88 in doubles.* On the premises is the Chart House, one of the best restaurants in St. Croix (it's noted for its salad bar). You can relax on the sun deck, shaded patio, or in the freshwater pool. The staff will make arrangements for golf, tennis, horseback riding, and sightseeing tours, and there's a beach just a few hundred yards across the harbor, reached by ferry. Mile Mark Charters watersports center, run by Betty's two sons, offers daily trips to Buck Island's famous snorkeling trail as well as a complete line of watersports. Special events are organized on request.

King's Alley Hotel, 55 King St., Christiansted, St. Croix, USVI 00820 (tel. 809/773-0103, or toll free 800/843-3574), stands at water's edge, surveying Christiansted Harbor's yacht basin. The hotel, a series of 23 air-conditioned bedrooms, is furnished with a distinct Mediterranean flair. Many of its units overlook a swimming pool terrace, with its oval pool surrounded by tropical plants. The galleries opening off the bedrooms are almost spacious enough for entertaining. *In summer, the meticulously cared-for rooms rent for $50 to $90 daily single or double,* the charge rising to $80 to $120 single or double in winter. All the rooms, incidentally, have twin or king-size beds. The Marina Bar features nightly entertainment by the pool. Right outside your door are boutiques and restaurants.

Hotel Caravelle, Queen Cross Street, Christiansted, St. Croix, USVI 00820 (tel. 809/773-0687, or toll free 800/524-0410). This establishment, biggest of the downtown hotels, usually caters to a clientele of international business people who prefer to be near the center of town. There's an Andalusian-style tile fountain splashing near the rectangular bar in the middle of the ground-floor reception area. The restaurant Banana Bay Club is a few steps away. Many resort activities, such as sailing, deep-sea fishing, snorkeling, scuba, golf, and tennis, can be arranged from the reception desk. A swimming pool and sun deck face the water, and all the shopping and activities of the town are close at hand. Accommodations, each with color TV, air conditioning, a phone, and a private bath, are priced according to their views. In winter, doubles cost $79 to $105 daily, *doubles renting for $68 to $88 in summer.* In each case, singles cost $10 less per day.

Holger Danske Hotel, 1 King Cross St., Christiansted, St. Croix, USVI 00820 (tel. 809/773-3600), named after World War II's Danish resistance movement, is a pleasant garden-style hotel stretching along a concrete walkway leading from the outlying reception area. A restaurant and a pool are on the premises. The decor of each of the 44 accommodations is unfussy, spacious, and comfortable, and most have simple kitchens, patios or verandas, air conditioning, TV, phones, and radios. Best Western, the management company, charges winter rates of $84 to $110 daily in a single, $94 to $130 in a double, and $15 for each additional person lodged in a double room. *In summer, single rates are $54 to $80 daily, and doubles rent for $64 to $90.*

Small, Select Hotels

Moonraker Hotel, 43A Queen Cross St., Christiansted, St. Croix, USVI 00820 (tel. 809/773-1535), is a charming blend of the old and the new in the heart of Christiansted, run by the Hemeon and Abbott families. The hotel has been completely renovated and redecorated in a tropical motif. Bedrooms surround an old Danish courtyard shaded by a flourishing mango tree. All 15 of the units have private baths, TV, refrigerators, phones, and air conditioning. In winter, doubles cost $70 daily, and singles go for $65. *Charges off-season are $50 daily in doubles, $45 in singles.* An extra person in a double pays $10. The hotel's Moonraker Lounge on the second floor is a favorite rendezvous for tourists and locals alike. Live entertainment is offered nightly in season. The Moonraker is close to the waterfront, free-port shopping, excellent dining, and nightlife.

Danish Manor Hotel, 2 Company St., Christiansted, St. Croix, USVI 00820 (tel. 809/773-1377), is built around an old Danish courtyard and a freshwater pool right in the heart of town. It's a compound that combines the very old and the very new. The hotel was erected on the site of a Danish West Indies Company's counting house. An L-shaped three-story addition stands in the rear, with spacious, air-conditioned rooms with encircling balconies, ceiling fans, cable TV and HBO, and private baths. All units overlook an intimate courtyard, dominated by an ancient mahogany tree. The entrance to the courtyard is through old arches. *The owner charges $50 to $60 daily in a double in summer.* Tariffs rise in winter to $75 to $85 in a double. Prices include morning coffee and a continental breakfast. The hotel has a freshwater pool. Reservations can be made by calling toll free 800/778-8233.

The Waves at Cane Bay, P.O. Box 1749, Kingshill, St. Croix, USVI 00851-1749 (tel. 809/778-1805), is an intimate and tasteful property run by John and Betty Silander. The location is about eight miles from the airport, midway between the island's two biggest towns, on a well-landscaped plot of oceanfront property, which is somewhat like you'd find on the coast of southern Italy. Accommodations rise in angular two-story units with screened-in verandas. The Silanders welcome their guests as part of their extended family, hosting twice-weekly cocktail and barbecue parties on the oceanside terrace and adding many homelike touches to their accommodations. Each of these is high-ceilinged, with fresh flowers, well-stocked kitchens, comfortable and tasteful furnishings, private libraries of paperback books, and thick towels. A two-room villa next to the main house has a large oceanside deck. In winter, units rent for $95 to $145 daily for single or double occupancy. *In summer, singles cost $50 to $95, and doubles go for $60 to $95.* The establishment's social center is the beachside bar, ringed with stone. Don't overlook the possibility of a game of golf or tennis at the nearby Rockresort course, Carambola.

Cathy's Fancy Beach Hotel, P.O. Box 1668, Christiansted, St. Croix, USVI 00820 (tel. 809/773-5595 or toll free 800/524-5004), advertises itself accurately as "the Caribbean the way it used to be." This 21-unit hotel lies three miles west of Christiansted on a sandy four-acre plot of beachfront property covered with palm trees, where hammocks have been strung. Each unit has a ceiling fan, veranda, comfortable tropical furniture, kitchens for self-catering (supplies can be bought nearby), and a "barefoot on the beach" kind of feeling. In winter, studios and one- or two-bedroom apartments for two to four people rent for $137 to $185 daily. *In summer, prices are reduced to $70 to $95 daily for the same accommodations.* There is no formal restaurant, but snacks and drinks, including tasty piña coladas, are sold near the beach, and a Sunday West Indian barbecue is held.

OTHER FROMMER GUIDES TO THE CARIBBEAN: In addition to the guide you are now reading, Frommer publishes four other guides that cover the Caribbean. Each provides information for travelers with particular needs: those looking for great shopping, those needing a secret place in the sun, those searching for the right cruise vacation, and those seeking the perfect honeymoon.

Every serious shopper knows that there's more to do in the Caribbean than soak up the sun. The islands offer an incredible opportunity for shopping and acquiring some of the best of the world's merchandise, often at substantial savings off U.S. prices. *Frommer's Shopper's Guide to the Caribbean* tells you how and where to find the very best in quality and value and also in those items that reflect the islanders' cosmopolitan heritages and skills.

In *Caribbean Hideaways,* well-respected author and editor Ian Keown selects the 100 best, ultra-romantic places to stay throughout the Caribbean from Anguilla to Virgin Gorda. You won't find any chain hotels and fast-paced gambling resorts here. What you will find are tranquil oases with tropical gardens, havens of peace offering the finest service and cuisine, world-class resorts offering every conceivable kind of diversion—in short, establishments that care about what's authentic and what's not.

Frommer's Cruises is the guide to the best cruise travel values in all price ranges —deluxe, moderate, and budget—written by Marylyn Springer and Donald A. Schultz. Their painstaking work has won them the Best Travel Guide Award from the Society of American Travel Writers. This award-winning guide is reliable and detailed, giving full reports on each ship's public rooms, ambience, cabins, attractions, and special programs, as well as schedules, itineraries, and costs (including specific cabin prices). It covers more than 100 cruise ships—including the newest ones— that depart from North American harbors to such ports as Martinique, Barbados, Antigua, as well as to many ports outside of the Caribbean.

In *Frommer's Guide to Honeymoon Destinations,* the travel editor of *Modern Bride,* Risa Weinreb, has compiled a guidebook to the greatest honeymoon destinations throughout the Caribbean, as well as in the United States, Canada, and Mexico. Choose any destination and this book will enable you to plan all the details of your honeymoon. Each entry describes Romantic Interludes, places to go to share those quiet moments and those more adventurous, fun-filled times; Hotels and Hideaways, from the deluxe hotels to the small, quaint country inns; Romantic Restaurants, where you can linger over lavish candlelit dinners; and After-Dark Rendezvous, nightspots for dancing and romancing 'til dawn.

For information on how to purchase these and other Frommer guides, turn to the last two pages of this book.

Chenay Bay Beach Resort, P.O. Box 24600, Christiansted, St. Croix, USVI 00824 (tel. 809/773-2918 or toll free 800/548-4457), is a resort with a rustic and "barefoot casual" ambience. The 20 cottages of the complex rise in 30 acres of property, with one of St. Croix's finest beaches for swimming, snorkeling, windsurfing, and strolling, about four miles west of the town. Each cottage contains a kitchenette, private bath with shower, and ceiling fans. Some units have optional air conditioning.

Cottages rent for $115 to $125 per day for two guests in winter, *$75 to $85 for two in summer.* Rates include a welcome cocktail, use of beach lounge chairs and towers, and use of snorkeling equipment. The resort houses the Mistral Windsurfing Center of St. Croix. The Beach Pavilion Restaurant serves from 11 a.m. to 9 p.m., and Thursday night beach barbecues with entertainment are a popular feature. The resort is managed by Richard Locke, a veteran operator of Caribbean and Bahamian hotels.

Plantation Life

Sprat Hall Plantation, P.O. Box 695, Rt. 63, Frederiksted, St. Croix, USVI 00840 (tel. 809/772-0305 or toll free 800/843-3584), one mile north of Frederiksted, can never be duplicated. It is the oldest plantation "great house" in the Virgin Islands and the only French plantation house left intact. Dating back to the French occupation of 1650 to 1690, it's set on 20 acres of grounds, with private white sandy beaches.

The units in the great house have been designated for nonsmokers because of the value of the antiques. Converted slave quarters have been redecorated and carpeted. They're all air conditioned and have a view of the sea. Room service is available to guests in either the great house or the slave quarters. If you want more privacy and to be pretty much on your own, you might choose one of the Arawak suites, redecorated and with front porches for lounging or outdoor dining. There is full maid service daily, and guests have a choice of suites with king-size, double, or twin beds. All rooms have radios, and some have TV (available in any unit on request). Some of the Arawak group are two-bedroom cottages accommodating four to six people. These are also air-conditioned and completely equipped for tropical living by the sea. In the slave quarters, single rooms rent in winter for $100 daily doubles or twins going for $110, and nonsmoking rooms in the great house for $120. All these are on the EP. Arawak cottage rates are $140 for one or two persons in two-room suites, $240 for up to four persons in two-bedroom cottages. *Summer prices are $70 for singles, $80 for doubles in the slave quarters, and $90 in the great house, all EP. Cottage rates are $100 and $140, respectively.*

You can be sure of warm hospitality and good food, either at the Beach Restaurant at lunch or in the Sprat Hall great house restaurant, recommended below under Dining Near Frederiksted. On the grounds is the best equestrian stable in the Caribbean (see "The Sporting Life" below). The Hurd family runs the operation and offers hiking and birdwatching, as well as water sports such as snorkeling, swimming, and shore fishing. Scuba diving, deep-sea fishing, jet skiing, and water skiing can be arranged for you.

Self-Sufficient Units

If St. Croix's high hotel tariffs deflate your budget too severely, there is an alternative. In general, condominiums are rented at half or a third the going hotel rates. Particularly in the Frederiksted area, you'll find some excellent bargains. And if you wait until after April 15, prices are often half what they are in high season. My recommendations follow.

Tamarind Reef Beachside Inn, Estate Southgate, Christiansted, St. Croix, USVI 00820 (tel. 809/773-0463 or toll free 800/524-2036), named after the lace-leafed tamarind trees growing on the property, sits behind a hedge of allamanda on the north coast of the island. Accommodations are clustered on flat, sandy ground, in semiprivate cabañas and low-lying bungalows, partially sheltered by trees and flowering shrubs. Each of the 16 units has a TV, kitchenette, computerized safe, ceiling fan, and comfortable but spartan furniture. In winter, depending on the week and the size of the unit, prices range from $135 daily in a single to $155 in a double. *In the off-season, they cost from $75 daily in a single, $85 in a double.* There's a swimming pool on the premises, and a nearby tropical bar, The Deep End, is often peopled with escapees from Christiansted who enjoy the ambience. The bar serves light food and tropical drinks from 11:30 a.m. to 7 p.m. The Green Cay Marina, under the same ownership and adjacent to the inn, offers gourmet cuisine at The Galleon restaurant. Children are welcome here and can enjoy spending most of their day on the half-moon-shaped beach which has a view of an uninhabited cay just across the water. Complimentary features at the inn include welcoming cocktails, snorkeling gear, and a continental breakfast served poolside every morning.

Sugar Beach Condominiums, Golden Rock Estate, Christiansted, St. Croix, USVI 00820 (tel. 809/773-5345 or toll free 800/524-2049), is a row of modernized, stylish one-, two-, and three-bedroom apartments strung along the famous white Sugar Beach. When you tire of its white sands, you can swim in the curvy freshwater swimming pool nestled beside a sugar mill where Virgin Islands rum was made three centuries ago. Under red-tile roofs, the apartments are staggered, with patios set back to provide privacy. The units, opening toward the sea, are complete with kitchens and are tastefully furnished. In winter, a studio for two costs $135 daily, ranging upward to $225 for a two-bedroom unit for four people. *In summer, studios for two go for $75 daily, two-bedroom villas for four costing $125.* Maid service costs extra, but the charge is nominal. The property has two lit tennis courts with Laykold playing surfaces. The Carambola Golf Course is only a short drive away.

Colony Cove, 221A Estate Golden Rock, Christiansted, St. Croix, USVI 00820 (tel. 809/773-1965 or toll free 800/524-2025). Of all the condo complexes of St. Croix, this one is perhaps the most like a full-fledged hotel, lying about a mile west of Christiansted next to a palm-dotted beach. It's composed of a quartet of buff-colored three-story buildings whose angular façades ring a kidney-shaped swimming pool. Each unit contains its own clothes washer and dryer (rare for St. Croix), a kitchen, cable color TV, enclosed veranda or gallery, floors layered with cool rows of ceramic tiles, two air-conditioned bedrooms, and a pair of bathrooms. Winter rates, based on double occupancy, are $185 daily. A third or fourth person sharing pays an extra $20 each. *Summer rates, double occupancy, run $110 daily, a third or fourth party paying $15 each.*

Cane Bay Reef Club, P.O. Box 1407, Kingshill, St. Croix, USVI 00851 (tel. 809/778-2966). Nine suites overlook the surf, each with a fully equipped kitchen, bedroom, living room, bath, and balcony where you can dine. The living room couches make into two single beds, so one suite can become a family accommodation. From your own private balcony you'll have a view of the surf of the Caribbean. *In summer, one person pays $50 daily, two persons being charged $60.* In winter, only weekly rentals are accepted, costing $546 for two persons, each additional person paying $15 daily. There are two new luxurious condo suites, still budget priced at $130 for doubles in winter, *$80 in summer.* Joining other guests in an outdoor barbecue or 40-foot swimming pool. The hotel lies within walking distance of Cane Bay Plantation, where you can dine if you make a reservation. According to *Skin Diver* magazine, the club is one of the ten best dive spots in the Caribbean. It's also the closest resort to the famed Carambola championship golf course.

WHERE TO DINE: Don't limit yourself to the mainly continental places in Christiansted, but head also for Frederiksted, not just for food but for what might be called "dining adventures" in establishments reeking with character.

In Christiansted
Kendricks, 52 King St. (tel. 809/773-9199), is a fine restaurant in the heart of old town, in an old brick building. Climb a flight of brick stairs to the second-floor dining room, with a view of old Christiansted, the distant sea peeking out from above the rooftops. Full meals cost $30 and up and might include any of the following specialties of David and Jane Kendricks: grilled breast of duck with a molasses and black peppercorn sauce, grilled rack of lamb with roasted garlic and thyme sauce, and grilled fresh fish served with sun-dried tomatoes and a basil-flavor cream sauce. Desserts vary according to the whims of the chef, but among them might be fresh apple crisp and a richly caloric version of mud pie. The restaurant is open only for dinner, from 6 to 10:30 p.m. seven days a week.

Top Hat, Company St., opposite Market Square (tel. 809/773-2346), represents the culinary adventure of two Scandinavians, Bent and Hanne Rasmussen. They took this second-floor space over an arcade, creating the aura of a Danish *kro* (inn). Only dinner is served, offered Monday to Saturday from 6 to 10 p.m. from November to May. Appetizers range from smoked eel to cheese croquettes, as well as small Ping-Pong meatballs so popular in Denmark. A favorite soup is the homemade split pea. From the sea you might try filet of plaice Hanne (served with a white wine sauce). I'd also suggest the crêpes stuffed with shrimp from Greenland and topped with a white wine sauce. You can also order a herring platter, steak tartare, and tournedos béarnaise. A good selection of desserts is offered, or else you might finish with their Viking coffee. Dinners begin at $35 per person.

Comanche, 1 Strand St. (tel. 809/773-2665), is one of the best-liked restaurants on the island. Even though relaxed, it is quietly elegant in its own way. It's a very busy place, and you'll really need a reservation. Lunch is served from 11:30 a.m. to 2:30 p.m. and dinner from 6 to 10 p.m. The menu of West Indian and continental specialties is eclectic—an assortment of mouthwatering delicacies likely to include everything from fish and conch chowder to Cantonese shrimp balls. Each night a different special is featured (mine most recently was roast chicken with an oyster stuffing). Desserts include a bread pudding with rum sauce. Dinner tabs average around $30 per head.

Anchor Inn, 58A King St. (tel. 809/773-0263), is downtown in Christiansted, right on King's Wharf, but it reminds some diners of a Sausalito bistro. It's on the second floor with a covered terrace, so from your dining perch you can see the boats in the harbor. It's an ideal place to meet your friends for a late breakfast, enjoying their custardy French toast topped with sliced ripe bananas covered in real whipped cream. The cost is $4.50. You might also try their beer buttermilk pancakes. "Creative" omelets, 14 in all, are quite good too. At lunch the menu is predictable—burgers, chef's salad, and soups. At dinner the menu improves considerably. I'd suggest a variety of fresh island fish, such as lobster and conch, which are brought in almost daily from the local charter boats and fishermen. The catch of the day is usually prepared West Indian style (sautéed in butter, then stewed with fresh onions, green peppers, tomatoes, and spices). Count on spending from $22 to $28 for dinner. Open daily, breakfast is served daily from 7:30 to 11 a.m. (from 8 a.m. Saturday and Sunday); lunch from 11 a.m. to 2:30 p.m., and dinner from 6:30 to 9:30 p.m. The bar is open from 4 p.m. to midnight.

Dino's, 4C Hospital St. (tel. 809/778-8005), lying one block east of Fort Christiansvaern, this bistro, decorated in the Mediterranean style, is housed in a 200-year-old brick building. It has two distinct sections: an air-conditioned interior and an open-air terrace. The terrace lies within a commercial arcade in the heart of town. Only dinner is served, costing from $30, and it is offered nightly from 6 to 10. You might begin with one of the homemade pasta dishes, then go on to veal piccata or perhaps scallops Serafino. Many guests end their meal with one of the luscious Italian desserts or else settle happily for an ice-cold espresso.

Golden China, 28 King Cross St. (tel. 809/773-8181), serves food as fine as that enjoyed in the Chinatowns of New York or San Francisco. The best experience is to get a group of six couples and arrange for the special Chinese banquet. You'll hardly believe it. If you don't know that many people, you can still enjoy many specialties, including those from the Hunan and Szechuan kitchens. Each dish is prepared to order, and only the finest-quality ingredients are used. Of course, from time to time certain ingredients may not be available because of the vagaries of supply in St. Croix. Dinner is likely to run around $12 per person. However, lunches, served Monday to Friday from 11:30 a.m. to 2:30 p.m., go for only about $6.

Tivoli Gardens, 39 Strand St., upstairs over the Pan Am Pavilion (tel. 809/773-6782), is a favorite local rendezvous, run by Gary Thomson. From this large second-floor porch festooned in lights you get the same view of Christiansted Harbor that a sea captain might. White beams hold up the porch, and trellises and hanging plants help to evoke its namesake, the pleasure gardens of Copenhagen. The menu is international, everything from gazpacho to pâté to a country terrine to escargots provençale, to a goulash inspired by a recipe concocted in the day of the Austro-Hungarian Empire. For dessert, those in the know order a wicked, calorie-heavy chocolate velvet cake. Save room for it, and count on spending from $30 to dine here or $15 for lunch, served from 11:15 a.m. to 2:30 p.m. daily except Sunday. Dinner hours are 6 to 9:30 nightly. Often there is live dancing from 7 p.m., when reservations are advised.

The **Chart House,** 59 King's Wharf (tel. 809/773-7718). This nautically decorated waterfront restaurant opens onto the waterfront in Christiansted. It has a classy look of Oriental carpets and wicker chairs. Normally I don't like chain restaurants. However, when I'm on an island such as St. Thomas or Puerto Rico, I always head for a Chart House, knowing that I am likely to get one of my finest meals. To begin with, it has the best salad bar on the island, and many come here just for that. However, I always order their celebrated prime rib, which is a huge slab of meat. You might prefer instead their lobster, or barbecued beef ribs. Regardless, try their baked potato: it's a palate-pleaser. The mud pie is justly renowned. Telephone for a reservation and visit only for dinner, seven nights a week from 6 to 10. Meals cost from $25.

Bombay Club, 5A King St. (tel. 809/773-1838). Its plant-encircled ambience is concealed from the street by the foundations of an 18th-century building. The food, while not overly fancy, is some of the best in Christiansted and reasonable in price: full dinners cost from $25 to $30. Menu items include the catch of the day, chicken Bombay, and sautés of shrimp, beef, or chicken. Meals are served from 11:30 a.m. to 2:30 p.m. and 6 to 11 p.m. daily. No lunch is served on Saturday and Sunday.

Ritz Café, Bar, and Deli, Queen Cross St. (tel. 809/773-2985), is a neighborhood enclave of convivial locals, owing its success to New York–born Mike Harris. Its beamed ceiling and brick walls were originally part of an 18th-century great house. Lunches, costing around $8, might include shrimp salad, lobster salad, and Black Forest cake. A fixed-price steak dinner is served nightly for about $12. Sandwiches, cold cuts, and drinks are readily available. Breakfast is a daily ritual as well. The café is open without interruption Monday through Saturday from 7:30 a.m. to 10 p.m., on Sunday from 4 to 10 p.m. The bar remains open until midnight.

King's Alley Café, 55 King St. (tel. 809/773-0468), is a popular place to eat right in the heart of Christiansted activity. In a breezy, open-air setting, you'll have a view of the harbor from one of its tables. If you wish, you can patronize only the bar, which specializes in calypso daiquiris. Many of these are consumed at happy hour from 4 to 7 p.m. Actually the place opens for breakfast at 7:30 a.m., serving until 11 a.m.; it also presents a special Sunday breakfast from 8 a.m. to 2 p.m. featuring such dishes as eggs Benedict. Otherwise, lunch and dinner are served continuously from 11:30 a.m. to 10 p.m. During the day guests order from the extensive menu of sandwiches and burgers, paying from $10 for a light meal. At night they usually sample more elaborate fare, such as one of the barbecue dishes (ribs or chicken), or the catch of the day. Buttered conch is a local favorite. Dinners cost $15 and up. Five large seawater fish tanks provide customers with the opportunity to see many fish, lobsters, and other reef creatures.

Dining Near Frederiksted

Outside of Frederiksted, 1½ miles to the north on Rt. 63, stands **Sprat Hall Plantation** (tel. 809/772-0305), which I have endorsed with enthusiasm as a place to stay. However, if that isn't possible, you might want to call the co-owner of Sprat Hall, Joyce Hurd, and tell her you'd like to come by for dinner. (Try to get there at 7 p.m.) That won't fluster her a bit. She and her West Indian cooks have been feeding guests for years, and they've won their own kind of fame on the island for dining in what is the oldest plantation great house in St. Croix. I even dropped in once for a good country breakfast, costing $6. The dinners here, going for around $18, are recommended by *Gourmet* magazine. Chances are, the vegetables you'll be served came right from the plantation gardens. Each night you face a choice of main dishes. It might be lobster, conch, or lamb. The roast beef is a winner. And you get "as much as you want to eat." Joyce will have made some soursop ice cream ("I think I invented it"). Dinners are served every night. "We never close," Joyce said. "People have to eat, don't they?" Yes, they do, and they eat very well at Joyce's table. For dining, women are requested to wear dresses, with long pants and sports jackets or dress shirts being required for men. No jeans or T-shirts, please.

Around the Island

Mahogany Room, Carambola Beach Resort Golf Club, Kingshill (tel. 809/778-3800), has an inviting, clublike ambience. With its soaring plantation-style wooden ceiling, it was designed to evoke the heyday of the sugarcane era. Fine ingredients are used in the latest culinary techniques. Traditional and classical dishes are always on the menu, but exciting and innovative Caribbean tastes are included as well. For example, you might start with red bean soup or something more exotic, perhaps a strawberry yogurt bisque. You could follow with grilled wahoo in a ginger lemon butter or grilled pork loin with a sauce of cinnamon and pumpkin. The table d'hôte menu is different every night. Much of the produce used here comes from the resort's own 20-acre farm. Nonresidents are charged $40 for dinner, served nightly from 6:30 to 9 p.m., by reservation only. The resort lies between Christiansted and Frederiksted on North Shore Road.

Cormorant Beach Club, Pelican Cove (tel. 809/778-8920), may well provide you with your most elegant beachside dining experience in St. Croix. The restaurant blends the cuisine of California with Cruzan specialties, along with providing a touch of continental flair. When available, fresh local seasonal ingredients are used, along with the finest imports such as select beef flown in from the New York markets. The menu changes nightly in high season, slightly less often in summer. You might be tempted, for example, with lamb marinated in fresh pomegranate juice (a natural tenderizer) or else a Créole-inspired dish such as tuna sautéed with Puerto Rican peppers. Dinners cost from $30 and are served nightly from 7 to 10. Always call for a reservation.

During the day, the hotel dining facilities are open only to residents. The exception to that is the Sunday brunch, costing $17 for all you can eat. It's served from noon to 2:30 p.m. and is rapidly becoming an island tradition, especially among locals.

The **Brass Parrot** is at the Buccaneer Hotel (tel. 809/773-2100), which was already previewed as a leading resort on the island. It also comes up with one of the fanciest—and best—dining choices. If you call to make a reservation, you can eat with the guests of the resort. Men should wear a jacket, and women should appear in their most chic resort wear. The restaurant has been completely redone and installed in the "great house" of the Buccaneer, a pink masonry building. Views of the hills are framed by large arched windows. Bamboo furniture and thick pile carpeting add to the atmosphere of elegance. Decor aside, the reason people come here is for the food. French cuisine and West Indian dishes are the chef's specialties. The kitchen is known for such delicacies as rack of lamb, chateaubriand for two, Caribbean lobster, and veal langoustina. All this glamor comes with a price: expect to spend from $35 per person. Go between 7 and 9 p.m.

The **Galleon,** Green Cay Marina (tel. 809/773-9949), in a setting overlooking the ocean, is a local favorite, and deservedly so. The best cooking in Europe is found in northern Italy and in France, and that is what is offered here, including carpaccio just as good as that served at Harry's Bar in Venice (but it's cheaper here). Freshly baked breads and brochettes accompany main dishes, which might include an osso buco in the tradition of the Lombardy kitchen. Whenever available, you can also order fresh local fish, perhaps grouper. Of course, those who prefer the classics might order a perfectly done rack of lamb (which is carved at your table). Each main dish, even the lobster Benedict, is prepared to your request. Meals cost from $30 and are served from 6 to 10 p.m. Brunch is offered Sundays from 10:30 a.m. to 2:30 p.m. and costs from $17. The place has been called "casual but elegant," which is what many visitors want, especially those visiting St. Croix in the winter months.

Duggan's Reef, Teague Bay (tel. 809/773-9800), lies at Reef Beach at the eastern end of St. Croix (take Rt. 82). The owner is Frank Duggan, who runs this place near the water and open to the sea breezes. The bar, which is the most attractive feature of the place, begins inside the restaurant and ends on a wharf constructed over the water. For dining, the most popular main dish (perhaps 20% of the diners ask for it) is Duggan's Caribbean lobster pasta. At night, you can also order a catch of the day, or perhaps you might choose veal piccata or a rack of lamb. Dinners cost from $35 and are served from 6:30 to 9:30 p.m. It's important to reserve a table. Lunch, costing from $15 and served from noon to 3 p.m., is simpler, the menu featuring soups, salads, and well-filled sandwiches. The place is open daily in high season, closing on Monday off-season.

Oskar's Bar and Restaurant, La Grand Princesse, Rt. 75 (tel. 809/773-4060), just outside of Christiansted, is a good, inexpensive restaurant. This Swiss-run place is often filled when other, better-known (and more expensive) establishments are empty. Meals, tasty and big ones, cost only $12. After beginning with a cup or bowl of soup, try the special of the day, which might be roast pork with gravy, accompanied by mashed potatoes and corn. To go continental, you may prefer bratwurst with sauerkraut, or even filet mignon. To finish your repast, why not Black Forest cake? Lunch is served from 11:30 a.m. to 2:30 p.m. and dinner from 6 to 9 p.m. daily except Sunday.

WHAT TO SEE: The picture-book harbor town of the Caribbean, **Christiansted** is an old Danish port, handsomely restored (or at least in the process of being restored). On the northeastern shore of the island, on a coral-bound bay, the town is filled with Danish buildings, usually erected by prosperous merchants in the booming 18th century. These red-roof structures are often washed in pink, ochre, or yellow. A blaze of bougainvillea adds its brilliance to the color scheme. Built of solid stone, these 18th-century buildings have such thick walls they form their own kind of air conditioning. Arcades over the sidewalks make ideal shaded colonnades for shoppers. To maintain what Christiansted had, Government House—in fact, the whole area around the harborfront—has been designated as a historical site, and is looked after by the National Park Service.

You might begin your tour at the bright yellow **Fort Christiansvaern,** the best preserved of the five remaining Danish forts in the U.S. Virgins. Cannons, dungeons, an officer's kitchen, and bastions from its old defensive days are displayed. The fort saw many additions in the 19th century, as the Danish army garrisoned here until 1878. For the most part the fort was built of bricks brought from Denmark as ballast.

As you leave the fort, walk through a park to Company Street, stopping at **Steeple Building,** which was once the Lutheran Church of the Lord of Sabaoth. This was the first church built by the Danes after they colonized the island in 1734. The steeple, for which it was named, was added around 1794.

Today it is the U.S. Post Office, a museum, and Customs House, but the **Danish West India and Guinea Company,** also on Company Street, dates from 1749. Once it was a military depot.

In the old days, the customs house was **Scalehouse,** near the bandstand at the Wharf. Built in 1835, it was the office of the Danish weighmaster. Troops were also housed here; today the premises are occupied by a Visitors' Bureau.

In the Steeple Building and the Scalehouse, exhibits develop important facets of West Indian history. Choice examples of pre-Columbian Indian artifacts depict the life of these early inhabitants of the West Indies. European discovery and colonization, with special emphasis on the rise and decline of the plantation sugar economy, are graphically re-created. A special exhibit on the particular Danish colonial architecture developed on this island also displays restoration techniques. A focus on black history acknowledges the important contributions these citizens have played in the life of the island. Hours are 9 a.m. to 4 p.m., Monday through Friday.

Government House, on King Street, was finished in 1747, and this cream-colored and white residence housed the Danish governor-general before America purchased St. Croix. You can still see the tiny red guardhouse at the foot of the staircase going up from the patio to the big ballrooms with crystal chandeliers. These chandeliers and mirrors were a gift of the Danish government in 1966, replacing the originals. This house was joined with another house built in 1794 for a wealthy planter merchant named Adam Sobotker.

The original **Alexander Hamilton House** was built at the end of 1750, and it is said that Hamilton worked here when he was a clerk. The present house is a reconstruction, the original having burned in the 1960s.

The next day, or that afternoon, you might go on a walking tour of **Frederiksted.** It is an important point to know that a fire in 1879 swept over this harbor town. The citizens later rebuilt, using wood construction on top of the old Danish stone and yellow-brick foundations. In the reconstruction, Victorian gingerbread embellished the stone arches that remained, forming an elaborate jigsaw pattern. The old Danish town lies at the western end of the island, about 17 miles from Christiansted. This is a sleepy port town, very Old-World looking, which comes to life only when a cruise ship docks at its shoreline.

Most visitors begin their tour at russet-color **Fort Frederik,** considered the first fort to sound a foreign salute to the U.S. flag, in 1776. (St. Eustatius in the Dutch Windwards makes a convincing rival claim.) It was here on July 3, 1848, that Governor-General Peter von Scholten emancipated the slaves in the Danish West Indies. The fort has been restored to its 1840 look, and you can explore the courtyard and stables. The location is at the northern end of Frederiksted. An exhibit area has been installed in what was once the Garrison Room.

Just south of the fort, the **Customs House** is an 18th-century building which has a two-story gallery built in the 19th century. Here you can go into the Visitors' Bureau and pick up a free map of the town.

Nearby, privately owned **Victoria House** is a gingerbread structure built after the fire of 1879. In the rebuilding, some of the original 1803 structure was preserved.

Along the waterfront Strand Street, you reach the **Bellhouse,** the old Frederiksted Public Library. One of its owners, G. A. Bell, ornamented the steps with bells. The house today is an arts and crafts center and a nursery. Sometimes a local theater group presents dramas here.

Other buildings of interest include the **Danish School,** giving way in the 1830s to a building designed by Hingelberg, a well-known Danish architect. Today it's a the police station and Welfare Department.

Two churches are of interest. One is **St. Paul's Episcopal Church,** founded outside the port in the late 18th century. However, the present building dates from 1812. **St. Patrick's Catholic Church,** on Prince Street, began in the 1840s.

North of Frederiksted you can drop in at **Sprat Hall,** the island's oldest plantation (see my hotel and dining recommendations), or else continue along to the **rain forest,** covering about 15 acres, including the **Creque Dam.** Mahogany trees and yellow cedar grow in profusion, as do wild lilies. The dam is 150 feet high. As you travel through the terrain, which is private property incidentally, you'll hear the call of the mountain dove. The owner graciously lets visitors go inside to explore.

Most people want to see **Salt River,** but there isn't much to see. That's where Columbus landed for a brief moment, sending a boat out to a village filled with naked natives. These inhabitants turned out to be Arawaks, peaceful Indians captured by the militant Caribs. On their return, one of the Spanish leaders captured a "very beautiful Carib girl" from a native canoe, later writing that she "seemed to have been raised in a school of harlots." Columbus himself didn't actually set foot on ground.

The **St. George Village Botanical Garden,** just north of Centerline Road, four miles east of Frederiksted, at Estate St. George, is a veritable Eden of tropical trees, shrubs, vines, and flowers. Built around the ruins of a 19th-century sugarcane workers' village, the garden is a feast for the eye and the camera, from the entrance drive bordered by royal palms and bougainvillea to the towering kapok and tamarind trees, the multicolored hibiscus and frangipani, and the vast poinsettia bed—almost a quarter acre of red and white blooms from December to March. Restoration of the ruins is a continuing project. Two sets of workers' cottages provide space for a gift shop, rest rooms, a kitchen, and offices. These have been joined together with a Great Hall which is used by the St. Croix community for various functions. Other completed projects include the superintendent's house, the blacksmith's shop, and various smaller buildings used for a library, a plant nursery, workshops, and storehouses. Visitors are welcome from early morning until late afternoon; however, maps are available at the Great Hall. The gift shop is open Monday through Saturday from 9 a.m. to 3 p.m.; and the nursery on Tuesday, Thursday, and Saturday from 9 a.m. to noon. Admission is $2 for adults, $1 for children under eight, and donations toward the continued development of the garden are welcome.

Out on West Airport Road, the **Cruzan Rum Factory,** P.O. Box 218, makes the famous Virgin Islands rum. Guided tours depart daily from the visitors' pavilion Monday through Friday from 8:30 to 11:15 a.m. and 1 to 4:15 p.m. For reservations and information, telephone 809/772-0799.

Estate Whim Plantation Museum (tel. 809/772-0598) is unique among the many former sugar plantations whose ruins dot the island of St. Croix. It was restored by the St. Croix Landmarks Society. The plantation owner's house is different from most typical "great houses" in that it is composed of only three rooms. With three-foot-thick walls made of stone, coral, and molasses, the house is said to resemble a luxurious European château. Also on the premises is a typical woodworking shop, kitchen, gift shop, and a reproduction of a typical town apothecary. The ruins of the plantation's sugar processing plant, complete with restored windmill, remain. The museum is on Centerline Road about two miles east of Frederiksted and is open from 10 a.m. to 5 p.m. daily. Admission is $4 for adults, $1 for children.

SHOPPING IN CHRISTIANSTED: In Christiansted, where the core of my shopping recommendations are found, the emphasis is on hole-in-the-wall boutiques, selling one-of-a-kind merchandise. Handmade items are strong. Of course the same duty-free stipulations, as outlined earlier, apply to your shopping selections in St. Croix.

Knowing it can't compete with Charlotte Amalie, Christiansted has forged its own creative statement in its shops, and by reputation it has now become the "chic spot for merchandise" in the Caribbean. All the shops are easily compressed into half a mile or so, so on a day's tour (or half day) you'll be able to inspect much merchandise before making your purchases.

Little Switzerland, King Street (tel. 809/773-1976), is the unquestioned elite shop on the island for prestige watches, jewelry, china, and crystal. Only the finest watches are sold here, only the best crystal. The watches are priced exactly as they are in Switzerland—which is quite a saving on such name brands as Rolex, Concord, Ebel, Girard-Perregaux, Rado, Vacheron & Constantin, and many others. Incidentally, the owners employ Swiss watchmakers to see that every watch is in perfect adjustment. It's validated for you. Names in chinaware—Rosenthal, Aynsley, Royal Doulton, and Wedgwood—are here. This is also the official Hummel and Lladró shop. In addition, the shop is the largest Waterford importer in the West Indies.

Casa Carlota, Chandler's Wharf Mall (tel. 809/778-8940), a boutique at Gallows Bay, just east of Christiansted, is owned by Jill Yohn, who, with her husband, Michael (formerly in the diplomatic service in Mexico City), works to make the establishment a success. She specializes in high-quality cotton garments for women, presenting a distinctive collection of lightweight fashions that feature fine fabrics, meticulous craftsmanship, and outstanding styling. Included are Anokhi hand-blocked prints from Jaipur, India. You can view the colorful and creative collection in this comfortable, air-conditioned shop.

Finesse Boutique, Company St. (tel. 809/773-5711), is owned by Mrs. Juan Luís, wife of the former governor. It's one of the best places in Christiansted to go for perfume, offering such designer fragrances as Oscar de la Renta, Van

Cleef and Arpel. The store also has a tasteful, elegant selection of designer dresses.

Lion in the Sun, Strand St. (tel. 809/773-1660), is one of the most sophisticated and expensive boutiques on the island, specializing in casuals for both women and men. Designer names are the strong draw, including Sonia Rykiel of France and Byblos of Italy for women. Byblos also designs for men. From England comes work by a designer with an interesting first name, Ghost Iabel. Yohji Yamamoto has fashions for both sexes. The boutique also sells an interesting collection of footwear.

Footprints in the Sand, 6 Company St. (tel. 809/773-8808), has not only an engaging name but also one of the best selections on the island of shoes for children and women. Always style-conscious, it offers fine imports from some talented designers.

Leather Loft, King's Alley (tel. 809/773-2931), bills itself as "the leather boutique." St. Croix's finest leather shop, it displays a stylish assortment of Italian leather including travel wear, attaché cases, portfolios, handbags, and dress and casual shoes, along with small items such as wallets, made of quality leather.

Island Sport, Club Comanche, Strand St. (tel. 809/773-5010), lies on an upper level. It caters to the whole family, offering Merona sportswear for both men and women as well as children. You get a good range of merchandise, including custom St. Croix T-shirts, probably the most popular item sold. Check out their selection of swimwear.

La Parfumerie, 43A Queen Cross St. (tel. 809/778-7799), offers Orlane B-21 and Fashion Bazaar cosmetics, along with a selection of perfumes and fragrances from around the globe. Many of its selections are difficult to come by except at this boutique.

Colombian Emeralds, 43 Queen Cross St. (tel. 809/773-1928), specializes in stunning emeralds, called "the rarest gemstone in the world." Rubies and diamonds also dazzle here. In addition, you face a large selection of other gemstones, including ametrine, blue topaz, opals, and amethyst. The staff will show you their large range of 14-karat gold jewelry, along with the best buys in watches, including Seiko quartz, Omega, and Porsche.

Gem Exposé, 2-3 Strand St. (tel. 809/773-8705), as its name suggests, offers a wide selection of stunning 14- and 18-karat gold jewelry with or without gemstones. It can be custom-made to your specifications. Loose stones are also sold.

Java Wraps, Strand and King St. (tel. 809/773-7529), sells what are perhaps the most avant-garde fashions in St. Croix. The dedicated owner is Twila Wilson, originally from Colorado, who spends six months of the year in Java and Bali overseeing the production of her resort designs made of hand-batiked prints. Twila, who naturally wears a slinky sarong herself, says her "designs and fabrics emphasize cool, easy-to-wear, clean good-looking things." You'll find kimonos, rompers, bikinis, shorts sets, sun dresses, and shirts for men and boys. But the bestseller is the one-size sarong. If you purchase it, you're given a sheet of instructions on how to wear it. Ask to see her antique Dorothy Lamour sarongs. She also has a collection of children's wear.

Only in Paradise, 5 Company St. (tel. 809/773-0331), is a spacious air-conditioned store offering a choice assortment of gifts, such as art glass, linens, real and costume jewelry, and decorative items, as well as pearls however you want them—cultured, freshwater, or baroque.

Violette Boutique, 38 Strand St., Caravelle Arcade (tel. 809/773-2148), is a small department store with many boutique areas carrying lines known worldwide. Besides the largest perfume inventory in St. Croix, including many exclu-

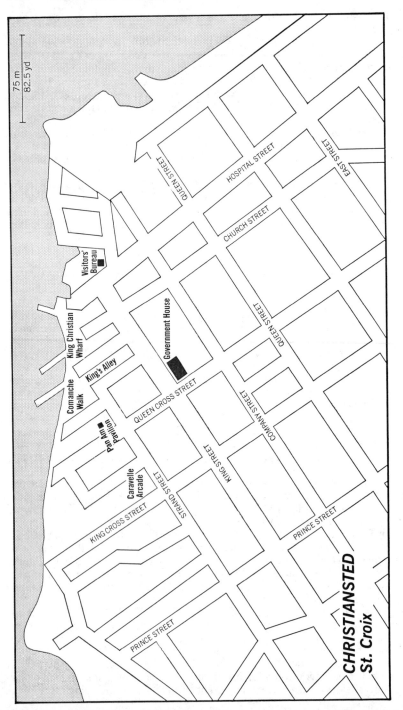

QUEEN STREET

HOSPITAL STREET

EAST STREET

CHURCH STREET

Visitors'
Bureau

King Christian
Wharf

Government House

QUEEN STREET

King's Alley

Comanche
Walk

QUEEN CROSS STREET

COMPANY STREET

Pan Am
Pavilion

Caravelle
Arcade

STRAND STREET

KING STREET

KING CROSS STREET

PRINCE STREET

CHRISTIANSTED
St. Croix

PRINCE STREET

75 m
82.5 yd

sive fragrances and hard-to-find bath lines, they also have the latest in Cartier, Seiko and Yves St. Laurent watches, all at duty-free prices. Clarins and Lancôme cosmetics have a private salon area. Upstairs, Gucci and Fendi accessories and the finest in women's fashions are shown year round.

The **Spanish Main,** Pan Am Pavilion (tel. 809/778-8711), off the Strand, is for those who favor handcrafted fabrics with style and integrity. The owner of this shop puts it most accurately when she says she offers "memories by the yard." You'll find bolts of hand-screened island prints on fabric that is 65% polyester, 35% cotton. The subjects are happy ones—a garden of native flowers, sails against the water, or flying birds against the sky. You can make your own apparel. Ready-to-wear dresses and evening wear are intriguing buys.

Pegasus, 57A Company St. (tel. 809/773-5241), is both the retail outlet and workshop of jewelers. They specialize in diamonds, gold, and gemstones, and can be trusted. In their undulating showcase they offer earrings, pendants, bracelets, and many one-of-a-kind pieces. Tariffs are based on the fluctuating price of gold. They also have a varied selection of handcrafted black coral, pink coral, and pearl jewelry.

Many Hands, Pan Am Pavilion (tel. 809/773-1990), is devoted exclusively to Virgin Islands handcrafts. There is also a collection of local paintings. You're invited to see their year-round "Christmas tree." Children get a lot of attention here, as there's an assortment of custom-made dresses and suits, along with stuffed toys. West Indian spices and teas are also sold, as are shellwork, stained glass, hand-painted china, and ceramic switch plates, as well as other ceramic objects and handmade jewelry.

Happiness Is, Pan Am Pavilion (tel. 809/778-8833). I was drawn to this shop by its catchy name. Inside, you'll find a collection of island-made handcrafts, along with jewelry, including some made out of black coral. There is also a collection of resort-style clothing. Ask for Jean.

Grog and Spirits Liquor Store, 59 King's Wharf (tel. 809/778-8400), in the King Christian Hotel building, is the place to go for choice beverages and snack foods. Larry S. Willett, a longtime resident of St. Croix, can advise you on how much you can take back home with you in the liquor, liqueur, wine, and champagne line. Many times the prices here are so low in comparison with those charged in the States that you will be well off to buy here and pay duty if you go over the U.S. Customs limit. If you're making a trip to Buck Island from the dock next to the grog shop, you can purchase grocery items for a picnic, as well as beer and soda. Cigarettes are also sold here. You can have everything packed in easy-to-carry boxes and delivered to your hotel ready for you to take home.

Larry Willett also operates **Portside Grog & Spirits,** Chandlers Wharf, Port St., Gallows Bay (tel. 809/773-8485), featuring the largest selection of wines available in St. Croix, with a walk-in cooler to ensure that you can always get plenty of cold beverages.

Land of Oz, King's Alley (tel. 809/773-4610), is the most enchanting store for children in the Caribbean. However, owner Joe Feehan says, "The store is for children of all ages." Variety is the keynote of this establishment, with emphasis on unusual items from around the world. An example is games, ranging from wahree, one of the world's oldest games, to the latest advertised on TV. Shipping is available if you want to avoid luggage cramp.

SHOPPING AROUND THE ISLAND: In your visit to the Estate Whim Plantation Museum, east of Frederiksted on Centerline Road, you might also want to browse through the **Whim Gift Shop.** Offering a good selection of gifts, appealing to a wide age spectrum, it has many imported items, but also many that are Cruzan made. Some were personally made for the Whim shop. And as any member of the staff will point out, if you buy something, it all goes to a worthy cause: the upkeep of the museum and the grounds.

On your tour of the island, especially if you're in western St. Croix in the vicinity of Frederiksted, you might want to stop off at the following offbeat shopping recommendations.

St. Croix Leap, Mahogany Rd., Rt. 76 (tel. 809/772-0421), is a fascinating adventure. You can visit the open-air shop, where you can see stacks of rare and beautiful wood being fashioned into tasteful objects. It is a St. Croix Life and Environmental Arts Project, dedicated to the natural environment through manual work, conversation, and self-development. The end result is a fine collection of Cruzan mahogany serving boards, tables, wall hangings, clocks, and sections of unusual pieces crafted into functional objects. They become a form of naturalistic art. St. Croix Leap is two miles up Mahogany Road from the beach north of Frederiksted. Large mahogany signs and sculptures flank the driveway. Visitors should bear to the right to reach the woodworking area and gift shop. For inquiries, write to Leap, P.O. Box 245, Frederiksted, USVI 00841-0245.

THE SPORTING LIFE: Beaches are the big attraction. The drawback is that getting to them from Christiansted, center of most of the hotels, isn't always easy. It can also be expensive, especially if you want to go back and forth during every day of your stay. Of course, you can always rent one of those housekeeping condominiums right on the water.

In Christiansted, if you want to beach it, head for the **Hotel on the Cay.** You'll have to take a ferry to this palm-shaded island.

Cramer Park, at the northeast end of the island, is a special public park operated by the Department of Agriculture. Lined with sea grape trees, the beach also has a picnic area, a restaurant, and a bar.

I highly recommended **Davis Bay** and **Cane Bay** as the type of beaches you'd expect to find on a Caribbean island—that is, palms, white sand, and good swimming, and snorkeling.

Snorkeling and Scuba

Spectacular sponge life, black-coral trees (considered the finest in the West Indies), and steep dropoffs into water near the shoreline have made St. Croix a diver's goal.

Buck Island, with an underwater visibility of more than 100 feet, is the site of the nature trail of the underwater national monument, and it's the major diving target. All the minor and major agencies offer scuba and snorkeling tours to Buck Island. Divers also like to go to **Pillar Coral,** with its columns of coral spiraling up to 25 feet; **North Cut,** one of the tallest, largest coral pinnacles in the West Indies; and **Salt River Dropoff,** plunging to well over 1,000 feet deep, as well as **Davis Bay Dropoff,** with its unique coral and rock mound structures in grotesque shapes.

Your best bed in Christiansted is **Caribbean Sea Adventures,** King's Wharf (tel. 809/773-5922). Write to them at P.O. Box 3881, Christiansted, St. Croix, USVI 00822. They have guided snorkeling tours to Buck Island. You can sail aboard a 40-foot catamaran for a full day including a beach barbecue, costing $40 per adult, $33 per child, or a half day for $30 for adults, $22 for children. The full-day sail in a 36-foot trimaran costs $45 for adults, $30 for children. If you prefer to go by motorboat, both the M/V *Deliverance* and the M/V *Scorpio* make trips from 9:30 a.m. to 1 p.m., costing $21 for adults, $15 for children. Sea Adventures offers the most complete scuba-diving facilities as a NAUI DREAM resort, a PADI, and an SSI facility for everyone from beginners to experienced divers.

Sea Shadows, P.O. Box 505, Cane Bay, St. Croix, USVI 00821 (tel. 809/778-3850), offers complete scuba programs as well as equipment for all purposes, plus snorkeling sets to rent. Tours go to the spectacular dropoff walls of the north shore of St. Croix. Business partners are Ohio-born Libby Wessel and Californian Steve Fordyce. They are involved in every aspect of scuba, including certification. A resort course for beginners costs $50 and spends a lot of time teaching the basics in a three-hour program. A one-tank dive for certified divers goes for $30, and a certification course, designed to make strong swimmers into competent divers, costs $300 and includes eight boat dives. Among dive packages offered are one for certified divers including three guided tours at different locations and one night dive, complete with scuba gear, for $125; and a resort introductory course for nondivers, with a resort introduction class and dive plus three guided dive tours, priced at $125, with all equipment included.

Tennis

Some authorities rate the tennis at the **Buccaneer Hotel** (tel. 809/773-2100, ext. 7360), as the best in the West Indies. This previously recommended hotel offers a choice of eight courts, two lit for night games. They are open to the public, nonguests paying only $4 per person per hour. However, you must call to reserve a court. A tennis pro is available for lessons, and there is also a pro shop.

A notable selection of courts is also found at the **Carambola Golf Club** (tel. 809/778-3800, ext. 254), which has five clay courts, two of which are lit for night games. Open to the public, it charges $20 per hour for nonguests, the fee going up to $28 at night. You must call to reserve. Both a pro shop and a tennis pro for lessons are available.

Golf

St. Croix has the best in the U.S. Virgins. In fact, guests at Caneel Bay Plantation on St. John, or visitors from St. Thomas, often fly over for a day's round. On the island are two 18-hole golf courses.

Carambola Golf Course (tel. 809/778-0747), on the northeast side of St. Croix, was designed by Robert Trent Jones, who called it "the loveliest course I ever designed." The course, formerly the Fountain Valley, with its bamboo, saman trees, and palms in many varieties, has been likened to a botanical garden. Its collection of par 3 holes is known to golfing authorities as the best in the tropics. The site of "Shell's Wonderful World of Golf," Carambola's course record of 66 was set by Tom Kite in 1987. Greens fees in winter are $40 per person for a day, which allows you to play as many holes as you like. The rental of a golf cart is mandatory at $25 per 18 holes. Summer greens fees are reduced to $20 per person for 18 holes, with carts costing $11 per person.

The other major course is at the **Buccaneer Hotel** (tel. 809/773-2100, ext. 7380), an 18-hole course that allows the player to knock the ball over rolling hills right to the edge of the Caribbean. Nonguests who reserve pay $20 greens fees, and carts rent for $10. Two miles east of Christiansted, the Buccaneer is a challenging 6,200-yard course, with spectacular vistas.

A final course is **The Reef** (tel. 809/773-9200), a 3,100-yard 9-hole course charging greens fees of $9, with carts renting for $10. On the east end of the island, the course is at Teague Bay and has its own loyal following. Its longest hole is a 579-yard par 5.

Horseback Riding

Jill's Equestrian Stables, P.O. Box 3251, St. Croix, USVI 00841-3251 (tel. 809/722-2880 or toll free 800/843-3584), is on the sprawling grounds of Sprat Hall Plantation, operated by Jill Hurd, daughter of the dynamic Joyce

Hurd, who runs the fine plantation hotel and restaurant. Jill's stables are known throughout the Caribbean for excellent horses and beautiful trail rides through the rain forest, past sugarmill ruins to the tops of the scenic hills of St. Croix. Beginners are offered reining and cantering instructions along the ride. Jill points out the massive kapok and baobab trees, mongooses, and fascinating termite nests. In season, riders get to sample the unique tropical fruits that grow in the area: sugar apple, soursop, mango, guava, tamarind, limeberry, and genep. Reservations must be made for rides at least a day in advance. Guests staying at Sprat Hall are given a discount on the prices. Jill says the best time to ride is mid-November to mid-December when it's cool and there are fewer riders per journey. September is also a slow season for tourists and therefore a better time if you're seeking a relaxed atmosphere with less hustle-bustle in St. Croix.

Fishing

The fishing grounds at **Lang Bank** are about ten miles from St. Croix. Here you'll find kingfish, wahoo, and dolphin. On light-tackle boats gliding along the reef, the catch is likely to turn up jack or bone fish. At Clover Crest, in Frederiksted, Cruzan anglers fish right from the rocks.

Serious sports fishermen can board the *Ruffian*, a 41-foot Hatteras convertible, available for half- or full-day charters with bait and tackle included. It's anchored at Kings Wharf, and reservations can be made during the day by calling 809/773-7165, or 809/773-0917 at night.

You can also try your luck aboard *Lady Mac-K*, a 32-foot Hatteras with towers that is available for half- or full-day charters, also with bait and tackle provided. Beginners are welcome. During the day, to reserve call 809/778-6118, and at night, 809/778-0487. It departs King's Alley Wharf in Christiansted.

Boating

Most boats move out to Buck Island. St. Croix has many boats for hire at widely varying rates, depending on the craft. **Llewellyn's Charter, Inc.** (tel. 809/773-9027), rents a 36-foot trimaran for sailing, fishing, and diving.

Windsurfing

The best place for this increasingly popular sport is the **Tradewindsurfing Water Sports Center** (tel. 809/773-2035), lying on a small offshore island in Christiansted harbor, part of the Hotel on the Cay. They give lessons and are open daily from 9:30 a.m. to 3:30 p.m. To rent a sailboard costs $15 per hour, $35 per half day, or $45 for a full day.

AFTER DARK: To find the action, you might have to hotel or bar-hop: nightlife in St. Croix is like a floating game of craps.

If he's playing, the one man to seek out is Jimmy Hamilton, Duke Ellington's "Mr. Sax." He and his quartet are a regular feature of St. Croix nightlife. Ask at your hotel to learn if he is appearing locally at the time of your visit.

The big treat of St. Croix is the **Quadrille Dancers.** Try to catch a performance if you can. You have to check at your hotel as to where you are likely to see one of their dances, little changed since plantation days. The women wear long dresses, white gloves, and turbans; and the men are attired in flamboyant shirts, sashes, and tight black trousers. When you've learned their steps, you're invited to join the dancers on the floor.

Bombay Club, 5A King St. (tel. 809/773-1838). The owners have managed to squeeze much miscellany into what is one of the most popular jazz clubs on the island. A large photograph of John Lennon greets visitors near the en-

trance. Other ornaments include original paintings, posters, and an array of tropical plants. You enter through a low stone tunnel and eventually find yourself
near a collection of bars and a courtyard garden with tables and chairs. Live jazz is
presented only on Friday from 9 p.m. to midnight. Drinks cost from $3. The
club is also recommended as a restaurant (see above).

I've also spent many a pleasant evening at the **Moonraker Lounge,** which
often has some very good guitar music. The location is on the balcony upstairs at
the Moonraker Hotel on Queen Cross Street (tel. 809/773-1535). Drinks cost
from $2. Open nightly from 8, Moonraker presents entertainment beginning at
8:30 p.m.

Bogart's Bar and Grill, Pan Am Shopping Center (tel. 809/773-1559). At
the water's edge, at the most distant end of the city's shopping centers, this horseshoe-shaped bar is little more than a celebration of the open air and the balmy
climate. Many of the sightlines focus on a big TV screen. Drinks are strong and
frothy. You can feast on steaks, fresh fish, chicken, or shrimp. These basic ingredients are prepared every style from Cajun to Créole. The homemade pasta dishes
are also good, including linguine with clam sauce. Meals cost from $15, and live
music is presented on Saturday from 6 to 9 p.m. It's open daily from 11 a.m. to
midnight (on Sunday from 5 p.m. to midnight).

Rumors, 54B Company St. (tel. 809/773-6602), can be a lot of fun.
Surrounded by bentwood chairs, hanging fans, potted plants, and raftered pink
ceilings, you can enjoy casual Caribbean dining from an eclectic menu, with
meals costing from $8. They also feature jazz and top-40 bands from the main-
land and several local reggae bands that "jam up" on Friday and Saturday from
10:30 p.m. to 2 a.m. Locals like the eight-by-six-foot maxi-video screen used for
Monday night football and MTV. Beer costs $2.50, and a $3 cover charge is
sometimes made. The place is open daily from 11 a.m. to 3 a.m.

Hondo's Backyard, 53 King St. (tel. 809/773-8187), offers a casual patio
atmosphere attracting people of all ages and all walks of life who come here to
enjoy hamburgers, barbecued chopped beef, hot dogs, or grilled chicken. Meals
cost from $10 and are served daily from 11:30 a.m. to 11 p.m. or midnight. Up-
stairs, a disco draws a more animated crowd of young dancers, converging nightly from 9 p.m. to 3 or 4 a.m. Sometimes there is a small cover charge for the disco
on weekends, but "that depends."

BUCK ISLAND: The crystal-clear water and the white coral sand of Buck Island, a satellite of St. Croix, are legendary. Now the National Park Service has
marked an underwater snorkeling trail. The park covers about 850 acres, including the land area, which has a sandy beach with picnic tables set out and pits for
having your own barbecues. There are two major underwater trails for snorkeling
on the reef, plus many other labyrinths and grottoes for more serious divers.

Slithering through its undergrowth of days of yore, you were likely to run
into Morgan, LaFitte, Blackbeard, or even Captain Kidd.

A barrier reef of elkhorn coral, the calm waters of Buck Island shelter many
reef fish, including the queen angelfish and the smooth trunkfish. Buck Island
lies only 1½ miles off the northeast coast of St. Croix. Uninhabited, it is only a
third of a mile wide and a mile long.

Now a parkland, the island was inhabited for a long time—since the 1750s
in fact. It's been a place of residence and a garden for growing crops. It's also been
used for pasturage, and its timbers have been cut to build houses on St. Croix. It
became a park in 1948, and the goats were eliminated in the 1950s. The attempt
was to return Buck Island to nature, and it's been successful. Even the endangered brown pelicans are producing young here.

Small boats run between St. Croix and Buck Island, charging from $20 to

$35, and snorkeling equipment is furnished. You head out in the morning, and nearly all charters allow an hour and a half of snorkeling and swimming.

One company well versed in transporting nature lovers to the Buck Island underwater trail is **Mile Mark Charters,** King Christian Hotel, 59 King's Wharf, P.O. Box 3045, Christiansted, St. Croix, USVI 00820 (tel. 809/773-2628). Owned and operated by two enterprising brothers, Miles and Mark Sperber, the company offers twice-daily tours to the aquatic wonders of Buck Island. Water-watchers can pick one of two ways to reach the reefs: One is aboard a glass-bottom boat departing twice daily from a point in front of the King Christian Hotel from 9:30 a.m. to 1 p.m. and 1:30 to 5 p.m., costing $20 per person. All snorkeling equipment is included. A more romantic journey is aboard one of the company's wind-powered sloops or catamarans, which for $10 more per person offers the sea breezes and the thrill of wind power to reach the reef. A full-day tour in the sailboat costs $40, and either Miles or Mark is happy to explain the fine points of underwater nature-watching.

Captain Llewellyn (tel. 809/773-9027) has been sailing to Buck Island for more than 20 years, and he'll take you there on *Charis,* a 36-foot trimaran, which is the only charter boat sailing from the east end. Both half-day and full-day sails are arranged, as are sunset sails.

Captain Heinz (tel. 809/773-3161 or 809/773-4041) is an Austrian-born skipper with some 20 years of sailing experience. His trimaran, *Teroro II,* leaves Green Cay Marina "H" Dock at 9 a.m. and 2:30 p.m., usually filled with small groups, never more than 24 passengers, who pay $35 per person. All gear and safety equipment are provided. The captain sailed the first *Teroro* across the Atlantic, and he's not only a skilled sailor, but a very considerate and concerned host while you're aboard. He will even take you around the *outer* reef, which the other guides do not, for an unforgettable underwater experience.

On the island, you can take a hiking trail through the tropical vegetation that covers the island. There are rest rooms, plus a small changing room for visitors.

CHAPTER VI

THE BRITISH VIRGIN ISLANDS

□ □ □

1. ANEGADA

2. JOST VAN DYKE

3. MARINA CAY

4. PETER ISLAND

5. TORTOLA

6. VIRGIN GORDA

7. MOSQUITO ISLAND (NORTH SOUND)

8. GUANA ISLAND

With its small bays and hidden coves, once havens for pirates, the British Virgin Islands are considered among the world's loveliest cruising grounds by the yachting set.

Strung over the northeast corner of the Caribbean are some 40 islands, although skeptics might consider many of these rocks, perhaps cays, and in some cases, "spits of land." Only a trio of the British Virgins are of any significant size: Virgin Gorda (the "Fat Virgin"), Tortola ("dove of peace"), and Jost Van Dyke.

Other islands have such names as Fallen Jerusalem and Ginger. Norman Island is said to have been the prototype for Robert Louis Stevenson's *Treasure Island*. On Deadman Bay, a rocky cay, Blackbeard marooned 15 pirates and a bottle of rum, which gave rise to the ditty.

Columbus came this way in 1493, gazing upon beautiful harbors and green hills, but the British Virgins apparently made little impression on him. Sir Francis Drake sailed into the channel in 1595, seeking Spanish treasure ships. Drake's arrival here was commemorated by having the channel named after him. Less than a generation later the British claimed the island, and the Spanish and Dutch contested it. Tortola was officially annexed by the English in 1672.

The British Virgin chain lies some 60 miles east of Puerto Rico. These islands, craggy and volcanic in origin, are just 15 "air minutes" from St. Thomas. There is regularly scheduled ferry service between St. Thomas and Tortola as well.

The vegetation is varied. In some parts of the British Virgins palms and mangoes grow in profusion, while other places are arid and studded with cactus. Everything depends on the rainfall.

Even though there are predictions that mass tourism is on the way, the British Virgins are still a paradise for escapists. The British Home Office, according to a report I once read, listed them as "the least important place in the British Empire."

GETTING THERE: There are no direct flights from New York to Tortola, but you can make good connections through San Juan, St. Thomas, or St. Croix, each of which is serviced by such major carriers as **American, Pan American,** and **Eastern.**

Your best bet is to take an **American Eagle** flight from San Juan to Tortola. This superb little carrier has daily trips from San Juan to Beef Island/Tortola, and you can also return to San Juan from Tortola on American Eagle. The airline also has daily flights from San Juan to Virgin Gorda and from St. Thomas to Virgin Gorda.

Eastern Metro is another possibility. It has daily flights from San Juan to Beef Island/Tortola, as well as daily flights from San Juan to Virgin Gorda.

If you're on one of the other islands, you can often make good connections on **Air BVI** or **LIAT.** For example, those two lines wing in to Tortola from St. Kitts, St. Maarten, Antigua, and St. Thomas. However, some of these connections are not daily, so check with a travel agent of the airline.

Another flight possibility is **Virgin Island Seaplane Shuttle,** which has three-times-a-week service from St. Croix to Tortola and the same service from St. Thomas.

If you're on Tortola, the most popular trip is to fly to Virgin Gorda. Air BVI makes daily flights from Beef Island/Tortola to Virgin Gorda, a short hop.

From Canada it's best to fly to a U.S. city, such as Miami, and make a connecting flight to San Juan.

Passengers arriving from Europe can best make connections through Antigua. Antigua is serviced directly from London on **British Airways.**

You can also go from Charlotte Amalie (St. Thomas) by **public ferry** to West End and Road Town on Tortola, a quiet, 45-minute voyage along Drake's Channel through the islands. Ferries shuttle between Road Town and Peter Island seven times a day, and there are also daily trips connecting Road Town, Tortola, and Spanish Town on Virgin Gorda.

PRACTICAL FACTS: The British Virgin Islands are a British colony, with their own elected government and a population of about 11,000.

Currency: The U.S. dollar is the legal currency, much to the surprise of arriving Britishers who find no one willing to accept their pounds ("but this is a British colony," they protest, to no avail). Note: All prices in this chapter are given in U.S. dollars.

Documents: U.S. and Canadian citizens need produce only an authenticated birth certificate or a voter registration card to enter the British Virgin Islands. On that evidence, they are welcome for a stay of up to six months, but must possess return or ongoing tickets and show evidence of adequate means of support and prearranged accommodations during their stay.

Electricity: Your U.S.-made appliances can be used here, as the electrical current is 110 volts AC, 60 cycles.

Language: English is the tongue spoken in this British colony.

Medical care: Thirteen doctors practice in Tortola, and there is a hospital with X-ray and laboratory facilities. One doctor practices on Virgin Gorda. Your hotel will put you in touch with the islands' medical staff.

Prohibitions: Unlike some parts of the Caribbean, nudity is an offense punishable by law in the BVI. Drugs, their use or sale, are also strictly prohibited.

Taxes: A government tax of 7% is imposed on all hotel rooms. There is no sales tax. A $5 departure tax is collected from all persons leaving by air, $3 for those departing by sea.

Telephone: You can call the British Virgins from the continental U.S. by dialing area code 809, then seven digits. Each phone number in the islands begins with 49. However, once you are here, you can omit both the 809 and the 49 to make local calls, dialing only the last five digits of the numbers given in this chapter.

Time: Watch your clock. The island operates on Atlantic Standard Time. In the peak winter season, when it's 6 a.m. in the British Virgins, it's only 5 a.m. in Miami. However, when Miami and the rest of the east coast goes on Daylight Saving Time, the clocks are the same in both places.

Weather: The islands, covering about 59 square miles, have a perfect year-round climate, with temperatures of 75° to 85° Fahrenheit, and the prevailing trade winds keep the islands from being too humid. Rainfall is infrequent, but even during the rainy season, precipitation is generally heavy for only about 10 or 15 minutes and stops just as abruptly as it began.

1. ANEGADA

The most northerly and isolated of the British Virgins, 30 miles east of Tortola, Anegada has more than 500 wrecks lying off its notorious Horseshoe Reef. It's different from the other British Virgins in that it's a coral and limestone atoll, flat with a 2,500-foot airstrip.

At its highest point its land mass reaches a height of 28 feet, and hardly appears on the horizon if you're sailing to it. At the northern and western ends of the island are some good beaches, which might be your only reason for coming here.

The population numbers about 250, many of whom have looked for (but not found) the legendary hidden treasure on such sunken ships as the *Paramatta,* which has been at rest for a century. If you decide to come here, know that you're at a remote little corner of the Caribbean: don't expect one frill and be prepared to put up with some hardships, such as mosquitoes.

The only major accommodation on the island is the **Anegada Reef Hotel,** Anegada, B.V.I. (tel. 809/494-3425 Marine Operator and ask for Anegada Reef). As the saying goes, it isn't for everyone. It's one of the most remote little places recommended in this guide, and guests who stay here are in effect "hiding out." It's not for first-time visitors to the Caribbean either, and attracts those who can settle for its barebone life in one of 12 motel-like rooms with only the simplest of amenities. The beach is not that desirable but it's still a favorite of the yachting set, who like to stop off here to enjoy hospitality provided by Lowell Wheatley. Naturally in such an isolated place guests book in here on the American plan, paying $105 daily in a single and $160 in a double in winter. *Off-season tariffs on the AP are $95 daily in a single, $150 in a double.* Fishing, both inshore and deep sea, along with diving, snorkeling, and of course swimming, are possible, even a little beachcombing. On party nights Mr. Wheatley brings in a fungi band, or he might stage a barbecue right on the beach with tall rum punches. If you're going over just for the day, you can order lunch at the beach bar. The cook specializes in conch fritters. At night, barbecued lobster is a favorite at dinner. In addition to lobster you'll find fresh fish, beef, and poultry, along with the inevitable conch. If you're over touring for the day and want to dine at the Reef, drop in early and make a reservation. Dinner, at $16 to $24, is served at 7 p.m.

While on the island, you may want to visit **Neptune's Treasure** (tel. 809/494-3425), a seaside restaurant run by the Soares family, who serve fresh fish and fresh lobster they catch themselves. One reader writes, "I had my first dogfish

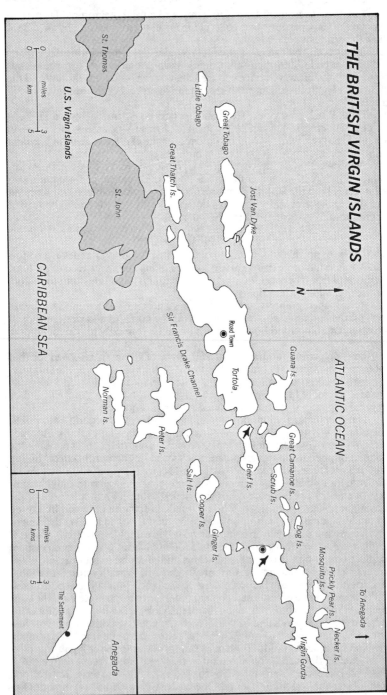

THE BRITISH VIRGIN ISLANDS

ATLANTIC OCEAN

CARIBBEAN SEA

U.S. Virgin Islands

St. Thomas

St. John

Little Tobago

Great Tobago

Great Thatch Is.

Jost Van Dyke

Road Town

Tortola

Sir Francis Drake Channel

Guana Is.

Norman Is.

Peter Is.

Beef Is.

Scrub Is.

Great Camanoe Is.

Dog Is.

Sail Is.

Cooper Is.

Ginger Is.

Mosquito Is.

Prickly Pear Is.

Necker Is.

Virgin Gorda

To Anegada

Anegada

The Settlement

N

shark at this restaurant, and it was great!" Lunch costs $5, and dinner goes for $8 to $20. The place is open seven days a week for breakfast, lunch, and dinner from 8 a.m. to 9 p.m. The people are helpful in explaining to you how to explore their island. Their radio contact in the B.V.I. is on Tortola Radio, Channel 16 or 68.

The family also rents tents with single or double air mattresses if you'd like to stay on the island—and don't mind roughing it a bit. You can take a taxi to one of their sandy beaches and go snorkeling along their reefs.

2. JOST VAN DYKE

This rugged island, on the seaward side of Tortola, was probably named for some Dutch pirate. About 130 people live in four square miles. On the south shore of this mountainous island are some good beaches at White Bay and Great Harbour. In the 1700s a Quaker colony settled here to develop sugarcane plantations. One of the colonists, William Thornton, won a worldwide competition to design the Capitol in Washington, D.C.

Smaller islands surround the place, including Little Jost Van Dyke, the birthplace of Dr. John Lettsome, founder of the London Medical Society.

The island has only a handful of places to stay but several dining choices, as it's a popular stopping-over point for the yachting set.

WHERE TO STAY: A perfect retreat for escapists, the **Sandcastle,** White Bay, Jost Van Dyke, B.V.I. (tel. 809/494-3502), is a four-villa colony with cottages built in an octagonal style and surrounded by flowering shrubbery and bougainvillea. Nestled among the palms, these individual cottages take advantage of the tropical breezes and gain every inch of the view. This is a small, personalized place, catering to only a handful of guests. You're allowed to mix your own drinks at the beachside bar, the Soggy Dollar, but you'll also have to keep your own tab. Visiting yachting people often drop in here for a while, enjoying the beachside informality and ordering a drink called a "Painkiller." In the guest book you'll find this quotation: "I thought places like this only existed in the movies." In winter, two people can stay here on the full-board plan at a cost of $240 per day; a single person pays $180. *Also on the full-board plan, a couple in summer need pay only $180 per day, and a single costs $150.* Tax and service are added to all tariffs. The manager will pick up guests at West End in Tortola. Fly to Beef Island and take a taxi from there. Or else you can take the ferry from St. Thomas, which goes to the West End three times a day. There's a transportation charge for stays of less than six nights.

Sandy Ground, Box 594, West End, Tortola, B.V.I. (tel. 809/494-3391), offers eight villas with self-sufficient housekeeping units of the type you might see along Spain's Costa del Sol. The estates, as it is called, is built on a 17-acre hill site on the eastern part of Jost Van Dyke. The colony rents out two- and three-bedroom villas. One of my favorites was constructed on a cliff that seems to hang about 60 or so feet over a good beach. If you've come all this way to reach this tiny outpost you might as well stay a week, which are the rates quoted. In winter, two people are charged $950 weekly, each additional person paying another $150. *However, in summer, the charge is lowered to $750 for two people weekly, with each additional person paying only $100.* The airy villas are each privately owned, and each unit is fully equipped with such necessities as refrigerators and stoves. They have their own electric generator. The managers help guests with boat rentals and water sports.

WHERE TO EAT: Explorers on Jost Van Dyke don't have to bring a packed lunch before heading out. The previously recommended **Sandcastle** on White

Bay (tel. 809/494-3502), has good food, but it does require a reservation, as supplies in the kitchen are limited. At night, you dine by candlelight right on the beach. Naturally, attire is casual. Lunch costs from $10, and dinner, featuring fresh fish when available, is from $25. Try rack of lamb, stuffed grouper, or duck à l'orange. Lunch is served daily at 1:30 p.m. and dinner is offered at 7:30 p.m.

Yachtsmen like to drop in at **Ira's-by-the-Sea,** at Little Harbour (no phone). Perhaps that's because a free welcoming drink awaits the captain (the rest of us have to pay). The food is simply prepared and inexpensive. Conch is always available, prepared in several ways. A fish dinner of whelks is more expensive. A catch of the day is always featured, and it might even be lobster. Then, the price "depends." Otherwise count on spending around $20 with drinks. Lunch is served from noon to 3 p.m.; dinner, from 7 to 9:30 p.m. Ira's is open seven days a week.

Abe's by the Sea is a native bar and restaurant on Little Harbour where the cook knows how to please the sailors with a menu of fish, lobster, conch, and chicken. Prices are low too. Most diners escape for around $20, money well spent, especially when a fungi band entertains you with its music and plays for dancing. For the price of the main course, you get peas and rice, along with coleslaw and beans, plus dessert. Sometimes Abe's has a pig roast, and these turn out to be festive nights. Approaching the harbor, you'll see Abe's restaurant on your right. Seven days a week, lunch is served from noon to 3 p.m. and dinner from 7 to 9:30 p.m. For reservations, call Abe's, VHF Channel 16 Marine Radio.

3. MARINA CAY

Near Beef Island, Marina Cay is a tiny islet of six acres. Its only claim to fame was as the setting of the Robb White book *Our Virgin Island,* which was filmed with Sidney Poitier and John Cassavetes. The island lies only five minutes away by launch from Trellis Bay, adjacent to Beef Island International Airport.

The reason I'm mentioning such a tiny cay is because it's the site of a cottage hotel, previewed below:

Marina Cay Hotel, Marina Cay, B.V.I. (tel. 809/494-2174; for reservations, write to P.O. Box 76, Road Town, Tortola, B.V.I., or First Resorts International, 116 Radio Circle, Mount Kisco, NY 10599, tel. 914/241-8770 or toll free 800/235-3303). This small hotel, opened in 1960 and extensively renovated, still has its original charm and conviviality. It can house 24 guests in units that include chalets, villas, and A-frames, all overlooking a fine reef and Sir Francis Drake Channel, dotted with islands. Marina Cay is a tropical garden, with frangipani, almond, flamboyant, tamarind, hibiscus, oleander, and bougainvillea in abundance. Dining is casual, with a good cuisine featuring continental and West Indian dishes. Winter rates are $235 to $395 per day in doubles, MAP. *Summer rates are 30% less.* Activities include snorkeling on adjacent Mother Turtle Reef, sailing on Sunfish, windsurfers, and the J-24 sloop, scuba diving (with certification courses taught by a resident divemaster), castaway picnics on secluded beaches, and deep-sea fishing.

4. PETER ISLAND

Half of the 1,050-acre island, with its good marina and docking facilities, is devoted to the yacht club described below. A ferry makes the run across Sir Francis Drake Channel to Peter Island. Leaving from the CSY Dock, the craft takes from 20 minutes to half an hour. The CSY Dock is approached before you reach Road Town on the road from Beef Island Airport. Beach facilities are found at palm-fringed Deadman Bay, which faces the Atlantic but is protected by a reef.

The island is so private that except for an occasional mason at work and the endless vegetation, about the only creature a guest will encounter is an iguana or a wild cat whose ancestors were abandoned generations ago by shippers (they are said to have virtually eliminated the rodent population).

Peter Island Hotel and Yacht Harbour, P.O. Box 211, Road Town, Tortola, B.V.I. (tel. 809/494-2561 or toll free 800/346-4451; for reservations, write Peter Island, 220 Lyon St., Grand Rapids, MI 49503) is a maritime village resort on a 675-acre site created by Peter Smedvig, the Norwegian shipowner, and now owned by Amway of Michigan. In eight harborfront units, 32 air-conditioned rooms are rented. The upper-floor units have front and rear balconies, and the lower-floor rooms have private patios, each with a view. Special touches include built-in refrigerators, his-and-hers washbasins, and pull-out magnifying mirrors. To add to the room count, 20 units were constructed overlooking Deadman Bay. In all, there are five beachfront villas, each with four rooms. They were built from locally quarried stones in blues, sand-bleached grays, taupes, and browns.

The beach-house units, on the MAP, cost from $450 for two people. It's cheaper for two guests to stay at one of the harborfront units. There MAP rates are $380 daily. *In summer, MAP tariffs are reduced: two persons pay $290 to $340 daily.* Special package plans are also offered. The Crow's Nest, overlooking Deadman Bay, crowns the peak above the hotel. This four-bedroom villa, with its own saltwater swimming pool, is rented for $2,400 for up to eight people per day in high season, *for $2,000 off-season.* In addition, Peter Island offers Sprat Bay villa on the water's edge. It has three bedrooms, two baths, a kitchen, a terrace, and a living room, with a rustic wooden interior. The daily AP rate for Sprat Bay is $800 for up to six people. Naturally, there is a main swimming pool, and the club's marina facilities are considered among the best equipped in the Virgin Islands. Horseback riding, tennis, and sailing are easily arranged, as are such water sports as scuba-diving, snorkeling, and skiing. An international clientele has included actors Nick Nolte, Robert Shaw, and Jacqueline Bisset, who stayed here during the filming of *The Deep.*

For dining, the **Peter Island Hotel and Yacht Harbour** (tel. 809/494-2561) serves food that is considered among the best in the British Virgins. Even if you aren't staying in one of the previously recommended accommodations, you can go over just for the cuisine. Boats depart from CSY Baughers Bay at 10 a.m. and noon for lunch and at 6:30 p.m. for dinner, when reservations are required. Lunch is offered daily at the Beach Restaurant from 12:30 to 2 p.m., and dinner is presented in the main dining room nightly from 7:30 to 9:30. Barbecue lunches and dinners are featured on the beach, or you can eat in the main dining room decorated in a nautical motif. The prix-fixe dinner, served nightly except Saturday, costs $30, plus service. Both European and local chefs prepare specialties. On Saturday evening, a big smörgåsbord is prepared, the accent on local seafood. Meat or grilled fish is served from the rôtisserie. A prime rib is carved right at your table, and you can enjoy one of the best and most varied wine lists in the Virgin Islands, with some rare clarets. In season a jacket is required in the main dining room.

5. TORTOLA

On the southern shore of this 24-square-mile island, **Road Town** is more like a village. Still, it's the capital of the British Virgin Islands, the seat of Government House and other administrative buildings. The landfill at Wickhams Cay, a 70-acre town center development and marina in the harbor, has brought in a massive yacht-chartering business and has transformed the sleepy capital into more of a bustling, sophisticated center.

On the same southern coast as Road Town, Tortola is characterized by rugged mountain peaks which contain yellow cedar and frangipani, among other foliage. On the northern coast, however, are white sandy beaches, banana trees, mangoes, and clusters of palms.

No visit to Tortola is complete without a trip to **Mount Sage,** a national park rising 1,780 feet. Here on its slopes you'll not only find traces of a primeval rain forest, but you can enjoy a picnic, overlooking neighboring islets and cays. The mountain is reached by heading west from Road Town.

Also west from Road Town for about 4½ miles, you come to **"The Dungeon,"** the island's oldest fort, erected by the Dutch in 1640. Botanists should look for the rare wild West Indian cherry tree growing on the unkempt grounds.

Nearby you can view the ruins (and I mean ruins) of **Thornton Great House.** Here lived Dr. William Thornton, the Quaker I've mentioned previously who won the competition to design the Capitol in Washington, D.C.

Close to Tortola's eastern end, **Beef Island** is the site of the main airport for passengers arriving in the British Virgins. The airstrip is 3,600 feet long and can accommodate the Avro 748 turbo-jet 48-seaters.

The tiny island is connected to Tortola by the Queen Elizabeth Bridge, which the queen dedicated in 1966. The one-lane bridge spans the 300-foot channel which divides the little island from its bigger sister, Tortola. On the north shore of Beef Island is a good beach, Long Bay.

GETTING AROUND: In this remote part of the Caribbean, getting around can be a bit of a problem. However, there are **taxis,** which meet every arriving flight. Your hotel can also call a taxi, and one will soon arrive at your doorstep. The fare from the Beef Island Airport to Long Bay is $7 per person. A tour lasting 2½ hours costs $35 for one to three persons. To call a taxi in Road Town, dial 809/494-2322, in Beef Island, 809/495-2378.

Car Rentals

Driving in the B.V.I.'s is only for those who like hairpin turns on a Coney Island Cyclone terrain. You'll need a Canadian or American driver's license, and in addition, you must pay $10 at police headquarters for a temporary British Virgins driving permit, good for three months.

Both **Budget Rent-a-Car** and **Avis** operate out of Road Town on Tortola, offering cars for $35 to $45 per day or $210 to $270 per week in winter. Summer rates are $24 to $35 daily, $135 to $180 weekly. Budget is at 11 Wickhams Cay, Road Town, Tortola (tel. 809/494-2639), and Avis has its offices opposite Prospect Reef Resort (tel. 809/494-2832).

Driving is on the left, as I'd like to remind the policeman who nearly killed me recently as he came speeding down the pike on the right!

Sightseeing Tours

This is probably your best bet for taking a look at Tortola. **Travel Plan Tours** (tel. 809/494-2348) will pick you up at your hotel (a minimum of four persons required) and take you on a 2½-hour tour of the island, for $30 per person. At night you can call 809/494-2154 and arrange for a morning tour.

Bicycle Rentals

If you can handle the rugged terrain, you'll find single and tandem bicycles for rent at **Hero's Rental,** P.O. Box 372, Main St., Tortola, B.V.I. (tel. 809/494-3536) in Road Town in Tortola. Rates start at $4 per hour.

WHERE TO STAY: Most of the places are small—"mom and pop" operations —and informality is the keynote at these inns. My favorites follow:

Frenchman's Cay Hotel & Yacht Club, P.O. Box 1054, West End, Tortola,

B.V.I. (tel. 809/495-4844), is a luxury resort on the windward side of the little island of Frenchman's Cay that is connected to Tortola by a bridge. Its location provides it with year-round cooling breezes and panoramic views of the Sir Francis Drake Channel and the outer Virgins. The hotel, set in 12 acres of handsomely landscaped waterfront land, has one- and two-bedroom detached villas, elegantly furnished, each with a shady terrace, a full kitchen, a dining room, and a sitting room with a queen-size sofa bed suitable for two persons. The two-bedroom units have two full baths. *In summer, one-bedroom villas, housing up to four guests, cost from $73 to $94 per day. Two-bedroom villas, holding up to six people, cost $105 for three, going up to $134 for six.* Winter charges in one-bedroom villas are $130 for single occupancy, $140 for use as a double. Three people in a two-bedroom unit pay $195 per day, four occupants paying $210. Additional guests using the queen-size sofa beds are billed at the rate of $10 per person per day.

The Clubhouse restaurant and lounge bar, overlooking the freshwater pool, is between the beach and the tennis court. It's a true island structure, with a distinctive open-beam roof. Lunch is served from 11 a.m. to 2:30 p.m. and dinner from 6:30 to 9 p.m. You can enjoy a drink while you watch the chef prepare one of the barbecue specialties of the restaurant. The hotel can arrange day sailing, scuba diving, fishing tours, and horseback riding, as well as island tours and car rental. For reservations or information, get in touch with E and M Associates, 45 W. 45th St., New York, NY 10036 (tel. 212/719-4898 or toll-free 800/223-9832).

Long Bay Hotel, P.O. Box 433, Road Town, Tortola, B.V.I. (tel. 809/495-4252 or toll free 800/537-4252), on the north shore, about ten minutes from the West End, is a low-rise hotel complex set in a 50-acre estate with nearly a mile of white sand beach. It is the first port of entry to Tortola. Escapists who want a far-away corner of a half-forgotten island come here. Units are available in a wide range of styles, shapes, and sizes. Suites, including regular and superior, as well as cottages are scattered up the side of a hill planted with such flowery shrubbery as hibiscus. Cottages come with two bedrooms, a bath and shower, a kitchen, and a living room overlooking the ocean. Some elevated beachfront rooms are set at the edge of the white sands, with twin beds, a bathroom, and a kitchenette, as well as a deck overlooking the ocean with a patio at beach level. In winter on the EP, these rent for $160 double, $140 single. *In summer, rates are $95 double, $85 single.* In winter, suites range in price from $95 to $150 for double occupancy, EP. Cottages housing four persons peak at $200 daily, *this rate being lowered to $120 in summer. Doubles can book a suite here in summer at tariffs ranging from $70 to $90 and singles for $55 to $85.* Suites, called hillside studios, are air-conditioned and have a dressing area with vanity.

The beach restaurant offers breakfast and luncheon and, in the winter, informal à la carte suppers. The Garden Restaurant serves dinner by reservation only, and the food is of excellent quality. Boats can also be rented for sailing, diving, and exploring the out islands. If the surf is too rough for you, an oceanside saltwater swimming pool adjoins the beach house (which was once a distillery, incidentally).

The Sugar Mill, P.O. Box 425, Apple Bay, Tortola, B.V.I. (tel. 809/495-4355 or toll free 800/223-9815 for reservations), is set in lush foliage, on the north side of Tortola, a long $24 haul from the airport. Built on the site of a 300-year-old sugar mill, the cottage colony sweeps down the hillside to its own little beach, with jasmine, oleander, hibiscus, avocados, plantains, citrus trees, gardenias, bougainvillea, mangoes, bananas, pineapples, and sugar apples brightening the grounds. The estate is owned by Jeff and Jinx Morgan, formerly of San Francisco, who are travel, food, and wine writers. They provide a warm greeting and atmosphere, and make one feel immediately welcome.

Comfortable apartments climb up the hillside. At the center is a circular swimming pool for those who don't want to go down to the beach. Accommodations are contemporary and beautifully thought out, ranging from suites and cottages to studio apartments, all self-contained with kitchenettes and private terraces with views. In winter, mid-December to mid-April, standard singles rent for $100 standard doubles for $110. Deluxe accommodations are priced at $150 in singles, $160 in doubles, $175 in triples, and $190 in quads. *Summer rates in standard units are $70 in singles, $80 in twins. For deluxe units, singles pay $85, doubles $95, triples $110, and quads $125.* Prices are quoted on the EP. The four suites rented are each suitable for four family members. Ceilings are sloped, made of native lumber, and to keep the sea breezes moving, you can turn on a ceiling fan. Lunch is served down by the beach, and dinner in the old Sugar Mill Room, its stone walls decorated with Haitian paintings (see my dining recommendations). Breakfast is on the terrace. The bars are open all day, and snorkeling equipment can be used free. The estate is closed in August and September.

Treasure Isle Hotel, P.O. Box 68, Road Town, Tortola, B.V.I. (tel. 809/494-2501 or toll free 800/221-4588 for reservations), is the most complete and central resort on Tortola, built at the edge of the capital on 15 acres of hillside overlooking a marina. The core of the hotel is a rather splashy and colorful lounge and swimming pool area, with 40 rooms, all with phones and some with TV, on two levels along the hillside terraces, a third level being occupied by condominiums. Winter EP rates are $100 to $110 daily in singles, $105 to $115 in doubles, and $112 to $130 in triples, with an extra $30 per person charged for MAP. *Summer prices are $65 daily single, $75 double, and $87 triple, with $28 extra per person charged for MAP.*

Adjoining the lounge and pool area is a covered open-air dining room overlooking the harbor. The cuisine is respected here, with barbecue, carvery, and full à la carte menus offered at dinner, 7 to 9 p.m. daily except Wednesday. On Wednesday, a West Indian buffet is served, including callaloo soup and fish ceviche as appetizers, followed by conch rôtis, barbecued fish, roast beef and Yorkshire pudding, papaya and cheese, plantain, sweet potatoes, and much more. That night, entertainment and dancing are also part of the fun. The hotel has a fully equipped dive facility, handling beginning instruction and ranging up to full certification courses. Daily package tours are offered to beaches and secluded islands nearby, and there are also dive and other packages offered for your entire vacation.

Prospect Reef Resort, P.O. Box 104, Road Town, Tortola, B.V.I. (tel. 809/494-3311 or toll free 800/223-0888 for reservations), British-owned, is the largest and most up-to-date resort in the British Virgins. From this village built on a coral reef, panoramic views of Sir Francis Drake Channel unfold. Attractively modern buildings have been set tastefully on landscaped grounds of 38 acres, opening onto a bustling little private harbor. Built as condominiums, rental units consist of suites, town houses, villas, and apartments. In winter, guests on the EP are charged $110 to $170 in a single or double. A two-bedroom villa costs $400 daily for four persons. Breakfast and dinner carry a supplement of $39 per person daily. *In off-season, EP singles or doubles cost $60 to $100. Two-bedroom villas suitable for four persons go for $250 daily.* Accommodations include private balconies or patios, private baths or shower, good-size living and dining areas, plus separate bedrooms or sleeping lofts. There's a pool to swim in, another to dive in, plus sea pools for snorkeling or just fish watching. Six tennis courts with lights are available to buffs. There's also a pitch-and-putt course. Food at the Prospect Restaurant, a combination of continental specialties and island favorites, was praised by *Gourmet* magazine. Diners usually begin their meals with an apéritif at the Drop Inn Bar by Prospect Harbour. The chef's specialties include duckling in orange sauce and lobster in champagne. Count on spending about $25 at dinner, if you don't order lobster. The water-sports desk can fill you in on what's available in day sailing, dinghy rental, snorkeling, scuba-diving, or sports fishing.

The Moorings/Mariner Inn, P.O. Box 139, Road Town, Tortola, B.V.I. (tel. 809/494-2332, or toll free 800/835-8530 for reservations), is the Caribbean's only complete yachting resort, outfitted with 100 sailing yachts, some worth around $500,000. On an eight-acre resort, the inn was obviously designed with the yachting crowd in mind. These yachting people find not only support facilities and service but also shoreside accommodations: lanai hotel rooms, a dockside restaurant, Mariner Bar, a swimming pool, a tennis court, a beach club, a gift shop, and a dive shop that has underwater video cameras available for rent. In winter, you can stay in a single room on the EP for $80 per day or in a double for $105. *Off-season, singles are lowered to $55, and doubles go for $65.* Suites cost $135 in winter, *$85 in summer.* Rooms are spacious and all have kitchenettes.

WHERE TO EAT: Most guests dine at their hotels, but if you want to break the monotony of that, I have a few suggestions.

Sugar Mill Room, Apple Bay (tel. 809/495-4355). You dine in an informal room which was transformed from a three-centuries-old sugar mill (see my hotel recommendations). Your hosts are Jeff and Jinx Morgan, formerly of San Francisco. They know much about food and wine. Together they write a monthly column, "Cooking for Friends" in *Bon Appétit,* have published their recent cookbook, and have another ready to go. Works by Haitian painters have been hung on the old stone walls of the dining room, forming a gallery of primitive art. Big copper basins once used in the distilling of rum have been planted with tropical flowers. Before going to the dining room, once part of the old boiling house, I suggest a visit to the charming little bar, everything open air in the true West Indian fashion. Jinx Morgan supervises the dining room and is an imaginative cook herself. One of their most popular creations, published in *Bon Appétit,* is a curried banana soup. They are likely to prepare delectable chicken breasts in a number of ways, seafood Créole, lobster crêpes, and a cold rum soufflé. Everything here is homemade, including many island specialties. Ingredients for the crisp salads come mostly from the hotel's extensive herb and vegetable garden. Breakfast begins at 8 a.m. (the house specialty: rum French toast), lunch is served on the beach from noon to 2 p.m., and dinner in the dining room begins at 7:30 p.m. At dinner, the cost is around $25, and you must call for a reservation.

The Cloud Room (tel. 809/494-2821) provides a unique dining experience in Tortola. This restaurant and bar sits at the top of Butu Mountain, overlooking Road Town. When weather permits, which is practically every day of the year, the roof slides back, allowing you to dine under the stars. The catch is that the road there is bad (and there's no place to park), so the owner, Paul Wattley, prefers to arrange to pick you up when you make your reservation for dinner, served nightly from 7:30 to 9:30 p.m. For anywhere from $20 to $30, including wine, you'll get a selection of juicy sirloin steaks, fresh fish in season, shish kebab (the house specialty), and shrimp in Créole sauce. The restaurant is open for dinner only, daily except Sunday from November to May.

Brandywine Bay Restaurant, P.O. Box 151, Road Town (tel. 809/495-2301). Marti and Ben Brown over the years have developed quite a few fans in the Virgin Islands. You'll find them in a garden-like atmosphere on the south shore of Tortola, overlooking Drake's Channel, about ten minutes by taxi from Road Town. The setting may be romantic, but it is mainly the food that attracts the patrons. Very fresh ingredients are used, and the menu is both West Indian and continental. That is, you might prefer cracked conch Bahamian style, but you can also get a perfect Wiener schnitzel or a veal piccata. If the caviar crêpes don't tempt you, perhaps the chicken Kiev will. Meals cost from $20, and are served nightly except Sunday from 6:30 to 9:30 p.m. Always make a reservation.

If you're staying in one of the efficiency apartments on Tortola and don't want to cook, I suggest you go over to **Carib Casseroles,** on Main Street, near the post office in Road Town (tel. 809/494-3271). Even *The New York Times* praised its "excellent frozen meals," which are called "Meals on Keels." Persons aboard yachts who don't want to be galley slaves drop in here, selecting from a choice of 30 international dishes, including such West Indian specialties as beef and green banana curry, red snapper in fresh lime butter, shrimp with garlic, and Cuban picadillo. Meals begin at $15. Some of these dishes were featured in *Cuisine* magazine. You can purchase these fast-food pouches which you cook by dropping in hot water. If you're in town for lunch or dinner, you can go over to the little garden restaurant and "splice the mainbrace" with a rum punch. You can enjoy memorable soups, including Créole fisherman's stew, tomato and eggplant, peanut Créole, and pumpkin. For dessert, try the sugar Bum Bum pie (with custard and cream). The garden restaurant is likely to be closed for two months beginning in August. Otherwise, hours are 11 a.m. to 3 p.m. and 7 to 10 p.m. daily except Sunday.

The Pub, Fort Burt Marina (tel. 809/494-2608) stands at water's edge, and locals on Tortola like to go here for a sundowner. It's a British-style pub in the Fort Burt Marina complex, with a good view of the sailing scene. Boat owners like to visit at opening time, 10:30 a.m., for drinks, and a few might make it to the midnight curfew, depending on how thirsty they are or how long at sea. Lunches are simply prepared and inexpensive, featuring dishes such as chicken and chips, hamburgers, and a special of the day. At dinner there is more of a choice, with shrimp, chicken, and prime ribs flown in from Puerto Rico on Thursday. Fresh local fish includes dolphin, swordfish, and snapper. Meals cost around $15. Lunch is served from noon to 2:30 p.m., and dinner hours are 7 to 9:30 p.m. daily. The atmosphere of the Pub is relaxed, dress is casual, and reservations are not required. On Friday and Saturday nights, entertainment is provided all year with dancing to some of B.V.I.'s most popular bands, and there is a dartboard for daily use.

EXCURSIONS FOR THE DAY: If you've decided to risk everything and navigate the roller-coaster hills of the B.V.I., then you need a destination. **Cane Garden Bay** is one of the choicest pieces of real estate on the island, long discovered by the sailing crowd. Its white sandy beach is a cliché of Caribbean charm, with sheltering palms. It is nearly always semi-deserted. No one crowds you here.

Rhymer's, P.O. Box 570, Cane Garden Bay (tel. 809/495-4639) is the place to go for food and entertainment. The success of the place depends very much on James E. Rhymer himself, who, to judge from the size of him, likes his own food a lot. Skippers of any kind of craft are likely to stock up on supplies here; but you can also order cold beer and refreshing rum drinks. Conch and whelk show up regularly on the bill of fare. If you're tired of fish, maybe James will make you some of his barbecued spareribs. The beach bar and restaurant is open seven days a week from 8 a.m. to 9 p.m., serving not only breakfast, but lunch and dinner, which costs from $18 up. On some nights a steel drum band will entertain the mariners, and maybe the host himself will show you what a limbo dance is all about! Ice and freshwater showers are available (there are towels to rent as well), and you can ask about renting Sunfish and windsurfers.

Skyworld, Ridge Rd. (tel. 809/494-3567), is all the rage, certainly the worthiest excursion on the island. At one of the loftiest peaks on the island, a breezy 1,337 feet, it offers views of both the U.S. and British Virgins. The french fries and onion rings have been praised by *Gourmet* magazine. If you're here at sundowner time, order some conch fritters, which are considered the best on the island. Guests come here for the view at lunch and dinner, when an elegant, classic French-inspired menu is offered. Main dishes include lamb, quail, and fresh fish. Lunch costs from $6, dinner from $18. Hours are from 10 a.m. to 10 p.m. daily. Reservations are recommended for dinner.

For the best and most authentic West Indian cuisine, check out **Mrs. Scatliffe's Restaurant,** Carrot Bay (tel. 809/495-4556). She offers meals at her island home. Some of the vegetables you'll be served come right from her garden. For dinner, served from 7 to 9 p.m. daily, you must always call in advance so she'll be prepared for you, but you can just pop in for lunch, from noon to 2 p.m. daily. Meals cost from $20. You can begin with one of the best daiquiris on the island, made from fresh tropical fruit. While munching a breadfruit stick, you'll be told what's cooking, perhaps a spicy papaya soup to begin your repast, followed by chicken in a coconut shell, even fresh "old wife," a fish. After dinner, your hostess's family will join her for a fungi performance for your entertainment.

WHERE TO SHOP:
Most of the shops are on Main Street, Road Town, on Tortola, but know that the British Virgins have no duty-free-port shopping. British goods are imported without duty, and the wise shopper will be able to find some good buys among these imported items, especially in English china. In general, store hours are from 9 a.m. to 4 p.m. Monday to Friday, 9 a.m. to 1 p.m. Saturday.

The Cockle Shop, Main St., Road Town (tel. 809/494-2555), carries jewelry handmade in the British Virgins, including many gift and souvenir items, and pieces of Wedgwood, too.

Go to **Past and Present,** over the J&C Department Store (tel. 809/494-2747), to see china and pewter, as well as a collection of antique silver. They sell some unusual books, too.

The **Shipwreck Shop,** Main St., Road Town (tel. 809/494-2587), depending on what "washed up" on its premises, usually has a collection of West Indian handcrafts, including placemats, sandals, grass rugs, straw bags, shell jewelry, and wooden bowls, all for sale in one of the more traditional structures in Road Town.

Pusser's Company Store, at Main St. and Waterfront Rd. in Road Town (tel. 809/494-2467) is equally divided between a long, mahogany-trimmed bar accented with many fine nautical artifacts and a souvenir store selling T-shirts, postcards, and upmarket gift items. Pusser's Rum is one of the best-selling items here, or perhaps you'd prefer polished brass mementoes of your visit.

Sunny Caribbee Spice Company, Main St., Road Town (tel. 809/494-2178), in a lovely old West Indian building which was the first hotel on Tortola, specializes in Caribbean spices, seasonings, teas, condiments, and handcrafts. Most of the products are blended and packaged on the island. You can buy two world-famous specialties here: West Indian hangover cure and Arawak love potion. A Caribbean cosmetics collection, Sunsations, is also available, including herbal bath gels, West Indian bay rum, island perfume, sunshine lotions and the like.

Little Denmark, Main St., Road Town (tel. 809/494-2458), is your best bet for famous names in gold and silver jewelry and china: Spode, Royal Copen hagen, and Georg Jensen. Here you'll find many of the well-known designs from Scandinavian countries. There's also a collection of watches but not at duty-free prices.

THE SPORTING LIFE: Tortola boasts the largest fleet of bareboat sailing charter boats in the world, and is also one of the finest diving areas anywhere.

Snorkeling and Scuba

Marina Cay is known for its good snorkeling beach, and the one at Cooper Island is another honey. Divers are attracted to Anegada Reef, which is the site of many shipwrecks, including the *Paramatta* and the *Astrea*. However, the one dive site in the British Virgins that lures them over from St. Thomas is the wreckage of the R.M.S. *Rhone,* near the western point of Salt Island. *Skin Diver* magazine called this "the world's most fantastic ship wreck dive." It teems with beautiful marine life and coral formations, and was featured in the motion picture *The Deep.*

Baskin in the Sun, P.O. Box 108, Road Town (tel. 809/494-2858, or toll free 800/233-7938). For a good swimmer interested in taking his or her first dive under careful supervision, this well-equipped outfit is the best choice in Tortola. The establishment offers a resort course for beginners which includes lessons in a pool and a one-tank reef dive lasting a full afternoon. The cost is $80. The operators provide expeditions to many dive sites, including the R.M.S. *Rhone* which sank in 1867, and have a solid working knowledge of the best offshore dive sites.

Boating

The best for this is Charlie and Ginny Cary's **The Moorings,** P.O. Box 139, Road Town (tel. 809/494-2331), whose eight-acre waterside resort I've already previewed as a dockside hotel recommendation. This place, along with others, makes the British Virgins the cruising capital of the world. The Carys started the first charter service in the British Virgins. From their beautiful fleet of sailing craft, you can choose your own design, including a Moorings 50 and a Morgan 46, considered the queens of the Caribbean charter fleet. They can accommodate three couples in comfort and style. Arrangements can be made for bareboating or going out with a skipper.

They have a staff of some 60 mechanics, electricians, riggers, and cleaners. In addition, if you're going out on your own, you'll get a thorough briefing session about Virgin Island waters and anchorages. To make reservations in the U.S., call 800/535-7289, toll free.

The *Shadowfax,* Treasure Isle Hotel Jetty, Tortola (tel. 809/494-2175), is a catamaran whose double-hulled construction permits smooth sailing even in rough seas, with an experienced crew taking the boat out for a day of snorkeling off reefs rich in marine life. Snorkel equipment, a buffet lunch, and an open bar are covered by the fee of $60 per person. The highlight of the outing is a tour through weirdly angled granite formations of Virgin Gorda "Baths." These shelter tidal pools, massive tree roots, exotic fish, and caches of soft white sand. Considered haunted by the native Indians, these massive boulders offer one of the most bizarre expeditions in the islands.

AFTER DARK: There isn't much nightlife. Your best bet is to ask around and find out which hotel might have entertainment on any given evening. Fungi, steel bands, and scratch bands appear regularly. Nonresidents are usually welcome.

6. VIRGIN GORDA

The second-largest island in the cluster of British Virgins, Virgin Gorda ("Fat Virgin") remains truly virginal. However, seen from the sea, it doesn't look virginal at all—rather, like a pregnant woman lying on her back.

Virgin Gorda is ten miles long and two miles wide, with a population of some 1,100. It lies 12 miles east of Road Town, and is reached by frequent flights from Beef Island off the shores of Tortola. Virgin Gorda is also frequently visited from St. Thomas, which lies only 26 miles away. Speedy's Fantasy (tel. 809/495-5240) operates a ferry service between Road Town and Virgin Gorda, the trip taking only half an hour. The ferry makes several trips daily.

The northern side of Virgin Gorda is mountainous, a peak reaching 1,370 feet. However, the southern half is flat, with large boulders appearing at every turn. The best beaches are at Spring Bay, Trunk Bay, and Devil's Bay.

Among the places of interest, **Coppermine Point** is the site of an abandoned copper mine and smelter. Because of loose rock formations, it can be dangerous to explore and caution should be used if you're going there. Legend has it that the Spanish worked these mines in the 1600s. However, the only authenticated document reveals that the English sank the shafts in 1838 to mine copper.

The Baths are on every visitor's list to Virgin Gorda. These are a phenomenon of tranquil pools and caves formed by gigantic house-sized boulders. As these boulders toppled over one another, they formed saltwater grottos, suitable for exploring.

The best way to see the island if you're over for a day trip is to call Andy Flax at Fischers Cove Beach Hotel (tel. 809/495-5252). He runs **Virgin Gorda Tours Assoc.,** which will give you a tour of the island for about $30 per person. The tour is operated twice daily from the hotel's parking lot.

Kilbride's Underwater Tours, Saba Rock, P. O. Box 40, Virgin Gorda, B.V.I. (tel. 809/494-2746), is run by the Kilbride clan. Among them they have been diving for more than a century. The Kilbride family members have done everything from spending two weeks under the sea as "aquanauts" to underwater demolition work. They'll take you on underwater tours of the dive sites in the area, ranging from coral forests and wall-to-wall fish to wrecks (the *Rhone* among others). A one-tank dive costs $40; two-tank dive, $60. A half day's snorkeling costs $25 per person. Saba Rock is an island on the eastern end of Gorda Sound.

THE RESORT HOTELS: An embodiment of understatement in luxury is **Little Dix Bay Hotel,** P.O. Box 70, Virgin Gorda, B.V.I. (tel. 809/495-5555 or toll free 800/223-7637), a 102-room resort discreetly scattered along a crescent-shaped private bay on a 500-acre preserve. It has the same quiet elegance as its fellow Rockresort, Caneel Bay Plantation on St. John in the U.S. Virgins. All rooms, built in woods of purpleheart, mahogany, locust, and ash, have private terraces, with a view of the sea or of gardens. Some units are two-story rondavels raised on stilts to form their own breezeways. On the outside they may appear like South Seas huts, but on the inside intelligent decorating has brought contemporary styling with all the conveniences. *From mid-April until May 31 and November 1 through December, doubles rent for $345, the price including three meals daily. June 1 to the end of October, doubles cost $300 AP. Plans such as tennis specials and honeymoon packages are also offered in summer.* In winter, full AP rates are $495 daily for two persons. Trade winds come through louvers and walls of screens, the air mixture further cooled by ceiling fans. In the rondavels, hammocks swing from the stilts.

At the Pavilion, with its peaked roofs, you can dine in the open, or else enjoy meals in the Sugar Mill Restaurant with its adjoining bar. If you're coming over for lunch at Sugar Mill, you can order such light fare as an Antilles fresh fruit salad with coconut sherbet or sandwiches. Little Dix offers many extras. Guests have the use of Sunfish, floats, and snorkeling gear. They also have Boston whalers that take you to the beach of your choice with a picnic lunch, and horseback riding is also available (extra). On Thursday all the guests at Little Dix are transported by car or Boston whaler to Spring Bay for a barbecue luncheon with a steel band.

Biras Creek Estate, P. O. Box 54, Virgin Gorda, B.V.I. (tel. 809/494-3555), is a magnificent resort lying at the northern end of Virgin Gorda. It stands like a hilltop-crowning fortress, not to keep away pirates, but to welcome the sun and views. On a 150-acre estate with its own marina, it occupies a narrow neck of land, flanking the sea on three sides. To create their Caribbean hideaway, Norwegian shipping interests carved out this resort in a wilderness, but wisely protected the natural terrain. The estate is well planted with flowering trees and bushes, and there is a greenhouse on the grounds to keep the resort supplied in foliage and flowers. Along the way, you might also see iridescent hummingbirds and the friendly little bananaquit. Scattered along the shore, 16 cottages and 32 suites shelter guests. Cooled by ceiling fans, suites have well-furnished bedrooms and divan beds with a sitting room and private patio, plus a refrigerator. You can open your windows to enjoy the sea breezes. There are three sets of rates. *The cheapest is during the summer period from April to December 18. At that time, double AP rates are $280 a day.* Highest tariffs are charged from December 19 until April 15: from $370 to $570 in a double. There are no singles. These tariffs include three meals a day, plus use of facilities and equipment, such as a pool, snorkeling gear, Sunfishes, paddleboards, and tennis courts. Also provided are free trips to nearby islands and beach barbecues twice a week. Special honeymoon packages are also offered off-season.

The food has won high praise. You never know what you're going to be served. Take the soups—it might be gazpacho, or even curried apple or grapefruit soup. Grouper baked in a shell, moussaka with banana bread, and pheasant flown in from the British Isles are just some of the dishes you are likely to be served during your stay. The wine cellar is also good. At the peaked-roof hilltop main house, the dining room and its connecting drinking lounge are quietly elegant, with heavy hewn beams and a ceramic tile mural. There's always a table with a view. A barbecued lunch is often served on the beach. Guests arriving in Virgin Gorda can be met by a taxi and taken to the hotel's motor launch for a speedy trip to Biras Creek.

Bitter End Yacht Club, P.O. Box 46, John O'Point, North Sound, Virgin Gorda, B.V.I. (tel. 809/494-2746 or toll free 800/223-1108 for reservations), is a rendezvous point for the yachting set cruising through the British Virgins. Guests have included treasure hunter Mel Fisher and Jean-Michael Cousteau. Bitter End offers an informal yet elegant life, guests taking one of the hillside chalets or well-appointed beachfront and hillside villas overlooking the sound and yachts at anchor. For something novel, you can stay aboard one of the 27-foot yachts, yours to sail, with dockage including daily maid service, meals in the Yacht Club dining room, and overnight provisions. Marina rooms are the same rates as live-aboard yachts, a good saving. Daily winter rates for hillside villas or chalets are $210 single, $260 double, $330 triple, and $400 for a family of two adults and two children 6 to 16 years old. Beachfront villas cost $250 in singles, $300 in doubles, $370 in triples, and $440 for a family of four. Yacht live-aboards or marina room occupants pay $170 single, $220 double, $290 triple, and $360 for four. *Summer charges, May to mid-November, are $170 single, $220 double, $285 triple, and $350 for a family of four in hillside villas. Beachfront villas* *and hillside chalets cost $210 single, $260 double, $325 triple, and $390 for four. Marina rooms and yacht live-aboards pay $130 for singles, $180 for doubles, $245 for triples, and $310 for quads.* Special packages are offered for longer stays, prices varying with the season. Rates include all meals, with dining in the Clubhouse Steak and Seafood Grille or the English Carvery. The social hub of the place is the bar, where you're likely to find everybody from the publisher of *Yachting* magazine to the sun-streaked Flying Dutchman and the Barefoot Contessa.

If you're not a sailor, the helpful staff gives free on-the-beach instruction to get you started. Formal lessons are also available. A sailboat practically comes with your room, as rates include unlimited use of the club's fleet of Lasers, Sunfish, Rhodes 19s, and J-24s, as well as windsurfers and outboard skiffs. Or you can charter a CAL 2-27 for an overnight trip. There are great sheltered-water sailing, reef snorkeling as you hunt for that doomed Spanish galleon, expeditions to neighboring cays, shelling, endless beachcombing possibilities, marine science participation, whatever, all included in the rates.

Olde Yard Inn, P.O. Box 26, The Valley, Virgin Gorda, B.W.I. (tel. 809/ 495-5544), is a charmer. It's got a lot going for it, namely its owner, Carol Kaufman, a New Yorker in the restaurant business in Fort Lauderdale, Florida, for 13 years before coming here. This little 14-room Caribbean inn is beautifully run, with good food, good beds, and hospitality that ranks among the best in the British Virgins. Near the main house are two long bungalows with large renovated bedrooms, each with its own bath and patio. Scattered about are a few antiques and special accessories. On the MAP in winter, guests pay $140 daily in singles, $215 in doubles, $275 in triples, and $335 in quads. *From mid-April to mid-May and again from mid-November to mid-December, MAP bookings are accepted at $115 in singles, $155 in doubles, $205 in triples, and $255 in quads. The EP charge is $55 per person daily. However, from mid-May to mid-November, you can stay here for $55 daily in a single, $85 in a double, and $115 in a triple, with a buffet breakfast included.*

When you arrive you'll be asked about your interests. Perhaps you'll find a saddled horse waiting for a before-breakfast or a moonlight ride. Or you'll go for a sail on a yacht or a snorkeling adventure at one of 16 beaches, with a picnic lunch provided (perhaps lobster, pâté, champagne, or peanut butter sandwiches). Under a banana-leaf thatched roof, the meals served here are one of the reasons for coming over. Steaks cut at the inn are from the finest fresh sirloin. Meals have a decided French accent. If you're just visiting for the day, you can enjoy a lunch from noon to 2 p.m., costing from $10. Dinners, from 7 to 9 p.m., begin at $15 but could run up to $30 if you want lobster. Movies are shown at 9 p.m. daily in the library, and there is live entertainment twice a week in the dining room. On the premises is a small boutique full of bright, intriguing items such as local silkscreened clothes, arts and crafts, painting and sculpture, as well as other fun items such as Chinese and American kites in silk, nylon, cotton, and paper.

Fischers Cove Beach Hotel, P.O. Box 60, The Valley, Virgin Gorda, B.V.I. (tel. 809/495-5252), is a group of cottages nestled near the beach of St. Thomas Bay, with swimming at your doorstep. Erected of native stone, each house is self-contained, with one- or two-bedroom units having a combination living and dining room with a kitchenette. At a food store near the grounds, you can stock up on your provisions if you're doing your own cooking. A two-story unit (12 rooms) has been added to the resort. These are pleasant but simple rooms, offering a view of Drake Channel. Each has its own private bath (hot and cold showers) and private balcony. In winter, one-bedroom cottages housing two guests go for $135 daily, and a two-bedroom cottage suitable for four costs $200. *In summer, one- and two-bedroom cottages for two to four persons are in the $105 to $185* *daily range*. The hotel rooms are rented for $185 daily in a double and $130 in a single in winter, both MAP tariffs. *In summer, it's possible to stay in one of the hotel rooms at a charge of $85 daily in a double, $65 in a single.*

Lunch, from noon to 2 p.m., costs around $12 and up, and dinner, from 7 to 10:30 p.m., ranges from $22. A resident steel band provides entertainment most nights, and periodically a local scratch band plays.

Guavaberry Spring Bay Vacation Homes, P.O. Box 20, Virgin Gorda, B.V.I. (tel. 809/495-5227) are clusters of hexagonal redwood, white-roofed houses built on stilts and available for daily or weekly rentals. It's like living in a treehouse, with screened and louvered walls open to let in sea breezes. Each home has one or two bedrooms, and all have private baths, with a small kitchenette and dining area. The hosts are Betty Roy and Tina and Ludwig Goschler, her daughter and son-in-law. They'll show you to one of their unique vacation homes, each with its own elevated sundeck overlooking Sir Francis Drake Passage. Two people in winter pay $110 daily for a one-bedroom house, the rate rising to $165 per day for four people in a two-bedroom house, plus service and tax. An extra person pays $20 per day. *In summer, a one-bedroom house costs $70 per day; the two-bedroom house, $105 per day, also plus tax and service.* Within a few minutes of the cottage colony is the beach at Spring Bay. It's also possible to explore the "Baths" nearby. The owners provide a complete commissary for guests, and such tropical fruits as tamarind and soursop can be picked in season or else bought at local shops. They will make arrangements for day charters for scuba-diving or fishing, and will also arrange for island Jeep tours and saddle horses.

7. MOSQUITO ISLAND (NORTH SOUND)

The sandy, 125-acre Mosquito (also spelled Moskito) Island just north of Virgin Gorda wasn't named for those pesky insects we all know and few if any love. It took its name from the Mosquito (or Moskito) Indians, who were the only known inhabitants of the small land mass before the arrival of the Spanish conquistadors in the 15th century. Archaeological relics of these peaceful Indians and their agricultural pursuits have been found here.

Today the privately owned island is uninhabited except for **Drake's Anchorage,** P.O. Box 2510, North Sound, Virgin Gorda, B.V.I. (tel. 809/494-2254 or toll free 800/624-6651; in Massachusetts, 617/661-4745), which many repeat patrons consider their favorite retreat in the British Virgins. The hotel offers only ten comfortable rooms and two villas. All the accommodations are decorated with Haitian art, and each contains a private bath and sea-view veranda. The villas have private kitchens. Units at this idyllic oasis are managed by Peter and Jamy Faust. In winter, charges are $285 daily for a double room, $210 for a single, and $85 for a third person lodged in a double, all AP. *Summer rates are $195 in a double, $145 in a single, with a third person in a double paying $70 daily, AP.* The resort provides free use of windsurfers, snorkeling equipment, and bicycles. For additional fees, you can go scuba-diving, take boat trips to a nearby deserted island or to the "Baths" at Virgin Gorda, go deep-sea fishing, make day sails, go horseback riding, or try your skill at waterskiing. The snorkeling and scuba here are considered so good that members of the Cousteau Society spend one month each year exploring local waters. There are four beaches on Mosquito Island, each with different wave and water conditions, so guests can choose what suits them. The resort's restaurant is attractively tropical in design and conscious of both French and Caribbean culinary styles. It faces the water and offers a superb cuisine which features local and continental dishes, lobster, a fresh fish of the day, and a weekly pig roast in winter, with a live band for entertainment.

Getting here requires taking a plane to the Virgin Gorda airport and Speedy's Taxi from there to the Leverick Bay Dock. The taxi driver will "radio" ahead, and a boat will be sent from Drake's Anchorage to take you on the five-minute ride from the dock to the resort. The fare is complimentary if you stay at least seven nights. Otherwise, it will be added to your room bill upon checkout.

8. GUANA ISLAND

This 850-acre island, a nature sanctuary, is one of the most private hide-aways in the Caribbean. Don't go here seeking resort action, but if you want to retreat from the world, to envelop yourself in a natural setting where intrusion by people has been wisely controlled, then Guana Island might be for you. It lies right off the coast of Tortola. To reach it, the **Guana Island Club,** P.O. Box 32, Road Town, Tortola, B.V.I. (tel. 809/494-2354), will send a boatman to meet arriving guests at Beef Island airport. Of course, you must give the club fair warning of your arrival. You should advise their office in New York of your arrival. For reservations, write or call Guana Island Club, Timber Trail, Rye, NY 10580 (tel. 914/967-6050, or toll free 800/54GUANA).

After your arrival on Guana Island, a Nissan Patrol with an open surrey top will transport you up one of the most scenic hills in the region. You arrive at a cluster of whitewalled cottages that were built as a private club in the 1930s on the foundations of a Quaker homestead. The stone-trimmed bungalows never hold more than a total of 30 guests. Since the dwellings are staggered along a flower-dotted hillside, the sense of privacy is almost absolute. The panoramic sweep from the terraces is spectacular, particularly at sunset. When guests hunger for company, they'll find a convivial atmosphere at the rattan-furnished club-house. Dinners by candlelight are served family-style on the veranda, with menus which include home-grown vegetables and continental and Stateside specialties. Dinner is a casually elegant sit-down affair, whereas lunch is served buffet style every day. The bars are self-service, and the hotel bills clients according to the honor system.

Each guest cottage has a shower (but don't use too much water). In high season, two people on AP pay $385 daily, and a single is charged $295. *Shoulder season rates are in effect from November 1 to December 15: $275 daily in a double, $185 in a single, both AP. In off-season, AP tariffs in a double range from $240 to $275 daily, with singles paying $150 to $185.* Sports lovers and/or beachcombers will find seven beaches, some of which require a boat to reach. There are two clay tennis courts, all water sports including fishing and snorkeling, a fleet of small sailing craft, and a network of nature trails.

CHAPTER VII

HAITI

□ □ □

Sights, sounds, tastes, and smells come together uniquely in the oldest black republic in the western hemisphere. In the heart of the Caribbean, Haiti is the size of the state of Maryland and shaped like the claw of a large Maine lobster. Bizarrely exotic, inescapably moving, it is the most flamboyant island in the Caribbean, a French-speaking land with a pure African cast.

These people speak their special Créole tongue and maintain the songs and dances of their African past. They still very much practice voodoo with its richly symbolic ceremonies.

Haiti occupies the western part of the island of Hispaniola, lying some 643 air miles southeast of Miami, and even though it's on the same island, it bears almost no resemblance to the Spanish-speaking Dominican Republic.

A primitive rhythm seems to pulsate through Haiti, this teeming, turbulent land of stark contrasts and subtle blending. Its poverty is often masked in the blossoms of the flamboyant tree and the bougainvillea vine.

Just how poor is Haiti? To illustrate, one family lives in a tin-roofed hovel, only seven feet square, some of its rotting wooden boards missing. The family members, seven in all, sleep huddled together on a bed made of banana leaves. Yet they are considered rich enough to employ a servant.

The landscape is dominated by a trio of mountain ranges, the major ones of which are the Cibao Mountains and the Cordillera Central, their peaks climbing to 8,000 to 9,000 feet above sea level.

Some six million people live in Haiti, about 90% are black. In addition to a scattering of whites, many of the remaining 10% are Haitian Créoles, descendants of the early French colonists who mixed with Africans.

TRAVELER'S ADVISORY. It is with deep regret that the author of this guide-book, long a promoter of tourism to Haiti, feels that pleasure and vacation travel in Haiti is no longer recommended, as of this writing. The suspension of our coverage of the tourist facilities of Haiti, its hotels, shops, and attractions, follows a 1988 traveler's advisory by the U.S. State Department, advising U.S. citizens to defer non-essential travel to Haiti because of its changing political situation and resulting uncertainties about security there.

That advisory was allowed to expire as a conscious decision by the State Department. Yet, at presstime, travel conditions have not improved. The author of this guide fears that the country's continuing underlying unrest, its bitter poverty, reports of street hostilities, and violently changing governments make a problem-free vacation there impossible.

This disrecommendation of Haiti as a tourist destination is made with a full understanding of the artistic and cultural wealth which has always made Haiti one of the Caribbean's most passionately interesting travel destinations.

We look forward to reinstating our coverage of one of the world's most fascinating islands in a future edition when political and social circumstances warrant it.

A VIOLENT HISTORY: The first tourist, the Haitians say, was Columbus, who sighted the island of Hispaniola on his maiden voyage to the New World on December 5, 1492. In time, Spain was to conquer the island, killing nearly one million peaceful Arawak Indians who made up the native population.

Under Spanish rule, a decree called for the importation of African blacks as slaves. When Spain failed to colonize the entire island, French buccaneers, from their base in Tortuga off the northwest coast, moved into what is now Haiti. Eventually they took control in the western part of Hispaniola, a move legalized by treaty in 1697. Spain officially ceded the territory to France.

In May 1801 a former slave and coachman, Toussaint-L'Ouverture, was elected governor. Considering this secession, Napoleon ordered the rebellion quelled. Defeating the Haitians, the French took L'Ouverture prisoner.

However, revolutionists led by Jean-Jacques Dessalines and Alexandre Pétion, two Haitian generals, eventually defeated the French army, whose troops returned to Paris in 1803. Dessalines proclaimed Haitian independence on January 1, 1804. He also proclaimed himself emperor, a title he held until his death in 1806.

Henri Christophe, the prototype of Eugene O'Neill's *Emperor Jones,* was named as first president of the republic. But he proclaimed himself king. Pétion was to succeed him. However, Christophe's action divided the nation, and the north and west were ruled as an empire until the self-proclaimed king shot himself in 1820.

At the overthrow of Haitian president Guillaume Sam in 1915, the Americans, fearing a German invasion, occupied the country and didn't leave until 1934. After much turmoil and many leaders, Dr. François Duvalier ("Papa Doc") was elected president in 1957, launching an iron-fisted dictatorship until his death in 1971. He was succeeded by his less militant son, Jean-Claude ("Baby Doc") Duvalier, as "president-for-life." However, the title was a misnomer. The pudgy dictator, along with his wife and family, fled Haiti in February of 1986 to a life of exile in Europe. Unfortunately, he and his wife looted much of the treasury. A period of unrest, killings, upheaval, and random violence has followed in the wake of their departure. The present Haitian government faces an uncertain future, and its once-flourishing tourist industry has come to a virtual standstill.

CHAPTER VIII

THE DOMINICAN REPUBLIC

□ □ □

Five centuries of culture and tradition converge in the mountainous country of the Dominican Republic, the fastest-growing tourist destination in the Caribbean. The 54-mile-wide Mona Passage separates the República Dominicana from Puerto Rico. In the Dominican interior, the fertile Valley of Cibao (this is rich sugarcane country) ends its upward sweep at the Pico Duarte, formerly Pico Trujillo, the highest mountain peak in the West Indies, soaring to a height of 10,417 feet.

Nestled amid Cuba, Jamaica, and Puerto Rico, the island of Hispaniola (Little Spain) consists of both Haiti (which takes up the westernmost third of the island), and the Dominican Republic, which has a lush land mass equal to that of Vermont and New Hampshire combined.

Columbus sighted the coral-edged Caribbean coastline on his first voyage to the New World—"There is no more beautiful island in the world." The first permanent European settlement in the New World was founded on November 7, 1493, the ruins still remaining near Montecristi in the northeast. Primitive Indian tribes had called the island Quisqueya, "mother earth," before the Spaniards arrived to butcher them.

Much of what Columbus first saw still remains in a natural, unspoiled condition, but that may change. The country is building and expanding rapidly, launching itself in the Caribbean resort race as fast as time and money will allow.

Gulf+Western created and subsequently sold a fabulous resort on the southeastern coast of La Romana; and the northern shore, centered around Puerto Plata and Sosúa, is still a vast sweep of shimmering surf and sand, and is itself currently the scene of heavy resort development.

In the heart of the Caribbean archipelago, the country has an 870-mile coastline, about a third of which is given to magnificent beach. The average temperature is 77° Fahrenheit. August is the warmest month and January the coolest period, although even then it is still warm enough to swim at the beaches and enjoy the tropical sun.

That being so, you may ask why the Dominican Republic has been relatively undiscovered by visitors. The answer is largely political. The country has been steeped in misery and bloodshed almost from the beginning, climaxed by the infamous reign of Rafael Trujillo and the civil wars that followed.

The seeds of trouble were sown early. Hispaniola is divided today largely because a 1697 treaty with Spain granted the western part of the island to France. In 1795 another treaty between France and Spain granted the eastern part to France too.

But the French weren't in control for long. Their possession gave rise to the War for Reconquest in which the French colonials were defeated, the country returning to Spanish domination. José Nuñez de Caceres in 1821 proclaimed the "Ephemeral Independence," but after that Charles Boyer, the Haitian president, declared the Dominican Republic a part of Haiti, an occupation that lasted for nearly a quarter of a century.

It wasn't until February 27, 1844, that "La Trinitaria" was founded. This freedom movement, begun by Juan Duarte, made him the father of the Dominican Republic.

The country's problems weren't solved easily, as it once more became a pawn in the colonial possession game. The Spanish claimed the country until they were ousted.

In 1916 the United States established a military occupation which lasted until July 12, 1924. After their departure, Rafael Trujillo eventually overthrew the elected president in 1930, gaining power and dominating the country until his assassination in 1961. He wanted to be known as "El Benefactor," but more often his oppressed people called him "The Goat," because of his revolting excesses.

Now, with much of their often notorious past a subject of history books, the Dominicans are rapidly rebuilding and restoring their country. It does offer the visitor a chance to enjoy the sun and sea as well as an opportunity to learn something historically or even politically if the problems of a developing society should interest you.

GETTING THERE: **American Airlines** offers many flights to the Dominican Republic. Passengers departing from the northeastern U.S. or eastern Canada can make easy connections through New York on one of three nonstop daily flights into the Dominican Republic. Added to this are at least two (and sometimes more) connections through American's hub in San Juan. American's flights to San Juan also depart from dozens of North American cities several times a day.

Depending on the time of year, American's round-trip passage to Puerto Plata, for example, can cost as little as $263 in low season and $345 per person in midwinter, if certain conditions are met. Prices, of course, are subject to change.

These low fares require seven-day advance purchase and a Saturday night stop-over in the Dominican Republic.

The least expensive tickets are usually non-refundable if changes are made in the itinerary. Lower fares are usually offered for flights departing between Monday and Thursday with weekend travel costing a bit more.

American is not alone in servicing the Dominican Republic. **Pan Am** offers daily nonstop service to Santo Domingo, where passengers bound for Puerto Plata make a touchdown before continuing. Depending on their city of origin, other passengers reach Puerto Plata through Miami. From Miami, Pan Am offers several daily flights to both Santo Domingo and Puerto Plata. Likewise, **Eastern** flies into the Dominican Republic from New York's La Guardia Airport. **Air Canada** flies once a week (every Saturday in both directions) between Toronto and Puerto Plata.

A recent addition to the airlines on this route, **Continental Airlines,** offers a daily nonstop flight from New Jersey's Newark Airport to Puerto Plata. Flying time on most New York runs is about 3 ½ hours.

For up-to-date prices and departure schedules, contact one of the airlines or your travel agent.

GETTING AROUND: This is not always easy if your hotel is remotely perched. The most convenient means of transport is provided by taxis, rental cars, públicos, and guaguas.

Taxis

Taxis aren't metered, and determining the cost in advance (which you should do) may be difficult if you and your driver have a language problem. Taxis can be hailed in the streets, and you'll definitely find them stationed outside the major hotels, most definitely outside the airport as you emerge from Customs.

Car Rentals

The best way to see the Dominican Republic is by car, particularly since intra-island transportation by bus tends to be erratic, hot, and overcrowded. Rail transportation is nonexistent. Chartering a small plane is sometimes an expensive option. Most visitors take to the roads in self-drive cars. A word of warning, however. Although the major highways are relatively clear of obstacles, the country's secondary roads, especially those in the east, are disturbingly potholed and rutted. Plan a generous amount of transit time between destinations, and drive carefully. Your Canadian or American driver's license is suitable. And unlike many places in the Caribbean, you drive on the right.

Because of close business links to the United States, at least five U.S.-based car-rental firms maintain branches in the Dominican Republic, usually at Puerto Plata, Santo Domingo, La Romana, and other places. **Budget Rent-a-Car** is a well-run operation, maintaining late-model Daihatsus, Hondas, and Isuzus at strategic locations. At Puerto Plata, for example, high season rentals of the least expensive car, a Daihatsu Cuore, cost $205 per week with unlimited mileage, reserved one week in advance, without air conditioning or automatic transmission. For those latter conveniences, the least expensive car rents for $262 to $327 per week with unlimited mileage.

I strongly advise readers to buy the optional collision damage waiver, which, for around $6 per day, reduces your collision liability from full financial responsibility to $750.

If no cars are available at Budget, you'll still get a quality car (but will pay more) at Hertz or Avis, both of which have offices at Santo Domingo and Puerto Plata. National, another worthy contender, offers air-conditioned Nissan Sunnys

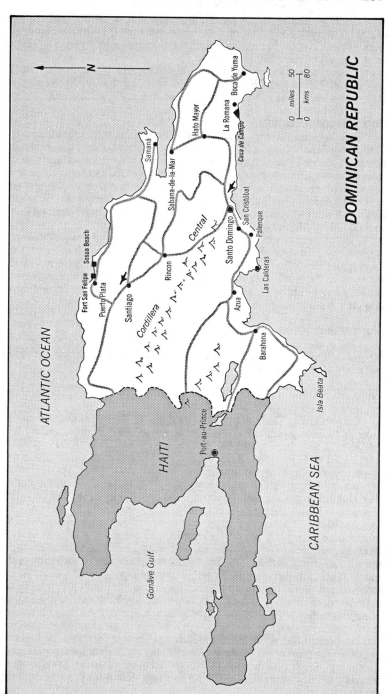

with automatic transmissions for $273 weekly with seven-days advance purchase. Be warned, however, that cancellation runs you 25% of the cost of the weekly rental. National's mandatory collision damage waiver is priced at $28 per week, but still carries a $300 deductible.

For reservations and more information, call the rental companies toll free at least a week before your departure. Budget is at 800/527-0700; National at 800/328-4567; Hertz at 800/654-3001, and Avis at 800/331-2112.

Public Transportation

Cars that transport the public in Santo Domingo, as well as elsewhere in the Dominican Republic, are called **públicos.** They are a kind of multipassenger taxi that travels on main thoroughfares, stopping to pick up persons waving from the side of the street, motioning the direction they want to go. You must tell the driver your destination when he stops to pick you up. If he doesn't go to the place you are headed, he'll let you know, and you can wait for another público. Watch for cars with a white seal on the car's front door. Fares range from 60 centavos (12¢) to RD$1 (20¢), depending on your destination.

Public buses, called **guaguas,** provide the same service as públicos, but you're likely to be somewhat more crowded in the buses, as conductors hang out the side and hop off to try to get riders for their vehicles in competition with the públicos. In the towns the guagua fare is usually 45 centavos (9¢). Larger buses provide service outside the towns, charging from RD$2.10 (42¢), depending on how far you go.

Sightseeing Tours

One of the leading tour operators is **Prieto Tours,** 125 Francia Ave. (tel. 809/682-9000), who will arrange a number of sightseeing excursions for you in and around Santo Domingo.

PRACTICAL FACTS: A few helpful hints may ease your entry into this country, so reminiscent of old Spain in many ways.

Currency: The Dominican peso is legal tender. The Dominican monetary units are the peso (symbol: RD$) and the centavo. Coin denominations are 1, 5, 10, 25, and 50 centavos, and bill denominations are RD$1, RD$5, RD$10, RD$20, RD$50, RD$100, RD$500, and RD$1,000. Price quotations in this chapter appear sometimes in American and sometimes in Dominican currency, depending on the policy of the establishment, but the use of any currency other than Dominican pesos illegal. This means that even if a payment you are to make is quoted in U.S. dollars, it must be translated into pesos and paid therewith. All foreign visitors are asked to comply with this provision under penalty of fine, imprisonment, or both. As of this writing, you get about RD$5 to $1 U.S. (RD$1 equals about 20¢ U.S.), but this rate will probably fluctuate many times during the lifetime of this guide. You should always check with your bank or the tourist office before planning your budget for the Dominican Republic. At the international airports and major hotels, there are bank booths where you can get your American currency converted into Dominican pesos at the rate of exchange prevailing in the free market. You will be given a receipt for the amount of foreign currency you have exchanged. If you don't spend all your Dominican currency, you can present the receipt with the remaining pesos at the Banco de Reservas booth at the airport and receive the equivalent in American dollars to take out of the country. Payments by credit card are charged to you at the rate of exchange of the free market. Commercial banks can exchange dollars for pesos but not the reverse.

Note: All currency quotations in this chapter are in U.S. dollars unless RD$ is specifically designated.

Documents: To enter the Dominican Republic, citizens of the U.S. and Canada need only proof of citizenship, such as a passport or an original birth certificate, although citizens may have trouble returning home without a passport. A reproduced birth certificate is not acceptable. Upon your arrival at the airport, you must purchase a tourist card for $10 U.S.

Electricity: The country has the same electricity as the U.S.—that is, 110 volts AC, 60 cycles—so adapters are not necessary.

Embassy: The U.S. Embassy is on Cesar Nicolas Penson Street, Santo Domingo, Dominican Republic (tel. 809/541-2171).

Holidays: The Dominican Republic celebrates the usual holidays, such as Christmas and New Year's, but also has some of its own. They include January 21 (Our Lady of La Altagracia); January 26 (Duarte's Birthday); February 27 (National Independence Day); Movable feast (60 days after Good Friday, a Corpus Christi holiday), August 16 (Restoration Day); and September 24 (Our Lady of Las Mercedes).

Language: The official language is Spanish, but English is making inroads. Even if they can't understand you (too often the case with waiters in hotels), they'll give you a smile.

Taxes: A departure tax of $10 U.S. is assessed. This must be paid in U.S. currency. The government imposes an 11% tax on hotel rooms, 6% on food and beverages.

Telephone: You can call the Dominican Republic from mainland U.S. by dialing area code 809, then the local number. When you're on the island, the area code isn't necessary.

Time: It's Atlantic Standard Time throughout the country. When New York and Miami are on Eastern Standard Time, and it's 6 a.m. in either city, it is 7 a.m. in Santo Domingo. However, during Daylight Saving Time, when it's noon on the east coast mainland, it is the same time in Santo Domingo.

Tips and service: In most restaurants and hotels, a 10% service charge is added to your check to include service. Most well-bred citizens of the country usually add from 5% to 10% more, especially if the service has been good.

Once the hassle of Customs (you get a very thorough check!) is over, some four million Dominicans extend a *bienvenido.*

SANTO DOMINGO

Bartholomeo Columbus, brother of Christopher, founded the city of New Isabella on August 4, 1496, later renamed Santo Domingo. That makes it the oldest city in the New World, a haven for history buffs, built on the banks of the Ozama River.

On the southeastern Caribbean coast, Santo Domingo—known as Ciudad Trujillo from 1936 to 1961—is, of course, the capital of the Dominican Republic. It has had a long, sometimes glorious, more often sad, history. At the peak of its power, Diego de Valásquez sailed from here to settle Cuba; Ponce de León went forth to discover and settle Puerto Rico and Florida; and Cortés was launched in the direction of Mexico.

The city today still reflects its long history—French, Haitian, and especially Spanish.

I'll first review its modern (for the most part) hotels and restaurants before picking up the sightseeing trail.

1. HOTELS IN SANTO DOMINGO

I'll lead off with the most expensive choices, but even the most pricy hotels in Santo Domingo might be classified as medium priced in most of the Caribbean. In off-season, some of their rooms are definitely inexpensive. So here is your chance to live it up a bit, enjoying luxury that might be out of your price range elsewhere. *Remember:* Taxes and service will probably be added to your bill.

THE UPPER BRACKET: Called "the pride of the Dominican Republic," **Jaragua Resort, Casino, & European Spa,** 367 Avenida George Washington, Santo Domingo, Dominican Republic (tel. 809/686-2222), was built on the 14-acre site of the old Jaragua, popular in Trujillo's day. The new "Ha-ra-gua" is a splashy waterfront palace, with the largest casino in the Caribbean and a 1,000-seat Las Vegas–style showroom. Convenient to the major attractions and shops of Santo Domingo, the centrally located hotel, which officially opened in 1988, spreads its accommodations across two separate buildings: the ten-story Jaragua Tower and the two-level Jaragua Gardens Estate.

In this complex are 355 luxuriously appointed rooms with central air conditioning, including 18 suites. Seemingly no expense was spared, as reflected by marble bathrooms with large makeup mirrors and hairdryers, three touch-tone phones with direct dialing, mini-bars and refrigerators, and computerized door locks. Yet all this luxury is comparatively inexpensive, at least *in off-season when two persons are charged from $65 to $110 daily in standard rooms.* In winter, two persons pay from $160 to $210 daily, still remarkable value. Suites are far more expensive, of course. Depending on the season, MAP is another $35 to $42 per person daily. Guest services include 24-hour room service, a beauty parlor, and a barber, plus butler service in the deluxe floors of the Jaragua Tower.

Surrounding a swimming pool are 12 private cabañas, a snack bar, and an outdoor bar. The hotel has one of the best tennis centers in Santo Domingo, with four clay courts lit for night games. There is also a pro shop. Major attention focuses on the spa with all the latest exercise equipment, as well as saunas, Jacuzzis, and whirlpool baths. A medical staff supervises the activity, and guests can avail themselves of any number of massages, facials, herbals wraps, and beauty treatments. Also there are classes in aerobics. These spa facilities are considered the most complete in the Caribbean.

Hotel Santo Domingo, Avenida Independencia, Santo Domingo, Dominican Republic (tel. 809/535-1511), run by Premier Resorts & Hotels, has a tasteful extravagance, the designs of William Cox, and the styling of the famed Dominican haute couturier, Oscar de la Renta. Their flair has made this ochre stucco structure, 15 minutes from the downtown area, a prestigious address in Santo Domingo, often attracting presidents of other Latin American countries. Opening onto the sea, the deluxe hotel stands on 14 acres of landscaped grounds of tropical planting, some of which forms a pleasing backdrop for an Olympic-size swimming pool area.

Air-conditioned rooms are spread out in two structures, three stories tall, these framing latticework loggias, one dedicated to orange trees. Most of the rooms open onto views of the water, but some face the garden, which isn't bad either. A superior room—that is, extra-large with two double beds—rents for $125 daily in winter, the price for a deluxe unit with a balcony overlooking the Caribbean being $175. Rates are for with double or single occupancy. *In summer, these rates are reduced to $100 and $130 daily.* Just off the lobby, guests enjoy dinner at El Alcazar (see my dining recommendations). At a fountain is the informal restaurant El Cafetal, and you can also enjoy a poolside lunch at Las Brisas.

The piano bar, Las Palmas, draws a lively crowd at night. The hotel has three professional tennis courts lit for night games.

Hotel Hispaniola, Avenida Independencia, Santo Domingo, Dominican Republic (tel. 809/533-7111), has done an amazing Cinderella act, emerging from the shell of the Trujillo-era Hotel Pax (which once housed Juan Peron) into its present reincarnation. Now operated by Premier Resorts & Hotels, it was practically rebuilt and completely transformed. The location is across from its sister establishment, the deluxe Hotel Santo Domingo, already recommended. On ten beautifully landscaped acres, it is a six-story structure, with an attractive swimming pool and a thatched coffeehouse (a bohío), where you can order breakfast, lunches, or drinks. The top-floor rooms, which are preferable, offer seaside views. A standard room with balcony costs $86 daily in winter, and there are more than a dozen garden rooms going for $96 daily, either single or double occupancy. *In summer, these tariffs are considerably reduced, a standard unit going for only $70 daily, a garden room for $80, either single or double occupancy.*

The hotel's restaurant, La Piazzetta, serves Italian specialties. The evening hot spot is not only the casino but also the disco Neon 2002, attracting a great deal of local trade. Guests at the Hispaniola are entitled to use the facilities at the Hotel Santo Domingo, including its professional tennis courts.

Santo Domingo Sheraton Hotel & Casino, 365 Avenida George Washington, Santo Domingo, Dominican Republic (tel. 809/542-5151), is a high-rise right on the Malecón, standing behind a rather forbidding black wall. However, once you go along a tree-lined drive, you arrive at a vast lobby that is really a solarium. There are 260 rooms, all doubles, and eight suites. *In summer, single or double occupancy costs from $80 to $85 daily.* In winter, singles or doubles rent for $120 to $130 daily. Suites are more expensive. Units are equipped with color TV with remote control, direct-dial phones, hairdryers, and 24-hour room service. Except for those on the third floor, all units have ocean views. At the plant-filled Petit Café, overlooking the lobby, you can enjoy a sundowner before heading for Yarey's Lounge, a piano bar with entertainment. Dining is at Antoine's (see the recommendations to follow), an elegant continental place. Breakfast or lunch is taken at La Terraza coffeehouse, which opens onto a terrace surrounding the large pool opening onto views of the sea. Other additions to the hotel are La Canasta, a restaurant featuring Dominican food, and the Omni Disco, plus the handsome casino. The hotel is a good bet for the commercial traveler, as it offers babysitters, laundry and dry-cleaning services, secretarial and translation services, and mail and telegram service, as well as an Avis car rental on the premises.

The Moderate Range

Plaza Naco Hotel, Plaza Naco Mall, P.O. Box 20338, Santo Domingo, Dominican Republic (tel. 809/541-6226), is another ideal accommodation for commercial travelers or for visitors seeking a lot of space and facilities. It offers 220 accommodations, every unit a suite, handsomely decorated and equipped with such amenities as computer safe lock doors, central air conditioning, guest safes in every unit, kitchenettes with utensils, dining rooms, and cable TV. A standard suite has not only two phones but also a hairdryer. In winter, single or double occupancy costs from $80 to $100 daily. *In summer, you pay $60 to $80 daily for either single or double occupancy.* There is a good restaurant, Gourmet, although you can also patronize the terrace or pool cafeteria, or else order room service 24 hours a day. Those who want their own supplies for their suites can use the deli or the mini-market. Residents of the hotel are admitted free to the disco. You can stay in shape here, as the hotel has a sauna with massages available, plus a Jacuzzi, solarium, and gym. Other facilities on the premises include a rent-a-car desk, a tour desk, laundry and dry cleaning services, and, for the business traveler, bilingual secretaries and legal translators.

Dominicana Concorde, Avenida Anacaona, Mirador del Sur, Santo Domingo, Dominican Republic (tel. 809/562-8222), is a complete resort with a casino outside the city, about half an hour's drive from the airport. The Paseo de los Indios is a five-mile park right outside the hotel's grounds. The only ingredient missing at the Concorde is a beach. Instead it places emphasis on its geometrically designed swimming pool which includes a bar jutting out into the pool with underwater seats. The main building is a high-rise, with many built-in playground facilities. The pool is placed adjacent to eight tennis courts, which are lit at night. The bedrooms, 337 in all, plus 21 cabañas near the pool, utilize island colors and furnishings, and each has a double or twin bed, a radio, and an intimate sitting area, plus a private balcony from which you have a view of faraway mountains or of the nearby sea. In winter, singles or doubles cost $80 to $100 daily. *Off-season, singles or doubles go for $55 to $75 daily.* Service and taxes are added to all bills. Even more expensive suites are available.

The lobby is in pastel hues, and the most advanced design is El Mercado coffeeshop, which uses wooden packing cases in its decor. You can order everything from such Stateside specialties as a hamburger to such local delicacies as pumpkin bisque. The main dining room, La Casa, was decorated to evoke a colonial Dominican mansion. Both seafood and international dishes are offered here, including lobster thermidor. The rooftop lounge, L'Azotea, offers a view at night. You'll want to have at least a drink here. Other facilities include eight lit tennis courts, basketball, volleyball, a health club, and a sauna.

Hotel Lina, Avenidas Maximo Gomez and 27 de Febrero, Santo Domingo, Dominican Republic (tel. 809/689-5185), is the modern, six-story outgrowth of the restaurant that was begun by Lina Aguado, a Spanish woman who came to Santo Domingo to cook for Trujillo. The restaurant has grown into one of the best known in the Caribbean (see my dining recommendations to follow). The hotel has attracted everybody from Julio Iglesias to David Rockefeller to Latin American presidents. After a much-needed renovation, its facilities have been considerably upgraded, including a gym and sauna for women only. There is also a piano bar, a Kiosko Bar, and a gambling casino. There are also a swimming pool and tennis courts. The hotel offers 217 well-furnished rooms, each with private bath and air conditioning. *On the EP, standard singles or doubles in summer cost $75 to $105 daily.* In winter, standard singles or doubles cost from $100 to $122 daily. Suites are more expensive.

El Embajador Hotel Casino, 65 Avenida Sarasota, Santo Domingo, Dominican Republic (tel. 809/533-2131), was created by Trujillo as a concrete-and-glass deluxe hotel with a luxury penthouse for his own use. It was built at the western outskirts of the city on the grounds of a horse-racing track, but today modern high-rise buildings have made inroads on the land where, in the Trujillo era, playboy Porfirio Rubirosa and El Jefe's son, Ramfis Trujillo, once played polo. Perhaps no hotel in Santo Domingo has undergone such a metamorphosis in spirit as this place. The Oriental owners, however, have given it a major refurbishing, and affiliated it with the HUSA chain. The seven-story modern building has 309 air-conditioned bedrooms, French provincial in style, with both king- and queen-size beds, walk-in closets, color TV via satellite, and private terraces. Singles in winter cost $65 daily, and doubles go for $75. *Off-season, singles rent for $55 and doubles for $65.* Among the best restaurants in Santo Domingo are the Jade Garden, featuring Chinese cuisine, and the Embassy Club, the deluxe restaurant with an international cuisine, which is known for its flambé dishes. You can drink and dance in La Fontana lounge. On the grounds are tennis courts and an undulating swimming pool with a waterside terrace for refreshments. Its casino is previewed in the After Dark section.

Hotel El Napolitano, 51 Avenida George Washington, Santo Domingo, Dominican Republic (tel. 809/687-1131), is a safe haven—and a good bargain—along the Malecón, which is usually lively until the wee hours. Popular with Dominicans, El Napolitano rents 73 comfortably furnished units, many of which are family rooms. There is a swimming pool on the second floor. The units have central air conditioning, and most rooms are equipped with two double beds. Year round, the charge is $30 for one person, going up to $35 for two. All accommodations open onto the sea. The café is open 24 hours a day, and the hotel also has a good restaurant, specializing in seafood, especially lobsters. There is also a disco and a piano bar, with both live and recorded music. If you like crowds, lots of action, and informality, El Napolitano may be for you.

Hotel Cervantes, 202 Avenida Cervantes, Santo Domingo, Dominican Republic (tel. 809/688-2261), has long been a favorite among budget-conscious American travelers. A family hotel, with a security guard, the Cervantes offers 180 comfortably furnished bedrooms in four floors. It may not be the most tasteful hotel in Santo Domingo in terms of decor, but it is nevertheless clean and efficient, with a pleasant staff. Each unit is equipped with air conditioning, phone, TV, and refrigerator. *In summer, singles pay $36.30 daily, with doubles going for $39.93.* In winter, the single rate is $43.92, and doubles rent for $47.55. The hotel has a swimming pool and is also known for its bronco Steak House, featuring both imported and local charbroiled beef.

2. WHERE TO DINE

In Santo Domingo, guests are not forced to dine every night in their hotels. The city has a host of restaurants serving good food. Dining rooms offering European cuisine, especially Italian, abound. Most of the restaurants stretch along the seaside, bordering Avenida George Washington, popularly known as the Malecón.

The national dish is *sancocho,* a thick stew made with meats (maybe seven different ones), vegetables, and herbs, especially marjoram. Another national favorite is *chicharrones de pollo,* pieces of fried chicken and fried green bananas flavored with pungent spices. One of the most typical of Dominican dishes is *la bandera* (the flag), made with red beans, white rice, and stewed meat. Johnnycakes and mangú, the latter a dish inherited from people called *cocolos* who came to the Dominican Republic from the Windward and Leeward islands, are frequently eaten. Johnnycakes can be bought on the street corner or at the beach, but you must ask for them as *yaniqueques.* Mangú, often included with breakfasts of local foods at hotels, is a purée of green plantains.

Everything tastes better with a good local beer known as Presidente. Wines, under strict and limited control by Customs, are imported, and the prices tend to run high. Dominican coffee is compared favorably with that of Colombia and Brazil.

THE LEADING RESTAURANTS: In a residential sector of the capital, **De Armando,** Calle Santiago Esq. Jóse J. Perez, Gazcue (tel. 809/689-3534), operated by restaurateur Armando Rodriguez, offers dining indoors or outdoors. As an hors d'oeuvre, you might order seafood au gratin or else the pumpkin soup. Señor Rodriguez named filete Armando after himself, and he is justifiably proud of the dish. The meat is served in a brandy-laced, herb-flavored mushroom sauce. Lamb, another good dish, is offered with a red wine sauce, and many chicken recipes are featured, including pollo merengon, served in its own juices along with steamed vegetables and olives. Desserts are made fresh every day, and the wine list is well chosen, ranging from French to Iberian. Meals cost from RD$75 ($15), and reservations are needed. The restaurant is open daily from noon to midnight, but it is at its best in the evening, when there is live piano music.

The restaurants of **Jaragua, Casino, & European Spa,** 367 Avenida George Washington (tel. 809/686-2222), make for a dining festival. Four of the most unusual theme restaurants in the Dominican Republic radiate from a central core, a granite-covered, postage stamp-size wine-tasting bar.

First, there is **Latino,** featuring not only Dominican specialties but those of other Latin countries as well. You might begin with the increasingly popular Spanish *tapas* (hors d'oeuvres), then follow with such classic dishes as a Dominican favorite, "goat-in-rum." Homemade pasta may attract you to **Figaro,** which features the cuisine from both the north and south of Italy, along with delectable pastries and cappuccino. The **Manhattan Grill** isn't confined just to New York–type chow. Food ranges from New England (creamy clam chowder) to Louisiana (shrimp gumbo Cajun-style). Meat cuts are imported from the U.S. All these restaurants are open to the casino, but for a "closed-door policy," you can patronize **Lotus,** which roams the Orient for inspiration. As you can see from the open kitchen as you enter, its woks are black and well-seasoned with use. You might select a dish from Korea or the Philippines, but the Chinese concoctions are the most popular. There is also a selection of Japanese dishes, including sushi. Meals in any of these restaurants cost from RD$75 ($15), and service is from 7:30 to 11 p.m. daily.

If you're playing at the casino, you can go to **The Deli** on the premises overlooking the hotel garden and falls. This busy place, open 24 hours a day, features sandwiches such as corned beef and pastrami, along with the kind of fare associated with New York delis. It also does some Dominican dishes, including peeled shrimp in a hot spicy sauce. Many visitors drop in here just for the homemade ice cream and egg creams, with meals costing from RD$35 ($7).

Il Buco, 152-A Arzobispo Meriño (tel. 809/685-0884), is one of the most popular dining choices in the capital, drawing haut Santo Domingo to its precincts, where they are served an array of countrywide Italian and international specialties. Giuseppe Storniolo is the guiding light behind this successful enterprise in a restored 16th-century house accented with brick, stucco, and flowered tablecloths. All in-the-know diners request his antipasti, an array of both hot and cold Italian-style hors d'oeuvres. Follow with a pasta if you have the appetite, as it's homemade and likely to be served in a savory sauce. Fresh seafood, including bass and lobster, are served as well, depending on what looked good that day at the market. Award-winning dishes include green lasagne and stuffed veal rollatine. The waiters are polite and efficient, and often there is entertainment, all of which makes for a romantic dining choice. On Friday and Saturday nights call for a reservation. Count on spending around $20 or more for one of your finest meals in the capital. Open noon to midnight daily.

Reina de España, 103 Avenida Cervantes (tel. 809/685-2588), offers the Spanish, international, and Créole cuisine of Jesus Ramiro, who has made a sensation of his restaurant on San Juan's El Condado. You can stop for an apéritif at the long bar. Try such culinary specialties as frogs' legs Romana or quail stew with herbs. Another interesting dish is roast duck with mango sauce, instead of the usual orange. Lobster is prepared almost any way you like it, and most fish dishes are excellent, including the seafood casserole. Local dishes aren't neglected, and you might, for example, ask for a Dominican shrimp soup. For dessert, corn ice cream (that's right) is the dish to order for a new taste sensation.

Meals cost from RD$130 ($26), among the most expensive in the capital, but patrons are usually satisfied, knowing they are getting quality ingredients handled by master chefs.

El Alcazar, Hotel Santo Domingo, Avenida Independencia (tel. 809/535-1511), was created by Dominican designer Oscar de la Renta in a Moroccan motif, with aged mother-of-pearl, small mirrors, and lots of fabric. All of this forms a setting for showing off the culinary skills of the restaurant's chef. The preparation of dishes from the extensive international menu is always good, and sometimes excellent. Good materials are used, and well-made sauces add further zest to dining. The presentation of the food, as well as the service from a well-trained staff, provides yet another reason to dine here. Appetizers include onion soup and lobster bisque. The kitchen is known for its steaks and grills, such as filet mignon with béarnaise sauce. There is also a good selection of seafood, including grilled shellfish. Dinner, served nightly from 7 to 11:30 p.m., costs from RD$80 ($16). Lunch, from noon to 3 p.m., features international buffets: one day it might be Chinese; another day, Italian. These cost from RD$32 ($6.40) and provide one of the best food buys in the city. Call for a reservation.

Antoine's, Hotel Santo Domingo Sheraton, 361 Avenida George Washington (tel. 809/685-5151), is the place where the well-dressed Dominican family goes to celebrate a special occasion. Of course, the well-run restaurant in this deluxe hotel also draws an international crowd among the guests staying at the Sheraton. Unusual appetizers include squid in garlic dressing. The waiters often suggest the lobster thermidor, but I've found the red snapper Basque-style more interesting, and it costs less. If you don't want fish, perhaps the tournedos Rossini will intrigue you. For dessert, I happily settle for Spanish coffee, but the next table on my most recent visit preferred baked alaska. Tabs tend to be wide-ranging here, but count on at least RD$75 ($15). Dinner is served from 7 p.m. to midnight daily.

Lina Restaurant, Hotel Lina, Avenida Maximo Gomez (tel. 809/689-5185). Opened by Lina Aguado, whose influence still pervades the ambience and the cuisine, this restaurant is internationally renowned for its paella Valencian-style and its paella with seafood. Seabass is prepared in two different ways, both good—one flambéed with brandy, another in Lina's familiar Basque style. I'm also fond of the tempting mixed seafood au Pernod cooked in a casserole. Tender steak is also prepared in three different ways: roquefort, pepper, and mustard. Appetizers are large in number and unusual, more than just your regular shrimp cocktail. Naturally, the chefs will prepare a cold Andalusian gazpacho. One good main dish you might like is stewed lima beans, Asturian style. The menu is vast, and you may give up and order something before you finish reading it. For dessert, you can ask for flaming apples with Cointreau. Other classic desserts are also rewarding. Meals cost from $25, but the food is deserving. Reservations are suggested. It is open daily from noon to 3 p.m. and 6:30 p.m. to 1 a.m.

Vesuvio I, 521 Avenida George Washington (tel. 809/689-2141), is the most famous Italian restaurant in the Dominican Republic, possibly Santo Domingo's most heavily patronized dining facility. Both visitors and local business people crowd in here for tasty, reasonably priced Italian fare, about every dish you can think of from that country's vast culinary repertoire.

What to order? That is always a problem here, as the Neopolitan owners, the Bonarelli family, have worked since 1954 to perfect and enlarge their menu. Their homemade soups are excellent. From the north coast the restaurant receives such fresh fish as red snapper, sea bass, and oysters, and prepares them in interesting ways. The crowfish is one of their specialties, one variety being à la Vesuvio—grilled crowfish topped with garlic and bacon. The broiled seafood platter is a sample of all their seafood. The veal comes from the Bonarellis' own herd. A favorite dessert is tortelloni al vodka, but you may prefer a recent creation, choccolat fettuccine à la parra, a real chocolate pasta, only instead of sugar they've added salt. An average meal begins at RD$50 ($10). The restaurant is open daily all year from noon to 2 a.m., and you don't need a reservation as it's run on a first-come, first-served basis.

The owner of Vesuvio claims to be the pioneer of pizza in the Dominican Republic. He makes a unique one next door in **Pizzeria Vesuvio**—a yard-long pizza pie! If you want to try their other Italian place, go to **Vesuvio II, 17** Tiradentes (tel. 809/565-9797).

Juan Carlos, 7 Gustavo Mejía Ricart (tel. 809/562-5088), is a top-quality restaurant, handsomely decorated in pinks and mauves. Local paintings add to the attractiveness of the place. But it is the food that attracts the repeat clientele, mostly Dominicans. Several years ago the restaurant with a bodega was opened by Carlos Gil from Palencia, Spain. His specialties include tripe in the Madrid style, guinea hen in madeira, rabbit in a wine sauce, a seafood paella (prepared for at least two persons), roast lamb, and a seafood casserole. You can also order quail stew and seabass in orange sauce. Count on spending from RD$117 ($23.40) and up. The restaurant is open from noon to 3 p.m. and 7 to midnight seven days a week.

LESS EXPENSIVE CHOICES: One of the most attractive restaurants in Santo Domingo, **La Fromagerie,** Plaza Criolla (tel. 809/567-8606), has a regional tavern decor and is air-conditioned. The staff is accommodating, and the list of dishes is international, including Dominican specialties. At lunch, you may prefer to sample one of the crêpes, stuffed with a variety of fillings. Classic dishes include stuffed pot roast, duckling in an orange sauce, and bouillabaisse. More unusual fare is likely to feature a shellfish fondue, frogs' legs in a champagne sauce, and crabmeat in a red sauce. Meals cost from $15. Reservations are rarely needed. Open noon to midnight seven days a week.

Fonda La Atarazana, 5 Calle Atarazana (tel. 809/689-2900). For native food in a colonial atmosphere, with night music for dancing as well, this patio restaurant often has forkloric festivals. Just across from the Alcázar, the restored structure can easily be visited as you're shopping and sightseeing in the old city. This place retains plenty of character, without being deliberately self-conscious about it. A cheap, good dish is chicharrones de pollo, which is tasty fried bits of Dominican chicken. Otherwise, you might try curried baby goat in a sherry sauce. Sometimes the chef cooks lobster thermidor and Galician-style octopus. If you don't mind waiting half an hour, you can order the sopa de ajo (garlic soup). The pork dishes attract many fans, who come here especially for the fricassée pork chops. An average repast will cost from RD$50 ($10).

Café San Michel, 24 Avenida de Lope de Vega (tel. 809/562-4141), on a traffic-clogged street in a section of town called Naco, is a popular restaurant which may have its finest hour when live music is played in the evening, and friends and lovers gather in the bar that is open daily from noon to 12:30 a.m. Specialties from the French and international menu include many different kinds of beefsteak, seabass, red snapper, shrimp, lobster prepared in several ways, Caesar salad, spinach lasagne, soufflés of shrimp or spinach, cream of pumpkin soup, gazpacho, and a series of flavorful chicken breast dishes, each stuffed in a different way. A dessert spectacular is the chocolate soufflé. Full meals here cost around $20 per person.

Restaurant/Bar Jai-Alai, 411 Avenida Independencia, corner of José Joaquin Pérez (tel. 809/685-2409). The original owner of this cosmopolitan restaurant left his home in Bilbao, Spain, when he was 18. After running a successful eatery in Lima, Peru, he came to Santo Domingo, where he set up this restaurant named after the favorite sport of his Basque ancestors. Today the restaurant is directed by the founder's son, Luís Llaque Gordillo, and his wife, Goyi, who welcomes guests with a smile and a fluency in several languages. Shellfish is famous here, with such offerings as lobster Créole, shrimp Jai-Alai, seafood casserole, and oysters in red sauce. Other dishes include octopus Créole, garlic soup, Spanish-style pork chops, rabbit in garlic sauce, and seabass, both Basque and Breton style. As a before-dinner drink you might enjoy a glass of the Peruvian pick-me-up called *pisco*. Full meals cost from RD$60 ($12). The restaurant, which you'll find just back of the Sheraton Hotel, is open for lunch and dinner daily from 11:30 a.m. to 4 p.m. and 6:30 p.m. to midnight.

Restaurante El Bodegón, 152 Arzobispo Meriño (tel. 809/682-6864), occupies several elegant rooms in the heart of the oldest part of the city, opposite the cathedral. The building is a house whose oldest parts date from the 15th century, all of it decorated with heavy ceiling timbers, massive wrought-iron chandeliers, old furniture, and scores of pictures by well-known Dominican artists. Many of the artists are friends of the owner, Frank Salcedo, whose cuisine has won gastronomic awards and whose devotees include luminaries. The bar has received an international award for the house special, a rum caña. Full meals, costing from around RD$50 ($10), can include international dishes such as zarzuela de mariscos (fish and shellfish in a casserole), gazpacho, garlic soup, or a special cassoulet made with lamb, pork stew, sausage, and beans. For dessert you might like to try the pineapple custard. Meals are served daily except Sunday from noon to 3 p.m. and 7 p.m. to midnight.

Jade Garden, Hotel Embajador, 65 Avenida Sarasota (tel. 809/533-2131), is clearly in the front rank in Chinese cookery in Santo Domingo. The management even sent its cooks to Hong Kong to learn some of the secret methods of Peking and northern Chinese cookery, and they returned to please customers with an array of specialties, including such delectables as minced pigeon, soya-bean chicken, sweet-corn soup (superb), lemon duck (even better!), sweet-and-sour pork, deep-fried fish, and fortune chicken, finished off with a toffee banana. The pièce de résistance is the Peking duck, which the chef roasts in an open-fire stove. Your tab at dinner might be RD$60 ($12) or more. Luncheons are great buys, one set meal costing only RD$24 ($4.80). Hours are daily from noon to 3 p.m. and 7:30 to 11:30 p.m.

Restaurant Aubergine, Plaza México Edificio, Alma Mater Avenue, corner of México (tel. 809/566-6622). This is one of the smallest restaurants in Santo Domingo, with no more than eight tables, yet it offers 150 different dishes, many of which are inspired by German-Swiss recipes. Simple but stylish, the "Eggplant" (its English name) contains tones of pink, violet, and red, with hanging straw lamps and enlarged photos of Germany. The music might be a Strauss melody about the Blue Danube. Since 1979, the location has been in a residential neighborhood on the ground floor of a tall building. Full dinners, prepared by the owner-chef, Harald Mossle, cost from RD$50 ($10). These might include veal Zurich style, beef filet in a roquefort sauce, sauerkraut with sausage and pork chops, seabass with almonds, chicken Cordon Bleu, and stuffed eggplant, of course. For dessert, try a slice of the Black Forest cake. Open daily except Sunday, the establishment serves from noon to 3 p.m. and 7 p.m. to midnight.

La Bahia, 1 Avenida George Washington (tel. 809/682-4022), is an unprepossessing type of place right on the Malecón. You'd never know that it serves some of the best, and freshest, seafood in the Dominican Republic. One predawn morning as I passed by, early-rising fishermen were waiting outside to sell the chef their latest catch. Rarely in the Caribbean will you find a restaurant with such a diversity of seafood offerings. For your appetizer, you might prefer ceviche, seabass marinated in lime juice, or lobster cocktail. Soups come from the sea and are likely to contain big chunks of lobster as well as shrimp. See if any of these specialties tempt you—kingfish in coconut sauce, seabass Ukrainian style (a specialty—how did they get the recipe?), baked red snapper, and seafood in the pot. A lot of unusual offerings show up on the menu. Conch is a special favorite with the chef, who knows how to prepare it in many ways. After a big seafood dinner here, costing from RD$50 ($10), desserts are superfluous. No reservations are needed. Service is from 9 a.m. until the last customer departs for home in the early hours of the morning.

Ananda, 7 Casimiro de Moya, corner of Pasteur (tel. 809/682-4465), is a vegetarian restaurant where you can enjoy good food in an informal, cozy room with Oriental or classical music supplying the background effect. The menu here includes a dish of the day as well as other foods all combining natural products. You can feast on a salad made of cucumber, tomato, celery, and spinach, black beans and rice with vegetables, white rice cooked in Chinese or Hindu style with fruits or vegetables, or even a "grilled steak"—actually made of gluten and served with a tasty sauce. Try the ripe plantain pudding for dessert with a local flavor, or perhaps you'd like the peanut or whole-bread pudding. All the desserts at Ananda are made with brown sugar or honey. A meal will cost from RD$15 ($3) at this health-oriented restaurant, which is open daily from noon to 10 p.m.

La Canasta, Hotel Santo Domingo Sheraton, 365 Avenida George Washington (tel. 809/685-5151), is the best late-night dining spot in the capital. Between the Omni Casino and the Omni Disco (both recommended separately in the nightlife section), the restaurant is not only economical, but the best news is that the restaurant serves the most popular Dominican dishes, culled from favorite recipes throughout the country. A complete meal costs RD$30 ($6) and up. Among the favorite local offerings are sancocho, a typical stew with a variety of meats and yucca, and mondongo (tripe cooked with tomatoes and peppers). Unusual offerings include goatmeat braised in a rum sauce and pigs' feet vinaigrette Créole style. The Canasta is open from noon to 3 p.m. and 8 p.m. to 6 a.m. daily.

3. EXPLORING THE CAPITAL

Santo Domingo, a treasure trove, is part of a major government-sponsored restoration. The old town is still partially enclosed by remnants of its original city wall. Its narrow streets, old stone buildings, and forts are like nothing else in the Caribbean. The only thing missing is the clank of the armor of the conquistadores.

Old and modern Santo Domingo meet at the **Parque Independencia,** a big city square whose most prominent feature is its Altar de la Patria, a shrine dedicated to the three fathers of the country, Duarte, Sanchez, and Mella, all of whom are buried here. These men led the country's fight for freedom from Haiti in 1844. As in provincial Spanish cities, the square is a popular gathering point for families on Sunday afternoon. Old men sit in the sun and play dominoes. El Conde Gate stands at the entrance to the plaza. It was named in 1955 for Count (El Conde) de Penalva, the governor who resisted the forces of Admiral Penn, the leader of a British invasion. It was also the site of the March for Independence in 1844, and holds a special place in the hearts of Dominicans.

Heading east along El Conde Street—a microcosm of Dominican life—you reach Columbus Square, with a large bronze statue honoring the discoverer. The statue was made in 1882 by a French sculptor. On the south side of the plaza, the **Cathedral of Santa Maria la Menor** (tel. 809/689-1920) is the oldest cathedral in the Americas, begun in 1514 and completed in 1540. Characterized by a gold coral limestone façade, it is a stunning example of the Spanish Renaissance style, with elements of Gothic and baroque. In the 475-year-old nave, a neo-Gothic marble mausoleum supports a bronze sarcophagus believed to contain the remains of Columbus. (It must be pointed out that several other locations, including Seville, Spain, make this same claim.) The cathedral was visited by Pope John Paul II in 1979 and again in 1984, at which time he was shown work in progress for celebration of the 500th anniversary of the European Discovery of America to be marked in 1992. The cathedral will be the axis of the celebration. An excellent art collection of retables, ancient woodcarvings, furnishings, funerary monuments, and silver and jewelry of the Treasure of the Cathedral can be seen.

The most outstanding structure in the old city is the **Alcázar,** the palace built for the son of Columbus, Diego, and his wife, the niece of Ferdinand, king of Spain. Diego became the colony's governor in 1509, and Santo Domingo rose as the hub of Spanish commerce and culture in America. Constructed of native coral limestone, it stands on the bluffs of the Ozama River. For more than 60 years it was the center of the Spanish court, entertaining such distinguished visitors as Cortés, Ponce de León, and Balboa. After its heyday, it fell on bad days, or rather two disastrous centuries, as invaders pillaged it. By 1835 it lay in virtual ruins; and it wasn't until 1957, in Trujillo's day, that the Dominican government finally restored it to its former splendor. Its nearly two dozen rooms and open-air loggias are decorated with paintings and period tapestries, as well as 16th-century antiques. It is open from 9 a.m. to noon and 2:30 to 5:30 p.m. daily, except Tuesday, charging RD$5 ($1) admission. The same ticket entitles you to visit the **Museu Virreinal** or Museum of the Viceroys, adjacent to the Alcázar. It houses period furnishings and tapestries, as well as paintings dating from the colonial period.

The **Casa del Cordon,** or "Cord House," stands near the Alcázar at the corner of Calles Emiliano Tejera and Isabel la Católica. It was named for the cord of the Franciscan order which is carved above the door. Francisco de Garay, who came to Hispaniola with Columbus, built the casa in 1503–1504, making it the oldest stone house in the western hemisphere. Among important events that took place within the walls of the Casa del Cordon was the time it lodged the first Royal Audience of the New World which performed as the Supreme Court of Justice in the island and the rest of the West Indies. On another occasion, in January 1586, as a memorable gesture, the noble ladies of Santo Domingo gathered here to donate their jewelry as ransom demanded by Sir Francis Drake in return for his promise to leave the city. The restoration of this historical manor was financed by the Banco Popular Dominicano, where its executive offices are found.

Also in the shadow of the Alcázar, **La Atarazana** is a fully restored section which centered around one of the New World's finest arsenals, serving the conquistadores. It extends for a city block, catacombed with merchandise-loaded shops, art galleries (both Haitian and Dominican paintings), and boutiques, as well as some good native and international restaurants, some of which have been recommended previously.

Just behind river moorings, the oldest street in the New World is called **Calle las Damas,** or "Street of the Ladies." Some visitors assume this was a bordello district. Actually it wasn't. Rather, the elegant ladies of the viceregal court used to promenade there in the evening. It is lined with colonial buildings.

Across the street, the **National Pantheon**—a fine example of Spanish American colonial architecture—was originally a Jesuit monastery in 1714, although it was later used as a warehouse for storing tobacco. Once it was a theater as well, and its massive size is characterized by austere lines. Trujillo had restored it in 1955, projecting it as his burial place, but instead one chapel preserves the ashes of the martyrs of June 14, 1959, who tried in vain to overthrow the dictator. Admission is free, and it can be visited Monday through Saturday.

From here you can walk a few steps north to visit the chapel of **Our Lady of Remedies,** where the first inhabitants of the city used to attend Mass before the cathedral was erected.

The **Museo de las Casas Reales,** or Museum of the Royal Houses, also stands on the Calle las Damas (tel. 809/682-4202). Originally it was the Palace of the Royal Audencia and Indias Chancery and the Palace of Governors and Captain Generals. Through artifacts, tapestries, maps, and re-created halls, including a courtroom, it traces Santo Domingo's history from 1492 to 1821. Gilded, elegant furniture, arms and armor, and other colonial artifacts, all inspected by King Juan Carlos of Spain in 1976, make it the most interesting of all museums of Old Santo Domingo. It contains replicas of the three ships commanded by Columbus, and one exhibit is said to hold part of the ashes of the famed explorer. You can see, in addition to pre-Columbian art, the main artifacts of two galleons sunk in 1724 on their way from Spain to Mexico, along with remnants of another Spanish ship, the *Concepción* (18th century). Hours are daily except Monday from 9 a.m. to 5 p.m., and admission is RD$5 ($1).

On Padre Billini, formerly University Street, at the corner of Arzobispo Meriño, is the **Casa de Tostado** (Tostado House) whose beautiful Gothic geminate (i.e., double) window is the only one existing today in the New World. The house was first owned by the scribe Francisco Tostado, and inherited by his son of the same name, a professor, writer, and poet who was the victim in 1586 of a shot fired during Drake's bombardment of Santo Domingo. The Casa de Tostado, which at one time was the archbishop's palace, now houses the **Museum of the Dominican Family,** showing how life was in the 19th century for a well-to-do household. It can be visited daily except Monday from 9 a.m. to 5:30 p.m. Admission is RD$5 ($1).

Museo del Hombre Dominicano, Plaza de la Cultura, Calle Pedro Henríquez Ureña (tel. 809/687-3622), houses the most important collection in the world of artifacts made by the Taíno Indians, who greeted Columbus in 1492. Thousands of magnificently sculptured ceramic, stone, bone, and shell works are on display. Daily, except Monday, hours are 10 a.m. to 5 p.m., and admission is RD$5 ($1).

If time remains, try also to see the **Puerta de la Misericordia.** Part of the original city wall, this "Gate of Mercy" was once a refuge for colonists fleeing hurricanes and earthquakes.

The **Monastery of San Francisco** is but a mere ruin, lit at night. That any part of it still is standing must be counted as a miracle. It was destroyed by earthquakes, pillaged by Drake, and bombarded by French artillery.

In total contrast to the colonial city, modern Santo Domingo dates from the Trujillo era. A city of broad, palm-shaded avenues, its seaside drive is called **Avenida George Washington,** more popularly known as the **Malecón.** This boulevard is filled with restaurants, as well as hotels and nightclubs.

In downtown Santo Domingo, it is now possible to visit the **National Palace,** the three-story, domed structure ordered built by President Trujillo in 1939 and used as the seat of government since its inauguration in 1947. The edifice, considered an architectural triumph in the Dominican Republic, was designed by Italian architect Guido D'Alessandro. It stands in landscaped gardens, where concerts are sometimes held. Because the first floor is mainly occupied by staff offices, visits start on the second floor, where you'll see the Gallery of Presidents. Paintings of the Dominican coat-of-arms from the first design to the one now in use are also displayed. In this room too are the velvet-upholstered, carved mahogany chair used by Trujillo and a mammoth conference table. Of particular interest is the Hall of Caryatides on the third floor, surrounded by 44 marble columns topped by carvings of female figures, separated by mirrors. A presidential suite on this floor is used to house visiting dignitaries. Visitors are sure to be impressed by the extensive use of marble throughout the palace, most of it the country's own product. For a guided tour of the palace, call 809/689-1131, ext. 211. Admission is free.

Museo Nacional de Historia Geografia (Museum of History and Geography), Calle Pedro Henríquez Ureña (tel. 809/686-6677), near the National Library, contains personal belongings of Trujillo, such as clothing, handkerchiefs, French perfume, uniforms, combs, briefcases, and medals from Argentina, Spain, and Japan, as well as personal documents. A series of photographs traces the career of the former ruler. Also on exhibit at the museum are artifacts of the conquistadores, the early colonists under Spanish rule, the Haitian invasion of the Dominican Republic, and other highlights of the nation's history. Admission is RD$5 ($1), and English-speaking guides are available.

The former site of the Trujillo mansion, the **Plaza de la Cultura** has been turned into a large, attractive park, containing the National Library and the National Theater, which sponsors folkloric dances, opera, outdoor jazz concerts, traveling art exhibits, classical ballet, and music concerts. Also in the center, the Gallery of Modern Art has an exhibition of national and international paintings (the emphasis on native-born artists), as well as antiques.

I'd also suggest a visit to the **Paseo de los Indios,** that sprawling five-mile park with a restaurant, fountain displays, and a lake.

About a 20-minute drive from the heart of the city is **Los Tres Ojos** or "three eyes," which stare at you across the Ozama River from Old Santo Domingo. There is a trio of lagoons set in scenic caverns, with lots of stalactites and stalagmites. One lagoon is 40 feet deep, another 20 feet, and yet a third—known as "Ladies Bath"—only 5 feet deep. A Dominican Tarzan will sometimes dive off the walls of the cavern into the deepest lagoon. The area is equipped with walkways. The location is off the Autopista de las Americas on the way to the airport and the beach at Boca Chica.

In the northern sector of Santo Domingo, the **Botanical Gardens** at Arroyo Hondo are the biggest in all of Latin America. In 1.8 million square meters, flowers and lush vegetation of the Dominican Republic can be seen anytime from 9 a.m. to noon and 2 to 6 p.m., and admission is RD$3 (60¢). Seek out, in particular, the Japanese Park, the Great Ravine, and the floral clock. You can also tour the grounds by horse carriage or else take a boat. The gardens are closed Monday.

At the **National Zoological Park** (tel. 809/562-3149), in beautiful parkland with the Isabela River at its northern boundary, you can see one of the largest zoos in Latin America, home to both native and exotic animals and birds, in habitats closely resembling their home territories. An aquatic bird lake, a crocodile pond, an aviary, a snake exhibit, and a huge "African Plain" where fauna from that continent roam make the Santo Domingo zoo a fascinating place to visit. The zoo has a souvenir shop, snack bar, and rest areas. It is open from 9:30 a.m. to 5 p.m. daily, except Saturday and Sunday, when it closes at 5:30 p.m. Admission is RD$1 (20¢) for adults, 75 centavos (15¢) for children. Some of the exhibits cost extra, as does a little train that transports visitors through the grounds for 25 centavos (5¢) per person. To get to the zoo, take Avenida Tiradentes, the busy thoroughfare intersecting Avenida 27 de Febrero, running past Plaza Naco shopping center. Go past Avenida J.F. Kennedy until you reach the zoo at the city's remote outskirts.

4. SHOPPING, SPORTS, NIGHTLIFE

Typical of Latin cities, Santo Domingo has a pulsating life both day and night. I'll preview some of the action in the sections ahead, beginning with—

SHOPPING: The best buys are in handcrafted native items, especially amber jewelry, the national gem, a petrified fossil resin millions of years old. The pine from which the resin came disappeared from the earth long ago. The origins of amber were a mystery until the beginning of the 19th century when scientists determined the source of the gem.

Look for pieces of amber with trapped objects such as insects and spiders inside the enveloping material. Colors range from a bright yellow to black, but most of the gems are golden in tone. Amber deposits in the Dominican Republic were only discovered in modern times. Fine-quality amber jewelry, along with lots of fakes, is sold throughout the country.

A semiprecious stone of light blue (sometimes a dark-blue color), larimar, is the Dominican turquoise. It often makes striking jewelry, and is sometimes mounted with wild boar's teeth, but you may prefer to make a less obvious statement with silver or gold.

Ever since the Dominicans presented John F. Kennedy with what became his favorite rocker, visitors have wanted to take home a rocking chair, a piece of furniture popular throughout the country. To simplify transport, these rockers are often sold unassembled (you put them together when you get home).

Other good buys include Dominican rum, hand-knit articles, macramé, ceramics, and crafts in native mahogany. Always haggle over the price, particularly in the open-air markets. No stallkeeper expects you to pay the first price asked. The best shopping streets are El Conde, the oldest and most traditional shop-flanked avenue, and Avenida Mella.

In the colonial section, **La Atarazana** is filled with galleries and gift and jewelry stores, charging inflated prices. Duty-free shops are found at the airport, in the capital at the **Centro de los Heroes,** and at both the Hotel Santo Domingo and the Hotel Embajador. Shopping hours are generally from 9 a.m. to 12:30 p.m. and from 2 to 5 p.m., Monday through Saturday.

Head first for the **Mercado Modelo,** the National Market, on the Avenida Mella, filled with stall after stall of craft products. Of course, this is a workaday market, catering to the needs of the capital's citizens, so it also overflows with spices, fruits, and vegetables. The merchants will be most eager to sell, and you can easily get lost in the crunch. Remember to bargain for any item that strikes your fancy. You'll see a lot of tortoise-shell work here, but exercise caution, since many species, especially the hawksbill, are on the endangered-species list and could be impounded by U.S. Customs if discovered in your luggage. The already-mentioned rockers are for sale here, as are mahogany ware, sandals, baskets, hats, clay braziers for grilling fish, whatever.

If you're worried that that piece of amber you like may be plastic (and you don't want to strike a match to it in front of the stallkeeper), then you can be assured of the real thing at **Ambar Marie,** 9 Caonabo, Gazcue (tel. 809/682-7539). At this small shop, you can even design your own setting for your choice gem. Look especially for the tear-drop earrings and beautiful amber and gold necklaces. The shop is in the house of its owner, Marie Louise Taulé, who had a Dominican mother and a French father. In a residential area, the shop is open at regular business hours Monday to Friday (closed weekends).

Novo Atarazana, 21 La Atarazana (tel. 809/689-0582). Although its name would imply that it's new, this is actually one of the best-established shops in town. Inside you can purchase pieces of amber, black coral, leather goods, woodcarvings, and even rocking chairs. It's open seven days a week.

Ambar Tres, 3 La Atarazana (tel. 809/688-0474), lies in the colonial section of the old city. This shop sells jewelry made from amber, black coral, mahogany carvings, watercolors, oil paintings, and other Dominican products. The shop is open seven days a week, but it closes at noon on Sunday.

Galería de Arte Nader, 9 La Atarazana (tel. 809/688-0969), in the center of the most historical section of town, is a well-known gallery that sells so many Dominican and Haitian paintings that they're sometimes stacked in rows against the walls. There's an ancient courtyard in back if you want a glimpse of how things looked in the Spanish colonies hundreds of years ago. The gallery is open daily except Sunday from 10 a.m. to 1 p.m. and 4 to 7 p.m.

Tu Espacio, 102 Avenida Cervantes (tel. 809/686-6006), is one of the most charming shopping places in the capital. In a Dominican house, it is crammed with all sorts of goodies, including Taíno art (handcarved reproductions, of course), both Dominican and European antiques, monumental bamboo furniture, and those odds and ends with which Victorians used to clutter their homes. If you're looking for that special trinket, you're likely to find it here. The merchandise is always changing, so you never know what is on sale at any particular time.

The **Plaza Criolla** is a modern shopping complex, with a distinguished design theme. A complex of shops is set in gardens with tropical shrubbery and flowers, facing the Olympic Center on 27 de Febrero. The architecture makes generous use of natural woods, and a covered wooden walkway links the stalls together.

THE SPORTING LIFE: The Dominican Republic may have some great beaches, but they aren't in Santo Domingo. The principal beach resort in the area of the capital is at **Boca Chica,** less than 2 miles east of the international airport and about 19 miles from Santo Domingo. Clear, shallow blue water laves the fine white sand beach and a natural coral reef that protects the area from big fish. The east side of the beach, known as "St. Tropez," is popular with Europeans. The great beaches are at **Puerto Plata,** but that's a rough, three-hour drive from the capital, and at **La Romana,** a two-hour drive to the east. Most of the major Santo Domingo hotels have swimming pools.

For other descriptions of sporting activities, refer to the sections on La Romana and Puerto Plata.

Snorkeling and Scuba

Divers rate the Dominican Republic high for its virgin coral reefs, where you can explore ancient shipwrecks and undersea gardens with an endless variety of marine life.

Mundo Submarino, 99 Gustavo Mejía Ricart (tel. 809/566-0340), is the best in Santo Domingo. It offers a snorkel tour from 9 a.m. to 1:30 p.m. from the beach or a secluded cove. A minimum of four divers is required, paying $25 per head. Advanced scuba tours are featured at the same time—daily diving by boat, in both a shallow and a deep reef with steep walls. The possibilities for photography are excellent. All equipment is included at a cost of $25 for one dive.

Golf

Serious golfers head for **La Romana** or the course that Robert Trent Jones designed at **Playa Dorada,** in the vicinity of Puerto Plata. Golf is also available in the capital at the **Santo Domingo Country Club,** an 18-hole course which grants privileges to guests of most of the major hotels. The rule here is members first, which means it's impossible for weekend games.

Tennis

The major hotels have very good courts, especially at the **Santo Domingo Sheraton, Embajador, Lina,** and **Dominican Concorde** (with eight championship courts). Guests at **Hotel Jaragua** and **Hotel Santo Domingo** will find excellent courts set aside for residents. Some of these courts are lit for night games.

Polo

Made so famous during Trujillo's day, polo is still a popular sport. Polo fields are in Santo Domingo at **Sierra Prieta,** with games played on weekends, and in La Romana at Casa de Campo there are four fields.

Baseball

The national sport is baseball, and many of the country's native-born sons have gone on to the major leagues. From October through February, games are played at stadiums in Santo Domingo and elsewhere. Check the local newspaper for schedules and locations of the nearest game.

Horse Racing

Santo Domingo's race track, **Perla Antillana,** schedules races on Tuesday, Wednesday, Thursday, and Saturday. You can make it a day here, having lunch at the track's restaurant.

Cockfighting

Dominicans like this brutal "sport," but it offends many foreign visitors. However, if you want to see a cockfight, go to the **Santo Domingo Cockfighting Coliseum,** Avenida Luperton (tel. 809/565-3844), across from the Alas del Caribe Airport. This is a modern installation, and you'll see the spectators reach fever excitement. Stakes are high, and the cocks are well trained. The action is followed on closed-circuit TV, as guests sit in air conditioning on comfortable seats.

NIGHTLIFE: From a hectic night of merengue to gambling casinos to disco dancing, Santo Domingo has some of the most varied nightlife in the Caribbean.

Nightclubs

La Fiesta Showroom, Jaragua Resort, Casino, & European Spa, 367 Avenida George Washington (tel. 809/686-2222), brings splashy Las Vegas–type revues to the Dominican Republic. In a 1,000-seat showroom, a multi-million-dollar revue with performances by top-name entertainers is staged at 10 p.m. Thursday and Sunday and at 11 p.m. Friday and Saturday. The 1½-hour show costs $25. Against a backdrop of the largest waterfall on any stage in the world, the show is in four acts, with a four-piece orchestra as well as 40 dancers and an array of "pets," including tigers, leopards, lions, and a 12-foot python. The auditorium is equipped with a 40-foot magic screen enabling performers to step out of projected images and onto the stage. Always call for a reservation.

Meson de la Cava, Avenida Mirador del Sur (tel. 809/533-2818), is a charming restaurant and nightclub built in a natural cave 50 feet under the ground, providing live music for dancing. Shows with merengue music are offered. To reach it, you descend a perilous open-backed iron stairway. At first I thought this was a mere gimmicky club until I sampled the food, finding it among the best in the capital. Waiters bring in one good-tasting platter after another, placing them on your table perched under stalagmites and stalactites if you've been sent to the grottoes. For an appetizer you're faced with the usual selection—shrimp cocktail, onion soup, or gazpacho. Instead of those, however, you may go for the bisque of seafood or red snapper chowder. Among the main-course selections, you'll find "gourmet" beefsteak, fresh seabass in red sauce, tournedos, and coq au vin. You can finish off with a sorbet. Meals begin at RD$50 ($10) per person, plus the cost of your drinks. Hot food is served daily from noon to 4 p.m. and 6 p.m. to midnight. If you go just for the music and dancing, and many do, you'll be charged an entrance fee of RD$5 ($1) per person. After midnight, the waiters present a show of their own. The place is open every day.

Alex's Club, Avenida George Washington (tel. 809/532-1359), on the second floor of the Ocean Inn Building, offers a nightly program of new wave and merengue music for persons age 21 and up. Jackets are required for men. Admission is RD$10 ($2), and the establishment is open from 9 p.m. to 3 a.m. daily except Tuesday.

Pubs and Bars

Two of the leading rendezvous points of Santo Domingo are close to one another, in the oldest section of the city. The **Village Pub,** 350 Calle Hostos (tel. 809/699-7340), is a favorite nightlife spot for Dominicans. If you appreciate lively places, you may like it, too. You can drink in the tropical garden. A beer costs RD$7.50 ($1.50). The place is open from 4 p.m. to 3 a.m. daily.

When you're ready for a change, you can drop into **Raffles,** 352 Calle Hostos (no phone), next door to the Village Pub. Raffles is known around town as an American pub. You may have to hunt around for a table in the series of high-ceilinged Spanish-style rooms with heavy beams, masses of plants, and soothing candlelight. Any lone woman who ventures in here will probably be approached whether she's looking for it or not. The bar, boasting what has been called the most photogenic pool hall in the Western Hemisphere, is open from 6 p.m. to 4 a.m. daily except Sunday when its hours are from 8 p.m. to 4 a.m. You pay RD$4 (80¢) for most drinks.

Piano Bars

Most of the "chic stops" are in the big hotels. **Las Palmas,** at the Hotel Santo Domingo, Avenida Independencia (tel. 809/535-1511), was decorated by the country's best-known designer, Oscar de la Renta. Under a high-vaulted ceiling, mirrored walls are painted with palm fronds. This is the best piano bar in town. A terrace, open to the sea, adjoins the bar. Romantic music is often played, and you can hear, on occasion, jazz, samba, and the bossa nova. Dancing music is played on certain nights. There is never a cover charge, and hard liquor costs from RD$15 ($3). Waitresses wear Dominican colonial dress. Hours are from 5 p.m. to 1 a.m. daily, with happy hour from 6 to 8 p.m., when hors d'oeuvres are free.

Fontana Bar, El Embajador Hotel, 65 Avenida Sarasota (tel. 809/533-2131), is a place to enjoy good music whether it's by the piano player and vocalist early in the evening or the trio later, with a variety of tunes for listening or dancing. The rhythms range from Dominican folk songs to samba to the merengue. The bar, which faces the front door of the hotel's lobby, is inviting. The Fontana also looks out on a patio leading to a swimming pool. Hard drinks cost from RD$15 ($3), and it is open from 4 p.m. to 1 a.m. daily.

Disco Action

Disco-hopping in the Dominican Republic is an after-dinner ritual, although many couples postpone their almost-obligatory visits until after the end of a movie or whatever. At that time, even the most dedicated career woman may don sequins and other alluring garments for an evening out at such places as—

Neon Discothèque, Hotel Hispaniola, Avenida Independencia (tel. 809/535-7111), is one of the town's best-established discos. It offers Latin jazz with different guest stars each week, although disco dancing under flashing lights is one of the main reasons for its popularity. The clientele tends to be somewhat formal compared to that of other nightclubs of Santo Domingo. For example, men should wear jackets. You might see Oscar de la Renta and some of his friends among the well-dressed patrons, most of whom seem to be over 30. The Neon has a cover charge of RD$15 ($3). The place is closed on Monday. Otherwise, it opens at 9 a.m. and stays open until very late, depending on the crowd.

Omni Disco, Hotel Santo Domingo Sheraton, 365 Avenida George Washington (tel. 809/685-5151), is popular with visitors and some of the sons and daughters of the country's most prestigious families who come here to drink and dance. Hotel guests enter free, nonresidents paying a cover charge of RD$10 ($2). The club is open from 8 p.m. to 2 a.m., perhaps later, daily, closing time depending on the crowd.

L'Azotea, Dominican Concorde Hotel, Avenida Anacaona, Mirador del Sur (tel. 809/562-8222), has the most dramatic premises of any disco in town. On the top floor of this first-class hotel, it is one of the most attractive after-dark rendezvous points in Santo Domingo, with stunning views. Occasionally, live entertainment is featured, and there is always recorded music. The entrance fee ranges from RD$10 ($2) to RD$25 ($5), depending on the act booked. The club is open from 9 p.m. to 1 a.m. daily except Sunday.

Casinos

Santo Domingo has several major gambling casinos. The most spectacular is **Jaragua Casino,** Jaragua Resort, Casino, & European Spa, 367 Avenida George Washington (tel. 809/686-2222), whose brightly flashing sign is the most dazzling light along the Malecón at night. You'll think you're on the Strip in Las Vegas. You step into the action, a high-rolling world of croupiers and dealers wearing black ties and wingtip collars. This is the most glamorous casino in the country, fittingly housed in the capital's poshest hotel. Action—blackjack, baccarat, roulette, slot machines—is from 4 p.m. to either 2 or 3 a.m., depending on business, seven days a week. You can gamble in either Dominican pesos or U.S. dollars.

Other casinos include **El Embadajor Casino,** 65 Avenida Sarasota (tel. 809/533-2131), where you'll hear the whirr and clicks from the gaming tables. The popular games of blackjack, craps, and roulette are offered from 4 p.m. to 5 a.m. In between gaming sessions, you can spend an intimate moment at La Fontana, their casual bar where hors d'oeuvres are served.

One of the most stylish casinos is at the Hotel Santo Domingo Sheraton, 365 Avenida George Washington (tel. 809/685-5151), the **Omni Casino,** with a bilingual staff offering blackjack, craps, baccarat, and keno, among other popular games. It's open from 3 p.m. to 7 a.m. daily.

Yet another casino, a bit far from the heart of the city for my taste, is the **Dominican Concorde Casino,** Avenida Anacaona, Mirador del Sur (tel. 809/562-8222), which is about half an hour's drive from the airport, bordering the Paseo de los Indios. If you're a high roller, you'll find that it has the highest limits in the city. The most popular games are wheel of fortune and keno, along with blackjack, baccarat, and roulette. It is open daily from 4 p.m. to 4 a.m.

One of the newer casinos is at **Hotel Hispaniola,** Avenida Independencia (tel. 809/535-7111), open from 4 p.m. to 5 a.m. daily.

5. EAST TO LA ROMANA

On the southeast coast of the Dominican Republic, La Romana was once a sleepy sugarcane town that also specialized in cattle raising. Unless one had business here with either industry, no tourist bothered with it. But when Gulf+ Western opened and later sold a tropical paradise resort of refinement and luxury, the Casa de Campo, on its outskirts, La Romana soon became a word known in the jet-set vocabulary.

If you're already in Santo Domingo, you can drive here in about an hour and 20 minutes from the international airport. (Allow another hour if you're in the center of the city.) Of course, everything depends on traffic conditions (watch for speed traps).

If you're going just to Casa de Campo from North America, you'll find the easiest routing via San Juan, which has the most convenient connections from the mainland (see "Getting There" under Puerto Rico, Chapter IV). Once in San Juan, an **American Eagle** plane flies daily from San Juan to La Romana, departing San Juan at 1:45 p.m. and arriving in La Romana at 2:48 p.m. Depending on conditions and the time of the year, the round-trip fare ranges from $98 to $140 per person. Return flights depart La Romana at 3:10 p.m., and these are coordinated with American's trans-ocean jet service at its hub in San Juan.

THE ULTIMATE RESORT: Translated as "House in the Country," **Casa de Campo,** La Romana, Dominican Republic (tel. 809/523-3330 or toll free 800/223-6620; in Florida, 305/856-5405 collect) offers the greatest resort in the entire Caribbean area—and the competition is stiff. It brings a whole new dimension to a holiday. Gulf+Western took a vast hunk of coastal land, more than 7,000 acres in all, allowing enough breathing space for everyone, and carved out this stunningly chic resort, which today is operated by Premier Resorts & Hotels. The ubiquitous Miami architect, William Cox, helped create it, and Oscar de la Renta provided the style and flair. Tiles, Dominican paintings, and louvered doors, as well as those flamboyant de la Renta patterned fabrics, characterize most of the interiors. The main buildings form a network, constructed of native-grown unpainted wood, each connected by walkways and sheltered by roofs. Gardens blossom with flowering shrubbery and scenic vistas confront you in every direction.

Red-roofed casitas are two-story structures around the main building. *In summer, charges are $95 to $110 daily, based on either single or double occupancy.* In the high season these same accommodations rent for $210 to $230, daily, either single or double occupancy. Villas cluster along the golf course, using the broad Bermuda fairways as common lawns; and there are more villas built along the sea. The tennis village cluster of villas at La Terraza is perched high on the hills, looking out across the cane, fairway, and meadows to the Caribbean. Villas, furnished with a kind of rustic Dominican elegance, come with bath and shower, a large living room, kitchen, refrigerator, and balcony. Each villa offers either a private terrace or veranda overlooking some land or sea vista. The charge is reasonable. For example, a two-bedroom villa for four persons cost $440 daily in winter, but *the price is lowered to $230 off-season.* At the core of everything is a wonderland swimming pool—four, in fact—each on a different level, with thatch huts on stilts to provide beverages and light meals. Perched over the pool is La Cana, the two-level bar and lounge, with a thatched roof but no walls. Dinner is on a rustic roofed terrace. The food is among the best in the Dominican Republic, and the chefs always make it interesting. Perhaps they'll throw a roast suckling pig barbecue right on the beach. Most of the beef used is grown right on the plains of La Romana.

Dining at Casa de Campo

To reach any of the dining spots recommended below by telephone, call the Casa de Campo resort complex number, 809/523-3333, and then the four-digit extension number given for each of the restaurants listed.

Tropicana (ext. 3000) is the most glamorous restaurant at the complex. It's a breeze-filled pavilion known for its innovative seafood market, where diners leave their tables to browse through some of the freshest seafood in the region. Displayed on ice near sizzling woks and smoking grills, the offerings are described by a polite maître d'. Any one of 20 or so spices can be used in the way you decide. Choices depend on whatever is fresh at the sea market. Lobster and giant shrimps are always available. Your meal might begin with selections from a salad bar whose ingredients are displayed beneath the dragon-shaped prow of a fantasy version of a war canoe. If you prefer meat or chicken, a mouthwatering choice of tempura, Szechuan, and Polynesian specialties are also offered, including lobster Canton and chicken teriyaki. Full meals cost RD$150 ($30) and are served daily from 7 to 11 p.m. Reservations are necessary.

El Patio (ext. 2265). Originally designed as a disco, this high-ceilinged room now contains a shield of lattices, banks of plants, checkerboard tablecloths, and a pleasantly familiar battalion of enthusiastic waiters. Technically, its format is that of a glamorized coffeeshop, but you can order some substantial platters from a list of daily specials. Full meals, costing from RD$75 ($15), include ceviche, Cuban-style black-bean soup, sandwiches, salad bowls, sirloin steaks, and several pasta dishes. Full meals are served from 7 a.m. to midnight daily.

Lago Grill (ext. 2266). Whether or not you enjoy its favors later in the day, this place is ideal for breakfast. It has one of the best-stocked morning buffets in the country. It's so popular that residents of the resort's hundreds of secluded villas sometimes break their self-imposed code of privacy to come here to sample its offerings. Your view is of a lake, a sloping meadow, and the resort's private airport, with the sea in the distance. Serve yourself from a fresh juice bar, where a Dominican employee in colonial costume will extract juices from one of 25 different tropical fruits in any combination you prefer. Then select your ingredients for an omelet from several overflowing bowls, give them to a man in a toque, and he'll whip them into an omelet as you wait. The fixed-price breakfast costs RD$38 ($7.60), and is served daily from 7 to 11 a.m. Lunch is from noon to 4 p.m., costs RD$50 ($10), and includes sandwiches, burgers, sancocho (the famous Dominican stew), and fresh conch chowder, along with cold avocado soup in a half pineapple. There is also a well-stocked salad bar.

SPORTS: At La Romana, on 7,000 acres of lush turf, you'll find three Pete Dye golf courses, a stable of horses with twice-weekly polo, a private marina with deep-sea and river trips, snorkeling on live reefs, and clay target, skeet, and trap ranges, plus 13 tennis courts.

Golf

The **Casa de Campo** courses are known to dedicated golfers everywhere—in fact, *Golf* magazine called it "the finest golf resort in the world." The course, Teeth of the Dog, has also been called "a thing of almighty beauty," and it is. It is a ruggedly natural terrain, with seven holes skirting the ocean. Opened in 1977, the Links is the inland course, built on sandy soil away from the beach. Québec-born Gilles Gagnon, the head golf professional, will answer your questions (call him at ext. 3115). Hours are from 7 a.m. to 7 p.m.

Beaches

Bayahibe is a large, palm-fringed sandy crescent reached by a 20-minute launch trip or else by road, a 30-minute drive from La Romana. In addition, **La Minitas** is tiny, but nice, an immaculate little beach and lagoon. Transportation is provided on the bus, or else you can rent a horse-drawn buckboard.

Tennis

A total of 13 clay and four hard-surface courts at Casa de Campo, the best on the island, are lit for night play. Tennis pro Paco Hernandez of the Beverly Hills Country Club is available for lessons and frequently arranges some of the biggest tennis tournaments in the Caribbean. The courts are available seven days a week from 7 a.m. to 10 p.m., and an hour of daylight net time costs $13.50, while 60 minutes of nighttime play is $16.50.

Water Sports and Fishing

Casa de Campo (tel. 809/523-3333) has one of the most complete water-sports facilities anywhere in the Dominican Republic. Reservations and information on any seaside activity can be arranged through the resort's concierge. A sampling of what's available includes the following:

You can charter a boat for a cruise to snorkel or go deep-sea fishing. The resort maintains eight charter vessels, with a minimum of eight persons required per outing. Only four can fish at a time. A half-day cruise costs $250; a full day going for $350.

Patrons interested in river fishing on the Chavón can arrange trips there through the hotel as well. Some of the biggest snook ever recorded have been caught here. Half-day trips, lasting from 8 a.m. to noon or noon to 4 p.m. daily, cost $16.50 per person. This is a more private form of activity, as only two persons are permitted in any single boat.

If you only want a look at the famous river which gave Altos de Chavón its name, Casa de Campo arranges river tours from 5 to 7 p.m. daily, costing $13.50 per person. Each boat holds a maximum of four.

If all you're looking for is a secluded beach with everything from palm trees to sailboats for rent, you'll appreciate Minitas Beach, where the following rental items are available: snorkeling gear, sunfloats, canoe, Sunfish sailboats, windsurfers, and Hobie Cats. Windsurfing costs $10, and snorkeling is $3.50 per hour. Sunfish and paddleboats can be rented for anywhere from $13.50 per hour. The center can be reached by calling extension 2293, and it's open from 9 a.m. to 5 p.m. daily. The resort offers free transportation to the beach by horse-drawn buckboard every hour.

There are no on-site arrangements for scuba-diving, but the hotel will put interested clients in touch with a nearby place which leads such trips.

Polo and Horseback Riding

Ever since the grand days when Dominican playboy Porfirio Rubirosa mounted some of the finest horses in the world, the Dominican Republic has prided itself on its prowess as a polo-playing mecca. The Casa de Campo has always prided itself on the polo traditions it has kept alive since it was first established. For many years the resort employed a nephew of the Maharajah of Jodhpur, the late Jabar Singh, whose pupils included Ramfis Trujillo, son of the former dictator.

Today Casa de Campo is the best place in the Caribbean for playing, learning, and watching the fabled sport of kings and princes. On the premises are three full-size polo fields (one a practice field), a horse breeding farm, and scores of polo ponies, as well as a small army of veterinarians, grooms, and polo-related employees. If during your visit you hear that a polo match will be played, by all means go.

The man who spearheads this reverence for polo-related traditions is a retired brigadier-general in the British army, Arthur Douglas-Nugent. Rarely will a man combine sophisticated charm and polo-playing skill the way Mr. Douglas-Nugent does, attracting devotees from South and North America and Europe. As equally gifted at the social arts is Mr. Douglas-Nugent's charming and stylish wife, Diana.

Most serious polo players arrive with their own equipment, but beginners learn by watching more experienced players and participating in trail rides (which last from one to three hours), as well as riding lessons at the resort's dude ranch. These cost $23.50 each.

Adventure in Bloodless Shooting

A shooting facility for sportsmen, the **Sporting Clays,** has been developed by the owners of Casa de Campo, the Fanjuls, aided by Michael Rose, longtime instructor at the West London Shooting School, where he made a worldwide reputation for his expertise. The facility simulates hunting conditions in the field, with shooting stations (ten at presstime) projecting the natural environment of the quarry represented by clay targets—game and birds. The targets' trajectories and speed vary, some even "flying" out of the 110-foot tower erected on the course.

It costs about $48 to go around with one of the instructors. The double-barreled shotgun is provided free, but you pay for the ammunition you use. You can take a lesson from Rose for $60 from December through April, but his instruction will be much in demand. Whether you're a veteran shooter or a beginner, this is an exciting new sport to try.

Fitness Center

Casa de Campo operates one of the most complete fitness centers in the country. It also has one of the very few squash courts in the Dominican Republic, costing $11.50 per hour. Aerobics sessions cost $3.50 per class, and there is also a collection of weights and exercise machines which are free. A whirlpool and sauna bath costs $8.50 for 30 minutes. The place is best known for its masseuses, who will massage away your tensions for $16.50 an hour.

ALTOS DE CHAVÓN: Again under the daring guiding eye—and purse—of Gulf+Western, an international arts center known as Altos de Chavón was created at a point six miles from La Romana and just east of Casa de Campo. At the edge of its acreage, on the high banks of the Chavón River, an entire town was built to house artisans, both local and international, who come here on a rotating basis, teaching sculpture, pottery, silkscreen printing, weaving, dance, and music, among other artistic pursuits.

A two-year college of the arts has its campus here. Here they can work in their craft shops and display their finished wares for sale. The construction was under the energetic guidance of an Italian builder, who was seemingly inspired by a hill town in the Tuscan countryside. He did a stunning job of creating an old-world village. To many, the village already looks as if it has stood there for centuries. It almost suggests a Hollywood movie set, except that everything here is real.

In the center is the red-tile Church of St. Stanislaus. Surrounding it are "old" houses, along with restaurants on the main plaza, an inn, and other buildings, all overlooking the valley with its river. Arcaded shops sell merchandise, and stairways lead to studio apartments for the artisans and their private loggias.

Frank Sinatra inaugurated the 5,000-seat auditorium, an ampitheater modeled after the Greek antiquity at Epidaurus. Local and international artists appear here frequently. "Sunset performances" are usually on Friday and Sunday evening.

In addition, the museum, **Museo Arqueologico Regional**, open from 9 a.m. to 9 p.m., is devoted to the legacy of the vanished Taíno Indian, displaying artifacts found along the banks of the river.

A narrow walk leads down over a small arched bridge, wending its way to the river below. Before you arrive at the village, there's a large parking area. A bus runs between Casa de Campo and Altos de Chavón every hour.

Accomplished professional artists compete for 20 three-month residencies here each year. Representing many countries and artistic disciplines, the residents live and work in the village and hold exhibitions throughout the year.

Where to Dine in Altos de Chavón

All telephones in Altos de Chavón operate through Casa de Campo switchboard. To reach one of the extensions given below, just dial 809/523-3330 and then the extension number.

Casa del Río (ext. 2345) is the most glamorous and interesting restaurant at Altos de Chavón. It occupies the basement of a re-creation of an Iberian house whose towers, turrets, tiles, and massive stairs are gracefully entwined with strands of bougainvillea. Inside, artfully textured brick arches support oversize chandeliers, suspended racing sculls, and wine racks filled with bottles of champagne. Piano music might accompany your meal. You could begin with an unusual presentation of escargots and gnocchi, or else a soup, perhaps hearts of palm vichyssoise. Main courses are likely to include honey-flavored breast of duck or lobster lasagne. Dinners cost from RD$225 ($45) and are served nightly from 7. Reservations are essential.

La Piazzetta (ext. 2339) snuggles happily within the 16th-century-style "village" set high above the Chavón River. Well-prepared Italian dinners are served here. You might begin with an antipasto misto, following with filet of seabass with artichokes and black olive sauce, chicken saltimbocca, or beef brochette with a walnut and arugula sauce. Your fellow diners are likely to be guests from the deluxe Casa de Campo nearby, enjoying a respite from living in Eden. You'll spend RD$175 ($35) and up for dinner, but this tab could rise much higher if you order a costly wine. Dinner is served daily except Monday from 7 to 11 p.m.

Café de Sol (ext. 2346). If you want a pizza after your exploration of the mosaic-dotted plaza near the church, you'll probably enjoy this stone-floored indoor/outdoor café. To reach it, you climb a graciously proportioned flight of exterior stone steps to the rooftop of a building whose ground floor houses a jewelry shop. It is open from 7 a.m. to 9:30 p.m. daily. Meals cost from $10.

El Sombrero (ext. 2353) occupies a thick-walled colonial-style building whose jutting hand-hewn timbers and roughly textured plaster evoke a corner of old Mexico. There's a scattering of dark, heavy furniture and an occasional genuine antique, but the main allure comes from the spicy Mexican cuisine. Most guests dine outside on the covered patio, within earshot of a group of wandering minstrels whose sombreros accentuate their romantic lyrics. A margarita, laced with salt and tequila, is an appropriate accompaniment to the tortillas, nachos, enchiladas, and burritos that are the house specialties. Grilled steaks and brochettes are also popular. Full meals cost from RD$100 ($15.50) and are served at dinner only, every night of the week from 7 to 11 p.m. Because of its popularity, reservations are a good idea.

Shopping

Oscar de la Renta/Freya Boutique (ext. 2359). Other than an outlet in Miami, this boutique is reputed to sell the creations of Sr. de la Renta less expensively than anywhere else. Some dresses begin as cheaply as $150, but rise to hundreds of dollars for the more lavish designs. Also for sale is a striking collection of purses and boxes cunningly fashioned from tortoiseshell, bone, and cowhorn. Visitors are welcome daily except Sunday from 10 a.m. to 6 p.m.

Everett Designs (ext. 2331). Its designs are so original that many visitors mistake this place for a museum. Each piece of jewelry is handcrafted in a mini-factory at the rear of the shop. Minnesota-born Bill Everett is the inspirational force for many of these pieces, which include Dominican larimar and amber, 17th-century Spanish pieces-of-eight from sunken galleons, and polished silver and gold. The shop is open from 10 a.m. to 9 p.m. daily.

Bugambilia (ext. 2355). A staff of sales clerks will explain the origins of dozens of ceramic figures on display. Sculpted in positions ranging from bearing water to carrying flowers to posing as brides, the female figures are crafted in the industrial city of Santiago as part of a long tradition of presenting peasant women without faces. Look, however, for an expression of dignity in the bodies of the figurines. The largest are packed but not shipped. The store also has a winning collection of grotesque papier-mâché carnival masks. It's open daily from 9 a.m. to 9 p.m.

After Dark

Genesis Disco (ext. 2340) features just about every kind of music at least once each evening. Clients are wide-ranging in tastes, from the most avant-garde artists to relatively conservative visitors from the corporate world. In any event, if you've always wanted to dance your way through the gamut from rock, blues, salsa, merengue, to a good dose of romantic "music for lovers," this is the place for you. The illuminated and translucent dance floor is studded with multicolored pieces of coral. Open at 9 each night, the disco levies a cover charge ranging from RD$10 ($2) to RD$15 ($3). It is closed on Sunday in summer.

Legends (Bill's Bar) (ext. 2380). To the right of the cathedral (as you face its front entrance), this is the premier gathering place for the assembled artists, masons, literati, and students of Altos de Chavón. Owned and managed by American-born Bill Bakas, it's an alluringly simple milieu of framed art posters, exposed wood, and animated conversation. Only drinks are served, averaging RD$8 ($1.60). The bar is open seven days a week from 4 p.m. to 2 a.m. (and often much later).

6. PUNTA CANA

Continuing east from La Romana, you reach Punta Cana, site of several major tourist developments, including Club Med. More are projected at the easternmost tip of Hispaniola. It perhaps will one day become a formidable rival of Puerto Plata.

The area is known for its white sand beaches and gin-clear waters, that Caribbean cliché that is nonetheless true, with coconut palms to complete the picture. This is an escapist's retreat, although resorts compete to have enough activities around the clock to keep guests on the premises.

When white sand bores you, head inland to the typical Dominican city of **Higüey,** 27 miles from Punta Cana, which hasn't been made pretty for tourists. There, you can see the **Basilica Nuestra Señora de la Altagracia,** with the largest carillon in the Americas. The founders of the church conceived the basilica to honor Our Lady of Altagracia, the patron saint of the Dominican Republic. The church is said to represent the best modern architecture on the island. It is reputedly the site of miracles.

Higüey was founded in 1494 by the conqueror of Jamaica, Juan de Esquivel, with immigrants brought in between 1502 and 1508 by Ponce de Léon to populate the land. It was from the castle he built here that the tireless seeker of the Fountain of Youth set out in 1509 to conquer Puerto Rico and in 1513 to check out Florida.

Toward the southern coast is **Saona Island,** where some one thousand people live on 80 square miles of land, surviving primarily by fishing and hunting for pigeons and wild hogs, a healthy way to live, as attested by the fact that Saona has the lowest mortality rate in the Dominican Republic.

Plans call for the completion of an international airport here, so check its status before going there. At presstime, the Punta Cana airport was accepting DC-8 charters. Up to now, most guests arrive at Las Americas International Airport in Santo Domingo, then take a bouncing, three-hour bus ride to Punta Cana. It is also possible to fly to San Juan, then make connections with an American Eagle flight to La Romana, where an overland transfer to Punta Cana can be arranged.

INCLUSIVE RESORTS: At a point 145 miles east of Santo Domingo, **Club Méditerranée** Punta Cana, Cabo Engaño, Higüey, Dominican Republic (tel. 809/567-5228), opened in 1981, and it can be said that it put the far eastern tip of the island of Hispaniola on the tourist map. The 600-bed village lies along a reef-protected white sandy beach, which offers some of the best diving areas on the islands. It was here that the crews of *Pinta, Niña,* and *Santa Maria* are believed by some to have put ashore. Columbus wouldn't recognize the place today. Three-story clusters of bungalows are strung along the beach, containing twin beds and opening either on the sea or onto a coconut grove. Each is air-conditioned with red-tile floors and a private shower-bathroom. Rates depend on the time of year. The most expensive time to book is over Christmas and New Year's, when the per person cost goes up to $1,200 weekly based on double occupancy. *In summer per person rates are around $650 weekly.* In winter they rise to around $750 per person weekly. The Punta Cana airport lies about five minutes from the village.

Sports include sailing, windsurfing, snorkeling, waterskiing, swimming, archery, and tennis on 10 courts, four of which are lit for night games. You get the usual Club Med activities here, including picnics, boat rides, nightly dancing, shows, and optional excursions. There's even a computer workshop. Activities spin around a combined dining room/bar/dance floor and theater complex facing the sea in the center of the village. In front of this activity center is a big swimming pool. A small restaurant and disco, nearby, are built beside the sea. The club has a Mini-Club for juniors, highlighting circus training, computer workshops, and other activities. There is a separate area in the village for activities for the even younger set. For reservations and information in New York, call 212/750-1670; otherwise dial toll free 800/CLUB MED nationwide.

Bavaro Beach and **Bavaro Garden Hotels,** P.O. Box 1, Punta Cana, Higüey, Dominican Republic (tel. 809/682-2161), a massive resort colony, lies on one of the best beaches in the Caribbean, with some 26 miles of white sands stretching in either direction. It contains a total of 1,001 rooms divided between two resorts. Opening in 1985, the Bavaro Beach Resort is spread across four different low-rise buildings, each of which lies parallel to the beachfront for a maximum view of the sea. In 1987, because of the success of the first enterprise, a new complex, containing 401 additional rooms, was added and called Bavaro Garden Hotel. The garden hotel shares the water sports and dining facilities of the original resort.

Each room is air-conditioned, containing a terrace, phone, ocean view, cable TV, and a safety deposit box, along with a double bed and a single or two doubles. Most stays here are sold on a week-long basis and are priced with MAP included (but not lunch or drinks). Also included in the package are taxes, service, transfers from Santo Domingo in a bus or van, entertainment, and many different water sports and such activities as tennis, aqua gym, water polo, and aerobics. *In summer per person rates, based on double occupancy, are $480 per week.* In winter, per person week-long stays go up to $760, based on double occupancy. The popular beach bar is the most active spot during the day, giving way to a disco at night. In the club you can learn the merengue. There are at least five different restaurants on the grounds, along with four bars and two lounges.

For information, contact Barcelo Tours, 150 S.E. Second Ave., Suite 806, Miami, FL 33131 (tel. toll free 800/336-6612 nationwide but in Florida call 800/367-3100). If passengers can arrange it directly with the Miami sales office, they can participate in charter flights from San Juan directly to Punta Cana. Departures are Saturdays only in both directions.

Punta Cana Beach Resort, Punta Cana, Higüey, Dominican Republic (tel. 809/541-2724 for information), is a formidable rival of Club Med and the Bavaro complex. Privacy gets priority here on 105 acres of tropical vegetation opening onto its own 2,300 feet of sandy beaches. Accommodations range from villas to studios, along with various suites, each with air conditioning and cable TV. Studio hotel rooms contain kitchenettes, as do one-bedroom suites (built on one or two levels). The most luxurious units are two- and three-bedroom villas where you can settle in, as in a private home, with a dining room and living room area, along with a kitchen and a patio in the rear. In winter single occupancy of a studio is from $105 to $113 daily, going up to $140 to $156 in a suite. Double occupancy of a studio is from $126 to $140 daily, rising to $162 to $180 in a suite. A two-bedroom apartment, suitable for four occupants, costs from $345 to $383 per day. All rates are MAP. *In summer, studio singles cost $112 per day, or $146 in a suite, whereas double occupancy of studios and suites ranges from $156 to $224 daily, with a two-bedroom apartment for four occupants costing $292. These charges include MAP.*

The resort has a 3,000-square-foot pool with a bar where you can swim up for a fast daiquiri. Children have their own more protected pool. A host of sports (on land and sea, as the expression goes) include tennis, scuba, windsurfing, horseback riding, and snorkeling. Several excursions can be arranged, even to a local cattle ranch. La Tortuga Beach Club perches under a thatched roof and looks out through a magnificent archway to the water. It is a veritable beehive of life here with a piano bar and a restaurant. It's senseless to give a room count, as the resort has many "phases" projected and big, big plans. To book a room call toll free at 800/223-9815.

7. NORTH TO PUERTO PLATA

Originally it was Columbus's intention to found America's first city at Puerto Plata, naming it La Isabela. But a tempest detained him, and it wasn't until 1502 that Nicolas de Ovando founded Puerto Plata, or "port of silver," lying 130 miles northwest of Santo Domingo. The port in time became the last stop for ships going back to Europe, their holds laden with treasures taken from the New World.

From Santo Domingo, the 3½-hour drive directly north passes through the lush Cibao Valley, home of the tobacco industry and Bermudez rum. You pass through Santiago, the second-largest city in the country, 90 miles north of Santo Domingo. Most of the hotels are not in Puerto Plata itself but in a special tourist zone called **Playa Dorada.** The international airport is actually not in Puerto Plata but lies east of Playa Dorada on the road to Sosúa.

Puerto Plata shows signs of offering a broad-based appeal to a market which may shun more expensive resorts, with some hotels boasting a nearly full occupancy rate almost all year. It is already casting a shadow on business at longer-established resorts throughout the Caribbean, especially in Puerto Rico.

The backers of this usually sun-drenched spot have poured vast amounts of money into a flat area between a pond and the curved and verdant shoreline. (It rains a lot in Puerto Plata during the winter, while the south and Punta Cana are drier.) Major hotels have been constructed, as well as a scattering of secluded condominiums and villas and a Robert Trent Jones–designed golf course, plus a riding stable with a complement of horses for each of the major properties.

Fort San Felipe, considered to be the oldest fort in the New World, is a popular attraction. Philip II of Spain ordered its construction in 1564, a task that took 33 years to complete. Built with eight-foot-thick walls, the fort was virtually impenetrable, and the moat surrounding it was treacherous. The Spaniards sharpened swords and embedded them in coral below the surface of the water to discourage use of the moat for entrance or exit purposes. The doors of the fort are only four feet high, another deterrent to swift passage. During Trujillo's rule Fort San Felipe was used as a prison. Standing at the end of the Malecón, the fort was restored in the early 1970s. Admission is 75 centavos (15¢). Open from 9 a.m. to noon and 3 to 5 p.m. daily except Thursday.

Isabel de Torres, a tower with a fort built when Trujillo was in power, affords a magnificent view of the Amber Coast from a point near the top, 2,595 feet above sea level. You reach the observation point by cable car *(teleférico),* a seven-minute ascent. Once there, you are also treated to seven square acres of botanical gardens. The round trip costs RD$5 ($1). The aerial ride is operated daily except Wednesday from 8 a.m. to 5 p.m. Be warned: There is often a long wait in line for the cable car.

You can see a collection of rare amber specimens at the **Museum of Dominican Amber,** 61 Duarte St. (tel. 809/586-2848), owned and operated by Didi and Aldo Costa. The museum, open Monday to Saturday from 9 a.m. to 5 p.m., is near Puerto Plata's Central Park. Guided tours in English are offered. Admission is RD$2 (40¢).

A chain of ocean banks off the northeast coast is a Zona Economica Exclusiva (ZEE), established by the Dominican Republic for conservation of important living and nonliving natural resources in the waters and on the ocean bottom. Lobsters, conchs, and various fish abound there, but La Plata and La Navidad banks are a stopover for some of the most important winter visitors to the area—**humpback whales,** who make annual visits as they travel thousands of miles in their migrations. You may be fortunate enough to see some of these huge sea mammals cavorting in the water if you go to the banks by boat. Dolphins (the mammals) also frequent the area. The banco de la Plata is a marine life sanctuary.

GETTING AROUND: If you prefer to be free to come and go as you wish, you

may choose to rent a **car.** For information on this, see the discussion of car rentals in the Santo Domingo introduction. You might even find that a **motor scooter** will be suitable for transportation in Puerto Plata or Sosua.

If you take a **taxi,** make an agreement with the driver on the fare before your trip starts, as the vehicles are not metered. You'll find taxis in Central Park. At night it's wise to establish your cab ride on a round-trip basis. If you go in the daytime by taxi to any of the other beach resorts or villages, check on reserving a vehicle for your return trip.

For a much cheaper ride, take a **concho,** a multipassenger taxi or van that travels on the main roads. If you take one from Central Park, be sure it's really a concho and not a regular taxi. You can also flag down these vehicles on the highway, but you have to wave at all cars as the conchos are not designated on the outside. If it is one, and has room for another passenger, it will stop for you.

WHERE TO STAY: The combined Aztec and Moorish design of **Eurotel,** P.O. Box 337, Playa Dorada, Puerta Plata, Dominican Republic (tel. 809/586-3663), makes this property the most imaginative and stylish on the coast. It sits amid a garden of flowering plants, flagstone walkways, and a roughly textured rock wall from which a dozen artificial springs feed water pool. Each of the comfortable and stylish bedrooms has its own Spanish-style *mirador* (sheltered balcony) and the aura of a comfortable private apartment. Rooms are rented as either singles or doubles. In winter, a standard room costs $98 daily, *lowered to $90 daily in summer.* Junior and superior suites are the same price year round, costing $130 to $150 daily for two guests. Outside, if you follow the flowing tropical stream (which empties the pool), you reach a palm-thatched beachside entertainment center with its own bubbling whirlpool, an offering of water sports, a music platform for live entertainment, and a cluster of dining and drinking facilities. The resort has five different restaurants, each with distinctive character. These include The Americas, the most formal and elegant, where men should wear ties and jackets in high season. The most popular, the Bergantin near the beach, is so casual that guests show up in wet swim suits. There's even a pizzeria, Piccolo Mondo. The hotel opened a casino in 1989, and it also operates the leading nightclub of Puerto Plata.

Playa Dorada Hotel & Casino, P.O. Box 272, Puerto Plata, Dominican Republic (tel. 809/586-3988), a theatrically designed hotel, opened in 1983, and it's one of the few hotels in all the Caribbean which can boast nearly full occupancy during most of the year. It offers one of the biggest swimming pools in Puerto Plata, around which the hotel management hosts barbecues, buffet suppers, and weekly entertainment which includes singers and dancers known throughout the Spanish-speaking world. The reception area is an air-conditioned oasis of Victorian latticework set beneath the soaring ceiling. The 253 bedrooms are arranged along rambling corridors which, at the end of a long day on the beach, may seem almost endless. More than two-thirds of the hotel's units are set into red-roof wings which face the sands of the 1½-mile beach. In high season, rooms cost $120 daily for single or double occupancy, with each additional person in a room paying $20. *Summer prices are $50 for single or double occupancy, $10 for an additional person.* A sports package is included in all tariffs. The hotel also has specially designed rooms for handicapped patrons. In addition to La Palma restaurant and the many bars and entertainment facilities, guests have access to a full range of boating, water sports, and golf activities. Three tennis courts are lit for night games. There's a cocktail lounge, Las Olas, where live entertainment is presented every night, as well as one of the hottest discos in town on the premises. Among the amenities are a babysitting service, laundry and valet service, and video movies.

Radisson Golf, Tennis, & Beach Resort, Puerto Plata, Dominican Republic (tel. 809/586-5386), is one of the best of the modern complexes springing up in resort-studded Puerto Plata. It offers suites and villas as well as standard rooms that have many amenities, including individually controlled air conditioning, direct-dial phones, fully stocked mini-bars, color TV with cable programming, and bed turn-down service. In high season, rooms cost from $135 daily for single or double occupancy, with junior suites, suitable for two guests, renting for $140. *In summer, prices go down to $65 daily for single or double occupancy of a standard room, $80 for two in a junior suite.* As its name suggests, the resort is sports-oriented. You can play golf on the nearby 18-hole course, participate in a variety of water sports, ride horseback, and do aerobics. The hotel has a number of dining facilities, including the terrace overlooking the pool or at La Condesa, where a more refined cuisine is served from 7 to 10 nightly. The beach club, La Tortuga Loca, has full facilities, including a barbecue area. There's beach shuttle service from the hotel.

When **Dorado Naco**, P.O. Box 162, Puerto Plata, Dominican Republic (tel. 809/596-2019), was built in 1982, there was only one other hotel in the entire Playa Dorada area. After registering, you'll be ushered past the poolside bar and restaurant complex, down a series of flowered walkways into one of the 150 units. A wide range of sports and entertainment is available to guests. A beach bar and grill lie a short walk from every room. The hotel has live music every night and live shows twice weekly. Throughout the week in season, guests find a full range of planned activities. A nightly buffet is served under a portico near the pool, and à la carte meals are available in a covered dining room.

Each unit contains comfortable furniture, a kitchen, and a creative arrangement of interior space. Many guests choose to spend some of their evenings *en famille,* cooking at home, although a popular weekly meal plan includes seven breakfasts and four dinners for around $69 in high season. Many of the units are clustered along parapets or around well-planted atriums, and some of the larger ones include duplex floor plans and about as much spacious luxury as a vacationer could hope for. *In summer, the price is $100 daily in a one-bedroom suite for one to two persons. A one-bedroom penthouse suite, housing up to four persons, costs $130 daily, and a two-bedroom suite, also suitable for four, goes for the same price.* In winter, a one-bedroom suite for one or two persons rents for $150, the cost rising to $200 for up to four persons in either a one-bedroom penthouse suite or a two-bedroom suite.

Villas Doradas Beach Resort, P.O. Box 1370, Playa Dorada, Puerto Plata, Dominican Republic (tel. 809/586-3000), opened in 1984, is a pleasant collection of town houses arranged in landscaped clusters, usually around a courtyard. There's no beachfront here. Rather, part of your experience will be almost a community feeling, with neighbors all around in the groups of small villages set up around a series of green areas. The complex is within walking distance of sand beaches and golf facilities. A focal point of the resort is the restaurant, Las Garzas, where a musical trio entertains guests every evening beneath the soaring pine ceiling. The management also features barbecues around the kidney-shaped pool area, where a net is sometimes set up for volleyball games. Of course, it would be tempting never to leave the shade of the cone-shaped thatch-roofed pool bar, which is one of the most attractive and popular parts of the whole resort. Each unit is pleasantly furnished and attractively unpretentious, with louvered doors and windows to make your temporary home either open or closed to the outside world. There's a TV in each villa, as well as air conditioning and a phone. Single or double occupancy costs $90 daily in winter, with junior suites for two going for $110. *In summer, single or double occupancy becomes a real bargain at only $45 daily, with suites for two costing $60.*

Jack Tar Village, P.O. Box 368, Playa Dorada Beach, Puerto Plata, Dominican Republic (tel. 809/586-3800 or toll free 800/527-9299). Purchased by an investment group from Texas, this all-inclusive resort may represent the shape of things to come. Set at the edge of the sea and clustered around two swimming pools, the facility offers drinks, all meals, most water sports, and entertainment within its compound, so that you need never leave the grounds. In the central, cement-covered core of the resort, you'll find dozens of vacationing adults and children playing shuffleboard, cards, table tennis, or volleyball, or just whiling away the time. If you simply prefer to linger beside one of the indoor/outdoor bars, where everything is free (even cigarettes), you'll have plenty of company. If you're more energetic, many water and land sports are offered, most of them included in the overall price of your accommodation in one of the white-walled villas. The 284 units rent for $120 per person double occupancy in high season, for $170 single occupancy. *In summer, the charge is $110 daily per person for double occupancy, $150 for single occupancy.* One child age 2 to 12 may stay in the parents' double room for $50 in either season. Four nights a week, dinners are sit-down affairs in the high-ceilinged dining room, with waiter service and frequent musical entertainment. The rest of the time, and often at lunch, meals are buffet style.

Montemar, Avenida Circunvalación del Norte, P.O. Box 382, Puerto Plata, Dominican Republic (tel. 809/586-2800), is a glistening hotel complex that plays a double role: it's one of the pioneer resorts in the area, and it houses the local hotel school. The lobby is one of the most distinctive in the area. Large bamboo chandeliers illuminate the upholstery, where images of birds flit across the comfortable couches and the naturalistic mural behind the reception desk. Your needs will be cared for by a battalion of students. A lounge nearby engages a merengue band which plays every night beside the illuminated palms. The hotel offers a total of 95 units, most with views of palms and the sea. *Off-season, singles rent for $30 daily, and doubles go for $35.* Rates in winter are $45 daily in singles, $50 in doubles. The resort's restaurant, La Isabella (see my dining recommendation), is one of the best decorated and most sophisticated restaurants in town. There are three tennis courts in the hotel complex.

WHERE TO DINE: Perhaps the most distinguished restaurant in Puerto Plata is **De Armando,** Calle Separación Esq. Antera Mota (tel. 809/586-3418), launched by Armando Rodriguez in 1981. (He opened another one in Santo Domingo in 1987.) In an elegant setting, his international cuisine has been pleasing diners for years. You can select an appetizer such as escargots bourguignonne or else one of half a dozen soups, including lobster bisque. He serves excellent fish dishes. For that Dominican flavor, there is moro choncho, rice and black beans served with pork fritters. Each day, a dessert is freshly made. Meals cost from RD$75 ($15). Service is daily from noon to midnight, and reservations are advised. At night, a guitar trio entertains.

One of the loveliest buildings in downtown Puerto Plata, **Jimmy's,** 72 Calle Beller (tel. 809/586-4325), is an alluring establishment, serving some of the best food. It lies behind lacy rows of cast-iron balustrades in a century-old building. Full meals are priced from RD$75 ($15) and are served daily from 11 a.m. to 11 p.m. The internationally inspired menu includes lobster "Jimmy's style" which is flambéed at your table with cream sauce, along with such steaks as tournedos, and filet mignon. The kitchen turns out a delectable version of a local cream of fish soup called *sopita,* along with several versions of chicken (including one with lemon) and such spectacular desserts as bananas flambé and crêpes suzette.

Valter's, Las Hermanas Mirabal Boulevard (tel. 809/586-2329). Its low-slung Victorian porch, with its adjacent garden, seems like the ideal place for a romantic candle-lit dinner. Built about a century ago as a private home, it has ring-around gingerbread painted in vivid shades of lime green, an oversize veranda laden with dozens of tables, and a neo-Victorian bar. Open seven days a week from 11 a.m. to 3 p.m. and 7 to 11 p.m., it serves meals from RD$75 ($15). Surf and turf is the house specialty, and you'll also find an array of classic pasta dishes. The owner, Valter Tapparo, is from Vicenza, Italy. Reservations are necessary, particularly on weekends when many local residents make dining a special event.

Jade Garden, Villas Doradas, Playa Dorada (tel. 809/586-3000). Contained on the grounds of the previously recommended Villas Doradas in the hotel zone, this is a high-ceilinged and airily modern restaurant specializing in Chinese food. You can enjoy a Chinese buffet on Monday, Wednesday, and Friday, costing RD$49 ($9.80). Set evening meals for two persons begin at RD$78 ($15.60), with à la carte dinners going for RD$50 ($10) and up per person. Typical menu items include barbecued Peking duck, sautéed diced chicken in chili sauce, and fried crab claws. The restaurant is open seven days a week, serving dinner from 6 to 11 p.m. Lunch is offered only in winter, from noon to 3 p.m.

Porto Fino, Hermanas Mirabal Boulevard (tel. 809/586-2858), is a good Italian restaurant just across from the entrance of the Hotel Montemar. The owner's Italian dishes have made this place popular in the Puerto Plata area. Parmesan breast of chicken, eggplant parmesan, ravioli, and pizzas are served in generous helpings. Expect to pay from RD$50 ($10) for a complete meal, although you'll get off much cheaper if you only order pizza. The restaurant is open daily from 11 a.m. to 11 p.m.

Los Pinos Restaurant/Bar La Chispa, Hermanas Mirabal Boulevard (tel. 809/586-3222). Within the rough-hewn walls of this intimate retreat lies a warmly decorated restaurant created by an expatriate Québecois, Monique Leveiller. Styled a bit like something you'd come across in the South Seas, it's a convenient perch for daiquiri drinkers; however, many customers prefer the comfortable banquettes ringing the tables looking out over the forest. Food is served from 3 p.m. to midnight daily except Sunday. Meals, costing from RD$75 ($15), include seafood paella, pepper steak, pastas, seabass, wine-baked chicken, and grilled lamb chops.

Restaurant La Isabella, Hotel Montemar (tel. 809/586-2800). Because many of the staff of this restaurant are students at the adjoining hotel school, the service is probably better than at places where the help has become jaded. The decor is one of the most elegant in Puerto Plata. You enter a spacious, split-level room with subtle lighting, where the combined effect is like a page from a fashion magazine. Only dinner is served here, from 6 to 11 p.m., with a polite staff of uniformed waiters looking after you. The food items are likely to change, but throughout the year feature such dishes as a paella for two persons, oysters, veal kidneys Beefeater style, and a chicken suprême in a cream sauce. Meals cost from RD$75 ($15).

Dominican Joe's, 60 Beller St. (tel. 809/586-1277), serves some of the best local cuisine in town in an atmosphere described as "family style." It's housed in one of the gingerbread-style Victorian buildings in the downtown section. Dominican Joe isn't Dominican at all. He's Joe Lombardi, an Italian-born refugee from Boston. Try, if featured, stone crabs from Turks and Caicos which are boiled in beer. Full meals cost from RD$45 ($9) and are served daily from 11 a.m. to midnight.

Roma II, Beller Street at Emilio Prud'homme (tel. 809/586-3904), is an air-conditioned restaurant staffed by an engaging crew of well-mannered young employees, who work hard to converse in English. You can order from a selection of 13 varieties of pizza beginning at RD$10 ($2) and containing tempting combinations of cheese, shrimp, and garlic. Full meals cost from RD$60 ($12) and include a full array of seafood such as paella, seafood casserole, several preparations of lobster, seabass, and octopus prepared Créole style or with vinaigrette.

Beef dishes include Stroganoff or tenderloin. Hours are from 11 a.m. to midnight daily.

WHERE TO SHOP: Unless otherwise cited, most shops are open from 9 a.m. to 6 p.m. Monday to Saturday. The largest shopping center on the north coast, **Plaza Turisol**, is a shopping mall with a multicolor roof and about 80 different outlets. Each week, or so it seems, a new store opens. You may want to head here to get a sampling of the merchandise available in Puerto Plata before going to any specific recommendation. The plaza lies about five minutes from the centers of Puerto Plata and Playa Dorada on the main road heading east.

The best-established place for fine gold jewelry is **Harrison's**, 14 J. F. Kennedy (tel. 809/586-3933). The shop also sells silver and black coral jewelry.

The best place in town to purchase fairly priced samples of the two stones for which the Dominican Republic is noted is the **Factory Gift Shop**, 27 J. F. Kennedy (tel. 809/586-3834). Amber from the island's north shore and larimar turquoise from the south shore are sold in a wide and attractive variety, or you can buy black coral, bull's horn, or Dominican pictures. Ramón Ortiz and his family will show you their workshop, where they polish different grades of their raw material into cunningly shaped figures, representing everything from frogs to rabbits. Some of the rare (and expensive) pieces contain well-preserved insects, and one even has in it a (petrified) lizard. Anything you buy can be mounted in silver or gold.

Tourist Bazaar Boutique, 61 Calle Duarte (tel. 809/586-2848), is a neoclassical house sheltering the Amber Museum, but it also contains the densest collection of boutiques in Puerta Plata. Merchandise is literally packed into seven competing establishments. A generous percentage of the paintings is from neighboring Haiti, but the amber, larimar, and mahogany woodcarving are from the Dominican Republic. On the premises is a patio bar.

Centro Artesanal, 3 Calle Kennedy (tel. 809/586-3724). This is a nonprofit school for the training of future Dominican crafts people, and it's also a promotion center for local crafts and jewelry. Selected student projects are for sale. The establishment is open weekdays from 8 a.m. to noon and 2 to 5 p.m.

SPORTS: The north coast is a water-sports scene, although the sea here tends to be rough. Snorkeling is popular, and windsurfing is among the best in the Caribbean. The resort of Cabarete, east of Puerto Plata (see below) is notable as the host of an annual windsurfing tournament.

Tennis is a popular pastime. Some of the best facilities in the Playa Dorada area are available at the **Radisson Golf, Tennis, & Beach Resort** (tel. 809/586-5386). It offers seven all-weather courts as well as a pro shop and club. Depending on the season, courts for nonresidents rent for RD$10 ($2) to RD$20 ($4) per hour.

Robert Trent Jones, Jr., designed the par-72, 18-hole **Playa Dorada championship golf course** which surrounds the resorts and runs along the coast. Even nongolfers can stop at the clubhouse for a drink or a snack to enjoy the views. Instead of trying to call the course, it's best to make arrangements at the activities desk of your hotel.

You'll find superb **beaches** to the east and west of Puerto Plata. Among the better known are Playa Dorada, Sosúa, Long Beach, Cofresi, Jack Tar, and Cabarete.

AFTER DARK: The major nighttime activity takes place in the casinos. A recent addition is the **Eurotel**, Playa Dorada (tel. 809/586-3663), one of the splashiest and most elegant casinos in the Dominican Republic, suitable to the resort to which it belongs. Dealers from Santo Domingo worked overtime teaching the inexperienced crew the intricacies of craps, roulette, and blackjack before the casino opened. Action is from 4 p.m. to 4 a.m. daily.

Playa Dorada Casino, Playa Dorada Hotel, Playa Dorada (tel. 809/586-3988), is also open from 4 p.m. to 4 a.m. daily. No shorts are permitted inside the premises after 7 p.m., and beach attire is never allowed. The casino's entrance is flanked by plum-color columns, leading to an airy garden courtyard. Inside, mahogany gaming tables are reflected in the silver ceiling and ringed with mauve and pink walls.

Puerto Plata Beach Resort & Casino, Malecón (tel. 809/586-4243), was the first casino in Puerto Plata, but it was just the bellwether, as more and more have followed. One of the most charming casinos in Puerto Plata, with high ceilings and tall French windows, this one is open from 4 p.m. to 4 a.m. daily. Guests find crap tables, 16 blackjack setups, roulette wheels, and two "big six" layouts. Gamblers can play in either pesos or U.S. dollars.

In 1989, **Jack Tar Village,** Playa Dorado (tel. 809/586-3800), joined the gaming flock by opening a casino and disco along with a European-style gourmet restaurant. It is built in Spanish Mediterranean colonial style with a terracotta roof. Between bouts at the games tables, guests quench their thirst at one of five bars. No shorts or bathing suits are allowed in the casino which is open daily from 4 p.m. to 4 a.m.

La Hispaniola, Eurotel, Playa Dorada (tel. 809/586-3663), is the leading nightclub in the Playa Dorada area. It offers first-class revues like those staged in Puerto Rico. It is open nightly from 9 p.m. to 3 a.m., usually charging an entrance fee of RD$20 ($4), although that could vary, depending on the entertainment. Guest stars and show girls round out a night of drinking and dancing. The club is richly decorated with velvet walls and a mirrored ceiling.

A heavily patronized disco is **Vivaldi's,** corner of Hermanas Mirabal Boulevard and the Malecón (tel. 809/586-3752). Many non-Dominicans wouldn't think of coming back to Puerto Plata without rendezvousing with their acquaintances here. There's a restaurant on the upper floor, but most of the people who stream in head for the ground-floor disco, where a combination of everything from salsa to reggae to New York City's recent dance releases is played practically all night. The interior is ringed with what you might call wrap-around neon. If you want a breath of cool air, there's a little-used terrace in front. There's a cover charge of RD$10 ($2) to RD$15 ($3), depending on the night of the week.

The disco at the **Playa Dorada Hotel,** Playa Dorada (tel. 809/586-3988), is among the most animated nightspots in Puerto Plata. Head for the central core of the hotel on the ground level and pass through the orchid-colored lobby to reach it. The entrance fee is RD$10 ($2) on Friday and Saturday night; otherwise it's free. Once inside, you're faced with a dance floor (which is usually packed by the end of the evening) and lots of banquette seating, tiny tables, and flashing lights. Open from 10 p.m. to 3 a.m. daily.

8. SOSÚA

About 15 miles east of Puerto Plata lies one of the finest beaches in the Dominican Republic, Sosúa Beach, a strip of white sand more than half a mile wide in a cove sheltered by coral cliffs. The beach connects two communities, which together make up the town known as Sosúa.

At one end of the beach is **El Batey,** an area with quiet residential streets, gardens, restaurants, shops, and hotels that can be visited by those who can tear themselves away from the beach. Real estate transactions have been booming in El Batey and its environs, where many streets have been paved, and fine villas with manicured lawns are maintained by eminent Dominicans.

At the other end of Sosúa Beach lies **Los Charamicos,** a sharp contrast to El Batey. Here you'll find tin-roofed shacks, vegetable stands, chickens scrabbling in the rubbish, and warm, friendly people. This community is a typical Latin American village, recognizable through the smells, sights, and sounds in the narrow, rambling streets. All this may be changed even by the time you visit, however, as developers are eyeing the entire Sosúa area.

Sosúa isn't very old, as history records time. It was founded in 1940 by European Jews seeking refuge from the growing destruction of their race by Adolf Hitler. Trujillo invited 100,000 Jews to settle in his country, where they would escape Nazi terror on a banana plantation. One of the reasons behind the offer was allegedly to "whiten the blood of the islanders." Actually, only 600 or so Jews were allowed to immigrate, and of those, only about a dozen or so remain. However, there are some 20 Jewish families living in Sosúa. For the most part they are engaged in the dairy and smoked-meat industry which the refugees began during the war. Nowadays, with the dwindling Jewish population, many German expatriates are found in the town. There is a local one-room synagogue, rescued from the termites, where biweekly services are held. Many of the Jews intermarried with Dominicans, and the town has taken on an increasingly Spanish flavor. Women of the town are often seen wearing both the Star of David and the Virgin de Alta Gracia.

Taxis, charter buses, and públicos from Puerto Plata and Playa Dorada let passengers off at the stairs leading down to Sosúa Beach from the highway.

WHERE TO STAY: In business since 1987, **Playa Chiquita Beach Resort,** Sosúa, Dominican Republic (tel. 809/571-3431), the "big hotel on the little beach" (*playa chiquita* means "little beach" in Spanish), has a total of 90 rooms completed and more on the way. A harlequin façade of vivid Caribbean colors greets guests who arrive in this relatively isolated spot, once a grazing field for cattle, on a private beach.

The private accommodations are bright, large, and cheery, opening for the most part onto ocean views. Room amenities include satellite TV, tiny kitchens, well-stocked mini-bars, big baths, and little verandas. Prices are right. *In summer, two persons pay $65 daily, and one guest is charged $55.* In high season, a single or double rents for $86 daily. MAP costs another $17 per person per day. Units are arranged around a lagoon-shape pool. The hotel's formal air-conditioned restaurant, Bacchus, is considered one of the finest in the resort. Its wines come from places as far apart as Chile and Italy. Tables are set with highly polished silver. Dominican and continental specialties are served.

Sosúa by the Sea, P.O. Box 361, Sosúa, Puerto Plata, Dominican Republic (tel. 809/571-3222), has a blue and white concrete main building softened with wooden lattices that make it gracious and inviting. Accommodations lie on either side of meandering paths of well-planted tropical gardens. The pool area opens onto Sosúa Bay, and the resort stands between two beaches. From the open-air rooftop lounge, you have a view of Mount Isabel de Torres (referred to earlier). A formal restaurant serves both Dominican specialties and an international cuisine. At lunch, you can patronize the poolside bar and grill. Reached by elevator, the light, airy bedrooms are either well-furnished studios or one-bedroom suites—all rooms have air conditioning, cable TV, a compusafe, and phone. *In summer, the price for one or two persons in a studio is $40 daily, the cost going up to $60 daily for two to four persons in a suite.* In winter, one or two guests pay $70 daily for a studio, with two to four guests being charged $95 daily in a suite. The hotel has many activities, including a sports clinic and a beauty salon.

Villas Los Coralillos, Sosúa, Dominican Republic (tel. 809/571-2623), in the center of the nighttime activity, was begun in 1986 and completed in 1989.

Its 81 well-furnished accommodations are in a series of terracotta-tiled Iberian villas cantilevered over a bougainvillea-draped hillside. The action centers around the pool and main restaurant overlooking Sosúa Bay. Guests, depending on their needs, can request one- or two-bedroom villas, set in the midst of tropical planting and walking paths. The views from some of the villas are among the most spectacular in Sosúa.

In high season, a single or double rents for $55 daily, *this tariff being lowered to $40 in summer*. Each standard unit has air conditioning, twin beds, and a small veranda. Some of the larger villas containing kitchenettes are suitable for four to five guests. A friendly quartet or family can occupy one of these units for $125 daily in high season, *$100 in summer*. Dining at the hotel's El Coral Restaurant is recommended separately. Los Coralillos is the only hotel in town with direct access to the main Sosúa beach, and if you tire of the pool, you can stroll to the sea through century-old mahogany and almond trees. For reservations, write to the hotel in care of P.O. Box 851, Santo Domingo, Dominican Republic.

Hotel Yaroa, El Batey, Sosúa, Dominican Republic (tel. 809/571-2651), was named after a long-ago Indian village, within whose boundaries many of the hotel's staff still live. Opened in 1986, it encompasses views of dozens of leafy trees that ring its foundations. Inside are such decorative touches as an atrium illuminated by a skylight shaped like a Star of David, lots of exposed wood and stone, and a well-designed garden ringing a sheltered swimming pool. Each of the two dozen bedrooms has a Spanish-style mirador with a planter filled with local ferns, pine louvers for privacy, terracotta floors, lots of airy space, and a private bath. Two of the accommodations are designed like private cabañas at poolside. Singles or doubles cost $45 in winter, *$25 in summer*. Breakfast, light lunches, and French cuisine at night are served in the dining room, Sonya, recommended separately.

Hotel Sosúa, Calle Alejo Martinez, El Batey, Sosúa, Dominican Republic (tel. 809/571-2683), is in a suburban community about two minutes by car from the center of town. Its simple and attractive layout includes a reception area designed to conceal a flagstone-rimmed pool from the street outside. The bedrooms are strung along a wing extending beside the pool. The rooms contain air conditioning, ceiling fans, and an occasional pine balcony. *In summer, the 37 double rooms rent for $25, the three apartments going for $30*. In winter, the cost is $45 in a double, $50 in an apartment.

Auberge du Village Inn, 8 Dr. Rosen, El Batey, Sosúa, Dominican Republic (tel. 809/571-2569). Low slung, low-key, and unpretentious, this pleasant country inn was purchased late in 1985 by a Swedish-born couple, Ninni and Hans Magnusson. You pass beneath a grape arbor to reach the concrete walls of the reception area, which encircles an almost oval swimming pool. Only breakfast is served here, but drinks and snacks are available throughout the day at the tranquil poolside veranda. Each of the seven accommodations has its own ceiling fan, air conditioning, and private bath. Single or double rooms cost $45 daily in winter, *$35 in summer*. The establishment lies about a five-minute walk from the beach.

WHERE TO DINE: The best and arguably the most pleasant restaurant in town is **El Coral,** El Batey (tel. 809/571-2645). It's in a Spanish-style building roofed with red tiles and set at the bottom of the cultivated garden near the end of Sosúa Beach. It offers a spacious area with terracotta tiles, wooden accents, and stark white walls opening onto a panoramic view of the ocean. If you look out over the rear garden from one of the flowered terraces or through one of the big windows, you see an elliptical pool midway down the hill leading to the ocean. There's a bar in a room adjoining the dining room. The specialties include conch

Créole-style, pork chops with pineapple, octopus Créole-style, shrimps with garlic, and flan. Full meals begin at around RD$50 ($10). It opens daily for breakfast at 7 a.m. and serves dinner till 11 p.m.

Restaurant Sonya, Hotel Yaroa, El Batey (tel. 809/571-2651), has a good quality menu, not overly large but select, with well-chosen ingredients and fine service. The food is both Dominican and international, with an emphasis on French cuisine. For example, at dinner you might be served poached kingfish in a white butter sauce, or filet steak with roquefort. For dessert, the crêpes suzette are an experience. Full evening meals, costing RD$60 ($12) are served from 6 to 11 p.m. daily except Sunday. Lunches, costing RD$25 ($5), served from 11:40 a.m. to 4 p.m. daily except Sunday, are simpler affairs, with such dishes as spaghetti Dominicana and chicken brochettes likely to be on the menu.

Marco Polo Club, El Batey (tel. 809/571-3600), opens onto one of the most spectacular views of any restaurant in the Caribbean. While sipping a rum punch or one of the mixed drinks, called "shooters," you can enjoy Sosúa Bay from your cliffside perch. The restaurant is ideal for either a meal or just a drink. It has not one but two bar happy hours daily—from 4 to 6 p.m. and 10 to 11 p.m. Meals are served from 8 a.m. to midnight daily. Breakfast is in fact available until 2 p.m., and you might order a health breakfast or perhaps a smoked herring omelet. The chef's specialty is a seashell paella, but you can ask for grilled Atlantic fish of the day. Meals cost from RD$50 ($10) unless you order more expensive types of seafood. At night, there's dancing under the stars.

Restaurant Morua Mai, 5 Pedro Clisante, El Batey (tel. 809/571-2541). Its patio, facing a popular intersection, is the closest thing to a European sidewalk café in town. Inside, where occasional live entertainment is an important attraction, is a high-ceilinged, double-decked, and stylish space filled with touches of neo-Victorian gingerbread, upholstered banquettes, and wicker furniture. Don't overlook the possibility of a sun-washed drink or cup of afternoon tea in this establishment's side courtyard, where a cabaña bar serves drinks from beneath a palm-thatched roof. The café is open throughout the day, and lunch is served daily from 11:30 a.m. to 3 p.m. except in summer, and dinner is on from 7 to 11 nightly year round. Pizzas, sandwiches, and light meals at lunch cost from RD$18 ($3.60), while full dinners go for RD$65 ($13). Menu specialties include charcoal-grilled lobster, fish platters (with oysters, octopus, conch, and seabass), Valenciana paella, and daily specials such as grilled chicken with orange sauce.

AFTER DARK: Italian Giovanni Mercurio grabs the spotlight with his **Casa del Sol** (tel. 809/571-2979), open from 9 p.m. to 4 a.m. seven days a week. It not only has the largest dance floor in Sosúa, but it is also air-conditioned and has a first-rate sound system and a big video screen. Under a thatch roof, a pyramid structure was built on the outskirts of town. For a cover charge ranging from RD$15 ($3) to RD$20 ($4) per person, the disco welcomes an international crowd along with Dominicans.

9. CABARETE

This little village, lying between Sosúa and Río San Juan on the east coast, has in the past few years become known as one of the best windsurfing locations in the world, drawing devotees from around the globe. Even if you don't windsurf you might want to consider it for an inexpensive holiday by the sea. An offshore coral reef shields the white sandy beach from the breakers. The water temperature never falls below 80° F even in January and February. It usually takes 40 minutes by car, even less, to reach Cabarete from the heart of Sosúa. But, of course, everything in the Dominican Republic depends on road conditions.

The leading resort is **Punta Goleta,** Cabarete, Dominican Republic (tel. 809/571-3030), whose ochre walls and green gingerbread stand fantasy-like in the hot Caribbean sun. Lying three miles west of Cabarete, this 100-acre property, opened in 1986, fronts the Atlantic. It offers 128 rooms in a modified Caribbean Victorian style of architecture. There are plenty of activities around the big swimming pool or in the trio of bars and the Jacuzzi. Sports include 24-hour tennis and horseback riding. Most guests check in only to go windsurfing, and techniques are improved at the Mistral School of Windsurfing. Each unit contains a private bath and phone, and many of them also have private patios or balconies.

Rates are "mostly inclusive"—that is, they include taxes, service, horseback riding, all meals, and a free shuttle bus service to and from Sosúa. The package does not include windsurfing, liquor, or rental of motorscooters. In high season, a seven-night package costs $980 weekly in a single, $607 per person in a double, $567 per person in a triple, and $547 per person in a quad. Higher prices are quoted at Christmas and Easter and on certain other holidays. *In summer, the weekly package costs $799 in a single, $399 per person in a double, and $299 per person in a triple or quad.*

Buffet breakfasts are followed by daily barbecues at the beach bar, then dinner in the formal Green House, with a Dominican and international cuisine. To cap the evening, guests head for the Breeze Club, the hotel's disco. For reservations and information, call toll free at 800/874-4637.

Cabarete Beach Hotel, Cabarete, Dominican Republic (tel. 809/571-2551), is a small Caribbean inn, a Swiss venture, standing on the highway running through the center of the village. The windsurfers' choice, it contains a total of 20 bedrooms, with more planned.

Opening onto a bathing beach, the hotel offers simple but comfortable accommodations, each with toilet and shower. Many also have terraces or balconies fronting the sea. In high season, single or double occupancy costs $45 to $75 daily. *Tariffs are lowered in summer to $30 to $45 daily for either one or two persons.* For half board, add another $10 per person per day to the prices. The cuisine is both Swiss and Dominican. Even if you're just touring the east coast, you can stop for a meal any time from 7 a.m. to midnight daily. The restaurant opens onto a sea view.

10. RÍO SAN JUAN

The best reason for going to this sleepy town is to explore the Laguna Gri-gri (see below), requiring a 1½-hour drive from Puerto Plata. If you decide to spend the night or even a few relaxing days, the **Hotel Río San Juan,** Río San Juan, Dominican Republic (tel. 809/589-2379) is an attractive hostelry which usually caters to a Dominican and Canadian clientele. The various sections of the structure are connected by catwalks and breezeways, most of which are raised above a series of cultivated gardens, the centerpiece of which is a large pool. The building is outfitted in a modern interpretation of a plantation style and contains a piano bar. Here, amid a color scheme with red accents and exposed wood, the management hosts Friday- and Saturday-night combo entertainment. Each of the 38 rooms has a private bath, painted cinderblock walls, mahogany trim, wall-to-wall carpeting, and air conditioning. *In summer, single or double occupancy costs $26 daily,* the charge in winter going to $40 for one or two persons. The hotel lies five miles from a good beach, Playa Grande. The owner, Orlando Alvarado, called the "poet farmer," worked his way up to his present status. He was 14 before he wore his first pair of shoes, and he rode to school on a donkey. He still owns his own farm with livestock and grows much of the produce used in the hotel's restaurant.

LAGUNA GRI-GRI: Lots of people dream about embarking (safely, of course) on a tour of a prehistoric swamp, but few realize that in the Dominican Republic the opportunity exists for one of the most exotically beautiful trips anywhere in the Caribbean. Near the spot where the waters of the Arroyo Grande feed into the ocean, a wilderness of mangrove swampland has thrived in isolation for centuries.

Today, almost completely unspoiled, it's a refuge for hundreds of tropical and migrant birds, with surprisingly few insects in residence. At a well-marked departure point in Río San Juan, you can negotiate for the services of a motorboat and its crew for between one and ten persons. The well-maintained, wide-bottomed boats embark on tours of an area that is reminiscent of the most secluded sections of the Florida Everglades.

You might suggest that the end point of your tour be **La Cueva de las Galondrinas,** which lies beyond the mouth of the river several miles along the rocky coastline. The cost will be around RD$100 ($20) per boatload. Along the way, note the soaring gri-gri trees, whose roots descend like tentacles into the water, plus the bizarre rock formations along the coast. Their forms include everything from natural arches to configurations resembling skulls. The end point of the tour, the Cave of the Galondrinas, was formed by a rockslide in 1846. Today the grotto takes its name from the bird, the galondrina, resembling the swallow, which migrates to South America in winter. If the water isn't too rough, a boat can be navigated right into the azure waters of the eerily echoing grotto, which some visitors say is just as blue as, and much less crowded than, anything along the Neapolitan coast of Italy.

Heading South Along the Coast

El Farallon, La Catalina de Cabreta, Sanchez (Nagua), Dominican Republic (no phone), is a Canadian-owned complex of Mediterranean-style stucco villas set high above a luxuriant hillside overlooking the Atlantic coast less than 12 miles from Río San Juan. Only 12 bedrooms are rented, each with balconies overlooking the sea, and cooling by ceiling fans. Guests book in here for a week at inexpensive prices: *$206.46 per person weekly in summer, based on MAP double occupancy.* In winter, the tariff goes up to $246 per person weekly, MAP, for double occupancy. Even if these prices rise, and they surely will, you'll still be getting a bargain. The superb cuisine comes as a surprise for this area. The secret of the success is that the tres belle table is one of the finest in Québec. Chefs of the famous Le Mitoyen fly to the island for cooking vacations, and they serve marvelous food, unique on the north shore. If you're not staying here, you can enjoy dinner, served from 7:30 to 8:30 nightly. For reservations, write to Louise Lalande, 12190 James Merrice, Montréal, Québec H3M 2H1, Canada.

11. SAMANÁ

Lying on the remote Samaná Peninsula in the eastern part of the island, Samaná overlooks a large bay surrounded by outstanding natural beauty. Columbus arrived on the peninsula's beaches on January 12, 1493, and witnessed the first battle in the New World between Spaniards and the Indian population, Ciguayos. In his diary, he recorded that he had never "seen so many arrows fly over a vessel." He called the bay "Gulf of Arrows."

The little town was founded in 1756 by Canary Islanders sent here by the Spanish government, which was seeking to protect the area from seizure by French pirates. France had its eye on the place as a site for a projected Fort Napoleon, showcase for France's New World colonies. The Gallic bubble burst, and the Spanish colonists kept their foothold in Samaná. They were joined by slaves from

America who had fled the cotton plantations of the South. The U.S. government had designs on Samaná Bay and its harbor in the late 19th century and tried to lease the area. This effort was thwarted by the somewhat shaky Dominican Republic.

The beauty of this part of the country is made up of high hills sloping gently to the ocean, tree- and shrub-covered valleys, and little harbors and coves with white sand beaches. The seaside fishing town of Samaná was targeted for development by the government in the mid-'70s, but construction of a large resort hotel failed to bring visitors flocking to the place.

There are beautiful beaches around the bay, some of which can be reached only by boat. Many activities are possible here, among them scuba-diving, snorkeling, swimming, sailing, deep-sea fishing, and hiking.

The most popular excursion, which hotels can arrange, is to **Cayo Levantado,** nicknamed "fantasy island," lying about an hour's boat ride from Bahia beach. On the island are lush tropical growth and at least two good sandy beaches. Most excursions provide for lunch on the beach, where fish is grilled over an open fire. It takes about an hour to follow the walkways around the island that connect cabañas on the cay.

Because of all the natural beauty of Samaná Peninsula, you might want to consider some organized sightseeing tours, since getting about on your own can prove difficult. Your best bet is to go to **Samaná Tourist Service,** 5 Avenida La Marina, Samaná (tel. 809/538-2541), and ask that agency (the best on the peninsula) about what is being planned for the time of your visit.

Today, the town of Samaná has wide boulevards and several good restaurants. It is the major settlement on the southern shore, currently reached by a long and circuitous detour from the northern settlements of Portillo and Las Terrenas. The drive from Portillo takes about an hour and a half. If you drive to Samaná from Puerto Plata, allow at least four hours, maybe more, depending on road conditions. Likewise, it is at least a five-hour drive from Santo Domingo, 152 miles away. Many visitors charter planes and arrive at Arroyo Barril Airport, which has a 5,000-foot runway. Flying time from Santo Domingo is only 30 minutes.

FOOD AND LODGING: The best and most up-to-date accommodations on Samaná Peninsula are not in the town of Samaná but on the north shore outside Las Terrenas, a fairly long drive away. There, a cluster of neo-colonial buildings, reminiscent of similar structures in Costa Rica, is **El Portillo Beach Club,** El Portillo, Las Terrenas, Provincia de Samaná, Dominican Republic (no local phone). This is a tranquil and unspoiled place, popular with Canadian and German tour groups, occupying a beachfront setting of rustic charm. The 99 accommodations come in different sizes, most of them in tile-roofed, two-story bungalows set apart from the main building. Each has its own private porch or upstairs balcony. Rates are complicated, depending on the booking, and charges are all-inclusive. That means everything from sports activities to liquor, cigarettes, all meals, and your room. If you'd like to stay here just for one night, *the daily rates in summer are $80 in a single, $130 in a double, and $165 in a triple.* Winter charges are $100 daily in a single, $170 in a double, and $210 in a triple. These prices are estimated and subject to change. When booking, check to see what special packages might be offered at the time of your visit.

The place is fairly active day and night, with a host of sporting events regularly scheduled, such as sailing clinics, horseback riding, snorkeling tours, tennis clinics, beach volleyball, even sack races. Guests can spend most of the day at the beach or else retreat to the shade of a sea grape or almond tree to relax. At night, after a bountiful buffet of Dominican specialties, including on occasion grilled freshly caught lobster, entertainment is provided. Perhaps a trio will perform, a bonfire will be lit on the beach, or a fire-eater will be brought in to amuse.

Until the hotel situation in the town of Samaná improves, you may want to confine your visit there to a dining stop. A surprisingly good restaurant is **La Mata Rosada,** 5 Avenida Malécon (tel. 809/534-2400). The surprise is, first, that it serves such a sophisticated menu, and second, that in this remote part of the island, it resembles the kind of *le bistro* you are more likely to encounter on the French Riviera, all due to the work of Nice-born Jean-Pierre DeLeuse.

Monsieur DeLeuse, with all his Gallic finesse, will show you to one of the bamboo tables placed around a reflecting pool, where you'll be served the best food on the peninsula. You might begin with salade niçoise, the famous dish of the host's homeland, or else the chef's pâté or Burgundy-style snails. For your main course, you might try duck with orange sauce, rabbit provençale, or the catch of the day. Meals cost from RD$75 ($15), with dinner offered daily except Sunday. Reservations are advisable. Lunch is served in winter, from 11 a.m. to 3:30 p.m. except Sunday. It's wise to check to see if the restaurant is open when you plan to go there, as it is likely to be closed from mid-September until the first of November.

CHAPTER IX

BRITISH LEEWARD ISLANDS

□ □ □

1. ANTIGUA AND BARBUDA
2. MONTSERRAT
3. ST. KITTS
4. NEVIS
5. ANGUILLA

Once a British colony, all the Leeward Islands except Montserrat and Anguilla have moved into more independent seas. The language of the Leewards, however, remains English.

An aviator once said that these islands look like "a fleet of cockleshells set afloat in the sea." Between French-controlled Guadeloupe and the U.S. Virgins, at a bend of an archipelago, the British Leewards consist of Antigua (in association with isolated Barbuda), Montserrat, the twin state of St. Kitts and Nevis, and little Anguilla. Of them all, Antigua with its many beaches and resort hotels is the best equipped for mass tourism. In fact, not too long ago only Antigua and St. Kitts were visited by tourists—the rest were braved only by the most adventurous voyagers. Today the opening of more hotels and the providing of modern tourist facilities draw thousands to Montserrat, Nevis, and to more remote Anguilla. The latter island is also becoming increasingly chic as an address.

It must be added that Antigua, with its advantageous geographical location, has the further merit of making a good base for going almost anywhere in the West Indies.

U.S. and Canadian citizens do not have to have a passport, but they will be asked for some means of identification such as a birth certificate or voter registration card. An outbound ticket for transportation is also required.

All the islands in this chapter use the Eastern Caribbean dollar (EC$). However, no one faints if you give them a U.S. dollar. Nearly all hotels bill you in U.S. dollars. Only certain tiny restaurants present their prices in EC dollars. Make sure you know which dollars are referred to when you inquire about the price of something. The EC$ is worth about 37¢ in U.S. currency (EC$2.70 to $1 U.S.). Unless otherwise specified, rates quoted in this chapter are given in U.S. dollars.

1. ANTIGUA AND BARBUDA

Antigua boasts a different beach for every day of the year—365 of them. Most of these beaches are protected by coral reefs, and the color of the sand is often sugar-white.

Antigua, Barbuda, and Redonda form the independent nation of Antigua and Barbuda, within the Commonwealth of Nations. (Redonda is an uninhabited rocky islet of less than one square mile, located 20 miles southwest of Antigua; and sparsely populated Barbuda is previewed at the end of this section.)

From a poverty-stricken sugar island, Antigua has risen to the position of a 20th-century vacation haven. Yankee millionaires seeking British serenity under a tropical sun turned Antigua into a citadel of elegance around the exclusive Mill Reef Club, where you will be accepted only if recommended by a member. The island has now developed a broader base of tourism—attracting not just the rich, but the middle-, even lower-income voyager.

Rolling, rustic Antigua (pronounced An-*tee*-ga) has as its highest point Boggy Peak, 1,360 feet above sea level. Stone towers, once sugar mills, dot the landscape; but in inland scenery Antigua isn't as dramatic as some of the British Leewards such as St. Kitts. But, oh, those beaches!

Discovered by Columbus on his second voyage in 1493, Antigua has a population of about 75,000 and an area of 108 square miles. The average all-year temperature ranges from 75° to 85° Fahrenheit.

Independence has come, but Antigua is still British in many of its traditions. English planters settled Antigua in 1623. In 1666 the French occupied the island, but Antigua was ceded to England the following year by the Treaty of Breda.

The summer carnival takes place on the first Monday and Tuesday in August and the preceding week. Included in this festival of fun and spectacle are a beauty competition, as well as calypso and steel-band competitions. Carnival envelops the streets in exotic costumes that recall the people's African heritage. The spring highlight is Antigua's annual sailing week in late April or May.

The capital is **St. John's,** a neatly laid-out large town, six miles from the airport and less than a mile from the deep-water Harbour Terminal. The port is the focal point of commerce and industry, as well as the seat of government and tourist shopping. Trade winds keep the streets fairly cool, as they were built wide just for that purpose. Protected in the throat of a narrow bay, the port city consists of cobblestone sidewalks, weather-beaten wooden houses, corrugated iron roofs, and louvered West Indian verandas.

GETTING THERE: Because of its role as a hub of transport to several other islands, Antigua is considered an important air link. Most passengers in the northeastern U.S. opt for the **American Airlines** nonstop service to Antigua from New York's JFK Airport. Departing every day around 9 a.m., it leaves late enough for passengers from Boston, Providence, Hartford, and other cities to make early-morning connections. Winging in to Antigua at 2 p.m., the flight lands in time for passengers to enjoy a late-afternoon sunbath. Likewise, American's relatively late (4:35 p.m.) daily departure from Antigua for New York permits another half day of vacation in the Caribbean.

American's rate structure is cheaper when a Caribbean-bound vacationer books his or her hotel reservation simultaneously with air transport. (American's tour desk will provide this service.) Many of the hotels that an American Airlines reservation clerk will propose are reviewed in this guide. If, however, you prefer to book your hotel independently, American's cheapest travel option for high-

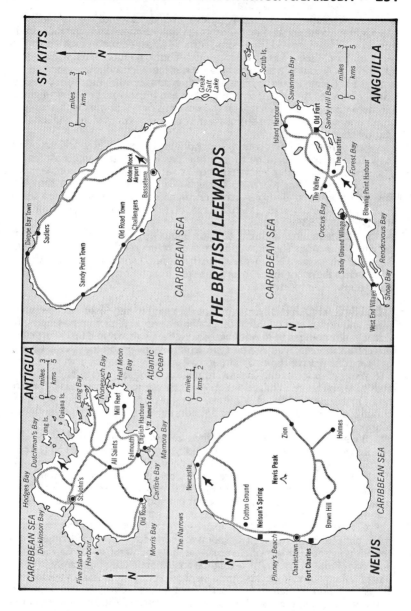

ST. KITTS

N

0 miles 3
0 kms 5

Great
Salt
Lake

Dieppe Bay Town

Sadlers

Sandy Point Town

Old Road Town

Challengers

Golden Rock
Airport

Basseterre

CARIBBEAN SEA

ANGUILLA

N

0 miles 3
0 kms 5

Scrub Is.

Savannah Bay

Island Harbour

Old Fort

Sandy Hill Bay

The Quarter

Forest Bay

The Valley

Blowing Point Harbour

Crocus Bay

Sandy Ground Village

Rendezvous Bay

West End Village

Shoal Bay

CARIBBEAN SEA

THE BRITISH LEEWARDS

ANTIGUA

N

0 miles 3
0 kms 5

Hodges Bay

Dutchman's Bay

Dickinson Bay

Long Is.

Guiana Is.

Long Bay

Nonesuch Bay

Half Moon
Bay

Mill Reef

St. James's Club

Atlantic
Ocean

St. John's

All Saints

Falmouth

English Harbour

Mamora Bay

Old Road

Carlisle Bay

Morris Bay

Five Island
Harbour

CARIBBEAN SEA

NEVIS

N

0 miles 1
0 kms 2

The Narrows

Newcastle

Zion

Holmes

Cotton Ground

Nevis Peak

Nelson's Spring

Brown Hill

Pinney's Beach

Charlestown

Fort Charles

CARIBBEAN SEA

season travel (subject to change) requires a seven-day advance purchase, a Saturday night stayover, and carries a $25 penalty for alteration of itinerary. Depending on availability, round-trip passage costs $408 per person in high season for weekday travel (defined as Monday through Thursday) and $425 for passage on other days. Of course, these fares are lower in shoulder and low season and are subject to change. Passengers flying to Antigua from other American cities are usually funneled through American's hub in San Juan. From there, two flights a day depart for Antigua. A telephone reservations clerk will work with a complicated array of flight patterns to ensure the quickest, most efficient, and least expensive connections.

Pan American offers routings to Antigua, but passengers originating in New York are required to wait for as much as four hours in either Dutch St. Maarten or Miami before being transferred to a flight on a regional airline.

Passengers willing to transfer through Miami often select the **Eastern Airline** daily nonstop flight from there to Antigua. However, at presstime a strike has curtailed Eastern service, and the future of the airline is uncertain. Its toll-free number is 800/535-6660.

Air Canada offers Saturday nonstop flights from Toronto to Antigua, but only in high season. The flight connects with planes coming in from Montréal. Most Canadians fly to New York, where they connect with another carrier.

Each of the major airlines maintains a toll-free number for reservations, tariff quotations, and information.

GETTING AROUND: Transportation isn't hard to find. **Taxis** meet every airplane, and drivers wait outside the major hotels hoping to pick up passengers. In fact, if you're going to be in Antigua for a few days, you may find that a particular driver has "adopted" you. A typical fare from, say, the airport to Halcyon Cove is $10 for a one-way trip. From the airport to Curtain Bluff, however, will cost from $18.25, as it's a long run. The government of Antigua fixes the rates, and the taxis have no meters. While it's costly, the best way to see Antigua is by private taxi. Drivers are also guides. Most taxi tours, taking in all the major sights, including lunch at Admiral's Inn, last 3½ hours and cost $15 per hour for one to four passengers.

Buses are not recommended for the average visitor, although they do exist. Service seems erratic and undependable along impossibly bumpy roads. The official hours of operation between St. John's and the villages are 5:30 a.m. to 6 p.m., but don't count on it. However, if you're adventurous, you'll find buses the cheapest means of transport, costing EC$1.60 (60¢) for most fares. In St. John's, buses leave from the West Bus Station for Falmouth and English Harbour, the major goal of most travelers.

Car Rentals: A self-drive car may be practical for some visitors, although many prefer to be driven from one point to another by taxi. Considering the notoriously pot-holed roads of Antigua—among the worst in the Caribbean—with one of the Caribbean Basin's highest accident rates, this is certainly an excellent idea for many visitors. Still, if you insist on driving, note that as a holdover of British tradition, Antiguans *drive on the left*. Many car-rental agencies operate in Antigua. However, there is one important requirement. You must obtain a driver's license, costing $12. To obtain one, you must produce a valid U.S. or Canadian license. It is no longer necessary to go to the police station to obtain this license. Most car-rental firms are authorized to issue it to you in exchange for a fee. Car-rental firms in Antigua are sometimes precariously financed local operations, although two or three are affiliated with major car-rental firms in the United States. **Avis** is represented (see below), and you also have a choice of some very local and often small operations (one of which I recommend). However, several local firms rent cars that aren't in the best of condition, and with the pot-holed roads of Antigua you need the best-maintained vehicle you can get.

Operating under its own banner, **Budget Rent-a-Car** maintains a local office in Antigua at Powell's Estates (tel. 809/46-14522). When you arrive at Coolidge Airport, a Budget representative will see that you are delivered to Budget's island headquarters. Head for the Budget kiosk in the arrivals hall. The cheapest car available is usually a manual-transmission Nissan March without air conditioning. In high season, it rents for $216 per week, with each additional day costing $36. However, you must notify Budget at least two business days in advance to get this rate. You must also be at least 25 years old. If you're looking for a car with air conditioning and automatic transmission (either two- or four-door, seating four passengers comfortably), the charge for a Nissan Sunny with these options is $288 weekly, with each additional day costing $48.

Budget charges $10 per day for a collision damage waiver, but—and this is a serious *but*—clients must pay up to the first $1,000 worth of damage in case of an accident. To reserve a car before going to Antigua, call toll free 800/527-0700.

Avis has an office at the island's international airport. Holders of a collision damage waiver with Avis are not responsible for any liability, but it usually charges higher rates.

Carib Car Rentals, P.O. Box 1258, Hodges Bay, Antigua, W.I. (tel. 809/46-22062), will pick you up and deliver you anywhere on Antigua. It rents vehicles that are clean, modern, and reliable. For one day expect to pay from $42, with a free choice of automatic or stick shift. If you keep the car from two to six days, it costs $42 per day, and for seven days, the charge is $230. Air conditioning costs slightly more. Hours are from 8 a.m. to 5 p.m. seven days a week.

PRACTICAL FACTS: An independent nation since 1981, Antigua and Barbuda has a system of government modeled after the British Parliamentary system, with the administration of the state conducted by a Cabinet of Ministers headed by the Prime Minister.

Banks: Bank hours are usually Monday to Thursday from 8 a.m. to 1 p.m. and Friday from 8 a.m. to 1 p.m. and 3 to 5 p.m.

Customs: Arriving visitors are allowed to bring in 200 cigarettes and one quart of liquor, plus six ounces of perfume.

Electricity: Most of the island's electricity is 220 volts AC, 60 cycles. However, the Hodges Bay area and some hotels are supplied with 110 volts, 60 cycles.

Embassy: You can receive help in some emergencies at the **U.S. Embassy,** Queen Elizabeth Hwy., St. John's, Antigua, W.I. (tel. 809/46-23511).

Information: For information about Antigua and Barbuda, get in touch with **Antigua and Barbuda Department of Tourism,** 610 Fifth Ave., Suite 311, New York, NY 10020 (tel. 212/541-4117); or 121 S.E. First St., Suite 508, Miami, FL 33131 (tel. 305/381-9762). In Canada, information is available at the **Antigua and Barbuda Department of Tourism & Trade,** 60 St. Clair Ave. East, Suite 205, Toronto, Ontario MT4 1N5 (tel. 416/961-3085).

Medical care: The principal medical facility is **Holberton Hospital,** Queen Elizabeth Hwy., Antigua, W.I. (tel. 809/46-20251).

Taxes and service: A departure tax of $8 (U.S.) is imposed. In addition, a 7% government tax is added to all hotel bills. Most hotels also add a 10% service charge.

Telephone: The dialing code to Antigua and Barbuda is 809/46, followed by five digits. Direct dialing is possible from the North America. A 24-hour-a-day telephone service links Antigua to all parts of the world. Calls can be made from hotels or from the office of **Cable & Wireless** in St. John's.

Time: Antigua falls within the Atlantic Time Zone, placing it one hour ahead of Eastern Standard Time, except when Eastern Daylight Time takes over. Then Antigua's time is the same as in the eastern United States.

Water: Water generally is safe to drink here, but many visitors prefer the bottled variety, either plain or carbonated.

HOTELS: Antigua's hotels are among the best and most plentiful in the eastern Caribbean, and generally they are small—a 100-room hotel is rare on the island. Check summer closings, which often depend on the caprice of the owners who will decide to shut down if business isn't good. Incidentally, air conditioning, except in first-class hotels, isn't as plentiful as some visitors think it should be. Chances are, your hotel will be on a beach. You can also rent an apartment or cottage if you want to cook for yourself.

Reminder: A 7% government tax and 10% service charge will probably be added to your hotel bill. Check first to save yourself a shock at the end of your stay.

In a Class by Itself

Curtain Bluff, Old Road, P.O. Box 288, Antigua, W.I. (tel. 809/46-31115), is the premier resort of the island, opened in 1961, and for understated elegance and refined resort living, it is virtually without peer in the Caribbean. (If I awarded stars, which I don't, and five were the maximum, I'd give Curtain Bluff six.) This oasis of serenity and comfort, the home of Sailing Week, lies in southwest Antigua 15 miles from the airport, the most tropical-looking section of the resort-studded island. Its founding father is Howard W. Hulford, the chairman or, as he is sometimes called, the boss. Once a pilot for Texaco, he discovered his Shangri-la back in the '50s while flying over it.

In a setting like a subtropical forest, the resort offers 61 beautifully furnished accommodations, including superior units with king-size beds, deluxe rooms with double beds, five suites with two bedrooms, and one suite with one bedroom. Ceiling fans and trade winds keep the rooms cool, and individual terraces open onto the water. Many thoughtful amenities and luxuries are provided, such as wall safes, marble or tile floors, terrycloth robes, bidets, tubs and showers, and fresh flowers daily (there's a plant nursery on the grounds). The resort operates on the Full American Plan, with rates including all meals (superb ones, at that), wine by the glass, soft drinks, tennis, water sports, laundry, and postage. *In shoulder season, mid-October to mid-December and mid-April to mid-May, you're charged $365 to $595 daily in a double, $265 to $495 in a single.* In winter, doubles cost $465 to $695 daily, and singles go for $365 to $585. An executive suite is more expensive, of course.

One reason guests check in here is for the food. The cuisine doesn't just aspire to excellence, it achieves it. Swiss-born Ruedi Portmann keeps his menu limited, so that all the food will be freshly prepared and artistically arranged on your plate. Mr. Portmann imports the finest ingredients for his continental meals, supplementing them with fresh staples and vegetables from the island. Curtain Bluff boasts the most extensive wine selection in the Caribbean, the creation of Mr. Hulford, who is justifiably proud of his collection that includes every major red bordeaux. After dinner, guests can dance under the stars to a live band. Men are required to wear jackets and ties after 7 p.m. Once a week, the resort hires a steel band to entertain guests down at the beach with a splendid buffet, where you can have the best conch and/or lobster salad you are likely to taste anywhere.

Curtain Bluff is a sporting paradise, offering at no extra charge sailing, waterskiing, skindiving, scuba diving (for certified divers only), tennis (four championship courts plus a pro shop and a full-time pro), and other activities such as aerobics classes. The resort closes June 1 to mid-October, during which time it seems busier than ever, because a great deal of money is poured back into it to have it shiny like new when it reopens. Thus, it has remained the connoisseur's choice, perhaps drawing more repeat business than any other resort in the Caribbean. It has long been popular with writers, such as novelists Evan Hunter and Herman Wouk.

Other Leading Resorts

St. James's Club, P.O. Box 63, St. John's, Antigua, W.I. (tel. 809/46-31113, in New York 212/485-2575 or toll free 800/275-0008), is a luxurious resort on Mamora Bay. Accommodations include elegant ocean-view rooms and suites, all with complete baths, phones, and radios. Satellite TV from the U.S. is provided in all villa accommodations. In high season on MAP doubles cost $400 to $500, suites for two going for $550 to $750. *Off-season doubles on MAP rent for $300 to $350, suites for two persons costing $450 to $600.* For single guests, the club deducts $75 from the rates charged in doubles. More expensive villas and hillside homes are also rented.

The best of local and international dishes, freshly caught seafood, salads, barbecue grills, and tropical fruit are accompanied by cool white wine or dark rum cocktails. You can relax in elegant surroundings in the Rainbow Garden Restaurant or eat al fresco by candlelight at the Docksider Café overlooking Mamora Bay, enjoying lobster, barbecued chicken, and ribs. Take a little pasta in Piccolo Mondo, the hillside trattoria with views of sunset over the bay. Lunch at the poolside Reef Deck is a social occasion when you can help yourself to salads, burgers, and local delicacies.

The resort's leisure facilities are among the best in the Caribbean. A variety of water sports is available, offering sailing boats (Sunfish and Hobie cats), sailboards, aqua bikes, deep-sea fishing, waterskiing, and snorkeling. The more adventurous may prefer to don scuba tanks for an ocean dive. A scuba certification school offers American and European certification. The club has seven day-and-evening-play hard tennis courts with a center court for tournaments, and offers the Martina Navratilova tennis program. The St. James's stables house Texas quarterhorses, on which guests can ride along hillside trails. There are also a complete Universal-equipped gymnasium, a Jacuzzi, massage parlor, beauty salon, and a croquet court. The Jacaranda nightclub will top off an evening for more active guests. Many enjoy gambling in the high-ceilinged European-style casino, whose walls are covered in a combination of Italian art deco columns and vertical stripes.

Jumby Bay, P.O. Box 243, Long Island, Antigua, W.I. (tel. 809/46-32176), is an exclusive little island resort, 300 acres in all, lying off the eastern coast of Antigua and reached after a 12-minute motor launch ride. The site was selected for its white sandy beaches, along a coastline protected by coral reefs. In gin-clear waters, guests can snorkel, go scuba-diving, or swim when they're not playing tennis, going fishing or sailing, or perhaps waterskiing. The grounds have been handsomely landscaped in part with loblolly and white cedar trees. The resort at its peak can accommodate about 110 guests. The hotel is on the site of what had been the private home of a plantation owner who grew sugarcane. In the 200-year-old vastly restored estate house, there is now a lounge, a library and games room. Dinner is served here, often attracting the yachting crowd who put into the 750-foot dock. The food is excellent, and picnic lunches can be arranged.

Pampered guests are housed in cottage rooms, each with a large master bedroom and its own patio overlooking the water, or else in a unit fronting the ocean on Jumby Bay Beach. These latter accommodations have a living and sitting area as well as a wet bar. Some of them even have a private "no curtains" shower courtyard which can provide entertainment to your roommate if you've kept your figure in shape. From November 1 to April 30, two persons can stay here on the AP at rates ranging from $525 to $675 daily. *Off-season is from the first of April to the end of May, when two persons are charged $525 daily, AP, and from the first of June until the first of September when tariffs are $425, AP, for two guests.* The hotel is closed in September and October. For reservations, consult your travel agent or get in touch with Jumby Bay, U.S.A., 1111 Cedar Swamp Rd., Old Brookville, NY 11545 (tel. 516/626-9200, 718/895-9868 in New York City, or toll free 800/437-0049).

The Royal Antiguan Resort & Casino, P.O. Box 1322, St. John's, Antigua, W.I. (tel. 809/46-23733, in New York City 212/661-4540, toll free in the U.S. 800/223-1588, or toll free in Canada 800/531-6767), owned by Savoy Resorts, opened in 1987. It occupies 150 acres on the crescent-shaped shores of Deep Bay on the northwest coast of Antigua. It is only a 25-minute ride from the airport and 15 minutes from St. John's. Set between Deep Bay and a lagoon, the resort creates the feeling of being on a private tropical island. Another attractive aspect of the property is that the main nine-story building is hidden by palm trees from view when you lie on the beach, adding to the feeling of seclusion. But should you want certain facilities, such as a beauty salon, dry cleaning/laundry service, newsstand/drugstore, or bed turn-down service, to name a few, they are available.

The resort has a total of 282 accommodations, including guest rooms, one- and two-bedroom suites, and one-bedroom cottages with private patios or terraces. Every unit has air conditioning, remote-control TV and VCR, radio, mini-bar with refrigerator, direct-dial phone, and terry robes, all in a decor of custom-designed Italian furnishings, marble counters, and ceramic tile floors. Winter EP rates are $200 daily for a minimum double to $850 for a two-bedroom suite. *In summer, minimum doubles rent for $100 daily, and two-bedroom suites go for $680.* Note that there are several categories of accommodations: standard, superior, and deluxe rooms, one-bedroom suites, and one-bedroom cottages, all falling between the prices quoted above. MAP is an additional $50 per day per person.

Guests need not venture outside the resort for dining and evening entertainment. There are four restaurants, including Andes on Deep Bay Beach, resting on stilts over the water, which specializes in fresh Caribbean catches and prime meats for lunch or dinner in an open-air, casual setting. Live entertainment and dancing is offered in the evening. For formal dining, La Regence serves French continental cuisine with impeccable service in sophisticated surroundings. The Lagoon Café, known for its breakfasts, is for those who want casual al fresco dining in a tropical setting. The resort also has Barrington's Bar and the Atrium Lobby Bar. The calm waters in Deep Bay are ideal for the many water sports available here including snorkeling, scuba diving, fishing, sailing, waterskiing, paddle boat rides, and windsurfing. Or you may head to the free-form swimming pool with swim-up bar set between Deep Bay and the lagoon. There are eight all-weather tennis courts, four lit for night play, plus a 400-seat tournament grandstand court.

First-Class Hotels
Halcyon Cove Beach Resort and Casino, P.O. Box 251, Dickenson Bay, Antigua, W.I. (tel. 809/46-20256, toll free in New York 800/223-1588, and toll free in Canada 800/531-6767), is a total resort with plenty of glamor and a casino. There are 150 stylish bedrooms, equipped for discerning guests, each

with a private furnished veranda. *Off-season, single or double occupancy costs $105 to $165 daily, with suites for two going for $250.* In winter, single or double accommodations rent for $195 to $275 daily, and suites for two cost $350. MAP in any season is an extra $45 per person per day.

The Arawak Terrace, the hotel's main dining room, is open for breakfast and dinner. You can also lunch or dine on the elongated Warri Pier, standing on stilts 200 feet from the shore. It's reached by a boardwalk over the sea. You dine and drink under a thatched and shingled open-air café. There's nearly half a mile of beach, and at one end is one of the major centers of Antigua's water-sports program. Often there are buffet dinners. Other activities include playing tennis on the hotel's own courts and horseback riding. The hotel is on an elevation, and it's but a three-minute walk down to the beach. Deck chairs and umbrellas are placed around a bar built right at the freshwater swimming pool, and a large airy dining room has a view of the sea. The hotel also has an ice-cream-parlor–coffeeshop as well as a cocktail lounge that occasionally has entertainment. Tennis players will find three courts lit for night play. In season, the management brings in a steel band to provide poolside entertainment on Sunday. The location is 1½ miles from the airport and 7 miles from St. John's, about a 15-minute taxi ride.

Blue Waters, P.O. Box 256, Soldier Bay, Antigua, W.I. (tel. 809/46-20292), curves around a private sandy beach, where you can lie in a hammock as a waiter serves you a strawberry rum punch. The location is four miles (about a 15-minute ride) from St. John's, to which the management provides a shuttle service at $3.50 per person. All rooms are beachfront and air-conditioned, surrounded by luxurious flowers and shrubs with coconut palms and shade trees in the extensive grounds. The property was extensively renovated in 1986, and eight two- and three-bedroom villas were built. In winter, doubles or singles pay from $280 to $340, MAP daily. The resort is likely to be closed from mid-May to mid-July. *Otherwise, the single rate off-season is $85 to $105, going up to $110 to $140 in a double, plus another $30 per person for MAP.* The Sunday brunch is deservedly praised; and on Tuesday and Friday, outdoor barbecues with continental and West Indian dishes, among the best in Antigua, attract a lively crowd. In season, you can dance to combos, steel bands, or disco music, and every Tuesday night the management throws a house party featuring crab racing. Water sports, tennis, sailing, and fishing are all complimentary, or you may prefer just to relax in the clear freshwater pool or enjoy a sundowner from the gazebo. Deep-sea fishing and coastal trips to nearby islands are available.

Jolly Beach Resort, P.O. Box 744, Antigua, W.I. (tel. 809/462-0061), is certainly jolly all right—in fact, it's the liveliest and most action-oriented hotel in Antigua, especially in water sports. Five miles from St. John's and 11 miles from the airport, it is set amid 38 acres of grounds on a mile and a half sandy beach, with plenty of vendors. It's the most popular hotel on the island, with a total of 475 accommodations, making it the largest in Antigua, as well as in the whole eastern Caribbean.

Whether you like this place or not may depend a great deal on your room assignment: some are spacious, others quite cramped. Many units are built in the Moorish style, lying in landscaped gardens. All contain private bath or shower with either queen, king, or twin beds, a ceiling fan, and air conditioning. Most guests book in here on weekly package deals. *In summer, singles cost from $385 to $420 weekly, with doubles going for $455 to $490 per person.* In winter, singles pay $595 to $630 weekly, and doubles are charged from $560 to $630 per person. All tariffs are per person for seven days and include MAP, service, transfer from the Antigua airport, watersports, and tennis. Drinks, lunch, and departure tax are not included.

The free-form freshwater swimming pool is connected at its narrowest part by a wooden footbridge. Guests from all over the world enjoy animated splashing, gossiping, and partying here. In the older section, guests spend time around the beach bar, Coconut Wharf, later enjoying dining in the Flamboyant Restaurant which has music for dancing. In the newer section, the Palm Grill and the Palm Restaurant are popular dining spots, serving a continental fare, Stateside specialties, and West Indian dishes. Buffets and barbecues are regular features. Night-owls dance until the early hours at Jaybee's Disco. The hotel offers a range of outside water sports such as scuba diving and deep-sea fishing which can be arranged at extra cost. Free activities include use of the tennis courts, Sunfish, sailboats, windsurf boards, paddleboats, rowboats, and waterskiing and snorkeling equipment.

Hawksbill Beach Resort, P.O. Box 108, St. John's, Antigua, W.I. (tel. 809/46-21515), takes its name from an offshore rock locals say resembles a hawksbill turtle. On the grounds is a former sugar mill, now turned into a boutique. The resort is ten miles from the airport and four miles from St. John's. Set on four beaches (one reserved for those who want to go home sans tan-lines), it is a magnet for the sporting set, with a swimming pool, tennis court, Sunfish sailing, surfing, and snorkeling. There's even waterskiing for a nominal charge. There are two restaurants (one on the beach) and two bars. It's usually lively here if the crowd is right, and entertainment, such as limbo dancers and calypsonians, is featured five nights a week.

Frankly, this isn't the newest or freshest-looking property around, but it is a long-enduring favorite. It revolves around an open-air, breezy central core, with 88 comfortably furnished bedrooms spread about the grounds. A lot of your enjoyment at this resort depends on your room. The most expensive units are the beachfront cottages, while the least costly rooms open onto a garden. In winter, two people pay $275 to $330 daily, with singles costing $230 to $270. *In summer, singles pay $120 daily and doubles $135 in standard rooms, while beachfront cottages, either single or double occupancy cost $160.* Units contain ceiling fans and showers. Dinner is another $25 per person per day.

Pineapple Beach Club, P.O. Box 54, St. John's, Antigua, W.I. (tel. 809/46-32006; in New York City 212/840-6636, toll free in the U.S. 800/223-9815; toll free in Québec and Ontario 800/468-0023), opened in 1986. The property lies on 45 acres of forested land, sloping down to a beach and a peninsula. Furnished with woven cane furniture, the units contain two double beds or one queen-size bed as well as private baths. Rates are all-inclusive, covering room, meals, sports, and drinks. In high season, charges per person are $150 to $175 daily, *lowered to $125 per person daily in summer.* On the premises are two restaurants and bars, a freshwater pool, tennis courts, and a windsurfing school with both sailboat and board instruction.

Small, Special Inns

The **Copper and Lumber Store,** P.O. Box, Nelson's Dockyard, English Harbour, St. John's, Antigua, W.I. (tel. 809/46-31058), is an 18th-century building originally occupied by purveyors of wood and sheet copper for the construction and/or repair of sailing ships of the British fleet plying the waters of the Caribbean. Today the louvered and shuttered windows of its dignified Georgian façade look out on increasing numbers of guests who recognize that in many ways this is the most understatedly elegant hotel in Antigua. The store and its adjacent harbor structures were built of brick brought from England in the holds of ships as ballast, to be replaced on return voyages by sugar, rum, and other rich products of the West Indies. These bricks imbue the building with 18th-century

English charm and sometimes serve to conceal its necessary modern amenities. Each of the brick-lined period accommodations has its own design and is named after one of the ships that fought at the battle of Trafalgar. Each is a well-proportioned study in high-quality 18th-century decorating. They're filled with fine Chippendale and Queen Anne reproductions, antiques, gleaming brass chandeliers, hardwood paneling, and hand-stenciled floors, all with a curator's eye for detail. Even the showers look like cabinetry in a sailing vessel, being lined with thick paneled slabs of mahogany accented with polished brass fittings, then carefully shielded with many coats of waterproofing. All the 14 suites have kitchens, private baths (with showers only), and ceiling fans. *In summer, rents are $80 daily in singles, $130 for two occupants.* Winter prices are $90 daily in singles, $250 in doubles. Contemporary suites are also available for up to four persons. A traditional English pub adjoins the hotel, offering food daily from 10:30 a.m. to 9:30 p.m. The restaurant provides lunch and dinner.

Admiral's Inn, P.O. Box 713, English Harbour, St. John's, Antigua, W.I. (tel. 809/46-31027), as a building, was planned in 1785, the year Nelson sailed into the harbor as captain of the H.M.S. *Boreas.* Completed in 1788, the building's ground floor was used to store lead, turpentine, and pitch, with offices for dockyard engineers upstairs. Today it has been converted into one of the most atmospheric inns in Antigua. In the heart of Nelson's Dockyard, and loaded with West Indian charm, the hostelry is constructed of weathered brick brought from England as ships' ballast. The façade is eye-captivating, with shutters, dormers, and a terrace opening onto a centuries-old garden. The ground floor, with its brick walls, giant ship beams, and island-made furniture, has a tavern atmosphere, with decorative copper, boat lanterns, and old oil paintings, everything lit at night by wrought-iron chandeliers.

Antilles ambience collectors will find that whatever room they're assigned will be full of character. There are three types of accommodations. Highest tariffs are charged for some ground-floor rooms in a tiny brick building—on the site of a provisional warehouse for Nelson's troops—across the pillared courtyard from the main structure. Each of these rooms has a little patio and a garden entry. Ceiling fans and optional air conditioning keep these spacious rooms cool. The same superior rate applies to front rooms on the first floor above the ground floor of the main building, with a view out over the lawn and harbor. A medium rate applies to the back rooms on this floor, all of which have air conditioning. The least expensive rate is for smaller chambers on the top floor, which may get warm during the day in summer but are quiet, with dormer-window views over the yacht-filled harbor. All rooms have ceiling fans and private baths and showers. Only 14 twin-bedded rooms are rented. So reservations are imperative. *In summer, singles on the EP stay here at rates that range from $48 to $56 daily, and doubles cost $56 to $68.* In winter, EP rates go up—$68 to $78 for a single, $80 to $94 for a double. The inn is closed in September. Rates entitle you to use the inn's snorkeling equipment and Sunfish craft. Free transportation is also provided to two nearby beaches. On Saturday night a steel band plays. For the inn's restaurant, refer to the section on where to dine.

Galley Bay Surf Club, P.O. Box 305, Five Islands, Antigua, W.I. (tel. 809/46-20302). When she created this place west of St. John's, Edee Holbert, now gone, had a fantasy of Gauguin and Polynesia—grass roofs and lily ponds. The world beat a path to her door, including Greta Garbo, who was caught unaware by a nosy magazine photographer who snapped her photograph in the nude on the beach. All that was a long time ago and the Galley Bay has now become part of Caribbean legend. It's still around, still offering its "just for fun" accommodations, but the fickle "big names" have gone elsewhere. Horses suitable even for beginning riders are available, and there are also hard-surface tennis courts, snorkeling (a sunken schooner is nearby), and a dinghy for fishing. In season, dancing is nightly to West Indian bands, particularly at the barbecues. The food is especially good, and *Gourmet* magazine has published some of the recipes. Outstanding are the Caribbean fish chowder, flambé desserts, coq au vin, and lobster thermidor.

A variety of accommodations is offered. For tranquility seekers, the Gauguin Village, with 12 units, is 150 feet off the beach, built around a salt pond under a leafy coconut grove. Each of these units consists of two villas—one with a spacious bedroom, the other with a good-sized bath and dressing room. Directly on the beach, advertised as "four seconds from bed to sea," are a dozen beach rooms, each with a sunken tub in the bathroom and private lanai and palm-woven leaf shutters. In addition, a quartet of executive beach rooms are also on the beach. These are big double rooms, decorated with style and imagination, including a private lounge, private bar, dining porch, and kitchen. The price depends not only on the season, but the accommodation you select. In winter, a single in a beach room pays $200 daily, a double going for $210. In Gauguin Village, prices are $170 daily in singles, $180 in doubles. *In summer, a single can rent a beach room for $105 daily, a double costing $135. One person pays $90 daily in Gauguin Village, and doubles are rented for $120.* All these are EP tariffs. A five-day minimum stay is required at Christmas and in February.

Sandpiper Reef Resort, Crosbies Estate, P.O. Box 569, St. John's, Antigua, W.I. (tel. 809/46-20939), is set in an isolated corner of the island's north coast, between a rolling meadow and a sandy beach, yet it is near casino action and some of the finest restaurants in Antigua. The resort rents 22 superior accommodations cooled by ceiling fans and two junior executive suites on a stretch of beach guarded by a coral reef. Two persons can stay here in winter for $180 to $240 daily. *In summer, prices drop to $80 to $150 daily for two persons.* For the latter prices, you get a one-bedroom suite. Add another $40 per person daily for breakfast and dinner. Guests lounge around the freshwater swimming pool or else enjoy the free water sports.

The Inn, P.O. Box 187, English Harbour, St. John's, Antigua, W.I. (tel. 809/46-31014), owned by Peter and Ann Deeth, stands in a corner of Freeman's Bay. Guests have a choice of pleasingly furnished hillside studios and suites, or else beachfront units, the latter naturally costing more money. In winter, hillside singles on the MAP rent for $250 daily, rising to $270 on the beach. A MAP double on the hillside goes for $285, increasing to $310 to $340 daily on the beach. *Regular off-season rates are $80 to $95 daily in singles, $95 to $110 in doubles.* Suites are always more expensive. The Inn has one of the finest sites in Antigua, with views over Nelson's Dockyard and English Harbour from its terrace. Have a before-dinner drink in the old-style English Bar, with its stone walls and low-overhead beams. Lunch is served both at the beach house and in the main dining room, and the Inn is known for the quality of its cookery. Water sports include Sunfish sailing, waterskiing, snorkeling, rowing, deep-sea fishing, and scuba diving. Tennis can be played on courts, lit at night, five minutes away.

Long Bay Hotel, P.O. Box 442, Antigua, W.I. (tel. 809/46-32005 or toll free 800/223-9868), is dramatically situated on a spit of land between the open sea and a sheltered lagoon, on the eastern shore, beyond the hamlet of Willikie's. It has been owned and operated by the Lafaurie family since 1966. Many repeat visitors consider it more of an inn than a large-scale hotel. It features 20 breeze-filled rooms as well as five furnished cottages for more reclusive guests. High-season rates range from $90 to $150 per person double occupancy on the EP. *However, from mid-October to December 20 and from mid-April to mid-June, tariffs* *go from $75 to $120 per person on the EP, based on double occupancy*. The service charge is added to your bill. The hotel is closed from mid-June to mid-October. The resort is centered around a hip-roofed clubhouse whose stone-walled dining room and artifact-dotted bar provide a relaxing environment. There's a championship tennis court, plus complete scuba facilities and a full array of rental sailboats on the premises. Golf is nearby. Babysitters are available when needed, and there is a special dinner sitting just for children. The hotel has a library and games room, a separate building for the dining room, and a beach house restaurant and bar.

Lord Nelson Club, P.O. Box 155, Antigua, W.I. (tel. 809/46-23094), is a self-contained resort about a mile from the airport, some five miles from St. John's. The club occupies 19 acres, opening onto its own private sandy beach. The pink-walled hotel may look a bit ramshackle in places, but it has a lot of character. Expatriates, both English and American, flock here. The inn has American owners, the Fuller family. One of its members, Nick, was a former U.S. consul. Rooms vary widely, and I prefer the pleasantly decorated twin-bedded rooms, each with a private tile bath and a terrace with a view of the water. The trade winds keep it cool at night. In season, two persons can stay here on EP for $85 daily, a single person paying $65 daily. *From mid-April to mid-December, reductions are granted: $65 daily for two on EP, $55 for one person.* The hotel is closed in September and October. The old-fashioned dining room offers a cuisine that includes some of the island specialties, as well as the partial hull of a beached dinghy set up in its center as a serving station. Set directly on the sand, the stone-walled bar is ready to serve you a tropical drink at your request. The club specializes in windsurfing for intermediate and advanced board surfers.

Best for the Budget

Barrymore, P.O. Box 244, Fort Rd., St. John's, Antigua, W.I. (tel. 809/46-21055), has its own special niche in resort-crowded Antigua. First, it's a good bargain. Second, it's Antiguan, run by the LaBarries, and offers an inexpensive holiday in an unpretentious setting. A small bungalow colony with a freshwater swimming pool, it stands on three acres of private grounds, about a mile from the nearest beach and the capital. Free transportation is provided to the beach. Waterskiing, horseback riding, and windsurfing facilities are available. The place does a good family business, and children are free to romp on the lawn planted with poinsettia bushes. Rooms and efficiencies are in white-sided modern bungalows scattered about the grounds, bordered by flowering shrubbery. Bedrooms have modern appointments motel style, private baths, and patios. Some, not all, contain air conditioning. In winter, singles on the EP cost $60 to $68 daily, and doubles go for $78 to $86. *Off-season, singles rent for $48 to $56 and doubles for $63 to $70 daily.* The LaBarries enjoy a good reputation on the island for serving West Indian dishes, especially Antiguan lobster, at their popular restaurant, Dubarry's (see "Where to Eat," below). You can dine inside or out on the porch, enjoying the breezes if there are any. The LaBarrie family is descended from Madame du Barry, and their French heritage is evident in the charm and grace with which they run this inn.

Falmouth Harbour Beach Apartments, P.O. Box 713, Antigua, W.I. (tel. 809/46-31094), might be what you're looking for, if you'd like to be near the historic English Harbour. On, or just above, a small sandy beach, it offers an informal Antiguan atmosphere, renting 28 twin-bedded studio apartments. Each unit has a private bath with shower and a ceiling fan along with an electric stove, refrigerator, and oven if you'd like to prepare your own meals. After cooking, you can eat your food on your own terrace while overlooking the water. For what it offers, the prices are very reasonable: *only $62 to $66 daily in a twin and $48 to $52 in a single (effective May 1 to December 15)*. Winter rates are still a good buy at $84 to $88 daily in a twin and $72 to $74 in a single. Children are accommodated for $15 per night extra. A dozen units are directly on the beach, while the others lie on a hillside just behind. You can dine at Admiral's Inn in the vicinity (see restaurant section following).

Self-Sufficient Accommodations

Antigua Village, P.O. Box 649, Dickenson Bay, Antigua, W.I. (tel. 809/46-24299), set on a peninsula stretching into the turquoise waters around it, is more of a self-contained condominium community than a holiday resort. A freshwater pool, a restaurant, a bar, and a mini-market are on the premises, with a casino and more restaurants within walking distance. You can use the neighboring tennis court, and there's an 18-hole golf course nearby. Water sports are free. The Village has studio apartments and villas, all of which have kitchenettes, patios or balconies, twin beds in the bedrooms, and sofa beds in the living rooms. In winter, studios rent for $170 to $195 daily, single or double occupancy. One-bedroom apartments cost $210 to $245 daily, also single or double occupancy. Prices vary according to the view. *Low-season rates in studios are $90 to $110 per day, single or double, and one-bedroom apartments cost $110 to $135, also single or double.*

Siboney Beach Club, P.O. Box 222, St. John's, Antigua, W.I. (tel. 809/46-23356). Its Australia-born owner, Tony Johnson, arrived in Antigua in 1959 and has lived here ever since. His hotel, named after the Amerindian tribe predating the Arawaks, is set into a thickly foliated acre of beachfront. It's shielded on the inland side by what may be the tallest and most verdant hedge on the island. The club's social center is the Coconut Grove restaurant. The dozen comfortable suites are in a three-story balconied building draped with bougainvillea and other vines. Some suites have optional air conditioning, and all have fans and louvered windows for natural ventilation. There is no TV, but some suites have phones. All the units have separate bedrooms, living rooms, and balconies or patios, plus tiny kitchens behind movable shutters. Apart from the suites, there is a tree house—a single room with a king-size bed and jungle decor perched high in a ficus Benjamina tree. In winter, singles rent for $170 to $200 daily, and doubles go for $190 to $225. *Summer charges are $90 to $120 daily in singles, $110 to $140 in doubles.* The tree house price is negotiable. MAP can be arranged for another $40 per person per day.

Hodges Bay Club, P.O. Box 1237, Antigua, W.I. (tel. 809/46-22300). Set beside a well-managed restaurant, the Pelican Club, this neo-Mediterranean town-house complex lies between the seaside road and the beach. Although decorated differently, each unit is stylish and attractively personalized, with a fully equipped kitchen, daily maid service, two balconies, ceiling fans, air conditioning, cable TV, and phone. Some have high cathedral ceilings, and all lie a few steps from a stretch of sandy beachfront where the snorkeling is said to be particularly good. In winter, a one-bedroom villa for two persons rents for $240 daily, *dropping to only $150 in summer.* Winter prices for a two-bedroom villa for four persons are $320 to $360 daily, *summer tariffs for the same accommodation being $195 to $230.* The resort's facilities include water sports, tennis courts, and a freshwater swimming pool.

Dian Bay Resort, P.O. Box 231, St. John's, Antigua, W.I. (tel. 809/46-32003). Set on a sun-washed hilltop in an area filled with expensive private villas and flowering shrubs, this is a remote hideaway. Completed in 1985, it contains 32 units. Each has a veranda, a fully equipped kitchenette, and ceiling fans. Only two of the units are air-conditioned, but no one seems to mind because of the cooling trade winds. In winter, one-bedroom suites, suitable for two persons, cost $118 to $130 daily, and two-bedroom suites for up to four persons go for $210 a night. *In summer, one-bedroom suites go for $70 to $85 daily and two-bedroom suites for $140.* Children under 12, staying with paying adults, are housed free. A mini-market on the premises provides food staples for those interested in cooking within their units. The in-house restaurant is recommended separately. A labyrinth of masonry walkways leads past a swimming pool to a sheltered lagoon, where windsurfing and snorkeling equipment is provided free to guests. The establishment lies on the windswept eastern end of the island.

Pillar Rock Resort, Deep Bay, P.O. Box 1166, St. John's, Antigua, W.I. (tel. 809/46-20559), is one of the most modern condo resorts in Antigua, its buildings spread on the side of a hill overlooking a sandy beach and the Royal Antiguan Hotel. At present, there is a cluster of 60 well-furnished villas, suites, and studios, each opening onto sea views. At a location about ten minutes from St. John's, Pillar Rock was developed by Jim Brodie and Phillip Cotroneo. The resort rents self-sufficient units equipped with private kitchenettes. Furnishings are in contemporary rattan. Every bedroom has a private patio or terrace. Many of these villas are privately owned, but they're rented when the owners are not in residence. Accommodations come in a wide range, so agree on facilities before booking. Depending on the place you choose, winter rates are $180 to $350 for two persons daily. *Summer prices for two persons are $150 to $200 daily.* Some of the villas are suitable for four persons, at an extra charge of $10 per person per day. The hotel has a freshwater pool, bar, and a restaurant which merits a separate recommendation.

Galleon Beach Club and Hotel, P.O. Box 1003, English Harbour, St. John's, Antigua, W.I. (tel. 809/46-31024), is built on a flat sandy area dotted with palms, only a few feet above the level of the nearby harbor. Accommodations are in a handful of low-slung cottages with big verandas and large plate-glass windows. Because of the isolated position of some of the cottages, you should never leave valuables in your room. In winter, one-bedroom studios for two cost $145 to $170 daily, one-bedroom cottages for two going for $190, and two-bedroom cottages renting for $240. Two-bedroom deluxe villas cost $300. *In summer, one-bedroom studios are $85 to $100 daily, cottages run $115, and two-bedroom deluxe villas rent for $190.* Guests socialize on the veranda of the hotel's Colombo's Restaurant, recommended separately.

WHERE TO DINE: Traditionally, hotels were the answer if you wanted to dine out in Antigua. That is no longer true. In addition to the hotel facilities, many independently operated restaurants have opened in and around St. John's, serving West Indian food not readily available in the hotel dining rooms. Many dishes, especially the curries, show an East Indian influence. Lobster is a specialty. In the 1980s "gourmet" restaurants, charging inflated prices in some cases, started sprouting up on the island. Several of these are previewed in the section called "Elsewhere on the Island."

Fine Dining Around

Clouds, Halcyon Cove Beach Resort and Casino, P.O. Box 251 Dickenson Bay (tel. 809/46-20256), is the gourmet restaurant of this previously recommended hotel. Aptly named, you dine on a bluff overlooking the bay, enjoying the magnificent view at night while partaking of the chef's specialties. Reservations are absolutely essential, and only dinner is served; the restaurant is open every evening, except Sunday, from 7 to 10:30. You can begin with one of the soups of the night, perhaps zucchini and carrot or else the more classic lobster bisque. Then you can march through the continental dishes, including many cuisine moderne touches, such as breast of chicken stuffed with duck and a pistachio mousse or filet of grouper steamed with leeks and shitake mushrooms. Another good dish is a medley of seafood blended with saffron cream and white wine. Meals cost from $50.

Le Bistro, Hodges Bay, P.O. Box 390, St. John's (tel. 809/46-23881), is an authentic French bistro, the best on the island. Raffaele and Philippa Esposito run this little enclave of French cuisine on the north shore. Recognized by many international magazines, including *Gourmet,* for its superb fare, it has a Lyon-born chef, Pascal Milliat. He named the fettuccine Raffaele, made with cream, parmesan, and mushrooms, after his patron. Other dishes include vol-au-vent with seafood (lobster, shrimp, and scallops), and a rack of lamb (imported from Iowa) for two. Only dinner is served, costing $50 and up, and reservations are vital in high season. Hours are from 7 to 10:30 p.m. daily except Sunday. The restaurant shuts down from the first of May to the first of August.

The Pelican Club Restaurant, Hodges Bay Club, P.O. Box 1237, St. John's (tel. 809/46-22300), is well recommended for its fine cuisine with local touches. This quiet and intimate restaurant, with modern country touches like stone columns and brass ceiling fans, lies behind a low white wall on a sloping plot of land between the road and the sea. The restaurant is run by an Irish chef, Gerard Allen, who presents a sophisticated and creative cuisine, drawing on many culinary traditions.

You might choose lobster bisque laced with aged cognac, tournedos of beef with onion marmalade and ginger and lime sauce, or perhaps you'd like to try the fish specialties that are created daily. Scrumptious desserts include a dark chocolate mousse with a crème de cacao sauce and a special coconut and grenadine frozen soufflé with a strawberry sauce. Any of these dishes can be served to diet-conscious customers without sauce. Dinner, served from 6:30 to 9:30 p.m. in high season (closed Sunday off-season), costs $50 and up. Lunches, offered from 11:30 a.m. to 2:30 p.m. daily, are less elaborate, costing from $15. The bill of fare is likely to include pan-fried red snapper, thick club sandwiches, and an array of pasta and curried salads. If you're in the neighborhood for breakfast, from 7 to 10:30 a.m., you can enjoy American-inspired eye-openers for $7 and up.

Dubarry's, Barrymore Hotel, P.O. Box 244, Fort Road (tel. 809/46-21055), is one of the best restaurants in town. In a modern, low-slung building adjacent to the Barrymore Hotel, it's divided into two distinctly different dining rooms and a pleasant paneled bar. On a chilly evening you'll be seated inside in a modern room capped with a well-finished ceiling of Douglas fir and pitch pine. In warm weather and during informal lunches, diners are seated behind an iron railing on an al fresco terrace overlooking the blue rectangle of an outdoor pool. Local vegetables are often used as accompaniments to the specialties served by candlelight. They include lobster bisque (from Antiguan lobster), several beef dishes, the best catch of the fisherman's haul—and poulet au Dubarry's, the house specialty, a breast of chicken stuffed with shrimp, wrapped in spinach leaves, and then baked before being topped with lobster sauce. Meals cost from EC$100 ($37), and are served from noon to 2 p.m. and 7 to 9:30 p.m. daily except lunch Sunday. Reservations are needed.

L'Auberge de Paris, Trade Winds Hotel, P.O. Box 1390, Dickenson Bay (tel. 809/46-21223). Among all the restaurants of Antigua, this one offers the most sophisticated decor. It's reminiscent of a bistro in the south of France, although both the accents and the attitude of the staff are pure Parisian. There is a glossy collection of cocktail tables, low-slung sofas, and soft lights of the bar area, where a pianist (sometimes imported from Paris) creates music on certain nights. Most guests enjoy a drink in the bar before heading for the slope-ceilinged dining room. Meals, costing from $50, are likely to include grilled lamb chops with onions and herbs, medallions of veal with fruit and curry, and grilled lobster with cocktail sauce. You might begin with snails in garlic butter, finishing with a champagne sorbet. It's open only for dinner, which is served nightly except Sunday from 7 to 10:30 p.m. It's on a hillside on the northern end of the island, not far from the Halcyon Cove Hotel.

Lathefield Restaurant, Hodges Bay, P.O. Box 1138, St. John's (tel. 809/46-22560). Personal, intimate, and charming, this unusual restaurant occupies a yellow-and-white Victorian house about eight miles northeast of St. John's. Set on 11 acres of what used to be a cotton plantation, the house was for several years the home of a Moravian bishop. It contains only 13 tables. Prepared by American-born Paul Corroon, the fare might include char-broiled strips of filet mignon, chicken Chesapeake (stuffed with lobster, green onions, and mushrooms and served with spinach), chicken Cordon Bleu (stuffed with ham and cheese), and red snapper New Orleans style (with lobster chunks and béchamel sauce). A house specialty is California cioppino, a delectable fish stew whose recipe originated in San Francisco. Full meals cost from EC$100 ($37) and are served only at dinner from 7 to 11 every night except Wednesday and from mid-July to mid-October. Reservations are suggested in high season, and jackets and ties are discouraged. The restaurant is occasionally patronized by guests of the ultra-exclusive Mill Reef Club.

Pavilion Restaurant, Pillar Rock Resort, P.O. Box 1166 (tel. 809/46-22325), lies about three miles south from St. John's. A refreshing find, it is especially pleasant in the evening, when the chef prepares his excellent continental fare, including Antiguan fresh lobster or the catch of the day. You might begin with a Caesar salad, then go on to one of the continental dishes such as veal français or chicken Cordon Bleu. Everybody's favorite dish is linguine with lobster sauce. Full meals cost from $40 per person, and service is from noon to 4 p.m. and 6 to 11 p.m. daily. Guests dine with a view of the resort's swimming pool, overlooking The Royal Antiguan Resort to which you can later retire for casino action.

Colombo's Restaurant, Galleon Beach Club. P.O. Box 1003, English Harbour (tel. 809/46-31450), is a Polynesian-style open-air terrace sheltered from the sun and rain by a ceiling crafted from woven palm fronds suspended on top of vertical posts. It's only a few steps across the flat sands to the water. Lunches in this sprawling place cost EC$65 ($24.05) and might include spaghetti marinara, lobster salad, and sandwiches. Dinners are more elaborate, around EC$100 ($37), and include daily specials from a classic Italian inventory of veal scallopini, veal pizzaiola, and lobster mornay. These can be accompanied by a wide assortment of French or Italian wines. Lunch and dinner are offered daily, except for the annual vacation from early September to early October. Lunch is served from 12:30 to 2:30 p.m. daily and dinner from 7:30 to 10 p.m. Live music, including reggae, rock and roll, jazz, or calypso, is often presented.

Admiral's Inn (tel. 809/46-31027) has already been previewed in the hotel selections, a historic building in Nelson's Dockyard. In a 17th-century setting, lobster, seafood, and steaks are served, a lunch costing $9 to $14, the price rising to about $22 for a full dinner, plus service and tax. For your main course, you're usually given four or five choices daily—perhaps broiled kingfish, or lamb chops with mint sauce. Before dinner, have a drink in the bar. There you can read the names of sailors carved in wood more than a century ago. The service is agreeable, and the setting is heavy on atmosphere. In season, you should make a reservation for dinner. It's open seven days a week, serving breakfast from 7:30 to 10 a.m., lunch from noon to 2:30 p.m., and dinner from 7:30 to 9:30 p.m. It's closed during all of September.

Shirley Heights Lookout, Shirley Heights (tel. 809/46-31785). In the 1790s this was the lookout station for advance warning of unfriendly ships heading toward English Harbour. To strengthen Britain's position in this strategic spot, Nelson ordered the construction of a powder magazine which, by the time the property was leased from the government, had fallen into almost total ruin. Today the panoramic spot is one of the most romantic in Antigua. This is my favorite lookout point in the Caribbean. Visitors sometimes prefer to be served on the stone battlements below the restaurant. A far more desirable experience to me is to dine under the angled rafters of the upstairs restaurant, where large, old-fashioned windows surround the room on all sides. Specialties include pumpkin soup, grilled lobster in lime butter, garlic-flavored shrimp, and good desserts, such as banana flambé and carrot cake. Full meals cost about EC$80 ($29.60), although less expensive hamburgers and sandwiches are available from the pub downstairs. Friday is Caribbean night when a buffet of local and Caribbean dishes is served. There is live entertainment. Reservations are required. A tradition with residents and visitors alike is Sunday at the Heights. The "end of the week" barbecue that begins at 3 p.m. features six hours of nonstop entertainment, with a steel band concert from 3 to 6 p.m. and a reggae band from 6 to 9 p.m. The establishment is open from 9 a.m. to 10 p.m. daily. However, avoid it when cruise ship passengers take over. It's best at lunch.

Crabbs Pier 5, Crabbs Slipway & Marina (tel. 809/46-32144). Interesting for anyone who enjoys evaluating the attributes of boats, this pleasant open-air restaurant sits at the edge of a particularly opulent marina. You can drink at the thick mahogany bartop and then dine in a simple modern room whose menu is written on a blackboard. Full lunches, costing from EC$50 ($18.50), include hamburgers, salads, and grilled fish along with less expensive snacks. Dinners from EC$80 ($29.60) include more elaborate fare such as veal Cordon Bleu, leek soup, and the catch of the day, along with Antiguan lobster. Breakfast is served daily (often to residents of the moored yachts) from 9 to 11:30 a.m., lunch from 11:30 a.m. to 3 p.m., and dinner from 7:30 p.m. until "late." The location is in the center of a sun-flooded marina complex on the windswept eastern coast of the island.

Casuarina Restaurant, P.O. Box 1309, Anchorage Rd. (tel. 809/46-23751), is in a once-private home set in a garden rife with West Indian plants and trees, including, of course, the casuarina. Owner/chef Jean-Paul Michel Palhories and his partner and hostess, Antiguan Sonia Kelsick, serve fine French cuisine and local seafood. You might begin with the chef's terrine and then order the house specialty, a deboned leg of lamb stuffed with spinach and veal kidneys. You can also order a superb bouillabaisse or else Antiguan lobster. Daily specials are offered, depending on what Jean-Paul finds on his daily trips to the market. Expect to spend from EC$150 ($55.50) for dinner, the only meal served. The restaurant is intimate and exclusive, so reservations are important. Service is from 6:30 to 11 p.m. daily except Sunday.

Coconut Grove, Siboney Hotel, Dickenson Bay (tel. 809/46-23356), opens right onto the beach. You dine at simple tables set on a flagstone floor beneath a thatch roof. In a coconut grove and cooled by sea breezes, the restaurant is run by Bob and Julia England. They specialize in fresh lobster, fresh fish, and other seafood but also offer good steaks and ribs in a spicy barbecue sauce. Continental dishes, such as osso buco, also appear on the menu, and shrimp fritters are a specialty. Lunches cost from EC$50 ($18.50), with dinners priced at EC$120 ($44.40). The restaurant is open daily from noon to 3 p.m. and 6:30 to 10:30

p.m. Reservations for dinner are a good idea. Live music is presented several nights a week.

In and Around St. John's

Antigua House, Newgate St. (tel. 809/46-20818), combines local Antiguan cuisine with a romantic island setting in an old house. Daily luncheon specials are likely to include fish chowder, peanut chicken, or conch salad, costing EC$60 ($22.25). At night, menu offerings are more extensive, and you might choose from Antiguan lobster (sometimes lobster from Barbuda), pineapple chicken, or rum-marinated beef. Those green fig salads on the menu aren't made of figs at all but of bananas. Dinners cost from EC$100 ($37). A string or steel band usually is brought in to play for the guests on Friday and Saturday nights.

Big Banana Holding Company, Redcliffe Quay (tel. 809/46-22621), serves some of the best pizza in the Eastern Caribbean, in what was once slave quarters. With its ceiling fans and laid-back island atmosphere, it has come of the aura of a place where Sydney Greenstreet might have stopped for a drink, called "dwinks" on the menu. The libations, coconut or banana crush, are practically desserts all by themselves. Not only can you order zesty pizza but also such other delights as overstuffed baked potatoes, fresh fruit salad, or conch salad. Light meals cost from EC$15 ($5.55). Hours are from 8:30 a.m. to 10 p.m. Monday to Saturday, from 5 to 10 p.m. Sunday.

Brother B's, Long St. and Soul Alley (tel. 809/46-20616), is preferred for West Indian food, attracting a faithful crowd as well as a scattering of visitors. You can dine on the patio, enjoying lobster caught fresh daily, plus fresh vegetables from Antiguan farms. The restaurant serves meals from 11:30 a.m. to 5 p.m. and 6 to 10 p.m. daily except Sunday. Antiguan specials, prepared from recipes known for a century or two by oldtime island cooks, are served. For example, on Monday you might enjoy dumplings and mackerel, or pepperpot and fungi the following day. At night, hot plates include grilled lobster and breaded pork chops, Antiguan style. Bottles of hot sauce are placed on every table. Expect to spend from $20 up. Sometimes a little jazz band plays on weekends.

The Victory, 3 Redcliffe St. (tel. 809/46-24317), stands near the shopping center of Redcliffe Quay. The owners invite you to "come lime with us." This big restaurant, open to the breezes, is an especially good choice if you're in town on a shopping expedition. Lunches, costing from EC$35 ($12.95), feature sandwiches and fresh salad plates of lobster or tuna. At dinner, costing from EC$80 ($29.60), the fare is more elaborate, featuring black Angus steak, pan-fried snapper, and Antiguan lobster. The old stone-and-timber building also has a popular bar. In summer, the place is open from 8 a.m. to 7 p.m., but in winter, it extends its hours until 11 p.m. as it offers dinner then.

18 Carat, Church St., St. John's (tel. 809/46-20016), is one of the best lunchtime stops in town. Its location is in the center, under a lattice-trimmed parapet which the owners have built at the edge of a sheltered garden. The blackboard menu appeals to a wide array of local residents. The kitchen produces flavorful versions of chicken and corn chowder, cheeseburgers and hamburgers, seafood platters, and chicken-stuffed baked potatoes. Full meals cost EC$40 ($14.80) and are served from 11:30 a.m. to 3:30 p.m. and 6:30 to 10 p.m. It's closed Sunday all year and also closed Saturday during off-season.

Cockleshell Inn, Lower Fort Rd. (tel. 809/46-20471), may be hard to find, but it's one of the most economical and best dining spots on the island. Established in 1978, and known throughout the island, it occupies a building which served as the nerve center for Antigua's first airport until it was abandoned in 1945. You can dine on a covered veranda overlooking a pleasant garden. Its chef-owner, Winston Derrick, who once lived in Canada, uses the produce of Antigua

—potatoes, eggplant, papaya, pineapple, but mainly freshly caught fish. Of course, you'll want to order one of three different cockle preparations after which the restaurant is named. These include steamed cockles, cockles with garlic butter, and cockles stuffed with bread crumbs. His rolls are homemade: "You've got to cook for people so they come back." A complete dinner costs around $18, although up this to $25 if you want lobster. The inn is open daily except Thursday from 6 p.m. until midnight.

EXPLORING ANTIGUA: In the southern part of St. John's, the **market** is colorful and interesting, especially on Saturday morning. Hucksters busy selling their fruits and vegetables bargain and gossip. The semi-open-air market lies at the lower end of Market Street.

Also in town, **St. John's Cathedral,** the Anglican cathedral, has had a disastrous history. Originally built in 1683, it was replaced by a stone building in 1745. That, however, was destroyed by an earthquake in 1843. The present pitch-pine interior dates from 1847. The interior was being restored when, in 1973, the twin towers and structure were badly damaged by another earthquake. The towers and the southern section have been restored, but restoring the northern part is estimated to cost thousands of dollars, for which contributions are gratefully received. At the entrance, iron gates were erected by the vestry in 1789. The figures of St. John the Baptist and St. John the Divine, at the south gate, were said to have been taken from one of the Napoleonic ships and brought to Antigua by a British man-of-war. The cathedral is between Long and Newgate Streets at Church Lane.

After leaving St. John's, the average visitor heads for one of the biggest attractions in the eastern Caribbean, **Nelson's Dockyard.** It's open seven days a week from 8 a.m. to 6 p.m., charging an admission of EC$3 ($1.10).

One of the safest landlocked harbors in the world, the restored dockyard was used by Admirals Nelson, Rodney, and Hood. It was the home of the British fleet at the time of the Napoleonic wars. From 1784 Nelson was the commander of the British navy in the Leeward Islands, having his headquarters at English Harbour. English ships used the harbor as early as 1671, finding it a refuge from hurricanes. The era of privateers, pirates, and great sea battles in the 18th century revolved around the dockyard.

Restored by the Friends of English Harbour, the dockyard is sometimes known as a Caribbean Williamsburg. Its colonial naval buildings stand now as they did when Nelson was there (1784–1787). However, Nelson never lived at the Admiral's House—it was built in 1855. It does, however, contain what may have been his bed, a four-poster of gilded ivory-colored wood. The house has been turned into a museum of nautical memorabilia. (For accommodations at English Harbour, refer to my earlier recommendations.)

A footpath leads to **Fort Barclay,** the fort at the entrance to English Harbour. The path starts just outside the dockyard gate and it's about half a mile away. The fort is interesting, a fine specimen of oldtime military engineering.

If you're at English Harbour at sunset, head for **Shirley Heights,** named after General Shirley, governor of the Leeward Islands in 1781. He fortified the hills guarding the harbor. Standing are Palladian arches, once part of the barracks. The Block House, one of the main buildings, was put up as a stronghold in case of siege. The nearby Victorian cemetery contains an obelisk monument to the officers and men of the 54th Regiment.

On a low hill overlooking Nelson's Dockyard, **Clarence House** was built by English stonemasons to accommodate Prince William Henry, later known as the Duke of Clarence, even later known as King William IV. The future king stayed here when he was in command of the *Pegasus* in 1787. At present, it is the country home of the governor of Antigua, and is open to visitors when His Excellency is not in residence. A caretaker will show you through (it's customary to tip him, of course), and you'll see many pieces of furniture on loan from the National Trust. In days of yore, Princess Margaret and Lord Snowdon stayed here on their honeymoon.

On the way back, take **Fig Tree Drive,** a 20-some-mile circular drive across the main mountain range. It passes through lush tropical hills and fishing villages along the southern coast. You can pick up the road just outside Liberta, north of Falmouth. Winding through a rain forest, it passes thatched villages, and every hamlet has a church with lots of goats and children running about. However, don't expect fig trees. Fig is an Antiguan name for bananas.

About half a mile before reaching St. John's you come to **Fort James,** which was begun in 1704 as a main lookout post for the port. It was named after James II in whose reign efforts were made to build the fort on the point known as St. John's.

Other places on the island worth seeking out include the following:

Parham Church: The origin of this church is unknown. However, a church stood on this spot in 1755. The church, overlooking Parham Town, was destroyed by fire, and the present structure was erected in 1840 in the Italian style. Richly adorned with stucco work, it was damaged by an earthquake in 1843. Much of the ceiling was destroyed and very little of the stucco work remains, but the octagonal structure is still worth a visit.

Potworks Dam: This is the largest man-made lake in Antigua, surrounded by an area of natural beauty. The dam has a capacity of a billion gallons of water, protection for Antigua in case of a drought.

Indian Town: One of Antigua's national parks, Indian Town, is at a northeastern point on the island. Over the centuries Atlantic breakers have lashed the rocks, carving a natural bridge known as Devil's Bridge. It's surrounded by numerous blowholes spouting surf.

Megaliths: At Greencastle Hill, a long climb will reveal these megaliths, said to have been set up by human hands for the worship of a sun god and a moon goddess. Some experts, however, believe that the arrangement is an unusual geological formation, a volcanic rockfall.

Antigua Rum Distillery: This production plant at Rat Island turns out a fine rum, Cavalier. Check at the tourist office about arranging a visit. Established in 1932, the plant is next to Deep Water Harbour. Its annual production rate is in excess of 250,000 imperial-proof gallons.

SHOPPING: Most of the shops are clustered on St. Mary's Street or High Street in St. John's. Some shops are open daily except Sunday from 8:30 a.m. to noon and 1 to 4 p.m., but this rule varies greatly from store to store. Antiguan shopkeepers are an independent lot. Many of them close at noon on Thursday.

There are many duty-free items for sale, including English woolens and linens, and you can also purchase several specialized items made in Antigua. These include original pottery, local straw work, Antigua rum, and silkscreened, hand-printed local designs on fabrics, as well as mammy bags, floppy foldable hats, and shell curios.

If you want an island-made bead necklace, don't bother to go to any shop. Just lie on the beach—anywhere—and some "bead lady" will find you.

Sea island cotton products are good buys, and some of the best are found at the **West Indian Sea Island Cotton Shop,** St. Mary's Street (tel. 809/46-22972). The shop is an outlet for the Romney Manor workshop on St. Kitts. The

Caribelle label consists of batik and tie-dye, offering beach wraps, swimwear, and head ties.

Coco Shop, the "brown house on St. Mary's Street" (tel. 809/46-21128), is one of the best-equipped marts in town. It's a West Indian beach and shore fashion center, utilizing sea island cottons, even prints from Liberty of London. You can purchase these fabrics either made up or by the yard. Men's shirts have a tropical flair, and some of the carefree clothes are hand-embroidered. Men, women, and children will find a selection of shirts, dresses, blouses, and bikinis. Placed on the counters are hand-crafted ceramics, all made in Antigua. The most popular are the famous steel bandsmen. Ask for Antiguan Frangipani Perfume. There is a Coco Shop at the airport.

The **Industrial Workshop for the Blind,** All Saints Rd. (tel. 809/46-20663), stands next to the public market in downtown St. John's. On sale here are pieces of straw work including floormats, doormats, baskets, chairs, stools, hats, clothes hangers, serving trays, and souvenir wall plaques of Antigua. All products are made by the blind.

Sugar Mill Boutique, St. Mary's St. (tel. 809/46-24523), set amid a collection of other clothing stores and shops, sells garments whose fabrics have been silkscreened by Antiguan artists. The designs include depictions of birds, fish, flowers, and shells indigenous to the region. The store sells a wide array of vibrantly colorful swimwear, evening wear, and casual clothes for men and women. Everything sold here is advertised as hand- or machine-washable.

Quin Farara's Liquor Store, Long St. and Corn Alley (tel. 809/46-20463). Antigua has some of the lowest liquor prices in the Caribbean, and this shop has one of the largest collections of wines and liquors on the island. Often you'll save up to 50% on what you'd pay in the States. The staff will show you how to take home a "gallon," pay the duty, and still save. Don Diego (originally Cuban) cigars are also on sale.

Shoul's Chief Store, St. Mary's St. opposite Barclays Bank (tel. 809/46-21139), is an Ali Baba's cave of treasures. The store sells household items and appliances, a wide range of local and imported souvenirs, Antigua T-shirts, and fabrics of all colors, designs, and textures will be shown to you by the helpful and friendly staff.

Shipwreck Shops Ltd. (tel. 809/46-21322) has five convenient locations: St. Mary's Street at Kensington Court, and at Jardine Court, the Jolly Beach Hotel, the Halcyon Cove Hotel, and Heritage Quay. Their walls, ceilings, and counters are loaded with merchandise either from Antigua or some neighboring island. They carry everything from A to Z—T-shirts, coverups, swim suits, dresses, photo supplies, beach accessories, jewelery, wooden bowls, figurines of wood and ceramic, glassware, hats, bags, postcards, and more. They also have daily newspapers, magazines, and many paperback books.

Custom Made Garment, Inc., Vivian Richards St. (tel. 809/46-22845), features Jim Tillet silkscreen prints, plus other materials, in either ready- or custom-made garments. Doris George designs and makes clothing for you, as well as helping make sure the fit is right on ready-made clothing.

Redcliffe Quay

This historic complex is the best corner for shopping (or dining) in St. John's, except that the duty-free merchandise is sold at Heritage Quay (see below). Once, Redcliffe Quay was a slave-trading quarter, but those unfortunate times are long gone. After the abolition of slavery, the quay was filled with grog shops and merchants peddling various wares. Now it has been redeveloped and contains a number of the most interesting shops in town, some in former warehouses.

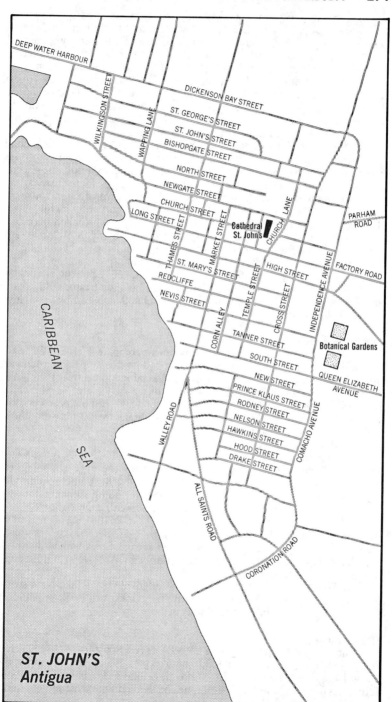

ST. JOHN'S
Antigua

I'll provide a few recommendations, just to get you started.

Serendipity, Redcliffe Quay (tel. 809/46-22026), sells merchandise from England, Scotland, and Ireland, including handmade Scottish teddy bears, crofter's handwoven lambswool blankets and shawls, scrimshaw, and a small selection of Irish pewter. They also sell items made of Montserrat sea island cotton.

Island Woman, 7 Redcliff Quay (tel. 809/46-24220), is considered one of the best of the unusual stores in the shopping labyrinth of Redcliffe Quay. Specializing in casual sportswear, usually for women, it also has a limited selection for men and children. A few of the garments are hand-blocked and batiked in tropical colors and designs, and are often made in Antigua.

A Thousand Flowers, Redcliffe Quay (tel. 809/46-24264), sells Indonesian batiks, crafted on the island into sundresses, knock-'em-dead shirts, sarongs, rompers, and swimwear. Many of the garments are designed into a one-size-fits-all motif of knots and flowing expanses of cloth appropriate for the tropics.

Jacaranda, Redcliffe Quay (tel. 809/46-21888), is worth a visit. You might be tempted by the art of John Woodland or placemats and prints by Jill Walker. The shop also stocks cosmetics from the islands along with herbs and spices.

Windjammer Clothing Company, Redcliffe Quay (tel. 809/46-20746), offers casual dress for women, children, and men. The lightweight clothing was made in the West Indies, the designers using natural fibers and cotton.

The Goldsmitty, Redcliffe Quay (tel. 809/46-24601), presents the designs of Hans Smit in precious stones and gold. Each item is a treasure. Buyers can select from a wide array of merchandise, including necklaces, earrings, and rings, in 14K or 24K gold.

Heritage Quay

Antigua's first shopping and entertainment complex, Heritage Quay is a multimillion-dollar center featuring a variety of duty-free shops, some 40 in all, and a vendor's arcade in which local artists and craftspeople display their wares. Restaurants in Heritage Quay offer a range of cuisine and views of St. John's Harbour, while a "food court" serves visitors who prefer to feast on local specialties in an informal setting. Plans call for a 200-seat dinner theater featuring shows and local talent, plus a casino and supper club.

Leading shops include the following:

Colombian Emeralds, Heritage Quay (tel. 809/46-23462), is the largest retailer of Colombian emeralds in the world, with branches at key shopping centers in the West Indies and The Bahamas. It offers an excellent variety of emeralds along with jewelry made from precious stones, including sapphires and diamonds. The store claims significant savings on prices charged back home.

Little Switzerland, Heritage Quay (tel. 809/46-23108), is a name familiar to frequent travelers to the Caribbean. It sells the best selections of Swiss-made watches in Antigua, all the big brand names such as Rolex and Vacheron & Constanin. It also displays china and crystal made by Wedgwood and Baccarat, among other fine houses.

SunSeekers, 13 Heritage Quay (tel. 809/46-23618), is an elegant swim- and sportswear shop for women and men. They stock such designer names as Gottex, Jantzen, Caralina, and Triumph.

Island Arts

The best gallery on the island is **Island Arts** (tel. 809/46-13332), which is open Monday to Saturday from 9:30 a.m. to 5 p.m. Island Arts is found at the Alton Place Gallery, on Sandy Lane, directly behind Hodge's Bay Club, about four miles from St. John's. It is the home and studio to the artist and collector,

Nick Maley, who allows visitors to roam through some 1,500 feet of exhibition space. Many paintings are very reasonable in price—even the expensive ones. He is an expert on Caribbean artists, and has staged many exhibitions. His growing fame has led to his issuing several of his own fine art reproductions, including the provocative *Windkissed & Sunswept.* Previously he was a makeup artist, working in illusions on such productions as *Star Wars* and *The Empire Strikes Back.*

Near Freetown

Harmony Hall, Brown's Mill Bay (tel. 809/46-32057), is a recent structure of cut-stonework, in the same architectural theme as a restored sugar mill, both with views over Nonsuch Bay. Harmony Hall aims at promoting excellence in Caribbean art and craft by providing a special showcase in a distinctive setting. The original complex is in a Victorian great house near Ocho Rios, Jamaica. The old Brown's Bay Mill here in Antigua contains a circular bar, a large barbecue with seating in the shaded garden or the cut-stone dining room, and a small sitting area on top with a panoramic view.

Harmony Hall houses an art gallery, with regular exhibitions showing collections by top Caribbean artists and sculptors. In the gift shop, you can choose from a wide range of such objects as Annabella boxes (Annabella is the founder of Harmony Hall), objets d'art from the 19th century, hand-decorated wood carvings of birds and fruit, books, cards, ceramics such as hand-painted Caribbean cottages, jewelry of indigenous materials done by the region's top designers, and many other craft items by local artisans.

The establishment is open from 10 a.m. to 6 p.m. daily. To get there, you can follow signs along the road to the Mill Reef and Half Moon Bay.

THE SPORTING LIFE: Beaches, beaches, and more beaches—Antigua has, as mentioned, some 365 of them. Some are superior. There's a lovely beach at **Pigeon Point,** in Falmouth Harbour, about a four-minute drive from Admiral's Inn. The beach at **Dickenson Bay,** near the Halcyon Cove Hotel, is also superior, and for a break, you can enjoy meals and drinks on the hotel's Warri Pier, built on stilts in the water (this beach is also a center for water sports). Chances are, however, you'll swim at your own hotel.

Golf

In golf, Antigua doesn't have the facilities of some of the other islands such as Puerto Rico. But what it has is good. The 18-hole, par 72 **Cedar Valley Golf Club** (tel. 809/46-20161) is three miles out of St. John's, near the airport. The island's largest, with panoramic views of Antigua's northern coast, it was designed by the late Richard Aldridge to fit the contours of the area. Visitors can play on this semi-private course by prior arrangement with the manager. Daily greens fees are $16. Caddies charge $4 for nine holes, $8 for 18 holes. Carts for 18 holes cost $20. Equipment can be rented for $5 per day.

The other course of note is the one at **Half Moon Bay** (tel. 809/46-22138), on the southeast corner of Antigua. It's a nine-holer. In season, guests of the hotel are guaranteed a space—and you may not be. Greens fees are $8 per day for the nine holes, and clubs rent for $5. In theory, the caddy charge is $4, but it's advisable to pay yours more than that.

Horseback Riding

Antigua Riding Stables (tel. 809/46-11946), located in the meadows at Yepton's Beach Resort, near The Royal Antiguan Resort, offers supervised rides on some of the best horses on the island, exploring the nature trails on the northeast side of Antigua. A qualified riding instructor is on hand.

Tennis

Tennis buffs will find courts at most of the major hotels. Some are lit for night games. I don't recommend playing tennis at noon in Antigua unless you're a "mad dog or an Englishman." It's just too hot! If your hotel doesn't have a court, you'll find them available at the **Halcyon Cove, Half Moon Bay, Cedar Valley Golf Club, Jolly Beach,** and **The Royal Antiguan** (the latter two have eight courts each). If you're not a guest, you'll have to book a court, paying charges that vary from hotel to hotel. Residents of a hotel usually play free.

Water Sports

Scuba diving is best arranged through **Dive Antigua,** Halcyon Cove Beach Resort and Casino, Dickenson Bay (tel. 809/46-23483, ext. 217), Antigua's longest established and most experienced dive operation.

You can also arrange scuba-diving trips at the **Jolly Beach Hotel** on Morris Bay (tel. 809/42-20061, ext. 111).

Long Bay Hotel (tel. 809/46-32005), on the northeastern coast of the island at Long Bay, is good location for various water sports—swimming, sailing, waterskiing, deep-sea fishing, windsurfing, and scuba-diving. The hotel has complete scuba facilities. Both beginning snorkelers and experienced divers are welcomed. One-tank dives for already-certified divers cost $50 per person. Two persons diving together pay only $40 per person for a one-tank dive. Long Bay doesn't offer scuba courses for beginners. You're taken on snorkel trips by boat to Green Island at a cost of $25 per person (if there are two or more) and to Great Bird Island for $25 per person (minimum of four). The shallow side of the double reef across Long Bay is ideal for the neophyte, and the whole area on the northeastern tip has many reefs of varying depths.

The **Blue Waters Beach Hotel,** Soldiers Bay (tel. 809/46-20290), has one of the best water-sports programs on the island. Waterskiing is available at about $10 for 15 minutes or five pulls per person. In addition, they offer snorkeling gear, fishing rods, windsurfers, pedaloes, Sunfish, Hobie cats, and canoeing, all complimentary to Blue Waters guests.

Windsurfing

Patrick's Windsurfing School offers lessons for beginners at Halcyon Cove Beach Resort and Casino, Dickenson Bay (tel. 809/46-20256), with a full range of boards and sails available, together with radio-assisted rescue facilities.

Patrick's also operates **High Winds Center** at Lord Nelson Beach Club, Dutchmans Bay, P.O. Box 155, Antigua (tel. 809/46-23094). The center accepts only intermediate and advanced windsurfers because of its gusty Atlantic coast breezes. Instruction in jibing and other advanced windsurfer techniques is offered, as well as a Windsurfer Certification Course. The charge is $50 per day, and the same range of boards and sails, plus radio-assisted rescue facilities, is available here as at the Halcyon Cove facility. Classes are offered from 10 a.m. to noon and 2 to 4 p.m.

Parasailing

This sport is gaining in popularity in Antigua. Facilities are available during the day except Sunday on the beach at Dickenson Bay (tel. 809/46-10945).

There are also facilities at the previously recommended Jolly Beach and Royal Antiguan Hotels.

Fishing

Deep-sea fishing can usually be arranged at your hotel desk. If you want to negotiate on your own, check out **Long Bay Hotel** (tel. 809/46-32005), which offers a half-day inshore fishing at $30 per person if there are two or more in your party. For deep-sea fishing, including guide, bait, and tackle, the cost is $135 per half-day trip.

Sailing

Since Admiral Nelson's day, sailing has been popular in Antigua. I prefer the **Servabo Fun Cruise** taken in a character-type vessel, the last constructed of a British sailing fishing trawler popular from 1750 to 1927. Based off the shores of Dickenson Bay, the 64-ton *Servabo* celebrated her 50th anniversary some time back. She even appeared before the cameras, in the Omar Sharif film *The Mysterious Island*. The vessel's barbecue cruise costs $50 per person. Out at sea you're given barbecued steak and lobster, and you're gone from 10 a.m. to 4 p.m. The cruise departs from Antigua Village. The day is filled with calypso music, snorkeling, and rum punches. Telephone 809/46-21581 for reservations.

All major hotel desks can book you on a day cruise on the 108-foot "pirate ship," the *Jolly Roger.* For $40, you are taken sightseeing on a fun-filled day, with drinks and a barbecue steak chicken, or lobster. The *Jolly Roger* is the largest sailing ship in Antiguan waters. Lunch is combined with a snorkel trip. Dancing is on the poop deck, and members of the crew teach passengers how to dance calypso. Everything's a little corny, but most passengers love it. If you want to make reservations on your own, telephone 809/46-22064.

NIGHTLIFE: Most nightlife revolves around the hotels, unless you want to roam Antigua at night looking for that "hot native club." If you're going out for the night, make arrangements to have a taxi pick you up—otherwise you could be stranded in the wilds somewhere. Antigua has some of the best steel bands in the Caribbean.

After dinner, you might also want to patronize the **Halcyon Cove Casino** (tel. 809/46-20256). It offers all the games of chance, giving you an opportunity to try your luck at roulette, blackjack, American craps, and super-jackpot slots. It is open nightly at 9, staying in business "till the last person leaves."

Maione's Casino Royal Antiguan, The Royal Antiguan Resort & Casino (tel. 809/46-23733), is a 6,000-square-foot international casino with American games, including black jack, baccarat, roulette, craps, and slot machines. It is open daily from 8 p.m. "until."

Flamingo Antigua Hotel and Casino, Michael's Mount (tel. 809/46-21266), is a gambling complex that's part of the hotel of the same name, about half a mile from the center. It offers blackjack and craps tables, plus a large assortment of slot machines and roulette. Open daily from 9 p.m. "until."

Tropix, Redcliffe Quay (tel. 809/46-22317), is the leading disco on the island, considered one of the most popular nightclubs in Antigua. Dress is semiformal or sort of casually elegant. It is open nightly, from 9 to whenever, Tuesday to Sunday, charging an admission of $6. The place, once a warehouse used for the storing of tamarinds and sheepskins, now has a hi-tech format.

BARBUDA: Known by the Spanish as Dulcina, sparsely populated Barbuda, part of the independent nation of Antigua and Barbuda, is considered the last frontier of the Caribbean. Charted by Columbus in 1493, the island lies 26 miles to the north of Antigua, and is about 15 miles long by 5 miles wide with a population of some 1,200 hardy souls, most of whom live around the unattractive village of Codrington.

Don't come here seeking lush, tropical scenery, as flat Barbuda consists of coral rock. There are no paved roads, fewer than 60 hotel rooms, only a handful of restaurants, and pastel-colored beaches, the most famous of which stretches for more than 17 miles.

Hunters, fishermen, and just plain beachcombers are attracted to the island, as it has some fallow deer, guinea fowl, pigeon, and wild pig. Those interested in fishing for bonefish and tarpon negotiate with the owners of small boats which hire them out.

The most impressive sight on Barbuda is the **frigate bird sanctuary,** one of the largest in the world, where visitors can see the birds, *Fregata magnificens,* sitting on their eggs in the mangrove bushes. The mangroves stretch for miles in a long lagoon accessible only by a small motorboat. Tours to the sanctuary can be arranged in Antigua at various hotels and resorts and cost about $100 for a day-long trip, which may include a flight from Antigua, a sanctuary visit, sightseeing, and a Barbudan lobster lunch. Caribbean Link Ltd., a high-speed ferry service, provides day trips on Sunday, costing $95 which includes round-trip fare, a tour, and a beach party. Besides the frigate bird, the island attracts some 150 species of birds, including pelicans, ibis, herons, kingfishers, tropical mockingbirds, oyster catchers, and cormorants.

The main town is named after Christopher Codrington, who was once the governor of the Leeward Islands. He is believed to have deliberately wrecked ships on the reefs circling Barbuda. What is known is that he used the island, which he'd received in 1691 from the Crown, for the purposes of breeding slaves. He was given the island in return for "one fat pig per year, if asked."

Barbuda has a temperature that seldom falls below an average of 75° Fahrenheit.

The island is reached after a 15-minute flight from Antigua's Coolidge Airport. It has two airfields, one at Codrington, the other a private facility, "Kelly Field," at Coco Point. To reach Barbuda from Antigua, contact Frank DeLisle, owner of **Carib Aviation** (tel. 809/46-23147), who charges $15 each way for scheduled Antigua/Barbuda flights three times a week. Once you're on Barbuda, you should hire a Jeep and a mandatory driver, costing around $80 per day for an island tour, at a small house owned by Bernard Thomas (no address, no phone). Just ask at the airport. LIAT also flies from Antigua to Barbuda. Call 809/46-20700 for details.

Those trippers over just for the day usually head for **Wa'Omoni Beach Park,** where they can visit a frigate bird sanctuary, snorkel for lobster, and eat barbecue.

Curiosities of the island include a **"Dividing Wall,"** which once separated the Codrington family from the black people, and the **Martello Tower,** which predates the known history of the island. Tours also cover interesting underground caves on the island. Stamp collectors might want to call at the **Philatelic Bureau** in Codrington.

To book an excursion to Barbuda and/or accommodations, get in touch with **Claudia Richards,** The Earl's Complex, P.O. Box 57, St. John's, Antigua, W.I. (tel. 809/46-24488). There are few available accommodations on the island, however.

The Earl's Villa, housing up to eight guests, can be rented for $130 per day or $890 per week year round. This includes maid and laundry service. They also rent efficiencies and cottages for two, costing $50 per day, $350 per week all year. Some of the units are outside Codrington, some in the village. Meals can be arranged.

Another affordable option is **Sunset View Resort,** costing around $75 per day for two in winter, *$55 in summer.* Rooms are modest but clean and adequate.

An Exclusive Retreat

Coco Point Lodge (tel. 212/696-4750 in New York City for reservations) is a private club, occupying a 164-acre peninsula with more than 2½ miles of white sandy beach at the southern tip of Barbuda. The allure of this place was summed up in a long-ago chance encounter on the beach with Greta Garbo. She looked sternly at me and, taking in my flash of recognition, said, "You know who I am, and I know who I am, so we'll keep it our little secret." Secrecy and privacy, a screen pulled down against the prying eyes of the world — that's what this place is all about. It doesn't want or need publicity. Most of its guests return year after year, making it very difficult for newcomers to book rooms. Guests are housed either in the main building or in one of the newer cottages such as Spanish Point, Martello Tower, or Sea Crescent, a total of 32 accommodations with beachfront patios. Coco Point caters to everybody from a small-town banker to titans of industry or actresses who want to escape from it all, even Princess Margaret. A lot of wicker is used, making the lodge evoke a summer home in the Hamptons. The designer did the exclusive Mill Reef Club on Antigua. The inn is definitely understated, and that's how its clients like it. The social hub is the clubhouse. The lodge receives only from November 15 to May 1. Usually there are rarely more than 50 guests at one time, perhaps 60 at the very most. Dress is casual, and ties and jackets are certainly not required.

All tariffs include air transfer from Antigua, three meals a day, and free liquor. In high season, charges are $475 to $750 for two persons daily. *In summer, rates are $375 to $600 per day for two persons.* Occupants of singles receive a $50 reduction from the prices listed above. There is also a $150 surcharge levied on all guests, which is a membership fee, as this place is really a private club. The food is flown in from Miami, except some fresh produce which may be shipped in from Dominica and St. Kitts. Their seafood and homemade bisques are superb. About 40% of the guests come here to enjoy the good fishing. A 43-foot motor sailer is placed at the disposal of guests. Guests who land on the lodge's own 3,000-foot strip are picked up quickly, and 15 minutes later are found sitting on the beach with a rum punch. Included in the rate is air transportation from Coolidge Airport in Antigua. Other facilities include waterskiing and two very fine all-weather tennis courts. The owner Bill Kelly, who once lived next door to the Kennedys in Hyannis Port. Frankly, Mr. Kelly prefers to keep the crowds out. Therefore if you're planning to drop in for a drink or a meal, forget it, unless you're a paying guest. Many a visiting yachtsman has been turned away disappointed.

2. MONTSERRAT

To see "the way the Caribbean used to be," a good choice for a visit is Montserrat. Vacationers often fly to the volcanic island just for the day and later are sorry they hadn't booked more time. Called "The Emerald Isle of the Caribbean," Montserrat is some 27 miles southwest of Antigua, lying between Guadeloupe and Nevis. The pear-shaped island is mountainous with lush green forests, much tropical vegetation, and some licorice beaches of volcanic sand that are powdery but black.

Montserrat was sighted by the ubiquitous Columbus in 1493 and named after the famous sawtoothed mountain near Barcelona. However, it wasn't until 1632 that Irish settlers colonized the island, when Oliver Cromwell, it is believed, shipped out a band of reluctant colonists who'd been captured after a rebellion. Sending the unwilling band to the ruggedly beautiful island was Cromwell's way of getting rid of them. Montserrat also became home to Irish settlers who fled their new homes on St. Kitts because of religious persecution. The Irish influence is shown in names of places on the island and in the surnames of present-day residents.

The flag of Montserrat is the British Union Jack, but the official badge is the very Irish "Lady with the Harp." The shamrock can be seen on the center gable of Government House, which can be visited, and it's also on the stamp with which Montserrat immigration people stamp your passport. The island even marks March 17 as a public holiday, but this is because the slaves in the early days staged a rebellion on St. Patrick's Day. By 1648 there were more than 1,000 Irish families living on Montserrat, a place that had become known as a sanctuary from religious persecution.

Today Montserrat's more than 12,000 hard-working, friendly people, most of whom were descended from African slaves, often speak with an Irish brogue as a heritage left by those early settlers.

The island was captured by the French in 1644, restored to England in 1668, and retaken by the French in 1782, who ceded it to Britain in 1783. Popular as a retiree resort, the island has political stability, its officials having elected to remain a British Crown Colony, as they don't have the financial independence to go it alone. The capital, **Plymouth,** is reputed to be one of the cleanest in the Caribbean. It's best viewed on Saturday market day, when gossip is traded along with fruit.

George Martin, best known as the producer of the Beatles, has launched a contemporary electronic studio in a Belham Valley estate, and he uses Olveston House, the residence of an early lime-juice magnate, as a private residence for the Aire recording company (tel. 809/491-5656). Therefore don't be surprised if, when exploring Montserrat, you encounter such artists as Paul McCartney or Elton John, both of whom have been known to come here for weeks at a time to record music and to "wind down." Among celebrities who have stayed on the island in years past have been Ringo Starr, Jimmy Buffet, and Stevie Wonder.

GETTING THERE: Antigua is the "gateway" to Montserrat. There is no direct flight from North America to Montserrat. Most visitors fly here by going first to Antigua (see "Getting There" under Antigua, above). Once in Antigua, you can book a **LIAT** flight (Leeward Islands Air Transport), as there are several morning and afternoon hops daily, the number increasing in winter. The passage from Antigua to Montserrat is only 15 minutes.

GETTING AROUND: There are 150 miles of surfaced roads, and taxis and buses are the most popular means of transport. **Taxi** drivers meet every plane. Typical fares from the airport to Vue Pointe are EC$35 ($13) one way, EC$26 ($9.50) from the airport to Montserrat Springs Hotel. Sightseeing tours cost about $10 per hour. Motor **buses** run between Plymouth and most areas at fees ranging from $1 to $2.

You can rent a car in Montserrat, although you must go to the police station where you'll be given a temporary driver's license upon presentation of a valid U.S. or Canadian license and payment of EC$30 ($11.10). It is possible to obtain a license at the airport. Rental cars, ranging in price from $40 per day, unlimited mileage, are generally booked at your hotel, or you can get in touch with **Pauline's Car Rental** at Amersham (tel. 809/491-2345) or **Jefferson Car**

Rental at Dagenham (tel. 809/491-2126). Incidentally, car rentals aren't allowed to operate out of the airport, so one must board a taxi for the cross-island trip to Plymouth. It's important to bear in mind that there are only two gasoline stations (they call it petrol here) in Montserrat. One is the Texaco station, north of Plymouth, and the other is opposite the public market, N & B Servicentre.
Remember: Drive on the left.

PRACTICAL FACTS: Montserrat is still a Crown Colony, as are the Cayman and British Virgin Islands. This means that the British monarch, represented by a governor, is head of state.
   Currency: All of the British Leeward Island use the EC$, although most prices are given in U.S. dollars.
   Electricity: You'll need an electrical adapter for all U.S.-made appliances, as the island supplies 220–230 volts AC, 60 cycles.
   Information: For information and assistance, see the **Department of Tourism,** P.O. Box 7, Plymouth, Montserrat, B.W.I. (tel. 809/491-2230).
   Taxes: The government charges a hotel tax of 7%. In addition, it imposes a $6 departure tax when you leave the island.
   Telephone: Montserrat can be dialed directly from mainland North America by using the Caribbean area code of 809, then 491 (the prefix for all numbers on the island), then the four-digit local number. Of course, when you're on Montserrat, you can dispense with the area code when calling.
   Time: Montserrat is on Atlantic Standard Time. When it's 6 a.m. in Plymouth, it's 5 a.m. in New York or Miami. However, island clocks match those of the Eastern Standard Zone on the mainland when Daylight Saving Time is in effect in the U.S.
   Tips and service: Most hotels add a 10% surcharge to your final tab to cover tips. If they don't, it's customary to tip from 10% to 15%.
   Weather: The mean temperature of the island ranges from a high of 86.5° to a low of 73.5° Fahrenheit.

HOTELS: Montserrat has a wide variety of accommodations. Although limited in number, they vary greatly in style—plantation guesthouses, modest inns, condominium colonies, small resort complexes, and luxury villas. The trade winds, more than air conditioning, will keep you cool. Informality is the keynote.
   Don't forget that the government imposes a 7% room tax on hotels, and usually a 10% service charge is also added. To save yourself a shock when your tab is presented, check about this when you register.
   Vue Pointe Hotel, P.O. Box 65, Old Towne, Montserrat, B.W.I. (tel. 809/491-5211), is a family-run cottage colony of 28 hexagonal, shingle-roofed villas, plus a dozen interconnected town houses. They're set on five acres of sloping land near a black sand beach. Most of the accommodations are constructed with natural lumber, having open-beamed ceilings, and they're furnished with bamboo and modern pieces. Each has a private bath, a sitting room area, and twin beds. The staff are unobtrusive, but so well trained they seem to anticipate your needs. When they can, they offer music and dancing to a steel-band beat. They'll even show movies.
   In winter, two persons pay $205 daily in a cottage, while a single person is charged only $160, all on the MAP. A double room, also on the MAP, rents for $170 daily, a single for $125. *In summer, tariffs are lowered, with two persons on the EP paying $62 daily: and a single charged $50.* A natural breeze sweeps through accommodations in lieu of air conditioning. Besides the freshwater swimming pool, there are two tennis courts, lit for evening games. The cuisine is the best on

the island, and as proof of that, everybody seems to show up for the West Indian barbecue on Wednesday night. Food is served family-style, which means that no one faints if you ask for second helpings. However, the first helpings are usually generous enough to suffice. There are two attractive bars, one at the rambling main house, the other, called the Nest, at water's edge. The location is just 11 miles from the Montserrat airport and about two minutes from the challenging seaside Montserrat Golf Club. The staff will arrange for fishing, sailing, and snorkeling. Dress is informal, except on Monday and Saturday nights in season, when custom dictates that the men spruce up a bit.

Montserrat Springs Hotel, P.O. Box 259, Richmond, Montserrat, B.W.I. (tel. 809/491-2481), is a 29-room inn nestled on a hillside, with a superb view of Plymouth, a mile away. The manager runs a quiet, subdued, small hotel, welcoming you into a split-level house with its trade-wind-swept, open-air terrace built around a swimming pool that juts out on the hill. Guest rooms extend down a breezy corridor. Your air-conditioned room has a picture window with a small patio. Baths are big and tiled. The hotel has a Jacuzzi and a hot-water mineral bath. In the open-air lounge, you can enjoy a before-dinner drink before walking up to the mezzanine for a big, hearty West Indian dinner. In winter, singles on the EP pay $90 to $145 daily. Doubles are $105 to $160. *Off-season, singles are $60 to $90, while doubles cost $75 to $105.* A third adult in a room pays $25, but there is no charge for children up to 12 sharing a room with adults. The beach is 100 yards away. On some nights there is live music and entertainment, perhaps crab racing.

Coconut Hill Hotel, P.O. Box 337, Plymouth, Montserrat, B.W.I. (tel. 809/491-2144), in the residential suburbs half a mile outside Plymouth. This antique Montserratian mansion has roots deep in the soil of the island. The son of the original owner converted the property into a hotel way back in 1908, adding rooms on the top floor. Other renovations have been carried out to improve the facilities. It's classic in style—the façade has remained the same over the years, with a long upper and lower balcony across the front. Across the rear of the building, a dining room, serving island-style meals, offers an unmarred view. All but one of the nine bedrooms have private baths, and are furnished with a mixture of the old and new. Each room also has a phone, but don't expect air conditioning. However, you may sleep blissfully in a four-poster bed. In winter, guests on the MAP are charged $75 daily in a single, $99 in a double. *Off-season reductions drop the prices to $57 daily in a single, $80 in a double, both MAP tariffs.*

Flora Fountain Hotel, Lower Dagenham Rd., P.O. Box 373, Montserrat, B.W.I. (tel. 809/491-3444), is popular with business travelers who appreciate its central location in Plymouth. This hotel is built around a circular courtyard centered on a fountain whose illumination is computerized. Each of its 18 bedrooms is concealed behind mahogany doors. There isn't much of a view, but each unit has its own balcony nonetheless. Rooms have private baths and air conditioning. In winter, singles cost $65 daily, and doubles run $90, with breakfast included. *In summer, singles rent for $44 daily, and doubles go for $54, also with breakfast include.* The hotel offers a fixed-price lunch from 11 a.m. to 2:30 p.m., costing only EC$12 ($4.45) per person. Try to visit for their Saturday morning West Indian buffet breakfast, when you can feast on such local dishes as salt fish, bananas, breadfruit, souse, and blood pudding. Of course, you can order bacon and eggs if you prefer.

SELF-SUFFICIENT VACATIONS: The island's most luxurious villa complex, **Villas of Montserrat,** P.O. Box 421, Plymouth, Montserrat, B.W.I. (tel. 809/491-5513), offers three deluxe villas, each with three bedrooms, three baths (one with a Jacuzzi), a large living room with color TV and stereo, a spacious dining area, and a gourmet kitchen with microwave oven and dishwasher. They also have their own swimming pools, and there are washer and dryer facilities. The villas, accommodating up to six persons, rent for $1,950 per week in winter, *$1,650 in summer.* Prices provide inclusive services, including air transport from Antigua, transportation to the your villa (after you have been assisted through Customs and Immigration), rum punch drinks, and a cold lobster and champagne dinner. Your breakfast will be served on the patio, followed by a tour of the island. Maid service is covered in the rates, and you can arrange for a private cook if you wish. The handsome villas are on a hillside, with views of Isle Bay and the Caribbean Sea as well as the Montserrat golf course.

A condominium hillside colony, **Shamrock Villas,** P.O. Box 221, Plymouth, Montserrat, B.W.I. (tel. 809/491-2431), suggests an Iberian village of white, balcony-studded houses. Owners have arranged for their villas to be rented in their absence. From all villas there are views of the sea, the black sandy beaches, and Plymouth. Up for rent are one- and two-bedroom apartments as well as penthouses. In season (December to April), the rates for one-bedroom/one-bath apartments are $400 weekly. A two-bedroom unit, suitable for four, costs $500 weekly. *In off-season, a one-bedroom unit for two persons is only $300 weekly. A two-bedroom accommodation for four persons rents for $350 weekly.* Linen and cutlery are included, even for short-term rentals. Maid service is available at an extra cost. Services are close by. Bread comes fresh from the baker, and at the local market you can sample the produce grown on the island, especially the abundant tomatoes, carrots, and pineapples. A beach and tennis court are adjacent.

Lime Court Apartments, P.O. Box 250, Plymouth, Montserrat, B.W.I. (tel. 809/491-3656), is an apartment colony right in the center of town, a short walk from the beach, shops, and restaurants. The property is walled in, making the gardens private. Fully furnished one- and two-bedroom apartments are available with well-equipped kitchens and electric cooking. Each unit has a hot-water shower for the bedroom, and all utilities and maid service are included in the tariffs. The most luxurious unit is No. 9, a penthouse apartment offering a magnificent view of the harbor; it's well furnished, and has a private patio. This rents for $225 weekly year round. Four one-bedroom accommodations with private patio cost $150 weekly. Some two-bedroom units with private patios go for $215. The manager, Neville Bradshaw, advises that in winter all bookings should be made at least two months in advance.

Belham Valley Hotel, P.O. Box 420, Montserrat, B.W.I. (tel. 809/491-5553), is a series of cottages on a hillside overlooking the Belham Valley and its river. The beach is about a seven-minute walk, and you can also stroll over for an evening at the already-previewed Vue Pointe Hotel. The Frangipani studio cottage, surrounded by tropical shrubs and coconut palms, is a showpiece, consisting of a large bed-sitting room, a fully equipped kitchen, a private bath, and a balcony. *In low season, it rents for $250 weekly for two persons,* increasing to $350 weekly in high season. The Jasmine studio apartment, contains a large bed-sitting room, a small dinette, a private bath, and a fully equipped kitchen. There is also a small private patio with views of the sea or the distant mountains. *It rents for $175 weekly for two in low season,* $225 in winter. A newer apartment, the Mignonette, has two bedrooms, a bath, and a living area with fully equipped kitchen, plus a large patio facing the golf course and the sea. Four people can stay here for *$240 weekly off-season,* $400 in season.

WHERE TO DINE: Some of the best fruit and vegetables in the Caribbean are grown in the rich, volcanic soil of Montserrat. The island is known for its tomatoes, carrots, and mangoes; and "goat water" (a mutton stew) is the best-known local dish. Another island specialty is "mountain chicken," as locally caught frogs' legs are called.

Belham Valley Restaurant, near the Vue Pointe Hotel (tel. 809/491-5553), is the premier restaurant of Montserrat. Among the island dishes, you can enjoy a Créole callaloo soup or perhaps Montserrat conch fritters. In addition, you can try such delectable items as escargots à la bourguignonne, or a combination of seafood served in a rich vermouth cream sauce, or that ubiquitous Montserrat "mountain chicken" or frogs' legs. Desserts are mouthwatering, including a coconut cream cheesecake, velvety smooth mango mousse, and fresh coconut pie. Meals cost around EC$80 ($29.60). Lunch is served Tuesday to Saturday from noon to 2 p.m. and dinner daily except Monday from 6:30 to 9 p.m. Reservations for dinner are encouraged. During the summer, the place is open Thursday, Friday, Saturday, and Sunday.

The setting is tropical romantic, the restaurant is in a former private home, standing on a hillside overlooking the Belham River and its valley. It is convenient for guests at the Monserrat Golf Course, and of course those at Belham Valley Hotel.

Vue Pointe Restaurant, Vue Pointe Hotel (tel. 809/491-5211). Graciously elegant and surrounded with lawns and shrubbery of this previously recommended hotel, this is one of the best-directed restaurants on the island. Fixed-price dinners cost from EC$60 ($22.25), and are served nightly from 7 to 9:30. The Wednesday-night barbecue is an island event, the evening enlivened by a steel band. The kitchen turns out such fare as "mountain chicken," filet of kingfish, Créole-style red snapper, roast leg of pork with apple compote, West Indian curried chicken with condiments, and filet of sole caprice. Dessert might be a slice of lime cheesecake or a tropical fruit salad. Reservations are suggested if you're a nonresident.

The Gallery, in Wapping (tel. 809/491-2579), across from the Yacht Club, opened in 1985. Matt Hawthorne and Bruce Munroe of Toronto came over from Antigua on a day trip and fell in love with Montserrat. They stuck around to open this place, where some readers have found what they claim is "the best pizza in the Caribbean." The hosts also prepare an array of other dishes, including escargots, snapper stuffed with crab, and beef cooked in beer. There's always a special of the day as well. Lunch costs from EC$12 ($4.45), and dinner runs from EC$25 ($9.25). In season, the restaurant serves lunch daily from noon to 2 p.m. and dinner from 7 to 10 p.m. Happy hour is from 6 to 7 p.m. In off-season, they're closed on Tuesday and Wednesday. Sunday hours are from 6 p.m. "until." Guests can dine outside, enjoying the breeze. Live bands are occasionally brought in for dancing on weekends.

Sugar Daddy's, at Wapping (tel. 809/491-3354), is a black-and-white building set beside the sea. Its origins go back to 1652, and it was once used as a fortification. There is no printed menu, but different dishes are offered every night, including kingfish, lobster, and shrimp. You can count on such items as goat water, souse, salt fish (only on Friday), and the inevitable "mountain chicken." At lunch you can enjoy such simple fare as sandwiches and hamburgers along with one hot special, costing from EC$20 ($7.40). Go between 11:30 a.m. and 2:30 p.m. Dinner, served from 7:30 to 10:30 p.m., costs between EC$30 ($11.10) and EC$50 ($18.50). The restaurant is closed on Sunday and Monday.

Village Place, Salem (tel. 809/491-5202). If you weren't looking for it, you might think its encircling hedges and thatch fences concealed a private house. Local lore says that Elton John proposed marriage to his future wife at one of the outdoor tables. You can stand beneath the white cedar beams of the indoor bar admiring the musical memorabilia (owner Andy Lawrence is a former disc jockey), or you can claim a table in the courtyard and listen to tree frogs. A three-course fixed-price meal costs from EC$30 ($11.10) and might include chicken, an array of salads, pumpkin or callaloo soup. If you just want a snack, then order some of the most delectable barbecued chicken wings in the West Indies. In high season the place is open daily from noon to midnight. In the off-season it opens at 5 p.m., closing "whenever guests decide to leave."

Blue Dolphin Restaurant, Parsons (tel. 809/491-3263). A meal within its painted concrete walls offers the advantage of contact with a kind-hearted staff, whose spokesperson is Richard Skirrey. The Blue Dolphin sits on the side of a steep hillside near the medical school amid a lush landscape of plants. In theory, lunch is from noon to 2 p.m., and dinner's on from 5 to 9 p.m. seven days a week. But if you don't call in advance, it's possible the restaurant will not be open to receive you. Full meals, costing from EC$30 ($11.10), include pumpkin soup, lobster, kingfish, "mountain chicken," pork chops, and breaded boneless breast of chicken, followed by coconut cream pie with ice cream.

The Attic, Marine Drive (tel. 809/491-2008), is on the third floor of the Runaway Travel building in the heart of Plymouth. On what is actually a modified rooftop, you are welcome to sit beneath a palm-thatch sun screen, surrounded by plants and cooled by breezes from three sides. Open from 8 a.m. to 3 p.m. daily except Sunday, the place offers breakfast, lunch, and snacks. Rôtis, quesedillas, hamburgers (they claim, the best on the island), and a daily special which might be local beef, fish, or a surprise, depending on the day of the week. Sandwiches are available. Snacks and lunches cost from EC$7.50 ($2.80) to EC$20 ($7.40). The bar and restaurant are also open from 6 to 10 p.m. daily except Sunday in high season, Tuesday and Thursday in summer. Two persons can enjoy a full dinner with wine for less than EC$100 ($37).

The Iguana, Old Fort Rd., Wapping (tel. 809/491-3637). Set in a tropical garden near a cluster of other restaurants, this establishment serves some of the most creative cuisine in the neighborhood. Its core was originally built 200 years ago as a cotton mill, but today its dark stone-walled interior contains a nautical, somewhat spartan bar where you can have a before-dinner drink. Guests dine beneath a palm-thatched sun screen in the back garden. The establishment remains open Wednesday through Sunday from 11 a.m. to 10 p.m. Lunch, costing from EC$30 ($11.10), includes a local version of lobster salad, and pasta with clam sauce. Dinners are more elaborate, at EC$60 ($22.20), and require a reservation. Specialties include "mountain chicken," fresh tuna, kingfish Créole, red snapper, and sautéed chicken breast. Dessert is likely to be a freshly made batch of homemade ice cream.

Yacht Club Bar & Restaurant, Wapping (tel. 809/491-2237). Its stucco-sided premises could hardly be less pretentious, but some of the most famous rock 'n' roll personalities of Britain—including Sting and Boy George—have swilled their beer on its oceanside veranda. Eddie Edgecombe is the kind-hearted owner of this popular place near the sands, across from the Gallery Bar and Restaurant. In addition to drinks, lunches are served from 11 a.m. to 2 p.m. Monday to Friday. There's no lunch on Saturday and Sunday (only members are admitted then). Dinner is nightly except Sunday from 7 to 10 p.m. Lunch, costing from EC$14 ($5.20), includes lasagne, boiled fish, broiled kingfish, hamburgers, salads, and sandwiches. Dinner, from EC$25 ($9.25) features such items as lobster, roast beef with Yorkshire pudding, and several kinds of chicken. On Sunday from November to March, only club members and guests are admitted, and a barbecue lunch is usually served.

The Oasis, Wapping Rd., Plymouth (tel. 809/491-2328), is nestled on the ground floor of an 18th-century stone house, and separated from the sea by a road, a copse of sea grape coconut palms, and hibiscus. If you select a table inside, you'll be ringed with stone walls craftsmen assembled more than 200 years ago.

Dinner is served from 5 to 8 p.m. Monday to Saturday, and reservations should be made. The cuisine is simple but full of flavor. Depending on the night of the week, you might be served boneless breast of chicken in a light batter and accompanied by "Oasis sauce," or a filet mignon wrapped in bacon, perhaps red snapper sautéed with lime-flavored butter. Meals cost from EC$29 ($10.75). Paul Coughlan, the owner, keeps everything low-key and laid-back, frequently performing magic and making balloon animals at your table. He is also an internationally read personal-business newspaper columnist.

EXPLORING MONTSERRAT: The island is small, only 11 miles long and 7 miles across at its widest point. Its gently rolling hills and mountains reach their zenith at **Chances Peak,** rising to 3,000 feet. From its vantage point, a panoramic vista of the island unfolds. To climb the mountain, even serious hikers need a guide, which your hotel can arrange.

Galway's Soufrière, in the south-central region of the island, is a crater which bubbles and steams with sulfur smoke. A journey of exploration here is recommended for nature lovers. The government has a shortcut path, a mountain road lined with tree ferns, allowing you to drive up to within a 15-minute walk of the vents. Look also for the exotic incense tree. Yellow sulfur spills over the side in stark contrast to the green of the forest. Again, you should have your hotel arrange a mountain guide.

On the way there, you can stop to explore **Galway's Plantation,** an archeological project directed by the Montserrat National Trust. In the 1660s David Galway, an Irishman from Cork, settled the land with Irish indentured servants who were later replaced by African slaves. He established a sugar plantation which reached its peak a century later; however, the plantation declined after the slaves were freed. The ruins remain today, including the old sugar boiling house and the sugar mill.

Another natural wonder, the **Great Alps Waterfall,** is reached by first taking a 15-minute taxi ride south from Plymouth. After the driver lets you off, the waterfall lies a leisurely hour's walk through a lush interior. You come upon a horseshoe-shaped formation with crystal water plunging some 70 feet into a mountain pool. The noonday sun turns the mist into rainbow colors, reflecting the shadows of the rich surrounding foliage, a mystical effect of great beauty and worth the trek.

On the outskirts of Plymouth, **St. Anthony's Church**—the main Anglican church on the island—was built between 1632 and 1666, then rebuilt in 1730. Freed slaves, upon their emancipation, donated two beautiful silver chalices, on display. Next to the church is a gnarled tamarind tree two centuries old.

About a 15-minute drive from town, the ruined **Fort St. George** dates from the 18th century, and from it a magnificent panorama unfolds. The fort is 1,184 feet above sea level. Another ruin is **Fort Barrington,** also built in the 18th century.

At yet another fortification, **Bransby Point,** you can see restored cannons. The early earthworks date from 1640 to 1660. In 1693 a gun battery was built on this site, but it was destroyed by the French in 1712. In 1734 the British constructed a gun platform. By 1983 the restoration had been completed after 200 years of destruction.

The **Montserrat Museum,** in Plymouth, is housed in an old sugar mill at Richmond Hill. Here is displayed a collection of Montserratian artifacts, including pictures of island life at the turn of the century. Some of the artifacts relate to the island's pre-Columbian history. The featured exhibit is a small replica of a wind-driven sugar mill. Admission is free, but donations maintain the museum.

Hours are 2:30 to 5 p.m. on Wednesday and Sunday. Curator Edward Laroussini will answer your questions. He can be reached at his home phone (tel. 809/491-5443).

Government House is one of the most interesting buildings on the island. The older parts date back to the 1700s. In 1906, a few years after a disastrous hurricane, it was substantially rebuilt in the traditional gingerbread style. The attractive terraced grounds may be visited from 10:30 a.m. to noon Monday to Friday. The house is sometimes open to the public on Wednesday morning.

SHOPPING: There is no duty-free shopping, but some interesting locally made handcrafts are for sale. Straw goods and small ceramic souvenirs predominate, along with sea island cotton fabrics. Most shops are open daily except Sunday from 8 a.m. to noon and 1 to 4 p.m. They usually observe early closing on Wednesday, shutting down at 12:30 p.m.

The **Montserrat Sea Island Cotton Company** sales outlet, at the corner of George and Strand Sts. (tel. 809/491-2556), offers exclusive locally handwoven West Indian Sea Island cotton products and such souvenir items as leather goods and ceramics. The outlet is open from 8 a.m., closing at 4 p.m. on Monday, Tuesday, Thursday, and Friday, and at noon on Wednesday and Saturday.

Outside of town, the government-owned and -operated **Montserrat Leather Craft** (tel. 809/491-2378) is in an actual leathercraft shop at the Groves. There, artistic handcrafted leather goods are offered for sale. All items—belts, wallets, handbags, sandals, purses—are made from locally tanned genuine leather. See in particular the batik belts. The factory is closed on Saturday and Sunday.

The **Spinning Plant** (tel. 809/491-2825) and **Hand-Weaving Studio** (tel. 809/491-2915), both owned and operated by the government, are at sites on the Industrial Estate. Sea island cotton yarn and roving (a step in turning fiber into soft yarn), manufactured by the plant, are hand-woven into a variety of end products. Clara Davidson, who came from Nova Scotia, founded the Hand-Weaving Studio, teaching the young women of Montserrat the craft. The products are unique, and the spun cotton is locally grown. Various designs of placemats, tablecloths, skirt-length material, clutch bags, stoles, scarves, baby blankets, and belts are offered for sale.

Tapestries of Montserrat (The John Bull Shop), Parliament St., P.O. Box 500, Plymouth (tel. 809/491-2520), over the bridge in Wapping just outside Plymouth, sells handcrafted rugs, wall hangings, tote bags with Caribbean designs, and kaleidoscopes made of brass. Products are handmade by skilled artisans, whom you can watch at work in the shop, operated by Mr. and Mrs. Gerald Handley.

Carol's Corner, Vue Pointe Hotel (tel. 809/491-5211), lies in a high-ceilinged public room of this previously recommended hotel. This shop offers one of the most concentrated collections of Montserrat-related memorabilia on the island. They sell the famous stamps of Montserrat and copies of the difficult-to-obtain flag. There's a version of a Montserrat cookbook, *Goatwater,* which describes "how to skin and clean a fat female iguana." There's also a collection of roadmaps, summery dresses of sea island cotton, and a selection of local jams and honey. If you forgot your toothbrush, there are cosmetics and sundries as well.

Dutcher's Studio, P.O. Box 130, Plymouth (tel. 809/491-5253) is a glass and ceramic studio in Olveston just outside Plymouth. Items are made of hand-cut and hand-painted glass, with many signed and collectors' pieces. Featured are wind chimes made of bottles, hand-painted dishes, mobiles, dolls, and ceramic works of art, all made on Montserrat. Studio hours are 8:30 a.m. to 2:30 p.m. Monday to Friday. If you wish to go there on Saturday, Sunday, or holidays, you must call for an appointment. The studio is near the Vue Pointe Hotel and Salem.

THE SPORTING LIFE: There are many isolated areas for **swimming** and sunning; and perhaps you'll like black sand. Most hotels have pools and lounging areas, however.

People interested in **fishing** should ask at their hotel about the availability of small boats for rent.

Tennis buffs will find two lit asphalt courts at the previously recommended Vue Pointe Hotel. There are also two courts at Montserrat Springs, which are lit for night games. Residents play free, but nonresidents are charged EC$10 ($3.70) for daytime play, EC$16 ($5.90) for night games.

The **Montserrat Golf Club,** while only nine holes, is considered one of the finest in the eastern Caribbean. Even though it has only 11 greens, a full round of 18 holes can be played, by doubling up. Greens fees are $12.50 per person per day. The second hole, the best known, is about 600 yards across two branches of the Belham River. It covers an area of some 100 acres.

Shamrock Watersports, Vue Pointe Hotel (tel. 809/491-5211). After Danny Sweeney taught the British rock star Sting to windsurf, Sting used Danny's name in the lyrics of one of his hit songs. Today Danny still teaches windsurfing techniques from a kiosk on the black sand crescent of the Vue Pointe Hotel's beach. Windsurfers rent for $10 per hour, an introductory lesson costing $8. You can rent Sunfish at $10 per hour, or a day's snorkeling equipment for $5.

You can relax and enjoy a day's sail aboard the 46-foot trimaran **John Willie,** leaving Vue Pointe Beach at 10 a.m. and returning at about 4:30 p.m. Captain Martin Haxby takes you along the northwest coast of Montserrat to the white sands of Rendezvous, where you can snorkel on Montserrat's only reef, swim, and dive. The return trip, to the accompaniment of Capt. Martin singing sea chanteys and telling folk tales, is past the island's natural pyramid in Little Bay, Soldiers' Ghaut where the French landed in the 1700s, Bunkem Bay, woodlands, lime kilns, and a vista of lovely villas on the rolling hillsides. You can fish from the boat if you wish. A bar is open all day, included in the price of $40 per person (children under ten go free). Reservations can be made at the Vue Pointe Hotel Montserrat Springs Hotel, or by calling 809/491-5738. Capt. Haxby can be reached through P.O. Box 375, Plymouth.

The 15-foot speedboat **Buff** will take passengers from Vue Pointe to Rendezvous for $20 per person, waterskiing at Little Bay or Rendezvous for $25 per person, or fishing for $40 per hour. For information or reservations, call Hubert Buffonge (tel. 809/491-2613).

AFTER DARK: Montserrat may be sleepy during the day, but it gets even quieter at night. The most activity is at the **Vue Pointe Hotel,** Old Towne (tel. 809/ 491-5210), where a steel band plays every Wednesday night, and there is nightly entertainment by local musicians in season. At the Wednesday-night bash, a barbecue dinner is cooked, costing EC$60 ($22.20) per person.

If you've never seen a West Indian disco, attracting just the local crowd, then you can drop in at **La Cave,** Evergreen Drive (no phone). In Plymouth, it is a modest little place, playing records for dancers. The disco charges an entrance fee of EC$5 ($1.85).

The Plantation, Wapping Rd., Plymouth (no phone). Much less formal and a bit more raucous than its neighbor, the previously recommended Oasis downstairs, this establishment occupies the upper story of a 200-year-old stone-walled house. It's one of the most popular bars for visiting musicians and local medical students. Only a bar, with no food service, it's open daily from 7:30 p.m. until very late. Video movies are sometimes shown as an accompaniment to the beer and rum drinks.

3. ST. KITTS

The volcanic central island of the British Leewards is not really a resort mecca in the way Antigua is. Its major crop is sugar, and has been since the mid-17th century.

At some point in your visit you'll want to eat sugar directly from the cane. Any St. Kitts farmer will sell you a huge stalk, and there are sugarcane plantations all over the island. Just ask your taxi driver to take you to one. You strip off the hard exterior of the stalk and bite into it, chewing on the tasty reeds and swallowing the juice. It's best with a side glass of rum.

The Caribs, the early settlers, called St. Kitts *Liamuiga,* or "fertile isle." Its mountain ranges reach up to nearly 4,000 feet, and in its interior are virgin rain forests, alive with the sound of hummingbirds and the chatter of wild green vervet monkeys. The monkeys were brought in as pets by the early French settlers and turned loose in the forests when the island became British in 1783. The native African animals have proliferated and can perhaps best be seen at the Estridge Estate Behavioral Research Institute. Another import, this one British, is the mongoose, brought in from India as an enemy of rats in the sugarcane fields. The people of the island say the only trouble with that plan is that the mongooses and rats operate on different time cycles, the rats committing their depredations while the mongooses sleep. Wild deer are found in the St. Kitts mountains.

Sugarcane climbs right up the slopes, and there are palm-lined beaches around the island as well. As you travel around St. Kitts, you'll notice ruins of old mills and plantation houses. You'll also see an island rich in trees and vegetation —frangipani, bougainvillea, hibiscus, and flamboyant trees (the treasured poinciana was first cultivated in the Caribbean by Count de Poincy).

St. Kitts is 33 miles long and 6½ miles wide, riding the crest of that arc of islands known as the northerly Leeward group of the Lesser Antilles. It is separated from its sister state of Nevis by a two-mile-wide strait. Its administrative capital is Basseterre.

In 1967 St. Kitts was given internal self-government and, along with Nevis, became a state in association with Britain. (Anguilla, included in this associated state at the time, broke away.)

On his second voyage in 1493, Columbus spotted St. Kitts, naming it Saint Christopher, but the English later changed that to St. Kitts. In 1623 the Europeans colonized St. Kitts when Sir Thomas Warner landed with his wife and son and a party of 14 farmers. This settlement made St. Kitts the first British colony in the West Indies. When the island later sent out parties of settlers to neighboring islands, St. Kitts became known as "the mother colony of the West Indies."

Shortly after their arrival, the English were joined by the French. In 1627 they divided the island between them and, united, they withstood attacks from the Caribs and the Spanish. But in time the British and French fought among themselves, and the island changed hands several times until it was finally given to the British by the Treaty of Versailles.

The capital, **Basseterre,** an 18th-century-print port with its waterfront intact, lies on the Caribbean shore near the southern end of the island, about a mile from Golden Rock Airport, where you will land. With its white-painted colonial houses with toothpick balconies and wide, palm-lined streets, it looks like a Hollywood version of a West Indian port.

The bustling harbor is filled with schooners from Antigua, St. Martin, and Nevis which carry the rich produce to St. Kitts to neighboring islands. You'll also spot freighters from the U.S. and Canada. The men of St. Kitts are known as good sailors, and it's interesting to see them in action, skillfully handling their boats.

This British colonial town is built around a so-called Circus, the town's round square. A tall green Victorian clock tower stands in the center of the Circus. In the old days, wealthy plantation owners and their families used to promenade here.

At some point, try to visit the marketplace. There, country women bring baskets brimming with mangoes, guavas, soursop, mammy apples, and wild strawberries and cherries just picked in the fields. You can see the vegetables you may eat later in the day—yams, breadfruit, hearts of palm, pumpkins, christophines. Tropical flowers abound.

Another major square is called Pall Mall, once a thriving slave market. It is surrounded by private homes of Georgian architecture.

GETTING THERE: St. Kitts is 2,000 miles southeast of New York or four hours by direct jet flight. Miami is 1,300 miles away, about three hours direct flight time. **BWIA** flies twice weekly from New York to St. Kitts, on Thursday and Sunday, returning the same day. If you want to go there any other day, BWIA connects with **LIAT** in Antigua. LIAT makes a 90- to 180-minute wait in Antigua. From Miami, BWIA flies to Antigua, where it also connects with LIAT for the flight on to St. Kitts.

You can fly from Boston, Chicago, Miami, New Orleans, New York, Philadelphia, Baltimore, or Washington to San Juan, St. Thomas, St. Croix, St. Maarten, or Antigua on **American Airlines, Eastern Airlines, Pan Am, Capitol Air,** or **Delta.** You then connect with LIAT to fly to St. Kitts or Nevis. Most passengers, however, fly from any of dozens of points in North America, taking, for example, **American Airlines** to its hub in San Juan. There they can make connections with one of **American Eagle's** three daily flights from Puerto Rico to St. Kitts. Only one of these is nonstop, although the others allow visitors to island-hop throughout the Caribbean chain, stopping for brief touchdowns on (and aerial views of) other islands.

If you're already on the Dutch island of St. Maarten and want to visit St. Kitts (with perhaps a side trip to Nevis), you can do so aboard one of the most remarkable little airlines in the Caribbean. **Windward Islands Airways International** (known by its nickname, Winair) formed in 1961, makes several flights from St. Maarten to St. Kitts and Nevis a week. This little airline carries passengers and freight, and does so well, to nearly a dozen destinations in the Antilles. Chances are you'll fly to either St. Kitts or Nevis aboard a Twin Otter. For the best methods of flying to St. Maarten (if that is the first leg of your journey), refer to Chapter X.

In addition, consult your travel agent for direct charter flights to St. Kitts from New York and other major U.S. cities.

From Montréal or Toronto you can go to St. Kitts via San Juan or Antigua on **Air Canada** and BWIA.

GETTING AROUND: A good road encircles the island. I'll preview the major means of transport.

Car Rentals

Delisle Walwyn & Co. Ltd., Liverpool Row (tel. 809/465-2631), operates Economy Car Rental, with cars and scooter bikes available. Suzuki sedans cost $28 per day, $170 weekly; Mazda standard vehicles run $32 daily, $196 weekly; and Mazda automatics go for $35 per day, $210 per week. A scooter bike rents for $14 daily, $84 weekly. The minimum age for car rental is 25. A valid St. Kitts and Nevis driver's license is necessary, but this can easily be obtained at the police station. Rental rates include public liability, property damage, and fire and theft insurance. If the car is involved in a collision, the renter's responsibility for damage will be up to $400. This responsibility will be waived if you elect to pay $5 per day. There is no extra charge for leaving your vehicle at the airport or at your hotel if you notify the company in advance.

Holiday Car Rentals, South Independence Square, Basseterre (tel. 809/ 465-6507), has late model Nissan cars to rent with both manual and automatic transmission. Prices range from $28 daily, $168 weekly, for a Nissan March with manual shift to the Nissan Stanza, $40 per day, $240 per week, with automatic transmission, air conditioning, and power steering. Unlimited mileage is included. Other requirements for rental of a car are the same as those given for Economy Car Rental above.

Reflecting British tradition, *driving is on the left!* However, you'll need a local driver's license, which can be obtained at the Traffic Department in Basseterre for EC$30 ($11.10).

Taxis

Since most taxi drivers are also guides, this is the best means of getting around. You don't even have to find a driver at the airport (one will find you). Drivers also wait outside the major hotels, so getting around is fairly easy. Before heading out on an expedition, however, you must agree on the price—taxis aren't metered. Also, ask if the rates quoted to you are in U.S. dollars or the EC dollar. Taxi rates may have risen considerably by the time you read this, so check the fares. At the time of writing, you could go from the airport to, say, Frigate Bay for EC$18 ($6.65), or all the way to Sandy Point for EC$29 ($10.75).

Sightseeing Tours

You can negotiate with a taxi driver to take you on a tour of the island for about $25 for a three-hour trip. Most drivers are well versed in the lore of the island, and all of them of course speak English. Lunch can be arranged either at the Rawlins Plantation Inn or the Golden Lemon.

Inter-Island Ferries

Most visitors to St. Kitts or Nevis like to spend at least one day on the sister island, and the government passenger ferry M.V. *Caribe Queen* provides such an opportunity. The schedule permits departures from either island between the hours of 7:30 and 8:30 a.m. daily except Thursday and Sunday, returning at 4 and 6 p.m. (check the time at your hotel or the tourist office). The cost is EC$10 ($3.70) one way. Passengers are allowed one hand package free, with a minimal fee for additional pieces.

Local Air Service

LIAT (Leeward Islands Air Transport) provides daily morning and afternoon flights to and from Nevis at a cost of $15 per person. Make reservations at the LIAT office on Fort Street in Basseterre (tel. 809/465-2286) instead of at the airport.

PRACTICAL FACTS: Entry requirements, money, and language were previewed in the introductory section to this chapter.

Banks: If you want to exchange your dollars into Eastern Caribbean currency, you'll find banks open Monday to Friday from 8 a.m. till noon (also on Friday from 3 to 5 p.m.).

Customs: You are allowed in duty free with personal belongings.

Drugstores: For getting prescriptions filled and finding the regular drugstore merchandise you need, **The Medic's Pharmacy,** corner of Cayon and Fort Sts., Basseterre (tel. 809/465-2228; 809/465-2810 after closing), is open from 8 a.m. to 6 p.m. Monday, Tuesday, Wednesday, and Friday, to 1 p.m. Thursday, and to 8 p.m. Saturday.

Electricity: St. Kitts electricity is 230 volts AC, 60 cycles, so you will need an adapter for U.S.-made appliances.

Emergencies: In case of an emergency, telephone 99 from Basseterre main exchanges and 999 from all other exchanges.

Information: Tourist information can be obtained from the **Tourist Board,** P.O. Box 132, Basseterre (tel. 809/465-2620), and from the **St. Kitts-Nevis Tourist Board** Stateside office, 414 E. 75th St., New York, NY 10021 (tel. 212/535-1234).

Taxes: The government imposes a 7% tax on rooms and meals, plus another EC$13.50 ($5) airport departure tax (but not to go to Nevis).

Telecommunications: Telegrams and Telexes can be sent from Cable & Wireless, Cayon St., Basseterre (tel. 465-2219), from 8 a.m. to 6 p.m. weekdays, 8 a.m. to 2 p.m. on Saturday, and 6 to 8 p.m. on Sunday and public holidays. International telephone calls, including collect calls, can also be made from the cable office. To call direct from the mainland, dial the 809 area code, then the local number. Don't use the area code once you're in St. Kitts.

Time: St. Kitts is on Atlantic Standard Time, and its clocks never change all year. That means that in winter when it's 6 a.m. in Basseterre, it's 5 a.m. in Miami or New York. When the U.S. goes on Daylight Saving Time, Basseterre and the East Coast mainland keep the same time.

Tips: Most hotels add a service charge of 10% to cover tipping. If not, tip from 10% to 15%.

Water: The water supply of the island is good and generally safe.

Weather: St. Kitts lies in the tropics, its warm climate tempered by the trade winds. The average air temperature is 79° Fahrenheit and the average water temperature is 80°. Average rainfall is 55 inches. Dry, mild weather is usually experienced from November to April; May through October are hotter and rainier.

HOTELS: This is no resort-studded island like Antigua. Rather, the island has hotels of character, small and special, ranging from plantation-style living to retreats so remote they're accessible only by a bumpy boat ride.

If you're planning a budget for your trip, don't forget the government tax on hotel rooms, plus the service charge that will probably be added to your bill.

Ocean Terrace Inn, P.O. Box 65, Fortlands, St. Kitts, W.I. (tel. 809/465-2380), is affectionately known as the O.T.I. If you want to be near Basseterre, it's the best hotel around the port (it also has an excellent cuisine and is the chief center for water sports, all detailed in the section to follow). The O.T.I. commands a view of the harbor and the capital, with oceanfront verandas. With its many terraces and different levels, it's so compact that a stay here is like a house party on a great liner. Terraced into a well-landscaped hillside above the edge of Basseterre, the hotel has particularly beautiful gardens and grounds, as well as two pools and a Jacuzzi.

All the handsomely decorated, air-conditioned bedrooms overlook the "great open-air living room"—that is, a well-planted terrace with a flagstone-edged swimming pool (which has a row of underwater stools where you'll be served well-made drinks while still immersed). My favorite bar is in the shadow of an elaborate aviary. The furnishings are color coordinated, with a light, tropical feeling. In winter, singles on the MAP range from $92 to $147 daily, while doubles cost $134 to $224. *Off-season MAP rates range from $88 to $184 in a single, from $135 to $182 in a double.* Some more expensive suites are available, and guests can stay here on the EP if they wish, for somewhat lower prices. A third person in a room on the MAP costs $65 year round. In addition to its stylish rooms in the hillside buildings, the hotel offers the Fisherman's Wharf and Village, a few steps from the nearby harbor. These wooden units are filled with most of the comforts of home. In winter, two persons can rent a one-bedroom apartment for $180 daily, and a two-bedroom apartment for four persons for $260, EP. *In summer, a one-bedroom apartment rents for $132 daily for two persons, a two-bedroom unit for four guests costing $176 daily, EP rates.* Colin Pereira, who is a Kittitian is your host at Ocean Terrace, and he runs a tight ship.

Fairview Inn, P.O. Box 212, St. Kitts, W.I. (tel. 809/465-2472), was originally the 18th-century great house of a wealthy French plantation owner. Set on the rise of a hill, and surrounded by tropical flowers and flamboyant trees, it is only five miles from the jetport and three miles west of the city, about a ten-minute run by taxi. It has its own swimming pool and sundeck, and there is a secluded beach just a 12-minute walk from the inn. Prince Charles once danced the carnival queen around the pool. The manor house has plenty of character, with its lacy front verandas, louvered windows, and long, covered loggia. Some of the bedrooms are in the main building, and others are in cottages in the rear garden where the plantation outbuildings of yesteryear used to stand. Each of the 30 twin-bedded rooms has a private bath as well as its own patio. You can ask for air conditioning (available in some of the rooms), but trade winds usually suffice. I prefer the bedrooms that have been converted from stone stables. Natural-stone walls have been incorporated into the scheme. The rooms are clean and comfortable. In winter, for about four nights a week a calypso band will come in to entertain. In season, singles rent for $78 to $88 daily on the EP and doubles for $88 to $98. *Off-season, a single pays only $50 to $60; two persons, $60 to $70.* Breakfast and dinner carry an additional daily supplement of $28 per person. In my opinion, the Fairview Inn is one of the best tourist buys in the Caribbean.

What makes Fairview Inn such a success, drawing repeat visitors, is its ownership. A Trinidadian, Freddy Lam, and his wife, Betty (she's from St. Kitts), extend old-fashioned hospitality. Betty's island background is reflected in her cuisine. For example, she grows her own papaya, making green papaya pie to delight her diners. The Lams also grow their own vegetables and pineapples, and often use breadfruit as well as making a superb callaloo soup.

Jack Tar Village Royal St. Kitts Resort & Casino, P.O. Box 406, St. Kitts, W.I. (tel. 809/465-8651, 210/670-9800 in the U.S., or toll free 800/527-9299), is the largest-scale hotel on St. Kitts and is certainly the showcase hotel of the much-touted Frigate Bay development. Set on a flat sandy isthmus between the sea and a saltwater lagoon, this is a lot like a private country club. The resort is almost completely self-contained, with a built-in incentive never to leave its perimeter. It has the island's only casino and a helpful scattering of signposts indicating the direction to the dozens of sports-related activities. Thoughtful touches include the designation of one swimming pool area for quiet reading, another for such active sports as volleyball. Four tennis courts are illuminated for nighttime play, and a golf course is nearby.

The resort has no fewer than four restaurants, a number of bars, and a rate structure that includes everything (meals, drinks, and golf) in one all-inclusive price. *Single rooms cost $160 daily in summer, doubles go for $120 per person, and triples rent for $110 per person.* In winter, the charge is $180 for singles, $140 per person for doubles, and $130 per person for triple occupancy. The rent for a child two to 12 years old is $50 year round. Accommodations are separated into two groupings, one at either end of the resort. Each of the almost 300 units has individually controlled air conditioning, a patio or balcony, and tropical furniture. Most visitors prefer the second-floor rooms because of their higher ceilings. When you check in, I.D. tags are usually issued in an effort to help you get acquainted with your fellow guests quickly. Throughout the day an enthusiastic staff will keep anyone who's interested hopping from one organized activity to another. These include everything from Scrabble and shuffleboard tournaments to scuba lessons to toga ("it's time to get crazy") contests.

Golden Lemon, Dieppe Bay, St. Kitts, W.I. (tel. 809/465-7260), was created by Arthur Leaman, one-time decorating editor of *House & Garden* magazine. With his taste and background, he has formed a tiny oasis that is a citadel of charm in the British Leewards, in a place that was once a busy French shipping port named for a more famous bay in its home country. Mr. Leaman found this then-ramshackle 17th-century house, set back from a coconut grove and a black volcanic sand beach on the northwest coast of St. Kitts. The original French manor house has a Georgian upper story added in the 18th century. The two-story building, with its covered galleries looks like pictures from *House & Garden*. Flanking the great house, Mr. Leaman has added 16 villas of one and two bedrooms, each with its own pool and furnished in the style of the main house. The spacious rooms are furnished with antiques, and always contain fresh flowers, and you are waited on by a well-trained staff. Overhead, slow-turning ceiling fans keep the air moving. "Sophisticated" and "elegant" are the words most often used to describe the Golden Lemon and its clientele.

A minimum stay of four nights is required in season, and Mr. Leaman limits guests to a maximum stay of two weeks, perhaps fearing that they may get restless even in Paradise. In winter, the MAP rates are $185 to $225 daily in a single, $275 to $310 in a superior or deluxe double or twin, and $385 in one-bedroom suites. *Off-season, on the MAP, singles rent for $145 to $185 daily, superior doubles and twins for $225 to $245, deluxe doubles and one-bedroom suites for $295 to $310.* There's a tennis court for the use of guests.

Fort Thomas Hotel, P.O. Box 407, Basseterre, St. Kitts, W.I. (tel. 809/465-2695), has a sweeping view of the sea from its position above the town, offering beautiful panoramas. The spacious air-conditioned rooms all have two double beds and private balconies. In winter, singles are $80 daily, and doubles pay $95. *Summer rates are $55 daily in singles, $65 in doubles.* The hotel's restaurant, carvery, and barbecue are known for their relaxed atmosphere, excellent cuisine, and seasonal evening entertainment. Tennis and free transportation to the beach can be arranged at the front desk. From the Olympic-size freshwater pool and the terrace bar, you have a clear view of the neighboring island of Nevis.

Rawlins Plantation, P.O. Box 340, Mount Pleasant, St. Kitts, W.I. (tel. 809/465-6221), is a small, family-owned hotel, set on a former plantation among the remains of a muscovado sugar factory. Near Dieppe Bay on the northeast coast, the former plantation is 350 feet above sea level, enjoying cooling breezes from both ocean and mountains. Behind the grounds the land rises to a rain forest and Mount Misery. Rawlins is unique on St. Kitts, evoking certain plantation hotels on neighboring Nevis. A 17th-century windmill has become converted into a charming suite, complete with private bath and sitting room; and the boiling houses, formerly a caldron of molasses, have been turned into a cool courtyard where guests dine, enjoying the flowers and tropical birds. Accommodations are rented in the main house, as well as pleasantly decorated cottages which have been equipped with modern facilities. The plantation is run by Mr. and Mrs. Philip Walwyn, who graciously let you swim in their pool (fed from their own mountain spring), or eat at their table, offering peace and tranquility for the discriminating few who find their way to their door. Vegetables usually come from their own gardens. *On the MAP, singles are welcomed off-season for*

$170 daily and doubles for $270. In winter, prices rise to $220 in a single, $330 in a double, all on the MAP. In season, a minimum stay of four days is required.

Frigate Bay Beach Hotel, P.O. Box 137, Frigate Bay, St. Kitts, W.I. (tel. 809/465-8935), is set on a verdant hillside above a point where English settlers used to watch the passing frigates. Accommodations are in white condominiums administered as hotel units for their absentee owners. The villas housing these "second homes" have alternating red and yellow tile roofs. The central core of the resort contains a pair of round swimming pools and a cabaña bar where you can enjoy a drink while partially immersed if you choose. Green hills rise up behind the hotel, while on either side are beaches lined with rugged cliffs. An 18-hole golf course and tennis courts are within walking distance. Units are nicely furnished to the taste of the owner and painted in an array of pastel colors. They have cool tile floors, ceiling fans, sliding glass doors leading onto verandas, private baths, and air conditioning. Winter rates are $95 to $120 daily for a double, $190 for a one-bedroom suite suitable for two persons, and $310 for a two-bedroom suite for up to four persons. *In summer, doubles go for $60 per day, a one-bedroom suite for $90, and a two-bedroom suite for $150.*

OTI Banana Bay Beach Resort, P.O. Box 65, St. Kitts, W.I. (tel. 809/465-2754), is a secluded gem accessible only by boat. Guests are met at the airport and taken to OTI Pelican Cove Marina where the M.V. *Banana Peel* waits to take them on the scenic cruise to Banana Bay. The creativity put into the physical side of this 20-room hideaway is evident immediately: the use of colors and attention to details captures the perfect setting for a Caribbean vacation. The spiritual side is no less a factor, for the accent is on tranquility, allowing one to walk quietly along sandy beaches and absorb the beauty of surrounding landscape. Activity focuses on the beach. Snorkeling, windsurfing, or Sailfish sailing is complimentary. If you wish, you can take the hotel's regular boat service to the Ocean Terrace Inn's Pelican Cove Marina, where an island tour of St. Kitts or shopping in downtown Basseterre can be arranged. Reading and good conversation have priorities, or just laze away the day in a hammock slung between palm trees, sipping an exotic elixir of tropical flavors from the Booby Bird Beach Bar. The food is excellent, served without fanfare, providing a good balance of fresh local seafood and continental dishes. MAP rates, including the cost of transportation on arrival and departure, are $175 in a single and $240 in a double from mid-December to mid-April. *Summer MAP rates, from mid-April to mid-December, are $140 in a single, $180 in a double.*

Leeward Cove Condominium Hotel, P.O. Box 123, Frigate Bay, St. Kitts, W.I. (tel. 809/465-8030), has apartments for rent, in addition to its condos that are lived in by their owners. Overlooking a championship golf course in the scenic Frigate Bay area of St. Kitts, the units are self-catering, with apartments of one and two air-conditioned bedrooms, adjoining baths, dining areas, completely equipped kitchens and living rooms with convertible sofas, making them suitable for four to six people. Winter rates are $155 daily for one-bedroom apartments occupied by one or two guests, $250 for two-bedroom units for up to four people. *Summer prices are $110 and $155.* An extra person over the maximum covered by the tariffs is charged $22 per night. Also offered are standard bedrooms rented for $75 daily for doubles in winter, *$55 in summer.* Added conveniences are daily maid service, a mini-mart next door, water sports, and nearby restaurants and casino. A special feature is a complimentary car for each week's stay in one of the apartments.

WHERE TO DINE:
Most guests eat at their hotels; however, St. Kitts has a scattering of good restaurants where you are likely to have spiny lobster, crab back, pepperpot, breadfruit, and curried conch.

I'd recommend that you dine with a local family at least once. That way, you'll get to meet Kittitians in their homes as well as enjoy a good local cuisine. Your hotel will often make such arrangements.

Georgian House, South Square St., Basseterre (tel. 809/465-4049), fronts Independence Square. As the name suggests, this is a restored Georgian manor, decorated with Queen Anne reproductions, and said to be the oldest habitable building in St. Kitts. Long, long before its present reincarnation as the leading restaurant on the island, it was the exclusive Planters' Club. New Yorker Georgiana Bowers, the owner and chef, offers a well-prepared and sophisticated menu that changes nightly. You may be there on the night peanut soup is served, but you also might settle happily for chilled cucumber soup. Main courses are likely to include roast leg of lamb, chicken breasts in garlic, and lobster thermidor. Desserts are luscious here. Maybe it'll be Tía Maria mousse. The menu is à la carte. With a drink or two, count on spending from $30 per person. Hours are 6:30 to 9 p.m., except Sunday. Dinner is served in the beautifully restored dining room. The restaurant shuts down in summer when business in St. Kitts is at a minimum.

In Basseterre, some of the finest cuisine is found at the **Ocean Terrace Inn,** Basseterre (tel. 809/465-2754). It also offers the best view, especially at night when you can sit and watch the lights in the harbor. Regional food is featured every night, and standard dishes from the international repertoire are invariably included as well. My most recent dinner, costing from $25, began with curried chicken broth, followed by sliced hardboiled eggs in a mushroom sauce served on the half shell. Then came an order of tasty fish cakes, accompanied by breaded carrot slices, creamed spinach, a stuffed potato, johnnycake, a cornmeal dumpling, and a green banana in a lime butter sauce, topped off by a tropical fruit pie and coffee! Dining is on an open-air veranda. On Sunday there's a chicken luncheon barbecue around the pool, costing from $8. Lunch is served daily from 11 a.m. to 2 p.m. and dinner from 6 p.m. "until."

Fisherman's Wharf Seafood Restaurant and Bar, Fortlands, Basseterre (tel. 809/465-2380) is between the sea and the white picket fence surrounding its neighbor, the Ocean Terrace Inn. Its heart and soul lies near the busy buffet grill, where a quartet of hard-working chefs prepare fresh seafood in an organized and rapid-fire clockwork manner. The grill and picnic tables around the grill are supported by the stout planks of a seaside wharf. An employee hovers to take your drink order, but food orders should be requested personally at the buffet grill. Specialties (usually cooked at the grill while you stand and watch) are grilled lobster, shrimp in garlic sauce, shark steak with local herbs and spices, and grilled catch of the day. Full meals go for $20 per person and up. Lunch is served Monday to Friday, from noon to 2 p.m. You can dine seven days a week from 7 until at least 10:30 p.m. On Wednesday and Friday there's a Calypso seafood all-you-can-eat buffet costing a reasonable $18 per person, with live entertainment.

Jong's, Conaree Beach (tel. 809/465-2062), is an Oriental restaurant combined with Cisco's Hideaway Bar. It serves the best Oriental food in St. Kitts, the dishes well prepared, the service friendly and efficient. Main courses include chicken, beef, lobster, conch in garlic butter sauce, and ginger chicken. A complete meal costs about $20. The bar opens at 11 a.m., remaining so until midnight. Lunch is daily from noon to 2:30 p.m., and dinner from 6:30 to 10 p.m. It's important that you call and make a reservation. Closed Monday.

Victor's, Stainforth St., Basseterre (tel. 809/465-2518), is a totally Kittitian neighborhood restaurant set in concrete-sided quarters behind Basseterre's Church of the Immaculate Conception. It serves lunch from noon to 3 p.m. and dinner from 7 to 10 p.m. daily except Sunday. December to April, Sunday service is done by reservation. Full meals cost from EC$45 ($16.65) and might include deep-fried or steamed fish, boneless beef, mutton, spare ribs, and a local specialty known as goat water. The restaurant provided fast service.

For West Indian food, you might try **Avondale House,** George St. (tel. 809/465-2487), a 200-year-old wood-frame house with an accommodating and well-used veranda. Its interior could hardly be simpler, having as a focal point a sturdy bar and clusters of rickety tables. Meals are served every day except Sunday from 10 a.m. to 10 p.m. (on Sunday, usually from 2 to 10 p.m.). Only about half a dozen dishes are offered, written in block letters above the bar. Items include cheeseburgers, chicken and chips, chicken and rice, fish and rice, and fish and corn. A simple meal costs around EC$25 ($9.25).

If you're touring St. Kitts, the best luncheon stop is at the **Golden Lemon,** Dieppe Bay (tel. 809/465-7260), the 17th-century house converted into a hotel by Arthur Leaman, former decorating editor of *House & Garden* magazine (see the description above). Always call in advance for a reservation. Lunch is in a lush tropical setting of ferns, bougainvillea, and ginger under a breadfruit tree. The food is very good, and the service is polite. A complete luncheon costs around $15. Dinner costs from $20 to $30, table d'hôte, and is served in an elegant, candlelit dining room. The cuisine features Créole, continental, and American dishes, with locally grown produce, and the menu changes daily. Dress is casual chic. Lunch is served from noon to 3 p.m. and dinner from 7 to 10 p.m.

Ballahoo Restaurant, The Circus (tel. 809/465-4197), is about a block from the sea on the second story of a wood-frame Victorian building with lots of gingerbread. Its wide veranda is one of the coolest places in town on a hot afternoon, thanks to the sea breezes and the high ceiling. Meals cost from $15. They serve such specialties as chicken kebab, "blue parrot" fish filets, chicken pie, and curried conch. It's open every day except Sunday from 10 a.m. to 11 p.m. As you dine, you can admire the dome of the nearby Treasury Building.

The Patio, Frigate Bay (tel. 809/465-8666), is at the private home of a likeable Kittitian family, the Peter Mallalieus. Only dinner is served, daily from 7:15 to 11 p.m. Because each dish is prepared to order, it is imperative that you phone ahead to announce your arrival. Cocktails are served in the lush flower garden just a few feet from the rear terrace of the house. The family's high-ceilinged modern living room is transformed with tablecloths and kerosene lanterns into a dining room. Meals cost around $35 per person, and they include home-grown vegetables and a fresh seafood menu that changes nightly. If you have any special menu requests, Mr. Mallalieu will probably follow them.

The Anchorage, Frigate Bay (tel. 809/465-8235), is an isolated beachfront restaurant on the rolling acres of Frigate Bay, in the shadow of an enormous leafy tree. The restaurant's many-peaked roof shelters its concrete-slab floor from sudden showers. Pansy and Ewart Martin (who come from Nevis and Bermuda respectively) prepare rum-based drinks and seafood every day of the week from 8 a.m. to midnight. The menu offers four different salads, broiled or thermidor lobster, steak, hamburgers, 13 kinds of sandwiches, fresh fish, and ice cream. Full meals cost EC$50 ($18.50) to EC$75 ($27.75). If you're looking for an unspoiled beach with a casual restaurant nearby, this may be a good selection for you.

EXPLORING ST. KITTS: The chief sight is **Brimstone Hill,** which was once known as the "Gibraltar of the West Indies." In size, this 18th-century fortress rivaled the pyramids of Egypt. A car can be driven up the winding road, almost to the top. When your driver lets you out, you have to climb stairs to the main fortifications. A bronze plaque, unveiled by Queen Elizabeth II on a visit here, proclaims the citadel a national park. There's a $2 admission fee. Brimstone Hill is open daily from 9:30 a.m. to 5:30 p.m. (on Thursday and Sunday from 2 to 5:30 p.m.). The history of St. Kitts from the Stone Age is traced in a small museum.

In 1782 the fort was besieged and captured by the French, but Britain regained it the following year. Although the hurricanes of 1834 and 1852 brought great damage, the citadel has been partially reconstructed, its guns remounted. Today you can see the ruins of the officers' quarters, barracks, the ordnance store, a cemetery, and the redoubts.

Thousands of slaves worked for more than a century to complete this fortress. From its precincts there is a magnificent view with a radius of 70 miles. You can see Saba and St. Eustatius to the northwest, St. Barts and St. Maarten to the north, and Montserrat and Nevis to the southeast. The fortress dominates the southwest of St. Kitts.

Rugged visitors also make the eight-hour excursion to **Mount Liamuiga** (at least you'll get a lot of exercise). A Land Rover will take you part of the way, and you should hire a guide. After that, it's a long, steady climb to the lip of the crater at 2,600 feet (the peak is 3,792 feet). Hikers can descend into the crater, clinging to vines and roots.

At the hamlet of **Half-Way Tree,** a large tamarind marked the boundary in the old days between the British-held sector and the French half.

It was near the hamlet of **Old Road Town** that Sir Thomas Warner landed with the first band of settlers, establishing the first permanent colony, to the northwest at Sandy Point. Sir Thomas's grave is in the cemetery of St. Thomas Church.

A sign in the middle of Old Road Town points the way to **Carib Rock Drawings,** all the evidence that remains of the former inhabitants. The markings are on black boulders, the pictographs dating back to prehistoric days.

Two commercial tours interest visitors. Get your driver to take you to the **Sugar Factory,** which is best seen from February through July, when the cane is ground. You don't need a reservation, and you'll see the process from when the raw cane enters the factory until it emerges as bulk sugar.

Guests are also allowed to visit the **Carib Beer Plant,** an English lager beer-processing house. Carib Beer is considered the best in the West Indies, if sales are any indication. At the end of the tour through the plant, visitors are given a cold Carib in the lounge. The plant doesn't always operate, so check before heading there to see if it's open.

SHOPPING: The good buys here are in local handcrafts, including leather items made from goatskin, baskets, and coconut shells (the locals know how to make almost anything from these items). Some good values are also to be found in clothing and fabrics, especially sea island cottons. Store hours are 8 a.m. to noon and 1 to 4 p.m. except Sunday, although this is likely to vary greatly, depending on the individual shopkeeper.

Caribelle Batik, at Romney Manor (tel. 809/465-6253), qualifies as a sightseeing attraction as well as a shopping expedition. Its workroom and sales showrooms are in the most romantic setting of any shopping recommendation in this guide—the entire Romney Manor, a plantation established in the 17th century. You'll need a car, as it's reached via a short, steep road off the coast. It's right off Old Road, in the shade of a flamboyant tree. On the way to the manor, ask your driver to show you the Carib petroglyphs carved on stones (right near Old Road Town).

In the showroom a chart explains the batik process. You can watch as island workers apply different layers of molten wax and color, both required in the printing process. Also there are facilities for tie-dye fabrics. Items include wall hangings made of West Indian sea island cotton. Take your time and you'll usually find someone willing to explain the process to you. The shop offers beautiful caftans, T-shirts (pre-shrunk), and batik pictures. U.S. citizens may make duty-free purchases here. If you want to create your own ensemble, you can do so by purchasing lengths of fabric. Visiting hours are Monday to Friday from 8 a.m. to 4 p.m.

Losada's Antiques and Things, Wigley Ave., Fortlands (tel. 809/465-2564), near the Ocean Terrace Inn and the Fort Thomas Hotel, is a cozy "antiques and everything" shop in premises with access to a flower and shrub garden. It's owned by Mrs. Ghislaine Cramer, who keeps her eye on anything on the island that could be classified as an antique. She's at every estate sale and knows value. Her boutique has a collection of old gold watches, silver service, antique and contemporary jewelry in gold and silver, decanters, and teapots. She always has some antiques on consignment, and also offers local craftware such as bamboo fans and fabric hats. She encourages young, talented craftspeople on St. Kitts to sell their creations at her store.

You'll find the **Spencer Cameron Art Gallery** (tel. 809/465-4047) by the Circus, with its entrance on Bay Road. Here, a British woman, Rosey Cameron-Smith, produces watercolors and limited-edition prints of scenes from St. Kitts and Nevis. She arrived here about ten years ago and was captivated by the island's charms. She made an effort to reproduce in art some of the essence of true West Indian life, particularly the humor that sneaks into all its aspects. Rosey is well known on the island for her paintings of Kittitian Carnival clowns, showing all the color and excitement of this old island tradition. Exclusive Spencer Cameron designs form another facet of the gallery interest with a range of T-shirts and dresses silkscreened by hand in the gallery's workshop. The wide selection of artwork ranges from small prints to large ones, hand-colored prints to original paintings. Rosey also produces a variety of greeting cards, postcards, and calendars, as well as first-day cover issues of the Christmas stamp editions of Carnival clowns and masqueraders she painted for the government.

For the most luxurious shopping at affordable prices, I suggest **A Slice of the Lemon,** in the Palms Arcade at the Circus in Basseterre (tel. 809/465-2889), cool white and mirrored, with green carpeting. In 1979, Martin Kreiner opened a duty-free shop at the already-previewed Golden Lemon, thus the name. The Slice offers duty-free perfumes, watches, jewelry, and crystal.

The shop at the Golden Lemon moved across the street from the hotel on Dieppe Bay and is now called **Lemonaid** (no phone). It stocks the unusual in jewelry, plus clothes by Southern Cross Designs of Nevis (handmade) and noted couturier John Warden of Canada in the original fabrics of Cinnamon Hill, Nevis, as well as gifts and antiques.

Palmcrafts, Princes St., Basseterre (no phone), is one of several shops at Palms Arcade. It sells locally produced jams and jellies made from natural ingredients, skin oils and lotions made from coconut oil scented with tropical fragrances, spices, herb teas and condiments from Sunny Caribee, straw items, local handcrafts, and wall hangings.

Craftshouse (tel. 809/465-3241), is an outlet for the handcrafts of St. Kitts and Nevis made by craftsmen working through the National Handicraft and Cottage Industries Development Board. They offer items in copper, wood, coir, and coconut as well as furniture. You'll find Craftshouse shops at the Golden Rock International Airport; Ponds Pasture Industrial Site, Bay Rd., Basseterre; the Treasury Pier, Bay Rd.; and the Deep Water Port. Shops are open during normal business hours.

Stamp collectors interested in what is essentially a new stamp-issuing country can find distinctive stamps bearing the name of St. Kitts at the **St. Kitts Phila-**

telic Bureau, Social Security Building, Bay Rd., Basseterre (tel. 809/465-2874). When St. Kitts and Nevis formed their own government, they had independent stamp bureaus established on both islands.

THE SPORTING LIFE: Sporting activities aren't as developed on St. Kitts as they are on more tourist-oriented islands, but the outlook is improving. Beaches are the primary concern of most visitors, who find the swimming best at Conaree Beach (two miles from Basseterre), Frigate Bay, and Friar's Bay. The narrow peninsula in the southeast that contains the island's salt ponds also boasts its best beaches.

Water Sports

A variety of activities is offered by **Dive St. Kitts,** Pelican Cove Marina Ltd., Ocean Terrace Inn (tel. 809/465-2754). From Fisherman's Wharf, you can swim, sail, float, paddle, or go on scuba-diving and snorkeling expeditions.

Scuba trips, including all gear and guided dive trips by boat, cost $30 for one tank per person, $50 for two tanks per person per day, and $170 for eight tanks per person over four days. Total training in theories and practical applications to safe and enjoyable scuba-diving are offered in a full certification course, including all gear, text, and certification. The cost for this course is $200.

Snorkel trips, in a safety-equipped boat with an experienced boatman, take you to good spots to see the underwater life around St. Kitts. Mask, fins, and snorkel are included in the cost of $25 per person per half day for a minimum of two persons. A trip to Cockleshell or Banana Bay takes you down the uninhabited southern peninsula of St. Kitts, past the Nag's Head to the Banana Bay Beach Hotel or the Cockleshell Hotel. You can have a lazy lunch, hunt seashells, and explore the clear water. All snorkeling gear is included. The price of this full-day excursion is $35 per person, with a minimum of two persons required. Another snorkeling expedition is a beach picnic. You're taken on a scenic ride to the southern peninsula, where the beaches are inviting to swimmers and snorkelers. A camp-style lunch of freshly caught fish or lobster, plus white wine, is served. You leave the dock at 10 a.m., returning at 4 p.m. The charge is $40 per person, with a minimum of four persons required.

Waterskiing and windsurfing are also provided by Dive St. Kitts. Instruction in waterskiing is available for novices, and you can also be taught the fundamentals of windsurfing. Waterskiing prices are $30 per half hour, $50 per hour, while windsurfing costs $10 per hour. However, if you need instruction in this latter sport, the charge is $15 per hour.

Deep-Sea Fishing

Again, you must turn to Dive St. Kitts at the Ocean Terrace Inn (tel. 809/465-2754). If six persons want to go out, a half-day fishing jaunt can be arranged at a cost of $50 per half day, tackle and bait included.

Golfing

At **Frigate Bay** there is an 18-hole championship golf course, and there's a nine-hole course at **Golden Rock.** Robert Trent Jones designed the course at the Jack Tar at Frigate Bay. Greens fees are $20 for 18 holes, $12 for 9 holes. Caddies get $8 per 18 holes.

Tennis

The **Olympic Club,** just around the corner from the Ocean Terrace Hotel, has tennis courts on which visitors can play. Also downtown, at the **St. Kitts**

Lawn Tennis Club you can arrange for a temporary membership. Call 809/465-2754 for details.

NIGHTLIFE: There isn't much. A moonlight cruise, offered by **Dive St. Kitts,** Pelican Cove Marina Ltd., Ocean Terrace Inn (tel. 809/465-2046), takes you from Fisherman's Wharf at about 6:30 p.m. You can enjoy rum punch, beer, and soft drinks as you relax under the moon. The cruise costs $25 per person, with a minimum of four persons required.

If you're in the mood to gamble, St. Kitts's only **casino** is at the Jack Tar Village, Frigate Bay (tel. 809/465-8651). It's open to all visitors, who can try their luck at roulette, blackjack, craps, and slot machines. The casino opens at 8 p.m. There is no entrance fee.

The best all-around place for entertainment is the **Ocean Terrace Inn** (tel. 809/465-2754), which has entertainment two nights weekly off-season and more frequently in season. There's no cover charge, and guests pay EC$3.75 ($1.40) per drink. Who knows what's likely to be happening on any given night? Often you dance to live bands. Perhaps you'll hear a West Indian group or watch an African dance. On several occasions carnival queens model batik bathing suits. And it's always a good idea to introduce yourself to the longtime bartender, Marcus Payne, who'll show you the aviary and aquarium behind the bar. Watch the "love birds." Also consider attending the Wednesday- or Friday-night buffets at the previously recommended Fisherman's Wharf, which lies on the waterfront down from the Ocean Terrace.

If you decide to venture into one of the local bars around the island, you just might be served a concoction known as "Halfway Three." It's made of bootleg and white lightning, along with moonshine, and is to be drunk at your own risk.

4. NEVIS

Two miles south of St. Kitts, Nevis (pronounced *Nee*-vis) was sighted by Columbus in 1493. He called it *Las Nieves,* Spanish for "snows," because its cloudcapped mountains reminded him of the snow-capped range in the Pyrenees. The island, almost circular, appears like a perfect cone when viewed from St. Kitts, its sister state. The cone rises gradually to a height of 3,232 feet. A saddle joins the mountain to two smaller peaks, Saddle Hill (1,250 feet) in the south, and Hurricane Hill (only 250 feet) in the north. Coral reefs rim the shoreline, and there is mile after mile of palm-shaded white sandy beaches.

Columbus may have been the first European to see the island, but it was settled by the British in 1628. The volcanic island is famous as the birthplace of Alexander Hamilton, drafter of the U.S. Constitution and first U.S. Secretary of the Treasury. Nevis claims he was born January 11, 1757, but reference books differ. It was also at Nevis that Admiral Nelson harbored his fleet in Napoleonic days, marrying a rich, young widow, Frances Nisbet. His best man was the Duke of Clarence, later King William IV of England.

In the 18th century Nevis, "The Queen of the Caribees," was the leading spa of the West Indies, made so by its hot mineral springs.

Once Nevis was peppered with prosperous sugarcane estates, which are gone now (many converted into some of the most intriguing character hotels in the Caribbean). Sea island cotton is the chief crop today.

As you drive around the nostalgic island, going through tiny villages such as Gingerland (named for the spice it used to export), you'll reach the heavily wooded slopes of Nevis Peak. From that vantage point there are magnificent views of the neighboring islands. Nevis is an island of exceptional beauty and has remained unspoiled. Its people, in the main, are black descendants of slaves. Nevis is usually approached by ferry boat or air from **St. Kitts.**

On the Caribbean side, **Charlestown,** the capital of Nevis, was very fashionable in the 18th century, as sugar planters were carried around in carriages and sedan chairs. Houses are of locally quarried volcanic stone, often supporting a clapboard second story, encircled by West Indian fretted verandas. A town of wide, quiet streets, this port only gets busy when its major link to the world, the ferry from St. Kitts, docks at the harbor. Then it becomes a cascade of activity.

GETTING THERE: You can fly to Nevis on **LIAT** (tel. 809/469-5238) on scheduled service from St. Kitts, Antigua, or Montserrat. No flight takes more than 25 minutes. There is direct service from St. Croix, St. Barts, and Anguilla. **Carib Aviation** is available for charters and will fly two to five passengers. The trip by air from St. Kitts takes only five minutes. The cost for a charter is $60 for the whole plane (five to nine passengers). For information, call 809/469-5295 in Nevis.

You can also use the **inter-island ferry** service from St. Kitts aboard the government passenger ferry M.V. *Caribe Queen.* For information on this service, see the section on St. Kitts, under "Getting Around."

GETTING AROUND: Your small plane arrives at the airport a half mile from Newcastle in the north of the island. Or if you're coming by ferryboat from St. Kitts, you'll be delivered right to the heart of the capital, Charlestown.

Rental Cars

If you're prepared to face the rocky, pot-holed roads of Nevis, you can arrange for a rental car from a local firm. Avis, Budget, National, and Hertz maintain no offices in Nevis. Once on the island, ask at your hotel about arranging for a car rental.

To drive in Nevis, you must obtain a permit from the Traffic Department, costing about $12 and is valid till December 31 no matter when it's purchased. Remember, all the vehicles must be driven *on the left-hand side of the road.*

Taxis

You can also rent a taxi with a driver (who also doubles as a guide). You'll find them waiting at the airport at the arrival of every plane. As an example of fares charged: a taxi ride between Charlestown and Newcastle Airport costs EC$20 ($7.40); between Charlestown and Old Manor Estate, EC$15 ($5.55); and from Charlestown to Pinney's Beach, EC$5 ($1.85). You can hire a taxi to or from Charlestown Pier and Bath Hotel or Bath Village for EC$5 ($1.85). To take a sightseeing tour around the island, a 3½-hour excursion, you'll pay EC$90 ($33.30). Between 10 p.m. and 6 a.m., 10% is added to the prices for Charlestown trips. The average taxi holds up to four persons, so when the cost is sliced per passenger, it's a reasonable investment. No sightseeing bus companies operate on Nevis, but a number of individuals own buses which they use for taxi service.

PRACTICAL FACTS: Language, currency, and entry requirements have already been discussed in this chapter's introductory section. Most visitors will clear Customs in St. Kitts, so arrival in Nevis should not be complicated.

Banks: Banking hours are from 8 a.m. to noon Monday to Saturday. However, most of them reopen from 3:30 to 5:30 p.m. Friday. Closed Sunday.

Electricity: As in St. Kitts, an electrical transformer will be needed for most U.S. and Canadian appliances. The electricity is 230 volts AC, 60 cycles.

Information: One of the best sources is the **Tourist Bureau** on Main Street in Charlestown (tel. 809/469-5521). The St. Kitts-Nevis Tourist Board in the U.S. is at 414 E. 75th St., New York, NY 10021 (tel. 212/535-1234).

Post office: The post office is open from 8 a.m. to 3 p.m. daily, except Thursday when it closes at 11:30 a.m.

Taxes: The government imposes a 7% tax on hotel bills, plus a departure tax of EC$13.50 ($5) per person. You don't have to pay this tax in Nevis if you're returning to St. Kitts, since Nevis and St. Kitts are the same country. However, if you're flying from either Nevis or St. Kitts to some other destination in the Caribbean, the tax will be assessed.

Telecommunications: Telegrams and Telexes can be sent from **Cable & Wireless** offices, Main St., Charlestown (tel. 809/469-5000). International telephone calls, including collect calls can also be sent from the cable office. Hours are from 8 a.m. to 6 p.m. Monday to Friday, to noon Saturday. Closed Sunday and public holidays. To call Nevis from the mainland, dial the area code, 809, then the local number.

Time: As in St. Kitts, Nevis is on Atlantic Standard Time, which means it's usually one hour ahead of the U.S. East Coast, except when the mainland goes on Daylight Saving Time. Then clocks are the same.

Tips and service: A 10% service charge is added to your hotel bill. In restaurants, it is customary to tip from 10% to 15% of the tab.

Water: The water of Nevis is generally safe to drink and in good supply.

Weather: The information given in "Practical Facts" for St. Kitts regarding climate is also true for Nevis.

HOTELS: Several of the inns of Nevis have been adapted from long-abandoned sugar plantations. The style and amenities may transport you back to a bygone era. In addition, there are a scattering of air-conditioned motel-type accommodations for those who prefer that.

Old Manor Estate, P.O. Box 70, Gingerland, Nevis, W.I. (tel. 809/465-5445, 212/840-6636 in New York City), has an old-world kind of grace that makes it the most desirable hotel on Nevis and one of the most unusual and delightful hostelries in the entire Caribbean. When Nevis was settled in the 17th century, the forested plot of land on which the hotel sits was granted to the Croney family in 1690 by the King of England. Construction of a plantation whose main house, now in ruins, has been dubbed "the best example of Georgian domestic architecture in the Caribbean" continued in a gradual expansion throughout the 18th and 19th centuries. Until 1936 the estate was a working sugar plantation. On the grounds you can see the rusted flywheels of cane-crushing machines whose bases are engraved "Glasgow—1859–1861." For a dark and better-forgotten period of its history, this burgeoning plantation served as a stud farm for the breeding of slaves. When the last of the Croney line, Bertie, died in 1967, he left vacant the longest continually lived-in great house in the West Indies.

The entire complex, including the main house and stone outbuildings, sits at a cool and comfortable elevation of 800 feet. In 1981 a spunky, competent, and gracious Ohio widow, Vicki Knorr, purchased the property and embarked on its restoration. Everything about her regime has encouraged a nonplastic, solidly grounded foundation in architectural and culinary excellence. Mrs. Knorr has a creative and professional relationship with her hard-working and talented son, Greg. Living on the premises, he handles long-range administrative planning as easily as he tends bar. Although rehabilitation of the great house will require years of patient labor, the hotel occupies a trio of stone outbuildings that are almost as beautiful as the house. The estate workers' clapboard huts were replaced by the kind of structures sometimes seen on 800-year-old estates in the south of France. Gracefully proportioned stone stairs are flanked by ancient trees and vines, giving the place a dignified, colonial ambience of filtered sunlight. The former smokehouse and jail were replaced by a rambling villa called the Overseer's Building.

Each of the 15 accommodations contains wide-plank floors of such tropical hardwoods as greenheart, plushly comfortable colonial-reproduction furniture, and high-ceilinged space. In high season, with MAP, singles cost $145 daily, and doubles go for $210. *In low season, singles on the MAP rent for $105 daily, and doubles run $150.* The resort is not recommended for children under 12. A big part of the success of Croney's is the culinary inspiration of Mrs. Knorr. Her Cooperage dining room, recommended separately, is the finest on the island. Breakfast is served every day in guests' bedrooms. Lunch is in the raftered dining room or beside the most unusual swimming pool on Nevis. Chiseled from fitted blocks of volcanic rock, it was crafted from a 150-year-old cistern. You serve yourself from a buffet table and a century-old grill in the plantation's colonial kitchens. Every Friday night, the natural stone amphitheater near the kitchen serves as the perfect acoustical setting for some of the best-attended parties on the island. In the rear is a swimming pool made with natural cut stone gathered from Mount Nevis.

Nisbet Plantation Inn, New Castle, Nevis, W.I. (tel. 809/469-5325), is a gracious estate house on a coconut plantation where gentility and a respect for fine living prevail. This is the former home of Frances Nisbet, who married Lord Nelson at the age of 22. (Enamored of Miss Nisbet at the time, he later fell in love with Lady Hamilton, and Frances Nisbet died a bitter old woman in England, one of history's piteous figures.) The present main building on the 30-acre plantation was rebuilt on the foundations of the original 18th-century great house. The ruins of a circular sugar mill stand at the entrance, covered with cassia, frangipani, hibiscus, and poinciana. Set in the palm grove are the guest cottages with covered verandas, all with private baths with showers and two with ornate four-poster beds. On the MAP, winter rates are $285 to $345 in a double, $195 to $230 in a single. *In summer, the rates in a double are $175 to $230, and in a single, $110 to $230, also on the MAP.* These rates are for standard and superior rooms.

Breakfast is served on a veranda with a view down a wide grassy lawn lined with sentinel palm trees which leads to a half-mile-long sandy beach, one of the best in Nevis. Two neighboring bays combine to make a total of three miles for beachcombing and shelling. An offshore reef protects the swimming area, providing good snorkeling, with spearfishing and snorkeling equipment available free at the hotel. At the end of the day a tranquil evening meal is served in the dining room of the main house, furnished with English antiques. Local fish and lobster as well as continental and American cuisine are featured, and Créole dishes are offered on occasion. Complimentary wine is served at dinner. This is always a social event: the guests gather first on the veranda for "sundowners," then are seated at tables for four to six people (if you want a different arrangement, ask in advance). Sunday is barbecue time on the beach, enjoyed to the accompaniment of a steel band. If visitors drop in, they are charged $25. The managers are easy-going and hospitable, and with the assistance of their well-trained staff, they see to your needs. There is a library in the main house, but if you want more energetic pursuits, horseback riding can be arranged, and you'll find a hard court for tennis near the main house. Racquets and balls are provided. Fishing, sailing, and surf-jetting are available about five miles from the hotel and can be arranged through the management. Car rentals are provided at the inn. All reservations for stays here are taken in the Duluth, Minnesota, area office (tel. 218/722-5059).

Zetland Plantation, P.O. Box 448, Gingerland, Nevis, W.I. (tel. 809/469-5454), originally a sugar plantation, was converted into an exceptional hotel, occupying a 750-acre site with good views of both the Atlantic and the Caribbean Sea. The former plantation lies 1,000 feet up on the slopes of Mount Nevis, from which you can view Antigua and Montserrat. Its name is derived from Scotland's Shetland Islands. Today Zetland is more like a country-club lodge. More than a dozen plantation suites (square one-story houses) are rented, containing spacious lounges and bedrooms. Hotel-type maid service is included in the tariffs. Scattered about the grounds, all rental units are within easy walking distance of the main complex. Because of its mountain perch, trade-wind breezes keep the plantation cooled. *In summer, EP doubles cost $85 to $125 daily, rising to $100 to $150 in a triple.* In winter, tariffs go up to $165 to $250 in a double and $195 to $280 in a triple. Some of the newer units, really mountainside suites, have their own plunge pools. Rates include wake-up coffee and transportation to the hotel beach hut. When making reservations, inquire about package rates and family plans. The Sugar Mill has been transformed into a family unit, housing up to six people.

As only 44 guests can be accommodated at a time, everybody quickly gets to know everybody else. The manager will outline the sports program to you, including hikes through tropical forest, tennis, horseback riding, or swimming at the plantation pool. Or you can drive to Zetland's beach for ocean swimming. A place for the discriminating traveler, Zetland also serves good food. Most of it is grown on the plantation. People staying here on EP rates are charged extra for gas for cooking in their units.

Hermitage Plantation, St. John Figtree Parish, Nevis, W.I. (tel. 809/469-5477), a much-photographed, frequently copied historians' delight, is said to be the oldest all-wood house in the Antilles, built amid the high-altitude plantations of Gingerland in 1740. It probably wouldn't offer the bucketloads of meticulously researched charm of today without the careful supervision of a former Philadelphian, Richard Lupinacci. He and his wife, Maureen, have assembled one of the best collections of antiques on Nevis. Each piece corresponds with taste and flair to the wide-plank floors, intricate latticework, and high ceilings of this beautiful hotel. The ten accommodations are in five glamorous outbuildings designed like small plantation houses. Many contain huge four-poster beds, antique accessories, and colonial louvered windows. With MAP, winter rates are $150 daily in a single, $225 in a double. *In summer, rooms with MAP are $120 daily in a single, $155 in a double.* Laundry service is one of this place's many fringe benefits. The property is protected by parallel rows of dry retaining walls. In the center, amid stands of very old mango trees, is a pleasant rectangular swimming pool.

Golden Rock Estate, P.O. Box 493, Gingerland, Nevis, W.I. (tel. 809/469-5346), a sugar estate built in 1815, high in the hills of Nevis, has been converted into one of the most charming and atmospheric inns in the Caribbean. You walk through a 25-acre garden in a tropical setting of about 150 acres. The original windmill, a stone tower, has been turned into a duplex honeymoon retreat (or else accommodations for a family of four or five), with an elaborate four-poster bed. The inn has 15 double rooms in all, spread about the garden, shaded by hibiscus and allamanda, yet within a minute's walk of the freshwater swimming pool and shady terrace where tropical rum punches are served. Each villa has been decorated with flair, and the king-size beds are four-posters made of bamboo. The fabrics used are island made, with tropical flower designs. In addition, the rooms have large porches for relaxing, reading, or just looking out at the sea. In winter, a single rents for $100 daily, and a double goes for $150, plus another $25 per person for breakfast and dinner. *In summer (April 1 to December*

20), a single costs only $50 daily, a double renting for $75, plus $25 if you also want breakfast and dinner. Children under age 2 stay free. Wine is included at dinner, which is likely to be a West Indian meal (ever had stuffed pumpkin?) served at the 175-year-old "long house." Before dinner you can enjoy a tall drink in the hotel's bar. A facility at Pinney's Beach, the Carousel Bar, serves lobster, shrimp, grilled fish, and hamburgers with coconut-husk flavor. It's open daily except Sunday during the winter season. Otherwise you can have a picnic lunch prepared in the hotel's kitchen. To find the beach bar, turn at the sign of the hand-carved horse's head.

The owner-manager, Pam Barry, will show you to the tennis court or start you on a hike through a rain forest, where you might spot a wild monkey. The hotel's bus takes guests to one of Golden Rock's beaches every day at no extra cost. The estate owns one beach on the leeward side, part of Pinney's Beach, and another on the windward side where you can surf. The shuttle runs round trip to both beaches, with a shopping stop in Charlestown if you want it. In addition, a 16-foot Boston whaler is offered for waterskiing, light offshore fishing, and snorkel and scuba-diving. Scuba is available to accredited divers only. Two windsurfers can be used free by guests (lessons cost extra). A private car, either a Mini-Moke or a Volkswagen, is available for one or two couples, including insurance and mileage.

Montpelier Plantation Inn, P.O. Box 474, Montpelier, Nevis, W.I. (tel. 809/469-5462), 700 feet up the slopes of Mount Nevis, offers sixteen rooms with private terraces and baths in modern cottages kept cool and fresh by the almost-constant light breeze. Other portions were set on the foundations of the ruins of the great Montpelier estate. Much use has been made of local stonework and traditional architectural styles. The magnificent and extensive gardens have, at their center, the 18th-century sugar mill, a mammoth swimming pool and pool bar, and at the periphery a hard tennis court. The hotel concentrates on the quality of its food, using when possible fresh local produce. Winter rates on the MAP are $200 daily in a single and $280 daily in a double. *Off-season, MAP rates are $100 daily in a single and $150 in a double.* The inn has its own speedboat, a 17-foot Boston whaler with 85-hp outboard engine for waterskiing and snorkeling. Horseback riding, sailing, and deep-sea fishing can be arranged. In season, several nights a week there are dances at nearby establishments. Montpelier occasionally has a grand affair, featuring a local scratch band.

Pinney's Beach Hotel, P.O. Box 61, Charlestown, Nevis, W.I. (tel. 809/469-5207), is the only hotel on one of the most spectacular beaches in Nevis. A miniature resort, it is a bungalow colony, 48 double rooms, including six family-type units, clustered around a waterside patio where you can have cooling drinks, lunch, or take a dip. Rooms are modestly equipped, yet supplied with the basic necessities. Some are air-conditioned. Each unit comes with a private bath and a patio, and a view of the palm-fringed coastline is thrown in as well. The cheaper bungalows are set back a bit, overlooking an inner flower garden, while the others have their own direct entrance onto the beach. In winter, double rooms rent for $150 daily on the MAP, and singles go for $90. *In summer, the manager reduces the tariffs to $60 daily in a single, $100 in a double, all MAP.* Horseback riding, sailing, and deep-sea fishing can be arranged by the hotel, and there's a tennis club about 50 yards from Pinney's.

Rest Haven Inn, P.O. Box 209, Old Hospital Road, Charlestown, Nevis, W.I. (tel. 809/469-5208), is a collection of bungalows standing on 2½ acres of grounds. I prefer the newer units which the soft-spoken owner, Almon Nisbett (with two t's—no relation to Frances), has built at water's edge. Each with a private patio opening onto the Caribbean, these are his deluxe units—spacious, air-conditioned, containing twin-size and single beds. For these, of course, he charges his highest tariffs. The older rooms containing twin beds are set back a bit, located within the pool and dining area compound, facing each other with private patios. Some of these have simple efficiency units for light cooking. *Summer rates, depending on the accommodation, range from $40 to $60 daily in a single, from $60 to $80 in a double, EP.* In winter, EP tariffs are $55 to $75 daily in a single, from $65 to $100 in a double. For half board, add $20 per person daily. The hospitality is what counts here, not the grand surroundings, and you are close to Charlestown, a five-minute walk away. The location is also near Pinney's Beach. Mr. Nisbett has a reputation for serving good island dishes, and if you want to go hiking, one of his staff will pack a picnic lunch for you. There is also a snackbar, where light lunches, including lobster, are served daily to those who don't want to leave the grounds. Tennis is available on the hotel's own courts.

WHERE TO DINE: When you can get it, the native food is good. If you request sea urchin, the chef won't be surprised. (*Note:* you may see turtle on some menus, but remember that this is an endangered species.) Suckling pig is roasted with many spices, and eggplant is used in a number of tasty ways, as is the avocado. Most people dine at their hotel. To break what could be monotony, many guests "hotel-hop," taking their lunch or dinner at one of the other hotels on the island.

If you find yourself in Charlestown at midday, you might do better gathering the makings for your own picnic lunch. One way to do this is to go to the **market-place,** buying fresh fruit, such as mangoes, from the stallkeepers. Then head for the **Nevis Bakery,** where you can order coconut tarts, and fresh-baked bread. The friendly people at **Main Street Grocery Store** will provide the rest of the makings for your lunch, including canned pâté.

For those who are interested in spending the day on the three-mile, white-sand Pinney's Beach, to get a suntan and not be burdened with packing a lunch, then **Pinney's Beach Hotel** (see previous recommendation) offers the finest in local cuisine, ranging from sandwiches to a sumptuous three-course meal. Ms. Nicholls, the sprightly and charming manager, will welcome you.

The Cooperage, Old Manor Estate, Gingerland (tel. 809/465-5445), is the previously recommended hotel's dining room, in a reconstructed building where coopers once made barrels for the sugar mill. Built in the 17th century, it had a tilted floor so that the coopers could roll their completed barrels from the enormous forge to a storage area at the building's opposite end. The floor has been leveled, but the colonial aura has been retained under the sophisticated guidance of Ohio-born Vicki Knorr. Dinner is served under the high, raftered ceiling surrounded by thick walls of local stone. In addition to having a fascinating history, the Cooperage is also the best restaurant on an island where there's plenty of stiff competition.

Lunch, served daily from noon to 3 p.m., includes such light-textured specialties as spinach salad, stuffed Caribbean lobster, and fruit desserts. The cost is from $12. Dinner, with wine included, costs from $30, and you can choose from a changing list of specialties based on the daily availability of ingredients. Examples are shrimp with coconut served on spinach, an array of soups, curried chicken breasts "Old Manor style" with homemade noodles, local fish bought fresh each morning, and a succulent variety of local shrimp. Reservations are suggested, especially for nonresidents. Dinner is served from 7 to 9:30 nightly.

Hermitage Plantation, St. John Figtree Parish (tel. 809/469-5477), is a place to combine an excellent dinner with a visit to the oldest house on Nevis, now one of the island's most unusual hotels, recommended previously. Meals are served on the latticed porch of the main house, amid candles and good cheer. Maureen Lupinacci, who runs the place with her husband, Richard, is the skillful hostess who sees to combining continental recipes with local ingredients. Menu specialties include snapper steamed in banana leaves, plus carrot and tarragon soup, brown bread, ice cream, and a delectable version of rum soufflé. Full dinners with wine and drinks cost around $35 per person. Dinner is served daily at 8 p.m., but first you must have a before-dinner drink in the colonial-style living room of the Lupinacci family. Nonresidents are accepted as dinner guests.

Montpelier Plantation Inn, at Montpelier (tel. 809/469-5462), was previously recommended as a hotel, but it offers some of the finest dining on the island as well, and will accept nonresidents who make a reservation. At this grand old West Indian mansion, you can dine on the veranda, enjoying a three-course table d'hôte dinner for $25, plus wine and drinks. For that, you're given an appetizer, main course, and dessert. Lobster and fish such as red snapper are served the day the catch comes in. The menu is eclectic, and sometimes you'll find roast beef and Yorkshire pudding on the menu. The candlelit dinner has an 8 p.m. seating, so try to show up on time. A buffet lunch, costing $12, is offered daily from 1 to 2 p.m. One of the local bands comes in to entertain about every ten days.

Oualie Beach Club, Oualie Bay, Nevis, W.I. (tel. 809/469-9735), offers dishes made from lobster, conch, fish, and shrimp, cooked by West Indian recipes with a hint of American or European influence. Daily specials are posted on the notice board. Lunch is served from noon to 3 p.m. and 6 to 9 p.m., with meals costing from $10. The beach club also has six hotel rooms right on the beach. The club, offering outstanding water sports, is owned by the Yearwood family.

EXPLORING NEVIS: When you arrive at the airport, it's best to negotiate with a taxi driver to take you around Nevis. The distance is only 20 miles. You may find yourself taking much longer if you stop to see specific sights. The people will often engage you in conversation.

The major attraction is the **Birthplace of Alexander Hamilton,** on Main Street overlooking the bay (tel. 809/469-5786). Mr. Hamilton was the illegitimate son of a Scotsman, James Hamilton, and Rachel Fawcett, a Nevisian of Huguenot ancestry. The family left the island in 1782 and never returned to Nevis. The lava stone house by the shore has been restored, and a small museum, dedicated to Nevis History and Hamilton, has been established. The Archives of Nevis are housed there. The museum is open from 8 a.m. to 4 p.m. Monday to Friday and 10 a.m. to noon Saturday from mid-December and April. No admission is charged, but donations are accepted.

At Bath Village, about half a mile from Charlestown, stands the **Bath Hotel,** in serious disrepair, and its **Bath House,** which has been restored to use. The hotel was built in 1778 by John Huggins to accommodate some 50 guests, mostly wealthy planters in the West Indies who were afflicted with rheumatism and gout. The hotel had five hot baths built in which temperatures ranged up to 108° Fahrenheit. It shut down in 1870. Intermittently through the years since, efforts were made to restore the complex to use, but mainly, for more than a century, the hotel, patched and proud, has stood as a reminder of Nevis's heyday, but with goats treading the tired verandas instead of fancy, if ailing, gentlemen who strolled about with their ladies when young Alexander Hamilton was making his name known in the American colonies. Both the hotel and the Bath House were acquired by the Nevis Island government in 1983, and the Bath House has been renovated and reopened for use under the management of the Ministry of Tourism, quickly becoming popular with both islanders and tourists. A feasibility study has been authorized with a view to restoration of the Bath Hotel, with the aim of using it for the promotion of industrial development and tourism.

Nearby, **St. John's Church** stands in the midst of a sprawling graveyard in Fig Tree Village. It is said to have been the parish church of Lady Nelson, wife of

Horatio Lord Nelson. A church of gray stone, dating from the 18th century, it contains the record of Nelson's marriage to Frances Nisbet in the church register.

At Morning Star Plantation nearby, the **Nelson Museum** contains a large collection of Nelson memorabilia gathered by Robert D. Abrahams, a Philadelphia lawyer. The museum can be visited free. Among other items displayed is a faded letter written by Nelson with his left hand, after he lost his right one. Also displayed are paintings depicting Nelson's romance with Lady Hamilton, plus dining chairs from the admiral's flagship, the *Victory*. See also a grandfather clock that was deliberately (and permanently) stopped the moment Queen Elizabeth entered the museum on February 22, 1966, the most recent big event that has happened on Nevis. The museum is open daily from 9:30 a.m. to 1 p.m.

Ashby Fort is now overgrown, but it was once used by Lord Nelson to guard his ships in Nevis while they took on fresh water and supplies. Nearby is **Nelson's Spring,** near Cotton Ground Village. In the 18th century, Nelson is said to have watered his ships here before they left to fight in the American Revolution. The fort, in sad disrepair, overlooks the site of **Jamestown,** an early settlement that was devastated by a 1680 tidal wave.

The **Eden Brown Estate** lies about a mile and a half from New River and it's said to be haunted. Once it was the home of a wealthy planter, whose daughter was to be married, but her husband-to-be was killed in a duel at the prenuptial feast. The mansion was then closed forever and left to the ravages of nature. A gray solid stone still stands, and only the most adventurous go here on a moonlit night.

Outside the center of Charlestown, the **Jewish Cemetery** was restored in part by an American, Robert D. Abrahams, the Philadelphia lawyer already mentioned. At the lower end of Government Road, this necropolis was the resting place of many of the early shopkeepers of Nevis. At one time Sephardic Jews coming from Brazil made up a quarter of the population. It is believed that Jews introduced sugar production into the Leewards. Most of the tombstones date from between 1690 and 1710.

SHOPPING: Normal store hours are from 8 a.m. to noon and 1 to 4 p.m. except Thursday, when some places are closed in the afternoon, and Saturday, when some stay open to 8 p.m. Most are closed Sunday.

Everybody, including Prince Charles, heads for **Eva Wilkins' Studio** on the grounds of the old sugar mill plantation her father owned. She is the most famous artist of Nevis, and invites visitors to come by her studio and home during the day, except from noon to 3 p.m. "when I need rest." A spry, elderly lady who doesn't "understand modern ways," she displays both black-and-white and color prints. Her studio is at Clay Ghaut Estate near Montpelier in Gingerland. She paints island people (using real models), local flowers and scenes. On the grounds near her house is a miniature reproduction of the original sugar factory. Ask your driver if she's in residence before starting out. Everybody knows when Miss Wilkins is on the island.

For one of the most bizarre shopping expeditions in this book, head for the home of **Mrs. Jones,** the last house on the right going east out of New Castle, a tumbledown old village near the airport. Mrs. Jones doesn't put out a sign "because I don't need one." She candidly admits, "I'm known all over the world, but I've been no place from Nevis." An elderly peanut farmer, she turns out unglazed pottery: "I make every creature but man, and only God can put life into him." Her specialty is terracotta birds, and she also makes oversize clay pots, but mostly her assistants do the work today.

The Sand Box Tree, Chapel St. (tel. 809/469-5662), offers the complete line of Cinnamon Hill fabrics, the beautiful cottons designed and silk-screened by hand on Nevis. The fabric is available by the yard and is suitable for garments, slipcovers, and curtains. Custom-made clothing is available, and you can order any type of garment for men, women, and children, made to measure with next-day service. Also at this shop is a ready-to-wear collection designed for Cinnamon Hill by John Warden, award-winning designer from Montréal. Mr. Warden has combined silk-screened prints with hand embroidery to create a high quality and sophisticated line of high-fashion clothing and accessories, produced on Nevis from the first stitch to the last. The shop also carries a wide range of jewelry, gift items, and postcards. To aid visitors, The Sand Box Tree offers "Nevis Happenings," an up-to-date bulletin board with notices of what's going on on the island, such as special nights at hotels, houses for rent, babysitting services, and information on where to get what.

The Sand Castle at Oualie Beach (no phone) is the place to shop on your way to the beach. It offers a full line of bathing suits for men, women, and children, plus cover-ups and beach bags. Suntan lotions, sun glasses, snorkeling gear, and sand toys make this the most complete beach store on Nevis.

The **Nevis Handicraft Cooperative Society, Ltd.,** Cotton House, Charlestown (no phone), in a stone building, is about 200 feet from the wharf, near the colorful marketplace. The handcraft shop contains locally made gift items, including unusual objects of goatskin, local wines made from a variety of fruits grown on the island, hot pepper sauce, guava cheese, jams, and jellies. The shop is open from 8:30 a.m. to 12:30 p.m. and 1:30 to 4 p.m. Monday to Friday, 8:30 a.m. to 12:30 p.m. Saturday.

Heading up Government Road, you reach the **School for the Blind** (no phone), where the Nevisians make handcrafts for sale. Visiting hours are 9 a.m. to noon and 1 to 4 p.m. Monday through Wednesday (9 a.m. to noon on Saturday). Go only if you want to buy something, as it seems cruel to disturb these unfortunate people who have very little money and few prospects.

The National Handicraft and Cottage Industries Development Board has a branch of its **Craftshouse** sales outlets, offering a variety of handcrafted articles, at Pinneys Industrial Site, Charlestown (tel. 809/469-5505).

Persons interested in stamp collecting can go to the **Nevis Philatelic Bureau,** Head Post Office, Market St., Charlestown (tel. 809/469-5388). The bureau, fully air-conditioned, invites stamp collectors to see the wide range of colorful stamps. Hours are from 8 a.m. to 4:30 p.m. Monday to Friday.

The best for last—**Caribbee Clothes** are sold in the RDC Mall on Main Street (no phone), featuring hand-embroidered styles. Nevis themes often form the motif in the patterns. Resort-type shirts and skirts are sold, and they're quite beautiful—and expensive. The little industry provides work for many craftspeople on the island, and Caribee Clothes are sold in many fine West Indian boutiques and in America.

THE SPORTING LIFE: The best beach on Nevis—in fact, one of the best beaches in the Caribbean—is the reef-protected **Pinney's Beach,** with its clear water and gradual slope. Just north of Charlestown, you'll have three miles of sand (often virtually to yourself), culminating in a sleepy lagoon that evokes a scene south of Pago Pago.

In sports equipment, it's best to bring your own. However, hotels are stocked with limited gear (but equipment may often be in use by other guests).

Snorkeling

Again, head for Pinney's Beach. You might also try the waters of Fort Ashby, where the settlement of Jamestown is said to have slid into the sea, and legend has it that the church bells can still be heard and the undersea town can still be seen when conditions are just right. So far, no diver, to my knowledge, has ever found the conditions "just right."

Water Sports

Scuba Safaris Ltd., Oualie Beach (tel. 809/469-9518), offers scuba diving and snorkeling in an area rich in dive sites. Single-tank boat scuba dives cost $35, two-tank boat dives going for $60, and night dives for $45. They also offer resort and certification courses, dive packages, and equipment rental. Glass-bottom boat and snorkeling trips take you from Nevis across the narrows to St. Kitts. The 30-foot glass-bottom boat takes you at a leisurely pace, and masks, fins, snorkels, snorkel vests, rum punch, and drinks are provided during the 2½-hour cruise. Boat charters to Basseterre, Banana Bay, Cockleshell Bay, and other beaches are offered, as well as deep-sea fishing trips on request. Scuba Safaris operates in conjunction with **Oualie Beach Club,** Oualie Bay, Nevis, W.I. (tel. 809/469-9735).

The fishing is excellent, not only for snapper and grouper, but for bonita and kingfish as well. The best hotel for making boating arrangements is the **Golden Rock,** P.O. Box 493, Nevis, W.I. (tel. 809/469-5346). It supplies a diesel boat, *Explorer,* to take fishermen out, charging $100 for four persons for the chance to hook a dolphin (the fish), wahoo, or Spanish mackerel. The Golden Rock has its own 16-foot Boston whaler for waterskiing, light offshore fishing, and snorkel and scuba-diving.

Tennis

Most of the major hotels have courts.

Golf

Devotees of this sport are invited to go to St. Kitts, a 45-minute boat ride or a 10-minute air hop, for a game.

Mountain Climbing

This is strenuous, recommended only to the stout of heart. Ask first at your hotel for a picnic lunch, and also the desk, to arrange a guide for you (he'll probably request about $25 for two hikers). Hikers climb Mount Nevis, 3,500 feet up to the volcanic (extinct) crater and enjoy a hike to the rain forest to watch for wild monkeys.

Horseback Riding

Horseback riding is available at the **Nisbet Plantation** (tel. 469-5325), previewed earlier. Naturally, you ride English saddle. The cost is $15 per person for one hour, $10 for each hour to follow. With a guide, you are taken along mountain trails, and along the way you visit the site of long-forgotten plantations.

5. ANGUILLA

It's small, serene, secluded, and special. The most northerly of the Leeward Islands in the eastern Caribbean, Anguilla (rhymes with *vanilla*) is only 16 miles long, with a maximum of 35 square miles in land area. Columbus may have spotted the island, calling it *anguilla* (Spanish for "eel") because of its shape. The little island has a population of some 7,000 people, predominantly of African descent but also some European, particularly Irish. Anguilla lies five miles north of St. Maarten. Flat as a pancake, long and slender, Anguilla has very little rainfall. The soil is unproductive, with mainly low foliage and sparse scrub vegetation, but the beaches of white coral sand around the island are outstanding.

Anguilla was once part of a federation with St. Kitts and Nevis, but it gained its independence from that association in 1980 and has since been a self-governing British possession. A constitution adopted in 1976 provides for an autonomous elected government. English, of course, is the official language. Most of the men on the island work in the tourist industry or as lobster fishermen.

The island was first colonized by the British, in 1650. The colony was subjected to sporadic raids from Irish and French freebooters. In 1745 a French expedition of two frigates and some 700 soldiers launched an attack, but were repulsed by the governor and his militia. The French invaders landed again in 1796, an attack bravely resisted by heroic Anguillans who fed their cannons with lead balls from their sprat nets. The invasion failed and Anguilla went back to sleep under Britain's protection. It is said that the sea-island cotton seed which spread to Georgia and the Carolinas in 1889 came originally from Anguilla.

One of the most popular beaches is Road Bay, framed by the crescent-shaped village of Sandy Ground and a large salt pond. There you can negotiate with one of the local fishermen to take you to **Sandy Island,** studded with palms, just 20 minutes from port. You can also go farther out to Prickly Pear Cay, stretching like a sweeping arc all the way to a sand spit populated by sea birds and rusty-brown pelicans.

Other good beaches include Shoal Bay, which apart from its silver sands boasts some of Anguilla's best coral gardens, the habitat of hundreds of tiny fish with iridescent, brilliantly colored markings. Crocus Bay is a long, golden beach, where a fisherman might take you out in search of snapper or grouper, or ferry you to such wee islands as Little Scrub.

At Island Harbour's horseshoe bay, fishermen bring in the lobster catch. On the beach they caulk colorful boats and mend their nets. You'll want to take plenty of pictures. Schooners are built on the shore at this hamlet, which lies at the east end of the island.

Boat trips can also be arranged to **Sombrero Island,** 38 miles northwest of Anguilla. This mysterious island, with its lone lighthouse, is 400 yards wide at its broadest point, three-quarters of a mile in length. Phosphate miners abandoned it in 1890; and limestone rocks, now eroded, rise in cliffs around the island. The treeless, waterless terrain evokes a moonscape. Once an 1869 lighthouse which stood here served the ships of the world.

Anguilla used to be for the adventurous explorer, attracted by its unspoiled nature. With the opening of some super-deluxe (and super-expensive) hotels, however, Anguilla in the 1980s was suddenly "discovered," becoming one of the most chic targets in the Caribbean. And it is its very isolation that attracts them.

One of Anguilla's most festive, and certainly most colorful, annual festivals is **Carnival,** held jointly under the auspices of the Ministries of Culture and of Tourism. The island's people display the culture, drama, creativity, and love of their land in a burst of fun. The festival begins on the Friday before the first Monday in August, lasting one week. Carnival harks back to Emancipation Day, or August Monday as it's called, when all enslaved Africans were freed.

GETTING THERE: International airports serving Anguilla are San Juan, Dutch St. Maarten, St. Kitts, Antigua, and St. Thomas. Anguilla is served by more than 50 scheduled flights per week in addition to charter flights and extra sections. The coming of **American Eagle** service from San Juan to Anguilla in 1987 signaled a new day in tourism for the island. American Eagle is the commuter partner of American Airlines in the Caribbean. The airline offers nonstop service to Anguilla on 19-seat Casa aircraft from its modern airline hub in San Juan, leaving Puerto Rico daily at 2:05 and 8:45 p.m. Return flights from Anguilla depart for San Juan at 9:15 a.m. and 4 p.m. But all flight schedules are subject to change, so check with the airline or a travel agent. The 2:05 p.m. flight from San Juan is particularly recommended, as it connects with American Airlines flights from the entire east coast of the U.S. as well as from Montréal and Toronto.

If you're already in Dutch St. Maarten, you may want to consider one of the three scheduled flights a day on **Windward Islands Airways International (Winair).** This little airline, formed in 1961, usually flies Twin Otters. It is an easy and convenient connection.

Several other airlines also provide service. **Air BVI** wings in on three scheduled flights weekly from San Juan, and **LIAT** has five scheduled flights weekly from St. Kitts and three from Antigua. St. Thomas is another gateway. Air BVI operates three scheduled flights a week from St. Thomas to Anguilla, but more convenient connections are available on Winair, which has daily scheduled flights from St. Thomas to Anguilla.

Air Anguilla and **Tyden Air** are air taxi services offering several daily flights to Anguilla from Dutch St. Maarten, St. Thomas, Tortola, and St. Kitts. Charters are available on both carriers. Flying time from St. Maarten to Anguilla is seven minutes, from San Juan and Antigua one hour, from St. Thomas 45 minutes, and from St. Kitts 30 minutes.

Ferries leave the ports of Marigot Bay, French St. Martin, and Blowing Point, Anguilla, at approximately 45-minute intervals Sunday to Friday. The first ferry leaves St. Martin at 8:10 a.m. and the last at 5:40 p.m. From Blowing Point, the first ferry leaves at 7:30 a.m. and the last at 5 p.m. Saturday ferries depart at half-hour intervals. There are two night ferries at 7 and 10:45 p.m. The one-way fare for a day ferry is $8, rising to $12 for a night ferry. There is a $1.50 departure tax. No reservations are necessary.

GETTING AROUND: The best way to see the island is a **taxi** tour. In about two hours, one of the local drivers (all of them are guides) will show you everything. A driver costs about $40 for this service. If you're visiting just for the day (as most sightseers do), you can be let off at your favorite beach after a look around, then picked up and returned to the airport in time to catch your flight back to wherever.

To explore the island, it's best to **rent a car.** There are many rental agencies on the island which can issue temporary drivers' licenses. These are also issued at police headquarters in The Valley and at ports of entry, costing about $6. To qualify for this local driver's license, you must possess a valid license from your home country. The temporary license is good for three months. *Remember to drive on the left.*

Many visitors prefer the independence that only their own car can bring. **Budget Rent-a-Car** might be the best bet for a trouble-free car rental. You can make an advance reservation from North America before you leave home (tel. toll free 800/527-0700). Rentals are available by the day, although they usually work out to be less expensive if you keep the car for a full week. Local taxi unions prevent any car-rental company from maintaining an office at the airport, so you'll have to take a taxi to Budget's headquarters in a concrete building at the Quarter (tel. 809/497-2217).

Drivers must be at least 21 years old to rent a car, and they must present a valid U.S. driver's license and either a credit card or a cash deposit. More adventurous drivers consider a Mini-Moke as the most dashing possibility, with its powerful engine and open body not unlike an army Jeep. They rent for $214 per week, with unlimited mileage. More conservative cars, with sides, such as a Hyundai Pony with manual transmission, rent for about $146 per week. The same car with air conditioning costs only $16 more weekly. Rental of any of Budget's cars carries the understanding that you'll pay all damages if there's any damage to the vehicle. To lessen the responsibility, you can purchase an insurance policy (known as a collision damage waiver) that reduces your financial responsibility to $500 if there's an accident. It costs around $5 per day.

If you'd prefer, you can rent an automatic- or standard-shift car from **Connor's Car Rental,** P.O. Box 65, South Hill, Anguilla, B.W.I. (tel. 809/497-6433). Daily rates are $30 to $50 (the more expensive tariff is for air conditioning). Mileage is unlimited, but gas is extra. For reservations, write to Maurice Connor at the address given. Don't be surprised to find a vintage Japanese car waiting, as Connor's 57 cars are Toyotas, Hondas, and Isuzus.

PRACTICAL FACTS: Although the islands categorized as the British Leewards have many similarities because of their long British heritage, there are some points of information that may help you settle into and enjoy Anguilla.

Currency: The Eastern Caribbean dollar is the official currency of Anguilla, although U.S. dollars are widely circulated. There are four banks in Anguilla, and the official exchange rate is EC$2.70 to $1 (U.S.), or 37¢ to EC$1.

Customs: Duties are levied on goods imported into the island at varying rates: from 5% on foodstuffs to 30% on luxury goods, wines, and liquors.

Documents: Visitors to Anguilla require a valid passport or other form of identification bearing a photograph. All visitors must have an onward or return ticket.

Electricity: Except in The Valley area, electricity is provided by privately owned generators. Current is 110/220 volts.

Holidays: Special holidays include Anguilla Day (May 30), August Monday (the first Monday in August), August Thursday (the Thursday after August Monday), Constitution Day, (the Friday after August Monday), and Separation Day (December 19).

Information: Tourist information is available at the **Anguilla Department of Tourism,** P.O. Box 104, The Valley, Anguilla, B.W.I. (tel. 809/497-2759). In the U.S., the **Anguilla Tourist Information Office** is at 1208 Washington Dr., Centerport, NY 11721 (tel. 516/673-0150). Information is also available in Manhattan by calling 212/869-0402. The **Anguilla Hotel and Tourism Association,** P.O. Box 104, The Valley, can be reached by calling 809/497-2944.

Medical care: In medical services, there is a **Cottage Hospital,** The Valley (tel. 809/497-2551), plus several district clinics.

Police: Crime is not a problem in Anguilla. If you do need to call the police, however, telephone police headquarters in The Valley (tel. 809/497-2333) or the substation at Sandy Ground (tel. 809/497-2354).

Post Office: The main post office (tel. 809/497-2528) is in the Valley. Collectors consider Anguilla's stamps valuable, and the post office there also operates a philatelic bureau. Hours are 8 a.m. to noon and 1 to 3:30 p.m. Monday through Friday, and 8 a.m. to noon on Saturday. Hotel owners on Anguilla have told me that mail directed to them often ends up (for reasons known only to postal authorities) in either Bombay, India, or Sydney, Australia.

Radio: A daily broadcast service is provided by **Radio Anguilla,** which operates on a frequency of 1505 kHz (200 meters) with a power of 1,000 watts.

Taxes: The government collects a departure tax of EC$8 ($2.96) if you go by air and an 8% tax on rooms.

Telecommunications: Telephone, cable, and Telex services are offered by Cable and Wireless (W.1) Ltd. Calls can be placed direct from the U.S. (dial 809/497 plus four digits) and may be made 24 hours a day. The company's hours are 7:30 a.m. to 10:30 p.m. weekdays, from 10 a.m. to 8 p.m. Sunday.

Time: Anguilla is four hours behind Greenwich Mean Time and one hour ahead of Eastern Standard Time.

Weather: The hottest months in Anguilla are from July to October; the coolest, from December to February. The mean monthly temperature is about 80° Fahrenheit.

ACCOMMODATIONS: Sleepy Anguilla has awakened to tourism, but the island still has a long way to go. In fact, it definitely doesn't want to become another Dutch St. Maarten. Development is being controlled. Some of the resorts recommended below are still under construction. Villas and cottages are being added. Most of the operations are small and informal, and there's more than just a "touch of class" as well, as reflected by the elegant and expensive resorts with which I'll lead off. *Don't forget:* An 8% government tax will be added to your hotel bill, plus in most 10% for service.

The Deluxe Choices

Cap Juluca, Maunday Bay, P.O. Box 240, Anguilla, B.W.I. (tel. 809/497-6779), is the creation of Sue and Robin Ricketts, who also co-developed Malliouhana (see next listing). Occupying a 179-acre site on the island's best beach, Cap Juluca quickly moved to the forefront of Caribbean properties. The villas are a happy blend of West Indian and Mediterranean styling, and each unit is designed to take advantage of the trade winds. It also has the best restaurant on the island, Pimms (see listing). Named after the rainbow god of the Arawak Indians, Juluca, the resort currently offers 18 spacious units which can be divided into deluxe doubles, one- or two-bedroom suites, or, if you're very rich, rented as private houses. The units front the beach and grant their privileged guests privacy, comfort, and elegance, even if a visitor is a movie star (many are).

Of course, all the expected amenities are here, including air conditioning (or ceiling fans if you prefer), mini-bars, safety deposit boxes, ice-makers, and king-size beds. Marbled and mirrored bathrooms are spacious, each set in a landscaped garden. A continental breakfast is served daily on your terrace. Depending on the accommodation, two persons in winter pay from $250 daily in a beachfront luxury double to $625 for a beachfront suite with two adjoining bedrooms, a sitting/dining room, kitchenette, three baths, dressing room, covered terrace, and open patio or roof sun terrace. Beachfront villas are available at much higher prices. *In summer, the cheapest double rents for $150 daily, beachfront suites costing $440.* Water sports are offered, including waterskiing, fishing, windsurfing, Sunfish sailing, and snorkeling. One championship tennis court was open at presstime, but more are to come.

Malliouhana, P.O. Box 173, Meads Bay, Anguilla, B.W.I. (tel. 809/497-6111), is named for the Carib Indian word for Anguilla, but that's all that is primitive about this deluxe and glamorous hotel. A surprise in "sleepy" Anguilla, this is one of the few places in the Caribbean basin where you will be coddled in such splendor and comfort—for a price, of course. Everywhere you go, you see burnished mahogany, enough that it probably required the destruction of a small forest to provide. The many examples of sophisticated Haitian art were chosen by the famed "Boston Brahmin" decorator, Lawrence Carleton Peabody II. Some of my favorites are the oversize triptychs by a Haiti-born artist named Brésil.

The hotel has 51 bedrooms and suites distributed among the main buildings and outlying villas. They're set in the center of 25 arid acres and two miles of white sand beaches. Each room has expanses of closets crafted from Brazilian walnut and mahogany, spacious bathrooms of marble, tropical furnishings, and wide private verandas. Each of the villas can be rented as a single unit or subdivided into three comfortable accommodations. Now the bad news: You must pay the piper. In high season, rooms rent for $400 daily, single or double occupancy. Suites for two begin at $450 per day, stretching up to as much as $1,450 per day for an entire villa. *In the off-season, singles or doubles cost from $200 daily, with suites for two beginning at $250 per day.* These prices are EP. There's a water-sports center, plus three tennis courts. The food is appropriately good and described separately.

Coccoloba Plantation, P.O. Box 332, Barnes Bay, Anguilla, B.W.I. (tel. 809/497-6871), is one of the top resorts in this part of the Caribbean, a 51-room honey set on 30 acres of land overlooking two of the finest beaches on the island. The Caribbean feeling is achieved here with clear, bright colors, as seen in the air-conditioned detached private villas, all of which have a good ocean view, with such luxury touches as an oversize bathroom and a step-up bedroom with two double beds. Only 20 minutes from the airport, the resort is justly proud of its cuisine, which has been called a celebration "of the natural gifts of the Caribbean." Guests are tempted by the Caribbean/Créole and French-American cuisine. The emphasis is on fish and shellfish.

Before booking, ask your agent about tennis, honeymoon, and family plans. Otherwise, *single or double occupancy from April 15 to November 3 costs $160 to $210 daily, rising in shoulder season (November 4 to December 15) to $290 to $330 daily.* In winter, single or double occupancy costs $290 to $375 daily. A suite is more expensive. The resort has a freshwater Olympic pool and adjacent Jacuzzi with a swim-up bar. In addition to tennis on two Omni courts, both lit at night, Coccoloba offers deep-sea fishing, sunset cruise trips, and nearby waterskiing. For reservations and information, contact Resorts Management toll free at 800/225-4255 (in New York, 212/696-4566).

First-Class Selections

The Mariners, Road Bay, P.O. Box 139, Sandy Ground, Anguilla, B.W.I. (tel. 809/497-2671), is the kind of place a vacationer may be tempted to return to again and again. It occupies a flat sandy area beside an isolated beach whose access road winds between flowering shrubs and hillocks. Accommodations are contained in three two-story buildings and cottages delightfully embellished with gingerbread. All of the 51 rooms have ceiling fans, modern tile baths, and decor reminiscent of New England summer cottages in the 1930s. Singles cost $150 to $170 daily in winter, doubles renting for $180 to $190, and one-bedroom suites suitable for four persons go for $285. *In summer, the price of singles is $120 to $125 daily, with doubles costing $130 to $135, and one bedroom suites renting for $240.* MAP is an additional $45 per person per day. The resort's restaurant is recommended separately. There are two tennis courts, lit at night. For information and reservations, contact the Mariners Reservation Office, P.O. Box 756, Lewisville, AR 71845 (tel. toll free 800/223-0079; in Arkansas or Alaska, 501/921-4237.

Cul de Sac, Blowing Point, Anguilla, B.W.I. (tel. 809/497-6461), advertises itself as a place for those who seek "sun, sea, and tranquility." You get all that and a lot more around here. There are six handsomely appointed and beautifully decorated studio apartments perched on the Caribbean at Blowing Point overlooking the mountains of St. Maarten. Each apartment has a bedroom/sitting room, bathroom, and kitchen/dining room with a large terrace opening onto the sea. In the winter, a studio cottage rents for $150 to $185 daily, EP; *the tariff drops to $135 daily for two people in summer.* There is full maid service. A swimming pool opens onto those mountains of St. Maarten already referred to. There is, as well, a private beach with a jetty, known for its snorkeling possibilities. Guests at Cul de Sac can spend a lazy morning in the swimming pool placed in a garden setting, later enjoying a champagne and lobster picnic at one of the offshore cays. The food at Cul de Sac is among the best on the island. It is also an entertainment center. An added advantage is that guests of Cul de Sac are entitled to enjoy the same benefits as the pampered residents of Malliouhana.

Cinnamon Reef Beach Club, Little Harbour, Anguilla, B.W.I. (tel. 809/497-2727 or toll free 800/223-1108), is one of the most sophisticated resorts in the British Leewards. Ringed with plants, its architectural style is a combination of ultramodern lines with a vaguely Moorish motif. Accommodations are contained in white stucco villas, the porticos of which are pierced by enormous portholes and large archways leading onto private terraces. Inside the units, guests climb several steps to reach the well-appointed bedrooms and dressing rooms, which look down on a spacious living room filled with comfortable furniture. Ample quantities of water—both hot and cold—are available, since a giant cistern is part of the property. Since there are only 18 accommodations (garden suites, beach suites, and villas), guests have the feeling of being in a wealthy private home, a feeling enhanced by the ministrations of the manager, Mike Emmanuel, the owner. Winter rates on the EP range from $200 per couple in a garden suite to $275 per couple in a villa. *Summer prices per couple run $100 to $150 EP, and November 1 to mid-December, couples pay $150 to $200.* The supplement for MAP is $40 per person. Children under 12 are not accepted at the club.

The dining room and bar areas are the focal points of this glamorous retreat, which has already attracted celebrities. The views over the veranda are of the reef-sheltered harbor where boats ride at anchor. Some form of live entertainment and occasional dancing is offered at night. On the premises is a freshwater rectangular pool big enough to swim laps in, two championship tennis courts, free sailboats, paddleboats, snorkeling equipment, windsurfers, and fishing equipment for the use of guests. Scuba-diving can also be arranged. The beach, sheltered by a reef, has tons and tons of fine coral sand which marine geologists pumped in over many seasons.

Anguilla Great House, P.O. Box 157, Rendezvous Bay, Anguilla, B.W.I. (tel. 809/497-6061), offers a luxuriously modernized form of West Indian hospitality, in buildings constructed in a typical Anguillan style with gingerbread trim and painted shutters. A gracious informality pervades the place. Cooled by ceiling fans, the bedrooms have either twin or queen-size beds and are well appointed, decorated in a traditional style with Victorian reproductions made in Jamaica. All accommodations open onto their own verandas. They are classified as standard rooms, studios, and suites, on a rising price scale. *In summer, singles cost $105 to $215 daily, with doubles going for $115 to $295.* In winter, singles rent for $160 to $300 daily, with doubles costing $185 to $300. The higher prices are for two-bedroom suites. Some suites have their own living rooms and dining areas, plus fully equipped kitchenettes. Guests enjoy food at the Great House Beach Bar & Restaurant, where both West Indian and a continental cuisine are served. A variety of water sports can be arranged.

The Budget Range

Rendezvous Bay Hotel, P.O. Box 31, Anguilla, B.W.I. (tel. 809/497-6549), surrounded by a buffer of its own 60 coconut-covered acres, is an unpretentious resort that was the first hotel to open on the island, back in 1962. It sits on one of the most beautiful bays in the Caribbean, its sweep of shoreline having hardly any indentations or protrusions as seen from the hotel's concrete jetty. French cannons, retrieved from their watery graves occupied since the 17th-century battle of Rendezvous Bay, dot the surrounding garden. Most of the accommodations are in the cement, motel-like annexes set amid a forest of tropical trees. Seven two- and three-bedroom villas on the beach are the most recent additions. On the MAP, singles cost $105 daily in winter, with doubles priced at

$135. *Summer rates are $65 daily in a single, $95 in a double, all MAP.* When you're ready to socialize, head for the deep and wide porch in front of the dining room. Its concrete overhang is supported by stout columns that barely interrupt the almost constant breeze. Filled with rickety furniture, this porch is the preferred hangout of Jeremiah Gumbs, the Anguilla-born patriarch-proprietor. He and his wife, Lydia, created their dream from a tropical wilderness many years ago. Even though there are many grander addresses on the island, and a lot more expensive choices, many faithful guests still prefer the Rendezvous.

Guesthouses (The Best Buys)

Inter-Island Guest House, Lower South Hill, Anguilla, B.W.I. (tel. 809/ 497-6259), is a two-story residential style villa with upper and lower covered verandas, overlooking the sea and neighboring French St. Martin. It lies some three miles from the beach at Sandy Ground. You'll definitely need a car. The guest house offers about a dozen simple but comfortable bedrooms, each with a private bath. Everything is kept sparkling clean. *In summer, singles cost only $25 a day MAP, and doubles go for $40.* Winter prices for MAP are $35 daily in singles, rising to $50 in doubles. They also rent one- and two-bedroom apartments. The food is a good West Indian cuisine, with freshly caught fish.

Lloyd's Guesthouse, The Valley, P.O. Box 52, Anguilla, B.W.I. (tel. 809/ 497-2351), is a simple Anguillan guest house named for a local politician David Lloyd, the founder of this place, who represented Anguilla when his country was part of a federation with St. Kitts and Nevis. Guests are welcomed into a family home with a quiet, congenial atmosphere, where 14 modestly furnished bedrooms are rented. *In summer, singles cost $40 daily, doubles going for $64, all MAP.* Charges in winter, also MAP, are $45 in a single, $65 in a double. Boats can be arranged for waterskiing and fishing.

Apartments and Villas

Carimar Beach Club, P.O. Box 327, Anguilla, B.W.I. (tel. 809/497-6881), opens onto beautiful Meads Bay. It's considered the best of the small apartment hotels on the island, where you get the privacy of an apartment, yet some of the comforts of a hotel. The 23 well-appointed units are in two-story Mediterranean-style villas, each with a large living room, dining area, and patio or balcony overlooking the sea. *In summer, a one-bedroom apartment for two people rents for $200 daily, costing five guests $250 in a two-bedroom accommodation, while six people pay $375 in a three-bedroom unit.* These tariffs go up in winter: $260 daily for two, $350 for five, and $525 for six people. For dinner, if you can afford it, you can go over to the deluxe Malliouhana nearby for a gourmet French meal.

Sunshine Villas in Anguilla, P.O. Box 142, Anguilla, B.W.I. (tel. 809/ 497-6149, or 215/565-3462 in the U.S.), is a widely scattered collection of elegant villas organized into one rental pool by the entrepreneurial skill of a team of Canadian expatriates, Jim and Judy Henderson. Currently they have keys and access to several houses, each of which has a set of its own particular virtues. If you write to them, the Hendersons will send detailed information and sometimes photos, even a videotape, advertising special features of this villa or that. Each comes with daily maid service. Daily rentals for two usually range from $120 to $300, depending on the size and location.

The Seahorse, P.O. Box 17, Anguilla, B.W.I. (tel. 809/497-2751), near Shaddick Point on Rendezvous Bay, features five one-bedroom apartments. Each unit is spacious and well furnished, with fully equipped kitchen, bath, and private gallery where you can view the sunset. The apartments are on the water on a small but ideal beach. At water's edge is a barbecue area for outdoor cooking or enjoying a drink. *The weekly rate in summer is $480 for two people,* going up to $620 in winter, rates including maid service.

Easy Corner Villas, P.O. Box 65, South Hill, Anguilla, B.W.I. (tel. 809/497-6433), are owned by Maurice E. Connor, the same man who rents out most of the cars on the island. The 12 one-, two-, and three-bedroom units are in landscaped settings with sunset views from the private porches, and you can also watch sailboats and beach frolickers. All units have full kitchens, combination living-dining rooms, porches, large and airy rooms, ceiling fans, bright and light rattan furniture, and TV. Children over the age of 2 are welcome, and daily maid service is available at an extra charge. *In summer, one-bedroom accommodations for two cost $125 daily, two-bedroom units for four go for $155, and three-bedroom cottages for six, are priced at $195.* In winter, one-bedroom units cost $160, two-bedroom facilities rent for $195, and three-bedroom accommodations go for $240.

WHERE TO DINE: Order spiny lobster if you can get it. It's very good here and invariably fresh (many of the neighboring islands get their lobster from the fishermen of Anguilla). For seafood lovers, there is no end to the enjoyment of the island's specialties, such as crayfish, whelk, yellowtail, and red snapper. But the gustatory delights in Anguilla are not limited to seafood, as the following round-up of restaurants reveals. Home-grown vegetables, such as christophines and yams, accompany many local dinners, with the ubiquitous rice. Of course, the major resorts serve some of the most elegant continental fare in the West Indies.

The Upper Bracket

Pimms, Cap Juluca, Maunday Bay (tel. 809/497-6779), is the most elegant restaurant on Anguilla and one of the best in the Caribbean. It is vaguely Moorish, with a dome soaring over the bar. The tents, arches, and columns may make you think you're in Marrakesh. At Rocky Point, this fashionable rendezvous opens right onto the bay. It is open for lunch daily from noon to 2:30 p.m., when you can order chilled creamy soups, salads, and fresh fish. Or why not have a lobster club sandwich? Lunches cost around $20. The place takes on an added glamor and allure in the evening, serving dinner from 7 to 10 p.m. You can order a special menu degustation at $40. The menu features a tantalizing array of dishes from appetizers such as crab beignet and lobster tabbouleh to main dishes including seafood pot-au-feu and locally caught fish. For dessert, try "The Devil Made Me Do It" mousse. In winter, entertainment is often presented.

Malliouhana Restaurant, Meads Bay (tel. 809/497-6111). Who would ever expect the celebrated Jo Rostang to turn up in such a remote outpost as Anguilla? Monsieur Rostang runs that deluxe citadel of haute cuisine, La Bonne Auberge, at Antibes on the French Riviera. The restaurant's nouvelle cuisine served there is ranked among the best along the Riviera. Mr. Rostang also operates this restaurant at Malliouhana. Admittedly, not all the same ingredients from France are available here. Their cuisine is still very French, but they also provide a Caribbean flair, making use of local ingredients not likely to be found in France. What they do with Anguillan fish, particularly red snapper, is amazing. They also have a French pastry chef who is among the finest in the Caribbean. You get good food, ideal service, and glamorous surroundings. Meals can easily cost $50 and up, particularly with wine. The wine cellar has at least 30,000 carefully selected bottles from which you can make your choice. Reservations are imperative. Plan to make an evening of it. Hours are 12:30 to 3 p.m. and 7 to 10 p.m.

Coccoloba Plantation Restaurant, Coccoloba Plantation Hotel, Barnes

Bay (tel. 809/447-6871), has been targeted by gourmet clients who want to taste the food and wine inspired by the ideas of consultant Jean-Yves Loizance, of Boston's Food and Wine Research Inc. You can visit for lunch daily from 12:30 to 2:30 p.m., when a $25 buffet is featured that is lavish in quantity and quality. Try the exotic fruit sherbets. Dinner, costing from $40, is served nightly from 7 to 9:30, and you can make your selections from an à la carte menu that highlights freshly caught fish and other seafood. Sometimes there is entertainment, but on any night guests can enjoy a light but sophisticated cuisine.

Less Expensive Choices

Hibernia, Sandy Ground (tel. 809/497-3180), is a lovely little spot with a garden setting that might enchant even the most demanding Parisian. It's the personal statement of a French chef, Raoul Rodriguez, and Irish-born Mary Pat O'Hanlon. Whether you start with the conch torte or pasta with smoked salmon and vodka, the choice is likely to be satisfying. Local ingredients, such as freshly caught lobster, go into many of the dishes. Raoul even makes his own bread and ice cream. Meals cost from $30, and the place is open daily from noon to 2:30 p.m. and 7 to 9:30 p.m.

The Mariners, Sandy Ground (tel. 809/497-2671), is one of the neo-Victorian out-buildings of the previously recommended hotel, is a wood-sided restaurant offering a comfortable indoor bar and a naturally ventilated outdoor veranda for dining. Full dinners might include Anguilla fish soup with rouille, Mariners pepperpot soup, filet of beef with peppercorn sauce, and fresh lime cheesecake with cinnamon and coconut crust. Lunches, served daily from noon to 2:30 p.m., cost $15 and up. Dinner, costing from $30, is offered from 7:30 to 9:30 p.m.

Lucy's Harbour View and Restaurant, South Hill (tel. 809/497-6253), not only has the most attractive view on the island, but offers imaginatively prepared food. What makes it special is its owner, Lucy Halley, who lived in the French part of St. Martin, learning many secrets of the cuisine there. She features both French and West Indian cookery, and her place is open seven days a week for lunch and dinner (she closes it when "the last person is served"). The restaurant is placed like a converted home on a cliff, overlooking the salt ponds, with a view of three islands. Lucy has renovated and added to her place so that her 60-seat dining room offers everyone a spectacular view of Sandy Ground and Road Bay. When you call or just arrive, ask Lucy what she has in the larder, or tell her what kind of food you like. If the catch is right, her staff will make a lobster stew. She serves fish filet, grilled lobster, Créole dishes, conch, shrimp, and the island's zestiest curried goat "just like mama made." Meals cost from $15 up. Lunch is served daily from 11:30 a.m. to 3 p.m. and dinner from 6:30 p.m. "until." This is a lively, fun spot, particularly on Tuesday with live entertainment and on Saturday night when a steel band sets the tempo.

Best for the Budget

Barrel Stay Beach Bar & Restaurant, Sandy Ground (tel. 809/497-2831), is open all day, and full meals are served from 11 a.m. to 3 p.m. and 6:30 to 10 p.m., costing $15 and up. A favorite is the fish soup served in the French fashion. The chef is noted for his fresh Anguilla seafood, including lobster, yellowtail, and conch. You can also order prime steaks, smoked ham, and chicken brochette. All dishes are served with a variety of fresh local West Indian vegetables. Desserts include homemade chocolate mousse and French ice cream. A selection of French wines is offered at reasonable prices.

Trader Vic's Beach Bar and Restaurant, Shoal Bay (tel. 809/497-2091), is a breeze-cooled restaurant beside the sands of one of the island's northern beaches, designed somewhat like a big gazebo. Fritz Smith, the friendly owner, opens for the breakfast crowd daily at 7 a.m., remaining open until midnight. You can always drink and snack in the gazebo, which many guests wouldn't think of abandoning in favor of a more formal dining room. However, there is a dining room in a concrete structure, available for more formal meals during the flexible lunch and dinner hours. Menu items include char-broiled lobster, ribs, and hamburgers. Full meals cost $25 to $30. The house lobster is usually caught by Fritz. Live entertainment is presented on the beach on Thursday, Friday, and Sunday from 2 to 5 p.m.

Roy's Place, Crocus Bay (tel. 809/497-2470), has absolutely no chic or elitist characteristics. What you'll find is an extension of the kind of pub you might find in Yorkshire or Devon. Owners Roy and Mandy Bossons come from those two counties of England, so the similarity is only natural. There's an indoor bar which has a constantly busy trade whether the restaurant is full or not. Dining is outside on a covered veranda overlooking the beach, with subdued lighting and music in the evening. Meals cost around $25 and include a wide selection of seafood and meat dishes: lobster soup, fish and chips, conch Créole, and tenderloin steak. Not all dishes listed on the menu will be available on the day of your visit. Lunch is served daily from noon to 2:30 and dinner from 6 to 10 p.m.

Happy Jack's Restaurant, Shoal Bay Villas (tel. 809/497-2051), lies on a white sand beach, with apartments hidden behind a screen of palms and aloe plants. At the edge of the sand, a cabaña-style thatch-roofed restaurant and bar with wooden tables sits on a cement slab. Open daily from 8:30 a.m. to 5 p.m. in low season, from 7:30 a.m. to 10 p.m. in high season, it serves lobster, fish, and conch dinners for $25 each. Lunch costs about half that.

The Old House, George Hill (tel. 809/497-2228), is a pleasant restaurant with a reputation for good food and polite service, occupying a white-fronted plantation-style house overlooking the airport. Built in the 1950s as a private vacation home, the building is today the domain of a dedicated Rotarian and restaurateur, Kenneth Rogers. The place opens for the breakfast trade at 7 a.m. daily, closing its doors at 11 p.m. after a full day spent catering to lunch and dinner crowds. Lunch costs from around $12 and includes fresh preparations of fish Créole, London broil, chef's salad, freshly caught Anguillan pot fish, fish on a bun, and home-style barbecued beef. Dinner, costing from $20, might have among its offerings native lobster, West Indian breast of capon, fresh conch, barbecued steaks, and a limited selection of wine.

SHOPPING: Efforts have been made in recent years to develop handcrafts among the islanders.

The best known is the **Local Gift Shop** in the Quarter (no phone), a tiny little place where every item is homemade. Gifts made of shells are displayed, along with wooden dolls. The hand-crocheted mats are quite beautiful, and tablecloths and bedspreads are woven with awesome patience into spidery lace designs; but many of these are grabbed up by shops on neighboring islands and sold there at high prices. Baskets and mats are made from stripped corn husks and sisal rope. Model schooners and small pond boats are also for sale. Anguillan handcrafts are simple, an emerging industry deserving support.

Judy Henderson's **Sunshine Shop,** P.O. Box 142 (tel. 809/497-6149), co-owned by the already-mentioned Maurice Connor, is in South Hill opposite Connor's Car Rental agency. Judy stocks fine cotton wear, including dresses, coverups, shirts, shorts, and pareos from Thailand.

For men, there are unusual batik shirts and bathing trunks. The shop also has hand-painted wooden items from Bali as well as an assortment of interesting and ingenious silkscreened items and lithographs of island houses, ready to frame when you return Stateside. Look for the large color photographs of the island's famous "Butterfly Wing" boats, postcards, and note cards of island homes. The shop is full of many worthwhile carry-home items and contains a few hidden surprises.

La Romana, at Malliouhana Hotel (tel. 809/497-2111), is a showcase of the best European fashion and jewelry designers, whose products are offered at duty-free prices. Names such as Misani from Milan, La Nouvelle Bague from Florence, Carlo Weingrill, Petochi, and Jolanda Marini are among the fabulous jewelry designers represented. Women's and men's fashions are by Armani, La Perla, Fendi, Chanel, Byblos, and other top figures in the world. The shop is open daily from 9 a.m. to 1 p.m. and 4 to 8 p.m.

Stamp collectors will head for the already-mentioned **Valley Post Office,** The Valley (tel. 809/497-2528), if they want to acquire unusual stamps from Anguilla.

THE SPORTING LIFE: The major activity is swimming and lying on one of Anguilla's magnificent beaches (see the introduction). When you tire of that, the following are recommended:

Water Sports

Most of the coastline of Anguilla is fringed by coral reefs, and the island's waters are rich in marine life. Off the shore are sunken coral gardens and brilliantly colored fish. Fish include the torpedo-headed wrasse, the striped squirrelfish, and the sleek garfish. Conditions for scuba-diving and snorkeling on the island are ideal.

Tamariain Watersports Ltd., P.O. Box 247, The Valley (tel. 809/497-2020), has a shop on the beach at Sandy Ground. It is a PADI five-star training facility and offers a complete line of scuba-diving classes and PADI Certification Courses. They carry several lines of equipment for rent or sale. Deep-sea fishing and day sail charters can also be arranged.

Fishing

Fishing excursions can be made with the local fishermen. Your hotel can make the arrangements for you. You should bring your own tackle. Absolutely agree on the cost, however, before setting out, as some misunderstandings have been reported.

A more organized form of this activity is available at **Tamariain Watersports,** P.O. Box 247, The Valley (tel. 809/497-2020). Here, deep-sea fishing trips can be arranged.

Malliouhana, Meads Bay (tel. 809/497-6111), can also make arrangements for guests to go deep-sea fishing. They also go on day trips to neighboring islands. The deluxe hotel has its own 34-foot cruiser, plus a sailing yacht at its disposal.

Tennis

Malliouhana, Meads Bay (tel. 809/497-6111), has four championship Laykold tennis courts with a tennis pro and shop, with a pro year round.

There are also two courts at **Cinnamon Reef,** Little Harbour (tel. 809/497-2727). The cost to nonresidents is $20 per hour.

ENTERTAINMENT: Of special interest is **Johnno's Beach Bar,** Sandy Ground (tel. 809/497-2728), which is a favorite of Michael J. Fox and other Hollywood grandees who have discovered Anguilla. They, along with regular people, flock to this place during the daytime for its rustic allure. It enjoys somewhat the same style as the famous Basil's Beach Bar on the exclusive island of Mustique in The Grenadines. From 10 a.m. to 6 p.m. daily, you can order a Beck's beer on the beach as well as spare ribs nicely barbecued, grilled chicken, or freshly caught fish. Meals cost from $15. "Jump-up time" is on Friday and Saturday (go after 9 p.m. and stay late) or on Sunday afternoon (hit it around 3 p.m.) when native bands draw an interesting mixture of locals and visitors.

CHAPTER X

DUTCH WINDWARDS IN THE LEEWARDS

□ □ □

1. ST. MAARTEN
2. ST. EUSTATIUS
3. SABA

The Dutch Windwards have the same orientation to the northeast trades as do the British Leewards, documented in the previous chapter. However, the islands of Sint Maarten, Sint Eustatius (called "Statia"), and Saba—no more than dots in the Antilles—are called "The Dutch Windwards." This is confusing to the visitor, but it makes sense in the Netherlands. The Dutch-associated islands of Aruba, Bonaire, and Curaçao, lying off the coast of South America, go by the name of "The Dutch Leewards."

The Windwards in the Leewards were once inhabited by the fierce Carib Indians who believed that one acquired and assimilated the strength of his slain enemy by eating his flesh!

Columbus, on his second voyage to America, is said to have sighted the group of small islands on the name day of San Martino (St. Martin of Tours), hence the present name of Sint ("Saint") Maarten.

Cooled by trade winds, the Windwards are comfortable to visit at any time of the year. The three Windward Islands, along with Bonaire and Curaçao, form the Netherlands Antilles. Aruba is now a separate entity.

1. ST. MAARTEN

It's small, only 37 square miles, about half the area of the District of Columbia. A split-personality island, St. Maarten is half Dutch, half French (who call their part St. Martin).

The divided island is considered the smallest territory in the world shared by two sovereign states (for a preview of St. Martin, refer to Chapter XII on the French West Indies). The only way you know you're crossing an international border is when you see the sign, *"Bienvenue, Partie Française"*—attesting to the peaceful coexistence between the two nations on the island.

The island was divided in 1648, and visitors still ascend Mount Concordia,

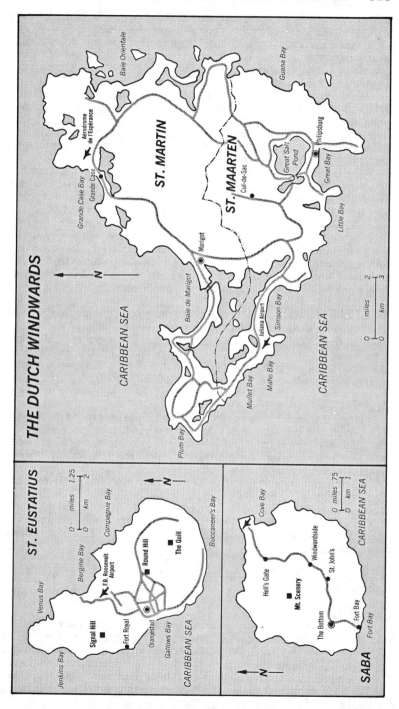

near the border, where agreement was reached. Even so, St. Maarten was to change hands 16 times before becoming permanently Dutch.

Legend has it that a gin-drinking Dutchman and a wine-guzzling Frenchman walked around the island to see how much territory each could earmark for his side in one day. The Frenchman outwalked the Dutchman, but the canny Dutchman got the more valuable piece of property.

Northernmost of the Netherlands Antilles, St. Maarten lies some 150 miles southeast of Puerto Rico. A lush island, rimmed with bays and beaches, it has a year-round temperature of 80° Fahrenheit.

In addition to some 36 beaches—long, languorous coral strands—duty-free shopping and gambling casinos draw visitors to St. Maarten where there has been a rush of hotel building in the past few years.

The Dutch capital, **Philipsburg,** curves like a toy village along Great Bay. The town lies on a narrow sand isthmus separating Great Bay and Great Salt Pond. The capital was founded in 1763 by Commander John Philips, a Scot in Dutch employ. To protect Great Bay, Fort Amsterdam was built in 1737.

The town still retains some of its unique shingled architecture. The main thoroughfare is the traffic-clogged Front Street, stretching for about a mile. It's lined with stores selling international merchandise, such as French designer fashions and Swedish crystal. If you don't find what you want, you can take one of the little lanes, known as *steegjes,* that connect Front Street with Back Street, running parallel to it. Back Street is another shoppers' mart.

GETTING THERE: St. Maarten's airport is the second busiest in the Caribbean after San Juan's. **American Airlines** features one daily nonstop flight to St. Maarten from New York's JFK Airport, as well as four additional daily flights (two from JFK, two others from New Jersey's Newark Airport), that make connections through American's modern hub in San Juan. A network of cities throughout Canada and the U.S., as well as about a dozen islands in the Caribbean, use either New York or San Juan as their primary hubs, so getting to St. Maarten is rarely a problem.

If you stay for between 3 and 21 days, and if you reserve and pay for your ticket seven days in advance, your ticket will cost less. In high season, round-trip passage from New York costs $395 per person on a weekday and $425 on a weekend. Fare options change, of course, with the seasons and the availability of space, so check with American Airlines or a travel agent.

Continental Airlines flies from Newark, New Jersey, to St. Maarten, and **Pan Am** offers service from New York. Some visitors, especially those from the west and southwest find it convenient to connect to St. Maarten through American's Dallas–Fort Worth hub. Passengers originating in Florida often select either **Eastern Airlines** or American Airlines, which both offer flights from Miami to St. Maarten.

GETTING AROUND: Transportation is not difficult, with a variety of methods available.

Taxis

Taxis are unmetered, but St. Maarten law requires drivers to have a list which details fares to major destinations on the island. Typical fares, say, from Juliana Airport to the Mullet Bay Resort and Casino are $4; from Philipsburg to Juliana Airport, $7. There are minimum fares for two passengers, and each additional passenger pays another $1. Passengers are entitled to two pieces of luggage free, and each additional piece is assessed 50¢ extra. Fares are higher by 25% between

10 p.m. and midnight, and 50% higher between midnight and 6 a.m. Even if you're renting a car, taxi regulations require you to take a cab to your hotel, where your car will be delivered.

Buses

This is a reasonable means of transport in St. Maarten if you don't mind inconveniences, and at times overcrowding. The fare is only 85¢, and buses run from 7 a.m. to midnight, serving most of the major locations in St. Maarten. The most popular run is from Philipsburg to Marigot on the French side.

Car Rentals

Unlike some of the islands in the Caribbean, car rentals in St. Maarten are a practical means of transport, particularly if you're staying at an isolated hotel or else on the French side.

Budget Rent-a-Car (the least expensive at press time) maintains a booth at the airport, although because of local regulations the cars are kept at a different place, within a building on Airport Road. After you clear immigration and claim your luggage, a counter attendant at Budget will help you with the necessary forms. St. Maarten law requires that cars be delivered directly to your hotel (a demand of the union of taxi drivers). Most experienced visitors head immediately for their hotel by taxi, bypassing the long lines at the rental kiosks. A phone call to Budget's local office (tel. 011-599-5/44275) will bring an employee to your hotel with the necessary paperwork.

Drivers must be between 21 and 70 years of age and must present a valid driver's license and either a major credit card or a cash deposit. Clients who do not arrange for additional insurance at the time of rental pay up to the first $5,000 worth of damage to a car in the event of an accident. Additional insurance costs around $10 per day.

For the best rates, clients should reserve seven days in advance through Budget's reservations system. In the U.S. the toll-free number is 800/527-0700. The company's least-expensive car in high season (and subject to change) is a manual transmission Suzuki Fronte (without air conditioning), going for $144 per week with unlimited mileage, plus tax. Budget's least expensive car with air conditioning and automatic transmission costs $216 per week, with unlimited mileage, plus tax.

Avis and **Hertz** are also represented on St. Maarten, but charge more for their least expensive cars than Budget. Of course, conditions could change, so we may want to check on their current offerings by calling their toll-free numbers: Hertz at 800/654-3131 and Avis at 800/331-1212.

Drive on the right. International road signs are observed.

Sightseeing Taxi Tours

If you don't want to drive, you can negotiate with a taxi driver who will also serve as your guide. One or two passengers are charged $30 for a 2½-hour tour, and an additional passenger pays around $7.50. For service, call tel. 011-599-5/24019.

PRACTICAL FACTS: A few helpful hints about St. Maarten may make your visit here more pleasurable.

Banks: Most banks are open from 8:30 a.m. to 1 p.m. Monday to Friday, reopening on Friday from 4 to 5 p.m.

Currency: The legal tender is the NAf (guilder), and the official rate at which the banks accept U.S. dollars is $1.79 NAf equals $1. Regardless, U.S. dollars are easily, willingly, and often eagerly accepted in the Dutch Windwards, especially St. Maarten. *Note:* Prices in this chapter are given in U.S. currency unless otherwise designated.

Documents: To enter the Dutch-held side of St. Maarten, U.S. citizens should have proof of citizenship in the form of a passport (preferably valid but not more than five years expired), or else an original birth certificate with a raised seal or a photocopy with a notary seal, or, finally, a voter's registration card. Naturalized citizens may show their naturalization certificate, and resident aliens must provide the alien registration "green" card or a temporary card which allows them to leave and reenter the U.S. All visitors must have a confirmed room reservation before their arrival on the island. A return or ongoing ticket must also be shown.

Electricity: The Dutch side of the island operates on 110 volts AC (60 cycles) of electricity, and chances are, you won't need an adapter (unless you're staying on the French side).

Emergencies: Emergency telephone numbers include the police at 2299 and an ambulance at 2299 also.

Information: If you want information before you go, you can ask at the **St. Maarten Tourist Office,** 275 Seventh Ave., 19th Floor, New York, NY 10001 (tel. 212/989-0000).

Language: Even though the language is officially Dutch, most people speak English.

Medical care: If you need medical assistance, ask at your hotel. There is one hospital (tel. 011-599-5/22300) on the Dutch side and another on the French side.

Taxes and service: A $5 departure tax is charged when you're leaving the island. A 5% government tax is added to hotel bills, and in general, hotels also add a 10% or 15% service charge. Unless service has not been added (unlikely), it is customary to tip around 15% in restaurants.

Telephone: From Dutch St. Maarten, if you want to call French St. Martin, dial 06 plus the French number. It's also possible to dial St. Maarten direct from the United States by using the area code, 011-599-5, then the five-digit local number. However, once you are on the island, use only the last five digits of numbers given below or others called within the Dutch side of the island.

Time: St. Maarten is on **Atlantic Standard Time.** In winter, when the U.S. is on Eastern Standard Time, it will be 6 a.m. in Philipsburg when it's only 5 a.m. in New York. During Daylight Saving Time, the island keeps the same time as the U.S. East Coast.

HOTELS: Hotels in St. Maarten run the gamut—from big-time resort hotels, some with tennis courts and gambling casinos, to motel-like efficiency units where guests prepare their own meals, to simple West Indian guesthouses. (For my selection of inns and hotels on St. Martin, refer to Chapter XII.)

As I mentioned in "Practical Facts" above, a government tax of 5% and a 10% to 15% service charge is likely to be added to your hotel bill. It's wise to ask about this when you book a room, to save yourself a shock when you check out.

Resort Hotels

Mullet Bay Resort & Casino, St. Maarten, N.A. (tel. 011-599-5/42801), has been called "an island within an island." It's so vast and complete, set on 172 acres, that many guests never leave the grounds of this condo-cum-resort hotel. On the westernmost tip of St. Maarten, just a five-minute ride from Juliana Airport, it boasts the island's only golf course, an 18-hole layout designed by Joseph

Lee. It is also a tennis resort, with 14 courts, some of which are lit for night games. During the day, in addition to golf and tennis, water sports are offered, including windsurfing, snorkeling, Sunfish sailing, waterskiing, or swimming in one of the two large pools. At night, there's gambling at Grand Casino at Mullet Bay, plus dancing at Le Club.

Twins and doubles are well furnished and comfortable, but you may prefer a one- or two-bedroom apartment in a one- or two-story building or one of the villas spread across the grounds. All accommodations are air-conditioned and have color TV, phones, and refrigerators. The apartments are especially luxurious, with complete living rooms, patios or balconies, and kitchens. (There's a food market on the grounds.) *Off-season, twin rooms range from $125 to $175 daily. For oceanfront suites, add another $35 per day to the higher tariff. Two persons can rent a one-bedroom suite for $185 to $250 daily.* In winter, twin rooms rent for $205 to $245 daily, with one-bedroom suites going for $285 to $335. The surcharge for one-bedroom, oceanfront units is $50 per day. Of course, far more expensive, spacious, and luxurious accommodations are available for those willing to pay substantially higher tariffs than those quoted here. MAP (breakfast and dinner) costs an additional $45 per person per day year round.

The dining facilities of the resort are exceptional. The Shipwreck and The Deli offer both breakfast and lunch, and there is also Little Italy. The Little Oceanreef features seafood and Créole cookery among other selections. The Frigate offers steaks and salads for dinner, and the Bamboo Garden, open only for dinner, is one of the premier restaurants of St. Maarten, serving cuisines from the four regions of China. Some outstanding packages are available for stays here, ranging from golf to honeymoon, so you might want to inquire about these when you consider booking here. For reservations, call toll free 800/468-5538.

Maho Beach Hotel & Casino, Maho Bay, St. Maarten, N.A. (tel. 001-599-5/42115, 212/969-9220 in New York, or toll free 800/223-0757), opened in a vitally renovated format late in 1985, after more than $15 million had been lavished on its stylish interior. It's set about half a mile from the airport in a greenbelt which seems to showcase its pink-and-white façade. Inside the soaring lobby, a series of gracefully curved laminated beams peak pagoda style into an airy summit. Its Casino Royale is the largest on the island. A hexagonal freshwater pool is surrounded by a tile deck looking out over Maho Bay. A crescent of sandy beach, with water sports, lies at the bottom of the hill. On the premises are a trio of stylish restaurants. One is the Lotus Flower, a branch of the well-known restaurant of that name in San Juan, and another, the Ristorante Roma, has, of course, an Italian cuisine. About a third of the 247 rooms contain kitchenettes, and each has wicker furniture, air conditioning, TV, phone, Italian tiles, and plush upholstery. A few are in a separate cluster near the resort's tennis courts. In winter, depending on the accommodation, singles cost $155 to $235 daily, and doubles go for $175 to $255. *In low season, depending on the time of year, singles rent for $70 to $135 daily and doubles for $80 to $155.*

Le Plage at Royal Islander Club, P.O. Box 2000, Maho Bay, St. Maarten, N.A. (tel. 011-599-5/42388), is a time-share resort operated in part as a luxury hotel, with access to Maho Beach facilities next door. All units face the bay and feature fully furnished one- and two-bedroom apartments with Italian marble floors, balconies, satellite color TV, direct-dial phones, baths, and vanities, as well as fully equipped kitchens with microwave ovens and marble counter tops. The apartments are centrally air-conditioned. In winter, single or double occupancy of a studio or one-bedroom facility costs from $230 to $290 daily. *In summer, prices are $98 to $165 daily for two persons.* In all seasons, more expensive accommodations than those I've cited are rented. A freshwater swimming pool, a car-rental service, and an activities desk are on the premises. Dining facilities, water sports, tennis courts, a casino, disco, nightclub, and shopping arcade are nearby.

Pelican Resort and Casino, P.O. Box 431, Philipsburg, Simpson Bay, St. Maarten, N.A. (tel. 011-599-5/42503, 212/840-6636 in New York City, or toll free 800/223-9815), is a seaside resort whose architectural styles are about as varied as its clientele. The village-style sections are well separated with buffers of bougainvillea and hibiscus. The largest cluster contains only 20 units and, like all the others, is tucked into a hillside, with a sweeping view of the sea. Scattered among the 12 acres are a lily pond, many small waterways, an orchid garden, a Jacuzzi, tennis courts, a swimming pool, 1,400 feet of oceanfront, and a marina. Guests can arrange water sports through the hotel or outside agencies. There's a convenience deli on the premises to make shopping easy, and a casino and restaurant, the Suisse Chalet, add to vacationing pleasure. All accommodations are privately owned and leased through the hotel management to vacationing guests. Each has one or two bedrooms, a kitchen, a 24-hour color TV with satellite reception, a phone, and a cassette tape player. Rates for the accommodations vary widely with the season and the exposure. Guests are required to remain for a minimum of seven nights during the most popular periods of the winter season. In winter, studios for one or two persons range from $150 to $170 daily, with one-bedroom units, again for one or two guests, costing from $170 to $250. *In summer, two persons can stay here in one of the studios for $80 daily, the price going up to $100 and above in a one-bedroom unit.* The hotel has a revitalization center (but more about this later).

Belair Beach Hotel, P.O. Box 140, Philipsburg, St. Maarten, N.A. (tel. 011-599-5/23362), is on Little Bay Beach. One of the most surprising things about this breezy, all-oceanfront hotel is the size of the accommodations, all suites. Each of the suites contains a bedroom and a half, two full baths, a fully equipped kitchen including a microwave oven, satellite color TV, a 21-foot patio or veranda with a sweeping view of the sea, two phones, full air conditioning, and many extras, such as nightly turn-down of beds and fresh-daily beach towels.

EP rates in winter are $245 daily for single or double occupancy, rising to $375 during the peak periods around Christmas and in February. Suites accommodate a maximum of six people, each additional guest sharing the unit paying $30 per day. *Off-season, the charge is from $135 to $165 per day single or double. Each additional person up to the maximum of six per suite, pays $15 per day. Children under 12 are accepted free in off-season.* The Sugar Bird Café serves breakfast, lunch, and dinner in a casual atmosphere. Grocery and gift shops are on the premises, and there are desks for car rental and water sports arrangements. For vacationers who want more activities, the Divi Little Bay Resort & Casino is just a short walk down the beach.

Great Bay Beach Hotel & Casino, P.O. Box 310, Front St., Philipsburg, St. Maarten, N.A. (tel. 011-599-5/22446), is a complete modern resort at the southwestern corner of the Great Bay of downtown Philipsburg. In fact, all the shops and restaurants of the old town are walkable from the hotel. Its five floors of cellular rooms—225 air-conditioned, suitably furnished units—have walk-in closets and tile baths, each with a balcony and view of either the sea or hills. On the grounds are abundant facilities. Near the main building is a terracotta sun terrace, surrounded by palm trees and lounge furniture. At one end set in among the shrubbery is a poolside refreshment area. The main dining room has water-view windows, and features local foods in addition to Stateside cooking plus continental specialties from Great Bay's chef. *Summer EP rates in a single are $75 to $100 daily and $85 to $110 in a double.* In winter, guests are accepted on EP for $140 to $175 daily in a single, $150 to $185 in for two people. Suites are more expensive. Below the swimming pool terrace is a wide sandy beach, and skiing boats can be had at your request. Across the road are tennis courts. There is also a water-sports center on the premises. Saturday evenings are enlivened by a steel band, with calypso entertainment. Many gamblers flock here to one of the important casinos on the island, which has one-arm bandits in addition to roulette and baccarat.

Smaller Resort Hotels

St. Maarten Beach Club Hotel & Casino, P.O. Box 465, Philipsburg, St. Maarten, N.A. (tel. 011-599-5/23434), is ideal for those high-rolling casino-oriented visitors who want to be part of the action. For fun and amusement more than as a tranquil retreat, the hotel boasts the famous Peacock Casino, the only major gaming establishment in the downtown area. The club is actually a condo hotel, broken into two separate sections, each bordering Front Street. One side opens onto the beach, its rooms fronting the harbor of Great Bay. Each accommodation, 78 in all, is a well-furnished and air-conditioned suite, with satellite TV, phone, and daily maid service. Beachview units are the most expensive. One-bedroom accommodations suitable for two persons cost from $125 to $150 daily in winter, with two-bedroom suites suitable for four or even five going for $195 to $250 daily. *Rates are slashed in summer, a one-bedroom unit renting for $69 to $79 daily for one or two persons, a two-bedroom condo for up to four guests costing $110 to $135.*

The club's restaurant, Fandango, is one of the island's most popular, and it serves an American cuisine—dishes include fresh seafood and good beef recipes. There's no time limit on happy hour at the Heartbreak Bar, where two-for-one specials are offered all day, along with free hot and cold hors d'oeuvres.

Dawn Beach Hotel, P.O. Box 389, Oyster Pond, St. Maarten, N.A. (tel. 011-599-5/22929), stands on the Atlantic side of the island, near the Dutch-French border. It cuddles next to a tall mountain at Oyster Pond. The location is about eight miles from Philipsburg, reached by a scenic but twisting road. Each of the 155 individual villas along the beach and on the mountain offers a choice of air conditioning or ceiling fans. *Summer EP rates for two persons range from $90 to $105 daily in a double,* going up in winter to $205 to $295. It's really villa condo living, and the owners of this resort complex have emphasized luxury and style. Beds are big enough to stretch out in and units are equipped with small kitchenettes. A large Bali-style restaurant, capped by a pagoda roof, is a potent lure, serving good meals. There is also a bar on the premises. The Oriental gardens use such Japanese-like touches as a bridge over the swimming pool. Sprawling sea grape trees provide cover from the sun, as do umbrellas around the freshwater pool with a cascading waterfall. The hotel has made many improvements, including two composition tennis courts lit for night play. A water-sports desk will make arrangements for cruising, windsurfing, waterskiing, snorkeling, and sailing, including all-day charters to St. Barts, Saba, and Anguilla. A shuttle to and from Philipsburg operates three times a day.

Divi Little Bay Resort & Casino, P.O. Box 61, Little Bay, St. Maarten, N.A. (tel. 011-599-5/22333), the first of the island's resort hotels, is a very complete resort, with its private 1,000-foot beach, within a short distance of the shops and restaurants of Philipsburg. The hotel opened in 1955 with only 20 rooms, and Queen Juliana, and her husband, Prince Bernhard, were the first guests. Princess Margaret came here on her honeymoon. Other royalty has visited as well, including Queen Beatrix. You'll find everything you might need on the premises, whether it's water sports, a beauty parlor, a Las Vegas–style casino, or a freshwater pool. There are three tennis courts, plus regular local entertainment. At a beach bar, you can order those long, cool, intoxicating drinks, and a snackbar is appealing for a light lunch. Continental dishes, Stateside favorites, and authentic Dutch and West Indian specialties are served in the historic Peter Stuyvesant Lounge opposite the casino. Diners enjoy a candlelit atmosphere with light music for listening or dancing. Guests gather at Le Café to enjoy the disco bar. A late-night coffeeshop, La Primavera, is open from 6 p.m. to 1 a.m. The decor of the bedrooms is warm and inviting, with private bath and terrace or balcony, as well as air conditioning and wall-to-wall carpeting. The best rooms are the beachfront accommodations. *In summer, singles or doubles cost $97 to $159 daily.* Winter prices are $220 to $270 single or double, the higher tariffs for beach-level accommodations. Another $36 per day per person is charged year round for breakfast and dinner.

Treasure Island Hotel & Casino at Cupecoy, P.O. Box 14, St. Maarten, N.A. (tel. 011-599-5/44297). One end of this imaginatively designed resort stands on a rocky bluff above a beach whose edges are dotted with caves. Other accommodations lie across a busy road and stretch up a hillside ablaze with bougainvillea. The resort's focal point is a piazza whose wrap-around arcade evokes a city in southern Europe. In the center, a splashing fountain sets the tone for the Treasure Island casino. The resort's most expensive units lie, of course, near the beach in stylish buildings with sloping roofs. Each of the units contains Caribbean colors, wicker furniture, cable color TV, private bathrooms, and private terraces. The 300 accommodations rent in winter for $125 to $225 daily for two persons. *In summer, accommodations range from $65 to $200 daily for two.* On the premises are tennis courts, a trio of swimming pools (one near the beach and two on the hillside), and a concierge and staff who can help arrange various water sports and outside excursions.

La Vista, Pelican Key Estates, St. Maarten, N.A. (tel. 011-599-5/43005), is one of the golden nuggets of St. Maarten, although it's not well known. The resort offers 24 large and handsomely furnished junior suites, penthouse suites, and what it calls Antillean cottages. Each accommodation opens onto a sea view and contains a kitchenette with the necessary equipment, a generous living and dining area, and a good-size balcony. Other amenities are color cable TV and direct-dial phones. In winter, two persons are charged from $190 to $290 daily, these tariffs raised by $25 daily during Christmas holidays. *In summer, two persons pay from $80 to $135 daily, a bargain considering the style level of this place.* The complex features a freshwater pool and lounge area, as well as an open-air restaurant offering buffet breakfasts and casual lunches. The resort is about a ten-minute drive from Philipsburg, longer if the traffic is heavy.

Holland House, P.O. Box 393, Front St., Philipsburg, St. Maarten, N.A. (tel. 011-599-5/22572), shares the beach and water-sports center with the St. Maarten Beach Club, to which you also retire when you want some casino action. It rents 54 cozy apartments decorated with furnishings from the Netherlands. Each unit contains a tiny kitchenette, ideal for cooking an omelet but not a big dinner. You're right on the beach, where you can order drinks at the bar. An open-air dining terrace fronts Great Bay. Some people like it, and maybe you will too. You're certainly near everything, including all the major restaurants and shops of Philipsburg. EP rates in a double in winter are $125 to $145 daily, singles paying $110 to $130. *Summer tariffs are $88 to $90 daily for a double room EP, and $72 to $83 for a single.* Even if you're not staying here, you might want to call and reserve a table for dinner. This is one of the few hotels that serves authentic Dutch specialties.

Inns of Character

Oyster Pond Yacht Club, P.O. Box 239, St. Maarten, N.A. (tel 011-599-5/22206), is splendidly chic, a Caribbean Shangri-La, eight miles from Philipsburg, reached by a twisting, scenic road. On the windward side of the island, a circular harbor on the eastern shore near the French border, the fortress-like structure stands guard over a 35-acre protected marina. Catering to a select clientele, it is not unlike a small parador in southern Spain, unflawed in architecture and decoration. With its own harbor for yachts, it also has a private half-moon sandy beach reached by passing along beautiful landscaped grounds. There is also a swimming pool 44 feet by 22 feet, decorated with blue and gray French tiles. Its central courtyard is open to the skies, and the living room, also al fresco, has an elegant touch, with white wicker, fine paintings, an understatement of good taste. Off the courtyard, and opening onto the sea, is a bar/lounge, as warm and comfortable as one's private home. The dining room is exceptional, the chef turning out a well-prepared continental cuisine intermixed with some Créole dishes. The service is superb, and the tables are set with the finest of china and linen. All dining is à la carte. After dinner, guests sip coffee on the outer terrace under palm trees, watching the sea and listening to the waves crash against the cliff.

The hotel is furnished in part with nautical antiques, mostly white wicker, like a great country house. It offers only 20 rooms, and these are accommodations of character. Some are duplexes, and the decoration is often in the West Indian buccaneer style. Bedrooms open onto arches with a wooden balustraded balcony overlooking the pond or sea. In winter, two persons can stay here in units ranging from standard to deluxe at prices going from $330 to $350 daily. The most elegant accommodations are the tower suites, costing $370 daily for two persons. *In off-season, two persons are charged $190 to $210 daily with tower suites for two renting for $230.*

Caravanserai, P.O. Box 113, Maho Bay, St. Maarten, N.A. (tel. 011-599-5/44214), is an elegant oasis on its private coral promontory close to the airport, six miles west of Philipsburg. An occasional jet lands or takes off, but otherwise it's quiet around here. A long time ago, it was the creation of an exiled New Yorker, Dave Crane, who turned it into one of the most urbane inns in the West Indies. Both Juliana and Beatrix, from the Dutch royal family, have stayed here. The architecture utilizes natural woods and stone, with moorish arches, wooden frame octagonal structures, all decorated with tropical furnishings such as peacock bamboo and rattan chairs. There are two tennis courts, every kind of water sport, a private beach, and two swimming pools. The larger pool opens onto a long, arched loggia, where you can have an American breakfast or an evening meal. The cuisine is international. The octagonal peak-roofed Ocean View bar is on the tip of the promontory. Accommodations come in a wide range—one-bedroom apartments and studios facing the Caribbean, 15 superior rooms also facing the sea, and 5 standards opening onto the courtyard, plus a quartet of villas, ideal for lovers. In winter, rooms rent for $205 to $280 daily, either single or double. *In summer, prices for either single or double occupancy are $115 daily in a standard bedroom, $215 in a studio.*

Mary's Boon, P.O. Box 2078, Simpson Bay, St. Maarten, N.A. (tel. 011-599-5/44235), really a small casual inn, is a string of 12 oversize apartments with kitchenettes designed as private villas, with personalized style, directly on a three-mile sandy beach, just south of the Juliana Airport and 15 minutes from Philipsburg. It's near the airport, but big planes are rare, and when they do land, they do so only in the daytime. There's a dining gallery fronting Simpson Bay in case you decide to take the half-board arrangement. The cuisine is Dutch-French West Indian. In the bar you fix your own drinks on the honor system. The rooms are done in rattan and wicker, louvered windows open to sea breezes, and there is an occasional tile and flagstone antique floor. Most of the rooms are in separate cottages, but there are two units in the main house. The efficiencies have ceiling fans. *On the EP, two persons are charged $75 daily in summer.* Rates go up in winter to $130 daily. Rooms are rented only to two guests—no third parties. No children under 16 are accepted.

Pasanggrahan, P.O. Box 151, Front St., Philipsburg, St. Maarten, N.A. (tel. 011-599-5/23588), is the Indonesian word for guesthouse, and this one maintains a clientele which favors old-style West Indian living. It's a marvelous bargain in high-priced St. Maarten. A small, charming, informal guesthouse, it's right on the busy, narrow main street of Philipsburg. It's set back under tall trees, with a building-wide white wooden veranda. The interior still has many old features, such as peacock bamboo chairs, a pair of Indian spool tables, and a gilt-framed oil portrait of Queen Wilhelmina. In fact, so many guests asked to see the bedroom where the queen and her daughter, Juliana, stayed in World War II that the management turned it into the Sydney Greenstreet Bar. Set among the wild jungle of knep trees, coconut palms, and flowering shrubbery, is the dining area, Sarai Seaside Restaurant, named after the daughter of the owner, Oli de Zela. She brings remarkable charm and graciousness to the running of this property, which dates from 1905. Even if you aren't staying here but want a "breath of fresh air," a retreat from the shoppers' mall of Front Street, you might enjoy a reasonably priced meal here. Service is from 11:30 a.m. to 4 p.m. and 6:30 to 11 p.m. daily. You reach the private beach, only 50 feet away, through the jungle filled with hummingbirds, yellowbirds, and mockingbirds. There are 30 newly renovated bedrooms with king-size beds and beautiful Saban bedspreads, each with a private bath, some in the main building, others in an adjoining annex. All accommodations have ceiling fans, and air conditioning is available. *In summer, singles and doubles range in price from $64 to $82 daily, including breakfast.* In winter, tariffs range from $95 to $125 daily in a single or double. MAP costs another $30 per person daily.

Efficiency Units and Guesthouses

Horny Toad Guest House, Butterfish Road, P.O. Box 397, St. Maarten, N.A. (tel. 011-599-5/44323), was once an island governor's residence. The present owners, Betty and Earle Vaughan, continue the tradition of hospitality found there in former days: hosts and guests are soon on a first-name basis. What you get here for your money makes it desirable, as it opens directly onto the beach at Simpson Bay. The second floor of their white frame building has an encircling covered West Indies balcony, and their efficiency units, eight in all, have kitchen areas and private baths. Two have separate bedrooms housing three guests per unit. Daily maid service is included. Everything is casual. *In summer, the efficiencies rent for $95 daily. EP, double occupancy.* In winter, double or single occupancy costs $165. An extra person is charged $35 per day year round. *Note:* The guesthouse is near the airfield and does have noisy moments. To make reservations before traveling to the island, get in touch with Betty and Dave Harvey, 7 Warren St., Winchester, MA 01890 (tel. 617/729-3171).

The Beach House, P.O. Box 211, 160 Front St., Philipsburg, St. Maarten, N.A. (tel. 011/599-5/22456), is a little eight-unit guesthouse, one minute from the windward beach at Great Bay. One-bedroom, air-conditioned apartments, with fully equipped kitchenettes, daily maid service, and private balconies, are furnished in a simplified Caribbean motif. *In summer, a single person pays $42 daily, with two persons charged $48 to $58.* In winter, single or double occupancy costs $85 to $95 daily. Several of the best restaurants of St. Maarten are virtually at your doorstep.

The Town House Villas, 175 Front St., P.O. Box 347, Philipsburg, St. Maarten, N.A. (tel. 011-599-5/22898), is a group of ten two-story apartments at the edge of the restaurant and shopping district of Philipsburg. At your doorstep is Great Bay Beach, dotted with palms—it's all shut off from the main street by a rugged stone wall and a wrought-iron gate. The town houses are handsome, rather formal with slanted shingled mansard roofs, and set-in second-floor windows. Each apartment has two large bedrooms and 1½ baths. There's a completely equipped kitchen, plus raised dining area in the long and well-furnished living room. Wide glass doors open onto a private terrace with lounge chairs. Whether dining or having conversation in the living room or drinks on your terrace, you can enjoy a view of the bay. *In summer, two persons pay $80 daily, with three or four persons paying $100.* In winter, up to four persons can rent one of these units for $175 per day.

RESTAURANTS: Half-Dutch, half-French St. Maarten/St. Martin has dozens of good international restaurants, and visitors on each side must decide each night if they want to "cross the border" to dine. Specialties range from Créole through continental, with a decided French accent. Dutch cooking is harder to come by.

Upper Bracket Dining
L'Escargot, 84 Front St. (tel. 011-599-5/22483), is my favorite French bistro, right in the heart of Philipsburg where the competition is keen. It's perched in a gaily decorated 100-year-old Antillean house, with a red tin roof, celebrating its namesake by serving snails in pâté à choux, with mushrooms, in omelets, or in the more traditional escargots à la provençale. For good-tasting *bonne cuisine française,* and some of the nicest, friendliest people around, you'll do well here, and the prices, although not cheap, seem reasonable to most diners. If you arrive before your reservation, you can relax in the bar to your left before being shown to your candlelit table. Not one bit of space is undecorated, and the decor may appear too gimmicky to some. But that shouldn't make you suspicious of the food. It's first rate—caviar blinis, duck in a pineapple and banana sauce, snapper in papillotte, lobster thermidor, coq au vin. If you can still manage it after all that, the waiter will serve you a chocolate mousse to finish your repast, which should cost from $43. In season, reservations are necessary. It is open daily from 11:30 a.m. to 2:30 p.m. and 6:30 p.m. to "very late," perhaps 11:30 p.m. in season.

Antoine's, Front St. (tel. 011-599-5/22964), offers *la belle cuisine* in an atmospheric building next to the Little Pier in the center of Philipsburg. Wear your casual-chic resort wear here at night and be sure to make a reservation in season. You can enjoy an apéritif in the cocktail bar. If the crowd is right (usually in winter), Antoine's takes on worldly sophistication, and the staff will prove that you don't have to cross the border for impressive wines, top-quality service, and a long list of Gallic specialties. Fresh local fish is always available, but well-sauced beef and chicken dishes are also served, at a cost of around $40 for dinner, perhaps $20 for lunch. Every restaurant owner seems to specialize in the increasingly hard-to-get lobster, and Antoine's is no exception. The spiny Caribbean langouste is regularly featured and well prepared. Other main dishes are likely to include frogs' legs in garlic butter, grouper in cream and white wine sauce, and escalope of veal dijonnaise. Hours are from 11:30 a.m. to 4 p.m. and 6:30 to 11 p.m. daily.

The Red Snapper, 93 Front St. (tel. 011-599-5/23834), is one of the premier restaurants of Philipsburg. Operated by Antoine's (see previous recommendation), it is a French restaurant on the sea, reached by passing through a narrow alleyway. You can cool your thirst with an apéritif at a mahogany bar before going into the restaurant, open to a view of the harbor. The chef's specialties are prepared with flair, and only quality ingredients are selected. You might enjoy baked gratin of mussels, chicken breast with raspberry vinegar, or marinated sea scallops with hot goose liver. Fresh lobster is sautéed in a vermouth-flavored spinach sauce. Full dinners cost from $45, lunches from $25. Hours are from noon to 3 p.m. and 6 to 11 p.m. daily except on Monday in summer.

Bilboquet, Pointe Blanche (no phone). For specialties unique in the Caribbean, this private house provides cookery that is imaginative and prepared with flair. Bilboquet provides two prix-fixe dinners for about $45 nightly. The five-course meals are served from 7:30 to 8:30 p.m., except Monday. The trick is, you must visit the place first to make a reservation (24 hours in advance). Perhaps this proves you can find it at night. Follow the road to Pointe Blanche, turning left at the *Chronicle* newspaper building, then taking another left at Taiwan Food Supply. It's the first uphill left turn (Pigeon Road) after that. Once there, you write your name on a waiting list. Their cuisine is completely international, and they can travel from Thailand to Greece with little problem in translation (after all, they are language experts). For example, one meal might begin with a Cuban black-bean soup or callaloo soup with crabmeat, follow with scampi fritti, then a Greek moussaka with a green salad, topped off by a southern pecan pie. The view is of St. Barts.

Le Perroquet, Airport Rd. (tel. 011-599-5/44339), only a short walk from the airport, is the domain of a French chef of exceptional ability, Monsieur Pierre Castagne. The name of this restaurant comes from the famed Chicago restaurant. The St. Maarten version is in a typical West Indian house with shutters open to the trade winds blowing around Simpson Bay Lagoon. Monsieur Castagne made his reputation quickly on St. Maarten by offering such dishes as ostrich breast (yes, that's right) and filet of boar. You can also order more familiar fare, beginning with a savory fish soup or else a fresh mâche salad, and moving on to mussels marinara, duck with a Grand Marnier orange sauce, or red snapper in a garlic sauce. Castagne wheels a table with some of the specialties of the night from which you can make your visual selection, a nice touch. Meals are expensive, costing from $60 per person. Reservations are necessary, and dinner, the only meal served, is offered nightly from 6 to 10. Closed in June and September.

Spartaco, Almond Grove Plantation Estate (tel. 011-599-5/45379), lies in a residential suburb midway between Philipsburg and the airport. Its limestone walls were originally built in 1803 as part of the West Indian manor house, but the decor today includes strong doses of 1930s art deco and some hi-tech design. Guests sit in the main dining room with its discreet lighting or on a breeze-filled wrap-around veranda. The restaurant is the creation of an Italian entrepreneur from Siena, Spartaco Sagantoni, who is assisted by a handful of Italian chefs. They offer one of the most sophisticated menus on the island, with full meals costing from $50 per person. Only dinner is served, from 6:30 to 10 p.m. daily, except on Monday in summer, and reservations are suggested. Specialties include fresh black tagliolini (angel-hair pasta flavored with squid ink, served with shrimp, parsley, and garlic sauce). The chef also prepares fresh green gnocchi with gorgonzola cheese. Among the main dishes, you might sample swordfish Mediterranean, composed of parsley, garlic, capers, and olive oil which Mr. Sagantoni imports from his relatives who produce it on a farm outside Florence. The antipasto makes a fine beginning, especially a divine version of squid salad.

Ristorante Da Livio, Front St. (tel. 011-599-5/22690), is the place to go for the classic Italian cuisine. The best of its kind in St. Maarten, it is run by Livio Bergamasco, who was the maître d' of the Great Bay Beach Resort before going into business for himself. A traditional dinner here might include linguine alle vongole (clams) or perhaps saltimbocca alla romana, a popular Roman specialty that literally means "jump in your mouth." It's made with ham and veal. The pasta specialty, fettuccine alla Livio, is prepared right at your table. For dessert, save room for the spumone salsa cioccolato, followed by café stravagante. He also has a good wine selection. Expect to spend from $35 for dinner, served nightly from 6:30 to 10:30, and in season, a reservation is wise. Lunch, from noon to 2 p.m. daily, costs around $20. However, specific seatings are at 6:30, 7:30, and 9 p.m. You can dine al fresco, overlooking Great Bay.

West Indian Tavern, 8 Front St. (tel. 011-599-5/22965), is like a primitive island painting, exploding with vibrant colors such as turkey red and lime green. A buccaneerish place, it was built from local cedar early in the 1800s on the site of a Jewish synagogue, making it St. Maarten's oldest restaurant. After 5 p.m., everybody in St. Maarten seems to gather for a sundowner. The place has plenty of atmosphere—bamboo and rattan chairs, big potted ferns, tropical plants, slow-turning overhead fans, and old-world nautical prints. If conversation slackens, a noisy parrot keeps it lively. The chef specializes in fresh local lobster, which he does in endless ways, all a treat. Some of his other delectable dishes include fresh local grouper sautéed with bacon, hazelnuts, and served in a cream sauce; yellowtail with medallions of lobster in a mornay sauce; and fisherman's pie (lobster, crab, shrimp, and snapper in champagne). The dessert specialty is real Key lime pie. An average meal will cost about $25 to $30, unless you order lobster. You dine in a garden patio, shaded by tamarind, frangipani, and lime trees. Dinner is nightly from 6 p.m. to midnight. Backgammon is played until 2 in the morning, and there is live entertainment on most nights.

Félix Restaurant, Pelican Key (tel. 011-599-5/42797), is one of the island's best choices for an al fresco meal, opening onto the sea. Margaret and Richard (Félix) Ducrot, who describe their cuisine as "typically French," are the owners. This place is at its most romantic during candlelit dinners when seating choices range from intimately sheltered booths to outdoor tables set within sight and sound of the sea. Many of the seafood specialties come from the lobster tank whose waters bubble at ground level near the lounge. Full dinners can total $40 per person and might include chateaubriand for two, rack of lamb, fish caught locally that day and sometimes served with an exquisite sorrel-flavored hollandaise, a wide selection of lobster dishes, and a Felix salad. Open daily except Wednesday from November 1 to May 1, the restaurant serves only dinner from 7 to 10 p.m.

The Moderate Range

The **Café Royal** (tel. 011-599-5/23443), in the atrium of the Royal Palm Plaza, a few blocks from the Main Square in Philipsburg, is a local favorite. You can order lunch, dinner, and lavishly packed picnic baskets. You can eat for about $20. French pâtés and pastries, Dutch hams and cheeses, the local Caribbean spiny langouste, and fresh fruits, along with American favorites, including hamburgers and cheesecake, make up the regular fare. The café opens for breakfast at 8 a.m., serving until 11 a.m. In fact, it's the best place along Front Street for breakfast if you don't eat at your hotel. You can order a continental or a "millionaire's breakfast." The kitchen quickly prepares for lunch, serving it from 11 a.m. to 5 p.m., offering shrimp, herring, lobster, soups, salads. Happy hour is from 5 to 6 p.m. Dinner, offered from 6 to 10 p.m., is candlelit, and guests are offered a choice of a fixed-price meal or à la carte. The café is open daily.

In the rear section of the Café Royal you'll discover a gourmet shop, "Eat Royal." This small shop is brimful of local and international delicacies, and has had many a satisfied customer, including Princess Margaret. If given notice, you'll be prepared an elegant picnic basket for two, costing $32. In addition to gift items, most of them packable, you'll be tempted with smoked salmon, pâté, caviar, lobster, and fresh croissants.

Paradise Café, Maho Village (tel. 011-599-5/42842). Set at the top of a hill close to the airport, across from the Maho Beach Hotel, this has become a chic enclave. Near the bar, an elegant swimming pool is fed by a source splashing out of a terracotta urn. Visitors select a large peacock chair which, along with the caged birds and mahogany sheathing, create an aura much like you'd find in a colonial outpost of France. Lunch is served daily except Monday from noon to 4 p.m. Dinner is nightly from 6 p.m. to midnight in high season and from 6:30 to 11 p.m. in off-season. The menu features occasional "creative outbursts from the chef," as well as always available Mexican specialties, T-bone steaks, banana flambé, and frothy tropical drinks. A separate listing includes those dishes temptingly grilled over mesquite wood, including kingfish steak, catch of the day, chicken, and beef dishes. Full meals, costing from $30, might conclude with one of the specialty coffees.

Chesterfields, Great Bay Marina, Pointe Blanche (tel. 011-599-5/23484), has a special attraction other than its good food—which, incidentally, is among the best served on the Dutch side. It offers pierside dining with a view of the harbor, on a trade-wind–swept veranda right close to Great Bay Marina. When the yachting set gathers here (everybody seems to know everybody else), the atmosphere becomes almost like that of your friendly "local." The setting and the dress are both casual, and you dine on several international specialties, with fresh seafood and French-inspired cookery a highlight. Try, for example, the prime rib served with sautéed mushrooms or the red snapper Créole or broiled. Dinners cost from $30. In season, there's always some lively activity going on, such as champagne brunches on Sunday when you can feast on eggs Benedict or Florentine or seafood omelets. It's open from 11 a.m. to 3:30 p.m. and 6:30 p.m. to midnight every day. This is the place where Barbara Walters invited veteran actor Robert Mitchum for an interview for her TV program.

De Hollandia, Airport Rd. (no phone), is a turn-of-the-century yacht riding at anchor on the waters of Simpson Bay Lagoon, welcoming guests to dine aboard beneath the sky. Specializing in provençale dishes, French-born owner/chef Regis Carrom prepares charcoal-broiled meats, grilled lobster, and a hearty bouillabaisse. He purposely keeps the menu small to ensure quality. Diners sip apéritifs in the yacht's cozy paneled bar, then ascend to the main deck where meals are served on tables set up under a canopy. Dinner costs from $35. After dinner, a band entertains with calypso, reggae, and the béguine, with snacks and light meals being available. *De Hollandia* is open from 6 p.m. to 4 a.m. daily except Tuesday. It is on the lagoon next to Simpson Bay Bridge.

The Greenhouse, Veterans Drive, Bobby's Marina (tel. 011-599-5/22941), open to a view of the harbor, is filled with plants, as befits its name. It's the best restaurant in the marina area, and probably one of the finest in its price category. As you dine, breezes filter through the dozens of lattices separating its perimeter from the waterfront outside. Lunch is served daily from 11 a.m. to 4 p.m., and dinner from 5 to 10 p.m. Live entertainment is offered nightly from 10 p.m., when the copious rectangular bar fills up. Lunches, costing from $15, include the catch of the day, a wide selection of burgers, icy gazpacho, and frittatas. Dinners, from $25, might feature chunks of lobster in wine sauce, or a whole red snapper.

La Rosa Ristorante (tel. 011-599-5/23832), on the premises of the St. Maarten Sea Palace, in a setting overlooking Great Bay Harbor, captures the essence of fine Italian cuisine, offering a reasonably priced dining experience complemented by music and a candlelit setting. La Rosa's chef prepares southern Italian cuisine, featuring house specialties such as rigatoni La Rosa and aragosta al cartoccio. Meals cost from $25. There are two dinner seatings, 7 and 9 p.m. daily December through April, being closed Monday from May to November. Reservations are suggested.

Pinocchio, Italian Village, 57 Front St. (tel. 011-599-5/22166), has other entrances, but the preferred way to go in is through an authentically restored tunnel-shaped cistern leading into the Italian patio. In the heart of town, it can also be entered from the beach, luring diners to its terrace swept by trade winds and its al fresco patio bar, which is known for its frozen fruit daiquiris. The intricate latticework in the dining room frames the harbor, and you take a seat at a large community table. Most guests seem to prefer pasta, but you can also order many other Italian specialties, as well as fresh local seafood such as blackened snapper. Try the cold mango soup, or one of the Cajun-Créole specialties served daily from 11 a.m. to 4 p.m. The luncheon offering includes the usual array of burgers, sandwiches, and salads, along with tropical fruit drinks. Naturally, you can order a café espresso, and children's specials are also offered. Dinner is served every night from 6 to 11 p.m. This place usually stays active until 2 a.m. with live entertainment.

Sam's Place (tel. 011-599-5/22989), at the end of Front Street, is where Bogie might land if he were alive and in St. Maarten today. Locals and tourists alike use Sam's "front porch" as a rendezvous point, practically at any time of the day. Boatmen come in here at breakfast ordering steak and eggs, vacationing southerners like the pancakes in syrup, and homesick New Yorkers ask for a toasted bagel with cream cheese. At lunch the item to order is one of the locally well-known "Samburgers." Dinner on the upper deck turns to heartier fare, such as charcoal-broiled steak. When available, try the fresh local fish or the Caribbean spiny langouste. The place is inexpensive: you can get by for around $25 unless you order the expensive lobster or steak. The open-air bar serves hors d'oeuvres at happy hour. It's open from 8:30 a.m. to 2 a.m. daily. There's live entertainment nightly.

The Wajang Doll, 125 Front St. (tel. 011-599-5/22687), housed in a wood-fronted West Indian building on the main street of town, is considered one of the best Indonesian restaurants in the Caribbean. There's a low-slung front porch where you can watch the pedestrian traffic outside, and big windows in back overlooking the sea. The restaurant is best known for the way a waiter will bring 20 little dishes to your table, the combined total of which is known as a *rijsttafel.* The cuisine varies from Bali to Java, and each dish carries a distinctive culinary touch. The chef crushes his spices every day for maximum pungency, according to an ancient craft. A four-course meal costs $15.95 per person, a 19-course dinner going for $19.95. Specialties in addition to the rijsttafel include fried snapper in a chili sauce, marinated pork on a bamboo stick, and Javanese chicken. The restaurant is open for dinner only, every night except Sunday, from 6:45 to 10 p.m. Reservations are suggested since the place has only 16 tables.

Callaloo, Promenade Arcade, Front St. (no phone), is where the locals go to eat. It doesn't bother with credit cards and such but concentrates on serving good food at the best prices in town. Service is daily from noon to 3 p.m. and 7 to 11 p.m. for main meals. However, you can drop in for breakfast at 7 a.m. and continue drinking until 2 a.m. Usually the first seating for dinner at 7 is full so you may want to go later. Meals cost less than $20 per head and are likely to include chicken teriyaki, pork sautéed with a peanut sauce, seafood lasagne, or a T-bone steak. You can order quiches or hamburgers at lunch, along with freshly made salads. At night, many guests, especially late arrivals, like the individual pizzas.

Zachary's, Pointe Blanche (tel. 011-599-5/22260), offers rib-sticking fare at inflation-fighting prices. If you don't mind the ride out to Pointe Blanche, you can enjoy the best ribs in town from Zachary's barbecue pit. Favorites are the baby back rack of ribs. Of course, you can also ask for barbecued chicken or combinations along with such deep-fried specialties as a seafood platter. The main dishes are served with a choice of cole slaw, french fries, baked potato, or Boston baked beans. The elegant part of the menu is reserved for the prime rib, offering either a giant cut or a junior cut. Zachary's barbecue fantasy buffet is served every Monday and Thursday night, and the restaurant is open seven days a week from 6:30 to 10:30 p.m. Meals cost around $20.

Calypso Restaurant, Airport Rd., Simpson Bay (tel. 011-599-5/44233), lies just east of the airport, and don't be deceived by its dusty parking lot and concrete façade. The place serves excellent Créole food in a blue-and-white setting which is airy. Melford Hazel and a polite staff offer meals any time you want them from 11 a.m. to midnight daily except Monday. Lunch starts at $12, including pizzas, sandwiches, a calypso salad (with peppers, avocados, pineapple, cheese, and hard-boiled egg), and five different local dishes. Dinners are more elaborate, costing from $23. Featured are crab backs, conch fritters, fish soup, and flambé custard with brandy. There's a steel band playing some nights. The specialty drink of the house is a Calypso Treat, concocted from Galliano, apricot brandy, coconut cream, and rum.

SHOPPING: St. Maarten is not only a free port, but there are no local taxes. Prices are sometimes lower than anywhere else in the Caribbean. However, the problem is that you must know what you're looking for—what is actually a bargain. Too many cruise-ship passengers have returned home to find the same Japanese camera selling for less in their local discount store. Many well-known shops in Curaçao offer branches here, in case you're not going on to the ABC islands.

Except for the boutiques at resort hotels, the main shopping center is in downtown Philipsburg. Most of the shops are on two leading streets, Front Street (called Voorstraat in Dutch), which is closer to the bay, and Back Street (Achterstraat), which runs parallel. Shopping hours in general are from 8 a.m. to noon and 2 to 6 p.m. weekdays. If a cruise ship is in port, many shops open even on Sunday.

I'll only mention a few shops to get you started, as nearly every building in Philipsburg seems to be a store ready to sell.

Specialty Stores

Shipwreck Shop, Front St. (tel. 011-599-5/22962), is a West Indian store selling hammocks, beach towels, steak plates and salad bowls, baskets, handmade jewelry, T-shirts, postcards, stamps, books, and much more. It's the home of woodcarvings, native art, seasalt, cane sugar, and spices. In all, it's a treasure trove of Caribbean handcrafts.

Java Wraps, Mullet Bay Hotel Shopping Arcade (tel. 011-599-5/42801, ext. 2789), is all white with Javanese straw matting on the walls and decorated with exotic Balinese woodcarvings. Locals and visitors alike buy the hand-batiked resortwear line, specializing in shorts, shirts, sundresses, and children's clothing. Java Wraps is known for its sarongs. You can have a demonstration of how to tie them in at least 15 different ways.

New Amsterdam Store, 54 Front St. (tel. 011-599-5/22787), in business since 1925, offers novelty items, T-shirts, and costume jewelry, hand-embroidered blouses for women, and porcelain figurines from Italy and Spain. They also feature St. Maarten's largest linen department. Beachwear for women is also on display, including on my latest rounds Gottex and Oberson swimwear from Israel. They sell men's and women's elegant sportswear from leading French and Italian designers, as well as accessories and shoes. You'll find everything from jogging suits to watches to 14- and 18-karat gold and silver jewelry.

Gulmohar's, Front St. (tel. 011-599-5/22956), could save you a shopping trip to the Orient. It's a real bazaar. On display are linen and drip-dry tablecloths,

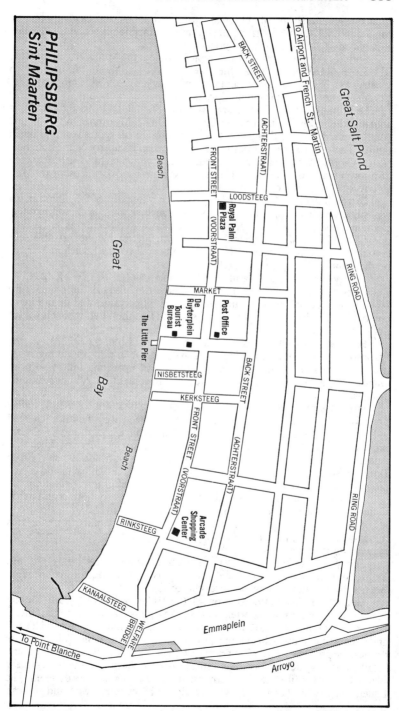

PHILIPSBURG
Sint Maarten

batik dresses and shirts, silk blouses, Japanese kimonos, and elegantly beaded handbags. Look for meerschaum pipes, music boxes, fine silk scarves, souvenirs, and, of course, liquor at duty-free prices.

Spritzer & Fuhrmann, in the shopping arcade at the Mullet Bay Resort (tel. 011-599-5/44381), are called "the jewelers of the Caribbean." In addition to jewelry, watches, china, crystal, and giftware, they provide a wide range of other elegant creations in a wide range of prices.

La Romana, Royal Palm Plaza, 61 Front St. (tel. 011-599-5/22181), is arguably the most chic international boutique in St. Maarten. On two floors, you'll find a display of designer wares, including Italian sportswear and beach outfits. Their shoe salon, for both men and women, is superb. Name designers such as Giorgio Armani are regularly featured here with merchandise that is often 25% lower than it is in the United States. La Romana has two other shops at Mullet Bay Resort and Porsche Design, Juliana Airport.

Oro de Sol, Piazza Treasure Island at Cupecoy (tel. 011-599-5/22602), is a well-stocked shop offering one of the most imaginative watch and jewelry collections on the island. Its inventory includes an array of gold watches as well as European-style high-fashion jewelry studded with precious stones. It also sells crystal by Lalique and Baccarat. The establishment also has a branch in Marigot on the French side if you're going there.

Yellow House (Casa Amarilla), Wilhelminastraat (tel. 011-599-5/23438). Residents of the Dutch-speaking islands know this place as the branch of a century-old establishment in Curaçao. All kinds of perfumes and luxury items are sold here, including fine porcelain dishes and figurines. Everything is sold at duty-free prices.

H. Stern Jewellers, 56 Front St. (tel. 011-599-5/23328), is the Philipsburg branch of a worldwide firm that engages in mining, designing, manufacturing, exporting, and retailing jewelry for all occasions and in all price ranges. They use precious gems to create pieces in contemporary and traditional designs.

Little Switzerland, 42 and 69 Front St. (tel. 011-599-5/23530), offers fine-quality European imports made even more attractive by the prices charged in Philipsburg. Elegant and finely crafted watches, china, crystal, and jewelry are on display. Watches include Rolex, Chopard, Baume & Mercier, Ebel, and Audemars Piguet, and other famous names. You can purchase Aynsley, Royal Doulton, Wedgwood, what have you, from the stock of fine china, or add crystal pieces by Lalique, Waterford, Daum, Baccarat, and Orrefors to your collection.

Colombian Emeralds International has a store on Front Street and in the Olde Street Arcade (tel. 011-599-5/22438), where you can find stones from collector to investment quality. Unmounted duty-free emeralds from the rich mines of Colombia, as well as emerald, gold, diamond, ruby, and sapphire jewelry, will tempt your eye and pocketbook.

For your camera needs, try **Caribbean Camera Centre,** Front St., Philipsburg (tel. 011-599-5/25259), which has a wide range of merchandise. But it's always wise to know the prices charged back home.

Guavaberry Company, 10 Front St. (tel. 011-599-5/24497), sells the rare island folk liqueur of St. Maarten. For centuries, this has been made in private homes, but it is now available to everyone. You may want to stop in at their shop and free-tasting house, which is open from 9 a.m. to 5 p.m. daily. Sold in square bottles, the product is made from rum that is given a unique flavor by use of rare, locally grown berries. These berries usually grow in the hills in the center of the island. Do not confuse the guavaberries with guavas. They are very different. The liqueur is aged and has a fruity, woody, almost bittersweet flavor, and you can blend it with coconut for a unique guavaberry colada to dazzle your friends and keep them guessing. Another way to serve it is to pour a splash into a glass of icy champagne.

As you're leaving, you might drop in at **Antillean Liquors,** at Juliana Airport (tel. 011-599-5/44267). This duty-free shop which attracts the last-minute shopper is open seven days a week, 365 days a year, from 8 a.m. to 7 p.m. It has a complete assortment of all the leading brands of liquor and liqueurs, as well as cigarettes and cigars.

Shopping Centers

Museum Arcade, 119 Front St. (tel. 011-599-5/22976), is a gallery of specialty shops designed in an authentic old West Indian style and built around St. Maarten's first museum. The museum is part of a foundation designed to promote excavations and other explorations on the island, as well as to carry out other projects related to the island's history and its cultural and artistic past. The museum is housed in a cottage on Front Street, built in the West Indian gingerbread style, dating from 1888.

The Museum Arcade with its specialty shops, constructed around the cottage, features six shops, a French café, and a French restaurant. The variety of items available ranges from Italian leather goods to French perfumes to novelty souvenirs. Crystal from the Scandinavian countries is also sold. If you're interested in unique gift items reflecting West Indian culture, then visit my favorite in the complex, **Museum Classics,** run by an American, Gail B. Knopfler, who has long been a promoter of St. Maarten. The arcade is next to the Sea Palace Hotel and has access from Front Street as well as Great Bay Beach. Visitors can enjoy the open-air terrace, breezy courtyard, and, importantly, the public bathrooms.

Olde Street Shopping Center, in the heart of Philipsburg, is across from the St. Maarten Beach Club and Holland House Hotel, with entrances from both Front and Back Streets. Built in West Indian–Dutch style with fretwork and pastel structures, it features 22 shops, including chic boutiques and an open-air bar/restaurant/café. Several branches of famous stores have smaller outlets here, including Java Wraps and Colombian Emeralds, already previewed. One of the best is **Dalila Boutique,** 106 Old St. (tel. 011-599-5/24623), which is run by a charming Frenchman, Claude Chereau, who makes frequent trips to Bali to restock his supply. In fact, many of the designs are the work of Monsieur Chereau. You'll find a wide assortment of batik clothing for both men and women as well as unusual and imaginative decorations for your home.

Amsterdam Shopping Center is geared more for the local trade than for visitors, but many intrepid shoppers drive out here, at Madame Estates, just outside Philipsburg, to scan the wares, hoping for a bargain. There are nearly 50 shops in the center, including a laundromat (not easy to find in the Caribbean), a leather goods shop, a beauty spa, and many others. You can also dine at restaurants inspired by everywhere from Africa to Surinam, featuring such dishes as peanut soup and fried banana satay. There's even a Pizza Hut.

THE SPORTING LIFE: Regardless of what hotel you select in St. Maarten, you're never far from the water. On the Dutch side you'll find a magnificent collection of white sandy beaches, perhaps your own hidden cove. If you're a beach-sampler, you can often use the changing facilities at some of the bigger resorts for a small fee. (Nudists should head for the French side of the island, although the Dutch side is getting more liberal about those who prefer to take their sun in skimpy attire.)

Windsurfing and jet-skiing are especially popular on St. Maarten. The unruffled waters of Simpson Bay Lagoon, the largest in the West Indies, are ideal for these sports, as well as for the more traditional waterskiing. For the daring, parasailing is also available.

Water Sports

Both the serious snorkeler and the scuba-diver are attracted to St. Maarten's crystal-clear bays and the countless coves that honeycomb the island. Underwater visibility reportedly runs from 75 to 125 feet. The biggest attraction for scuba-divers is the 1801 British man-o-war, H.M.S. *Proselyte,* which came to a watery grave on a reef a mile off the coast. Divers today can see her cannons and anchors. Most of the big resort hotels have facilities for scuba-diving, and someone on the staff will provide information about underwater tours, for photography as well as night diving.

One of the major water-sports centers, **Maho Watersports,** Mullet Bay Resort, P.O. Box 309, Philipsburg, St. Maarten, N.A. (tel. 011-599-5/44387), is the longest-established dive operation on the island. The center provides scuba lessons. A resort course, including beach instruction, all equipment, and a beach dive, costs $45. PADI or NAUI certification is available for $350, including 40 hours of instruction. A one-tank dive for certified divers is priced at $40. Dive packages are available on request. For snorkelers, there are half-day coral-reef trips to Pinel Island, including an island tour, a short boat ride, instruction, all equipment (life jackets and beach umbrellas included), soft drinks, rum punch, and the sea. You can rent snorkel equipment and other dive items. Owned and operated by Adrienne Gonia and Mike Myers, Maho Watersports is open seven days a week from 8:30 a.m. to 5 p.m.

Trade Winds Dive Center, Great Bay Marina, near Chesterfield's Restaurant in Philipsburg, St. Maarten, N.A. (tel. 011-599-5/44387), is owned and operated by the owners of Maho Watersports at Mullet Bay Resort (previewed above). Trade Winds has a 25-foot Mako with twin 155-horsepower outboards for its diving trips. Two dive masters accompany a maximum of eight divers on each trip. One-tank dives, costing $40, take about 1½ hours dock to dock, and two-tank-dive trips, for $70, are about three hours. For beginners, a two-hour introductory scuba course is offered for $45. Both NAUI open water and advanced certification courses are offered, costing $350. All equipment is included. Reservations are necessary for dives or courses. Like Maho Watersports, Trade Winds Dive Center is open seven days a week from 8:30 a.m. to 5 p.m.

Sint Maarten Divers, Great Bay Hotel, Front St., P.O. Box 310, Philipsburg, St. Maarten, N.A. (tel. 011-599-5/23008, ext. 536), provides a good dive service and water sports. The staff knows some exciting and colorful spots to dive among reefs, wrecks, and a maze of tunnels and coral valleys. They also make interesting night-dive trips. The staff is licensed by PADI, ACUC, and CMAS. A one-tank dive including equipment costs $40, a three-dive package going for $100. A resort course (introductory scuba lesson) is priced at $30, and a snorkeling adventure, including gear and drinks, is $25. Advance reservations are necessary.

Red Ensign Watersports, Oyster Pond Hotel, P.O. Box 427, Philipsburg, St. Maarten, N.A. (tel. 011-599-5/25310), is one of the best on the island, offering a full array of water sports. Waterskiing here costs $25 for 15 minutes of fun or $40 for half an hour, but special package deals are offered. Run by Maria Harris from New York, the center staff will explain the various offerings, including the basic price of going sailing. For example, you can rent a Sunfish for $10 per hour or a catamaran at $30 per hour. Windsurfing is possible for $10 per hour, and you can also rent snorkeling gear for $10 per day. They conduct a barbecue and snorkeling trip departing daily at 10 a.m. and returning at 3 p.m. The net price is $50 per person.

Parasailing

Lagoon Cruises & Watersports N.V., on the lagoon at Mullet Bay Resort (tel. 011-599-5/42898, ext. 337), offers a parasailing thrill—a 10-minute flight for about $25 per person. Combining the lift of a kite with the drag of a parachute, parasailing gives you a view of the island from above on closer terms than you get from an airplane. No experience is required, and Lagoon Cruises is open daily.

Deep-Sea Fishing

Half-day deep-sea bottom fishing excursions are offered aboard the *Wampum,* operating out of **Bobby's Marina** in Philipsburg (tel. 011-599-5/22366). The vessel departs from the marina at the head of Front Street at 9 a.m., returning at 1 p.m., Tuesday to Saturday. All bait and tackle are furnished, plus instructions for novices and an open bar. The cost of a half-day trip is $35 per person.

Picnic Sails

One of the most popular fair-weather pastimes for vacationers to St. Maarten is to sign on for a day of picknicking, sailing, snorkeling, and sightseeing aboard one of several boats providing this service. The sleek sailboats usually pack large wicker hampers full of victuals and stretch tarpaulins over sections of the deck to protect sun-shy visitors.

A picnic sail is offered on the *Gabrielle,* which sails from Bobby's Marina, leaving at 9 a.m. and returning at 5 p.m. year round. The *Gabrielle* is a 46-foot ketch, with a spacious cockpit and large decks. Its $55-per-person price includes lunch, beer, French wine, and use of all equipment. You're taken to a secluded cove on a small island where you can sunbathe, swim, and snorkel. Call 011-599-5/23170 after 6 p.m..

In most cases you can make reservations for any of these cruises at the activities desk of your hotel.

Sailing to Other Island Countries

Vacationers to St. Maarten have the opportunity to visit other inhabited Caribbean islands on day trips. Experienced skippers make voyages to St. Barts in the French West Indies and to Saba, another of the Dutch Windwards in the Leewards, stopping long enough for passengers to familiarize themselves with the island ports, to shop, and to have lunch if they wish, returning to St. Maarten the same day.

The *Quicksilver,* a 61-foot motor-sailing catamaran, leaves from Great Bay, Chesterfield's Marina daily at 9 a.m., returning around 5 p.m. It makes a two-hour run to the French island of St. Barts, where you can visit the little capital, Gustavia, shop, and tour the island at your leisure. The $45 fare includes an open bar. A $5 departure tax is required. You can visit the *Quicksilver* at the dock before or after a cruise. Telephone 011-599-5/22167 for reservations.

On the power yacht *Maison Maru,* passengers sail along the shoreline while the captain, Larry Berkowitz, points out landmarks and regales his listeners with amusing tales of island life. During a day-long excursion, lunch with wine is served. An hour's layover in Marigot allows time for shopping and sightseeing on the French side of the island. You can even go swimming and snorkeling in secluded coves. The 57-foot *Maison Maru* (tel. 011-599-5/22188) departs from the Little Pier in Philipsburg at 9:30 a.m.

The *Eagle,* one of the most beautiful catamarans home-ported in Philipsburg, measuring 67 feet long and 30 feet wide, sails for St. Barts daily at 9:30 a.m., returning to St. Maarten at 5 p.m. The boat, with double hulls painted black with gold trim and propelled by a billowing spinnaker, takes passengers on the cruise which includes snacks, open bar, use of snorkeling gear, and spectacular views. The cost is $45 per person, plus $5 departure tax. The *Eagle* docks at Great Bay Marina.

The *Style,* which also overnights at Great Bay Marina, sails daily except Monday at 9 a.m. for Saba, returning the same day at 3:15 p.m. The cost is $45 for a round trip. There is no departure tax, as Saba is a Dutch-held island.

The *White Octopus,* a 75-foot motor-driven catamaran, offers spacious upper and lower decks for passengers going from St. Maarten to St. Barts, a trip lasting 1½ hours. The boat leaves Philipsburg every Monday to Saturday at 9 a.m., returning at 5 p.m. The cost is $45 per person, plus $5 departure tax. The boat docks at Bobby's Marina, P.O. Box 383, Philipsburg, St. Maarten, N.A. This is said to be the island's fastest waterborne method of reaching St. Barts. There's an open bar, and snacks are served on the way back.

Trips to deserted Sandy Beach on Prickly Pear Island near the British island of Anguilla, are offered by Lagoon Cruises & Watersports N.V., Mullet Bay Resort (tel. 011-599-5/42898, ext. 337) aboard the 50-foot catamarans, *Bluebeard I* and *Bluebeard II* for a day's recreation, charging $55 per person for the sail, an open bar, snacks, a barbecue lunch (fish, chicken, ribs, or even lobster, although it's $9 extra), snorkeling, and underwater photography. Equipment for the latter two activities is complimentary.

El Tigre, a 60-foot catamaran, sails daily from Great Bay Marina at 9:30 a.m., cruising to St. Barts where you can spend the day touring, shopping, and going to the beach. *El Tigre* arrives back on St. Maarten around 5:30 p.m. The fare, including an open bar, is $45 per person, plus $5 departure tax. For information, write to P.O. Box 346, Philipsburg, St. Maarten, N.A.

You can circumnavigate St. Maarten on *Cheshire Cat,* a luxurious catamaran, leaving from Bobby's Marina in Philipsburg (tel. 011-599-5/22366) at 9 a.m. and returning by 5 p.m. The sail takes you on a trip "down island" in the lee of St. Maarten, then rounds Basse Terre, the most westerly part of the island, and sails into the Anguilla Channel, allowing views of bays and islands. *Cheshire Cat* then takes passengers to the deserted island of Tintamarre (Flat Island), where for 30 years beginning in 1902, the locally dubbed "King of Tintamarre" and his 100 workers operated a cotton plantation. Here, you can relax on the long beach, swimming and snorkeling, with lessons given to beginning snorkelers. A lunch of barbecued local fish, spare ribs, or chicken is served with salads, French bread, and French wine. The homeward journey is along the windward side of the island. The trip includes lunch, open bar, sodas, snacks, and snorkeling gear, all for $60, plus $5 departure tax, for adults, $30 for children.

Tennis

You can try the courts at any of the large hotels, but **Mullet Bay Resort** (tel. 011-599-5/42801, ext. 376), is the undisputed champion of both the French and Dutch sides of the island, with 14 tennis courts. Residents of the resort pay $4 per person hourly, and nonresidents are charged $7 per person per hour. Rackets are rented for $4 per hour. Two of the courts can be illuminated for night games, costing $22 per hour.

Golf

Mullet Bay Resort & Casino (tel. 011-599-5/42801, ext. 370), has an 18-hole course, one of the most challenging in the Caribbean, designed by Joseph

Lee. The greens stretch along Mullet Pond and Simpson Bay Lagoon, providing both beauty and hazards. Greens fees are $30 for 18 holes or $20 for nine holes, including use of a cart. There are no caddies, but there are pros to help you improve your game, a 30-minute lesson costing $25. Only residents of the resort are permitted to play on the course.

Revitalization Center
Health, beauty, and relaxation programs are offered at **Pelican Resort and Casino,** Simpson Bay (tel. 011-599-5/42426), where you can enter into one or all of the processes, ranging from facials to electroridopuncture to anti-cellulitis treatments to plastic and reconstructive surgery. Revitalization is offered through weekly, monthly, or yearly programs, with rejuvenation processes followed.

Horseback Riding
Crazy Acres, Wathey Estate, Cole Bay (tel. 011-599-5/22061). Riding expeditions here invariably end on an isolated beach where the horses, with or without their riders, enjoy the cool waters in an after-ride romp. Two experienced escorts accompany eight-person outings which begin at 9 a.m. every weekday, returning about noon. The price is $40 per person, lunch included. Riders of all levels of experience are welcome, with the single provision that they wear bathing suits under their jeans for a grand finale on the beach. It's recommended that reservations for any activity be made at least two days in advance. On weekends, families wishing to picnic together can arrange horseback outings *en famille* through the stable.

NIGHTLIFE: On the Dutch side of St. Maarten, there are few real nightclubs. After-dark activities begin early here, as guests select their favorite nook for a sundowner, perhaps the veranda of the **West Indian Tavern** or the beautiful garden patio of **Pasanggrahan,** both of these establishments having been previously recommended.

A fun spot is **The Blue Note,** at the Pinocchio Restaurant, 57 Front St., Philipsburg (tel. 011-599-5/22166). It offers live entertainment every night and is open from 6 p.m. to 4 a.m. Drinks go for half price at happy hour from 6 to 7 p.m. The club features rock 'n' roll, country and western, funk, pop, jazz, reggae, whatever. There is no admission charge.

A favorite spot for sunset watching is at the **Caravanserai,** a luxury hotel also previously recommended. An airy octagonal gazebo caps a rocky outcropping at Burgeaux Bay. From here, guests watch for the legendary "green flash," an atmospheric phenomenon written about by Hemingway that sometimes occurs in these latitudes just as the sun drops below the horizon. Each evening guests wait expectantly, and have been known to break into a round of applause at a particularly spectacular sunset.

Most of the combos and **gambling casinos** as well are in the big hotels such as the **Mullet Bay Resort and Casino,** the **Maho Reef Beach Resort** (with its glittering Casino Royale), **Divi Little Bay, Great Bay,** and the **St. Maarten Beach Club** (refer to the previous recommendations for descriptions and locations). Casino action is usually from 8 p.m. till 3 a.m., but the casino at the St. Maarten Beach Club opens at 1 in the afternoon. A newer casino is at the **Pelican Resort** (tel. 011-599-5/42503), built to a Swiss design incorporating a panoramic view of Simpson Bay. It features Las Vegas rules.

Treasure Island Casino, at Treasure Island Hotel & Casino (tel. 011-599-5/42500), is one of the most lighthearted casinos in the Caribbean. Its gaming tables and sharp-eyed staff are everything you'd expect them to be, and 17th-century figures ring the trompe l'oeil gallery on the ceiling. Peering down (presumably into your cards) is a cast of raffish and humorous characters. There's no cover charge to enter.

The big hotels, and some of the smaller ones too, sponsor **beachside barbecues** (particularly in season), bringing in steel bands and offering native music and folk dancing. Outsiders are welcomed at most of these events, but call ahead to see if it's a private catered affair.

Le Club, Mullet Bay Resort & Casino (tel. 011-599-5/42801), is the most glamorous club of this sprawling resort. It stands next to the Shopping Plaza and Grand Casino and is open from 10 p.m. "until." The joint rocks nightly except Monday. Every night, happy hour is from 10 to 11 p.m. when drinks sell at half price. "Friends," St. Maarten's number one recording band, might put in an appearance while you are here. Admission is $5 per person.

Studio Seven Nightclub and Disco, Maho Beach Hotel (tel. 011-599-5/42115). Glittering, electronic, and contemporary, this disco is just above the lobby level of this previously recommended hotel. Open from 10 p.m. to 5 a.m. nightly, it offers a water view, changeable lighting, danceable music, and a pair of video screens showing unusual films. There's no cover charge on weeknights, but on Friday and Saturday a $8 door charge is assessed.

2. ST. EUSTATIUS

Called "Statia," this Dutch-held island is just an eight-square-mile pinpoint in the Netherlands Antilles, still basking in its 18th-century heritage as the "Golden Rock." One of the true backwaters of the West Indies, it is just awakening to tourism. The location is 150 miles east of Puerto Rico, 90 miles east of St. Croix, 38 miles due south of St. Maarten, and 17 miles southeast of Saba.

Two extinct volcanoes, the Quill and "Little Mountain," are linked by a sloping agricultural plain, growing yams and sweet potatoes, forming the topography of Statia. The valley is known as De Cultuurvlakte.

Overlooking the Caribbean on the western edge of the plain, Oranjestad (Orange City) is the capital and the only village, consisting of both an Upper and Lower Town, connected by stone-paved, dogleg Fort Road.

Statia was sighted by Columbus in 1493, on his second voyage, and the island was claimed for Holland by Jan Snouck in 1640. The island's history was turbulent before it settled down to peaceful slumber under Dutch protection. From 1650 to 1816, Statia changed flags 22 times!

Once the trading hub of the Caribbean, Statia was a thriving market, both for goods and for slaves. Benjamin Franklin directed his mail to Europe through Statia.

Before the American Revolution, the population of Statia did not exceed 1,200, most of whom were slaves engaged in raising sugarcane. When war came and Britain blockaded the North American coast, Europe's trade was diverted to the West Indies. Dutch neutrality lured many traders, which led to the construction of a mile and a half of warehouses in Lower Town. The Americans obtained gunpowder and ammunition shipped through Statia.

Statia's historical links are strong with the United States. Its Fort Oranje was the first fortress to salute the Stars and Stripes, flying from the 14-gun brigantine *Andrew Doria*. The date was November 16, 1776. Statia paid for such early recognition of a revolutionary government. In reprisal, in 1781 Great Britain's Admiral Rodney seized and sacked Statia, luring unsuspecting vessels into anchorage by continuing to fly the Dutch flag. It is estimated that when Rodney sailed away, he carried from $15 to $20 million of booty from Statia.

Contrary to legend, Statia was not destroyed by Rodney. After his forces left, the island bounced back to reach the pinnacle of its prosperity in 1790, with a population put at 8,125 persons. Its gradual decay came about when it was no longer needed as a transit port for the American colonies. Also it was bled by the exorbitant demands of interim French and English governments. Its unprotected warehouses eventually tumbled into the sea, and only their barest shells and raw foundations remain, skeletal stone walls that one historian dubbed "the Pompeii of the Caribbean."

GETTING THERE: St. Eustatius can be reached from Dutch St. Maarten's Juliana Airport via **Windward Islands Airways International** (called Winair). The flying time to Statia is only 20 minutes from St. Maarten, with flights five times a day. Once there, connections can be made on Statia for flights either to Saba or St. Kitts. There are often as many as four flights per day.

The little airline, launched in 1961, has an excellent safety record and has flown such passengers as David Rockefeller. Chances are you will fly to Statia on a Twin Otter with 20 seats. The flight is called STOL (short take-off and landing). At present it costs only $40 per round trip. You can visit just for the day, but it's recommended that you spend more time to savor the special flavor of Statia.

In St. Maarten, telephone 011-599-5/44230 to make a reservation on this flight, and always be certain that you reconfirm your return passage once you are on Statia.

Daily flights from St. Kitts to St. Eustatius via Winair or Leeward Islands Air Transport (LIAT) are also offered.

Connections can be made on Statia for Saba. Telephone 011-599/34210 or 011-599/34237 for schedules. There are often as many as four flights per day. LIAT flies in from Antigua and St. Kitts.

GETTING AROUND: Taxis are your best bet. They meet all incoming flights and will drive from there to your hotel. On the way to the hotel, I assure you that your driver will offer himself as a guide during your stay on the island. Taxi rates are inexpensive, probably no more than a $3 ride to your hotel from the airport. If you book a 3½-hour tour later in the day (and in that time you should be able to cover all the sights on Statia), the cost is about $35 per vehicle.

Avis Rent-a-Car is represented through a local dealer, **Rouse Enterprises** at 1 Lampeweg (tel. 011-599/32311). It's your best bet if you're preplanning your trip and want to reserve a car in advance. The cheapest vehicle is a Daihatsu Cuore, which, with unlimited mileage included, costs $36 per day. Drivers must be 21 years old to rent a car. For more information, call toll free anywhere in the U.S. by dialing 800/331-1212.

PRACTICAL FACTS: To help make your stay in St. Eustatius more enjoyable, the following data may be important.

Banks: For financial matters, the **Banco Popular Antiliano** is open from 8:30 a.m. to 1 p.m. Monday to Friday and also from 4 to 5 p.m. on Friday.

Crime: This is a place in the world where crime is almost nonexistent. If there is any trouble at all, it is likely to be caused by your fellow tourists, not by the locals.

Currency: The official unit of currency is the Netherlands Antilles guilder (NAf), but nearly all places will quote you prices in U.S. dollars.

Customs: Arrival is at **Franklin Delano Roosevelt Airport,** where there is no customs, as the island is a free port.

Documents: U.S. and Canadian citizens need proof of citizenship, such as a passport, voter registration card, or a birth certificate, along with an ongoing ticket.

Electricity: It is the same as the U.S., 110 volts AC, 60 cycles.

Information: For information before you go, ask at **St. Eustatius Tourist Office,** 275 Seventh Ave., New York, NY 10001-6788 (tel. 212/989-0000). On the island, the **Tourist Bureau** is at 3 Fort Oranjestraat (tel. 011-599/32433). Hours are from 8 a.m. to noon and 1 to 5 p.m. Monday to Friday.

Language: Dutch is the official language, but English is commonly spoken.

Medical Care: A licensed physician is on duty at the **Princess Beatrix Hospital,** 25 Prinsesweg (tel. 011-599/32211), in Oranjestad.

Taxes: There is no departure tax if you are returning to the Dutch-held islands of St. Maarten or Saba. If you're going elsewhere, you'll leave them $5 richer.

Telephone and Telegraph: Ask at your hotel if you need to send a cable. St. Eustatius maintains a 24-hour-a-day telephone service to the world, and sometimes it takes about that much time to get a call through! When dialing from the United States, use the complete numbers given, including the prefixes 011-599. However, when dialing locally, you need not use the area codes.

Time: The island is in the Atlantic Time Zone, which is the same as Eastern Daylight Saving Time year round.

Tips and Service: Tipping is at the visitor's discretion, and most hotels, guesthouses, and restaurants include a 10% service charge.

Water: The water here is safe to drink.

Weather: Once on the island, visitors find a climate with an average daytime temperature of 78° to 82° Fahrenheit. The annual rainfall is only 45 inches.

HOTELS: Don't expect deluxe hotels or high-rises. Statia is strictly for escapists. Sometimes guests are placed in private homes. There are, as well, some small guesthouses on the island.

The Old Gin House, Bay Road, P.O. Box 172, Lower Town, St. Eustatius, N.A. (tel. 011-599/32319), is a two-in-one hotel, with half a dozen rooms facing the beach in Oranjestad, the other 14 built across the street and opening onto a pool. What used to be known as the "Mooshay Bay Public House"—the hotel set back from the beach—is of more recent vintage than the Old Gin House. However, it was built on the ruins of 18th-century warehouses once used to store molasses. It is run by John May and Marty Scofield, two expatriate Americans. In their inn, they have mixed antiques with practical and well-chosen pieces. They have shown a healthy respect for the past but were not trapped by it, remembering that this was an inn to be used and enjoyed by modern-day travelers. From a decaying cistern a small pool was shaped, and an old cannon was discovered while digging the swimming hole. It's been retired to a peaceful nook. The rooms at the Publick House are set in a brick building with a double row of balconies. An overseer's gallery has been turned into a library and backgammon room. Cooled by overhead fans and sea breezes, each accommodation has sophisticated touches, including paintings and wrought-iron wall hangings from Haiti.

Across the street, the Old Gin House originally began as a hot-dog stand in 1972, but it just grew and grew, becoming a six-room inn of character, small but special. The decision to build grew out of a response from clients who came here to eat and stayed around looking for a place to stay. A two-story unit faces the sea, the rooms cooled by breezes. The ceilings are high, and balconies open onto the waterfront. In winter, the oceanfront deluxe double accommodations rent for $130. *Single or double occupancy in summer is $100 daily.* For breakfast and dinner (with complimentary wine), there is an additional charge of $32 per person daily.

La Maison sur la Plage, P.O. 157, Zeelandia Bay, St. Eustatius, N.A. (tel. 011-599/32256), is nestled on a secluded hilltop overlooking two miles of private beach on the eastern coast of the island. It contains only ten bedrooms, a pleasant swimming pool, and a restaurant which is recommended separately.

The hotel's collection of green-and-white outbuildings and its sloping lawn are set near the hollow of a verdant and rocky glen. The rooms are angular and a bit spartan, and residents use their private front verandas for reading and talking. Each unit contains a private bath and a fan, renting for $75 daily, either single or double, in winter. *In summer, single or double units cost $55 daily.* Tariffs include a continental breakfast. The social center, where you'll get a glimpse of island life, is a long and comfortable bar where the sound of the sea is never far away.

Golden Era Hotel, Lower Town, St. Eustatius, N.A. (tel. 011-599/32345). Set directly on the water, this modern 20-room hotel is clean and serviceable. Less elegant than its next-door neighbor, the Old Gin House, it is sincere in its welcome and is air-conditioned and comfortable. It and its simply decorated bar and dining room are operated by Hubert Lyfrock. Eight of the accommodations don't have a water view, but the remaining dozen offer a full or partial exposure to the sea. Tasteful and spacious, these units rent for $70 daily in a single, $88 in a double, and $104 in a triple in winter. *Summer tariffs are $60 single, $75 double or triple.* Nonresidents of the hotel who want a meal should phone for a reservation at least 30 minutes before their arrival. Lunch is from noon to 2 p.m. and costs from $15 per person. Dinner, from 7 to 9 p.m. daily, goes for $20 and up per person and is likely to include stewed fish, curried lobster, and ice creams such as passion fruit and mango. The fruit punch, with or without rum, is delectable.

Henriquez Apartments, Oranjestad, St. Eustatius, N.A. (tel. 011-599/32299), has two locations: nine apartments in the Golden Rock area near the airport and four others in Upper Town Oranjestad, Princess Weg. The accommodations in the Golden Rock area all have fans, TV, compact refrigerators, coffeemakers, and private baths. They consist of five one-bed apartments housing one or two persons and four two-bed units for up to four persons. Rates year round are $25 in a single, $35 in a double. On the premises are a bar/restaurant and an outdoor patio with barbecue facilities. In Upper Town, the accommodations consist of two three-bedroom units holding up to nine guests and two two-bedroom apartments for up to four persons. They all have kitchens, living rooms, dining rooms, and baths and rent for $20 in a single, $30 in a double year round.

WHERE TO DINE: Overlooking the beach, the **Old Gin House and Mooshay Publick House,** Lower Town (tel. 011-599/32319), provides a nostalgic atmosphere where guests at lunch can enjoy the shady treillage terrace. Perhaps you'll begin with a soursop or strawberry daiquiri. If featured, I'd suggest the peanut soup (so good its recipe once was published in *Gourmet* magazine). The secret is dry-roasted peanuts and a dollop or so of *ketjap bentang.* Recipes are the creation of American expatriate Marty Scofield. Some of his luncheon specialties include lobster Antillean, skewered chicken with peanut sauce, and red snapper mousse, although you can also order a hamburger if you're so inclined. Fresh pineapple is the preferred dessert. Expect to spend $15 to $20, depending on your selection. For dinner all you have to do is walk across the street.

Try to arrive before the dinner setting, so you can enjoy a drink in the pub, a structure of wooden beams and old ship-ballast bricks. The chefs are likely to feature a delicate quiche niçoise with a light, flaky crust, or perhaps fish chowder. Specialties include the bisque de homard with rouille, made with lobster legs, perfectly balanced with Mediterranean spicing. Complimentary wine is included, and the total cost is $35, well-spent money. In homage to the 18th century, Delft and pewter are used generously. Dining is by candlelight in either of two rooms, connected by brick arches with an eclectic collection of ship models, old clocks, and primitive paintings. Lunch is from noon to 2 p.m., and dinner from 6 to 9 p.m.

La Maison sur la Plage, Zeelandia Bay (tel. 011-599/32256), is contained in a greenhouse-style wing of the previously recommended hotel. Beneath a high ceiling whose walls are open to the wind, you enjoy full meals, costing $20 at lunch, $35 at dinner. These are served from noon to 2 p.m. and 7 to 9 p.m. daily, except in September. Lunch might consist of fish soup, lobster salad (served in a shell), and marinated fish Tahiti style. Dinner is more elaborate, featuring such choices as fish mousse with chives, stuffed chicken, and lamb with tomatoes, mushrooms, and thyme. French-born Michelle Greca is your host, seeing that her cuisine reflects Gallic flair.

Talk of the Town Bar & Restaurant, L.E. Saddlerweg, St. Eustatius, N.A. (tel. 011-599/32236), is in the Golden Rock area on the edge of town, about five minutes' walk from the airport. Nora and Koos Sneek, the owners, offer lunch from 11:30 a.m. to 2 p.m. and dinner from 6 to 10 p.m. daily. The bar is open from 11 a.m. "until." They serve local and international dishes such as red snapper, lobster, and a variety of steaks. Specialties, which should be ordered in the morning, are lobster stew, stewed papayas, eggplant soufflé, spice crab backs, goat meat, and bullfoot soup. Meals cost from $15. Eight bedrooms above the restaurant are rented, costing $55 per couple in high season, *$45 in low season.* Prices include breakfast. All the rooms are air-conditioned and have private baths, phones, and TV.

L'Etoile, 6 Van Rheeweg (tel. 011-599/32299), is a second-floor local restaurant with a few simple tables. Caren Henriquez has had this place for some time, and she is well known in Statia for her local cuisine, but you don't run into too many tourists here. In fact, it's one of the few places on the island that quotes menu prices in Netherland Antillean guilders. Favored and recommended main dishes include the ubiquitous "goat water" (a stew), stewed whelks, as well as tasty spareribs. Caren is also known for her pastechis, deep-fried turnovers stuffed with meat. Expect to pay from $18 for a complete and very filling meal. Lunch is from noon to 2 p.m.; dinner, 7 to 10 p.m. (on Sunday, from 8 a.m. to 6 p.m.).

The **Stone Oven Bar & Restaurant,** 15 Faeschweg, Upper Town, Oranjestad (tel. 011-599/32247), is a small house with a garden patio with a cozy Caribbean decor. Myrtle V. Suares, the manager, serves a variety of local and West Indian dishes, with meals costing from $18. The place is open daily for lunch from 11 a.m. to 2 p.m. and for dinner from 7 to 10:30 p.m. The bar is open from 11 a.m. This is the liveliest place in town during "Jolly Time" every Friday from 9 p.m. until they decide to close the doors.

SEEING THE SIGHTS: The capital, **Oranjestad,** stands on a cliff looking out upon a beach and the island's calm anchorage, where in the 18th century you might have seen 200 vessels offshore. **Fort Oranje** was built in 1636 and restored in honor of the U.S. Bicentennial celebration of 1976. Today it is perched like one of the island's seabirds atop the cliffs. Its terraced rampart is lined with old cannons. You'll see a bronze plaque honoring the fact that "Here the sovereignty of the United States of America was first formally acknowledged to a national vessel by a foreign official." The plaque was presented by Franklin D. Roosevelt. The fort is now used for government offices.

One of the island's most attractive buildings stands across from the square. Once this house belonged to Johannes de Graaff, Statia's most famous governor. It was de Graaff who ordered the salute to the Stars and Stripes. The plundering Rodney also stayed here in 1781. Today **Statia Museum,** Doncker de Graaff House, Upper Town (no phone), the island's most impressive museum, is contained inside the 17th-century walls of the governor's house. It lies in the center of town, amid a dusty garden, with a 20th-century wing crafted from mahogany.

Open weekdays from 9 a.m. to 5 p.m. and weekends from 1 to 4 p.m., it charges an entrance fee of $1 for adults, 50¢ for children. Exhibits demonstrate the process of sugar refining, archeological artifacts from the precolonial period, and a pair of elegantly beautiful reproductions of 18th-century rooms. On the upper floor is a massive piece of needlework by an American, Catherine Mary Williams, showing the flowers of Statia.

A few steps away, a cluster of 18th-century buildings is called **Three Widows' Corner,** surrounding a quiet courtyard.

Nearby are the ruins of the first **Dutch Reformed church.** To reach it, turn west from Three Widows' Corner onto Kerkweg. Tilting headstones record the names of the characters in the island's past. The St. Eustatius Historical Foundation recently completed restoration of the church. Visitors may climb to the top level of the tower and see the bay as lookouts did many years before.

In the center, **Honen Dalim,** a Jewish synagogue, the second in the western hemisphere, can be explored, although it is in ruins. Once Statia had a large Jewish colony of traders. This house of prayer was begun about 1740 and was damaged by a hurricane in 1772. It fell into disuse at the dawn of the 19th century. The synagogue stands beside Synagogpad, a narrow lane whose entrance faces Madam Theatre on the square.

The walls of a ritual mikvah rise beside the **Jewish burial ground** on the edge of town. The oldest stone in the cemetery is that of Abraham Hisquiau de la Motta, who died in 1742. The inscription is in both Portuguese and Hebrew. The most recent marker is that of Moses Waag, who died February 25, 1825. Most poignant is the memorial of David Haim Hezeciah de Lion, who died in 1760 at the age of "2 years, 8 months, 26 days." Carved into the baroque surface is an angel releasing a tiny songbird from its cage.

In addition, a short ride from Oranjestad takes you to the road's end at White Wall. There on your left is **Sugarloaf,** a mini-replica of Rio's famed cone. On the right is a panoramic view of **St. Kitts.**

At the base of the pink-gray cliff beneath Fort Oranje, **Lower Town** was the mercantile center of Statia in the 18th century. Bulging with sugar, rum, and tobacco, Lower Town was once filled with row upon row of brick warehouses. Part of the rich cargo of some of these warehouses was human, slaves held in bondage awaiting shipment to other islands in the Caribbean. You can wander at leisure through the ruins, stopping later at the Old Gin House for a drink.

The Quill is an extinct volcano, called "the most perfect" in the Caribbean, sheltering a lush tropical rain forest, a botanical wonderland, in its deep wide crater. The Quill rises to 1,960 feet on the southern edge of the island. Hikers climb it. Birdwatchers come here for a glimpse of the blue pigeon, a rare bird known to frequent the breadfruit and cottonwood trees in the mountains.

SHOPPING: Merchandise is very limited, but you may want to pick up a local item or two as a reminder of a pleasant stay. Most shops, what few there are, are open from 8 a.m. to noon and 1:30 to 5:30 p.m. weekdays, from 10 a.m. to noon and 2:30 to 5:30 p.m. on Saturday. Of course, this could vary widely.

Mazinga Giftshop, Upper Town (tel. 011-599/32245), sells an array of souvenirs of the island, T-shirts, liquor, costume jewelry, handbags, Delft from Holland, and paperback romances. You may have seen more exciting stores in your life, but this is without parallel the best Statia offers.

The Hole in the Wall, Upper Town, Oranjestad (tel. 001-599/32265), is literally built into a wall adjacent to the Catholic Church grounds. It features local handcrafts, designed and hand-sketched by the owners. Available are block-printed wall hangings and clothing, postcards, jewelry made from natural local plants and some from "blue slave beads" from the 18th century. Also stocked are authentic 17th-century clay pipestem earrings. The shop is open from 10 a.m. to 5 p.m. Monday to Saturday.

THE SPORTING LIFE: There are few organized sports activities. Life here is casual.

Water Sports

On the Atlantic side of the island, at Concordia Bay, surfing possibilities are best. However, there is no lifeguard protection.

Snorkeling tours through the Caribbean Sea to explore the remnants of an 18th-century man-of-war and the walls of warehouses, taverns, and shops that sank below the surface of Oranje Bay more than 200 years ago are available.

Dive Statia (tel. 011-599/32348) is a fully equipped diving center operating in a former warehouse next to the Old Gin House Hotel, with packages offered for accommodations and dives connected with the hotel. Dive Statia's professional staff guides divers of all levels of experience to the historic shipwrecks and ruins of 18th-century seaports sitting on the ocean bottom. The establishment offers one-tank beach dives and one- and two-tank boat dives, plus night dives. All dives include all necessary equipment. Certification cards are required. Snorkel trips are also offered, with your own gear required. Underwater camera rental and film processing are available. Package tours for three, five, or seven nights, in connection with the Old Gin House Hotel can be reserved through Go Diving (tel. 612/942-9687 or toll free 800/328-5285).

Tennis

Tennis can be played at Madam Estate at the **Community Center.** The court has a concrete surface and is lit for night play. Changing facilities are also available. It should cost about $2 or less to use the court. The center and the tennis facilities were dedicated on Statia-American Day, November 16. Bring your own equipment.

Crab Catching

I'm perfectly serious. If you're interested in this sport, you can join Statians in a crab hunt. The Quill's crater is the breeding ground for these large crustaceans. At night they emerge from their holes to forage, and that's when they're caught. Men, either with flashlights or else relying on moonlight, climb the Quill, catch a crab, and take the local delicacy back to their favorite cooks on the island who prepare stuffed crab back.

Hiking

Perhaps this is the most popular sporting activity. Those with the stamina can climb the slopes of the Quill. Hikers make their way through a lush rain forest which grew when volcanic activity died down. The trip takes about half a day, and you can ask the tourist office to arrange for a guide for you. He'll expect at least $20.

Swimming

On the southwestern shore of Statia are the best volcanic beaches for swimming. Any taxi driver can take you to what he or she thinks is the best spot.

3. SABA

An extinct volcano, exotic, cone-shaped Saba is five square miles of rock carpeted in lush foliage such as orchids (which grow in profusion), giant elephant ear, and Eucharist lilies. At its zenith it reaches a height of 2,900 feet at Mount Scenery, which the locals call simply "The Mountain." The Dutch settled the island in the mid-17th century, and out of such an unusual piece of jagged geography they created an experiment in living that has continued to grow.

Saba is in the Netherlands' Windward Islands at the top of the Lesser Antilles arc. The location is 150 miles east of Puerto Rico and 90 miles east of St. Croix. Most visitors fly over from the Dutch-held section of St. Maarten (Saba is 28 miles to the south).

Columbus is credited with sighting Saba in 1493. Before it became permanently Dutch, it was passed back and forth among other European masters a total of 12 times. At one time it was English, then French, then Spanish, and so forth.

Sabans have been known in days of yore to take advantage of their special topography—that is, they pelted invaders from above with rocks and boulders. Because of the influence of English missionaries and Scottish seamen from the remote Shetland Islands who settled on the island, Saba has always been English speaking. The official language, however, is Dutch.

Because of those early settlers from Europe, 60% of the population is white. Don't be surprised to run into locals with red hair and freckled fair skin.

On Saba, tidy white houses cling to the mountainside, and small family cemeteries adjoin each dwelling. Lace-curtained gingerbread-trimmed cottages give a Disneyland aura.

The first Jeep arrived on Saba in 1947. Before that, Sabans went about on foot, climbing from village to village. Hundreds of steps had been chiseled out of rock by the early Dutch settlers in 1640.

Engineers told them it was impossible, but Sabans built a single cross-island road by hand. It's filled with hairpin turns, zigzagging from Fort Bay, where a deep-water pier accommodates large tenders from cruise ships, to a height of 1,600 feet. Along the way it has fortress-like supporting walls.

Past storybook villages, the road goes over the crest to **The Bottom.** Derived from the Dutch word *botte,* which means bowl-shaped, this village is nestled on a plateau and surrounded by rocky volcanic domes. It occupies about the only bit of ground, 800 feet above the sea. It's also the official capital of Saba, a Dutch village of charm, with chimneys, gabled roofs, and gardens.

From The Bottom you can take a taxi up the hill to the mountain village of **Windwardside,** perched on the crest of two ravines at about 1,500 feet above sea level. This village of red-roofed houses, the second most important in Saba, is the site of the two biggest inns and most of the shops. From Windwardside, you can climb steep steps cut in the rock to yet another village, **Hell's Gate,** teetering on the edge of a mountain. Only the most athletic go from here to the lip of the volcanic crater.

In Windwardside, the **Harry L. Johnson Memorial Museum** is in an old sea captain's home, with antique furnishings, evoking an 1890s aura. Filled with family memorabilia, the house can be visited throughout the day, and admission is $1. The surprise visit of Jacqueline Kennedy Onassis is still vividly recalled. It is open from 10 a.m. to noon and 1 to 3:30 p.m. Monday to Friday.

GETTING THERE: You can leave New York's JFK Airport in the morning and be at Captain's Quarters in Saba for dinner that night. To do that, you can take a direct flight on any of several major carriers from JFK to St. Maarten. From Juliana Airport there, you can fly to Saba on **Winair** (Windward Islands Airways International). Flying time is 20 minutes, and round-trip fare is $40.

Many guests at hotels on St. Maarten fly over to Saba on the morning flight, spend the day sightseeing, then return to St. Maarten on the afternoon flight. Air connections can also be made in Saba to St. Kitts and Statia.

For information about flights, call **Windward Islands Air Transport** at 011-599/42255.

Arriving by air from St. Maarten, the traveler steps from Windward Island Airways' 20-passenger STOL (short takeoff and landing) plane onto the tarmac runway of the Juancho Yrausquin Airport. The airstrip stretches 1,312 feet along the aptly named Flat Point, one of the few level areas on the island. From there the road rises in 20 serpentine curves to the village of Hell's Gate which, despite its name, nestles in the shadow of the island's largest church.

Trips can be made aboard MV *Style*, a high-speed, 52-foot power yacht that makes the one-hour journey between St. Maarten and Saba Tuesday to Saturday, departing at 9 a.m. from St. Maarten's **Great Bay Marina** (tel. 011-599-5/22167) and returning at 5 p.m. Round-trip fare is $45. The *Style* has comfortable seating, an open bar, and taped music.

GETTING AROUND: Transport is mostly on foot, but taxis and a few rental cars are available. In the unlikely event you should dare want to drive a car on Saba, your hotel can make arrangements for you at a cost of about $35 a day. The danger of driving must be emphasized though.

Taxis

Taxis meet every flight, and you can use one to take you to your hotel or to make a sightseeing tour. The cost of a two-hour tour is $7 per person if there are more than four passengers making the trip. One to four persons pay $30.

Hitchhiking

Now frowned upon in much of the world, hitchhiking has long been an acceptable means of transport in Saba, where everybody seemingly knows everybody else. On recent rounds, my taxi rushed a sick child to the plane and picked up an old man to take him up the hill because he'd fallen and hurt himself—all on my sightseeing tour! I welcomed this cooperative spirit. At least by hitchhiking, you'll get to know everybody else.

Walking

The traditional means of getting around on Saba is still much in evidence. But I suggest that only the sturdy in heart and limb walk from The Bottom up to Windwardside. Many do, but you'd better have some shoes that grip the ground, particularly after a recent rain.

PRACTICAL FACTS: As mentioned in the introduction to this chapter, Saba, like the other islands of the Netherlands Antilles, uses as legal tender the Netherlands Antilles guilder (NAf), valued at $1.79 to the U.S. dollar at press time. However, prices given here are in U.S. currency unless otherwise designated, U.S. money being accepted by almost everybody here.

Banks: The only bank on the island is Barclays, Windwardside (tel. 011-599/42216), open from 8:30 a.m. to 12:30 p.m. Monday to Friday.

Customs: You do not have to go through customs when you land at Juancho Yrausquin Airport, as this is a free port.

Documents: The government requires that all U.S. and Canadian citizens show proof of citizenship, such as a passport or voter registration card. An on-going ticket must also be produced.

Electricity: Saba uses 110 volts AC, 60 cycles, so most U.S.-made appliances do not need converters.

Information: Whatever your problems, you can take them to Glenn C. Holm, who is the chairman of the Saba Tourist Board. He operates out of a small office, the Tourist Bureau (tel. 011-599/42231), next door to the post office in Windwardside. Hours are from 8 a.m. to noon and 1 to 5 p.m. Monday to Saturday.

Medical care: A.M. Edwards Medical Centre, The Bottom, Saba, N.A. (tel. 011-599/43239), is Saba's hospital complex. To call the doctor's office, phone 011-599/43288.

Taxes: The government imposes a 5% tourist tax on hotel rooms. If you're returning to St. Maarten or flying over to Statia, you must pay a $2 departure tax. However, if you're going anywhere else, a $5 departure tax is imposed.

Telephone and cables: Cables and international telephone calls can be placed at the Cable and Wireless office in Windwardside (tel. 011-599/42225). To telephone direct from the United States, dial 011-599, then the local five-digit number, all of which begin with a 4 for Saba.

Time: Saba's time is the same as Eastern Daylight Time.

Tips and service: Most restaurants and hotels add a 10% or 15% service charge to your bills to cover tipping.

Weather: Once you get off an airplane, you encounter a temperature of 78° to 82° Fahrenheit. The annual rainfall is 42 inches.

WHERE TO STAY: The island has a few inns of character, extremely limited in accommodations, yet special and charming for that reason. If you check into an address here, you could safely say you're "hiding out."

Captain's Quarters, Windwardside, Saba, N.A. (tel. 011-599/42201), is a restored 19th-century sea captain's house converted into a guesthouse where many visitors spend secluded holidays. Just off the village center of Windwardside, it's a complex of several wood-frame guesthouses surrounding the main house with its traditional verandas and covered porches. You make your way here by going down a narrow, steep lane. Thrust out toward the water, almost as if ready to tumble down to the sea, is a freshwater swimming pool surrounded by a terrace where you can sunbathe or order refreshments from an open-air bar. The manager, Rudolph Hassell (nearly everybody on Saba seems to be named Hassell), handles the inn with style, and he's rightly proud of the chef, well known in the islands as "Sugar." The cool and refreshing dining room is nestled behind the main house amid a screen of plants. Service is polite and attractively formal at the candlelit dinners.

The main house was built by a Saban sea captain and serves as office, library, sitting room, and kitchen on the first floor, with two private accommodations above (one is a honeymoon suite). The house is furnished with antiques gathered from many ports of the world. About half of the ten bedrooms contain four-poster beds, and each is complete with a private bath and balcony overlooking the sea and Mount Scenery. Well-designed and cozy studio rooms stand in the garden. Everything seems a quaint reminder of New England. The hotel, open all year (except in September), *charges $60 in a single in summer, $75 in a double, and a third or fourth person sharing a room is assessed another $25.* In winter, the single tariff is $75, going up to $95 in a double. These are tariffs for rooms only. For breakfast and dinner, add another $27 per person daily. Modern comfort and infinite charm combine to form a tasteful, distinctive Saban atmosphere.

Scout's Place, Windwardside (tel. 011-599/42205), right in the center of the village, is hidden from the street. It's set on the ledge of a hill, giving every table a view of the sea. The place is owned by Diana Medora, who makes guests feel right at home in the inn to which she has added new rooms for a total of 14, making it the largest on the island. It is sheltered in an old house, with a large covered but open-walled dining room. It's an informal-type place, with a highly individualistic decor that might include everything from Surinam hand-carvings to peacock chairs in red-and-black wicker to silver samovars. Don't be surprised either if you see a plastic chair or two. Rooms open onto an interior courtyard filled with flowers, and each unit has a view of the sea. Furnishings are fairly coordinated, unpretentious, and very informal. Most of the rooms have private baths; others must share. Rates are the same all year—$60 daily for two people with private bath, $55 for a single. Tariffs include breakfast.

Juliana's Apartments, Windwardside, Saba, N.A. (tel. 011-599/42269), is a small group of charming guestrooms operated by Juliana and Franklin Johnson. Modern and immaculate, the rooms have private baths and balconies. In winter, singles are charged $45 daily, with doubles paying $65. *Summer rates are $40 daily in singles, $50 in doubles.* A spacious apartment with a complete kitchenette, dining/living room, separate bedroom, bath, and a large porch facing the sea rents for $95 per day in winter, *$65 in summer* for single or double occupancy. Guests at Juliana's can enjoy the facilities of Captain's Quarters nearby, including use of the pool and other amenities.

Cranston's Antique Inn, The Bottom, Saba, N.A. (tel. 011-599/43203), is a frame inn standing near the village roadway, with a front terrace where everyone congregates for rum drinks and gossip. It's an old-fashioned house, more than 100 years old at least, and every bedroom has antique four-poster beds. Mr. Cranston, the owner, will gladly rent you the same room where Queen Juliana once spent a holiday. It's on the second floor, on your left, facing the rear garden. Aside from the impressive wooden beds, the furnishings are mostly hit or miss. Rates, in effect all year, are $40 daily in a single, rising to $55 in a double, including breakfast. Local dishes are offered, such as roast pork from island pigs, red snapper, and broiled grouper. Mr. Cranston has a good island cook, who makes use of locally grown spices. Meals are served on a covered terrace in the garden. The house is within walking distance of Ladder Bay.

WHERE TO EAT: For visitors over for the day, **Scout's Place,** Windwardside (tel. 011-599/42205), is a popular dining spot, but you should have your driver stop by early and make a reservation for lunch there. Food at Scout's is simple and good, rewarding and filling, and the price is low too, about $12 for lunch. Dinner is more elaborate, and because of the limited staff reservations are definitely necessary. For your evening meal, expect to pay about $18. Tables are placed on an open-side terrace, the ideal spot for a Heineken at sundown. Local vegetables, homemade bread, and fruit are served. Lunch is at one sitting, 12:30 p.m., and dinner is also at one sitting, 7:30 p.m.

Captain's Quarters, Windwardside (tel. 011-599/42201), is an alternative choice for dinner, and again you must reserve a table. Dining is al fresco; however, if it rains, don't worry—they have a roof. Large, hearty appetites are catered to here, at a cost averaging around $18 for dinner. Perhaps you'll be there on the night they have fresh grouper. It's one of the best selections in the Caribbean. Soups are homemade and often quite good. Because of the limited supplies on Saba, vegetables are often frozen. Likewise, the wine list is very limited. Lunch will cost much less, about $10, and you can also stop in here for a very filling breakfast at around $6. The dining room is open every day of the year except during the June closing. Lunch is at one sitting: 12:30 p.m. daily. Likewise there is one sitting for dinner, at 7:30 p.m.

Saba Chinese Restaurant (Moo Goo Gai Pan), Windwardside (tel. 011-599/42268), occupies a house lying amid a cluster of residential buildings on a hillside above Windwardside. Operated by a family from Hong Kong headed by Yu Yuk Choi, it offers some 100 dishes, an unpretentious decor of plastic tablecloths and folding chairs, and a style of cookery so popular that many residents claim this to be their most frequented restaurant. Full meals cost from 30 NAf

($16.80) and include an array of Cantonese and Indonesian specialties. Among them are lobster Cantonese, Chinese chicken with mushrooms, sweet-and-sour fish, chicken with cashew nuts, conch chop suey, several curry dishes, roast duck, and nasi goreng. The establishment is open daily except Monday from 11 a.m. to 10 p.m.

SHOPPING: After lunch you can go for a stroll in Windwardside, stopping at the boutiques, which often look like someone's living room (sometimes they are). Most stores are open daily except Sunday from 9 a.m. to noon and 2 to around 5:30 p.m.

Stitched by Saban wives when their fishermen husbands were off to sea, the traditional drawn threadwork of the island is famous. You don't even have to go to a shop to find it. Chances are, your driver will stop along the road as women, mostly descendants of Europeans, crowd around. You'll find out later that the shy woman selling the drawn threadwork is the sister of your taxi driver.

Sometimes this work, introduced by a local woman named Gertrude Johnson in the 1870s, is called Spanish work, because it was believed to have been perfected by nuns in Caracas. Selected threads are drawn and tied in a piece of linen to produce an ornamental pattern. It can be expensive if a quality linen has been used, not to mention the amount of painstaking human detail that went into its creation.

The **Island Craft Shop,** Windwardside (no phone), has a good selection of drawn threadwork if you didn't buy some along the road. Owned by Bob and Ruth Beebee, it also sells items in linens, and you can purchase many souvenirs as well as black coral jewelry.

The **Saba Artisan Foundation,** The Bottom (tel. 011-599/43260), in recent years has made a name for itself in the world of fashion with hand-screened resort fashions. The clothes are casual and colorful. Among the items sold are men's bush jacket shirts, numerous styles of dresses and skirts, napkins, and placemats, as well as yard goods. Island motifs are used in many designs, and you might like a fern or casava-leaf print. Also popular are the famous Saba drawn lace patterns. The fashions are designed, printed, sewn, and marketed by Sabans. Mail-order as well as wholesale distributorship inquiries are invited.

As a final shopping note, try to come home with some "Saba Spice," an aromatic blend of 150-proof cask rum, with such spices as fennel seed, cinnamon, cloves, and nutmeg, straight from someone's home brew. It's not for everyone (too sweet), but will make an exotic bottle to show off at home.

SABA MARINE PARK: Stretching around the entire island to 200 feet below the highwater mark, the Saba Marine Park has been established by the Saba government and the Netherlands Antilles National Parks Foundation to preserve the island's marine environment. The park is zoned for various purposes. There is an all-purpose recreational zone for boating, fishing, swimming, snorkeling, and diving, including Saba's only little beach. A large multiple-use zone has no restrictions on fishing or diving except as covered by overall park regulations. Four recreational diving zones have been set up, with line- and spearfishing prohibited, and there is an anchorage and harbor, called the commercial zone. The park is intended to guarantee that coral reefs and the marine environment will be safeguarded for the future.

Information is available from **Saba Marine Park,** Fort Bay, P.O. Box 18, Saba, N.A. (tel. 011-599/43295).

THE SPORTING LIFE: Don't come here for beaches. Saba has only one sand beach, and it's about 20 feet long. Sports here are mostly do-it-yourself. John F.

Kennedy, Jr., likes to visit Saba to enjoy the underwater scenery and dark, volcanic sands and coral formations.

Saba, according to some divers, offers "some of the most spectacular diving in the Caribbean." **Saba Deep Dive Center,** Fort Bay, P.O. Box 22, The Bottom, Saba, N.A. (tel. 011-599/43347), right at the water's edge, can treat you to excellent scuba diving and snorkeling. Also available are NAUI and PADI certification courses, introductory scuba lessons, tank fills, equipment rental or sale, snorkel rental, and trips. Complete dive packages include dives, accommodations, meals, and taxi/bus service.

Sea Saba Dive Center, Windwardside (tel. 011-599/42246), is where Joan and Lou Bourque share with clients their knowledge of the underwater elkhorn forests and giant boulder gardens that make Saba "the unspoiled queen of the Caribbean," with regard to the sea world. The Bourques offer packages covering a variety of interests, including underwater photography, slide shows, marine biology seminars, and all PADI certification and resort courses.

Tennis buffs will find a public court in The Bottom. It's a cement court and doesn't charge players.

The island is as beautiful above the water as it is below. Mountain walking is therefore actually the major sport, and the top of **Mount Scenery** is a wildlife reserve, the goal of eager bands of hikers. Allow more than a day and take your time climbing the 1,064 concrete steps up to the cloud-reefed mountain. One of the inns will pack you a picnic lunch. The higher you climb, the cooler it grows, about a drop of 1° Fahrenheit every 328 feet. On a hot day this can be an incentive. The peak is 2,855 feet high.

If you don't want to set out on your own, **Botanical Tours** are offered, as well as other hikes with your special interests in mind, arranged by the Saba Tourist Office (tel. 011-599/42231) or Captain's Quarters (tel. 011-599/42201), costing $7.50 per person for up to four participants, $5 per person for larger groups. The Botanical Tour takes you to the top of Mt. Scenery into the tropical rain forest where orchids bloom in winter and golden heliconia in spring. A shorter hike is possible to **Maskehorne Hill,** where huge rock formations covered with orchids and bromeliads lead to a view of Windwardside. You can walk up the steps and cut through the terraced fields and forest of Big Rendezvous to an overlook of Crispeen. For a different view of the island, hike along Sandy Cruz, starting at Upper Hell's Gate and walking along the Deep Gut, with its blend of cultivated fields and windswept forest.

Others not so athletic may settle for a hike up Bobby Hills, 66 terraced steps leading to a peak of 1,500 feet. Beautiful views unfold in every direction.

CHAPTER XI

JAMAICA

□ □ □

Jamaica, 90 miles south of Cuba, is the third largest of the Caribbean islands, with some 4,400 square miles of predominantly green land, a mountain ridge peaking at 7,400 feet above sea level, and on the north coast, many beautiful white sand beaches with clear blue sea.

First populated in A.D. 700 by Arawak Indians, gentle people from South America who named the island "Xaymaca," Jamaica was sighted by Christopher Columbus, who called it "the fairest isle eyes have seen," in 1494—Jamaicans will tell you that he was their first tourist and was a repeat visitor, like so many others to follow him. Spain settled the island in 1509. In due course, Africans were imported by the Spanish as slaves to supplement the Indian labor force, which was gradually depleted by European disease and overwork. By 1655, when the English captured the island, there were no Arawaks left.

Until 1962 Jamaica was a Crown Colony of Great Britain but has now achieved full independence within the Commonwealth. The island's motto is, appropriately, "Out of Many, One People." The islanders are mostly of African or Afro-European descent, with a minority of British, Chinese, Indians, Portuguese, Germans, and people from other West Indian islands, all intermarried to create one people. The government is similar to that of Great Britain, the queen being represented by a governor-general appointed on the advice of the prime minister of Jamaica, who is elected. English is the official language, but with delightful adaptations, and you'll probably hear "Jamaica talk" when you take your *bankra* (basket) and *dunny* (money) to the market or have a meal of fish tea, rundown, and skyjuice.

Tourism has become the biggest industry in Jamaica, surpassing the traditional leaders, bauxite and aluminum.

The average Jamaican is friendly, and responds to a smile and a cheerful hello with kindness. Of course, there are rogues in every country, and common sense has to prevail when you travel.

In general, if you like people, you will like the Jamaicans. Don't call them natives, however. They feel it's insulting, and they are proud of just being called Jamaicans.

GETTING THERE: The most popular routings to Jamaica are from New York or Miami. The national airline, **Air Jamaica,** and **Eastern** fly several times a day from Miami to both Kingston and Montego Bay (Eastern, of course, has many connections throughout the U.S. via Miami).

Air Jamaica flies direct to Jamaica from Atlanta, Miami, Tampa, Los Angeles, New York, Philadelphia-Baltimore, and Toronto. **Air Canada** flies five times a week in high season to both Montego Bay and Kingston with connections from Toronto to other major Canadian cities. In low season, there are three flights per week.

American Airlines departs daily from John F. Kennedy Airport for both Montego Bay and Kingston. The plane usually stops in Montego Bay for refueling before continuing on to Kingston.

A wide array of fares is available. The cheapest ones are contingent on the availability for the particular day of travel of whatever block of seats American has set aside for its promotional fares. Currently, round-trip high-season fares from New York to Kingston are as low as $264 for weekday travel (Monday through Thursday), or $284 at other times (Friday through Sunday). A limited number of these rock-bottom fares are available to the public only if reservations are made in advance and if the return half of the round-trip ticket is used within 3 to 21 days of the original departure date.

If American's quota of inexpensive seats to Jamaica is filled by the time of your hoped-for departure date, it might be necessary to book a regular excursion ticket for which no advance reservations are necessary. From New York to Kingston in high season, the regular round-trip coach-class fare reaches a high of $584, but because of a complicated series of price reductions that are granted to travelers who reserve far enough in advance, it's possible, based on the availability of seats on the day of your departure, to pay less. The prices of regularly scheduled excursion tickets in low season are substantially less.

So many ticket options are available that you should always call ahead.

GETTING AROUND: Many people like to see more of Jamaica than just their resort hotel. If so, I have the following suggestions for seeing the countryside:

By Air

The bulk of travelers to Jamaica, particularly tourists, enter Jamaica via Montego Bay. The island service is by **Trans-Jamaican Airlines Ltd.** (tel. 809/993-2405 in Port Antonio, 809/923-9498 in Kingston, and 809/952-5403 in Montego Bay). The international **Air Jamaica** handles sales and provides information overseas. Trans-Jamaican flies between the major towns of the island. Fares are reduced slightly in low season. Incidentally, there are two Kingston airports, which are connected by taxi. One, Tinson Pen, in the heart of downtown Kingston, is for domestic flights, the other for international. Car-rental facilities are only available at the international airport.

By Car

Jamaica is big enough and public transportation is unreliable enough that a car is not really a luxury but is almost a necessity if you plan to do any sightseeing beyond the confines of your hotel. Over the years, I have tried and recommended

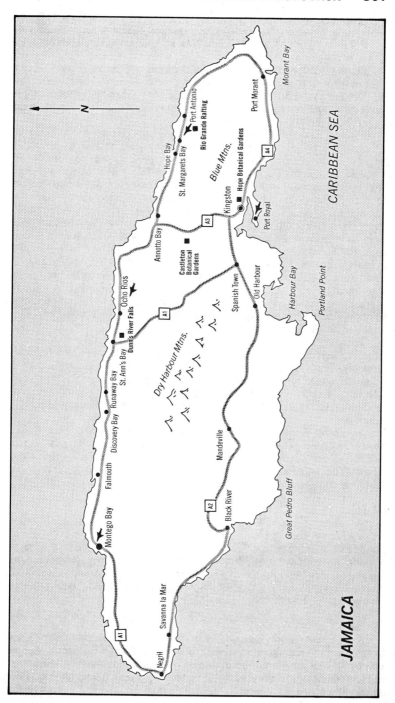

JAMAICA

CARIBBEAN SEA

N

Morant Bay

Port Morant

Port Antonio
Rio Grande Rafting
Blue Mtns.
Hope Bay
St. Margarets Bay
Hope Botanical Gardens
Kingston
Port Royal
A4
A3
Annotto Bay
Castleton Botanical Gardens
Spanish Town
Old Harbour
Harbour Bay
Portland Point
Ocho Rios
A1
Dunns River Falls
St. Ann's Bay
Runaway Bay
Discovery Bay
Dry Harbour Mtns.
Mandeville
Falmouth
A2
Black River
Montego Bay
Great Pedro Bluff
Savanna la Mar
A1
Negril

all the major car-rental firms. On my most recent trip, I used the **Budget Rent-a-Car** subsidiary. Budget has three offices in Jamaica—at the Norman Manley Airport in Kingston, at 14 Waterloo Road, New Kingston, opposite Terra Nova Hotel, and in downtown Ocho Rios.

Renting a car in Jamaica is easy, but there are several things you should be aware of before starting out. Drivers must be between the ages of 25 and 70 and must present a valid driver's license and a credit card when filling out the forms. Travelers without a credit card must pay a $500 to $1,000 security deposit in cash at the time of rental.

Budget's insurance policies declare that any driver is responsible for the first $500 of damage to the car, if he or she accepts a collision damage waiver. (The potential liability is even greater with several other car-rental companies.) If a driver decides to purchase such a waiver, costing $9 per day, his or her eventual liability in the event of an accident will be limited to the first $500 damage. If the driver forgoes the waiver, he or she must pay the entire bill for the damage.

Budget offers a wide variety of vehicles, mainly Japanese. Any rental is cheaper by the week, although daily rentals are also possible. The following prices apply to vehicles reserved at least two full business days in advance through Budget's toll-free reservation system. A Toyota Starlet, with manual transmission and a seating capacity of four, costs $265 per week, with each additional day costing an extra $38. Rentals of less than a week cost $49 per day. Unlimited mileage is included in all rates, but a 10% government tax is added. Automatic-transmission cars with air conditioning are also available: a Nissan Sunny costs $330 per week with this equipment, and extra days cost an additional $47. Daily rentals of less than a week cost $60 per day.

There are numerous car-rental agencies in Jamaica in addition to Budget, including **Avis** and **Hertz.** For the same type of cars, prices and terms of rental vary only slightly. It is best to book your car in advance of your arrival with the airline or your travel agent. Some agencies rent cars to persons 21 years of age with valid licenses. To compare prices, you could check with the following toll-free numbers: Budget, 800/527-0700; Hertz, 800/654-3131; and Avis, 800/228-0668.

As in other British-influenced countries, driving is *on the left.* Speed limits in town are 30 miles per hour; elsewhere, 50 mph. Gas is measured by the imperial gallon, the charge payable only in Jamaican dollars—no credit cards are accepted. (The cost of gasoline may be higher by the time you visit.) Your own valid driver's license is acceptable.

By Train

A leisurely sort of travel, but a marvelous way to see the country, is by rail. At each station, peddlers leap onto the train to sell their wares, jumping off at the last possible second as the train leaves the station. Expect to pay J$17 ($3.06) for second-class rail travel and J$26 ($4.68) for first-class journeys (available Saturday and Sunday only) for the trip between Kingston and Montego Bay, which takes about 4½ hours. There are two departures a day. Check at local stations to see when trains are expected to run.

By Taxi

Kingston has no city taxis with meters, so agree on a price before you get in. In Kingston and the rest of the island special taxis and buses for visitors are operated by JUTA (Jamaica Union of Travellers Association) and have the union's emblem on the side of the vehicle. All prices are controlled, and any local JUTA office will supply a list of rates. JUTA drivers do nearly all the ground transfers, and some offer sightseeing tours. I've found them pleasant, in the main knowledgeable, and good drivers. There are many companies offering sightseeing tours of the island. Most of the cabs are of U.S. origin, but they are old.

Moped and Honda Rentals

These two-wheel vehicles can be rented in Montego Bay, and you'll need a valid driver's license. **Montego Bike Rentals,** 21 Gloucester Ave. (tel. 809/952-4984), rents Hondas for $38 per day, requiring a $300 deposit. Scooters are $28 per day. Deposits are refundable if vehicles are returned in good shape.

PRACTICAL FACTS: To ease your orientation to an often bewildering island, I have some important information you should know in advance of your arrival. *Caveat:* Some Jamaicans dislike having their pictures taken, for various reasons. Ask permission first.

Banks: Banks islandwide are generally open from 9 a.m. to 2 p.m. Monday to Thursday, 9 a.m. to noon and 2:30 to 5 p.m. Friday.

Documents: U.S. and Canadian residents do not need passports but must hold a return or ongoing ticket and proof of citizenship. Other visitors need passports, for a maximum stay of six months.

Drugs: Hard drugs and *ganja* (marijuana) are illegal and imprisonment is the penalty for violation. Prescriptions are accepted only if issued by a Jamaican doctor. Hotels have doctors on call. If you need any particular medicine or treatment, bring evidence, such as a letter from your own doctor.

Electricity: Most places have the standard electrical voltage of 110, as in the U.S. However, some establishments operate on 220 volts, 50 cycles. If your hotel is on a different current from your U.S.-made appliance, ask for a converter.

Marrying: You can get a marriage license after 48 hours' residence on the island, and then marry as soon as it can be arranged. You will need your birth certificates, and where applicable, divorce documents. Apply to the Ministry of Justice, Kingston. Most Jamaican hotels will make arrangements for your license and for your wedding.

Nudity: Nude bathing is allowed at a number of hotels, clubs, and beaches (especially in Negril) which are signposted "Swimsuits Optional." Elsewhere, the law will not even allow topless sunbathing.

Stores: Hours vary widely, but as a general rule most business establishments open at 8:30 a.m., closing at 5 p.m. Monday to Friday (or in some places, earlier at 4:30 p.m.). Some shops are open on Saturday until noon.

Taxes: The government imposes a room tax, ranging from $4 to $8 in small hotels. This goes up to $8 to $16 in larger establishments, the higher price being for deluxe and first-class accommodations. Some hotels charge an energy tax. The tax is per room per night. On departure, you will be charged J$40 ($7.20) tax at the airport. It's payable in Jamaican dollars. (All air flights must be reconfirmed no later than 72 hours before departure.)

Telephone: All overseas telephone calls outside your hotel incur a government tax of 10%. To call Jamaica direct from North America, dial the area code, 809, then the local number.

Time: In winter, Jamaica is on Eastern Standard Time. However, when the U.S. is on Daylight Saving Time, when it's 6 a.m. in Miami it's 5 a.m. in Kingston.

Tips and service: Tipping is customary. A general 10% or 15% is expected in hotels and restaurants on occasions where you would normally tip. Some places add a service charge to the bill. Tipping is not allowed in the all-inclusive hotels.

Water: It's usually safe to drink piped-in water islandwide, as it is often filtered and chlorinated. Naturally, if available, it is much more prudent to drink bottled water.

Weather: Expect temperatures around 80° to 90° Fahrenheit on the coast. Winter is a little cooler. In the mountains, it can get as low as 40°. There is generally a breeze, which in winter is noticeably cool. The rainy periods are October to early November, and May to early June. Normally rain comes in short, sharp showers; then the sun shines.

MONEY: Be careful! There are Jamaican dollars and there are U.S. dollars. Unless it is clearly stated, either in shops or when agreeing to a rate with a taxi driver or in a restaurant, always insist on knowing which dollar they are quoting. Actually, tourists are required to pay their bills in Jamaican dollars, written J$. However, shopkeepers and hotel owners still, in many cases, quote tourists prices in U.S. dollars. Jamaica has adopted the policy of excluding U.S. currency from circulation. For purposes of clarification, in this book prices quoted in Jamaican dollars will be given as J$, with the U.S. conversion in parentheses after that quotation. Otherwise, the dollar figures given are in U.S. currency. As of this writing, the Jamaican dollar is still fluctuating. Any comment made by me will likely be out of date by the time you actually reach Jamaica. At the time of research for this edition, a visitor could get about J$5.40 to $1 U.S. (J$1 equals about 18¢). But that rate has fluctuated greatly, and is certainly likely to continue upward or downward during the lifetime of this edition. However, to give you a rough idea of what certain services will cost, I will convert at the prevailing rate at the time of research. But remember to check with your bank or a Jamaican tourist office to find what the prevailing rate of exchange will be during your visit.

You should use your immigration card when making bank transactions and also when converting Jamaican dollars back into U.S. dollars.

Jamaican currency comes in different sizes: J$1, J$2, J$5, J$10, and J$20. Coins are 1¢, 5¢, 10¢, 20¢, 25¢, and 50¢. There is no limit to the amount of foreign currency you can bring in, but it is illegal to import or export Jamaican currency. Duty-free shops, banks, and hotels change money. But wherever you change money, get a currency receipt—you must present it when changing your surplus Jamaican dollars at the end of your stay. Both international airports have banks.

MEET THE PEOPLE: The Jamaica Tourist Board operates the Meet-the-People program in Kingston and the island's five major resort cities and towns. Through the program, visitors get the opportunity to meet Jamaican families who volunteer to host them free for a few hours or even a whole day. More than 650 families are registered in the scheme with the Tourist Board, which keeps a list of their interests and hobbies. All you have to do is give the board a rough idea of your own interests, and they will arrange for you to spend the day with a similar family.

Once with them, you just go along with whatever they plan to do, sharing their life, eating at their table, joining them at a dinner party. You may end up at a beach barbecue, afternoon tea with the neighbors, or just sitting and expounding theories, arguing, and talking far into the night. The program does not offer overnight accommodation.

If you have a particular interest—birds, butterflies, music, ham radio, stamp collecting, or spelunking (there are many caves to explore)—the tourist board will find you a fellow enthusiast. Many lasting friendships have been developed because of this unique opportunity to meet the people.

It is important to know that this service is entirely free. You need not even take your hostess a gift, but she will certainly appreciate a bunch of flowers after your visit.

In Jamaica, apply at any of the tourist boards: Tourism Centre, 21 Dominica Drive, Kingston 5 (tel. 809/929-9200); 21 Ward Ave., Mandeville P.O., Manchester (tel. 809/925-1072); Cornwall Beach, P.O. Box 67, Montego Bay, St. James (tel. 809/952-4425); Ocean Village Shopping centre, P.O. Box 240, Ocho Rios, St. Ann (tel. 809/974-2570); City Centre Plaza, P.O. Box 151, Port Antonio, Portland (tel. 809/993-3051); or Shop No. 20, Plaza de Negril, Negril P.O., Westmoreland (tel. 809/957-4234). In the U.S. and Canada: 866 Second Ave., 10th Floor, New York, NY 10017 (tel. 212/688-7650); Suite 1210, 36 South Wabash Ave., Chicago, IL 60603 (tel. 312/346-1546); 8411 Preston Rd., Suite 605, L.B. 31, Dallas, TX (tel. 214/361-8778); 3440 Wilshire Blvd., Suite 1207, Los Angeles, CA 90010 (tel. 213/384-1123); 1320 South Dixie Hwy., Suite 1100, Coral Gables, FL 33146 (tel. 305/665-0557); 1 Eglinton Ave., Suite 616, Toronto, Ontario M4P 3A1, Canada (tel. 416/482-7850); or Mezzanine Level, 1110 Sherbourne St., W. Montréal, Quebec H3A 1G9, Canada (tel. 514/849-6386).

FOOD AND DRINK: Because this is an island, there is great emphasis on seafood. Rock lobster is a regular dish on every menu, appearing grilled, thermidor, cold, hot. Saltfish and ackee is the national dish, a concoction of salt cod and a brightly colored vegetable that tastes something like scrambled eggs. Escovitch (marinated fish) is usually fried and then simmered in vinegar with onions and peppers. Curried mutton and goat are popular, as is pepperpot stew, all highly seasoned and guaranteed to reduce your body temperature.

Jerk pork is peculiar to country areas, where it is barbecued slowly over wood fires until crisp and brown. Apart from rice and peas (which are really red beans), usually served as a sort of risotto with added onions, spices, and salt pork, vegetables are exotic: breadfruit, imported by Captain Bligh in 1723 when he arrived aboard H.M.S. *Bounty;* callaloo, rather like spinach, used in pepperpot soup (not to be confused with the stew of the same name); cho-cho, served boiled and buttered or stuffed; and green bananas and plantains, fried or boiled and served with almost everything. Then there is pumpkin, which goes into a soup or is served on the side, boiled and mashed with butter.

Coconut milk is a refreshing drink, especially when you stop by the roadside to have a local vendor chop the top from a fresh nut straight from the tree. Sweet potatoes appear with main courses, but there is also a sweet potato pudding made with sugar and coconut milk, flavored with cinnamon, nutmeg, and vanilla. You'll meet the intriguing *stamp and go,* salt fish cakes to eat as an appetizer; *fall back,* salty stew with bananas and dumplings; and *rundown,* mackerel cooked in coconut milk, often eaten for breakfast. For the really adventurous, *manish water,* a soup made from goat offal and tripe, is said to increase virility. Patties (meat pies)—the best in the island are at Montego Bay—are another staple snack. Boiled corn, roast yams, roast saltfish, fried fish, soups, and fruits are sold at roadside stands.

Rum punches are everywhere, and the local beer is Red Stripe. The island produces many liqueurs, the most famous being Tía Maria, made from coffee beans. Rumona is another good one to take home with you. Bellywash, the local name for lemonade, will supply the extra liquid you may need to counteract the heat of the tropics. Blue Mountain coffee is the best, but tea, cocoa, and milk are usually available to round off a meal.

REGGAE FESTIVAL: The annual Reggae Sunsplash Festival, usually held the second week in August in Montego Bay, features Jamaican artists. Arrangements to attend can be made by May of every year. Many local hotels are fully booked for the festival, so advance reservations are necessary. The Jamaican Tourist Board's U.S. and Canadian offices (see above under "Meet the People") can give you information about packages and group rates for the festival. Other reggae concerts and festivals featuring top performers are held throughout the year in Jamaica. Ask the tourist board.

THE SPORTING LIFE: If sports are important to your vacation, you may want to review the offerings of Jamaica before deciding on a particular resort. Sports are so spread out, and Jamaica so large, that it isn't feasible to go on a long day's excursion just to play golf, for example. The cost of most activities is generally the same throughout the island.

Golf

In all the West Indies, Jamaica has the best courses. Montego Bay alone has four championship courses. Space does not permit a description of all these courses, but one in particular, the one at **Wyndham Rose Hall Beach Hotel and Country Club** (tel. 809/953-2650), has been called "one of the top five courses in the world." This seaside and mountain course is unusual and challenging. Built on the shores of the Caribbean, its eighth hole skirts the ocean, then dog-legs onto a promontory and a green thrusting 200 yards into the sea. The back nine is the most scenic and interesting, rising into steep slopes and deep ravines on Mount Zion. The tenth fairway abuts the family burial grounds of the Barretts of Wimpole Street, and the 14th passes the vacation home of singer Johnny Cash. The 300-foot-high 13th tee offers a rare panoramic view of the sea and the roof of the hotel, and the 15th green is next to a 40-foot waterfall, once featured in a James Bond movie. A fully stocked pro shop, a clubhouse, and a professional staff are among the amenities. In winter, rates are $25 for 18 holes, dropping to $20 in summer.

Others include the challenging **Tryall** (tel. 809/952-5110), in Hanover, 12 miles from town, where the Mazda Champions Tournament, with the biggest golf purse in the world, was played from 1985 through 1987 and the Jamaica Classic in 1989. It charges $50 in winter for 18 holes, lowering the price to $25 in summer.

The **Half Moon,** Montego Bay (tel. 809/953-2211), has a championship course designed by Robert Trent Jones that opened in 1961, opposite the hotel. The course has manicured and diversely shaped greens. In winter, you can play 18 holes for $50, the price dropping to $35 in summer. However, hotel guests can play free. Half Moon has a staff of golf professionals.

Montego Bay also has another 18-hole course, less well known than the others. It's the **Ironshore Golf Club** (tel. 809/953-2800), which charges $20 for 18 holes in winter, $15 in summer.

Golfers can continue along the north coast to Runaway Bay, near Ocho Rios, where the **Super Club's Runaway Bay Golf Club** (tel. 809/973-2436). Greens fees are $14 for 18 holes in winter, $12 in summer.

Upton Golf Course & Plantation, P.O. Box 178, Ocho Rios (tel. 809/974-2528), also welcomes visitors to play its 18 holes. It promises you're 700 feet up "and always cool." Golfers play amid beautiful scenery, paying greens fees of J$18 ($6.65) for 18 holes. There is a clubhouse and bar.

In Kingston, check out **Constant Spring Club** (tel. 809/924-1610), an 18-hole course in the foothills of the Blue Mountains, and **Caymanas Country Club** (no phone), near the Caymanas Race Course.

In Mandeville, there's the nine-hole **Manchester Golf Club** (tel. 809/962-2403), where championship tournaments are played annually.

Water Sports

Water options for the sports lover proliferate throughout Jamaica, with many activities offered as part of all-inclusive packages by the island's major hotels. However, there are other well-maintained facilities for water sports not connected to the hotel offerings.

Jamaica has some of the finest diving waters in the world. The average diving depth ranges from 35 to 95 feet. Visibility is usually from 60 to 120 feet. Most of the diving is done on coral reefs, which are protected by underwater parks where fish, shells, coral, and sponges are plentiful. Experienced divers can also see wrecks, hedges, caves, dropoffs, and tunnels.

Caribbean Amusements Co. (CAC), at the Trelawny Beach Hotel in Falmouth (tel. 809/954-2450), offers scuba-diving programs to the offshore coral reefs that are considered some of the most spectacular of the Caribbean. There are seven ACUC-certified dive guides, three dive boats, and all the necessary equipment for either inexperienced or already-certified divers. Guests of the Trelawny benefit from free introductory lessons and the availability of a free daily dive. Nonresidents are charged $30 per dive. Diving is conducted partly offshore of the hotel and partly near the reefs at Ocho Rios. Night dives are also offered, and transportation is provided to all dive sites. Night dives cost extra, even for guests of the hotel. Trelawny Beach also offers free snorkeling, Sunfish sailing, windsurfing, and glass-bottom-boat rides.

Seaworld Resorts, Ltd., Montego Bay (tel. 809/953-2180), has facilities at Rose Hall and Cariblue Beach for visitors interested in scuba-diving, either on a beginner basis or as an experienced diver. Snorkeling and other water sports, including waterskiing, are offered. Cruises aboard the M/V *Princess* are available for those who don't want to work too hard, although you can snorkel, swim, waterski, and parasail during the cruise if you wish. Trips to Negril and a dinner cruise are on the program.

The **Negril Scuba Centre,** Negril Beach Club Hotel (tel. 809/957-4425), is operated by a U.S. midwesterner, Karen McCarthy, whose staff of licensed PADI instructors and divemasters teach and supervise. A resort course and a beginner's dive are offered, as well as full certification courses. This is the most modern scuba operation in the center.

SunDivers Jamaica Ltd., Club Caribbean, Runaway Bay (tel. 809/973-2346), a five-star PADI dive training facility, offers classes for beginners up to instructors. Eleven dive boats with a trained water-sport staff take divers to fine scuba sites. Custom dive packages plus video vacation packages are available. The club has a full range of water sports, including sailing, windsurfing, snorkeling, waterskiing, fishing, parasailing, and glass-bottom boat rides.

For water sports in Port Antonio, visit the **Admiralty Club,** Navy Island, Port Antonio Tour Company, Ltd. (PATCO), P.O. Box 188, Port Antonio (tel. 809/993-2667). Snorkeling off Crusoe's Beach is offered, equipment rental including mask, snorkel, and fins; or you can go scuba-diving with certified divers, mask, fins, belt, and tanks provided. They also give scuba lessons. Windsurfing, sailing, and deep-sea fishing are also part of the water-sports program.

Many hotels offer some of the water sports cited above free to their guests. In general, prices are as listed below.

Waterskiing: It costs about $12 for a 15-minute ski run, and many hotels have training facilities. Apply locally.

A Sunfish: Many hotels and some public beaches have Sunfish sailboats for rent at about $10 per hour. Hotels with their own fleets will charge less.

Snorkeling: Equipment is available in many places, for $8 to $12 per day.

Windsurfing: Some hotels have boards for windsurfing available. The best place for this sport is Port Antonio. It usually costs about $10 per hour.

Horseback Riding

The best riding is in the Ocho Rios area. Jamaica's most complete equestrian center is **Chukka Cove Farm and Resort,** P.O. Box 160, Richmond Llandovery, near Ocho Rios (tel. 809/972-2506). A one-hour trail ride costs $20. The most popular ride is a three-hour beach jaunt where, after riding over trails to the sea, you can unpack your horse and swim in the surf. Refreshments are served as part of the $40 cost of this trip. A six-hour beach ride, complete with picnic lunch, goes for $60. Polo lessons are also available, costing $25 for a 30-minute lesson.

Also good is the program at **Rocky Point Stables,** Half Moon Club, Montego Bay (tel. 809/952-1526), offering trail rides and riding lessons. Charges are $26 for 1½-hour rides, $32 for a 2½-hour combined trail ride and ocean swim for you and your horse.

Tennis

Most hotels have their own courts, many floodlit for night games. If your hotel does not have a court, expect to pay about $6 to $8 per hour at another hotel.

All-Jamaica Hardcourt Championships are played in August at the **Manchester Club,** 1 Caledonia Rd., Mandeville (tel. 809/962-2403). The courts are open for other play the rest of the year. The cost is J$20 ($3.60) per person per game.

Deep-Sea Fishing

North Jamaica waters are world-renowned for their gamefish, including dolphin, wahoo, blue and white marlin, sailfish, tarpon, Allison tuna, barracuda, and bonito. The Jamaica International Fishing Tournament and Jamaica International Blue Marlin Team Tournaments run concurrently at Port Antonio every September or October. Most major hotels from Port Antonio to Montego Bay have deep-sea fishing facilities, and there are many charter boats.

At Port Antonio, **Coral Baby** (tel. 809/993-3511) takes out up to six persons for $180 per half day, $300 per day, with crew, bait, and tackle.

Seaworld Resorts Ltd., in Montego Bay (tel. 809/953-2180), operates flying-bridge cruisers, with deck lines and outriggers, for fishing expeditions. A half-day fishing trip costs $260.

At Ocho Rios, the **Sans Souci Hotel & Club** (tel. 809/974-2353) offers deep-sea fishing for $250 for six persons.

1. KINGSTON

Kingston, the largest English-speaking city in the Caribbean, is the capital of Jamaica, with a population of some 587,000 people living on the plains between Blue Mountain and the sea.

The buildings are a mixture of very modern, graceful old, and plain ramshackle. It's a busy city, as you might expect, with a natural harbor that is the seventh largest in the world. The University of the West Indies has its campus on the edge of the city. The cultural center of Jamaica is here, along with industry, finance, and government. Now covering some 40 square miles, the city was founded by the survivors of the 1692 Port Royal earthquake, and in 1872 it became the capital, superseding Spanish Town.

WHERE TO STAY: Kingston has accommodations in all price ranges, but I'll begin with—

The Leading Hotels

Security-conscious Kingston now provides all leading hotels with guards, not unlike the deluxe apartments in New York.

Wyndham Hotel New Kingston, 85 Knutsford Blvd., P.O. Box 112, Kingston 10, Jamaica, W.I. (tel. 809/926-5430 or toll free 800/822-4200, 800/631-4200 in Canada), rises in an imposing mass of pink-colored stucco pierced with oversize sheets of tinted glass. Each unit has a white metal balcony, emphasizing to viewers the distinctive rose tint (the designers call it "Wyndham Red Rock") that is the trademark of the Wyndham hotel chain. The designers of the hotel included lots of extras. The engineers added an on-site generator, activated during the occasional city power failure. The hotel contains around 400 rooms, three restaurants, four bars, an Olympic-size swimming pool, floodlit tennis courts, a fully equipped health club, and all the amenities to make what was a commercial hotel into an inner-city resort. Each of the bedrooms and suites contains cable TV. Year round, units capable of accommodating from one to two persons cost $105 to $140 daily, while suites usually begin at $200 per night. An additional person can stay in any double room for an extra $25 per night, while children under 18 stay free in their parents' room. MAP can be arranged for an additional $30 per person per day. Use of the tennis courts is free daily until 4 p.m., after which they rent for $12 per hour.

The hotel's Rendezvous Piano Bar is a gathering place where live entertainment is presented in a setting of plants and soft lights. Palm Court, on the mezzanine level of the main lobby, beside the Rendezvous, is a small, intimate restaurant created for business lunches. It offers Italian specialties, steaks, kebabs, and a generous salad bar. The desserts are sinful, and the wine list—*c'est formidable*. This is the perfect place for the power lunch and other civilized forms of tête-à-tête. Lunch and dinner, served daily except Sunday, cost from J$50 ($9) up. A disco called the Jonkanoo (see "Kingston After Dark,") is on the premises.

The **Jamaica Pegasus,** 81 Knutsford Blvd., Kingstown 5, Jamaica, W.I. (tel. 809/926-3690, 212/541-4400 in New York City, or toll free 800/223-5672 in the U.S. and Toronto), a Trusthouse Forte hotel, is a favorite with commercial travelers, lying in the banking and a fine residential area of Kingston. After its major renovation it is better than ever, and is the site of many conventions and social events. It competes with panache with any other hotel in town, combining English style with Jamaican warmth. Its 4 p.m. tea service at the Pavilion Restaurant is considered a bit of a social event among some residents. The hotel also makes an effort to provide vacation-related activities which in theory exist only in a resort. A jogging track, health club, tennis courts, an outdoor pool, and a staff willing to arrange water sports and sightseeing help the hotel compete for the vacationers' business. Each of its 350 well-furnished bedrooms is air-conditioned, containing satellite-connected color TV, coffee-making equipment, phone, radio, and private bath. Year-round rates for single or double occupancy cost from $150 daily. Several floors of luxuriously appointed suites form the Knutsford Club, with special executive services. Here two persons pay from $150 to $475. The Talk of the Town restaurant on the 17th floor is one of the most dramatic in town, and for a change of pace, the Surrey Tavern serves pub lunches and good beer.

Oceana Hotel and Conference Centre, corner of King Street and Ocean Boulevard, P.O. Box 986, Kingston 10, Jamaica, W.I. (tel. 809/922-0920, or toll free 800/526-2422). Traditionally considered a well-managed commercial hotel, the Oceana has competed for the resort market since its lavish refurbishment in 1986. It occupies an oceanfront neighborhood filled with prominent business and government buildings, a few steps from the cruise-ship piers in

Kingston's harbor. Rising 12 imposing stories, the hotel offers an array of vacation-oriented facilities in spite of its location in the center of town. It has a ten-sided freshwater swimming pool ringed with modern verandas and shingle-capped pavilions, a health club popular with the capital's weightlifters, and a staff who organize water sports, golfing, and tennis. Laundry, Telex services, newsstands, a hairdresser and barbershop, and an in-house drugstore provide big-city-hotel type services. The stylish and popular Fort Charles restaurant is reviewed separately. A lobby-level bar, which converts to an evening disco, combines navy-blue murals of 18th-century Jamaican life with cool jazz and tall drinks. The hotel is physically connected to Jamaica's largest and most modern conference center, and consequently houses delegates from the frequent international meetings conducted next door. Year-round rates range from $80 to $100 per night, single or double. Each of the comfortable blue bedrooms is air-conditioned and freshly painted in shades of blue and pink.

The Courtleigh, 31 Trafalgar Rd., Kingston 10, Jamaica, W.I. (tel. 809/926-8174), is housed in a symmetrical, white-painted, two-story building that stands amid a flowering garden set back from the busy street. Jamaican owned, the establishment contains a covered reception area with no exterior walls, a plantation-inspired series of verandas and gardens, and extended balconied wings containing the pleasant, simple yet comfortable accommodations. The central core of all this is the flower-bordered pool area, sheltered from the suburbs outside by the hotel as well as by shrubs and trees which a team of gardeners works to maintain. Recently annexed is a beautifully furnished all-suites complex, containing units with one, two, and three bedrooms, all with private baths, phones, color cable TV, air conditioning, and a swimming pool. They rent for $72 to $145 for two persons. The other rooms, each with a modern veranda or balcony of its own, a private bath, a phone, and air conditioning, cost $48.50 in a single, $65 in a double. On the premises is a popular disco, Mingles (see "Kingston After Dark," below), and the recommended Plantation Terrace Restaurant (see "Where to Dine").

Small Budget Hotels

Terra Nova Hotel, 17 Waterloo Rd., Kingston 10, Jamaica, W.I. (tel. 809/926-2211), is a gem among small, independently run hotels. Built in 1924 as a wedding present for a young bride, the house has had a varied career. It was once the family seat of the Myers rum dynasty, and the birthplace and home of Christopher Blackwell, promoter of many Jamaican singers and musical groups, among which were Bob Marley and the Wailers and Millie Small. In 1959 the house was converted into a hotel, and, set in 2½ acres of well-kept gardens with a backdrop of greenery and mountains, is now considered one of the best small Jamaican hotels. There is a swimming pool behind the hotel. Most of the 33 air-conditioned bedrooms are in a new wing. All have balconies or patios looking out onto the gardens. Year-round tariffs are the same in a single or double, $85 daily. Your à la carte breakfast is served on the balcony or in the dining room. Above the portico is a balcony roof bar. The Spanish-style dining room, a fairly recent addition to the old building, with a stone floor, wide windows, and spotless linens, offers some of the best international food on the island (see "Where to Dine").

Indies Hotel, 5 Holborn Rd., Kingston 10, Jamaica, W.I. (tel. 809/926-2952), is set in one of the small side streets of New Kingston opening onto a flower garden. The half-timbered building with double gables has a small reception area decorated with potted plants, a lounge, and a TV lounge. The bedrooms, restaurant, and bar are grouped around a cool patio, all spotless. The 16 rooms go year round for $27.50 to $35 daily in a single. All have shower and toilet and are air-conditioned. The Indies has a reputation among the locals for friendly atmosphere and good-quality, budget meals. Their fish and chips is renowned, although Jean claims that their specialty is pizza. They also serve steak with all the trimmings, and when they get fancy, prepare lobster thermidor.

Hotel Four Seasons, 18 Ruthven Rd., Kingston 10, Jamaica, W.I. (tel. 809/926-8805), is a nice old house with a colonial-style veranda along the front, looking onto mango trees and a pleasant wooded garden through which you drive. There is good car parking, and you enter through the columns of the veranda to the reception and dining areas of this hotel. Recently, a block of rooms with modern decor was added. The rooms are simple and air-conditioned, each having a phone, color TV, and a private bath or shower. Year round they rent for $50 daily for a single, $25 to $27.50 per person in a double, EP. All meals are served to both hotel guests and outsiders, either on the terrace or in the formal dining room. Monday to Friday, a buffet lunch has an interesting selection of hot dishes, vegetable salads, and desserts. The hotel has two bars (one inside, one out). There is an arrangement for swimming at one of the large hotels nearby.

A Hostel on the Outskirts

Up Blue Mountain, for back-to-nature buffs and backpackers, is **Whitfield Hall,** a hostel and coffee property about six miles from Mavis Bank. Usually people drive to Mavis Bank or Mahogany Vale, leave their cars at a farm, and walk or use a Land Rover for J$100 ($18) each way for up to eight people. You can be picked up in Kingston with this Land Rover for J$200 ($36) each way, also for a maximum of eight. The last four miles are rough and steep. Whitfield Hall is an old coffee plantation house, and is the last inhabited house before the peak, some 4,000 feet above sea level. It's a hostel, providing accommodations for some 30 people, in rooms containing two or more beds. Blankets and linen are provided, but no personal items such as towels, soap, or food. There is a deep-freeze and a refrigerator as well as good cooking facilities, crockery, and cutlery. All water comes from a freshwater spring, and all lighting is by kerosene pressure lamps (called *Tilleys*). Wood fires warm the hostel and its guests, for it gets cold in the mountains at night. The charge per night is $6 per person all year. You bring your own food and share the communal kitchen. You can stay here for one night, one week, or if you really want to get away from it all, for longer.

Most visitors tend to aim for seeing the sunrise from the summit of Blue Mountain, which means getting up at around 2 to 3 a.m. to walk the additional 3,202 feet to the summit along bridle paths through the forest. The route is clearly marked, and all you really need is a good flashlight and warm clothing to go with your hiking boots or strong shoes. It's a three-hour walk each way. It is possible to hire a mule or horse to make the jaunt, accompanied by a guide, for approximately J$120 ($21.60) round trip for the 13-mile journey. It is quite possible to spend a week or more in the mountains, just walking to see the vast variety of flowers and trees, the largest variety of ferns in the world, to listen to the crickets, and to watch the birds. There are many trails, and the hostel has information on various routes to take. However, visitors should not leave the bridle paths and wander into the forest without a guide, as it is easy to get lost. One can arrange for a guide, negotiable locally.

For reservations at the hostel, information, or a brochure, write or phone John Allgrove, 8 Armon Jones Crescent, Kingston 6, Jamaica, W.I. (tel. 809/927-0986, home).

WHERE TO DINE: Kingston has a good range of places to eat, whether you're seeking stately meals in plantation houses, hotel buffets, or fast-food shops.

Blue Mountain Inn, Newcastle Rd. (tel. 809/927-7400), is about a 20-

minute drive from downtown Kingston, an 18th-century coffee plantation house set on the slopes of Blue Mountain, surrounded by trees and flowers on the bank of the Mammee River. On cold nights, log fires blaze, and the dining room gleams with silver and sparkling glass under the discreet table lights. The inn is one of Jamaica's most famous restaurants, not only for food but for atmosphere and service. Men are required to wear jackets (ties are optional), but the effort is worth it and the cool night air justifies it. Women are advised to take a wrap. Menus change monthly and feature dishes of the Caribbean, fresh seafood, and U.S. steaks. All are served with a selection of fresh vegetables. Top off your meal with tropical fruit salad and cream, Tía Maria parfait, baked alaska, or a more ambitious banana or pineapple flambé. The wine list includes European varieties together with local beverages. A complete meal costs about $35. Reservations are essential, as it is popular all year. Go between 7 and 9 nightly.

In Devon House, 26 Hope Rd., is the **Port Royal Grogg Shoppe** (tel. 809/ 926-3580), with its weathered swinging sign, open for lunch, dinner, morning coffee, and snacks, from 9 p.m. to midnight. You can eat on patios under the trees, in sight of the royal palms and the fountain in front of the main building. The terraces are called either "mango" or "mahogany." Your meal will have a traditional Jamaican character, and the bar serves 11 different rum punches and 10 fruit punches, such as a tamarind fizz or a papaya (paw-paw) punch. Snacks include coffee and sandwiches. Lunch offers appetizers, among them a "tidbit" of jerk pork or a bowl of soup (perhaps Jamaican red pea—really bean—or pumpkin soup). The cost of the meal, ranging from J$40 ($7.20) to J$75 ($13.50), will depend on your selection, either a sandwich and soup or a complete hot meal. Main dishes include offerings such as Jamaican ackee and salt fish, barbecued chicken, or steamed snapper. Also tasty are their unusual homemade ice creams made of local fruits such as soursop. Blue Mountain tea or coffee is also served, and a 10% service charge is added to all bills.

Norma, 8 Belmont Rd. (tel. 809/929-4966), has a sophisticated cuisine and an open-air setting. It was established by Norma Shirley after a return to her native Jamaica from a 20-year residency in the Massachusetts Berkshires. The cuisine is an imaginative collection of creative recipes accumulated from throughout the world, each of which is strongly influenced by nouvelle cuisine. She holds forth in the rear garden of an unpretentious private house in Kew Kingston, about a five-minute drive from the Pegasus Hotel. The parsley, thyme, and oregano used in many dishes was cultivated in a garden behind a screen of ficus. Assisted by a trio of friends, Ms. Shirley serves only lunch, from noon to 3 p.m. except Saturday and Sunday. (The only dinner served is on the last Friday of each month when a classical guitarist is present.) Full meals cost from J$150 ($27) to J$175 ($31.50), consisting of menu items written on a blackboard. They might include fettuccine with chicken and shrimp, grilled baby lamb chops, and a fresh salad of the day. Reservations are suggested, because the place seems to be one of the preferred luncheon stopovers for a community of artists and gallery owners.

Terra Nova Hotel Restaurant, 17 Waterloo Rd. (tel. 809/926-9334), in one of the choice small hotels of Kingston, welcomes an enthusiastic crowd of local business people and other dignitaries at mealtimes into a formal dining room. Today the grandeur of the portico, the elaborate moldings of the hotel reception area, and the restaurant are souvenirs of the affluent one-time owners. The dining room serves a combination of international and Jamaican specialties, with emphasis on fish and shellfish dishes. These include mixed grill, pepper steak, seafood platters, and baked crab. The chef is also noted for his flambé dishes and his fondues. Complete lunches cost from around J$65 ($11.70), while dinners average J$125 ($22.50) per person.

The **Plantation Terrace,** in the Courtleigh Hotel, 31 Trafalgar Rd. (tel.

809/926-8174), is a pleasant place to dine and escape from the traffic of Kingston. Meals are served under a covered parapet lined with tropical plants near an outdoor cabaña-style poolside bar. Seated on iron armchairs you'll enjoy à la carte breakfasts, Sunday-night barbecues, Thursday Jamaican evenings, and popular lunches and dinners. The other guests may include a scattering of business people as well as the employees of the American and Australian consulates nearby. The uniformed staff will serve such specialties as pepperpot soup, chicken gumbo, pork piccata, chicken Cordon Bleu, baked crab backs, and many other dishes which vary according to the culinary culture being emphasized on a particular evening. There's even an occasional Chinese specialty, as well as Jamaican dishes of ackee and codfish, pig's tail, and stewed beef served on Thursday. Complete dinners begin at J$65 ($11.70), while lunches are slightly less expensive. Full Jamaican breakfasts are served even to nonresidents for J$15 ($2.70). The restaurant, which sometimes has live music in the evening, is open seven days a week: 7 to 10 a.m., noon to 3 p.m., and 7 to 11 p.m.

Jamaica Pegasus Hotel, 81 Knutsford Blvd. (tel. 809/926-3690), offers gourmet dining in its rooftop Talk of the Town restaurant from an à la carte menu which features an excellent four-course meal at about J$140 ($25.20). Discreet, attentive service is provided. Main dishes include red snapper in lime butter or grilled lobster in garlic butter, preceded by smoked salmon or pepperpot soup. It is open from 7 p.m. to 1 a.m. nightly, providing entertainment. Le Pavillon features nouvelle cuisine and is open Monday to Friday from 12:30 to 3 p.m. (on Saturday from noon to 6 p.m.). For snacks, high tea, cakes, or pastries, it is open Monday to Friday from 11 a.m. to 8 p.m. In short, there's something to suit everyone's taste. The **Surrey Tavern,** with its own entrance, is a pub with wooden tables and chairs, low lighting, and a long, wood-paneled bar in the English tradition. At lunchtime noon to 3 p.m. Monday to Friday, a cold pub buffet is served, featuring a daily hot special. Meals cost from $12. Enjoy a long glass of cold draft beer while tapping to a jazz beat. The pub is closed on Saturday and Sunday.

Fort Charles Restaurant, in the Oceana Hotel, 2 King St. (tel. 809/922-0920), is open seven days a week from 7 a.m. to 10 p.m. You can use it as a coffeeshop-style place for a quick snack or else as a more formal restaurant. Lunches cost from J$50 ($9.50). You can order a cold roast beef open-face sandwich. There is also barbecued chicken, and the more exotic lobster thermidor, seafood newburg, or rock lobster. From 7 p.m., the dinner menu includes a variety of appetizers, soups, steaks, and other meat dishes in addition to the daytime menu. Oceana seafood lasagna is a specialty, and you can also order such dishes as steamed filet of snapper in coconut milk and pork piccata. Their steaks are called the juiciest in town. Depending on your selection of a main course, dinner prices will begin at J$80 ($29.60) and range upward.

Indies Pub and Grill, 8 Holborn Rd. (tel. 809/926-2952), was designed around a garden terrace, which on hot nights is the best place to sit. Of course, you can always go into the inner rooms, which are haphazardly but pleasantly decorated with caribou horns, tortoise shells, half-timbered walls, an aquarium sometimes stocked with baby sharks, and even a Canadian moosehead. The establishment offers a full sandwich menu at lunchtime. In the evening you can enjoy grilled lobster, fish and chips, barbecued quail, chicken Kiev, or roast beef. You can eat here for about J$50 ($9) and up every day of the week from 11 a.m. to 1 a.m.

Chelsea Jerk Centre, 9 Chelsea Ave. (tel. 809/926-6322), lies between the New Kingston Shopping Centre and the Wyndham New Kingston Hotel. It is the city's most popular provider of the Jamaican delicacies known as jerk pork and jerk chicken. You can order food to take away, or eat in the dining room. A half pound of jerk pork or half a jerk chicken costs from J$15 ($2.70). You might order a side portion of what the scrawled blackboard refers to as "Festival," which is fried cornmeal dumplings. The place is open from 11:30 a.m. to 2 a.m. daily except Sunday.

WHAT TO SEE: Even if you're staying at one of the resorts, such as Montego Bay or Ocho Rios, you may want to come into Kingston for sightseeing, and for visits to nearby Port Royal and Spanish Town.

Devon House, 26 Hope Rd., was built in 1881 by George Stiebel, a Jamaican who, after mining in South America, became one of the first black millionaires in the Caribbean. A striking building of classical style, the house has been restored to its original beauty by the Jamaican National Trust. The grounds contain craft shops, boutiques, three restaurants and shops that sell the best ice cream in Jamaica in exotic fruit flavors, and a bakery and pastry shop with Jamaican puddings and desserts. The main house also displays furniture of various periods and styles. The former coach house is now the Port Royal Grogg Shoppe (described earlier). Admission to Devon House is J$5 (90¢). The house is open daily from 10 a.m. to 5 p.m., except Sunday.

Almost next door to Devon House are the sentried gates of **Jamaica House,** residence of the prime minister, a fine, white-columned building set well back from the road.

Continuing along Hope Road, at the crossroads of Lady Musgrave Road and King's House Road, turn left and you'll see a gate on the left with its own personal traffic light. This leads to **King's House,** the official residence of the governor-general of Jamaica, the queen's representative on the island. The outside and front lawn of the gracious residence, set in 200 acres of well-tended parkland, is sometimes open to view from 10 a.m. to 5 p.m. Monday to Friday. The secretarial offices are housed next door in an old wooden building set on brick arches. In front of the house is a gigantic banyan tree in whose roots, legend says, *duppies* (as ghosts are called in Jamaica) take refuge when they are not living in the cotton trees.

On Old Hope Road, behind the Colleges of Arts, Science, and Technology, are the **Hope Botanical Gardens** (tel. 809/927-1257), occupying 60 acres on the grounds of the Hope Sugar Estate. It was one of the three largest estates in this area. The others are King's House and the University of the West Indies. The aqueduct constructed in 1759 still brings water to the gardens and augments the city's supply. The pride of the gardens is the fine orchid house containing specimens of some 200 native Jamaican species. There are a cactus garden and more than 600 different types of trees, including an impressive palm avenue, flowering trees, fruit trees, and creepers. For those interested in the plants, a guide is available to escort you and answer your questions. The guide's services are free, as is admission to the gardens, but it is the practice to tip. A quick tour will take about an hour. You may find that you prefer to wander along the tree-lined paths among the flowers and listen to the incessant chirping of the birds hidden in the leaves. A fountain was constructed just to the front of the Palm Avenue, and several picnic structures were set up. The gardens are open daily from 8:30 a.m. to 6:30 p.m.

Coconut Park Funland (tel. 809/927-1076) is in Hope Gardens and next to the zoo. The establishment is owned and operated by the Polio Foundation and the Jamaica Association for Mentally Handicapped Children. The frontal canteen and the land on which the other buildings stand, as well as the small children's zoo, belong to the Ministry of Agriculture. The two charities lease the funland and buildings, while the ministry owns and operates the zoo. The admission fee is nominal. The canteen is open from 10 a.m. to 5 p.m. daily. The gates to the rides open at noon and close at 5 p.m.

Between Old Hope Road and Mona Road, a short distance from the Botanic Gardens, is the **University of the West Indies,** built in 1948 on the Mona Sugar Estate, the third of the large estates in this area. Ruins of old mills, storehouses, and aqueducts are jostled by the modern buildings on what must be the most beautifully situated campus in the world. The chapel, an old sugar factory building, was transported stone by stone from Trelawny and rebuilt on the campus close to the old sugar factory, the remains of which are well preserved and give a good idea of how sugar was made in slave days.

The **National Stadium,** Briggs Park, of which Jamaica is justly proud, has an aluminum statue of Arthur Wint, national athlete, at the entrance. The stadium is used for such activities as soccer, field sports, and cycling, and in 1966 was the site of the Commonwealth Games. Beside the stadium is the **National Arena,** used for indoor sports, exhibitions, and concerts, and there is an Olympic-size pool. Admission prices vary according to activities.

A mile above Kingston, if you go north on Duke Street, you come to **National Heroes Park,** formerly known as George VI Memorial Park. This was the old Kingston race course. An assortment of large office blocks, including the offices of the Ministries of Finance and Education, overlooks the park and the statues of Simón Bolívar and of national heroes, Nanny of the Maroons, George Gordon, and Paul Bogle, martyrs of the Morant Bay revolt. Norman Manley, and Alexander Bustamente, national heroes of Jamaica, are buried here, as is Sir Donald Sangster, a former prime minister.

Just north of Heroes Park, on Marescaux Road, is **Mico College** (tel. 809/929-5260), a tertiary coeducational teacher training institution. Lacy Mico, a rich London widow, left her fortune to a favorite nephew on the condition that he marry one of her six nieces. He did not, and the inheritance was invested, the interest being used to ransom victims of the Barbary pirates. With the end of piracy in the early 19th century, it was decided that the capital would be devoted to founding schools for newly emancipated slaves, and, among others, Mico College was established. The INAFCA Museum is also at Mico.

The central administrative offices of the **Institute of Jamaica,** founded in 1879, are between 12 and 16 East St. (tel. 809/922-0620), close to the harbor. Open from 8:30 a.m. to 5 p.m. Monday to Thursday, to 4 p.m. on Friday, the institute fosters and encourages the development of culture, science, and history in the national interest. The institute has responsibility for the following divisions and organizations, only some of which are at the East Street headquarters: a Junior Centre, the Natural History Division (which is the repository of the national collection of flora and fauna), and the National Library. Those located elsewhere are the Cultural Training Centre, 1 Arthur Wint Dr., with schools of music, dance, art, and drama; the African-Caribbean Institute, 12 Ocean Blvd., which conducts research on cultural heritage; the Museums Division, with sites in Port Royal and Spanish Town, which have the responsibility for the display of artifacts of relevance to the history of Jamaica; the National Gallery, 12 Ocean Blvd.; and the Institute of Jamaica Publications Ltd., 2A Suthermere Rd., which publishes a quarterly, the *Jamaica Journal,* as well as other works of educational and cultural merit.

The **National Library of Jamaica** (formerly the West India Reference Library), Institute of Jamaica, 12-16 East St. (tel. 809/922-0620), a storehouse of the history, culture, and traditions of Jamaica and the Caribbean, is the finest working library for West Indian studies in the world. It has the most comprehensive, up-to-date, and balanced collection of materials, including books, newspapers, photographs, maps, and prints, to be found anywhere in the Caribbean. Of special interest to visitors are the regular exhibitions which attractively and professionally highlight different aspects of Jamaica and West Indian life. It is open Monday to Friday from 9 a.m. to 4:30 p.m.

The Bob Marley Museum, formerly Tuff Gong Studio, 56 Hope Rd. (tel. 809/927-9152), is said to be the most-visited sight in Kingston, although unless you're a Bob Marley fan, it may not mean much to you. The clapboard house with its garden and high surrounding wall was Marley's home and recording studio until his death. The museum is open daily except Sunday from 9 a.m. to 5 p.m. Admission is J$10 ($1.80) for adults, J$5 (90¢) for children.

SHOPPING: Downtown Kingston, the old part of the town, is centered around Sir William Grant Park, formerly Victoria Park, a newly remodeled showpiece of lawns, lights, and fountains. North of the park is the Ward Theatre, the oldest in the New World, where the traditional Jamaican pantomime is staged from December 26 to early April. To the east is Coke Methodist Church and to the south, the equally historic Kingston Parish Church.

Cool arcades lead off from King Street, but everywhere there is a teeming mass of people going about their business. There are some beggars and the inevitable salesmen who sidle up and offer "hot stuff, mon," frequently highly polished brass lightly dipped in gold and offered at high prices as real gold. The hucksters do accept a polite but firm "no," but don't let them keep you talking or you'll end up buying. They are very persuasive!

On this street are the imposing General Post Office and the Supreme Court buildings.

New Kingston Shopping Centre, New Kingston, is one of the most modern shopping centers in Jamaica, known more for its assemblage of merchandise than for any particular merchant. Sleek, contemporary, and stylish, it offers boutiques centered around a Mayan-style pyramid, down the sides of which cascades of water irrigate trailing bougainvillea. Fast-food stores, ice-cream stands, whatever, are also found here. Free concerts are often presented in the open-air theater.

Sangster's Old Jamaica Spirits, 17 Holborn Rd. (tel. 809/926-8888), has a full array of unusual rum-based liqueurs available in this well-scrubbed factory outlet on a side street off the modern uptown New Kingston business area. The entrance isn't well marked, but once you enter the showroom, you know from the hundreds of bottles on display that you're in a rum lovers' mecca. The prices vary, based on the quality and size of the container, not on the contents. You can pay from J$26 ($4.70) to J$76 ($13.70) for such tempting flavors as coconut rum (my personal favorite); coffee-orange, wild orange, ortanique, pimento dram, coffee cream, coconut cream, and Blue Mountain coffee liqueurs; 100% rum; and their latest product, Gold Rum Cream. The store is open Monday to Friday from 8:30 a.m. to 4:30 p.m. There's a large trolley filled with samples of the various rums and liqueurs which you can sample from small cups before you buy.

Kingston Crafts Market, at the west end of Harbour Street, downtown, is a large, covered area of small stalls individually owned, reached through such thoroughfares as Straw Avenue, Drummer's Lane, and Cheapside. All kinds of island crafts products are on sale: wooden plates and bowls, trays, ashtrays, and pepperpots made from mahoe, the national wood of the island. Straw hats, mats, baskets are also on display. Batik shirts and cotton shirts with gaudy designs are sold. Banners for wall decoration are inscribed with the Jamaican coat-of-arms, and wood masks often have elaborately carved faces. Apart from being a good place to buy worthwhile souvenirs, the market is where you can learn the art of

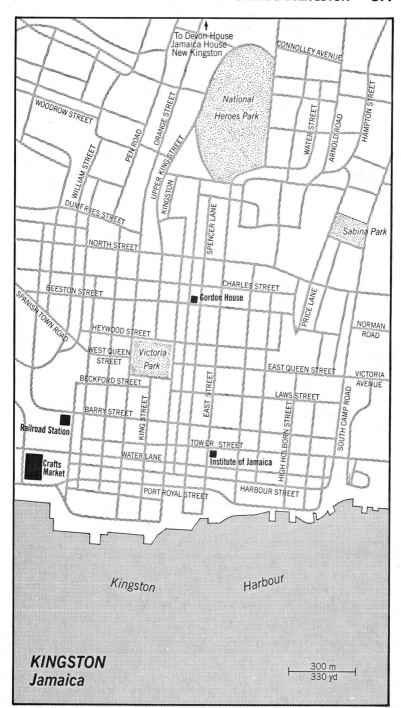

To Devon House
Jamaica House
New Kingston

CONNOLLEY AVENUE

National
Heroes Park

WOODROW STREET

WATER STREET

ARNOLD ROAD

HAMPTON STREET

PEN ROAD

ORANGE STREET

UPPER KING STREET

KINGSTON

WILLIAM STREET

DUMFRIES STREET

SPENCER LANE

Sabina Park

NORTH STREET

BEESTON STREET

CHARLES STREET

Gordon House

PRICE LANE

SPANISH TOWN ROAD

HEYWOOD STREET

NORMAN
ROAD

WEST QUEEN
STREET

Victoria
Park

EAST QUEEN STREET

VICTORIA
AVENUE

BECKFORD STREET

EAST STREET

LAWS STREET

KING STREET

BARRY STREET

HIGH HOLBORN STREET

SOUTH CAMP ROAD

Railroad Station

TOWER STREET

Crafts
Market

WATER LANE

Institute of Jamaica

PORT ROYAL STREET

HARBOUR STREET

Kingston   Harbour

KINGSTON
Jamaica

300 m
330 yd

bargaining and ask for a *brawta,* a free bonus. However, be aware that, unlike in Haiti and the Hispanic islands, bargaining is *not* a Jamaican tradition. Vendors will take something off the price but not very much.

Things Jamaican, Devon House, 26 Hope Rd. (tel. 809/929-6602), is a showcase of Jamaican handcrafts. Every item in the store is made in Jamaica, not only the paintings and sculpture, but the sauces and liquor, including the best of Jamaican rum, and items in straw. Look also for their collection of pewter knives and forks, based on designs of original pewter items discovered in archaeological exploration in the Port Royal area in 1965. In this collection you can buy items with the Tudor Rose Seal and Lion Rampant spoons, among others. This reproduced Port Royal collection, however, is leadless, unlike the original. Even the imperfections have been reproduced. There is an outlet in Montego Bay if you're not heading for Kingston.

Ital Craft, Twin Gates Plaza (tel. 809/926-8291), is a fashionable boutique which sells accessories made from natural products on the island. In Rastafarian, the name of the boutique means "something good," and that is what you get if you shop here. For example, accessories and pieces of jewelry are imaginatively concocted and creatively conceived from Jamaican corals and shells. The boutique is run by Cindy Breakspeare Tovares Finson, who was a former "Miss World."

Buying Art in Jamaica

For many years the richly evocative paintings of Haiti were viewed as the most valuable contribution to the arts in the Caribbean. There is within Jamaica, however, a rapidly growing perspective of itself as one of the artistic leaders of the Third World. An articulate core of Caribbean critics are focusing the attention of the art world on the unusual, eclectic, and sometimes politically motivated paintings being produced in Jamaica.

Mutual Life Gallery, Mutual Life Centre, 2 Oxford Rd. (tel. 809/926-9025). One of the country's most prominent art galleries is in the corporate headquarters of a major insurance company. After you pass a security check, you can climb to the corporation's mezzanine level for an insight into the changing face of Jamaican art. The gallery's array of exhibitions are organized by Pat Ramsey, who encourages developing unknowns and showcases established artists with panache and flair. Exhibitions change once a month, but there is usually a stable of long-term exhibits. The Mutual Life Insurance Company donates the space for free as part of its own attempts to improve the status of the arts in the Caribbean. The gallery is open on Monday to Friday from 10 a.m. to 6 p.m. and on Saturday from 11 a.m. to 3 p.m. It is a nonprofit institution.

The **Frame Centre Gallery,** 10 Tangerine Pl. (tel. 809/926-4644), is one of the most important art galleries in Jamaica. Its guiding force is a gracious connoisseur of Caribbean art, Margaret Burnall. This gallery was opened early in the 1970s and today has a changing array of some 300 paintings and pieces of sculpture. One of the best-known artists whose work is displayed here is the late Honorable Edna Manley ("the Jamaican Chagall"), whose other important role was as the wife of Norman Manley. The gallery is open from 8:30 a.m. to 5 p.m. Monday to Friday, from 9:30 a.m. to 1 p.m. Saturday and Sunday.

SIGHTS IN THE ENVIRONS: Not far from Kingston are two centers for sightseeing worth a visit—Port Royal and Spanish Town.

Port Royal

From West Beach Dock, Kingston, a ferry ride of 20 to 30 minutes will take you to Port Royal, or you can drive on the Palisadoes Road to this fishing village.

Port Royal, once the island's capital, conjures up pictures of swashbuckling pirates led by Henry Morgan, swilling grog in harbor taverns. This was once one of the largest trading centers of the New World, with a reputation of being the wickedest city on earth (Blackbeard stopped here regularly on his Caribbean trips). But the whole thing came to an end at 11:43 a.m. on June 7, 1692, when a third of the town disappeared under water as the result of a devastating earthquake. Nowadays, Port Royal, with its memories of the past, has been designated by the government for redevelopment as a tourist destination.

As you drive along the Palisadoes, you arrive first at **St. Peter's Church.** It's usually closed, but you may persuade the caretaker, who lives opposite, to open it if you want to see the silver plate, said to be spoils captured by Henry Morgan from the cathedral in Panama. In the ill-kept graveyard is the tomb of one Lewis Galdy, a Frenchman swallowed up and subsequently regurgitated by the 1692 earthquake.

Fort Charles, the only remaining one of Port Royal's six forts, has withstood attack, earthquake, fire, and hurricane. Built in 1656 and later strengthened by Morgan for his own purposes, the fort was expanded and further armed in the 1700s, until its firepower boasted more than 100 cannons, covering both the land and the sea approaches. After subsequent earthquakes and tremors, the fort ceased to be at the water's edge and is now well inland. In 1779, Britain's naval hero, Lord Horatio Nelson was commander of the fort and trod the wooden walkway inside the western parapet as he kept watch for the French invasion fleet.

Fort Charles Maritime Museum is in the former British naval headquarters where Nelson served. Scale models of the fort and ships of past eras are to be seen in the small museum. It's open from 10 a.m. to 4 p.m. Monday to Friday, to 5 p.m. Saturday and Sunday. Admission is J$1 (18¢) for adults (children, free).

Giddy House, once the Royal Artillery storehouse, is another example of what the earth movements can do. Walking across the tilted floor is an eerie and strangely disorienting experience.

On the land side of the fort is the **Old Naval Hospital,** which now houses the **Archaeological Museum and Research Centre.** This building was completed in 1818 and is the oldest cast-iron prefabricated building in the western hemisphere. It contains many artifacts unearthed from digs and underwater searches around Port Royal, including a watch that had stopped at the moment of the 1692 earthquake, now in pieces, but totally authentic; a Chinese porcelain madonna, of which only three exist in the world, recovered from the sea; Spanish armor; slave shackles; and much weaponry, together with models and descriptive tableaux of the Port Royal of the past. Admission to the upstairs museum is gained by ringing the 19th-century bell for the guide. You can see such things as Prince Henry's Polygon Battery, the Old Coaling Wharf, the Jail House, and the Victoria and Albert Battery complex, not to mention the Chocolata Hole. The museum was damaged in the September 1988 hurricane and was closed at press time awaiting repairs. Check its status at the time of your visit.

Spanish Town

From 1662 to 1872 Spanish Town was the capital of the island. Originally founded by the Spaniards as Villa de la Vega, it was sacked by Cromwell's men in 1655 and all traces of papism were obliterated. The English cathedral, surprisingly retaining a Spanish name, **St. Jago de la Vega,** was built in 1666 and rebuilt after being destroyed by a hurricane in 1712. As you drive into the town from Kingston, the ancient cathedral, built in 1714, catches your eye, with its brick tower and two-tiered wooden steeple, which was not added until 1831. As the cathedral was built on the foundation and remains of the old Spanish church, it is half-English, half-Spanish, showing two definite styles, one Romanesque, the other Gothic.

Of cruciform design and built mostly of brick, the cathedral is historically one of the most interesting buildings on the island. The black and white marble stones of the aisles are interspersed with ancient tombstones, and the walls are heavy with marble memorials that are almost a chronicle of Jamaica's history, dating back as far as 1662. Episcopalian services are held regularly on Sunday at 7 and 10:30 a.m. and at 6:30 p.m., sometimes conducted by the bishop of Jamaica, whose see this is.

Beyond the cathedral, turn right and two blocks along you will reach Constitution Street and the **Town Square.** This delightful little square is surrounded by towering royal palms.

On the west side is old King's House, gutted by fire in 1925. The façade was restored and a small museum built within. This was also damaged in the 1988 hurricane and was closed at press time. Again, check its status. This was the residence of Jamaica's British governors until 1972 when the capital was transferred to Kingston, and many celebrated guests—among them Lord Nelson, Admiral Rodney, Captain Bligh of H.M.S. *Bounty* fame, and King William IV, stayed here.

Behind the house is the **Jamaica People's Museum of Craft and Technology** (tel. 809/922-0620), open daily from 10 a.m. to 5 p.m. The garden examples of old farm machinery, an old water mill wheel, a hand-turned sugar mill, a coffee pulper, an old hearse, and a fire engine. An outbuilding contains a museum of crafts and technology, together with a number of smaller agricultural implements. In the small archeological museum are old prints, models (including one of King's House based on a written description), and maps of the town's grid layout from the 1700s.

On the north side of the square is the **Rodney Memorial,** perhaps the most dramatic of the buildings on the square, commissioned by a grateful assembly to commemorate the victory in 1782 of Baron George Rodney, English admiral, over the French fleet, which saved the island from invasion.

Opposite the Rodney Memorial was the **Court House,** the most recent of the four buildings. The court occupied the ground floor, and when in session, overflowed onto the pavement and road, an animated throng of court attendants, defendants, witnesses, and spectators, all apparently accompanied by relatives and friends. The courthouse was recently destroyed by fire, but it is to be rebuilt.

The final side of the square, the east, contains the most attractive building, the **House of Assembly,** with a shady brick colonnade running the length of the ground floor and above it a wooden pillared balcony. This was the stormy center of the bitter debates for Jamaica's governing body. Now the ground floor is the parish library, and council officers occupy the upper floor, along with the Mayor's Parlour.

The streets around the old Town Square contain many fine Georgian town houses intermixed with tin-roofed shacks. Nearby is the **market,** so busy in the morning you will find it difficult, almost dangerous, to drive through. It provides, however, a bustling scene of Jamaican life.

Driving to Spanish Town from Kingston on the A1 (Washington Boulevard), at Central Village you come to the **Arawak Museum,** on the right. The entrance appears to lead to a quarry, but don't be put off. Drive down to the museum, a hexagonal building on the site of one of the largest Arawak settlements on the island. It is open Monday to Thursday from 10 a.m. to 5 p.m. and Friday from 10 a.m. to 4 p.m. The small, well-planned museum contains drawings, pictures, and diagrams of Arawak life, plus old flints and other artifacts which help you to understand the early history or prehistoric period of Jamaica. Smoking of tobacco seems to have been a habit even in 1518, when Arawaks were recorded as lighting hollow tubes at one end and sucking the other. The visitor can also see signs of an original Arawak settlement at White Marl, around the museum building.

KINGSTON AFTER DARK: There are safer places to be. Use caution when going out.

Nightspots

The **Red Hills Strip** in downtown Kingston has a number of nightclubs, all of which I make it a point to avoid.

Illusions, 2-4 South Ave., Lane Plaza (tel. 809/926-7419), is one of the most popular discos in Kingston, in spite of its unchic location in a shopping center. It has a gray- and pastel-colored decor, cast-iron Corinthian columns, mirrors, and many hi-tech accessories, along with spinning ceiling fans and Caribbean planting. It also opens for a good-value lunch Monday to Friday from noon to 3 p.m., costing from J$40 ($7.20) and including an array of sandwiches, salads, and barbecued pork, chicken, or beef. After a two-hour siesta, the bar reopens at 5 p.m. on weekdays, at 6 p.m. on Saturday and Sunday, remaining so until the wee hours. At night, visitors pay a cover of J$35 ($6.30) for men, J$25 ($4.50) for women. In the course of the evening the crowd changes from office workers celebrating to a late-night crowd eager to mingle, mix, and mate.

Jonkanoo, Wyndham Hotel New Kingston, 77 Knutsford Blvd. (tel. 809/926-5430), chic, contemporary, and elegant, is a glamorous disco recently refurbished. Open Monday to Saturday, it provides a variety of entertainment, although disco is the mainstay. On Monday night, the emphasis is on sports on the big eight-foot video screen. Tuesday is dedicated to jazz, and the Friday afternoon "Happi Hour" is one of Kingston's most popular events. From time to time, cabaret stars perform. There is a cover charge of J$20 ($3.60) for jazz and on weekends. For special events, it varies from J$30 ($5.40) to J$50 ($9) per person.

Mingles Disco, Courtleigh Hotel, 31 Trafalgar Rd. (tel. 809/926-8174), is set into the innards of the hotel at the far end of the reception area. This popular disco is furnished with a dark-grained decor of movable tables, parquet floors, and large expanses of both bar space and dancing areas. Residents of Kingston sometimes pour in here for the live concerts that are held every weekend. On other evenings, disco is featured; there's no cover charge. Red Stripe beer costs around J$14 ($2.50). There's a J$30 ($5.40) cover charge for live concerts. Monday to Friday, the disco and bar are open from 5 p.m. to 2 a.m. and Saturday from 8 p.m. to 2 a.m. It's closed Sunday.

Live Theater

Kingston is called the cultural heart of the West Indies. There are several theaters presenting live performances: **Ward Theatre** on North Parade (tel. 809/922-0318), **Little Theatre** on Tom Redcam Drive near the National Stadium (tel. 809/926-6129), and the **Creative Arts Centre** at the University of the West Indies (tel. 809/927-7546). Most tickets cost J$20 ($3.60). All stage local or imported plays and musicals, light opera, and revues. You may be fortunate enough to catch a performance by the Jamaica National Dance Theatre or the Jamaica Folk Singers, whose vivid and spontaneous performances show the true Jamaican folk culture.

Most entertainment of this sort is listed in the daily press, along with one-time attractions and sporting activities.

2. PORT ANTONIO

Port Antonio is a seaport on the northeast coast of Jamaica, 63 miles from Kingston, where Tom Cruise filmed *Cocktails*. It has been called the Jamaica of 100 years ago. Port Antonio is the mecca of the titled and the wealthy—European royalty with titles of duchesses and barons, along with such film stars as Linda Evans and Raquel Welch. You are likely to encounter Whoopi Goldberg, who came here to film *Clara's Heart*, Peter O'Toole, or Tommy Tune.

To reach it from the capital, you have a choice between taking the A4 road through Port Morant and up the east coast, or driving north on the A3 through Castleton and approaching along the north coast, where Jamaica's tourist industry started. In other days, visitors arrived by banana boat and stayed at the Titchfield Hotel (which burned down) in a lush, tropical part of the island unspoiled by gimmicks. The small, bustling town of Port Antonio is like many on the island: both clean and untidy, with sidewalks around a market filled with vendors; tin-roof shacks competing with old Georgian and modern brick and concrete buildings; lots of people busy shopping, talking, laughing, and some just loafing, others sitting and playing Dominoes, loudly banging the pieces down on the table, which is very much part of the game.

The market is a place to browse among local craftwork, spices, and fruits. Captain Bligh landed here in 1793 with the first breadfruit plants, and Port Antonio claims that the ones grown in this area are the best on the island. Visitors still arrive by water, but now it's in cruise ships which moor close to Navy Island, and the passengers come ashore just for the day.

Navy Island and the long-gone Titchfield Hotel were owned for a short time by film star Errol Flynn. The story is that after suffering damage to his yacht, he put into Kingston for repairs, visited Port Antonio by motorbike, fell in love with the area, and in due course acquired Navy Island, some say in a gambling game. Later, he either lost or sold it and bought a nearby plantation, Comfort Castle, still owned by his widow, Patrice Wymore Flynn, who spends most of her time there and hopes to open a museum honoring Flynn (refer to "What to See," below). He was much loved and admired by the Jamaicans and was totally integrated into the community. They still talk of him in Port Antonio, especially the men, who refer to his womanizing and drinking skills in reverent tones.

WHERE TO STAY: About 2½ miles east along the coast toward Frenchman's Cove stands **Trident Villas & Hotel**, P.O. Box 119, Port Antonio, Jamaica, W.I. (tel. 809/993-2602), an elegant rendezvous of the rich and famous. This deluxe hotel complex, one of the most tasteful and refined on the north shore, is a good all-year bet for those who want a quiet, relaxing Jamaican holiday, away from the more publicized tourist areas of the north and northwest coasts. The complex sits regally above jagged coral cliffs with a seaside panorama. The hotel is the personal and creative statement of Earl Levy, scion of a prominent Kingston family. Nearby he has erected a multimillion dollar replica of a European château, where overflow guests of the hotel are sometimes grandly housed, sleeping in plantation beds.

The main building is furnished with many antique and well-chosen accessories, and flowers decorate the sea-breeze cooled lobby. After checking in, you'll be conducted to your lodgings by a uniformed porter, a holdover of British colonial charm. Your accommodations will be a studio cottage or tower, reached by a pathway through the gardens. In a cottage, a large bedroom with ample sitting area opens onto a private patio with nothing between you and the sea except grass and a low stone wall. All cottages and tower rooms have baths with tubs, showers, and toilets, plus ceiling fans and plenty of storage space. Jugs of ice and water are constantly replenished, and fresh flowers grace the dressing table. Singles are accommodated in either junior or deluxe villa suites, paying $250 to $350 in winter, *$110 to $150 in summer.* Doubles and triples are lodged in junior, deluxe villa, prime minister's, or imperial suites. Prices for two are $300 to $530 in winter, depending on the category of your room, *dropping to $130 to $330 in summer.* Triples pay from $370 to $660 in winter, *$180 to $380 in summer.*

There's a small private sand beach, and the immaculate gardens embrace a pool and a gingerbread gazebo. Lounges, tables, chairs, and bar service add to your pleasure. At lunchtime, you can go to the main building where there are two patios, one covered. Breakfast is also served there, or you can take it on your private patio, served by your own butler. At dinner, men are required to wear jackets and ties to the meal served in one wing of the main block. Silver service, crystal, and Port Royal pewter sparkle on the tables. Dinner is a many-course set meal, so if you are concerned with dietary restrictions or phobias, you should make your requirements known early so that alternative food can be served. Tennis, horseback riding, and such water sports as sailing and snorkeling are included in the tariffs.

Fern Hill Club, P.O. Box 100, Port Antonio, Jamaica, W.I. (tel. 809/993-4243, 800/423-2095 toll free in the U.S.; or 416/620-4666 in Canada). Attractive, airy, and panoramic, this resort occupies 45 forested acres high above the coastline. The hotel reservations are handled in Toronto, home of developer Bill Brennan, and rates include air fare from Toronto to Kingston. However, it is also open to visitors from other places during slack periods. Today, the establishment comprises a glistening colonial-style clubhouse and five outlying villas, plus a comfortable annex at the bottom of the hill. The club has three swimming pools, a tennis court, the well-maintained Blue Mahoe bar (named after the wood that sheathes it), a dining patio, and a collection of highly private accommodations. Prices are quoted per week for double occupancy (no singles). In winter, charges are $660 to $700 per person, with a two-bedroom villa or a one-bedroom villa suite going for $740 per person. *Off-season, rates are $545 to $575 per person weekly, going up to $650 per person in the villas or villa suites.* A $49 per person service charge is added to all tariffs. A shuttle bus makes infrequent trips down the steep hillside to one of a pair of beaches, Frenchman's Cove, and a wilder, less populated beach called San San. The resort is technically classified as a time-share property, but its accommodations are rented to one-time vacationers by a management company when investors are away.

Goblin Hill Villas at San San, P.O. Box 26, Port Antonio, Jamaica, W.I. (tel. 809/993-3286), occupies a green and sunwashed hillside once reputed to shelter goblins but is now filled with vacation homes on San San Estate. The swimming pool is surrounded by a vine-laced arbor, which lies just a stone's throw from an almost-impenetrable forest. On the premises are a pair of illuminated Laykold courts and a long flight of steps leading down to the crescent-shaped sands of San San beach. The resort contains 28 stucco-sided villas, each of which is set town-house style against its neighbors. Units contain air conditioning, a ceiling fan, and king-size beds. Each is staffed with a housekeeper who prepares and serves meals, cleans house, and attends to chores. In winter, a one-bedroom villa, suitable for two people, costs $1,480 per week, and a two-bedroom villa, suitable for six guests, goes for $1,880 per week. *Summer charges are $1,080 in a one-bedroom accommodation, $1,680 for a two-bedroom villa.* A rental car is included in all rates. For reservations, call 809/925-8108 in Jamaica, 800/423-4095 toll free in the U.S.

Admiralty Club, Navy Island, P.O. Box 188, Port Antonio, Jamaica, W.I. (tel. 809/993-2667), is Jamaica's only private island getaway, a resort and marina on that "bit of paradise" once owned by actor Errol Flynn who came here for some off-screen adventures. Today this cottage colony, with its yacht club and marina, is one of the best kept travel secrets in the Caribbean. In what had been the former swashbuckling movie star's garden of Eden, a memorabilia room has been set up, with stills from some of Flynn's pictures.

You can visit just for the day (see "Beaches," coming up), but it'd be much better to lodge here, enjoying a host of activities, including three beaches, one a secluded clothing-optional stretch of sand known as Trembly Knee Cove. A full range of water sports, such as scuba and windsurfing, is also offered. You can wander at leisure exploring the island, with its collection of hybrid hibiscus, bougainvillea, and royal and coconut palms (many of which were originally ordered planted by Flynn himself).

Large studio cottages and spacious villas branch out from the main clubhouse (some contain kitchenettes). In winter only MAP tariffs are quoted: $95 daily in a single and $130 in a double, going up to $150 to $192 for two in studios and one-bedroom villas. *In off-season, guest rooms, including a full breakfast, rent for $55 to $65 daily for one, $70 to $80 for two, with studio and one-bedroom villas for two renting from $95 to $140 daily.* Ceiling fans and trade winds keep the cottages cool, and mosquito netting over the beds add a plantation touch. In addition to the beaches, a swimming pool is on the grounds. The wood furniture used is made right on the island. At night, after enjoying drinks in the H.M.S. *Bounty* Bar, guests can dine on the Orchid Terrace. There they can order a six-course dinner, served nightly from 7 to 10, for J$85 ($15.30) to J$120 ($21.60). Lunch, daily from noon to 3 p.m., costs from J$65 ($11.70). The chef always has lobster, along with freshly caught fish such as dolphin and snapper, as well as Jamaican specialties such as stewed chicken and curried goat. Nonresidents should call to let the manager know that they're coming.

Bonnie View Hotel, P.O. Box 82, Port Antonio, Jamaica, W.I. (tel. 809/ 993-2752), a hillside hugger, opens onto Port Antonio, Navy Island in the middle of the harbor, and the Caribbean. Take "Mango Walk" to the pool and gardens of one of the oldest continuously operated hotels in the Caribbean, in business for more than four decades. The balcony of Bonnie View is famous. The bedrooms are simply but adequately furnished, with private baths. There is no air conditioning, as the hotel has the advantage of the mountain breezes which lower the temperature by some ten degrees. There are 23 rooms and one cottage. All year, rates are $44 to $49 daily in a single, $60 in a double. Add $24 per person per day for breakfast and a set dinner. All rooms have balconies, some toward the sea, others toward the mountains. The lounge patio and the veranda are pleasant places to sit and drink a rum punch or nibble a lunchtime snack.

Breakfast is served either in your room or in the dining room set back from the patio. At both lunch and dinner, a mixture of tasty Jamaican and international dishes is offered. On Saturday night during the season, a calypso band provides music for dancing after dinner. The pool has a bar and a large lounging area where you can relax under the sun with the mountains for company. Hotel guests can use the free staff bus down to Port Antonio and back at scheduled times. There are tennis courts, and most other sporting activities can be arranged for you. Bunches of bananas hang in the entrance, and guests can help themselves to a quick snack at will. You drive up a bumpy road for a sundowner in the Lookout Point Bar.

De Montevin Lodge Hotel, 21 Fort George St., Port Antonio, Jamaica, W.I. (tel. 809/993-2604), is probably the most ornate and best-maintained version of a gingerbread house in town. It stands on a narrow back street whose edges are lined with architectural reminders (some of them not well preserved) of the colonial days. Originally built as a sea captain's house in 1881, the hotel is really worth a photograph. Cast-iron accents and elongated red and beige balconies set a tone for the charm you find inside: cedar doors, art deco cupboards, a ceiling embellished with lacy plaster designs, and the most elaborate cove moldings in town. Don't expect modern amenities here: your room might be a study of another, not-yet-renovated era. In any season, a room with a shared bath costs $20 daily in a single, $30 in a double, and $49 in a triple. Units with private baths costs $25 to $55. Mrs. Mullings is the owner of this 13-room hotel.

Friends, P.O. Box 225, Port Antonio, Jamaica, W.I. (tel. 809/929-9430 in Kingston). Its mountaintop setting, coupled with the concerned attentions of its charming owner, create an aura more like a private home than a hotel. This is the panoramic eyrie of one of Port Antonio's most cultivated citizens, the articulate and elfin Ken Ramsay, set amid a thickly forested hillside whose view encompasses the multiple headlands and seacoasts of north Jamaica. Don't expect an easy arrival if you decide to stay here. Its access road is a challenge, rough and winding. Take courage in the belief that at the top a clearing will open to reveal twin chalets and a filling meal prepared by a cooperative employee. Rooms flow into one another around a central supporting column, and the villas are outfitted with Jamaican paintings and photographs. Year round, a one-bedroom chalet for two persons rents for $60, while a two-bedroom chalet for up to four persons goes for $100 daily. Maid service is optional at $5 per day. Mrs. Ramsay works in Kingston at the Mutual Art Gallery.

WHERE TO DINE: A surprising array of atmospheric choices awaits you. All hotels welcome outside guests for dinner, but reservations are required. Check with the hotel.

Trident Hotel Restaurant (tel. 809/993-2602) has for a long time been frequented by those seeking gourmet cuisine. Part of the main hotel building, the restaurant has an air of elegance. The high-pitched wooden roof set on white stone walls holds several ceiling fans which gently stir the air. The antique tables for two, four, or more are set with old china, English silver, and Port Royal pewter. Dinner is served at 8 o'clock, and men are required to wear jackets and ties. A butler shows you to your table, where warm bread, cold butter, and ice water await. A waiter, resplendent in uniform and white starched shirt, and, to complete the picture, pristine white cotton gloves, will help you choose your wine. The waiter whispers the name of each course as he serves it: Jamaican salad; coconut soup; dolphin with mayonnaise and mustard sauce; French salad with wine vinaigrette; steak with broccoli and sautéed potatoes; peach Melba and Blue Mountain coffee with Wild Orange, a Jamaican liqueur. The cost of the meal is around $50 per person. Tip at your discretion. Wine is extra. The six-course menu varies each day, but there is no à la carte service. The meal is expertly cooked and beautifully served. Reservations are required.

Fern Hill Club, P.O. Box 100 (tel. 809/993-3243), is one of the finest dining spots in Port Antonio, with a sweeping view of the rugged coastline. Sunset watching here is said to be the best at the resort. The food is not neglected for the view, but is a well-prepared combination of international dishes and Jamaican specialties. Service is daily from 1 to 2 p.m. and 7:30 to 9:30 p.m. A fixed-price lunch costs J$55 ($9.90), with dinners priced from J$120 ($21.60). On Monday, a beach-side buffet with a folklore and fashion show is staged from 7:30 p.m. to midnight, costing J$175 ($31.50). On Friday, there is buffet cabaret show when the housekeepers dance and sing. It's good fun.

The Rafters' Restaurant, Rafter's Rest (tel. 809/993-2778), lies at the edge of the river at the point where still waters provided a convenient resting point for the commercial raft operators who used to float goods downstream. Jean McGill and Beverley Dixon are the graciously softspoken managers of this establishment, where a flautist sometimes provides musical diversion through-out the day. The neoclassical pavilion housing the establishment was built in 1954 by a local architect. The house drink is the Río Grande special, combining four kinds of rum with fresh fruit juice. Food includes open-face sandwiches, burgers, an array of salads, curried goat or chicken, and grilled lobster. Fresh fish is served grilled, steamed, or pan fried. Meals cost J$25 ($9.25) and up. Hours are from 7:30 a.m. to 7 p.m. daily. The turnoff leading to this place lies about five miles west of Port Antonio.

De Montevin Lodge Restaurant, 21 Fort George St. (tel. 809/993-2604), is *the* place for a true Jamaican dinner. Start with pepperpot or pumpkin soup. Follow these with curried lobster and chicken Jamaican style with local vegeta-bles. Top the meal off with coconut or banana cream pie, washed down with cof-fee, a meal fit for a good trencherman or woman, for $6.50 to $8 and up. An ice-cold Red Stripe beer goes well with such a meal. The menu changes according to the availability of fresh supplies, but the standard of cooking and the full Ja-maican character of the meal are constant. Always call the day before to let them know you're coming. Mrs. Mullings is considered the best cook in Port Antonio. She was Errol Flynn's cook, incidentally. Meals are served daily from 12:30 to 2 p.m. and 7 to 9 p.m.

Huntress Marina Club, 16 West St. (tel. 809/993-3318). Set beneath a thatch-covered roof at the end of an industrial pier, this deliberately raffish bar and restaurant is a favorite of the expatriate yachting set. Many of the ultra-expensive yachts whose crews have dined here have pinned their ensigns on the roughly textured planks and posts. Verne Pettingill (who happens to own the adjacent marina as well) is the guiding force of this open-air watering hole. It opens for breakfast at 7 a.m. and remains in business through the day until at least 10 p.m., and often much later. A filling American-style breakfast costs J$15 ($2.70), lunch is from J$25 ($4.50), and a full dinner runs from J$35 ($6.30). Menu items include the usual array of tropical drinks, burgers, seafood ceviche, liver with bananas, and ackee with saltfish.

Mr. Pettingill also has yachts for charter, with crew and tackle, for those who wish to go deep-sea fishing. Prices are $33 to $46 per person for half a day. Call the number above for information.

WHAT TO DO: For the experience of a lifetime, most guests follow the lead of a legendary film star and go—

Rafting on the Río Grande

Rafting started on the Río Grande and on the Martha Brae River as a means of transporting bananas from the plantations to the waiting freighters. In 1871 a Yankee skipper, Lorenzo Dow Baker, decided that a seat on one of the rafts was better than walking, but it was not until Errol Flynn arrived that the rafts became popular as a tourist attraction. Flynn used to hire the craft for his friends and encouraged the drivers to race down the Río Grande, spurred on by bets on the winner. Now that the bananas are transported by road, the raft skippers make one or maybe two trips a day down the waterway.

The rafts are some 33 feet long and only about 3 feet wide, propelled by stout bamboo poles. There is a raised double seat about two-thirds of the way back for the two passengers. The skipper stands in the front, trousers rolled up to his knees, the water washing his feet, and guides the lively craft down the river, about eight miles between steep hills covered with coconut palms, banana plan-tations, and flowers, through limestone rock cliffs pitted with caves, through the Tunnel of Love, a narrow cleft in the rocks, then on to wider, gentler water.

The day starts at Rafter's Rest, a few miles west of Port Antonio at Burlington on St. Margaret's Bay. Trips last 2½ hours, and they're available from 8:30 a.m. to 5 p.m. daily, at a cost of $35 per raft. Leave your valuables in the specially provided lockers. A fully insured driver will take you to the starting point and pick you up again in your rental car. If you feel like it, take a picnic lunch. Bring enough for your skipper too, and he will find a peaceful spot for your meal and perhaps a swim, regaling you with lively stories of the river. For more information, call Río Grande Attraction Ltd., Port Antonio (tel. 809/993-2778).

A Trip to the Blue Lagoon

About five miles east of Port Antonio, at the end of a winding, gravel-colored road, lie some of the most iridescently turquoise-colored waters in all of Jamaica. The Blue Lagoon, known simply as the "blue hole," is one of the most photographed sights on the island. Driving, you follow the signs off the main road past Frenchman's Cove Hotel down to the beach. Believed to be a function of a 186-foot deep bottom, intense sunlight, and the effects of a freshwater tributary which makes the waters even bluer, the place has a parking lot ringed with an animated community of vendors. You can go for a look at the waters, perhaps negotiate with a salesperson over a local handcraft, or even indulge in a scuba or snorkeling exploration of the lagoon's bottom.

Many visitors can make a meal at the veranda-style **Blue Lagoon Restaurant,** San San (tel. 809/993-2495), the focal point of their afternoon. Open for drinks throughout the day and most of the evening, it serves buffet lunches and dinners whose ingredients are sometimes grilled or charcoaled. Dinner is especially romantic because of the water lapping at the piers. You can choose from lobster, crab backs, and jerk pork or chicken. Meals cost around $15. Food is served from 8 to 11 a.m., noon to 3 p.m., and 7 to 10 p.m. daily. The restaurant's dangling fish nets and parasols are set up to receive visitors seven days a week.

A Blue Lagoon Celebrity Voyage and Beach Party is held from 1:30 to 3:30 p.m. daily. You sail in flat-bottom boats to the Blue Lagoon, with an informed commentary on 21 points of historic interest and houses of celebrities seen from the sea. There is a cultural show on the beach to follow. On Tuesday, when the charge is $12.50, there is music, dancing, and unlimited rum punch and fruit drinks. For more information, get in touch with Verne Pettingill, Huntress Marina (tel. 809/993-3318).

Boat Cruises

Also sailing from Huntress Marina (tel. 809/993-3318) is a two-hour **historical tour cruise** aboard the *Lady Jamaica.* The cruise takes you to Port Antonio's twin harbors with narration on the town's history and 21 points of interest. The *Lady Jamaica* has a small glass viewing panel in its bottom. The tour, offered daily from 10:30 a.m. to noon, costs $6.50 per person and includes a free rum punch or soft drink.

The *Lady Jamaica* also makes **sunset cruises** on Thursday from 5 to 7 p.m., costing $12.50, with unlimited cocktails, disco, and snacks.

The Admiralty Club Resort on Navy Island also offers boat tours.

Beaches

Port Antonio has several white sand beaches open to the public, some free and some for a charge for use of facilities. **Boston Beach** is free, and often has light surfing, and there are picnic tables as well as a restaurant and snackbar. Before heading to this admission-free beach, which was donated in part by Robin Moore (of *The Green Berets* fame), stop nearby and get the makings for a picnic lunch at the most famous center for jerk pork and chicken in Jamaica. These crude, rustic shacks also sell the much rarer jerk sausage. A pound of any type, suitable for three to four persons, costs J$24 ($4.30). The dish was said to originate with the Maroons who lived in the hills beyond and occasionally ventured out to harass plantation owners. The location is east of Port Antonio and the Blue Lagoon.

Also free is **Fairy Hill Beach** (Winnifred), with changing rooms and showers. **Frenchman's Cove Beach** attracts a chic crowd to its white sand beach combined with a freshwater stream. Nonhotel guests are charged a fee.

Navy Island, once Errol Flynn's personal hideaway, is a fine choice for swimming (one beach is clothing optional) and snorkeling at Crusoe's Beach. Take the boat from the Navy Island dock on West Street across from the Esso station. It's a seven-minute ride to the island, a round trip costing J$11 (82¢). The ferry runs 24 hours a day. The island is the setting for the Admiralty Club (see above).

San San Beach was voted by men of the U.S. Navy some years ago to be one of the best beaches in the world. Adults pay J$4 (72¢) and children J$2 (36¢) to enter. There are changing rooms, showers, a picnic area with barbecuing facilities, a full dive shop, and trained and licensed lifeguards. There are full watersports facilities, including windsurfers, Sunfish sailboats, paddle boats, canoes, and snorkeling equipment available for rent. If you're interested in scuba, and you're a PADI- or NAUI-certified diver, a one-tank dive costs J$150 ($27). A shallow-water lesson for scuba beginners is also J$150 ($27).

WHAT TO SEE: Continuing our energetic activities, I have the following suggestions:

Somerset Falls is eight miles west of Port Antonio, just past Hope Bay on the A4. The waters of the Daniels River pour down a deep gorge through the rain forest, with waterfalls and foaming cascades. You can ride in an electric goudda to the hidden falls. This is one of Jamaica's most historic sites, used by the Spanish before the English capture of the island, and it is a stop on the daily Grand Jamaica Tour from Ocho Rios. Phone Verne Pettingill (809/993-3318) or check with your Ocho Rios hotel or travel agent. At the falls, you can swim in the deep rock pools and buy sandwiches, light meals, beer, soft drinks, and even liquor at the snackbar.

The **Caves of Nonsuch** and the **Gardens of Athenry,** P.O. 195, Port Antonio, Portland (tel. 809/993-3740), are east from Port Antonio past the Blue Lagoon. Turn right, and follow the signs about six miles up into the hills through small villages to the caves. It's an easy drive and an easy walk to see the stalagmites, fossilized marine remains, evidence of Arawak civilization, and signs of volcanic activity, adding up to 1½ million years of life on earth. From the Gardens of Athenry there are panoramic views over the island and the sea. The gardens are filled with coconut palms, flowers, and trees. Admission to the caves and gardens is $5 per person. The facilities are open seven days a week, and complete guided tours are given from 9 a.m. to 5:30 p.m. Rates include a guide for both the caves and gardens. Refreshments are available at the Athenry Pavilion, and one beverage is included in the tour.

The **Folly Great House** (no phone) lies on the outskirts of Port Antonio. The remains of the two-story mansion can be visited free. It was built, it is said, in 1905 by Arthur Mitchell, an American millionaire, for his wife, Annie, daughter of Charles Tiffany, founder of the famous New York store. Sea water was used in the construction, and the house began to collapse only 11 years after they moved in.

Because of the beautiful location, it is easy to see what a fine great house it must have been, but the years and vandals have not added to its attractiveness. Decay and graffiti mar the ruins.

Someone once said, "Anything is possible in Jamaica." Although I can't promise it, it is sometimes possible to arrange a trip to the **Errol Flynn Plantation,** Priestman's River P.O., Portland (phone 809/993-3294 for information). Of course, the more in your party, the better your chances of getting to see the land so beloved by the film star and author of the autobiography *My Wicked, Wicked Ways*. The widow of the film star, Patrice Wymore Flynn (you may remember her from several films she made in the '50s), is now the owner of the working plantation which lies in the area of Priestman's River, 13 miles east of Port Antonio. Sometimes she personally does cruise ship visitors about the property where coconut and pimiento are grown.

Privately owned **Crystal Springs** was part of a former plantation, lying on 156 acres of land. It's one of the newer attractions of Port Antonio. Visitors can explore its grounds, taking in the landscaping, the flowers, and the birds. It is open daily from 8 a.m. to 6 p.m. However, before heading to the western outskirts of town, check for the status of this attraction at Stuarts Travel Service, 23 Harbour St. (tel. 809/993-2609) in Port Antonio.

3. OCHO RIOS

A north-coast resort some two hours by road from either Montego Bay or Port Antonio, Ocho Rios was once a small banana and fishing port, but in recent years tourism has become the leading industry. It is now Jamaica's cruise ship capital. The bay is dominated on one side by a bauxite loading terminal and on the other by a range of hotels with sandy beaches fringed by palm trees. Runaway Bay, once only a satellite of Ocho Rios but now a resort area in its own right, is presented in the next section.

Ocho Rios and neighboring Port Antonio have long been associated with celebrities, its two most famous writers being Sir Noël Coward (who invited the world to his doorstep), and Ian Fleming, creator of James Bond (more about their homes later).

It is commonly assumed among Spanish-speaking people that Ocho Rios was named for eight rivers, which is its Spanish translation. But it doesn't mean that in Jamaican. In 1657 British troops chased off a Spanish expeditionary force who'd launched a raid from Cuba. The battle was near Dunn's River Falls, now the single most important tourist attraction of the resort. Seeing the rapids, the Spanish called the district *las chorreros*. That battle between the Spanish and the British forces was so named. The British and the Jamaicans weren't too good with Spanish names back then, so *las chorreros* was corrupted into "ocho rios".

Frankly, unless you are on a cruise ship, you may want to stay away from the major attractions on cruise ship days. Even the duty-free shopping markets are overrun, and the street hustlers become more strident in promoting their crafts, often junk souvenirs. Dunn's River Falls becomes almost impossible to visit at those times.

However, if you savor the unique flavor of Ocho Rios on other days, you may find it one of the most rewarding destinations in the Caribbean. Parasailing, waterskiing, boardsailing, and jetskiing have been sports added in recent decades, and Ocho Rios is the site of two fishing tournaments held in May and September of every year. Many prefer to stay at one of the all-inclusive resorts, such as Boscobel and the couples-only Couples or the couples-only Sandals. Others such as Jamaica Jamaica in Runaway Bay accept families with children under 16. Those interested in the elegant resort circuit may elect to stay at Sans Souci.

WHERE TO STAY: The area of Ocho Rios is a formidable rival of Montego

Bay. Some inns of character remain, holding out against the newer, all-inclusive developments that may sweep away what is left of the former colonial life of the resort.

The Luxury Leaders

Sans Souci Hotel, Club & Spa, P.O. Box 103, Ocho Rios, Jamaica, W.I. (tel. 809/974-2353), named French for "without a care," is the most luxurious and tasteful hotel in Ocho Rios. It's set four miles east of town on a forested plot of land whose rocky border abuts the sea. The site it occupies was valued for medicinal qualities of its sulfur-rich mineral springs in the 1930s. Erected, demolished, and erected again, the resort witnessed the visits of some gilt-edged titles of Britain in the 1960s when the premises were leased as private apartments. In 1984, after a financial shuffle, it reopened as a richly deluxe hotel. The resort is terraced into a steeply lush hillside whose manicured pathways and steps traverse a richly flourishing jungle. A cliffside elevator brings guests to a secluded outdoor bar whose perimeter includes rocks and an edging of greenery. There's a freshwater pool, plus a frothy and bubbling mineral bath big enough for an elephant, and a labyrinth of catwalks and bridges stretching over rocky chasms filled with surging water. Each of the 71 air-conditioned accommodations has its own veranda or patio, elegant copies of Chippendale furniture, plush upholstery, and a subdued kind of colonial elegance. In winter, EP singles cost $220 to $260 daily, and doubles go for $240 to $400. *In summer, a single goes for $115 to $155 daily, doubles renting for $135 to $250.* For a full American breakfast and a five-course à la carte dinner, the cost is $50 per person daily in winter, *$40 in summer.* Food is served from 7:30 a.m. to 9 p.m.

Charlie's Spa, named after the giant sea turtle that has lived in its own mineral spring by the mineral pool for the last two decades, is a fully equipped health spa that rivals the famous spas of Europe. It offers a six-day program, Monday to Saturday. This is a his-and-her spa, allowing couples to do things together and share an experience. Sports lovers appreciate the hotel's four Laykold tennis courts (two of them lit), and the nearby croquet lawn. Scuba, snorkeling, windsurfing, deep-sea fishing, and Sunfish and catamaran sailing are available at the beach. Guests can golf on the 18-hole Upton Country Club course and watch polo matches while they take afternoon tea at the St. Ann Polo Club, Drax Hall. For reservations and information, call Elegant Resorts of Jamaica (tel. 809/666-34566) in Miami, or toll free 800/237-3237.

Jamaica Inn, P.O. Box 1, Ocho Rios, Jamaica, W.I. (tel. 809/974-2514), is a long, low, U-shaped building set close to the sea, surrounded by grass and palm trees with oleander and bougainvillea. The cool, comfortable lounge with books, and the games room with cards and jigsaw puzzles, will provide you with something to do in case of rain, but it's the outdoor attractions that bring people to the inn. Lovely patios open onto the lawns, and the bedrooms, which face the sea, are reached along garden paths. Winter rates, including three meals a day and tea, are $250 in a single (not ocean view), rising to $300 to $350 in a double. *Summer tariffs cost from $125 daily in a single and from $185 to $195 in a double.* The expensive White Suite here was a favorite of Winston Churchill. There is a small pool almost at the water's edge, where a wide, white sand beach invites you to swim or lounge. The sea close in is almost too clear to make snorkeling an adventure, but farther out it is rewarding. For the nonaquatic there is tennis, with golf close by at the Upton Country Club.

The inn is proud of its cuisine. The chef was trained in Europe and lends his expertise to the production of dishes both international and Jamaican. You can have breakfast served in your room, selecting from kippers, an omelet, or pancakes with maple syrup, or you can enjoy it in the dining room. Lunch is a pleasant à la carte affair, with a wide menu choice. Dinner, for a charge of $30, may start with mango nectar, caviar on toast, or stuffed sweet peppers, followed by soup. For the main course, there may be lobster thermidor, broiled tenderloin with béarnaise sauce or fried chicken. You can finish with a dessert or cheese, and Blue Mountain coffee. The management requires men to wear a jacket and tie at night.

Plantation Inn, P.O. Box, Ocho Rios, Jamaica, W.I. (tel. 809/974-5601), is a magnificent hotel evoking a southern antebellum mansion, reached by a sweeping driveway and entered through a colonnaded portico, set above the beach in pleasant gardens. All bedrooms open off balconies and have their own patios overlooking the sea. The rooms are attractively decorated with chintz and comfortable furnishings, and are air cooled by revolving fans. On the MAP, two persons can stay here in winter at prices ranging from $290 to $545 daily, the latter for occupancy of a junior suite. *In summer, prices are reduced: the same MAP is offered for $195 to $310 daily for two persons.* For single occupancy in either season, deduct $40 per night. Apart from the regular hotel, there are two units that provide lodgings. Plantana Villa above the east beach sleeps two to six people. Blue Shadow Villa on the west side accommodates up to eight guests.

There is an inside dining room, but most of the action takes place under the tropical sky. English tea is served on the terrace every afternoon. You can have breakfast on your balcony. Lunch is outdoors, with a choice of chilled native nectars, followed by a sandwich, or perhaps you'll enjoy a shrimp curry. In winter, men are required to wear jackets at dinner, jackets and ties Friday and Saturday night. In summer, the dress code is more relaxed, calling for casual elegant with no jacket. Breakfast is served at 7:30 a.m., lunch from 1 to 2:30 p.m., and dinner from 8 to 9:30 p.m. On Thursday a Jamaica night buffet is offered, and you can feast, enjoy a local show, and dance to calypso music. The beach is 50 steps down from the garden, and seats on the way provide resting spots. Water sports are available: skindiving, Sunfish sailing, and windsurfing. There is a glass-bottom boat on one of the two private beaches, or you can just take it easy and get a tan while doing nothing at all. The hotel has a jungle gym offering exercise equipment, and there is a sauna as well as facials, massages, and waxing.

All-Inclusive Resorts

Couples, P.O. Box 330, Ocho Rios, St. Ann, Jamaica, W.I. (tel. 809/974-4271). Don't come here alone—you won't get in! You're asked to bring a "little love here," and that means your lover. The management defines couples here as "any man and woman in love." Everything is in pairs, even the double chairs by the moon-drenched beach. Once you've paid the initial fee, you have free use of all facilities—there will be no more bills. It's a taboo subject. Even the cigarettes and whisky are free. You get three meals a day too, including all the wine you want. And tips are not permitted. Every bedroom has either a king-size bed or two doubles, and furnishings are pleasantly traditional. Breakfast is bountiful. You can have it on the terrace, or a continental breakfast can be served on your private patio. Every room has a patio fronting either the sea or the beach; if not that, then gardens or the mountains. The hotel accepts bookings for eight, nine, and ten days, including seven, eight, or nine nights on a Friday-to-Monday basis. Different rate structures are offered, depending on the time of year. The highest winter tab is an ocean-view room at $2,300 per week per couple. *Summer prices are reduced to from $1,940 upward per person per week.*

Dinners are four courses, and afterward there is dancing on the terrace every evening, with a different kind of entertainment. The piano bar opens at 7 p.m., and stays that way until the last guest retires (this is sometimes at 7 a.m.). You can play tennis on one of the five world-class courts, three of which are lit, or else play squash on one of the two championship courts, cycle, go horseback riding, sail, waterski, scuba dive, surf, snorkel, or work out in the Nautilus gym. Golf is available at Runaway Bay, or you may want to slip away to their private island where you can bask in the buff. The only criticism I have of the resort is that it does away with the mating game, unless you cast a roving eye on someone else's other half.

Sandals Ocho Rios, Ocho Rios, Jamaica, W.I. (tel. 809/974-5453—but subject to change), is the newest addition in the ever-expanding "couples only" empire of Gordon (Butch) Stewart who pioneered similar properties in Montego Bay and Negril. The formula is the same: one price per male-female couple including everything. On nine well-landscaped acres, it offers 237 comfortably furnished rooms with either ocean or garden views. There are some cottage units, too. Each room is reasonably large and air-conditioned, with king-size beds, along with hairdryers, radio, and phones. Two people can stay here for four nights at rates ranging from $865 to $1,030, going up to $1,750 to $2,090 should a couple desire to spend a week. Special summer discounts may apply after July until mid-December. Check with a travel agent or call toll free in the U.S. and Canada at 800/327-1991.

Included in the package are all meals, "anytime" snacks, unlimited wine and drinks (some of which can be consumed at an oceanside swim-up bar), two freshwater pools, a private manmade beach along with a host of sporting activities including waterskiing, windsurfing, sailing, snorkeling, and scuba with equipment and instruction. Other amenities include paddleboats, kayaks, a glass-bottom boat, a Jacuzzi, saunas, a fully equipped fitness center, and tennis day or night. Nightly theme parties and live entertainment take place in a modern amphitheater. A unique feature of the resort is an open-air disco. Round-trip transfers from the airport are also included in the package. Special features, also thrown in, are tours to Dunn's River Falls and massages.

Eden II, P.O. Box 51, Ocho Rios, St. Ann, Jamaica, W.I. (tel. 809/972-2300), knew life as the Jamaica Hilton before becoming an all-inclusive couples resort. Set on the seafront between Ocho Rios and St. Ann's Bay, the resort is very sports oriented, with, among other facilities, a Nautilus Fitness Centre that features a hot tub and aerobic exercise classes. Tennis is played both day and night, and other activities include dance lessons, volleyball, and backgammon. You can go horseback riding about 2,000 feet above sea level, jog along a marked trail, and partake of such water sports as skiing, windsurfing, scuba-diving, snorkeling, and sailboat racing.

Rooms are attractively furnished, each with a private balcony if overhead or a patio if on ground level. As in most couples-only resorts in Jamaica, a client gets the works: that is, three meals a day, along with "happy hour" hors d'oeuvres, Sunday champagne brunches, and all bar drinks (even cigarettes). A choice of four wines is available at lunch and dinner. Transfers are arranged between the airport and the hotel. Rates are quoted on the basis of stays ranging from three to seven nights. Accommodations are in four categories: standard, superior, deluxe, and junior suite. Depending on your lodging assignment, the highest charges are from December 18 to January 6 and January 28 to March 31, when prices per person range from $485 to $605 for three nights, $975 to $1,248 for seven nights. From January 7 to January 27 and April 1 to August 31, the charge per person for three nights is $450 to $525, seven nights costing $880 to $1,060. The lowest rates are charged from September 1 to December 21, when each person pays $428 to $500 for three nights, $836 to $1,007 for a seven-night stay.

Boscobel Beach, P.O. Box 63, Ocho Rios, Jamaica, W.I. (tel. 809/974-3330), which is old Spanish for "beautiful gardens by the sea," and it is that and more. Set on 14½ acres of prime seafront property, it stands 10 miles east of Ocho Rios, with a total of 208 rooms.

Children aren't excluded here; rather, they are encouraged and welcomed, with a big program set aside for them, including a games room, even a mini-zoo, and other activities. The resort also makes special rates for single parents traveling with children and is unique in promoting a special program for grandparents and their grandchildren. Naturally, baby-sitting can be arranged, too. But adults with no children are also welcome and given plenty of incentive to visit. All the well-furnished and attractively decorated bedrooms are equipped with radios, TVs, phones, and refrigerators. Some of them feature large balconies and sunken bath-tubs. Oceanview and gardenview rooms are more expensive. Less costly is a series of 44 lanai rooms (these are smaller) which open right onto the beach.

Guests can book in here for three nights or seven nights. In winter, the per person rates for three nights range from $450 to $535, with seven-night book-ings costing from $1,050 to $1,250. Children under 14 years old sharing a room with parents are not charged, but singles must pay a supplement of $60 per night. *In summer, three-night bookings, depending on the accommodation, range from a low of $390 to a high of $425 per person. A booking of seven nights costs from a low of $910 to a high of $995 per person.* Included in the package are all meals (breakfast and a buffet lunch are served on the Jippi-Jappa Terrace). Dinner, also included, is of-fered in an open-air dining room (a special children's meal is served earlier). Throughout the day guests can order snacks at a bar on the beach. There are also four bars on the property, including the one at the beach as well as one around a large swimming pool, yet another around a piano, and a final one in a disco that opens at 11 p.m. Live local entertainment is a nightly feature.

For the prices quoted, guests will find an array of activities, including four tennis courts (two lit for night play), transfers to the golf course (with greens fees included), a fully equipped gym, exercise classes, aerobics, two Jacuzzis, reggae dance classes, and such water sports as windsurfing, sailing, waterskiing, and scuba diving. Transfers to and from the airport are included.

Club Americana, P.O. Box 100, Ocho Rios, Jamaica, W.I. (tel. 809/974-2151), is a 325-room citadel, opening onto a long, sandy beach, next door to the Mallards Beach Hotel in the heart of the resort. It is not a couples-only resort as it also accepts singles and families. It is a modern high-rise, with air-conditioned units, a large cool lobby, and a shopping arcade which is handy if you don't want to walk to the nearby Ocean Village Shopping Center. In what the club calls its all-inclusive party plan, it offers buffet breakfasts, lunches, and dinners, as well as unlimited beverages (yes, beer, liquor, and wine, too), and a burst of entertain-ment with shows and dancing, plus a disco that operates until early in the morn-ing. A wide range of sports programs is also offered, including windsurfing, snorkeling, and sailing with lessons for each, plus a glassbottom boat ride, a trip to Dunn's River Falls, and tennis day or night. No tipping is necessary.

Rooms, depending on their desirability, are divided into standard, superior, and deluxe. Even more expensive junior suites and deluxe suites are also offered. Weekly winter rates quoted are per person, single or double occupancy, with prices ranging from a low of $415 to a high of $965. *In off-season, weekly rates, per person, single or double occupancy, costs from a low of $400 to a high of $880.* Chil-dren 3 to 12 pay $25 per day in a room shared with two adults. Transfers to and from the airport are also included. The club has many amenities, including a freshwater pool, an activities desk, and an adult games room. All its meals are buffet.

First Class

Mallards Beach Hotel, P.O. Box 245, Ocho Rios, Jamaica, W.I. (tel. 809/974-2201), has known many lives, including time logged as both a Hyatt and a Sheraton and by the time you read this, might have been sold and launched under a new banner (check with a travel agent before booking in here). A high rise, it stands on the beach near its neighbor, Club Americana. Not for those seeking a small Caribbean inn, it contains a wealth of activities and amenities, including tennis courts, a swimming pool, on-site water sports, duty-free shopping, barber and beauty shops, a health club, and a sauna, along with an array of dining and drinking facilities, including four bars. Its central location allows you to walk to the duty-free shopping of Ocho Rios.

The hotel offers a total of 397 spacious, air-conditioned rooms and suites, opening onto private balconies with views either of the sea or mountains. *In off-season, singles range from $75 to $155 daily, with doubles costing from $80 to $160 (the higher tariffs are for one-bedroom suites).* Charges include a buffet breakfast. In winter prices in a single go from $120 to $240 daily, with two persons paying from $130 to $250, again the higher prices for one-bedroom suites. Children under 12 room free if they share a unit with a paying adult. For another $25 per person, guests can have MAP, including any of the hotel's theme dinners or else à la carte in the Vivaldi Grill Room and Piano Bar or the Garden Terrace Restaurant. Poolside barbecues and buffets are regular features of the hotel, and reggae and calypso music allow you to dance the night away.

Less Expensive Choices

Shaw Park Beach Hotel, P.O. Box 17, Cutlass Bay, Ocho Rios, Jamaica, W.I. (tel. 809/974-2552), is an elegant Jamaica Georgian property with all rooms directly on the beach, facing the ocean. It has three bars, two inside and the Beach Bar on the Caribbean Terrace under the sky. The reception area looks like a colonial version of a Georgian living room, and the terrace one floor below is built right up to the crashing waves. All rooms are air-conditioned and comfortably furnished. Most have full bathrooms, but some in the east wing contain showers. There is a swimming pool, and ocean water sports—sailing, fishing, windsurfing, waterskiing, snorkeling—are available from the beach at nominal charges. The hotel has its own tennis courts and reciprocity with Upton Golf Club. A resident band plays for dancing nightly, and floor shows are arranged most nights. The nightclub, Silks, vibrates to disco music and has an intimate Jockey Bar. *In summer, singles range in price from $96 to $108 daily, and doubles cost $107 to $121. Four persons can occupy a deluxe two-bedroom apartment suite for about $2.* Winter rates rise to $138 to $151 daily in a single, $150 to $163 in a double, with a two-bedroom apartment suite costing four persons about $371 daily. Shaw Park Gardens (described under "Boonoonoonoos") are owned and operated by the hotel and provide a pleasant afternoon's sightseeing.

Hibiscus Lodge Hotel, P.O. Box 52, Ocho Rios, Jamaica, W.I. (tel. 809/974-2676), offers more value for money than any resort at Ocho Rios. It is an intimate little 26-room inn, with character and charm, perched precariously on a cliffside. Each of the bedrooms has private baths and verandas open to the sea. All accommodations contain ceiling fans. In winter, EP doubles rent for $54 daily, going up to $79 in a triple. *However, in summer EP doubles are only $44 daily, with triples paying $64.*

After a day spent swimming in a pool suspended over the cliffs, with a large sundeck, guests can enjoy a drink in the unique swinging bar. On the three-acre site are a Jacuzzi and tennis court, along with conference facilities. The owners, Richard Powell and Alfred Doswald, can direct you to their restaurants, Almond Tree and Red Poll (reviewed separately). In a coast studded with large resorts, Hibiscus Lodge has maintained its unique personality, and guests like to return to it as they are attracted by its offbeat charm and gracious hospitality.

Inn on the Beach, P.O. Box 342, Ocho Rios, St. Ann, Jamaica, W.I. (tel. 809/974-2782), just behind the sprawling Ocean Village Shopping Centre, is a

Jamaican-run inn at the edge of a public beach in the center of town. Its accommodations are as comfortable as those in larger, more expensive resort hotels nearby. If you don't mind the absence of the varied on-the-premises entertainment facilities of the larger hotels, this may be the place for you. Open-air hallways lead to the sunny bedrooms, each of which has two double beds, large windows, a terrace, air conditioning, a tile bath, and attractive furnishings. There's no elevator, no bar, and no restaurant in the hotel, but you'll find a number of watering spots within walking distance, and two restaurants, under different management, are connected architecturally with the rear side of the inn. In winter, the 46 accommodations rent for $72 daily in a single, $80 in a double, $95 in a triple, and $105 in a quad. *In summer, rates go down to $48 daily in a single, $58 in a double, $68 in a triple, and $82 in a quad.*

WHERE TO DINE: One of the most captivating eating places anywhere in Jamaica is **Ruins Restaurant, Gift Shop and Boutique,** on DaCosta Drive on Turtle River (tel. 809/974-2442). You dine in a spot at the foot of a series of waterfalls that can be considered a tourist attraction in their own right. In 1831 a British entrepreneur constructed a sugar mill on the site, using the powerful stream to drive his water wheels. Today, all that remains is a jumble of ruins, hence the restaurant's name. After you cross a covered bridge, perhaps stopping off for a drink at the bar in the outbuilding first, you find yourself in a fairyland where the only sounds come from the tree frogs, the falling water from about a dozen cascades, and the discreet clink of silver and china. Tables are set on a wooden deck leading all the way up to the pool at the foot of the falls, where moss and other vegetation line the stones at the base. As part of the evening's enjoyment you may want to climb a flight of stairs to the top of the falls, where bobbing lanterns and the illuminated waters below afford one of the most delightful experiences on the island. Reservations are important, since in season this restaurant draws crowds. Menu items include a wide range of Chinese food, such as sweet-and-sour pork or chicken, several kinds of chow mein or chop suey, and a house specialty—lobster sautéed in a special sauce. International dishes include lamb or pork chops, chicken Kiev, and an array of fish. Full meals range from J$50 ($9) to J$100 ($18). Lunch is served daily except Sunday from noon to 2:30 p.m., and dinner is offered seven days a week from 6 to 9:30 p.m.

    Almond Tree Restaurant, P.O. Box 52, Hibiscus Lodge Hotel (tel. 809/974-2676), run by the lodge owners (their resort was previously recommended), Richard Powell and Alfred Doswald, is a two-tiered patio restaurant with a tree growing through the roof, overlooking the Caribbean. Lunches, costing J$75 ($13.50), are served daily from noon to 3 p.m., and dinner, priced from J$150 ($27) à la carte, is offered from 6 to 10 p.m. Almond Tree specialties include a wide range of continental dishes. Lobster thermidor is the most expensive item on the menu, but I prefer their bouillabaisse (not only pieces of conch, but lobster). Also excellent are the roast suckling pig, medallions of beef Anne Palmer, and a fondue bourguignonne. Jamaican plantation rice is a local specialty. The wine list offers a variety of vintages, including Spanish and Jamaican. Have an apéritif in the unique "swinging bar" (swinging chairs, that is).

    Red Poll Restaurant, P.O. Box 52, Hibiscus Lodge Hotel (tel. 809/974-2676), is run by the same owners as the Almond Tree. In Jamaican, *poll* means bull, and at this cliffside-hugging, open-air restaurant, you get some of the best beef in Ocho Rios. Sometimes it is grilled simply, as in the char-broiled T-bone steak, but at other times the chef prepares fancier concoctions such as tournedos Rossini and kebab à la Hibiscus. Other dishes come from the "pork pit." An interesting appetizer is either terrine du pork or else a classic onion soup. Meals are served at dinner only from 6 to 10 p.m., costing J$175 ($31.50).

The Casanova, Sans Souci Club, Spa & Resort, P.O. Box 103 (tel. 809/
974-2353), in the main building of this previously recommended hotel, is one of
the most elegant dining enclaves along the north coast of Jamaica. In the late
1960s Harry Cipriani (of Harry's Bar fame in Venice) taught the staff some of his
culinary techniques. The pasta is still made fresh daily along with many of the
other staples. Jazz from a lattice-roofed gazebo might accompany your meal,
served daily from noon to 3 p.m. and 7 to 9:30 p.m. Lunches cost from $20 each,
with dinners in the $30 to $50 range. Typical dishes, served by polite, formally
dressed waiters, include smoked marlin, lobster bisque, stuffed pork chops
served with a coconut-curry sauce, and chicken suprême flambéed with whisky.
Desserts are sumptuous, and might be followed by one of the house's four special
coffees. Reservations are suggested.

   Carib Inn Restaurant, off Main St. (tel. 809/974-2445), within walking
distance of most hotels, is nestled among crotons and coconut palms on 17 acres
of streams and manicured lawns. To begin your meal, you might order ackee on
toast, or a seafood crêpe. Soup, a grill, seafood, or a flambé specialty can follow.
For dessert, try a Tía Maria parfait (baked banana with coconut cream) or Irish
coffee. For lunch, I suggest one of the daily specials such as curried goat and
white rice, stewed beef, or ackee and codfish. A full dinner costs from J$125
($22.50); lunch goes for J$50 ($9) and up. It's open daily: try to go between
noon and 2 p.m. and 7 and 9 p.m. Bring your camera and swimwear and get
tanned on a private beach or dive into the water of the sea or the Olympic-size
freshwater swimming pool.

   Le Gourmand, Coconut Grove (tel. 809/974-2717), calls itself a "nice little French restaurant," and that is what it is. You can dine outside by the fountain
or else find a cozy table inside. Service is daily from noon to 3 p.m. and 6:30 to
10:30 p.m. The luncheon menu includes cold lobster salad (or else a salad made
with smoked marlin) or else stuffed crêpes and omelets, along with the soup of
the day and sandwiches. Expect to spend from J$50 ($9) and up. Dinner is more
elaborate, beginning with a selection of hors d'oeuvres such as smoked salmon or
escargots à la provençale. For your main course, you face a choice of such dishes
as beef stroganoff or filet mignon bouquetière. For dessert, the choice is sabayon
or perhaps crêpes suzette. The menu is wisely limited, and only quality ingredients are used. Dinners cost from J$175 ($31.50).

   "On the Bay," Fisherman's Point (tel. 809/974-5339), lies in the heart of
Ocho Rios, part of a complex of rental units (Fisherman's Point), in the vicinity
of Turtle Beach. The rather elegant dining spot, launched in 1987, is open all year
daily from 11 a.m. to 10 p.m. For dinner, you can always count on "today's
catch," perhaps Caribbean lobster and certainly seafood chowder and marinated
conch. A specialty is a flaming sword of seafood, and paella is also another praise-
worthy dish. You can also order steak and chicken dishes, finishing perhaps with a
chocolate soufflé. Meals cost from $25.

   Little Pub Restaurant, 59 Main St. (tel. 809/974-2324), is in a tropical
patio surrounded by souvenir shops bordered with gingerbread fretwork. This
indoor-outdoor pub's inner rooms focus on a small stage area for local bands. No
one will mind if you just enjoy a drink while you sit in one of the pub's barrel
chairs, but if you want dinner, you can proceed to one of the linen-covered tables
capped with cut flowers and candlelight. Menu items include barbecued chicken,
grilled steaks, grilled kingfish, brown fish stew with peppery brown gravy (a Jamaican specialty), and banana flambé. Dinners cost J$125 ($22.50) and up.
Breakfast is daily from 7 to 11 a.m.; lunch from 11 a.m. to 4:30 p.m., and dinner
from 6 p.m. to midnight. To add to the ambience of this already-colorful spot,
live music is offered during dinner, as well as a live show at 10 p.m. during high

season. During the show, limbo and cabaret acts are featured. Many guests find that the live music is better than that offered in similar places around town. The pub is immediately west of the Ocho Rios roundabout behind a crumbled fortification and lots of shrubs.

Harmony Hall Restaurant, Harmony Hall, P.O. Box 192 (tel. 809/974-4478), is both the leading art gallery in the area (refer to "What to Do"), and a good and moderately priced restaurant. It is open daily from 11 a.m. to 11 p.m., serving lunches for J$50 ($9) and dinners for J$100 ($18). Lunches are likely to begin with the soup of the day, then follow with a Jamaican specialty. Dinner is more elaborate, including, on one recent occasion, lobster cocktail, chicken Oriental, and rum cake. Diners can order food either inside the 19th-century building, which is decorated in the tavern style, or else on the patio, enjoying the breezes. A well-selected staff serves you.

Parkway Restaurant, 60 DaCosta Dr. (tel. 809/974-2667). This popular establishment in the commercial center of town couldn't have a much plainer façade. Inside it continues to be unpretentious, but many local families and members of the business community know you can get some of the best-tasting and least expensive local dishes here of any place in Ocho Rios. On clean napery, amid a serviceable decor, hungry diners are fed daily from 7:30 a.m. to 11 p.m. Full meals, costing from J$60 ($10.80), include Jamaican-style chicken, curried goat, sandwiches, filet of red snapper, and to top it off, banana cream pie.

WHAT TO DO: A pleasant drive out of Ocho Rios along the A3 will take you inland through **Fern Gully.** This was originally a riverbed, but now the main road winds up some 700 feet between a profusion of wild ferns, a tall rain forest, hardwood trees, and lianas. For the botanist, there are hundreds of varieties of ferns, and for the less plant-minded, roadside stands offer fruit and vegetables, carved wood souvenirs, and basketwork. The road runs for about four miles, sometimes with a large pool of sunlight, sometimes fingers of light just penetrating the overhanging vegetation. Then at the top of the hill, you come to a right-hand turn, onto a narrow road leading to Golden Grove.

You pass Lydford with the remains of **Edinburgh Castle,** built in 1763, the lair of one of Jamaica's most infamous murderers, a Scot named Lewis Hutchinson, who used to shoot passersby and toss their bodies into a deep pit built for the purpose. The authorities got wind of his activities, and although he tried to escape by canoe, he was captured by the navy under the command of Admiral Rodney and was hanged. Rather proud of his achievements (evidence of at least 43 murders was found), he left £100 and instructions for a memorial to be built. It never was, but the castle ruins remain.

Continue down the A1 to **St. Ann's Bay,** the site of the first Spanish settlement on the island, where you can see the **Statue of Christopher Columbus,** cast in his hometown of Genoa, erected near St. Ann's Hospital on the west side of town, close to the coast road. There are a number of Georgian buildings in the town. The **Court House** near the parish church, built in 1866, is most interesting.

Follow the A3 back toward Ocho Rios and you will pass **Dunn's River Falls.** There is plenty of parking space, and for a charge of J$3 (55¢) you can relax on the beach or else for J$5 (90¢) climb with a guide to the top of the 600-foot falls. Dressing rooms are available. You can splash in the waters at the bottom of the falls or drop into the cool pools higher up between the cascades of water. The beach restaurant provides snacks and refreshing drinks. You can visit from 8 a.m. to 5 p.m. daily. If you're visiting the falls, wear old tennis shoes, whatever, anything to protect your feet from the sharp rocks and to prevent slipping.

Cariñosa Gardens, P.O. Box 74, Ocho Rios (tel. 809/974-5346) over-looking the bay, a three-minute drive from the cruise ship docks, is a 20-acre trop-ical garden. Fourteen waterfalls provide a showcase of nature, as does a walk-in aviary on half an acre with 150 exotic birds of the tropics. Garden tours, lasting from 9 a.m. to 5 p.m. daily, cost $2.50 per person. Guests wander through a gar-den walk, taking in the beauty of such plants as anthurium, bromeliads, and im-patiens. It is also possible to order lunch here, served daily from noon to 3 p.m. Costing around $20, a menu offers such dishes as bay marlin smoked or Seville chicken julienne with Jamaican herbs. The restaurant is set in a pond fed by a 40-foot waterfall. Later you can visit the Hall of Master Crafts and shop for woodwork, ceramics, embroidery, jewelry, pewter, and perfumes.

Prospect Plantation, P.O. Box 38, Ocho Rios (tel. 809/974-2058), 4½ miles east of Ocho Rios, is a working property. A visit to this plantation com-bines the opportunity to take an educational, relaxing, and enjoyable tour. On your leisurely ride by covered jitney through the scenic beauty of Prospect, you'll readily see why this section of Jamaica is called "the garden parish of the island." You can view the many trees planted by such visitors as Sir Winston Churchill, Dr. Henry Kissinger, Charlie Chaplin, Pierre Trudeau, Sir Noël Coward, and many others. You will learn about and see growing pimento (allspice), bananas, cassava, sugarcane, coffee, cocoa, coconut, pineapple, and the famous leucaena "Tree of Life." You'll see Jamaica's first hydroelectric plant and Jamaica red poll cattle at the feedlot, and sample some of the exotic fruit and drinks. Your guide will be a graduate of **Prospect Training College,** founded more than 29 years ago by Col. Sir Harold Mitchell, Bt.

Horseback riding is available on four scenic trails at Prospect. The rides vary from 1 to 2¼ hours. Advance booking of one hour is necessary to reserve horses.

Tours, costing from $7.50, depart Monday through Saturday at 10:30 a.m. and at 2 and 3:30 p.m., and on Sunday at 11 a.m. and 1:30 and 3 p.m. Children under 12 go free.

Brimmer Hall Estate (tel. 809/994-2309) is farther east from Ocho Rios in the hills two miles from Port Maria, an ideal place to spend a day, where you can relax beside the pool and sample a wide variety of brews and concoctions, includ-ing an interesting one called "Wow!" The Plantation Tour Eating House offers typical Jamaican dishes for lunch, and there is a souvenir shop with a good selec-tion of ceramics, art, straw goods, woodcarvings, rums, liqueurs, and cigars. All this is on a working plantation where you are driven around in a tractor-drawn jitney to see the tropical fruit trees and coffee plants, and learn from the knowl-edgeable guides about the various processes necessary to produce the fine fruits of the island. The plantation tours are at 11 a.m. and 1:30 and 3:30 p.m. daily. The cost is $10.

Firefly, P.O. Port Maria, St. Mary, 20 miles east of Ocho Rios above Oracabessa, was the home of Sir Noël Coward and his longtime companion, Gra-ham Payn, who, as executor of Coward's estate, donated it to the Jamaica Nation-al Heritage Trust. Now open daily from 9 a.m. to 5 p.m. for an admission of J$10 ($1.80) the house has been kept exactly as it was on the day Sir Noël died in 1973, even to the clothes, including Hawaiian print shirts, hanging in the closet in his austere bedroom with its heavy mahogany four-poster. The library contains his large collection of books, and the living room is warm and comfortable with big armchairs and two grand pianos where he composed several famous tunes. Here the English Queen Mother was entertained. When the lobster mousse he was serving her melted, Coward opened a can of pea soup. Guests—Coward's "bloody loved ones"—who spent a night or more were housed in Blue Harbour, a villa nearer to Port Maria, where Sir Noël lived before building Firefly. Celebrated guests included Evelyn Waugh, Winston Churchill, Errol Flynn and his wife Patrice Wymore, Laurence Olivier, Vivien Leigh, and such theatrical and cinema greats as Claudette Colbert, Katharine Hepburn, and Mary Martin. Paintings by the noted playwright, actor, author, and composer adorn the walls. An open patio looks out over the pool and the sea, and across the lawn, on his simple, flat white marble grave is inscribed simply: "Sir Noël Coward, born December 16, 1899, died March 26, 1973."

Coward was a frequent guest of Ian Fleming at **Goldeneye,** on the north shore, made fashionable in the 1950s. It was here that the most famous secret agent in the world, 007, was born in 1952. Fleming built the house in 1946, and wrote each of the 13 original Bond thrillers in it. The island permeates many of the Bond thrillers. Through the large gates, with bronze pineapples on the top, came a host of international celebrities: Evelyn Waugh, Truman Capote, Graham Greene. The house was closed and dilapidated for some time after the writer's death. However, its present owner, Christopher Blackwell, the British music publisher, has restored the property. It is furnished with "just the basics," the way Fleming wanted it, and the beachfront house can be rented (at a rate to be negotiated). Otherwise, unless you're a guest of the tenant, you aren't allowed to visit as it is private property. However, all 007 fans in this part of the world like to go by, hoping for a look.

Harmony Hall, P.O. Box 192 (tel. 809/974-4233) was built near the end of the 19th century as another one of the "great houses" of Jamaica, this one connected with a pimento estate. Today, after a restoration, it's a center for a gallery selling paintings and other works by Jamaican artists. Arts and crafts are also sold, and some very good ones at that, not the usual junky assortment you often find on the beach. A bar in mahogany paneling has a collection of Victorian memorabilia. The gallery is open daily from 10 a.m. to 6 p.m.

If you'd like to dine there, refer to the restaurant recommendations for Ocho Rios. To reach it, you drive about four miles east of Ocho Rios on the main road to Oracabessa. Or else call and inquire about their free shuttle service.

Columbus Park Museum is a large, open area between the main coast road and the sea at Discovery Bay. Admission is free, and hours are 9 a.m. to 5 p.m. daily. You just pull off the road and then walk among the fantastic collection of exhibits, which range from a canoe made of a solid piece of cottonwood in the same way the Arawaks did it more than five centuries ago, to a stone cross, a monument originally placed on the Barrett estate at Retreat by Edward Barrett, brother to the poet Elizabeth Barrett Browning. You'll see a tally, used to count bananas carried on men's heads from plantation to ship, as well as a planter's strongbox with a weighted lead base to prevent its theft. Also among the exhibits are 18th-century cannons used in the French and Spanish hostilities and during the American Revolution, and a Spanish water cooler and calcifier, a fish pot made from bamboo, a corn husker, a manual grass chopper, and a waterwheel of the type used on the sugar estates in the mid-19th century for all motive power. You can follow the history of sugar since its introduction in 1495 by Columbus, who brought canes from Gomera in the Canary Islands, and see how Khus Khus, a Jamaican perfume, is made from the roots of a plant, and how black dye is extracted from logwood. Pimento trees, from which allspice is produced, dominate the park. There is a large mural by Eugene S. Hyde, depicting the first landing of Columbus at Puerto Bueno (Discovery Bay) on May 4, 1494. The museum is well worth a visit to learn of the varied cultures that have influenced the development of Jamaica.

To see a model Jamaican small farm, visitors can go to **Circle B Farm,** Liberty District, near Priory, St. Ann (tel. 809/972-2988), between Runaway Bay and

Ocho Rios. Hilma and Bob Miller open their property to walking guided tours, costing $12 per person, including a welcome rum or fruit punch, fruits in season, and a native buffet lunch. To look at the diversified farm operation and enjoy the Millers' hospitality takes about two hours. The farm is open to visitors from 10 a.m. to 5 p.m. daily.

Boonoonoonoos

Boonoonoonoos is Jamaican for "very nice" or "super," and also stands for a "happening" in Jamaica.

At **Shaw Park Gardens,** you can stroll through the magnificent gardens to Lookout Point, where a 17th-century cannon points you to a view over Ocho Rios and Turtle Bay. Other paths lead past rushing waterfalls and babbling streams, and a flight of 100 steps takes you up or down, through the trees and bushes that are a sanctuary for a rich variety of bird life. There is a saying about this path, that those who walk together here will never forget the experience. Don't forget your camera. Hours are 9 a.m. to 5 p.m. daily, and admission is $1. On most Tuesdays, a Boonoonoonoos Tea is served, along with a fashion show, followed by a band concert.

A **Reggae Lobster Party** at Coconut Grove Great House is a Jamaican experience you can enjoy Monday and Thursday from 7 to 11 p.m. Reggae music, a native floor show, an open Jamaican bar, and dinner are all part of the package, costing $29 for adults, $14.50 for children. For information, get in touch with Karl Young, Coconut Grove Great House Ltd., P.O. Box 282, Ocho Rios (tel. 809/974-2619).

Also presented by Karl Young's organization is an event promising "romance and adventure." All year on Sunday and Tuesday at 7 p.m. you can enjoy a **Jamaican Night on the White River,** a few miles to the east of Ocho Rios. The boat trip takes you up the torchlit river for a picnic supper on the banks. There is an open bar for as much as you can drink. A native folklore show precedes dancing under the stars. The cost is $31 for adults, $15.50 for children.

SHOPPING: There are three main shopping plazas—Ocean Village, Pineapple Place, and Coconut Grove—all open daily except Sunday from 9 a.m. to 5 p.m. Almost everything is offered, including food, clothing, and souvenirs.

At **Ocean Village Shopping Centre** (tel. 809/974-2683), there are numerous boutiques, food stores, a bank, sundries purveyors, travel agencies, service facilities—what have you. For example, you might shop at **Pretty Feet** shoe shop (tel. 809/974-5040), **Honey Bee Pastry Shop** (tel. 809/974-2829), or **Americana Enterprises Ltd.** (tel. 809/974-2248), where you can purchase Wedgwood, Royal Doulton, Royal Worcester, and the like for duty-free prices.

Passengers from cruise ships invariably head from the piers to **Americana & Nancy's,** Ocean Village Shopping Centre (tel. 809/974-2248), also with duty-free articles for sale. The outlet claims discounts of 40% to 60%. The shop displays all the big names such as Wedgwood and Waterford crystal, along with figures by Lladró and Hummel. They also carry Capodimonte, Coalport, Daum, Lalique, Royal Doulton, Royal Worcester, and Spode, along with a selection of French perfumes and jewelry in 14-karat gold or silver.

Ruth Clarage Ltd., Ocean Village Shopping Centre (tel. 809/974-2874), specializes in beautifully colored hand-silkscreened prints. Many are embroidered by hand in her Montego Bay workshops, and if you wish, you can buy ready-made dresses, evening wear, and sports clothes. Tasteful matching ceramic jewelry can be bought also.

Ocho Rios Laundry Mart, Ocean Village Shopping Centre (tel. 809/974-

2409), is where you can do your own laundry laundromat-style or else leave it and your dry cleaning to be done for you.

Ocho Rios Pharmacy, Ocean Village Shopping Centre (tel. 809/974-2041), sells most proprietary brands, perfumes, plasters for sore heels, and sun-tan lotions, among its many wares.

Pineapple Place Shopping Centre, just east of Ocho Rios, is a pleasant collection of cedar-shingle-roofed cottages set amid tropical flowers. Many shops are represented here.

Ocho Rios Craft Park is a complex of some 150 stalls through which to browse. At the stalls, an eager seller will weave you a hat or a basket while you wait, or you can buy from the mixture of ready-made hats, hampers, handbags, placemats, and lampshades. Other stands stock hand-embroidered goods and will make up small items while you wait. Alongside all this activity, woodcarvers work on bowls, ashtrays, native heads, and statues chipped from lignum vitae, and make cups from local bamboo. Even if you don't want to buy, the park is worth a visit for it is lively and colorful.

The **Coconut Grove Shopping Plaza** is a collection of low-lying shops linked by walkways and shrubs. The merchandise consists mainly of local craft items. Many of your fellow shoppers may be cruise-ship passengers looking for something to buy.

You can see and purchase work by Jamaican artists at the **Frame Centre Gallery,** above the Little Pub on Main Street (tel. 809/974-2374). Work of established painters and up-and-coming talent can be seen here.

AFTER DARK: Hotels often provide live entertainment to which nonresidents are invited. Ask at your hotel desk where "the action" is on any given night. Otherwise, you may want to patronize the club previewed below.

Silk's Nightclub, Shaw's Park Hotel, Cutglass Bay (tel. 809/974-2552). There are slot machines in one corner, well-upholstered banquettes, a smallish dance floor, and a green-and-red decor whose contrasting tones seem to add energy to the sometimes-animated crowd of drinkers and dancers. Nonresidents of this well-known hotel can enter for J$20 ($3.60) each. The club is open nightly from 10 p.m. until very early the next morning, depending on the crowd (or lack of one).

4. RUNAWAY BAY

Once this resort was a mere satellite of Ocho Rios. However, with the opening of some large resort hotels, plus a colony of smaller hostelries, Runaway Bay is now a destination in its own right.

This part of Jamaica's north coast has several distinctions: It was the first part of the island seen by Columbus, the site of the first Spanish settlement on the island, and the point of departure of the last Spaniards leaving Jamaica following their defeat by the British. Columbus landed at Discovery Bay on his second voyage of exploration in 1494, and in 1509, Spaniards established a settlement called Sevilla Nueva (New Seville) near what is now St. Ann's Bay, about ten miles east of the present Runaway Bay village. Sevilla Nueva was later abandoned, the inhabitants moving to the southern part of the island.

In 1655, an English fleet sailed into Kingston Harbour and defeated the Spanish garrison there. However, a guerrilla war broke out on the island between the Spanish and English. This ended with final defeat of the Spanish, and the remnants of the once-proud army, under Don Arnaldo de Ysassi, embarked for Cuba in 1660, thus ending the Spanish resistance. The departure was from a small fishing village on the north coast, and some believe that this "running away" from Jamaica gave the name Runaway Bay to the village whence the Spanish sailed. However, later historians believe that the name possibly came from the traffic in runaway slaves from the north coast plantations to Cuba.

FOOD AND LODGING: An original plantation great house has been restored and turned into a small hotel of charm and character, **Eaton Hall Beach Hotel & Villas,** P.O. Box 112, Runaway Bay, Jamaica, W.I. (tel. 809/973-3504). The brick foundation walls are probably those of an English fort dating from the 17th or 18th century. A subterranean passage, now bricked up, leads from the living room to the coral cliffs behind the house. The 52-room property is a successful coordination of the old blended with newer rooms added in wings that maintain the same architectural tradition. There are suites containing carved mahogany four-poster beds and other furnishings of the 18th-century period. Some of the bedrooms of the great house open onto an arched portico, and four units in the main house front the sea. On each side of the hall are bedroom wings with ocean views. These are furnished in a more restrained way, but with good judgment, utilizing tropical fabric designs and older mahogany pieces. Directly on the beach are the villas, with four bedrooms. Your veranda here will extend out over a rocky ledge, and the water is six feet below you. The mahogany trim used in parts of the hotel is beautiful. *Off-season MAP rates range from $95 to $145 daily in a single, $82.50 to $100 per person in a double.* In winter, prices go up to $125 to $170 daily in a single and $95 to $125 per person in a double. For all the tariffs quoted, you get not only your room but also a full breakfast and dinner daily, as well as transfers between Montego Bay airport and the hotel. Children under 12 are not accepted.

Each week a barbecue is offered, and once a week also, there is a Jamaican buffet with a show; otherwise, the piano bar provides nightly entertainment. The resident band plays six nights a week. The ambience of the great house and its surrounding garden is memorable. The entry lounge has smart styling, with old beams, an open fireplace, traditional wing chairs, and mahogany reproductions. The dining room is dignified yet warm as you sit on carved high-backed chairs. After your meal, you can walk to an adjoining lounge and terrace for a nightcap, watching the flickering lights from the swimming pool. On the grounds is a tennis court (unlit), plus two freshwater swimming pools.

Jamaica, Jamaica, P.O. Box 58, Runaway Bay, Jamaica, W.I. (tel. 809/973-2436, 516/868-6924 in New York, or toll free 800/858-8009), is one of the most interesting all-inclusive resorts in the region. A stylish incarnation of a resort which has known several identities since it was built, it operates on a price plan including three meals a day, all drinks, free cigarettes, and a galaxy of other benefits. Its long, low-lying clubhouse is approached by passing through a park filled with tropical trees and shrubbery. Inside the lobby is the best re-creation of the South Seas in Jamaica, with hanging wicker chairs and totemic columns. Live music emanates from a stylish bar every evening at 6:30 p.m., reggae exercise classes are held twice daily, and there's an open-air gym filled with Nautilus equipment. A nightclub offers live shows five nights a week at 10:30. Near the wide sandy beach, there's even a mini-jungle, with dangling hammocks. The nearby swimming pool is traversed by a wooden footbridge, and at a beachside restaurant and sports center, a complete list of sports-related activities are presented. There's even a nearby nude beach. Each of the 238 rooms has a view of a well-landscaped courtyard. Windows are angled toward the light, and each unit is air-conditioned with a private balcony overlooking the sea. Rates are based on double occupancy. For three nights in winter, prices range from a low of $460 to a high of $677 per person. The single supplement is $60 per person nightly. The seven-night package in winter costs from $1,080 to $1,580 per person. *In summer, the three-night package, based on double occupancy in a shared twin, ranges from $390 to $410 per person, rising to $860 to $950 per person for seven nights. The single supplement is lowered to $50 per person per night.* The resort does not accept those under the age of 16.

Runaway H.E.A.R.T. Country Club, P.O. Box 98, Runaway Bay, St. Ann, Jamaica, W.I. (tel. 809/973-2671), has been called "the best kept secret in Jamaica." It practically wins hands down as the bargain of the north coast. One of Jamaica's few training and service institutions, the club and its adjacent academy are operated by the government to provide a high level of training for young Jamaicans interested in the hotel trade. The hotel is very well run with a professional staff, intermixed with trainees, who are helpful and eager to please, and offer perhaps the finest service of any hotel in the area.

The rooms, only 20 in all, are bright and airy, and all are air conditioned with private bath, with either a king-size bed, a double bed, or twin beds. Each room also has a phone. Accommodations open onto private balconies with views of well-manicured tropical gardens or else vistas of the bay and golf course. In winter EP single rates are only $50 a day, with doubles costing $60, a remarkable bargain. At that rate, you might want to stick around a while and take a package of eight days and seven nights, including seven breakfasts and four dinners. For that, singles pay $595, with double occupancy costing $420 per person. *In summer, EP singles cost only $29 per night, with doubles going for $50. The off-season, eight-day, seven-night package, which includes seven breakfasts and three dinners, is only $460 for a single or $320 per person in a double.* All package rates include round-trip airport transfers, unlimited golf greens fees, and use of a chaise longue at the pool or at a private beach, which is reached by a free beach shuttle.

Guests enjoy taking a dip in the hotel swimming pool, later having a drink in the piano bar (ever had a cucumber daiquiri?), before heading for the dining room, the Cardiff Hall Restaurant, which has a combination of Jamaican and continental dishes. The young people give you classic European table service, as they've been taught. Nonresidents can also enjoy dinner served nightly from 7 to 9, a well-prepared table d'hôte costing J$90 ($16.20). The academy has won awards for some of its dishes, including "go go banana chicken" and curried codfish.

Caribbean Isle Hotel, P.O. Box 119, Runaway Bay, Jamaica, W.I. (tel. 809/973-2364), is a small hotel with eight superior and 15 standard rooms, offering personalized service in an informal atmosphere. The rooms all have ocean views with air conditioning, private baths, and showers, and the superior units all have private balconies. *Summer rates are $30 daily in singles and $40 in doubles for standard accommodations. Superior rooms rent in summer for $55 single or double occupancy.* In winter, standard singles cost $40 daily, standard doubles going for $50. Superior units go for $60 single or double. The hotel has a TV in the bar-lounge and a dining room leading onto a sea-view patio. Meals are served from 8 a.m. to 9:30 p.m. daily. Dinner includes lobster, fish, shrimp, pork chops, chicken, and local dishes prepared on request.

IN THE ENVIRONS: Not a hotel, **Lillyfield,** P.O. Box 20, Bamboo Post Office, St. Ann, Jamaica, W.I. (tel. 809/974-5508), is a private home with overnight accommodations available. After he left the Manley government as its minister of culture, Arnold Bertram and his wife, Claire, undertook the restoration of this 300-year-old plantation house. Today, Lillyfield is still "basically" a working coffee plantation, with a scattering of cattle to assist in the economic upkeep of the premises. Set high in the hills, it lies about seven miles over winding roads south of Runaway Bay. The Bertrams offer a quartet of simple yet elegant bedrooms, costing a year-round price of about $85 per person nightly, based on double occupancy, with breakfast and dinner included.

Chukka Cove Farm, P.O. Box 160, Richmond Llandovery, Ocho Rios, Jamaica, W.I. (tel. 809/972-2506), well known for its horse-riding tours, is also the most complete equestrian center in Jamaica for horse lovers who'd like to live on the grounds. It is often frequented by Captain Mark Phillips, husband of Britain's Princess Anne. On the estate's acreage lie six two-bedroom villas, each with a veranda, plank floors, and an architectural plan vaguely reminiscent of 18th-century models. With all meals and drinks, as well as a number of extras, including a staff to clean and prepare meals in one of the villa kitchens, *double occupancy costs $200 per night off-season, with a single rate priced at $160.* In winter rates only for double occupancy are quoted at $214 per night, with all meals and drinks. If you prefer only a villa with the staff accompanying it, and with no meals included (the staff will cook for you), double occupancy in winter is $128 per night, *lowered to $114 in summer.*

5. FALMOUTH

This port town, which lies on the north coast about 23 miles east of Montego Bay, is just beginning to be discovered by tourists. Of course, Trelawny (see below) has already put it on the tourist map. The town in itself is interesting but ramshackle. There is talk about fixing it up for visitors, but no one seems to have done that yet. If you leave your car at Water Square, you can explore the town in about an hour or so. The present courthouse was reconstructed from a building from the early 19th century, and fishermen—those men who go out for lobsters—still congregate on Seaboard Street. You'll pass the Customs Office and a parish church dating from the closing years of the 18th century. Later, you can go on a shopping expedition outside of town to Caribatik (see below).

AN ALL-PURPOSE RESORT: About a half-hour's drive from Sangster International Airport in Montego Bay, **Trelawny Beach Hotel,** P.O. Box 54, Falmouth, Jamaica, W.I. (tel. 809/954-2450), is a 350-room, self-contained resort in Falmouth, under Warwick International Hotels. Locally made materials, in keeping with the policy of the "New Jamaica," were used when possible, including wicker furniture along with Jamaican floral fabrics. The 1,400-foot beach area was achieved with the leasing of 1,100 feet of adjacent frontage. Bohíos were built around the pool area, and many new trees and flowers have been planted in the gardens to give everything a lusher look.

In winter, the daily MAP rates per person are $143 in a single, $112 in a double, and $100 in a triple. Children 14 and under may share a room with an adult at $25, MAP. Accommodations are in air-conditioned rooms with private balconies and an ocean or mountain view. *Daily MAP rates in summer are $103 in a single, $76 per person in a double.* A honeymoon package is available. Rates include complimentary tennis, water sports, live entertainment nightly, shuttle-bus service to Mo Bay, and parties. Free lessons are given in scuba-diving, snorkeling, Sunfish sailing, windsurfing, and waterskiing, even reggae dancing. The resort has four lit Laykold tennis courts, plus a swimming pool. A children's activity center offers supervised activities daily from 10 a.m. to 5 p.m., plus children's dinners on Monday, Wednesday, and Saturday at 5:30 p.m. The center is also open during the adults' dinner hour, 7 to 9 p.m. Your best bet for lunch or dinner is the Palm Terrace, where an à la carte selection is offered at midday. Dinner is also served in the Jamaican Room, although it's open only depending on occupancy of the hotel and never on barbecue nights. The Jamaican Room is an indoor, air-conditioned facility with wicker chairs, cedar tables, and carpeting.

You can order snacks and drinks at the Almond Tree coffeeshop, adjacent to the Palm Terrace, and at poolside.

WHERE TO EAT: A well-recommended dining place is **Glistening Waters Inn and Marina,** P.O. Box 133, Falmouth (tel. 809/954-3229). Residents of Montego Bay sometimes make the 22-mile drive out here just to sample an ambience of the almost-forgotten Jamaica of another era. The restaurant with a veranda overlooking the lagoon, is housed in what was originally a private clubhouse of the aristocrats of nearby Trelawny. The furniture here may remind you of a stage set for *Night of the Iguana.* Wicker chairs alternate with simple wicker tables. Menu items may include many local fish dishes such as snapper or kingfish, served with bammy (a form of cassava bread). Other specialties are three different lobster dishes, three different preparations of shrimp, three different conch viands, fried rice, and pork served as chops or in a stew. Meals cost from J$75 ($13.50). Hours are from 11 a.m. to 3 p.m. and 6 to 11 p.m. daily. Many guests look forward to coming here because the waters of the lagoon are memorable. They contain a rare form of phosphorescent microbes which, when the waters are agitated, glow in the dark. Ask about boat cruises.

WHERE TO SHOP: Two miles east of Falmouth on the north coast road is **Carabatik Island Fabrics,** at Rock Wharf on the Luminous Lagoon (tel. 809/954-3314). You'll recognize the place easily, as it has a huge sign painted across the building's side. This is the private living and work domain of Muriel and Keith Chandler, who escaped the snows of Chicago years ago to introduce a batik studio and clothing factory to Jamaica as a pioneer industry in 1970. Today the batiks of Muriel Chandler are viewed as stylish and sensual garments by chic boutiques from Padre Island, Texas, to fashion enclaves in the American Northeast.

There is also a full range of scarves and wall hangings, some patterned after themes such as a parade of the endangered animal species of the world, as well as abstract patterns reminiscent of a painting by Jackson Pollock. Original batik paintings are also sold. The shop, which contains a factory in back where either Muriel or Keith will describe the intricate process of batiking, is open daily except Sunday and Monday from 10 a.m. to 3 p.m. They are closed from mid-May to mid-November, but during that time, the place can be visited by telephone appointment.

A SIDE TRIP TO RÍO BUENO: I suggest a visit to this little village near Falmouth, to stop at **Gallery Joe James,** Río Bueno, Trelawny (no phone), halfway between Ocho Rios and Montego Bay, 30 miles each way. Joe is one of those rare, gentle men in whose company you could happily spend a day or a year, listening to his talk about art, his life in England and Jamaica, his enthusiasm for painting and carving, and his hopes for the future development of art in Jamaica. At the woodcraft workshop, he personally supervises production of the sculptures and woodcarvings which, with his own striking paintings, fill the gallery.

Enter the gallery from the parking lot. It is brilliant with portraits, landscapes, color, and life. Indigenous woods are used to create carvings of heads, small birds, or bowls. A carved crocodile, a crab, a turtle, or a turtle-shaped ashtray are among the interesting souvenirs.

Warning: Don't try to bargain for the items on sale here. Joe will voluntarily offer a discount if you buy a number of objects of reasonable value. Otherwise, the prices are as marked.

At the **Lobster Bowl Restaurant,** early visitors can have breakfast for J$25 ($4.50). Lunch, noon to 3 p.m., is served inside or on the patio with the water almost lapping your feet. For dinner, the cost of the main dish includes soup, salad, dessert, coffee, and a Tía Maria, plus a main course of grilled fish, broiled lobster, or sirloin steak. The wine list includes a wide variety, or you can order Red Stripe beer. The menu is kept small so that the quality of each dish is high. Lunch costs from $15 and dinner from $25. Hours are daily from 8 a.m. to 11 p.m.

6. MONTEGO BAY

Montego Bay first attracted tourists in the 1940s when Doctor's Cave Beach was popular with the wealthy who bathed in the warm water fed by mineral springs. The town, now Jamaica's second-largest city, is on the northwest coast of the island. In spite of the large influx of visitors, it still retains its own identity with a thriving business and commercial center, and functions as the market town for most of western Jamaica. It has cruise ship piers and a growing industrial center at the free port. The history of Mo Bay, as the islanders call it, goes back to 1494 when it was discovered as an Arawak settlement.

As Montego Bay has its own airport, the Donald Sangster International airport, those who vacation here have little need to visit Kingston, the island's capital, unless they are seeking the cultural pleasures of shows and concerts of all kinds, museums, and galleries. Otherwise, you have everything in Mo Bay, the most cosmopolitan of Jamaica's resorts.

WHERE TO STAY: Montego Bay offers accommodations in all brackets, from the luxurious Round Hill to guesthouses. I'll begin with—

The Luxury Leaders

Round Hill Hotels and Villas, P.O. Box 64, Montego Bay, Jamaica, W.I. (tel. 809/952-5150), is by now a Caribbean legend, one of the most distinguished hotels in the West Indies. The hotel and villa colony stands on a 98-acre peninsula, once part of Lord Monson's sugar plantation, lying eight miles west of Montego Bay. Everybody from the Kennedys to Sir Noël Coward to Cole Porter has driven up the casuarina-lined, curving driveway. Perhaps as they got out of the car, they'd hear Irving Berlin trying out one of his new show tunes. But that famous piano was given to a parish church (regrettably, I say).

Today there is a "new Round Hill" which has emerged from yesterday (it opened its doors in 1954). It still attracts a lively, sophisticated crowd, but the "new names" are likely to be Paul McCartney, Ringo Starr, even the Aga Khan. Unlike the past, all nights are informal except Saturday when a jacket and tie or black tie for men are required. Likewise, it is preferred that you wear all white on the tennis court.

Surrounded by beautifully landscaped and well-maintained tropical gardens, Round Hill accommodates some 200 guests, who enjoy its private beach, its swimming pool, the view of Jamaica's north shore, and the vista of the mountains. The least expensive accommodations are in Pineapple House, dubbed "The Barracks" by Adele Astaire. Don't be misled by that affectionate appellation. These rooms are comfortably and handsomely decorated, containing ceiling fans and opening onto views of the water and beach and costing from $260 to $270 daily double occupancy, including a full American breakfast. For full MAP, add another $25 per person daily. Pineapple House is open only from November 15 to April 15. In winter villa suites range from $295 to $435 daily for double occupancy, with a third person paying another $40. In all there are 27 private villas dotted over the hillside. Each villa has two, three, or four individual suites with a private living area and/or patio, and 17 contain their own swimming pools. Even though Pineapple House closes in winter, the villas remain open all year and are rented on a weekly basis from mid-April to mid-November.

A two-bedroom villa, suitable for four, for example, costs $1,400 per week, including a cook who will shop and prepare meals for you, maid service, linen, and electricity. Many of the owners of the villas have furnished them stylishly, including one-of-a-kind antiques, silk rugs, and brass beds topped with pineapple finials.

At a little sandy bay is an intimate straw hut and an open terrace where guests congregate for informal luncheons. Dining is on a candlelit terrace beneath a giant banyan tree, or else you'll be served in the roofed-over Georgian colonial room overlooking the sea. The cuisine is a mixture of Jamaican and continental dishes. The entertainment is varied—a bonfire beach picnic on Monday, a calypso barbecue on Wednesday, a Jamaican night on Friday, and Round Hill's gala night every Saturday. A program of water sports is also offered. Incidentally, women visiting in February should make a point of appearing every day in a different designer bathing suit: It's the thing to do here.

Tryall Golf, Tennis & Beach Club, Sandy Bay Post Office, Hanover Parish, Montego Bay, Jamaica, W.I. (tel. 809/952-5110), is a complex of elegant villas and a stately stone and glass great house built in 1834 and vastly rebuilt. The location is on a 2,200-acre sugarcane plantation, about 14 miles from the airport at Montego Bay and some 12 miles from the heart of the resort, a 20-minute drive. It has been called one of the grande dames of Jamaican resorts, and it is. A total of 52 recently refurbished units, all air-conditioned, are rented. The hotel offers large handsomely furnished guest rooms with picture windows and in some cases four-posters. The most expensive rentals are the luxuriously furnished villas, set in lush tropical foliage, and designed and placed on the grounds for privacy. Villas come with full-time staff, including a cook, maid, laundress, and gardener. It's the ultimate in luxury for the island, and very expensive. A two-bedroom villa, suitable for four persons, costs from $3,750 per week, EP, in winter, *$3,200 weekly in summer, also EP.* Regular guestrooms in winter cost from $240 to $32 daily in singles, doubles going for $280 to $360, including MAP. *In off-season, singles cost from $140 to $190 daily, with doubles going for $180 to $230, all MAP.*

The pride of the estate is the fairways of the 18-hole golf course, a 6,680-yard, par-71 course. Nine Laykold tennis courts, five lit for night games, are also offered. Horseback rides along century-old trails can also be arranged. The pool has a swim-up bar. For reservations and more information, get in touch with a travel agent or Scott Calder Int. (tel. 800/336-4571 in North America).

The **Half Moon Club,** P.O. Box 80, Montego Bay, Jamaica, W.I. (tel. 809/952-2211), lies about eight miles from Montego Bay's city center and some six miles from the international airport. It is considered one of the 300 best hotels in the world. Set in pleasant gardens, the resort complex consists of hotel rooms, cottages, apartments, and golf villas. One hotel critic called the cottages "divine; . . . Marie Antoinette would have liked them." Many have private swimming pools. Over the years, it has attracted distinguished guests, including President George Bush.

In off-season, singles range from $100 to $200 daily, with doubles costing $130 to $230. In winter, singles cost $180 to $450 daily, with doubles priced from $220 to $490. MAP is another $40 per person daily. Much made-in-Jamaica reproduction furniture is used, including some mahogany four-poster beds. All accommodations contain air conditioning and ceiling fans. Throughout, the resort blends 18th-century architectural details with the plantation colonial style of architecture.

The Sugar Mill restaurant has a personal touch, set as it is beside a working water wheel from a bygone sugar estate. For my comments on the cuisine served here, refer to the restaurant section. Connected to the main building, the Seagrape Terrace is also a choice place to dine. Meals are served on an outdoor terrace under the spreading branches of an 80-year-old sea grape tree. The club has a calypso group, a resident band, and nightly shows, or you can taxi into Montego Bay to sample the nightlife there. The Half Moon also has a shopping arcade with a pharmacy and boutiques, plus a beauty salon, as well as a sauna and massage facilities. From the west side of the property, which offers a mile of swimming beach, a guest can sail, windsurf, or snorkel, and from the east side it's possible to go scuba-diving or deep-sea fishing. One can swim in the club's two major freshwater pools or play tennis on one of the club's 13 courts (four of which are floodlit at night). There are also four lit squash courts (British tradition lives on), and of course the 18-hole Robert Trent Jones–designed golf course is another lure. Greens fees are included.

Inclusive Resorts

Sandals Montego Bay, P.O. Box 100, Montego Bay, Jamaica W.I. (tel. 809/952-5510), is a honeymoon haven, perhaps the one resort in the Caribbean with the highest occupancy rate. This 19-acre site of about 240 rooms is a couples-only (male and female) resort. This is an all-inclusive resort, including all meals, snacks, nightly entertainment (including those notorious toga parties), unlimited drinks night or day at one of four bars, taxes, service, tips, and round-trip airport transfers and baggage handling from the Montego Bay airport. *In off-season, per couple rates weekly range from a low of $1,775 to $2,350.* In winter, depending on the room, per couple prices by the week begin at $2,195 and go up to $2,160. The lower tariffs are for standard rooms, and the higher charges are for one-bedroom suites.

Accommodations are either in villas spread along 1,700 feet of white sandy beach or in the main house where all bedrooms face the sea and contain private balconies. All units are air-conditioned and well furnished, with king-size beds and such amenities as hairdryers, radio, and phone.

Activities fill the roster here, including waterskiing, snorkeling, sailing, scuba diving, and windsurfing. Paddleboats and a glass-bottom boat appeal to seafarers, while others select a spot around one of two freshwater pools, later going into one of three Jacuzzis. Tennis is available day or night. The Playmakers, as staff members are called, like to keep everybody amused and the joint jumping. Dinner is by candlelight on an al fresco terrace bordering the sea. Those who haven't tired themselves can head for the late night disco, Skydome, which often has rum and reggae nights. As guests seem to have a tendency to overeat and overdrink, there is a fully equipped fitness center to take off those excess pounds. Reserve as far ahead as possible. The location is near the airport.

Sandals Royal Caribbean, P.O. Box 167, Montego Bay, Jamaica, W.I. (tel. 809/953-2231), was, in 1966, the choice of Queen Elizabeth and Prince Philip when they visited the island. She'd be welcomed back today, but only if she brought her Prince with her, as this is an all-inclusive couples-only (male and female) resort. This is a reincarnation of what was once a prestigious Montego Bay hotel constructed in the Jamaican colonial style. The building lies on its own private beach (which, frankly, isn't as good as the one at Sandals Montego Bay). Some of the British colonial atmosphere overlay remains, as reflected by a formal tea in the afternoon, but there are modern touches as well, such as a private island reached by boat where clothing is optional.

The 165 spacious rooms come in a wide range, from standard to superior to deluxe. Even higher in price are the deluxe beachfront accommodations or a junior suite. Amenities include hairdryers, radio, and phone. *Shoulder and summer rates range from a low of $780 to $2,195 per couple per week.* Winter tariffs by the week cost from $2,195 to $2,610 for two persons. This inclusive package takes in a lot: three meals a day (unlimited snacks at the beach bar and grill as well), nightly entertainment and theme parties, and round-trip airport transfers. Royal Caribbean also offers a full range of sports programs and other recreational activities, including scuba diving (limited to one dive per day), sailing, snorkeling, canoeing, paddleboating, and windsurfing. Tennis is available day and night, and guests can swim to their delight in one of two freshwater pools, or check out the action in one of the Jacuzzis, or use the facilities of a health spa. After dining from an à la carte menu (lunch is buffet), guests enjoy disco action. If you're not married by the time you arrive, management can also arrange for your wedding.

Jack Tar Village, P.O. Box 144, Montego Bay, Jamaica, W.I. (tel. 809/952-4341, or toll free 800/527-9299), is called simply "The Village" in Mo Bay. Like its sister hotels in Puerto Plata and Grand Bahama, it offers one of those "all-inclusive" package deals, including, while you're here: all meals; unlimited wine with lunch and dinner; unlimited beer, wine, and liquor both day and night; daytime tennis; water sports such as windsurfing, waterskiing, snorkeling, and sailing; nightly entertainment; sauna and massages; free use of the tennis clinic; and even reggae dance lessons. Its policy, as of this writing, is to require no minimum stay. That means a rate in winter of $190 daily in a single, $150 per person in a double. *Rates go down in summer to $140 daily in a single, $90 per person in a double.* Private balconies open directly onto Montego Bay, and guests practically live in their swimsuits. A few steps from your private room lead directly to the beach. Lunch is served at beachside or in the main dining room.

Fantasy Resort, Gloucester Ave., P.O. Box 161, Montego Bay, Jamaica, W.I. (tel. 809/952-4150), in the heart of Montego Bay, is set between the seaside road and a steep, tree-covered cliff. In spite of its location, if you turn your back to the busy boulevard outside, and look only at the cliffs beyond, you'll think you're in the Jamaican countryside. The reasonably priced MAP package, offered in both summer and winter, includes round-trip transfers to and from the Montego Bay airport and breakfast and dinner daily. Guests are housed in rooms which are air-conditioned and contain for the most part an ocean view with private bath and balcony. *In summer daily MAP rates are $90 to $100 in a single, rising to $140 to $160 for two persons.* In winter prices go up to $110 to $132 daily in a single and from $150 to $174 in a double, all MAP. Access is provided to the Doctor's Cave Beach nearby. Facilities at the hotel include a freshwater pool, two tennis courts (day play), a disco, an exercise room, a Jacuzzi, and nightly entertainment. For reservations, call toll free 800/433-4643. It's one of the most reasonable resorts in Montego Bay.

Carlyle on the Bay (a Sandals Resort), Kent Ave., P.O. Box 412, Montego Bay, Jamaica, W.I. (tel. 809/952-4140), is separated from the sea by a main road. This couples-only (male and female) hotel is built around a large pool and patio, but you can also walk to the beach.

Of the 52 rooms, 38 open onto the swimming pool. Accommodations, for the most part, are air-conditioned, containing king-size beds and private baths along with such amenities as hairdryers, clock radios, and phones. Rates are all inclusive, and that means three meals a day, "anytime" snacks, unlimited drinks both day and night, along with nightly entertainment, plus round-trip airport transfers to and from the hotel. Even tips are included. *From March 25 to December 22, you can book in here for four days and three nights (the minimum time allowed) at costs ranging from $550 to $580 per couple.* Arrivals are accepted on any day of the week. *A full week—seven days and six nights—costs two people from $1,100 to $1,160.* At other times of the year, rates go up. Two people on a four-day (three-night) rental pay from a low of $645 to a high of $735. For seven days and six nights, the charge begins at $1,125, going up to $1,280 per couple. A full recreational and sports program is included in the price, and that means snorkeling, windsurfing, Sunfish sailing, and trips on an underwater vision boat. On the premises are an exercise room, saunas, a Jacuzzi, and tennis. Food is served in bountiful portions.

SeaGarden Beach Resort, Kent Ave., Montego Bay, Jamaica, W.I. (tel. 809/952-4780, or toll free 800/545-9001), about 1½ miles east of Montego Bay, stands near some of the most popular public beaches. Designed in a British colonial style of neo-Victorian gingerbread, tall columns, and white lattices, it is airy, comfortable, and stylish. A dining room is under a high arched ceiling sheathed in mahogany whose view opens onto a flagstone-covered courtyard. The 100 accommodations lie in sprawling motel-like units around the pool in back. Each unit is air-conditioned, containing a private balcony or patio, private bath, and simple mahogany furniture. Prices include three meals a day, all drinks, cigarettes, transfers from the airport, free tennis on a pair of illuminated courts, tax, and gratuities. Oceanview rooms always carry higher prices than standard accommodations. In keeping with the American tendency to take shorter holidays, three-night stays are possible, even in winter. Weekly packages are still a feature, however. For three nights in winter, all-inclusive singles cost $492 to $513 daily, doubles go for $327 to $338 per person, and triples rent for $294 to $301 per person. *In summer, a three-night package costs from $444 to $463 daily in a single, $295 to $304 per person in a double, and $265 to $271 in a triple.*

Lady Diane's Hotel, 5 Kent Ave., Montego Bay, Jamaica, W.I. (tel. 809/952-4415). Its motivating health-conscious philosophy makes guests think they've registered in a yoga and meditation retreat instead of a conventional hotel. In its center is the most charming plank-covered terrace in Montego Bay. From its surface you can enjoy a view of the sea and a popular beach just across the street. The hotel contains 15 stylishly antique bedrooms, dozens of pieces of wicker furniture, and lattices. Year-round prices are almost always quoted on a weekly basis: $770 in a single, $595 per person in a double, with meals, snacks, shiatsu massages, taxes, service, and airport transfers included. The kitchens are the only place I know of in Jamaica that have insistently adapted Jamaican ingredients to the rigors of a macrobiotic diet. All meals are "natural," served family style. Ingredients include only organic grains, beans, and flours, these ingredients concocted into all-vegetarian meals which the clientele appreciates. Call collect for reservations or information.

First-Class Choices

Wyndham Rose Hall Beach Hotel and Country Club, P.O. Box 999, Montego Bay, Jamaica, W.I. (tel. 809/953-2650, or toll free 800/822-4200), is a 500-room hotel on a former sugar plantation that once covered 7,000 acres. The hotel abuts the 200-year-old home of the legendary "White Witch of Rose Hall," now a historic site. Just nine miles east of the Montego Bay Airport, Wyndham Rose Hall is at the bottom of a rolling 30-acre site along the north-coast highway. Although it's popular as a convention site, the hotel also caters to a family-oriented market where children are considered an important part of the clientele. Behind the reception area at the bottom of a flight of stairs there are three pools —one for wading, one for swimming, and a third for diving. It's never more than a short walk to one of the many bars scattered around the hotel property, and a sandy beach, rental sailboats, and a top-rated golf course meandering over a part of the hotel grounds are here for the enjoyment of the guests. There are also five restaurants and a busy staff of social organizers. A seven-court lit tennis complex is headed by world-class professionals who offer a complete tennis program. The all-weather Laykold courts are at the side door of the hotel and within view of the ocean.

The seven-story, H-shaped structure ensures that nearly every room has a view of the sea. Most units have two oversize double beds. Singles are furnished with a Chesterfield that can convert to a double bed. All rooms have private balconies. The charges are $120 to $140 daily in high season for a single or double room. *Off-season, singles or doubles range in price from $70 to $80 daily.*

Holiday Inn, P.O. Box 480, Montego Bay, Jamaica, W.I. (tel. 809/953-2485), is an oceanside hotel whose stone façade is separated from the busy street outside by a screen of palm trees. The hotel ensures its guests' privacy by having a guard at the entrance to screen persons coming in. Inside you find numerous amenities, including a free-form pool whose narrowest section is spanned by an arched footbridge. A sandy beach, a variety of water sports (glass-bottom boats, sailboats, and scuba- and skindiving), a disco, a Jamaica nightclub, live entertainment by the pool nightly, and tennis courts are also available for the patrons' enjoyment. Other facilities are a children's playground and a choice of four bars—one in an inner atrium—plus four restaurants. In winter, singles range from $117 to $156 daily. Doubles go for $122 to $161. *In summer, singles are priced from $75 to $99 daily, and doubles cost $80 to $104.* MAP is available for $38 more per adult, $30 per child under 12.

Less Expensive Choices

Winged Victory Hotel, 5 Queen's Dr., Montego Bay, Jamaica, W.I. (tel. 809/952-3891). Glistening, tall, and modern, this hotel delays revealing its true beauty until you pass through its comfortable public rooms into a Mediterranean-style courtyard in back. There, urn-shaped balustrades enclose a terraced garden, a pool, fringes of plants, trees, and flowering shrubs, along with a veranda looking over the faraway crescent of Montego Bay. The veranda's best feature is the Calabash Restaurant, reviewed separately. The dignified owner, Roma Chin Sue, added about two dozen additional rooms to her already well-known restaurant in 1985. All but five have a private balcony or veranda, along with an attractively eclectic decor that is part Chinese, part colonial, and part Iberian. In winter, singles or doubles cost $80 to $100 daily. *In summer, single or double rooms rent for $60 to $80 daily.* MAP can be arranged for another $25 per person daily. By far the most luxurious accommodation is the four-bedroom penthouse. Designed as a duplex, it offers two levels of panoramic balconies, a view of the landscape, an industrial kitchen capable of serving a banquet, and a fine collection of Chinese art and furniture. Each bedroom, suitable for two persons, rents in high season for $150 daily, *dropping to $110 per bedroom in low season.*

Wexford Court Hotel, Gloucester Ave., P.O. Box 108, Montego Bay, Jamaica, W.I. (tel. 809/952-2854), is on the main road about ten minutes to downtown Mo Bay and close to Doctor's Cave Beach. The small hotel has a pleasant pool and a patio where in season calypso is enjoyed. The rooms are air-conditioned, and some have nice living/dining areas, bathrooms, and kitchenettes, if you wish to cook for yourself. All rooms have patios shaded by gables and Swiss chalet-style roofs. *In summer, singles range in price from $60 to $70 daily, doubles go for $65 to $75, and triples cost $75 to $85.* In winter, rates are $70 to $80 in singles, $75 to $85 in doubles, and $85 to $95 in triples. For breakfast and dinner, add another $28 per day for each adult, $24 for each child. The Wexford Grill includes a good selection of Jamaican dishes, such as chicken deep fried with honey. Guests can enjoy drinks in the Wayside Pub. The hotel is owned and operated by Godfrey G. Dyer, who has led an interesting life, being a former policeman, detective, and taxi business entrepreneur. When he felt his other ventures were getting too demanding, he settled for just running the hotel.

Royal Court Hotel, Sewell Ave., P.O. Box 195, Montego Bay, Jamaica, W.I. (tel. 809/952-4531), is a budget accommodation set on the hillside overlooking Montego Bay, with a swimming pool. The rooms are furnished with bright, tasteful colors. All have air conditioning, private bathrooms, and patios. The larger ones have fully equipped kitchenettes. *The charge in summer for a single is $30 to $58 daily; for a double, $40 to $68.* In winter, a single costs $45 to $69, a double $55 to $78, all EP. Meals are served in the Pool Bar, and dinner is a set meal. On Sunday evening, a Jamaican buffet is served around the pool. Nightly, a resident band plays soft music on the patio under the stars, for dancing or listening. Free transportation is provided to the town, the beach, and the golf course and tennis club, where special rates can be arranged for hotel guests. This hotel is clean, attractive, has a charming atmosphere, and is good value.

Ocean View Guest House, Sunset Ave., P.O. Box 210, Montego Bay, Jamaica, W.I. (tel. 809/952-2662), a super-bargain, is half a mile from the airport and the same distance from the public beach. Buses pass the door for the ride down into Mo Bay, and the owner runs his own bus to and from the airport. There is a small library and TV room. Nightly video movies are shown free, and satellite reception is also available. You can use a stock of Jamaican music tapes to provide background, or you might want to hurl a few darts. All the rooms are either air-conditioned or have fans. Each has hot and cold running water, and most open onto a veranda or the spacious front porch. It's quietest at the back. *In the off-season, room rates are $15 in a single, $12 per person in a double.* In winter, the costs rise to $20 in a single, $18 per person in a double. Breakfast at $3 and dinner from $5 are offered. The owner will arrange for you to play tennis or golf, and water sports can also be arranged.

Toby Inn, P.O. Box 467, Montego Bay, Jamaica, W.I. (tel. 809/952-4370), is a three-star accommodation. It's not on the sea, but famous Doctor's Cave Beach is a short walk away. All of the 60 bedrooms have private baths and air conditioning. In winter, single EP rates are $70 daily, and doubles cost $75. *In off-season, prices drop to $50 daily for a single, $65 for a double.* The hotel has two pools, a restaurant, a beauty salon, and the Cozy Tree Bar. In season, live entertainment and a manager's welcome party are presented once a week.

Doctor's Cave Beach Hotel, P.O. Box 94, Montego Bay, Jamaica, W.I. (tel. 809/952-4355), across the highway from the famous beach, is backed by lush vegetation and has a garden patio among the trees, with a dance floor. Meals are taken on the terrace surrounded by trees, which are floodlit at night. In the Cascade bar, with stone walls and waterfall, you can listen to music. *In summer, EP singles rent for $50 to $55 daily, with doubles going for $70 to $75.* Winter tariffs are $70 to $75 daily in singles, EP, rising to $90 to $95 in doubles. For breakfast and dinner, add $30 per person daily to the rates quoted. All the 80 bedrooms have air conditioning, private baths, and phones. There are ten suites with kitchenettes. In the Heroes' Lounge, you will see representations of national figures from Admirals Rodney and Nelson to the present prime minister. The hotel has a pool and a game room where you can play billiards, table tennis, and chess.

Richmond Hill, Union Street, P.O. Box 362, Montego Bay, Jamaica, W.I. (tel. 809/952-3859), is visited primarily by diners (see my recommendations to follow), but it's also an inn, a remodeled historic manor house built in the 1700s. The property was once owned by the Dewars, a Scottish clan from which the famous whisky takes its name, but today Captain Stanley Chin is in charge. Units are scattered in a series of outbuildings surrounding the pool. The bedrooms aren't spacious, but are in keeping with the character of the old house. A few of the accommodations have kitchens and air conditioning, and all open onto verandas. In winter, singles pay $73 daily; doubles, $107. *In summer, rates are lowered: singles cost from $67 and doubles from $81.*

FOOD IN MO BAY: The resort has some of the finest—and most expensive —dining on the island. But if you're watching your wallet, you'll find that food is often sold right on the street. For example, on Kent Avenue you might try jerk pork, a delicacy peculiar to Jamaica. Seasoned spareribs are also grilled over charcoal fires and sold with extra-hot sauce. Naturally, you order a Red Stripe beer to go with it.

Cooked shrimp are also sold on the streets of Mo Bay. They don't look it, but they're very hotly spiced, so be warned. If you have an efficiency unit with a kitchenette, you might also want to buy fresh lobster or the "catch of the day" from Mo Bay fishermen. It's easily and readily available.

Now, my more formal dining selections below.

The Georgian House, 2 Orange St. (tel. 809/952-0632), brings a grand cuisine and an elegant setting to the heart of town. The buildings date from the 18th century when they were constructed by an English gentleman, who later deserted Montego Bay for London following the death of his wife. You can select either the upstairs room, which is more formal, or the garden terrace, with its fountains, statues, lanterns, and cutstone exterior. Lunch is served in the Blue Room downstairs. Free pick up and return can be arranged for dinner only.

An international cuisine, backed by a fine wine list, is served at dinner every evening from 6 to 9:30 and at lunch Monday to Saturday from noon to 3 p.m. Lunches cost from $25, with dinners going for $40. You might begin with a typically Jamaican appetizer such as ackee and bacon, then follow with pan-barbecued shrimp (you peel the shrimp yourself but are given a scented fingerbowl). International dishes such as tournedos Rossini are also prepared with flair. For dessert, the temptations are great, including a baked banana in coconut cream.

Sugar Mill Restaurant, The Half Moon Club, Half Moon Golf Course (tel. 809/953-2314). After a drive through rolling landscape, you arrive at a stone ruin of what used to be a water wheel for a sugar plantation. In the comfortable, breeze-filled building, guests dine on an open terrace by candlelight, with a view of a pond, a working water wheel, and plenty of greenery.

Although he came from Switzerland, it was with the produce of the Caribbean that Chef Hans Schenk blossomed as a culinary artist. In time, he would entertain everybody from the British royal family to former King of Egypt, Farouk. Lunch here can be a relatively simple affair, perhaps an ackee burger with bacon, preceded by Mama's pumpkin soup and followed with a homemade rum and raisin ice cream. Meals cost from $20 and are served from noon to 2 p.m. daily. But at dinner the special touch of the chef is reflected any night from 7 to 10 when you are likely to get a bill of $40 or more. Smoked north coast marlin is a specialty. You might follow with stuffed pork chop with mango or breadfruit stuffed with curried crayfish. He is said to make the most elegant Jamaican bouillabaisse on the island. Should you prefer something less exotic, he also prepares today's catch, either broiled or meunière. You top your meal with a cup of Blue Mountain coffee. Reservations are needed, and a mini-van will be sent to most hotels to pick you up.

Brigadoon Restaurant, 2 Sewell Ave., off Queen's Drive (tel. 809/952-1723), offers free limousine service from and to your Mo Bay hotel. The restaurant is open from 5 p.m. to midnight daily. There is an inside dining room in case of bad weather, but most of the time you eat on the wide, half-covered patio between the tropical forest and the sea. The staff knows what good service is and makes sure you enjoy your meal. You might like the smoked dolphin with lemon sauce or escargots bourguignonnes before embarking on the main meal, which includes soup, hot bread and butter, salad, and fresh vegetables in the price of the main course. Among the main dishes, fresh fish, especially red snapper and king-fish, are the big drawing cards. One specialty is labeled simply "Jamaican National Dish," and the chef asks you to trust him. Among the desserts, try the

Jamaican banana flambé, followed by coffee from the Blue Mountain. Dining tabs come to $35. Dress at the Brigadoon is informal, and you can dance after dinner or just listen to calypso music or the latest reggae. There is no cover and no minimum.

The **Diplomat,** 9 Queen's Dr. (tel. 809/952-3353), offers a delightful, informal yet elegant evening. Hidden behind a long white wall, gates lead to a sweeping driveway through clipped lawns, old trees, and colorful flower beds to a gracious house, not as old as its columned style would suggest. The restaurant does not require ties and jackets for men, but shorts and T-shirts are frowned upon. Guests dine on the terrace overlooking a floodlit ornamental pool with fountains playing and trees silhouetted with lights leading down toward the sea. The calm efficiency of the waiters completes a pleasant evening. Liqueurs are served at your table or in the drawing room. Expect to spend $30 per person. The restaurant is open only for dinner, which it serves year round from 6:30 to 10:30 p.m. except on Sunday. Georg is in partnership with Ralph Chapman, a retired English businessman who built the house as his private home. This is a good place from which to watch Mo Bay's famous sunsets.

Julia's, Julia's Estate, Bogue Hill (tel. 809/952-1772). The winding jungle road you take to reach this place is part of the evening's before-dinner entertainment. After a jolting ride to a site high above the city and its bay, you pass through a walled-in park which long ago was the site of a private home. Today the building that is the land's focal point is a long, low-slung modern house whose fresh decor encompasses sweeping views. Go nightly from 5:30 to 10:30, and don't forget to make a reservation (a van will come to your hotel and pick you up). Raimondo and Julia Meglio, drawing on the cuisine of their native Italy, prepare chicken cacciatore, breaded milanese cutlet with tomato sauce and mozzarella cheese, filet of fresh fish with lime juice and butter, and seven different kinds of pasta, among other dishes. Meals cost from $35 per person.

Restaurant Ambrosia, Wyndham Rose Hall (tel. 809/953-2650). The cuisine it serves stresses northern Italian recipes. It sits across the highway from one of the largest hotels in Montego Bay, a few miles from the center. Its cedar-shingled design and its trio of steeply pointed roofs give the impression that the place is a clubhouse for some neocolonial country club. Once you enter the courtyard, complete with a set of cannons, you find yourself in one of the loveliest restaurants in the area. You'll enjoy a sweeping view over the rolling lawns leading past the hotel and down to the sea, interrupted only by buff-colored Doric columns. Only dinner is served, and it's offered nightly except Friday from 6:30 to 10:30 p.m. Full meals, costing from $20 per person, might include saltimbocca, veal piccata, manicotti with seafood, zuppa pavese, and an amaretto tart.

Marguerite's by the Sea, Gloucester Ave. (tel. 809/952-4777), is a well-known Mo Bay eatery, which, as its name implies, overlooks the sea. You can dine on a terrace overlooking the water, enjoying the fresh food which is usually well prepared and served, along with a tasteful atmosphere. Lobster salad and smoked marlin are popular for lunch. The menu changes, depending on the availability of fresh produce. You can, however, generally count on getting lobster or a grilled New York sirloin. Invariably there is a "catch of the day," and you can ask the chef to steam it in coconut milk if you prefer. International dishes include the likes of chicken chasseur or a seafood crêpe. For a complete dinner with wine, the tab is likely to be $40. It's best to call for a reservation. You may not need it, but why take a chance? The place is open nightly from 6 to 10:30.

Siam Restaurant and Jazz Club, 25 Leader Ave. (tel. 809/952-5727), has brought new spice and flair to the Montego Bay restaurant scene. It is especially beautiful at sunset, when guests enjoy their drinks on a candlelit terrace with a view of the coastline. A Thai chef prepares a refined cuisine which is served from 6 p.m. until around midnight, Tuesday through Sunday. You get not only food but entertainment, as this is also a jazz club (see "After Dark"). You might begin with one of the savory appetizers, such as lobster tempura or a spicy noodle salad, even a soup such as "bean thread." You can also look for a page listing the day's specials, which might include a Thai curry. Main dishes include chicken (try it with a spicy ginger root and string beans), beef (dare you try the hot chili?), or seafood such as sweet and sour fish. Meals cost from J$175 ($31.50). Arrangements can be made for you to be picked up and returned to your hotel if you call ahead. Chances are, a meal here will be one of your more memorable experiences in Jamaica.

Richmond Hill Inn, Union St. (tel. 809/952-3859), is an old plantation house above the bustle of the bay area. Music is muted and classical in the early evening, but calypso is introduced later on. You might begin your repast with a shrimp-and-lobster cocktail, which for many years I have found their best appetizer. Dolphin (the fish, that is) is regularly featured among the "catch of the day." If you're traditional, try the filet mignon or lamb chops, and don't plan to escape for less than $35 for dinner. Hours are daily from 11 a.m. to 3 p.m. and 6 to 10 p.m.

The **Calabash Restaurant,** 5 Queen's Dr. (tel. 809/952-3891). Perched 500 feet above the distant sea, this well-established restaurant has amused and entertained such luminaries as Peter O'Toole, Robert McNamara, Leonard Bernstein, Francis Ford Coppola, and Roger Moore. It was originally built as a private villa by a doctor in the 1920s. About 22 years ago Roma Chin Sue, its owner, established its Mediterranean-style courtyard and its elegantly simple eagle's-nest patio as a well-managed restaurant. Full meals cost from $40, featuring seafood, Jamaican classics, and international favorites. These include curried goat, surf and turf, the house specialty of mixed seafood en coquille (served with a cheese-and-brandy sauce), and a year-round version of a Jamaican Christmas cake. Meals are served daily from noon to 2 p.m. and 6 p.m. "until." Reservations are necessary. The previously recommended Winged Victory Hotel is the mother of the restaurant.

The **Cascade Room** at the Pelican, Gloucester Ave. (tel. 809/952-3171), in an intimate setting and relaxing atmosphere, is one of Montego Bay's finest seafood restaurants. Rushing waterfalls and cool tropical foliage blend with the natural cedar of the interior to make dining an enjoyable experience. Excellent service combines with the finest of seafood, such as lobster in the shell, shrimp Créole, filet of red snapper, and ackee and codfish, to name a few. There is bar service and an adequate choice of wines. Dinner costs J$150 ($30.50) per person. The restaurant is open from 6 to 10 p.m. daily.

Town House, 16 Church St. (tel. 809/952-2660), is a lovely old, red-brick house built in 1765. The restaurant has recommendations from, among others, *Gourmet* magazine. You find the bar and restaurant around at the back of the house in what used to be the cellars, now air-conditioned with tables set around the walls. Old ship lanterns give a warm light, and pictures of bygone days and of soldiers of the past adorn the walls. The place is a tranquil, cool luncheon choice, if you want to dine lightly, enjoying sandwiches and salads—or more elaborate fare if you're hungry—far removed from the noonday glare of Mo Bay. If you return for dinner, it becomes more atmospheric, and you're faced with a wide and good selection of main courses. Everybody seemingly talks favorably of red snapper en papillotte, that is, baked in a paper bag. You might also try stuffed lobster. I'm fond of the chef's large rack of barbecued spareribs with the owner's special Tennessee sauce. You'll easily spend from $25 for dinner and about $15 for lunch, which is not served on Sunday. Otherwise, it's best to go from noon to 2:30 p.m. and 7 to 9:30 p.m.

Pier I, "On the Waterfront" (that's it's official address) (tel. 809/952-2452), is one of the major dining and entertainment hubs of Mo Bay. Built on land fill in the bay, it is operated by Robert and Beverley Russell, whose Jamaican food is considered some of the best served at the resort. Fishermen bring fresh lobster to them which the chef prepares in a number of ways, including Créole style or curried. You might begin with one of the typically Jamaican soups such as conch chowder or red pea (which is actually red bean). At lunch their hamburgers are said to be the juiciest in town, or else you might find their quarter decker steak sandwich with mushrooms equally tempting. The chef also prepares such famous island dishes as jerk pork or chicken. You might also like their Jamaican red snapper, finishing your meal with a slice of moist rum cake. Lunch costs from J$75 ($13.50) with dinners priced from J$175 ($31.50) and up. The restaurant is open daily from noon to 3 p.m. and 6:30 to 11 p.m. You can drink or dine on the ground floor, open to the sea breezes, but most guests seem to prefer the more formal second floor. If you call, the Russells can arrange to have you picked up in a mini-van at most hotels (you're also returned).

WHAT TO DO: Rafting on the Martha Brae is an exciting adventure. To reach the starting point, drive east to Falmouth and turn approximately three miles inland to **Martha Brae's Rafters Village.** The rafts are similar to those on the Rio Grande, and charge about $28 per raft, with only two persons allowed on a raft, plus a small child if accompanied by an adult. The trips, lasting about an hour, operate seven days a week from 9 a.m. to 4 p.m. You sit on a raised dais on bamboo logs. The rafters supplement their incomes by selling carved gourds. Along the way you can stop and order cool drinks or beer along the banks of the river. There is a bar, a restaurant, and a souvenir shop in the village. Later you get a souvenir rafting certificate.

Cornwall Beach is Jamaica's finest underwater marine park and fun complex, a long stretch of white sand beach with dressing cabañas. Water sports, scuba-diving, and snorkeling are available. Admission to the beach is J$2 (35¢) per adult, J$1 (18¢) for children, for the entire day. A bar and cafeteria offer refreshment. Hours are 9 a.m. to 5 p.m. daily.

Doctor's Cave Beach, across from the Montego Bay Club, helped launch Mo Bay as a resort in the 1940s. Admission to the beach is J$4 (72¢) for adults, J$2 (18¢) for children. You can participate in water sports here. Dressing rooms, chairs, umbrellas, and rafts are available from 9 a.m. to 5 p.m. daily.

For a plantation tour and even a hot-air balloon ride to get a bird's-eye view of the countryside, go on a **Hilton High Day Tour** (tel. 952-3343), with an office on Beach View Plaza. Round-trip transportation on a scenic drive through historic plantation areas is included. Your day starts at the plantation, with the balloon ride if you choose, the next thing being a continental breakfast at the old plantation house on a patio overlooking the fields and hills. You can roam around the 100 acres of the plantation and visit the German village of Seaford Town or St. Leonards village nearby. A Jamaican lunch of roast suckling pig with rum punch is served at 1 p.m. The charge for the day is $46 per person (with the balloon ride optional at $15) for the plantation tour, breakfast, lunch, and transportation.

Jamaica Safari Village, outside Falmouth, is open from 8:30 a.m. to 5:30 p.m. daily, with continual conducted tours. The trek leads through a petting zoo area and breeding centers, and alongside crocodile ponds. An interesting thing about crocs is that a 750-pound adult is able to move at 40 miles per hour. You may get to hear the crocodile love call, which is original to say the least. Safari Village served as a film set for the James Bond thriller, *Live and Let Die.* Tours cost J$20 ($3.60) for adults, J$10 ($1.80) for children. Reservations can be made by calling 809/952-4415 or JADCO at 809/952-4425.

Rocklands Feeding Station, Anchovy (tel. 809/952-2009), otherwise called Rocklands Bird Sanctuary, was established by Lisa Salmon, known as the Bird Lady of Anchovy, attracting nature lovers and birdwatchers. It's a unique experience to have a Jamaican doctor bird perch on your finger to drink syrup, and to feed small doves and finches millet from your hand, plus watching dozens of other birds flying in for their evening meal. The feeding station is open every afternoon throughout the year from 3:15 until half an hour before sundown (varying with the time of year). Admission is $4. Do not take children age 5 and under, as they tend to worry the birds. Smoking and playing transistor radios are forbidden. Rocklands is about a mile outside Anchovy on the road from Montego Bay.

Montego Bay's most famous trip is the **Governor's Coach Tour,** a railway tour in a coach, which is a second-class European version. The trip takes you some 40 miles into the heartland, through banana and coconut groves and coffee plantations, stopping frequently at little villages. At one such stop, Catadupa, you can order men's Jamaican shirts and women's dresses made to measure in the style and material you select. You collect your garments on the return journey.

The tour visits the Appleton Estate Rum Distillery. You also pass Anchovy and Cambridge; and at Ipswich, a visit is made to the famous caves to see the fascinating rock formations. The tour, offered Tuesday to Friday, takes all day, from 9:30 a.m. until 5 p.m. The cost is $35 per person, which includes a picnic lunch with complimentary drinks. Telephone 809/952-1398 for reservations. The booking office is Jamaica Tours, 686 Half Moon St., Coral Gardens, P.O. Box 227, Montego Bay. Negril is also a starting point for the tour.

A tour aboard the **Appleton Express** is offered by Ragus Tours Ltd., P.O. Box 989, Montego Bay (tel. 809/952-3692). It takes you on an open-bar train journey into the interior of Jamaica. You ride in air-conditioned coaches through the spectacular scenery, stop at the Ipswich Caves, and then visit the Appleton Rum Distillery. There you can learn about the history of the oldest distillery of the island. Lunch is included in the price of $44 per person for the day's trip.

The **Croydon Plantation,** Catadupa, St. James (tel. 809/952-4137), a 45-minute ride from Montego Bay, can be visited on a half-day tour. Included are round-trip transportation from your hotel, a visit to the working parts of the plantation, tasting of pineapple varieties as well as fruit juices and sugarcane, plus a barbecued chicken lunch. This tour costs $35 per person. For information, call the above number or ask at your hotel desk.

A picnic on Wednesday and Saturday can be a highlight of your visit. The **Miskito Cove Beach Picnic,** which takes place at the cove of that name, leaves at 10 a.m., returning at 3:30 p.m., with pickups at Tryall and Round Hill. For $36 per person, you can enjoy an open Jamaican bar, buffet lunch, calypso band, a glassbottom-boat ride, a raft ride with a calypsonian singer on board, and water sports including snorkeling with a guide and equipment provided, Sunfish sailing with trained captains, jetskiing, and windsurfing. The picnic is arranged by Aqua Cove Centre, Montego Bay (tel. 809/952-1387).

Mountain Valley Rafting is offered at Lethe Property, about ten miles from Montego Bay, daily from 9 a.m. to 5 p.m. For $26, two persons can go rafting, and there are free donkey rides. The raft trip takes about an hour. This trip is operated by Great River Rafting & Plantation Tour Ltd., P.O. Box 23, Montego Bay (tel. 809/952-4706).

Touring the Great Houses

Occupied by plantation owners, the great houses of Jamaica were always built on high ground so that they overlooked the plantation itself and could see the next house in the distance. It was the custom for the owners to offer hospitality to travelers crossing the island by road. They were spotted by the lookout, who noted the rising dust. Bed and food were then made ready for the traveler's arrival.

The most famous great house in Jamaica is the legendary **Rose Hall** (tel. 809/953-2456), a nine-mile jaunt east from Montego Bay along the coast road. The subject of at least a dozen Gothic novels, Rose Hall was immortalized in the H. G. deLisser book *White Witch of Rosehall*. The house was built about two centuries ago by a John Palmer. However, it was Annie Palmer, wife of the builder's grandnephew, who became the focal point of fiction and fact. Called "Infamous Annie," she was said to have dabbled in witchcraft. She took slaves as lovers, killing them off when they bored her. Those servants called her "the Obeah woman" (*Obeah* is Jamaican for "voodoo"). Annie was said to have murdered several of her coterie of husbands while they slept, and eventually suffered the same fate herself in a kind of poetic justice. Long in ruins, the house has now been restored and can be visited by the public at a cost of $5 for adults, $3 for children. Hours are daily from 9 a.m. to 5 p.m.

Greenwood (no phone) is even more interesting to some house tourers than Rose Hall. On its hillside perch, it lies 14 miles to the east of Montego Bay and 7 miles west of Falmouth. Hours are 9 a.m. to 6 p.m. daily, and admission is J$25 ($4.50) for adults. Erected in the early 18th century, the Georgian-style building was once the residence of Richard Barrett between 1780 and 1800. He was of the same family as Elizabeth Barrett Browning. On display are the original library of the Barrett family, with rare books dating from 1697, along with oil paintings of the Barrett family, china made by Wedgwood for the family, and a rare exhibition of musical instruments in working order, plus a fine collection of antique furniture. The house today is privately owned but open to the public.

About five miles from Falmouth, you can take the **Good Hope Plantation and Great House** tour daily (appointments are necessary to tour the house). The house tour, costing $4, is worthwhile, as you see the interior of the Palladian great house, built in 1755—antique furniture, carpets, paintings, and collectors' items of all sorts. The riding tour, costing an additional $20, takes you along trails leading to Jamaica's most impressive remains of an 18th-century sugar plantation. You'll see the slave hospital, two overseers' cottages, a storehouse, shop, and assistant manager's house. The 2,000-acre plantation is now a working beef, coconut, and aloe vera farm. For information about the tour, get in touch with Patrick Thompson, owner, Good Hope, Falmouth (tel. 809/954-3289).

Boat Cruises

Fun cruises are offered aboard the *Mary-Ann* (tel. 809/952-5505). A morning cruise is at 10 a.m. At the sound of the conch trumpet, played by a quartet blowing conch shells, you set out aboard the 57-foot Australian ketch on a scenic cruise across the bay, with a stop where you can see colorful coral and reef fish in marine gardens, swim, snorkel, and collect shells. You have lunch ashore in a fishing village in the ship's special picnic grounds. The cruise costs $35 per person. The *Mary-Ann* also makes a sunset dinner cruise, leaving at 3 p.m. Sailing is from Sandals Resort. You sail around the bay, sip drinks, and enjoy dinner under the stars by candlelight at the Almond Terrace Restaurant by the sea. The dinner cruise costs $35 per person. For both of these jaunts aboard the *Mary-Ann,* free pickup and return service is provided.

Day and evening cruises are offered aboard the *Calico,* a 55-foot gaff-rigged wooden ketch, sailing from Pier 1 on the Montego Bay waterfront. You can be transported to and from your hotel for either cruise. The day voyage, departing at 10 a.m. and returning at 3 p.m., provides a day of sailing, sunning, and snorkeling (with equipment supplied), plus a Jamaican buffet lunch served on the beach, all to the sound of reggae and other music. The cruise, costing $40 per person, goes daily except Monday. The *Calico*'s evening voyage, costing $20 per person, is from 5 to 7 p.m. Wednesday to Saturday. Cocktails and wine are served as you sail through sunset. For information and reservations, call Capt. Bryan Langford, North Coast Cruises Ltd., White Sands Post Office, Montego Bay (tel. 809/952-5860).

MONTEGO BAY SHOPPING: You can find good duty-free items for purchase here, including Swiss watches, Irish crystal, Japanese perfumes, English china, Danish silverware, Portuguese linens, Italian handbags, Scottish cashmeres, Indian silks, and liquors and liqueurs. Jamaican arts and crafts are available throughout the resort and at the Arts and Crafts Market (see below).

The main shopping areas are at **Montego Freeport** within easy walking distance of the pier, **Sam Sharpe's Square** (where most of the in-bond shops are, aside from at the large hotels), **Overton Plaza, Holiday Village Shopping Centre,** and **Westgate Shopping Centre.**

In 1987, the **Old Fort Craft Park,** a shopping complex with 180 vendors (all licensed by the Jamaica Tourist Board), opened in the heart of Montego Bay on the site of Fort Montego. The location fronts Howard Cook Boulevard up from Gloucester Avenue. A market with a varied assortment of handcrafts, it is ideal browsing country not only for that little souvenir of Jamaica but for some more serious purchases as well. You'll see a selection of wall hangings, hand-woven straw items, hand-carved wood sculpture, and you can even get your hair braided if that is your desire. Fort Montego, now long gone, was constructed by the British in the mid-18th century as part of their defense of "fortress Jamaica." But it never saw much action, except for firing its cannons every year to salute the monarch's birthday.

Blue Mountain Gems Workshop (tel. 809/953-2338), at the Holiday Village Shopping Centre, offers a tour of the workshops to see the process from raw stone to the finished product you can buy later.

Throughout the island, Appleton's overproof, special, and punch rums are excellent value. Tía Maria and Rumona (the one coffee-, the other rum-flavored) are the best liqueurs. Khus Khus is the local perfume.

Things Jamaican, 44 Fort St. (tel. 809/952-5605), affiliated with the government and set up to encourage the development of Jamaican arts and crafts, it is a showcase for the talents of the artisans of this island nation. Here is displayed a wealth of the products of Jamaica, even food and drink, including rums and liqueurs along with jerk seasoning and such jellies as orange pepper. Look especially for Busha Browne's fine Jamaican sauces. These recipes are prepared and bottled by the Busha Browne Company in Jamaica just as they were 100 years ago. Try especially their spicy chutneys such as banana or their planters spicy piquant sauce or their spicy tomato (called *love apple*) sauce, which is not to be confused with catsup. Many items for sale are carved from wood, including not only sculpture but salad bowls and trays. Some shoppers take large handwoven Jamaican baskets to the airport with them. You'll also find women's handbags made of banana bark (in Jamaica, these are known unflatteringly as "old lady bags").

Look also for reproductions of the Port Royal collection. Port Royal, once described as "the wickedest city on earth," was buried by an earthquake and tidal wave in 1692. After resting in a sleepy underwater grave of 275 years, beautiful pewter items were recovered and are living again in reproductions (except the new items are leadless). Some of the pewter came from the Netherlands, other items from Britain. Impressions were made, and molds were created to reproduce them. They include Rat-tail spoons, a spoon with the heads of the monarchs William and Mary, Splay-Footed Lion Rampant spoons, and spoons with Pied-de-Biche handles. Many items were reproduced faithfully, right down to the pit marks and scratches. To complement this pewter assortment, Things Jamaican created the Port Royal Bristol-Delft Ceramic Collection based on original pieces of ceramics found in the underwater digs. Items in this collection include onion bottles and "Quaker Man" chocolate pots.

At the **Arts and Crafts Market** near Harbour Street in downtown Montego Bay you can find a wide selection of handmade souvenirs of Jamaica, including straw hats and bags, wooden platters, straw baskets, musical instruments, beads, carved objects, and toys. That "jippa jappa" hat is important if you're going to be out in the island sun.

Neville Budhai Paintings, Reading Main Rd. (no phone), lies five miles west of Montego Bay, along the side of the road leading to Negril. This well-known gallery sells original paintings by Jamaican and Puerto Rican artists. Woodcuts, batiks, and lithographs are also sold. The gallery is open daily from 8:30 a.m. until some time in the early evening.

AFTER DARK: There are a lot more activities to pursue in Montego Bay in the evenings than going to the discos, but the resort certainly has those too. Much of the entertainment is offered at the various hotels.

Siam Restaurant and Jazz Club, 25 Leader Ave. (tel. 809/952-5727), lets you combine a meal of Thai food, considered the haute cuisine of the Orient, with the best jazz in Montego Bay. The restaurant of this establishment has been recommended, but the jazz played here is often as hot as the chili peppers in the sauce. Meals cost from J$175 ($31.50), which means you get not only well-prepared food but some of the best jazz artists in the area as well. Douglas Wachholz is in charge of hiring the musicians, and he showcases their talents Tuesday through Saturday from 8 p.m. to midnight. If you call for a dinner reservation, arrangements can be made to have you picked up at your hotel.

Pier I, "On the Waterfront" (tel. 809/952-2452), already previewed as an excellent selection for Jamaican cookery, might also be your entertainment choice for a night on the town. On Saturday night a live band, usually reggae, is brought in from 7:30 to 10 p.m., when a cover charge of J$100 ($18) is imposed. On Sunday it's oldies night, when your favorite records of yesterday are played. There's usually a congenial crowd on those evenings. Friday night sees disco action from 10 p.m. "till daybreak." Usually a J$20 ($3.60) cover charge is assessed on most disco nights. But entertainment schedules are always variable, so you should call first.

The **Junkanoo Lounge and Disco,** at the Wyndham Rose Hall Beach Club (tel. 809/953-2650), is one of the liveliest spots in the Mo Bay area. The recently improved 180-seat club has an inviting atmosphere and one of the best sound systems in Jamaica. There is no admission or cover charge, and drinks begin at $2.50. It's open from 8:30 p.m. until "very late" seven days a week.

For some "life-seeing" adventures, I have the following recommendations: Every Sunday, Tuesday, and Thursday, there's an **Evening on the Great River,** during which you ride in a fishing canoe up the river ten miles west of Montego Bay. A torchlit path leads to a re-created Arawak Indian village, where you eat, drink as much as you like at the open bar, and watch a floor show. The Country Store offers jackass rope (tobacco by the yard), nutmeg, cinnamon, brown sugar, and all sorts of country items for sale. The cost, with transportation, is $36 per person. The operator is Hartley Morris, Great River Productions, 29 Gloucester Ave., Reading, St. James (tel. 809/952-5047).

An interesting Jamaican experience is **Lollypop on the Beach,** at Sandy Bay, Hanover, half a mile west of Tryall, held every Wednesday from 7:30 to 11 p.m. (on Saturday also if the demand is heavy). Your $35 includes round-trip transport to the beach from Mo Bay hotels, a glassbottom-boat ride with a calypso band, dinner of seafood and jerk meats, and traditional dance groups performing cumina, reggae, the basket dance, the bamboo dance, the limbo, and dancing on the beach. The festivities are run by Sunmar Enterprise Ltd., Montego Bay (tel. 809/952-4121).

Boonoonoonoos Beach Party is held on Friday from 7 to 11 p.m. on Walter Fletcher Beach, Montego Bay, costing $29 (not recommended for children). A live band, three-course Jamaican dinner, open Jamaican bar, and a native floor show make for a festive evening. For information, call the Coconut Grove Great House Ocho Rios (tel. 809/974-2619).

7. NEGRIL

Jamaica's newest resort, on the western tip of the island, is famed for its seven-mile beach, the pride of the area. A place of legend, Negril recalls Buccaneer Calico Jack (his name derived from his fondness for calico undershorts) and his carousings with his infamous women pirates, Mary Read and Ann Bonney.

Emerging Negril is 50 miles and about a two-hour drive from Montego Bay's airport along a winding road, past ruins of sugar estates and great houses. From Kingston, it's about a four-hour drive, a distance of 150 miles.

This once-sleepy village has turned into a tourist mecca, visitors drawn to its beaches along three well-protected bays—Long Bay, Bloody Bay (now Negril Harbour), and Orange Bay. Negril became famous in the late 1960s when it attracted laid-back American and Canadian youth, who liked the idea of a place with no phones, no electricity. They rented modest digs in little houses on the West End where the local people extended their hospitality. But those days are long gone. Today visitors speak of a "new Negril," with its all-inclusive resorts such as Hedonism II and Sandals Negril. New, more sophisticated hotels have been built, and all in all, a better-heeled and less rowdy crowd is drawn today to Negril, including hundreds of European visitors.

At some point you'll want to explore Booby Cay, a tiny islet off the Negril Coast. Once it was featured in the Walt Disney film *20,000 Leagues Under the Sea,* but now it's rampant with nudists from Hedonism II.

Chances are, however, you'll stake out your own favorite spot along Negril's seven-mile beach. You don't need to get up for anything, as somebody will be along to serve you. Perhaps it'll be the "banana lady," with a basket of fruit perched on her head. Maybe the "ice cream man" will set up a stand right under a coconut palm. Surely the "beer lady" will find you as she strolls along the beach, a carton of Jamaican beer on her head, a bucket of ice in her hand, and hordes of young men will seek you out peddling illegal "ganja" whether you smoke it or not. Negril has the dubious distinction of being called the marijuana resort of the Caribbean.

There are really two Negrils: The West End, site of many little eateries such as Chicken Lavish and cottages that still receive visitors, including the famous Rockhouse, a covey of thatched rondavels (see below). The other Negril is on the east end, the first you approach on the road coming in from Montego Bay. It is the site of the best hotels that enjoy some of the most panoramic beachfronts, such as Negril Gardens. These modern resorts are giving Negril a touch of class.

A WIDE RANGE OF RESORTS: My favorite nest in Negril, **Negril Gardens,** Westmoreland, Negril, Jamaica, W.I. (tel. 809/957-4408), rests amid

tropical verdure on the famous seven-mile stretch of beach. The two-story villas, each of which is accented with Chippendale-style crosshatch balconies, are well furnished and air-conditioned with satellite TV and private baths. Rooms open onto a front veranda or else a balcony with either a beach or a garden view. In winter, a single or double unit rents for $100 to $110 daily, *the rates lowered in summer to $74 to $80 daily, again either single or double.* A maximum of two children are allowed free in each room shared with their parents. The units on the garden side are cheaper, and many guests prefer this location because it is the site of a beautiful swimming pool with a beach bar and a tennis court.

Directly on the beach is a Tahiti-style bar where you can observe the ever-changing scene night and day. Right behind it stands an al fresco restaurant serving some of the best food in Negril. Nonresidents are also invited to patronize this facility, where they are likely to get good Jamaican cookery along with a scattering of international dishes. Memorable dishes include various versions of conch, lobster, and other seafood, plus curried goat and stew peas, or chicken fricassé. It's more economical to arrange to stay here on MAP, paying another $25 per person daily for breakfast, lunch, or dinner. Dinner is from 7 to 10:30 nightly. A disco adjoining a bank is also on the grounds (the garden side), and it's open only to members or else residents of the hotel.

Poinciana Beach Villas, Norman Manley Blvd., Negril, Jamaica, W.I. (tel. 809/957-4256 or toll free 800/468-6728), is set amid verdant landscaping in its own gardens, the centerpiece of which is a small L-shape pool set on a terrace above the ocean. The resort contains 16 functionally modern, two-story villas, any of which can be rented as an entire unit. If you're interested in less expansive living, each villa has a labyrinth of halls, doors, kitchens, and baths, so that sections or rooms within the villas can be rented as relatively modest lodgings. Opened in 1983, the resort offers a beachfront bar, a restaurant, a watersports kiosk, and a tradition of live reggae and calypso music on some nights. Most, but not all, accommodations have air conditioning, and a few of the more expensive ones contain kitchens or refrigerators. *Two people in a hotel room pay from $40 (very basic units) to $75 daily in summer, the cost rising to $77 to $135 for two in a studio, one-bedroom villa, or one-bedroom suite.* In winter, standard and superior hotel rooms for two cost $50 to $110 daily, whereas the charge is $120 to $179 for two in a studio or a one-bedroom villa or suite. Some units are big enough to house four to six people, but these cost more.

Charela Inn, P.O. Box 33, Negril, Jamaica, W.I. (tel. 809/957-4277), is a seafront inn reminiscent of a Spanish country-style hacienda. It's not the place for social types on the see-and-be-seen circuit, but for those wanting genuine hospitality where they're treated like one of the family. Homey meals and an informal atmosphere attract a loyal following to this site, on the A1, north of Negril. The main house and its addition have a row of arches with air-conditioned bedrooms, all with a tropical architecture and decorative details. In winter, singles can stay here on half-board terms ranging from $120 daily; doubles (also half-board) cost from $80 to $95 per person. *In summer, MAP singles range from $85 to $100 daily, doubles costing from $60 to $65 per person.* At sunset most guests gather at the fountain terrace to sample the various rum drinks. At this time your hosts like to introduce fellow guests. Ask about snorkeling, waterskiing, fishing, boating, tennis, golf, horseback riding, and sightseeing.

Negril Beach Club Hotel, P.O. Box 7, Negril, Jamaica, W.I. (tel. 809/957-4220), is a casual, informal resort designed around a series of white stucco cubes adorned with exterior stairways and terraces. The entire complex is clustered like a horseshoe around a rectangular garden whose end abuts a sandy beach. There's ample parking on the premises and easy access to a full range of sporting facilities including snorkeling, a pool, volleyball, table tennis, and windsurfing. Other activities can be organized nearby, and beach barbecues and buffet breakfasts are ample and frequent. Accommodations range from simply furnished units to one-bedroom suites with kitchens. *In summer, singles range from $40 to $65 daily, doubles from $50 to $75, and triples from $60 to $85.* In winter, singles go for $72 to $100 daily, doubles for $80 to $110, and triples for $90 to $120. MAP can be arranged for $25 per person per day. The Seething Cauldron on the beach serves barbecues, seafood, and such Jamaican specialties as roast suckling pig and ackee and codfish.

Negril Tree House, P.O. Box 29, Negril, Jamaica, W.I. (tel. 809/957-4386), is a desirable little escapist retreat with an ideal beachfront location. Each accommodation contains a tile bath, and suites, as an added bonus, also have kitchenettes. Rental units are scattered across the property in octagonal buildings, 11 in all. Owner Gail Jackson offers a total of 44 comfortably furnished rooms, plus 12 suites, each with air conditioning or ceiling fans. In winter single or double occupancy costs from $80 to $105 daily. Family suites, for up to four guests, rent from $190 to $250 daily. *In summer prices are lowered to $55 to $85 daily for one to two persons, with family suites for up to four persons costing $120 to $140 daily.* The resort features a number of water sports, including parasailing, snorkeling, and scuba diving.

Negril Cabins, Negril, Jamaica, W.I. (tel. 809/957-4350), the bargain of the resort, it is a Robinson Crusoe–type place but far more elegant than you might expect. At least more elegant than its prices indicate. *In summer tariffs are only $40 daily either single or double,* rising to $55 in winter. Set on the eastern approach to Negril, the highway coming in from Montego Bay, the resort stands across the road from a beach called Bloody Bay, where the infamous 18th-century pirate, Calico Jack, was done in by the British.

The place consists of small villas, none more than two stories high, rising on stilts. There are ten timber cottages, each containing two bedrooms with private baths and balconies. The so-called cabins are set in a four-acre garden, with Royal Palms, Bull Thatch, and other vegetation including a rare mango tree (its fruit is called simply "number eight"). You can order a tropical punch, a medley of fresh Jamaican fruits, before enjoying a good-tasting Jamaican dinner at night. Families, friends, or couples are invited to call toll free at 800/526-2422 (the Jamaica Reservations Service).

THE INCLUSIVE RESORTS: Devoted to the pursuit of pleasure, **Hedonism II,** P.O. Box 25, Negril, Jamaica, W.I. (tel. 809/957-4200), is called the "home of hedonism." It includes "the works" in a one-package deal, except at Hedonism they even give you all the booze you want to drink. Some abuse the privilege, but most guests seemingly drink in moderation. The resort is closed to the general public. There is no tender of any sort, and tipping is not permitted. In two-story clusters, 280 rooms are stacked, dotted around a gently sloping 22-acre site. You enter under a cedar-roofed portico to find a miniature "city," totally equipped with everything and a staff usually willing to serve your needs. There is a large covered area filled with rest tables, bars, and at the end, a swimming pool. Most of the guests, who must be above 16 years of age, are Americans, with a significant number of Canadians, some Europeans, and a few South Americans. A minimum stay of one week is required. Rates given below are per person weekly, based on double occupancy. This is not a "couples-only" resort. Singles are accepted, but the rooms are doubles. Therefore you are likely to be assigned a same-sex roommate if you should arrive alone. Arrivals are on Friday, Saturday, Sunday, or Monday. Weekly tariffs in winter range from $1,160 per person double occupancy. *In summer, $840 to $940 per person is charged weekly for double occupancy, all inclusive.* In the open-sided dining room, Jamaican and international buffets are served.

If your pursuit of pleasure covers sports activities, you can enjoy the use of all sports facilities, equipment, and instruction, including sailing, snorkeling, water skiing, scuba-diving, windsurfing, embarking on the underwater vision boat, using the Jacuzzi, and swimming in the hotel pool. There are six tournament-class tennis courts (lit at night) and two badminton courts, and if you prefer, you can play basketball, squash, volleyball, or table-tennis. Hedonism has Nautilus and free-weight gyms, areas for aerobics, and an indoor games room. If you want to get out and about, you can go bicycling or horseback riding. If all that activity—or even a portion of it—leaves you any energy, nightly entertainment is presented, along with a live band, show disco, and piano bar. On one section of the beach "clothing is optional," as the management states. On some nights guests dress up in sheets which they like to think of as Roman togas. Provocative beauty contests are staged as well, including one with wet T-shirts. The resort also has a secluded beach on nearby Booby Key (originally *Cay*) where guests are taken twice a week for a picnic.

Sandals Negril, Negril, Jamaica, W.I. (tel. 809/957-4332), is an all-inclusive, couples-only (male-female) resort, part of the expanding "empire" of the enterprising Gordon "Butch" Stewart, who pioneered similar operations in Montego Bay. The word "Sandals" in Jamaica has come to stand for a "no problem, mon" vacation, as they say locally. The resort occupies some 13 acres of prime beachfront land about an hour and a half drive (maybe more) from the Montego Bay airport. Round-trip transfers to and from Montego Bay are part of the package deal.

The developers linked two hotels by a complex, forming a unified whole. The crowd is usually convivial, decidedly informal, and often young. Its beach-oriented clientele likes the lazy lifestyle here. The new resort offers a total of 187 well-furnished bedrooms, including some loft suites which are the highest priced category of units. There are five divisions of accommodations, rated standard, superior, and deluxe, plus deluxe beachfront rooms or one-bedroom suites. Rooms are casually furnished in a tropical motif, with hairdryers, radios, and phones. *In shoulder and summer seasons, all-inclusive weekly prices range from a low of $780 to a high of $2,210 per couple.* In winter two persons pay from a low of $985 to a high of $2,530 weekly. Certain holiday periods are subject to restrictions of a $125 surcharge per couple per week. Rates include all meals, even snacks, and unlimited drinks day or night at one of four bars (a swim-up pool bar is a special feature). Nightly entertainment, including theme parties, is also included.

An extensive range of recreational activity is also part of the package, and that means scuba diving, snorkeling, Sunfish sailing, windsurfing, canoeing, a glassbottom boat, and a fitness center with saunas and Universal exercise equipment, along with two freshwater pools. Tennis is available day or night.

Negril Inn, Negril, Jamaica, W.I. (tel. 809/957-4371), in the heart of the seven-mile beach stretch, is an all-inclusive resort, but is not confined to couples only. The resort offers 46 delightful guest rooms, each air-conditioned and with private balcony, spread through a series of two-story structures in a tropical garden setting of flowering hibiscus, coffee rose, and night jasmine.

Couples or singles are welcomed here year round, but children are not accepted in winter. In the off-season, children 12 and under stay free if they share a room with two full-paying adults. Offering a host of activities, day or night, this resort has thoughtfully employed a helpful staff. The all-inclusive rate in winter is $165 daily in a single, $130 per person in a double, and $120 per person in a triple. *In off-season, the single all-inclusive rate is $140 daily, $105 per person in a double, and $90 per person in a triple.* Included in this package are all meals, all alcoholic drinks (except champagne), nightly entertainment (including disco action), windsurfing, waterskiing, scuba diving, snorkeling, hydrosliding, aqua bikes, a glassbottom boat, two floodlit tennis courts, a piano room, a Universal weight room, and, most important, round-trip transfers to and from the airport at Montego Bay. Filtered water comes from a 10,000-gallon plant on the premises. For brochures, information, and reservations, contact Medhurst & Associates, 1208 Washington Dr., Centerport, NY 11721 (tel. 516/673-0150 or toll free 800/634-7456).

A RUSTIC HIDEAWAY: On the lighthouse road, 1½ miles south of Negril, **Rockhouse,** P.O. Box 24, Negril, Jamaica, W.I. (tel. 809/957-4373), looks, as you approach it, like a remote African village ready to be photographed for *National Geographic.* Frankly, this place isn't for everyone. It caters to surf lovers who like its lack of phones. Kerosene lamps, which are still available, used to be the only form of illumination at night, but now the place has electricity, ceiling fans, refrigerators, and hotplates. The thatched rondavels, rustic style, with their peaked roofs, cling to the trees and cliffs above coves and pools. On the water doesn't mean on the beach. You go swimming "off the rocks." Your particular hut might be perched on a rock formation just ten feet above the water. A lot of divers like to lodge here, exploring the crystal-blue coves.

The cottages may look primitive from the outside, but actually they have the desired amenities tucked away. There are studios and villas for two guests, with a sleeping loft for additional beds. The beach house has two bedrooms, a living and a dining room, plus a bath and a kitchen with a two-burner gas plate. There's a private shower with palm trees and sky for a ceiling. This is primarily an adult retreat, but children over 12 are welcomed. In winter, two persons pay from $80 daily in a studio, $120 in a villa. *In off-season, two persons are charged from $70 to $90 daily.* For the beach house, meals are prepared in your room, or else you can go to Rick's on the beach. If you'd like to have supper at the complex, ask the management, giving them a 24-hour notice. For reservations, write to P.O. Box 78, Park Ridge, IL 60068 (tel. 312/296-1894).

WHERE TO DINE: Many visitors eat at their hotels. However, there are several other most atmospheric and intriguing possibilities.

Whether you have a meal or not, everybody in Negril at sundown seems to head for the rebuilt **Rick's Café** (tel. 809/957-4335), the name inspired by the old watering hole of Bogie's *Casablanca.* The "Rick" in this case is owner Carl Newman. Here the sunset is said to be the most glorious at the resort, and after a few fresh-fruit daiquiris (pineapple, banana, or papaya) you'll give whoever's claiming that no argument. At this cliffside proximity to nature, "casual" is the word in dress. The location where you order your eggs Benedict, Jamaican style, or fresh lobster is right on the westernmost promontory. Ham omelets are good here, and there are lots of Stateside specialties. The fish is always fresh, and you might have red snapper or grouper. Try the chef's Jamaican fish chowder. Expect to pay from $25 for dinner. You can also buy plastic bar tokens at the door, which you can use instead of money à la Club Med. Open noon to 9 p.m. daily.

Le Vendôme, Charela Inn, P.O. Box 33, Negril Beach (tel. 809/957-4277), enjoys a good reputation for its food, and nonresidents are invited to visit to sample the cuisine that is a combination of, in the words of the owners, Daniel and Sylvia Grizzle, a "dash of Jamaican spices" with a "pinch of French flair." Their wine and champagne are imported from France. You dine on a terracotta terrace, enjoying a view of the palm-studded beach. Lunch is from 11 a.m. to 3 p.m., costing from J$60 ($10.80), with dinners served from 6:30 to 10 or 11 p.m., going for J$125 ($22.50) and up. Service is daily all year. You can order a homemade pâté, perhaps a vegetable salad to begin with. You can follow with such dishes as baked snapper, duckling à l'orange, or a seafood platter.

Mariners Inn and Restaurant, West End, P.O. Box 16, Negril, Jamaica, W.I. (tel. 809/957-4348). The main reason most guests come here is for the boat-shape bar and the adjoining restaurant whose access is through a tropical garden which eventually slopes down to the beach. As you drink or dine, the breezes will waft in under the most pleasant and relaxed experiences in Negril. Curried chop suey and chicken are available, as are cheese omelets, homemade pâté, and—if you really want to dine properly—lobster thermidor. Look also for the chef's specialty of the day. Open seven days a week from 11 a.m. to 3 p.m. and 5 to 11 p.m. There are also rooms and apartments for rent, 50 units in all. Charges in doubles are $60 daily for double bedrooms in winter, $95 for apartments, also double occupancy. *In summer, double rooms rent for $45 daily, apartments for $65.* Activities can include swimming in the boat-shape pool, scuba diving, snorkeling, and horseback riding.

Cafe au Lait/Mirage Cottages, Lighthouse Rd., West End, Negril, Jamaica, W.I. (tel. 809/957-4471), is run by Daniel and Sylvia Grizzle, the Jamaican/French couple who prepare the cuisine as well as directing the smooth operation of the place. Menu items include quiches, escargots, lobster, and an unusual crêpe made with cheese and callaloo. There are four kinds of pizza, roast lamb, pork, and chicken, and there is a wine list stressing French products. Dessert may be lime tart with fresh cream, concluding a full meal that will cost from J$100 ($18). The restaurant is open only for dinner, from 5 to 10 p.m. daily.

Set in 4½ acres of tropical garden, the property flanks two sides of the road. On the land side, there are two two-bedroom cottages, ideal for four to six people. On the sea side, where high cliffs dominate the coastline, they have one one-bedroom cottage, one duplex, and four large studio rooms with big balconies and views of the coast. All accommodations have private baths and ceiling fans. The studios are air-conditioned. Winter rates are $65 to $90 per person daily, and *summer tariffs are $40 to $70 per person daily.* There are beautifully appointed sunning areas, three access ladders to the sea, and a gazebo for relaxing in the shade.

Negril Tree House, P.O. Box 29, Norman Manley Blvd. (tel. 809/957-4386), an informal beachfront place, takes its name from a mamee tree which grows through the main building of this resort hotel. Dining is on the second floor, but guests can come early and have a drink in the beachfront bar. This is a lively center both day and night, and it is open daily from 6:30 a.m. to 10 p.m. Lunches cost from J$60 ($10.80), with dinners going for J$150 ($27) and up. At lunch you can ask for a homemade soup, perhaps pepperpot, or a sandwich or else more elaborate fare such as a typically Jamaican dish of escovitched fish. Some of the produce comes from the owner's own farm in the country. At night, Gail Jackson, your hostess, brings out her full repertoire of dishes to amuse her guests, including a lobster spaghetti "worth a detour." You might begin with a callaloo quiche and later follow with roast chicken (a specialty) or conch steak. Try the Tía Maria parfait for dessert. In the past, Gail Jackson has been known for importing reggae bands, but you'll have to check to see if anything is happening at the time of your visit.

Cosmo's Seafood Restaurant & Bar, P.O. Box 32, Norman Manley Blvd. (tel. 809/957-4330), is one of the best places to go for local seafood. Centered around a Polynesian thatched bohío open to the sea and bordering the beachfront, this is the dining spot of Cosmo Brown, who entertains locals as well as visitors. He's known in these parts for his conch soup, and you can order that or else conch in a number of other ways, including steamed or curried. He's also known for his savory kettle of curried goat. You can also order freshly caught seafood and fish as well, depending on what the catch turned up. His rustic establishment is open daily from 9 a.m. to 9 p.m. Prices are among the most reasonable at the resort, with meals costing from J$50 ($9).

I've found that **Chicken Lavish,** West End (tel. 809/957-4410), whose name I love, is the best of the lot. Just show up on the doorstep and see what's cooking. Curried goat is a specialty, as is fresh fried fish. Fresh Caribbean lobster is prepared to perfection here, as is the red snapper caught in local waters. But the main reason I've recommended the place is because of the namesake. Ask the chef to make his special Jamaican chicken. He'll tell you, and you may agree, that it's the best on the island. Along with a salad and dessert, expect to spend around J$75 ($13.50) for a complete meal. Dinner is from 7 to 10 p.m. daily. What to wear here? Dress as you would to clean up your backyard on a hot August day.

6. MANDEVILLE

The "English Town" Mandeville lies on a plateau more than 2,000 feet above the sea in the tropical highlands. The commercial part of the town is small, surrounded by a sprawling residential area popular with the large North American expatriate population mostly involved with the bauxite-mining industry. Much cooler than the coastal resorts, it's a possible center from which to explore the entire land.

Shopping in the town is a pleasure, whether in the old center or in one of the modern complexes such as Grove Court. The market in the center of town teems with life, particularly on weekends when the country folk bus into town for their weekly visit. The town has several interesting old buildings. The square-towered church built in 1820 has fine stained glass, and the little churchyard tells an interesting story of past inhabitants of Mandeville. The Court House was built in 1816, a fine old Georgian stone-and-wood building with a pillared portico reached by a steep, sweeping double staircase.

Among the interesting attractions, **Marshall's Pen** (tel. 809/962-2260) is one of the great houses, an old coffee plantation home some 200 years old and filled with antique furniture, fine grandfather clocks, beautiful carpets, and valuable rugs. The house is a history lesson in itself, as it was once owned by the Earl of Balcaris, the island's governor. It has been in the hands of the Sutton family since 1939. They farm the 300 acres, breeding mainly Jamaican red poll cattle. They have a large collection of seashells, some fine Arawak relics, and a large general stamp collection. This is very much a private home and should be treated as such. Guided tours can be arranged, costing 50¢ per person. For information or appointments to see the house, get in touch with Robert L. Sutton, P.O. Box 58, Mandeville (tel. 809/962-2260).

WHERE TO STAY: My top choice for a stay in this area is the **Hotel Astra,** 62 Ward Ave., Mandeville, Jamaica, W.I. (tel. 809/962-3265). It's a family-run hotel, operated by the McIntyres, who do all they can to ensure that visitors and local people alike are satisfied. Diana McIntyre-Pike, known to her family and friends as Thunderbird (she is always coming to the rescue of guests), happily picks up people in her own car, taking them around to see the sights and organizing introductions to people of the island. The hotel has 20 double rooms and two suites, mainly in two buildings reached along open walkways. The tariff all year is J$283 ($50.95) to J$495 ($89.10) daily, double occupancy.

The Zodiac Room, entered from the lounge area, offers excellent meals. Lunch or dinner is a choice of a homemade soup such as beef-and-vegetable or pumpkin, followed by shrimp rice, meatballs Italiano, or braised steak. All main dishes are served with a selection of rice, buttered cho-cho, scalloped potatoes, and other vegetables. A large salad bowl is also included at dinner. The kitchen is under the personal control of Diana, who is always collecting awards in Jamaican culinary competitions, and someone is on hand to explain to you the niceties of any particular Jamaican dish. A complete meal costs J$45 ($8.10) to J$75 ($13.50). Dinner is served from 6:30 to 9:30 p.m. Monday to Friday, from 7 to 10 p.m. Saturday and Sunday. Friday is barbecue night, when guests and townfolk gather around the pool to dine. Spareribs, chicken, and steak are delectable. The Revival Room is the name of the bar, where everything including the bar stools is made from rum-soaked barrels. Try the family's own homemade liqueur and "reviver," a pick-me-up concocted from Guinness, rum, egg, condensed milk, and nutmeg—guaranteed not to fail. There is a dart board for a game, if the locals haven't beaten you to it. Hours are from 11 a.m. to 11:30 p.m. daily. Bar snacks, including pizzas, are served if you don't want a full meal. In addition to the pool, there is a sauna, or you can spend the afternoon at the Manchester Country Club, where tennis and golf are available. Horses can be provided for cross-country treks from Dalkeith Riding School or John Nightingale.

Mandeville Hotel, 4 Hotel St., Mandeville, Jamaica, W.I. (tel. 809/962-2138), is a modern place with a large outdoor bar and a spacious lounge. Recently refurbished, the hotel offers good food and service. Activity centers mainly around the pool and the coffee shop, where substantial meals are served at moderate prices. Room rates range from $40 to $90 daily, double occupancy, year round. There are attractive gardens with many fine old trees and beautiful plants. Golf and tennis can be played at the nearby Manchester Country Club. Horseback riding can also be arranged.

WHERE TO EAT: Standing 100 feet above Mandeville, **Bill Laurie's Steak House,** Bloomfield Gardens, P.O. Box 150 (tel. 809/962-3116), a long, two-story wooden house with a veranda stretching the length of the upper floor. Outside you are likely to find 14½ cars, none less than 30 years old, including an old London taxi which used to take customers home after a heavy meal. The front end of an old Wolseley makes up the total count. Going upstairs to the bar and restaurant, you meet even more examples of Bill's squirrel-like habits—more than 500 vehicle license plates decorate the walls, pictures of cars fill all available extra space, along with visiting cards by the thousand, beer mats, and model cars vying for space among pewter tankards left there permanently by regulars who are set in their ways. The kitchen still has a wood-burning stove in excellent condition, carefully blacked but no longer used. Bill came from Scotland 34 years ago and loves his island highland home in the sun, where he can indulge his love of old cars and collecting things.

The food consists of appetizers such as fruit punch or mango nectar, soups, and steaks varying in size and cut. Ground beef steak, mixed grill, and lamb chops are among the main-dish offerings. All meals are cooked to order and come with french fries, salad, and vegetables. You'll spend about $20. Dinner is served from 7 to 9 p.m. daily.

Mandeville Hotel, 4 Hotel St. (tel. 809/962-2460), is close to the city center and popular with local business people who use the coffeeshop by the pool for a quick, appetizing luncheon stop. A wide selection of sandwiches is available. You can order milkshakes, tea, or coffee. In the hotel restaurant, open for lunch (you must reserve for dinner but not necessarily for lunch), the à la carte menu offers such foods as Jamaican pepperpot soup, lobster thermidor, fresh snapper, and kingfish. Potatoes and vegetables in season are included in the main-dish prices. A complete meal can cost from $9. If you happen to be there at breakfast, a full Jamaican meal costs from $7. Hours are daily from 7 to 10 a.m., noon to 2 p.m., and 7 to 9 p.m.

WHAT TO SEE AND DO: Mandeville is the sort of place where you can become well acquainted with the people and feel like part of the community.

For the Speleologist
One of the largest and driest caves on the island is at Oxford, about nine miles northwest of Mandeville. Signs direct you to it after you leave Mile Gully, a village dominated by St. George's Church, some 175 years old.

Birdwatching
At **Marshall's Pen** cattle estate and nature reserve, near Mandeville, 89 of Jamaica's 256 species of birds (including 23 endemic species and many North American winter migrants) can be seen. Groups can arrange guided birding tours of the scenic property *in advance,* for early morning or evening (to see nocturnal birds) or to go to other outstanding birding spots in Jamaica, at rates to be negotiated.

For further information, get in touch with **Robert L. Sutton,** P.O. Box 58, Mandeville (tel. 809/962-2260).

Taking the Waters
Milk River Mineral Bath, Milk River, P.O. Clarendon (tel. 809/924-9544), lies nine miles south of the Kingston–Mandeville highway. It boasts the world's most radioactive mineral waters, recommended for the treatment of arthritis, rheumatism, lumbago, neuralgia, sciatica, and liver disorders. These mineral-laden waters are available to guests of the hotel as well as casual visitors to the enclosed baths or the mineral swimming pool. The restaurant offers fine Jamaican cuisine, health drinks, and special diets in an old-world atmosphere of relaxation. The nearby Milk River affords boating and fishing. Accommodations are available at year-round MAP rates, ranging from J$130 ($23.40) to J$168 ($30.25) daily in a single, J$232 ($41.75) to J$244 ($43.95) in a double.

Huntingdon Summit Tour
On Knockpatrick Road, 1½ miles from Mandeville, you can visit the octagonal, hilltop home of Mr. Cecil Charlton (tel. 809/962-2432), daily except Wednesday and Saturday from 10 a.m. to 6 p.m. Mr. Charlton also has a collection of rare birds. There is no admission charge, but visitors may tip guides or give a donation.

CHAPTER XII

FRENCH WEST INDIES

□ □ □

1. MARTINIQUE
2. GUADELOUPE
3. ST. MARTIN
4. ST. BARTHÉLEMY

French charm and tropical beauty combine in the great curve of the Lesser Antilles. A long way from Europe, France's western border is composed mainly of Guadeloupe and Martinique, with a scattering of tiny offshore dependencies, such as the six little clustered Îles des Saintes.

Almond-shaped Martinique is the northernmost of the Windwards, while butterfly-shaped Guadeloupe is near the southern stretch of the Leewards. These are not colonies, as many visitors wrongly assume, but the westernmost *départements* of France, meaning that these *citoyens* are full-fledged citizens of la belle France.

Other satellites of the French West Indies include St. Martin (which shares an island with the Dutch-held St. Maarten; see Chapter X), St. Barthélemy, Marie-Galante, and La Désirade, a former leper colony.

Unlike Barbados and Jamaica, the French West Indies are Johnny-come-latelies to tourism. Although cruise-ship passengers had arrived long before, mass tourism began in these islands only in the 1970s. Before that, Jacques Cousteau or David Rockefeller could retreat here, enjoying a hideaway, but no longer. Créole customs make these islands unique in the Caribbean. The inhabitants also serve some of the best food. Don't be afraid if I've sent you to a dilapidated wooden shack. You may find the *New York Times* food editor there too, sampling a sumptuous meal.

Traveler's Advisory: As of this writing, U.S. and Canadian citizens can visit the French West Indies without a visa, even though Martinique and Guadeloupe are part of France, which *does* demand a visa. But in a fast-changing world, policies can change overnight, and prospective visitors should check with tourist boards or airlines flying to a particular destination to determine the latest information.

For more information, get in touch with the French West Indies Tourist Board, 610 Fifth Ave., New York, NY 10020 (tel. 212/757-1125).

1. MARTINIQUE

France's anchor in the Caribbean world, Martinique is the land of the Empress Joséphine. In her youth, Madame de Maintenon, mistress of Louis XIV, also lived here in the small fishing village of Precheur.

Martinique still has remarkable women, considered the most beautiful in the West Indies. A mingling of African and French blood has produced a classic Créole beauty. In days gone by, she was famous for her *madras et foulard* costume, a dress reserved now more for special occasions. Presumably, the flair of the knots of the madras reveals whether the girl is engaged, married, or available (or any combination of the above).

Columbus first charted Martinique, and the French settled the island when the king's gentleman, Belain d'Esnambuc, took possession in the name of Louis XIII. The year was 1635. In spite of some intrusions by British forces, the French have remained in Martinique ever since. Emigration from France produced sugarcane plantations and rum distilleries.

Early in the beginning of their colonization, the French imported black slaves from Africa to work the plantations, but at the time of the French Revolution, slavery began to decline on Martinique. But it wasn't until the mid-19th century that its abolition was obtained by Victor Schoelcher, a Paris-born deputy from Alsace. Since 1946 Martinique has been a part of France.

Martinique is part of the Lesser Antilles and lies in the semitropical zone, its western shore facing the Caribbean, its eastern shore the livelier Atlantic. It is some 4,340 miles from France, 2,000 miles from New York, 2,300 miles from Montréal, and 1,450 miles from Miami.

The surface of the island is only 420 square miles—50 miles at its longest dimension, 21 miles at its widest point.

The ground is mountainous, especially in the rain-forested northern part where Mount Pelée, a volcano, rises to a height of 4,656 feet. In the center of the island the mountains are smaller, Carbet Peak reaching a 3,960-foot summit. The high hills rising among the peaks or mountains are called "Morne." The southern part of Martinique has only big hills, reaching peaks of 1,500 feet at Vauclin, 1,400 feet at Diamant. The irregular coastline of the island provides five bays, dozens of coves, and miles of sandy beaches.

The climate is relatively mild, and the heat is rarely uncomfortable, the average temperature in the 75° to 85° Fahrenheit range. At higher elevations it's considerably cooler. The island is cooled by a wind the French called *alizé,* and rain is frequent but doesn't last very long. From late August to November might be called the rainy season. April to September are the hottest months.

The early Carib Indians, who gave Columbus such a hostile reception, called Martinique "the island of flowers," and indeed it has remained so. The vegetation is lush, including hibiscus, poinsettias, bougainvillea, everything enhanced by such trees as the flamboyant, the royal palm, coconut, giant bamboo, mango, orange, and the locust tree. Almost any fruit that can grow in the ground sprouts out of Martinique's soil—pineapples, avocados, bananas, papayas, and custard apples.

Birdwatchers are often pleased at the number of hummingbirds, while spotting the mountain whistler and blackbird as well. The mongoose is common, and multicolored butterflies add to the panorama of nature. After sunset, there's a permanent concert of grasshoppers, frogs, and crickets.

GETTING THERE: Most airlines route North American passengers to the French departments of Martinique and Guadeloupe in roughly the same patterns. Therefore much of what you read here about getting to Martinique applies equally to its sister island.

Most vacationers in the New York and New Jersey area select a daily flight from JFK Airport, and change in San Juan or Miami. **American Airlines** offers efficient transfer via its hub in San Juan and continues service on American's partner, **American Eagle,** to Guadeloupe or Martinique.

A phone call to a package-tour operator is always a good idea before booking your reservations because often, reductions are awarded to passengers who book their air fare and hotel reservations at the same time.

Service is also available on **Air France.** In the winter season, daily service is offered to Guadeloupe and Martinique. Every afternoon, an Air France plane flies from San Juan to the French islands. On Monday, Wednesday, Saturday, and Sunday, the plane goes first to St. Martin and then to Guadeloupe and Martinique. On Tuesday and Thursday, a 727 takes off for Guadeloupe and Martinique, and on Friday a 747 from Paris flies to San Juan and on to Guadeloupe.

Continental Airlines provides daily service from Newark Airport to French St. Martin, via Queen Juliana Airport on Dutch St. Maarten. A 727-200 leaves at 9:35 a.m., arriving in St. Martin at 2:35 p.m., with a 3:15 p.m. return flight getting to Newark at 6:30 p.m.

These schedules could—and probably will—change by the time of your departure for the islands. For more information, call the airlines directly or your travel agent.

GETTING AROUND: Travel by **taxi** is the most popular method, and rates are expensive. Most of the cabs aren't metered, and you'll have to agree on the price of the ride before getting in. Most visitors arriving at Lamentin Airport head for one of the resorts along the peninsula of Pointe du Bout. To do so costs about 142F ($22.01) during the day, about 200F ($31) for two in the evening. Night fares are in effect from 8 p.m. to 6 a.m.

If you want to rent a taxi for the day, it's better to have a party of at least three or four persons to keep costs low. Depending on the size of the car, expect to pay from 550F ($85.25) for a five-hour trip. Only a few of the drivers will be able to speak English, however.

Ferry

The least expensive way to go between Fort-de-France and Pointe du Bout is by ferry, costing 15F ($2.33) per passenger. However, service is not as frequent as it should be, so check departure points and times before relying on this means of transport.

Ferry service has been expanded between Fort-de-France and the little beach resorts of Anse Mitan and Anse-à-l'Âne, which are across the bay and are home to many small hotels and a multitude of Créole restaurants. The boat, called *Madinina,* after the island's original name, has a capacity of 100 and a crew of three. It departs daily from Quai d'Esnambuc in Fort-de-France every 30 minutes from 6 a.m. to 7 p.m. daily. The piers at Anse Mitan and Anse-à-l'Âne are departure points for those areas. The trip takes only about 15 minutes, a round-trip ticket costing about $2.50.

Buses

There is no railway system in Martinique, but buses are operated from Fort-de-France, linking every single village on the island. Depending on the distance, fares run from 50¢ to $3. However, for those taking this local means of transport, I must point out that mama, her kids, or even a chicken may ride on your lap.

"Taxis collectifs" are preferred. These are usually limos or vans holding from about eight to ten passengers, charging fares in the 5F (78¢) to 20F ($3.10) range, depending on where you're going. They are faster than the buses and much less crowded. In Fort-de-France, the departure point for these CTs is at Pointe Simon on the harborfront.

Car Rentals

If you rent a car in Martinique, you must be at least 21 or in some cases 25 years old, depending on the company. Even companies renting to drivers aged 21 will usually refuse them a collision damage waiver (eliminating the financial obligation of a renter to pay for damages in the event of an accident).

To those 25 or over, **Hertz, Avis,** and **Budget** will welcome them at their airport kiosks. All three companies maintain late model cars. Of the big three, **Budget Rent-a-Car** has the most consistently inexpensive cars, as well as a well-planned airport facility with minibus service and computerized rapid returns.

Winter rates for Budget's least expensive vehicles are $237 weekly, as opposed to $272 at Hertz and $296 at Avis. Cars with air conditioning and automatic transmission cost more. The French government adds 14% tax. For reservations and information, call toll free within the U.S. by dialing Budget at 800/527-0700, Avis at 800/331-2112, and Hertz at 800/654-3001.

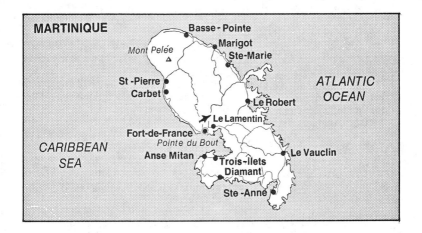

Scooter Rentals

"Funny" (tel. 011-596/63-42-82), with four agencies in Martinique, offers a variety of motorcycles and motor scooters for rent. For a Peugeot 50, Peugeot 80, or Vespa 80, the charge per day is 91F ($14.11). A Vespa 125 costs 96F ($14.88). The rent for a Yamaha 125 or Honda 125 is 215F ($33.33). Rates are for unlimited mileage, and tax is included. A 1,500F ($232.50) minimum deposit is required unless you pay by a major credit card. Call the number given above to find out the "Funny" location nearest to you and to reserve the vehicle you wish.

PRACTICAL FACTS: French is the official language, spoken by almost everyone. The local Créole patois uses words borrowed from France, England, Spain, and Africa. In the wake of increased tourism, English is occasionally spoken in the major hotels and restaurants. But don't count on driving around the countryside and asking for directions in English. The Martiniquais aren't that bilingual yet.

Consulate: The U.S. Consulate is at 14 rue Blenac (tel. 011-596/63-13-03), in Fort-de-France.

Currency: The French franc is legal tender here. You should exchange your money at banks as they give much better rates than the hotels. Currency quotations in this chapter are both in U.S. dollars and French francs, as hotels often publish their rates in American dollars to visitors from North America. Of course, exchange rates are subject to dollar fluctuations. Exchange rates quoted are only for your general guidance, and may not actually be in effect at the time of your visit. One franc is presently exchanged for 15½¢ U.S. (6.40 francs equal $1 U.S.).

Documents: U.S. and Canadian citizens need proof of identity for stays of less than 21 days. After that, a valid passport is required. A return or ongoing ticket is also necessary.

Electricity: Electric current is 220 volts AC, 50 cycles. You'll need a converter or adapter for U.S. appliances.

Information: A helpful address on the island: **Office Départemental du Tourisme** (Tourist Office), Boulevard Alfassa (Bord de Mer), B.P. 520, 97206 Fort-de-France, Martinique, F.W.I. (tel. 011-596/63-79-60).

Medical Care: Health services and medical equipment are both modern and comprehensive (there are some 18 hospitals and clinics). In an emergency, your hotel can put you in touch with the nearest one.

Telephone: When calling Martinique from North America, dial 011-596, then the six-digit number you are calling on the island. It is not necessary to use the area code for local calls—just the six-digit number.

Time: Martinique time is one hour later than Eastern Standard Time, except when Eastern Daylight Saving Time is in effect. Then Martinique time is the same as in the Eastern Time zone of the United States.

Water: Potable water is found throughout the island.

CARNIVAL: If you like masquerades and dancing in the streets, you should attend carnival, or "Vaval" as it is known here. The event of the year, carnival begins right after the New Year, as each village prepares costumes and floats. Weekend after weekend, frenzied celebrations take place, reaching fever pitch just before Lent.

Fort-de-France is the focal point, and the spirit of the carnival envelops the island, as narrow streets are jammed with floats. On Ash Wednesday the streets of Fort-de-France are filled with *diablesses,* or she-devils (portrayed by members of *both* sexes). They are costumed in black and white, crowding the streets to form King Carnival's funeral procession. As devils cavort about and the rum flows, a funeral pyre is built at La Savane. When it is set on fire, the dancing of those "she-devils" becomes frantic (many are thoroughly drunk at this point).

Long past dusk, the cortège takes the coffin to its burial, ending carnival until another year.

FORT-DE-FRANCE: A mélange of New Orleans and Menton (French Riviera), Fort-de-France is the main town of Martinique, lying at the end of a large bay, surrounded by evergreen hills. Iron-grillwork balconies overflowing with flowers are commonplace here.

The people of Martinique are even more fascinating than the town. Today the Créole beauties are likely to be seen in jeans instead of their traditional turbans and Empress Joséphine-style gowns, but they still have the same walk. Heads held high, shoulders up, they have a jaunty spring. They're a proud, sprightly people, and I miss their massive earrings that used to jounce and sway as they sauntered along.

Narrow streets climb up the steep hills on which houses have been built to catch the overflow of the capital's more than 100,000 inhabitants.

At the center of the town lies a broad garden planted with many palms and mangoes, **La Savane,** a handsome savannah with shops and cafés lining its sides. In the middle of this grand place stands a statue of Josephine, "Napoleon's little Créole," made of white marble, the work of Vital Debray. With the grace of a Greek goddess, she poses in a Regency gown. She looks toward Trois-Îlets where she was born.

After viewing her, you can head for the **St. Louis Roman Catholic Cathedral,** built in 1875. It's an extraordinary iron building, which someone once likened to "a sort of Catholic railway station."

There's another statue of the island's second main historical figure, Victor Schoelcher (you'll see his name a lot in Martinique). As mentioned, he worked to free the slaves more than a century ago. This statue stands in front of the Palais de Justice.

The **Library Schoelcher** also honors this popular hero. It was first displayed at the Paris Exposition of 1889. However, the Romanesque portal, in red and blue, the Egyptian lotus-petal columns, even the turquoise tiles, were imported piece by piece from Paris, reassembled finally in this West Indian setting of royal palms and tamarinds.

Guarding the port is **Fort St-Louis,** built in the Vauban style on a rocky promontory. In addition, **Fort Tartenson** and **Fort Desaix** stand on hills overlooking the port.

The **Musée Départemental de la Martinique,** 9 rue de la Liberté (tel. 011-596/71-57-05) is the one bastion on Martinique that preserves its pre-Columbian past, the relics left from the early settlers, the peaceful Arawaks and the cannibalistic Caribs. Exhibits depict in artifacts and garments the life of these Indians. The location is along the rue de la Liberté, at the same location as the government-sponsored Caribbean Art Center, facing the Savane. The museum is open Monday to Friday from 9 a.m. to 1 p.m. and 2 to 5 p.m. (from 9 a.m. to noon on Saturday), charging adults 8F ($1.24), children 3F (47¢).

Sacré-Coeur de Balata Cathedral, also overlooking Fort-de-France, is a copy of the one looking down upon Montmartre in Paris—and this one is just as incongruous, maybe more so.

A few minutes from Fort-de-France, **Balata Garden** (Le Jardin de Balata) (tel. 011-596/64-48-73), some six miles north of the capital, is a tropical botanical park. The park was created by Jean-Philippe Thoze on land the jungle was rapidly reclaiming around a Créole house that belonged to his grandmother. He has also restored the house, furnishing it with antiques and engravings depicting life in other days, with bouquets and baskets of fruit renewed daily. The garden contains flowers, shrubs, and trees growing in profusion and offering a vision of tropical splendor. Balata is open daily from 9 a.m. to 6 p.m. Admission is 30F ($4.65) for adults, 10F ($1.55) for children.

Hotels In and Around Fort-de-France

Rates are sometimes advertised in U.S. dollars, sometimes in French francs, and sometimes in a combination of the two currencies. It depends on the individual hotel.

Hôtel La Batelière, 97200 Schoelcher, Martinique, F.W.I. (tel. 011-596/61-49-49), stands on the west coast. The 18-acre estate lies in La Batelière, a residential suburb about a mile from Fort-de-France. This waterside French-modern hotel is a 200-room, air-conditioned white stucco structure, set back in a garden from its wide private beach. The hotel lacks super-glamor but serves successfully as a center of many water sports, social activities, dining choices, and nightlife activities with its casino and disco action. Each unit contains a tile bath, but best of all are the room-wide glass doors opening onto your own water-view terrace. In winter, you can stay here (with a continental breakfast included) in a single for 810F ($125.55) to 1,300F ($201.50) daily, for 1,050F ($162.75) to 2,500F ($387.50) in a double. *Off-season, singles are accepted for $118 to $140 daily and doubles for $148 to $170.* In the Lafitte dining room, French, international, and Créole cuisine is served, and there's a pizzeria near the swimming pool. You may enjoy a span of dredged sand or the round swimming pool. You can order a drink under the canopied bar as you sit comfortably on cushions. Sports such as scuba-diving, snorkeling, windsurfing, sailing, and waterskiing are available at rates which depend on the season and duration. Tennis is free, however, except at night when there's a surcharge. On the premises are a beauty salon and barber-shop and a sauna.

Hôtel l'Impératrice, Place de la Savane, rue de la Liberté, 97200 Fort-de-France, Martinique, F.W.I. (tel. 011-596/63-06-82), favored by business people, faces a landscaped mall. Named for Josephine, it's a 1950s "layer-cake" stucco hotel, with encircling balconies overlooking the traffic at the west side of the Savane. The lounge has large, white wickerwork chairs. Adjoining is a bar with white furniture set on its tile floor. If you don't like to perch there, you may prefer the bar on the next level, with its harmonious green-and-white decor. The bedrooms are modern and functional, each air-conditioned with private bath. The front rooms tend to be noisy; yet, to compensate, windows overlook the life along the Savane. Since this is not a resort hotel, rates stay more or less the same year round. Singles pay 275F ($42.63) to 327F ($50.69), with doubles costing 350F ($54.25) to 402F ($62.31) daily. If you're in Fort-de-France on a shopping excursion, you might want to consider dining at Le Joséphine.

Le Lafayette, 5 rue de la Liberté, 97200 Fort-de-France, Martinique, F.W.I. (tel. 011-596/73-80-50), is a modern 23-room hotel right on La Savane. You enter through the rue Victor-Hugo, reaching the reception hall after climbing a few steps of terracotta. The dark-brown wood doors are offset by the soft beige walls. Inside the bedrooms, Japanese wall tapestries form the decorative motif, and most rooms contain twin beds in a dark-brown wood. The windows have small panes, and the curtains are color coordinated with the bedspreads. Bathrooms are in pure white, and the overall impression is of a neat, clean, but simple, hostelry. *In off-season, rooms range from $43 daily in a single. Doubles go for $60.* In winter, EP singles rent for 340F ($52.70) and doubles for 380F ($58.90) daily.

Le Bristol, 20 km. rue Martin-Luther-King, 97200 Fort-de-France, Martinique, F.W.I. (tel. 011-596/63-66-79), was originally built on a hillside as the center of a plantation that surrounded it in 1890. Later, when the encroaching suburbs of Fort-de-France threatened its agriculture, it was converted in 1925 into the first hotel in town. The hotel's ornate gables are seen at the top of a steep road about a five-minute drive from the center of town, within its own ten-acre garden. The ten bedrooms, with air conditioning and private baths, are decorated in a Créole style with colonial furniture. *They rent for $42 to $75 daily for two persons in low season,* $50 to $85 for two in high season. The restaurant is one of the most outstanding in the area.

Hôtel Victoria, Rond Point de Didier, 97200 Fort-de-France, Martinique, F.W.I. (tel. 011-596/60-56-78). Its central core was built in 1888 by a French

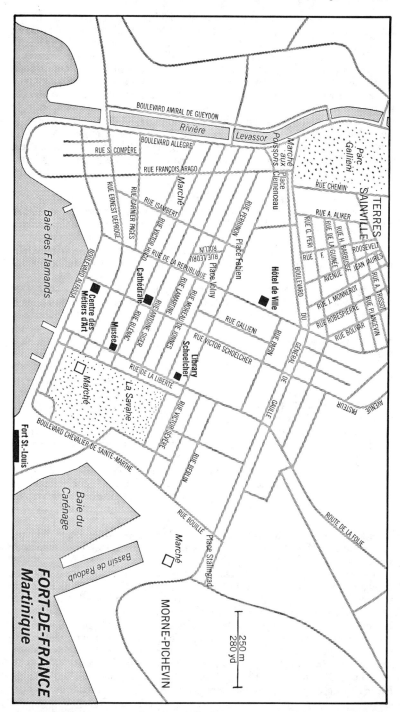

FORT-DE-FRANCE
Martinique

Fort St.-Louis

Baie des Flamands

Baie du
Carénage

Bassin de Radoub

MORNE-PICHEVIN

250 m
280 yd

BOULEVARD AMIRAL DE GUEYDON

Rivière   Levassor

BOULEVARD ALLEGRE

RUE S. COMPÈRE

RUE FRANÇOIS ARAGO

Marché aux Poissons

Place Clemenceau

Parc
Galliéni

TERRES-SAINVILLE

RUE CHEMIN

RUE A. ALIKER

RUE G. PÉRI

RUE H. BARBUSSE

RUE DE LA GUINÉE

RUE F

RUE J. F

ROOSEVELT

AVENUE

JEAN JAURÈS

RUE A. FRISSO

RUE J. MONNEROT

RUE ROBESPIERRE

RUE PLANGEVIN

RUE BOLIVAR

BOULEVARD DU GÉNÉRAL DE GAULLE

AVENUE PASTEUR

RUE ISAMBERT

RUE GARNIER PAGÈS

RUE ERNEST DEPROGE

BOULEVARD ALLEGRE

RUE VICTOR HUGO

RUE DE LA RÉPUBLIQUE

RUE PERRINON

Place Fabien

RUE FÉDON

RUE EDRU

ROLLIN

Place Voltry

RUE LAMARTINE

RUE MOREAU DE JONNÈS

RUE GALLIENI

RUE ANTOINE SIGER

RUE BLÉNAC

RUE VICTOR SCHOELCHER

RUE PAPIN

Cathédrale

Centre des
Métiers d'Art

Musée

RUE DE LA LIBERTÉ

Library
Schoelcher

La Savane

Marché

BOULEVARD ALLEGRE

BOULEVARD CHEVALIER DE SAINTE-MARTHE

RUE VICTOR-SIGER

RUE BERLIN

RUE BOUILLE

Place Stalingrad

ROUTE DE LA FOLIE

Marché

Hôtel de Ville

Baie des Flamands

slave owner. Today it occupies a residential neighborhood north of the center of Fort-de-France, behind rows of seven-foot-tall hibiscus hedges. The place is far from being plush, and the hillside location may be difficult to find, but still its accommodations are clean and simple. Motel-like units huddle into a sprawling series of outbuildings and satellite wings whose focal point is a swimming pool. From its terrace and from the windows of some (but not all) of the rooms, you can enjoy a sweeping view over the city to the sea. Each of the 27 accommodations has its own tile bath, big window, and relatively banal modern furniture. In winter, singles cost $43 to $55 daily, and doubles go for $60 to $80. *In summer, singles rent for 290F ($44.95) to 310F ($48.05), and doubles cost 340F ($52.70) to 360F ($55.80).* The Victoria's restaurant, L'Arc en Ciel, is one of the finest in the Fort-de-France area, best enjoyed in the evening when you can look out at the lights in the harbor below.

Dining in and Around Fort-de-France

Many travel-wise visitors wing in to Martinique just to sample its Créole cookery. The food served here, at least in my opinion, is the best in the Caribbean. The island's chefs and Créole mamas have been called "seasoned sorcerers." They took not only their native talent for good cooking, but have borrowed freely from Spain and Africa. They've even thrown in a bit of Hindu and a touch of Asian cuisine.

In honor of its African roots, Créole cooking is based on seafood, often bought by the chef "fresh from the Caribbean Sea." Out in the country, every cook has his or her own herb garden, as the Martinique cuisine is highly seasoned with herbs and spices. Except in the major hotels, most restaurants are family run, offering real homemade cooking. Best of all, you usually get to dine al fresco.

Stuffed, stewed, skewered, or broiled langoustes, turtles, clams, conchs, oysters, and octopuses are presented to you with French taste and subtlety but with martiniquais skill and invention. Every good chef knows how to make *colombo,* a spicy rich stew of poultry, pork, or beef, served with rice, herbs, sauces, and a variety of seeds. Another Créole favorite is *calalou* (callaloo in English), a soup flavored with savory herbs. Yet another traditional French West Indian dish is *blaff,* fresh seafood poached in clear stock and usually seasoned with hot peppers. Incidentally, watch those Sunday closings.

Tiffany, La Croix Bellevue, route de Bellevue (tel. 011-596/71-33-82), is an elegant little restaurant that's my personal favorite. It may be the best table on the island, and there are those who suggest that it's one of the best restaurants in all the Caribbean. Four miles north of town, it faces the Institut Vivioz. Its owner, Claude Pradines, who also owns an antique shop in Paris, has created an enticing atmosphere in which to serve his exquisite French specialties. It's an old pink-and-white gingerbread house. Louvered windows let in the sea breezes, which are then whirled about by the ceiling fans.

I suggest you let Monsieur Pradines propose a dinner for you. It might be baby pullet in a tarragon or a Créole sauce, perhaps duck magret with raspberry vinegar. The choice depends on what fresh produce was imported from France. I recently dined on filet mignon with a buttery roquefort sauce. That was preceded by asparagus in puff pastry with a herb cream sauce. A menu is offered including three appetizers, filet mignon, fish, veal, and dessert. The finish came with velvety chocolate cake and a Martinique coffee. To improve his culinary skills, he journeys to France every year to learn "what's cooking." Dining here as well as speaking to him is a pleasure, especially if you're sipping his first-class wine. In the garden are lime trees, banana, and papaya loaded with fruit, and darting trips are made there to gather produce for some of the dishes served. When Monsieur Pradines is in a good mood, he'll entertain guests with magic and card tricks. The typical price of an à la carte menu is 280F ($43.40). It is open for lunch from noon to 3 p.m. and for dinner from 7:30 to 10 p.m. It is closed on Saturday for lunch and all day Sunday.

Le Lafayette, 5 rue de la Liberté (tel. 011-596/63-24-09), in a previously recommended hotel, is elegant, expensive, and good with a refined cuisine. With it china, silver, and crystal, a profusion of beautiful flowers, and walls hung with original art, it is considered the most fashionable place to dine in Fort-de-France. The chef, Henri Charvet, a maître cuisinier formerly of Aix-en-Provence, combines traditional Créole recipes in a light version with new and light renditions of classic French cuisine. The result is a modern and imaginative selection of dishes that have won critical plaudits. Try, if featured, the shrimp in puff pastry with spinach, salmon gros sel in olive oil, veal kidneys, or one of the four or more different Créole dishes prepared daily. Meals cost from 300F ($46.50) and are served from 12:30 to 2:30 p.m. and 7:30 to 10:30 p.m. The place is closed Saturday at lunchtime and all day Sunday.

La Grand'Voile, Pointe-Simon (tel. 011-596/70-29-29), set near the water at the geographical center of town, occupies the second story of an angular concrete building. Many guests prefer a seat outdoors on the veranda with a view of the water. The Migliorini family, your hosts, offers a cuisine that is a delightful blending of French and Créole recipes. You might try, for example, sea urchin fricassée, a whole duck with foie gras (flavored with honey and vinegar), or a roast lobster with Créole sauce. Desserts include glacé chocolate terrine and raspberry sauce. The bargain is the weekday lunch (Monday to Friday), costing 130F ($20.15). Otherwise an elaborate table d'hôte menu, containing the chef's specialties, costs 290F ($44.95). Regular à la carte meals go for 225F ($34.88) and up. Hours are daily from noon to 2:30 p.m. and 7:30 to 10:30 p.m.

D'Esnambuc, rue de la Liberté (tel. 011-596/71-46-51), is small, select, and elegant, the domain of Josette Kleinpeter since 1981. You climb to the third floor, enjoying not only good food but a view of the bay and a refreshing atmosphere. The cuisine here is imaginatively French, with hints of West Indian spices added in. A noonday fixed-price lunch costs 90F ($13.95), and at least three other fixed-price meals are more expensive. If you order à la carte the tab could run to as much as 200F ($31). The list of French and Créole specialties includes fish soup, sea urchin quiche, octopus with red beans, rabbit chasseur (with red wine and mushrooms), and a colombo of chicken. Lunch is served daily from noon to 3 p.m.; dinner, 7 to 10:30 p.m. Closed Sunday.

El Raco, 23 rue Lazare-Carnot (tel. 011-596/73-29-16), lies in a commercial and residential neighborhood where life seems little changed since 1945. For such a small place, the menu is astonishingly elaborate, with a medley of both French and Spanish dishes. You can ask the chef to prepare you a classic paella, perhaps preceded by gazpacho or Catalán eggs. There is also a limited Créole menu of fresh shellfish, including stuffed oysters, or you might ask for stingray in black butter or wild duck with pineapple. Wine, a selection of sophisticated vintages, can be selected by the glass. Meals, costing from 200F ($31), are served from noon to 2 p.m. and 7:30 to 10 p.m. The restaurant is closed Saturday and Monday at lunch and all day Sunday.

La Biguine, 11 route de la Folie (tel. 011-596/71-40-07), has been rated by some food critics as one of the finest restaurants in Martinique. It's the personal statement of a master chef, Gérard Padra, who for a long time was associated with the Bakoua. He found this clapboard colonial-style house and installed a restaurant, bar, and tea salon (dining is on the second floor). Few who try his gastronomy are disappointed. It is a showcase for the many fine dishes for which he is known, including a Créole mutton soup, shrimp fricassée, blaff, coq au vin, and shark in tomato sauce. For a perfect ending to one of his repasts, try one of his sorbets (sherbet) made with local fruits. Reservations are essential. Meals are served from noon to 2 p.m. and 7 to 11 p.m. He is closed on Saturday for lunch and all day Sunday. Meals cost from 200F ($31).

Le Coq Hardi, 52 rue Martin-Luther-King (tel. 011-596/71-59-64). If the chef/proprietor isn't too busy, he might take time out to tell you about his days of serving in the French Foreign Legion in Algeria and Indochina. Le Coq Hardi is a steakhouse, known for its meats grilled over a wood fire. You'll find it beside a steeply inclined traffic artery which crisscrosses a residential hillside just outside the center of town. This is a place for hearty eaters who don't mind spending about 200F ($31) for a worthy dinner. In some ways Le Coq Hardi is the type of bistro that the famous food critic Waverley Root was always discovering in some working-class arrondissement of Paris. It is open every day except Wednesday from noon to 1:45 p.m. and 7:15 to 10:45 p.m.

Typic Bellevue, 83 Boul. de la Marne (tel. 011-596/71-68-87), a few minutes from the center of town, is a rustic rural house, with shutters and an outdoor terrace. Operated by Jacky Grillot, it's frequented by local residents because of its well-prepared Créole dishes, which are served at reasonable prices. As you dine on the terrace, you'll get the feeling of stopping over at a roadside inn. Among the specialties are seafood such as lobster and local shrimp, fricassee of goat, fish soup, steamed baby shark, and frogs' legs with green pepper sauce. A meal of Créole specialties will lead to a tab in the neighborhood of 100F ($15.50) to 180F ($27.90). A set lunch costs only 65F ($10.08). It shuts down on Saturday afternoon and Sunday. Otherwise, meals are served from noon to 3 p.m. and 7:30 to 10 p.m.

Shopping in Fort-de-France

Your best buys in Martinique are French luxury imports, such as perfumes, fashions, Vuitton luggage, Lalique crystal, or Limoges dinnerware. Sometimes (but don't count on it) prices are as much as 30% to 40% below Stateside levels.

A cautious reader who is nobody's fool sounds a warning to all readers. He points out that if you pay in dollars, store owners supposedly will give you a 20% discount, which is the "Value Added Tax" imposed on countries of Europe that are members of the Common Market. He proposes a hypothetical example. That is, a shopper will make a purchase for 1,000F. Less 20%, that becomes 800F. However, when you pay in dollars the rates vary considerably from store to store, and almost invariably they are far lower than that proposed at one of the local banks. He writes: "The net result is that you received a 20% discount, but then they take away from 9% to 15% on the dollar exchange, giving you a net savings of only 5% to 11%—not 20%." He further notes, "Actually, you're probably better off shopping in the smaller stores where prices are 8% to 12% less on comparable items and paying in francs that you have exchanged at a local bank."

The main shopping street is rue Victor-Hugo. The other two leading shopping streets are the rues Schoelcher and St-Louis.

Facing the tourist office and alongside Quai d'Esnambuc is an open market where you can purchase local handcrafts and souvenirs. Many of these are tacky, however.

Far more interesting is the display of vegetables and fruit, quite a show, at the open-air stalls along rue Isambert. Don't miss it for its local ambience, and you can't help but smell the fish market alongside the Levassor River.

Try to postpone your shopping trip if a cruise ship is in town.

Hours at most shops are weekdays from 7:30 a.m. to 12:30 p.m. and 2:30 to 5:30 p.m., on Saturday from 8 a.m. to noon; closed Sunday.

Roger Albert, 7 rue Victor-Hugo (tel. 011-596/71-71-71), offers all the big names in perfumes from Paris as well as crystal from Baccarat and Lalique, chinaware from Limoges, figurines by Lladró, and sportswear by Lacoste and Fila. The merchandise is of the highest quality, providing one of the finest selections in the Caribbean. Long established, just off the Savane, this is the best known store in Martinique.

Merlande, 10 rue Schoelcher, near the cathedral (tel. 011-596/71-30-92), is one of the finest department stores in the Caribbean. French fashions are sold, along with china, crystal, and Baccarat, and such famous names in perfume as Lanvin, Chanel, Jean Patou, and Guerlain.

The best place to go for handcrafts and souvenirs is the **Caribbean Art Center,** rue Ernest-Deproge (tel. 011-596/70-25-01), facing the Savane, next to the tourist office and Air France. Everything here is handmade. All the craftwork of the island is represented here, particularly basketwork and clay crafts. You'll find madras, napkins, and table settings; bags in coconut husks, moon fishes, and boubous (large multicolored gowns), the latter at much lower prices than in the hotel shops. Look also for the Martiniquais doll in her *madras et foulard.*

For the ubiquitous local fabric, madras, there are shops on every street with bolts and bolts of it, all colorful and inexpensive. So-called haute couture and resortwear are sold in many boutiques dotting downtown Fort-de-France.

Crazy Boutique, 17 rue Victor-Hugo (tel. 011-596/73-26-68), likes to set a mood that it calls très parisienne. I'd call it the most outrageous fashion in Fort-de-France. The boutique certainly lives up to its name. It also sells an array of sportswear.

Cadet-Daniel, 72 rue Antoine-Siger (tel. 011-596/71-41-48), which opened in 1840, sells Christofle silver, Limoges china, and crystal from Daum, Baccarat, Lalique, and Sèvres. Like some nearby stores, it also offers island-made 18-karat gold baubles, including the beaded *collier chou,* or "darling's necklace," long a required ornament for a Créole costume.

La Fontaine Fleurie (tel. 011-596/60-23-21) is a "sweets shoppe" on the corner of rues Victore Severe and Gallieni in the heart of Fort-de-France. Run by Any Chalono, the kitchen makes its own candies from fresh regional fruits and also sells popular French chocolates, marzipan *calissons* from Aix-en-Provence, *betises* mint candies from Cambrai, and, of course, local coconut bars called *doucelettes* and *lotchios.*

Before leaving Martinique, you may want to purchase some rum, considered by aficionados to be one of the world's finest distilled drinks. Hemingway in *A Moveable Feast* lauded it as the perfect antidote to a rainy day. I suggest you try Vieux Acajou, a dark, mellow Old Mahogany, or else a blood-red brown liqueur-like rum bottled by Bally. The best place for browsing is **La Case à Rhum,** Galerie Marchande, 5 rue de la Liberté (tel. 011-596/73-73-20).

Gourmet chefs will find all sorts of spices in the open-air markets of the capital, or such goodies as tinned pâté or canned quail in the local *supermarchés.*

Shopping Elsewhere on the Island

If you're staying at one of the hotels on the peninsula of Pointe du Bout, you'll find that the Marina complex there has a number of interesting boutiques. Several sell handcrafts and curios from Martinique. They are of good quality, and are quite expensive, regrettably, particularly if you purchase some of their batiks of natural silk and their enameled jewel boxes.

North of the capital in the village of Bezaudin near Ste-Marie, Madame

Nogard's little *boutique gourmande,* **Ella** (tel. 011-596/69-30-75), specializes in exotic home-grown spices, homemade preserves of island fruits, and original syrups.

There are the sturdy, attractive straw food baskets in the shops of nearby Mornedes-Esses, the *vannerie* (basket-making) capital of Martinique.

Another homemade delicacy that makes a distinctive gift is bloc de foie gras, prepared and put up in glass jars by Mme Beatrice de Meillac at her 1,500 duck farm, **Habitation Durocher** (tel. 011-596/51-13-60), near Lamentin. At Christmas, her specialty is a terrine of foie gras made with armagnac and presented in a lovely crock made by the **Poterie de Trois-Îlets** (tel. 011-596/68-03-44), an excellent place on Martinique to buy ceramics.

A Side Trip to Trois-Îlets

Marie-Josèphe-Rose Tascher de la Pagerie was born here in 1763. As Joséphine, she was to become the wife of Napoleon I and empress of France from 1804 to 1809. She'd been married before to Alexandre de Beauharnais, who'd actually wanted to wed either of her two more attractive sisters, taking her as a consolation prize. Six years older than Napoleon, she pretended she'd lost her birth certificate so he wouldn't find out her true age. Although some historians call her ruthless and selfish (certainly unfaithful), she is still revered by some in Martinique as an uncommonly gracious lady. Others have less kind words for her, because Napoleon is said by some historians to have "reinvented" slavery. Some see the influence of Joséphine in that hideous practice.

After 20 miles of driving from Fort-de-France, you reach Trois-Îlets, a charming little village. One mile outside the hamlet, you turn left to **La Pagerié,** where a small museum of mementos relating to Joséphine has been installed in the former estate kitchen. Along with her childhood bed in the kitchen, you'll see a passionate letter from Napoleon. The collection was compiled by Dr. Robert Rose-Rosette. Here Joséphine gossiped with her slaves and played the guitar.

Still remaining are the partially restored ruins of the Pagerié sugar mill and the church (in the village itself) where she was christened in 1763. The plantation was destroyed in the 1766 hurricane. The museum is open daily, except Monday, from 8:30 a.m. to 5:30 p.m., charging 5F (78¢) for admission.

A botanical garden, **Parc des Floralies,** is adjacent to the Golf de l'Impératrice Joséphine, as is the museum devoted to Joséphine described above.

Maison de la Canne (tel. 011-596/68-32-04) stands at Pointe Vatable on the road to Trois-Îlets. It was created in 1987 to house a remarkable permanent exhibition that tells the story of sugarcane with panels, models, tools, a miniature slave ship, an ancient plow tethered to life-size models of two oxen, a restored carriage, and a copper still. Hostesses guide visitors through the exhibition. It's open from 9 a.m. to 5:50 p.m. Thursday to Sunday.

POINTE DU BOUT: Pointe du Bout is a narrow, irregularly shaped peninsula across the bay from Fort-de-France. Over the past few years it's become the major resort area of Martinique. This is because of four major hotels—PLM Azur Carayou, PLM Azur Pagerié, Bakoua, and the Méridien.

In addition to these hotels and others, you'll find a Robert Trent Jones–designed golf course, a dozen tennis courts, several restaurants, a marina, a gambling casino, discos, swimming pools, facilities for horseback riding, waterskiing, scuba-diving, snorkeling, and volleyball courts.

To drive there from Fort-de-France, leave by Rt. 1, which takes you for a few minutes along the autoroute. You cross the plain of Lamentin, the industrial area of Fort-de-France and the site of the international airport. Very frequently the air is filled with the fragrance of caramel because of the large sugarcane factories in the area.

After 20 miles of driving, you reach Trois-Îlets, Joséphine's hometown. Three miles farther on your right, take the D38 to Pointe du Bout.

For those who want to reach Pointe du Bout by sea, there's a ferry service as mentioned, running all day long (until midnight) from Fort-de-France for 15F ($2.33) fare.

The Resort Hotels

Bakoua Beach Hotel, Pointe du Bout, 97229 Trois-Îlets, Martinique, F.W.I. (tel. 011-596/66-02-02), has buildings that are not overpowering, allowing the natural beauty of the landscape to survive. The 140-room hotel consists of three hillside buildings in the center of the garden of frangipani and coconut palms, plus another building, a bungalow type, right on the beach. The hotel often draws a list of celebrities, including Paul McCartney and Mike Douglas. Of course, they book the imperial suite, with its green marble sunken bathtub and four-poster bed. The style of the rooms is more or less colonial. All the units are comfortable, with a refined polish. In the high season, a double, including a full American breakfast costs 1,400F ($217) to 2,250F ($348.75) daily, with singles going for 1,200F ($186) to 1,700F ($263.50). *In summer, tariffs are lowered to 980F ($151.90) to 1,140F ($176.70) daily in a double, 765F ($118.58) to 840F ($130.20) in a single.* A convivial bar, crafted into a perfect circle out of exotic Caribbean hardwood, is one of the ideal rendezvous points at Pointe du Bout. If you want a snack, you can have it on the beach, but for an elegant repast, I suggest Le Chateaubriand, with its French chef. Dinner is from 7 to 10 p.m. daily. The hotel has an oval swimming pool perched on a terrace right over the beach. Sports are free here, including tennis, volleyball, snorkeling, and sailing. The hotel closes in September. In high season it provides dancing every night (only four times a week in the off-season). The Ballets Martiniquais usually show up at some point during the week.

Hôtel Méridien Trois-Îlets, P.O. Box 894, 97245 Fort-de-France CEDEX, Martinique, F.W.I. (tel. 011-596/66-00-00, 212/245-2920 in New York City, 416/598-3838 in Toronto, or toll free 800/543-4300 in the U.S. and Canada), is really a miniature village, an Air France property offering first-class accommodations in 297 rooms. It has excellent facilities, including a dramatically designed reception area open to the palm-fringed swimming pool and the waters of the bay. Among the restaurants and bars of this hostelry, the Casa Créole offers gourmet meals served by Créole waitresses dressed in regional costume. The Vonvon disco features electronic rhythms for the international crowd, while the casino provides glitter. The hotel is slightly angled to follow the line of the shore. Because of that, all units benefit from a view of either the Caribbean or the bay, at the far end of which you'll be able to see the lights of Fort-de-France. Around the huge block of rooms are a water-side garden, a 100-foot marina, and a cabaña bar near the swimming pool.

The bedrooms provide much comfort, with luxurious baths, private balconies, and attractively modern furnishings. Room service is available 24 hours a day. In winter, singles range from $135 to $325 daily on the EP, with doubles going for $175 to $325 and triples for $225 to $450. *In summer, also on the EP, singles rent for $95 to $125 daily, doubles for $110 to $170, and triples for $144 to $192.* On certain nights of the week, the hotel hosts the vibrant Ballets Martiniquais near the pool. A Créole buffet supper follows this folkloric show, costing hotel guests $34, nonresidents paying $37. Farther out on the point is an old fort where you can stroll, breathing air filled with tropical fragrances.

PLM Azur Carayou, Pointe du Bout, 97229 Trois-Îlets, Martinique, F.W.I. (tel. 011-596/66-04-04). One of the advantages of staying here is that you don't realize you're entering a hotel. Rather, you think you've come for a walk in a tropical garden. It's easy to forget that behind the scenes are 200 bedrooms. The buildings are encircled by large lawns planted with coconut or palm trees and many flowering bushes. The rooms are in two-story bungalows, each having a balcony. The view from your abode will be of gardens, a marina, or the bay of Fort-de-France. In the center of everything is a circular swimming pool, also with a view of the bay. The curving beach provides safe swimming as well. Also taking advantage of that bay view, La Paillote, a bar, is nicely decorated and lit by original cord lamps. Rates include free use of the sports equipment, except for waterskiing. However, you're admitted free to the hotel's disco, Vesou. On the EP in winter, singles cost 715F ($110.83) to 965F ($149.58) daily, with doubles going for 1,000F ($155) to 1,520F ($235.60). *Tariffs in summer are $71 to $87 daily in singles, $84 to $106 in doubles.*

In the Café Créole, you can order a quick snack lunch, without interference with your suntanning schedule. It connects the beach to the pool and acts as an open passage. On the buffet, you'll have a choice of salads and desserts and can select the plat du jour. The café is also open for dinner. It serves some of the best food on Pointe du Bout, tasty and attractively presented. La Boucau is the principal restaurant, created with an island atmosphere of white ceilings and wooden beams. The view over the bay is dramatic at night. In the background is a stage where a local combo plays during dinner. While the atmosphere is quite exotic, the restaurant may also be noisy at times. Fish is the specialty, and Créole cookery is done with flair here. Main dishes include red snapper, stuffed crabs, conch ragoût, or a blaff (stew) of sea urchin. The cuisine is first class, the portions rather generous.

PLM Azur La Pagerié, Pointe du Bout, 97229 Trois-Îlets, Martinique, F.W.I. (tel. 011-596/66-05-30), gives you a chance to have the independence of your own personal apartment. In neat, efficient, streamlined designs, the club offers 98 air-conditioned rooms, some with kitchenettes and balconies opening onto a view of the bay. The location is across the road from the action swirling around the Bakoua. Units are not only comfortable but attractive, with tile floors and white walls, in contrast to the bright pastel draperies and bedspreads. Furnishings are in a clean-cut contemporary style. In winter, EP rates are 520F ($80.60) to 620F ($96.10) daily in a single, 640F ($99.20) to 740F ($114.70) in a double, with full hotel services. *In summer, prices are $50 daily in a single, $54 in a double.* If you don't want to cook, you can order a meal at one of several restaurants at your doorstep. There is also a large swimming pool.

Small Inns (Budget to Moderate)

Auberge de l'Anse Mitan, Anse-Mitan, 97229 Trois-Îlets, Martinique, F.W.I. (tel. 011-596/66-00-98). Many of its guests prefer its location at the isolated end of a road whose more commercial side is laden with restaurants and a bustling nighttime parade. The hotel was originally built in 1930, but it's been renovated several times since then by the hospitable Athanase family. What you see today is a three-story concrete-box–type structure with 19 rooms, plus six other accommodations strung along the beach in one-bedroom cottages. Each unit is air-conditioned and has a private bath. In winter, singles cost 275F ($42.63) daily, and doubles go for 370F ($57.35), with studios for two persons renting for 375F ($58.13). *In summer, singles are charged 240F ($37.20) daily, with doubles paying 290F ($44.95), and two persons in a studio being billed 350F ($54.25).* For an additional 50F ($7.75) per person, half board can be arranged.

Outsiders are welcome to have a fixed-price meal if they phone ahead. Dinner is served every night from 7:30 to 9. The hotel also has a cozy bar.

La Matadore, Anse Mitan, 97229 Trois-Îlets, Martinique, F.W.I. (tel. 011-596/66-05-36), is a simple inn where you might spend most of your vacation in your bathing suit. It was launched by François, the former Bakoua chef, and Raymonde. They rent out 11 pleasant rooms, which are comfortable in spite of their simplicity. In season, a single, with breakfast included, ranges from 315F ($48.83) daily, a double going from 430F ($66.65). *Off-season, tariffs are lowered to 310F ($48.05) in a single, 420F ($65.10) in a double, also with breakfast.* The food served here is among the best on the island (see my dining recommendations).

Dining Outside "The Big Four"

La Villa Créole, Anse Mitan (tel. 011-596/66-05-53). Even with a reservation, in high season you'll sometimes be requested to wait in the bar for up to an hour before a table becomes available. Events like this are evidence of the vast popularity of what's probably the most original restaurant in Martinique. The entertainment that keeps the guests coming back is produced by the owner himself, Guy Bruere-Dawson. A pop musician, he designed his restaurant with an L-shaped rear veranda whose arms encompass a thatch-roofed bandshell-cum-gazebo. From its gingerbread-laden confines, he sings and plays the guitar, often between taking orders for the Créole dishes emerging from the kitchen. Guy's wife, Ghislaine, supervises the food, which includes such specialties as salade de morne Créole (codfish with avocado, tomato, and cucumbers), a three-meat colombo, a blaff of sea urchin (sea urchins poached in clear stock), fricassée of conch, and for dessert, chocolate mousse and banana flambé. Full meals, costing from 200F ($31), definitely require a reservation; no matter how late it is eventually honored. The establishment is open for lunch from noon to 2 p.m. and for dinner from 7 to 10 p.m. The restaurant, closed all day Sunday and Monday for lunch, stands in a cluster of less popular places in a cozy West Indian home.

Au Regal de la Mer, Anse Mitan, Trois-Îlets (tel. 011-596/66-04-00), sits in a cluster of competing restaurants on a quiet lane which looks a bit like a raffish version of St-Tropez. Créole waitresses in traditional costume serve full meals beginning at 200F ($31). A specialty is a seafood platter, where a tangle of seaweed shelters a selection of rock lobster, freshwater crayfish, and shrimp. Many French diners adore this. If you're in the mood for something else, you can order a rock fish soup, gourmet veal tidbits in pastry, filet of Caribbean salmon with a mussel-flavored cream sauce, and an array of desserts. The establishment prefers reservations. Meals are served daily from noon to 3 p.m. and 7 to 10:30 p.m.

L'Amphore, Anse Mitan (tel. 011-596/66-03-09), lies at the end of a bumpy road which begins near the outermost gates of the Bakoua Hotel. The restaurant specializes in seafood, and its ambience is a bit Tahitian, a bit Polynesian, and intimate. Horizontal wooden louvers partially conceal a view of palms and flowering shrubs. It was designed around one of the most exotic-looking lobster tanks on the island. Lobster is the most visible ingredient on the menu, and it's offered in many different varieties. You can also order conch stew, octopus stew, and a savory version of a three-meat curry stew. Desserts are light, including an exotic version of fruit soup. Full meals, costing from 250F ($38.75), require a reservation. The restaurant is open daily except Monday from noon to 2 p.m. and 7 to 11 p.m. No lunch is served on Tuesday.

La Mouïna, km. 2.5, route de Redoute (tel. 011-596/79-34-57), whose name is a Créole word for a house of reunion, is a restaurant offering one of the finest luncheon stops on the island. Sitting next to the police station in the suburb of Redoute, this 50-year-old, white-walled colonial house shelters the culinary domain of one of the island's most experienced chefs. It was converted into a restaurant by Swiss-born Magdeleine Karchesz and her French husband, Guy. Your meal might include snapper in coconut sauce, roast squab, Portuguese oysters, tête (head) of veal, or filet bordelaise. To top it off, you can try one of the luscious desserts, such as raspberry cake. Full meals cost from 250F ($38.75). Lunch is served from noon to 4 p.m. and dinners from 7:30 to 9:30 p.m. daily except Sunday. Always reserve a table. Ask at your hotel for good directions before setting out, because it's a bit hard to find.

Le Cantonnais, Pointe du Bout la Marina (tel. 011-596/66-02-33), is decorated in the classic Chinese fashion of red and gold. Your host, a Martiniquais, Tien-You Guy, offers not only excellent change-of-pace fare, but his tariffs are also kept low. For example, I'd suggest broiled shark fin (I'm perfectly serious). His sliced duckling with plum sauce is excellent too. Soups include braised bird's nest with minced chicken. A set meal is offered daily for 85F ($13.18). Otherwise, count on spending from 150F ($23.25). Either meal is a fine bargain. The restaurant is open from 6:30 to 11 p.m. seven days a week. Lunch is served only on Sunday from noon to 2 p.m. Closed in September.

La Matadore, Anse Mitan (tel. 011-596/66-05-36), has long enjoyed a position as one of the best Créole restaurants in Martinique, and I want only to add to that well-deserved reputation. François and Raymond Crico, your sophisticated hosts, will present you a selection of such savory dishes as crabes farcis (this is a land crab which has been deviled and flavored with a hot seasoning and tossed in breadcrumbs, then baked in its own shell). Try the classic red snapper, which they simmer in a well-flavored court bouillon. For a main course, the most obvious choice is a colombo of mutton, which is a Créole version of curry. La Matadore lies across the bay from Fort-de-France near the hotels of Pointe du Bout which include the Bakoua Beach and the PLM Azur Carayou. The Cricos like to take Wednesday off, but are there every other night, serving you a fine repast for 200F ($31) to 250F ($38.75). Hours are noon to 2:30 p.m. and 7:30 to 10 p.m.

Incidentally, the Matadore in the title has caused some to believe this might be a Spanish restaurant. Actually, the name is Créole for "arrogant woman in full dress."

THE SOUTH LOOP: We now leave Pointe du Bout, heading south for more sun and beaches. Centers here include Le Diamant, Sainte-Anne, and Le François.

From Trois-Îlets, you can follow a small curved road which brings you to Anse-à-l'Âne, Grande Anse, and Anse d'Arlet. At any of these places are small beaches, quite safe and usually not crowded.

At Anse d'Arlet, for example, the scenery is beautiful. Fishing boats draw up on the beach, the men drying their nets in the sun.

From Anse d'Arlet, two winding roads may be chosen to take you to Diamant. One follows the coastline, the other forcing its way through the hills. Both of them offer pleasant scenery.

Anse-à-l'Âne

Reflet de la Mer, Anse-à-l'Âne, 97229 Trois-Îlets, Martinique, F.W.I. (tel. 011-596/68-32-14), has as its charming maître cuisinière Créole Mme Pauline Achille, assisted by her daughter Paulette. A ferryboat from Fort-de-France lands every hour at a spot a few steps away from a simple cement building at the edge of the beach housing this restaurant and small hotel. Menu items include blaff of fish and conch, blaff of sea urchin, conch fricassée, colombo of chicken and mutton, stuffed crabs, and fish soup. Full meals, costing 150F ($23.25), are served from noon to 3 p.m. and 6 to 9 p.m. daily except Monday. If you want to make a day of it, you can bring your beach clothes for an after-lunch swim. The owners also rent six simple rooms which, with half board included, cost 220F ($34.10) daily in a single, 350F ($54.25) for a double. The rooms contain sinks, showers, and toilets as part of the bedroom, not set off in a separate bathroom.

Grande Anse

Le Tamarin Plage, 97217 Anse d'Arlet, Grande Anse, Martinique, F.W.I. (tel. 011-596/68-67-88), is a place little changed since the time when Paul Gauguin visited this part of Martinique. Sugarcane leaves cover the ceiling, and a rough-textured veranda overlooks the beach. Locals sit at the bar most of the day, while Mr. Perronette, the owner, mixes drinks. The renovated restaurant has an aquarium with fish and spiny lobster. Set meals cost 80F ($12.40), and à la carte repasts go for 150F ($43.25) and up. Service is included. Menu items include several kinds of accras, fish soup, stuffed crab, chicken fricassée, sea crab fricassée, and grilled lobster. This restaurant opens every day at 6 a.m., remaining in business until after the last diner has gone home. If you'd like to stay over here, bedrooms with half board rent for 500F ($77.50) daily for two persons, with full board for 900F ($139.50) for double occupancy.

Anse d'Arlet

La Case à Cha-Cha (tel. 011-596/76-42-28) is an intensely local kind of restaurant which developed when Ginette Adé, her husband, André, and their children expanded their bakery to include an adjacent eating place. Today the bakery is still in business, yet the main focus of the family's energy is the restaurant's kitchen. Frankly, the building is a makeshift affair filled with the simplest of accessories. Your fellow diners are likely to be Martiniquais rather than tourists. You reach the dining room by going through a corridor bar. Menu choices usually include pork with pineapple, coconut and pumpkin flan, soup z'habitant, seafood tart, boudin, fish blaff, grilled fish, goat colombo, grilled lobster, and conch fricassée. Full meals cost from 130F ($20.15). You'll find this place near the center of town. It's open daily except Monday from noon to 2:30 p.m. and 6 to 9 p.m.

Le Diamant

Here is a village with quite a good beach open to the winds from the south. **Diamond Rock** just from the sea rising to a height of 573 feet. In a daring maneuver in 1804, the British carried ammunition and 110 sailors to the top. There, in spite of French coastal artillery bombardment, they held out for 18 months, commanding the passage between the rock and Martinique. You can visit it, but the access by small boat is considered risky.

Diamond Beach is excellent, with surf and bathing possibilities. It's lined with the familiar groves of swaying palms.

Novotel Le Diamant, 97223 Le Diamant, Martinique, F.W.I. (tel. 011-596/76-42-42), stands two miles outside the village on a half island. Architecturally, it's an aesthetic success. The reception opens onto a large pool which you cross on a Chinese-style wooden bridge to connect with the buildings where the rooms are located. The bedroom units face either the pool or the coast with its expansive view of the famous Diamond Rock. The furniture in the bedrooms is functional and comfortable. *The prices off-season are $100 to $120 daily in a single, $120 to $143 in a double, both on the EP.* In winter, EP rates, are 750F ($116.25) daily for a single, 990F ($153.45) for a double. Outside of the hotel, the neighboring beaches aren't too crowded, and the view of the Caribbean is splendid in most directions. If you don't want to leave the hotel, you can of course relax around the pool, sipping your rum punch at the bar. Lawns and gardens, as well as tennis courts, surround the hotel. Water sports and many divertissements are also offered by management. The trip from the airport to the hotel in a taxi will take half an hour.

Hôtel Diamant les Bains, 97223 Le Diamant, Martinique, F.W.I. (tel. 011-596/76-40-14), is a small, beachfront, family-style hotel, with a cluster of cottages, and a swimming pool. Close to the water, everything rests under palm trees. The cultivated gardens surrounding the bungalows have lounge chairs, where you can sit and enjoy the view of Diamond Rock. The main building, with its upper-deck bedrooms, houses the restaurant where you can dine on the terrace with a view of the sea. The cuisine is mostly Créole, with some French dishes. The chef pays liberal attention to locally caught fish. A special menu is offered at 175F ($27.13). You can sample classic Créole specialties, such as stuffed sand or sea crabs, spicy black pudding, a fish blaff, finishing with a coconut flan. However, if you're touring the island, you should note that the restaurant is closed on Wednesday. The air-conditioned beachside bungalows have red-tile floors, light beamed ceilings, and built-in fruitwood headboards, set on a raised level. Baths have tiles and French showers. In high season, a single can stay here, with breakfast and dinner included, for 380F ($58.90) to 480F ($74.40) daily, two persons paying 570F ($88.35) to 670F ($103.85). *In off-season, EP rates are $43 daily in a single, $60 in a double.* Closed early September to mid-October.

As you follow the road south to Trois Rivières you'll come to **Sainte-Luce,** perhaps one of the island's most charming villages. Beautiful beaches surround the town, and it's the site of the Forest Montravail. Continuing, you'll reach Rivière Pilote, quite a large town, and Le Marin, at the bottom of a bay of the same name. From Le Marin, a five-mile drive brings you to—

Sainte-Anne

At the extreme southern tip of Martinique, this is a sleepy little village, with white sand beaches. It opens onto views of the Sainte Lucia Canal, and nearby is the site of the Petrified Savannah Forest. The French call it **Savane des Pétrifications.** It's a field of petrified volcanic boulders in the shape of logs. The eerie, desert-like site, no man's land, is studded with cacti. The region is so barren you'll not want to linger long.

Before reaching Sainte-Anne, on your right as you head south is the route des Boucaniers which brings you to the only hotel on the beach, **Les Boucaniers/Club Méditerranée,** Pointe-Marin, 97227 Sainte-Anne, Martinique, F.W.I. (tel. 011-596/76-72-72). Nestled on a peaceful cove, designed like a Créole village, the club is set on the 48-acre site of a former pirate's hideaway at Buccaneer's Creek. It stands in a forest of coconut palms. In the typical Club Med style, it features around-the-clock activities. Sports such as sailing, waterskiing, and snorkeling are provided for the overall package cost. In a domed two-level building in the heart of the resort, you'll find the dining places, an amusement center, a theater, dance floor, and bar. On one part of the white sandy beach you can go in the buff. A walk along rue du Port (the main street of Club Med) leads to a conically roofed circular Tour du Port, a bar which overlooks the sailboat fleet anchored in the marina. Accommodations are in comfortable, air-conditioned bungalows which are booked for double or triple occupancy, each with twin beds and private shower baths. *In summer and fall, one-week land rates with everything included run from about $590 to $650 per person.* Winter and spring land rates range from around $750 to $1,100 per person weekly (it's most expensive at Christmas, of course). Activities include day-long picnics, basketball, volleyball, softball, water polo, aerobics, stretching, and disco dancing at the opposite end of the village.

Nonguests on a tour of Martinique are welcome to stop in here for a meal, enjoying a large buffet for 200F ($31), with Créole specialties where you help yourself to all you want. Other facilities include the Café du Port, a small café for afternoon drinks and leisure talk, and the Maison Créole, a restaurant annex opening every night with a different menu.

If you want to stay right in Sainte-Anne, I recommend **La Dunette,** 97227 Sainte-Anne, Martinique, F.W.I. (tel. 011-596/76-73-90), a motel-like structure on the water. It's near the Club Med and the white sandy beaches of the Salines as well. It has only 18 rooms, all of which are air-conditioned. The seaside inn is protected by a garden filled with flowers and tropical plants. Mme Marie-Louise Kambona is the owner. In winter, a single ranges in price from 345F ($53.48), with doubles going for 500F ($77.50). *In summer, singles cost 250F ($38.75), and doubles run from 360F ($55.80).* The furnishings are in casual modern, and some of the units are quite small. In the evening guests gather for drinks on the terrace above the sea. Water sports and excursions can be arranged for you, even a jaunt to watch a mongoose fight a snake. The restaurant is closed off-season.

Aux Filets Bleus (tel. 011-596/76-73-42), set on a flat area close to the beach, is a family-run restaurant flanked by canopies and separated from the road by a hedge. Once you've entered, the seaside exposure of the al fresco dining room and its terrace make you feel like you're in an isolated tropical retreat, where the only sound is the splash of waves and the tinkling of ice in glasses. What you think is a glass-covered reflecting pool set into the floor is actually a lobster tank. From it come many specialties, which include several preparations of lobster. Also featured are stuffed crab, fried sea urchins, and many kinds of grilled fish. Meals begin at 150F ($23.25). The Anglio family, the owners, serve lunch from 12:30 to 3 p.m. and dinner from 7:30 to 10 p.m. The place is closed Monday in summer.

At the end of the main street of Sainte-Anne, turn on your left and head for the **Manoir de Beauregard,** 07227 Sainte-Anne, Martinique, F.W.I. (tel. 011-596/76-73-40), an 18th-century manor house where Madame Marcelle Saint-Cyr, the owner, has brought a tasteful, personalized touch. The present relais was built somewhere between 1700 and 1720, and the name probably comes from one of its early owners, a settler named d'Orient, whose daughter married a knight called "de la Touche de Beauregard." While its location is near some of the most beautiful beaches on the island, most guests seem to prefer to splash around the swimming pool. The manoir is a white building under a tile roof, its arches evoking Spain. The interior has been adapted to make it a comfortable place for paying guests, yet the old architectural features have been respected. The lounge hall is not grand—rather, it's furnished in a Créole style, with pieces handmade by local artisans from island-grown timber. Ornate wrought-iron reredos rescued from a cathedral at Fort-de-France serve as room dividers.

Your bedroom will probably have a four-poster bed made from island trees. Each room is air-conditioned, containing a private bath (each one individually decorated). In high season, singles or doubles pay 500F ($77.50) daily for bed and breakfast. *Off-season, the rate is reduced to 395F ($61.23) daily single or double.* The main dining room is an enclosure of a long terrace with handmade chairs. Another room is used mainly for informal breakfasts, although most guests prefer the terrace. Even if you don't stay here, know that many guests make a reservation for meals just to sample the Créole cookery. A table d'hôte luncheon or dinner costs from 100F ($15.50), rising to 200F ($31) à la carte. Food is served daily from 12:30 to 2:30 p.m. and 7:30 to 9:30 p.m.

After passing Le Marin, you reach **Vauclin,** a fishing port and market town that is pre-Columbian. If you have time, stop in at the Chapel of the Holy Virgin, dating from the 18th century. Visitors like to make an excursion to **Mount Vauclin,** the highest point in southern Martinique. There they are rewarded with one of the most scenic panoramas in the West Indies.

THE NORTH LOOP: As we swing north from Fort-de-France, our main targets are Le Carbet, St-Pierre, Montagne Pelée, and Leyritz. However, I'll sandwich in many fascinating stopovers along the way.

From Fort-de-France there are three ways to head north to the Montagne Pelée. The first way is to follow Rt. N4 up to St-Joseph. There you take the left fork for three miles after St-Joseph, turning onto the D15 toward Marigot.

At Morne des Esses, you might want to stop for lunch at **Le Colibri** (The Hummingbird), Allée du Colibri (tel. 011-596/69-32-19), which is the private Créole home of Madame Clotilde Paladino and her daughters. She has been called a sorceress in the kitchen. If the terrace fills up with weekenders from Fort-de-France, you'll be seated on another smaller veranda where you can survey the cooking. The place is decidedly informal, and it exudes the warmth of madame. The typically Créole cookery is first class. For example, you might begin with a calalou soup with crab or a sea urchin tart. Among the dishes I recommend are a buisson d'ecrevisses (crayfish), stuffed pigeon, chicken with coconut, and roast suckling pig. For dessert, try a coconut flan. The tab comes to about 150F ($23.25) for a complete meal. The French wines are inexpensively priced. Hours are noon to 3 p.m. and 7 to 11 p.m. daily except Monday.

Alternative Routes

Another way to Montagne Pelée is to take the N3 through the vegetation-rich Mornes until you reach Le Morne Rouge. This road is known as "Route de la Trace," and is now the center of the Parc Naturel de la Martinique.

A different way to reach Montagne Pelée is to follow Rt. N2 along the coast. Close to Fort-de-France, the first town you reach is **Schoelcher.**

Farther along Rt. N2 you reach Case Pilote, and then Bellefontaine. This portion, along the most frequented tourist route in Martinique—that is, Fort-de-France to St-Pierre—will remind many a traveler of the French Riviera. Bellefontaine is a small fishing village, with boats stretched along the beach. As an architectural curiosity, note the many houses also built in the shape of boats.

Leaving Bellefontaine, a five-mile drive north will deliver you to—

Le Carbet

Columbus landed here in 1502, and the first French settlers arrived in 1635. In 1887 Gauguin lived here for four months before going on to Tahiti. You can stop for a swim at an Olympic-size pool set into the hills, or else look upon flocks of native women scrubbing clothes in a stream.

The **Centre d'Art Musée Paul Gauguin,** Anse Turin, Carbet Martinique (tel. 011-596/77-22-66), is near the beach represented in the artist's two paintings, *Gord de Mer.* The landscape has not changed in 100 years. The museum, housed in a five-room building, commemorates the French artist's stay in Martinique in 1887, with books, prints, letters, and other memorabilia. There are also paintings by René Corail, sculpture by Hector Charpentier, and examples of the artwork of Zaffanella. Of special interest are faïence mosaics made of once-white pieces which were turned pink, maroon, blue, and black in 1902 when the fires of

Montagne Pelée devastated St-Pierre. There are also changing exhibits of works by local artists. The museum is open daily from 10 a.m. to 5 p.m., charging an admission of 10F ($1.55).

If you'd like to have lunch here, try **L'Imprévu,** Grande Anse (tel. 011-596/78-01-25). It would be difficult to find a less formal restaurant than this, although it's a preferred stopover for many residents who return to it every time they're in the area. Vertical sections of bamboo support the palm-frond roof, below which groups of friends play an unusual form of tarot. Unlike many card players, they're usually happy to decipher the symbols for visitors. Everard Miré is the owner. You can order a drink at the stand-up bar or choose a table under the sunshield overlooking the beach. The house specialty is a libation called golden apple *(prune de cythère)* juice. Menu items include accras made with codfish, titiris (a small river fish), blaff (seafood poached and seasoned,) grilled conch, and pigeon with sauce Imprévu. Several dishes require a 24-hour advance notice. Full meals range from 150F ($23.25). Open daily from 10 a.m. to 4 p.m. and 7 p.m. to midnight.

St-Pierre

At the beginning of this century St-Pierre was known as the "Little Paris of the West Indies." Home to 30,000 inhabitants, it was the cultural and economic capital of Martinique. On May 7, 1902, the citizens read in their daily newspaper that "Montagne Pelée does not present any more risk to the population than Vesuvius does to the Neapolitans."

However, on May 8, at 8 a.m., the southwest side of Montagne Pelée exploded, raining down fire and lava. At 8:02 a.m. all 30,000 inhabitants were dead —that is, all except one. A convict in his underground cell was spared, saved by the thickness of the wall. When islanders reached the site, the convict was paroled, leaving Martinique to tour in Barnum and Bailey's circus.

St-Pierre never recovered its past splendor. Now it could be called the Pompeii of the West Indies. Ruins of the church, the theater, and some other buildings can be seen along the coast.

The **Musée Volcanologique** (tel. 011-596/77-15-16) was created by an American volcanologist Franck Alvard Perret, who turned the museum over to the city in 1933. Here in pictures and relics dug from the debris you can trace the story of what happened to St-Pierre. Dug from the lava is a clock that stopped at the exact moment the volcano erupted. The museum is open from 9 a.m. to 12:30 p.m. and 3 to 5 p.m., charging an entrance fee of 5F (78¢).

A good luncheon stop is **La Factorerie,** Centre de Formation Rurale (tel. 011-596/77-12-53). Many patrons of this restaurant, which was built by a young people's co-op, make it a point to stop in the stone church a few paces away either before or after a meal. Both buildings are set near the top of a steep hill high above the town, with a view that sweeps out over a well-kept lawn, a forest, and the sea. In an al fresco setting under a beamed ceiling, you'll be able to choose Créole specialties such as grilled fish with spicy sauce, fish soup, brochette of conch, grilled lobster, accras of shrimp, and the local recipes for blaff and chicken colombo. Set meals are offered for 90F ($13.95) and up. The restaurant is open only for lunch daily from noon to 2:30 p.m.

From St-Pierre, you can continue along the coast north to—

Le Prêcheur

Once the home of Madame de Maintenon, mistress of Louis XIV, Le Prêcheur is the last village along the northern coast of Martinique. Here you can see hot springs of volcanic origin and the **Tombeau des Caraïbes** (Tomb of the Carib Indians), where, according to legend, the collective suicide of many West

Indian natives took place after they returned from a fishing expedition and found their homes pillaged by the French.

The best dining in the area is at **La Belle Capresse** (tel. 011-596/53-02-90), a small, open-air restaurant across the road from the water but within hearing distance of the surf. This may be a *petit* restaurant, but it has a *grande* cuisine. Meals cost from 150F ($23.25) and are likely to include filet of fish poached in coconut milk, a crab soufflé, or a fluffy mound made with sea urchins. Crab is also served stuffed as a main course, and you can order lobster prepared three different ways, fricassée of conch, or pork with pineapple. Service is from noon to 5 p.m. and 7 to 10 p.m. daily except Sunday night and Wednesday.

Montagne Pelée

A spectacular and winding road takes you through a tropical rain forest. The curves are of the hairpin variety, and the road is twisty and not always kept in good shape. However, you're rewarded with tropical flowers, baby ferns, plumed bamboo, and valleys so deeply green you'll think you're wearing cheap sunglasses.

You reach the village of Morne Rouge, right at the foot of Montagne Pelée, a popular vacation spot for Martiniquais. From there on, a narrow and unreliable road brings you to a level of 2,500 feet above sea level, 1,600 feet under the round summit of the volcano that destroyed St-Pierre. Montagne Pelée itself rises 4,656 feet above sea level.

If you're a trained mountain climber, you can scale the peak, reaching Grand Rivière—that is, if you don't mind four or five hours of hiking. Realize that this is a mountain, that rain is frequent, and that temperatures drop very low. Tropical growth often hides deep crevices in the earth, and there are other dangers. That's why if you're really serious about this climb, you should hire an experienced guide. As for the volcano, its death-dealing rain in 1902 apparently satisfied it, at least for the time being!

Upon your descent from Montagne Pelée, you can drive down to Ajoupa Bouillon, which likes to describe itself, perhaps with justification, as the most beautiful town in Martinique. Abounding in flowers and shrubbery with bright yellow and red leaves, this little village is the site of the remarkable **Gorges de la Falaise.** These are mini-canyons on the Falaise River up which one can travel to reach a waterfall. Ajoupa-Bouillon also makes a good lunch stop.

Abri Restaurant (tel. 011-596/53-32-13), at the northern terminus of the village, is housed in a large cement building not unlike an aircraft hangar, whose rough edges are softened by potted plants. Originally a cockfight stadium, this is the domain of Ms. Hardy Dessources. Meals cost from 200F ($31) and might begin with a glass of freshly squeezed sugarcane juice. Lunch only is served, from noon to 3 p.m. daily. The kitchen is known for its fricassée of crayfish, which is served to you and two or three others in a large bowl with herbs. You must shell the fish, then dip it into the sauce. It's a messy—and expensive—affair. You might prefer instead to order fish stuffed with sea urchins and cooked in coconut fronds. To begin, you can order *calalou* soup with crab or many kinds of accras, ranging from sea urchins to pumpkin.

You can continue east toward the coast, reaching the town of Basse-Pointe in northeast Martinique. A mile before Basse-Pointe, turn left and follow a road that goes deep into sugarcane country to—

Leyritz

Here you can explore the best restored plantation in Martinique, perhaps stopping by for lunch.

Hôtel Plantation de Leyritz, 97218 Basse-Pointe, Martinique, F.W.I. (tel. 011-596/78-53-92), the pride of Martinique, was built around 1700 by a plantation owner, Bordeaux-born Michel de Leyritz. It was the site of the "swimming pool summit meeting" in 1974 between Presidents Gerald Ford and Valéry Giscard d'Estaing. It's still a working banana plantation, which (since 1970) has been restored by Charles and Yveline de Lucy de Fossarieu to its original and authentic character. There are 16 acres of tropical gardens, and at the core is an 18th-century stone great house. From the grounds, the view sweeps across the Atlantic taking in fearsome Montagne Pelée. The owners have kept the best of the old, such as the rugged stone walls (20 inches thick), the beamed ceilings, and the tile and flagstone floors. They have created a cozy setting of mahogany tables, overstuffed sofas, and gilt mirrors. A few of the outbuildings, former slave quarters with bamboo roofs and stone walls, now house guests, and new ones have been added. I prefer the units—ten in all—in the manor, because they are probably the most attractive, certainly the most authentic. You can also stay in the carriage house across the lawn. Don't expect luxury—that's not the style here. In winter, guests can stay here on the continental plan, paying 500F ($77.50) to 800F ($124) daily in a single and 630F ($97.65) to 940F ($145.70) in a double. *In off-season, with breakfast included, singles cost 368F ($57.04) to 560F ($86.80) daily, and doubles go for 420F ($65.10) to 630F ($97.65).*

The dining room is in a rum distillery, incorporating the fresh spring water running down from the hillside. Eating here is dramatic at night, and the cuisine is authentically Créole. Afternoon tea or apéritifs are served in the salon, with flickering lights from a 19th-century bronze and globed chandelier. You sit on Martinique rockers. On the surrounding walls are gilt-framed portraits, plus scenic views of the island and Paris. Tour bus crowds predominate at lunch. Most guests visit just for lunch, heading south for the night. If that's the case with you, expect to pay from 120F ($18.60) to have lunch here. On my most recent rounds, I enjoyed a first-class Créole lunch, which was really like a dinner. The main course was grilled chicken covered in coconut milk sauce, along with *oussous,* a freshwater crayfish which came in a herb sauce. Vegetables consisted of sautéed breadfruit and sautéed bananas. Dinners go for 175F ($27.13) and up. Lunch is served from 12:30 to 2 p.m., and dinner, from 7:30 to 9 p.m., seven days a week. Dinner is more elaborate, with both French and Créole dishes, including duck with pineapple, a colombo of lamb, and *boudin* (blood pudding) Créole.

Basse-Pointe

At the northernmost point on the island, Basse-Pointe is a land of pineapple and banana plantation fields, covering the Atlantic-side slopes of Mount Pelée volcano.

Chez Mally Edjam (tel. 011-596/78-51-18) is a local legend. Many visitors prefer to drive all the way from Pointe du Bout to dine with her instead of at the Leyritz Plantation. Of course, never arrive without calling for a reservation—it's like visiting a private home, which is what it is. You sit out on one of a handful of tables on her side porch. You can also eat in the main dining room. Grandmotherly Mally Edjam is busy in the kitchen, turning out her Créole delicacies. She knows how to do all the dishes for which the island is known: stuffed land crab with a hot seasoning, small pieces of conch in a tart shell, and a classic colombo de porc, the Créole version of pork curry. She is known also for her lobster vinaigrette, her papaya soufflé (which must be ordered in advance), and her highly original confitures, which are tiny portions of fresh island fruits, such as pineapple and guava, that have been preserved in a vanilla syrup. Expect to spend from 170F ($26.35) for lunch, which is generally served from noon to 3 p.m. seven days a week.

Grand Rivière

After Basse-Pointe, the town you reach on your northward trek is Grand Rivière. From there, you must turn back. Before doing so, you may want to stop at **Chez Vava,** Boulevard de Gaulle (tel. 011-596/55-72-72), a good restaurant right at the entrance to the town. With its bright-orange tiling, it's easy to spot. You'll also find plenty of space to park your car. The style is like a simple country inn. It is actually the *maison privé* of Laurence Viellot. For 150F ($23.25), you can order a tomato salad, broiled fish with rice, and a dessert. À la carte menu items include Créole soup, a blaff of sea urchins, lobster, and various colombos. An old rum punch, a specialty of the house, is also offered. If you order the most elaborate items on the menu, your tab could climb to 175F ($27.13). Hours are from 7 a.m. to 6 p.m. daily.

Lorrain

Lorrain, called the "kingdom of bananas," is a charming hamlet on the northeastern coast, but it might not keep your attention for very long. That is, unless you knew about the restaurant recommended below.

Relais des Îles, rue Chaumereau-Lamotte (tel. 011-596/53-43-85), is one of the least known restaurants on the island. Its lack of fame is undeserved, since its Créole food is among the best in Martinique. It's as if it's just awaiting discovery by the major food magazines. It's housed in an old Martiniquais house with shutters, clapboard siding, gingerbread fretwork, and a large veranda looking down on a curve in the road near the center of town. Antoine and Gabrielle Duventru are the hospitable owners of this refreshingly simple place, where specialties vary with the availability of ingredients and where much of the art depends on the inspiration Mme Duventru might feel at the moment. Since she was born within a few miles of this spot, she's been able to pick up many gems of culinary lore. Your meal might include pâté en pot (which, despite its name, is a kind of lamb soup), soup with crabs, six kinds of soufflé and a unique and original recipe of stuffed cucumbers and onions. Other possibilities are four kinds of tarts (made with sea urchins, onions, crayfish, or conch), stuffed crab, and a soupe d'habitants made with such vegetables as cabbage, leeks, onions, celery, and locally grown leaves. Set meals cost from 75F ($11.63), while à la carte menus cost from 150F ($23.25). The restaurant is open every day from 6 a.m. till after dinner. Reservations are a good idea.

Sainte-Marie

Heading south along the coastal road, you bypass Marigot, coming to a sightseeing stop in the little town of Sainte-Marie where you can visit the attraction previewed below.

Le Musée du Rhum Saint James, at the Saint James Distillery (tel. 011-596/69-30-02), displays engravings, antique tools and machines, and other exhibits tracing the history of sugarcane and rum from 1765 to the present. Guided tours of the museum also include a visit to the distillery and storage area, and a session of rum tasting. Hours are 9 a.m. to 6 p.m. Monday to Friday, to 1 p.m. on Saturday and Sunday.

Trinité

If you head back south along the coastal route, you'll pass through the small village of Trinité on the Atlantic side of Martinique. It would hardly merit a stopover were it not for the following hotel.

Saint-Aubin Hôtel, 97220 Trinité, Martinique, F.W.I. (tel. 011-596/69-34-77) is one of the loveliest inns in the Caribbean basin. A former restaurant owner, Normandy-born Guy Forêt has sunk his fortune into restoring this three-story Victorian house and turning it into a three-star hostelry. Painted a vivid pink with fancy gingerbread, it was once a plantation house, sitting on a hillside above sugarcane fields and Trinité's bay. A long excursion from Pointe du Bout or Fort-de-France, it would make the perfect luncheon stopover or the ideal retreat for a vacation in Martinique. The location is 14½ miles from the airport, 19 miles from Fort-de-France, and 2 miles from the seaside village of Trinité itself. There are 800 yards of private beach as a further enticement, plus a swimming pool on the grounds. All rooms are air-conditioned, with wall-to-wall carpeting and modern (not antique) furniture. There are some family rooms as well. After dinner you can sit on the veranda on the first and second floors, enjoying life as lived long ago. Rooms have a view of either the garden or the sea. In winter, two persons can stay here for 450F ($69.75) daily, with breakfast included, while singles pay 320F ($49.60). *In summer, the charge is $43 daily in a single, $60 in a double.* The restaurant and bar are reserved for use of hotel guests.

South of Trinité, you might consider stopping for dinner outside the little town of—

Le Robert

Nestled in the curve of a sumptuous bay with many little islands, Le Robert is a prime center for fish-breeding.

Tong-Yen, sur la route du Robert (tel. 011-596/65-17-89), lies right outside town on the main road south to François. Its chef prepares a savory Vietnamese and French cuisine, and the restaurant is one of the better bargains on the island, with meals costing from 125F ($19.38). The specialty is lacquered duck, but you can also try many kinds of shrimp, including with a hot pepper sauce, or sole with ginger. Hours are from noon to 3 p.m. and 7 to 10:30 p.m. daily except Sunday night and Monday. The restaurant is in a low-slung pink building across a flowery courtyard.

Le François

The fertile lands of this essentially agricultural community have been improved by an irrigation system from Manzo dam. The town is known for its off-shore shoals, many little islands, and white sandy sandbars, all making for good sea trips.

At Morne d'Acajou near Le François on the Atlantic coast, the **Clement Rum Company** (tel. 011-596/54-79-59) has been revitalized, with an attractive little rum-tasting room and a historical exhibit. The plantation house, called Domaine d'Acajou, has been restored. Hours are from 9 a.m. to 5 p.m. Monday to Saturday, to 4 p.m. Sunday.

Le François also enjoys a reputation for cookery, which is best at **Club Nautique,** Pointe Bateau (tel. 011-596/54-31-00). Every morning you can see the owner, Jacqueline Amalis, out checking over the early-morning catch. Her keen eye selects only the best. To get to the club, you cross the main street, heading for the sea. Stay along the shoreline until you reach Nautique. Before you order, you can sample various rum punches at a bar on the terrace. Then you descend a few steps to the simple but scrubbed-clean dining room. The food is very fresh, the kitchen clean. You can even dip your feet in water if you've just emerged from the sands. Set menus are offered for 130F ($20.15) and 220F ($34.10), which include such delectable items as sea urchin fritters, sweet clams, shellfish, lobster, or broiled fish. Meals are served from noon to 4 p.m. and 7 to 9:30 p.m. seven days a week.

Lunch might be preceded by a boat trip to the nearby coral reefs where Joséphine used to bathe. Boat excursions leave every day at 11 a.m.

After dining in Le François, you can return to Fort-de-France by passing through Le Lamentin, or you can go to the Pointe du Bout route through Ducos and Rivière Salée.

THE SPORTING LIFE: The Martiniquais often don't work at their sports as hard as many North Americans do. Yet they have an active sports program.

Scuba-diving, snorkeling, fishing, and waterskiing can be enjoyed all along the coastline. Golf clubs are at your disposal in all the first-class hotels, where prices are obtainable (tariffs vary considerably, depending on the duration and season).

Tennis

This game is widely played on the island, and each large hotel has courts. Residents play free during the day, and night games usually require a 40F ($6.20) surcharge for lighting for 30 minutes. Nonguests are faced with a playing-time charge that could range from $8 to $10 per half hour.

Your best bet is to play at one of the three courts on the grounds of **Golf de l'Impératrice Joséphine** at Trois-Îlets (tel. 011-596/68-32-81), a five-minute drive from one of the major hotels at Pointe du Bout. The setting here is one of the most beautiful in Martinique.

Scuba-Diving and Snorkeling

Scuba-divers come here to explore the St-Pierre shipwrecks sunk in the 1902 volcano eruption and the Diamond Rock caves and walls. Small scuba centers operate at many of the hotels.

Snorkeling equipment is usually available free to hotel guests, who quickly learn that coral, fish, and ferns abound in the waters around the Pointe du Bout hotels.

To the south, **Bathy's Club** in the Hôtel Méridien (tel. 011-596/66-00-00), is the scuba center for Pointe du Bout, serving neighboring hotels Bakoua and PLM Azur Carayou. Daily dive trips leave from the Méridien pier. Prices include equipment rental, transportation, guide, and drinks on board. Dives are conducted twice daily, from 8 a.m. to noon and 2 to 6 p.m., and full-day charters can be arranged. The dive shop on Méridien's beach stocks everything from weight belts and tanks to partial wetsuits and underwater cameras.

Buccaneer's Creek/Club Med (tel. 011-596/76-72-72) has long made scuba a part of its weekly packages, costing from $550 to $1,200, depending on the week. The dive school goes to the reefs around Ste-Anne at the southern tip of Martinique, where the club is situated.

Two other Martinique hotels also have scuba centers. La Batalière (tel. 011-596/61-49-49) houses the **Tropicasud International Diving Center,** headed by a fully licensed and certified divemaster. The boat leaves directly from the hotel.

Facing historic Diamond Rock off the southwestern coast is Diamant-Novotel (tel. 011-596/76-42-42), which boasts scuba facilities at **Pointe de la Chery,** where a resort conducted in the swimming pool for beginning divers is free. After that, a one-tank dive costs 200F ($31), a package of three one-tank dives goes for 500F ($77.50).

Windsurfing

This is the most popular sport in the French West Indies. Equipment and lessons are available at all hotel water-sports operators, especially the **Hôtel**

Méridien (tel. 011-596/66-00-00), where the cost is 85F ($13.18) for a one-hour rental.

Waterskiing
This is available at every beach near the large hotels, the cost about $10 for 10- to 15-minute rides.

The Beaches
The beaches south of Fort-de-France are white, while the northern strands are composed mostly of gray sand. Outstanding in the south is the **Plage des Salines,** near Ste-Anne, with palm trees and miles of white sand, and **Diamant,** with the landmark Diamond Rock offshore. Swimming on the Atlantic coast is for experts only, except at **Cap Chevalier** and **Presqu'île de la Caravelle Nature Preserve.** Public beaches do not as a rule have changing cabins or showers. Some hotels charge nonguests for the use of changing and beach facilities, and request a deposit for rental of towels.

Hiking
Inexpensive and guided excursions in which tourists can participate are organized by the personnel of the Parc Régional de la Martinique year round. Special excursions can be arranged on request of small groups by getting in touch with the **Parc Naturel Régional de la Martinique,** Caserne Bouillé, Fort-de-France (tel. 011-596/73-19-30). A folder is available at the Martinique Tourist Office.

The Presqu'île de la Caravelle Nature Preserve, a well-protected peninsula jutting into the Atlantic Ocean, has safe beaches and well-marked trails to the ruins of historic Château Debuc and through tropical wetlands.

Serious hiking excursions to climb Montagne Pelée and explore the Gorges de la Falaise or the thick coastal rain forest between Grand'Rivière and Le Prêcheur are organized with local guides at certain times of the year by the park staff.

Camping
Camping is permitted in some places, including in the mountains and forests and on many beaches. It is advisable to check with the local mayor's office or property owner before setting up camp. Campsites are usually basic, although comfortable camps with cold showers and toilets are on the southeast coast at Macabou; at Ste-Luce, Le Marin, and Ste-Anne on the south coast; and Anse-à-l'Âne near Trois-Îlets. One of the best spots is **Courbaril Camping** Anse-à-l'Âne, 97229 Trois-Îlets, Martinique, F.W.I. (tel. 011-596/68-32-30). Separated from the public beach by a fence, this campground jumbles together spaces for tents with some three dozen unpretentious, no-frills bungalows. If you bring your own tent, you can use the showers and toilets for 33F ($5.12) per day for two people. No tents are rented. Many guests opt for the cramped accommodations in the bungalows where doubles pay 131F ($20.31) daily for units without air conditioning, 160F for those with air conditioning. Air-conditioned triples cost 185F ($28.68) per day. Next door, an indoor/outdoor restaurant and bar, the Nid Tropical, serves fast food and beer throughout the day.

Horseback Riding
Ranch Jack, Anse d'Arlet (tel. 011-596/68-63-97) offers daily horseback rides for both experienced and novice riders, at a cost of 270F ($41.85) per half day. This is an ideal way to discover both botanical and geographical Martinique.

They'll arrange for you to be picked up at your hotel and delivered back after your outing. Créole horses are used for the rides.

Another horseback riding center, **La Cavale,** is near the Diamant-Novotel (tel. 011-596/76-22-94). It boasts more than a dozen horses and offers a wide range of activities, including introductory lessons, manège riding, walks, and games for beginners and children. Experienced riders can try the obstacle course, cross-country riding, and horseback sightseeing excursions. Three hours of riding on the beach or on one of the mountain paths costs 230F ($35.65) per person. The horses rest on Monday and Wednesday.

Golf

The famous golf course designer, Robert Trent Jones, visited Martinique and left behind the 18-hole **Golf de l'Impératrice Joséphine** at Trois-Îlets (tel. 011-596/68-32-81), a five-minute, one-mile drive from the leading resort area of Pointe du Bout and about 18 miles from Fort-de-France. The course unfolds its greens from the birthplace of Empress Joséphine for whom it is named, across rolling hills with scenic vistas down to the sea. Amenities include a pro shop, a bar, a restaurant, and three tennis courts. Greens fees are 180F ($27.90) per day for one person for 18 holes.

Sailing

This is a big pastime in Martinique. It's also a big cost unless there are enough in your party. Only a select few can afford yacht charters, either crewed or bareboat. If you want to see the waters around Martinique, it's better to go on one of the sailboat excursions in the bay of Fort-de-France and the southeast coast of the island.

A 79-foot ketch, **Captain Cap,** sails regularly from the Méridien Hôtel at Pointe du Bout. Reservations can be made by calling any local travel agent or at most hotels. A full-day excursion with lunch is offered, and no more than 60 passengers go out at a time. Also, sunset cruises are scheduled as well. The day excursion is on Wednesday and Friday, with a 9 a.m. departure, returning at 5 p.m. The cost is 320F ($49.60) per person. The sunset cruise, with music and rum punch, is on Friday at 5 p.m., returning at 7:30 p.m., at a cost of 80F ($12.40) per person.

A Look at Marine Life

L'Aquascope, at the Marina at Pointe du Bout (tel. 011-596/68-36-09), offers visitors a skindiver's view of marine life at a cost of 80F ($12.40). Reservations can be made at the boat dock for the trip, which lasts less than an hour. In a genuine helicopter cockpit, one is taken along the ocean floor for a view of coral colonies, starfish schools, sponges, and sea urchins. You ride in armchair comfort while a fantastic underwater world unfolds around you. *L'Aquascope* is one of the few vessels of its kind in the world.

Deep-Sea Fishing

Increased facilities for deep-sea fishing have been developed in Martinique because of the demand created by fine catches of tuna, barracuda, dolphin, kingfish, and bonito. Most hotels will help make arrangements for the sport if given a day or two advance notice, and the **Meridien Hotel,** for example, has daily trips.

Bathy's Club at the Meridien (tel. 011-596/66-00-00) sends out its 37-foot *Egg Harbor* every day at 6 a.m. for a 3½-hour trip. The excursions, primarily for recreational fishermen, cost 1,200F ($186) for the boat, including gear and breakfast. Two trolling rigs allow four persons to fish at one time, which the boat can accommodate up to six. Barracuda is the most common catch on these trips.

The Mongoose vs. the Snake

Some people say you've not really seen Martinique until you've attended a match between a mongoose and a snake. Said to have been imported by East Indian workers, this is a to-the-death struggle. If you attend such an event, you're to remain deadly still. Even lighting a cigarette is supposed to break the concentration of the combatants. Incidentally, the mongoose almost always wins. Some taxi drivers or small innkeepers on the island will tell you where to go to watch this "sport." Frankly, I prefer to skip it.

AFTER DARK: Everybody who goes to Martinique wants to see the show performed by **Les Grands Ballets de la Martiniquais,** a bouncy group of about two dozen dancers, along with musicians, singers, and choreographers. Many members of the troupe look no more than 17 years old. Launched in the early '60s, this group performs the traditional dances of Martinique and has been acclaimed in both Europe and the States. With a swoosh of gaily striped skirts, a gentle swaying of hips, and clever acting, dancers capture all the exuberance of the island's soul.

The group has toured abroad with great success, but they perform best on home ground. Dressed in traditional costumes—madras headdresses, gold earrings, lace blouses, silk scarves, billowing skirts, and crisply starched petticoats—the island girls are led by their young men through such dances as the spirited mazurka, which was brought from the ballrooms of Europe, and the exotic béguine. The Grands Ballets is considered one of the best ensembles in the Caribbean.

Cole Porter, incidentally, did not invent the béguine. It's a Martinique dance—some would call it a way of life. Instead of having me try to explain it, it's best to see it. Or dance it, if you think you can.

The group presents tableaux that tell of jealous brides and faithless husbands, demanding overseers and toiling cane cutters. There's a dreamy "Créole Waltz" and an erotic "Calenda," danced to the beat of an African drum. The "Parasol Dance" and "Carnival" add sparkle to the performance, and the show may end with the last mentioned dance or with "Adieu Foulard, Adieu Madras," a tale of a Créole girl's hopeless love for a French naval officer who must leave her.

Les Grands Ballets perform Monday at the Hôtel Diamant-Novotel, Wednesday at the PLM Azur Carayou, and Friday at the Bakoua Beach, but this can vary so check locally. In addition, the troupe gives mini-performances aboard visiting cruise ships. The Ballets Martiniquais can be seen Thursday at the Méridien Trois-Îlets and Saturday at the Hôtel La Batelière. To enjoy a buffet dinner and a ballet show at one of the hotels costs from 250F ($38.75).

There's also a lot of nightlife revolving around the four major hotels at Pointe du Bout—**Bakoua Beach, PLM Azur Carayou, Méridien Trois-Îlets,** and **PLM Azur La Pagerié.** As mentioned, on certain nights you can watch Les Ballets Martiniquais. In addition, musicians, some of them quite young, play nightly in the larger hotels.

Hotel guests are allowed in free at three of the nightclubs, **Vesou** in the PLM Azur Carayou, **Vonvon** in the Méridien Trois-Îlets, and **Hutte** in Bakoua. If you're not a resident of one of the hotels, you'll be charged an entrance fee of around 80F ($12.40), including your first drink. Most of these clubs are open nightly except Sunday from 10:30 p.m. It's hard to say which club is the best, as a mainly young crowd wanders from one to the other on a warm night. My preference, however, is for **Vesou.**

The **Casino Trois-Îlets,** on the premises of the Méridien Trois-Îlets, Pointe du Bout (tel. 011-596/66-00-30) is open every night from 9 a.m. to 3 a.m. Here you can try to win the cost of your vacation by playing roulette, blackjack, or chemin-de-fer. Some form of identification with picture is required at the entrance. You present it along with 55F ($8.53).

You might also try your luck at the **Hôtel La Batelière Casino** (tel. 011-596/61-49-49), Schoelcher, outside Fort-de-France. Not as glamorous as Las Vegas, it attracts a leisure crowd who play roulette, French chemin-de-fer, craps, or blackjack. An identity card such as a passport is required. The entrance fee is 58F ($8.99), and hours are 9 p.m. to 3 a.m.

I'd advise you to spend your nights in the big hotel clubs. There are other native clubs frequented by the Martiniquais. However, some "incidents" have been reported when tourists strayed in. If you insist on going to one of these clubs "to see the real béguine," I suggest you go there with some local friends, if you've made any, who know the island.

2. GUADELOUPE

"The time is near, I believe, when thousands of American tourists will come to spend the winter among the beautiful countryside and friendly people of Guadeloupe." Or so Theodore Roosevelt accurately predicted on February 21, 1916. Guadeloupe isn't the same place it was when the Rough Rider himself rode through, but the natural beauty he witnessed, and certainly the people, are still there to be enjoyed.

Guadeloupe is part of the Lesser Antilles, lying about 200 miles north of Martinique, closer to the United States than its sister island. In addition to tourism, sugar production and rum beef up the local economy. The total surface of Guadeloupe and its satellite islands is close to 700 square miles. There is a lot of similarity in climate, animals, and vegetation between Martinique and Guadeloupe. So no one is surprised coming from one island to the other.

Guadeloupe is, in fact, formed by two different islands, separated by a narrow seawater channel, known as Rivière Salée. **Grande Terre,** the eastern island, is typical of charm of the Antilles, with its rolling hills and sugar plantations.

On the other hand, **Basse Terre,** to the west, is a rugged mountainous island, dominated by the 4,800-foot volcano La Soufrière, which is still alive. Its mountains are covered with tropical forests, impenetrable in many places. Bananas grown on plantations are the main crop. The island is ringed by beautiful beaches which have attracted much tourism.

Among the celebrities from the island, Saint-John Perse (alias Alexis Saint Leger) was born in St. Leger des Feuilles, a small islet in Pointe-à-Pitre bay, in 1887. The French diplomat was better known as a poet, the Nobel Prize winner in 1960. During all his life he wrote a constant song to the beauty of his island.

Guadeloupe was first called *Karukera* by the Arawaks, meaning "the island of the beautiful waters." On November 3, 1493, Columbus landed, naming the island *Santa Maria de Guadelupe de Estramaduros,* which in time became Guadeloupe. The island's modern history is very much related to that of Martinique. Guadeloupe was settled by Sir Lienard de l'Olive and Sir Duplessis d'Ossonville, who were detached from Martinique by its commander, Belain d'Esnambuc. These men arrived with a group of some 500 settlers on June 18, 1635.

The British seized the island in 1759. They gave it back, but took it once more in 1794. A mulatto, Victor Hugues, attacked them with his revolutionary army of blacks and whites, but he faded after Napoléon came to power, allowing the British to move in again in 1810. The island returned to French hands in 1815.

For 100 years Guadeloupe was a dependency of Martinique. In 1946 Guadeloupe became a full-fledged French *département* (the French equivalent of

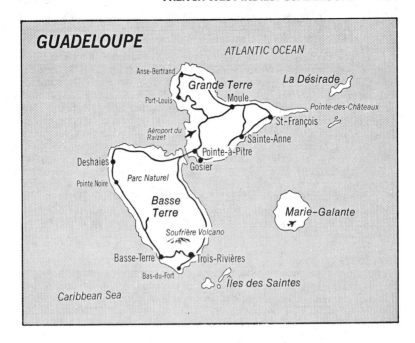

an American state), and its people are citizens of France with all the privileges therein.

GETTING THERE: Information on getting to Guadeloupe is the same as for getting to Martinique. See the "Getting There" section on Martinique, earlier in this chapter.

GETTING AROUND: You'll find **taxis** when you arrive at the airport, but no limousines or buses waiting to serve you. After 9 p.m., until 7 a.m., cabbies are legally entitled to charge you 40% more. In practice, either day or night, the taxi drivers charge you whatever they think the market will bear. Always agree on the price before getting in.

Buses

As in Martinique, there is no rail service. But buses link almost every hamlet to Pointe-à-Pitre. However, you may need to know some high school French to use the system. From Pointe-à-Pitre you can catch one of these jitney vans, either at the Gare Routière de Bergevin if you're going to Basse Terre, or the Gare Routière de Mortenol if Grande Terre is your destination. The cost, for example, from Pointe-à-Pitre to Basse-Terre is only 30F ($4.65).

Car Rentals

Your access to a car enables you to circumnavigate Basse Terre, which many aficionados claim is one of the loveliest drives in the Caribbean. Car-rental kiosks at the airport are usually open to meet international flights. Rental rates at local companies might appear less expensive, depending on the agency, but several readers have complained of mechanical problems and bill irregularities. If you want to be sure to get a car when you arrive, it's often best to reserve one in advance through the nationwide toll-free numbers of North America's largest car-rental companies: **Hertz, Avis,** and **Budget,** each of which is represented on the island.

Budget is consistently the least expensive. The cheapest rates at all three companies are awarded to renters who reserve their cars at least two business days before pickup. Budget's least expensive vehicle, a four-passenger Toyota Starlet with manual transmission and without air conditioning, costs $180 per week, plus a whopping 14% tax imposed by the French government. Avis and Hertz charge $241 and $282 for similar cars, plus tax. If you require air conditioning, Budget again offers the best rental. Its cheapest car is $265 per week, as opposed to $334.37 at Hertz and $366 at Avis. Younger drivers, however, need be only 21 before renting from Hertz, whereas they must be 22 at Budget and 25 at Avis.

All three companies offer additional insurance. Budget, for example, charges an extra $6.65 per day, but you're protected in case you have an accident. For more information, call Budget toll free at 800/527-0700, Hertz at 800/654-3131, and Avis at 800/331-2112. Drive on the right, and drive defensively.

Driving is on the right side, and there are several gas stations along the main routes.

Taxi Tours

If you're traveling with people or imaginative in putting a party together, it's best to sightsee by taxi. Usually the concierge at your hotel will help you make this arrangement. Depending on the size of car you order, you can expect to pay from 700F ($108.50) a day for this service. Split four ways, the tab is much easier to handle, of course, but it's cheaper to rent a car.

PRACTICAL FACTS: An important note to remember is that the people of Guadeloupe do not like to be photographed unless they are camera-ready in their best clothes. Tourists should always ask permission before photographing anybody, and don't be surprised if the answer is a flat and resounding no.
  Currency: The official monetary unit is the French franc, and some shops will take U.S. dollars.
  Customs: Items for personal use, "in limited quantities," can be brought in tax-free.
  Documents: For stays of less than 21 days, proof of identity is needed, plus a return or ongoing plane ticket. For a longer stay, a valid passport is required.
  Drugstores: The pharmacies carry French medicines, and most over-the-counter American drugs have French equivalents. Prescribed medicines can be filled if the traveler has a prescription.
  Electricity: The local electricity is 220 volts AC, 50 cycles, which means you'll need an adapter. Some of the big resorts lend these to guests, but don't count on it. One hotel I know had only six in stock, and a long, long waiting list (and of the six, two were broken!). Clients should take their own.
  Information: The major tourist office in Guadeloupe is called the **Office Départemental du Tourisme,** corner of rue Schoelcher and Délgrés, in Pointe-à-Pitre (tel. 011-590/82-09-30).
  Language: The official language is French, and Créole is the unofficial second language. As in Martinique, English is spoken only in the major tourist centers, rarely in the countryside.
  Medical care: There are five modern hospitals in Guadeloupe, plus 23 clinics. Hotels and the Guadeloupe tourist office can assist in locating English-speaking doctors.
  Police: If you have a police emergency, call 011-590/82-00-05 in Pointe-à-Pitre or 011-590/81-11-55 in Basse-Terre.

Taxes: A departure tax, required on scheduled flights, is included in the air fares.

Telephone: To telephone Guadeloupe from North America, the area code is 011-590, and then you dial the digits of the number on the island. However, when you're here, you do not dial the area code, only the six-digit local number.

Time: Guadeloupe **time** is one hour later than Eastern Standard Time (when it's 6 a.m. in New York, it's 7 a.m. in Guadeloupe). When Eastern Daylight Saving Time is in effect, Guadeloupe and New York keep the same clocks.

Tips and service: Hotels and restaurants usually add a 10% to 15% **service charge,** and most taxi drivers who own their own cars do not expect a **tip.** Surprisingly, neither do hotel porters.

Tobacco: American tobacco and cigarettes are available at hotel shops, and Guadeloupe also has some **café-tabacs,** selling foreign cigarettes.

POINTE-À-PITRE: The port and chief city of Guadeloupe, Pointe-à-Pitre lies on Grande Terre. Unfortunately, it doesn't have the old-world charm of Fort-de-France in Martinique. What beauty it does possess is often hidden behind closed doors.

Having been burned and rebuilt so many times, the port has emerged as a town lacking in character, with modern apartments and condominiums forming a high-rise backdrop over jerry-built shacks and industrial suburbs. The rather narrow streets are jammed during the day with a colorful crowd creating a permanent traffic tie-up. However, at sunset the town becomes quiet again and almost deserted.

The real point of interest in Pointe-à-Pitre is shopping. It's best to visit the town in the morning—you can easily cover it in a half day—taking in the waterfront and outdoor market (the latter is livelier in the early hours).

Open-air stalls surround the **covered market** at the corner of rue Frébault and rue Thiers. Here you can discover the many fruits, spices, and vegetables which are enjoyable just to view if not to taste. A deep fragrance of a Créole market permeates the place. In madras turbans local Créole women make deals over their strings of fire-red pimientos. The bright fabrics they wear compete with the rich tones of oranges, papayas, bananas, mangoes, and pineapples. The sounds of an African-accented French fill the air.

The town center is the Place de la Victoire, a park shaded by palm trees and poincianas. Here you'll see some old sandbox trees said to have been planted by Victor Hugues, the mulatto who organized a revolutionary army of both whites and blacks to establish a dictatorship. In this square he kept a guillotine busy, and the death-dealing instrument still stood there (but not in use) until modern times.

Sloops that travel through the islands, as well as fishing schooners, tie up at the old port, La Darse. Farther out, Caribbean cruise ships drop anchor to allow their passengers to go on shopping expeditions. We might as well follow suit.

Shopping

Frankly, if you're going on to Fort-de-France in Martinique, I suggest you skip a shopping tour of Pointe-à-Pitre, as you'll find far more merchandise there, and perhaps friendlier service. However, if you're not, I'd recommend the following shops, some of which line the rue Frébault.

Of course, your best buys will be anything French—perfumes from Chanel, silk scarves from Hermès, cosmetics from Dior, crystal from Lalique and Baccarat. I've found (but not often) some of these items discounted as much as 30% lower than Stateside or Canadian prices.

Shops, which most often will accept U.S. dollars, give these discounts only to purchases made by traveler's check. Purchases are duty free if brought directly from store to airplane. In addition to the places below, there are also duty-free shops at Raizet Airport, selling liquor, rums, perfumes, crystal, and cigarettes.

Most shops open at 9 a.m., closing at 1 p.m., then reopening between 3 and 6 p.m. They are closed on Saturday afternoon, Sunday, and holidays. When the cruise ships are in port, many eager shopkeepers naturally change these hours, stretching them out, even on weekends, much to the regret of the clerks.

One of the best places to buy French perfumes, at prices often lower than those charged in Paris, is **Phoenicia**, 8 rue Frébault (tel. 011-590/83-50-36) and 121 rue Frébault (tel. 011-590/82-25-75).

Rosébleu, 5 rue Frébault (tel. 011-590/82-93-44), has one of the biggest stocks in Pointe-à-Pitre of jewelry, crystal, perfumes, gifts, and fashion accessories. If you pay with traveler's checks, you'll get discounts. Closed Monday.

Vendôme, 8–10 rue Frébault (tel. 011-590/83-42-84), has imported fashions for both men and women, as well as a large selection of gifts and perfumes, including the big names. Usually you can find someone who speaks English to sell you a Cardin watch.

Actually, if you're adventurous you may want to seek out some native goods found in little shops along the back streets of Pointe-à-Pitre. Considered collector's items are the straw hats or salacos made in Les Saintes islands. They look distinctly related to Chinese coolie hats and are usually well designed, often made of split bamboo. Native doudou dolls are also popular gift items.

Where to Stay

For convenience to terminals, if you'd like to seek lodgings in Pointe-à-Pitre, I have the following suggestion:

Hôtel Bougainvillée, Angle des rues Delgrès et Frébault, 97110 Pointe-à-Pitre, Guadeloupe, F.W.I. (tel. 011-590/90-14-14), is a concrete-walled, unfrilly, but clean and serviceable hotel whose location on a busy street corner guarantees a regular clientele of commercial travelers. Guests register in a wood-trimmed, renovated lobby before taking a cramped elevator to one of the 36 bedrooms. The units are well maintained, with white walls and heavy dark furniture, like something you'd find in Iberia. Each contains air conditioning, a private bath and shower, and a phone. In winter, singles rent for 440F ($68.20) daily and doubles for 500F ($77.50). *Off-season, rates are 320F ($49.60) in singles, 350F ($54.25) in doubles.*

Where to Dine

La Canne à Sucre, 17 rue Jean-Jaurès (tel. 011-590/83-58-48), is one "sugarcane" that has created a local sensation, and in spite of its youth has already become the most select rendezvous for a superbly prepared Guadeloupean cuisine in Pointe-à-Pitre. Gérard Virginius, along with his wife, Marie, have restored this pink-and-white colonial house, with a kitchen from which emerge all the tempting dishes of the Créole cuisine. You dine in a parlor setting with a choice of two rooms.

For an appetizer, try one of their fritters made with *malange,* which tastes like sweet potatoes to me, and another with a vegetable known as *giraumon,* a squash-like pumpkin. Their stuffed land crabs (called *crabes farcis* here) are among the best sampled on the island. Conch is queen around here, and it's likely to be served in a variety of ways, put in everything from a tart to soup. I consider it best here when it's cooked with eggplant. For a main course, try leg of lamb stuffed with local mint, pigs' feet Antillean style, or tournedos Canne à Sucre. Desserts are lavish and sinful: a soursop sherbet or a coupe Canne à Sucre (a rondelle with old rum, coconut sherbet, whipped cream, banana, caramel, and a touch of cinnamon). It's traditional to begin your meal with a small rum punch. The restaurant is closed on Saturday for lunch, all day Sunday, and in October, but open otherwise for those who make a reservation. Hours are noon to 2 p.m. and 7:30 to 10 p.m. Expect to spend from $35 per person for dinner.

Saint-John Perse once wrote about the fine old time sailors had when they arrived in Pointe-à-Pitre when it was used as a stopover anchorage on the famous Route du Rhum. But since that day is long gone, you may not want to linger; you can take a different route instead, this one to the "South Riviera," from Pointe-à-Pitre to Pointe de Châteaux.

LE BAS DU FORT: The first tourist complex, lying just two miles from Pointe-à-Pitre, is called Le Bas du Fort, in the vicinity of Gosier.

The **Aquarium de la Guadeloupe,** Place Créole, Marina Bas-du-Fort (tel. 011-590/90-92-38), is rated as one of the three most important of France and is the largest and most modern in the Caribbean. Just off the main highway near Bas-du-Fort Marina, the aquarium houses a series of tanks containing tropical fish, coral, underwater plants, and huge sharks and other sea creatures. The exhibits are all clearly labeled. Open daily from 9 a.m. to 7 p.m. Admission is 30F ($4.65).

Where to Stay

PLM Azur Marissol, Le Bas du Fort, 97190 Gosier, Guadeloupe, F.W.I. (tel. 011-590/90-84-44), is a secluded bungalow colony of two- and three-story structures, set away from the main road, occupying grounds from a secondary route to the shoreline. In a setting of banana trees and lawns, it offers first-class comfort in 200 air-conditioned rooms, either in bungalows or in the two wings, which open onto a view of the park-like grounds or the water. The furnishings are in "sober modern," and the floors are tiled, the baths having a separate toilet. In winter, singles rent for 700F ($108.50) daily and doubles for 900F ($139.50). The charge for a bungalow for two persons is 1,350F ($209.25). *Summer prices are 425F ($65.88) to 625F ($96.88) in singles or doubles, 550F ($89.25) to 760F ($117.80) in bungalows for two persons.* All units have either twin or double beds. The beach is small, but you'll have the use of a large swimming pool. The hotel is a complete resort with lots of sports activities. A beauty and fitness center offers such features as a "hammam" steam room, exercise lessons called "gymnastique douce," a beauty care salon, calisthenics in the sea or pool, relaxation exercises based on yoga, and hot water baths with algae or oils. Next to the pool is a circular bar, Le Wahoo. The hotel's deluxe restaurant, Le Grand Baie, opens onto a terrace where you can order both local Créole specialties and the traditional French cuisine. The set menu of four courses costs from 155F ($24.03). Sicali is an open grill lying halfway between the beach and the pool, providing simple but savory meals, with grilled meat or fish, as well as a serve-yourself salad bar and a dessert buffet. The hut-shaped restaurant enjoys much favor from guests.

Fleur d'Épée Novotel, Le Bas du Fort, 97190 Gosier, Guadeloupe, F.W.I. (tel. 011-590/90-81-49), one of France's most successful resort hotels, stands beside a duet of crescent bays whose white sands are shaded from the direct sunlight by palms and sea grape trees. Gauguin might have felt at home amid the rustic beachside pavilions where each of the 186 bedrooms is a well-scrubbed, carefully tiled enclave of air-conditioned quiet, with color TV, bath, phone, and a floor plan duplicated with great success in Novotels around the world. In high season, doubles cost 1,350F ($209.25) daily, and singles go for 1,100F ($170.50). *In summer, doubles rent for 600F ($93) daily and singles for 500F ($77.50).* There's a pleasant, breeze-filled restaurant on the premises, as well as about a dozen indoor/outdoor eating places within walking distance, many with views of the beach.

Where to Dine

La Plantation, Bas du Fort, Galeríe Commerciale de la Marina (tel. 011-590/90-84-83), is a stylish but unremarkable establishment in a marina complex that could easily be on Long Island. Hidden in this ordinary scene is one of the finest dining places on Guadeloupe. In an intimate, modern, air-conditioned setting, French and nouvelle cuisine are presented by Gianni Ferraris, the owner and chef de cuisine, who hails from Italy. For a beginning, try either a superb hors d'oeuvre of mixed clams and scallops with lobster sauce or zucchini spaghetti with seafood. Main dishes include a côte de boeuf rôtie, filet of tuna with bone marrow sauce, and mixed white meat of chicken and conch (lambi) with spicy sauce. It's easy to spend from $45 for a meal, including wine. Hours are from noon to 2:30 p.m. and 7 to 10:30 p.m. daily except Sunday. Reservations are important.

L'Albatros, Bas du Fort (tel. 011-590/90-84-16), is the challenger to La Plantation's crown. It has a far more romantic location, as its terrace opens onto the water near the already recommended Azur Marissol. Dinner is served from 7 to 11:30 p.m. daily. You might begin your meal with seafood soup or a "salad of the ocean," then follow with either fresh lobster, grilled red snapper, fricassée of conch, or one of the various meat and poultry dishes which include a confit of duckling. Various set menus are offered for 95F ($14.73) to 170F ($26.35). However, if you order à la carte, expect to spend from 200F ($31). In season, reservations are necessary.

Escale à Saigon, route des Fleurs d'Épées, Bas du Fort (tel. 011-590/90-95-75), is one of the best Oriental restaurants in Guadeloupe with a polite staff and a terrace setting designed to evoke a sense of peacefulness. Its only drawback is its location at the top of a long, steep, one-lane driveway where you might have to jockey for position with an advancing car. Full meals, costing from 175F ($27.13), are served daily except Monday from noon to 2 p.m. and 5 to 10:30 p.m. The Vietnamese and Chinese specialties include the fish of the day with ginger sauce, Vietnamese pâté with crabmeat, shrimp-and-chicken Saigon soup, asparagus-and-crabmeat soup, beef sautéed with onions, and several versions of duck (including one with "five perfumes"), along with grilled sea urchins with curry and coconut.

GOSIER: Some of the biggest and most important hotels of Guadeloupe are found at this holiday center, with its nearly five miles of beach, stretching east from Pointe-à-Pitre.

For an excursion, you can climb to **Fort Fleur d'Épée,** dating from the 18th century. Its dungeons and battlements are testaments remaining of the ferocious fighting between the French and British armies in 1794 seeking to control the island. The well-preserved ruins command the crown of a hill. From there you'll have good views over the bay of Pointe-à-Pitre, and on a clear day you can see the neighboring offshore islands of Marie-Galante and Îles des Saintes.

Where to Stay

Auberge de la Vieille Tour, Montauban, 97190 Gosier (tel. 011-590/84-23-23), is a harmonious combination of the old and the practical new, where you get vintage charm and an authentic Créole quality. Directed by the Pullman interests, the complex encircles an 1835 sugar mill whose thick-walled tower (which looks like a lighthouse) is the reception area. To that original structure, 80 rooms of first-class standard, with balconies overlooking the gardens and a small private beach, have been added. As you enter the driveway, you pass old mechanical parts of the former mill—dented wheels, the furnace, whatever. The modern bedroom extensions flow out into the tropical garden. For those who want even more privacy than that provided by the regular units, there are three intimate bungalows. At Christmas, singles cost 1,088F ($168.64) to 1,362F ($211.11) daily, and doubles go for 1,720F ($266.60) to 2,110F ($327.05). The rest of the winter, depending on the particular month, singles rent for 938F ($145.39) to 1,240F ($192.20) and doubles for 1,374F ($212.97) to 1,768F ($274.04). *In summer, singles are charged 625F ($96.88) to 788F ($122.14), with doubles paying 872F ($135.16) to 1,088F ($168.64),* all with breakfast and taxes included. The waterfront garden is the social center, with its large swimming pool. If you'd like to eat at the hotel, refer to the recommendations in "Dining at Gosier." Sometimes limbo dancers are brought in, and buffets and barbecues are planned. Most sports are available at the hotel, and on the premises is a shop providing local handcrafts at reasonable tariffs. The hotel has a freshwater pool. Tennis is played on three composition courts, which are floodlit for night play.

PLM Azur Callinago Beach Hotel and Village, 97190 Gosier, Guadeloupe, F.W.I. (tel. 011-590/84-25-25), named after a Carib Indian hero, stands along the Gosier beachfront, between the Auberge de la Vieille Tour and the Salako. It's run like a small resort inn along the Mediterranean and has a helpful staff. In buildings of white stucco, some 40 rooms, with private baths, air conditioning, and private balconies, are rented. In high season, the cost is 650F ($100.75) daily in a single, 800F ($124) in a double, with breakfast. *In off-season, the single tariff is 303F ($46.97) daily, with doubles costing 416F ($64.48).* In the residential village complex, next to the hotel, the management offers 115 studios and duplex apartments. The studios, for example, are spacious with a combination living room and bedroom furnished in Nordic modern, with complete kitchens and baths. A sliding glass wall opens onto a small private balcony overlooking Gosier Bay. The duplexes, of course, are larger. You ascend a spiral staircase to your upstairs bedroom, with a private bath and another small terrace. On the premises is a little, well-stocked market if you'd like to do light housekeeping. In winter, rates are 620F ($96.10) for a studio single, 740F ($114.70) for a studio double, and 1,200F ($186) for a duplex suitable for three or four persons. *In summer, one person pays 260F ($40.30), two pay 416F ($64.48), and a duplex for three or four costs 620F ($96.10).* The prices are for rooms only. If you want to dine out, you can eat in the hotel's restaurant, offering both French and Créole foods, a good meal costing 120F ($18.60) and up.

The hotel opens onto a white sand beach, and on the grounds is a freshwater pool. Such sports as waterskiing, sailing, snorkeling, pedalboating, windsurfing, and rides on a 36-foot sailing boat are available, but you'll pay extra for these. There are two tennis courts as well.

Ecotel Guadeloupe, 97190, Gosier, Guadeloupe, F.W.I. (tel. 011-590/84-20-20), is a restful retreat surrounded by gardens. Within an eight-minute drive of the capital and ten minutes from the airport, the hotel is maintained by students from the local hotel school. It's modern in styling, yet its restaurant, bar, and bedrooms are French West Indian in feeling. Each of the accommodations, 44 in all, opens onto a view of the pool, the gardens, or the adjoining forest. The units contain many built-in pieces. The air conditioning is occasionally not strong enough for some guests, but it is silent. Breakfast is served on an al fresco extension of the comfortably furnished reception area. To stay here costs 456F ($70.68) daily in a single in high season, 642F ($99.51) in a double, breakfast included. *These prices drop to 283F ($43.87) daily in a single off-season, doubles going for 393F ($60.92).* At the restaurant, Le Galion, serving dinner only, you get not only student waiters but also student cooks, the latter under the tutelage of a trained chef from France. Among the specialties is a filet de machoiran, a fleshy fish shipped in from Guyana. Also try their local red snapper done in a variety of ways. They also do a gâteau de langouste (spiny lobster) with whisky. Snails come with Pernod and walnuts. Expect to pay from 150F ($23.25) for a meal. If you choose, you can dine on lighter fare alongside the swimming pool at Pap-Pap.

La Créole Beach Hotel, Pointe de la Verdure, 97190 Gosier, Guadeloupe, F.W.I. (tel. 011-590/84-26-26), has the nicest hotel design of any of the Gosier establishments. Half New Orleans, half colonial, the hotel stands alongside two beaches in a setting of lawns and trees, as well as hibiscus and bougainvillea. The bedrooms, 156 regular ones plus six duplexes, are traditional in tone, with dark wood pieces, carpeted floors, direct phones, TVs, mini-bars, and individually controlled air conditioning. Your balcony will be large enough to be your breakfast spot or a perch for your sundowner. High-season rates, including a full American breakfast, are 950F ($147.25) daily in a single, 1,250F ($193.75) in a double. *In summer, the cost of a single is 460F ($71.30), that of a double being 595F ($92.23).* The gourmet restaurant is called Sainte-Anne, and it is attractively decorated with plants. Many local specials are served here, along with a more familiar international cuisine. During the day guests enjoy drinks at the poolside bar, St-Tropez, or a lunch at the beach snackbar named Beethoven. The restaurant Les Alizés stands on an airy terrace near the pool and is full of handsome greenery. Many water sports as well as tennis are provided.

Serge's Guest House, 7 Périnette, 97190 Gosier, Guadeloupe, F.W.I. (tel. 011-590/84-10-25), right in the middle of town, gives you a chance to live in a Créole family house with an encircling garden awash with tropical flowers and vegetation. Each of the 25 modestly furnished rooms in this Logis de France contains air conditioning and a private bath, while several of the units have verandas and kitchenettes. A swimming pool is set amid the greenery. Meals are consumed in a sunny room whose glass louvers open onto a view of the garden. There, an octagonal gazebo serves as a daytime bar and a nighttime rendezvous for occasional live entertainment. Serge Helene is the helpful owner. Year-round rates in rooms without kitchenettes range from 205F ($31.78) daily single or double. Studios with kitchenettes cost 230F ($35.65) to 240F ($37.20) single or double. The white concrete structure lies just over a mile from the nearest beach, and there's a tennis court on the grounds.

Dining at Gosier

In addition to the hotels, many small restaurants are found in Gosier and the vicinity. At some of these places you'll get Créole cookery with a relaxed atmosphere, and often relaxed service too. Many of these places you may discover on your own. I'll suggest the following. First, I'll document the best in-hotel dining, then the independent places.

Auberge de la Vieille Tour, Montauban, Gosier (tel. 011-590/84-23-23), is one of the finest restaurants on the island. The main dining room is decorated in the French country style, with beamed ceilings, paneled walls, and chandeliers. The service from a staff hired by the Pullman chain in France is among the best on the island. The menu will probably change many times during the lifetime of this edition, but you'll get, in whatever form, French nouvelle cuisine here. The fish soup with fennel will get you going, then you are likely to be faced with such temptations as veal sweetbreads delicately braised with honey or roast lamb with a saffron sabayon. The locally caught red snapper is likely to be accompanied by cucumber balls and mango butter (yes, mango butter). The price is high, about $35 per head, but it's worth it. Hours are from noon to 2 p.m. and 7 to 10 p.m.

Chez Violetta, Périnette Gosier (tel. 011-590/84-10-34) stands at the far eastern end of Gosier Village, en route to Ste-Anne. Of all the Créole restaurants on the island, this is the most formally decorated. It has Louis XIII–style velvet-covered chairs, striped wallpaper in rich but somber colors, and a decor that looks as if it were transported from Burgundy. In spite of its neocolonial trappings, this is the domain of the high priestess of Créole cookery, who, though aged, still presides in the kitchen. Her name is Violetta Saint-Phor, whose skill has become almost a legend on the island. She serves lunch from noon to 3 p.m. and dinner from 7 to 10:30 p.m. every day of the year. On the à la carte menu, try her stuffed crabs, her blaff of seafood, and her fresh fish of the day (perhaps red snapper). For an appetizer, you might ask for cod fritters or beignets called "accra." The classic blood sausage, boudin, is also served here. In addition, she does a fine conch ra-goût, superb in texture and flavor. It's best when served with hot chilis grown on Guadeloupe. On occasion she'll even prepare a brochette of shark, if available. Fresh pineapple makes an ideal dessert, or you can try her banana cake. For a real-ly fine meal on the à la carte menu, expect to pay from 185F ($28.68). Waitresses dress in *madras et foulard*.

Chez Rosette, Lotissement des Gisors, route de Gosier (tel. 011-590/84-11-32), is centered near many of the previously recommended hotels whose guests, even though on the half-board plan, come here for dinner. They know they'll get Créole cookery that is zesty and beautifully flavored with spices and herbs. Chez Rosette is one of the largest Créole places in Guadeloupe. It grew from a "front porch" restaurant made famous by Madame Rosette, whose suc-cessors carry on today. The restaurant has grown over the years, keeping up to the size of the kindly and vivacious family who own it. The guiding force is a gracious Créole matron, Marie-Louise Limol, whose pretty daughters help keep the kitch-ens running smoothly. The location is in a sprawling wood-sided building with several wings, a handful of dining rooms, and a garden with outside tables. Lunch is daily from noon to 3:30 p.m. and dinner from 7 to 11:30 p.m. Known for its fish platters, which are often stewed or curried, the restaurant also serves such dishes as seafood stew and colombos of goat, chicken, or conch. A fixed-price meal is popular at 90F ($13.95) to 120F ($18.60), while à la carte dinners cost from 175F ($27.13). Service is performed by a bevy of Guadeloupiennes dressed in the traditional *madras et foulard*. If you're interested in renting one of the comfortable, clean bedrooms upstairs, in winter singles cost 250F ($28.75) daily, and doubles go for 300F ($46.50). *Tariffs are reduced 30% in summer.* Each unit contains air conditioning and a private bath.

La Chaubette, route de la Riviera (tel. 011-590/84-14-29). Begin with a rum punch, made with white rum and served with a lime wedge and sugar. But don't order too much—it's lethal, and you won't be able to get through the rest of dinner. This is a "front porch" Créole restaurant with lots of local color. About a 12-minute run from Pointe-à-Pitre, it's almost like the Guadeloupe ver-sion of a roadside inn, with its red-checked tablecloths and curtains made of bam-boo. Mme Gitane Chavalin is in charge, and she's known in the area for her Créole recipes, using, whenever possible, the fish and produce of her island. When it's available, her langouste is peerless, as is her hog's-head cheese with a minced-onion vinaigrette. She's closed Sunday, but otherwise will top off a fine meal for you by serving either coconut ice cream or a banana flaming with rum. For her trouble, expect a bill around $25 per person for a complete meal. Service is from noon to 4 p.m. and 7 to 11 p.m. Monday to Saturday.

PETIT HAVRE: This sleepy hamlet lies between Gosier and Ste-Anne, and is just starting to emerge as a tourist destination. I'll offer both an accommodation and a top-notch restaurant here.

Hôtel Cap Sud Caraïbes, Chemin de la Plage, Petit Havre, 97190 Gosier, Guadeloupe, F.W.I. (tel. 011-590/85-96-02), is an intimate hotel resembling a pink-walled inn in the south of France. Designed in an octagonal shape which effectively shows off its pleasant swimming pool, walled garden, and planting, it offers a dozen rooms to guests who want to avoid the larger and more impersonal hotels. Each of the accommodations has air conditioning, lots of sun-flooded space, Mediterranean-style contrasts of white plaster with dark wood, and a tile baths. In winter, with breakfast included, singles rent for 500F ($77.50) and doubles for 650F ($100.75). *In summer, the cost is 300F ($46.50) per person per day.* Breakfast and light meals are served in a Tahitian-style cabaña bar a few steps from the swimming pool. A mini-forest of banana plants separates guests from the gates, which lie about a five-minute walk from the beach.

Le Bistrot, rue de la Plage, Petit Havre (tel. 011-590/85-91-82), made a quantum leap forward when Guy Laurent Piquion took over. A fascinating man who's had a widely varied career (he once appeared in the buff in the musical, *Hair*), he brings style and elegance to this place. The restaurant stands at the bottom of a sloping pathway leading past tall trees from the main road to Petit Havre. You might begin your meal with clams from nearby Le Moule. The broth is savory, a delight to drink. You can make selections from such dishes as stuffed crab or conch, a rillette of rabbit or a fisherman's casserole. They also know how to prepare lamb well. For dessert, try something tempting, perhaps an apple tart "upside down." Meals cost from 200F ($31). Service is from noon to 3 p.m. and 8 to 10 p.m. daily except Sunday and Monday.

STE-ANNE: About nine miles from Gosier, little Ste-Anne is a sugar town and a small resort, offering many fine beaches and lodging facilities. In many ways it's the most charming of the villages of Guadeloupe, with its town hall in pastel colors, its church, and its principal square, Place de la Victoire, where a statue of Schoelcher commemorates the abolition of slavery in 1848.

Where to Stay

Its best-known resort is **Club Med–Caravelle,** 97180 Ste-Anne, Guadeloupe, F.W.I. (tel. 011-590/88-21-00, or toll free 800/258-2633), covering 45 acres along a cape covered with palm trees. Its beach is one of the finest in the French West Indies. Beads are legal tender here. Club Med vacations are open to members only, but membership is available. An all-inclusive vacation package is offered, with one price, which depends on the time of year and the city from which you depart. It includes all-you-can-eat meals daily, with unlimited wine at lunch and dinner, plus use of all sports facilities, with expert instruction and equipment. The Med-Caravelle accommodates its guests in air-conditioned double-occupancy rooms with private baths. The weekly rate not including air fare is *$610 per person in summer,* from $820 to $1,350 in winter and spring (highest at Christmas).

Food is a specialty at the resort, the breakfast and lunch buffet tables groaning with French, continental, and Créole delicacies. Dinner is served in the main dining room, which has been enlarged and remodeled into a series of small, comfortable sections, or in La Maison Créole annex restaurant. At the north end of the beach, this jewel-like dining spot is set above the sand and decorated with bright, white gingerbread trim. You'll be welcomed at the pleasant bar and covered open-air dining area overlooking the sea. There's a weekly folklore night when the dinner features specialties of the region, along with a performance by the Guadeloupe folklore ballet. Also in the evening, guests gather around the bar and dance floor, which becomes the theater for nightly entertainment. Afterward you can dance at the midnight disco. The center of daytime activities is the wide stretch of beach. Windsurfing, sailing, and sunbathing have many devotees, and snorkeling trips leave daily from the dock. There are also sea excursions to explore the island's coastline. Other sports include tennis (six courts), archery, calisthenics, volleyball, basketball, and table tennis. The Med-Caravelle offers a complete line of programs in its computer workshop, with 25 computers available. A special beginners course is available.

Hôtel La Toubana, P.O. Box 63, Durivage, 97180 Ste-Anne, Guadeloupe, F.W.I. (tel. 011-590/88-25-78) is a hostelry centered around a low-lying stone building on a cliff overlooking the bay. Many guests come here just for the view, which on a clear day encompasses Marie-Galante, Dominica, La Désirade, and the Îles des Saintes, but you'll quickly learn that there's far more to this charming place than just a panorama. The 32 rooms and 32 red-roofed bungalows lie scattered among the tropical shrubs along the adjacent hillsides. (*Toubana* is the Arawak word for "small house.") In winter, depending on the particular month of occupancy and depending on the level of luxury of the unit occupied, singles pay 599F ($92.85) to 1,024F ($158.72) daily, and doubles are charged 374F ($57.97) to 625F ($96.88) per person. *In summer, singles or doubles rent for 410F ($63.55) to 500F ($77.50).*

The manager of this resort is Patrick Vial-Collet, who studied innkeeping in Switzerland and trained in London. His ideas contributed to the designer's inspiration of lining the dining room walls with illuminated aquariums from which schools of fish and crayfish stare back at curious visitors. The dining room, painted in shades of aqua and white, offers both indoor and al fresco dining stretching right up to the edge of the pool. The beach is only a five-minute walk from any lodging, while tennis courts are on the premises. Deep-sea fishing and other water sports can be arranged.

Incongruously named, the ten-room **Hôtel Le Grand Large,** 97180 Ste-Anne, Guadeloupe, F.W.I. (tel. 011-590/88-20-06), at the edge of town, is close to the municipal beach. It's nestled in the midst of tropical greenery, including coconut palms, on a two-acre site. Life here is informal and casual, everything beach oriented. The hostess is the charming Mme Georges Damico (her English is not strong, so maybe you could try your French). Accommodations are white bungalows with twin beds and private baths, all air-conditioned. That may not really be necessary as they're exposed to the trade winds. Guests can stay here in winter for a charge of 565F ($87.58) daily in a single, 600F ($93) in a double. *Summer prices are 365F ($56.58) daily in a single, 400F ($62) in a double.* Of the ten rooms, four contain kitchenettes, and these are rented only by the week, *costing 1,750F ($271.25) in summer*, rising to 2,450F ($379.75) in winter, single or double occupancy. Only breakfast is served, but there are many independent restaurants nearby, so clients always have a choice.

Le Relais du Moulin, Chateaubrun, 97180 Ste-Anne, Guadeloupe, F.W.I. (tel. 011-590/88-23-96). The 19th-century stone tower that gives this place its name juts boldly above the hilly countryside. It required the entrepreneurial skill of two energetic sisters, Patricia and Florence Marie, to transform it into the centerpiece of their well-landscaped hotel. After passing between huge hedges of crimson poinsettia, guests register in the circular confines of the tower. Later they are ushered to one of the hotel's 40 accommodations, about half of which are contained in private red-roofed bungalows. The others are clustered into quartets whose sides are covered with trumpet vines and bougainvillea. Each of the units is air-conditioned and has a private bath, terrace with a hammock, and refrigerator. Duplexes are more expensive than bungalows. With breakfast included, winter rates are 470F ($72.85) to 510F ($79.05) daily in a single, 570F ($88.35) to 660F ($102.30) in a double. *In summer, with breakfast included, singles go for 310F ($48.05) to 410F ($63.55) and doubles for 400F ($62) to 425F*

($65.88). Guests congregate at the breeze-filled bar whose stout timbers overlook the rectangular sapphire of the swimming pool. Free bicycles are available, and facilities for archery are on the premises. A few guests check into this hotel primarily for its horseback riding. For a recommendation of its restaurant, Tap-Tap, see below.

Where to Dine
Tap-Tap, Le Relais du Moulin, Châteaubrun, Ste-Anne (tel. 011-590/88-23-96). An excursion to this restaurant gives visitors a chance to see the rolling horse country nearby. You dine in the shadow of a soaring mill, originally built in 1848, beneath a ceiling crisscrossed with heavy beams. Oversize windows flood the interior with sunlight at lunch from 12:30 to 2 p.m. At night, the flickering candles give the room the aura of a Norman farm at dinners served from 7:30 to 9:30 p.m. seven days a week. The kitchen turns out a blend of Antillean-inspired French food. A Créole-inspired fixed-price meal costs 135F ($20.93), while à la carte dinners go for around 200F ($31). Specialties include a navarin of fish, lamb with green pepper sauce, and scallop casserole with saffron.

L'Amour en Fleurs, Ste-Anne (tel. 011-590/88-23-72). If anyone can lure guests from the groaning buffet tables at the nearby Club Med, it's Mme Trésor Amanthe, who is considered a "sorceress" of Créole cookery. Assisted in her advanced years by her charming daughter, Maggie, this Créole mama has attracted a great amount of attention over the years from some of the most discerning visitors to Guadeloupe. The building is little more than a blue-painted concrete shell, open to the echoes of the whizzing traffic outside, with dime-store chairs, scarred wooden tables, and strings of paper lanterns and streamers. Guests receive a warm-hearted welcome and are served well-prepared Créole food seven days a week from 11 a.m. to 11 p.m. Full meals, costing from 125F ($19.38), include copious portions of accras, blood pudding, blaff, court bouillon, ragoûts of goat, pork, or chicken, and spicy colombos (curries). Dessert might be a portion of coconut ice cream.

ST-FRANÇOIS:
Continuing east from Ste-Anne, you'll notice many old round towers named for Father Labat, the Dominican founder of the sugarcane industry. These towers were once used as mills to grind the cane. St-François, 25 miles east of Pointe-à-Pitre, used to be a sleepy fishing village, known for its native Créole restaurants. Then Air France discovered it and opened a Méridien hotel with a casino. That was followed by the promotional activities of J. F. Rozan, a native, who invested heavily to make St-François a jet-set resort. Now the once-sleepy village possesses first-class accommodations, as well as an airport available to private jets, a golf course, and a marina.

Where to Stay
In hotels, **Méridien St-François,** 97118 St-François, Guadeloupe, F.W.I. (tel. 011-590/88-51-00) is one of the first Méridien hotels built for Air France, standing alongside one of the best beaches in Guadeloupe on 150 acres of land. The climate, quite dry here, is refreshed by trade winds. A four-star hotel, it offers 272 rooms either overlooking the sea or the Robert Trent Jones–designed golf course. The rooms are fully equipped with many amenities to add to your comfort, and furnishings are in a modern style combined with Créole overtones. The hotel was refurbished in 1984. *In low season, a single pays 770F ($119.35) daily, and a double costs 960F ($106.95).* However, in high season, prices go up to 1,080F ($167.40) daily in a single, 1,230F ($190.65) in a double. Included in the tariffs are use of the swimming pool, tennis courts, and windsurfers. Club

Caraïbe, which offers only an à la carte menu, is in the style of a deluxe restaurant, charging from 250F ($38.75) for a good meal, either from the French cuisine or the Créole repertoire. Or perhaps you'll prefer Balaou, a terraced restaurant in a more relaxed and exotic mood. In addition, the hotel has a grill and barbecue snackbar, Le Casa Zomar, right on the beach, where the prices are quite high, especially if you order lobster. Alongside the swimming pool, Lele is a tropical bar serving punches and other drinks. At night you can dance at Le Bête à Feu, the hotel's disco.

For people who care for more independence, I suggest a bungalow at Guadeloupe's poshest property, **Hamak,** 97118 St-François, Guadeloupe, F.W.I. (tel. 011-590/88-59-99), a quarter of a mile from the Méridien. Its sandy beach along the lagoon and its proximity to golf and a tiny airport make it popular with jet-setters from Europe and the U.S. "Les amis" like to be elegant, but informally so. It was the site of the 1979 international summit that brought President Carter and Giscard d'Estaing, among others, here. Spread on a 250-acre estate, accommodations are in villas (each with two individual tropical suites with twin beds opening onto a walled garden patio where you can sunbathe *au naturel*). Each bungalow houses one to four guests. In peak season, a single ranges in price from 1,680F ($260.40) to 2,290F ($354.95) daily, and a double goes for 1,850F ($286.75) to 2,460F ($381.30), with an American breakfast. *In off-season, charges are 960F ($148.80) to 1,360F ($210.80) daily in a single, 1,170F ($181.35) to 1,580F ($244.90) in a double.* MAP is an extra 200F ($31) per person daily. These prices include the suite, tennis, taxes, and service. Hamak has two two dining rooms, one opening onto the beach, the other onto an enclosed garden. Service at lunch is limited to hotel guests, but outsiders can dine here if they reserve in advance. Crayfish is the house specialty, prepared for both hot and cold dishes. Hamak has an 18-hole Robert Trent Jones golf course at its front door, with a full-service clubhouse and snackbar. A spa Jacuzzi pool, windsurfing, and other water sports facilities add to the pleasure of staying here. The hotel is closed from early September to early October.

Trois Mats Hotel (Three Masts), 97118 St-François, Guadeloupe, F.W.I. (tel. 011-590/88-59-99), a less expensive annex of the Hamak, is only about a mile from the center of town, although many of its occupants never leave the area surrounding its marina. The hotel is a trio of modern buildings that sit directly on the water a short walk from the Hôtel Méridien. Each of the 36 accommodations has its own kitchen, although cooking facilities are on either a balcony or a large terrace. In winter, studio apartments cost 515F ($79.83) daily in singles, 650F ($100.75) to 860F ($133.30) in doubles. *Summer prices are 410F ($63.55) in singles, 535F ($82.93) in doubles.* All tariffs are EP. Taxes and service are included in the rates. Beaches, tennis courts, golf, discos, and restaurants are all easily accessible.

Where to Dine

Restaurant Les Oiseaux, Anse des Rochers, 97118 St-François, Guadeloupe, F.W.I. (tel. 011-590/88-56-92), is probably the best imitation of a Provençale farmhouse on the entire island. It stands on a seaside road about 3½ miles west of St-François on a scrub-covered landscape whose focal point is the sea and the island of Marie-Galante. Its walled-in front garden frames a stone-sided, low-slung building which produces the perfumes of a southern French and Antillean cuisine worth the detour. This is the domain of Arthur Rollé and his wife, Claudette, who charge from 200F ($31) for full à la carte meals. Fixed-price dinners cost 80F ($12.40) to 100F ($15.50). These repasts include a fish mousse, Créole-style beef, and a filet en croûte with red wine sauce. Try also the marmite Robinson, inspired by the tale of Robinson Crusoe, a delectable fondue of fish and vegetables which you cook for yourself in a combination of bubbling coconut and corn oil. Dessert might be a composite of four exotic sherbets or a crêpe. Full meals are served from noon to 3 p.m. and 7 to 10:30 p.m. No meals are served on Thursday, and no evening meal is served on Sunday. Les Oiseaux also offers a quartet of small, simply furnished bedrooms, suitable for anyone looking for isolation, sea views, and superb food on the premises. A room rents for 120F ($18.60) daily single, 150F ($23.25) double. The prices are even more reasonable if you rent by the week: 750F ($116.25) for one person, 900F ($139.50) for two. With half board, singles rent for 200F ($31) per day, doubles for 280F ($43.40). The establishment is closed in September and early October.

La Louisiane, Quartier Ste-Marthe, outside St-François (tel. 011-590/88-44-34). The century-old plantation house that encloses this restaurant is sheltered from the road by trees and shrubbery. The French owners, Daniel and Muriel Hugon, brought with them when they emigrated some of the best parts of the cuisine of their native regions, Provence and the Vosges. Full meals cost from 200F ($31) and might include a filet of turbot with passion fruit garnish, a gratin of lobster, veal escalope with shrimp, and scallops with ginger and lemon butter. The restaurant is open daily from noon to 2 p.m. and 7 to 10 p.m. except Monday. Reservations are needed.

POINTE DES CHÂTEAUX: Seven miles from St-François is Pointe des Châteaux, the easternmost tip of Grand Terre, at the point where the Atlantic meets the Caribbean. Here, where crashing waves sound around you, you'll see a cliff sculptured by the sea into castle-like formations, the erosion typical of France's Brittany coast. The view from here is splendid. At the top is a cross put there in the 19th century.

If you wish, you can walk to the Pointe des Colibris, the extreme end of Guadeloupe. From there you'll have a view of the northeastern sector of the island, and to the east a look at La Désirade, another island which has the appearance of a huge vessel anchored far away. Among the coved beaches found around here, Pointe Tarare is the *au naturel* one.

Restaurant La Mouette, Pointe des Châteaux (tel. 011-590/88-62-52). Set near the end of a sand-bordered road stretching to Pointe des Châteaux, this veranda restaurant is built like an enlarged version of a Victorian gazebo. Amid turquoise-colored walls and gracefully turned balustrades, you can enjoy fresh seafood from the kitchen. Full meals cost from 130F ($20.15) and are served daily from noon to 3 p.m. and 7:15 to 10:30 p.m. No food is served on Sunday night and all day Tuesday. Your dinner might include a savory colombo of goat, lamb chops, a blaff of fish, accras, or shellfish.

To go back to Pointe-à-Pitre from Pointe des Châteaux, you can use an alternative route, the N5 from St-François. After a nine-mile drive, you reach the village of—

LE MOULE: Founded at the end of the 17th century, Le Moule was known long before Pointe-à-Pitre. It used to be a major shipping port for sugar. Now a tiny coastal fishing village, it never regained its importance after it was devastated in the hurricane of 1928, like so many other villages of Grand Terre. Because of its more than ten-mile-long crescent-shaped beach, it is developing as a holiday center. Modern hotels, built along the beaches, have opened to accommodate visitors.

Specialties of this Guadeloupian village are *palourdes,* the clams which thrive in the semi-salty mouths of freshwater rivers. Known for being more tender and less "rubbery" than saltwater clams, they often, even when fresh, have a distinct sulphur taste not unlike that of over-poached eggs. Local gastronomes prepare them with saffron and aged rum or cognac.

Nearby, the sea unearthed some skulls, grim reminders of the fierce battles fought among the Caribs and the French and English. It's called "The Beach of Skulls and Bones."

The **Edgar Clerc Archeological Museum** (tel. 011-590/23-57-57) shows a collection of both Carib and Arawak Indian artifacts gathered from various islands of the Lesser Antilles. The admission-free museum is open Monday, Tuesday, Thursday, and Friday from 9:30 a.m. to 12:30 p.m. and 2:30 to 5:30 p.m.

To return to Pointe-à-Pitre, I suggest you use the D3 toward Abymes. The road winds around as you plunge deeply into Grand Terre. As a curiosity, about halfway along the way, a road will bring you to **Jabrun du Nord** and **Jabrun du Sud.** These two villages are inhabited by white people with blond hair. They are said to be survivors of aristocrats slaughtered during the Revolution. Those members of their families who escaped found safety by hiding out in Les Grands Fonds. The most important family here is named Matignon, giving its name to the colony known as "les Blancs Matignon." These citizens are said to be related to Prince Rainier of Monaco.

Pointe-à-Pitre lies only ten miles from Les Grand Fonds.

THE ROAD NORTH: From Pointe-à-Pitre, head northeast toward Abymes, passing next through Moren à l'Eau, reaching **Petit Canal** after 13 miles. This is Guadeloupe's sugarcane country, and a sweet smell fills the air. It is worth stopping over in the charming but sleepy town of Petit Canal to sample the following restaurant.

Restaurant Le Barbaroc, rue Schoelcher, Petit Canal (tel. 011-590/84-72-71). One of the most dedicated cooks in Guadeloupe is Mme Félicité Doloir. In the 1983 edition of the *Annual Book of Cooks* by H. J. Heinz, she was featured as "one of the ten outstanding cooks in the world." She has researched local recipes since her youth and has made trips to such cities as New York to teach her lore to audiences of enthusiastic students. Her restaurant, not far from her birthplace, lies on the main street of town in an unpretentious concrete building whose terrace is reached by climbing a flight of stairs. The daily specials are written on a chalkboard hanging over the street. One of Madame Doloir's goals, which she describes fervently, is the promotion of locally produced ingredients in their most flavorful combinations. Her unique recipes are served in an upstairs room whose decor includes country-French furniture, flowers, wooden balustrades, and large, prominently displayed slogans advocating the dignity of mankind with special stress on the rights of women. Go here as much for an experience as for a good meal. The restaurant is open every day for lunch and dinner from noon to 3 p.m. and 7 to 10 p.m., serving such dishes as codfish accras (whose pastry shell is made from carrots, eggplant, pumpkins, wheat flour, and breadfruit), *burgots* (sea snails) gratinée, purée of breadfruit, crab pâté, *poulet du pays cuit fumé* (smoked chicken), and sweet potato noodles. Even homemade beer is served here, as well as a house drink, *maby,* made from ingredients which include tree bark and which tastes a little like absinthe. Meals cost from 200F ($31).

Continuing northwest along the coast from Petit Canal, you come to **Port Louis,** well known for its beautiful beach, La Plage du Souffleur, which I find best in the spring. Then the brilliant white sand is effectively shown off against a contrast of the flaming red poinciana. During the week, the beach is an especially quiet spot. The little port town is asleep under a heavy sun, and it has some good restaurants.

Le Poisson d'Or, 2 rue Sadi-Carnot, Port Louis (tel. 011-590/22-58-63), is a little Antillean house, entered by going down a narrow corridor, emerging into a rustic room. You can climb the steps to the second floor, an open terrace overlooking the sea and the fishing boats gently swaying in the water. It's run by Mme Eleanore Boulate and her daughter, Esther Madel, who apprenticed at her mother's apron from the age of eight. In spite of its simple setting, the food is excellent. Try, for example, the stuffed crabs, the court-bouillon, topped off by coconut ice cream, which is homemade and tastes it. With a bottle of good wine, your bill will come to about 125F ($19.38). The place is a fine choice for an experience with Créole cookery. Meals are served from 9 a.m. to 4:30 p.m. and 6 to 9 p.m.

Also in Port Louis, you may want to patronize **Chez Odette,** rue Gambette (tel. 011-590/22-92-40). On a weekend, residents of Guadeloupe are likely to drive all the way from Basse Terre to sample the Créole viands offered by Rose Mozar, the *cuisinière patronne,* the daughter of founding mother, Odette. The *accras* (fritters) here are not made with just saltcod, but also from *giraumon,* the local pumpkin. They're a savory treat. Her colombos, made with either curried local goat or chicken, are among the best in this part of Guadeloupe. She also stuffs and seasons crabs to perfection. Among the local vegetables served is a delectable christophine (a chayote) gratinée. The dining room is exposed to the trade winds, if there are any, and the place is aggressively simple—and that's how the local diners like it. Meals cost from 100F ($15.50) to 125F ($19.38) and are served from noon to 3 p.m. and 7 to 10 p.m.

About five miles from Port Louis lies **Anse Bertrand,** the northernmost village of Guadeloupe. What is now a fishing village was the last refuge of the Carib tribes, and a reserve was once created here. Everything now, however, is lazy and sleepy.

Le Château de Feuilles, Campèche, Anse Bertrand (tel. 011-590/22-30-30), is set inland from the sea, amid eight rolling acres of greenery and blossoming flowers. A gastronomic hideaway, it is owned and established by a Norman-born couple, Jean-Pierre and Martine Dubost. To reach their place in Guadeloupe, motorists must pass the ruins of La Mahaudière, an 18th-century sugar mill. A gifted chef making maximum use of local ingredients, Monsieur Dubost prepares such specialties as pâté of warm sea urchins, sautéed conch with Créole sauce, gigot of shark with fresh pasta and saffron sauce, and a sauerkraut of fresh fish with papaya. Full meals cost from 250F ($38.75) and are served daily except Monday in winter from 11:30 a.m. to 3 p.m. and 7:30 to 10:30 p.m. Reservations are advised, especially in summer when meals will be especially prepared in anticipation of your arrival. No food is served in October.

Folie Plage (also known as Chez Prudence; tel. 011-590/22-11-17) lies directly north of Anse Bertrand at Anse Laborde. Its owner, Prudence Marcelin, is another *cuisinière patronne,* who enjoys much local acclaim for her Créole cookery. She too draws people from all over the island, especially on Sunday when this place is its most crowded. Island children frolic in the pool, and in between courses, diners can shop for handcrafts, clothes, and souvenirs sold locally. Her court-bouillon is excellent, as is either her goat or chicken (curried) colombo. The way she handles *palourdes* (clams) also attests to her imagination. She also knows how to make a zesty sauce to serve with fish. Her crabes farcis are done to perfection as well. The place is relaxed and casual, and the bill rarely comes to more than $15. Service is from noon to 3 p.m. and 7 to 10 p.m.

From Anse Bertrand, you can drive along a graveled road heading for **Pointe de la Grande Vigie,** the northernmost tip of the island, which you reach after four miles of what I hope will be cautious driving. Park your car and walk carefully along a narrow lane which will bring you to the northernmost rock of Guadeloupe. The view of the sweeping Atlantic from the top of rocky cliffs is remarkable—you stand at a distance of about 280 feet above the sea. If the day is clear, you can see the island of Antigua, about 35 miles away.

Afterward, a four-mile drive south on quite a good road will bring you to the **Porte d'Enfer** or "gateway to hell." Once there, you'll find that the sea comes violently against two narrow cliffs.

After this kind of awesome experience in the remote part of the island, you can head back, going either to Morne à l'Eau or Le Moule before connecting to the road taking you in to Pointe-à-Pitre.

A BASSE TERRE ROUND-UP: Leaving Pointe-à-Pitre by Rt. N1, you can explore the lesser windward coast. After a mile and a half, you cross the Rivière Salée at Pont de la Gabarre. This narrow strait separates the two islands that form Guadeloupe. For the next four miles, the road runs straight through sugarcane fields.

At the sign, on a main crossing, turn right on the N2 toward **Baie Mahault.** Leaving that town on the right, head for **Lamentin.** This village was settled by corsairs at the beginning of the 18th century. Scattered about are some old colonial mansions.

Ste-Rose

From Lamentin, you can drive for 6½ miles to **Ste-Rose,** where you'll find several good beaches. On your left, a small road leads to Sofaia, from which you'll have a splendid view over the coast and forest preserve. The natives claim that a sulfur spring here has curative powers.

Chez Clara (tel. 011-590/28-72-79) is the culinary statement of Clara Lesueur and her talented and charming mother, Justine. Clara, her hair tightly braided with flashing gold thread, has the manner and appearance of a chic Parisienne, a role she filled when she lived in the French capital and appeared as a model in fashion layouts in *France-Soir.* She said good-bye to that life, however, when she returned to Guadeloupe, her home, and set up her breeze-cooled restaurant. Try for a table on the open patio, where young palm trees complement the color scheme. Clara and Justine artfully meld the French style of fine dining with authentic, spicy Créole cookery. Specialties listed on the blackboard menu may include crayfish, curried skate, lobster, clams, *boudin* (blood pudding), *ouassous* (local crayfish), brochette of swordfish, *palourdes* (small clams), even *crabes farcis* (red-orange crabs with a spicy filling). The *sauce chien* served with many of the dishes is a blend of hot peppers, garlic, lime juice, and "secret things" that go well with the house drink, made with six local fruits and ample quantities of rum. To further cool your palate, your dessert might be a choice of sherbets such as guava, soursop, or passionfruit. Full meals cost around 150F ($23.25) and are served daily except Sunday night and all day Wednesday. Hours are noon to 2:30 p.m. and 8 to 10 p.m. The place is closed in October.

At Deshaies/Grand Anse

A few miles farther along, you reach Pointe Allegre, the northernmost point of Basse Terre. At Clugny Beach, you'll be at the site where the first settler landed in Guadeloupe.

A couple of miles farther will bring you to **Grand Anse,** one of the best beaches in Guadeloupe. It's very large and still secluded, sheltered by many tropical trees.

Next to the beach is a good restaurant, **Le Karacoli** (tel. 011-590/28-41-17). To get here, you turn off the main highway onto a secondary road leading to the tree-shaded beach. The restaurant stands behind a wall and a large parking lot. There's a pleasant high-ceilinged dining room, but my preferred spot is on the jungle-like terrace. There, dozens of tropical trees almost erupt out of holes in the concrete, allowing shafts of sunlight to dapple the napery of the tables. This is the domain of Mme Lucienne Salcède, a beautiful Créole woman, and her brother, Robert Salcéde. Born in Guadeloupe, they were taught to cook by their mother, using on occasion 200-year-old recipes. The accras (saltcod fritters) are considered some of the best on the island. They are also known for, among other dishes, a superb version of curried chicken colombo. A specialty called simply La Créole consists of farina dumplings, crayfish, shrimp, conch, and ten different spices. The place is open from noon to 4 p.m. daily except Friday. À la carte meals cost from 150F ($23.25). No dinner is served. In winter, an adjacent disco attracts local residents at night. Le Karacoli shuts down in October.

Le Mouillage, Deshaies (tel. 011-590/28-41-12), standing right at the natural harbor, has long been a sought-after address among the yachting crowd who come here for the excellent Créole cuisine. Try the spicy accras as an appetizer. At this seafood restaurant, Fred Racine offers 16 different dishes from which to choose. The à la carte meals cost from 150F ($23.25) up. Hours are from noon to 3 p.m. and 6 to 9 p.m. daily. Reserve in advance if you don't want to spend time over too many cocktails.

At Deshaies, snorkeling and fishing are popular pastimes. The narrow road winds up and down and has a corniche look to it, with the blue sea underneath, the view of green mountains studded with colorful hamlets.

Nine miles from Deshaies, **Pointe Noire** comes into view. Its name comes from black volcanic rocks. Look for the odd polychrome cenotaph in town.

Route de la Traversée

Four miles from Pointe Noire, you reach Mahaut. On your left begins the Route de la Traversée, the Transcoastal Highway. This is the best way to explore the scenic wonders of **Parc Naturel de Guadeloupe** when traveling between the capital, Basse-Terre, and Pointe-à-Pitre. I recommend going this way, as you pass through a tropical forest.

To preserve the Parc Naturel, Guadeloupe has set aside 74,100 acres or about one-fifth of its entire terrain. Reached by modern roads, this is a huge tract of mountains, tropical forests, and magnificent scenery.

The park is home to a variety of tame animals, including Titi (a raccoon adopted as its official mascot), and such birds as the wood pigeon, turtledove, and thrush. Small exhibition huts, devoted to the volcano, the forest, or to coffee, sugarcane, and rum, are scattered throughout the park.

The Parc Naturel has no gates, no opening or closing hours, and no admission fee.

From Mahaut you climb slowly in a setting of giant ferns and luxuriant vegetation. Four miles after the fork, you reach **Les Deux Mamelles** (The Two Breasts), where you can park your car and go for a hike. Some of the trails are for experts only; others, such as the Pigeon Trail, will bring you to a summit of about 2,600 feet where the view is impressive. Expect to spend at least three hours going each way. Halfway along the trail you can stop at Forest House. From that point, many lanes, all signposted, branch off on trails that will last anywhere from 20 minutes to two hours. Try to find the **Chute de l'Écrevisse,** the "Crayfish Waterfall," a little pond of very cold water which you'll discover after a quarter of a mile. Male hikers are likely to encounter some local beauties swimming here. If so, you can join them for a cooling dip.

After the hike, the main road descends toward Versailles, a hamlet about five miles from Pointe-à-Pitre.

However, before taking this route, while still traveling between Pointe-

Noire and Mahaut on the west coast, you might consider the following luncheon stop.

Chez Vaneau, Mahaut/Pointe-Noire (tel. 011-590/98-01-71) offers a wide, breeze-filled veranda overlooking a gully, the sight of local neighbors playing cards, and steaming Créole specialties coming from the kitchen. This is the unquestioned domain of Vaneau Desbonnes, who is assisted in the many culinary tasks by his wife, Marie-Gracieuse. Depending on business, meals are served from noon to midnight daily, with an early closing on Sunday. Fixed-price meals begin at 70F ($10.85), and à la carte dinners at 120F ($18.60). Specialties include oysters with a piquant sauce, crayfish bisque, ragoût of goat, different preparations of octopus, and roast pork.

If you don't take the route de la Traversée at this time but wish to continue exploring the west coast, you can head south from Mahaut until you reach the village of **Bouillante,** which is exciting for only one reason: you might encounter Brigitte Bardot, as she's a part-time resident.

Try not to miss seeing the small island called **Îlet à Goyave** or **Îlet du Pigeon.** Jacques Cousteau often explores the silent depths around it.

Facing the islet is the best choice for a luncheon on the whole island:

La Touna, Malendure (tel. 011-590/98-70-10), is built on a narrow strip of sand between the road and the sea, its foundation almost touching the water. This gives patrons of this charming restaurant a marine panorama which complements the seafood specialties that Francis and Françoise Ricart and their son, Emmanuel, concoct so skillfully in the kitchen. Most of the dining tables are in a side veranda whose ceiling is covered with palm fronds. Despite its allure, many of the guests delay a meal until after a drink in the sunken bar whose encircling banquettes give the impression of the cabin of a ship. One of the most appealing rituals in Guadeloupe has become a habit here: you are brought a tray on which are seven or eight carafes, each filled with a rum-soaked tropical fruit such as guava, maracoja, pineapple, and passion fruit. You select the ingredients you prefer and mix your own drink. This you can savor as you observe your fellow diners or look out at the waves. Of course if you prefer the house specialty, you'll have a combination of fruit with or without rum, one of the most refreshing drinks on the island. Menu items make use of the freshest ingredients, many of them brought in daily by the Ricarts' deep-sea fishing business (see my discussion of Fishing Club Antilles in "The Sporting Life," below). Full meals cost from around 150F ($23.25) and might include a mousse of smoked swordfish, calamari provençale, avocado stuffed with crayfish, stuffed crabs, stuffed sea urchins, kingfish steak, kingfish au poivre, cassoulette of shark with cream sauce, and stingray with black-butter sauce. Lunch, the only meal served, is offered from noon to 3 p.m. daily. Reservations are important on Sunday.

After a meal at La Touna, you can explore around the village of Bouillante, the country known for its thermal springs. In some places if you scratch the ground for only a few inches you'll feel the heat.

Another good choice for lunch is **Chez Loulouse** (tel. 011-590/98-70-34), at Malendure Plage, also opposite Pigeon Island. Many guests prefer their rum punches on the panoramic veranda, overlooking a scene of loaded boats preparing to depart and merchants hawking their wares. A quieter oasis is the equally colorful dining room inside, just past the bar. There, beneath a ceiling of palm fronds, is a wrap-around series of Créole murals which seem to go well with the reggae music emanating loudly from the bar. This is the creation of one of the most visible and charming Créole matrons in this end of the island, Madame Loulouse Paisley-Carbon. Assisted by her children, she offers fixed-price meals for 135F ($20.93) when her langouste Loulouse or house-style Caribbean lobster is the main course. Without lobster, full meals cost from 85F ($13.18). Food is served from noon to 3:30 p.m. and 7 to 10 p.m. Specialties in addition to lobster include spicy versions of fish, conch, octopus, accras, grating of christophine (squash), and savory colombos of chicken or pork.

Vieux Habitants

The winding coast road brings you to Vieux Habitants (Old Settlers), one of the oldest villages on the island, founded back in 1636. The name comes from the people who settled it. After serving in the employment of the West Indies Company, they retired here. But they preferred to call themselves inhabitants, so as not to be confused with slaves.

Basse-Terre

Another ten miles of winding roads bring you to Basse-Terre, the seat of the government of Guadeloupe, lying between the water and La Soufrière, the volcano. Founded in 1634, it's the oldest town on the island, and still has a lot of charm, its market squares shaded by tamarind and palm trees.

The town suffered heavy destruction at the hands of British troops in 1691 and again in 1702. It was also the center of fierce fighting during the Revolution. The story of Colonel Delgres blowing himself up in 1802, along with his troops, is like a Guadeloupe Fort Alamo.

In spite of its history, there isn't much to see except for a 17th-century cathedral and Fort St-Charles, which has guarded the city (not always well) since it was established.

Le Houëlmont, 34 rue de la République (tel. 011-590/81-35-96), is set in the monumental heart of town, across a boulevard from a massive government building, the Conseil General. It is the oldest and best-established restaurant in the island capital. After climbing a flight of stairs to the paneled second story, diners enjoy a sweeping view over the hillside, sloping down to the sea one block away. Mme Boulon, the owner, an oldtime Guadeloupienne restaurateur, offers fixed-price meals beginning at 110F ($17.05) or à la carte dinners at 135F ($20.93) and up. Food is served from noon to 3 p.m. and 7 to 10:30 p.m. Specialties include a medley of Créole food such as accras, court-bouillon of fish, grilled fish, steaks, shellfish, and blood sausage. Closed for dinner in October.

La Soufrière

The big attraction of Basse Terre is the famous sulfur-puffing La Soufrière volcano, which is still alive, but dormant—for the moment at least. Rising to a height of some 4,800 feet, it is flanked by banana plantations and lush foliage.

After leaving the capital at Basse-Terre, you can drive to **St-Claude,** a wealthy suburb, four miles up the mountainside to a distance of 1,900 feet. It has an elegant reputation for its perfect climate and luxurious tropical gardens.

An excellent place for a stopover is **Relais Bleu de la Soufrière,** 97120 St-Claude, Guadeloupe, F.W.I. (tel. 011-590/80-01-27). Originally built in the 1860s as the island residence of one of Guadeloupe's governors, Governor Favtier, this charming Créole mansion was reopened in 1987. Graced with verandas, a flowering garden, high ceilings, and thick walls, the hotel offers 22 comfortable bedrooms and a pleasantly old-fashioned dining room. Each of the accommodations has a private bath, air conditioning, and a view either of the garden, an inner courtyard, or the faraway sea. All year singles or doubles rent for 300F ($46.50) to 400F ($62) per day, with breakfast included. Reaching the beach requires a ten-minute car ride, although the mansion's location in the north-central residential section of St-Claude places it near most of the town's architectural points of interest. Even if you're a nonguest, you can visit for a meal served daily in the dining room from noon to 2 p.m. and 7 to 9:30 p.m. Fixed price meals costing from 80F ($12.40) to 130F ($20.15), with à la carte dinners going for 170F ($26.35). Specialties include recipes from both the classic French cuisine as well as adaptations of Créole dishes.

Instead of going to St-Claude, you can head for **Matouba,** in a country of clear mountain spring water. The only sound you're likely to hear at this idyllically quiet place is of birds and the running water of thousands of springs. The village was settled long ago by Hindus.

You'll find good food at **Chez Paul de Matouba,** Rivière Rouge (tel. 011-590/80-01-77), on the banks of the small Rivière Rouge (Red River). The dining room on the second floor is enclosed by windows, allowing you to drink in the surrounding dark-green foliage of the mountains. The cookery is Créole, and crayfish dishes are the specialty. However, because of the influence of the early settlers, Hindu meals are also available. By all means, drink the mineral or spring water of Matouba. Expect to pay around 135F ($20.93) for what one diner called "an honest meal." Specialties include stuffed crab, colombo (curried) chicken, as well as an array of both French, Créole, and Hindu specialties. It is open only for lunch from noon to 4 p.m., but not on Monday. Regrettably, if you're an independent traveler, you're likely to find the place overcrowded in the winter season with the tour-bus crowd.

Back in St-Claude, you can now begin the climb up the narrow, winding road the Guadeloupeans say leads to hell—that is, **La Soufrière.** The road ends at a car park at La Savane à Mulets, at an altitude of 3,300 feet. That is the ultimate point to be reached by car. Hikers are able to climb right to the mouth of the volcano. However, in 1975, the appearance of ashes, mud, billowing smoke, and earthquake-like tremors proved that the old beast was still alive.

In the resettlement process, 75,000 inhabitants were relocated to Grande Terre. However, no deaths were reported. But the inhabitants in Basse Terre still keep a watchful eye on the smoking giant.

Even in the parking lot, you can feel the heat of the volcano merely by touching ground. Steam emerges from fumaroles and sulfurous fumes from the volcano's "burps." Of course, fumes come from its pit and mud cauldrons as well.

The Windward Coast

From Basse Terre to Pointe-à-Pitre, the road follows the east coast, called the Windward Coast. The country here is richer and greener than any I've seen so far on the island.

To reach **Trois Rivières** you have a choice of two routes. One goes along the coastline, coming eventually to Vieux Fort, from which you can see Les Saintes archipelago. The other heads across the hills, Monts Caraïbes.

Near the pier in Trois Rivières you'll see some pre-Columbian petroglyphs carved by the original inhabitants, the Arawaks. They are called merely *Roches Gravées,* or "carved rocks." In this archaeological park, the rock engravings are of animal and human figures, dating most likely from A.D. 300 or 400. You'll also see specimens of plants, including the calabash, cassava, cocoa, pimento, and banana, that the Arawaks cultivated long before the Europeans set foot on Guadeloupe. From Trois Rivières, you can take boats to Les Saintes.

After leaving Trois Rivières, you continue on Rt. 1. Passing through the village of Banaier, you turn on your left at Anse Saint-Sauveur to reach the famous **Chutes du Carbet,** a trio of waterfalls. The road to two of them is a narrow, winding one, along many steep hills, passing through banana plantations as you move deeper into a tropical forest.

After three miles, a lane, suitable only for hikers, brings you to Zombie Pool.

Half a mile farther along, a fork to the left takes you to Grand Etang, or large pool. At a point six miles from the main road, a parking area is available and you'll have to walk the rest of the way on an uneasy trail toward the second fall, Le Carbet. Expect to spend around 20 to 30 minutes, depending on how slippery the lane is. Then you'll be at the foot of this second fall where the water drops from 230 feet. The waters here aren't too cold, averaging 70° Fahrenheit, which is pretty warm for a mountain spring.

The first fall is the most impressive, but it takes two hours of rough hiking to get there. The third fall is reached from Capesterre on the main road by climbing to Routhiers. This fall is less impressive in height, only 70 feet. When the Carbet water runs out of La Soufrière, it is almost boiling.

After Capesterre, you can go along for 4½ miles to see the statue of the first tourist who landed in Guadeloupe. It stands in the town square of Ste-Marie. The tourist was Christopher Columbus, who anchored a quarter of a mile from Ste-Marie on November 4, 1493. In the journal of his second voyage he wrote, "We arrived, seeing ahead of us a large mountain which seemed to want to rise up to the sky, in the middle of which was a peak higher than all the rest of the mountains from which flowed a living stream."

However, when Caribs started shooting arrows at him, he left quickly, heading for new adventures.

If you want to lunch in the area, try **Le Crépuscule** (Chez Dollin), in the village of Habituée, en route to Carbet Falls (tel. 011-590/86-34-56). It features the Créole cookery of a native Guadeloupean, Serge Dollin, who is assisted by a staff whose members live, for the most part, within a few steps of the restaurant's front veranda. The building lies about two miles east of the waterfall in a concrete building flanked by hibiscus hedges. You can dine well for 110F ($17.05) from noon to 4 p.m.

After Ste-Marie, you pass through Goyave, then Petit Bourg, seeing on your left the Route de la Traversée before reaching Pointe-à-Pitre. You will have just completed the most fascinating scenic tour Guadeloupe has to offer.

THE SPORTING LIFE: Most visitors come to Guadeloupe for swimming and sunning. There are many well-sheltered beaches where you can enjoy not only this, but fishing, skindiving, and waterskiing. Chances are, your hotel will be built right on a beach, or else will lie no more than 20 minutes from a good one. There is a plenitude of natural beaches dotting the island from the surf-brushed dark strands of western Basse Terre to the long stretches of white sand encircling Grande Terre. Public beaches are generally free, but some charge for parking. Unlike hotel beaches, they have few facilities. Hotels welcome nonguests, but charge for changing facilities, beach chairs, and towels.

Sunday is family day at the beach. You'll see how the local folk enjoy their day off. Topless sunbathing is common at hotels, less so on village beaches.

Snorkeling is not a major activity on Guadeloupe, and if that's your main interest, look to other Caribbean islands.

Golf

The **Golf de St-François** (tel. 011-590/88-41-87) is at St-François, opposite the Méridién Hôtel, about 22 miles east of Raizet Airport. The golf course runs alongside an 800-acre lagoon where windsurfing, waterskiing, and sailing prevail. The course, designed by Robert Trent Jones, is a 6,755-yard, par-71 course, which presents many challenges to the golfer, with water traps on 6 of the 18 holes, massive bunkers, prevailing trade winds, and a particularly fiendish 400-yard par-4 ninth hole. The par-5 sixth is the toughest hole on the course. Its

450 yards must be negotiated into the constant easterly winds. Greens fees are 200F ($31) per day per person.

Scuba Diving

Hot on the trail of Jacques Cousteau, who has spent much time in local waters, scuba-divers are drawn to Guadeloupe. Cousteau described Guadeloupe's Pigeon Island as "one of the world's ten best diving spots." During a typical dive, sergeant majors become visible at 30 feet, spiny sea urchins and dazzling green parrotfish at 60 feet, and magnificent finger, black, brain, and star coral come into view at 80 feet.

Other dive sites are Mouton Vert, Mouchoir Carré, and Cay Ismini. They are close by the major hotels, in the bay of Petit Cul-de-Sac Marin, south of Rivière Salée, the river separating the two halves of Guadeloupe. North of the Salée is another bay, grand Cul-de-Sac Marin, where the small islets of Fajou and Caret also boast fine diving.

A leading proponent of the sport is divemaster Alain Verdonck whose **Aqua-Feri Club** is based at La Créole Beach Hotel in Gosier (tel. 011-590/84-26-26), 15 miles east of Pointe-à-Pitre. Verdonck's underwater journeys explore the remains of two sunken ships, Pointe-à-Pitre Bay, coral reefs, and Pigeon Island.

A second dive center is operated at Bas du Fort. It's **Cabane de Loisirs,** Fleur d'Épée Novotel, Bas du Fort (tel. 011-590/90-81-49, ext. 398). Arrangements for diving are made at a wood-sided hut along a palm-fringed beach at this previously recommended hotel.

Nautilus Club, facing Pigeon Island from the beach at Malendure (tel. 011-590/98-70-34), has four boats for divers. Two dives a day are offered from the beach: at 9:45 a.m. and 2:45 p.m.

Another diving facility at Malendure is **Chez Guy** (tel. 011-590/98-81-72). Guy Genin has three boats, and regular dives are at 9:45 a.m. and 2:45 p.m., with a 12:30 p.m. dive available on request. Guy also has a diving center on Les Saintes. Both centers are open all year.

Sailing

Sailboats of varying sizes, crewed or bareboat, are plentiful. Information can be secured at any hotel desk. Sunfish sailing can be done at almost every beachfront hotel.

Deep-Sea Fishing

The season for barracuda and kingfish is January to May. For tuna, dolphin, and bonito, it's December to March.

Fishing Club Antilles, Section Poirier-Pigeon, 97125 Bouillante, Guadeloupe, F.W.I. (tel. 011-590/98-73-77), at Bouillante, isn't a club in the usual sense, more like a deep-sea fishing company. Some avid sport fishermen rent one of the establishment's bungalows so they can be at the pier when the first boat leaves at 5 a.m. Bungalows rent throughout the year for 410F ($63.55) in a single, 550F ($85.25) in a double. A six-hour boat rental, with equipment and crew, costs 2,500F ($387.50) from 5 to 11 a.m. An afternoon expedition from 3 to 7 p.m. goes for 2,000F ($310). Francis Ricart and his wife, Françoise, the French-born owners, also operate the previously recommended La Touna.

Waterskiing

Most seaside hotels can arrange this at a cost of $13 for 30 minutes' boating time.

Windsurfing

This is the hottest sport in Guadeloupe today, and it's available with lessons at all the major beach hotels.

Tennis

All the large resort hotels have tennis courts, many of which they light at night for games. The noonday sun is often too hot for most players. If you're a guest, tennis is free at most of these hotels. But you will be charged for night play. If your hotel doesn't have a court, you might consider an outing to **Le Relais du Moulin,** Châteaubrun, near Ste-Anne (tel. 011-590/88-23-96). There you can play tennis at 45F ($6.98) per hour.

Horseback Riding

Relais du Moulin Hôtel, at Châteaubrun, near Ste-Anne (tel. 011-590/88-23-96), the most complete stables on the island, has English thoroughbred horses which it rents for accompanied tours through sugarcane fields and the local countryside, at a cost of 150F ($23.25) per hour. Closed Monday.

Hiking

The **Parc Naturel de Guadeloupe** is the best hiking grounds in the Caribbean, in my opinion (please refer to the touring notes on Route de la Traversée). Marked trails cut through the deep foliage of rain forests until you come upon a waterfall or perhaps a cool mountain pool. The big excursion country, of course, is around the volcano, La Soufrière. However, because of the dangers involved, I recommend that you go out only with a guide. Hiking brochures are available from the tourist office. Guided hiking tours, such as a four-hour climb of La Soufrière, cost 300F ($46.50). Hotel tour desks can arrange this activity.

Warning: Hikers may experience heavy downpours. The annual precipitation in the higher slopes is 250 inches per year, so be prepared.

Camping

Campsites are basic, except at **Les Sables d'Or,** Plage de Grande Anse, 97126 Deshaies, Guadeloupe, F.W.I. (tel. 011-590/28-44-60), which has good facilities and rents tents. Camping areas separated by trees have water, shaded eating places, toilets, bathrooms, and kitchens. To rent a camp area and a tent costs 42F ($6.51) for one person, 62F ($9.61) for a two-person tent. Bungalows are also available, costing 62F ($9.61) for one renter, 82F ($12.91) for two. Simple bedrooms cost 120F ($18.60) per night, single or double.

AFTER DARK: Guadeloupeans claim that the béguine was invented here, not on Martinique. Regardless, the people dance the béguine as if they truly did own it. Of course, calypso, the merengue, whatever, moves rhythmically along, as the people of the island are known for their dancing.

Ask at your hotel where the folkloric **Ballets Guadeloupeans** will be appearing. This troupe makes frequent appearances at the big hotels, although they don't enjoy the fame of the Ballets Martiniquais, the troupe already described on the sister island.

Le Foufou is a disco on the grounds of the Hôtel PLM Azur Marissol, Le Bas du Fort, Gosier (tel. 011-590/90-84-84), two miles from Pointe-à-Pitre. It's open only from Tuesday to Saturday, and the action begins at 10 p.m. You're charged an entrance fee of 50F ($7.75) which entitles you to your first drink. After that, drinks cost from 35F ($5.43). Closed in summer.

Guests from surrounding hotels often head for the **Hôtel Salako,** Pointe de la Verdure (tel. 011-590/84-22-22). The after-dark attraction is the Disco Berdy, a disco nightclub. If the crowd is right, the place can be fun. For your first drink you pay 70F ($10.85), which includes the price of your entrance fee. Open daily except Monday from 10:30 p.m. to 4 a.m.

Casino de la Marina (tel. 011-590/88-41-44) stands near the Hôtel Méridien St-François. It is open from 9 p.m. to 3 a.m. to persons over 25 providing they have proof of identity in the form of a driver's license with a photo (or else a valid passport). The entrance fee is 60F ($9.30), and once inside, you can play American roulette, chemin-de-fer, and blackjack. Dress is casual. The nightclub in the open garden offers dancing under the stars to a live band or disco. A free buffet is spread Saturday night.

Another casino is **Gosier-les-Bains,** on the grounds of the Hôtel Arawak (tel. 011-590/84-18-36) in Gosier. Entrance fee is 60F ($9.30). Coat and tie are not required, but dress tends to be casually elegant. An identity card with photo is required for admission. It opens at 9 p.m., and the most popular games are blackjack, roulette, and chemin-de-fer. There is not only a restaurant, but a disco. Closing time is 3 a.m.

ÎLES DES SAINTES: A cluster of eight islands off the southern coast of Guadeloupe, the Îles des Saintes are certainly off the beaten track. The two main islands and six rocks are Terre-de-Haut, Terre-de-Bas, Îlet-à-Cabrit, La Coche, Les Augustins, Grand Îlet, Le Redonde, and Le Pâté. Of all those Saints, only Terre-de-Haut ("land of high") and to a lesser extent Terre-de-Bas ("land below") attract visitors, mostly Guadeloupeans wanting an escape.

If you're planning a visit, Terre-de-Haut is the most interesting Saint to call upon. It's the only one with facilities for overnight guests.

Some claim Les Saintes has one of the nicest bays in the world, a lilliput Rio de Janeiro with a sugarloaf. The isles, just six miles from the main island, were discovered by Columbus (who else?) on November 4, 1493, who named them "Los Santos."

The history of Les Saintes is very much the history of Guadeloupe itself. In years past the islands have been heavily fortified, as they were considered Guadeloupe's Gibraltar. The climate is very dry, and until the desalinization plant opened, water was often rationed.

The population of Terre-de-Haut is mainly white, all fishermen or sailors and their families who descended from Breton corsairs. The fishermen are very skilled sailors, maneuvering large boats called "saintois." They wear coolie-like headgear called a *salaco,* which is shallow and white with sun shades covered in cloth built on radiating ribs of thick bamboo. Frankly, they look like small parasols. Of course, all visitors want to photograph these sailors, and they seem to resent that. If you can't resist taking a picture, please make a polite request (in French, no less; otherwise they won't know what you're talking about). Women like to buy these hats (if they can find them) for use as beach wear. They are often likened to inverted saucers.

Terre-de-Haut is a place for discovery and lovers of nature, many of whom stake out their exhibitionistic space on the nude beach at Anse Crawen.

Part of the fun of Les Saintes is in getting there. The airport is a truncated strip that accommodates nothing larger than 20-seat Twin Otters. Air Guadeloupe has two round trips daily from Pointe-à-Pitre, which take 15 minutes.

There is daily ferryboat service, two boats going from Pointe-à-Pitre (a 50-minute trip) and three from Trois Rivières or Basse-Terre (25 minutes). Primary service to Marie-Galante and Les Saintes runs from Pointe-à-Pitre, the ferryboats leaving from the Gare Maritime des Îles, on the Quai Gatine across the harbor from the open-air market. Departure for Terre-de-Haut is at 8 a.m. daily (7:30 a.m. Sunday), with return at 4 p.m. Service to Marie-Galante operates Monday to Friday at 8 a.m. and Saturday at 7:30 a.m., with returns at 4:30 p.m. On Sunday, there are two return times—at 4 and 6 p.m. The fare to either Marie-Galante or Les Saintes is 70F ($10.85) one way or 130F ($20.15) round trip.

On an island that doesn't have a single car-rental agency, you get about by walking or renting a bike or motorscooter. Bikes cost around $18 per day and motorscooters around $36. They can be rented at hotels and in town near the pier. There are also minibuses called *Taxis de l'Île* (eight in all) which take from six to eight passengers and charge 30F ($4.65) for a 1½-hour tour, including a stop at Fort Napoléon.

At Terre-de-Haut, you'll find the main settlement at **Bourg,** a single street which follows the curve of the fishing harbor. A charming hamlet, it has little houses with red or blue doorways, balconies, and Victorian gingerbread gew-gaws. Donkeys are the beasts of burden, and everywhere you look are fish nets drying in the brilliant sunshine. You can also explore the ruins of Fort Napoléon, which is left over from those 17th-century wars, including the famous naval en-counter known in European history books as "The Battle of the Saints." You can see the barracks and prison cells, as well as the drawbridge and art museum. Occa-sionally you'll spot an iguana scurrying up the ramparts. Directly across the bay, atop Îlet-à-Cabrit, sits the fort named in honor of the Empress Joséphine.

You might also get a sailor to take you on his boat to the other main island, Terre-de-Bas, which has no accommodations, incidentally. Or you can stay in Terre-de-Haut and go on a hike to Le Grand Souffleur with its beautiful cliffs, and to Le Chameau, the highest point on the island, rising to a peak of 1,000 feet.

Scuba-diving centers are not limited to mainland Guadeloupe. The under-water world off Les Saintes has attracted deep-sea divers as renowned as Jacques Cousteau, but even the less experienced may explore its challenging depths and multicolored reefs. Intriguing underwater grottoes found near Fort Napoléon on Terre-de-Haut are also explored.

Where to Stay

The best place to stay at Terre de Haut is **PLM Azur Los Santos,** Vieille-Anse, 97137 Terre-de-Haut, Les Saintes, Guadeloupe, F.W.I. (tel. 011-590/99-50-40), at the foot of Fort Napoléon, managed by one of France's largest hotel conglomerates. An attractive oasis, with red roofs, gingerbread trim, and lots of vegetation, it is the largest hotel on the island. You don't get luxury here, but the rooms are comfortable and well maintained, 54 in all, each with private shower. Accommodations are in bungalows, about half of which are air-conditioned (these are naturally grabbed up first). You can also get a unit with kitchenette, as 16 are equipped with them. Try for an accommodation with a balcony overlook-ing the sea. In high season, depending on the accommodation, singles cost 580F ($89.90) to 620F ($96.10) daily, and doubles rent for 640F ($99.20) to 800F ($124). *In summer, singles pay 325F ($50.38) to 355F ($55.03) daily, with doubles being charged 460F ($71.30) to 500F ($77.50).* Breakfast is included in all the tariffs. MAP is another 135F ($20.93) per person daily. The hotel has a good restaurant and the most complete resort amenities of any establishment on the island. It also attracts those interested in water sports and underwater photogra-phy à la Cousteau.

Hôtel La Saintoise, 97137 Terre-de-Haut, Les Saintes, Guadeloupe, F.W.I. (tel. 011-590/99-52-50), is a modern, two-story building across from the prin-cipal plaza, with its almond trees and widespread poinciana. As in a small French village, the inn places tables and chairs on the sidewalk, where you can sit out and observe what action there is. The owner will welcome you, showing you through his uncluttered lobby to one of his modest bedrooms, of which he has only ten, each outfitted with a tile bath. Eight are air-conditioned. They are on the second floor, and the furnishings are admittedly modest. Everything is kept immaculately clean. In winter or summer, the single rate is 230F ($35.65), going up to 290F ($44.95) in a double. If you're over just for the day, you'll find the hotel perched at water's edge, near where the boat from Trois Rivières on Basse Terre comes in. You can make arrangements to have lunch here, costing from 75F ($11.63) per person, plus 10% service. The restaurant at La Saintoise serves a Créole cuisine on an open-air terrace at the water's edge.

Bois Joli, 97137 Terre-de-Haut, Les Saintes, Guadeloupe, F.W.I. (tel. 011-590/99-52-53), lies in the western part of the islands, overlooking a fine beach. In confectionery white, the stucco block sits on a palm-studded rise of a slope, the home of Monsieur and Madame Fred Blandin. Accommodations are spread between the main house and in some cottages on the hillside. Bold patterned fabrics are used on the beds, and the rooms are furnished in basic modern. About half the units are air-conditioned, with various combinations of shower bath arrangements. The inn offers 23 rooms in all. *In summer, the single MAP rate in a bathless single is 450F ($66.55) daily, going up to 450F ($69.75) in a unit with bath. Likewise, doubles on the MAP cost from 540F ($83.70) to 580F ($89.80).* In winter, the single MAP rate ranges from 450F ($69.75) to 520F ($80.60) daily, and doubles cost 590F ($91.45) to 660F ($102.30). Dinner is another 120F ($18.60) per person, but tax, service, and a continental breakfast are included in the rates quoted. Her food is good Créole-style cooking. Mr. Blandin can arrange for waterskiing, sailing, boat trips to some of the islets or rocks that form Les Saintes, and snorkeling. The place is for those who like their Caribbean holidays remote.

Village Créole, Point Coquelet, 97137 Terre-de-Haut, Les Saintes, Guadeloupe, F.W.I. (tel. 011-590/99-53-83), sits on the northern side of town, near the harbor, within view of the sea. There is no restaurant, but each of the 22 units has either one or two bedrooms and an efficiently organized kitchenette whose meals can be enhanced by owner Ghislain Laps's ability to procure fresh fish for his satisfied guests. Each unit contains a washer-dryer, a flower-filled patio, and comfortable summery furniture. Daily maid service is also included. The owner prefers weekly rentals, but shorter or longer stays are possible. In winter, depending on the view, doubles pay 450F ($69.75) to 560F ($86.80) per day, and triples are charged 580F ($89.90) to 720F ($111.60), with quads costing 680F ($105.40) to 800F ($124). *In summer, doubles cost 380F ($58.90) to 440F ($68.20) daily, and triples go for 450F ($69.75) to 545F ($84.48), with quads costing 600F ($93) to 645F ($99.98).* Organized activities arranged by the hardworking Monsieur Laps include bicycle rental, day trips, and tours of nearby Guadeloupe.

Jeanne d'Arc, 97137 Fond du Curé, Terre-de-Haut, Les Saintes, Guadeloupe, F.W.I. (tel. 011-590/99-50-41), lies on a beach in a village, less than a mile from the airport. This ten-room, two-story concrete building lies at the edge of the water. Units are modest in style, but they compensate with private showers (likely to be cold) and views of the water. English is spoken, and pedalboats and windsurfing on the beach can be arranged. Year-round prices are 250F ($38.75) daily for a single, 270F ($41.85) for a double, with breakfast included. Fresh fish and other seafood and Créole dishes are served on the simple seaside terrace restaurant.

Kanaoa, 97137 Terre-de-Haut, Les Saintes, Guadeloupe, F.W.I. (tel. 011-590/99-51-36), is a modern structure, utterly plain, that was erected on a little beach at Pointe Coquelet. Théo Giorgi owns this 14-room inn, including five units with views of the sea and Anse Mire Cove. All accommodations contain private showers, and a limited amount of English is spoken. The location is 1¼ miles from the airport, or about five minutes on foot from town. The furnishings are spartan. With breakfast included, singles year round rent for 280F ($43.40) daily and doubles for 320F ($49.60). A good Créole meal, costing 125F ($19.38), is served in the open-air restaurant at the water's edge.

Where to Eat

Many French-speaking guests used to come to Terre-de-Haut to eat roast iguana, the large but harmless lizard found on many of these islands. It is quite a tasty treat, somewhat like chicken. But now that the species is endangered, it is no longer recommended that this dish be consumed. Instead, you'll find lots of conch (called lambi), Caribbean lobster, and fresh fish. Prices are reasonable, among the least expensive meals of any place in France. For your dessert, you can sample the savory island specialty, *tourment d'amour* ("agony of love"), a coconut pastry available in the restaurants but best sampled from the barefoot children who sell the delicacy near the boat dock.

La Redonde (tel. 011-590/99-51-10) is one of the best places to go for a Créole-style paella. The owner of the establishment, "Chicken" Georges, calls his popular dish, "La Redonde," named after the restaurant. It's made with the best of the local catch every day, including conch, clams, and crayfish. Two persons must order it, paying 150F ($23.25). Grilled crayfish is the other most popular dish. Service is informal. The restaurant serves from noon to 2 p.m. and 7 to 9 p.m. daily except Friday.

Les Amandiers, Place de la Mairie (tel. 011-590/99-50-06), is perhaps the most traditional bistro setting of any restaurant at Terre-de-Haut. You can order a set menu for only 65F ($10.08). Conch (lambi) is prepared to perfection whether in a fricassée or a colombo, a savory curry stew. The cook knows how to prepare an excellent court bouillon of fish, and you can always count on grilled crayfish, a staple of the island. The catch of the day is also grilled the way you like it (rarely allowed to dry out on the grill). In addition to fish stews, banana stew (yes, that's right) and christophine (chayote, to many readers) stew are also served. A knowledge of French would be helpful around here. The island-born owner, Charlot Brudey, keeps the place open daily from 8 a.m. to 3 p.m. and 6 to 9 p.m. The location is across from the town hall in the center of Terre-de-Haut.

Chez Jeannine, Fond-de-Curé, Terre-de-Haut (tel. 011-590/99-53-37), has one of the most ambitious menus on the island. For example, often you have a choice of nearly a dozen appetizers, ranging from avocado stuffed with crabmeat to a *gâteau de poissons* (literally "fish cake"). The main courses are often adventurous, including goat stew. Crayfish and grilled fish (the ubiquitous catch of the day) appear daily on the menu. Local vegetables are used. Therefore you're likely to see christophine au gratin on the listings, perhaps a purée of pumpkin that's eaten like squash. Expect to pay around 100F ($15.50) for a meal prepared by the Créole chef, Mme Jeannine Bairtran. The place is open from 8 a.m. to 3 p.m. and 6:30 to 9 p.m. daily except Monday. The ambience is that of a Créole bistro—in other words, a hut with nautical trappings and bright tablecloths.

MARIE-GALANTE: The island, an offshore dependency of Guadeloupe, is an almost-perfect circle of about 60 square miles. Possessing much rustic charm, it lies 20 miles to the south of Guadeloupe's Grand Terre.

Columbus noticed it before he did Guadeloupe, on November 3, 1493. He named it for his own vessel, but didn't land there. In fact, it was 150 years later that the first European came ashore.

The first French governor of the island was Constant d'Aubigne, father of the Marquise de Maintenon. Several captains from the West Indies Company attempted settlement, but none of them succeeded. In 1674 Marie-Galante was given to the Crown, and from that point on its history was closely linked to that of Guadeloupe.

However, since 1816 the island settled down to a quiet slumber. You could hear the sugarcane growing on the plantations, and that was about it. Many windmills were built to crush the cane, and lots of tropical fruits were grown.

Now, some 30,000 inhabitants live here, making their living from sugar and rum, the latter said to be the best in the Caribbean. The island's climate is rather dry, and there are many good beaches. One of these stretches of sand covers at least five miles—brilliantly white, a real paradise. Swimming, however, can be dangerous in some places. The best beach is at Petite Anse, 6½ miles from Grand-Bourg.

Air Guadeloupe will bring you to the island in just 20 minutes from Pointe-à-Pitre.

Les Basse airport on Marie-Galante lies about two miles from **Grand-Bourg,** the main town with an 1845 baroque church. The 18th-century Grand Anse rum distillery can be visited, as can the historic fishing hamlet of Vieux Fort. The island is almost exclusively French speaking.

You can also go over by boat, as there is daily service on *Le Madras,* connecting Grand-Bourg to Pointe-à-Pitre. The one-way fare is 120F ($18.60). Call 011-590/83-12-45 for departure times. There are two sailings in each direction every day.

A limited number of taxis are available at the airport, and prices are to be negotiated.

Food and Lodging

There are only a few little accommodations on the island, which, even if they aren't very up-to-date in amenities, are clean and hearty. At least the greetings are friendly. They may also be bewildering if you speak no French.

I prefer the **Auberge de Soledad,** 97112 Grand-Bourg de Marie-Galante, Guadeloupe, F.W.I. (tel. 011-590/97-75-45), which lies about two miles from the airport on the outskirts of Grand-Bourg. In a setting of sugarcane fields, it rents out 20 simply furnished, air-conditioned rooms, each with private shower. Rooms are also equipped with refrigerators and TV sets (the latter of little use to most English-speaking guests). The hotel also rents bicycles and small motorcycles to guests. On the grounds are tennis courts. Mme Emma Avril prefers her guests to stay at least a week, but if you're rushed, she'll probably charge by the day. *In summer, either single or double occupancy will cost from 120F ($18.60) to 150F ($23.25) daily.* Winter rates are 150F ($23.25) to 250F ($38.75) single or double occupancy. More expensive units offer air conditioning. Meals are extra in the Créole restaurant.

L'Auberge de l'Arbre à Pain, rue Jeanne d'Arc, 97112 Grand-Bourg, Marie-Galante, Guadeloupe, F.W.I. (tel. 011-590/97-73-69), near the harbor in the middle of town, offers respectable accommodations to guests interested in a view of old colonial France. Each of the seven rooms contains simple furnishings, air conditioning, a private bath, and easy access to nearby beaches. Year-round rates, single or double occupancy, range from 220F ($34.10) to 260F ($40.30) per day. The hotel's restaurant is open continuously throughout the day for breakfast, lunch, and dinner, turning out such dishes as a court bouillon of fish, a soufflé of sea urchins, and a tempting array of fresh grilled fish. Full meals cost from 125F ($19.38) and you're welcome to have a meal here if you're visiting only for the day. Should you want a room, however, in winter, it is advised to book well in advance.

LA DÉSIRADE: The ubiqutous Columbus spotted this *terre désirée* or "sought-after land" after his Atlantic crossing in 1493. Named La Désirade, the island, which is less than seven miles long and about 1½ miles wide, lies just five miles off the eastern tip of Guadeloupe. This former leper colony is often visited on a day's excursion (Club Med types like it a lot).

The island has fewer than 2,000 inhabitants, including the descendants of Europeans exiled here by royal command. Tourism has hardly touched the place, if you can forget about those "day trippers," and there are almost no facilities for overnighting, with an exception or two.

The main hamlet is **Grande Anse,** which has a lovely small church with a presbytery and flower garden, and the homes of the local inhabitants. Le Souffleur is a village where boats are constructed; and at Baie Mahault are the ruins of an old leper colony from the early 18th century.

From Pointe-à-Pitre, Air Guadeloupe flies to La Désirade three times daily on a 20-minute flight. The airstrip on La Désirade accommodates up to 19-seat aircraft. Should you ever go by sea, the crossing is likely to be rough. A ferry leaves from La Darse in Pointe-à-Pitre, the crossing taking 1½ hours and costing 120F ($18.60) for a round-trip ticket. Telephone 011-590/83-12-45 for departure times.

On Désirade, three minibuses run between the airport and the towns. To get around, you might negotiate with a local driver. Bicycles are also available.

The best beaches are Souffleur, a peaceful and tranquil oasis near the boat-building hamlet, and Baie Mahault, a small beach that is a Caribbean cliché with white sand and palm trees.

For food and lodging, go to **La Guitoune,** 97127 Grande Anse, La Désirade, Guadeloupe, F.W.I. (tel. 011-590/20-05-07), where Mme Jeanville will welcome you to her native-style hotel. She rents out five modest rooms with private cold-water showers (toilets in the hallway) for around $30 per night. Her local restaurant is good, serving Créole meals for about 100F ($15.50), with the emphasis on fresh fish. It is 7½ miles from the airport and is exceptionally basic, but it's all that's available here.

3. ST. MARTIN

Partitioned between the Netherlands and France, the divided island of St. Martin (Sint Maarten in Dutch) has a split personality. The 37-square-mile island is shaped like a lazy triangle. The northern part of the island, a land area of about 21 square miles, belong to France, the southern part to the Netherlands.

The island has two jurisdictions, but there is complete freedom of movement between the two sectors. If you arrive on the Dutch side and clear Customs there, you need not worry anymore with red-tape formalities when crossing over to the French side—either for shopping, perhaps a hotel, and certainly for eating, as it has the best food (with some notable exceptions).

French St. Martin is governed from Guadeloupe and has direct representation in the government in Paris. Lying between Guadeloupe and Puerto Rico, the tiny island has been half French, half Dutch since 1648.

The principal town on the French side is **Marigot,** the seat of the subprefect and municipal council. Visitors come here not only for shopping, as the island is a free port, but also to enjoy the excellent cookery in the Créole bistros.

Marigot is not quite the same size as its counterpart, Philipsburg, in the Dutch sector. It has none of the frenzied pace of Philipsburg, which is often overrun with cruise-ship passengers. In fact, Marigot looks like a French village transplanted to the West Indies. The policeman on the beat is a gendarme. If you climb the hill over this tiny port, you'll be rewarded with a view from the old fort there.

About 20 minutes by car beyond Marigot takes you to **Grand Case,** a small fishing village, an outpost of French civilization that has some very good local Créole restaurants and a few places to stay.

St. Martin hardly has the attractions of St. Thomas, Puerto Rico, Jamaica, or whatever. You may ask, "Why come here?" There are no dazzling sights, no spectacular nightlife. Even the sports program on St. Martin isn't as organized as it is on most Caribbean islands, although the Dutch side has golf and other diversions.

Most people come to St. Martin just to relax. They can do that on the island's many fine beaches. In spite of its many drawbacks, the island has become such a popular tourist destination in the past few years that it's practically impossible to get a room in winter without reserving in advance.

Not just the beaches, but the hospitality of St. Martin is important too. This is a friendly island whose local population welcomes visitors. Some 70% of the residents work in the tourist business. In spite of its lack of great scenic beauty, the island has been called "civilized."

GETTING THERE: Most arrivals are at the Dutch-controlled **Queen Juliana International Airport,** St. Maarten. For a more detailed description of transportation to that side of the island, refer to the "Getting There" section of St. Maarten in Chapter X.

French St. Martin has **Espérance Airport** at Grand Case (tel. 011-590/87-51-21), used by **Air Guadeloupe** for its daily ten-minute flights to St. Barts (coming up).

GETTING AROUND: For visitors, the most common means of transport is the taxi. A **Taxi Service & Information Center** operates at the port of Marigot (tel. 011-590/87-56-54). Always agree on the rate before getting into an unmetered cab. Here are some sample fares, subject to change: From Juliana Airport on Dutch St. Maarten to Marigot costs $7 or $13 to Grand Case. From Philipsburg, capital of Dutch St. Maarten to Marigot is $7. These fares are in effect from 7 a.m. to 9 p.m. After that, they go up by 25% until midnight, rising by 50% after midnight.

You can also book 2½-hour sightseeing trips around the island, either through the organization listed above or at any hotel desk. The cost is $30 for one or two passengers, plus $7.50 for each additional guest.

It's much cheaper to go by one of the island's **buses,** which run from 6 a.m. until midnight. For example, one departs from Grand Case to Marigot every 20 minutes. There's a departure every hour from Marigot to the Dutch side. The one-way fare from Marigot to Philipsburg on the Dutch side is only 85¢, increasing to $1.50 from Grand Case.

Several **car-rental companies** operate on the island, but vehicles can't be picked up at the Dutch Juliana Airport and have to be delivered free to your hotel. Chances are, you'll make your car-rental arrangements at Juliana Airport before going over to your hotel by taxi on the French side. If so, you may want to refer to the transportation section for St. Maarten in Chapter X. **Budget, Avis, Hertz**—all the big names—are represented in the Dutch side.

Most hotels will reserve a car for guests in advance, and this is highly recommended in winter, when there is often a shortage of rental cars. Most companies

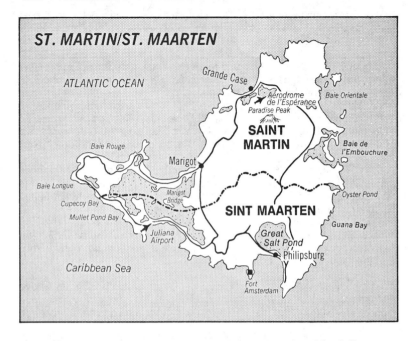

insist that drivers be at least 23 to 25 years old. All foreign driver's licenses are honored. One tank of gas should last a week.

PRACTICAL FACTS: English is widely spoken in St. Martin, although it is a French possession. A patois is spoken only by a small segment of the local populace.

   Banks: They generally are open from 8:30 a.m. to 1 p.m. Monday to Thursday. On Friday they're open during the day but also from 4 to 5 p.m.

   Currency: The currency, officially at least, is the French franc, yet U.S. dollars seem to be preferred wherever you go and are favored over francs. Canadians should convert their money into U.S. dollars and not into francs.

   Documents: U.S. and Canadian citizens should have either a passport, voter registration card, or a birth certificate, plus an ongoing or a return ticket.

   Electricity: The electric current is 220 volts, 50 cycles, which of course will necessitate a converter or adapter if you plan to use your appliances such as a hair dryer.

   Information: The tourist board, called **Syndicat d'Initiative,** is at Mairie de Saint-Martin at Marigot (tel. 011-590/87-53-26).

   Medical care: There is a hospital in Marigot (tel. 011-590/87-50-07), and hotels will help visitors in contacting English-speaking doctors.

   Tax: A departure tax of 10F ($1.55) at Espérance Airport is included in Air Guadeloupe's published fare.

   Telephone: French St. Martin is linked to the Guadeloupe telephone system, which can place calls to and from the U.S. In the U.S., dial 011, then 590, then the local number. To call Dutch St. Maarten from the French side, dial 93 plus the four digits of the St. Maarten number. To call from the Dutch side to the French side, dial 06, then the six-digit French number.

   Time: The island is on Atlantic Standard Time, which means that the only time the U.S. East Coast and St. Martin are in step is during the Daylight Saving Time of summer.

Tips and service: Your hotel is likely to add a 10% to 15% service charge to your bill to cover tipping. Likewise, most restaurants include the service charge on your bill.

Water: The water of St. Martin is safe to drink. In fact, most hotels serve desalinated water.

WHERE TO STAY: Most of the hotels are on the Dutch side. The French side seems to specialize in efficiency apartments with kitchenettes, and the hotels that do exist are more continental in flavor than some of the beachside hostelries bordering the sands outside of Philipsburg in St. Maarten.

At a few of the smaller St. Martin inns, guests are likely to be French speaking—so be duly warned if you fear a language problem.

The Luxury Leaders

Hotel La Samanna, Baie Longue, P.O. Box 159, 97150 St. Martin, F.W.I. (tel. 011-590/87-51-22), admits it's "not for everyone." However, if you're Mick Jagger, or just a person devoted to good, whole-hearted, unabashed sybaritism—and have lots of money—you should fit in beautifully here. Set on a landscaped 55-acre piece of choice property, the confectionery La Samanna opens onto a mile and a half of white sandy beach, filled with some of the best-stuffed bikinis you're likely to see this side of St-Tropez. In fact, the resort, like so many places in St. Martin, is more evocative of the Côte d'Azur or Morocco than the Caribbean. The place is what the French call *intime, tranquille, et informal.* Yes, *informal,* like *le weekend,* is creeping in to bastardize the French language. Around the blue-green waters of the Moorish-style pool you are likely to see some chic guests.

The hotel is a mélange of styles. At one minute you'll think you're in Fez, yet another look convinces you you're in a setting typical of Arizona (even Beverly Hills), and still another glance makes you think you've stopped off at a hotel somewhere in the Aegean Sea. Arches and balconies in pure "Greek fishing village white" are set off effectively by the use of stunning royal-blue doors and umbrellas. Splashes of bold fabrics are used on the puffy cushions on the Haitian furniture which is mostly in wicker and rattan. The colors are like a flamboyant flower garden. The choice of rooms is complicated. In the main building you'll find more than a dozen twin-bedded rooms. These have balconies and are screened from the terrace by a thatched ramada roof. Otherwise, you can ask for one of the two dozen one-bedroom apartments, one of the 16 two-bedroom units, or one of the six villas with three bedrooms each—each with fully equipped kitchens, living rooms, dining areas, and large patios. People often speak in awe of the rates charged here. On the EP in winter, La Samanna charges $485 to $670 daily, either single or double occupancy, and $650 to $1,550 daily in one of the two- or three-bedroom villas. *Two persons can stay here in summer in a twin-bedroom unit, paying from $280 to $380 daily or from $600 daily in a two-bedroom villa.* The hotel is closed in October. MAP is another $78 per person daily.

Before dinner, enjoy an apéritif in the bar, where an Indian wedding robe serves as the ceiling. Dining is al fresco with a French and Créole cuisine prepared by some of the best chefs on the island. You eat out on a candlelit terrace overlooking Baie Longue. After dinner, the bar becomes a disco. Down below at the beach, snorkeling, waterskiing, sailing, and island exploring can be arranged. Scuba-diving and other sports are always available, as is tennis.

La Belle Créole, P.O. Box 118, Pointe des Pierres a Chaux, 97150 Marigot, St. Martin, F.W.I. (tel. 011-590/87-58-66), lies two miles from Marigot and five miles from Juliana Airport (on the Dutch side). The deluxe Mediterranean-style resort, modeled after a typical French Riviera fishing village, lies on a peninsula within view of the capital of Marigot and is surrounded by three white beaches. Walkways paved in stone connect the central square of the resort to the accommodations, housed in 27 separate villas, one story to three stories high.

There are 156 spacious rooms, including 14 suites. Most units have private terraces and all are equipped with individually controlled air conditioning, mini-bars, direct-dial phones, and TV. Three types of guestrooms are rented, including those with king-size beds, double beds, and suites. Five are specially equipped for the handicapped. In winter, single or double occupancy costs from $255 to $535 daily *Summer prices are $150 to $390 daily*. Suites are more expensive, of course. All tariffs include a full American breakfast. Seating 200 patrons, the hotel's gourmet restaurant offers both a continental and a Créole cuisine. Four tennis courts, plus a pro shop, are on the grounds, and a full array of water sports is featured, including windsurfing and scuba diving. For reservations call toll free 800/445-8667.

L'Habitation, P.O. Box 230, Marcel Cove, 97150 St. Martin, F.W.I. (tel. 011-590/87-33-33, 212/757-0225 in New York City, or toll free 800/847-4249). Owned and developed by a consortium of French insurance companies, this is ambitious real estate. Its isolated location was considered almost inaccessible until a crew of engineers cut a two-mile road through some of the most rugged terrain on the island. It stands on a 150-acre flat and sandy patch of palm-dotted land between a saltwater pond and the beach, about 11 miles from Marigot. Accommodations are contained beneath the cedar-covered roofs of the deliberately overscale neo-Victorian buildings ringed with lattices, elaborate gingerbread, and shaded verandas. Each of the more than 250 accommodations has its own kitchenette, soundproofing, air conditioning, balcony, two-sink bathroom, phone, radio, color TV, internal video system, and stylish decor of tropical furniture. In winter, daily EP rates for single or double occupancy are $284 to $422, the latter for the marina suite. At Christmas and New Year's and in February, a seven-night minimum stay is required. *In off-season, the cost for single* or double occupancy is $170 to $259 daily. On the premises is a swimming pool whose twin circles appear like the interconnected petals of an expanding lotus. Near it, a pool bar resembles a tile-sheathed gazebo on stilts at the edge of the water. For casual dining, there is Le Balaou restaurant or Le BBQ on the beach. However, for a night of haute cuisine, along with crystal and silver, head for the formal dining room, La Belle France. Right next door, Le Privilège is on a mountainside overlooking the hotel. It is both a sports and fitness center and a dining and nightclub complex (but more about this later). L'Habitation closes in September.

First Class
Club Le Grand, P.O. Box 582, Marigot, 97150 St. Martin, F.W.I. (tel. 011-590/87-57-91), is French St. Martin's first all-inclusive resort for couples only. To reach it, you have to negotiate a confusing labyrinth of back streets at the edge of Marigot. Sunk into flat but lush acreage, the hotel has a rectangular pool, considered large by St. Martin's standards, a wrap-around terracotta terrace, and access to a wide sandy beach. The bedrooms are contained in a duet of elongated hip-roofed buildings whose verandas are accented with fretwork. Each accommodation contains air conditioning, a veranda or balcony, cable color TV, a private bath, and tropical furniture.

The club opened officially in December, 1988. *In off-season, prices range from $260 to $320 per couple nightly.* A minimum stay of three nights is usually required. In winter, tariffs go up to $300 to $375 per couple nightly. During certain peak periods, December 22 to January 2 and February 11 to 25, a seven-night minimum stay is required. The package deal include all meals, French wines with lunch and dinner, unlimited drinks, entertainment, taxes, and service charges, as well as snacks and transfers between the airport and the hotel. Tipping is not permitted. Other activities, also included, are sailing, tennis, exercise classes, snorkeling, and windsurfing. Call toll free 800/221-1831.

Grand Case Beach Club, Grand Case, 97150 St. Martin, F.W.I. (tel. 011-590/87-51-87) is a beachfront condominium hotel, run by the Acciani family from New York City and lying within walking distance of Grand Case. The two-story buildings are elongated, and most units open onto ocean-view terraces. You have a choice of several studios, one-bedroom apartments, and two-bedroom town houses and duplexes. Each apartment contains a fully equipped kitchen, bath, and a private patio. Units are airy, with tile floors, air conditioning, rattan furnishings, and daily maid service. Accommodations, from studios to two-bedroom duplexes, in winter cost $175 to $290 for one or two persons daily. *Off-season, prices are $88 to $164 for one or two persons.* There are two beaches and water-sports facilities, including scuba-diving, snorkeling, and sailing. The club has the first artificial grass tennis court in the Caribbean. Le Panoramique Restaurant, an architectural gem, extends out on a bluff overlooking Grand Case. The ambience at the hotel is informal. This is the type of place where you make friends with other guests and plan to see them the "same time next year."

The Moderate Range
La Résidence, rue du Général-de-Gaulle, Marigot, 97150 St. Martin, F.W.I. (tel. 011-590/87-70-37), in the commercial center of town, has a concrete façade enlivened with a neo-Victorian fretwork of gingerbread. Each of the rooms is arranged around a landscaped central courtyard, where a fish-shaped fountain splashes water into a bowl. A bar with a soaring tent, inspired by a Napoleonic campaign, serves drinks to clients relaxing on wicker and bentwood furniture. Each of the 22 bedrooms is air-conditioned, containing a minimalist decor, a TV, a mini-bar, and phone. All but a few have sleeping lofts and a duplex design of mahogany-trimmed stairs and balustrades. In winter, singles cost 500F ($77.50) to 800F ($124) daily, and doubles go for 600F ($93) to 900F ($139.50). An extra bed can be set up in any unit for 200F ($31) daily per person. *In summer, the single rate is $400F ($62) to 600F ($93) daily, with doubles costing 500F ($77.50) to 700F ($108.50). Another bed goes for 100F ($15.50) per person per day.* All tariffs include breakfast.

Le Royale Louisiana, rue du Général-de-Gaulle, Marigot, 97150 St. Martin (tel. 011-590/87-86-51), a 68-room hotel, occupies a prominent position in the center of Marigot. It's designed in a hip-roofed French-colonial Louisiana style whose rambling balconies are graced with geometrically ornate balustrades. Each accommodation contains air conditioning, TV hookup, bathroom, big sunny windows, a phone, and modern furniture. Standard rooms have either king- or queen-size beds. Fourteen of the accommodations are duplexes. Ideal for families, these units have a bedroom and bath on the upper level and a sitting room with a fold-out sofa on the lower floor. Duplex rates are not based on occupancy count, so a family of six, for example can rent a duplex for $170 daily in winter, *only $150 in summer.* Otherwise, the winter price in a single is $89 daily, rising to $110 in a double and $145 in a triple. *In summer, singles rent for $73 daily, doubles for $96, and triples for $116.* The hotel, a member of the French-owned Accor group, has a restaurant and bar, Le Hammock, serving breakfast and lunch. For dinner, patrons can go to one of the nearby French restaurants in Marigot.

Laguna Beach Hotel, Baie Nettle, 97150 St. Martin, F.W.I. (tel. 011-590/87-91-75), lies on the road between Marigot and the Lowlands. It offers 64 bedrooms in a pair of two-level buildings overlooking the swimming pool. The accommodations for the most part are large and provided with air conditioning, color TV, radios, video, terraces, phones, private safes, and hairdryers. *In off-season, a single costs 460F ($71.30) daily, rising to 510F ($79.05) in a double.* In winter, only double rates are quoted and in U.S. dollars: $180 per night. Standing across from the also-recommended Hotel Royal Beach, Laguna has a central swimming pool area and a dining room open to the breezes. It opened late in 1988, and its public rooms are furnished in part with rattan and decorated with Haitian art.

Hotel Royal Beach, P.O. Box 571, Baie Nettle, 97150 St. Martin, F.W.I. (tel. 011-590/87-89-89), is set beside the highway stretching from Marigot to the Lowlands. Although a modern building, it has softened its angles with rows of gingerbread and neo-Victorian accessories. Opened in 1988, it offers attractively decorated and comfortably furnished bedrooms at reasonable tariffs. *In summer, singles pay from 200F ($31) to 380F ($58.90) daily, with doubles costing from 270F ($41.85) to 480F ($74.40).* The least expensive units open onto either garden or ocean views. The most expensive accommodations have private terraces. The 80-room hotel also has a good restaurant, Le Cayali, serving a wide range of fare, including, for example, a Créole specialty, blood sausage; a French dish, onion soup; and even an American entry, fried chicken. The hotel is a member of Pullman International Hotels.

Le Pirate, P.O. Box 296, Marigot, 97150 St. Martin, F.W.I. (tel. 011-590/87-78-37), lies on the main road leading from Marigot to the Lowlands, set on a narrow strip of sandy land between the open sea and a salt pond. The aim of this 105-room hotel, as voiced by the management, is to combine "French savoir-vivre with Créole color." Each of its comfortably furnished bedrooms has air conditioning, a kitchenette, private bath, color TV, and a balcony opening onto views over the harbor or marina. Studios and duplexes are rented, the latter suitable for four guests. In high season, singles cost 600F ($93) to 950F ($147.25) daily, with doubles costing 700F ($108.50) to 1,050F ($162.75). *In off-season, singles rent for 350F ($54.25) daily, with doubles going for 450F ($69.75) to 540F ($83.70).* The hotel has a small swimming pool a few paces from the beach.

Hotel Captain Oliver, Oyster Pond, 97150 St. Martin, F.W.I. (tel. 011-590/87-40-26), is named for Oliver Lange, a Paris restaurateur for nearly a quarter of a century before coming to this place. Originally, he opened a restaurant on the site (reviewed separately). At the French-Dutch border, near the prestigious Oyster Pond Hotel on the Dutch side, he constructed 25 pink bungalows in a labyrinth of outlying cottages, each ringed with a suggestion of gingerbread and interconnected with boardwalks. High on a hill, the cottages command excellent views, and from the large terraces you can gaze over to St. Barts. Each unit is furnished in white rattan and decorated with local prints. The accommodations come with kitchenettes, marble baths, double sinks, large double closets, and many amenities including direct-dial phones and color TV. Each bungalow is provided with two beds, plus a sofa bed, which makes them possible family rentals. In winter, singles range from $170 to $200 daily, with doubles costing from $200 to $230. The more expensive units are for ocean-view rooms. *In off-season, singles cost from $95 to $115 daily, and doubles are $110 to $130.*

Sol Hotel Ambiance, Oyster Pond, 97150 St. Martin, F.W.I. (tel. 011-590/87-38-10), is a pastel-ornamented building overlooking the yachts bobbing in Oyster Pond right at the French-Dutch border. Built in 1987, this remote outpost consists of eight bungalows in the traditional West Indian style. Although small, this property aims to provide all the services of a large hotel, including a good-size pool, daily maid service, and Telex and Telefax. Each unit, offering either king-size or twin beds, has a kitchenette, air conditioning, and a terrace. *In summer, singles rent for $87 daily, with doubles costing $92.* In high season, singles cost $170 daily, and doubles go for $175. A continental breakfast, tax, and service are included.

Bertine's, La Savana, Grand Case, 97150 St. Martin, F.W.I. (tel. 011-590/ 87-58-39). A description of this place appears in the dining section of Grand Case. In addition to its dining facilities, it offers a quintet of comfortable but simple accommodations whose ambience is a lot like that of a lighthearted private home. Guests are given the use of a residents' lounge filled with wall-mounted fans and louvered windows. The location is isolated, the rooms not glamorous, and you'll need a car to get to the beach, but some guests return year after year. Rooms, single or double occupancy, rent for $65 daily in high season, *dropping to only $45 for two in summer.* An apartment is available for $20 additional per day. A continental breakfast is included. The little hotel is closed in October.

WHERE TO DINE: The classic French haute cuisine, with a big touch of the West Indies, is waiting to greet your taste buds. St. Martin has some of the finest food in the Caribbean.

Baie Longue

Even though you may not be staying at **La Samanna,** you might want to make a reservation to enjoy a meal on the resort's dining terrace. Judges of this cuisine, created by Jean-Pierre Jury, have declared it among the best in the Caribbean. The high prices reflect its image. Your meal could include à la carte specialties such as filet mignon sautéed with walnuts, medallions of lobster with spinach, or sliced filet of grouper in a red wine sauce. Items starred on the menu are low calorie, which is especially important to many of the figure-conscious patrons of this place. Meals, served from 12:30 to 2:30 p.m. and 7 to 9:30 p.m. daily, cost from ($69.75) per person. Lunches, where a theatrically prepared steak tartare is a favorite, are less expensive. Reservations are almost essential at any time. Call 011-590/87-51-22.

In and Around Marigot

Le Nadaillac, Galerie Périgourdine, rue de la Liberté (tel. 011-590/87-53-77). On the waterfront side of this gallery, a little terrace restaurant is like a transplanted pocket of France in the Caribbean. The chef-owner, Fernand Malard, a native of the Périgord region of France (which is famous for its truffles and foie gras), operates a splendid but expensive restaurant, with meals costing from 250F ($38.75). His skilled touch is seen in such dishes as giblet salad (it appears as *salade de gésiers aux lardons*) and in his preserved goose, or *confit d'oie.* Portions of goose are cooked in goose fat and preserved in stoneware pots. He gets many of his products from France, but also has imaginative touches with what emerges from local waters, such as red snapper. You might also try filet mignon with green peppercorns. The service is polite and often quite stylish. Dinner is served nightly (it's best to go between 7 and 9 p.m.) except Sunday, and reservations are recommended. In high season, the restaurant is open for lunch as well, serving from noon to 2:30 p.m., and it also offers dinner on Sunday night.

La Calanque, Boulevard de France, along the Baie de Marigot (tel. 011-590/87-50-82), has a devoted clientele, some of whom acclaim it as the finest French restaurant on the island. Dispensing haute cuisine, this bistro primarily features the cookery of Provence, with cuisine moderne variations. *Calanque* is "Mediterranean French" for "the bay." The decor is Marseille-style, and specialties include snails sautéed with fennel, red snapper with cream of watercress, roast rack of lamb, and breast of duck with corn crêpes. For dessert, ask for a Grand Marnier soufflé. However, expect to pay for what you get, with meals costing $60. Food is served from noon to 2 p.m. and 7 to 10 p.m. daily.

L'Aventure, Harborfront (tel. 011-590/87-72-89), is in a high-ceilinged building which was once a movie theater on the harbor. The owners have covered the ceiling with palm fronds to give the interior a tropical note to complement the mainland France touches. There's an airy bar area, accented with blue and white tiles and cooled with ceiling fans. The real soul of the restaurant, however, is on the narrow second-floor veranda overlooking the market and the yachts in the harbor. About 70% of the establishment's tables are there.

The house salad is made of avocado, shrimp, artichoke hearts, and marinated salmon. A fish terrine is filled with pieces of salmon and yellowtail. Shellfish lovers might order the lobster rolls in cabbage leaves, served with a fricassée of sweet red peppers. Other specialties include a fricassée of chicken in a lobster cream sauce, a 2,000-year-old recipe for duck with orange honey (sweet and spicy), and fresh trout stuffed with mushrooms. To top it off, your dessert could include a fruit or tea-flavored sherbet, iced pear soufflé with passionfruit sauce, or warm chocolate puff pastry with cold cacão sauce. Lunch, costing from $40, is served from noon to 2 p.m. daily and dinner from $50, is presented from 6 to 10 p.m. The restaurant is open seven days a week, except Monday off-season.

Le Mini Club, rue de la Liberté (tel. 011-590/87-50-69). After parking, you'll pass behind the building, climb a sloped flight of wooden stairs, and find yourself in an environment once described as a treehouse built among coconut palms. Suspended on a wooden deck above the sands of the beach, this establishment is filled with such accessories as Haitian murals, and grass carpeting. You might begin your meal with a glass of kir royale, made with a healthy dose of champagne. The French and Créole specialties include lobster soufflé (made for two or four persons), an array of fish and vegetable terrines, red snapper with Créole sauce, sweetbreads in puff pastry, and many kinds of salad, including one with fresh hearts of palm. Dessert might consist of bananas flambéed with cognac. Dinner is served nightly, while lunch is offered every day except Sunday. However, it is closed from May to September. The owners of the Mini are Claude and Pierre du Plessis, who hold lavish buffets every Wednesday and Saturday night, with unlimited wine included, for $35 per person. À la carte lunches cost around $15, while dinners go for $25 on the fixed-price offering. An à la carte dinner costs from $45. Hours are noon to 3 p.m. and 7 to 11 p.m.

La Vie en Rose, Boulevard France (tel. 011-590/87-54-42), is a balconied second-floor restaurant whose cozy dining room, with ceiling fans and candlelight, evokes for many observers the nostalgia of the 1920s. If you don't like the parlor, you can gravitate to one of the tables on a little veranda overlooking the harbor, providing you requested one when you made a reservation. A French gourmet rendezvous, the restaurant offers dinner costing a steep $75 per person. At lunch, you might get by for 200F ($31) or more. The chefs turn out such dishes as lobster fricassée, boneless chicken breast with capers, and entrecôte in red wine sauce. Red snapper is bedded in a spinach mousse. The soupe de poisson is served with a rouille sauce and garlicky croutons. The desserts are some of the best made on the island. La Vie en Rose serves lunch (from noon to 2:30 p.m.) and dinner (from 7 to 9:30 p.m.) seven days a week in high season, but is closed on Sunday off-season.

Restaurant Jean Dupont, Port La Royale (tel. 011-590/87-71-13), is operated by Monsieur Dupont, the proprietor who made his reputation at the very expensive Le Santal. This newer version is not quite as pricy, less formal, and romantically located in this shopping and dining complex in Marigot. The food is just as good here as it is at Le Santal and the service is excellent. Try, for example, a changing repertoire of dishes that might include sautéed scallops and shrimp in a light curry or a chicken suprême. For an appetizer, try the lobster soufflé on a bed of spinach with caviar. Meals cost from 250F ($38.75), and it is open daily from noon to 3 p.m. and 7 to 10 p.m.

La Maison sur le Port, Harborfront (tel. 011-590/87-56-38) attracts many guests at sundown to watch the yachts bobbing in the harbor. Lunch is a refreshing indoor/outdoor experience, where you are seated at tables placed between crisscross balustrades of the covered terrace. Christian Verdeau and his staff also welcome people to dinner in a refined atmosphere and elegant surroundings, with a view of a waterfall in the garden, with spotlights showing the flowers and plants around the restaurant. The tables are dressed with snowy tablecloths and Limoges china. For lunch, which is simpler than dinner, you can choose from a number of salads as well as fish and meat courses. The cost is around $25. A fixed-price dinner menu, costing $40, gives a choice of an appetizer, a main dish, and a dessert. Among the menu choices, you may be offered fresh fish such as snapper, salmon, or lobster; homemade pâté de foie gras; and filet of lamb, veal, or steak, each with a light sauce. Duck has always been a specialty of La Maison. You can order from a wine list with an extensive selection of imported French products at moderate prices or you may want to try the house cocktail, made with blanc de blanc wine, fresh orange juice, Grand Marnier, and a splash of lemon juice. The establishment is open daily for lunch from 11:40 a.m. to 3 p.m. and for dinner from 6 to 10:30 p.m. Reservations are necessary.

Davids, rue de la Liberté in Marigot (tel. 011-590/87-51-58), attracts visiting yachting people to its casual expatriate ambience. A red, white, and blue spinnaker hangs from the rafters. Appetizers include everything from conch fritters to potato skins, and good soups are served too, especially fish chowder and baked onion. Fresh dorado is prepared in different ways, and local lobster is done by the chef any way you want it. The specialty of the house is beef Wellington, served with a red wine sauce. Chicken Kiev, is a more recent addition, as is the Wiener schnitzel. The steaks are prime quality and can be served with dijonnaise or black pepper sauce. Your final bill will probably run from $25 per person at dinner, $12 at lunch. Light lunch is served daily from 11:30 a.m. to 3 p.m. and dinner from 6 to 10:30 p.m. The bar is open until midnight seven days a week.

La Brasserie de Marigot, rue du Général De Gaulle (no phone at presstime), is where the real French eat. Recently opened in a former bank, it has a marble and brass decor, a sort of retro 1950s style with green leather banquettes. Full meals cost from 130F ($20.15) and include all your old favorites: pot-au-feu, choucroute (sauerkraut garni), blanquette de veau, cassoulet, even chicken on a spit and steak tartare. Naturally, you can order interesting terrines here, and wine is sold either by the glass, carafe, or bottle. The place, located in the center of town, is air-conditioned, with a terrace overlooking the pedestrian traffic outside. It also features the most glamorous "takeout" service in St. Martin. Hours are daily from 7 a.m. to 3 a.m.

Native food? Try **Cas' Anny** (tel. 011-590/87-53-38), which used to be known as Chez Lolotte. It's on the rue de la Liberté in Marigot. The chef has shown expertise in turning out a French Antillean cuisine. If you break bread here, you enter an enclosed courtyard, eventually dining in a pavilion with a sweeping view of the sea. Mme Anne-Marie Boissard came from Martinique to open this restaurant, which serves both lunch and dinner, costing 120F ($18.60) at lunch and 180F ($27.90) or more at dinner. Here you can order such local dishes as boudin Créole, a Créole blood sausage. You might also try her conch in the style of Provence (it appears on the menu as lambi), and crabe farci or stuffed crab backs. Even if that weren't reason enough to recommend the place, it's possible to ask for more traditional dishes from the French repertoire, including such as soupe de poisson. Desserts are also good. It is open daily for lunch and dinner from noon to 3 p.m. and 6:30 to 11 p.m.

In and Around Grand Case

This beach town, a scant mile-long brush stroke, has the greatest concentration of fine dining spots in the Caribbean. On the town's one and only street there are more than 18 restaurants, serving the cuisines of at least half a dozen cultures.

Le Ritz Café, Grand Case (tel. 011-590/87-81-58). Its humorously irreverent owner, born of French parents in Vietnam, is perhaps the quintessential French colonial and an astute businessman. With his English-born wife, Sonya, Joel Morand established this restaurant amid one of the most stylish decors on the island. Originally built as a private house, it is now encased in a motif of black, gold, and salmon, with tasteful accents of art deco, along with ornate balustrades, a scattering of antiques, and a neo-Grecian arbor facing the sea. A place like this is so sophisticated that it can be all things to many people. It is open daily, serving meals from noon to 2:30 p.m. and 6:30 to 11 p.m. The staff dresses formally and gives superb service. Menu items combine French and Créole cuisine moderne for full dinners, costing 300F ($46.50) and up. Menu specialties include snails in red wine sauce, filet of turbot imaginatively sauced, and a fresh salad of asparagus garnished with truffles. The wines all come from France's famed Rothschild vineyards. The high standards of professionalism at the café are reflected in the many thoughtful touches which make guests feel welcome: valet parking is provided; complimentary beach chairs and towels are supplied to lunch guests upon request, and lively piano music accompanies dinner dancing. Reservations are suggested. Try it for Sunday brunch as well.

La Nacelle, Grand Case (tel. 011-590/87-53-63), has an elegant atmosphere with a whimsical pink trim and a selective menu, which was created by Charles Chevillot of New York's La Petite Ferme. He handsomely restored a *gendarmerie* built at the turn of the century, across from the pier. Lying about a ten-minute ride from Marigot, La Nacelle is expensive but worth it. At dinner here, your leek bisque, followed by lobster Caribbean style, is served under an almond tree in a flower-filled garden. Outside the courtyard, shaded by palm fronds, is a bright mural of a balloonist (a *nacelle* is the basket of a hot-air balloon). You can also dine inside, enjoying the immaculate service and fine tableware. Dinner, from 6:30 to 9 p.m. daily except Sunday, is likely to cost around $45. A winter-only restaurant, La Nacelle wisely employs masters of the French cuisine. For dessert, try, if featured, a sherbet made with guava. It's necessary to make a reservation.

L'Auberge-Gourmande, Grand Case (tel. 011-590/87-55-45), has generated a lot of local excitement, and deservedly so. You have to go to a bit of trouble to dine here, but it's worth it. The chef-owner, Burgundy-born Daniel Passeri, runs this small romantic dining room that is like a little country inn, perhaps somewhere in the heartland of France. Both classic French dishes, plus some with a touch of Burgundy, are served in this old Antillean home. Begin with a duck pâté with walnuts. The salads are well made here, using crisp fresh greens, often mixed with bits of ham, cheese, and walnuts. For a main course, the langouste is the most preferred and expensive selection, and the red snapper in port wine sauce is equally as good. You might also try duck breast with three-berry sauce or scallops and shrimp with fresh sauce. For dessert, try apple crêpe drenched in Calvados. For a complete meal, expect to spend from $35. The restaurant serves dinner six nights a week, closing Wednesday. Hours are 6:30 to 10 p.m. Trade winds cool the place in lieu of air conditioning. Closed in August and September.

Chez Martine, Grand Case (tel. 011-590/87-51-59). Diners sit at a well-set table on a gingerbread terrace overlooking the sea. This is a very French Antillean place, and the staff has been well selected, giving capable service. You get a number of dazzling choices in cuisine. To begin your meal, you're faced with such appetizers as uncooked salmon (marinated in a sauce of fresh herbs), snails in garlic butter, or foie gras in a jellied turnip concoction. The most tempting part of the menu is that listed under *poissons*. You can order grilled island lobster flambéed with cognac or beef tenderloin apple-roasted and seasoned with cider and bleu cheese. Meals cost around $20 for lunch, $40 for dinner. For dessert, try a French pastry. Hours are daily from noon to 3 p.m. and 6:30 to 10 p.m. Closed Tuesday in summer.

Hévéa, Grand Case (tel. 011-590/87-56-85), is a small and intimate restaurant, with only ten tables, whose owner is Jacqueline Dalbera. Here, you can enjoy French cookery in pleasant formal surroundings of French furniture and avant-garde paintings. The only meal is served from 6:30 to 10 p.m. daily. There are two fixed-price menus, one at $29 and another at $38. Dishes might include a marinated fresh raw salmon and sea scallops in lime juice and dill, sliced duck breast in a wine sauce with black currant, and a dessert specialty of chocolate marquise.

Mark's Place, Cul de Sac (no phone) lies on a road between Orléans and Grand Case. From the outside it appears like a cozy red-and-white cottage flanked with shrubbery. Inside you find a well-scrubbed and well-lit ambience of trestle tables, wide-plank floors crafted from Guyanese cedar, and a high ceiling. Lunch is served from 12:30 to 2:30 p.m., and dinner from 7:30 to 9:30 p.m. daily except Monday. You can enjoy a glass of kir, kir royale, or a pastel-colored but potent drink called a sternwheeler before your meal. After that, you might try such Créole specialties as stuffed crab, accras (spicy shrimp fritters), conch or octopus stew, grilled lobster, and strawberry Melba. There's a small list of international specialties, even hamburgers and snacks. The food is well prepared, a meal costing from $35.

Bertine's, La Savana, Grand Case (tel. 011-590/87-58-39), was previously recommended for its simple accommodations, but it's better known as an unusual and pleasant restaurant. It's contained in an angular concrete building atop a steep hill 1½ miles from Grand Case. Its two separate sections are joined by a wide veranda whose hardwood sheathing is kept spotlessly polished by Bernard and Christine Poticha. Born in Chicago, they moved to a warmer climate, took up cooking, and today are known for their copious portions, good humor, and charm. The restaurant is open nightly (except in October) at sunset and remains so until the last client is satisfied. Bernie does the cooking, while Christine serves and creates an ambience like a private dinner party. Between courses, guests watch the sunset glimmering over the sea between two hills. Full dinners, costing from $25, might include conch stew, crab au gratin, hickory-smoked pork ribs Chicago style (with Bernie's special sauce), and a homemade chocolate mousse pie. A novel house specialty is "steak on a hot rock." No reservations are necessary, but it's always wise to call in advance. The location near the farming hamlet of La Savana is at the top of a steep driveway.

Inland to Colombier

Minutes from Marigot, in the tiny hamlet of Colombier, is one of the best Créole restaurants on St. Martin, **La Rhumerie** (tel. 011-590/87-56-98). Owner West Indies–born Francillette Le Moine continues a tradition established by her late husband, Yannick, from Brittany, in serving with finesse dishes that influence many residents on the island to declare this their favorite restaurant. For years, I recommended the Le Moines' Chez Lolotte, which they ran in Marigot before taking a private home in this country setting. They transformed this home into a charming Créole restaurant that also serves traditional French dishes. These include stuffed crab back, escargots, and onion soup gratinée, but the place is best known for Créole cuisine, offering such dishes as curried goat, a salad of coffre (a local fish), conch in fresh herbs, and poulet boucanne Créole (home-smoked chicken served with baked green papayas and christophine au gratin). There are two servings every day at dinner, one at 7 and another at 9 p.m. Full meals cost $35 and up per person.

Anse Marcel

La Belle France, L'Habitation (tel. 011-590/87-33-33), is a beautifully appointed gourmet restaurant tucked away in a remote corner of St. Martin (its accommodations have been previewed earlier). You might begin with such delectable appetizers as Caribbean lobster soufflé before going on to a delightful salad with quail and flap mushrooms. La Marmite Caraïbe is a steamed selection of local fresh fish and seafood, braised fresh duck liver is sautéed in raspberry vinegar, and you can also order steamed young guinea fowl with a sherry sauce. Meals cost from 250F ($38.75). Only dinner is served, and it is offered nightly from 6:30 to 10, when reservations are needed.

Oyster Pond

Captain Oliver Restaurant, Hotel Captain Oliver (tel. 011-590/87-30-00), partially built on piers above the bay right at the Dutch border and overlooking a yacht-filled harbor, it is reached from either Marigot or Philipsburg along a difficult road. Once there, you'll find favorites such as West Indian conch, "fish soup of the captain," a fisherman's platter, tuna steak grilled with caper sauce, and fresh grilled lobster. Meals, served daily from noon to 3 p.m. and 7 to 11 p.m., cost $15 at lunch, $30 for dinner. This place has been known to island gourmets since it opened in 1983. It adjoins a previously reviewed bungalow colony facing the island of St. Barts, with a marina adding to its appeal, particularly at night.

SHOPPING: Many day-trippers come over to Marigot from the Dutch side just to look at the collection of boutiques from here. Marigot's streets, lined with neat little boutiques and shopping arcades, invite you to walk and browse.

It is a duty-free port, and because of that you'll find some of the best shopping in the Caribbean. There is a wide selection of French goods, including crystal, perfumes, jewelry, and fashions at 25% to 50% less than in the U.S. and Canada. There are also fine liqueurs, cognacs, and cigars. If you're seeking anything from jewelry to perfume to St-Tropez bikinis, you'll find most of the boutiques, often in mellow old buildings, along the rue de la République and rue de la Liberté in Marigot.

Most of the boutiques on the French side are open from 9 a.m. to noon or 12:30 p.m. and from 2 to 6 p.m., Monday to Saturday. When cruise ships are in on Sunday and holidays, some of the larger shops open again.

Prices are often quoted in U.S. dollars, and salespeople frequently speak English. Credit cards and traveler's checks are generally accepted.

Look especially for French luxury items, such as Lalique crystal, Vuitton bags, and Chanel perfume.

At Marigot

At harborside in Marigot, there is a frisky morning market with vendors selling spices, fruit, shells, and local handcrafts.

At **Port La Royale,** the bustling center of everything, mornings are even more alive: schooners unloading produce from the neighboring islands; boats boarding guests for picnics on deserted beaches; a brigantine setting out on a sightseeing sail. And throughout the handsome complex, the owners of a dozen different little dining spots are setting the stage for the daily ritual of a leisurely lunch. This is the *French* Caribbean, so meals are very important.

La Romana, rue de la République (tel. 011-590/87-73-69), in the heart of Marigot, occupies a handsome landmark building transformed into a showcase for the French fashion and jewelry designers represented by La Romana International Boutiques. Customers can also enjoy champagne cocktails offered by the shop at the clients-only café on the overhanging balcony, which provides an unobstructed view of the area.

The largest shopping arcade in St. Martin, Port La Royale has many boutiques, some of which come and go with great rapidity. Try **Lipstick,** Port La Royale (tel. 011-590/87-73-24), for the largest assortment of duty-free fragrances and cosmetics, as well as beauty preparations by such name designers as Dior and Yves St. Laurent. You can also get facial cleaning and massages here. There's another branch of Lipstick along rue de la République in Marigot (tel. 011-590/87-53-92).

Havane (tel. 011-590/87-70-39), Port La Royale, offers exclusive collections of French clothing, both in sports and high-fashion designs for men and women.

Should the heat of the day get to you, stop in at **Etna Ice Cream Per Dolce Vita,** Kennedy Avenue (tel. 011-590/87-72-72), in Port La Royale. Here, Paolo and Betty Smiroldo operate a gelateria-pasticciere, with homemade ice creams created from fresh fruit, their specialties costing from $1.50 to $3. You get such delights as a tartufo as good as the one served on the Piazza Navona in Rome, as well as spumoni, cassata, espresso, along with French croissants and mouthwatering pastries. A fresh-fruit drink, Frullato, is prepared in front of you so you can see what goes into it. The "sweet life" holds forth here from 9 a.m. to 7 p.m. daily (on Sunday from noon to 6 p.m.).

If you opt for a housekeeping holiday in St. Martin, know that the best food is at **K'Dis,** rue du Général-de-Gaulle, in Marigot (tel. 011-590/87-52-23). This is a French *supermarché* where you can order pâté, elegant mustards (especially from Dijon), fine French cheese and wine, and all sorts of fresh and canned goodies.

At another shopping complex, the **Galerie Périgourdine,** facing the post office, stands another cluster of boutiques. Here you might pick up some designer wear for both men and women, including items from the collection of Ted Lapidus. If you're interested in dining here, the Malards own the waterfront terrace restaurant, Le Nadaillac, part of the complex, which has been previously recommended.

Sandrine Boutique, rue de la Liberté (tel. 011-590/87-53-77), across from the post office in Galerie Périgourdine, features the latest fashions for men and women, as well as exclusive beachwear.

Maneks, rue de la République (tel. 011-590/87-54-91), is worth a stopover, as it has a little bit of everything: hand-carved figurines, tobacco products, liquors, gifts, souvenirs, cameras, radio cassettes, Kodak film, watches, and T-shirts.

Little Switzerland (tel. 011-590/87-50-03), also in Marigot, has a better-known branch in Philipsburg on the Dutch side. But the shop here is a fine one too. In fact it's one of the best places in the country if you're seeking European imports at prices lower than Stateside. You get not only name china and crystal, but precision Swiss watches. There is also a large selection of jewelry. The jewelry collection in both the Dutch and French stores is perhaps the biggest in the West

Indies. There are many gift items as well, and you can pick up your favorite fragrance.

Spritzer & Fuhrmann (tel. 011-590/87-59-62), the famous jewelry chain, has a branch in Marigot on the rue de la République, just off the bay. It offers a wide range of merchandise. Included in its collection are crystal, china, clocks, and a superb array of 14- and 18-karat gold jewelry.

Oro de Sol, rue de la République (tel. 011-590/87-57-02), whose branch in Dutch St. Maarten was already previewed, offers high-fashion jewelry styled with continental elegance. Many of its items are one-of-a-kind designs. Walk into the glittering world of diamonds and emeralds, rubies and rock crystal. You'll also find a selection of watches and clocks in the Cartier boutique, along with French porcelain and china.

Since you are not likely to be going to Haiti these days to purchase art, you'll find a good selection of native paintings at the **Gingerbread Gallery,** Port La Royale (tel. 011-590/87-73-21).

Grand Case

Pierre Lapin (tel. 011-590/87-52-10) is a *tiny* store selling original T-shirts made from hand-printed fabrics, paintings, books, and gifts. It's well known and *intime*.

Orléans

Local artist **Roland Richardson** (tel. 011-590/87-32-24), who lives in Orléans, welcomes visitors into his house to view and purchase his original watercolors and prints of island vistas. It's open Monday through Friday from 9:30 a.m. to 1 p.m.

THE SPORTING LIFE: The island as a whole has 32 perfect white sandy beaches. The hotels, for the most part, have grabbed up the choicest sands, and usually for a small fee nonguests can use their beach and changing facilities. Topless sunbathing is practiced commonly at the beaches on the French side. Club Orient Hôtel (tel. 011-590/87-53-85) has the only nudist beach on the island, but nude or mono-kini (as opposed to *bi*kini) is relatively common, even though total nudity is not officially endorsed.

Îlet Pinel, a tiny island off St. Martin, is perfect for beach recluses. Le Galion Beach Hôtel (tel. 011-590/87-51-77) will take visitors over to Pinel on request. The trip can also be made by negotiating with a passing fisherman to provide transport back and forth.

Scuba-Diving

Scuba is excellent around St. Martin. The types of diving are reef, wreck, night, cave, and drift, and the depth of dives is from 40 to 50 feet. Off the northeast coast on the French side, dive sites include Îlet Pinel for shallow diving, Green Key, a barrier reef; Flat Island for sheltered coves and geologic faults; and Tintamarre, known for its shipwreck. To the north, Anse Marcel and neighboring Anguilla are good choices. Most hotels will arrange for scuba excursions on request.

Snorkeling

The calm waters ringing the shallow reefs and tiny coves found throughout the island make it a snorkeler's heaven. The waters off the northeast shores of St. Martin have been classified as a regional underwater nature reserve, **Reserve Sous-Marine Régionale.** The area, comprising Flat Island (also known as Tintamarre), Pinel Islet, Green Key, and Petite Clef, is thus protected by official government decree. The use of harpoons is strictly forbidden. Snorkeling can be enjoyed individually or on sailing trips. Equipment can be rented at almost any hotel.

At **Grand Case Beach Club** (tel. 011-590/87-51-87), a one-hour snorkeling trip costs $10 to $15 per person, depending on the destination.

Waterskiing
This activity can be organized at most beachfront hotels.

Windsurfing
Almost every beachfront hotel has facilities for this sport, and many offer instructions for beginners.

Tennis
Tennis buffs heading for French St. Martin this year can keep in practice at most hotels. Once a rarity on the French side of the island, tennis is now a regular amenity.

L'Habitation has six courts, all lit for night play, and **La Belle Créole** has four, also lit. The Omnisport (artificial grass) court at **Grand Anse Beach Club** is also lit. There are three unlit courts at the exclusive **La Samanna** and two at **Le Galion.**

Horseback Riding
It is possible to ride horseback through the green hills of St. Martin or along its sand beaches. A riding facility, **Caid & Isa,** is operated by islanders Alain and Brigitte Duzant, longtime professional riders, next to L'Habitation. The horses cost $40 for a half-hour ride with an itinerary taking you into the hills of Anse Marcel and to the secluded beach of Petites Cayes (also known as Anse de la Pomme d'Adam, or Adam's Apple Cove). For reservations, phone 011-590/87-32-92).

Sports, Food, and Disco
A trek up a steep road leads to a beautifully landscaped hillside complex overlooking the resort of L'Habitation. Here you discover **Le Privilège,** Anse Marcel (tel. 011-590/37-33-38), the largest sports complex in French St. Martin, with six tennis courts, two squash courts, two racquetball courts, a weightlifting and fitness center (aerobics), a sauna and steamroom with massages, and a swimming pool. There is also a collection of nearly two dozen boutiques.

La Privilège offers two restaurants, one of them, Le Privilège Grill, a 24-hour operation. You can begin in the morning with café au lait, croissants, or omelets, stick around for lunch with onion soup and sandwiches, and enjoy grillades of fish, lobster sausage, and sorbets at night. At the formal dining room, Bagatelle, only dinner is served, nightly from 7 to 10, costing around $40. You might try the lobster cannelloni in truffle sauce or loin of veal in a creamy artichoke sauce. In keeping with its fitness image, a gourmet low-calorie menu is also offered.

To cap the evening, head for Boîte Privilège which is open every day from 10 p.m. to 3 or 4 a.m. (closed Tuesday in summer). A DJ holds court in his eagle's nest, and beer costs from 5F (78¢).

NIGHTLIFE: Some French St. Martin hotels have dinner-dancing, cocktail-lounge music, and even disco dancing, but the most popular after-dark pastime is leisurely dining. The best disco on the island is **Boîte Privilège,** at Le Privilège complex (see "Sports, Food, and Disco" previewed above). There is casino gambling on the Dutch side (refer to Chapter X).

4. ST. BARTHÉLEMY

New friends call it "St. Barts," while oldtime visitors prefer "St. Barths." Either way, it's short for St. Barthélemy—named by its discoverer Columbus in 1493 and pronounced "San Bar-te-le*mee.*" The uppermost corner of the French West Indies, it is the only Caribbean island with a touch of Sweden in its personality.

French adventurers first occupied it, selling out to the Knights of Malta in 1651. When the Caribs pushed the knights out in 1656, France regained control, eventually ceding her rights to Sweden, which ruled from 1784 to 1877.

Louis XVI had traded the island and its people to Sweden in exchange for trading rights in Hothenburg.

Once, in the 19th century, Britain also held control. However, in 1878 a plebiscite returned permanent control to France, and today St. Barts is a dependency of Guadeloupe.

For a long time the island was a paradise for a few millionaires, such as David Rockefeller who has a magnificent parabolic-roofed hideaway on the northwest shore, or Edmond de Rothschild who occupies some fabulous acres at the "other end" of the island. The Biddles of Philadelphia are in the middle. Nowadays, however, St. Barts is developing a broader base of tourism as it opens more hotels.

For the most part, St. Bartians are descendants of Breton and Norman fisher folk. The mostly white population is small, about 3,500 living in some eight square miles, 15 miles southeast of St. Martin and 140 miles north of Guadeloupe.

Occasionally you'll see St. Bartians dressed in the provincial costumes of Normandy, and when you hear them speak Norman French, you'll think you're back in the old country—except for the temperature. In little Corossol more than anywhere else you can see the following of traditions brought from 17th-century France. Here, if you are near the church before or after early-morning mass, you can probably see the barefoot elderly women who wear the starched white bonnets known as *quichenottes* or the *calèche.* This special headgear, brought from Brittany, was called *quichenotte,* a corruption of "kiss-me-not," and may well have served as protection from the close attentions of Englishmen or Swedes on the island. The bonneted women, who usually stay close to their homes, can also be seen at local celebrations, particularly on August 25, St. Louis' Day. The old women of Corossol are camera-shy, but they offer their homemade baskets and hats for sale to tourists.

Many of the people of St. Barts are long-limbed and attractive, of French and Swedish ancestry, the latter showing in their fair skin, blonde hair, and blue eyes.

The island's capital town is **Gustavia,** named after a Swedish king. In fact, Gustavia is St. Barts' only town and seaport. It's a landlocked, hurricane-proof harbor, looking like a little dollhouse-scale port.

GETTING THERE: From the U.S., the principal gateways are St. Maarten (see Chapter X), St. Thomas (see Chapter V), and Guadeloupe (included in this chapter). At either of these islands, connections to St. Barts can be made on interisland carriers.

It is just a ten-minute flight from Juliana Airport on Dutch-held St. Maarten. From St. Maarten, the best way to go is on a flight of **Windward Islands Airways International** (known as Winair). It operates an active passenger network, usually flying "Twin Otters" and doing it well. In St. Maarten, phone

011-599/5-44230 to make a reservation. This airline, which has carried such passengers as Queen Beatrix of Holland and Jacqueline Onassis, will fly you over to St. Barts in the morning and back around 5 in the afternoon. But I recommend that you spend more time, of course, to savor the special flavor of St. Barts. The current one-way fare is $26 per person.

If you're in Guadeloupe, you can fly in aboard **Air Guadeloupe,** a one-hour trip. Air Guadeloupe also has regular service to St. Barts from the small Espérance Airport on the French side of St. Martin.

It's also possible to fly with **Air St. Barts** and **Virgin Air,** which have regular service to St. Barts from San Juan (costing about $250 round trip) and St. Thomas (about $140 round trip). For information about these flights, phone Air St. Barts at the St. Jean Airport on St. Barts (tel. 011-590/27-61-20) or Virgin Air at the St. Barts Airport (tel. 011-590/27-71-76). The latter airline also has a toll-free reservation number: 800/522-3084.

Many jokes have been made about the makeshift landing strip at St. Barts. It's short to begin with, accommodating small craft. The biggest plane it can land is a 19-seat STOL (short takeoff and landing craft). As a chilling sight, a cemetery adjoins the strip! Locals pray to the white cross that stands between two hills flanking the field. Your plane has to make a curving swoop through a hilltop pass. Others suggest that a good belt of scotch should be downed before takeoff. No matter, everybody seems to arrive in one piece.

GETTING AROUND: The principal means are taxis, car rentals, sightseeing tours, even bikes, all of which are outlined below.

Taxis

They meet all flights. Once you've gone through the minor check at Customs, you can take one of these cabs to your St. Jean Bay hotel or go into Gustavia. Taxis are not very expensive, mostly because no one destination is all that far from any other.

Car Rentals

The hilly terrain, and perhaps the sense of adventure of the residents, combine to form a car-rental situation unique in the Caribbean. Never have I seen as many open-sided Mini-Mokes as I have in St. Barts. Painted in vivid primary colors, and designed along lines midway between those of a miniature tank and a World War II Jeep, they're fast, fun, and very windy. You can easily get into the swing of driving one if you're handy with a stick shift and don't care at all about your coiffure.

Budget Rent-a-Car offers them as their least expensive model, dispensing them out of offices at the airport and in Gustavia (tel. 011-590/27-67-43). The cheapest rate is awarded to clients who reserve at least two business days before their arrival and who plan to keep their car for at least five days. With unlimited mileage included, Mokes rent for $270 weekly in winter, $150 weekly in summer.

It's a good idea to buy additional insurance for $8 per day regardless of the model rented. Otherwise, you'll be responsible for the first $1,000 of damage to the car (with the insurance you're liable for only $100 of damage). For reservations and information in the U.S., call Budget toll free at 800/527-0700.

Budget's most aggressive competition, **Hertz,** operates in St. Barts through a local dealership, Henri's Car Rental. With branches at the airport and in St-Jean (tel. 011-590/27-71-14), it offers VW Beetles and open-sided Mini-Mokes for prices roughly comparable to those at Budget. Reservations and information are available by calling toll free in North America at 800/654-3001.

Avis is also represented on the island, but you'll need a reservation a full month in advance in high season, a requirement many visitors find cumbersome. Even with a month's advance reservation, its Mini-Mokes and Beetles usually cost more per week than the cars at Budget or Hertz. However, this could have changed by the time of your visit. For reservations and information, dial toll free 800/331-2112.

Regardless of which you select as your agency, remember that no one will mind if you honk your horn furiously while going around the island's blind corners, a practice that avoids many sideswiped fenders. Drive slowly, carefully, and with consideration.

Gas is extra. Tanks hold enough to get you to a gas station, of which there are three; but only one, the Shell station at the airport, is open on Sunday, and then only from 8 to 11 a.m. All valid foreign driver's licenses are honored.

Sightseeing Tours

Group tours are scaled to the island's size: eight passengers per minibus. The cost is about $30 for two passengers. Operators include **Constant Gumbs** (tel. 011-590/27-61-93), **Claude Lédée** (tel. 011-590/27-60-54), and Hugo Cagan's **St. Barth Tours** (tel. 011-590/27-61-28).

Motorbikes

These are plentiful, with Yamahas renting for about $25 per day. A driver's license is required. Call **St. Barth Moped Rental** (tel. 011-590/27-70-95) if you're interested in this means of transport.

Boat Service to St. Maarten

There is a variety of service between St. Barts and St. Maarten, but schedules vary with the season, so it's best to check on the spot. Contact the skippers of the *White Octopus* or *El Tigre,* who arrive in St. Barts around 11 a.m. after a one-hour, often turbulent, crossing from St. Maarten. They depart the same afternoon, usually at 3 p.m.

PRACTICAL FACTS: St. Barts, as mentioned, is a dependency of Guadeloupe, which in turn is an overseas *département* of France. As such, the citizens of St. Barts participate in French elections. It has its own mayor (elected every seven years), a town constable, and a security force of six policemen and at most a dozen gendarmes.

Banks: There are two banks on the island, both in Gustavia. The Banque Française Commerciale, rue du Général-de-Gaulle (tel. 011-590/27-62-62), is open from 8 a.m. to noon and 2 to 3:30 p.m. The Banque Nationale de Paris, rue du Bord-de-Mer (tel. 011-590/27-63-70), is open from 8:15 a.m. to noon and 2 to 4 p.m.

Currency: The official monetary unit is the French franc, but most stores and restaurants prefer payment in U.S. dollars. Most hotels also quote their rates in American currency at a discount from the rates as quoted in francs.

Customs: You are allowed to bring in items for personal use, including tobacco, cameras, and film.

Documents: If you're flying in, you'll need to present your return or on-going ticket. A valid passport is needed, or else a photo identification.

Electricity: Voltage is 200 AC, 50 cycles; therefore, American-made appliances require French plugs, converters, and transformers.

Information: For information while on the island, go to the **Office du Tourisme**, Mairie de St-Barth, rue August-Nyman, in Gustavia, 97133 St. Barthelemy, F.W.I. (tel. 011-590/27-60-08).

Language: French is the official language, and the type spoken by St. Bartians is a quaint Norman dialect. Some of the populace speak English, however, and there is seldom a language problem at major hotels, restaurants, and shops.

Medical care: Gustavia has one clinic, five doctors, and three dentists. Your hotel reception desk will put you in touch with one if the need should arise.

Tax: An airport departure tax of 15F ($2.33) is assessed.

Telephone: To make a direct telephone call from the U.S., dial 011-590, then the St. Barts six-digit number for station-to-station calls. Only the six-digit number need be used for calling within St. Barts.

Time: There is a one-hour time difference between St. Barts and the East Coast of the U.S. when Standard Time is in effect in the U.S. and Canada. Thus, when it's 7 p.m. in St. Barts, it is only 6 p.m. in New York or Toronto. The island tells time the French way: 1 p.m., for example, is 13 hours; midnight is 24 hours.

Weather: The climate of St. Barts is ideal: it's dry with an average temperature of 72° to 86° Fahrenheit.

WHERE TO STAY: With the exception of such places as Les Castelets, most places here are homey, comfortable, and casual. Everything is small, as tiny St. Barts is hardly in the mainstream of tourism. Some furnished hillside and beach cottages are rented out by the week or month. In March it's often hard to get in here unless you've made reservations far in advance. Rates throughout the island, with some exceptions, tend to be exceptionally expensive, and a service charge and tax are likely to be added to your bill. Ask about this beforehand to save yourself a parting surprise.

The Upper Bracket

Les Castelets, P.O. Box 60, Morne Lurin, 97133 St. Barthélemy, F.W.I. (tel. 011-590/27-61-73), is a luxurious private retreat perched on a hillside commanding spectacular views of Gustavia harbor and the offshore islands. Built in the Provençale style, it is exclusive, exceptional, and graciously conscious of its status as the most durably chic resort on the island. It lies a steep 1.7 miles from the airport, about three-quarters of a mile from Gustavia. Do not expect a beach and the seaside at your doorstep. However, you'll find a small triangular swimming pool with a view on the grounds. The beach at St-Jean is a five-minute drive down the steep hill to the sea.

A fashionable hideaway, this retreat of quiet comfort and relaxed luxury houses its guests in a number of different accommodations, including two small bedrooms in the main building. Villas have two bedrooms, a gracious two-story living room with a marble floor, complete kitchens, baths with bidets, and a wide private terrace for that view. Each villa has a tapedeck. The price of this style comes high. *Single or double occupancy of its rooms costs $100 to $130 daily, and villas for one or two persons rent for $120 to $295 from October to mid-December (the hotel is closed from early May to the end of September).* In high season, single or double occupancy of rooms costs $140 to $185 daily, with villas for two persons renting for $150 to $285. Even more expensive accommodations are available. Even if you're not staying here, you might try to nail down a reservation for dinner, as the place serves the finest food on St. Barts (see my dining recommendations to follow). For reservations or information, call or write to Jane Martin, Castelets, 717 Fifth Ave., 13th Floor, New York, NY 10022 (tel. 212/319-7488).

Hotel Manapany Cottages, P.O. Box 114, Anse des Cayes, 97133 St. Barthélemy, F.W.I. (tel. 011-590/27-66-55), with a wide range of spa facilities, climbs a steep, well-landscaped hillside on the northwest side of the island. This is one of the most luxurious and stylish hotels in the Caribbean (the name, translated from Malagese, means "small paradise"). It offers a cluster of 20 cottages on the hillside and a dozen or so along the water. Each is lavishly ornamented with patterns of gingerbread, and has a red roof and a rambling veranda open to a view of the sea. Wicker furniture combines tropical comfort with Gallic style. Behind sliding glass doors, either one or two air-conditioned bedrooms has a phone connection to a hard-working concierge, a large-screen TV with in-house video movies, ceiling fan, and tile bath. Each unit also has a kitchenette. In peak season, singles cost $120 to $180 daily, doubles going for $280 to $360, and one-bedroom suites renting for $360 to $470. *Summer rates are $85 to $100 in singles, $155 to $200 in doubles, and $230 to $280 in one-bedroom suites.* You register in a villa at the base of a hill.

Ouanalao is a crescent-shape terrace overlooking the sea, featuring casual dining with light lunches and candlelit romantic dinners. Italian dishes and fresh pastas are the specialties. More formal meals are served in an elegant raftered dining room, the Ballahou, which is recommended separately. The swimming pool is a perfect oval. Room service arrives on Mini-Mokes, and the sound of the surf is never far away. The spa facilities provide treatments that include massage, acupuncture, nerveotherapy, vertebrotherapy, lymphatic drainage, curative magnetism, and reflexology (foot massage), among other care.

Hotel Guanahani, Anse du Grand Cul-de-Sac, 97133 St. Barthélemy, F.W.I. (tel. 011-590/27-66-60), in New York 212/838-3110, or toll free 800/223-6800), opened with Gallic fanfare in 1987, immediately becoming the largest hotel on the island. The location, next to the Rothschild estate on St. Barts, is studded with pastel-hued West Indian cottage accommodations, all trimmed in gingerbread. It occupies a beachfront site flooded with sunlight, containing 76 stylish units clustered spread across a hillside, totaling seven acres. They range from deluxe rooms to lavish two-bedroom suites, all with private balconies or patios with sea views. Each room or suite has individually controlled air conditioning as well as ceiling fans, and most of them offer kitchens. In winter, two persons pay $325 to $415 daily, the cost rising to $465 to $525 in a junior suite with private pool. *In the shoulder and summer season, two persons pay from $180 to $230 for a room, while junior suites with private pools cost two persons $275 to $300 daily.*

Expensive, exclusive, and very, very French, the hotel offers fine dining in two restaurants, the Bartolomeo and l'Indigo, each open to sea views. The more formal Bartolomeo will be recommended separately. l'Indigo is a beachfront poolside café. The hotel has one large swimming pool, and 11 smaller ones are scattered throughout the property for use of occupants of junior suites. It also has two tennis courts with artificial grass, lit for night games, plus a refreshing set of water sports available at additional cost to residents.

Filao Beach, St-Jean, P.O. Box 167, 97133 St. Barthélemy (tel. 011-590/27-64-84), is a crescent-shape, 30-unit white stucco bungalow hotel, where each room is named after a château in France. This is the only *Relais & Châteaux* in the French West Indies. Right on the beach, the Filao stands across the road from the Village St-Jean and next to the Eden Rock. Try to get bungalow 10 or 40, near the beach. Regardless of which room you get, however, each is modern and elegantly simple, plushly carpeted, and well upholstered. Each contains an old-fashioned engraving of the château for which it is named, plus mahogany closets, air conditioning, direct-dial phone, private safe, radio, TV, ceiling fan, and a sun-flooded terrace big enough to enjoy a leisurely breakfast. Winter rates for two are 1,700F ($263.50) to 2,100F ($325.50) daily depending on the time of year. *The summer rate for two is 900F ($139.50).* The service charge is included in the rates. Airport shuttle and breakfast are included in the rates. The light meals served here at lunch are superb, including French omelets, stuffed land crabs, cold cuts, and fresh, crisp salads. They are served either at the café/bar or around the fresh-water swimming pool overlooking St-Jean Beach. The establishment is closed from the end of May to July 10.

François Plantation, Colombier, 97133 St. Barthélemy, F.W.I. (tel. 011-590/27-78-82), re-creates the plantation era, a sort of colonial à la française style. Set inland, in a tropical garden (not on the beach) the complex consists of 12 pavilions, each decorated in an elegant West Indian style, with reproduction antique four-poster beds. Each has air conditioning, ceiling fan, satellite TV, safe, phone, and bar. In winter, the charge is $250 to $350 daily for single or double occupancy, with an American breakfast included. *The off-season price, single or double, is $125 daily.* Eight of the bedrooms open onto sea views, while others front a garden vista. Bungalows are attractively decorated in pastel shades of pink, green, and blue. A spacious swimming pool commands a hill site, with a stunning view. The hotel, which opened the Christmas of 1987, also has an exceptional restaurant that deserves and gets a separate writeup. The owners are Françoise and François (you heard right) Beret, longtime residents of St. Barts. The plantation is closed from the end of August to the first of November.

The Expensive to Moderate Range

El Sereno Beach Hotel, Grand Cul-de-Sac, P.O. Box 91, 97133 St. Barthélemy, F.W.I. (tel. 011-590/27-64-80). Four miles from Gustavia, its low-slung blue-and-white façade and its isolated location create the aura of St-Tropez in the Antilles. A lot of the Riviera crowd is attracted to it, partly because of its Lyon-born owner, Marc Llepez, and his wife, Christine. A total of 20 accommodations are scattered over a carefully landscaped interior. On the premises are 17 bungalows with garden views, plus a trio of units overlooking the sea. In winter, singles cost $183 to $216 daily; doubles, $216 to $266. *In summer, depending on the view, singles rent for $100 to $120 daily, and doubles run $120 to $150.* Each unit contains two beds, an individual safe, a refrigerator, air conditioning, and color TV with video movies. The garden has a freshwater pool, in the center of which is a verdant island. The feeling is a bit like a private compound, whose social center is an open-air bar and poolside restaurant, La Toque Lyonnaise. There, full meals cost 300F ($46.50) and are served from 11:30 a.m. to 2 p.m. and 7 to 9 p.m. seven days a week.

L'Hibiscus, rue Thiers, 97133 St. Barthélemy, F.W.I. (tel. 011-590/27-64-82), is dramatically terraced into one of Gustavia's steep hillsides, a fact which gives visitors the lordly feeling of surveying the entire town from a private panoramic terrace. Its social center is in an imaginatively rambling modern building whose floor space was extended by a hardwood deck surrounding a circular and deep swimming pool. The adjacent bar is an open-air breezy kind of place, encompassing lattices, greenery, and that view of the port. This lovely place and its 11 cottages stand immediately beneath a 200-year-old clock tower in the uppermost region of town. Set amid a labyrinth of terracotta walkways on steeply sloping ground, each cottage has its own veranda, kitchenette, living room, TV with video, and tasteful accessories. *The bungalows rent for $85 daily in summer for two people,* the charge going up in winter to $230 to $260 for two occupants. The hotel offers a fine French cuisine, served on an attractive dining terrace. Many guests come early to enjoy the cocktail hour, as L'Hibiscus is considered one of the best spots in Gustavia for a sundowner.

La Banane, l'Orient, 97133 St. Barthélemy, F.W.I. (tel. 011-590/27-68-25), about a mile from the airport on the outskirts of the village of l'Orient, is a four-room hotel—small, intimate, well furnished, and filled with some of the most stylish antiques on the island. The complex is ringed by a fence whose boundaries lie within a three-minute walk from the beach. My favorite accommodation contains a large mahogany four-poster bed, whose trim was made from a little-known Central and South American wood called *angélique*. The trio of other units are less spacious, but each has a TV with video, some Haitian art, a mixture of antique and modern designs, a refrigerator, a private terrace, and louvered windows overlooking the garden. The owner is Jean-Marie Rivière, formerly a cabaret producer at the Alcázar in Paris. In winter, singles cost $200 to $280 daily, and doubles rent for $220 to $300. *In off-season, singles are charged $110 to $130 daily, with doubles paying $130 to $150.*

PLM Azur Jean Bart, St.-Jean Bay, 97133 St. Barthélemy F.W.I. (tel. 011-590/27-63-37), a two-minute walk from the beach, on a forested hillside above the bay, is a 50-unit hotel owned by a large French hotel chain. Well maintained, the hotel offers its own many-sided swimming pool, whose hibiscus-bordered terrace overlooks the sea and a labyrinth of well-landscaped walkways meandering among stone retaining walls. Each rental unit has air conditioning, a spacious balcony or terrace (but not necessarily with a sea view), phone, terracotta floors, and thick plaster walls. Twenty of the units offer self-contained kitchenettes. In winter, singles cost $111 to $159 daily, and doubles run $139 to $198, depending on the accommodation. *In summer, singles rent for $67 to $84 daily, and doubles cost $85 to $105, with a continental breakfast included.*

Tropical Hotel, P.O. Box 147, St-Jean, 97133 St. Barthélemy, F.W.I. (tel. 011-590/27-64-87), is a little picture-postcard-type inn, trimmed in gingerbread, offering an intimate and restful atmosphere. It's perched on a hillside spot, about 50 yards above St. Jean Beach (a mile from the airport and a mile and a half from Gustavia). The hotel (almost a bungalow inn) rents out some 20 air-conditioned, twin-bedded units, each with private shower, tile floor, color-coordinated schemes, plus a phone and a refrigerator to cool your tropical drinks. Nine of the units come with a sea view and balcony, and 11 contain a porch opening onto a garden which is so lush it looks like a miniature jungle. There's a hospitality center, where guests read, listen to music, or order drinks at a carefully paneled, inviting bar ringed with antiques. The freshwater swimming pool is small, but water sports are available on the beach. Breakfast is served at the poolside terrace. In season, a minimum stay of four days is required. For that privilege, guests pay $130 to $170 daily in a single in winter, $140 to $180 in a double. *Summer rates are $75 in a single, $95 in a double.*

Marigot Bay Club, 97133 St. Barthélemy, F.W.I. (tel. 011-590/27-75-36), is an intimate club run by Jean-Michel Lédée who offers six superb, bougainvillea-surrounded suites on a hillside. Each is well furnished in a modern, simplified style, with one bedroom, a private bath, living room, daily maid service, and kitchen facilities. Units open onto a private terrace overlooking the ocean. In winter, the single rate is $150 per day, going up to $180 in a double and $205 in a triple. *In summer, a single is reduced to $75 a day, rising to $90 in a double and $105 in a triple.* Down below, opening onto the sea, the Marigot Bay Club Restaurant is one of the most distinguished in St. Barts, offering fresh seafood along with fine French wines.

A sister property, **Marigot Sea Club,** 97133 St. Barthélemy, F.W.I. (tel. 011-590/27-75-36), presents 10 attractive suites overlooking the bay. It also has a large swimming pool. The accommodations are large and set in a landscaped garden. Facilities include a bedroom, with private bath, a living room, a kitchenette, and a private terrace opening onto the ocean. There is daily maid service. In winter, a single rents for $150 daily, going up to $180 in a double and $205 in a triple. *In summer, prices are lowered to $75 daily in a single, $90 in a double, and $105 in a triple.*

Eden Rock, St-Jean, 97133 St. Barthélemy, F.W.I. (tel. 011-590/27-72-94). When the rock it sits on was purchased many years ago by the island's former mayor, Remy de Haenen, the seller was an old woman who laughed at him for paying too many francs for it. Today it's part of the lore of the island, offering some of the best panoramas. The building capping its pinnacle looks like an idealized version of a Provence farmhouse. It's surrounded on three sides by the waters of St. Jean Bay. I prefer the terracotta terrace, especially in the glare of noon, when the frigatebirds are wheeling and diving for fish in the turquoise waters. Inside the stone walls is a collection of French antiques and paintings, including a few drawings by Monsieur de Haenen's father, a well-known turn-of-the-century illustrator. The de Haenen family prefers not to accept outside dining guests anymore. However, they still rent six rooms in the main house, along with a trio of red-roofed outbuildings scattered amid the cactus of a rocky garden. Each unit contains a sea view, refrigerator, air conditioning or ceiling fan, and plenty of unfussy, severely decorated charm. In winter, depending on the accommodation, rooms for two cost $110 to $165. *In summer, a single or double ranges from $85 to $100, including a continental breakfast.*

Hostellerie des 3 Forces, Vitet, 97133 St. Barthélemy, F.W.I. (tel. 011-590/27-61-25), is a "new age inn." Its cedar-sided accommodations are scattered over a dry and sandy slope whose panorama encompasses rolling hills near the village of Vitet, three miles from Gustavia. Twelve bungalows have been built, each graced with the name of one of the signs of the zodiac. Each is ringed with neo-Victorian gingerbread, containing a consciously simple decor of exposed wood and roughly textured fabrics, big windows, and private bathrooms. Most units have terraces and air conditioning, and all guests benefit from the gracious attention of the owner and resident astrologist, Hubert de la Motte. In high season, single occupancy of a cottage costs $120 daily, rising to $140 in a double. A suite for two persons is $220 daily. *In low season, single occupancy of a cottage is $75 daily, going up to $90 for two persons. One of the best bargains in low season is to check in here on MAP tariffs which are $110 daily in a single, $150 in a double.* On the premises is a swimming pool. The establishment closes in June and in October. Its restaurant is recommended separately.

Best for the Budget

Economy is not a word you hear used much in St. Barts. However, considering the relatively high price structure of the island, the following recommendations are easier on the pocketbook.

Le Village Saint-Jean, P.O. Box 23, St. Barthélemy, F.W.I. (tel. 011-590/27-61-39), is a cottage colony, 25 units in all, clustered beyond the previously recommended Tropical Hotel. The cottages and studios, built of stone and wood, contain kitchens, sundecks or gardens, and terrace living rooms, along with balconies, private baths, phones, air conditioning, and ceiling fans. Depending on your choice of accommodation, two persons in winter pay 660F ($102.30) to 1,510F ($234.83) daily. *In off-season, two persons are charged 360F ($53.84) to 770F ($119.35) daily.* The Jacuzzi suite is the most expensive. Although the rate structure is modest compared to some places on the island, don't be surprised to see an occasional French movie star among the clients. After all, they like to save money, too. The complex has a restaurant bar, Le Patio, with a terrace, serving good food. It's a long walk down to the beach, and, because of its location, it's best to arrive at Le Village in your Mini-Moke, as you'll need transportation.

Auberge de La Petite Anse, P.O. Box 117, 97133 St. Barthélemy, F.W.I. (tel. 011-590/27-64-60), promises peace and tranquility, and a good value. Eight clean, comfortable bungalows are offered, and your Mini-Moke will take you to some good beaches nearby. Eight two-story buildings, containing 16 apartments, were constructed 2 miles from the airport and 2½ miles from

Gustavia, above the beach at Petite Anse. Built into a cliffside, the studios have double beds, air conditioning, private baths, and kitchenettes with daily maid service. *In off-season, singles cost from $40 daily, doubles from $60, and triples from $80.* In winter, the single rate rises to $100 daily, the double to $120, and the triple to $150.

Les Mouettes, l'Orient, 97133 St. Barthélemy, F.W.I. (tel. 011-590/27-61-66), is what the French call an *auberge Antillaises*. Set inland, a good haul from the beach, it offers only eight bedrooms of casual comfort (two are air-conditioned, and the rest contain ceiling fans). Depending on the room assignment, year-round rates are 220F ($34.10) daily in a single and from 250F ($39.75) to 420F ($65.10) in a double. A modest, family-owned hotel, it presents a row of painted louvers to the street outside. A swimming pool with a terrace is found in the rear.

WHERE TO DINE: For the most part, you're served an essentially French cuisine with local adaptations, reflecting the island's unusual mixed European heritage. I've found few truly local dishes. However, at a private home I was once served "Madame Jackass," a red fish dish with hot peppers. As a warning, I'd like to note that many of these restaurants shut down on a whim if there's no business. This is true particularly in the autumn.

Most guests will want to swim and have lunch at one of the clubs right on the beach. See my recommendation of Chez Francine, below, as an example. Most of these clubs are rustic lean-tos, built of wood, more Tahiti in style than St. Barts. From tiny cooking galleys, battle-trained chefs often turn out an amazingly good cuisine, and not just hamburgers either. You might get breast of duck or charcoal-grilled lobster. A favorite specialty is puffy fritters of salt cod.

In Gustavia

L'Ananas, rue Courbet (tel. 011-590/27-63-77) in Gustavia. In 1980 what was originally built as a low-slung private house was gutted and converted into one of the most elegant restaurants on the island. It sits near the historic clock tower above the town on the side of a steeply sloping hill which permits sweeping views over the bay. Guests usually enjoy a drink near the thick mahogany surface of the bar before heading to one of the embroidery-covered tables. Full meals cost from 250F ($38.75) and are served only at dinner, from 7 to 10 p.m. No meals are offered on Tuesday off-season, and reservations are suggested. Specialties include fresh salmon, seabass, lobster salad with mango, followed by lemon pie. Often, the jazz played here draws a music-loving crowd (more about this later).

Au Port, rue Sadi-Carnot (tel. 011-590/27-62-36). From the outside it looks like a consciously raffish harborfront building, with a narrow veranda jutting above the bumpy road outside. You climb a steep and tiled flight of stairs to reach its second-floor dining room, where a simple decor of blue-and-white walls and neocolonial charm act as the appropriate foil for the cuisine of Breton-born chef Jean-Pierre Delage. With the restaurant's owner, Gérard Balageas, he prepares a satisfying classic French cuisine. No lunch is served, and dinner is offered throughout the winter from 6:30 to 10:15 p.m. every night of the week. The establishment is closed from June 1 until early November. Full meals cost from 250F ($38.75) and might include ragoût of seafood steamed in a coconut, filet of poached salmon with sage sauce, homemade foie gras, and a refreshing hot apple tart. Reservations are suggested, especially if you want one of the tables on the narrow veranda.

La Crémaillère, rue du Général-de-Gaulle (tel. 011-590/27-63-89), is easily one of the island's finest restaurants in all respects—service, the menu (in the classic French tradition), carefully selected ingredients, and a fine wine list. It's in a 200-year-old Swedish house which the French-born owner, Michel Brunet, transformed into a chic, elegant country hideaway with an undeniable tropical flair. You can dine on an eyrie-style balcony, but my favorite corner is inside the air-conditioned inner room. The cuisine benefits from the education Mr. Brunet received during his career at Maxim's in Paris. Queen Elizabeth II has been his most prestigious diner. Dinners at his place cost 300F ($46.50), and lunches are about half that much. Specialties include crayfish bisque, lobster thermidor, steak au poivre, and house-style lobster, with chocolate cake for dessert. Lunch is served only in high season, from noon to 3 p.m. daily; otherwise, dinner is from 6:30 to midnight seven days a week.

Restaurant aux Trois Gourmands, La Pointe (tel. 011-590/27-71-83), sits on the less congested side of the harbor behind a gingerbread-laden façade whose pink and white awnings flutter at boats moored nearby. Diners enjoy a drink on the wicker sofas near the bar, where each of the framed prints seems to evoke the same tropical theme. Christophe Gasnier, a much experienced chef de cuisine, serves lunch daily except Sunday from noon to 2 p.m. and dinner every evening from 7 to 10. No meals are served from mid-August to the end of September. Lunches, costing from 150F ($23.25), include fish soup, filet of red snapper, lobster salad, and faux filet with mustard sauce. Dinners, at 275F ($42.65), might include mussel soup with saffron, fish pâté in a tarragon sauce, homemade pasta with fresh foie gras, breast of duck with a cassis sauce, boneless chicken breast in a truffles sauce, and lobster medallions sautéed with sweetbreads.

Le Sapotillier, rue Sadi-Carnot (tel. 011-590/27-60-28), is a West Indian house on the less-visited side of Gustavia harbor. Here Austrian-born Adam Reiner runs one of the finest restaurants in the capital. Meals costing from 225F ($34.88), are served daily from 7 to 10 p.m. However, the place is closed on Sunday in low season and in June and September. Try such dishes as lobster stew with baby filet of turbot in a potato croûte with pistou, feuilleté of snails with an aged mustard cream sauce, or a panachée of fish paella with a saffron sauce.

Rôtisserie Bertrand, rue Lafayette and rue du Roi-Oscar-II (tel. 011-590/27-63-13), right in the heart of Gustavia, has been called "the best take-out service in the western hemisphere." The much-overworked owners, a French couple, are Pierre-Marie L'Hermite and his wife, Evelyne. If you don't want to cook, they'll prepare dinner for you. Order it in the morning, give them time to cook it, then pick it up later in the day. They turn out everything from French pizzas to many types of tarts (such as onion), to langouste mayonnaise, to pâté de campagne, to canard à l'orange. If you're here during the Yule season, you can enjoy oysters flown in from Brittany and fresh foie gras. It's no ordinary "deli." It's favored by locals (read that "well-heeled" locals), and it's the best place in St. Barts to pick up items if you're planning a picnic or a boat excursion to a neighboring island. Their casseroles to go include beef bourguignonne. Cooked platters cost from $5 to $8. The place is open from 8 a.m. to 1 p.m. and 4 to 7 p.m. daily.

La Langouste, rue du Roi-Oscar-II (tel. 011-590/27-69-47), used to be known as "Annie's." Annie, of the island family of Ange, is still around, but she prefers to name her place in honor of the clawless Caribbean lobster instead of herself. In a century-old building, erected during the Swedish domain over the island, her zesty little restaurant is near the Gendarmerie. You get down-to-earth Créole cookery here, and that means stuffed land crabs, conch ragoût, cod fritters (called *accra de morue*), the namesake langouste, always fresh fish, and curried chicken. Expect to spend about 175F ($27.13) for a filling repast. Lunches are light, but dinner is a Créole delight. Hours are noon to 2 p.m. and 7 to 10 p.m. daily except Thursday.

Anse des Cayes

Restaurant Ballahou, Hôtel Manapany Cottages, Anse des Cayes (tel. 011-590/27-66-55). Named after a small variety of swordfish, this is one of the best and most elegant restaurants on the island. To reach its sun-flooded pink-and-white interior, you pass beneath a portal dripping in fanciful Caribbean gingerbread. Dining is under a high ceiling whose rafters curve around the perimeter of an oval swimming pool. The restaurant presents fixed-price lunches for 140F ($21.70) and 175F ($27.13), and set dinners for 175F ($27.13) to 315F ($48.83), as well as à la carte menus. Lunch, served beside the pool in less formal circumstances, lasts from 12:30 to 3 p.m., and includes salads, stuffed land crabs prepared Créole style, air-dried alpine beef with lentils, and many variations of crayfish. Dinners, from 7:30 to 10 p.m., are served by candlelight inside and are attractively elaborate. They require an advance reservation for nonresidents. Meals, which are accompanied by live music, include such specialties as bisque of lobster, roast pigeon with watercress, braised sweetbreads, duck with a sweet orange sauce, and kidneys cooked with Armagnac and chicory, as well as an iced soufflé with old dark rum sauce.

In the St-Jean Beach Area

Le Pélican, Plage de St-Jean (tel. 011-590/27-64-64). The ambience and cuisine are so different here during the day and night that you'd almost think you were in two different restaurants. Lunch is served outdoors in the shade of an elongated parasol, within earshot of the nearby surf. From 11:30 a.m. to 4 p.m. it features full meals costing from 175F ($27.13). While sipping French wine in the Antillean sunshine, you can enjoy such specialties as fish soup, lobster bisque, and a generously portioned Créole platter laden with accras, shellfish, blood pudding, and grilled fish. Dinners are more elaborate, more expensive, and more formal. Full meals cost from 300F ($46.50) and are a showcase for the culinary specialties of Denis Bernard and Denis LaPlace. From 7 to 10 p.m. (except on Sunday), they prepare cold chopped rabbit with herbs and duck cooked in red wine with honey and cinnamon. The setting incorporates a trio of high-ceilinged dining rooms with pastel colors, a view of the sea, and candle light. Evening reservations are suggested.

Chez Francine, Plage de St-Jean, St-Jean Beach (tel. 011-590/27-60-49), maintains a delightfully informal atmosphere. The women at an adjoining table are likely to be dining topless. Checking out the action in winter, you might see Sylvester Stallone or Alain Delon. People from all over the island come here for lunch, served from 11:30 a.m. to 3:30 p.m. daily. The place is really little more than a boardwalk terrace built on top of the sand a few feet from the beach. Its overhead awnings and blackboard menu encourage an attire of bathing suits, or less, and no one even attempts to be formal. Typical meals, often preceded by a frothy piña colada, usually cost around $25 per person. They might include chilled lobster, grilled chicken or fish, a selection of wine or beer, and a choice of homemade tortes and cakes. The establishment is a busy focal point of beach life daily except for a two-week vacation sometime in midsummer.

Morne Lurin

Les Castelets (tel. 011-590/27-61-73) was already previewed as the most chic place to stay in St. Barts. Likewise, this eagle's-nest retreat is the most elegant dining choice. The elite meet in luxury, as celebrities from both sides of the Atlantic enjoy their apéritif on the terrace, said to have the best view on the island.

The dining room turns out a classic French and moderne cuisine, and the food is backed up by a fine wine cellar, considered one of the finest in the Caribbean. The chef, Michel Viali, was born in Marseilles, but he has long gone beyond the cookery of Provence. An artist of considerable skill, his cookery is not only beautifully prepared (he makes his own pasta and smokes his own fish), it is also well served.

Guest Jessica Lange preferred a salad named for Aphrodite (cubed lobster with mayonnaise and peach bits), while the late Tennessee Williams found a local yellowtail snapper (baked en papillote) his favorite. It's served with a shrimp and lobster sauce. I personally gravitate to a warm salad of walnut-flecked goose giblets. Whatever you select, it will usually be superb, especially the tarte maison, often presented with homemade ice cream. Les Castelets is closed all day Tuesday and for lunch on Wednesday. It is imperative to telephone for a reservation, and for the privilege of dining here, expect to pay from $50 per person. Dining hours are daily from noon to either 2 or 2:30 p.m. and 7 to 10 p.m.

If you're in the area late in the day, head up to the **Santa Fé Bar Restaurant** (tel. 011-590/27-61-04), which lies high up beyond Castelets. Here you'll get the best American-style hamburgers on the island, juicy ones at that. You can take in the view for free. Most checks are under $10 unless you have a lot to drink. Hours are 5:30 to 10 p.m. daily.

Colombier

François Plantation Restaurant (tel. 011-590/27-78-82) is the domain of Françoise and François Beret who take justifiable pride in their traditional cuisine of French gastronomy. The dining room, part of the old plantation that stood here, is attractively decorated and inviting. Even if you're not staying here, you may want to call and make a reservation for a meal. Only dinner is served, and it's offered nightly from 7 to 9. In off-season the restaurant is also closed on Sunday, and it shuts down in September and October. The chef might tempt you with a chilled cream of avocado soup or salmon in puff pastry with a mushroom cream sauce. You might also be drawn to a salad of conch (called lambi). Many main courses are presented to wake up the palate, including a noisette of lamb with fresh mint, chicken with coriander, and filet of beef with green peppercorns. For dessert, if featured, try the pineapple mousse. Meals cost from 225F ($34.88), and the service and the quality of ingredients used in the dishes presented are topnotch.

Anse du Grand Cul-de-Sac

Bartolomeo, Hôtel Guanahani, Anse du Grand Cul-de-Sac (tel. 011-590/27-66-60), is the deluxe dining choice for one of the most exclusive and expensive hotels on the island. It serves dinner only every night from 7 to 11 p.m. Non-residents of the hotel are welcome if they phone ahead for a reservation. The menu specialties, which are orchestrated by French chefs from Paris, cost from 350F ($54.25) for full meals. The menu frequently changes, but elegant dishes might include shrimp with herb-flavored oils, shark meat with vermicelli and soya sauce, crabmeat in puff pastry with a sweet-pepper sauce, climaxed by millefeuilles of pineapple and passion fruit.

Grande Saline

The favored place in the sun is **Le Tamarin** (tel. 011-590/27-72-12), which picks up the beach traffic—many in stunningly revealing bikinis—from the nearby Plage de Saline. It's isolated amid rocky hills and forests, in a low-slung cottage whose eaves are lined with gingerbread. Inside, you'll see Haitian paintings, exotic hardwoods, and wicker armchairs. If you'd like either lunch or dinner on the beach, paying $20 to $30 for the privilege, join the hungry diners at Le

Tamarin. I've never seen more than two dozen guests here at the same time, each eagerly reading the blackboard menu for the chef's suggestions. If you have to wait, diners can order an apéritif in one of the lazy hammocks stretched under a tamarind tree (hence the name of the restaurant). Fresh fish is invariably featured, but meat dishes and poultry also are cooked well. Service can be hectic, but if you're in a rush you shouldn't be here. It's for a lazy afternoon on the beach or a relaxed dinner under the stars. Lunch is served daily from 12:30 to 3 p.m. In winter, dinner is offered on Friday and Saturday from 7 to 9:30 p.m.

Grand Cul-de-Sac

Le Toque Lyonnaise, El Sereno Beach Hotel (tel. 011-590/27-64-80), is one of the premier restaurants of the island. It fronts a swimming pool and is partially open to the sky. Most guests come here for the *menu Lyonnais,* reflecting the culinary background of Christine and Marc Llepez, the owners. They invite chefs from Lyon, the gastronomic capital of France, to visit St. Barts. Their set menu costs 230F ($35.65), and you'll spend about the same ordering à la carte. Menu specialties are likely to include salade Lyonnaise, lobster ravioli, herb-flavored lamb, or magret of duckling with ginger. But all that depends on the whim of the latest chef, of course. The wine list is among the finest on the island. The restaurant is open to sea breezes and contained within an angular modern pavilion decorated in a tropical style with lattices. It is open nightly from 7 to 10, except from June to the end of September.

Restaurant Flamboyant (tel. 011-590/29-64-09). On the western edge of the island lies what many residents consider the best restaurant on the island. It's on the veranda level of the isolated home of Albert Balayn, a young chef who studied cuisine in France before returning to his native island. The preferred seating is on the panoramic terrace, where the hillside location contributes to a view over fields, forest, and sea. Only dinner is served, every night except Monday from 6:30 to 10 p.m. Full meals without wine cost from 250F ($38.75) and might include a succulent version of French onion soup, christophine (a kind of squash) stuffed with crayfish, a creamy version of fish soup, lobster in puff pastry, a salad of filet of duck breast with foie gras, a cassolette of crayfish, a filet of red snapper with a tomato- and rosemary-flavored cream sauce, filet of chicken with aged rum, and scallops with curry sauce. Dessert is appropriately elaborate, perhaps a savarin with rum and chantilly cream. Reservations are strongly suggested.

Club Lafayette (tel. 011-590/27-62-51), El Sereno Beach Hôtel, lies at a cove on the eastern end of the island. Lunching here daily from noon to 3 p.m. is like taking a meal at your own private beach club. After a dip in the ocean or a pool, you can order a *planteur* in the shade of a sea grape, and later proceed to lunch itself: a roquefort-and-walnut salad, a Créole version of *boudin noir* (black sausage), charcoaled langouste, grilled fresh fish, and breast of duck. In other words, this is no hamburger fast-food beach joint. Afterward, have a refreshing citrus-flavored sherbet. Prices begin at $25 for a good and satisfying meal. In winter, dinner is served daily from 7 to 10 p.m.

Vitet

Hostellerie des 3 Forces, Vitet (tel. 011-590/27-61-25), has a resident astrologist, a French provincial decor, well-scrubbed surfaces, and food with a genuine allure. The food is well prepared and beautifully served, and for dessert you get an astrological forecast thrown in. The heart and soul of the place is Hubert de la Mott, who arrived from Brittany with his wife and sister to create a hotel (recommended separately) where happiness, good food, comfort, and conversation could be a way of life. Even if you don't stay here, many diners drive out for a meal, enjoying it on a sun-washed, scrub-covered landscape. Food is offered from noon to 3 p.m. and 7:30 to 9:45 p.m. Evening meals are more formal, although each repast costs about 200F ($31) per person. Menu items depend on the availability of ingredients. However, the bill of fare might include salade niçoise, fish pâté, beef shish kebab with curry sauce, grilled fresh lobster, veal kidneys flambé with cognac, chicken livers fried with parsley and garlic, a cassolette of snails, filet of beef with béarnaise sauce, and such succulent desserts as crêpes suzette flambé. "Each dish takes time," in the words of the owner, because it's prepared fresh. Count on a leisurely meal and relax with the flow of the experience.

Public

Maya's (no phone) is the kind of place you might find in Martinique. That's because its French-Créole chef, Maya Veuzelin-Gurley, is from that island. To St. Barts, she brought her classic Créole dishes. You might begin with the salad of tomatoes, arugula, and endive, then follow with grilled fish in sauce chien (hot) or else a grilled filet of beef. She also prepares what she called "sailor's chicken" with soya sauce and coconut milk. For dessert, the coconut tart is a taste treat. Meals cost from 200F ($31), and only dinner is served, nightly except Sunday from 7 to 10. Since you can't call, you might go by during the day and sign a board at the entrance. The restaurant is closed in June, July, and September.

SHOPPING: You don't pay any duty in St. Barts. Everything is out-of-bond. The island, then, is a good place to buy liquor and French perfumes, among the lowest priced in the West Indies. Perfume, for example, is cheaper in St. Barts than it is in France itself. Champagne is cheaper than in Epernay, France. St. Barts is the only completely free-trading port in the world, with the exception of French St. Martin and Dutch St. Maarten.

Only trouble is, selections are limited. However, you'll find good buys in sportswear, crystal, porcelain, watches, and other luxuries.

If you're in the market for some island crafts, try to find those convertible-brim, fine straw hats St. Bartians like to wear. *Vogue* once featured this high-crown headwear in its fashion pages. They also have some interesting block-printed resort clothes in cotton.

La Romana, the famous international boutique chain representing renowned Italian and French designers of fashions and jewelry, has a shop at the Hibiscus Hôtel (tel. 011-590/27-64-82), open from 10 a.m. to noon and 5 to 11 p.m.

Gucci, Boulevard du Front de Mer, Gustavia (tel. 011-590/27-69-46), has dignified St. Barts with its presence, carrying the standard array of chic and expensive merchandise. Here you can get the real item, not the imitation from Asia.

The **Atelier** (tel. 011-590/27-61-72) at Colombier, two miles north of Gustavia, is Jean-Yves Froment's shop and studio, recently completely redecorated and reorganized. Visitors can watch the hand-dyed and block-printed decorations and tropical fashion prints being made.

La Calèche boutique, rue du Général-de-Gaulle (tel. 011-590/27-62-38), is an attractive place to purchase bathing suits, shoes, hats, St. Barts T-shirts, jewelry, and gifts. It serves such shoppers as Barbara Goldsmith, author of *Little Gloria . . . Happy at Last.*

Dick and Lenore Wulff operate the **Shell Shop,** rue du Général-de-Gaulle (no phone), a small shop offering shell and coral jewelry in original designs unique to St. Barts and the Caribbean. Shells and coral from all over the world, local handcrafts and block printing, free paperbacks, and U.S. sports information are available here.

Samson & Co., Nya Gatan (tel. 011-590/27-60-46), in Gustavia, stocks art from the Philippines and Bali and sells batiks and handpainted clothing for both men and women.

Smoke and Booze, rue du Général-de-Gaulle (tel. 011-590/87-60-24), is where to go for wine, liquor, liqueurs, and tobacco, as well as for toys and souvenirs. They'll package your beverage purchases for you to take home.

La Fonda Hermès, rue de la République (tel. 011-590/27-66-15), is the only outlet in the Caribbean of the famous Parisian haberdasher. It stands, basking in a pool of self-generated chic, across the street from the port. Be warned, you'll pay dearly for some French allure: a beach towel signed with the exalted Hermès name costs from $150, for example.

Little Switzerland, rue de la France (tel. 011-590/27-64-66). Behind glistening arrays of glass-frosted cases is an array of untaxed crystal, jewelry, and luxurious frill merchandise.

Boutiques Chamade, rue de la République (tel. 011-590/27-62-21). Its interior glistens with the reflection from dozens of Lalique vases, arrays of crystal, bottles of perfume, Christofle silver, and a selection of wristwatches. Both the merchandise and the attitude are very French.

Loulou's Marine, rue de la République (tel. 011-590/27-62-74). Some of its merchandise could come from any general store in France and some of it is so specialized that only a yacht owner could appreciate it. This is possibly the most gregarious rendezvous point in town, and amid pulleys, coils of rope, and folded sailcloth, you'll find T-shirts and unusual hardware.

THE SPORTING LIFE: Unlike the other French islands in the West Indies, total nudism is illegal on St. Barts. However, women can bathe topless in most places. Bikinied casualness seems to be the rule. The most popular beach is St-Jean, which has some waterfront cafés where you can get drinks and meals. Grand Cul-de-Sac, with its St. Barths Beach Hôtel, and Anse des Flamands are other attractive beaches. (Golfers please note: There are no golf courses on the island.)

Water Sports

Marine Service, Quai du Yacht Club (tel. 011-590/27-64-50). There aren't many watersports facilities in St. Bart's, but of them all, this is the most complete. It operates from a one-story building set directly on the water at the edge of a marina, on the opposite side of the harbor from the more congested part of Gustavia. One of its most popular outings is a sunset cruise offered daily from 5:30 to 7 p.m. for 210F ($32.55). It also conducts one-hour dives for 250F ($38.75) or else night dives for 300F ($46.50). Fishermen can go out for a half day of deep-sea fishing for 2,000F ($310). Sailing and snorkeling trips depart on a catamaran from 9 a.m. to 4 p.m. daily, costing 400F ($62) per person.

People who like **fishing** are fond of the waters of St. Barts. March through July they catch dolphin; in September, wahoo. Atlantic bonito, barracuda, and marlin also turn up with great frequency. I suggest you ask at your hotel to help arrange a trip out with one of the local fishermen, who prefer the handline, incidentally. It's best to bring your own speargun or rod and reel.

In addition, good charter boats are available each season. Names are posted on the pier at Marine Service, Quai du Yacht Club.

Sailing jaunts also can be arranged at many of the hotels, parties booked for trips to neighboring islands. Sometimes these are combined with fishing trips. Some of the hotels, such as Baie des Flamands, have Sunfish craft which they offer free to guests. Yachting isn't organized, however. Yet, in winter, anything's negotiable when stray yachts sail into Gustavia harbor.

Île Fourchue (Forked Island) is a popular rendezvous point for boats. Named for its configuration, with rocky peaks separated by valleys, Île Fourchue is horseshoe-shaped, with a protected anchorage. Its only permanent residents are goats, but a few ruins bear witness to the fact that it was once the home of a Breton who lived a Robinson Crusoe-style life here for many years. A charter to Île Fourchue and other nearby places can be had on the *Zavijava,* from Quai du Yacht Club, leaving at 1 p.m. You can swim and snorkel, then return to Gustavia at 5 p.m., all for $40 per person. For reservations, call **Le Calèche Yacht Charter Agency** (tel. 011-590/27-62-38) in Gustavia from 9 a.m. to noon and 2:30 to 5:30 p.m. Monday to Saturday.

Waterskiing is authorized from 9 a.m. to 1 p.m. and again from 4:40 p.m. to sundown. Because of the shape of the coastline, skiers must remain 80 yards from shore on the windward side of the island and 110 yards off on the leeward side.

Windsurfing is one of the most popular sports practiced on St. Barts. Try **St. Barth Wind School** at the Tom Beach Hôtel on Pelican Beach near Chez Francine. It's open from 9 a.m. to 5 p.m. daily. Windsurfing costs $12 per hour. Professional instructors are on hand.

Tennis

It's mainly for hotel guests. There's a court at the **St. Barths Beach Hôtel,** Grand Cul-de-Sac (tel. 011-599/27-62-73).

One of the best courts is at the **Hôtel Manapany** (tel. 011-590/27-66-55), previously recommended. Use of the court is free to residents both day and night. Nonresidents pay 100F ($15.50) per hour during daylight, 150F ($23.25) for nighttime illumination.

It's also possible to play on the courts of the previously recommended **Hotel Guanahani** (tel. 011-590/27-66-60), at Grand Cul-de-Sac. Court time costs 60F ($9.30) per hour, 90F ($13.95) for night games after 7.

NIGHTLIFE: Most guests consider a French Créole dinner under the open stars near the sea (or with a view of the twinkling stars) enough of a nocturnal adventure. After that, there isn't a lot of excitement.

In Gustavia, the most popular gathering place is **Le Select,** rue du Général-de-Gaulle (no phone), apparently named after its more famous granddaddy in the Montparnasse section of Paris. It's utterly simple, and a game of Dominoes might be under way as you walk in. In the open-air café garden, near the port, tables are placed outside on the gravel. The outdoor grill promises a "cheeseburger in Paradise." You never know who might show up here, perhaps Mick Jagger, perhaps Jimmy Buffet. Beer costs from 10F ($1.50), and the place is open daily except Sunday from 10 a.m. to 11 p.m. The locals like it a lot, and outsiders are welcomed but not necessarily embraced until they get to know you a bit. If you want to spread a rumor and have it travel fast across the island, start it here. In an adjoining garden the talk is of the sea.

Also in Gustavia, overlooking the harbor, is the **Hôtel Hibiscus,** rue Thiers (tel. 011-590/27-64-62), popular with visiting yachting people.

L'Ananas Jazz Bar, rue Courbet (tel. 011-590/27-63-77) in Gustavia is on the ground floor of the previously recommended L'Ananas restaurant. Drinks are expensive, from $7 per libation, but that gives you the right to listen to some of the best live music played on the island. Music begins at 8:30 p.m., lasting until midnight. In high season there is music every night, at least in theory. In the off-season, no entertainment is offered on Tuesday.

CHAPTER XIII

THE BRITISH WINDWARDS

□ □ □

1. DOMINICA
2. ST. LUCIA
3. ST. VINCENT
4. THE GRENADINES
5. GRENADA

These windward islands lie in the direct path of the trade winds, which swoop down from the northeast. British affiliated (now mainly independent), they are Gallic in manner, West Indian in outlook.

French habits often persist because of early Gallic invaders, as the islands changed hands many times before coming into Britain's orbit. On such islands as St. Lucia, and especially Dominica, you'll hear a Créole patois. English, however, is commonly spoken.

The British Windwards are made up of four main islands—St. Lucia, St. Vincent, Grenada, and Dominica—along with a scattering of isles or spits of land known as The Grenadines. Truly far-out islands, The Grenadines are a chain stretching from St. Vincent to Grenada. Some people group Barbados and Trinidad and Tobago in the British Windwards, but I have preferred, for convenience's sake, to treat these independent island nations separately in the following chapters.

Topped by mountains, bursting with greenery, the British Windwards in this chapter are still far enough off the mainline tourist circuit to make a visit to them something of an adventure. At some of the more remote oases, you'll have the sand crabs, iguanas, and sea birds to enjoy all by yourself.

For the most part the islands are small and volcanic in origin. They have no glittering casinos and dazzling resort hotels, but you'll not have a dull time, at least visually.

The islands use the same currency, the Eastern Caribbean dollar, worth about 37¢ U.S. *Note:* Prices in this chapter are given in U.S. dollars unless otherwise indicated. Most of the inhabitants live on their crops. There's little or no industry, and tourism is not overly developed, especially in Dominica.

1. DOMINICA

It has been called "the most original island in the Caribbean." Covered by a dense tropical rain forest that blankets its mountain slopes, including cloud-wreathed Morne Diablotin at 4,775 feet, it has vegetation unique in the West

Indies. Untamed, unspoiled Dominica (pronounced Dom-in-*ee*-ka, and not to be confused with the Spanish-speaking Dominican Republic) is known for its crystal-clear rivers and waterfalls, its hot springs and boiling lakes. According to myth, it has 365 "rivers," one for each day of the year. This is the most rugged of Caribbean islands.

Environmental pollution does not exist in Dominica. The island offers hiking, mountain-climbing, river bathing in crystal clear waters, and just plain rambling, while the underwater world of coral reefs and submerged wrecks attract more and more scuba divers. For the botanist and ornithologist, Dominica is a natural haven. The flora is extremely rich, with tropical plants, orchids, lianas, and ferns found in few other places in the world. There is also a wealth of medicinal plants, and tropical fruits grow in profusion. Among its varied fauna Dominica boasts two species of parrots—the red-necked Amazon and the Amazon Imperialis (*sisserou* is the local name)—found only on this island.

Dominica's rich cultural heritage is interwoven with history. The Carib Indians, the indigenous people of the Caribbean, live as a community on the northeast of the island. They are the descendents of the fierce and cannibalistic Caribs, who managed to hold out against Europe's two grand armies of the 18th century. The art and craft of today's Carib community are unique.

Some important island cultural events include Carnival, a colorful event with calypso and queen shows, steel bands, and street dancing; National Day celebrations from mid-October to Community Day, November 4; and Dominica Festival of Arts, Domfesta, an exposition of music, art, crafts, and theater.

SOME BACKGROUND: Largest of the British Windwards, Dominica (or Sunday Island) was sighted by Columbus in November of 1493. For centuries British and French troops fought each other for its domination. The deadly game eventually turned in Britain's favor, and it had to pay a ransom of $65,000 to France to get that country to leave. In 1805 Britain assumed control, yet it still had to deal with Carib uprisings, including an Indian war which broke out as late as 1930.

On March 1, 1967, Dominica got a new constitution and was declared a state in association with Britain. On November 3, 1978, it became independent and today is a republic and a member of the Commonwealth of Nations (formerly the British Commonwealth).

Dominica, with a population of some 80,000 souls, lies in the eastern Caribbean, between Guadeloupe to the north and Martinique to the south. English is the official language, but a French patois is widely spoken.

The mountainous island is 29 miles long and 15 miles wide, with a total land area of 290 square miles, many of which have never been seen by explorers other than, presumably, the Carib Indians.

Most Dominicans earn their living from agriculture. The government is making a strong bid for tourism—but not the type that would expect miles of white sandy beaches, which the island does not have. Rather, Dominica is known for its river swimming and natural attractions. Because of the many shipwrecks around the island, scuba-diving is popular, particularly off the west coast.

Rainfall varies from a dryness along the coast to a tropical rain forest downpour in the mountainous interior.

Clothing is casual, including light summer wear most of the year; however, take along a sweater for those trips into the mountains. Bikinis and swimwear should not be worn in the capital city, Roseau, or in the villages.

To sum up, go here for the beauties of nature more than *la dolce vita*.

Portrait of a Great Lady

One of Dominica's most valuable assets is its very human and intelligent prime minister, Miss **Eugenia Charles.** She's credited almost single-handedly with focusing world resolve on the U.S. military action that prevented Grenada from being taken over by Cuba in 1985. Her articulate presentation of the danger of Soviet influence in the Caribbean has placed her near the top of the region's leaders, and probably the most beloved by the media. Firmly allied with the U.S., and a personal friend of Ronald Reagan and Margaret Thatcher, she is known for her ability to listen creatively to the complaints and suggestions of her compatriots.

Once a week she returns to her private offices which she used during her long career as a lawyer and leader of the opposition. A discreet plaque on the door reads simply, "Eugenia Charles, Barrister at Law and Solicitor." Inside you are likely to see as many as 50 people, each with a cause to plead before the island's social and political grande dame.

Born of a prominent Dominican family, and educated in Canada and Britain, she is the island's ambassador to the world at large, and its most influential spokesperson.

When faced with the myriad possibilities of how to spend development money from the European Community and the U.S., she insisted that the island's notoriously pot-holed roads be widened into the smooth thoroughfares that crisscross the island today. Her rationale was to improve transportation infrastructures so that industries besides tourism could develop in Dominica's lush interior.

As for tourism, Miss Charles foresees that because of the frequent rainfall over Dominica, the island will never have the kind of "fun in the sun" holidays that other neighboring islands have fostered more or less successfully. Rather, she envisions the development of a series of spas in the jungle-covered interior, profiting from the profusion of mineral and hot springs.

Her birthday, May 15, is somewhat of a national event, at least observed by her political allies. One coup which Miss Charles is said to have engineered happened in 1985, when the island's hundreds of government employees went on strike for more pay. She went on the radio to announce in clear, articulate, and rational terms that the government simply had no additional money to pay for salary increases and that such an expenditure could bankrupt the country. Everyone returned to work without incident.

Gracious, hard-driving, and relentlessly realistic, she is indeed a Lady with a capital L, and the most memorable democratic leader of the entire Caribbean.

GETTING THERE: There are two airports in Dominica, neither of which is large enough to handle a jetliner. Therefore, there are no direct flights from North America, but demand continues to grow. The **Melville Hall Airport** is on the northeast coast of the island, almost diagonally across the island from the capital, Roseau, on the southwest coast. Should you land at Melville Hall, there is a 1½-hour taxi ride into Roseau, a tour across the island through the forest and coastal villages. The fare from Melville Hall to Roseau is EC$33 ($12.20) per person, and the driver has the right to gather up at least three passengers in his cab. A taxi may be rented for exclusive use for EC$120 ($44.40).

The newer **Canefield Airport** is about a five-minute taxi ride to the north of Roseau. The 2,000-foot airstrip accommodates smaller planes than those that can land at Melville Hall.

For many North Americans, the easiest way to reach Dominica is to take a flight to Antigua (see "Getting There" in Chapter IX). From there, you can take a LIAT flight to Dominica.

It is also possible to fly into Guadeloupe (see "Getting There" in Chapter XII). Once in Guadeloupe, you can make a connection on Air Guadeloupe or LIAT to Dominica. Air Martinique and LIAT also fly in from Fort-de-France, and connections on that airline are also possible from Barbados and St. Lucia. Air BVI flies in from St. Thomas and St. Maarten, and Air Caribe brings passengers from Puerto Rico and St. Maarten.

GETTING AROUND: Roseau is the capital, and many of the places to stay are found there.

At either airport, you can rent a **taxi,** and prices are regulated by the government.

If you rent a car, a fee of EC$20 ($7.40) is charged to obtain a driver's license. These are available at the airports. There are 310 miles of newly paved roads, and only in a few areas is a four-wheel drive necessary. *Driving is on the left.*

Car-rental establishments in Dominica include:

Valley Rent-a-Car, Goodwill Road in Roseau (tel. 809/448-3233), and at Portsmouth (tel. 809/445-5252).

Wide Range, 81 Bath Rd., Roseau (tel. 809/448-2198).

S.T.L. Rent-a-Car, Goodwill Road, Roseau (tel. 809/448-2340).

Rates range from $35 to $45 daily, $196 to $252 weekly. Drivers must be between 25 and 65 years of age, and a deposit of $100 is required. A collision damage waiver (CDW) is available on cars at a daily rate of about $6. A comprehensive insurance with a deductible clause of $300 for any damage or loss to the vehicle is applicable.

The **public transportation** system consists of private minibus service between Roseau and the rest of Dominica. These minibuses are filled mainly with school children, workers, and country people who need to come into the city. Taxis may be a more reliable means of transport to visitors, but there are hotels at which buses call during the course of the day.

Dominica Tours, Anchorage Hotel, Castle Comfort (tel. 809/449-2638), run by Mrs. Janice Armour, offers among the best tours on the island, including hiking, birdwatching, and photo safaris. The most popular tour is to the Carib Reservation and to Emerald Pool, a grotto in the heart of the rain forest. With lunch included, the six-hour safari costs $30. The two-hour tour to the Sulphur Springs and a visit to the Botanical Gardens goes for $15. I also recommend a combined tour of Trafalgar Triple Waterfalls, Sulphur Springs (via the Morne and Botanical Gardens), and Freshwater Lake, including a picnic lunch and rum punch, lasting six hours and going for $30.

Rainbow Rover Tours (tel. 809/448-8650), run by Ivor and Helene Rolle, offers air-conditioned Land-Rover tours personalized to suit your wishes. Whole-day tours, inclusive of lunch and drinks and costing $50 per person, and half-day jaunts, including drinks and costing $30 per person, are arranged to Dominica's many attractions to meet individual requirements. Activities such as diving, swimming, photography, and painting are catered for.

Paradise Tour (tel. 809/448-5999), a tour company geared to organizing for your enjoyment, is run by experienced, reliable, and well-informed drivers. Trips are arranged to historic sites and scenic spots. Various routes are available.

Otherwise you can negotiate your own terms with the taxi drivers eagerly

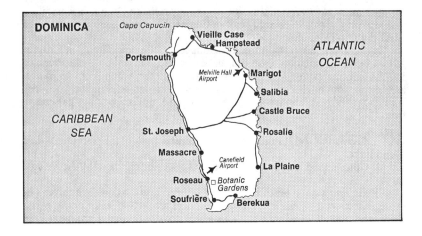

awaiting your business at the airport when the plane lands. Rates are about $15 per car for each hour of touring. As many as four passengers can go along at the same time.

PRACTICAL FACTS: An independent nation, Dominica, with 25 village councils and two town councils, is governed by a president as head of state and a prime minister who is head of government.

Banks: They're open from 8 a.m. to 1 p.m. Monday to Friday, reopening on Friday from 3 to 5 p.m.

Currency: Dominica uses the East Caribbean dollar, worth about 37¢ in U.S. currency.

Customs: Dominica is lenient, allowing you personal and household effects, plus 200 cigarettes, 50 cigars, and 40 ounces of liquor or wine.

Documents: To enter, U.S. and Canadian citizens must have proof of citizenship such as a passport, voter registration card, or a birth certificate. In addition, an ongoing or return ticket must be shown.

Electricity: For U.S.-made appliances, take along an adapter. The electrical current is 220 to 240 volts AC, 50 cycles, so a transformer is necessary. It's advisable to take a flashlight with you to Dominica, in case of power outages.

Information: A good source of assistance and information is the **Dominica Tourist Information** office, in the Old Market Plaza, Roseau, with administration offices at the National Development Corporation offices, Valley Road (tel. 809/448-2186). Information office hours are from 9 a.m. to 1 p.m. and 2 to 4 p.m. Monday to Friday, from 9 a.m. to 1 p.m. Saturday. Information and assistance can also be obtained from the Information Bureau at Melville Hall Airport (tel. 809/445-7051) and Canefield Airport (tel. 809/449-1242).

Taxes: A 10% government room tax is added to every hotel accommodation bill, plus a 10% tax on alcoholic beverages served in hotels and restaurants and a 3% tax on non-alcoholic drinks and food items. Anyone who remains in Dominica for 24 hours must pay a $6 departure tax.

Telecommunications: Dominica maintains phone, telegraph, teletype, Telex, and Telefax connections with the rest of the world. International direct dialing (IDD) is available as well as U.S. direct service through AT&T. The system is modern and reliable. To call Dominica from the U.S., dial the area code, 809, then the seven digit number, the first two being 44 and then the five digits. To call a number while you're on the island, it is only necessary to dial the last *five* digits (not the *44*).

Time: Dominica is on Atlantic Standard Time; that is, one hour ahead of Miami and New York in winter. However, they do not observe Daylight Saving Time, so that in summer, Dominican time is the same as U.S. cities in the eastern zone.

Tips and service: Most hotels and restaurants add a 10% service charge to all bills. Where this charge has not been included, tipping is up to you.

Water: The water is drinkable from the taps and in the high mountain country. Pollution is hardly a problem here.

Weather: Daytime temperatures average between 70° and 85° Fahrenheit. Nights are much cooler, especially in the mountains. The rainy season is from June to October, when there can be warnings of hurricane activity.

HOTELS IN DOMINICA: There are several places to stay, but none of them is very large. Only small groups of people or individual travelers can be accommodated at one time. Air conditioning may be found in some hotels, but most establishments on Dominica are simple. The cost of living here is low, and tariffs throughout the island entice the bargain seeker. However, don't forget that the government imposes taxes on hotel rooms, beverages, and food, which will probably be added to your hotel bill. Ask about this when you register to save yourself a surprise at the end of your visit.

In Roseau and Castle Comfort

Reigate Hall Hotel, Reigate, Dominica, W.I. (tel. 809/445-4031). Remotely lying on a steep hillside about a mile from Roseau, it was originally built in the 18th century as a plantation house. Some parts of the original structure are left, but the hotel has been substantially altered. Most of the old has been replaced with a comfortably airy design of hardwood floors and exposed stone. The establishment contains 17 rooms curving around the sides of a rectangular swimming pool. Each has a private bath, air conditioning, and phone. EP rates year round are $50 daily in singles, $80 in doubles. Suites rent for $110 for singles, $140 for doubles. The hotel has a sauna, an outdoor tennis court, a gym, and a good restaurant, recommended separately.

Fort Young Hotel P.O. Box 462, Roseau, Dominica, W.I. (tel. 809/448-5000), which opened in 1988, grew from the ruins of the 1770 Fort Young. I first knew this hotel in 1979, before it was wiped out by a hurricane. Now it has come back better than before. Attracting both commercial travelers and tourists, it offers a total of 32 comfortable bedrooms and one suite. All accommodations are air-conditioned, with ceiling fans and a balcony, the most desirable of which opens onto the sea. Each unit is air-conditioned. Singles rent for $80 daily, with doubles costing from $110 year round. The modern hotel's core is embraced by the crescent-shaped sweep of the historic walls of the old fort. There is an outdoor pool, and water sports can be arranged upon request. Events sometimes get lively here, as there is a weekly manager's punch party as well as disco action. Tours of the area can be arranged. On the premises is a health club.

Anchorage Hotel, P.O. Box 34, Dominica, W.I. (tel. 809/449-2638), is skillfully terraced so that its true beauty is only visible once you're inside. Lying at Castle Comfort, half a mile south of Roseau, the hotel is an EC$5 ($1.85) ride into town. Carl and Janice Armour provide 36 air-conditioned rooms, each with two double beds, all with shower or bath, plus a balcony overlooking their private pool. Mr. and Mrs. Armour are the most helpful hosts I've encountered on the island. For a peaceful holiday hideaway, year round the Anchorage rents a single for $40 nightly, a double going for $50, both EP. For breakfast and dinner, a supplement of $20 per person is tacked on. Children under 12 are granted reductions of 50%. In the bedrooms, draperies and bedspreads are often in florid prints. In spite of its location on shore, there is little or no beach available, so guests spend their days around the plant-ringed rectangular pool. However, the hotel does have its own jetty and a pebble beach for saltwater bathing. If you own a yacht, you can moor it here or use the dinghy to come over for a meal at the roof restaurant, with its view of the sea and Roseau Harbor. The hotel also has a squash court. They keep a fresh supply of ginger lilies and anthurium daily in the public rooms. The hotel's French and Caribbean cuisine is the best on the island. The food is simple but good, with an emphasis on fresh fish and vegetables. A table d'hôte luncheon or dinner costs $15. But you can dine much lighter, perhaps ordering only fish, a salad, and rice for $5. Nonresidents aren't allowed to use the swimming pool, but they can drop in for meals. A West Indian band plays music twice a week for dancing. On Tuesday night, there is a weekly buffet accompanied by piano music.

Excelsior Hotel, P.O. Box 413, Canefield, Dominica, W.I. (tel. 809/449-1501), is one of the most popular hotels in Dominica. Lying about two miles from the center of Roseau, but only a two-minute drive from Canefield Airport, the hotel contains only 14 well-scrubbed bedrooms, each with private bath, comfortable furniture, and access to a veranda. This is the only hotel in Dominica with its own specially designed conference room, making it the center of the island's business and commercial life. Guests are usually met at the airport, then redeposited there at the end of their visit. Even the clean and bright in-house restaurant is worth a special visit. Year-round prices are $45 daily in a single, $65 in a double, with MAP included.

Standing next to the Anchorage, **Sisserou Hotel,** P.O. Box 134, Castle Comfort, Dominica, W.I. (tel. 809/448-3111), is named after the island bird that is on the endangered-species list. It offers about the same class and comfort of accommodations as the Anchorage. The management lodges guests in one of 20 rooms, each with private bath, air conditioning, and a balcony overlooking the sea. The hotel stands right on the shoreline, but instead of swimming there, most guests dive into the hotel's pool. There's also a breeze-filled wooden bar sitting beneath a sun screen beside the pool. The hotel has a good restaurant. The public areas are mostly sheathed in two full-grained tropical hardwoods known as *samaan* and *gommier.* Year-round rates are $50 daily in a single, $60 in a double, breakfast included.

Evergreen Hotel, P.O. Box 309, Castle Comfort, Dominica, W.I. (tel. 809/448-3288). Built in 1986, this pleasant family-run hotel looks a bit from the outside like a Swiss chalet. It contains only ten rooms, a few of which have access to wrap-around tile-floored verandas. It sits amid a cluster of other hotels about a mile south of Roseau. A stony beach is visible a few steps beyond the garden. Inside and out, the airy, spacious, comfortably modern place was trimmed with the richly textured local gommier wood. Mena Winston, the Dominican-born owner, assists in the preparation of each of the well-flavored meals. With MAP included, singles year round cost $50 daily, and doubles run $70, plus service and tax. Each room has stone accents, air conditioning, and a private bath. Laundry service and scuba-diving can be arranged.

A Beachfront Resort

The **Castaways Beach Hotel,** P.O. Box 5, Roseau, Dominica, W.I. (tel. 809/449-6244), is the island's first major resort along the coast north of Roseau, some 13 miles from the capital. Nestled between the tropical forest and a mile-long black sand beach and ringed on the inland side with huge tamarind trees, the hotel has 27 concrete-walled rooms shaded by tall coconut palms. Each accommodation has a private bath and is spacious, well ventilated, and filled with simple contemporary furniture. Linda Harris, the managing director, charges from $100 daily for doubles in winter and $80 for singles. *In summer, prices are $80 in a double, $60 in a single.* A continental breakfast is included. On the beach is an open-air bar built in a fashion similar to the *chikees* of the Seminole Indians in the Florida Everglades, thatched with palmetto fronds. Water sports can be arranged through the reception desk, as can guided excursions to the island's principal sights. The hotel dining room serves some of the best food I've found on Dominica (see my recommendation below). A tennis court is available.

Rain Forest Retreats

Springfield Plantation, P.O. Box 41, Roseau, Dominica, W.I. (tel. 809/449-1401). It doesn't sit on any beach, and its access roads are winding (though newly paved). Still, it's one of the most unusual and raffishly charming hotels in Dominica. Set in a rain forest about seven miles north of Roseau, it occupies a wood-framed plantation house whose U-shaped design embraces a poinsettia-ringed front courtyard. Its dignified premises includes a richly gabled annex and the imposing private house of the estate's absentee owner, John Archbold, who is descended from the original chairman of Standard Oil.

It contains only six rooms and four apartments, each of which has a kitchen. None needs air conditioning, because of the constant mountainside breezes. Year round, with MAP included, singles cost $65 daily, and doubles go for $95. The establishment's social center is a panoramic veranda, from which you can see the sea between the cleft of two mountains. Furnishings throughout are an eclectic mix of 1950s tropical with a few antiques. Mostly, the place offers a simple, unpretentious, slightly eccentric oasis. If you want to go swimming, the Anthurium River, 200 feet from the hotel, offers a safe cold-water river pool secluded from prying eyes by the overhang of nearby trees. Luncheon visitors are welcome to the plantation, but only if they phone in advance. Mountain chicken is a specialty, as is crayfish from the river. Lunches for nonresidents cost EC$50 ($18.50). The gentlemanly manager, Tommy Coulthard, and his wife, Jane, are gracious and charming people.

Papillote Wilderness Retreat, P.O. Box 67, Roseau, Dominica, W.I. (tel. 809/448-2287), is a hotel and restaurant run by the Jean-Baptistes—Cuthbert, who handles the restaurant, and his wife, Anne Grey, a marine scientist. Their place, four miles to the east of Roseau, stands right in the middle of Papillote Forest, at the foothills of Morne Macaque. In this remote setting they have created a unique rain-forest resort that is somewhat primitive. You can spend an Adam and Eve life here, surrounded by exotic fruits, flowers, and herb gardens. In a wood-sided outbuilding, six rooms and two suites, all with baths. With MAP included, year-round rates are $65 daily in a single, $100 in a double, plus service and taxes.

Don't expect constantly sunny weather, since this part of the jungle is known for its downpours. Their effect, however, keeps the orchids, begonias, and brilliantly colored bromeliads lush. The 12 acres of sloping and forested land are pierced with a labyrinth of masonry walls and trails, beside which flows a network of freshwater streams, a few of which flow from hot mineral springs. Natural hot mineral baths are available, and you'll be directed to a secluded waterfall where you can swim in the river. The Jean-Baptistes also run a boutique in which they sell Dominican products, including appliquéed quilts, made by local artisans. Even if you don't stay here, it's an experience to dine on the thatch-roofed terrace (see "Where to Dine," below).

WHERE TO DINE: The local delicacy is the fine flesh of the *crapaud* (a frog), called "mountain chicken." Freshwater crayfish is another specialty, as is *tee-tee-ree*, fried cakes made from tiny fish. Stuffed crab back is usually a delight. The backs of red and black land crabs are stuffed with delicate crabmeat and Créole seasonings. The fresh fruit juices of the island are divine nectar, and no true Dominican spends the day without at least one rum punch.

La Robe Créole, 3 Victoria St. (tel. 809/448-2896), is considered the most important independent restaurant in the capital. It's contained inside the masonry walls of a low-slung colonial house, sitting beside a sunny plaza on a slope above the sea, behind a façade draped with flowering vines. Waitresses dressed in madras Créole costumes serve full meals costing from EC$65 ($24). In a long and narrow dining room capped with heavy beams and filled with nostalgia-laden reminders of the 19th century, you can enjoy pumpkin pimiento soup, callaloo with cream of coconut soup, crab back, pizzas, mountain chicken in beer batter, and shrimp in coconut with garlic sauce. For dessert, you can try banana or coconut cake or ice cream. The establishment and its bar are open daily except Sunday from 9 a.m. to 11 p.m. The number of tables is limited, so reserve.

A section of the restaurant, The Mouse Hole (tel. 809/448-2396), a good place for food on the run. From its take-out service, you can enjoy freshly made sandwiches and salads. Light meals cost $5. They make good Trinidad-inspired rôtis here. This is burrito-type food, a wheat pancake wrapping beef, chicken, or vegetables. In Dominica, these rôtis are most often flavored with curry.

The **Orchard Restaurant,** 31 King George V St. (tel. 809/448-3051). Late in 1986 this restaurant opened in its new home, a clean, wood-lined oasis of calm on a busy, centrally located street of the capital. There's a bar, as well as a large dining room and a lattice-covered courtyard to one side for outdoor dining. You can order take-out food here, but most clients come for the bar and the sit-down meals. Lunch is served daily except Sunday from 11:30 a.m. to 4 p.m., and dinner is nightly except Saturday and Sunday from 7 to 9. Full meals, costing from EC$50 ($18.50), include mountain chicken, callaloo soup with crabmeat, fish court-bouillon, coconut shrimp, black pudding, blood sausage, goat water, several pumpkin dishes, and breadfruit puffs. Friday night features barbecued meat dishes.

Reigate Hall Restaurant, Reigate Hall Hotel (tel. 809/445-4031), lies only a mile from the center of Roseau, but it seems so much longer because of the tortuous road leading up to it. Contained on the second story of this previously recommended hotel, the restaurant is an intimately lit enclave of such polished tropical hardwoods as greenheart along with exposed stone. A masonry spillway splashing water onto the paddles of a water wheel adds an old-fashioned accent. Lunch is from 1 to 3 p.m., and dinner is served from 7 to 10 p.m. daily. Menu items are derived from both French and Créole recipes, costing from EC$75 ($27.75) for a full meal. On any given night the bill of fare might include fish soup, beef curry, coq au vin, prawns in garlic sauce, seafood au gratin, and "mountain chicken" in a champagne sauce. Reservations are suggested if you're not a resident of the hotel.

The restaurant at the **Excelsior Hotel,** Canefield (tel. 809/449-1501), on the ground floor of one of the newest hotels of Dominica, serves well-prepared food at reasonable prices. Guests dine in a clean, inviting room with white walls and straw-bottomed chairs of island cedar. Meals are served without a break from 7 a.m. to 11 p.m. daily. A polite employee will offer you a glass of soursop juice before you order, unless you prefer something stronger from the bar. Lunch costs from EC$35 ($12.95) and dinner from EC$75 ($27.75). The bill of fare might include opossum (manicou), delectable preparations of mountain chicken, T-bone steak, fresh crayfish from one of the island's hundreds of freshwater streams, and fish "any style." Anthony Williams is the restaurant's manager.

The World of Food Restaurant and Bar, Vena's Hotel, 48 Cork St. (tel. 809/448-3286). In the 1930s the garden containing this restaurant belonged to a well-known novelist, Jean Rhys. Today it's the patio for one of the most charming Créole restaurants in Roseau. Some say that its owner, Vena McDougal, is the best Créole cook in town. You can have a drink at the stone-walled building at the far end of the garden if you want, but many guests select one of the rickety tables in the shadow of a large mango tree. Open from 7:30 a.m. to 10 p.m., seven days a week, the World of Food serves a fixed-price meal costing from EC$11 ($4.05) to EC$15 ($5.55). Specialties include steamed fish or fish steak, curried goat, chicken-filled rôti, black pudding, mountain chicken, breadfruit puffs, callaloo and watercress soup, crab backs, conch, and tee-tee-ree (fried fish cakes). She's said to make the best rum punches on the island as well—they're a concoction of rich fruits blended with local rums. The restaurant is attached to Vena's Hotel (really a guesthouse). If you want to reach the restaurant without passing through Vena's, its entrance is on Field's Lane.

Guiyave, 15 Cork St. (tel. 809/448-2930). Near the private office of the prime minister, this airy restaurant occupies the second floor of a wood-framed West Indian house. Rows of tables almost completely fill the narrow balcony overlooking the street outside. You can enjoy a drink at the stand-up bar on the second floor. The establishment is open only for breakfast and lunch. Hours are from 8 a.m. to 5 p.m. Monday to Friday, from 8 a.m. to 2 p.m. Saturday. It's closed all day Sunday. Full meals cost from EC$19 ($7) to EC$36 ($13.30). Specialties include different preparations of conch and rabbit, octopus and lobster, spareribs, chicken, Saturday-only rôtis, crab backs, mountain chicken, goat stew, and an array of sandwiches. The place is known for its juices, including refreshingly tropical glasses of soursop, tamarind, sorrel, cherry, and strawberry.

Papillote Wilderness Retreat (tel. 809/448-2287), previously recommended for its lodgings, is also one of the most alluringly located restaurants in Dominica. Even if you're not staying there, call for a reservation, negotiate with a taxi driver, and ask to be taken there for lunch. Amid nature trails rife with exotic flowers, century-old trees, and filtered sunlight, you dine on a masonry terrace a few steps from a sociable bar topped with a slab of samaan wood. The owners are Cuthbert Jean-Baptiste and his wife, Anne Grey. The array of health-conscious food includes flying fish, river shrimp, mountain chicken, dolphin, kingfish, dasheen puffs, breadfruit puffs, and a tempting array of tropical salads. Lunch and soothing drinks are served daily except Sunday from 10 a.m. to 4 p.m., costing from EC$35 ($12.95) for a full meal. Don't forget to bring sturdy walking shoes and a bathing suit. Near the dining terrace, Cuthbert built a Jacuzzi-size masonry basin which is constantly filled with the mineral-rich waters of a hot spring.

If you're touring north along the coast, consider stopping in for a meal at the already-recommended **Castaways Beach Hotel,** P.O. Box 5 (tel. 809/449-6244), 13 miles north of Roseau. In this resort setting, the managing director, Linda Harris, welcomes nonguests to her hotel dining room with its waterfront setting. Guests dress in casual resortwear and dine informally, enjoying the warm hospitality of the staff. Here you get the cuisine for which Dominica is known, including the crapaud or mountain chicken. Prepared in a number of ways, it is almost always delicious. They have a delicacy most often compared to quail. You can also get lambi (conch), as well as island crab mixed with a savory Créole stuffing. All dishes are garnished with the fruits and vegetables of Dominica's rich soil. For example, you might have glazed ham with passion fruit. Count on spending around $20 for dinner, less for lunch. Before dining, try a rum punch in the lounge or beach bar. Go from noon to 2 p.m. or 7 to 9 p.m.

TOURING THE ISLAND: Those making day trips to Dominica from other islands will want to see the **Carib Indian Reservation,** in the northeast. In 1903 Britain got the Caribs to agree to accept boundaries on 3,700 acres of land set aside for them. Hence, this is the last remaining domain of this once-hostile tribe (now subdued) who gave their name to the archipelago—Caribbean.

Their look is Mongolian, and they are no longer "pure-blooded." Blacks and others have married into the tribe. Today they survive by fishing, growing food, and weaving baskets and vertivert grass mats which they sell to the outside world. They still make dugout canoes too.

It's like going back in time when you explore **Morne Trois Pitons National Park,** a primordial rain forest, "me Tarzan, you Jane" country. Mists rise gently over lush, dark-green growth, drifting up to blue-green peaks that have earned for Dominica the title of "Switzerland of the Caribbean." Framed by banks of giant ferns, rivers rush and tumble. Trees sprout orchids, and everything seems blanketed with some type of parasitic growth. Green sunlight filters down through timeless trees, and the roar of a waterfall creates a blue mist.

Exploring this green heart of Dominica is for serious botanists and only the most skilled hikers, who should never penetrate unmarked trails without a very experienced guide.

Deep in the park is the **Emerald Pool Trail,** a half-mile nature trail that forms a circuit loop on a footpath passing through the forest to a pool with a beautiful waterfall. Downpours are frequent in the rain forest, and at high elevations cold winds blow.

Five miles up from the **Roseau River Valley,** in the south-central sector of Dominica, **Trafalgar Falls** can be reached after your vehicle passes through the village of Trafalgar. There, however, you have to approach by foot, as the slopes are too steep for vehicles. After a 20-minute walk, you arrive at the base of the falls. A trio of falls converge into a rock-strewn pool. Boulders sprout vegetation, and tree ferns encircle the flowing water. On the way there you pass growths of ginger plants or vanilla orchids.

The **Sulfur Springs** are evidence of the island's volcanic past. Jeeps or Land Rovers get quite near. Not only Sulfur Springs but also the **Boiling Lake** are bubbling evidence of underground volcanic activity, north and east of Roseau. It's like a bubbling pool of gray mud. Sometimes you hear a belch of smelly sulfurous fumes—the odor is like a rotten egg. Only the very fit should attempt to go to Boiling Lake. Some Dominicans fear that volcanic activity will erupt again. Freshwater Lake lies at the foot of Mount Macaque.

On the northwest coast, **Portsmouth** is Dominica's second-largest settlement. Once there, you can row up the Indian River in native canoes, visit the ruins of old Fort Shirley in Cabrits National Park, and bathe at Sandy Beach on Douglas Bay and St. Ruperts Bay.

The **Cabrits National Park** on the northwest coast of Dominica (tel. 809/448-2733), is a 650-acre protected site containing mountain scenery, tropical forests, swampland, volcanic sand beaches, coral reefs, and the ruins of a fortified 18th-century garrison of British, then French construction. The Cabrits Park's land area is a spectacular promontory formed by twin peaks of extinct volcanoes, overlooking fine beaches, with Douglas Bay on one side and Prince Rupert's Bay across the headland. Part of Douglas Bay forms the marine section of the park. Fort Shirley, the large garrison last used as a military post in 1854, is being wrested from encroaching vegetation. A small museum highlights the natural and historic aspects of the park. The name *Cabrits* comes from the Spanish-

Portuguese-French word for goat, because of the animals left there by early sailors to provide fresh meat on future visits.

SHOPPING: Store hours are usually from 8 a.m. to 4 p.m. Monday to Friday, 8 a.m. to 1 p.m. Saturday. In Roseau, the Old Market Plaza, of historical significance as a former slave trading market and more recently the Friday and Saturday morning vegetable market, now houses three craft shops, each specializing in coconut, straw, and Carib craft products.

Tropicrafts Ltd., at Queen Mary Street and Turkey Lane (tel. 809/448-2747), offers the well-known grass rugs handmade and woven in several intricate patterns at Tropicrafts' factory. They also have for sale handmade bags, shopping bags, and placemats, all appliquéed by hand. The handmade dolls are popular with doll collectors. The Dominican vertivert-grass mats are known throughout the world.

Caribana Handicrafts, 31 Cork St. (tel. 809/448-2761). Some island residents claim that the entire straw-weaving industry on Dominica was established by the store's dignified owner, Iris Joseph. You'll be able to see a few of the products being crafted at wooden tables. Near the front, stacks of a lengthy array of baskets in all sizes and shapes are stocked. Mrs. Joseph is usually pleased to explain the dying processes which turn the straw into one of three different earth-related tones. When straw is buried in the earth, it turns black; when it's soaked in saffron, it turns yellow; and when it's boiled with the bark of a tang tree, it turns purple. A selection of other goods, including Bello Hot Pepper (said to be the finest by island connoisseurs), is available.

THE SPORTING LIFE: Serious hikers find Dominica a major challenge. Guides should be used for all unmarked trails. You can reach one by going to the office of the **Dominica National Park** in the Botanical Gardens in Roseau (tel. 809/448-2732) or the Dominica Tourist Board.

As for **beaches,** some are in the northwest of the island around Portsmouth, the second town. There are also secluded beaches in the northeast, along with spectacular coastal scenery. But all of these are hard to reach, and you might settle instead for a freshwater swimming pool or river swimming.

The best water-sports center is **Dive Dominica,** Castle Comfort Guest House, P.O. Box 63, Dominica, W.I. (tel. 809/449-2188). Introduction to scuba-diving (resort course) costs $65, with all equipment provided. Open-water certification (NAUI) instruction is given. Snorkeling is also possible, with equipment for rent.

Dive Dominica also offers **boat charters,** with a 24-foot Aquasport taking a maximum of ten persons for $60 per hour. Trips are made to such destinations as Douglas Bay, Rodney's Rock, Soufrière, and Portsmouth, with prices depending on the distance traveled and the time consumed.

NIGHTLIFE: It's not very sophisticated, but there is some. A couple of the major hotels, such as **Castaways** (tel. 809/449-6244) and **Reigate** (tel. 809/448-4031), have entertainment on weekends, usually a combo or "jing ping" (traditional local music).

The **Anchorage Hotel** at Castle Comfort (tel. 809/449-2638) also has live entertainment and a good buffet at least one night a week.

Warehouse Disco in Roseau (no phone) provides entertainment on Saturday from 9 p.m. to 2 a.m. weekly for an entrance fee of $2.

If you're in Dominica at the right time, don't miss the **Korné Korn-La,** a street party usually held on the second Saturday of the month at Soufrière or Scotts Head Village. The name of the celebration means "blow the conch shell," a traditional sound that summoned plantation workers to the fields or home, announced the return of fishermen to shore with their catch, and signaled village get-togethers. Today's festivities include a row of candlelit stalls placed along the shore, where you can buy freshly barbecued lamb chops and grouper steaks for about $1.30 each and tasty little hotcakes for less than 10¢. There's recorded popular music blaring out, but my favorite is the live melodies of an accordion, a tambou, a boom-boom, a shack-shack, and a gwage. A small entrance fee is charged to pay for cleaning up the village.

2. ST. LUCIA

Second largest of the Windward Islands, St. Lucia (pronounced *Loo*-sha) is a checkerboard of green-mantled mountains, gentle valleys, wide beaches, banana plantations, a bubbling volcano, giant tree ferns, wild orchids, and fishing villages. There's a smell of the South Pacific about it. With its mixed French and British heritage, it has year-round temperatures of 70° to 90° Fahrenheit.

The actual discovery of this football-shaped island is shrouded in conjecture, some maintaining that Columbus landed on December 13, 1502. However, this widely held opinion is considered inaccurate. Records reveal that the explorer was far from St. Lucia on that date. It is often conceded that Spanish seamen discovered the island in some unknown year.

St. Lucia lies some 20 miles from Martinique. An English party coming from St. Kitts settled here in 1605, but the island was to change hands a total of 14 times, as the French and English fought intermittently for its control, their battles lasting for more than a century. Slaughter parties led by cannibalistic Caribs often deterred permanent settlements for years.

The island was a British colony from 1803 to 1967, when it became an associated state within the British Commonwealth. St. Lucia arrived at its full sovereignty on February 22, 1979.

A mountainous island of some 240 square miles, St. Lucia counts some 120,000 inhabitants. The capital, **Castries,** is built on the southern shore of a large, almost landlocked harbor—a "reliable shelter for ships"—surrounded by hills. The approach to the airport is almost a path between hills, and it's very impressive.

The capital was named after an 18th-century French secretary of state to the foreign colonies, Marshal de Castries. Fires have swept over the town many times, destroying its wooden buildings. The last catastrophe occurred in 1948. As a result, don't expect too many vintage structures.

GETTING THERE: Thanks to the increasing popularity of St. Lucia in recent years, getting there is now easier than ever. Airline routings from many North American cities, will require at least a touchdown in one or another Caribbean island before continuing on to St. Lucia. Because of its hub in San Juan, **American Airlines** is a good carrier to choose for a jaunt down to St. Lucia. Several flights depart daily from San Juan to both of the airports of St. Lucia.

Round-trip tickets from New York to St. Lucia in midwinter, depending on availability, can cost as little as $375 (subject to change). To qualify, passengers cannot travel on a weekend (defined as Friday, Saturday, or Sunday), and they must stay for between 3 and 21 days. Passengers can also use an airline's tour desk to secure reductions, sometimes substantial ones, if hotel reservations are made simultaneously with flight reservations.

It's wise to compare prices and options before booking a ticket, of course. **BWIA,** the official airline of Trinidad and Tobago, flies to St. Lucia from New York, Miami, and Boston. And, if you're already on one of St. Lucia's neighbors,

Leeward Island Air Transport (LIAT) makes frequent runs into St. Lucia from many islands.

Airports

St. Lucia has two airports. Most international flights land at Hewanorra Airport in the south, 45 miles from Castries. If you fly in here and you're booked into a hotel in the north, you'll have to spend up to about an hour and a half going along the pot-holed East Coast Highway. The average taxi cost is $35. Once this airport was known as "Beane Field," when Roosevelt and Churchill agreed to construct a big air base there.

However, inter-island flights land at Vigie Airport in the northeast, which is much more convenient as it brings you down just outside Castries. LIAT Airways with its small prop planes flies into Vigie.

GETTING AROUND: A good way to travel on St. Lucia is by **taxis,** which are ubiquitous on the island, and most drivers are eager to please. The drivers have to be quite experienced to cope with the narrow, hilly, switchback roads outside the capital. Special programs have trained them to serve as guides. Their cars are unmetered, but tariffs for all standard trips are fixed by the government.

In asking the fare for a ride, make sure you determine if the driver is quoting a rate in U.S. dollars or the EC$. Leisure drives cost about $20 per hour. One of the most popular runs—from Castries to Marigot Bay—goes for EC$40 ($14.75).

Car Rentals

First, remember to *drive on the left.* You will need a St. Lucia's driver's license. This can most easily be obtained at either airport upon arrival or at car-rental locations. Present your valid home license to the immigration officer for the car-rental company and pay a fee of EC$30 ($11.10).

Avis is the island's most visible car-rental company, with no fewer than eight locations, many in the large hotels. From a headquarters known as Sundrive Rentals, Vide Boutielle, P.O. Box 1010 (tel. 809/452-2202), in Castries, it delivers cars to the airports. Its cheapest cars, with manual transmission and no air conditioning, cost from $35 per day.

National Car Rental also has a representative on the island, St. Lucia Car Rental Services Ltd., P.O. Box 542, Castries, with several locations, including Hewanorra Airport (tel. 809/454-4669) and Vigie Airport (tel. 809/452-3050).

Local Buses

Minibuses, with names like "Lucian Love," and jitneys connect Castries with such main towns as Soufrière and Vieux Fort. They are generally overcrowded and often filled with produce on the way to market. Schedules are also unreliable. However, since taxis are expensive, it might be a reliable means of transport. At least it's cheap, usually from EC$1 (37¢) to EC$5 ($1.85) per ride. Buses for Cap Estate, the northern part of the island, leave from Jeremy Street in Castries, near the market. Buses going to Vieux Fort, Soufrière, leave from Bridge Street in front of the department store.

Sightseeing Bus Tours

Most hotel front desks will make arrangements for excursions, taking in all the major sights of St. Lucia. For example, **St. Lucia Representative Services,** P.O. Box 879, Castries (tel. 809/452-3762), offers many island tours, such as a half-day tour, Shopping Around the Island, every Monday and Friday, costing $12; a full-day Monday Round the Island Tour, costing $34, with lunch and drinks included as well as a stop at one of the old Choiseul plantations; a Rain Forest Tour for $27 on Wednesday; and a half-day North Island Tour costing $16 on Monday and Thursday. Tours leave if enough people want to go (usually a minimum of four passengers), and the journey can be simultaneously sweaty and charming. The minibuses hold either 14 or 25 seats, depending on the demand. The company has representatives making stops at most of the major hotels.

Sea Excursions

This type of tour can usually be arranged at your hotel's activities desk. One of the most popular tours, costing EC$140 ($51.80) per person, is aboard the *Brig Unicorn,* which takes you on a day's sail to Soufrière and the Pitons. The *Unicorn* starred as the slave ship in the TV series "Roots," among other movie roles. Built in 1948, it is a 140-foot vessel with 16 square-rigged sails, carrying a crew of 13. You sail southward from Coal Pot, near Castries, at 9 a.m., heading for Soufrière's Sulfur Springs. On the return voyage you're served a lunch aboard. Later, you swim at Anse Cochon and sail into Marigot Bay. You're back at dock at 4 p.m., where coaches await to return you to your hotel. To make reservations on your own, call 809/452-6811.

PRACTICAL FACTS: With its mixed French and British heritage, St. Lucia has interesting speech patterns. Although English is the official tongue, St. Lucians probably don't speak it as you do. Islanders also speak a French-Créole patois, similar to that heard in Martinique.

Currency: The official monetary unit is the Eastern Caribbean dollar, or EC$. It's about 37¢ in U.S. currency. However, most of the quotations will be in American dollars, as they are accepted by nearly all hotels, restaurants, and shops.

Customs: At either airport, Customs may be a hassle if there is the slightest suspicion, regardless of how ill-founded, that you are bringing illegal drugs into St. Lucia.

Documents: U.S. and Canadian citizens need proof of citizenship, such as a passport, voter registration card, or birth certificate, plus an ongoing or return ticket.

Electricity: This is a problem. Bring a converter, as St. Lucia has 220 to 230 volts AC, 50 cycles.

Information: For information while you're on the island, get in touch with the tourist information bureau on Jérémie Street, next to Customs Castries or the **St. Lucia Tourist Board** at P.O. Box 221, Castries, St. Lucia, W.I. (tel. 809/452-5968). In the United States, the office is at 820 Second Ave., New York, NY 10017 (tel. 212/867-2950).

Post office: The General Post Office is on Bridge Street in Castries. It's open from 8:30 a.m. to 4 p.m. Monday to Friday.

Service: Most hotels add a 10% service charge, and restaurants do likewise.

Taxes: The government imposes an 8% occupancy tax on hotel room rentals. If you're flying on to one of the islands in the Caribbean Commonwealth (English-speaking islands), you must pay a departure tax of EC$10 ($3.70). That is true also for the French West Indies and the U.S. Virgin Islands. However, if you're returning to the U.S. mainland or going elsewhere, the airport tax is EC$20 ($7.40). This tax must be paid in EC dollars.

Telephone: Cable & Wireless provides international telecommunications and also operates a dial phone system throughout the island. Cables may be handed in at hotel desks or at the offices of Cable & Wireless in the George Gordon Buildings on Bridge Street in Castries. To call St. Lucia from the U.S., dial the area code, 809, then the seven-digit local number. When you're on the island, you need dial only the last *five* digits of the number (not the 45 that precedes them).

Time: In winter, watch your clock. St. Lucia is on Atlantic Standard Time, placing it one hour ahead of New York or Miami. However, during Daylight Saving Time it matches the clocks of the U.S. East Coast.

Weather: This little island, lying in the path of the trade winds, has year-round temperatures of 70° to 90° Fahrenheit.

WHERE TO STAY: Most of the lead hotels on this island are in the same price range. You have to seek out the bargains (begin at the bottom of my list). Once you reach your hotel, chances are you'll feel pretty isolated, but that's what many guests want. Many St. Lucian hostelries have kitchenettes where you can prepare simple meals. Prices are quoted in U.S. dollars.

The Leading Hotels

Cunard Hotel La Toc, P.O. Box 399, St. Lucia, W.I. (tel. 809/452-3081), some 2½ miles south of Castries, bills itself as tropical, tranquil, and luxurious, and here's one place that delivers what it promises. The site, about a ten-minute drive from the capital on half a mile of curved beach, is on 100 secluded acres at the edge of the island, and the hotel consists of 158 handsomely furnished rooms. Each accommodation includes a private bath, air conditioning, plus balconies or patios offering views of the ocean or the exotic gardens, planted with red ixora and pink-purple eranthemum. *In summer, twins range in price from $130 to $160 daily, and singles cost $110 to $140.* In winter, two people pay $200 to $230 daily, and one person is charged $180 to $210. For breakfast and dinner, add another $42 per person. Le Toc Suites are like little dollhouses in pastel colors. *Town and Country* called this "one of the ten most luxurious villa complexes in the Caribbean." Set apart, each of the villas nestled against the mountainside facing the sea. They are connected by frequent shuttle service to the main building. In winter, a superior two-bedroom villa costs $325 daily, rising to $425 in a deluxe two-bedroom villa with a private plunge pool. *In summer, these same villas cost $190 to $265 daily.*

All guests have a choice of two swimming pools, one so big it has its own palm-studded island. Among the shops you'll find a beauty salon, souvenir shop, boutique, and a drugstore. Dining is at the Terrace Restaurant, the casual entertainment center; at Les Pitons Restaurant, which has some of the best food on the island; or at the Quarterdeck, which has classic grills and operates only in the winter season. On the grounds is a manicured nine-hole golf course with a resident pro. Tennis buffs enjoy any of La Toc's three Hartru courts (lit for night games) or the two hard-surface courts with a resident tennis pro. The front-desk personnel can arrange for you to go fishing for dorado (dolphin), swordfish, cavalle, or barracuda. Water sports include Sunfish sailing, windsurfing, snorkeling, and waterskiing, all free to La Toc guests. The private 120-foot brig, the *Unicorn,* sails twice weekly. There is live entertainment nightly, plus two floor shows a week. On the hotel grounds is a fitness center, for an entire body workout.

The St. Lucian Hotel, P.O. Box 512, Reduit, St. Lucia, W.I. (tel. 809/452-8351), 6½ miles from Castries, has not only the best program of water sports on the island but it opens onto the most spectacular beachfront, Reduit Beach. It has a total of 220 rooms, making it one of the largest on St. Lucia. The grounds are well landscaped, with swaying palms, latticed breezeways, and flowering shrubs. Bedrooms are attractively furnished with a number of amenities, including air conditioning, queen-size beds, and private baths. In winter, singles rent for $130 to $160 daily, doubles for $160 to $190), and triples for $220 to $260. *Summer* *prices (mid-April to mid-December) are $70 daily in singles, $90 in doubles, and $120 in triples.* All tariffs include breakfast.

Dining facilities here are among the finest north of Castries. Many clients book in on MAP, taking their meals in the Hummingbird Restaurant. However, if you wish to partake of an à la carte selection from both Caribbean and international food, you can head for the Flamingo. Not only that, but if you'd like to put more dining variety into your vacation, you'll find yourself on the doorstep of some of the finest independent restaurants on the island, including Capone's. During the day, the beach takes up most of the time of the guests. Those seeking an active vacation can enjoy a variety of water sports, among them scuba diving and windsurfing. Most water sports are free to hotel guests, but nonresidents can also participate in the program (see "The Sporting Life," coming up). The St. Lucian not only has the best disco on the island, it also has entertainment almost nightly, including floor shows, limbo dancing, fire-eaters, and a steel band. Some guests find the activities and food here so rich and varied they never leave the grounds, although I'm not recommending that.

Halcyon Beach Club, P.O. Box, Choc Bay, St. Lucia, W.I. (tel. 809/452-5331), a four-mile drive outside Castries, is almost the classic concept of a modern Caribbean hotel today. It offers the perfect vacation for the entire family. Set in landscaped tropical gardens, with caged parrots and free iguanas, the hotel contains 180 air conditioned rooms with ocean, beach, or garden views. In winter, singles range in price from $110 to $145 daily, with twins costing $140 to $165. *In summer, a single costs $70 to $90 daily, and twins are priced from $90 to $115.* Water sports, including waterskiing, windsurfing, Sunfish sailing, and snorkeling, are free to guests, as is use of the tennis courts in the daytime (two are floodlit at night, with a charge for their use) and of the two swimming pools, volleyball, shuffleboard, and a host of indoor games. There is also a children's playground.

You have a choice of two restaurants for dining, one of which, the Wharf Chanticleer à la carte restaurant, is built sea style over the ocean for cool evening enjoyment. Danish manager Peter Richard Kouly, who trained at the leading hotel in Copenhagen and then owned a disco and restaurant on Jutland, offers one of the most copious kitchen outputs on the island. The evening menu is filled with an international cuisine, including Danish and French specialties. A barbecue, bar, and disco with the latest sound equipment extends on a platform out into the sea, creating a kind of manmade island. There is also a piano bar.

The All-Inclusive Resorts

Couples, P.O. Box 190, Malabar Beach, St. Lucia, W.I. (tel. 809/452-4211), is an unusual hotel, where all meals, drinks, cigarettes, entertainment, and most incidental expenses are included in the initial price. The center of the complex is under a gridwork of peaked roofs floored with tasteful terracotta tiles. Set on the edge of a beach bordered with palm trees, the hotel has a sprawling garden centered around a 150-year-old samaan tree. A freshwater swimming pool is graced with a lattice-sheltered bar area. This is a resort for couples only, with no children allowed. (A couple, according to the sophisticated owner, Craig Barnard, and his beautiful wife, Penny, can be any two mutually interested persons.) Singles and triples are not accepted, which contributes to the relaxed ambience of lovers enjoying each other, making friends with other couples, and celebrating the beautiful physical plant as well as their relationships. A member of the staff will meet your plane at the airport with a chest of cold beer and rum punches when you arrive. The bar opens early and closes late. Most of the lunches are buffet style, and there's even a cold-cut buffet offered every evening after the end of the dinner hour. Evening action is fun, including a weekly pajama party the likes of which you may always have wanted to attend but never had the chance. The price for a bedroom for a couple for a week's stay is *$1,790 in summer* and $2,200 per week in high season. There are several price categories, depending on the season and the accommodation, with top prices charged for ocean-front luxury suites for two: *$2,420 weekly in summer,* $2,850 at the height of the winter season. The resort is at the end of the Vigie airport, near Castries.

Club Med, St. Lucia, W.I. (tel. 809/454-6647), is a resort set on a 90-acre property. The carefree lifestyle holds forth on the southernmost tip of St. Lucia, opening onto Savannes Bay, just five minutes from the international airport. Completely refurbished, the club offers eight tennis courts, much beachside living, and horseback riding. The usual array of Club Med's sports is featured, including volleyball, archery, soccer, basketball, calisthenics, and softball. In addition, the club's Sailing Center, near the main building, offers two large sail boats, which takes about two dozen sailors on full-day or overnight sailing trips. There is also a well-equipped Workout Center.

Land rates (without air fare) in summer range from $550 per week per person, based on double occupancy, with all activities and meals included. In winter, the cost is generally $650 to $850 per person for land rates for one week, but at Christmas, it rises to $1,100 per person weekly. Each unit is air-conditioned, with a private balcony overlooking the sea. Some 512 members are accommodated in four-story buildings in a coconut grove. The twin-bedded rooms offer double occupancy, each with a private shower. In the heart of the complex is an open-air bar, a freshwater swimming pool, and a dance and theater area. At meals, served in the second-floor dining room with a panoramic view, guests enjoy unlimited wine at lunch and dinner. Membership, costing $30 per family for a one-time initiation plus $50 for adults and $20 for children in annual dues, is open to all. For more information, call the club's toll-free number, 800/258-2633 Monday to Saturday, or in New York City you can visit their sales and information office at 3 E. 54th St. (tel. 212/750-1670).

Club St. Lucia, Cap Estate, St. Lucia, W.I. (tel. 809/452-0551), is the most economical of the all-inclusive resorts on the island. In Cap Estate, an area near Le Sport, it opens onto a curved bay where smugglers of yore used to bring in brandies, cognacs, and cigars from Martinique. The club's core is a wooden building with decks from which you can look down on a free-form pool. Bungalow accommodations are scattered over landscaped grounds. They feature one king-size or two twin beds, air conditioning or ceiling fans, and private baths, as well as patios or terraces. The inclusive package the resort puts together is an impressive one, offering all meals during your stay, even snacks, along with unlimited beer, wine, and mixed drinks both day and night. Winter rates fall into four different categories, ranging from $110 to $175 per person daily in a double, $160 to $235 in a single. *Off-season tariffs are lowered to $90 to $110 per person daily in a double, $135 to $165 in a single.*

The emphasis is on sports and entertainment. For the prices quoted, you can get day or night tennis, unlimited water sports (waterskiing, Sunfish sailing, windsurfing, snorkeling, and pedal boats), unlimited golf greens fees, and horseback riding at nearby stables. Other activities include everything from free movies to nightly entertainment. There's even a children's Mini Club with a playground and a supervised activities program. A regular shuttle bus carries adventure-seeking guests to Rodney Bay and Reduit Beach.

A "BODY HOLIDAY": Le Sport, Cariblue Beach, P.O. Box 437, St. Lucia, W.I. (tel. 809/452-8551), is, as the heading suggests, a resort that "cares for your body." An all-inclusive "body holiday" resort, Le Sport is a citadel of first-class living and pampering, on a 1,500-acre beachfront estate at the northern-

most tip of the island. You're an eight-mile run from Castries, and guests seem to prefer this isolation. The resort makes a promise faithfully kept: Everything "you do, see, enjoy, drink, eat, and feel" is included in the price. That means not only accommodation, three meals a day, all refreshments, and bar drinks, but also use of all sports equipment, facilities and instruction. This encompasses a full program of daily scuba diving, windsurfing, waterskiing, snorkeling, sailing, pool-swimming, golf, use of three floodlit tennis courts, fencing, archery, riding, and transfers to and from the airport. Live entertainment is provided, and a piano bar is popular until late at night. But emphasis is placed on the rejuvenating experience of European body tonics. The tonic part of the stay is based on Thalassotherapy, involving the healthful pampering of seawater massage, thermal jet baths, toning, physical culture, and beauty treatments for both sexes.

Accommodation is in 128 air-conditioned bedrooms, all overlooking the sea and each with private bath containing shower, bath, and hairdryer. The units fall into four categories: deluxe, oceanview, oceanfront, and beachfront-balcony. In winter, based on double occupancy, rates are $175 to $215 per person daily. *Off-season, all-inclusive prices for double occupancy are $160 to $200 per person daily.* The single supplement is $20 per day year round. The food is cuisine légère, modeled after the cookery pioneered by the famous French chef, Michel Guérard, in his Basque retreat. The point is not to make cuisine and dieting contradictory. However, in order not to get completely carried away on a non-caloric wave, the chef also prepares "sin dishes." The hotel's director is Craig Barnard, who has proved such a success with his Couples. He has thoughtfully employed a Scotsman, Nigel Nicol, as manager.

Unique Hideaway Resorts
Anse Chastanet, P.O. Box 216, Soufrière, St. Lucia, W.I. (tel. 809/454-7000), my favorite retreat on the island and one of the few places around that truly merit the cliche, "tropical paradise," is not only St. Lucia's premier dive resort but also an exceptional Caribbean inn, combining warm service, excellent food, a beach location, and first-class facilities. Set on a forested hill, above palm-fringed, lava-ash Anse Chastanet Beach, it lies two miles outside Soufrière. You're surrounded by coffee trees, mangoes, papayas, banana plants, breadfruit, grapefruit, coconut palms, flamboyants, and hibiscus. The core of the house is a main building decorated in a typical island style, with a relaxing bar and dining room. These assets come in handy, as it's a 129-step climb down to the sands.

Guests have a choice from among 37 well-designed units. They can stay on the beach in spacious accommodations styled like West Indian plantation villas, with four rooms each, two up and two down. (By the time of your visit, plunge pools may have been installed.) Other units are constructed like octagonal gazebos, cooled by ceiling fans. These have views of the Pitons, St. Lucia's famous twin peaks. Each accommodation is large and comfortably appointed. They contain locally made furniture crafted from island woods such as greenheart, wild breadfruit, and red cedar. *EP rates in summer range from $70 to $100 daily in a single, $45 to $65 per person in a double.* In winter, EP doubles cost $65 to $90 per person, singles going for $115 to $160. All prices rise during the Christmas period. For dinner and breakfast, add another $30 per person daily.

You can dine or drink on a wind-cooled terrace built like a tree house over the tropical landscape. The food is exceptional. Créole, continental, or American —the cuisine reflects the diversified backgrounds of the operators of the resort. Lobster is freshly caught in the bay. Anse Chastanet is 18 miles from Hewanorra International airport. If notification is given, it can be arranged for a car to pick you up on arrival.

Marigot Bay Resort, Marigot Bay, P.O. Box 101, Castries, St. Lucia, W.I.

(tel. 809/452-4357), is a blanket name to cover a complex of inns, cottages, restaurants, bars, boutiques, and yachting berths lying about a 45-minute drive along the west coast. Much favored by the yachting set, the lagoon setting was described by author James Michener as "the most beautiful bay in the Caribbean." On a low-lying spit of the palm-dotted island, the complex, part of which is reached only by ferry service, is the most idyllic spot on St. Lucia. A cluster of colonial-style cottages is called Marigot Hillside Villas, and they are spread along a hillside. Some are privately owned, others controlled by the hotel. Most are one- or two-bedroom buildings, attractively making use of both their indoor and outdoor areas. In winter, a one-bedroom cottage or a studio apartment for two rents for $140 per day, and a two-bedroom cottage for four costs $155. *Off-season, a one-bedroom unit goes for $85 to $105 daily, a two-bedroom accommodation costing $100 to $120.* The yachting set often stays at the Marigot Inn, which is decorated in the West Indian style. The double rooms here are comfortable and attractive, opening onto verandas where the occupants can look at their yachts. There's also a Hurricane Hole, a cottage hotel on the southeastern shore. It offers the only swimming pool in the complex. In season, hotel rooms cost $120 daily in a single, $125 in a double. Off-season rents are $65 to $85 in singles, $70 to $90 in doubles. The lunch restaurant is Doolittle's, built out over the water on stilts. Across the way, the Hurricane Hole's restaurant is The Rusty Anchor. Both will be recommended later.

The Best Bargains
   The Islander, P.O. Box 907, Rodney Bay, Castries, W.I. (tel. 809/452-0255, 212/840-6636 in New York City), is near Pat's Pub, the St. Lucian Hotel, and Reduit Beach. This well-recommended hotel has an entrance whose walls are festooned with hanging flowers. Botany-minded guests will appreciate the plaques attached to plants throughout the property, giving the names of the various species that grow here in abundance. Many of the accommodations were completed in 1988, making them among the newest facilities on the island. All of this was open savanna before it became the Islander. A brightly painted fishing boat serves as a buffet table near the pool, and there's a spacious covered bar area perfect for socializing with the owner, Greg Glacé. Units are named after different Caribbean islands. Of the 60 accommodations, 20 are self-contained, with kitchenettes and private baths/showers, while 40 have private showers and small bars with mini-refrigerators. Guests walk a few hundred feet to the beach and to shop in nearby markets if their lodgings are equipped for cooking and entertaining. In winter, apartments cost $85 for single occupancy and $95 for two persons, while rooms go for $75 single, $85 double. *Summer prices drop to $50 for single occupancy of an apartment, $60 double. Rooms are $45 single, $50 double.* Children under 12 stay in their parents' room free. Taxes and service are extra. Accommodations look over a grassy courtyard sheltered with vines and flowers, with a network of walkways leading to the convivial restaurant. There, the Friday-night manager's rum punch party is popular, as well as the barbecue, costing EC$45 ($16.65) per person for grilled fish, steak, pork, and chicken. The Monday night Caribbean buffet, going for EC$45 ($16.65) per person, draws an enthusiastic crowd.
   Green Parrot Hotel, Red Tape Lane, Morne Fortune (Good Luck Hill), St. Lucia, W.I. (tel. 809/452-3167). Connected to the Green Parrot restaurant, this hillside series of balconied accommodations winds sinuously up the side of one of the steepest slopes in Castries. Flanking both sides of the pathways are masses of flowering shrubs and vines. Near the top of the complex, the landscape architects designed a terraced swimming pool, where guests lounge in comfortable chairs with views of the harbor far below. A courtesy bus makes runs to the beach

daily except Saturday. A sunken bar is set into the floor of the Pool Room restaurant, where no one minds if patrons show up in their bathing suits. The 33 accommodations include a handful of apartments with kitchens. All of them are reached via brick-lined hallways whose sides are pierced with breezeway arches that open onto a view of the forest. In winter, singles cost $68, while doubles go for $85. *In summer, singles are $45, and doubles rent for $60.*

Harmony Apartel, P.O. Box 155, Castries, St. Lucia, W.I. (tel. 809/452-8756), is a small resort opening onto a marina near some of the finest restaurants of St. Lucia. Five miles north of Castries, this 21-unit complex offers studio efficiency apartments ideal for two persons, as well as two-bedroom units which can sleep four to six persons comfortably. The latter contain separate living rooms, plus a choice of one or two bathrooms. Some guests ask to be located on the ground floor, while others prefer to go upstairs. Each accommodation comes with a fully equipped kitchenette and a balcony overlooking the marina. Daily maid service is available. In winter, studio efficiencies rent for $76 daily, a superb bargain for two persons, with two-bedroom units, suitable for four to six guests, costing $108 to $120 daily. *In summer, these accommodations become the bargain of St. Lucia at $53 daily for two persons in a studio, $74 to $84 for four to six persons in an apartment.* For MAP, add $25 per person daily. The place is about 200 yards from the nearest beach, and a fine little restaurant, Mortar & Pestle, recommended separately, is on the grounds. There is also a swimming pool, and if you'd like to cook in, you can obtain supplies at the mini-mart on the premises.

WHERE TO DINE: If possible, try to break free of your resort hotel and dine in one of St. Lucia's little character-loaded restaurants. The local food is excellent, including such West Indian specialties as pumpkin soup, fried flying fish, stuffed crab back, and stuffed breadfruit, as well as the inevitable callaloo soup.

In Castries

San Antoine, Morne Fortune (tel. 809/452-4660), considered by many to be the finest restaurant in St. Lucia, is operated by Michael and Alison Richings in a historical setting. It was constructed in the 19th century as a great house, lying up the Morne, offering superb vistas over the capital and the water. Some time in the 1920s it was turned into the first hotel in St. Lucia by Aubrey Davidson-Houston, the British portrait painter whose subjects have included W. Somerset Maugham. However, in 1970 it was destroyed by fire. When it was restored in 1984, whatever could be retained, including the original stonework, was given a new lease on life, cleaned, and repaired. The owners wanted to make the place look as authentic as possible. Candles and oil lamps provide the illumination. The food is both continental and West Indian. You might begin with a fritto misto or ceviche, perhaps a seafood bisque, then follow with fettuccine carbonara, fish Créole, or lobster thermidor. Meals cost EC$90 ($33.30). The restaurant serves lunch from 11:30 a.m. to 2:30 p.m. Monday to Friday, dinner from 6:30 to 10:30 p.m. Monday to Saturday. It's closed Sunday from April to November.

Green Parrot, Red Tape Lane, Morne Fortune (tel. 809/452-3399), about a mile and a half from the center, overlooks Castries harbor. Your ascent from downtown will take about 12 minutes. Once you get there, the effort will have been worth it, as this is an elegant choice for dining. It's the home of its chef, Harry, who got his long years of training in prestigious restaurants and hotels in London, including Claridges. Guests take their time and make an evening of it. Many enjoy a before-dinner drink in the Victorian-style salon near a talkative green cockatoo (caged) which Harry claims has been here almost as long as he has. The price of a meal in the English-style dining room includes entertainment:

Harry can not only cook, he is also an entertainer of some note. Show nights are Wednesday and Saturday, beginning at around 10:30 p.m. They feature limbo dancers and fire-eaters, followed by music for dancing. Another special night is Monday: Ladies' Night. A woman who wears a flower in her hair, when accompanied by a man in a coat and tie, receives a free dinner. Everybody can listen to the music of the Shac-Shac band.

All of this may sound gimmicky, but the food doesn't suffer because of all the activity. There's an emphasis on St. Lucian specialties, using home-grown produce when it's available. The countertop of a stone platform in the dining room usually overflows with almost a week's supply, decoratively displayed like a Renaissance still-life. Try the christophine au gratin (a Caribbean squash with cheese) or the Créole soup made with callaloo and pumpkin. There are also five kinds of curry with chutney, as well as a selection of omelets and sandwiches at lunchtime. Some of the American guests seem to go for the steaks or the daily specials. Full meals cost from $25 up. Try to go between noon and 2 p.m. or 8 and 10 p.m. It's open daily. To precede your meal you might enjoy a house special, the Grass Parrot (made from coconut cream, crème de menthe, bananas, white rum, and sugar). If you choose it instead of a more conservative drink, you'll be in good company, since it's rumored to have been sampled by Michael Caine, Princess Margaret, and many of the prime ministers of the Caribbean islands.

Rain, Columbus Square (tel. 809/452-3022), has a touch of nostalgia: it's named for that old Somerset Maugham story made into a film in which Joan Crawford with her alarmingly enlarged lips did away forever with the rosebud mouth. Going behind its palm green and white façade and under its tin roof, you expect any of the actresses who played Sadie suddenly to come through the door —Gloria Swanson, June Havoc, Jeanne Eagles, Tallulah Bankhead, Rita Hayworth. The inspired creation was the idea of Al Haman, a former advertising man. "Under one roof" he installed a bar, restaurant, and boutique, the latter selling batiks, sarongs, custom-designed bikinis, whatever. A popular rendez-vous point, particularly with expatriates on the island. Rain keeps to the Maugham décor of ceiling fans, louvered doors, peacock chairs, and oil lamps. Try to head for the second-floor balcony—a gingerbread-frilled upper gallery—if you're dining. There you can not only order food, but can enjoy a view over the town square and its famous spreading samaan tree.

Menus are chalked up on blackboards. If you don't dine on the candlelit upper floor, you might prefer a nook in the garden courtyard, where an array of pizzas, burgers, and local foods are available in casually informal surroundings at bargain prices. A nightly feature is "the Champagne Banquet of 1885," a re-creation of the seven-course, four-wine dinner served on Columbus Square the year Rain's landmark house was built. Good cooks turn out a repertoire of other home-cooking in the evening that includes not only Stateside dishes, but West Indian specialties such as dolphin St-Jacques, pepperpot, stuffed crab, beef curries, and shrimp Créole. The salads are crisp and fresh with tangy dressing. The homemade ice creams are mouthwatering, especially soursop, which is featured in season. Aside from wine, expect to pay about $25 per person for dinner. Lunches cost from $8. Among drinks, I recommend such rum refreshers as Sadie's Sin and the Reverend's Downfall! Rain is closed Sunday and holidays but open from noon to 11 p.m. otherwise.

At Vigie Marina

Coal Pot, Gantner's Bay (tel. 809/452-5643), enjoys a waterside perch at historic Vigie Marina, and from that position attracts the yachting set or any stray boaters in the area. Set on its own wharf, the Coal Pot opens onto harbor views. Nautical touches abound, as in the fishnet-draped bar. The Cordon Bleu and Créole menu leans, naturally, to fresh seafood dishes, which are well prepared here, depending on what's available from the local catch. Lobster thermidor and flying fish are traditionally featured. You might begin your meal by ordering the bartender's special, a Naked Virgin, made with a blend of orange juice, rum, Galliano, and cream of coconut. One, I assure you, is enough. You can order something French—perhaps roast duck à l'orange—or something West Indian—curried chicken in a coconut shell. Meals cost from EC$70 ($25.90). Service is from noon to 2 p.m. and 6:30 to 10:30 p.m. daily except Sunday.

AT CHOC BAY

Pisces Restaurant, Choc Bay (tel. 809/452-5428), serves some of the best native food on the island, in an unlikely location at the top of a forbiddingly steep flight of steps from the road just opposite the Halcyon Beach Club. Tables are set on a terraced balcony of a stucco building high above the graveled parking lot near the sea. Opened in 1980, it is now run by Tony Victor, who learned much about the art of catering when he worked for Harry at the famous Green Parrot (previously recommended). His specialties include curried goat or lamb, barbecued fish or chicken, and souse. Try, if offered, his salad of locally grown "green figs," the St. Lucian term for bananas. Many of the accoutrements here are shaped like fish. All of the produce and practically everything except the shrimp (from Guyana) and the sirloin is locally produced. A luncheon special is featured for only EC$10 ($3.70), whereas a three-course dinner goes for EC$60 ($22.20). Meals are served daily except that no lunch is offered on Sunday. Hours are from noon to 3 p.m. and 6:30 p.m. to midnight (or much later on weekends, depending on business).

Rodney Bay

Capone's, Rodney Bay (tel. 809/452-0284), in vivid pink and green, could have been inspired by the old Billy Wilder film, *Some Like It Hot,* starring Marilyn Monroe. Actually, this is an art deco rendition of a speakeasy along Miami Beach in the 1930s. Near the lagoon and The St. Lucian Hotel, it is brightly lit at night. If you tell the waiter, "Al sent me," he'll know that you don't mean the gangster Al Capone but Al Haman, a former advertising man who created this place as well as the equally successful Rain, a restaurant already previewed.

At the entrance is a self-service pizza parlor that also serves burgers and well-stuffed pita bread sandwiches. However, it is my recommendation that you go into the back for a really superb Italian meal, beginning with a drink, perhaps "Prohibition Punch" or a "St. Valentine's Day Massacre," served by "gangster" barmen. A player piano enlivens the atmosphere as you peruse the menu. You might begin with a pasta (the lasagne is always a favorite, especially when accompanied by a "Little Caesar" salad). For your main course, try fresh chicken breast in the Valdostana style (that is, with ham and cream cheese) or batter-fried Antilles shrimp with a vodka-spiked cream sauce. You can get some of the best steaks on the island as well, seared over the coals, retaining their juice and flavor. Finish off with an Italian espresso before getting a bill of around EC$75 ($27.75). Hours are 11 a.m. to midnight daily except Monday.

Across the street is **Sweet Dreams,** Rodney Bay (tel. 809/452-0688), which is called "the ultimate sweet shop." For dessert lovers, there is no finer establishment on the island. For example, it offers 25 flavors of Italian ice cream and tropical fruit sorbets, including passion fruit. Frozen yogurt is also a feature, and you can get cookies and doughnuts as well. Unusual flavors are kiwi and guava, among others. Cones cost from EC$1.65 (61¢). Hours are from 10 a.m. to midnight daily except Monday.

Charthouse, Rodney Bay (tel. 809/452-8115), is set in a large grange-like building with a skylit ceiling and mahogany bar. It's built several feet above the bobbing yachts of Rodney Bay, without walls, to allow an optimum view of the water. Its exterior is crafted from weathered planking into a series of soft angles whose corners are masked with masses of hanging plants. Nautical charts of the region adorn the walls. Full meals, costing from EC$60 ($22.25), might include callaloo soup, St. Lucian crab backs, hickory-smoked baby back spare ribs, surf and turf, shrimp Créole, local lobster (in season), a choice of local fish, and well-prepared steaks. The restaurant is open daily except Sunday. Try to go from noon to 2:30 p.m. and 7 to 10:30 p.m.

Mortar & Pestle, part of the Harmony Apartel complex on Rodney Bay Lagoon (tel. 809/452-8756), mixes superb Caribbean cuisine with a fine view of the marina. The menu features more than 30 à la carte gourmet specialties such as baked Antigua clams, Guyana casareep pepperpot, frogs' legs Dominica, lobster Créole Guadeloupe, and lambi (conch) St. Lucia. The specialty of the house is red snapper Martinique, filets of red snapper sautéed in garlic butter with onions and mushrooms, simmered in a white wine cream sauce. It's served with breadfruit balls and christophine au gratin. If you're not in the mood for "haute cuisine des Caraïbes," they also have a European, a Chinese, and an Indian menu. A good selection of wines from Germany, France, Portugal, and California is offered. A complete meal will cost EC$20 ($7.40) at lunch to EC$55 ($20.35) at dinner. The restaurant is open Monday to Saturday for breakfast from 7:30 to 10:30 a.m., for lunch from noon to 2:30 p.m., and for dinner from 7 to 10:30 p.m. Reservations are advised in the evening.

The Lime, Rodney Bay (tel. 809/452-0761), stands in an area opposite The St. Lucian Hotel that is becoming known as restaurant row. Some of these places are rather expensive, but The Lime continues to keep its prices low, its food good and plentiful, and its service and welcome among the finest on the island, all of which attracts both locals and visitors. West Indian in feeling, The Lime has an open-air setting. In honor of its namesake, the restaurant features a lime special as a drink. Lunches cost from EC$12 ($4.44) with a fixed three-course dinner going for EC$35 ($12.95), although you can also order à la carte. Specialties are stuffed crab backs and fish steak Créole, and they also serve shrimp, steaks, lamb and pork chops, and rôti. The steaks are done over a charcoal grill. The Lime is open from 11 a.m. to 2 or 3 a.m. daily except Tuesday, the closing time depending on business.

At Gros Islet

Banana Split, Gros Islet (tel. 809/452-8125), lying between Castries and Cap Estate, is a huge barn-like wooden building, with its sides open to a view of the sea. One diner suggested that it is "not unlike an American Legion hall set up for a Sunday chicken dinner." Dining at a simply set, long wooden table, you might begin with one of the soups made with local ingredients. Lobster soup is the most elegant choice, but you can also order pumpkin or callaloo. Or perhaps you'd prefer a crab back appetizer, followed by chicken Créole. Lobster also appears as a main dish, either boiled and served with lime butter or else curried or offered thermidor-style. For dessert, you can order the namesake banana split. Meals, costing from EC$40 ($14.80), are served daily except Sunday from noon to 2 p.m. and 7:30 to 10:30 p.m. On Friday, there are Jamaican jump-up and reggae shows, when a band arrives.

Marigot Bay

Dolittle's and **The Rusty Anchor,** Marigot Bay Resort (tel. 809/453-4357), are the two restaurants that form the dining facilities of the famed resort recommended previously. On the far side of the bay, reached by frequent ferry-boat connections, Dolittle's can be visited daily for lunch from noon to 2:30 p.m. The Rusty Anchor, at the Hurricane Hole, is open only for dinner nightly from 7 to 10:30. Dolittle's was named for the Rex Harrison movie which created a lot of local excitement but didn't generate that much interest from worldwide audiences. But it's a name that still means a lot around here. This popular restaurant is right on the water. You can swim or snorkel before lunch or dinner. Before your meal, try the bartender's specialty, called a "Love Bird." This is a mixture of fresh *paw-paw* ("papaya to us"), Sabra orange liquer, cream, Cherry Heering, and a local rum. A yachting crowd drops in here, and the place has a congenial atmosphere. You might begin with callaloo soup (made with seafood) or else St. Lucian onion soup. A selection of hamburgers and sandwiches is offered, or you could select a chicken rôti. The catch of the day, perhaps dolphin, will be grilled for you and served with flavored rice. Meals cost from EC$35 ($12.95).

Later that evening, you can enjoy a dinner costing from EC$70 ($25.70) at The Rusty Anchor back across the water. It has an open-air setting, also overlooking the bay, with ceiling fans creating a typical West Indian atmosphere. Lobster is a specialty, prepared in several ways. Other main dishes are shrimp calypso and baked Cornish hen Créole style. You can also order the catch of the day grilled, sautéed, or poached.

In Soufrière

The Still (tel. 809/454-7224) is the first thing you'll see as you drive up the hill from the harbor of Soufrière. It's a very old rum distillery set on a platform of thick timbers. The front garden blossoms with avocado pears, and a mahogany forest is a few steps away. All of this contributes to the country ambience of this stone-walled restaurant where Michael and Monica Du Boulay serve their freshly cooked specialties. The bar near the front veranda is furnished with glossy tables cut from cross sections of tropical tree trunks. A more formal and very spacious dining room is nearby. A three-course lunch costs around EC$25 ($9.25) and might include chicken, pepperpot, pork chops, or fish. A buffet, when available, costs EC$20 ($7.40) per person. Lunch is served daily from noon to 3 p.m., but if you're coming with a big party, it's wise to phone ahead. Dinner, however, is by appointment only.

The Hummingbird (tel. 809/454-7232) was named for the tiny, darting birds that fly around this restaurant and its adjoining boutique, which sells fine art batiks. An outdoor pool is free for use by persons who drop into the restaurant for a meal or just a drink. Patrons have included everyone from Mick Jagger to the late Christina Onassis. The ceiling is covered with seafan coral. A few larger-than-life wooden statues of mermaids support the thatch roof in back, and near the entrance is a rock garden with a woodcarving made from the stump of a poinciana tree that was removed when its roots started interfering with the foundations of the building. The wide-ranging menu features many tempting drinks (for example, a Hummingbird Hangover made of sambuca, golden rum, orange juice, and bitters) as well as such international food specialties as curry, English, Indian, or West Indian dishes including seafood crêpes, ceviche (raw marinated fish), beef Stroganoff, steak Diane, and chateaubriand. Full meals cost around EC$60 ($22.25). Hours are from noon to 3 p.m. for lunch, 7 and 10 p.m. for dinner. It's open daily.

WHAT TO SEE: Lovely little towns, beautiful beaches and bays, mineral baths, bananas—even a volcano is here to visit.

Castries

The capital city has grown up around its harbor, which occupies the crater of an extinct volcano. Charter captains and the yachting set drift in here, and large cruiseship wharfs welcome vessels from around the world. Because of those devastating fires mentioned earlier, the town today has a look of newness, with glass-and-concrete (or steel) buildings replacing the French colonial or Victorian look typical of many West Indian capitals.

The **Saturday-morning market** in the old tin-roof building on Jeremy Street in Castries is my favorite "people-watching" site on the island. Country women dress up in their traditional garb of cotton headdress and come into town for the occasion, which makes it all seem carnival-festive. The number of knotted points on top reveals their marital status (ask one of the locals to explain it to you). The luscious fresh fruits and vegetables of St. Lucia are sold, as again, weather-beaten men sit close by playing *warrie,* which is a fast pre-video game of pebbles on a carved board. You can also pick up St. Lucia handcrafts, such as baskets and unglazed pottery.

Government House is a charming late Victorian building. A Roman Catholic cathedral stands on Columbus Square, which has a few restored buildings.

Beyond Government House lies **Morne Fortune,** the name meaning "Hill of Good Luck." No one had much luck here, certainly not the battling French and British fighting for Fort Charlotte. The barracks and guard rooms changed nationalities many times. You can visit the 18th-century barracks complete with a military cemetery, a small museum, the Old Powder Magazine, and the "Four Apostles Battery" (the apostles being a quartet of grim muzzle-loading cannons). The view of the harbor of Castries is spectacular. You can see north to Pigeon Island or south to the Pitons.

Pigeon Point

This island is connected to the mainland of St. Lucia by a man-made causeway off Gros Islet Bay, on the west coast. Pirates such as "Old Wooden Leg" used it as a retreat, as did Admiral Rodney's British fleet much later. It was from here that Rodney sailed to defeat De Grasse at the Battle of the Saints. Historic ruins of forts can still be seen. The island is named after the pigeon in honor of Rodney's hobby of breeding the birds here. There are also remnants of the Arawak Indians on the island. It's a perfect place for a picnic, after which you can go for a swim from its white sandy beaches.

You can visit the **Pigeon Island Museum,** with its artifacts of the years of conflict between France and Britain.

It is open daily except Sunday from 9 a.m. to 4 p.m., charging EC$3 ($1.15) admission.

Marigot Bay

Movie companies such as those for Rex Harrison's *Dr. Dolittle* or Sophia Loren's *Fire Power* like to use this bay, one of the most beautiful in the Caribbean, for background shots. It's narrow yet navigable by yachts of any size. Here Admiral Rodney camouflaged his ships with palm leaves while lying in wait for French frigates. The shore, lined with palm trees, remains relatively unspoiled, but some building sites have been sold. Again, it's a delightful spot for a picnic if you didn't take your food basket to Pigeon Island.

Soufrière

This little fishing port, St. Lucia's second-largest settlement, is dominated by two pointed hills called **Petit Piton** and **Gros Piton.** These two hills, "The

Pitons," have become the very symbol of St. Lucia. They are two volcanic cones rising to 2,460 and 2,619 feet. Once actively volcanic, they are now clothed in green vegetation. Their rise sheer from the sea makes them a spectacular landmark visible for miles around. Formed of lava and rock, they are the remains of St. Lucia's once-active volcanos. Waves crash around their bases.

In the vicinity of Soufrière lies the famous "drive-in" volcano. Called **Mount Soufrière,** it's a rocky lunar landscape of bubbling mud and craters seething with fuming sulfur. You literally drive your car into an old (millions of years) crater, parking the vehicle and walking between the sulfur springs and pools of hissing steam. A local guide is usually waiting beside them shrouded with sulfurous fumes that are said to have medicinal properties. For a small fee, he'll point out the blackened waters, among the few of their kind in the Caribbean.

Nearby are the **Diamond Mineral Baths,** surrounded by a tropical arboretum. Constructed on orders of Louis XVI in 1784, whose doctors told him that these waters were similar in mineral content to the waters at Aix-les-Bains, they were intended for recuperative effects for French soldiers fighting in the West Indies. Later destroyed, they were rebuilt after World War II. They have an average temperature of 106° and lie near one of the geological attractions of the island, a waterfall which changes colors (from yellow to black to green to gray) several times a day. For EC$3.50 ($1.30), you can bathe and benefit from the recuperative effects. This boiling caldron has not rained down any catastrophes to date, unlike its neighbors in St. Vincent and Martinique.

From Soufrière in the southwest, the road winds toward Fond St. Jacques where you'll have a good view of mountains and villages as you cut through St. Lucia's **Moule-à-Chique** tropical rain forest. You'll see the Barre de l'Isle divide.

Moule-à-Chique

At the southern tip of the island, Moule-à-Chique is where the Caribbean Sea merges with the Atlantic. This is the southernmost tip of St. Lucia, and the town of Vieux Fort can be seen, as can the neighboring island of St. Vincent, 26 miles away.

Banana Plantations

Bananas are the island's leading export. As you're being hauled around the island by a taxi driver, ask him to take you to one of these huge plantations which allow visitors to come on the grounds. I suggest a sightseeing look at one of the trio of big ones—the Cul-de-Sac, just north of Marigot Bay; La Caya, in Dennery on the East Coast; and the Roseau Estate, south of Marigot Bay.

SHOPPING: Stores are generally open from 8 a.m. to 4 p.m. to Friday, from 8 a.m. to noon Saturday—but watch those early closings at some shops on Wednesday. Most of the shopping is in Castries, where the principal streets are William Peter Boulevard and Bridge Street. Many stores will sell you goods at duty-free prices (providing you don't take the merchandise with you but have it delivered instead to the airport). There are some good buys—not remarkable—in bone china, jewelry, perfume, watches, liquor, and crystal. Souvenir items include bags and mats, local pottery, and straw hats, again nothing remarkable.

The **West Indian Sea Island Cotton Shop,** Bridge St. (tel. 809/452-3674), designs and creates original batik artwork entirely by hand. Wall hangings and clothing are among their merchandise which is exclusively available in the West Indies. They also stock a full range of Kokonuts designer T-shirts; Sunny Caribbee herbs, spices, and perfume products; hand-painted jewelry; and St. Lucia souvenirs.

Bagshaws, just outside Castries, at La Toc (tel. 809/452-2139), are the leading handprint silkscreeners. An American, Sydney Bagshaw, and family have devoted their considerable skills to turning out a line of fabric that is as colorful as the Caribbean. The birds and flowers of St. Lucia are incorporated into their designs. Linen placemats, men's shirts, women's skirts, wall hangings, and dress kits are good buys. Each creation is an original Bagshaw design.

Rain Boutique, Columbus Square (tel. 809/452-3022; see my restaurant recommendation), is fashionable and petit. In the corner of this virtual landmark restaurant, the boutique promises that you can "sip and sup while you shop." Chicly styled cotton clothing is offered. Even Sophia Loren bought some of her clothes here, and O.J. Simpson dropped in for some resortwear.

Y. de Lima's, William Peter Boulevard (tel. 809/452-2898), has a good range of jewelry in gold and silver, as well as an array of Swiss watches, cameras, and binoculars, all at duty-free prices.

Noah's Arkade, Post Office Lane, Bridge St. (tel. 809/452-2523), has an array of Caribbean handcrafts and gifts. Many of these are routine tourist items, yet you'll often find something interesting if you browse enough—local straw placemats and rugs, wall hangings, sandals, maracas, steel drums, shell necklaces, and warri boards. Many of the hotels have branches of this emporium.

Eudovic Art Studio, P.O. Box 620, Goodlands, Morne Fortune (tel. 809/452-2747). Vincent Joseph Eudovic is a master artist and woodcarver whose sculptures have been exhibited in the O.A.S. headquarters in Washington, D.C., and have gained an increasing island fame. He usually carves his imaginative free-form sculptures from local tree roots, such as cobary, mahogany, and red cedar, and follows the natural pattern, sanding the grain until it's of almost satin smoothness. Some of his carvings are from lourier cannea trees, which have disappeared from the island, although their roots often remain in a well-preserved state. Native to St. Lucia, he teaches pupils the art of wood carving. In the main studio, much of the work of his pupils is on display. However, ask to be taken to his private studio, where you'll see the remarkable work of this extraordinary artist. His studio is open daily from 7:30 a.m. to 4:30 p.m.

Caribelle Batik, Howelton House, P.O. Box 37, Old Victoria Road, The Morne (tel. 809/452-3785), is a workshop just five minutes' drive from Castries, where you can watch St. Lucian artists at work creating intricate patterns and colors for the ancient art of making batik. At the workshop you can purchase batik in cotton and silk, some made up in casual and beach clothing, plus wall hangings and other gift items reflecting the Caribbean. Drinks and snacks are served in the Dyehouse Bar and Terrace in the renovated Victorian-era building.

A Shopping Complex

Built with an eye to the cruise-ship passenger, **Pointe Seraphine Shopping Centre** has the best all-around collection of shops. Under red roofs in a Spanish-style setting, the complex requires the presentation of a cruise pass to the shopkeeper when purchasing goods. However, the visitor arriving by air can also shop here by presenting a passport or identification card, as well as an airline ticket. Visitors can take away their purchases except liquor and tobacco which will be delivered to the airport. In season, the center is open Monday to Saturday from 9 a.m. to 6 p.m. Off-season hours are from 9 a.m. to 5 p.m. Monday to Friday, 9 a.m. to 4 p.m. Saturday. It is also open when cruise ships are in port.

Among the shops represented are **Windjammer Trading Company** (tel. 809/452-7460), has casual clothing for all the family. Items using cotton and natural fabrics were designed and manufactured in St. Lucia.

Images (tel. 809/452-6883) offers a wide selection of perfumes, including such brand names as Estée Lauder, Oscar de la Renta, and Yves St. Laurent.

A good shop for luxury goods is **J.Q. Charles** (tel. 809/452-7591), with its offering of fine china, crystal, glassware, jewelry, perfumes, liquor, and local arts and crafts.

THE SPORTING LIFE: Since most of the island hotels are built right on the beach, you won't have far to go for swimming. I prefer the beaches along the western coast. On the windward side, a rough surf makes swimming at least potentially dangerous. Pigeon Island, off the north shore, is a fine beach, as is Vigie, just north of the harbor of Castries. For a novelty, you might try the black volcanic sand at Soufrière. The beach there is called **La Toc.**

Scuba Diving

In Soufrière, **Scuba St. Lucia,** Anse Chastenet Hotel, P.O. Box 216, St. Lucia (tel. 809/454-7354), established in 1981, offers one of the world's top dive locations. At the south end of Anse Chastanet's quarter-mile-long, soft, secluded beach, it offers great diving and comprehensive facilities for divers of all levels. Some of the most spectacular coral reefs of St. Lucia—many only ten to 20 feet below the surface of the water—lie a short distance from the beach. A great range of corals, such as finger, brain, boulder, leaf, flower, and soft, and sponges including tube, barrel, vase, and encrusting give an unparalleled mix of color and texture to the reef, providing shelter for many of its denizens and a dramatic backdrop for schools of reef fish.

Many professional PADI instructors who offer dive programs two or three times a day, of the most spectacular coral reefs in St. Lucia—some only 10 to 20 feet below the surface of the water—lie a short distance from the hotel's beach. Photographic equipment is available for rent (film can be processed on the premises), and instruction is offered in picture taking in price ranges depending on the time and equipment involved. Experienced divers can rent the equipment they need on a per-item basis. The packages include tanks, backpacks, and weightbelts. Through participation in the establishment's "specialty" courses, divers can obtain PADI certification. A two- to three-hour introductory lesson, including a short theory session, equipment familiarization, development of skills in shallow water, and a tour of the reef, with all equipment included, costs $50.

Water Sports

The best all-round center is **St. Lucian Watersports,** The St. Lucian Hotel, Reduit Beach (tel. 809/452-8351), which offers an array of activities, including parasailing, waterskiing, snorkeling, and windsurfing, as well as Sunfish sailing. Windsurfing, increasingly popular in St. Lucia, costs $10 per hour for a regular boat, $15 per hour for a speedboat. Sunfish sailing is EC$20 ($7.40) per hour, and snorkeling costs only $7 per hour. For $10, you'll be taken twice around the bay on waterskis. Parasailing is possible for $20 to $18 per person.

Horseback Riding

You can hire a horse at **Cas-En-Bas and Cap Estate Stables,** P.O. Box 1159, Castries. (To make arrangements, call Rene Trim at 809/452-8273). The cost is EC$35 ($12.95) per 1½ hours. As an added feature, you can ask about a picnic trip to the Atlantic, with a barbecue lunch and drink included. Departures are on horseback at 10 a.m. Nonriders can be included, as they are transported to the site in a van. They pay half price.

Tennis

Most of the big hotels have their own courts. If yours doesn't, ask at the front desk for the nearest one. Some of the courts on St. Lucia are lit for night games for those who'd like to avoid the midday sun.

Golf

St. Lucia has two nine-hole golf courses. One is at the **Cap Estate Golf Club,** P.O. Box 328, Castries (tel. 809/452-8317), at the northern end of the island. Greens fees are EC$30 ($11.10) per day. You can rent clubs for EC$15 ($5.55), and a trolley costs EC$5 ($1.85). There are no caddies. Hours are daily from 7:45 a.m. to sunset.

You can also play at **Cunard Hotel La Toc,** P.O. Box 399, Castries (tel. 809/452-3081), which has a resident pro. Greens fees are EC$25 ($9.25), but guests of the hotel play free. Golf clubs rent for EC$8 ($2.95) for nine holes, with caddies available for EC$4 ($1.50) for the nine. However, you should also tip your caddy. The course is open from 8 a.m. to 4 p.m. seven days a week.

Deep-Sea Fishing

The waters around St. Lucia are known for their gamefish, including blue marlin, sailfish, mako sharks, and barracuda, with tuna and kingfish among the edible catches. Most hotels can make arrangements for you to go on a fishing expedition, or you might prefer to make your own plans with **Michael Hackshaw,** P.O. Box 8, Castries, St. Lucia, W.I. (tel. 809/452-0216), whose family has been boating and fishing for generations. Born in St. Lucia, he operates three fishing boats out of Vigie Bay (near the Coal Pot restaurant). For a half-day of fishing with all equipment included, he will rent a 20-foot Bertram, suitable for four persons, for $170. Up to six persons can rent a 26-foot Bertram for $200 for half a day, although parties of that size usually prefer the greater comfort of his 31-foot Bertram, renting for $250.

NIGHTLIFE: There isn't much except the entertainment offered by hotels. If your hotel is silent and you're in the mood for action, ask at your front desk what other hotel might be planning entertainment that evening. In the winter months, at least one hotel offers a steel band, calypso music, whatever, at least every night of the week. Otherwise, check to see what's happening at **Rain** (tel. 809/452-3022), **Capone's** (tel. 809/452-0284), and the **Green Parrot** (tel. 809/452-3167)—see my restaurant recommendations.

Splash, The St. Lucian Hotel, Reduit Beach (tel. 809/452-8351), is the best disco on the island, with a large dance floor in a roomy, air-conditioned area. The disco plays an assortment of music from local reggae and calypso to American and European disco. There is a cover charge of EC$20 ($7.40) per person, and you must be 18 or over to enter. Hotel guests are admitted free. Splash is open daily except Sunday from 9 p.m. until the patrons all depart. Theme nights are: Monday, free entry; Tuesday, Oldie Goldie night; Wednesday, women admitted free; Thursday, men wearing ties admitted free; and Friday and Saturday, party hearty weekend. The disco has a nightly happy hour from midnight to 1 a.m.

3. ST. VINCENT

An emerald island 18 miles long and 12 miles wide, St. Vincent was charted by Columbus in 1498 on his third voyage. If the explorer had gone on a field expedition, and assuming he hadn't been devoured by the cannibalistic Caribs, he would have discovered an island of extraordinary natural beauty.

Amazing for such a small area, St. Vincent has fertile valleys, rich forests, lush jungles, rugged peaks, waterfalls, foam-whitened beaches, outstanding coral reefs (with what experts say is some of the world's clearest water), a volcano nestled in the sky and usually capped by its own private cloud, and 4,000 feet up, Crater Lake.

The tenacious Caribs held out longer on St. Vincent against the tide of European colonization than they did almost anywhere else. However, in a 1763 treaty the British won the right to possess the island. In 1779 French troups invaded. At the Treaty of Versailles in 1783 they gave it back to His Majesty's colonists.

A few years later Captain Bligh set off on the *Bounty* from England, going to Tahiti. There he loaded his vessel with breadfruit seedlings. Faced with mutiny, and after great difficulties (described in many historical novels), the captain in 1793 reached St. Vincent with his seedlings. The breadfruit trees took fantastically to St. Vincentian soil, earning for the island the title of "the Tahiti of the Caribbean."

In 1795, during the French Revolution, St. Vincent suffered yet another invasion. French revolutionaries, allied with the Caribs, burned British plantations and made a fierce war, only to be defeated by British forces the following year. The British decided St. Vincent was too small for both planters and Indians. The Caribs were rounded up and shipped off to British Honduras in Central America, where their descendants live to this day.

The island remained under "Rule Britannia" from that day until 1979, when, with The Grenadines, it achieved independent statehood within the Commonwealth. The governor-general is appointed by the Crown on the advice of the prime minister. Parliament consists of a House of Assembly elected every five years. The state of St. Vincent and The Grenadines has a population of about 120,000, mainly of African, East Indian, Carib, and European (especially Portuguese) descent.

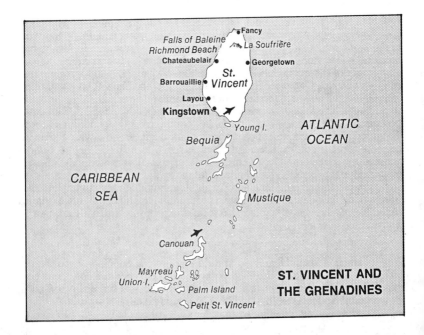

One of the major Windward Islands, St. Vincent is only now awakening to tourism, which hasn't yet reached massive dimensions. Sailors and the yachting set have long known of St. Vincent and its satellite bays and beaches in The Grenadines.

Much of its interior is inhabited and cultivated with coconut and banana groves. Arrowroot, often used as a thickening in baby foods, grows in abundance.

Unspoiled by the worst fallout which mass tourism sometimes brings, the people actually treat visitors like people: met with courtesy, they respond with courtesy.

Special events include the week-long Carnival in early July, one of the largest in the eastern Caribbean, with steel band and calypso competitions, along with the crowning of the king and queen of carnival.

GETTING THERE: In the Eastern Caribbean, St. Vincent—the "gateway to The Grenadines" (see the next section)—lies 100 miles west of Barbados, where most visitors from North America fly first, making connections that will take them on to St. Vincent and The Grenadines. For transportation from North America to Barbados, refer to the "Getting There" section of the next chapter.

From Barbados, you can connect with a **LIAT** flight to St. Vincent. The flight from Barbados takes just 35 minutes, and at least two of them go out daily. LIAT also flies in from Trinidad, St. Lucia, and Martinique.

There is an airport, of course, at St. Vincent, but also small ones at Mustique, Union Island, and Canouan.

Connecting flights to St. Vincent and The Grenadines are also available at the gateways of St. Lucia (Hewannora), Martinique, and Trinidad.

Air Martinique runs service between Martinique, St. Lucia, St. Vincent, Mustique, Canouan, and Union Island.

Increasing numbers of visitors to St. Vincent prefer the dependable service of one of the best-managed small airlines in the Caribbean, **Mustique Airways.** With advance warning, Mustique Airways will arrange a specially chartered (and reasonably priced) transport for you and your party to many of the surrounding islands. In fact, it's usually easier to make efficient connections through The Grenadines when an airline will work with you and personalize your itinerary. The price of these chartered transfers is less than you might expect. For example, one-way transport from Barbados to St. Vincent is $75 per person; from Barbados to Mustique, $83; and from Barbados to Union Island, $105. Although the airline is still classified as a charter service, it has two daily scheduled flights from St. Vincent to Mustique. Round-trip passage costs $90 per person, and flights depart St. Vincent daily at 7:30 a.m. and 4:30 p.m., landing on Mustique ten minutes later. Flights then head immediately back to St. Vincent.

Currently the airline owns four nine-passenger Islanders and one five-passenger Barons. Jonathon Palmer, the company's dynamic owner, can be reached through the touring company run by his wife, Marnie. For reservations, information, and up-to-the-minute prices, contact **Mustique Airways/ Grenadine Travel Company,** P.O. Box 1232, St. Vincent, W.I. (tel. 809/458-4380). Their office in Mustique is at the airport (tel. 809/458-4621).

GETTING AROUND: The government sets the rates for fares, but **taxis** are unmetered. The wise passenger, however, will always ask the fare and agree upon the charge before getting in. Figure on spending about EC$15 ($5.55) to go from the St. Vincent Arnos Vale Airport to your hotel, maybe more. Of course, you should tip about 12% of the fare.

If you don't want to drive yourself, you can also hire taxis to take you to the island's major attractions. Most drivers seem to be well-informed guides (it won't take you long to learn everything you need to know about St. Vincent). You'll spend about EC$30 ($11.10) per hour for a car holding two to four passengers.

Buses

Flamboyantly painted "al fresco" buses also travel the principal arteries of St. Vincent, linking the major towns and villages. The price is really low, depending on where you're going, and the experience will connect you with the people of the island. At least you'll get to see a preview of what's being taken to market, perhaps a burlap bag of arrowroot. The central departure point is Market Square. Fares range from EC$1 (37¢) to EC$4 ($1.50).

Car Rentals

Rentals can be arranged. However, driving on St. Vincent is a bit of an adventure because of the narrow, twisting roads and the *drive-on-the-left requirement*. To go motoring like a Vincentian, you'll soon learn to sound your horn a lot as you make the sharp curves and turns. If you present your valid U.S. or Canadian driver's license at the police department, and pay a EC$10 ($3.70) fee, you'll obtain a temporary permit to drive. Go to the police station on Bay Street in Kingstown.

Among the many leasing agents, **Car Rentals Ltd.,** on Halifax Street in Kingstown (tel. 809/456-1862), rents Mazdas and Fiat 125s. Try also **Kim's Rentals,** Grenville Street (tel. 809/456-1884), the local representative for **Hertz. Avis** has a branch at Kingston (tel. 809/458-4613). The cost is about $40 per day, but you usually get the first 50 miles free.

PRACTICAL FACTS: British customs are predominant, but with a distinct West Indian flair. Those invading French troops also left their legacy, and Gallic cultural influences remain as delightful traces. English is the official language, of course, yet there's a French patois spoken on a number of The Grenadines, including St. Vincent.

Banks: They're are open from 8 a.m. to noon Monday to Thursday and from 8 a.m. to noon and 3 to 5 p.m. on Friday (always check, as each bank may vary these hours slightly).

Currency: The official currency of St. Vincent is the Eastern Caribbean dollar, worth about 37¢ in U.S. money. *Note:* Most of the quotations in this chapter appear in U.S. dollars unless marked EC$. Most restaurants, shops, and hotels will accept payment in U.S. dollars or traveler's checks.

Documents: Visitors arriving should have proof of identity and a return or ongoing ticket, providing they are either Canadian or U.S. citizens.

Drugstore: For such needs, try **Deane's Pharmacy,** Middle St., Kingstown (tel. 809/457-1522).

Electricity: Electric current is 220 volts AC, 50 cycles, so you'll need an adapter. Some hotels have voltage converters, but it's best to bring your own.

Information: The local Tourist Board, Egmont St., Kingstown (tel. 809/457-1502). Inquiries in the U.S. can be made to the **St. Vincent and Grenadines Tourist Office,** 801 Second Ave., 21st Floor, New York, NY 10017 (tel. 212/687-4981).

Medical care: There are two hospitals on St. Vincent, **Kingstown General Hospital,** Kingstown (tel. 809/456-1185), and **Botanic Hospital,** New Montrose (tel. 809/457-1747).

Post office: The General Post Office on Halifax Street in Kingstown is open from 8:30 a.m. to 3 p.m. Monday to Friday, from 8:30 to 11:30 a.m. on Saturday. There are sub-post offices in 49 districts throughout the state, and these include offices in the Grenadine Islands of Bequia, Mustique, Canouan, Mayreau, and Union Island.

Taxes and service: The government imposes an airport departure tax of EC$15 ($5.55) per person. A 5% government occupancy tax is charged for all hotel accommodations. In addition, most hotels and restaurants add a 10% to 15% service charge.

Telephone: St. Vincent can be dialed directly from the mainland by using the Caribbean area code, 809, then the seven-digit number of the person or place you are calling. However, once on the island, you need dial only the last *five* digits of the number (not the *45*). The same is true for The Grenadines.

Time: Both St. Vincent and The Grenadines operate on Atlantic Standard Time: when it's 6 a.m. in St. Vincent, it's 5 a.m. in Miami. During Daylight Saving Time, St. Vincent keeps the same time as the U.S. East Coast.

Weather: The climate of St. Vincent is pleasantly cooled by the trade winds all year. The tropical temperature is in the 78° to 82° Fahrenheit range. The rainy season is May to November.

WHERE TO STAY: Accommodations range from tropical villas on their own private island to a guesthouse built back in the plantation era serving Créole cookery. Don't expect massive high-rise resorts here, as everything is kept small, and many Vincentians hope it will always be this way. The West Indian lifestyle prevails here. The places are comfortable, not fancy, and you usually get a lot of personal attention from the staffs.

Reminder: Most hotels and restaurants add government tax and service charge to your bill. Ask about this when you register at your accommodation, so that you will know whether there will be a surcharge on your final tab.

The Leading Resort

Young Island, P.O. Box 211, Young Island, St. Vincent, W.I. (tel. 809/458-4826), is a 25-acre resort that might have attracted Gauguin. Instead of that artist, it was supposed to be where a Carib Indian chieftain kept his harem. A paradise island promising barefoot happiness, it lies just 200 yards off the south shore of St. Vincent, to which it is linked by a ferry to the mainland from the pier right on Villa Beach, a five-minute ride. Tropical villas—25 deluxe, two luxury, and three suites—are set in a tropical garden of hibiscus, crotons, ferns, and white ginger, as well as giant almond, breadfruit, nutmeg, and mango trees. The beach, however, is of a brilliant white sand. Hammocks are hung under thatched roofs if you want to rest. Carib canoes and Sailfish await your use at the beach's edge. Island specials are served at the Coconut Bar, a thatched bohío on stilts which actually serves many of its drinks in fresh coconuts. The free-form pool, modeled on a tropical lagoon, is set into landscaped grounds. The hotel has one tennis court, which is lit for night games. All water sports, such as scuba-diving and waterskiing, are available. At the far end of the beach there's a saltwater lagoon-like pool where you can hear parrots and macaws chattering.

You're housed in Tahitian cottages with a bamboo decor and outdoor showers. Floors are of seashells and terrazzo, covered by rush rugs. *In low season, single guests on half-board arrangements pay $150 to $250 daily, the cost going up to $200 to $375 daily in a double.* In high season, half board is required. At that time a single person pays from $250 to $435 a day, the cost rising to $300 to $485 in a double. Ask about package rates for lovers, under the categories of "young lovers" and "lucky lovers." These are exceptional bargain deals offered during off-season periods. The food is well prepared, with an emphasis on lots of fresh fish and lobster and plenty of island-grown vegetables. Dining is by candlelight, and dress is informal. On some nights the hotel transports guests over to the rock on its other island, Fort Duvemette, for a cocktail party. There hors d'oeuvres are cooked over charcoal pits, and a local band plays under torchlight. Sometimes a steel band plays for dancing after dinner, and you're serenaded by strolling singers.

The Upper Bracket
Grand View Beach Hotel, P.O. Box 173, Villa Point, St. Vincent, W.I. (tel. 809/458-4811). The owner-manager, F.A. ("Tony") Sardine, named this place well. The "grand view" promised is of islets, bays, yachts, Young Island, headlands, lagoons, and sailing craft. Villa Point lies just five minutes from the airport and ten minutes from Kingstown. On well-manicured grounds, it is set on eight acres of tropical gardens, with bougainvillea and frangipani. Tennis and squash courts and a swimming pool are available. A converted private home, the hotel is a large, white, two-story mansion which has a dozen rooms with private baths to rent. Some of these are air-conditioned. Units are simply furnished, with flowery spreads and wood floors. Everything is maintained spotlessly, however. *In the off-season, singles rent for $68 daily and doubles for $86.* In winter, rates go up to $115 daily in a single, $165 in a double, with breakfast and included. For breakfast and dinner, add another $30 per person to the tariff quoted. For that you get a table d'hôte menu which changes every day. Most of the meals are based on fresh fish and island-grown vegetables. The cuisine is served in bountiful portions. The cookery is sometimes like a West Indian nouvelle cuisine style.

The Moderate Range
Sunset Shores Beach Hotel, P.O. Box 849, Villa Beach, St. Vincent, W.I. (tel. 809/458-4411), about four miles from Kingstown, is an attractively landscaped cluster of vacation accommodations set on terraces that descend to a sandy beach (the pleasant beach is fenced off from the lawn). An oblong swimming pool, flanked by a covered bar, is set just below the low-lying bedrooms. These contain comfortable beds, sliding glass doors, hanging wicker lamps, private baths, and air conditioning, and entrances are ringed with yellow-flowered trumpet vines. In winter, singles cost $85 to $100, daily, and doubles go for $105 to $120. *In summer, singles range from $60 to $75 daily, and doubles from $75 to $90.* All tariffs quoted are EP.

The Last Resort, P.O. Box 355, St. Vincent, W.I. (tel. 809/458-4231), is a hotel, restaurant, and bar, five minutes from the airport and 15 minutes from Kingstown. Its seaside setting is ideal for swimming, sunbathing, and watching the sunset from comfortable deck chairs on the large stone patio. Island tours, sailing through The Grenadines, diving and snorkeling, mountain climbing, and deep-sea fishing can be arranged for you by the hotel staff. Each of the spacious rooms is clean and tastefully furnished, freshly decorated in tropical colors. Each unit has its own bath and ceiling fans. Air conditioning is available in four of the rooms. From mid-December to mid-April, singles cost $35 daily, and doubles are $45. *The remainder of the year, rates are $30 daily in a single, $40 in a double.* Add $5 per day for air conditioning. Meal plans and discounts for stays of more than seven days are offered. Banana daiquiris, rum punch, and piña coladas are a few of the tropical drinks available in the beach bar just a few steps from the water's edge. The open-air restaurant features West Indian and Vincentian cooking prepared from local foods brought fresh each morning at the local market. Fish right from the sea, stuffed breadfruit, callaloo and pumpkin soup, as well as mango and coconut crème pies, are a few of the menu selections awaiting your taste You can enjoy live local folk music at the bar.

Villa Lodge Hotel, P.O. Box 1191, Indian Bay Beach, St. Vincent, W.I. (tel.

809/458-4641). Set at the side of a residential hillside a few minutes from the center of Kingstown, this is a favorite of visiting business people from the other islands. Because of its access to the beach and its well-mannered staff, it should be better known. Originally built as a white-sided private home, it still evokes in residents the feeling of being lodged in a well-proportioned, conservatively modern villa. It's ringed with plants growing in the gardens, which also contain a swimming pool. There's a pleasant wood-sheathed bar on the second floor, and a street-level dining room where good food is served, usually from a table d'hôte menu. Each of the air-conditioned rooms has a ceiling fan, a private bathroom, and a comfortable collection of simple furniture. In winter, MAP costs $120 daily in a single, $165 in a double. *In the off-season, MAP goes for $100 daily in a single, $145 in a double.* Near the bar is a spacious TV lounge.

CSY Hotel & Marina, P.O. Box 133, Blue Lagoon, St. Vincent, W.I. (tel. 809/458-4308), is a two-story grouping of rambling modern buildings crafted from local wood and stone. It's intricately connected to one of the best-known yacht-chartering businesses in the Caribbean, CSY, whose offices lie beneath the hotel's second-story reception area. There's a pleasantly breezy bar, with open walls and lots of exposed planking. As you relax, you'll overlook a moored armada of boats tied up at a nearby marina. A two-tiered swimming pool, terraced into a nearby hillside, offers two lagoon-shaped places to swim. Snorkeling, windsurfing, and daily departures on sailboats to Mustique and Bequia can be arranged through the hotel. Each of the 19 high-ceilinged accommodations has a balcony or patio, as well as a private bath. In winter, singles rent for $50 daily, doubles for $65, and triples for $75, all EP. *Summer charges are $45 in a single, $50 in a double, and $60 in a triple, also EP.*

Best for the Budget

The **Cobblestone Inn,** P.O. Box 867, Kingstown, St. Vincent, W.I. (tel. 809/456-1937). Originally built as a warehouse for sugar and arrowroot in 1814, the core of this historic hotel is made of stone and brick. Today it's one of the most famous hotels of St. Vincent, known for its labyrinth of passages, arches, and upper hallways. To reach its high-ceilinged reception area, you pass from the waterfront through a stone-sided tunnel into a chiseled courtyard. At the top of a massive sloping stone staircase you are shown to one of the simply decorated, slightly old-fashioned bedrooms. Each unit has air conditioning and walls covered with wide planks. Bathrooms were added long after the structure was built, so some of these units have regally proportioned windows opening over the rooftops of town. Year round, the 19 bedrooms cost from EC$115 ($42.55) in a single, from EC$150 ($55.50) to EC$175 ($64.75) in a double, with breakfast included, plus tax and service. Meals are served on a third-floor eagle's eyrie high above the hotel's central courtyard. Rows of glass windows and thick mahogany tables in its adjacent bar create one of the most unusual hideaways in town. The hotel is convenient for town; however, you'll have to drive about three miles to the nearest beach.

Mariner's Inn, P.O. Box 868, Villa Beach, St. Vincent, W.I. (tel. 809/458-4287). Its core is an old clapboard-sided West Indian house with an accommodating and well-used ring-around veranda. Most of its 20 accommodations are contained in two-story motel-like units which about the edge of the channel. Protecting moored yachts by its bulk, Young Island rises a few hundred yards offshore. Pleasant, informal, and slightly raffish, the hotel is unpretentious and a bit tatty, but with a West Indian kind of flair. There are lots of interesting touches, including an outdoor bar crafted from the hull of an old schooner, masonry walls flanked with croton, and an airy kind of indoor/outdoor living. It's not for everybody, but maybe you'll like it. With MAP included, singles cost $70 daily in winter, *$55 in low season.* Doubles on the MAP rent for $100 daily in winter, *$80 off-season.*

Heron Hotel, P.O. Box 226, Kingstown, St. Vincent, W.I. (tel. 809/457-1631), is one of those enduring favorites of people who like a guesthouse with a lot of West Indian flavor. In a bustling location in town, it's contained in a wood-framed warehouse which a century ago used to store vast quantities of copra (dried coconut) before it was shipped to Europe. Today its well-ventilated, big-windowed premises is a 15-room hotel that's more like a guesthouse. Mrs. Doreen McKenzie is the owner and manager (you'll meet her at the second-story reception area). You can always read quietly in an elegantly sparse living room whose high wood-framed ceiling evokes life of a century ago. Meals are served beneath the soaring ceiling of a room whose view encompasses a private court-yard encircled by some of the simple but comfortable accommodations. Each of these is air-conditioned, containing a private bathroom and simple pinewood furniture. Room 15, my favorite, is particularly spacious. With MAP included, singles cost $36 daily, and doubles rent for $57, year round.

WHERE TO DINE: Most guests eat at their hotels on the Modified American Plan. Unlike the situation on many Caribbean islands, many Vincentian hostel-ries serve an authentic West Indian cuisine. There are also a few independent eateries as well, but not many.

French Restaurant, Villa Beach (tel. 809/458-4972). Set in a clapboard house near the pier where the ferryboat from Young Island docks, this is one of the most consistently good restaurants on the island. It offers a long, semi-shadowed bar which you pass on your way to the rear veranda. There, overlook-ing the moored yachts off the coast of Young Island, you can enjoy well-seasoned, Gallic-inspired food. Surrounded with vine-laced lattices, you pay from EC$65 ($24.05) for full dinners, served daily from 7 to 9 p.m. Menu suggestions in-clude grilled Cornish game hen, curried conch, seafood cassoulette, fish and shrimp kebab, stuffed crab back, lobster crêpes, onion soup, followed by home-made ice cream or chocolate mousse. Lunch, from noon to 2 p.m. daily, is sim-pler, costing from EC$30 ($11.10). Its bill of fare includes quiche Lorraine, omelets, tunafish salads, and cheesecake. The establishment is closed for about two weeks every June.

The Dolphin, P.O. Box 651, Villa Beach (tel. 809/458-4238). Its waterside location, wide veranda, neo-Victorian gingerbread, and rambling front lawn make this unusual restaurant popular with the yachting crowd. Food is served in a casual European way, at outdoor tables in the shade of a huge tamarind tree. Caribbean lobster is often available. A salad bar is available, and a selection of rôtis and an array of pizzas (a favorite is the one studded with lobster) are also avail-able. Meals cost from $15. Open daily, the restaurant serves lunch from 11 a.m. to 3:30 p.m. and dinner from 6 to 10:30 p.m.

Basil's Bar & Restaurant, Bay St. (tel. 809/457-2713). This brick-lined en-clave is a newer and less famous annex of the legendary Basil's Beach Bar in Mustique. It lies in the early 19th-century walls of an old sugar warehouse, on the waterfront in Kingstown beneath the previously recommended Cobblestone Inn. The air-conditioned interior is accented with exposed stone and brick, soar-ing arches, and a rambling mahogany bar where you are likely to meet just about anyone. A daily luncheon buffet costs from EC$25 ($9.25), with an à la carte meal going for EC$35 ($12.95). The bill of fare could include lobster salad, shrimp in garlic butter, sandwiches, hamburgers, and barbecued chicken. Din-ners, from EC$70 ($25.90), feature grilled lobster, escargots, shrimp cocktail, grilled red snapper, and grilled filet mignon. The Friday night seafood buffet goes for EC$50 ($18.50), plus service. Lunch is from noon to 2 p.m., and dinner is on from 7 to 9:30 p.m., daily except Sunday. The bar remains open throughout the day, and on Sunday the place opens at 5 p.m., staying so "until very late."

Bounty, Back St. (tel. 809/456-1776), lies opposite Barclay's Bank in the center of Kingstown behind a green-and-white façade. The color scheme is repeated inside, with a raftered ceiling, clean napery, and large deli-style display case. Friendly faces help create a satisfying restaurant experience. Local people who work in the shops nearby come in for a typical British breakfast, costing from EC$8 ($2.95). Later the place jumps with business at lunch, when hamburgers and snack food are the most frequently ordered items. A snack costs from $5 (U.S.); a full meal, from $10. Everything is pleasantly casual, and it's open Monday to Friday from 8:30 a.m. to 4:45 p.m., on Saturday to 1:30 p.m.; closed Sunday.

Juliette's, Middle St. (tel. 809/457-1645). The alleyway that stretches from Middle Street to this restaurant is so narrow you might miss it. It will lead to a concealed courtyard and a flight of exterior steps which climb to a second-floor dining room. It's a clean, respectable West Indian dining room where only platters of food are served in place of more traditional three-course meals. Breakfast is from 8 to 10:30 a.m., and lunch is served from 10:30 a.m. to 2 p.m. daily except Sunday. The restaurant closes promptly at 4:30 p.m. after a busy day of feeding the office workers of Kingstown. Meals cost around $12. The menu consists of such island specialties as curried mutton, an array of fish, stewed chicken, and stewed beef. Many of the platters are garnished with fried plantain and rice.

WHAT TO SEE: In the capital, Kingstown, you can still meet oldtime beachcombers if you stroll on Upper Bay Street. White haired and bearded, they can be seen loading their boats with produce grown on the mountain, before heading to some secluded beach in The Grenadines. This is a chief port and gateway to The Grenadines, and you can also view the small boats, dinghies, and yachts that have dropped anchor here. The place is a magnet for charter sailors.

Kingstown

Lushly tropical and solidly British, the capital isn't as architecturally fascinating as St. George's in Grenada. Some English-style houses do exist, many of them looking as if they belonged in Penzance, Cornwall, instead of the West Indies.

At the top of a winding road on the north side of Kingstown, **Fort Charlotte** was built on Johnson Point, enclosing one side of the bay. Constructed about the time of the American Revolution, it was named after Queen Charlotte, the German consort of George III. The ruins aren't much to inspect. Instead, the reason to go here is for the view. The fort sits atop a steep promontory some 640 feet above the sea. From its citadel, you'll have a commanding sweep of the leeward shores to the north, Kingstown to the south, and The Grenadines beyond. A trio of cannons used to fight off French troops are still in place. Admission is 60¢, and for that you'll see a series of oil murals depicting the history of black Caribs. Hours are from 6 a.m. to 6 p.m. daily.

The second major sight is the **Botanic Gardens,** on the north side of Kingstown, about a mile from the center. Founded in 1765 by Gov. George Melville, they are the oldest botanic gardens in the West Indies. In this Windward Eden, you'll see 20 acres of such tropical exotics as teak, almond, cinnamon, nutmeg, cannonball trees, and mahogany. Some of the trees are more than two centuries old. One of the breadfruit trees, reputedly, was among those original seedlings brought to this island by Captain Bligh in 1793. There is also a large *Spachea perforata* (the Soufrière tree), a species believed to be unique to St. Vincent and not found in the wild since 1812. The gardens are open daily from 6 a.m. to 6 p.m. No admission is charged.

The **Archeological Museum,** in the Botanic Gardens, houses a good collection of stone tools and other artifacts in both stone and pottery. In front of it are shrubs which might have been found in the compound of an early Indian home.

In the heart of town, you might pay a visit to **St. Mary's Catholic Church,** on Grenville Street, with its curious mélange of architecture. Fancifully flawed, it was built in 1935 by a Belgian monk, Dom Carlos Verbeke. He incorporated Romanesque arches, Gothic spires, and almost Moorish embellishments. The result—a maze of balconies, turrets, battlements, and courtyards—creates a bizarre effect.

St. George's Cathedral has some beautiful stained-glass windows: the three on the east are by Kempe and the large one on the south is of Munich glass. The nave and lower part of the tower date from 1820, and the galleried interior is of late Georgian architecture.

After Kingstown, the following targets might intrigue you.

The Leeward Highway

The leeward or west side of the island has the most dramatic scenery. North from Kingstown, you rise into lofty terrain before descending to the water again. There are views in all directions. On your right you'll pass the Aqueduct Golf Course before reaching Layou. If you want to play golf, check its status as it often opens and closes. Here you can see the massive **Carib Rock,** with a human face carving dating back to A.D. 600. This is considered one of the finest petroglyphs in the Caribbean.

Continuing north you reach **Barrouallie,** where there is another Carib stone altar. Even if you're not a fisherman, you might want to spend some time in this whaling village where men still set out in brightly painted boats armed with harpoons, *Moby Dick*–style, to seek the elusive whale. However, "Save the Whale" devotees need not harpoon their way here in anger. Barrouallie may be one of the last few outposts in the world where such whale-hunting is carried on, but St. Vincentians point out that it does not endanger an already endangered species since so few are caught each year. If one is caught, it's an occasion for festivities and a lot of blubber.

The leeward highway continues to Chateaubelair, the end of the line. There you can swim at the attractive **Richmond Beach** before heading back to Kingstown. In the distance, the volcano, La Soufrière, looms menacingly in the mountains.

The adventurous set out from here to see the **Falls of Baleine,** 7½ miles north of Richmond Beach on the northern tip of the island, accessible only by boat. Coming from a stream in the volcanic hills, Baleine is a freshwater fall. If you're interested in making the trip, check with the tourist office in Kingstown about a tour there.

The Windward Highway

This road runs along the eastern Atlantic coast from Kingstown. Waves pound the surf, and all along the rocky shores are splendid seascapes. If you want to go swimming along this often-dangerous coast, stick to the sandy spots, as they offer safer shores. Along this road you'll pass coconut and banana plantations and fields of arrowroot, a crop that St. Vincent seems to monopolize.

North of Georgetown lies the **Rabacca Dry River,** which was the flow of lava from the volcano at its eruption at the beginning of the 20th century. The journey from Kingstown to here is only 24 miles, but it will seem like much longer.

For those who want to go the final 11 miles along a rugged road to **Fancy,** the northern tip of the island, a Land Rover, Jeep, or Moke will be needed.

La Soufrière

A safari to St. Vincent's hot volcano is possible. As you travel the island, you can't miss its cloud-capped splendor. On some occasions this volcano has captured the attention of the world.

The most recent eruption was in 1979, when the volcano threw ashes and spit lava and hot mud, covering the vegetation that grew on its slopes and sending thousands of Vincentians fleeing its fury. Without warning, belched-out rock and black curling smoke filled the blue Caribbean sky. Jets of steam spouted 20,000 feet into the air. About 17,000 persons were evacuated from a ten-mile ring around the volcano.

Fortunately, the eruption was in the sparsely settled northern part of the island. The volcano lies away from most of the tourism and commercial centers of St. Vincent, and even if it should erupt again, volcanologists do not consider it a danger to visitors lodged at beachside hotels along the leeward coast. The last major eruption of the volcano occured in 1902, when 2,000 people were killed. Until its 1979 eruption, the volcano had been quiet since 1972. The activity that year produced a 324-foot-long island of lava rock called Crater Lake.

Even if you're an experienced hiker, don't attempt to explore this volcano without an experienced local guide, many of whom will charge around $30 per person and up for the trip. Also, wear suitable hiking clothes and know that you're in the best of health before making such an arduous journey.

A guide will direct you in your car through a rich countryside of coconut and banana trees, coming to a clearing at the foot of the mountain. After you get there, you go on foot through a rain forest, following the trail that will eventually lead to the crater rim of La Soufrière. Allow at least three hours, unless you're an Olympic athlete.

At the rim of the crater you'll be rewarded with one of the most panoramic views in the Caribbean. That is, if the wind doesn't blow too hard and make you topple over into the crater itself! Extreme caution is emphasized. Inside, you can see the steam rising from the crater.

The trail back down is much easier, I assure you.

Marriqua Valley

Sometimes known as the Mesopotamia Valley, this land is considered one of the lushest cultivated valleys in the eastern Caribbean. Surrounded by mountain ridges, the drive takes you through a landscape richly planted with nutmeg, cocoa, coconut, breadfruit, and bananas. The road begins at Vigie Highway, to the east of the Arnos Vale Airport runway. At the town of Montréal you'll come upon natural mineral springs. Only rugged vehicles should make this trip.

Around Kingstown, you can also enjoy the **Queen's Drive,** scenic loop into the high hills to the east of the capital. From there, the view is magnificent over Kingstown and its yacht-clogged harbor to The Grenadines in the distance.

WHERE TO SHOP: You don't come to St. Vincent to shop, but once there, you might pick up some items in the sea island cotton fabrics and clothing that are specialties here. In addition, Vincentian artisans make pottery, jewelry, and baskets that have souvenir value at least.

Since the capital, Kingstown, consists of about 12 small blocks, you can walk and browse and see about everything in a morning's shopping jaunt. Try to be in town for the colorful, noisy **Friday-morning market.** You might not purchase anything. After all, you don't plan to bring fruit, fish, and poultry back on the plane with you, but you'll surely enjoy the riot of color.

Most shops are open Mondy to Friday from 8 a.m. to 4 p.m. Stores generally close from noon to 1 p.m. for lunch. Saturday hours are 8 a.m. to noon.

In the **St. Vincent Handicraft Centre** (tel. 809/457-1288), up the road from the wharf in Kingstown, you'll see a large display of the handcrafts of the island. On the site of an old cotton gin, this shop offers you a chance to see craftspeople at work, perhaps on macramé or metal-work jewelry.

Batik Caribe, Bay St., Kingstown (tel. 809/456-1666), contains some of the most unusual batiks in the Caribbean. This charming establishment justifiably considers its products more as artwork than as garments. This is the headquarters of a Caribbean-wide chain of high-quality shops making brightly colored cloth tinted in an Indonesian technique of lost-wax dye resistance, an item of high fashion. Mrs. Palmer is the Canadian-born entrepreneur who pours her artistry into the skillfully executed patterns. Designs are priced based on the number of colors (and consequently the amount of time) that go into their production. Many of the brightly colored scenes, like paintings, are suitable for framing. Others are better worn as scarves, shawls, or dresses. Sundresses, jumpers, and skirts for both men and women are sold, as well as amusing hats and children's clothing. Often one of the polite sales staff will unfold some of the original bolts of cloth like an Oriental rug.

Stechers Jewellery Ltd., Lot 19, Lane Bay St., Kingstown (tel. 809/457-1142), offers a good selection of crystal, quality watches, china, porcelain, and jewelry. The entrance is through the courtyard of the Cobblestone Inn.

The familiar **Y. de Lima Ltd.** , P.O. Box 187 (tel. 809/457-1681) also has a branch in Kingstown, well stocked with cameras, stereo equipment, clocks, binoculars, and jewelry. It is at the corner of Bay and Egmont streets.

Noah's Arkade (tel. 809/457-1513) is a little shop on Bay Street in Kingstown, selling handcrafts from the West Indies, including woodcarvings. It also offers locally made clothing. Noah's has shops at the Frangipani Hotel, Bequia, St. Vincent, and The Grenadines.

Stamp enthusiasts can visit **St. Vincent Philatelic Services, Ltd.,** Lower Bay St. (tel. 809/457-1911). This is the largest operating bureau in the Caribbean, offering for sale issues that are said to be the Caribbean's collectible.

Finally, as you're leaving you'll be able to purchase duty-free liquors and cigarettes at **Gonsalves Liquors** (tel. 809/458-4753) at Arnos Vale Airport.

THE SPORTING LIFE: In St. Vincent you skindive, fish, swim, or snorkel, and of course go sailing, mainly to The Grenadines.

All **beaches** on St. Vincent are public, and many of the best ones border hotel properties which you can patronize for drinks or luncheons. Most of the resorts are in the south, where the beaches have white or golden-yellow sand. However, many of the beaches in the north have sands that look like lava ash in color. The safest swimming is on the leeward beaches; the windward beaches can be dangerous.

Tennis

Short-term visitors to St. Vincent can play at the **Kingstown Tennis Club,** Murray Rd. Guests are charged a subscription of $6 per court per hour. You're asked to provide your own tennis balls and racquets and make arrangements through the chief steward in advance. Telephone 809/456-1288 for more information. Short-term visitors are allowed to play from 8:30 a.m. to noon.

Young Island and the **Grand View Beach** hotels (both previously recommended) also have tennis courts.

Snorkeling and Scuba-Diving

The best area for snorkeling and scuba-diving is the Villa/Young Island section on the southern end of the island.

Mariners Scuba Shop, P.O. Box 639, St. Vincent, W.I. (tel. 809/456-4228), is owned and operated by Earl and Susan Halbich, directly across from Young Island. They offer full diving service, and you can rent equipment here, going on guided reef trips in the warm, fantastically clear waters. The shop also offers night dives as well as beginner and advanced diving instruction, windsurfing, waterskiing, and yacht charters, including Freedom 35, Vanderstadt 45, and Gulfstar 43. The complete resort diving course costs $50 per person. If you're an experienced diver and want to go out on dive trips, the rental of the boat, tank, kit, and weights costs about $25 per person. A minimum of two divers is required.

Dive St. Vincent, P.O. Box 864, St. Vincent, W.I. (tel. 809/457-4714), on the Young Island Dock, has two dive boats and a capacity of 16 divers per trip. They specialize in dive tours and complete instruction from a staff of two certified instructors and three additionally trained dive guides. A one-tank dive costs $40, a two-tank dive going for $65, both including all equipment. Dive St. Vincent also offers water tours, such as one to Bequia and another to the Falls of Baleine, a popular trip.

Fishing

It's best to go to a local fisherman for advice if you're interested in this sport, which your hotel will usually arrange for you. The government of St. Vincent doesn't require visitors to take out a license. If you arrange things in time, it's sometimes possible to accompany the fishermen on one of their trips, perhaps four or five miles from shore. A modest fee should suffice. The fishing fleet leaves from the leeward coast at Barrouallie. They've been known to return to shore with everything from a six-inch redfish to a 20-foot pilot whale.

Sailing and Yachting

St. Vincent and The Grenadines are one of the great sailing centers of the West Indies. Here you can obtain yachts that are fully provisioned if you want to go bareboating, or else, if you're a well-heeled novice, you can hire a captain and a crew.

You can rent boats from **Caribbean Sailing Yachts (CSY),** at P.O. Box 491, Tenafly, NJ 07670 (tel. 800/631-1593 toll free in the U.S.), or in St. Vincent at its offices at the Blue Lagoon (tel. 809/458-4308). This company is in the full-service charter business. The cost of your craft will depend on the season. You'll be asked to prove what kind of sailor you are.

NIGHTLIFE: The focus is mainly on the hotels, and activities are likely to include nighttime barbecues and dancing to steel bands. In season, at least one hotel seems to have something planned every night during a week.

One of the liveliest spots is the **Mariner's Inn,** at Villa Beach (tel. 809/458-4287). Island calypso and steel-drum music are the featured attractions here, and local people show up to dance to good music.

The only casino on the island lies amid an isolated landscape whose rolling hills and surging freshwater streams evoke a tropical version of Scotland. Set in a glen, cradled by the surrounding hills, the **Emerald Valley Casino,** Penniston Valley (tel. 809/458-7421), is at the end of a rutted dirt road, about 45 minutes from Kingstown. Its stone-sided modern premises contain an array of gaming tables, slot machines, a duet of bars, a swimming pool, and landscaped lawns.

The casino is open every night except Monday from 8 to 3 a.m. The entrance fee is EC$5 ($1.85).

Next to the Young Island landing pier, the best-known spot for entertainment remains the **Aquatic Club** (tel. 809/458-4205), which "jumps up" with action, usually on Friday and Saturday nights. Guests from all the hotels come here to enjoy the music and sing-alongs. Drinks range in price from EC$3 ($1.10) up.

4. THE GRENADINES

South of St. Vincent, which administers them, this small chain of islands extends for more than 40 miles, offering the finest yachting area in the eastern Caribbean. They're strung like a necklace of precious stones, and have such wonderful names as Bequia, Mustique, Canouan, and Petit St. Vincent.

A few of the islands have accommodations, which we'll explore, but many are so small and so completely undeveloped and unspoiled that they attract only beachcombers and stray boating people in the area.

Populated by the descendants of African slaves, The Grenadines collectively add up to a land mass of only 30 square miles.

The islands are called The Grenadines because they lead to Grenada. These bits of land, often dots on nautical charts, may lack natural resources, yet they're blessed with white sandy beaches, coral reefs, and their own kind of sleepy beauty. If you're not spending the night in The Grenadines, you may at least go over for the day to visit one of them, enjoying a picnic lunch (which your hotel will pack for you) on one of the long stretches of beach.

GETTING THERE: The ideal way to go, of course, is to rent your own yacht, and many wealthy visitors do just that. If you'd like to consider that, refer to "The Sporting Life" in the previous section on St. Vincent. The least expensive method of going is on a mail, cargo, or passenger boat. However, to do this, you should be a free-wheeling person with lots of time and patience.

It's a unique experience for adventuresome travelers and for those who've never been on this type of vessel. You should carry along a raincoat to protect you from those quick Caribbean showers or that occasional big wave. Price and times might fluctuate, so you should check at the tourist office in Kingstown, St. Vincent.

The **government mail boats** leave St. Vincent on Monday, Wednesday, and Thursday at 9:30 a.m., stopping at Bequia, Canouan, and Mayreau, and arriving at Union Island at about 3:30 p.m. On Tuesday, Thursday, and Friday, a boat leaves Union Island at about 6:30 a.m., stopping at Mayreau and Canouan, reaching Bequia at about 11 a.m. and making port at St. Vincent at noon. One-way fares from St. Vincent are: to Bequia, EC$5 ($1.85); to Canouan, EC$10 ($3.70); to Mayreau, EC$12 ($4.45); and to Union Island, EC$15 ($5.55).

M.V. *Snapper* travels to and from St. Vincent and Bequia, Canouan, Mayreau, and Union Island on Monday, Tuesday, Thursday, and Friday, and only to and from Bequia on Saturday. These are all daytime trips, lasting from 7 a.m. to 3:05 p.m. Fares are the same as those given for the mail boat.

For information on other vessels making the sea trips, inquire at the tourist office in Kingstown or on the island you are visiting.

BEQUIA: Only seven square miles of land, Bequia (pronounced "Beck-wee") is the largest of St. Vincent's Grenadines. It's the northernmost island in The Grenadines, offering quite lagoons, reefs, and long stretches of nearly deserted beaches. Descended from seafarers and other early adventurers, its population of some 6,000 Bequians will probably give you a friendly greeting if you pass them along the road. Of the inhabitants, 10% are of Scottish ancestry, who live mostly in the Mount Pleasant region. A feeling of relaxation and informality prevails in Bequia.

The island lies nine miles south of St. Vincent. There is no airport, but you can travel here by government mail boat (see introduction to this section), by motor vessel, or by a three-masted island schooner, the *Friendship Rose*. This sailing vessel makes trips Monday to Friday, leaving Bequia at 6:30 a.m., arriving at St. Vincent at 7:45 a.m. It departs St. Vincent at 12:30 p.m. on the return, reaching Bequia at 1:45 p.m. M.V. *Snapper* comes to Bequia on Monday, Tuesday, Thursday, Friday, and Saturday.

Its main harbor village, **Port Elizabeth,** is known for its safe anchorage, Admiralty Bay. The bay was a haven in the 17th century for the British, French, and Spanish navies, as well as for pirates. Descendants of Captain Kydd (a.k.a. Kidd) still live on the island. Today the yachting set "from anywhere" puts in here, often bringing a kind of dazzling excitement to the locals.

No rental cars are available in the port, but you can hire a taxi at the dock to take you around or to your hotel if you're spending the night. Taxis are reasonably priced, but an even better bet are the so-called "dollar cabs," which take you anywhere on the island for a small fee. They don't seem to have a regular schedule. You just flag one down. Before going to your hotel, drop in at the circular Tourist Information Centre. You'll see it right on the beach. There you can ask for a driver who is familiar with the attractions of the island (nearly all of them are). You should negotiate the fare in advance. A three-hour tour with three or four passengers can probably be arranged for about $15 per hour.

If you want to see boats, just walk along the beach. There, craftsmen can be seen constructing vessels by hand, a method they learned from their ancestors. Whalers sometimes still set out from here in wooden boats with hand harpoons, just as they do from a port village on St. Vincent.

Frankly, after you leave Port Elizabeth there aren't many sights, and you'll probably have your driver, booked for the day, drop you off for a long, leisurely lunch and some time on a beach. However, you'll pass a fort with a harbor view, driving on to Industry Estates which has a Beach House restaurant serving a fair lunch. At Paget Farm, you can wander into a village of whalers, and maybe inspect a few jawbones left over from catches of yesterday.

At Moonhole, there's a vacation and retirement community built into the cliffs, really free-form sculpture. These are private homes of course, and you're not to enter without permission. For a final look at Bequia, head up an 800-foot hill which the local people call "The Mountain." From that perch, you'll have a 360-degree view of St. Vincent and The Grenadines to the south.

Where to Stay

Friendship Bay Hotel, P.O. Box 9, Bequia, The Grenadines, St. Vincent, W.I. (tel. 809/458-3222), is a beachfront resort offering 27 well-decorated rooms with private verandas nestled in 12 acres of tropical gardens. It sits on a sloping hillside with well-tended vegetation. The entire resort complex stands above a snow-white crescent of one of the best beaches on the island. Guests have a sweeping view of the sea and neighboring islands. The owners are Eduardo and Joanne Guadagnino. Eduardo moved from his homeland, Argentina, a number of years ago, going to California, where he went into the restaurant business and married native Californian Joanne. Joanne has seen to redecorating the hotel, using brightly colored curtains, bedspreads, and handmade wall hangings telling a picture story of life in Bequia, as well as grass rugs in the rooms, which are cooled by the trade winds. In winter, the MAP rate in a single is $85 to $135, rising to $150 to $200 in a double. *Summer MAP prices are $75 to $85 in a* *single, $100 to $150 in a double.* The Guadagninos have added a beach bar with swinging chairs in Caribbean style. They offer Saturday-night barbecues on the beach, with music provided by the hotel band, Exotica, a popular island combo. The food is good too, with many island specialties on the menu, along with Italian and Argentine cuisine. You can enjoy water sports and tennis here, or take an excursion aboard the hotel's classic yacht, built in 1920 in Cardiff, Wales, for Danish Lord Holstein Lebreborg, and completely restored by Mr. Guadagnino. The yacht makes trips to and from Mustique and St. Vincent, a one-hour sail, for about $45 per person per round trip. They also have a 27-foot Cigarette-type speedboat, *Guacho I,* that will take you to Mustique in just 15 minutes, for the same price as the yacht.

Sunny Caribee, P.O. Box 16, Admiralty Bay, Bequia, The Grenadines, St. Vincent, W.I. (tel. 809/459-3425), is built around an old colonial plantation house of wood-frame construction, set in ten acres of gardens. Accommodations consist of 17 West Indian cabañas painted in shades of pink and blue, each with its own private terrace, plus eight rooms in the main house. The property fronts a 700-foot white sandy beach, with a seafront bar and a kidney-shape beachside pool. The resort overlooks Admiralty Bay. The hotel rooms in the main building have twin beds and shared baths, while the cabañas have large double bedrooms, and modern showers, as well as ceiling fans. In winter, a hotel room rents for $40 daily in singles, $50 in doubles. Cabañas cost $90 daily for singles, $130 for two persons. *Summer tariffs in the hotel units are $30 daily in a single, $40 in a double. For a cabaña, one person pays $50, with doubles charged $70.* Rates quoted are EP. MAP costs an additional $25 per person per day. Breakfast and dinner are taken in the pleasant open-air restaurant. A wide-open veranda extends around three sides of the building, and guests sit here with nothing to do but unwind or have another beer, or both. You can also swim, snorkel, sail, waterski, or fish. There's also a tennis court if anybody has that much energy.

Spring on Bequia, Bequia, The Grenadines, St. Vincent, W.I. (tel. 809/458-3414). In the late 1960s the avant-garde design of this hotel won an award from the American Institute of Architects. Fashioned from beautifully textured honey-colored stone, it combines design elements from both Japan and Scandinavia. However, its flattened hip roof was inspired by the old plantation houses of Martinique. Constructed on the 18th-century foundations of a West Indian homestead, it sits in the middle of 28 acres of hillside orchards, producing oranges, grapefruit, bananas, breadfruit, plums, and mangoes. Because of the almost-constant blossoming of one crop or another, you get the feeling of springtime (hence the name of the establishment). Candy Leslie, the Minnesota-born owner, will welcome you and check you in. From the main building's stone-sided bar and open-air dining room, you might hear the bellowing of a herd of cows. On the premises is a swimming pool, along with a tennis court. There is access to a sandy beach at the bottom of a steep hill. Each of the ten units is ringed with stone and contains Japanese-style screens to filter the sun. *In the off-season, which is only from November to mid-December, one person pays $60 daily, and two people are charged $85, EP.* In winter, EP singles cost $90 daily, and doubles go for $125. For MAP, add $25 per person per day. For reservations write or call Spring on Bequia, P.O. Box 19251, Minneapolis, MN 55419 (tel. 612/823-1202); of call Scott Calder International toll free at 800/223-5581.

Julie's and Isola's Guest House, Port Elizabeth, Bequia, The Grenadines, St. Vincent, W.I. (tel. 809/458-3304). Charming, West Indian, and friendly, these twin establishments are owned by two of the most kind-hearted hoteliers on the island. Julie and Isola McIntosh are almost always on the premises, preparing meals or building extensions onto their family hotels. Julie, a mason, laid many of the bricks for both hotels, which lie across the street from one another about a block from the water. Isola's Guest House is the more modern and attractive, containing a total of 15 rooms, each with private bath. Julie's is slightly older. With MAP included, year-round rates at Julie's are $50 daily per person. Rates at Isola's, also with MAP, are $65 daily in a single, $115 in a double. Good West Indian food is served in the dining room which is a bougainvillea-covered veranda. The bill of fare is likely to include pumpkin fritters, very fresh fish, and curry dishes.

Where to Dine

The food is good and healthful here—lobster, chicken, and steaks from fish such as dolphin, kingfish, and grouper, plus tropical fruits, fried plaintain, and coconut and guava puddings fresh daily. Even the beach bars are kept spotless.

Friendship Bay Resort (tel. 809/458-3222) is contained in the welcoming precincts of the island's finest hotel, Friendship Bay. Guests eat in a candlelit room high above a sweeping expanse of seafront on a hillside rich with the scent of frangipani and hibiscus. Argentine-born Eduardo Guadagnino and his California-born wife, Joanne, prepare a tempting array of locally inspired dishes served by polite, uniformed employees. Lunch is served from noon to 3 p.m., costing from EC$15 ($5.55). Dinner, offered from 7:30 to 9 p.m., is more elaborate, costing from EC$49 ($18.15) to EC$65 ($24.05) and including such dishes as grilled lobster in season, curried beef, grilled or broiled fish (served Créole style with a spicy sauce), shrimp curry, charcoal-grilled steak flambé, and roast lamb. An island highlight is the Saturday-night jump-up and barbecue. Phone in advance if you're coming for dinner.

Frangipani (tel. 809/458-3255), the waterside dining room of the Hotel Frangipani, is one of the best restaurants on the island. Part of the dining room juts out onto a terrace wharf, whose foundations are sunk on piers into the harbor. Between the tables are clusters of tropical shrubs and a thatch-covered indoor/outdoor bar. With the exception of the juicy steaks imported for barbecues, only local food is used in the succulent specialties. Breakfast begins at 7:30 a.m., and lunches, served throughout the day until 6 p.m., cost from EC$20 ($7.40) and include sandwiches, salads, and seafood platters. Dinner, from 7:30 to 9:30 p.m., is by reservation. Specialties include baked chicken with rice and coconut stuffing, lobster, conch chowder, and an array of fresh fish. A fixed-price menu goes for EC$35 ($12.95), an à la carte meal costing from EC$45 ($16.65). A Thursday-night barbecue is an island event, costing EC$50 ($18.50) and including live entertainment.

In Port Elizabeth, the **Whaleboner Inn** (tel. 809/458-3233), has been an enduring favorite. It's still going strong in its new location next to the Hotel Frangipani. Inside, the bar is carved from the jawbone of a giant whale, and the bar stools are made from the vertebrae. It's open seven days a week, serving breakfast at 8 a.m. and offering food throughout the day until either 10 p.m. on midnight, depending on the crowd. Albert and Angie Hinkson, the owners, offer the best pizza on the island, along with a selection of fish and chips or well-made sandwiches for lunch. At night you may want one of the wholesome dinners prepared by a West Indian cook and including a choice of lobster, fish, chicken, or steak. Meals cost from EC$25 ($9.25) to EC$39 ($14.45). Favored by the yachting set, the restaurant has full bar service. The Whaleboner Boutique adjoins the restaurant, offering a variety of holiday items made from batik and silk-screen print Sea Island cotton, souvenirs, model whaling boats, and T-shirts.

Shopping

This is not a particularly good reason to come to Bequia, but there is some. At shops scattered along the water you can buy hand-screened cotton made by

Bequians. The best of these is **The Crab Hole** (tel. 809/458-3290), run by Carolyn and George Porter. Next door to the Sunny Caribee, they invite guests to visit their silkscreen factory in back. Later you can make purchases at their shop in front.

Noah's Arkade, Belmont (tel. 809/458-3424), owned and operated by island entrepreneur Lavinia Gunn, sells St. Vincentian and Bequian batiks, scarves, hats, T-shirts, dresses, and a scattering of pottery. There are also dolls, placemats, baskets, and homemade jellies concocted from grapefruit, mango, and guava, plus West Indian cookbooks and books on tropical flowers and reef fish. This place stands a few steps from the drinking terrace of the Frangipani Hotel.

Anyone on the island can show you the way to the workshops of **Sargeant's Model Boatshop Bequia** (tel. 809/458-3344). The place is the best known of its kind in the Caribbean, sought out by yacht owners looking for a scale-model reproduction of their favorite vessel. Mr. Lawson Sargeant is the self-taught woodcarver who established this business. Models are carved from a soft local wood called gumwood, then painted in brilliant colors of red, green, gray, or blue, whatever your fancy dictates. When a scale model of the royal family's yacht, *Britannia,* was commissioned in 1985, local newspapers photographed Queen Elizabeth II receiving the boat crafted in this studio. It required five weeks of work, meticulous blueprints, and cost $10,000. You can pick up a model of a Bequia whaling boat for $60 to $200. The Sargeant family usually keeps 100 model boats in inventory, and they come in many shapes and sizes. At least five workmen can be seen chiseling out the bodies of more in the backyard.

Water Sports

Dive Bequia, P.O. Box 16 (tel. 809/458-3504), specializes in diving, snorkeling, windsurfing, and waterskiing. Scuba dives cost $40 for one, $65 for two in the same day, $175 for a five-dive package, and $300 for a ten-dive package. Prices include all the necessary equipment. Introductory lessons cost $20 each per person. A five-dive open-water certification course is $300. A snorkeling trip is $10 per person.

MUSTIQUE: This island, 15 miles south of St. Vincent, is so remote and small it almost deserves to be unknown, and it would be if it weren't for the escapades of Princess Margaret. The princess has a cottage on this island of luxury villas which someone once called "Georgian West Indian."

The island is privately owned by a consortium of businessmen. When splashed on front pages in London, describing Princess Margaret's retreat, it was then owned by beer baron Colin Tennant, a millionaire Scottish nobleman, now Lord Glen Conner. An eccentric dandy, he was often photographed in silk scarfs and Panama hats. On the trail of Margaret, and her cousin the Earl of Lichfield, came a host of celebrities, including Truman Capote, Paul Newman, Mick Jagger, Raquel Welch, and Richard Avedon.

The island is only three miles long and one mile wide, and it has only one major hotel (see below). The best way to go to Mustique is by air charter on **Mustique Airways.** For a description of how to do that, refer to the "Getting There" section on St. Vincent. Chartered planes arrive on the small airstrip in the middle of the bird sanctuary. The airport closes at dusk, because there are no landing lights. Once there, you'll find no taxis. But chances are, someone at Cotton House will already have seen you land. After settling in, you'll find many good white sandy beaches against a backdrop of luxuriant foliage. My favorite is Macaroni Beach, where the water is like turquoise.

On the northern reef of Mustique you'll find the wreck of the French liner

Antilles, which went aground on the Pillories in 1971. Today its massive hulk, now gutted, can be seen cracked and rusting a few yards offshore, an eerie sight.

If you wish to tour the small island, you can rent a Mini-Moke to see some of the most elegant homes in the Caribbean. You can event rent *Les Jolies Eaux* (Pretty Waters)—that is, if you can afford it. This is the Caribbean home of Princess Margaret. A five-bedroom/five-bath house, it has a large swimming pool, naturally. Accommodating ten well-heeled guests, it is available only when HRH is not in residence. If you rent it, the princess will require references.

Where to Stay

The **Cotton House,** Mustique, The Grenadines, St. Vincent, W.I. (tel. 809/456-4777), operarted by Guy de la Houssaye, is an exclusive hotel, once operating as a private club, a place casually elegant, as is its clintele. The main house is an 18th-century structure, built of coral and stone. The house was painstakingly restored, rebuilt, and redecorated by Oliver Messel, uncle by marriage to Princess Margaret. The design of the hotel is characterized by arched louvered doors and cedar shutters. The antique loggia sets the style—everything from Lady Bateman's steamer trunks to a scallop-shell fountain on a quartz base. Guests sit here enjoying their sundowners. Perhaps earlier they played a game on the tennis court or had a swim at the pool surrounded by Messel's "Roman ruins" after a buffet lunch by the pool. Some of the rooms were also designed by Messel. Units are in two fully restored Georgian houses, a trio of cottages, a newer block of eight rooms, or a three-room beach house, all of which open onto windswept balconies or patios. Of course, you pay for all this—$384 daily in a double in winter, from $278 in a single, including full board and tea. *Off-season, the full-board tariffs are $242 to $260 daily in a double, $178 to $188 in a single.* The hotel enjoys an outstanding reputation for its food and service. The cuisine has a West Indian flavor. Nonresidents are allowed to dine here, but they must make reservations. Lunch ranges from $18, and dinner costs about $27 a head, plus wines.

Where to Dine

Nobody ever goes to this island of indigenous farmers and fisherfolk without spending a night drinking a **Basil's Beach Bar,** P.O. Box, Mustique (tel. 809/458-4621). A "South Seas island"–type establishment, it is more authentic than any reproduction in an old Dorothy Lamour flick. The gathering place for yachting people, as well as owners of those luxurious villas, the bar, but mainly its owner, has received a lot of newspaper publicity. Its greeter, Basil S. Charles, is a six-foot-four-inch heavily muscled charmer whom *Esquire* magazine called "the island's most famous product after its sandy beaches." Some people come here to drink and watch a beautiful view, but Basil's is also, by reputation, one of the finest seafood restaurants in the Caribbean. Both lunch and dinner are served daily at this establishment built on piers above the sea. You can dine under the open-air sun screens or with the sun blazing down on you. Expect to spend about $35 for a meal here, and a good one at that. On Wednesday night you can "jumpup" at a barbecue, and on Friday night there's limbo dancing, fire-eating, and folk dancing. Basil's is open daily from 8 a.m. until very late. There is also a boutique on the premises.

CANOUAN: In the shape of a half circle, Canouan is surrounded by coral reefs and blue lagoons, a virgin paradise. The island is only 3½ miles by 1½ miles in size, and is visited mainly by those who want to enjoy its splendid long beaches. Canouan has a population of fewer than 1,000 people, many of whom fish for a living.

You reach Canouan by first taking an international flight to Barbados. It's then 50 minutes by charter flight to Canouan. Alternatively, you can fly to St. Vincent on LIAT. There you'll be able to fly direct to Canouan on Inter-Island Air Services. There are also flights from Grenada.

Charters are also available from a three-seater plane in St. Vincent, which can fly to Canouan any day.

The cost of travel from St. Vincent to Canouan by the ferryboat M.V. *Grenadines Star* is usually EC$10 ($3.70).

The mother island, St. Vincent, lies 14 miles to the north and Grenada 20 miles to the south. Canouan rises from its sandy beaches to the 800-foot-high peak of Mount Royal in the north. There you'll find unspoiled forests of white cedar.

Food and Lodging

Canouan Beach Hotel, Canouan, The Grenadines, St. Vincent, W.I. (tel. 809/458-4413), is by far the best place to stay on Canouan. Opened in 1984, it offers attractive accommodations on its seven acres of beachfront. The location is about an eighth of a mile from the dirt landing strip of the hotel island's airport on a periwinkle-studded peninsula jutting out between the Atlantic and the Caribbean. The resort's social center lies beneath the sun screen of a mahogany-trussed parapet whose sides are open to a water view. A pair of lush but uninhabited islands lie offshore. Snorkeling, windsurfing, small sailboats, and a catamaran are available without charge to guests. All water sports, buffet lunches, barbecued suppers, and drinks are included in a weekly price. Depending on the accommodation, guests pay from $700 to $950, double occupancy, per week in high season, *$550 to $750 per week in low season.* Single occupants face a 75% surcharge. Each of the stone-sided accommodations is air-conditioned, with sliding glass doors, private baths, and comfortable furnishings.

UNION ISLAND: Midway between Grenada and St. Vincent, Union Island is the most southern of The Grenadines. It's known for its dramatic 900-foot peak, Mount Parnassus, which is seen by yachting people for miles away. If you're cruising in the area, Union is the port of entry for St. Vincent. Yachters are required to check with Customs upon entry.

Perhaps you'll sail into Union on a night when the locals are having a "big drum" dance. Costumed islanders dance and chant to the beat of drums made of goatskin.

The island is reached either by chartered or scheduled aircraft, by cargo boat, by private yacht, or by mail boat (see information under "Getting There" at the beginning of this section). M. V. *Snapper* stops at Union Island, arriving at 3:05 p.m. on Monday and Thursday, departing at 7 a.m. on Tuesday and Friday, on a voyage to and from St. Vincent, with stops at Bequia, Canouan, and Mayreau. The fare on both the motor vessel and the mail boat to and from St. Vincent is EC$15 ($5.55) per person each way.

Where to Stay

Accommodations are very limited and simple.

Anchorage Yacht Club, Clifton, Union Island, The Grenadines, St. Vincent, W.I. (tel. 809/458-4848). Built in the early 1970s and radically renovated in 1986, this is the leading hotel on the island, occupying a prestige position a few steps from the bumpy landing strip near a cluster of boutiques and shops. It combines a threefold function as a 15-room hotel, a pleasant restaurant and bar, and a marine service facility. The yachting club meets in the wood-and-stone bar. There you can order lunches for $12, and dinners for $18 and up. The bill of fare is likely to include fish soup, a wide array of fresh fish, and Créole versions of lamb, pork, and beef. Try the mango daiquari. The bar is open all day and into the night, but meals are served daily from 7:30 a.m. to noon for breakfast, noon to 2:30 p.m. for lunch, and 7 to 9:30 p.m. for dinner. Each of the pleasantly ventilated bedrooms has a pinewood ceiling, white tile floors, and a location midway between a pair of airy verandas. Units are furnished with modern pieces, and each is air-conditioned, with a private bath. In high season, singles or doubles cost $130 per night, *dropping to $100 per night in low season* with breakfast included. A two-bedroom villa, suitable for up to four persons, rents for $205 in high season, *dropping to $155 in low season.*

PALM ISLAND:
PALM ISLAND: Is this island a resort or is the resort the island? Casual elegance and privacy prevail on these 100 acres in the southern Grenadines. Surrounded by five white sand beaches, the island is sometimes called "Prune," so one can easily understand the more appealing name change.

A little islet in the sun, it offers complete peace and quiet with plenty of sea, sand, sun, and sailing. To reach the place, it's best to take a share-charter direct to Union Island (operated November through May), one mile west of Palm, where a launch will be waiting.

If you're visiting in summer, you can book a charter plane on your own; or first overnight in Barbados, then fly the next morning to St. Vincent with LIAT. There you can connect with Inter-Island Air Services' scheduled flight to Union Island, where you take the launch over to Palm Island.

Most people don't come to Palm Island to shop, but once there, you might see what's available at **La Boutique,** which has a collection of jewelry, local handcrafts, gifts, swimwear, plus other casual resort attire for both men and women.

Palm Island Beach Club, Palm Island, The Grenadines, St. Vincent, W.I. (tel. 809/458-4804) is the fulfillment of a long-cherished wish held by the Caldwells, John and his gracious, soft-spoken wife, Mary, to establish a hotel on an idyllic and isolated island. John is nicknamed "Coconut Johnny," because of his reforestation hobby of planting palms. At Prune Island, he planted hundreds upon hundreds of trees until its name was changed to Palm Island. An adventurer, this Texan once set out to sail by himself across the Pacific, coming to rest off the coast of Fiji. He made it to Australia, where he constructed his own ketch, *Outward Bound,* loaded his family aboard, and took off again. Eventually he made it to The Grenadines, where he operated a charter business. His exploits, including getting embroiled in an hurricane, were documented in the autobiographical book *Desperate Voyage,* an account of his 106-day, 8,500-mile journey at sea. After that exploit, he operated a charter business in The Grenadines, often taking guests to Palm (then Prune) Island. As his clients would swim or lie on the beach, he'd plant coconut palms.

Just right for the Grenadine frame of mind, he eventually built this cottage colony with enough room for 50 guests spaced under palms on the white sandy beach. Accommodations are in the Beach Club duplex cabañas or in one of the villas, which are equipped for housekeeping. Bungalows are built of stone and wood, with louvered walls as well as sliding glass doors that open onto terraces. The furniture was built by the Caldwells. All rooms are superior, with ceiling fans, window screens, rattan furniture, beach lounges. All have private showers, refrigerators, and outdoor walled patios on the oceanfront. In winter, a single with all meals rents for $190 daily, and a double costs $290. A third person in a double is charged $85. *Summer prices for rooms with all meals are $125 daily in a single, $175 in a double, a third person in a double paying $65.* Rates include afternoon tea served on the patio, a welcome drink, the manager's weekly punch par ty, airport transfers, TV, video, tennis, and snorkel gear. Dining is in a "South Seas island"-style pavilion where the food is good and plentiful. Nautically oriented guests like to have tall drinks at the circular beach bar.

The Caldwells also maintain a small charter fleet of yachts for day sails, with one of their amiable West Indian crewmen aboard to assist. These natives are experts on local history, customs, and tall tales.

PETIT ST. VINCENT: A private island four miles from Union, in the southern Grenadines, this speck of island is rimmed with white sandy beaches. On 113 acres, it's an out-of-this-world corner of the Caribbean that is only for self-sufficient types, who want to be away from just about everything.

To reach it, fly to Barbados, with luck arriving there before 4 p.m. If so, you can be on "PSV," as it is affectionately called, the same day. Passengers fly a charter or scheduled service. A common departure time will be scheduled for guests arriving that afternoon in Barbados for the 45-minute flight direct to Union Island. At Union Island, the PSV boat will meet you and take you on a half-hour ride to PSV. Connections can also be made through Martinique.

However, in such an offbeat oasis there exists **Petit St. Vincent Resort,** Petit St. Vincent, The Grenadines, St. Vincent, W.I. (tel. 809/458-4801), which has a kind of nautical chic. The resort was conceived by Haze Richardson, who had to do everything from planting trees to laying cables. The property was once owned by the archbishop of Trinidad. Open to the trade winds, this self-contained cottage colony was designed by a Swedish architect, Arne Hasselquist, who used purpleheart wood and the local stone, called blue bitch (yes, that's right), for the walls. This is the only place to stay on the island, and if you don't like it and want to check out, you'd better have a yacht waiting. But chances are, you'll be pleased. Cottages are built on a hillside or set close to the beach, in a 113-acre setting. Units open onto big outdoor patios, all with views. Winter AP rates, charged from mid-December to mid-April, range from $440 for one person, $570 for two. *In the off-season, November 1 to mid-December and mid-April to the end of August, AP tariffs drop to $235 daily in a single and $300 in a double.* The place is closed in September and October. Wicker and rattan along with khus-khus rugs set the Caribbean tone of the place. The units have no phones. When you need something, write out your request, place it in a slot in a bamboo flagpole, and run up the yellow flag. One of the waiters will arrive on a motorized cart to collect your order.

To make reservations, write to Petit St. Vincent, P.O. Box 12506, Cincinnati, OH 45212 (tel. 513/242-1333).

MAYREAU: A tiny cay, 1½ square miles of land in The Grenadines, Mayreau is a privately owned island shared by a hotel and a little hilltop village of about 170 inhabitants. It's on the route of the mailboat and M.V. *Snapper,* which ply the seas to and from St. Vincent, visiting also Canouan and Union Island.

Food and Lodging

Saltwhistle Bay Club, Mayreau, The Grenadines, St. Vincent, W.I. (tel. toll free 800/387-1752 in the U.S.) is a last frontier for people seeking a tropical island paradise. A young Canadian-German couple, Tom and Undine Potter, who for several years operated a beachside restaurant here catering to yachting visitors, have expanded their operation to a 20-room hotel complex, with six bedrooms, four one-bedroom suites, and ten deluxe duplex cottages sharing a rooftop gallery with tables, chairs, and hammocks. All the units contain private bath. They were built by local craftsmen using the stone of the island, floor tiles, and purple and green heartwood. They are all cooled by ceiling fans. In winter, single bedrooms rent for $230 daily and doubles for $320. *Summer rates are $130 to $150 single, from $210 double.* All these quotations are for MAP.

The dining room at the hotel is made up of circular stone booths topped by thatch canopies, and you can enjoy seafood fresh from the waters around Mayreau—lobster, curried conch, turtle steaks, and grouper. Guests can get acquainted at the bar. By day you can go snorkeling, fishing, windsurfing, cruising on a yacht, or just lolling in one of the hammocks strung among the trees in the 16-acre tropical garden, perhaps taking a swim along the expanse of white sand beach curving along the windward side of the island. One of the enjoyable excursions arranged by the Potters is a "Robinson Crusoe" picnic on a little uninhabited island nearby. Scuba-divers will be glad to know that there's a shipwreck to explore, a 1912 gunboat lying in 40 feet of water half a mile offshore.

5. GRENADA

The "Spice Island," Grenada is an independent three-island nation which includes Carriacou, the largest of the Grenadines, and Petit Martinique. The air in Grenada is full of the fragrance of spice and exotic fruits. The island has more spices per square mile than any other place in the world—cloves, cinnamon, mace, cocoa, tonka beans, ginger, and a third of the world's supply of nutmeg. "Drop a few seeds anywhere," the locals will tell you, "and you have an instant garden. The central area is like a jungle of palms, oleander, bougainvillea, purple and red hibiscus, crimson anthurium, bananas, breadfruit, birdsong, ferns, and palms.

Southernmost island of the Windward Antilles, Grenada (pronounced Gre-*nay*-dah) lies 60 miles southwest of St. Vincent and about 90 miles north of Trinidad. An oval-shaped island, it is 21 miles long and about 12 miles wide. Volcanic in origin, the island has an average yearly temperature of 83° Fahrenheit. Because of the constant trade winds, there is little humidity.

Like most of the Caribbean islands, it was sighted by Columbus, who sailed by it in 1498. Whether or not he landed is the subject of conjecture. Grenada was inhabited by the cannibalistic Carib Indians. The first Europeans who visited Grenada were probably London seafaring merchants, who ended up, no doubt, in the Carib stewing pot.

The French in 1650 were the first to establish relations with the Caribs, buying their favors for two bottles of brandy and some baubles. But those peaceful relations didn't last two long when the Indians tired of their trinkets. The conflict ended in 1651 at **Le Morne de Sauteur** (Leapers' Hill), as the last band of Caribs tossed their women and children into the sea, then in a suicide leap, plunged to their own deaths rather than submit to European domination.

After the inevitable British-French disputes and bloody wars for domination, Grenada settled down to British rule in 1783. In 1967 it became an associated state within the Commonwealth. Before it achieved independence in early 1974, political squabbles virtually shut down the island, bringing havoc to the tourist season in late 1973 and early 1974. A general strike shut down the port, as electricity and water were turned off.

Grenada was dominated by a volatile black leader, Eric Gairy, who had been considered a practitioner of black magic and a UFO believer, performing voodoo-like rituals to keep himself in power. On three separate occasions he proposed before a stunned United Nations that it undertake a study of UFOs.

For 12 years he oppressively ruled over the island until he was overthrown in the spring of 1979. The revolution cost only three lives, and boatloads of tourists, including a Soviet cruise ship, hardly noticed they were in the middle of a revolution.

The man who ousted Gairy was Maurice Bishop, along with his radical New

Jewel Movement. Bishop launched what is still a controversial 4½-year "revolution," cementing ties with the Soviet Union and Cuba. Dramatically, in 1983 Bishop was placed under house arrest. Later he was executed along with several key supporters. An even more radical Marxist-Leninist faction took over the government and installed a revolutionary military control.

President Reagan, however, looked upon these new leaders as "thugs." In October of that year, the U.S.—backed by other Caribbean countries—launched a successful invasion of Grenada, routing the military council and rounding up Cubans building the controversial Point Saline Airport.

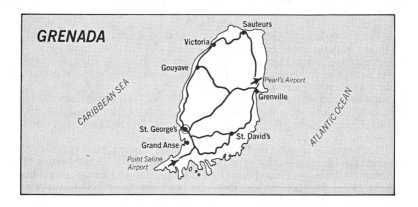

Beefed up by financial aid from the U.S., Grenada has revived a sagging tourist industry. The anti-American slogans have long been down. Instead you are likely to see billboards proclaiming "Thank God for U.S." Grenada is a safe destination, and American tourists are genuinely welcomed there.

Carnival time in Grenada is in August, lasting several days, with colorful parades, music, dancing—what have you. The festivities begin on a Friday, continuing practically nonstop to Tuesday. Steel bands and calypso groups perform at The Carenage, The Carnival finale, a gigantic "jump-up," takes place at St. George's. *Be warned:* if you dress in your good clothes to attend this event, you may get sticky from close body contact with the Djab Djab Molassi (devil-costumed figures daubed with molasses).

Grenada has a **People to People** program that allows you to meet the doctor, the waiter, or the spice-basket maker. The free program matches visitors to the island with Grenadians who share similar interests. For information, ask Grenada Tours and Travel, P.O. Box 46, St. George's.

GETTING THERE: The controversial Point Saline International Airport—financed in part by Cuba (and finished by the United States)—opened in October 1984, on the anniversary of the U.S. rescue mission of the island. At the southwestern toe of Grenada, the airport not only makes it possible for jumbo jets to land, it makes most of the major hotels accessible in only 5 to 15 minutes by taxi.

BWIA flies from Grenada to New York and Miami, and both BWIA and **LIAT** connect with international airlines, including British Airways, Air Canada, Eastern Airlines, American Airlines, Pan Am, and Air France, in Barbados, St. Lucia, Trinidad, Martinique, and Antigua. There is a Grenada Inter-Island Information Desk in the arrival section of the Grantley Adams International Airprt in Barbados.

British Airways flies from London to Grenada every Wednesday. From Grenada, LIAT has daily flights to Carriacou.

GETTING AROUND: You'll have to establish the price of a **taxi** before getting in. Most arriving visitors take a cab at the Point Saline Airport to one of the hotels near St. George's, at a cost of about EC$25 ($9.25).

You can also use most taxi drivers as a guide for a day's sightseeing, and the cost can be divided among three to four passengers. If so, count on paying EC$100 ($37) to EC$140 ($51.80) per day. Again, this figure is to be negotiated.

Car Rentals

The rates are fairly modest if you want this often-difficult means of transport through the length and width of Grenada. First, you must remember to *drive on the left.* A U.S. or Canadian driver's license is valid in Grenada, and a local driver's license can be obtained at a cost of EC$ ($11.10). Many car rental firms also issue local permits.

A word of warning about local drivers: There's such a thing as a Grenadian driving machismo where the drivers take blind corners with abandon. An extraordinary number of accidents are reported in the lively local paper.

Royston's Rent-a-Car, at Blue Horizons (tel. 809/444-4316), rents Daihatsus, Mazdas, and Charmants, among other vehicles. Rental fees, which include 50 free miles a day, are about $40 per day. Unlimited mileage is offered with a full week's rental.

Buses

There are two types. The most colorful and traditional ones are painted in red, blue, gold, whatever, and are just as crazy as their names (one, for example, is called "Oo-la-la"). On plank seats, you're bounced until you're squealing just as much as the live pig with which you're likely to be sharing the ride. Most of these buses depart from Market Square in St. George's.

Minibuses have been introduced as well, taking you on most short rides for EC$1 (37¢). They're not as colorful but are more comfortable.

Local Air Services

Many visitors like to fly over to Grenada's satellite island, Carriacou, for the day. **LIAT** makes the short takeoff and landing (STOL) flight in about 20 minutes at a round-trip cost of EC$112 ($41.44). To book a ticket, the LIAT telephone number is 809/440-2796. There are about three flights a day.

PRACTICAL FACTS: The State of Grenada is an independent entity, a member of the Commonwealth of Nations (formerly the British Commonwealth).

Banks: In St. George's, the capital, you'll find such banks operating as Barclays, Church and Halifax Street, St. George's (tel. 809/440-3232); Scotiabank, Halifax Street, St. George's (tel. 809/440-3274); and the National Commercial Bank (NCB), at the corner of Halifax and Hillsborough Streets, St.

George's (tel. 809/440-3566). There are branches of Barclays at Grenville, St. Andrew's; and on Carriacou. NCB has branches at Grenville, St. Andrew's; Gouyave; Thebaide Junction, St. David's; and Carriacou.

Currency: The official currency is the Eastern Caribbean dollar. Always determine which dollars—EC or U.S.—you're talking about when someone on Grenada quotes you a price. No restrictions are placed by Customs on the amount of money brought into the island.

Documents: Proof of citizenship is needed to enter the country. A passport is preferred, but a birth certificate or voter registration card for American, British, and Canadian citizens is accepted. However, in-transit passengers to Grenada need a valid passport. An ongoing or return ticket must be produced as well.

Drugstore: For your pharmacy needs, try **Benoit Pharmacy,** The Carenage, St. George's (tel. 809/440-3174).

Electricity: Not always reliable, electricity is supplied on the island by Grenada Electricity Services, and the current is 220/240 volts AC, 50 cycles.

Holidays: Grenada celebrates the usual holidays.

Information: Go to the **Grenada Tourist Department,** The Carenage in St. George's (tel. 809/440-2279). It's open Monday to Thursday from 8 a.m. to 4 p.m., and on Friday to 5 p.m. Maps, guides, and general information are available. In the U.S., the **Grenada Tourist Office** is at 141 East 44th St., Suite 701, New York, NY 10017 (tel. 212/687-9554 or toll-free 800/638-0852).

Language: English is commonly spoken on this island of 90,000 people, because of the long years of British influence. However, now and then you'll hear people speaking in a French-African patois handed down from long ago.

Medical care: There is a general hospital in St. George's, with an X-ray department and operating theater. Private doctors and nurses are available on call.

Newspapers and magazines: Among newspapers, the *Grenadian Voice* is published weekly. You'll also find *Time* or *Newsweek.*

Post office: The General Post Office in St. George's is open Monday through Thursday from 8 a.m. to 4 p.m., with a lunch break from 11:45 a.m. to 1 p.m. On Friday hours are 8 a.m. to 5 p.m. It's closed on weekends.

Radio: Radio Grenada, owned and operated by the government, broadcasts the news, and a lot of American pop and disco music.

Service: A 10% service charge is added to most restaurant and hotel bills.

Taxes: A 10% VAT (value added tax) is imposed on food and beverages. Upon leaving Grenada, you must fill out an immigration card and pay a departure tax of EC$25 ($9.25).

Telecommunications: All telecommunications services are provided by **Grenada Telecommunications Ltd.** (Grentel), a joint venture between the government of Grenada and Cable and Wireless Worldwide Communications Group. International telephone service is available 24 hours a day from pay phones. Public telegraph, Telex, and Fax services are also provided from Grantel's Carenage offices in St. George's (tel. 809/440-1000 for all Grental offices). Hours are from 7 a.m. to 7 p.m. Monday to Friday, 7 a.m. to 1 p.m. Saturday, and 10 a.m. to noon Sunday and holidays. To call a Grenada number from the U.S., you must dial area code 809, then a three-digit city code, and then a four-digit number. (City codes in Grenada vary.)

Weather: Grenada has two distinct seasons, dry and rainy. The dry season is from January through May; the rest of the year is the rainy season, although rainfall is not of long duration. The average temperature is 80° Fahrenheit.

WHERE TO STAY: Many of Grenada's hostelries evoke the Mediterranean more than the Caribbean in their architecture, perhaps in deference to the island's Spanish name. Innkeepers think small here. The Ramada Renaissance Hotel is the biggest place at which you can overnight, and nearly everything else is tiny, usually containing no more than a dozen rooms.

Don't forget: Your hotel or inn will probably add the service charge to your bill. Ask in advance about this, plus the government tax on food and beverage tabs you may run up. These charges are seldom included in the final total.

Ramada Renaissance Hotel, P.O. Box 441, Grand Anse Beach, Grenada, W.I. (tel. 809/444-4371, or toll free 800/272-6232), was radically renovated in 1986 and reopened as the most glamorous, tastefully executed, and stylish hotel on the island. It stands on a desirable stretch of beachfront, behind a cedar-shingle façade whose design might have been inspired by an 18th-century plantation house. Any comparison with another century, however, ends when visitors see the glistening interior. Guests register beneath the soaring octagonal roof of the entrance hall, then are ushered between a pair of manicured formal gardens to their rooms. Each of these is furnished with a formal blend of English reproduction pieces, thick carpeting, air conditioning, tile bath, phone, and radio/alarm. Each has a balcony or veranda, some of which open onto sun-flooded views of the beach. Depending on the exposure, high-season prices are $150 daily in a single or double. *Low-season charges are $95 daily* single or double. The hotel has two stylish restaurants, plus a lattice-encased gazebo for dancing the night away when there's live entertainment. On the premises is a swimming pool as well as a water-sports kiosk for the rental of sailboats, windsurfers, and snorkeling equipment.

Secret Harbour, P.O. Box 11, St. George's, Grenada, W.I. (tel. 809/444-4548), seen from the water of Mount Hartman Bay, reminds one of a Mediterranean complex on Spain's Costa del Sol—a tasteful one, that is, with white stucco arches, red tile roofs, and wrought-iron light fixtures. The design also has a Moorish touch in the tiles and terraces. From all over Grenada, including some island plantation homes, antiques were purchased, restored, and installed here. The bathrooms are also luxurious, with sunken tubs lined with color-rich Italian tiles, the lighting from unglazed medallion windows. Each of the 20 suites has a dressing room, living area, and patio overlooking the water. Steps lead down to the beach, as you pass among lime and papaya trees, palms, frangipani. Pathways take you to the tennis court, the free-form swimming pool, and the main building. Winter EP rates are $135 daily in a double, $115 in a single. *In summer, guests are quoted an EP rate of $85 daily in a double, $75 in a single.* In the dining room, decorated with style, a chef provides sumptuous meals. Arrangements can be made at the desk for car rentals, island tours, sports fishing, and golf.

Calabash, P.O. Box 282, St. George's, Grenada, W.I. (tel. 809/444-3234), built in the early 1960s, is today the best-established resort, and perhaps the most venerated hotel, on Grenada. Five miles south of St. George's and only minutes from the Point Salines International Airport, it occupies a landscaped eight-acre beach plot along an isolated section of Prickly Bay (L'Anse aux Épines). Many of the shrubs on the grounds, tiny when they were planted, make some of the stone outbuildings look diminutive. Foremost among the plants are the scores of beautiful calabashes (gourds) for which the resort was named. The social center of the place is a low-slung, rambling building whose walls are chiseled from blocks of dark gray wood. Above the bar, a massive beam of an almost-indestructible tropical hardwood called greenheart serves as a support for the masonry above. Two of the 22 hotel units have private swimming pools and entrances nearly concealed by the thunbergia (trailing orchid) vines. Rates in high season are $195 for a single, $220 for a double. *Off-season, charges are $85 in a single, $120 in a double.* All tariffs are for MAP. Rentals of sailboats and equipment for most other water-related activities are arranged by the staff.

Horse Shoe Beach Hotel, P.O. Box 174, St. George's, Grenada, W.I. (tel.

809/444-4410), is a little dream with vintage charm. Set on a hilltop, it is built in the Mediterranean style, a total of 18 cozily furnished terracotta cottages—each with a canopied four-poster bed—all with private balconies and air conditioning. Breathing in the fragrant shrubs, you stroll down the hill to the beach and sea. Constructed on a small promontory, the complex manages to capture the sea breezes at night, and you'll hear the rustling sound of wind blowing through acres of tropical gardens, filled with hibiscus and bougainvillea. Guests are so well coddled here that they keep returning year after year, enjoying the appealingly furnished rooms. Many of the furnishings came from buying antiques from old island family houses. The doorway to the Spanish stucco building is almost hidden by the foliage, including a towering banyan tree. You enter the Grenadian-Iberian dining pavilion and red-tile lounge, with its cozy nooks and original oil paintings. The dining room frames views of the beach and swimming pool, as well as of the gardens. A double costs $110 daily, and a single goes for $95. *In the off-season, it's possible to stay here at $85 daily in a double, $75 in a single.* Add $30 per person per day for MAP. The hotel has a full water-sports complex with scuba, snorkeling, windsurfers, Sunfish, pedal boats, and water scooters.

Spice Island Inn, P.O. Box 6, St. George's, Grenada, W.I. (tel. 809/444-4258), is on an estate overlooking the Caribbean and built along 1,200 feet of Grand Anse beach. The main house, reserved for dining and dancing, has a tropical aura and lots of nice touches, showing that taste and concern went into the design of the place. A total of 28 air-conditioned beach suites are offered, plus 14 pool suites, all pleasantly contemporary, stretched along the white sands. About ten of them are set back a bit and have their own private plunge pools, surrounded by high walls where guests can skinny-dip. In high season, the MAP rate runs $200 to $240 a day in a single, $210 to $275 for two persons sharing a double. *In low season, you can stay here on half-board terms at rates ranging from $120 to $155 daily in a single, from $140 to $190 in a double.* Furnishings in the rooms are not elaborate, with outdoor pieces such as wicker chairs. The waiter will arrive with your breakfast (a just-plucked red hibiscus resting on the tray), and you'll enjoy it (and, hopefully, who you're with) on a shaded patio, your very own. The place is known for its Sunday buffet, and the cooks do not only good Grenadian food, but also deftly turn out an international cuisine, including soursop ice cream (nutmeg is also a specialty), breadfruit vichyssoise, green turtle soup, and Caribbean lobster. Sometimes a combo plays for dancing.

Cinnamon Hill and Beach Club, P.O. Box 292, St. George's, Grenada, W.I. (tel. 809/444-4301), cooperatively owned, created by English expatriate Richard Gray, an actor, writer, producer, and architect, is a cluster of luxurious villas, like a Mediterranean-inspired village, surrounded by tropical gardens. Some 20 hacienda suites are clustered on the hillside overlooking Grand Anse beach, each fully air-conditioned, with a living room, terrace, fully equipped kitchenette, one or two bedrooms, private bath, and balcony opening onto the sea. *In the off-season, two people can rent either a one- or two-bedroom villa for anywhere from $77 to $160 daily.* In the high season, two guests are accepted for from $121 to $155 in a double with one-bedroom, from $153 to $213 daily in a two-bedroom villa. A one-bedroom villa or suite can sleep four persons, and a two-bedroom unit can shelter six guests. Breakfast is cooked right in your own villa. The Cinnamon Restaurant of the hotel specializes in the fresh seafood of Grenada. It serves breakfast from 8 to 10 a.m. and dinner from 7 to 10:30 p.m. No lunch is served. The tiles, stonework, and woodwork of the hotel are especially tasteful. A splash of red-tile roofs, white stucco arches, hand-hewn beams—everything is in keeping with the Spanish-Mediterranean theme. Sailing, snorkeling, waterskiing, skindiving, and fishing are arranged at the front desk. Guests can use the big health and fitness center.

Coyaba Hotel, P.O. Box 336, St. George's, Grenada, W.I. (tel. 809/444-4129), lies on a 2½-acre site on Grand Anse Beach, seven minutes from St. George's and the same distance from the Point Salines International Airport. The hotel, opened in 1987, has views of the town and the St. George's harbor. All the 42 units are air-conditioned and have double beds, plus verandas or patios. Each is equipped with a phone, and spacious baths with hairdryers. Laundry service is available. In winter, singles rent for $80 daily and doubles for $105, while *in summer, prices are $60 in singles, $80 in doubles.* An extra person in a double is charged $15 per day. For MAP, add $30 per person per day. The hotel has an open-air restaurant serving local and international cuisine with drinks offered at the main or pool bar. Activities include tennis on a Laykold court, volleyball, and water sports offered by the H.M.C. Diving Centre on the premises.

Twelve Degrees North, P.O. Box 241, St. George's, Grenada, W.I. (tel. 809/444-4580), lying on a very private beach, is operated by Joseph Gaylord, a former commercial real estate broker from New York, who greets visitors with a wide smile and an outstretched hand in front of a large flame tree on his front lawn. He owns this cluster of spotlessly clean efficiency apartments, not far from the airport at Point Saline. Many of the staff members have been with Mr. Gaylord since he opened the place many years ago, and are highly trustworthy. They'll cook breakfast, prepare lunch (perhaps pumpkin soup and flying fish), do the cleaning and laundry, go food shopping, and fix regional specialties for dinner (which you heat up for yourself later). The resort has its own tennis court, and a Sunfish and two sailing dinghies are provided free. A grass-roofed beach bar faces the water. Each unit (two with two bedrooms and six with one bedroom) comes with an individual uniformed attendant, who arrives at 8 o'clock each morning to perform the thousand small kindnesses that make Twelve Degrees North a favorite lair for returning guests from America and Europe. Each unit is equipped with an efficiency kitchen with a 12-cubic-foot refrigerator, large enough to prevent the need for food shopping daily. The large beds can be separated or pushed together, depending on the mood of the guests. The owner prefers to rent by the week, because, as he says, "a few days aren't enough to get to know Grenada." In winter, a two-bedroom apartment, suitable for four, costs from $200 daily, a one-bedroom unit for two persons goes for $130 a day, and each additional person pays $60. *In summer, four people in a two-bedroom apartment pay $160 per day, and two people in a one-bedroom unit pay $100.* Children under 12 are not accepted.

Blue Horizons Cottage Hotel, P.O. Box 41, Grand Anse, Grenada, W.I. (tel. 809/444-4316), was purchased by co-owners Royston and Arnold Hopkin from a bankrupt estate. Sons of the famous Grenadian hotelkeepers Audrey and Curtis Hopkin (now retired), they transformed the neglected property into one of the finest on the island, with an occupancy rate second only to that of Spice Island. The 32 suites and four studios are spread throughout a lush and flowering garden of 6¼ acres. Each bungalow has an efficiency kitchen and comfortable solid mahogany furniture. Children are welcomed, and they can watch the 21 varieties of native birds said to inhabit the grounds. High-season rates depend on the category of the cottage: standard, superior, or deluxe. On the EP, doubles in high season cost $90 to $110 daily, and singles go for $85 to $100. *In summer, rates are slashed to $65 to $80 daily in a double, EP, and $60 to $75 in a single.* Guests who prefer to cook in their rooms can buy supplies from a Food Fair at Grand Anse, a ten-minute walk away. Most important, Grand Anse beach is only five minutes away by foot. On the grounds is one of the best restaurants on the island, La Belle Créole (see my dining recommendations). Lunch is served around a pool bar.

La Sagesse Nature Center, P.O. Box 44, St. David's, Grenada, W.I. (tel.

809/444-6458), on a sandy, tree-lined beach, ten miles from Point Salines Airport, consists of a seaside guesthouse, restaurant, bar, art gallery and pottery, with watersports and satellite TV. Nearby are trails for hiking and exploring the area, a haven for wading and shore birds, hummingbirds, hawks, and ducks. Rivers, mangroves, and a salt pond sanctuary enhance the natural beauty of the place. The original great house of what was once La Sagesse plantation contains four apartments, each with a fully equipped kitchen. *Off-season, the price is $40 per couple daily.* From mid-December to mid-April, the rate is $50 per couple. The restaurant/bar specializes in lobster, fresh fish, and salads.

WHERE TO DINE: You may eat in all the restaurants of the hotels previously described, but you should call first to make a reservation, as food supplies are often limited if the chef doesn't know to expect you. I've found hotel food better in Grenada than in the other British Windward Islands. Many of the chefs are European or European trained, and local cooks are also on hand to prepare Grenadian specialties such as conch (called lambi here), lobster, callaloo soup (with greens and crab), conch-and-onion pie, and soursop or avocado ice cream. Turtle is also a favored dish, but please stick to nonendangered species in your menu selections.

It is estimated that some 22 kinds of fish, including fresh tuna, dolphin, and barracuda, are caught off the island's shores. Most are good for eating. Naturally, the spices of the island, such as nutmeg, are used plentifully. The cookery is often served family style in an open-air setting, opening onto a vista of the sea.

La Belle Créole, on the grounds at Blue Horizons, Grand Anse beach (tel. 809/444-4316), is one of the best restaurants in Grenada. Arnold and Royston Hopkin, who run it, are sons of "Mama" Audrey Hopkin, long considered the best cook on the island if you're seeking West Indian specialties. Archways frame views of the mountains and the beach. Lunch is served from noon to 2 p.m. every day, featuring such summertime snacks as soups, chicken, fish, or lobster salads. Lunch can be taken poolside. Dinner is table d'hôte, with a variety of choices featuring continental recipes with West Indian substitutions for foods not available on the island. A typical dinner might begin with dolphin (fish) mousse with callaloo, then conch chowder, followed by a main course such as Créole veal roll stuffed with ham, chicken livers, onions, and seasonings, baked in a wine sauce, and served with local vegetables such as a dasheen soufflé and christophines, along with candied plantain. This, plus a dessert of mango delight, would cost around $25. The walls and ceilings are covered with a type of island reed called *roseau,* which, strangely enough, must be cut only during a certain phase of the moon to provide a durable, long-lasting building surface. If cut at any other time of the month, experience has taught that the covering disintegrates into a powder within six months. Dinner begins promptly at 7 p.m. until the last order is accepted at 8:30. Each of the items on the table d'hôte is priced separately, to allow a guest to order only a main dish with coffee, for example.

Spice Island Inn, Grand Anse beach (tel. 809/444-4258). A favorite way to enjoy a meal in Grenada is on an uncrowded beachfront in the full outdoors, with only a well-designed parapet over your head to protect you from sudden tropical showers. At this inn, the view is of one of the best beaches in the Caribbean, miles of white sands, sprouting an occasional grove of sea grape or almond trees. The parapet looks like a Le Corbusier rooftop, built of imported pine and cedar, covering suntanned diners. An à la carte lunch, which you can eat in a swimsuit if you elect, costs from $15. Dinner menus change frequently and can be cooked to your specifications. They are usually table d'hôte, costing about $25 each and offering enough selections to make everyone happy. Meals are served seven days a week from 7:30 to 10 a.m., 12:30 to 2:30 p.m., and 7:30 to 9 p.m. Every Friday night there's a barbecue, costing EC$60 ($22.20), when a steel band is brought in. On Wednesday night, a buffet also costs EC$60.

Delicious Landing, The Carenage, St. George's (tel. 809/440-3948), is a popular restaurant at the entrance to the harbor, built on piers. Guests sit at tables supported by a mesh of beams, under a parapet of palm fronds. The setting is jauntily rickety and loaded with West Indian style. Some regular visitors argue that it offers yachting people one of the best views of whatever boat has just wandered into the harbor. The establishment is known for its soups, made with such fresh ingredients as callaloo, pumpkin, conch, and pigeon peas. You can select from the seafood salads and dinners made of ocean denizens that are probably only hours away from the fishing vessel. The restaurant is known for its conch steaks, cinnamon-fried chicken, sirloin sukiyaki, and fish pando simmered in local herbs and spices. One of the side dishes is a cheese-laden vegetable specialty called Grumby. My favorite drink is a cinnamon daiquiri. The place is open for food and drinks daily from 9:30 a.m. to midnight. Lunch is from 10:30 a.m. to 2 p.m., and dinner from 6:30 to 11:30 p.m. A three-course meal costs EC$35 ($12.95).

Rudolf's, The Carenage (tel. 809/440-2241), is a long-established restaurant overlooking this deep, U-shaped inner harbor lined with commercial establishments in St. George's. Some people claim this is the best place for dining on the entire island. You might call it "tropical Swiss." The restaurant is open for both lunch and dinner from 10 a.m. to midnight daily except Sunday. On the north corner of The Carenage, it's also a good spot for drinks in the late afternoon if you want to join the yachting machismo set. If you stick around for dinner, you'll find that the food is well prepared, with more choices offered on the menu than in most places at Grenada. You have a choice of about 13 different steak dishes, and if you're dining lighter, you're faced with a selection of some eight different omelets. Soups are both hot and cold, ranging from French onion to gazpacho. Try the lobster, fish, or conch. Specials are posted daily. Dinners begin at EC$35 ($12.95) but will range much higher if you order either steak or lobster as a main course.

The Nutmeg, also at The Carenage (tel. 809/440-2539), is right on the harbor, over the Sea Change Shop where you can pick up paperbacks and souvenirs. It's another rendezvous point for the yachting set and a favorite with just about everybody, both expatriates living on the island and visitors. It is suitable for a snack or a full-fledged dinner. from 11:30 a.m. to 11:30 p.m. Its drinks are very good. Try one of the Grenadian rum punches made with Angostura bitters, grated nutmeg, rum, lime juice, and syrup. An informal atmosphere prevails, as you're served your filet of fish with potato croquettes and string beans. There's always fresh fish, and usually callaloo soup, maybe lobster too, on most days. Lambi (that ubiquitous conch) is also done very well here. It can be so disguised you don't know what you're tasting. Lobster thermidor is the most expensive food item on the menu. Meals cost from EC$30 ($11.10). There's a small wine list with some California, German, and Italian selections. The sea view is good from the second-floor precincts, and you can drop in for just a glass of beer, staying as long as you wish. Sometimes, however, you'll be asked to share a table, but that's a good way to strike up a conversation. It is said that eventually, if you sit here long enough, everybody in Grenada will show up.

Coconut's Beach Restaurant, Grande Anse Beach (tel. 809/444-4644), at the bottom of a bumpy, sloping road, is actually more accessible by water than by land. Many of the guests come from yachts moored offshore. The restaurant occupies a ramshackle house with clapboard siding and a green roof. Set directly on the beach, it lies about half a mile north of St. George's. In the dining room you can watch the chefs prepare French and Créole specialties in the exposed kitchen.

The owners, Michel and Brigitte, open the place for bar service from 10 a.m. to 10 p.m. daily except Monday in low season. Meals are served from 10 a.m. to 3 p.m. and 7 to 10 p.m. This is probably the closest thing to Martinique you'll find on Grenada. Full meals cost from EC$50 ($18.50) and might include Tahitian-style fish, the catch of the day with a variety of sauces, curried conch with bananas, several barbecue dishes, T-bone steak, grilled lobster, pizzas, lobster gratin, and fisherman's platter.

Ristorante Italia, The Carenage (tel. 809/440-3986), is a pleasant restaurant on the second floor of a waterfront building in the geographical center of town offering a beautiful view of the inner harbor. The menu lists 15 varieties of pizza, costing EC$9 ($3.35) and up. Other offerings include eight types of spaghetti, four kinds of homemade fettuccine, eggplant parmigiana, cannelloni, and lobster thermidor. Full meals cost from EC$20 ($7.40). Lunch is served from noon to 2:30 p.m. Monday to Friday, dinner daily from 6 to 11 p.m. There is also full take-out service.

St. James Hotel, Grand Etang Rd., St. George's, Grenada, W.I. (tel. 809/440-2041), is a big, generously proportioned, old-fashioned, white-painted hotel on a hilltop overlooking the activity of St. George's. It caters to many local business people who consider it the best luncheon bargain in town. A fixed-price midday meal is offered every day except Sunday for EC$28 ($10.35), in an airy, light-filled dining room with good service. Dinner costs from EC$35 ($13) and includes an extra fish course not offered at the table d'hôte luncheon. Your meal might begin with an aromatic vegetable-and-chicken soup, then follow with a salad, along with conch casserole with tomatoes or a pungent beef stew with lots of hot peppers. An island dessert often featured is sopadilla delight. Lunch is from noon to 2 p.m. and dinner from 7 to 9 p.m. The 14-room hotel has some of the bargain rooms of the island for those devotees of little West Indian inns that rarely attract the beach-seeking tourist. Year-round rates EP are $30 to $40 in a single, $46 in a double.

Mamma's (tel. 809/440-1459) lies on the road leading to Grenada Yacht Services. Every trip to the Caribbean should include a visit to an establishment like Mamma's. Mamma (alias Insley Wardally) serves copious meals out of her private home to brawny local mechanics playing games of dominoes, quietly drunk fishermen stranded from nearby islands, Austrian yachtsmen, and groups of initially bewildered foreign tourists. She became particularly famous during the U.S. intervention in Grenada, as U.S. servicemen adopted her as their own island mama.

Mamma herself is as generous as her meals, which I was told came in two sizes: "the usual" and "the special." I telephoned ahead to order "the special," which, Mamma eventually told me, was really the same as "the usual." It included such dishes as callaloo soup with coconut cream, shredded cold crab with lime juice, freshwater crayfish, fried conch, and a casserole of cooked bananas, yams, and dasheen, along with ripe baked plantain, and tortillas made of curry and yellow chickpeas, followed by sugar apple ice cream. The specialty drink of the house is rum punch with cream, the ingredients of which are known only to Mamma. Dinner here must be reserved in advance, and it costs EC$36 ($13.30) per person, drinks extra. She is open seven nights a week, serving dinner from 7:30 p.m. to midnight. You must make reservations a day before you plan to go, and you'll be sure of having a choice from 26 to 30 different foods from Grenada, all locally done.

For change-of-pace dining, I suggest the **Bird's Nest,** Grand Anse (tel. 809/444-4264), in its own building with three palm trees at the entrance, opposite the Ramada Renaissance. This green-and-white restaurant is run by a Trinidadian-Grenadian couple, Derick and Lucy Steele, who give you a warm welcome. Their family business offers typical Chinese food, mainly Cantonese, along with Créole dishes. The most expensive main courses, of course, are those with a lobster base. You'll see the familiar shrimp eggrolls along with eight different chow meins. Sweet-and-sour fish is a favorite, and daily specials are posted. A take-out service is available. Expect to spend from $18 for a meal, served Monday through Saturday from 10:30 a.m. to 11 p.m. and on Sunday from 6 to 11 p.m.

Elsewhere on the island, I'd suggest the **Red Crab,** at L'Anse aux Épines (tel. 809/444-4424), which is popular with many Americans. It's a favorite Grenadian luncheon spot, set out under the trees. However, I always like to approach it in the evening, as your vehicle hurtles through an inky night. It's like an English pub in the mock Tudor style. Before taking your order, one of the waiters will bring you a draft beer, and you can settle back to enjoy the classic fish and chips prepared here. The chef also does some of the best stuffed crab backs on the island. You can also order a savory seafood chowder, or fried shrimp. Naturally, they offer callaloo soup. Dessert may perhaps be, say, blueberry pie à la mode. Your meal is likely to cost from EC$35 ($12.95). Hours are from 6 p.m. to midnight Monday, Wednesday, Thursday, and Sunday, from 6 p.m. to 1:30 a.m. Friday and Saturday. Closed Tuesday.

A Special Place

As you're touring north from the beach at Grand Anse and the capital at St. George's, one place is outstanding. It's Betty Mascoll's **Morne Fendue,** in St. Patrick's (tel. 809/440-9330). This 1912 plantation house constructed the year she was born, is her ancestral home. It was built of carefully chiseled river rocks held together with a mixture of lime and molasses, as was the custom in that day. Mrs. Mascoll and her loyal staff, two of whom have been with her for many, many years, always need time to prepare for the arrival of guests in advance, so it's imperative to call ahead. Lunch costs from EC$35 ($12.95) for nonresidents. The noonday repast is likely to include such local delights as yam and sweet potato casserole, curried port with lots of hot spices, and a hotpot of pork and oxtail. Because this is very much a private home, tipping should be performed with the greatest tact. Nonetheless, the hard-working cook and maid seem genuinely appreciative of a friendly gratuity.

Mrs. Mascoll has always lived in the house, except for a wartime stint in England. Her spacious living room is decorated with family portraits and heirlooms, including a patterned rug and heavily carved mahogany furniture. A collection of blue willow antique plates is displayed below the elaborate ceiling moldings. Mrs. Mascoll is known for introducing her house guests to her friends and neighbors on the long verandas beneath the hanging vines of her house. Her garden is host to several varieties of hummingbirds.

WHAT TO SEE: The capital city of Grenada, St. George's, is considered one of the most attractive ports, the picture-postcard variety, in the West Indies. Its landlocked inner harbor is actually the deep crater of a long-dead volcano, or so one is told.

In the town you'll see some of the most charming Georgian colonial buildings to be found in the Caribbean, still standing in spite of a devastating hurricane in 1955. The streets are mostly steep and narrow, and somehow this seems to enhance the attractiveness of the ballast bricks, wrought-iron balconies, the red tiles of the sloping roofs. Many of the pastel warehouses date back to the 18th century. Frangipani and flamboyant trees add to the palette of color.

The port, which some have compared to Portofino, is flanked by old forts and bold headlands. Among the town's attractions is an 18th-century pink-painted Anglican church, on Church Street, and a Market Square where colorfully attired farm women offer even more colorful produce for sale.

Fort George, built by the French, stands at the entrance to the bay, with subterranean passageways and old guardrooms and cells.

Everybody strolls along the waterfront, called **The Carenage,** where bustling activity is connected with the loading and unloading of schooners and the coming and going of the people in their little dinghies from moored yachts. The Carenage is best viewed on Tuesday afternoon when crates and bags of fruits and vegetables are loaded and bound for Trinidad.

On this side of town, the **Grenada National Museum,** at the corner of Young and Monckton streets, is set in the foundations of an old French army barrack and prison built in 1704. Small but interesting, it houses finds from archaeological digs, including the petroglyphs (the most recent discovery found in the autumn of 1980), native fauna, the first telegraph installed on the island, a rum still, and memorabilia depicting Grenada's history. The most comprehensive exhibit traces the Indian culture of Grenada. One of the exhibits shows two bathtubs—the wooden barrel used by the fort's prisoners and the carved marble tub used by Joséphine Bonaparte during her adolescence on Martinique. Hours are 9 a.m. to 3 p.m. Monday to Friday. Admission is 50¢ for adults, 10¢ for children.

The Outer Harbour is also called the **Esplanade.** It's connected to The Carenage by the Sendall Tunnel which is cut through the promontory known as St. George's Point, dividing the two bodies of water.

At the southern edge of town is the **Botanical Garden,** with a wide variety of tropical trees and flowers labeled so that you can identify them. Rare Caribbean animals and birds are kept in an adjoining zoo.

You can also take a drive up to Richmond Hill where **Fort Frederick** stands. The French built this fort in 1779, but before they could finish it, British troops had moved in. The English completed the structure in 1783. From its battlements, you'll have a superb view of the harbor and of the yacht marina.

An afternoon tour of St. George's and its environs should take you into the mountains northeast of the capital. About a 15-minute drive takes you to **Annandale Falls,** a tropical wonderland, where a cascade about 50 feet high falls into a basin. The overall beauty is almost Tahitian, and you can have a picnic surrounded by liana vines, elephant ears, and other tropical flora. Annandale Falls Center (tel. 809/440-2452) houses gift items, handcrafts, and samples of the indigenous spices of Grenada. Nearby, an improved trail leads to the falls where you can enjoy a refreshing swim. Swimmers can use the changing cubicles at the falls free. The center is open from 8 a.m. to 4 p.m. Monday to Friday.

A few miles away is **Grand Etang National Park,** encompassing the island's spectacular rain forest which has been made more accessible by hiking trails. Beginning at the park's forest center, the Morne LeBaye Trail affords a short hike along which you can see to the 2,309-foot Mt. Sinai and the east coast. Down the Grand Etang Road trails lead to the 2,373-foot summit of Mt. Qua Qua and the Ridge and Lake Circle Trail, taking hikers on a 30-minute trek along **Grand Etang Lake,** the crater of an extinct volcano lying in the midst of a forest preserve and bird sanctuary. Covering 13 acres, the water is a cobalt blue. All three trails offer the opportunity to see a wide variety of Grenada's flora and fauna. Guides for the park trails are available, but they must be arranged for in advance. The park's Nature Center on the shores of Grand Etang Lake is open daily from 8 a.m. to 4 p.m., featuring a video show about the park. Phone 809/440-7425 for more information or to arrange for guided trail walks.

The next day you can head north out of St. George's along the western coast, taking in beaches, spice plantations, and the fishing villages that are so typical of Grenada.

You pass through **Gouyave,** a spice town, the center of the nutmeg and mace industry. Both spices are produced from a single fruit. Before reaching the village you can stop at the Dougaldston Estate where you'll witness the processing of nutmeg and mace.

At the **Grenada Cooperative Nutmeg Association,** huge quantities of the spice are aged, graded, and processed. Most of the work is done within the ochre walls of the factory, which sprouts such slogans as "Bring God's peace inside and leave the Devil's noise outside." Women sit on stools in the natural light from the open windows of the aging factory, laboriously sorting the raw nutmeg and its by-product, mace, into different baskets for grinding, peeling, and aging.

Proceeding along the coast, you reach **Sauteurs,** at the northern tip of Grenada. This is the third-largest town on the island. It was from this great cliff that the Caribs leaped to their deaths instead of facing enslavement by the French.

To the east of Sauteurs is the palm-lined **Levera Beach,** an idyll of sand where the Atlantic meets the Caribbean. This is a great spot for a picnic lunch, but swimming can sometimes be dangerous. On the distant horizon you'll see some of The Grenadines.

The **River Antoine Rum Distillery** is where you can get an insight into the conditions under which "demon rum" was made 300 years ago. At the site, a series of hand-operated sluice gates set a water-operated sugarcane pulverizer into motion. At first glance the process is shockingly unsanitary (remember, this was the way it was done hundreds of years ago), but the finished product is distilled to a crystal clearness. It's reputed to be one of the best rums produced in the Caribbean. Don't be alarmed by the bats living in the top of the distillery's roof—they only attack insects. It might be advisable to contribute to the "retirement fund" of the employees after touring the premises.

Heading down the east coast of Grenada, you reach **Grenville,** the island's second city. If possible, pass through here on a Sunday morning when you'll enjoy the hubbub of the native fruit and vegetable market. There is also a fish market along the waterfront. A nutmeg factory here welcomes visitors.

From Grenville, you can cut inland into the heart of Grenada. Here you're in a world of luxuriant foliage, passing along nutmeg, banana, and cocoa plantations up to Grand Etang, previously mentioned. Your driver will then begin his descent from the mountains. Along the way you'll pass hanging carpets of mountain ferns. Going through the tiny hamlets of Snug Corner and Beaulieu, you eventually come back to the capital.

On yet another day, you can drive south from St. George's to the beaches and resorts spread along the already much-mentioned **Grand Anse,** which many people consider one of the most beautiful beaches in the West Indies. Water-taxis take you from The Carenage in St. George's to Grand Anse.

Point Salines, where the airport is now located, is at the southwestern tip of the island, where a lighthouse stood for 56 years. However, a sculpture of the lighthouse has been constructed on the grounds just outside the airside of the terminal building. A panoramic view ranging from the northwest side of Grenada to the green hills in the east to the undulating plains in the south can be seen from a nearby hill.

Along the way you'll pass through the village of **Woburn,** which was featured in the film *Island in the Sun,* and go through the sugar belt of **Woodlands,** with its tiny sugarcane factory.

This tour of the beaches and resorts is often called the "Royal Drive," named in honor of the route taken by Queen Elizabeth II and Prince Philip on their 1985 visit to the islands. In 1986, when President Ronald Reagan visited

Grenada, his tour took him along a newly constructed highway from the Airport into St. George's, via The Lagoon rood and on the Queen's Park, where a welcome rally was held in his honor.

SHOPPING: The one item everybody who visits Grenada comes home with is a basket of spices, better than any you're likely to find in your local supermarket. These hand-woven panniers of palm leaf or straw are full of items grown on the island, including the inevitable nutmeg, as well as mace, cloves, cinnamon, bay leaf, vanilla, and ginger. The local stores also sell a lot of luxury-item imports, mainly from England, at prices that are almost (not quite) duty free.

Store hours, in general, are 8 to 11:45 a.m. and 1 to 3:45 p.m. Monday to Saturday.

For your introduction to shopping on the island, head to **Grencraft,** Melville Street in St. George's (tel. 809/440-2655), which is the national outlet for all handcrafts made on the island. You'll find selections of straw, sisal, and khuskhus mats, along with the baskets, rugs, and hats for which Grenada is known. A fine selection of island-grown spices is sold, along with such condiments as nutmeg jam and jelly, hot sauce, and spice baskets. Many of the spices come in gift boxes. There are woodcarvings and utilitarian mahogany items, along with coral and coconut flex jewelry, plus calico dolls with spices inside. The shop enjoys a favorable waterside location which is reached by passing through Sendall Tunnel between The Carenage and the Esplanade.

One of the most interesting shops in St. George's is **Spice Island Perfumes Ltd.,** The Carenage (tel. 809/440-2006). This small store and workshop is open from 8:30 a.m. to 4:30 p.m. Monday through Friday, and from 9 a.m. to noon on Saturday. It produces and sells perfumes, potpourri, and teas made from the locally grown flowers and spices. If you desire, they'll spray you with a number of desired scents, helping you choose among such temptations as island flower, spice, frangipani, jasmine, patchouli, and wild orchid. The store also serves as the outlet for Spice Island cosmetics products, a range of high-quality Grenadian shampoos, conditioners, lotions, and other toiletries. It's also the exclusive distributor in Grenada for Caribelle Batik items and Kokonuts T-shirts. The shop stands near the harbor entrance, close to the Tourist Board, post office, public library, and Grencraft Handicraft Centre.

The most interesting shop for souvenirs and artistic items is **Yellow Poui Art Gallery,** Canash Hill, St. George's, in the next building after Barclays Bank. Here you can see oil paintings and watercolors, sculpture, prints, rare antique maps, engravings, and woodcuts, with prices beginning at $10 and going up. There is also a comprehensive display of newly acquired works from Grenada, the Caribbean area, and other sources, shown in four rooms, plus a continuous photography exhibition. The gallery is open from 8:30 a.m. to 4 p.m. Monday to Friday and from 9 a.m. to noon on Saturday. After hours, on weekends, and on holidays, phone 809/440-3001 for an appointment. Once there, you can check to see if their second gallery is open.

Noah's Arkade, Cross Street, St. George's (tel. 809/440-2482), in the center of town a block from the water, is a branch of the well-known chain of Caribbean gift shops. It sells handcrafts, straw articles, jewelry, stamps, film, postcards, books, and magazines.

Huggins, The Carenage (tel. 809/440-2031), deals in diamonds, precious stones, and gold and silver jewelry, plus china and crystal that includes world-renowned names such as Wedgwood, Aynsley, Blue Delft, Royal Doulton, Royal Brierley, Coalport, and Waterford. They also have such goods as designer sunglasses, scarves, and accessories.

Imagine, Grand Anse Shopping Centre (tel. 809/444-4028), offers an excellent line of Caribbean handcrafts in natural materials, including dolls, ceramics, straw items, clothing, and a good gift selection.

Tikal, Young Street (tel. 809/440-2310), is behind a narrow sidewalk at the side of a busy commercial street in an old-fashioned brick building. Inside is a collection of batik, terracotta, woodcarvings, wickerware, napery, and carved coconut shells.

THE SPORTING LIFE: The Spice Island can offer the kinds of diversions that urbanites yearn for, ranging from a few relaxing hours on a Sailfish cruising near the island's verdant coastline to a luxuriously catered week on a yacht. It could also include an afternoon in a small boat angling for the perfect dolphin, or a fiercely sunny day in search of that record-breaking big-game fish. Below the water's surface, other distractions appeal to sports lovers. Hundreds of varieties of fish and dozens of species of coral and sponges await your perusal, sometimes with underwater visibility stretching to 120 feet.

Beaches

Swimmers who simply enjoy the white sands of an almost-perfect island might want to spend their days at one of the best beaches in the Caribbean, **Grand Anse,** three miles of sugar-white sands extending into deep waters far offshore. Grenada, by the way, has a strictly enforced policy of public ownership of all beaches. Most of Grenada's best hotels are within walking distance of Grand Anse. In the unlikely event that you get bored there, you can take off and discover dozens more beaches on your own.

Water Sports

Along with many other water sports, Grenada offers the diver an underwater world, rich in submarine gardens, exotic fish, and coral formations. Off the coast is the wreck of the ocean liner *Bianca C,* which is nearly 600 feet long. Novice divers might want to stick to the west coast of Grenada, while more experienced divers might search out the sights along the rougher Atlantic side. Divers should know that Grenada doesn't have a decompression chamber for the relief of bends. Should this happen to you, it would require an excruciatingly painful air trip to Trinidad.

Grenada Yacht Services, P.O. Box 183, St. George's, Grenada, W.I. (tel. 809/440-2508), will arrange scuba-diving and snorkeling expeditions for beginners and intermediates. Resort-course dive packages are available. You can rent equipment, although it's supplied free for some activities. G.Y.S. also offers yacht charters, offshore fishing, and speedboat cruises.

Snorkeling and scuba-diving expeditions can also be arranged at **H.M.C. Diving Centre,** Coyaba Hotel, P.O. Box 336, St. George's, Grenada, W.I. (tel. 809/444-4129), as can a variety of other water sports.

Virgo Watersports, Horse Shoe Beach Hotel, P.O. Box 174, St. George's (tel. 809/444-4410), is a full-service operation offering water activities including scuba diving and chartering facilities from the hotel's beach for both guests and nonresidents. A PADI training facility offers dives at all levels. Prices, including equipment, range from $30 for one dive to $275 for 12 dives, including a night dive and visits to leading shipwreck sites. Courses, with a minimum of three persons required, range from a resort course for $65 to PADI certification courses for $325. Besides diving, activities available are snorkeling, waterskiing, parasailing. Such vehicles as waterscooters, pedal boats, Sunfish, and windsurfers are for rent. Deep-sea and bottom fishing, watertaxi trips, and sunset cruises can be arranged.

If you'd rather strike out on your own, take a drive to Woburn and negotiate with a fisherman for a ride to Glovers Island, an old whaling station, and snorkel away.

Golf

At the **Grenada Golf Course and Country Club,** you'll find a nine-hole course, charging greens fees of EC$15 ($5.55) for nine holes. The course is open Monday to Saturday from 8 a.m. to sunset (on Sunday from 8 a.m. to noon). From the course you'll have a view of both the Caribbean Sea and the Atlantic. Telephone 809/440-4128 for information.

Deep-Sea Fishing

Fishermen come here from November to March in pursuit of both blue and white marlin, yellowfin tuna, wahoo, sailfish, and other catches. Most of the bigger hotels have a sports desk which will arrange fishing trips for you.

Tennis

Tennis, like cricket and football, is a popular everyday sport in Grenada. Guests at the Secret Harbour, Calabash Hotel, and Twelve Degrees North can avail themselves of those well-kept courts. Otherwise, the **Richmond Hill Tennis Club** (no phone), which has two hard courts, will arrange a temporary membership for EC$20 ($7.40). Or as a nonmember you can play for EC$15 ($5.55) per person hourly. In addition, the **Tanteen Tennis Club** charges the same rates.

Boat Excursions

In St. George's, **The Loafer,** The Carenage (tel. 809/444-4371), an ocean-racing catamaran, departs Ramada Renaissance Beach every Thursday and Saturday, taking passengers for $20 per person on sunset and moonlight cruises weaving in and out of the coves and secret harbors of Grenada's coast. Private cruises can also be arranged. *The Loafer* was built in England for ocean racing. It's operated by Captain DeRoché, an enterprising young Grenadian.

Rhum Runner, P.O. Box 188, St. George's (tel. 809/440-3422), a metal-hulled catamaran with a parapet, moored at St. George's harbor, takes passengers on water tours for reef viewing, harbor trips, cocktail cruises, barbecue evenings, cruises up Grenada's coast, and all-you-can-drink punch cruises. Live, electronic, or steel-band music is offered. The cost is $20 per person.

Other charters can be arranged by getting in touch with **Grenada Yacht Services,** Lagoon Rd., P.O. Box 183, St. George's (tel. 809/440-2508). They'll arrange a charter on a 45-foot vessel between 9:30 a.m. and 4 p.m. on Saturday or Sunday, with rum punch and juice supplied. However, you're to bring your own lunch. The cost is $25 per person.

Hog Island is a convenient destination for anyone who presents a letter from his or her yacht club. An even more exotic destination would be to the so-called Bird Island, an unmarked and unnamed rocky island off the south shore of Grenada. There, thousands of white egrets nest each evening at dusk, flying away in one white mass at daybreak.

Another way to visit these islands is through **Henry's Woburn Tours** (tel. 809/443-5113), from 9 a.m. to 3 p.m. They go to the uninhabited Calivigny and Hog Islands just off the east coast of L'Anse aux Épines. You can enjoy the privacy of the beaches. Three-hour tours, such as one called "Southern Safari," cost EC$30 ($11.10) per person.

NIGHTLIFE: Regular evening entertainment is provided by the resort hotels. It includes steel bands, calypso, reggae, folk dancing, and limbo, even crab racing. But a lot of this activity depends on the house count at any given hotel. You'll have to ask at your hotel desk to find out what's happening at the time of your visit.

For those seeking culture, the 200-seat **Marryshow Folk Theatre,** Tyrell St. near Bain Alley, St. George's (tel. 809/440-2451), offers performances of Grenadian, American, and European folk music, drama, and West Indian interpretative folk dance. The theater is the home of the Tamarind Dance Troupe and the Vine Vwai La Grenada Dance Troupe. Check with Marryshow House or the tourist office to see what's on.

CARRIACOU: Largest of The Grenadines, Carriacou, "land of many reefs," is populated by about 8,000 inhabitants, mainly of African descent, who are scattered over its 13 square miles of mountains, plains, and white sand beaches. There's also a Scottish colony, and you'll see names such as "MacFarland." In the hamlet of Windward, on the east coast, villagers of mixed Scottish and African descent carry on the tradition of building wooden schooners. Large skeletons of boats in various stages of readiness line the beach where workmen labor with the most rudimentary of tools, building the West Indian trade schooner fleet. If you stop for a visit, a master boatsman will let you climb the ladder and peer inside the shell, and will explain which wood came from which island, and why he designed his boat in its particular way. The island's two peaks shoot skyward to almost 1,000 feet. Much of the population, according to reputation, is involved in smuggling. Otherwise, they are sailors, fishermen, shipwrights, and farmers.

The best time to visit Carriacou is in August in time for its **Regatta,** which was begun by J. Linton Rigg in 1965. It was started for work boats and schooners, for which The Grenadines are famous. Now work boats, three-masted schooners, and miniature "sailboats" propelled by hand join the festivities. Banana boats docking at the pier are filled with people rather than bananas, and sailors from Bequia and Union Island camp on tiny Jack-a-Dan and Sandy Isle, only 20 minutes away by outboard motor from Hillsborough. The people of The Grenadines try their luck at the greased pole, foot races, and of course the sailing races. Music fills the air day and night, and impromptu parties are held. At the three-day celebration, Big Drum dancers perform in the Market Square, as the sound of conga drums fills the air.

The **Big Drum dance** is part of the heritage of Carriacou brought from Africa and nurtured here more purely than perhaps on any other Caribbean island. The "Go Tambo," or Big Drum, is an integral part of such traditional events as stone feasts (marking the setting of a tombstone) and the accompanying rites. The feast, called *saraca,* and setting of the tombstone may be as long as 20 years after a death, marking the time when the grave is entombed, or formally marked with a gravestone. Another event involving the Big Drum and saracas is the *maroon.* This can involve a dream interpretation, but it seems actually to be just a regular festivity, held in various places during the dry season, with dancing and feasting. Boat launching may also be accompanied by the Big Drum and the saraca and usually draws crowds of participants.

Hillsborough is the chief port and administrative center, handling the commerce of the little island which is based mainly on growing limes and cotton. The capital bustles on Monday when the produce arrives, then settles down again until "mail day" on Saturday. The capital is nestled in a mile-long crescent of white sand.

The **Carriacou Museum** has a carefully selected display of Amerindian artifacts, European china and glass shards, and exhibits of African culture. In two small rooms it preserves Carriacou's history, which parallels that of its sister island, Grenada.

Also in Carriacou is the **Sea Life Centre,** created by the North American
Environmental Research Products organization and designed to educate both
the islanders and visitors about sea life, especially the lambi (conch) and turtle. It
features native paintings of fishermen at work, drawings of the life cycles of the
sea's inhabitants, and microscopes and incubators set up for visitors to view the
baby lambi and turtles that the center breeds.

The island attracts escapists, a sports-oriented crowd who spend their time
fishing, snorkeling, waterskiing, and sailing. Of course, you can just go beachcombing.

Getting There and Getting Around

Visitors arrive on the twice-weekly produce and mail **boats** from Grenada,
the trip taking five hours. A far faster method of transport is on a nine-seat **plane,**
which takes just 25 minutes from the Point Saline International Airport in Grenada. A terminal building opened officially in 1984 at Carriacou's Lauriston Airport. For information on air service between Carriacou and Grenada, see "Local
Air Services" in the Grenada section, above. Boat service, other than the mail
boat described in the section entitled "The Grenadines," is provided by *Alexia
II, Adelaide B,* and *Eastward,* which leave Grenada on Wednesday and Saturday
at 10 a.m., arriving at Carriacou at 2 p.m. The Carriacou-to-Grenada voyage
leaves at 10 a.m. on Monday and Thursday, reaching Grenada at 2 p.m. The fare
is EC$20 ($7.40) per person each way.

Food and Lodging

Prospect Lodge, Carriacou, Grenada, W.I. (809/443-7380), on the tranquil leeward side, is three-quarters of a mile from Bogles Village and two miles
north of Hillsborough. Guests at this comfortable lodge can engage in hiking,
snorkeling, fishing, boating, or just lounging around. Lee and Ann Katzenbach,
the owners, have pleasant rooms, a library guests can use, and the requisite binoculars, snorkel gear, small boats, helpful advice, and local guides to take you on
expeditions. Lee is a painter and sculptor, and Ann's a photographer and writer.
Both are knowledgeable about the activities possible on the island. Accommodations are in the main house, in an apartment addition connected to Prospect
House by a breezeway, and in a separate building, Orchard Cottage. Bedrooms
rent for $25 daily in a single, $30 in a double. The apartment costs $45 single,
$50 double, and the cottage goes for $50 for one or two persons, $65 for three or
four guests. Half board is priced at an additional $15 per person per day.

Silver Beach Resort, Beauséjour Bay, Carriacou, Grenada, W.I. (tel. 809/
443-7337), is a small hotel lying about a five-minute walk north of Hillsborough
on a mile-long white sand beach. Accommodations comprise eight villas, each
spacious with both a bedroom, a living room, a private bath, a fully equipped
kitchenette, and a patio; and there are also ten bedrooms, each with a sea view
from its own patio. In winter, the single EP rate is $60 daily, the price of a double
being $70. *In summer, singles cost $50 on EP, and doubles go for $55.* Charges for
housekeeping quarters are $60 for a single in a one-bedroom unit in winter, $70
for the same accommodations as a double. A two-bedroom apartment sleeping
four persons rents for $105. *In summer, the one-bedroom housekeeping unit costs
$50 single daily, $55 double, and $85 is charged for a two-bedroom self-contained
accommodation sleeping four.* The charges include gas, electricity, linen, cutlery,
and crockery. The bar and dining pavilion is found between the cottages and the
beach. At dinner you can sample some good local dishes prepared by native cooks
and including lobster, conch, and fresh fish. Locally grown vegetables and fruits
are served. Fishing, snorkeling, scuba-diving, windsurfing, and boating to near-

by islands can be arranged, including trips to World's End Reef in the Tobago Cays. Tennis is also available.

Cassada Bay Resort, Carriacou, Grenada, W.I. (tel. 809/443-7494), opened in 1988 on a site offering stunning views of the bay. Its accommodations of rough-cut timber, in nine cabins of two units, have pine furniture, bedrooms, living rooms, baths, and verandas, plus maid service. *Off-season, singles rent for $55 daily, MAP, and doubles go for $75.* In winter, the MAP price is $65 in a single, $85 in a double. The dining room serves traditional West Indian cuisine, and the resort has a bar. Water sports are available, with free ferry service to nearby islands for snorkeling, sunbathing, and exploring.

PETIT MARTINIQUE: The only inhabited one of Carriacou's offshore islands and also the largest is 486-acre Petit (pronounced *pitty*) Martinique, with a population of about 600. The chief occupation is listed as building and sailing fishing boats, but it's also famous as the center of the smuggling trade among the islands. Cigarettes and liquor from St. Barts' and St. Maarten's duty-free ports are popular smuggled goods.

BARBADOS

□ □ □

In the 19th century Barbados became famous as "the sanatorium of the West Indies," attracting mainly British guests suffering from the vapors who came here for the perfect climate and the relaxed, unhurried life.

In 1751 Maj. George Washington visited Barbados with his half-brother Maj. Lawrence Washington, who had developed tuberculosis. Regrettably, the future American president contracted smallpox there, which left him marked for life. Barbados is said to have been the only place outside what is now the United States that George Washington ever visited.

The smallpox danger long gone, Barbados still remains salubrious to the spirit, with its mixture of coral and lush green vegetation, along with seemingly endless miles of pink and white sandy beaches. The most easterly of the long chain of Caribbean islands, it still retains its Old World charm, an imprint of grace and courtesy left over from 300 years of British tradition.

Barbados is renowned for the friendliness of its hospitable people and for having the oldest parliament in the western hemisphere, with a British heritage unbroken since the first landing by Englishmen in 1625 until its independence in 1966. The 350th anniversary of the Barbados parliament was celebrated in 1989. And Barbados is one Caribbean island *not* explored by Columbus.

In a way, Barbados is like an England in the tropics, with its bandbox cottages with neat little gardens, its centuries-old parish churches, and a scenic, hilly district in the north known as "Little Scotland" where a mist rises in the morning. Narrow roads ramble through green sugarcane fields trimmed in hedgerows. Sugar is king, and rum is queen.

The first known inhabitants of Barbados were the Arawak Indians, who came over from South America. But they were gone by the time of the first British expedition in 1625. Two years later Capt. John Powell returned to colonize the island with 80 settlers who arrived at Jamestown (later renamed Holetown).

A thriving colony of Europeans and black slaves turned Barbados into a prosperous land, based on trading in tobacco and cotton, and by 1640, sugarcane. More and more slaves were imported to work these sugar plantations.

Many English families settled here in the 18th and 19th centuries, in spite of the usual plagues such as yellow fever or the intermittent wars. Because of the early importation of so many slaves, Barbados is the most densely populated of the West Indian islands, numbering some 258,000 souls.

Once Barbados was the most heavily defended fortress island in the Caribbean, as 26 forts ran along its 21 miles of sheltered coast. Perhaps for that reason, the island was never invaded. Slavery was abolished in 1834, and independence within the Commonwealth was obtained in 1966.

A coral island, Barbados is flat compared to the wild, volcanic terrain of the Antilles. It is 21 miles long and 14 miles wide. Most of its hotels are on the western side, a sandy shoreline. The eastern side, fronting the Atlantic, is a breezy coastline with white-capped rollers. Experienced surfers like it, but it's not safe for amateur swimmers.

It's a land of hills and dales, limousines (carrying such residents as Claudette Colbert) and donkey carts. You'll find hills, but not mountains. The highest point is Mount Hillaby at 1,115 feet. The island is shaped like a shoulder of lamb.

Barbados lies 200 miles from Trinidad and only 4½ jet hours from New York.

GETTING THERE: Flights are most often directed through New York's JFK Airport or through San Juan. From either of these cities, **American** has daily nonstop flights (and sometimes twice a day) to Barbados.

Currently, high-season round-trip prices from New York to Barbados are $395 per person for flights Monday through Thursday, going up to $425 for flights departing in either direction on Friday, Saturday, or Sunday. Passengers who opt for a transfer of aircraft in San Juan pay $20 less. Tickets at the prices cited require a seven-day advance purchase or a 14-day advance purchase if you opt to transfer in San Juan. A stopover ranging from 3 to 21 days is required in Barbados.

Pan Am flies daily nonstop from New York. **Air Canada** has nonstop service four times a week in midwinter (and three times a week in summer) from Toronto, with connections to dozens of cities in Canada. Eastern operates a nonstop daily flight from Miami departing at 5:30 p.m. in enough time for connections to be completed to most sections of North America.

Flying time from New York to Barbados is 4½ hours, from Miami to Barbados 3½ hours, and from Toronto to the Barbados around 5 hours.

GETTING AROUND: You're faced with a number of options: You can rent a taxi (expensive), rent a bike or scooter (inexpensive), take a bus (very inexpensive), rent a car (expensive), or walk around this island in the sun (very, very inexpensive).

Taxis

Typical of this part of the world, taxis aren't metered, but their rates are fixed by the government. Taxis on the island are identified by the letter "Z." One to five passengers are transported at the same time, and can share the fare among themselves. Overcharging is infrequent; most drivers have a reputation for courtesy and honesty. Taxis are plentiful, and drivers will produce a list of standard rates, outlining fares between Grantley Adams International Airport and the major hotels. For example, it costs $10 U.S. to be taken from the airport to Crane Beach. From the airport to the Barbados Hilton costs $11.

Buses

Unlike most of the British Windwards, Barbados has a reliable bus system. Haitian buses may be more colorful, but Bajan buses have springs and fan out from Bridgetown to almost every part of the island. On most of the major routes there are buses running every 15 minutes or so. Bus fares are $1 BDS (50¢) wherever you go. Exact change is required.

Car Rentals

If you don't mind *driving on the left,* as you'll have to do in all the British Windward Islands, you may find a self-drive car ideal for a Bajan holiday. A temporary permit is needed if you don't have an International Driver's License. Go to the police desk upon your arrival at the airport. You're charged a registration fee of $10 BDS ($5), and you must have your own license. The speed limit is 20 miles per hour within the city limits, 30 mph elsewhere on the island. The main police station is at Bridgetown (tel. 809/436-6600).

Sunset Crest Rent-a-Car, Sunset Crest, St. James (tel. 809/432-1482), launched in 1968, has the largest fleet of Mini-Mokes on the island. They rent for about $300 BDS ($150) per week. Most cars rent for $350 BDS ($175) to 400 BDS ($200) per week.

In addition to Sunset, another leading car-rental firm is **National Car Rental,** Strathclyde, St. Michael (tel. 809/426-0603), which offers a wide selection of Mokes and well-maintained cars. This company will deliver and pick up a car at your hotel.

Dear's Garage, Roebuck St., Bridgetown (tel. 809/429-9277), features 24-hour emergency road service, renting such vehicles as an Australian Moke, a Caribbean Cub, or a Suzuki (with manual or automatic transmission). If you want to rent a car, they will arrange to have you picked up free at your hotel.

All of these firms cited will issue you a visitor's driving permit so you don't have to make the trip to the police station.

Scooters and Bicycles

To rent a motor scooter—they call it "to hire" here—you must be 21 years of age and in possession of a valid motorcycle license or automobile driver's license with a motorcycle endorsement.

Mrs. Wells at **Jumbo Rentals** can rent you one for $200 BDS ($100) per week, with a $100 BDS ($50) deposit. You'll be supplied free with a helmet, compulsory by law.

Sightseeing Taxi Tours

Nearly all Bajan taxi drivers are familiar with the entire island, and usually like to show it off to visitors. If you can afford it, touring by taxi is far more relaxed than, and preferable to, taking one of the standardized bus tours. A 4½-hour tour of the island costs about $75 U.S. for a party of up to five persons.

Sightseeing Bus Tours

One of the leading minibus tour operators is **United Taxi Owners Association,** High St., St. Michael (tel. 809/426-0284). Almost any type of land tour can be organized and negotiated with these people. A five-hour island tour is likely to cost from $15 to $20 U.S. per person on a minibus.

PRACTICAL FACTS: Barbados is an independent sovereign state within the Commonwealth of Nations, of which Queen Elizabeth II is the symbolic head. British traditions are still strong.

American Consul: The United States Department of State maintains a Consular Section, first floor, Trident House, Bridgetown (tel. 809/426-3574).

Banks: Most banks in Barbados are open from 8 a.m. to 3 p.m. Monday to Thursday and from 8 a.m. to 1 p.m. on Friday, later reopening from 3 to 5:30 p.m.

Currency: The Barbados dollar (BDS) is the official currency, available in $100, $20, $10, $5, and $1 notes, as well as $1, 25¢, and 10¢ silver coins, plus 5¢ and 1¢ copper coins. The Bajan dollar is worth 50¢ in U.S. currency. Currency translations given in this chapter are only for the reader's convenience, and are subject to change. *Note:* Unless otherwise specified, currency quotations are in U.S. dollars. Most stores take traveler's checks or U.S. dollars. However, it's best to convert your money at banks and pay your bills in Bajan dollars.

Documents: A U.S. citizen coming directly from America to Barbados for a period not exceeding three months must have proof of identity and national status, such as an original birth certificate, citizenship papers, a driver's license with photograph, university or school ID card with photograph, job ID with photograph, or senior citizen card with photograph. For longer than three months, a passport is required. An ongoing or return ticket is also necessary.

Electricity: The electricity is 110 volts AC, 50 cycles, so at most establishments recommended you can use your U.S.-made appliances.

Holidays: Public holidays are January 1, Good Friday, Easter Monday, May Day (May 1), Whit Monday, Kadoment Day (a variable holiday), United Nations Day (first Monday in October), Independence Day (November 30), Christmas Day, and Boxing Day (December 26).

Language: The Barbadians, or *Bajans,* as they are called, speak English, but with their own island lilt.

Mail: Most hotel desks can attend to your mailing. Otherwise, the Main Post Office is in the Public Buildings of Bridgetown.

Medical care: A 600-bed hospital, the Queen Elizabeth (tel. 809/436-6450), is in Bridgetown. There are as well several private clinics, including the 135-bed St. Joseph Hospital (tel. 809/422-2232), operated by a Roman Catholic order in St. Peter Parish.

Taxes and service: When you leave, you'll have to pay a $16 BDS ($8) departure tax. Not only that, but when you go to pay your hotel bill, you'll find you've been charged an 8% government sales tax. And while I'm on the subject, most hotels and restaurants add at least a 10% service charge to your bill.

Telecommunications: You should have no trouble with telecommunications out of Barbados. Telegrams may be sent at your hotel front desk or at the **Barbados External Telecommunications Ltd.,** offices on Lower Broad Street in Bridgetown, which is open from 9 a.m. to 5 p.m. weekdays and 8 a.m. to 1 p.m. on Saturday. Telex and data-access services are also available. From the United States, you can call Barbados direct by dialing area code 809, then the local seven-digit number.

Water: Barbados has a pure water supply. It's pumped from underground sources in the coral rock which covers six-sevenths of the island, and it's safe to drink.

Weather: Daytime temperatures are in the 75° to 85° Fahrenheit range throughout the year.

1. HOTELS OF THE ISLAND

Per square inch, Barbados has the best hotels in the West Indies. Here you get elegant comfort; the atmosphere is often that of an English house party. Most of the hotels are small and personally run, with a quiet, restrained dignity.

Most of my recommendations are sited on St. James Beach, the fashionable sector. However, you'll have to head south from Bridgetown to such places as Hastings and Worthing for the best bargains, often in self-contained efficiencies or studio apartments where you can do your own cooking.

So as not to paint too rosy a picture, I'll give the bad news. Because of Barbados's long and continuing popularity, nowadays with back-to-back charter groups, the tariffs charged in these hotels often are, in my opinion, outrageous in high season. Many hotels will also insist that you take two meals at their establishments if you're there in the winter.

Barbados has some very good bargains as well, and I've surveyed the best of these too, on my most recent hotel hop around the island (see the end of this section). Prices cited in this section, unless otherwise indicated, are in U.S. dollars.

THE DELUXE RESORTS: A spectacular place to stay, **Royal Pavilion,** St. James, Barbados, W.I. (tel. 809/422-5555), a Pemberton hotel, is next door to Glitter Bay, which the chain also owns. The lavish and lush resort was built on the site of the former Miramar Hotel. The architects came up with a California hacienda style for their 72 waterfront junior suites and a villa consisting of three suites in eight acres of beautifully landscaped gardens. British grace and Bajan hospitality blend happily in this aristocratic property, which became one of the finest resorts in Barbados the moment it opened.

In shoulder and summer season, two persons pay from $140 to $240 daily, depending on their accommodation. The MAP supplement is $50 per person per day. Peak rates are charged in winter, when two persons pay from $280 to $390 daily, plus an MAP surcharge of $60 per person per day. Naturally, the villa for six persons and the one-bedroom oceanfront penthouse are far more expensive. Facilities include a freshwater swimming pool, two tennis courts (complimentary

for guests day and night), and two oceanfront restaurants. Tabora's, serves three meals a day. The Palm Terrace, with an open-air loggia, is open only for dinner, offering an à la carte menu of Caribbean and international fare. The chef specializes in flambé dishes, and on Wednesday night, a full international buffet is presented. The hotel offers a good water sports program and has duty-free shopping in its courtyard, featuring a Cartier shop, Yves St. Laurent, and Ferrari. There is also a beauty shop.

Glitter Bay, St. James, Barbados, W.I. (tel. 809/422-5555), places its emphasis on luxury. Of the 46 available Moorish-style units, 7 are three-bedroom penthouses, 29 are two-bedroom suites, which will convert into one-bedroom suites with kitchen, and the final 10 are one-bedroom suites. Each of the elegantly furnished accommodations has a private bath with double vanity, tub, and shower as well as an air-conditioned bedroom with a large private terrace. Suites feature fully equipped kitchens. The resort lies on a ten-acre site. All its units are on a series of descending terraces, giving guests a view from either patio or balcony. All rooms are doubles, rented as singles in summer only, and some of the biggest accommodations are suitable for four to six persons. *In summer, the single rate ranges from $125 to $185 daily, with a twin renting for $140 to $200. The MAP supplement is $50 per person per day.* In winter, a twin-bedroom rents for $280 to $305 daily, depending on the time of year, plus an MAP supplement of $60 per person daily. Of course, suites and penthouses are far more expensive.

The circular eatery here is Piperade, offering both classical and nouvelle cuisine, along with West Indian specialties. On Monday, a gala Bajan buffet is presented, and Friday is barbecue night. The Sunset Beach Bar is a popular rendezvous spot for a sundowner. Guests can dance under the stars and enjoy local entertainment such as a steel band or calypso. There is a full range of water sports provided on a complimentary basis, including waterskiing, windsurfing, snorkeling, and catamaran sailing. Many other activities, such as golf and horseback riding, can be arranged. Two tennis courts are lit at night.

Cobblers Cove Hotel, Cobblers Cove, St. Peter, Barbados, W.I. (tel. 809/422-2291), on the northwest coast, grew out of a beachfront mansion built, like a fort, with crenellations—which evidently appealed to someone's fancy. The home was erected over the site of a former British fort which used to protect vessels going into Speightstown, a mile away. Today, after its remake, the hotel is a favorite honeymoon retreat, offering 38 first-class suites in a phalanx of ten Iberian-style villas, each with air conditioning. Overlooking a white sand beach, each unit has a spacious living room, private balcony or patio, and a kitchenette. A full American breakfast appears daily in your suite, and late in the afternoon another waiter returns to take your dinner order. Beachfront units cost more than garden-view apartments. In winter, MAP twins range in price from $400 to $460 daily. *MAP couples in summer pay $195 to $215.* There are many acres of well-developed tropical gardens and lawns, including coconut palms and flowering shrubbery. A beach bar serves tropical drinks, which are more potent than you might think. The suites have been wisely placed throughout the gardens in horseshoe patterns, each making use of natural woods. The open-air, shingle-roofed dining room overlooks the sea, and the loggia living room reflects the taste of Richard and Jan Williams, who have owned and managed the property for many years.

Treasure Beach, St. James, Barbados, W.I. (tel. 809/432-1094), is a little resort that has the most loyal clientele of any hotel on the island. It's small but choice, known for its superb food and the comfort and style of its amenities. A gracious resort, Treasure Beach is indeed a treasure. Owner managed, it is both intimate and relaxed, with personalized service a mark of the well-trained staff. It is set in tropical gardens at the edge of a white sandy beach in St. James in the glitter "hotel belt" of Barbados. The bar is open to the gardens, and it is here that you can order tropical fruit drinks or whatever.

The accommodations are beautifully furnished in a tropical motif, and each of the 12 one-bedroom, air-conditioned units is a suite housed in one of the two-story villas that dot the property. They open onto private balconies or patios. Some guests prefer the upper level for more privacy. Amenities include valet and laundry service, safety deposit boxes, direct-dial phones, and a host of other thoughtful extras. In winter, two persons are charged from $195 to $270 daily, depending on the accommodation, plus an MAP supplement of $50 per person per day. *In summer, single or double occupancy costs from $95 to $140 daily, and the MAP supplement is $35 per person per day.* Even if you aren't staying here, try to sample some of its culinary specialties, including freshly caught seafood and island favorites from the Bajan culinary repertoire. The Monday night buffet, costing $50 BDS ($25), is an island event. You choose from an array of succulent dishes, such as roast prime rib and baked wholefish, along with delectable desserts. Lunch is served from noon to 2 p.m. and dinner from 7 to 9:30 p.m.

TRADITIONAL FAVORITES: A pocket of posh, **Coral Reef Club,** St. James Beach, Barbados, W.I. (tel. 809/422-2372), is one of the best and most respected resorts on the island. A Relais et Châteaux, its innkeepers, Budge and Cynthia O'Hara, are by now a virtual legend in Barbados, setting standards that are hard for their competitors to attain. Private cottages surround a main building, which is the lobby and reading room, with some guest rooms on the second floor. The cottages are scattered about a dozen handsomely landscaped acres with manchineels and casuarinas, fronting a long strip of white sandy beach, ideal for swimming. Rooms are air-conditioned and open onto private patios. There's a bath with each unit, and some of the rooms have separate dressing rooms as well. Lacy straw carpets evoke the West Indian touch. *In summer, MAP singles range from $90 to $140 daily and doubles from $158 to $270.* In winter, the single full-board rate is $180 to $269 daily, with doubles going for $290 to $460, also on the AP. When not on the sands, you can go for a dip in the pool before taking lunch in an open-air area, sharing your meal with the sugar birds. Dining and wining in the evening is most gracious, in an attractive room overlooking the ocean. A first-class continental chef is in the kitchen. There's a weekly folklore show and barbecue, and a Bajan buffet on Sunday evening, featuring a "Steamship Round of Beef," along with whole baked fish.

Sandy Lane, St. James, Barbados, W.I. (tel. 809/432-1311), is a great house–style Trust House Forte Hotel. The place represents luxury on a small scale, with beautiful suites and rooms, a private beach on one side, an 18-hole golf course on the other. In between are some fine all-weather tennis courts. The swimming pool is surrounded by Italianate gardens, Roman fountains, and colonnaded verandas. Sandy Lane was built on 380 choice acres of Bajan real estate on what had been a sugar plantation.

The suites and apartments are set in gardens extravagantly planted that attract many birds and rare butterflies. The buildings are in cut coral, with shingle roofs, baronial arches, high ceilings, and a porte-cochère—in all, grand-estatelike with tall gates, a driveway, and ornamental steps. All 112 rooms and suites have private baths and air conditioning. From December 19 to March 4, with MAP included, singles cost $410 to $525 daily, with doubles going for $480 to $575. Within this bracket, the higher prices are charged between Christmas and New Year's. *Off-season, EP singles cost from $300 to $340 daily, and doubles rent for $335 to $370.* You can order a cool salad at the pool at lunchtime, later enjoying a continental-inspired candlelight dinner. Groaning buffet tables are frequent, as is regular native entertainment such as calypso. You can also dine in the Seashell restaurant in winter only.

Colony Club, St. James Beach, Barbados, W.I. (tel. 809/422-2335). The entrance to this topnotch resort hotel is impressive, lined with Australian pines. This Bajan "residential club" lies about eight miles from Bridgetown on this well-known beach. An elegant feeling still prevails, even though the Colony has grown from a small "house party"–type establishment to a complex of some 75 rooms which look out on shaded verandas and handsomely landscaped grounds. Twenty-eight of the Colony's rooms are built in the vicinity of the beach, and all units have private patios and air conditioning. Accommodations are clustered in two- and three-story Mediterranean-style bungalows with red-tile roofs. The main building is the oldest, reflecting serenity and Bajan architecture. Sliding glass doors open onto sun terraces. Some units are so close to the pool you can almost dive in. *In summer, MAP singles range from $135 to $165 daily, and doubles go for $175 to $225.* In winter, MAP singles are priced at $210 to $270, while doubles pay $250 to $345. Both a continental cuisine and West Indian specialties are served on a covered terrace, a gracious setting for dining. The club's barbecues are well known here, and deservedly so. Entertainment, such as calypso, limbo, and dancing to a combo, is provided.

OTHER LEADING HOTELS: In more than 14 acres of elegantly landscaped gardens, **Barbados Hilton,** P.O. Box 510, Needham's Point, St. Michael, Barbados, W.I. (tel. 809/425-0200), is a self-contained resort, although it lies on the heavily populated southern edge of Bridgetown. Built in 1966 and overhauled and redecorated several times since then, it occupies the rugged peninsula where, in the 18th century, the English navy built Fort Charles, today little more than a crumbling but picturesque ruin. The Hilton's architecture incorporates porous blocks of bleached coral interspersed with jutting balconies and huge expanses of glass.

The bedrooms are arranged around a central courtyard filled with tropical gardens, and vines cascade from the skylit roof. Each of the comfortable units has air conditioning, color TV, mini-bar, well-equipped bath, and a balcony exposed to a view of Carlisle Bay on the north side or the Atlantic on the south. *Singles in summer on the EP rent for $89 to $109 daily and doubles for $98 to $108.* In winter, tariffs on the EP are $152 to $190 daily in singles, $170 to $208 in doubles. A popular restaurant, whose backdrop is a row of re-created clapboard Créole houses, serves Bajan and international specialties to the accompaniment of live music. The hotel has a small-stakes casino and both a beachfront day bar and an intimately alluring nighttime bar. Several kinds of water sports are included on the milk-white sands of the nearby beach, whose outermost edge is protected from storm damage by a riprap breakwater. On the premises are tennis courts, access to horseback riding, a sauna, a health club, and a masseur for tired muscles.

Grand Barbados Beach Resort, P.O. Box 639, Bridgetown, Barbados, W.I. (tel. 809/426-0890), lies on the outskirts of town on a flat and sandy plot of beachfront ringed by trees, not far from the Barbados Hilton. The lavishly renovated 133-room deluxe hotel is on Carlisle Beach about a mile from Bridgetown. The bedrooms all have air conditioning, balconies, mini-bars, satellite TV and in-room movies, hairdryers, safes, direct-dial phones in bedrooms and baths, and 24-hour room service. The two top stories of the hotel form the Aquatic Club Executive Floors, with certain extra amenities, such as complimentary cocktails, a continental breakfast, and pastries with coffee in the executive lounge at night. In winter, EP rates are $180 to $230 daily for singles, $200 to $260 for doubles. The top prices are for rooms in the Aquatic Club. Luxury pier suites with big balconies and panoramic views are $400 to $500 per day. *Off-season,*

singles rent for $110 to $130, doubles for $120 to $150, and suites for two for $210.
MAP can be arranged for another $50 per person per day. An extra person costs
$35 per day except for children under 12 who can share a room with two adults
free. Complete facilities are available for handicapped guests.

The hotel maintains its own 35-foot trimaran for ocean-going lunches and
sunset cruises, and provides an array of complimentary water sports. Perhaps best
of all, the hotel has a rambling pier jutting out into the sea, at the end of which is a
pleasant seafood restaurant, the Schooner, known for its buffets. Two other restaurants provide a range of menus, including the Golden Shell, the most elegant
and relatively formal dining room, the Coral Garden cocktail lounge, and a
coffeeshop, the Boardwalk Café on the pier, where nightly entertainment is
provided. Along with a variety of shops in the garden area, the Grand Barbados
has a massage room, an exercise room, a sauna, and a Jacuzzi.

Marriott's Sam Lord's Castle, St. Philip, Barbados, W.I. (tel. 809/423-
7350 or toll free 800/228-9290). If you lodge here in the "Regency Rascal's"
main house, it's like seeking an accommodation in a kind of Bajan Mount Ver-
non. The great house was built in 1820 and craftsmen were sent over from England to reproduce the queen's castle at Windsor. These ceilings look down on
the art of Reynolds, Raeburn, and Chippendale. According to legend, Samuel
Hall Lord built the estate on money acquired by luring ships to wreck on the
rocks of Cobbler's Reef by placing lanterns in the trees on his estate. He piled up a
fortune by looting the wrecked ships. Set on 72 imaginatively landscaped acres
with rare flowering trees, the estate has a wide, lengthy private sandy beach edged
by tall coconut trees, as well as seven professional tennis courts which are lit at
night. The location is about 14 miles out of Bridgetown, heading east beyond the
airport, which is a distance of 15 minutes by taxi. You can swim in any of three
pools which are built free form to look like small ponds or lakes. Other facilities
include a games room, exercise room, shuffleboard, table tennis, library, beauty
shop, and barbershop. Golf, sailing, horseback riding, snorkeling, waterskiing,
fishing, luncheon and nighttime cruises, and other outside activities are available
on the island and can be arranged by the activities director.

There are 256 guest rooms including 16 suites. All accommodations are air-
conditioned with private baths. There is a service charge and government tax
added to all bills. In high season, single or double occupancy costs $190 to $245
per day. The most expensive units are the castle rooms, in the main building. *In
shoulder season, March to May 14, single or double accommodations cost from $115 to
$135 daily, and in low season, singles or doubles go for $95 to $115.* There is a whole
list of dining and entertainment places, including the Sea Grill, open for breakfast, lunch, and dinner. Breakfast and dinner are also served in the Wanderer Restaurant, and you can order a hamburger at Sam's Place, right on the beach. There
are many bars as well. A Bajan Fiesta night in the hotel's Bajan Village is offered
once a week, as is a shipwreck barbecue and beach party with a steel drum band, a
limbo show, and fire-eaters on South Beach. Slot machines are available for play
every day, and goat races are held on the beach every Saturday.

Tamarind Cove, St. James Beach, P.O. Box 429, Bridgetown, Barbados,
W.I. (tel. 809/432-1332), a Mediterranean-style hotel with red tile roofs on a
site right on St. James Beach, has 76 rooms plus 12 suites. Tamarind offers style
and luxury, but informally so. Guests can enjoy the white sandy beach at their
doorstep or else lounge around the two palm-shaded pools. The modern
hacienda-style units are comfortable, with balconies overlooking the gardens or
ocean. Standard accommodations have a garden or pool view, and deluxe and
luxury units open onto the sea. *In summer, singles cost $115 to $160 daily, and
doubles go for $155 to $215 on the MAP.* Winter charges are $185 to $225 daily in
singles, $225 to $310 in doubles, also on the MAP. The food has a fine reputa-

tion. There is live entertainment most evenings. Water sports, such as waterskiing, windsurfing, catamaran sailing, and snorkeling, are provided free right off the hotel's beach. Golf, tennis, horseback riding, and polo are available nearby. Free transportation takes guests on shopping jaunts into Bridgetown once a day Monday to Friday.

Coconut Creek Club, St. James, Barbados, W.I. (tel. 809/432-0803), is an informal celebrity retreat on the fashionable coastline of Barbados. Rooms are snugly perched in a tropical garden overlooking two intimate sandy coves. Many of the bedrooms are built on the low cliff edge, overlooking the ocean. Others open onto the pool. Each has a private bath, and a veranda or balcony where your breakfast is brought to you. Rooms come in different classifications, the cheapest being labeled "moderate." From that, they rise to superior and deluxe on the oceanfront. *Off-season prices, with MAP included, are $95 to $115 daily in a single, $135 to $155 in a double. Shoulder season, November 5 to December 16, with MAP included, costs $120 to $140 daily in a single and $160 to $180 in a double.* High season, mid-December to the end of March, singles rent for $175 to $215 daily and doubles for $215 to $255, with MAP. The owners have created an outpost of Britannic nostalgia in the English pub, the Cricketers. Bajan buffets and barbecues are served on a vine-covered open pergola, overlooking the gardens and the sea. In the inn's cozy restaurant, the food has been praised by *Gourmet* magazine. Architecturally, the room has upside-down stucco arches and rough beamed dividers. There's dancing to West Indian calypso and steel bands. Swimming is in the bay or the freshwater pool, and complimentary water sports include waterskiing, windsurfing, snorkeling, and use of Hobie Cats.

Heywoods, St. Peter, Barbados, W.I. (tel. 809/422-4900), is a government-built collection of colonial-style buildings set amid palm trees. The complex stands on a 31-acre flat area near a mile-long sandy beach, a long haul north of Bridgetown. Although owned by the Barbados Tourism Corporation, the resort is managed by an independent company. On the premises are more than 306 rooms, clustered into seven architecturally different groupings, which contributes to a village-style ambience within each cluster. In winter, singles cost $185 to $205 daily, while doubles go for $200 to $220. *In summer, singles rent for $95 to $115, doubles for $110 to $130.* Some of the more expensive rooms contain kitchenettes. Children under 12 sharing a room with their parents stay free. The complex has five floodlit tennis courts, a nine-hole golf course, squash courts, and an assortment of boutiques. It also has a coffeeshop, an outdoor restaurant, a formal dining room, a seafood restaurant, and at least two bars. The resort's disco, Club Miliki, is recommended separately. There is also a wide selection of planned activities for guests and their children.

Crane Beach Hotel, Crane Beach, St. Philip, Barbados, W.I. (tel. 809/423-6220), is the most dramatic resort in Barbados. Its remote location on the southeast coast is on the edge of a rugged cliff, overlooking Cobblers Reef and its miles of unspoiled beach, yet it lies only two miles from Sam Lord's Castle and 12 miles from the capital, Bridgetown. Its core is an 18th-century mansion built of blocks of white coral. All has been carefully remodeled in the "estate mansion." One of Barbados's oldest hostelries, Crane has been known to generations of honeymooners from around the world. Both the hotel and the Crane Beach Club overlook a coconut grove, with a 1,000-foot ocean frontage on a white beach of coral sand. Sometimes young Bajans dive from this cliff as Mexican boys do in Acapulco.

Crane gives guests a choice of comfortably furnished rooms, well-equipped apartments, or else individually decorated, large-size deluxe suites, each one different, with a special character. In winter, EP rates for two people are $225 to $300 daily, the latter for a one-bedroom suite. A single stays here for $180 daily.

In summer, EP doubles cost $105 to $140 in the Estate Mansion, and a single goes for $95. The MAP supplement year round is $35 per person. All units have balconies, terraces, or sundecks, as well as private baths and phones. There are two swimming pools, the main one of Roman design. There is a brick terrace for sunbathing, and on the beach level is yet another pool. There are two refreshment bars, one cantilevered 60 feet above the beach.

Barbados Divi St. James Beach Resort, St. Lawrence, Barbados, W.I. (tel. 809/428-7178 or toll free 800/367-DIVI). Included within the embrace of the well-managed Divi chain, this hotel occupies a 20-acre plot beside the sea in St. Lawrence. Guests register in a round reception area lined with pine and native stone. The accommodations lie in three-story verandaed outbuildings ringing a lagoon-shaped pool. There, shaded by coconut palms, quiet drinking alternates with games of volleyball. The centerpiece is an airy restaurant and bar capped with a quartet of high cedar-shingled roofs. On the beach, flanking one end of the property, the array of free water sports includes waterskiing, snorkeling, Sunfish rentals, windsurfing, and Hobie Cats. Big signs warn swimmers to enter the water away from the patches of coral which sometimes come close to the water's surface. Each of the units contains air conditioning, a balcony, and tropical furniture. In winter, depending on the exposure, single or double rooms rent for $200 to $260 daily. Suites are more expensive. *In summer, singles or doubles cost $100 to $130 daily.*

Discovery Bay Beach Hotel, Holetown, St. James, Barbados, W.I. (tel. 809/432-1301), a member of Kuoni Hotel Management, Switzerland, is a first-class beachfront hotel on 4½ acres of tropical gardens. The main entrance is plantation style. The inn grew out of what had been a private beachside mansion built of coral stone. However, it's now firmly entrenched as a hotel on the casuarina-lined beach. Guest rooms are contained in a stretched-out, two-story wing that was built along the garden. If you don't want to be inspected by passersby, select a second-story perch with raftered ceilings. A more recently built block containing three floors of rooms fronts the sandy beach, with its cluster of thatch shade huts. All rooms have phones, radio, air conditioning and balconies or patios. Deluxe and junior suites have been recently refurbished and have TV and video. Of the 85 units, 55 are rated superior, having a garden or pool view, 21 are deluxe oceanfront accommodations, and nine are junior suites. Daily prices in winter for a single on the EP are $190, $225, and $255, depending on the rating of your room. Doubles cost $200, $240, and $275, while triples go for $250, $290, and $320. *In summer, the tariffs in singles are $95, $115, and $135; in doubles, $110, $135, and $160; and in triples, $140, $165, and $190.* The MAP supplement, both summer and winter, is $35 per person per day (half price for children under 12). A child sharing the room of two adults is free on EP. For MAP guests, exchange dining is offered at neighboring hotel restaurants at no additional charge. Otherwise, guests will enjoy a varied menu by candlelight at Discovery Bay as well as sumptuous buffets enhanced by impeccable service and outstanding presentation by the Swiss chef. In the center of the complex is a swimming pool, and adjoining are two well-tended tennis courts lit for night play. Free windsurfing, Sunfish sailing, and snorkeling are available for hotel guests, and complimentary transportation is provided to and from Bridgetown. In the entertainment area, a local combo often plays for dancing, and buffets are frequently spread under a covered portico.

Sandpiper Inn, Holetown, St. James, Barbados, W.I. (tel. 809/422-2251), has more of a South Seas look than most of the hotels of Barbados. Affiliated with the also-recommended Coral Reef, it is a self-contained, intimate resort on the waterside, lying along the fashionable west coast. Avoiding "sterile modern," it is Bajan in flavor, standing in a small grove of coconut palms and flowering trees. This cluster of rustic-chic rooms and suites surrounds the swimming pool, and some have a fine sea view. The hotel is right on the beach, and you can jog along the water's edge. The rooms open onto little terraces that stretch along the second story. Here you can order drinks or have breakfast. In winter, a MAP single ranges from $226 to $241 daily; a double or twin, from $252 to $376. *On the same MAP, a single in summer costs from $100 to $128 daily; a double or twin, from $132 to $223.* Ask about special rates for three to four people in one of the ocean-view suites. Dining is under a wooden ceiling, and the cuisine is both continental and West Indian. Sometimes big buffets are spread out for you, with white-capped chefs in attendance.

   Best Western Sandy Beach, Worthing, Christ Church, Barbados, W.I. (tel. 809/428-9033), is an 88-suite Bajan resort on the south shore of Barbados four miles from Bridgetown. It offers one- and two-bedroom suites, and features 16 honeymoon suites with queen-size beds and completely private patios for sunning or whatever. You may be impressed with the tastefully decorated and spacious accommodations. All units also have fully equipped kitchenettes, baths, and private balconies or patios, and all the furniture at this informal place is locally made. *Off-season rates are $90 to $110 daily in a single or double and from $130 to $145 for two-bedroom suites, suitable for four guests.* In winter, single or double occupancy costs from $170 daily, with two-bedroom units going for $250 daily. Facilities for the handicapped are provided in four of the ground-floor suites. Ron's Green House Restaurant, specializing in seafood and steaks, is under a wood-shingled palapa and opens out to the beach and swimming pool. The open-air design and use of wood and hanging plants give the restaurant a natural look by day that becomes romantic by candlelight at night. Every Tuesday the resort sponsors a Bajan Cohoblopot buffet for $20, when outsiders are welcome. Caribbean specialties such as flying fish, cou-cou, curries, plantains, and pepper-pot are served under the stars. Another restaurant, the Ocean Terrace, is a casual, open-air facility overlooking the beach, serving lighter, less expensive meals than the Green House.

   Water sports, which cost extra, include three-hour snorkeling trips, windsurfing, paddleboats, Sailfish, scuba lessons, air mattresses, snorkels, fins, and masks.

THE MIDDLE BRACKET: Repeat visitors to the two-part resort at **Divi Southwinds Beach Hotel,** St. Lawrence, Christ Church, Barbados, W.I. (tel. 809/428-7181), tend to have strong preferences for either its new or its old section, separated from one another by a busy road. The older section lies on the beachfront and consists of a collection of buildings surrounded by palms and sea breezes. The real showplace of the resort, however, is the newer building. It lies just behind what may be the most beautiful bearded fig trees in Barbados (the tree that inspired Portuguese sailors in discovery days to give this island the name it bears). This section looks like a tastefully interconnected series of urban town houses, with prominent wooden balconies and views of a large swimming pool. The renovated older section has the advantage of opening directly onto a wide and sandy expanse of beach. It also has an oval pool of its own, and visitors need only cross through two groves of palm trees and a little-used street to reach the resort's more stylish twin. *Off-season, single or double rooms for $120 to $150 daily, depending on the exposure, while a two-bedroom suite, suitable for up to four occupants, costs $190.* In winter, single or double occupancy costs $225 to $250 daily, while two-bedroom suites go for $290. MAP rates are from $36 to $38 per person extra per day.

Southern Palms, St. Lawrence, Barbados, W.I. (tel. 809/428-7171), is a seafront club with a distinct personality, lying on the Pink Beach of Barbados, midway between the airport and Bridgetown. The core of the resort is an old pink-and-white manor house, built in the Dutch style with a garden-level colonnade of arches. Spread along the sands are multiarched two- and three-story buildings, on grounds planted with oleander, bougainvillea, and hibiscus. Italian fountains and statues add to the Mediterranean feeling. In its more modern block, an eclectic mixture of rooms includes some with kitchenettes, some facing the ocean, others opening onto the garden, and some with penthouse luxury. On the EP, twin-bedded rooms in winter rent for $165 to $210 daily, single or double occupancy, and suites for two with kitchenettes cost $285. *In summer, EP rates, single or double, are $87 to $96 daily, two persons in a suite with kitchenette paying $134 daily.* Linking the accommodations is a cluster of straw-roofed buildings, including the Khus-Khus Bar and Restaurant, serving both a West Indian and a continental cuisine. A native orchestra often entertains, and you can dance the merengue to the music of a steel band. There's a terrace for sunning before you take a dip in the beachside freshwater swimming pool.

Cunard Paradise Village & Beach Club, Black Rock, St. Michael, Barbados, W.I. (tel. 809/424-0888, 212/880-7500 in New York City, or 800/528-6273 toll free). Built and operated by Cunard, this is one of the most sports-oriented resorts in Barbados. It sits on a hillside above a glistening white beach 2½ miles northwest of Bridgetown. Its clubhouse is attractively composed of lattices and chiseled stone in a sun-flooded position overlooking the sea. Within its elegant premises is a gazebo for dancing, an alluring indoor/outdoor restaurant, and two rounded swimming pools. Horseback riding, golf, sightseeing, and shopping trips to Bridgetown can be arranged by the staff. On the premises are a pair of Hartru tennis courts under the supervision of a pro. Accommodations are scattered among lattice-covered units rising amid a tropical collection of gardens and forests at the base of a steep hill. Each is air-conditioned, with a modern design of big windows and comfortable furniture. Depending on the exposure, singles rent for $190 daily in winter, doubles going for $210. *Summer and shoulder season prices are $120 to $140 in singles daily, $140 to $160 in doubles.* Children under 12 stay free in a room with two adults. MAP is an extra $42 per person per day.

Ginger Bay Beach Club, St. Philip, Barbados, W.I. (tel. 809/423-5810), contains a total of 16 suites, built on top of low, rocky cliffs extending into the sand-bottomed waters of the Atlantic. From your comfortable perch at poolside, you'd never guess how dramatic the setting really is. A walk onto the nearby cliffs will reveal exotic grottoes carved by the action of the waves. The focal point of the resort is the thatch-roofed restaurant called Ginger's, built inside the shelter of the pool area. Its decor includes a combination of tropical lattices set under a peaked roof whose open supports permit a free flow of air even when the ceiling fans are off. Although the villas seem to huddle close to one another, the façades are staggered to permit a feeling of privacy on each accommodation's veranda. Each contains its own hammock. *Off-season, singles are a bargain at $75 daily, with doubles costing $105.* However, in winter, single or double occupancy goes up to $220 daily.

Casuarina Beach Club, St. Lawrence Gap, Christ Church, Barbados, W.I. (tel. 809/428-3600). You'll approach this resort through a forest of palm trees which sway gracefully above a well-maintained lawn. The main building has a series of arched windows leading onto verandas, although to get to your accommodation, you pass through the outlying reception building and beside the pair of swimming pools. These are separated from the wide sandy beach by a lawn area dotted with casuarina and bougainvillea. On the premises is an octagonal roofed open-air bar and restaurant, as well as tennis and squash facilities. The front desk can arrange most seaside activities through outside agencies. Each of the 100 accommodations is air-conditioned and has a ceiling fan, a kitchenette, and wicker furniture. In winter, two persons are charged $105 to $120 daily. *In summer, two guests are housed for $70 to $80.* Children under 12 are accommodated free in their parents' room.

Settlers Beach, St. James, Barbados, W.I. (tel. 809/422-3052), is a seaside collection of well-appointed villas placed on four acres of beachfront property. Each air-conditioned apartment is self-contained, having two bedrooms with private bath, a spacious tile-floor lounge and dining room, plus a fully equipped kitchen. *In the shoulder and low season, an apartment for two costs $165 to $220 daily.* For breakfast and dinner, add a supplement of $35 per person daily. In high season, two persons stay here for $340 to $350 daily; three people, $380 to $400. The apartments have sunny colors, and the rates quoted include the services of a maid. Adjoining the buildings is a swimming pool surrounded by palms and lawn. The square-roofed dining room and lounge bar serves good food and drink, and at dinner you can select a table in the moonlight.

BEST FOR THE BUDGET: An oldtimer that seems just as good as ever, **Ocean View,** Hastings, Barbados, W.I. (tel. 809/427-7821), is the oldest hotel in Barbados, founded in 1901. It still maintains some vintage niceties too: Your bed is turned down at night and shoes left outside the door are waiting there polished the next morning. At dinner, vegetables are served from silver dishes. Built between the busy road and the beach, the pink-and-white Ocean View has some of the graciousness of a colonial English house, with an open staircase with an old balustrade and a seaside porch that's good for lounging. The location is on the south coast in Christ Church, with Bridgetown about 5 minutes away; the international airport, 15 minutes. Every bedroom is different—some large, some small and cozy—and an attractive use has been made of island antiques. In winter, singles range in price from $46 to $64 daily, a double costing from $67 to $81, all EP. *In summer, you pay $26 to $35 in a single daily, $45 to $55 in a double, EP.* MAP costs another $35 per person per day. This vintage hostelry also serves good food. You can dine at a table overlooking the sea, helping yourself at the well-known Sunday planters' brunch in winter. As in the olden days, they serve a big spread of Bajan specialties. Ernest Hemingway used to fill his plate high with flying fish and pepperpot, after having a bowl of callaloo soup. Lunches cost from $26 BDS ($13) to $30 BDS ($15), and dinners go for about $55 BDS ($27.50). Breakfast is from 7 to 9 a.m., lunch from 12:30 to 2 p.m., and dinner from 7 to 10 p.m. daily.

Bagshot House, St. Lawrence, Christ Church, Barbados, W.I. (tel. 809/428-8125), was built about a quarter of a century ago. Flowering vines tumble over the railing of the balconies. In front of the inn, the beach stretches out before you. Some of the well-kept, simply furnished units have views of the water. All rentals, however, contain private baths. Twins cost $134 daily in winter, and singles run $76, including breakfast and dinner. *In the off-season, these same twins go for $118 daily, singles for $70, both rates including half board as well.* A front sunbathing deck is perched right at the edge of a lagoon. This is actually the living room, but there is a deckside lounge decorated with paintings by local artists. Bridgetown is about a 15-minute drive to the west.

Chrizel's Garden, Gibbs, St. Peter, Barbados, W.I. (tel. 809/422-2403 or toll free 800/541-4065), is a quiet retreat that appeals particularly to those who enjoy a small hotel with a relaxed, informal atmosphere. Lying on the St. Peter coast in the northern part of Barbados where the sea is calm, it has no swimming pool, but Gibbs Bay, with its clear, warm water, is only a short walk away. The area has been called by some visitors one of the three most beautiful beaches in the world. Chrizel's is away from the rumble of main-road traffic and enjoys almost constant breezes. Guests are welcomed with a complimentary rum punch, and there is no charge for use of beach and snorkeling equipment. It offers a cozy bar near the dining room, overlooking the garden. The varied menu includes Bajan and continental specialties as well as vegetarian dishes. The accommodations are in three separate buildings, each with a veranda. All the units are on the ground floor, completely screened, with private baths and showers, plus ceiling fans to circulate the air. *In summer, two persons pay from $81 daily on the MAP or $45 for a room only.* MAP rates in winter for two persons are from $110. Chrizel's Garden is a good bargain in the Caribbean.

Fairholme, Maxwell, Christ Church, Barbados, W.I. (tel. 809/428-9425), is a converted plantation house lying five miles from the Grantley Adams Airport and six miles from Bridgetown. The main house with its original gardens is just off a major road, a five-minute walk to the beach, and across from its sister hotel the Sherringham Beach, with its waterfront café and bar which Fairholme guests are allowed to use. The older part has 11 double rooms with private baths, a living room area, and a patio overlooking an orchard and swimming pool. Beside the pool is a grassy lawn for sunbathing and a bar for island beverages. More recently added are 20 Spanish-style studio apartments, all with balcony or patio, built within the walls of the old plantation, with high cathedral ceilings, dark beams, and traditional furnishings. *In summer, rooms rent for $30 daily in double occupancy, $22 in a single, with apartments going for $40 daily for two persons.* In winter, rooms are $36 in a double, $24 in a single, with apartments costing $53 daily, double occupancy. Breakfast and dinner cost an additional $18 per person. The restaurant has a reputation for home-cooking—good, wholesome, nothing fancy, but the ingredients are fresh.

Barbados Windsurfing Club Hotel, Benston Beach, Maxwell, Christ Church, Barbados, W.I. (tel. 809/428-9095), attracts many of its guests just because it's one of the most fun places in town. If you're an avid windsurfer, this could be the perfect place for you, also. Set between the road and the sea, the accommodations at this young-at-heart resort are in a brightly painted three-story rectangular building with angled balconies. The 15 units are spacious and simple, including basic kitchens and baths. The highest rates are charged from mid-December through February, when two persons pay from $50 to $100 daily for a room, $120 to $150 for a suite. *In March, April, July, August, November, and the first two weeks of December, rooms for two cost $35 to $75 per day, with suites going for $90 to $110. The bargain season is May, June, September, and October, when rooms for two rent for $20 to $50 daily, with suites priced at $50 to $70.* The bedrooms are comfortable, but no one comes here for the decor. It's the youthful ambience and the camaraderie that makes this place noteworthy. Experts say that the windsurfing just off the hotel's sea wall is as good as that in Hawaii, which appeals to nearly fanatical followers of the sport who come from all over the western hemisphere. On a sunny day when the wind is right, observers on the hotel's grassy terrace can see flotillas of sailboards riding the waves, heading either out into the Atlantic or back to shore. For rates and details, see "The Sporting Life," below.

An informal restaurant on the premises serves simple lunches (sandwiches and hamburgers) during the day, while more complete evening dinners, with such main dishes as steak, chicken, and dolphin, cost about $25 BDS ($12.50). Several musical evenings are usually planned per week, drawing an energetic crowd of fun-loving participants. For information about the week's entertainment, call the hotel.

YOUR OWN APARTMENT: Shielded from the street, **Sichris Apartment Hotel,** 2 Worthing, Christ Church, Barbados, W.I. (tel. 809/427-5930, 212/355-6605 in New York City, or toll free 800/221-4588) lies behind a row of shrubbery and a high wall. It contains a sheltered pool area, 24 one-bedroom apartments, and a staff directed by David and Anne Walker. When they opened the hotel in 1978, the Walkers named it after their children, Simon and Christopher. Each of the accommodations contains air conditioning, direct-dial phone, a kitchenette, and a veranda with louvered doors. Beach lovers will find the ocean a short walk away, and visitors who prefer to cook in their own units can shop at supermarkets close by. The restaurant is an informal place with an adjoining cabaña bar and a series of scheduled barbecues and buffets with live music. *Summer rates in accommodations suitable for one or two people range from $75 to $85 daily,* while winter prices are $120 to $140, depending on whether your view is over the pool or over the road. Children under 12 stay free. MAP is available for a $45 supplement per person per day.

Travelers' Palm, 265 Palm Ave., Sunset Crest, St. James, Barbados, W.I. (tel. 809/432-7722), is designed for those who want to be independent, a choice collection of 16 well-furnished apartments with fully equipped kitchens and air conditioning. The apartments are filled with bright, resort colors and handcrafted furniture. They open onto a well-kept lawn with a swimming pool. Serviced by maids, apartments can house one to three people. The rate for one of these apartments runs from $50 daily in winter, *dropping to just $30 in summer.* Apartments also have a large living and dining room area, and a patio where you can have your breakfast or a candlelit dinner which you've prepared yourself.

Woodville Beach Apartments, Hastings, Christ Church, Barbados, W.I. (tel. 809/427-1498), is one of the best bargains in Barbados, ideal for families on a budget holiday. It is a U-shaped apartment complex built around a pool terrace overlooking the rocky shoreline of the sea. Functional minimalist in decor, it is nevertheless clean and comfortable. Each accommodation is fully equipped, and a variety of rental units are offered, ranging from a studio to a two-bedroom apartment. All have balconies or decks, private baths, and small kitchens where you can cook your own meals if you're keeping costs trimmed to the bone. There are supermarkets nearby. In winter, studios for two persons rent for $63 to $68 daily, a one-bedroom apartment for two costing $85, and a two-bedroom accommodation for four peaking at $116. *Off-season, a studio costs $38 to $42 daily for two persons, a one-bedroom apartment for two renting for $45, and a two-bedroom unit for four a real bargain at $72.*

ECONOMY ON THE EASTERN COAST: An unpretentious hostelry, **Atlantis Hotel,** Bathsheba, Barbados, W.I. (tel. 809/433-9445), is housed in a dilapidated green-roofed villa built by a wealthy planter in 1882. Set directly on the seacoast, the hotel has simple bedrooms—very simple—but all with private baths and toilets. Go for one of the more expensive units with a balcony. *Full-board rates are $30 daily in a single in summer, $55 in a double.* In winter, full board costs $35 in a single, $60 in a double, which makes the Atlantis one of the best bargains along the Atlantic coast of Barbados. But be warned: This place, even though it is one of the most famous hotels on the island, is not for everyone. The ocean at your doorstep can be turbulent, and even experienced swimmers can find trouble here. Nevertheless, the place has its devotees and staying here is definitely an offbeat adventure. Aside from inexpensive accommodations, this is the most popular luncheon spot on the east side of the island (but more about this later).

Kingsley Club, Cattlewash-on-Sea, near Bathsheba, St. Joseph, Barbados, W.I. (tel. 809/433-9422), fulfills a desire of many readers for a hidden-away little West Indian inn far removed from the bustle of the tourist-ridden west coast. In the foothills of Bathsheba, opening onto the often turbulent Atlantic, Kingsley Club lies on the northeast coast. A historical inn, with many associations, it offers seven simply furnished but clean and comfortable bedrooms. In winter, one person on EP pays $54 daily, two persons being charged $59. *In summer, an EP single costs $45, with a double going for $49 daily.* For MAP, add $28 per person daily to the EP rates. The place is a bargain, but it is only for those preferring isolation and an inexpensive retreat. At night, you can sit back enjoying a rum punch made from an old planter's recipe. The club enjoys a reputation for good cooking, and its Bajan food will be recommended later for those traveling to the east coast just for the day. Cattlewash Beach is one of the longest, widest, and, as the hotel brochure points out, "least crowded in Barbados." But please note: Swimming here can be extremely dangerous.

2. BARBADOS COOKERY

The famous flying fish jumps up on every menu, and when prepared right it's a delicacy, moist and succulent, nutlike in flavor, approaching the subtlety of brook trout. Bajans boil it, steam it, bake it, stew it, fry it, stuff it, or whatever.

Try also the sea urchin, or *oursin,* which you may have already sampled in Martinique and Guadeloupe. Bajans often call these urchins "sea eggs." Crab-in-the-back is another specialty, as is langouste, the Barbadian lobster. Dolphin and salt fish cakes are other popular items on the menu. Yams, sweet potatoes, and eddoes are typical vegetables. And Barbadian fruits are luscious, including papaya, passion fruit, and mangoes.

If you hear that any hotel or restaurant is having a "cohoblopot," call for a reservation. This is a Barbadian term which means to "cook up," and it inevitably will produce a host of Bajan specialties.

Bajan dishes are a blend of cookery styles: the British, and most definitely the East Indian and African. These recipes have been adapted to include the local meats, fruits, and vegetables. Pepperpot, stews, and curries are made with local chicken, pork, beef, and fish. The secret of the flavorful dishes, as any Bajan cook will tell you, is in the "seasoning up." It is said that seasoning techniques have changed little since the 16th century.

At Christmas, when many U.S. visitors come to Barbados, roast ham or turkey is served with jug-jug, a rich casserole of Scottish derivation that includes salt beef, ground corn flour, green pigeon peas, and spices. Cou-cou, a side dish made from okra and cornmeal, accompanies fish, especially the "flying fish" of Barbados.

If possible, escape the dining requirements of your hotel and sample the island's varied cuisine, which is interesting but not spicy exotic.

THE LEADING RESTAURANTS: Three miles from Sunset Crest, St. Thomas, **Bagatelle Restaurant,** Hwy. 2A (tel. 809/425-0666), is housed in a gubernatorial residence dating back to 1645. The secluded, remote, sylvan retreat lies in the hills in the center of the island, retaining the aura of colonial days. It has been transformed into one of the island's finest and most elegant choices for dining. Cooled by overhead fans, you can dine in rambling cellars, with candles and lanterns illuminating the menu as well as the white coral walls and the old archways. Service is very gracious, among the best I found on Barbados. You proceed first to a charming little bar where menu selections are made. Later you can select a cozy corner or dine outside, listening to the crickets. For $80 BDS ($40), you can select from the set menu, ordering perhaps salmon mousse, or going on to the callaloo soup or a fish chowder made mainly of flying fish, eddoes, and shrimp. For a main course, you might enjoy superbly cooked rack of lamb or a "sort of beef Wellington." Desserts are such luscious concoctions as key lime pie, or crème brûlée. Hours are 7 p.m. to midnight, seven days a week.

Reid's, St. James (tel. 809/432-7623), is one of the island's most fashionable dining spots. You might be tempted to order a drink in the darkly intimate brick-floored bar area before dinner. The dining room is in the breeze-filled extension of the main house under a raftered ceiling jutting out toward a sloping English garden with two fountains and a rockery. Only dinner is served here, every night except Sunday from 6 to 11 p.m. (last orders at 10 p.m.). Reservations are essential, especially on weekends. Full meals cost from $60 BDS ($30) and might include garlic-flavored shrimp, veal Cordon Bleu, pork en croûte, mixed seafood casserole, lobster tails, seafood crêpe, and beef kebabs.

La Cage aux Folles, Paynes Bay, St. James (tel. 809/432-1203), is the venture of Nick Hudson and Suzie Blandford. Nick earned his fame when he owned the popular Nick's Diner in London before coming to Barbados where, "in a fit of madness," he opened the Bagatelle Restaurant in 1971. He and Suzie decided to open La Cage aux Folles in 1982.

Try the sesame prawn pâté, sweet and sour shrimp, or Créole fish soup. Other courses include a fresh fish of the day, Malaysian beef and shrimp satay, and red-roast pork tenderloin. Hours are from 7 to 10 p.m. daily except Tuesday.

Belmore House, Holetown, St. James (tel. 809/432-1156), is the domain of Peter Staffner, a native of Kitzbühel, Austria, who operates this beachfront restaurant that has the ambience of a private home. You can dine on the terrace, listening to the sound of crashing waves. You might begin with a saffron-flavored fish soup or a chilled gazpacho. To follow, you can select a Wiener schnitzel or perhaps stuffed jumbo shrimp with walnut butter. There's always a fish of the day served with sauce Créole, or meat devotées might choose a cut of prime filet sautéed with peppercorns. For dessert, have one of the Austrian cakes or pastries. Meals cost from $75 BDS ($37.50) and are good value. This family-owned and -operated restaurant serves dinner from 6:30 to 9:30 p.m. daily except Sunday and Monday. They plan to have a Sunday buffet in winter from 11 a.m. to 2:30 p.m., but check on that. You should make dinner reservations.

Carambola, Derricks, St. James (tel. 809/432-0832), offers one of the most spectacular terraces for dining in the Caribbean. At this cliff-hugging place, with your table illuminated by candlelight, you can sample the savory viands of owners Robin and Hazel Walcott. An expanded Bajan house, the restaurant has quickly moved to the forefront of island dining experiences. The cuisine is creative with nouvelle touches, as reflected by such appetizers as kiwi mussels poached in white wine with shallots, or a "crock of conch, mussels, and squid," a soup given an added flavor by a touch of black rum. For your main dish, perhaps you'll be tempted by "Cajun-style blackened fish," the catch of the day served with jambalaya rice. Meals cost from 75 BDS ($37.50) and are served from 6:30 to 9:30 p.m. daily except Sunday. It is always necessary to make a reservation.

BAJAN COOKERY: Hidden behind lush foliage, **Brown Sugar,** Aquatic Gap, St. Michael (tel. 809/426-7684), is a beautiful al fresco restaurant at an island house. The ceiling is latticed, with slow-turning fans. There's an open veranda for dining by candlelight in a setting of hanging plants. The chefs prepare some of the tastiest Bajan specialties on the island. For an unusual and imaginative opening, try Salomon Grundy, a spicy-hot Jamaican favorite—a pâté of smoked herring, allspice, wine vinegar, onion, chives, and hot bonnie peppers, served with Jamaican water crackers. Among the soups, I suggest hot gungo-pea soup (pigeon peas cooked in chicken broth and zested with fresh coconut milk, herbs, and a touch of white wine). The price of the main course includes one of these appetizers, plus soup, vegetables, dessert, and coffee. Among the most recommendable main dishes, Créole orange chicken is popular, or perhaps you'd like stuffed crab backs. A selection of locally grown fresh vegetables is offered. For desserts, called confections here, I recommend the walnut rum pie with rum sauce. Your dinner tab will be $50 BDS ($25) or more. Dining is from 6:30 to 9:30 p.m. daily. The restaurant is also known for its superb luncheons, costing from $30 BDS ($15) and served from 11:30 a.m. to 2:30 p.m. Monday to Friday.

Koko's, Prospect, St. James (tel. 809/424-4557), is an award-winning restaurant, known for its excellent Caribbean cookery, a kind of Bajan *cuisine moderne.* The location alone is appealing, in a charming once-private house, built on coral blocks on a terrace overlooking the sea. You might begin with one of the homemade local soups, perhaps cohoblopot, made with "roots of the Caribbean," or stir-fried squid with lime and mayonnaise sauce as an appetizer. Shrimp and crab fritters are served with a fiery dip. Main dishes include the chef's catch of the day as well as island rabbit, west coast–style, served with a tamarind and ginger sauce. Each dessert is homemade and luscious. Meals cost from $60 BDS ($30) and are served nightly from 6:30 to 10.

Restaurant Château Créole, Porters, St. James (tel. 809/422-4116). In a spot near Glitter Bay, this stucco-and-tile house is set in a pleasant tropical garden dotted with statues of cherubs carrying lambs. After passing under a verdant arbor, you'll be invited to order a drink, served on one of the flowered banquettes filling various parts of the house. Meals are taken on the rear terrace, al fresco style, by candlelight. Barbara and Larry Tatem, formerly of Montréal, are the owners who welcome guests and direct the kitchens. Menu specialties include Créole dishes, which often make use of ample amounts of crabmeat, such as crab diablo and crabmeat au gratin. You might like Créole red-bean soup, New Orleans seafood gumbo, or chicken Pontalba. The establishment makes its own ice cream with local fruits. Full dinners, served every evening except Sunday, range from $45 BDS ($22.50) to $75 BDS ($37.50). The restaurant doesn't serve lunch. Dinner reservations are a good idea, especially in high season. Hours are 7 to 9:30 p.m.

David's Place, St. Lawrence (tel. 809/428-4537), promises "Barbadian dining at its best" and delivers on that promise. In a well-maintained West Indian clapboard house, the restaurant is run by David Trotman and his wife, Darla. Meals, costing from $50 BDS ($25), are served from 6 to 10 p.m. Tuesday to Sunday. You might begin with a hot and creamy pumpkin soup, then follow with a Bajan pepperpot or such freshly caught fish of the day as dolphin, kingfish, and red snapper. The chef might even prepare "Baxters Road chicken" in the way they do it on the famous nightlife street of Barbados. Desserts are tempting, including carrot cake with rum sauce.

The **Witch Doctor,** St. Lawrence Gap, Christ Church (tel. 809/428-7856), hides behind a screen of thick foliage. The decor, in honor of its name, features African and island woodcarvings of witch doctors. The place purveys a fascinating African and Bajan cuisine with some unusual concoctions which are tasty and well prepared, a big change from a lot of the bland hotel fare. For an appetizer, try the split-pea and pumpkin soup. You'll also be offered kingfish shango (cold, soused in lime). All main dishes are served with rice. Chef's specialties include flambé dishes, shrimp Créole, flying fish, and chicken piri-piri (from Mozambique). Dinner, the only meal served here, should run about $35 BDS ($17.50). Hours are 6:15 to 9:30 p.m. every night.

Pisces, St. Lawrence Gap, Christ Church (tel. 809/428-6558), is a private cottage, painted olive green, right on the waterfront. The front garden is dominated by coconut trees, and the dining rooms extend along the water's edge. Cooled by sea breezes, you can enjoy fish and seafood in a setting that is rustic yet has a subdued Caribbean elegance. With a name like Pisces, you expect and get well-prepared seafood dishes, including the famous flying fish of Barbados, served here stuffed with herbs. I'm very fond of the chef's blackened dolphin, curried kingfish, and his lobster chasseur. For dessert, I'd endorse the gooseberry coconut pie. Expect to spend around $55 BDS ($27.50) for a complete meal. Go for dinner only, from 6 to 9:30 p.m., and be sure to make a reservation. The place is open nightly in winter but closes on Sunday in summer.

THE MODERATE RANGE: In what used to be a private home, now considerably simplified, **Restaurant Flamboyant,** Hastings Main Rd., Christ Church (tel. 809/427-5588), has had many of the interior walls removed to allow ample space for dining. Mr. and Mrs. Brian Cheeseman, the owners, direct a kitchen where, because everything is prepared to order, the food may take a while to be served. Menu items include pumpkin and potato soup, a seafood crêpe Flamboyant, Wiener schnitzel, a half chicken stuffed Bajan style, shrimp in dill sauce, and apple pie à la mode. Full meals range upward from $60 BDS ($30) per person. Reservations are important, especially in high season. Hours are 6 to 11 p.m. daily except Sunday.

La Piperade, Glitter Bay, St. James (tel. 809/422-4111). Set at the back of the Glitter Bay Hotel, between a freshwater pool and a sandy beach, this restaurant is surrounded with lush and colorful vegetation. The restaurant is set in a series of contoured terraces leading on one side to the edge of the free-form pool. Specialties are tournedos Piperade, the chef's own chicken-liver pâté, whole Cornish game hen stuffed with wild rice and served with Périgueux sauce, a fresh fish of the day, and desserts such as Key lime pie. In addition, the chef prepares daily special dishes which vary with the season. Full meals cost from $70 BDS ($35). Reservations are a good idea at this excellent restaurant. Meals are served from 11:30 a.m. to 2:30 p.m. and 7 to 9:45 p.m. daily. The Sunday brunch, costing $20 BDS ($10), served from 11:30 a.m. to 4 p.m., features such succulent dishes as crêpes and omelets along with such main dishes as linguine with shrimp sauce.

Angry Annie's, Prospect, St. James (tel. 809/424-0425), is housed in an old West Indian home right along the glitter strip of Barbados containing its most exclusive and elegant hotels. It was named for Annie Matthews from Birmingham, England. If you ask her why she's angry, she replies, "Have you met my other half?" She's only joking, of course, and is really a gracious hostess who is intent on serving some of the best and most reasonably priced food in this rather high-priced area. You might begin with one of her homemade soups, but I prefer one of her fishcakes with a spicy sauce. For a main course, you can select the local fish of the day or perhaps a juicy sirloin steak. However, the ribs, either pork or beef, are most recommendable, and she'll also do a combination platter of chicken. For dessert, why not the coconut cream pie? Meals cost from $50 BDS ($25) and are served from 6 to 11 p.m. seven days a week.

The Steak House, St. Lawrence Gap, Christ Church (tel. 809/428-7152), is the island's first and finest steak house. Steaks of prime quality are flown in from the mainland, and will be served to you sizzling from the cast-iron grill where it is cooked to order as you watch. The menu also offers local fresh fish and seafood, plus the largest salad bar in Barbados. You might begin with crêpe da costa, a selection of seafood or beef marinated in fresh herbs and wrapped in a pancake. Besides T-bone steak and prime rib of beef au jus, the menu has such main dishes as shrimp Créole, and chicken Montrose (sautéed and cooked in a curry sauce). Dinners cost around $40 BDS ($20) and are served from 6 to 10 p.m. daily.

FRENCH CUISINE: Some of the finest French cooking on the island is at **île de France,** Windsor Arms Hotel, Hastings, Christ Church (tel. 809/436-2967). Place yourself in the hands of Michel, who will wish you *bon appétit* and serve you a menu that may evoke dishes you enjoyed in France in the '50s or '60s (if you were around then). You can order a complete meal consisting of such dishes as duck à l'orange, chicken provençale, or garlic shrimp. You might begin with a fish soup or a chicken liver mousse. The atmosphere is charming and traditional, and only dinner is served, costing from $60 BDS ($30). You must call for a reservation, and you'll be told that the first order is taken at 6:30 p.m., with the last seating at 8:30 p.m. daily except Monday.

ITALIAN FLAVOR: A classical Italian cuisine is served at **da Luciano,** "Staten," Hastings, Hwy. 7, Christ Church (tel. 809/427-5518), with a lovely setting—in a Barbados National Trust–designated building of architectural interest. They offer some of the finest Italian dining in the southern Caribbean. The restaurant has gained in popularity with its good service, top-quality ingredients, and skill and care in preparation. I recommend such specialties as cozze alla marinara (mussels in their shells sautéed in butter and parsley, with white wine and a lot of garlic). Try also the filetto battuto alla Luciano (flattened filet of beef flambéed in brandy, sautéed in butter, served with mustard, fresh cream, and mushrooms). The pièce de résistance is the quaglia nel nido alla wolfe (charcoal-broiled filet of beef topped with croutons of garlic bread, roast quail, and natural juice). For dessert, you can (in season) order fresh strawberries, finishing with an espresso. Your final bill will be from $60 BDS ($30). Hours are 6:30 to 10:30 p.m. daily.

Luigi's Restaurant, Dover Woods, St. Lawrence Gap (tel. 809/428-9218), is an open-air Italian trattoria with a Caribbean flavor. Since 1963 it has been operated in a well-maintained green-and-white house on a quiet road in the middle of a forest, making getting here somewhat of an expedition. From the rafters of this place are clustered hundreds of empty chianti bottles which, when a breeze blows, tinkle gently against one another like wind chimes. The dining areas include a shrub-lined veranda and several inside rooms. Meals are prepared to order and may require as much as a 30-minute wait. Three fixed-price meals are offered, at $20 BDS ($10), $22 BDS ($11), and $39 BDS ($19.50) per person. If you order à la carte, count on spending from $50 BDS ($25). Both the fixed-price and à la carte menus include such specialties as lasagne, vegetarian manicotti, filet mignon, seafood casserole, and grilled scampi with spaghetti. The restaurant serves only dinner, from 6 to 9:45 p.m. daily. However, in summer it closes on Tuesday.

BEST FOR THE BUDGET: In the Seaview Hotel, **The Virginian Restaurant,** Hastings Main Rd., Christ Church (tel. 809/427-7963), is known for its good home-cookery served in a restored manor house dating from the 18th century. Guests climb a flight of exterior stone steps to reach the high-ceilinged dining room. Only dinner is served, nightly from 6 to 11 p.m., costing $40 BDS ($20) per person, and reservations are suggested. Meals might include tenderloin steak pie, shrimp curry, fried flying fish, ragoût of beef, and house-style chicken.

During the day, if you're in the area you can have lunch at the **Tamarind**

Tree Club, also in the Seaview Hotel. Every day a luncheon special is featured for $15 BDS ($7.50), including soup, a main course, vegetable, and dessert or coffee. An à la carte menu is available as well. Service is from noon to 3 p.m.

The **Captain's Carvery,** the Ship Inn, St. Lawrence Gap, Christ Church (tel. 809/428-9605). In a wing of my favorite pub in Barbados, this paneled restaurant is one of the most richly atmospheric of any place on the island. It's in a square, high-ceilinged room with an unused wooden balcony and an Old English ambience. Against one wall stands a uniformed carver who serves generous portions to guests who line up for the heavily laden buffet table in the evening. Dinners cost $32.50 BDS ($16.25) and up. You can select from such soups as pepperpot or soup of the day and then ask the carver for your choice and size of cut of beef, pork, turkey, Canadian smoked ham, or leg of lamb, returning to replenish your plate as often as you wish. Lunch is less expensive, costing around $17 BDS ($8.50) for access to the buffet table. There is a uniformed carver, and the buffet selection is simpler. Still, at the price, it represents one of the best bargains in Barbados. Lunch is served from noon to 3 p.m. except Saturday and dinner from 6 to 10:30 p.m. daily. A popular spot for an apéritif is the lush tropical garden bar, and there is also an attractive outdoor dining room where you can enjoy your meals.

Waterfront Café, Cavans Lane, on the wharf of the Careenage, Bridgetown (tel. 809/427-0093), is an indoor/outdoor café, one of the best places to eat in town, set into a row of old warehouses on the harbor near the oldest bridge in town. Its long bar holds jars filled with pickled lemons, which everyone should try at least once, as well as the widest selection of beer (draft or bottled) in Barbados. The clientele may include anyone from a Swedish yachtsman to a Jamaican Rasta. Nightly, local musicians play here, specializing in jazz. No one will mind if you occupy one of the iron chairs while you have a drink or two. Menu choices include curry, seafood, flying fish, ceviche, gazpacho, and many local specialties. Dinners start at $20 BDS ($10), and lunches begin at $8 BDS ($4). The dining room is open from 10 a.m. to 10 p.m.

T.G.I. Boomers, St. Lawrence Gap (tel. 809/428-8439), offers some of the best bargain meals on the island. An American/Bajan operation, it has the largest and busiest lounge in Barbados. The cook prepares a special catch of the day, and the fish is served with soup or salad, rice, or baked potato, and a vegetable. You can always count on seafood, steaks, and hamburgers. A two-egg breakfast with bacon, toast, and coffee costs $6.95 BDS ($3.48). For lunch, you might have a daily Bajan special or a jumbo sandwich. Expect to pay from 12 BDS ($6). Dinners, depending on what you order, go for $19 BDS ($8.50) to $29 BDS ($14.50). Be sure to try one of the 16-ounce daiquiris, which come in six flavors. Breakfast is served daily from 8 to 11 a.m.; lunch, from 11:30 a.m. to 3 p.m.; and dinner, from 5:30 to 9:45 p.m.

EATING ON THE EAST COAST:
A mecca for food on the east coast, the slightly rundown **Hotel Atlantis,** Bathsheba (tel. 809/433-9445), is often filled with both Bajans and visitors. In the sunny, breeze-filled interior, with a sweeping view of the turbulent ocean, Enid I. Maxwell may be on hand to greet you. She's been welcoming visitors from all over the world ever since she opened the place in 1945. Her copious buffets are considered the best food value on the island. From loaded tables, you can partake of such dishes as pumpkin fritters, peas and rice, macaroni and cheese, chow mein, and souse, or a Bajan pepperpot. No one ever leaves here hungry. Lunch is from 1 to 2:30 p.m. daily, costing $28.75 BDS ($14.38). Those who stick around for dinner will find a full meal going for only $23 BDS ($11.50). The dinner serving (and don't be late) is at 7 p.m

Kingsley Club, Cattlewash-on-Sea, near Bathsheba, St. Joseph (tel. 809/433-9422), a historic inn recommended previously for its rooms, also serves some of the best Bajan food on the island in a turn-of-the-century house cooled by Atlantic breezes. You're greeted and shown to a table where you can order a four-course luncheon, costing $45 BDS ($22.50). They invite you to "come tuck in," enjoying your fill of such dishes as split pea and pumpkin soup, dolphin meunière, planters fried chicken, followed by one of their homemade desserts, perhaps coconut meringue pie. In the foothills of Bathsheba, about 15 miles from Bridgetown, the inn lies on the northeast coast of Barbados in an area called "Little Scotland." Lunch is from noon to 3 p.m. daily, and you should make reservations. It's also possible to order a dinner for the same price as the luncheon providing you let them know ahead. Service is from 6:30 to 8 nightly.

3. TOURING THE ISLAND

Barbados is worth exploring, either in your own car or else with a taxidriver guide. Unlike so many islands of the Caribbean, the roads are fair and quite passable. Usually they're well marked with crossroad signs. If you get lost, the people in the countryside are generally helpful and speak English.

Often hot and traffic clogged, the capital, **Bridgetown,** merits no more than a morning's shopping jaunt. An architectural hodgepodge, it was founded by 64 settlers sent out by the Earl of Carlisle in 1628.

You might begin your tour at the **Careenage,** from the French word meaning to turn vessels over on their side for cleaning. This was a haven for the clipper ship, and even though today it doesn't have its yesteryear color, it's still worth exploring. Maybe you'll see a "mauby woman" making her rounds. In colorful dress, she wends her way among the harbor traffic with her bittersweet brew called mauby. With one raised hand, she turns the tap from which the frothy liquid pours into a glass held in the other hand. To make the drink, dried bark is imported from neighboring islands. It is boiled until the water is dark brown and very bitter. This is the base of the drink to which sweetening, essences, and spices are added. Perhaps you'll also see a Bajan harbor policeman in his Nelsonian sailor suit, with a wide-brimmed straw hat and a blue-collared middy.

At **Trafalgar Square** the long tradition of British colonization is perhaps immortalized. The monument here, honoring Lord Nelson, was executed by Sir Richard Westmacott and erected in 1813. The **Public Buildings** on the square are of the great, gray Victorian Gothic variety that you might expect to find in South Kensington, London. The east wing contains the meeting halls of the Senate and the House of Assembly, with some stained-glass windows representing the sovereigns of England from James I to Queen Victoria. Look for the Great Protector himself, Oliver Cromwell.

Behind the Financial Building, **St. Michael's Cathedral** is the symbol of the Church of England transplanted. This Anglican church was built in 1655, but was completely destroyed in a 1780 hurricane. Reconstructed in 1789, it was also damaged by a hurricane in 1831, but was not completely demolished as before. George Washington is said to have worshipped here on his Barbados visit.

Some guides will tell you that the 18th-century "George Washington House" on Upper Bay Street is the spot where the future American president stayed during his Barbados journey. Historians doubt this claim.

The **Bridgetown Synagogue,** Synagogue Lane, in Bridgetown (telephone 809/432-0840 for information), is one of the oldest in the Western hemisphere, surrounded by a burial ground of early Jewish settlers. The present building dates from 1833. It was constructed on the site of an even older synagogue, erected by Jews from Brazil in 1651. Some time in the early 20th century, the synagogue was deconsecrated, and the structure served various roles. In 1983, the government of Barbados seized the deteriorating building, intending to raze it and build a courthouse on the site. An outcry went up from the small Jewish community on the island; money was raised for its restoration, the building was saved and is now part of the National Trust of Barbados and a synagogue once again.

At this point you can hail a taxi and visit **Garrison Savannah,** just south of the capital. Cricket matches and other games are played in this open-air space of some 50 acres. Horse races are also held at certain times of the year.

The **Barbados Museum** (tel. 809/427-0201), is housed in the former military prison at the impressive St. Ann's Garrison. In the exhibition, "In Search of Bim," extensive collections show the island's development from prehistoric to modern times. "Born of the Sea" gives fascinating glimpses into the natural environment. There are also fine collections of West Indian maps, decorative arts, and fine arts. The museum shop sells a variety of quality publications and handcrafts, and the Courtyard Café is a good place for a snack or lunch. The museum is open from 9 a.m. to 6 p.m. Monday to Saturday. It charges $4 BDS ($2) for adults, $1 BDS (50¢) for children.

Nearby, the russet-red **St. Ann's Fort,** on the fringe of the Savannah, garrisoned British soldiers in 1694. The fort wasn't completed until 1703. The Clock House survived the hurricane of 1831.

After Bridgetown, you pass through the middle-class resorts of Hastings, Rockley, Worthing, and St. Lawrence before arriving at **Oistin,** a former shipping port that today is a fishing village. Here the Charter of Barbados was signed at The Mermaid in 1652, as the island surrendered to Commonwealth forces. The inn, incidentally, was owned by a cousin of the John Turner who built the House of the Seven Gables in Salem, Massachusetts.

From here you can head on to **Sam Lord's Castle** (see my previous hotel recommendation). Although this is a hotel, it is also one of the major sightseeing attractions of Barbados. If you're not a guest, you'll have to pay $5 BDS ($2.50) to be admitted to the grounds. Built by slaves in 1820 and furnished with elegant Regency pieces, the house is like a Georgian plantation mansion. Take note of the ornate ceilings, said to be the finest example of stucco work in the western hemisphere. At the entrance to the hotel are shops selling handcrafts and souvenirs.

In the neighboring section, you can visit **Ragged Point Lighthouse,** built in 1885 on a rugged cliff. Since then the beacon has gone out as a warning to ships approaching the dangerous reef, called "The Cobblers." The view from here is spectacular.

Continuing north along the jagged Atlantic coast, you reach **Codrington College,** which opened in 1745. A cabbage-palm-lined avenue leads to old coral block buildings, and on the grounds you can enjoy a picnic lunch. Today the gray stone buildings are the home of the teaching Order of the Resurrection.

Before getting back on the coast road, ask in the neighborhood for directions to **St. John's Church,** perched on the edge of a cliff opening on the east coast, some 825 feet above sea level. The church dates from 1836 and in its graveyard rests a descendant of Emperor Constantine the Great, whose family was driven from the throne in Constantinople (Istanbul) by the Turks. He died in Barbados in 1678.

While in the area, you can go to **Villa Nova** (tel. 809/433-1524), built in 1834, a fine sugar plantation great house, furnished with period antiques in Barbadian mahogany and set in six acres of beautifully landscaped gardens, featuring wild orchids, flowering shrubs, mahoganies, palms, and tropical fruit trees. It's open from 10 a.m. to 4 p.m. Monday to Friday, charging $5 BDS ($2.50) for admission. To reach the place, take Hwy. 3B toward St. John's Church, but turn left by the fire station at Four Cross Roads, toward Mt. Tabor Church. Go less than a mile before turning left again. Almost immediately turn right, and up the hill you'll see the entrance.

Before the day is over, if you move fast enough, you can also visit **Andromeda Gardens** (tel. 809/433-9454). On a cliff overlooking Bathsheba on the rugged east coast, limestone boulders make for a natural eight-acre rock-garden setting, where thousands of orchids are in bloom in the open air every day of the year along with hundreds of hibiscus and heliconia. Other plants are more seasonal, including the flamboyant and frangipani, jade vine and bougainvillea, lipstick tree, candlestick tree, mammee apple, and many more. Many varieties of ferns, bromeliads, and other species that are house plants in temperate climates grow here in splendid profusion. A section is a palm garden, with more than 100 species. A simple guide helps visitors to identify many of the plants. The garden was started in 1954 by the present owner, Mrs. Iris Bannochie, on land that had belonged to her family for more than 200 years. On the grounds you'll occasionally see frogs, herons, guppies, and sometimes a mongoose or a monkey. Charging $5 BDS ($2.50) for admission, the gardens are open all day every day.

From the gardens, you can drive to the **Cotton Tower,** one of a chain of old landmark signal stations. English soldiers used these towers to warn when enemy ships were sighted along the coast. As the top of the tower is 1,000 feet above sea level, you'll have a panoramic view of the eastern sector of Barbados. Admission is $2 BDS ($1). It's open seven days a week from 9 a.m. to 5 p.m.

In the same area, **Hackleton's Cliff** also rises to a height of 1,000 feet, giving you another view of the rugged Atlantic coast. The attraction and the view were described in the book *Cradle of the Deep* by Sir Frederick Treves.

Eventually, you reach **Bathsheba,** the leading town along the east coast, where ocean rollers break, forming cascades of white foam. The same Sir Frederick compared this place to a "Cornwall in miniature." Today the old fishing village is a favorite resort among Bajans. For the best dining choice in the area, refer to the previously recommended Atlantis Hotel.

The trail north from Bathsheba takes in the **East Coast Road,** which runs for many miles with views of the Atlantic. Chalky Mount rises from the beach to 500 feet, forming a trio of peaks, and a little to the south, Barclays Park is a 15-acre natural wonder presented as a gift to the country by the banking people. There's a snackbar and picnic place here.

Stopping on the western side of Chalky Mount, you can visit Chalky Mount School, going out to see the **Potteries,** where potters turn out different products, some based on designs centuries old. Back on the north trail, you can see and perhaps take a picture of **Morgan Lewis Mill,** the only windmill remaining in Barbados with its arms and wheelhouses intact. The sight may remind you of the countryside of Holland. You can go inside for $2 BDS ($1). It's open seven days a week from 9 a.m. to 5 p.m.

The view from the top of **Cherry Tree Hill,** on Hwy. 1, is the finest in Barbados. You can look right down the eastern shore past Bathsheba to the lighthouse at Ragged Point, already described. The place is about 850 feet above sea level, and from its precincts you'll see out over "Little Scotland." The cherry trees from which the hill got its name no longer stand there, having given way to mahogany.

Most visitors to the area have come to go through **Farley Hill National Park,** which was used in the filming of *Island in the Sun.* The movie is now largely forgotten by the world, but it is still talked about a lot in Barbados. Paying $2 BDS ($1) per car to enter the park, you can explore the grounds and gracious ruins from 8:30 a.m. to 6 p.m. seven days a week. The filmmakers partially restored the shell of this once great house, but another fire destroyed the Hollywood remake.

The older section of the estate dates from 1818. Queen Elizabeth opened it as a national park in 1966.

The **Barbados Wildlife Reserve,** a project operated by the Primate Research Center, is in a lush mahogany forest across the road from Farley Hill National Park. From 10 a.m. to 5 p.m. daily, for an admission charge of $6 BDS ($3) for adults (half price for children under 12), you can stroll freely through what is primarily a monkey sanctuary. You can watch the uncaged monkeys of Barbados in their natural setting. Visitors can also see other Barbadian fauna on their home grounds, including wild hares, deer, tortoises, otters, pelicans, caymans, and a variety of tropical birds. For information, call 809/422-8826.

From Farley Hill you can head due west to **Speightstown,** which was founded around 1635 and for a time was a whaling port. The "second city" of Barbados, the town has some colonial buildings constructed after the devastating hurricane of 1831. The parish church, rebuilt in a half-Grecian style after the hurricane, is one of the places of interest. Its chancel rail is of carved mahogany.

South from Speightstown is what is known as the **Platinum Coast,** the protected western shoreline which opens onto the gentler Caribbean. Along the shoreline of the parishes of St. James and St. Peter are found the island's plushest hotels, which I've already previewed.

Holetown is the center of the coast, taking its name from the town of Hole on the Thames River. Here the first English settlers landed in the winter of 1627. An obelisk marks the spot where the *Olive Blossom* landed the first Europeans. The monument, for some reason, lists the date erroneously as 1605.

Nearby **St. James Church** is Anglican, rebuilt in 1872 on the site of the early settlers' church of 1660. In the southern porch is an old bell, bearing the inscription "God Bless King William, 1696."

Take Hwy. 2 from Bridgetown and follow it to **Welchman Hall Gully** (tel. 809/438-6671), in St. Thomas, a lush tropical garden owned by the Barbados National Trust. Here are to be found some specimens of plants that were here when the English settlers landed in 1647. Many of the plants are labeled—clove, nutmeg, tree fern, and cocoa among others—and occasionally you'll spot a wild monkey. Here you'll see a ravine and limestone stalactites and stalagmites, as well as breadfruit trees which are claimed to be descended from the seedlings brought ashore by Captain Bligh of the *Bounty*. Admission is $4 BDS ($2). It's open seven days a week from 9 a.m. to 5 p.m.

I also suggest a visit to **St. Nicholas Abbey** (tel. 809/422-8725), the Jacobean plantation great house and sugarcane fields which have been around since 1640. It was never an abbey. An ambitious owner in about 1820 simply christened it as such. More than 200 acres are still cultivated each year. In the parish of St. Peter, the structure—at least the ground floor—is open to the public Monday through Friday from 10 a.m. to 3:30 p.m., charging an admission of $5 BDS ($2.50) per person. The house is believed to be one of three Jacobean houses in the western hemisphere, and it's characterized by curved gables. Lt.-Col. Stephen Cave, the owner, is descended from the family who purchased the sugar plantation and great house in 1810. A movie made in 1934 with scenes of Barbados is shown at 11:30 a.m. and to 2:30 p.m. daily. Light refreshments are offered for sale.

Harrison's Cave at Welchman Hall in the parish of St. Thomas is the number one tourist attraction in Barbados, offering visitors a chance to view this beautiful natural underground world from aboard an electric tram and trailer. Before the tour, a color slide show of the cave is given in the presentation hall. During the tour, visitors see bubbling streams, tumbling cascades, and deep pools which are subtly lit, while all around stalactites hang overhead like icicles and stalagmites rise from the floor. Tours are daily from 9 a.m. to 4 p.m. except on Christ-

mas, Good Friday, and Easter Sunday. You should book in advance by calling
809/438-6641. Admission is $10 BDS ($5) for adults, $5 BDS ($2.50) for children.

The **Flower Forest,** P.O. Box 5T, St. Thomas (tel. 809/433-8152), at
Richmond Plantation, a mile from Harrison's Cave, is a recently established, 50-
acre area dedicated to preserving and encouraging growth of the flowering
shrubs, ferns, and trees native to the tropics, together with plantation crops on
which the island's economy was once based. Richmond is an old sugar plantation
with magnificent views of the Atlantic. The ruins are a relic of sugar cultivation.
Local handcrafts and fresh fruit are available, as well as light refreshments. Hours
are 9 a.m. to 5 p.m., and you can stay as long as you like. Admission is $8 BDS
($4).

Scattered attractions on the island include the following:

Morgan Lewis Sugar Windmill and Museum, St. Andrew, is typical of the
wind-driven mills that crushed the juice from the sugarcane in the 17th to the
19th centuries, producing sugar that made Barbados Britain's most valuable possession in the Americas. It was from the Barbados sugarcane that rum was first
produced. To reach the mill on the northeast coast of the island, follow Hwy. 1
past Farley Hill National Park to Hwy. 2. The mill and museum are open Monday through Saturday from 9 a.m. to 5 p.m. Admission is $2 for adults, $1 for
children under 14.

The 300-year-old **Sunbury Plantation and Museum,** St. Philip (tel. 809/
423-6270), on Hwy. 5, has been turned into a museum showing how a family
home looked in other days, with many Barbadian antiques in their collection. A
feature also is a collection of old horse-drawn vehicles used in daily living in a
bygone era. You may visit it from 10 a.m. to 4 p.m. Monday to Friday, 10 a.m. to
2 p.m. Saturday. Admission is $6 BDS ($3) for adults, $3 BDS ($1.50) for children.

Gun Hill Signal Station (tel. 809/429-1358), one of two such stations
owned and operated by the Barbados National Trust, is strategically placed on
the highland of St. George. It commands a magnificent view from the east to the
west. Built in 1818, it was the finest of a chain of signal stations and was also used
as an outpost for the British army stationed here at the time. Take Hwy. 3 from
Bridgetown and then go inland from Hwy. 4 toward St. George Church. Open
Monday through Friday from 9 a.m. to 5 p.m., it can be visited by adults for $4
BDS ($2), and children under 14 pay $2 BDS ($1).

Ronald Tree House, 2 Tenth Ave., Belleville (tel. 809/426-2421), is the
headquarters of the Barbados National Trust. Built in 1893, it's an example of a
typical Victorian Barbadian house. It is decorated with authentic furniture and
objets d'art of that period and is open to the public one afternoon a week. Hostesses dressed in Victorian costume will show you around if you call for an appointment. Hours are from 8 a.m. to 4 p.m. Monday to Friday. Admission is $4
BDS ($2).

SUBMERGED SIGHTSEEING: You no longer have to be an experienced
diver to see what lives 100 feet below the surface of the sea around Barbados.
Now all visitors can view the wonders that lie beneath the sea aboard *Atlantis II,* a
sightseeing submarine. The submersible seats 28 passengers, and, with two crew
members, makes 12 dives daily from 9 a.m. to 8 p.m. The ship is air-conditioned,
and both the day and the night dives offer striking views of the underwater world.
Passengers are transported from the Careenage in downtown Bridgetown
aboard the *Yukon II,* a 48-foot boat, to the dive site, about a mile from the west
coast of Barbados. The ride offers a view of the west coast of the island.

The underwater world is visible to submarine passengers through the ship's 16 two-foot wide viewing ports, eight on either side of the vessel, plus a 52-inch port at the front. Besides the rainbow of colors, tropical fish, and plants, you will see the *Stavronikita* at 150 feet down. This 350-foot cargo vessel was intentionally sunk and lies upright and intact below the surface. Tropical fish dart in and out of the ship's hatchways, masts, and rigging. Total time of the trip, including boarding and debarking and the trip to and from the dive site is about two hours. Fare for the day trip is $99 BDS ($49.50), going up to $115 BDS ($57.50) for the night voyage. Children 4 to 12 are charged half fare. For reservations, get in touch with Atlantis Ltd, Carlisle House, The Wharf, Bridgetown, Barbados, W.I. (tel. 809/436-8929, or a 24-hour number, 809/436-8932).

RUM TOURS: A luncheon tour, **The Story of Rum** tour, with guided visits to the home of Mount Gay, makers of Barbadian rum for some two centuries, is offered every Wednesday from 12:30 to 2:30 p.m. The trip includes a trek through various of Mount Gay's facilities and a buffet luncheon under the coconut palms. Steel band entertainment, free rum drinks featuring Mount Gay's rum cocktails, and free bus transportation from your hotel and back are included. The cost is $45 BDS ($22.50) per person. For reservations, phone 809/435-6900.

4. WHERE TO SHOP

Barbados merchants can sometimes treat you to duty-free merchandise at prices 20% to 40% lower than in the United States and Canada. Duty-free shops have two prices listed on items of merchandise, the local retail price and the local retail price less the government-imposed tax.

Some of the best duty-free buys include cameras (such as Leica, Rolex, and Fiji), watches (names like Omega, Piaget, Seiko), beautiful crystal (such as Waterford and Lalique), gold (especially jewelry), bone china (such names as Wedgwood and Royal Doulton), cosmetics and perfumes, and liquor (including Barbados rum and liqueurs), along with tobacco products and cashmere sweaters, tweeds, and sportswear from Britain.

The outstanding item in Barbados handcrafts is black coral jewelry made into attractive earrings, pendants, and rings. Clay pottery is another Bajan craft. In the touring section I recommend a visit to Chalky Mount and the Potteries, where this special craft originated. In Barbados you'll find a selection of locally made vases, pots, pottery mugs, glazed plates, and ornaments.

From local grasses and dried flowers, beautiful wall hangings are made, and the island craftspeople also turn out straw mats, baskets, and bags with raffia embroidery. Still in its infant stage, leatherwork is also found now in Barbados, particularly items such as handbags, belts, and sandals.

Shopping hours, in general are 8 a.m. to 4 p.m. Monday to Friday and 8 a.m. to noon on Saturday.

The best place to shop for duty-free merchandise in Barbados is **Cave Shepherd,** Broad St., Bridgetown (tel. 809/431-2121), with branches at Sunset Crest in Holetown, Speightstown, Heywoods Resort, Hastings, Grantley Adams Airport, and the Bridgetown Harbour. Cave Shepherd is the largest department store in Barbados and one of the most modern in the Caribbean. It was established in 1906, with the Cave family being sole owners, but after a disastrous fire in 1969, it was rebuilt with the financial assistance of more than 2,000 Barbadians and went public. The store offers perfumes, cosmetics from the world's leading houses, fine full lead crystal and English bone china, sweaters, cameras, gold and silver jewelry, swimwear, leather goods, and batik, handcrafts, and souvenirs. More than 70 brands of liqueurs are sold as well as other spirits. After you finish shopping, relax on the top floor in the cool comfort of the Ideal Restaurant.

While in Bridgetown, go down to the **Pelican Village** on Princess Alice Hwy., leading down to the city's Deep Water Harbour. A collection of island-made crafts and souvenirs is sold here in a tiny colony of thatch-roofed shops, and you can wander from one to the other. Sometimes you can see craftspeople at work. Some of the shops to be found here are gimmicky and repetitive, although interesting items can be found.

Batik Caribe sells original hand-dyed batik on quality 100% cotton and silk. Beautiful wallhangings are sold as well as a range of hand-hemmed scarves, beach and casual wear, and small gift items. Sales outlets are conveniently located: Nicholas House on Broad Street in Bridgetown, the Hilton Arcade, and the Handicraft Shop at Marriott's Sam Lord's Castle, to name a few. Visit their studio at Colleton Estate in St. John (tel. 809/433-1599) to see artisans working at this ancient craft.

Bridgetown's most modern shopping complex, **Mall 34,** on Broad Street, offers duty-free shopping in air-conditioned comfort. You can find watches, clocks, china, jewelry, crystal, linens, sweaters, and liquor, together with souvenir items and tropical fashions. A restaurant is on the top floor of the building, and shoppers can stop for a cool drink and a snack at the little café downstairs.

For a fine selection of Caribbean items, go to **Caribbean Creations,** Bridge House, Careenage, Bridgetown (tel. 809/427-0611). You'll find baskets, mahogany carvings, mats, bags, and other local souvenirs.

Harrison's, whose main shop is at 1 Broad St., Bridgetown (tel. 809/426-0720), has eight branch stores, all selling a wide variety of duty-free merchandise, including china, crystal, jewelry, leather goods, sweaters, and perfumes, all at fair prices. They've been in business since the 19th century.

Sea Nymph Dress Shoppe, at the Skyway Shopping Plaza in Hastings, South Coast (tel. 809/429-4242), specializes in swimwear (if you forgot your bathing suit), hostess gowns, blouses, shorts, slacks, and dresses made to order.

The Loomhouse, Skyway Plaza, Hastings, Christ Church (tel. 809/426-0442), is one of the showcases for the hand-weaving work of Roslyn of Barbados, a talented Barbadian artist and designer. On the outskirts of Bridgetown, this craft boutique displays work by Roslyn Watson. The government of Barbados has selected some of her pieces to present to such dignitaries as Pierre Trudeau, the former Canadian prime minister. Works by other craftspeople are displayed, in mahogany, clay, and straw. There is also a collection of coral.

Artemis, the Green Chattel House, corner of St. Matthias and Hastings Main Road, Christ Church (tel. 809/436-3216), has a pleasing selection of hand-painted and hand-dyed designs, local art and antiques, ceramics, shell jewelry, and souvenirs.

At **Da Costas Colonnade Shoppe,** Sunset Crest, St. James (tel. 809/432-1600), displays an excellent selection of fine china such as Aynsley and Belleek giftware, Waterford crystal, Lladró and Florence figurines, and other items, all at duty-free prices. French fragrances and locally made handcrafts are also sold. Its shop at Da Costas' Mall, Broad St. (tel. 809/429-4843), offers Royal Doulton, Wedgwood, and Aynsley fine china, plus articles from the other sources listed above.

Best of Barbados, Southern Palms Hotel, St. Lawrence Gap (tel. 809/428-7171), is perhaps the most attractive of an islandwide chain of stores selling only products designed and/or made in Barbados. It was established in 1975 by an English-born painter, Jill Walker, whose prints are best-sellers, and her husband,

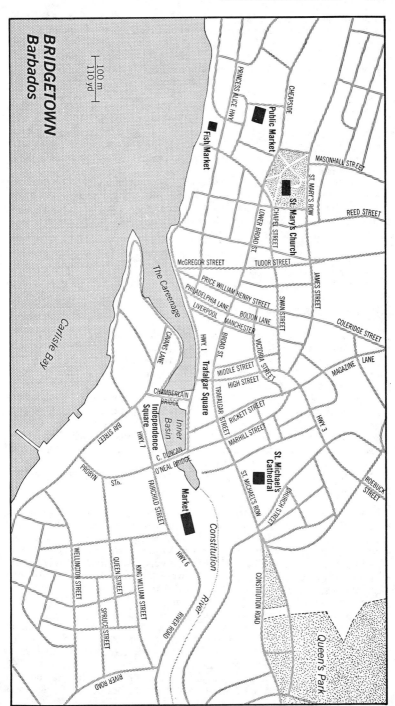

BRIDGETOWN
Barbados

100 m
110 yd

Carlisle Bay

The Careenage

Fish Market

Public Market

PRINCESS ALICE HWY.

CHEAPSIDE

MASONHALL STREET

ST. MARY'S ROW

St. Mary's Church

REED STREET

LOWER BROAD ST.

CHAPEL STREET

McGREGOR STREET

TUDOR STREET

JAMES STREET

PRICE WILLIAM HENRY STREET

PHILADELPHIA LANE

LIVERPOOL

BOLTON LANE

MANCHESTER

SWAN STREET

COLERIDGE STREET

CANN'S LANE

HWY 1

BROAD ST.

VICTORIA STREET

MAGAZINE LANE

Trafalgar Square

MIDDLE STREET

HIGH STREET

TRAFALGAR STREET

RICKETT STREET

HWY 3

CHAMBERLAIN BRIDGE

Inner Basin

MARHILL STREET

Independence Square

BAY STREET

HWY 7

C. DUNCAN

O'NEAL BRIDGE

St. Michael's Cathedral

ST. MICHAEL'S ROW

CHURCH STREET

ROEBUCK STREET

PROBYN STn.

FAIRCHILD STREET

Market

Constitution River

WELLINGTON STREET

QUEEN STREET

KING WILLIAM STREET

HWY 6

CONSTITUTION ROAD

SPRUCE STREET

RIVER ROAD

Queen's Park

Jimmy. Today the day-to-day administration of the boutiques is handled by their daughter, Sarah. They sell articles celebrating aspects of island life, including needlepoint pillows, blackface dolls, coasters and placemats with scenes of Bajan life, steel-band recordings, calendars, and recipe books. This tasteful place is in a pink-and-white building around the corner from the entrance to the Southern Palms Hotel. It's open from 9 a.m. to 5 p.m. Monday to Friday, 9 a.m. to 12:30 p.m. Saturday.

Boutiques abound in Barbados. One of the best is **The Petticoat Lane Boutique,** Bridgetown Complex (tel. 809/429-7037), run by Carol Cadogan, who designs tropical wear and is known for her one-of-a-kind items. For inspiration, she turns to the flora and fauna of the island and the world under the sea. She also sells the accessories to go with her apparel. Such magazines as *Vogue* and *Glamour* have praised her collection.

Bajan art, both in painting and sculpture, is now coming into its own. For a preview of what is happening in the art world, go to the gallery operated by the **National Cultural Foundation Gallery,** Queen's Park House, Queen's Park, Bridgetown (no phone). It is open from 10 a.m. to 1:30 p.m. and 2:30 to 6 p.m. Monday to Friday, 2 to 6 p.m. Saturday.

5. THE SPORTING LIFE

The principal activity is swimming and sunning, which, as has been discussed, is far preferable on the western coast in the clear, buoyant waters, though you may also want to visit the surf-pounded Atlantic waters in the east, which are better for viewing than swimming.

BEACHES: Barbadians will tell you that their island has a beach for every day in the year, and if you're there long enough you may be able to seek them out. If you're only visiting for a shorter time, however, you'll probably be happy with the ones that are easy to find. They're all open to the public, even those in front of the big resort hotels and private homes. The government requires that there be access to all beaches, via roads along the property line or through the hotel entrance. The beaches on the west, the so-called **Platinum Coast,** are the most popular. These include Paradise Beach, Paynes Bay and Sandy Lane Bay, Treasure Beach, Gibbs Bay, Heywoods Beach, Rockley, and Benson Beach. To reach the ones on the east, drive through the cane fields to **North Point, Cove Bay,** or **Archer's Bay,** or head down to the beautiful but more perilous one at **Bathsheba.** Crane Bay, Tent Bay, Long Bay—I could go on and on, but perhaps you'll try them all and then find your own.

SNORKELING AND SCUBA: The clear waters off Barbados have a visibility of more than 100 feet most of the year. More than 50 varieties of fish are found on the shallow inside reefs. On night dives, sleeping fish, night anemones, lobsters, moray eels, and octopuses can be seen. On a mile-long coral reef two minutes by boat from **Sandy Beach,** sea fans, corals, gorgonias, and reef fish are plentiful. *J.R.,* a dredge barge sunk as an artificial reef in 1983, is popular with beginners for its coral, fish life, and 20-foot depth. The *Berwyn,* a coral-encrusted tugboat that sank in Carlisle Bay in 1916, attracts photographers because of its variety of reef fish, shallow depth, good light, and visibility.

The **Asta Reef,** with a drop of 80 feet, has coral, sea fans, and reef fish in abundance. It's the site of a Barbados wreck sunk in 1986 as an artificial reef. **Dottins,** the most beautiful reef on the west coast, stretches five miles from Holetown to Bridgetown and has numerous dive sites at an average depth of 40 feet and dropoffs of 100 feet. The S.S. *Stavronika,* a Greek freighter, is a popular dive site for advanced divers. Crippled by fire in 1976, the 360-foot freighter was sunk a quarter-mile off the west coast to become an artificial reef in **Folkstone Underwater Park.** The mast is at 40 feet, the deck at 80 feet, and the keel at 140 feet. It's encrusted with coral.

The Dive Shop, Pebbles Beach, Aquatic Gap, Bay St., St. Michael (tel. 809/ 426-9947), offers some of the best scuba-diving in Barbados (costing about $33 each). Each day two dive trips go out to the nearby reefs and wrecks. In addition, snorkeling trips and equipment rentals are possible. A one-hour trip to a shipwreck with equipment goes for $8.

Sandy Beach Watersports, Worthing, Christ Church (tel. 809/428-9033, ext. 270), takes guests, both resident and nonresident, on scuba-diving and snorkel cruises daily to reefs and wrecks in both shallow and deep water.

Peter Hughes Underwater Barbados, St. Lawrence Gap (tel. 809/428-3504), is a branch in the wide-flung diving empire of Scottish entrepreneur Peter Hughes. In a wood-sided shed across the street from a sheltered bay, it is said to be the largest scuba facility on the island.

WINDSURFING: Experts say that the windsurfing off Bentson Beach is as good as any this side of Hawaii. Judging from the crowds of 20- to 35-year-olds who flock here, it's probably true. An establishment set up especially to handle the demand is the **Barbados Windsurfing Club,** Bentson Beach, Maxwell, Christ Church (tel. 809/428-9095). It rents boards and gives lessons to learners. Club Mistral, a company run by Mistral A.G. of Switzerland, manufacturer of the finest windsurfing boards in the world, provides the rental fleet for the Barbados facility. This fleet consists of up to 75 boards, all current models with a selection of 200 sails. Boards rent for $26 BDS ($13) per hour, and one-hour lessons cost $45 BDS ($22.50) per person.

PARASAILING: If you'd like to fly over Barbados with the sensation of being a bird, you can book a high-flying tour with **Chute the Moon,** Holetown Beach, near the Barbados Pizza House in St. James (for reservations, call 809/432-2058). This is a sensational ride, as you soar 200 feet into the air, taking in an aerial view of the resort-studded west coast. The cost is $50 BDS ($25) for a regular flight.

GOLF: Your best bet is the **Sandy Lane Hotel Golf Club,** St. James, on the west coast (tel. 809/432-1311). Greens fees in summer are $35 BDS ($17.50) for 18 holes, $25 BDS ($12.50) for nine holes. Rental of a gas-powered golf cart is $50 BDS ($25) for 18 holes, $30 BDS ($15) for nine holes. Clubs can be rented for $25 BDS ($12.50) for 18 holes, $15 BDS ($7.50) for nine. These prices are about 25% higher in high season.

A nine-hole executive course is at the **Rockley Resort Hotel,** Golf Club Road, Worthing, Christ Church (tel. 809/427-5896). Greens fees are $25 BDS ($12.50) for the nine holes. If you want to play 18 holes, you repeat the same course, paying $40 BDS ($20) for greens fees. You can rent a pull-cart and clubs for $20 BDS ($10).

At the **Heywoods Resort,** St. Peter (tel. 809/422-4900), there is an eight-hole golf course. Greens fees are $24 BDS ($12) for the eight holes, with clubs and a pull-cart costing $17 BDS ($8.50).

TENNIS: Most of the major hotels have their own tennis courts, some of which are lit for night games. Generally, if you're not a guest, these hotels charge anywhere from $12 BDS ($6) to $16 BDS ($8) per hour of court time.

At **Rockley Resort,** Christ Church (tel. 809/427-5890), courts are open from 8 a.m. to 10 p.m. At **Heywoods Resort,** St. Peter (tel. 809/422-4900), the courts are in play from 7 a.m. to 11 p.m. You can play at the **Sunset Crest Club,** St. James (tel. 809/432-1309), from 8 a.m. to 11 p.m.

HORSEBACK RIDING: A different view of Barbados is offered by **Caribbean International Riding Centre,** c/o Roachford, Sion Hill House near St. Patrick's, Christ Church (tel. 809/423-0007), with riding at Valley Hill Stables, Valley Hill House, Woodbourne, Christ Church. Trail riding in the countryside provides an hour's trip through plantations escorted by experienced guides, followed by relaxation over a cool drink in the clubroom. Experienced riders can follow more varied trails. Instruction is given to newcomers. The price, including transportation to and from your hotel and a complimentary drink, is $45 BDS ($22.50).

DEEP-SEA FISHING: The fishing is first-rate in the waters around Barbados, where fishermen pursue dolphin, marlin, wahoo, barracuda, and sailfish, to name only the most popular catches. There's also an occasional cobia.
    The Dive Shop, Pebbles Beach, Aquatic Gap, Bay Street, St. Michael (tel. 809/426-9947), can arrange half-day charters for one to six persons (all equipment and drinks included), costing $250 per boat. Under the same arrangement, the whole-day jaunt goes for $500. In other words, no discount.
    Jolly Roger Watersports, Sunset Crest and Colony Club, St. James (tel. 809/436-6424), offers deep-sea fishing on a cabin cruiser. You can fish for wahoo, dolphin, marlin, sailfish, yellowfin tuna, barracuda, and bonito. Prices are from $450 BDS ($225) for a half day.

BOAT TRIPS: Largest of the coastal cruising vessels, the *Bajan Queen,* is modeled after a Mississippi riverboat, and is the only cruise ship offering table seating and dining on local fare produced fresh from the on-board galley. There is also cover available from too much sun or rain. Day cruises include two anchor stops for swimming with snorkeling equipment provided, a buffet luncheon, water sports, open bar, and dancing to calypso music and international records. The *Bajan Queen* becomes a showboat by night, with local bands providing all kinds of music for dancing under the stars. You are treated to a dinner of roast chicken, barbecued steak, and seasoned flying fish with a help-yourself buffet of fresh side dishes and salads. Cruises are usually sold out, so you should book early to avoid disappointment. Each cruise costs $75 BDS ($37.50) and includes transportation to and from your hotel. For reservations get in touch with *Bajan Queen* Tours Ltd., Deep Water Harbour, Bridgetown (tel. 809/436-2149).
    Another popular cruise is aboard the *Jolly Roger,* a full-size replica of a fighting ship. You can enjoy drinks from an open bar, a full steak barbecue lunch, and nonstop music for dancing on the spacious sundeck. Later the boat stops at a sheltered cove where passengers can put on their bathing suits and go for a swim. Lunch cruises are from 10 a.m. to 2 p.m. Tuesday to Friday. At night passengers cruise and dance to the sounds of top local singing groups (in season only). The cost is $75 BDS ($37.50) day or night. Night cruises are Thursday and Saturday from 6 to 10 p.m. For information, telephone 436-6424, or visit the berth at Cavans Lane in Bridgetown.
    In addition, most of the big hotels have Sunfish and Hobie Cat craft for rent, costing $30 BDS ($15) to $50 BDS ($25) per hour for one or two passengers.

6. AFTER DARK IN BARBADOS
Most of the big resort hotels feature entertainment nightly, often dancing to steel bands and occasional native floor shows. Sometimes beach barbecues are staged. Otherwise, here's the lineup.

The best place to head if you're in Barbados on a Thursday or Sunday is **1627 And All That Sort of Thing** at the Barbados Museum in St. Michael's Parish (tel. 809/435-6900 for reservations). The show, from 7:30 to 10:30 p.m., is a historical celebration of Barbadian culture. At the museum, once a British military prison, the evening features a traditional Bajan buffet dinner, with a liqueur, followed by a folk-dance extravaganza by the Barbados Dance Theatre Company. For $70 BDS ($34), tax included, you are transported to and from the museum and are allowed to tour the exhibits. The drinks and hors d'oeuvres are complimentary as well. This is one of the best after-dark bargains in town, and you'll learn a lot as well as have fun.

The best dinner show on the island is **Barbados! Barbados!**, a two-act musical comedy based on the life of one of the island's most colorful characters, Rachel Pringle. This spectacular is staged every Tuesday in the Barbados Horticultural Society, original Boiling House at Balls Estate, Christ Church (tel. 809/435-6900 for reservations). The price of $65 BDS ($32.50) includes transportation to and from your hotel, hors d'oeuvres, complimentary drinks all evening, government tax, the show, and dinner. Hours are 6:30 and 10 p.m.

The **Plantation Restaurant and Garden Theatre,** Hwy. 7, St. Lawrence (tel. 809/428-5048), stages two of the most popular dinner shows on the island. On Tuesday the internationally known Merrymen sometimes perform their latest hits, and you can also see a Barbadian floor show featuring one of the island's top steel bands together with limbo dancing and fire-eating. The Merrymen are known to travel, so check with your hotel's activities desk to see if they are going to be performing. The buffet dinner starts at 7 p.m. and show time is 8:30 p.m. On nights when shows are staged, the cost, including dinner, is $65 BDS ($32.50). On Wednesday and Saturday, the **Plantation Tropical Spectacular II** is staged, a colorful cabaret dinner show with a cast of 30 dancers in scenes from the old marketplace, the mysteries of voodoo, and the splendor and excitement of carnival. A steel band provides dinner music. The dinner show, costing $34.50 (U.S.), is from 6 to 10 p.m. A Monday and Friday night dinner show, **Barbados by Night,** features the island's number one band, Spice, with pop, reggae, and calypso music, plus costume dancers, limbo, and fire-eating. The price of the show, which starts at 6:30 p.m., is $30 (U.S.), including dinner, the show, drinks, and tax.

The **Flambeau Bar,** at the Barbados Hilton on Needham's Point, St. Michael (tel. 809/462-0200), is an indoor-outdoor place. The bar is open from 5 p.m. to 1 a.m. daily, and happy hour, with free appetizers, is from 5:30 to 6:30 p.m. Live music is presented nightly, varying from small groups to solo entertainers.

The **Odyssey** nightclub, Palmetto Square (tel. 809/436-7455), offers entertainment for its customers on weekends, with a DJ in charge except when there's a live performance. On Thursday, at $5 per person, music starts at 9 p.m. Friday at 9 p.m. a live combo is the attraction, and admission is $10. Saturday hours are 10 p.m. to 5 a.m., $10 admission; and on Sunday, you can enter at 7 p.m. for $5. There's a dress code: no hats, shorts, sleeveless shirts (men), slippers, sneakers, or track shoes.

The **Warehouse,** Bridge House, Bridgetown (tel. 809/436-2897), is the island's leading disco, attracting a very youthful crowd. Spice, the island's leading band, often performs here. It is open nightly except Sunday from 9:30 p.m. until either 3 or 4 a.m. Live music begins at 11:30 p.m. The entrance fee ranges from $6 BDS ($3) to $12 BDS ($6), with a beer costing $3 BDS ($1.50).

Club Miliki, Heywoods, St. Peter (tel. 809/422-4900), translates as *welcome* in West African dialect. It plays disco music every evening except Sunday and Monday. There's a $12 BDS ($6) entrance charge, after which a beer costs $3

BDS ($1.50). The disco is in one of the many buildings (just follow the trail markers) at the government's Heywoods Resort, covered separately in the hotels section of this chapter.

The Beach Club, Sunset Crest, St. James (tel. 809/432-1309), is the social focal point for Sunset Crest. Happy hour at the Beach Bar is from 6 to 7 p.m., when drinks go for $2 BDS ($1). Fish fries, barbecues, or buffets are offered from 7 to 9 p.m. daily costing $7.50 BDS ($3.75) to 14 BDS ($7.50). Entertainment features live bands, amateur nights, films of Barbados, and local folk chorales. Monday is show night. Nondiners are charged $5 BDS ($2.50) to enter. Hours for entertainment are from 8 to 11 p.m. nightly. The club is also open for breakfast, from 8 to 11 a.m., and lunch, 11 a.m. to 3 p.m.

The Secret Garden Club, Hwy. 2A (tel. 809/425-2222), in the grounds of Bagatelle Great House, quite near Bagatelle Restaurant, three miles from Sunset Crest, St. Thomas, is a place where over-25s go to dance, drink, and chat. The bar, dancing, and drinking area is air-conditioned, and there is an outdoor section cooled by breezes. The place serves appetizers, desserts, and fondues until late. Backgammon boards are available, and the atmosphere is clubby and agreeable. The music, pitched at a noise level that allows conversation, is varied. The establishment is open from 8:30 p.m. "onwards" daily.

If you're in Barbados on a Thursday night, one of the most enjoyable evenings is to go to the **Barbados Hilton,** on Needham's Point, St. Michael (tel. 809/426-0200). There, a "night of the buccaneers" is staged at the gazebo. Dinner is at 7 p.m., a floor show at 8:30 p.m. The Bajan cuisine features roast suckling pig, barbecued spareribs, and grilled fish. The show that follows is lively. The cost is most reasonable as well: $60 BDS ($30) for adults, $32 BDS ($16) for children. There is also an evening of song and drama on Sunday night, costing $56 BDS ($28) for an international buffet and a program of Bajan folk ballads presented by Sing Out Barbados. On Tuesday a sumptuous buffet, costing $58 BDS ($29), is highlighted by a folkloric presentation in song and dance of life in a Barbadian fishing village.

Finally, for the most authentic Bajan evening possible and to top off your trip to Barbados, head for Baxters Road in Bridgetown, a street that reaches its peak of liveliness on Friday and Saturday after 11 p.m. In fact, if you stick around until dawn, the joints are still jumping. The street is safer than it looks, because Bajans come here to have fun, not to make trouble. Entertainment tends to be spontaneous. You might hear jazz on scratchy records, certainly the voice of Billie Holiday. Some oldtime visitors have compared Baxters Road to the back streets of New Orleans in the '30s. If you fall in love with the place, you can "caf crawl" up and down the street, where nearly every bar is run by a Bajan mama. All prices are about the same, but each place has its own atmosphere.

The most popular "caf" is **Enid's,** Baxters Road (she has a phone, "but it doesn't work"), a little ramshackle establishment where Bajans come to devour Enid's fried chicken at 3 in the morning. Her place is open daily from 8:30 p.m. to 8:30 a.m., when the last satisfied customer departs into the blazing morning sun and Enid heads home to get some sleep before the new night begins. You can also stop in for a Banks beer. In fact, if you want a totally Bajan experience, why not come here and occupy one of the oil-cloth clad tables in the dilapidated back room? You can order a complete dinner for about $7 BDS ($3.50).

A PUB CRAWL: A favorite of mine is **The Coach House,** Paynes Bay, St. James (tel. 809/432-1163). Fittingly, there are two antique coaches sitting on the lawn of this ochre-colored house which the owners say is 200 years old. Looking at it from the outside, it's difficult to guess the building's age because of its recently added veranda. However, once you're inside under the ceiling beams, the atmosphere is very much that of an English pub. Business people and habitués of the nearby beaches enjoy this establishment's buffet lunches, where Bajan food is served daily except Saturday from noon to 3 p.m. The price is $17.50 BDS ($8.75) per person for an all-you-can-eat assortment of chicken, baked fish, salads, and local vegetables. If you drop in between 6 and 11 p.m., you can accompany your drinks with bar meals such as flying fish and chips or steak and shrimp plus a fresh salad for a top $14 BDS ($7) to $20 BDS ($10) per person. There's also a more formal evening dining room on a lower floor, where meals, excluding service and drinks, cost around $38 BDS ($19). Menu specialties include homemade soup, fish Créole, and chicken béchamel. Even if you don't want to eat, you can enjoy drinks here. Live music is presented almost every night, featuring everything from steel bands to country to calypso. The pub is on the main Bridgetown–Holetown road just south of Sandy Lane.

The **Ship Inn,** St. Lawrence Gap, Christ Church (tel. 809/428-9605), contains an attractive rough decor of dark ceiling beams, ship engravings, and muted ship lanterns casting soft shadows. Many guests come for the darts, others for the drinks, and still others for meeting friends and/or enjoying the live music nightly. On weekends and late on weeknights the place is sometimes packed with diplomats and other VIPs (including the Bajan prime minister), as well as visiting sailors from the various navies that come into port here. The inn is both a pub and a restaurant, serving such food as steak-and-kidney pie, "bangers and mash," shepherd's pie, and flying fish and chips. Full meals cost from $14 BDS ($7) to $20 BDS ($10). More substantial meals are served in the Captain's Carvery, reached through a passageway. The inn is open from 6 p.m. to 2 a.m. daily.

TRINIDAD AND TOBAGO

□ □ □

Charted by Columbus on his third voyage in 1498, Trinidad has since then been peopled by immigrants from almost every corner of the world—Africa, the Middle East, Europe, India, China, and the Americas. It is against such a background that the island has become the fascinating mixture of cultures, races, and creeds that it is today.

Trinidad, which is about the size of Delaware, and its sister island, tiny Tobago, 20 miles to the northeast, together form a nation popularly known as "T & T." The islands of the new country are the southernmost outposts of the West Indies. Trinidad lies only ten miles from the Paria Peninsula in Venezuela, to which in unrecorded times it was once connected.

Trinidad is completely different from the other islands of the Caribbean, and that forms part of its charm and appeal. Visitors in increasing numbers are drawn to this island of many rhythms, where the great swinging sounds of calypso, limbo, and steeldrum bands all began.

The people are part of the attraction, the most cosmopolitan island in the Caribbean. Its polyglot population includes Syrians, Chinese, Americans, Europeans, East Indians, Parsees, Madrasis, Venezuelans, and the last of the original Amerindians, the early Indian settlers of the island. You'll also find Hindustanis, Javanese, Lebanese, slave descendants, and Créole mixtures. The main religions are Christianity, Hinduism, and Islam. In all there are a million-plus inhabitants, whose language is English, although you may hear speech in a strange argot, Trinibagianese.

Port-of-Spain, in the northwest corner of the island, is the capital, with the largest concentration of the population, about 120,000. Every costume and fabric is worn on the streets of this city.

One of the most industrialized nations in the Caribbean, and the third-largest exporter of oil in the western hemisphere, Trinidad, measuring 50 by 38 miles, is also blessed with a huge 114-acre Pitch Lake from which comes most of the world's asphalt. Further, it's also the home of Angostura Bitters, the recipe for which is a guarded secret.

The Spanish settled the island which the Indians had called *Iere,* or "land of the hummingbird." The Spaniards made their first permanent settlement in 1592 and held onto it longer than they did any of their other real estate in the Caribbean. The English captured Trinidad in 1797, and it remained British until the two-island nation declared its independence in 1962.

GETTING THERE: The three major contenders for passage from North America to Trinidad include **American Airlines, Pan Am,** and an airline based in Trinidad, **BWIA.** Frankly, your choice of airline should be influenced not only by price but also by your arrival time in Port-of-Spain. Trinidadian customs are notoriously slow and during the day, but late at night their irritation factor rises unbearably.

Pan American offers daily service to Port-of-Spain from New York's JFK Airport, with a connecting stop in Caracas, Venezuela en route. Many passengers pay a small surcharge to explore Caracas for a day or two. The lowest high-season fare Pan Am offers (but subject to change) is $395 on weekdays and $415 on weekends, each round trip, and requires a seven-day advance purchase and a delay of 3 to 21 days before using the return portion of your ticket. This fare is also dependent on advance bookings, with the lower-priced seats selling out long in advance. Pan Am flies daily from Miami to Port-of-Spain, with an intermediate stop in Barbados.

American Airlines also offers daily service to Port-of-Spain, with connections through dozens of U.S. cities. Each of its flights connects through American's hub in San Juan.

Finally, BWIA flies twice a day from New York's JFK to Port-of-Spain, making from one to three stops along the way in such places as Antigua, St. Kitts, Grenada, and/or Barbados, depending on the schedule. BWIA offers twice-daily flights from Miami to Port-of-Spain. BWIA's 1:15 p.m. flight makes up to four stops en route, while the 3 p.m. flight stops only once. BWIA also offers flights between Baltimore-Washington and Port-of-Spain every Saturday and Sunday in both directions.

For more information, call the reservations desk of the airlines or your travel agent.

GETTING AROUND: There are lots of **unmetered taxis,** in Trinidad. When inquiring about the fare, ask if the rates quoted are in U.S. dollars or Trinidadian dollars. It makes quite a big difference. A taxi ride from the airport into Port-of-Spain generally costs about $50 TT ($11.50) during the day, $75 TT ($17.25) at night. Most drivers also serve as guides. Their rates, however, are based on route distances, so get an overall quotation and agree on the actual fare before setting off.

There are also "pirate" taxis—private cars that take on passengers like a regular taxi.

The Route Taxi

Launched in World War II, a route taxi is like a bus, stopping and taking on passengers or letting them off as they proceed through Port-of-Spain and its environs. Drivers take a maximum of five passengers. Fares vary depending on the route, of course. A typical ride in a route taxi costs only $2 TT (46¢). There are also ten- and 20-seater route taxis.

Buses

All the cities of Trinidad are linked by regular bus service from Port-of-Spain. Fares are inexpensive, costing from 50¢ TT (12¢) for runs within the capital. However, buses are likely to be very overcrowded. Always try to avoid them at rush hours.

Car Rentals

Of all the Caribbean islands reviewed in this book, few present the car rental problems that Trinidad does. There are some 4,500 miles of good roads, so that while touring outside of Port-of-Spain goes quickly, the fierce traffic jams of the capital are legendary. And although your rental car will probably have a right-hand-mounted steering wheel, *you'll be required to drive on the left.* You'll also need a good map, but you'll find one hard to come by. All the major U.S. car-rental firms, at press time, had canceled their franchises in Trinidad. You can take a chance with local car-rental companies, but I have found none worthy of endorsement.

My strong advice is to avoid the anxiety of driving. You can rent taxis and local drivers for your sightseeing jaunts; if that is too expensive you can take an organized tour. Night driving can be especially hazardous.

Organized Tours

Sightseeing tours are offered by **Hub Travel Ltd.,** Suite 27, Bel Air Hotel, Piarco (tel. 809/664-4771, ext. 27). The tours are made in late-model sedans, with a trained driver-guide. Prices are quoted on a seat-in-car basis. Private arrangements will cost more.

A city tour, lasting two hours, will take you past the main points of interest of Port-of-Spain: White Hall, the President's House, Queen's Park Savannah, the Botanical Gardens, the National Museum and Art Gallery, the Emperor Valley Zoo, cathedrals, a mosque, temples, and through the commercial and residential centers, then to Lady Young Look-out for a panoramic view of the city. This trip leaves daily at 10 a.m.

You'll see tropical splendor at its best on a Port-of-Spain/Maracas Bay/Saddle Drive jaunt leaving at 1 p.m. daily, lasting 3½ hours. The tour begins with a drive around Port-of-Spain, passing the main points of interest listed above and then making one of the most beautiful drives of the island, through mountain scenery over the "Saddle" of the northern range to Maracas Bay, a popular beach. You return via Saddle Drive, Santa Cruz Valley, the village of San Juan, and the Lady Young Road for the panoramic view of Port-of-Spain.

An Island Circle Tour is a seven-hour journey which includes lunch and a welcome drink. Leaving at 9 a.m. daily, your car goes south along the west coast with a view of the Gulf of Paria, across the central plains, through Pointe-à-Pitre and San Fernando, and on eastward into rolling country overlooking sugarcane fields. Then you go down into the coconut plantations along the 14-mile-long Mayaro Beach. Here you're given time for a swim and lunch before returning along Manzanilla Beach and back to the city.

An especially interesting trip is to Caroni Swamp and Bird Sanctuary, a four-hour trek by car and boat into the sanctuary where you'll see rich Trinidad bird life, with vast flocks of exotic and colorful winged creatures gathering to feed (they nest here, also). Among the birds you can see the scarlet ibis, egrets, blue and white herons, roseate spoonbills, kingfisher, and other swamp birds. The tour leaves daily at 3 p.m.

PRACTICAL FACTS: The Republic of Trinidad and Tobago, which came into existence in 1976, is a parliamentary democracy, with a president and a prime minister.

Banks: They stay open from 9 a.m. to 2 p.m. Monday to Thursday, and from 9 a.m. to noon and 3 to 5 p.m. on Friday.

Currency: Trinidad and Tobago dollars are pegged to the U.S. dollar at an exchange rate of $1 U.S. to $4.25 TT. Ask what currency is being referred to when rates are quoted to you. I've used a combination of both in this chapter, depending on the establishment. U.S. and Canadian dollars are accepted in exchange for payment, particularly in places in Port-of-Spain, less so outside the capital. However, you'll do better by converting your Canadian or U.S. dollars into local currency.

Note: Unless otherwise specified, dollar quotations appearing in this chapter are in U.S. currency.

Customs: Going through **customs** in Trinidad is one of the worst procedures in the West Indies. Officials almost deliberately move at a snail's pace, causing endless delays, and local arriving families seem to transport entire households of goods, of which officials insist on examining every parcel. Even if you have nothing to declare and go through the green sign, you're still likely to be endlessly detained and questioned. Everybody seemingly knows about this situation, but nothing is done about it.

Documents: Visitors arriving in Trinidad and Tobago should have an ongoing or return ticket from their point of embarkation. You'll be asked to fill out an immigration card upon your arrival. The carbon copy of this should be saved, as it must be returned to immigration officials when you depart. Citizens of the U.S. and Canada do not need passports to enter Trinidad and Tobago for stays up to two months.

Electricity: The electric current is 110 or 220 volts AC, 60 cycles, but check before plugging in appliances.

Information: The Tourist Board, 122-124 Frederick St., Port-of-Spain (tel. 809/623-1932), provides information.

Post Office: The main post office is on Wrightson Road, Port-of-Spain, and is open from 7 a.m. to 5 p.m. Monday to Friday.

Taxes and service: The big hotels and restaurants add at least a 10% to 15% service charge to your final tab; if not, you should tip from 12% to 15%. In addition, the government also imposes a 3% occupancy tax on room rates. It also imposes a departure tax of $20 TT ($4.60) on every passenger more than 5 years old.

Telecommunications: To call Trinidad or Tobago from the U.S., dial the area code, 809, then the local number. On the islands, you do not need to dial the area code. Cables may be handed in at the Tourist Bureau, Piarco Airport, at a hotel desk, or at the offices of Textel, 1 Edward St., Port-of-Spain.

Time: Trinidad and Tobago time is the same as the U.S. East Coast, except when the States go to Daylight Saving Time. Trinidad does not, so when it's 6 a.m. in Miami, it's still 5 a.m. in Trinidad.

Weather: Trinidad has a tropical climate all year, with constant trade winds maintaining mean temperatures of 84° Fahrenheit during the day, 74° at night, with a range of 70° to 90°. The rainy season runs from May to November, but that fact shouldn't deter a visit at that time. The rain usually lasts no more than two hours before the sun comes out again.

CARNIVAL AND CALYPSO: Called "the world's most colorful festival,"
the Carnival of Trinidad is a spectacle of dazzling costumes and gaiety. Hundreds of bands of masqueraders parade through the cities on the Monday and Tuesday preceding Ash Wednesday. Traffic, except the human variety, comes to a stand-

still. The island seems to explode with music, fun-making, and dancing. It's been called a 48-hour orgy!

Hotel accommodations are booked months in advance, and most inns raise their prices at the time.

Some of the carnival costumes cost hundreds of dollars, and their owners spend all year making them, getting ready for next year's big event. For example, "bands" might depict the birds of Trinidad such as the scarlet ibis and the keskidee; or they might be a bevy of women coming out in the streets dressed as pussy cats. Others are dragons, devils, and demons. Costumes are also satirical and comical.

The top calypsonian is proclaimed king. On one occasion, the King of Carnival appeared dressed as a "Devil Ray" with a gigantic "delta wing," his eyes glinting behind a black mask, his body bound in black leather studded with silver.

Trinidad, of course, is the land of calypso, which grew out of the folksong of the Afro–West Indian. The lyrics command the greatest attention, as they are rich in satire and innuendo. The calypsonian is considered a poet-musician, and lines have often been considered libelous and obscene, capable of toppling politicians from office as they have in the past. In banter and bravado, the calypsonian reveals and gives voice to the sufferings, hopes, and aspirations of his people. At carnival time the artist sings his compositions to spectators in places called by the traditional name of "tents." There are five or six shows a night at the calypso tents around town, from 8 p.m. to midnight. Tickets for these are sold in the afternoon at most record shops.

Carnival parties, or fêtes, with three or four orchestras at each one, are public and are advertised in the newspapers. Tickets for these events, which go on for several weeks before carnival ends on Shrove Tuesday, cost $50 to $60. For a really wild time, attend a party on Sunday night before Carnival Monday.

You can attend rehearsals of steel bands at their headquarters, called *panyards,* beginning about 7 p.m. Preliminary band competitions are held at the grandstand of the Queen's Park Savannah in Port-of-Spain and at Skinners Park in San Fernando, beginning some three weeks before carnival.

The Tourist Board publishes a booklet, *Carnival in Trinidad & Tobago.* You can receive this guide and a calendar of carnival events from the **Trinidad & Tobago Tourist Board,** 118-35 Queens Blvd., Forest Hills, NY 11375 (tel. 718/575-3909).

1. HOTELS OF PORT-OF-SPAIN

The number of hotels is extremely limited. Almost every hotel in Trinidad has a completely different personality, ranging from such posh hillside hostelries as the Hilton to a turn-of-the-century nature preserve center up in the mountains. But don't check into any Port-of-Spain hotel expecting your room to open directly on a white sandy beach. The nearest beach is a long, costly taxi ride away.

When you're projecting your expenditures for your trip to Trinidad and Tobago, don't forget the tax and service charge that will be added to your hotel and restaurant bills.

Trinidad Hilton, P.O. Box 442, Port-of-Spain, Trinidad, W.I. (tel. 809/624-3211). On a hilltop, Trinidad's most distinguished hotel is called upside-down because the lobby is at the top and the rooms are staggered down below. You press the down button if you want to go to the tenth floor. Because of its location just above Queen's Park Savannah, most of its rooms have a view of the sea and mountains. You get a wide range of accommodations here, everything from a simple single to a suite with connecting doors. Rates, in effect all year, are

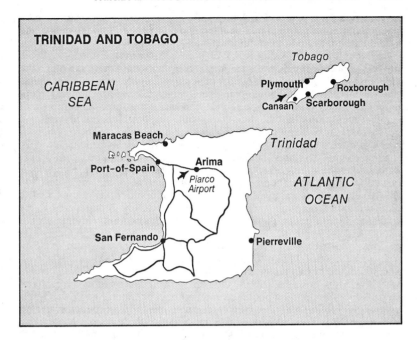

TRINIDAD AND TOBAGO

$105 to $142 daily in a single, from $120 to $156 in a double. All rooms are air-conditioned and have balconies. Most of the guests spend their time at the large tropical swimming pool, with its vast sunning areas and refreshment bar at the Gazebo where you can order the famous "rum and Coca-Cola." The main dining room is La Boucan, recommended separately, or you can congregate at the Pool Terrace, a tropical dining room with a two-story-high metal sculpture and lighting chandelier. Music is played for dancing in the Carnival Bar until 2 a.m. Some of Trinidad's best native entertainment is booked by the Hilton management. There's always plenty of activity, with pool barbecues featuring roast suckling pig, weekly fiestas, steel bands, limbo contests, whatever. The two all-weather tennis courts are lit for night games. Several shops, some offering handcrafts, are placed in the two-level arcade of the hotel. For the business traveler, the Hilton is the best choice of the island. Of particular interest are the 24-hour Telex and cable facilities, a worldwide courière service for documents, and secretarial and translation services.

Holiday Inn, Wrightson Road, P.O. Box 1017, Port-of-Spain, Trinidad, W.I. (tel. 809/625-3361), was wisely enough placed at the edge of the commercial area of the city, a combination of a business person's hotel yet with resort "trimmings." It is a white, streamlined block topped by La Ronde, its revolving 14th-floor restaurant where diners have a view of the coastline of Venezuela, nine miles across the sea. An international menu is offered. Adjoining the entrance lobby is a cloverleaf-shaped swimming pool and a thatched poolside bar. You forget, at least for a while, the traffic of the city. The pool has some submerged bar stools for those who want to drink while they swim.

Most of the hotel bedrooms, 235 in all, have a freshness to them, with colored fabrics on the beds and at the windows. The suites are more traditional, often with a decor inspired by the great house plantation style. Except for carnival, the year-round charge is $80 in a single, $92 in a double, but these are EP rates (no meals). Rooms have private balconies, two double beds, phones, radios, and individually controlled air conditioning.

Chaconia Inn, 106 Saddle Rd., P.O. Box 3340, Maraval, Trinidad, W.I. (tel. 809/628-8603), named for the country's scarlet national flower, is a miniature self-contained resort just north of Port-of-Spain in the cool mountain residential valley of Maraval. Its buildings are in simple style, and its furnishings in a contemporary motel idiom. Ken E. Duval, the managing director, runs one of Trinidad's finest small hotels, and does so with some flair. Personal hospitality is emphasized here by everybody from the management on down. You'll be housed in one of three accommodation categories: two-bedroom apartment suites (4), superior rooms (18), and standard rooms (9). All are equipped with private baths, air conditioning, phones, TV, and radios. The suites have kitchenette facilities. All year, tariffs are the same except during Carnival week. Singles cost $60 to $70 daily, doubles and twins going for $70 to $80, and triples renting for $80 to $90. Two-bedroom apartments are $120 to $140 daily. All rates are EP. For MAP, add $30 per person daily. In addition to the dining room/lounge, there is a Roof Garden Restaurant.

Hotel Normandie, 10 Nook Ave., P.O. Box 851, Port-of-Spain, Trinidad, W.I. (tel. 809/624-1181), originally built in the 1920s, was already a well-established hotel when its owners drastically modernized it in 1986. The two-story hotel rises around a banyan- and banana-filled courtyard in the center of which is a cool swimming pool accented with a jet of water. Inside, the 54 air-conditioned rooms each have a balcony or patio, and TV. Year-round prices for a single range from $60 to $80 daily, rising to $70 to $90 in a double. More elaborate accommodations, such as loft studios and suites, begin at $80 daily. Calm and cosmopolitan, the hotel sits next to one of the best art galleries in Trinidad, a skylit-covered shopping center, an attractive restaurant, and the botanical gardens of Port-of-Spain.

Kapok Hotel and Restaurant, 16-18 Cotton Hill, St. Clair, Trinidad, W.I. (tel. 809/622-6441), is a nine-floor modern little hotel at the corner of Queen's Park Savannah. From its lounge, you have not only a panoramic view of the park but of the Gulf of Paria. The lounge has been redecorated in pleasing, harmonious tones. Many guests who shun the Hilton seem to feel at home here, liking the slick neatness, the handsomely appointed bedrooms, and the rooftop restaurant serving Polynesian food. On the ground floor of the hotel is the Café Savanna, one of the finest restaurants in Trinidad. The location, in St. Clair, is in a pleasant and quiet residential area. They rent 71 well-furnished rooms, each with private bath, phone service, color TV, and air conditioning. The rooms have been refurnished with wicker, adding a tropical warmth to the spacious accommodations. Year-round rates (except during Carnival when they're higher) are $60 daily in a single, from $73 in a double, all EP. In the back is a small pool with a sunning area.

Moniques, 114 Saddle Rd., Maraval, Trinidad, W.I. (tel. 809/628-3334), is a bungalow in the lush Maraval Valley, about eight minutes from the downtown sector of Port-of-Spain. It's the home of Mike and Monica Charbonné. They have an informal, and most comfortable home where they have set aside eight rooms for paying guests. All units are air-conditioned, and each has its own bath. Singles range from $24 daily; doubles from $30, and triples from $37. These tariffs are in effect all year. Fellow guests like to gather on the tiny front lawn to exchange travel tips, and there is also a TV room. Arrangements are made for guests to go to a nearby swimming pool.

Zollna House, 12 Ramlogan Development, La Selva, Maraval, Trinidad, W.I. (tel. 809/628-3731), is on a hillside in the Maraval Valley with a view of

Port-of-Spain and the Gulf of Paria, two miles from the capital and a quarter of a mile off the Saddle Road. The two-story building has seven bedrooms and four spacious baths. Year-round rates are $22 for a single, $14 per person in a double, and $12 per person in a triple, EP. Tariffs go up by $8 per person during Carnival and $17 per person year round if breakfast and dinner are included. The house has two large porches, two indoor lounges, a beverage bar and games room, and dining areas on two floors, as well as a patio/barbecue setup outdoors. The garden is lush with flowering shrubs and fruit trees, home to a variety of birds. The house, white with black trim, is almost obscured by trees, but you can find it by going along the Saddle Road, turning into La Seiva Road, and going uphill for about a quarter of a mile. Owners are Gottfried Franz and Barbara Zollna, who also operate the Blue Waters Inn on Tobago.

Mount St. Benedict Guest House, Tunapuna, Trinidad, W.I. (tel. 809/662-4084), is a friendly, well-run guesthouse occupying a substantial building nestled on the ledge of a hill halfway between the airport and Port-of-Spain. It's really like a spiritual retreat and was once used as such for Catholic Dutch fathers. Capping the hillside are a church, monastery, and school, although the guesthouse is nonsectarian. Nine miles east of Port-of-Spain, this hilltop hostelry charges from $45 per person daily for a room and three meals. The neat, clean, uncluttered rooms have twin beds with cold water. Guests use the corridor baths, which have hot water. The food is above average, with an emphasis on local specialties. The dining room is spacious with two walls of windows providing a view of the valley, and meals are served family style. There's also a wide front veranda from which you can look out onto vistas of hibiscus, bougainvillea, and poinsettia. Bus transport is possible, but of course it's better to have your own wheels.

Asa Wright Nature Center, Spring Hill Estate, P.O. Bag 10, Arima, Trinidad, W.I. (tel. 809/622-7480 in Port-of-Spain). There really isn't anything like it in the Caribbean. Known by birdwatchers throughout the world, it sits on 190 acres of protected land near uplands where hummingbirds and rare varieties of toucans flourish. Trinidadian families sometimes arrive en masse for picnics, and it's a favorite outing for school groups. Devoted nature lovers can rent one of its 18 simple accommodations. Nine units are in the estate's original Edwardian house, with another nine in wood-frame outbuildings. Amenities are aggressively simple, the visual stimuli coming from the flocks of birds at the feeding stations. *The daily rate is $50 per person, double occupancy, from May to the end of November.* From December 1 to April 30, the price is $65 per person, also double occupancy. Singles are charged *$70 daily in summer,* $90 in winter. The tariffs include three meals a day, afternoon tea, and a complimentary rum punch each evening.

Visiting hours for nonresidents are 9 a.m. to 5 p.m., for an entrance fee of $5 TT ($1.15). The grounds contain dozens of carefully marked nature trails. The area has witnessed the arrival of 240 of the 660 species of butterflies known in Trinidad, and of more than 183 of the 418 species of native birds. Tours for birdwatchers, ecologists, botanists, ornithologists, entomologists, and photographers are arranged.

You can make toll-free reservations by calling 800/426-7781 (in New York, call 800/327-2753). Otherwise, write to Caligo Ventures, 387 Main St., Armonk, NY 10504.

2. FOOD IN TRINIDAD

The food in Trinidad is as varied and cosmopolitan as the islanders themselves. It was a British colony for years, yet the cookery of olde England never made much impression on Trinidadians. Red-hot curries remind one of the island's strong East Indian influence, and some Chinese dishes are about as good here as any you'd find in Hong Kong. Créole and Spanish fare, as well as French, are also to be enjoyed.

A typical savory offering is a rôti, a king-size crêpe, highly spiced, and rolled around a filling of chicken, shellfish, or meat. Of course, you may prefer to skip such local delicacies as opossum stew and fried armadillo. Naturally, your fresh rum punch will have a dash of Angostura bitters.

La Boucan, Trinidad Hilton (tel. 809/624-3211). Considered the finest restaurant in Trinidad, this establishment satisfies the eye as well as the palate. Against one of its longest walls stretches a graceful mural by Geoffrey Holder, the most famous (and most expensive) artist who came out of the Caribbean. Born in Trinidad, though living in New York most of his life, he painted this mural to honor the social gatherings which used to take place in Port-of-Spain's central park, the Savannah. Lunch is served on Monday to Friday only, from noon to 2:30 p.m.; dinner is offered every evening except Sunday and Monday from 7 to 10:30 p.m. Full meals cost from $160 TT ($36.80), slightly less at lunch, and require a reservation. Typical dishes include smoked breast of duckling with seasonal fruits, thinly sliced filet of shark (smoked on the premises over coals of guava wood), stuffed crab back, mushroom crêpes, West Indian curried boneless breast of chicken, flambéed pepper steak with Madagascar pepper, grilled kingfish steak with Créole sauce, and succulently smoked pork, beef, duck, and lamb dishes. Desserts are sumptuous. As you dine, live music from a lacquered piano on a central dais provides digestible entertainment.

Café Savanna, Kapok Hotel, 16-18 Cotton Hill, St. Clair (tel. 809/622-6441), on the ground floor of a previously recommended hotel, serves an excellent continental cuisine. You get refined service in a sophisticated and romantic setting. A complete dinner ranges from $20 to $30. Many of the specialties are prepared with flair, but they change seasonally so I can't recommend any particular dishes. There are always sizzling steaks, of course, and lobster when available. The café serves both lunch and dinner. Also in the same hotel is the equally popular Tiki Village (see below). The café is open Monday to Saturday. Lunch is Monday to Friday from noon to 2 p.m. and dinner from 7 to 10 p.m. On Saturday, only dinner is served.

La Fantasie, 10 Nook Ave., St. Ann's Village (tel. 809/624-1181), named after an 18th-century plantation which once stood here, is loaded with style and features a tempting version of nouvelle Créole cuisine. Open daily from 7 a.m. to 10 p.m., it charges around $40 TT ($9.20) for lunch, from $75 TT ($17.25) for dinner. On any particular day the changing menu might include chicken cocotte in a rich Créole sauce with herb dumplings, tournedos deluxe with wedges of apple and onion rings, stuffed crab back, and shrimp in a black-bean-and-ginger sauce, followed with a Trinidadian fruitcake with a rum-flavored custard.

Restaurant Singho, Long Circular Mall (tel. 809/628-2077). Lined with planks of cedar, this restaurant contains an almost mystically illuminated bar and aquarium. The restaurant is on the second floor of one of the capital's largest shopping malls. Open daily from 10 a.m. to 11 p.m., it's owned and operated by Roma Kim Sabeeney. Most guests order a fixed-price six-course meal, plus soup and one drink, for $60 TT ($13.80). A la carte dishes include shrimp with oyster sauce, shark-fin soup, stewed or curried beef, almond pork, and spareribs with black-bean sauce.

Tiki Village, Kapok Hotel, 16-18 Cotton Hill, St. Clair (tel. 809/622-6441), perches on the top floor of this hotel, offering a panoramic view at night. Polynesian creations with a Chinese flair are presented nightly, except Monday, from 5:30 to 10:30 p.m. You can also have lunch here, from 11:30 a.m. to 2:30 p.m. In the evening you should make a reservation. To get started, try the Polynesian delight, a combination of hors d'oeuvres. The eggroll is among the best I've ever ordered in the West Indies. Among the main courses, I'd recommend the Hawaiian luau fish. This is a whole fish coated with water-chestnut flour and fried crisply before it's engulfed in a sweet-and-pungent sauce. Chicken provincial is boneless cubes sautéed in a black-bean sauce. Desserts include an icebox cake, followed by Chinese tea, and then a bill of, say, $25.

Chaconia Inn, 106 Saddle Rd., Maraval (tel. 809/628-8603), recommended previously as a hotel, serves some of the best food of any hotel in Trinidad. Ken E. Duval, the managing director, has a good wine list and lots of continental specialties as well as Trinidadian dishes. The staff is helpful and the service good. In the dining room/lounge, meals are à la carte. There is a large selection of appetizers, steaks, seafood, poultry, salads, sandwiches, and desserts. Lunch, served from 11:30 a.m. to 2:30 p.m., costs $10 to $15, and dinner, from 7 to 10 p.m., goes for $12 to $25. The Roof Garden Restaurant is open for a barbecue dinner Friday and Saturday from 7 to 11 p.m., charging $13 to $20. Reservations are recommended for Friday and Saturday dinner. It is open daily.

Veni Mangé, 13 Lucknow St. (no phone), built in the 1950s of ochre stucco, lies on a tranquil street of private residences right off Western Main Road. If you can find this tiny home, you'll get a fine welcome from Allyson Hennessy and her sister, Rosemary Hezekiah. Considered a local media personality, Allyson runs a daily television talk show broadcast throughout much of Trinidad. Best described as articulate examples of a new generation of Créole women, Allyson and Rosemary dress in lavish neo-Victorian costumes, never without several pounds of fake amethysts, rhinestones, and jangling bracelets. Their conversational banter and tactfully exaggerated sense of theatricality have established this restaurant's lunch hour as the most interesting, lighthearted, and fun place to dine in all of Port-of-Spain. Because of local zoning laws, only lunch is served. Open Monday to Friday from 11:30 a.m. to 2:30 p.m., on Friday, they remain open until 9 p.m. as a bar and rendezvous point. No meals are served on Saturday or Sunday.

Start with their bartender's special, which is a coral-colored fruit punch, a rich, luscious mixture that combines the golden papaya with a banana whose skin is allowed to turn black so that its taste is most flavorsome. On some days they do an authentic callaloo soup, which, according to Trinidadian legend, can make a man propose marriage, even if the idea hadn't occurred to him before. Save room for one of the main courses, such as curried crab or West Indian hot pot (a variety of meat cooked Créole style), perhaps a vegetable lentil loaf. The helpings are large, and if you still have room, order their pineapple upside-down cake, unless you prefer fresh fruit or homemade ice cream with such tropical flavors as guava, mango, and coconut. For all this, you'll pay $22 or more for a fine meal and an example of local hospitality.

Sam's, 67 Western Main Rd., St. James (no phone), is probably the dining bargain of Port-of-Spain. Its ambience is very much like that of a Formica-covered West Indian version of a fast-food emporium. The specialty (and the only food offered) is an array of rôtis. Defined as an unsweetened pastry envelope stuffed with filling, it more often appears on a paper plate like a taco with the stuffing placed beside it. Rôtis cost from $10 TT ($2.30), including a variety of fillings, the most basic of which is *dhal purée* (a mash of boiled green peas). If you're adventurous, you can order such fillings as gizzard or goat, but most North Americans stick to shrimp, chicken, beef, or vegetarian. The establishment is open daily from 10 a.m. to midnight. There's another branch at 47 Richmond St.

J.B.'s, Valsayn Park (tel. 809/662-5837), is an informal restaurant managed by an enterprising Trinidadian family named Mowser. It is about 10 miles east of the center of Port of Spain and is open Monday to Friday from 11 a.m. to midnight, Saturday from 5 p.m. to midnight, and closed Sunday. The kitchen specializes in steaks and seafood, and no reservations are necessary. Full meals cost $25 each. There's a full bar, as well as a salad bar, along with an array of homemade ice cream and other desserts.

Rafters, 6a Warner St. (tel. 809/628-9258), is housed in a century-old stone building which was originally a shop. This attractive and popular restaurant lies on the corner of a busy commercial street. It is open Monday to Friday from 11 a.m. to 4 a.m. No lunch is offered on Saturday, but there is dinner service from 5 p.m. to midnight (closed Sunday). In addition to an à la carte menu, there is a carvery where cuts are served from roast joints along with vegetables and sauces. Full meals cost from $22. In the bar/lounge, music and busy crowds congregate on Friday and Saturday nights. When live music is performed, a cover charge of $5 is assessed; otherwise, it's free.

3. EXPLORING TRINIDAD

AROUND THE CAPITAL: One of the busiest harbors in the Caribbean, Trinidad's capital, Port-of-Spain, can be explored on foot. Most tours begin at **Queen's Park Savannah,** on the northern edge of the city. Called "The Savannah," it consists of 199 acres, complete with a race course, cricket fields, and vendors hawking coconut milk. What is now the park was once a sugar plantation until it was swept by a fire in 1808 which destroyed hundreds of homes.

Among the Savannah's outstanding buildings is the pink-and-blue Queen's Royal College, containing a clock tower with Westminister chimes. Today a school for boys, it stands on Maraval Road at the corner of St. Clair Avenue. On the same road, the family home of the Roodal clan is affectionately called "the gingerbread house" by Trinidadians. It was built in the baroque style of the French Second Empire.

In contrast, the family residence of the Stollmeyers was built in 1905 and is a copy of a German Rhenish castle. Nearby stands Whitehall, which was once a private mansion but today has been turned into the office of the prime minister of Trinidad and Tobago. In the Moorish style, it was erected in 1905 and served as the U.S. Army headquarters in World War II. These houses, including Hayes Court, the residence of the Anglican bishop of Trinidad, and others form what is known as "the magnificent seven" big mansions standing in a row.

On the south side of the park stands the **National Museum and Art Gallery,** 117 Frederick St. (tel. 809/623-6419). It's open from 10 a.m. to 6 p.m. daily, except Monday, charging no admission. On the ground floor you'll see some Amerindian artifacts, traces of Trinidad's early Indian settlers.

At the southern end of Frederick Street, the main artery of Port-of-Spain's shopping district, stands **Woodford Square.** The gaudy **Red House,** a large neo-Renaissance building built in 1906, is the seat of the government of Trinidad and Tobago. Nearby stands **Holy Trinity Cathedral,** whose Gothic look may remind you of the churches of England. Inside, look for the marble monument to Sir Ralph Woodford made by the sculptor of Chantry.

Another of the town's important squares is called **Independence Square,** dating from Spanish days. Now mainly a car park, it stretches across the southern part of the capital from the **Cathedral of the Immaculate Conception** to Wrightson Road. The Roman Catholic church was built in 1815 in the neo-Gothic style and consecrated in 1832.

The cathedral has an outlet that leads to the **Central Market** on Beetham Highway, on the outskirts of Port-of-Spain. Here you can see all the spices and fruits for which Trinidad is known. It's one of the island's most colorful sights, made all the more so by the wide diversity of people who sell their wares here.

At the north of the Savannah, the **Botanical Gardens** cover 70 acres. Once part of a sugar plantation, the park is filled with flowering plants, shrubs, and rare and beautiful trees, including an orchid house. Seek out also the raw beef tree—an incision made in its bark is said to resemble rare, bleeding roast beef. Licensed guides will take you through and explain the luxuriant foliage to you. In the garden is the President's House, official residence of the president of Trinidad and Tobago. Victorian in style, it was built in 1875.

One part of the gardens is the **Emperor Valley Zoo,** which shows a good selection of the fauna of Trinidad as well as some of the usual exotic animals. The star attractions are a family of mandrills, a reptile house, and open bird parks. You can take shady jungle walks through tropical vegetation. Adults pay $2 TT (46¢); children, $1 TT (23¢). Hours are 9 a.m. to 5 p.m. daily.

OUTSIDE PORT-OF-SPAIN: In the environs of Port-of-Spain, you may want to seek out the following sights. For one of the most popular attractions in the area, the Asa Wright Nature Center, refer to my hotel recommendations.

Fort George
On a peak 1,100 feet above Port-of-Spain, this fort was built by Gov. Sir Thomas Hislop in 1804 as a signal station in the days of the sailing ships. Once it could be reached only by hikers, but today it's accessible by an asphalt road. From its citadel you can see the mountains of Venezuela. The drive is only ten miles, but to play it safe, allow about two hours for the excursion.

Caroni Bird Sanctuary
At sundown, clouds of scarlet ibis, the national bird of Trinidad and Tobago, fly in from their feeding grounds to roost here. The 450-acre sanctuary couldn't be more idyllic, with blue, mauve, and white lilies, oysters growing on mangrove roots, and caimans resting on mudbanks. The sanctuary lies about a half hour's drive (actually seven miles) south of Port-of-Spain. Admission is $12 TT ($2.75) for adults, $6 TT ($1.40) for children.

Pitch Lake
One of the wonders of the world, its surface like elephant skin, the lake is 300 feet deep at its center. It's possible to walk on its rough hide, but I don't recommend that you proceed far. Legend has it that the lake devoured a tribe of Chayma Indians, punishing them for eating hummingbirds in which the souls of their ancestors reposed. The bitumen mined here has been used for paving highways throughout the world. This lake was formed millions of years ago, and it is believed that at one time it was a huge mud volcano into which mud asphaltic oil seeped. Churned up and down by underground gases, the oil and mud eventually formed asphalt. Sir Walter Raleigh, according to legend, discovered the lake in 1595, using the asphalt to caulk his ships. However, don't believe those legends that no matter how much is dug out the lake is fully replenished in a day. Actually, the level of the lake drops at the rate of about six inches a year. A tour of 120 miles around the lake lasts five hours.

The Saddle
This is a humped pass on a ridge dividing the Maraval Valley and the Santa Cruz Valley. Along this circular run you'll see the luxuriant growth of the island, as reflected by grapefruit, papaya, cassava, and cocoa. Leaving Port-of-Spain by Saddle Road, going past the Trinidad Country Club, you pass through Maraval Village with its St. Andrew's Golf Course. The road rises to cross the ridge at the spot from which "The Saddle" gets its name. After going over the hump, you descend through Santa Cruz Valley, rich with giant bamboo, into San Juan and

back to the capital along Eastern Main Road or via Beetham Hwy. You'll see splendid views in every direction. The tour recommended takes about two hours, covering 18 miles.

The North Coast Road

Nearly all cruise-ship passengers are hauled along Trinidad's "Skyline Highway" which opened in 1944. Starting at "The Saddle," previously recommended, it wends for seven miles across the Northern Range, and down to Maracas Bay. At one point, 100 feet above the Caribbean, you'll see on a clear day as far away as Venezuela in the west or Tobago in the east, a sweep of some 100 miles.

Most visitors take this route to **Maracas Beach,** one of the most splendid in Trinidad. Enclosed by mountains, it has the cliché charm of a Caribbean fantasy —white sands, swaying coconut palms, and crystal-clear water.

4. SHOPPING, SPORTS, NIGHTLIFE

In Trinidad, you'll find much to see and do in the capital itself, beginning with your morning shopping tour of the Port-of-Spain bazaars, going on to water sports, ending with some calypso entertainment in the evening.

WHERE TO SHOP: One of the large bazaars of the Caribbean, Port-of-Spain has luxury items from all over the globe, including Irish linens, English china, Scandinavian crystal, French perfumes, and of course, Swiss watches and Japanese cameras. More interesting than these usual items are the Oriental bazaars where you can pick up items in ivory or brass; perhaps a carved chest. Reflecting the island's culture are calypso shirts (or dresses), sisal goods, woodwork, cascadura bracelets, silver jewelry in local motifs, and saris. For souvenir items, visitors often like to bring back figurines of limbo dancers, carnival masqueraders, or calypso singers.

Most stores are open from 8 a.m. to 4 p.m. Monday to Friday (some shops remain open until 5 p.m.). Liquor and food stores close at noon on Thursday, and nearly all shops, except liquor and food, close at noon on Saturday.

For those luxury items mentioned, I suggest you pay a call at **Stecher's,** 27 Frederick St. (tel. 809/623-5912), which sells crystal, watches, jewelry, perfumes, Georg Jensen silver, handbags, Royal Copenhagen china, and other in-bond items which can be delivered to Piarco International Airport upon your departure. If you don't want to go downtown, there's a branch at the Hilton. Among the famous names represented here are Patek-Phillippe, Piaget, Girard Pérregaux, Royal Crown Derby, Bing & Grondahl, Belleek, Rosenthal, Lalique, Baccarat, and Swarovski. If you miss both shops, you can always pay a last-minute call at their tax-free airport branch, where they sell perfume, Cartier lighters, pens, leather goods, Hummel figurines, Swarovski crystal, local ceramics, cigarettes, and cigars.

Y. de Lima, 23A Frederick St. (tel. 809/623-1364), is another good store for duty-free cameras, watches, and local jewelry. Its third-floor workroom will make whatever you want in goldwork. You may emerge with everything from steel-drum earrings to a hibiscus blossom brooch.

Lakhan's Bazaar, 32 Western Main Rd. (tel. 809/622-4688), has an interesting selection of Indian merchandise, including beautifully designed saris, rugs, embroidered purses, as well as sandals. Go here also for ivory figurines, silk scarfs, and brass and copper ware.

Art Creators and Suppliers, Apt. 402, Aldegonda Park, 7 St. Anns Rd., St. Anns (tel. 809/624-4369). It's in a relatively banal concrete-sided apartment

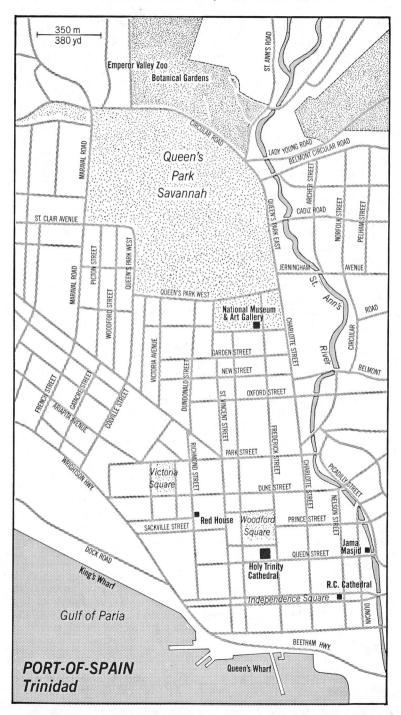

PORT-OF-SPAIN
Trinidad

complex, but the paintings sold inside are among the finest in the Caribbean. Clara Rosa De Lima, the creative force behind the gallery, is a recognized authority on Trinidadian art. The works sold here, however, are fairly priced examples of the very best of Trinidad. Among the artistic giants represented are the Holder brothers, both Geoffrey and Boscoe, along with Robert Mackie and Noël Vaucrosson. Ms. De Lima is usually candid about the relative merits of artists she represents, and maintains dialogues with a handful of artists in Brazil and Guyana as well. Paintings begin at $400 TT ($92), but could stretch up into the thousands of U.S. dollars. The gallery is open from 10 a.m. to 1 p.m. 4 to 7 p.m. Monday to Friday and on Saturday from 10 a.m. to noon. It is closed on Sunday.

Gallery 1-2-3-4, St. Anns Village (tel. 809/627-1673). Probably more iconoclastic and less conservative than any other gallery on the island, this art center displays its paintings in a space of minimalist walls and careful lighting. The gallery opened in 1985, and since then has attracted the attention of the art world. Its hours on weekdays are 10 a.m. to 6:30 p.m., on Saturday from 11 a.m. to 4 p.m., and on Sunday a variable schedule depending on a particular exhibit on display.

St. Anns Village, The Marketplace, 10 Nook Ave., St. Anns (tel. 809/624-1181), is one of the most fashionable shopping complexes in Trinidad, containing (perhaps at the time of your visit) 20 boutiques. Its client list includes some of the best jewelers, designers, and art dealers in Trinidad. Some of these shops come and go, so I won't recommend any one specifically. It's more a place for window-shopping and browsing at leisure. The complex forms an interconnected bride among three previously recommended establishments, the Hotel Normandie, the Restaurant Fantasie, and a top-notch art emporium, Gallery 1-2-3-4.

The **Trinidad and Tobago Blind Welfare Association,** Henry St. (no phone), makes everything from furniture to shopping baskets with rattan peel, rattan core, and sea grass. If you make a purchase here, you'll also be helping a sightless worker who is trying to help himself or herself.

The **Trinidad and Tobago Handicraft Cooperative** has its main shop at the Trinidad Hilton (tel. 809/624-3111). Here they offer items in fiber, straw, and wood, and they also sell small steel drums known locally as "ping pongs." Many other local products are sold, including everything from hammocks to salad bowls in purple heart.

THE SPORTING LIFE: Whatever your sporting pleasure—hunting an alligator or playing a simple game of tennis—Trinidad has many possibilities for athletic activities. However, no one surely ever arrived in Port-of-Spain seeking these endeavors alone. In Trinidad, sports are integrated into daily life, and for golf and tennis holidays one should read some of the previous chapters where much more emphasis is placed on such pursuits.

Beaches

Trinidad isn't thought of as beach country, yet surprisingly it has more beach frontage than any other island in the West Indies. The only problem is that most of its beaches are undeveloped and found in distant, remote places, far removed from Port-of-Spain. The closest of the better beaches, Maracas, is a full 18 miles from Port-of-Spain. (For lovely, inviting, and more accessible beaches, see the section immediately following, on Tobago.)

Tennis

The **Hilton** (tel. 809/624-3111) has the best courts, and you can also play at the **Trinidad Country Club** (tel. 809/622-3470) as well. On the grounds of the

Prince's building, there are public courts in Port-of-Spain (ask at your hotel for directions to these).

Fishing
All year long good catches are possible either in the deep sea or in inland Trinidadian waters. In the waters of the Gulf of Paria and on the north shore, you can pursue salmon, snapper, and grouper, or troll for Spanish mackerel, kingfish, wahoo, dolphin, or bonita. **Hub Travel,** 68-78 Maraval Rd., Port-of-Spain (tel. 809/622-0936), can arrange fishing trips.

Hunting
Hunters bag everything from an armadillo to an alligator in Trinidad, and there's wild game in the forest too, including agouti, wild hog (called *quenk*), or deer. Ask at the Trinidad Tourist Board for particulars about hunting licenses.

Golf
The oldest golf club on the island, **Moka** (tel. 809/629-2314), is in Maraval, about two miles from Port-of-Spain. This 18-hole course has a club-house that offers every facility to all visitors, and the course has been internationally acclaimed since it was the setting for the 1976 Hoerman Cup Golf Tournament.

AFTER DARK: At night in Port-of-Spain you'll hear the sounds of calypso and steel bands. Or hopefully you will.

Unfortunately, some of the best calypso is not in the capital, but at places such as **Sparrow's Hideaway** (no phone), my personal favorite. It costs $40 TT ($9.20) to enter, but it's a nine-mile taxi ride from the center of Port-of-Spain. Go only on a Saturday night. I recently asked three taxi drivers what it would cost to take me there and each one came up with a different figure, so I don't know what the going rate will be at the time of your visit. Of course, all collectors of calypso records know that "The Sparrow" is one of Trinidad's most famous singers. He is in fact known as the "calypso king of the world." If you're devotee enough to go, don't expect to see any fellow tourists. It's strictly a local crowd. Ask at your hotel reception desk for directions on how to get there. The club lies in Petit Valley at Diego Martin.

If you like your calypso in tamer surroundings than the famous but dangerous Independence Square, try the **Calypso Lounge** at the Holiday Inn, Wrightson Rd. (tel. 809/625-3361), in Port-of-Spain. A local band plays for dancing and some of the best calypsonians are brought in to entertain guests, especially in the winter months. Special shows are staged on Friday and Saturday when the minimum charge is $10 TT ($2.30).

Chaconia Inn, 106 Saddle Rd., Maraval (tel. 809/628-8603), becomes a "hot spot" on Friday and Saturday night when a Trinidadian band is brought in from 11 p.m. to 1 a.m. The charge is $10 TT ($2.30) per person.

Finally, you may want to attend the **Hilton Poolside Fiesta** at the already-recommended Trinidad Hilton, Port-of-Spain (tel. 809/624-3211). For about $85 TT ($19.55) per person, every Monday night at 10 the Hilton presents a traditional local show with limbo dancers and a steel band. A barbecue at 7 p.m. precedes the entertainment.

5. A SIDE TRIP TO TOBAGO
Unlike bustling Trinidad, its sister island of Tobago is sleepy. Trinidadians go there, especially on weekends, to enjoy its wide sandy beaches. The legendary home of Robinson Crusoe, Tobago is only 27 miles long and 7½ miles wide. The

people are quiet and friendly, and their villages are so tiny they seem to blend with the landscape.

Fish-shaped Tobago was probably sighted by Columbus in 1498 when he charted Trinidad, but the island was so tiny he paid no attention to it in his log. For the next 100 years it lay almost unexplored. In 1628 when Charles I of England gave it to one of his nobles, the Earl of Pembroke, the maritime countries of Europe suddenly showed a belated interest. From then on, Tobago was fought over no fewer than 31 times by the Spanish, French, Dutch, and English, as well as marauding pirates and privateers.

After 1803 the island settled down to enjoy a sugar monopoly unbroken for decades. Great houses were built, and in London it used to be said of a wealthy man that he was "as rich as a Tobago planter." The island's economy collapsed in 1884 and Tobago entered an acute depression. The ruling monopoly, Gillespie Brothers, declared itself bankrupt and went out of business. The British government made Tobago a ward of Trinidad in 1889, and sugar was never revived.

Tobago, "the land of the hummingbird," lies 20 miles to the northeast of Trinidad, from which it is reached by frequent flights. It has long been known as a honeymooner's paradise. The physical beauty of Tobago is stunning, with its forests of breadfruit, mango, cocoa, and citrus, through which a chartreuse-colored iguana will suddenly dart. Jungle brooks dance over rocks.

The island's village-like capital is **Scarborough,** which is also the main port. Most of the shops are clustered in streets around the market. From Scarborough one can either go cross-country toward Plymouth or head toward the southwest part of Tobago.

For "Practical Facts," refer to Trinidad. Essentially the same customs apply. The **Tobago Tourist Bureau,** Scarborough Mall, Scarborough (tel. 809/639-2125), provides general information about the island.

Nearly all passengers arrive from Trinidad, where they have already cleared Customs.

GETTING THERE: First, you go to Trinidad (see "Getting There" in the preceding section). Between Trinidad and Tobago, **BWIA** links the two sister islands with about 14 flights a day (sometimes they are impossibly overbooked). The first flight for Tobago leaves Trinidad at 6:40 a.m., and the last flight back to Trinidad departs Tobago at 8:45 p.m. You're airborne only 12 minutes. Inter-island flights tend to be crowded on weekends when Trinidadians themselves head to Tobago and its beaches. On certain BWIA flights to Trinidad, the side trip to Tobago can be included for no extra charge (ask a travel agent before flying to Trinidad how this works).

If you want to go to Tobago by boat, the **M.F. _Panorama,_** a coastal ferry with a bar and a trio of restaurants, makes the trip in about five hours. Tourist class is 30 TT ($6.90) one way.

Tobago's small airport is at its southwestern tip, Crown Point.

GETTING AROUND: From the airport to your hotel, take an unmetered taxi. The taxi fare from say, Crown Point Airport to the Arnos Vale Hotel is $45 TT ($10.35). You can also arrange (or have your hotel do it for you) a sightseeing tour by taxi. Rates have to be negotiated on an individual basis. For example, five passengers can take a four-hour tour going all the way to Charlotteville and back for a cost of $225 TT ($51.75).

For car rentals, get in touch with **Tobago Travel,** Milford Rd., Store Bay (tel. 809/639-8778), where the average cost of a small vehicle is about $45 TT ($10.35) to $50 TT ($11.50) per day, unlimited mileage. Gas, as of this writing, is $4.50 TT ($1.05) per liter. An international driver's license, if valid, entitles you to drive on Tobago's roads. *Don't forget that you must drive on the left.*

If you prefer to get around by motor scooter, **Banana Rentals,** Banana House, Kariwak Village, Scarborough (tel. 809/639-8441), offers Honda vehicles that are economical to operate. You can rent a scooter for as little as $12.

Public buses are modern and always very inexpensive. Buses travel from one end of the island to the other several times a day. Of course, expect an unscheduled stop at any passenger's doorstep, and never, but never, be in a hurry.

HOTELS OF TOBAGO: Quiet, tranquil oases, the hotels of Tobago are more for retreats, attracting those visitors who seek hideaways instead of action at high-rise resorts. Many of the hotels recommended below have been handsomely landscaped to blend into the natural terrain. Because of the shortage of restaurants on the island, it's best to take the MAP (breakfast and dinner) when booking a room.

Mount Irvine Bay Hotel, P.O. Box 222, Scarborough, Tobago, W.I. (tel. 809/639-8871), is Tobago's most expensive spa, built around an old sugar mill and bordering one of the finest golf courses in the Caribbean. On the north shore of the island, about a 20-minute drive from the airport, it brings to mind one of those luxurious country clubs, San Clemente style. The setting is on 150 acres of spread-out lawns, tropical gardens, areas for tennis, and an angular, free-form swimming pool with a swim-in bar and its surrounding terrace. It's like a resort community. Built L-shaped around the pool, a two-story hacienda wing of guest rooms is all air-conditioned, each with a private bath and its own terrace or balcony. These units open toward the green lawns with their brilliantly colored blossoms on flowery shrubbery. The rest of the cottages are in small square houses covered with such planting as beliconia. Each of these cottages has two rooms which are rented separately, each with a private bath and patio and a view of the fairways or the water. In winter, single rates in the main building range from $160 to $185 daily, with doubles costing $200 to $235, all half-board terms. *In off-season, it becomes cheaper, with singles going for $100 and doubles for $145, also MAP.*

The most impressive place to dine is the Sugar Mill Restaurant, built around the 200-year-old circular stone mill, under a shingled, raftered conical roof. While enjoying the smell of jasmine, you dine at a candlelit table. The cuisine is of an acceptable international standard. You can order drinks in the Cocrico Lounge, named after the national bird of Tobago. There's dancing almost every evening on the Sugar Mill Patio. Calypso singers are brought in, barbecues are held, and limbo dancers and occasional shows entertain you, particularly in season. Guests of the hotel also become temporary members of the golf club (see "The Sporting Life," below).

Arnos Vale, P.O. Box 208, Tobago, W.I. (tel. 809/639-2881), was once a sugar plantation, but you wouldn't know that now. On the north coast about a mile from Plymouth, Arnos Vale is one of the oldest hotels on Tobago, an unusual retreat tucked away on 400 tropical acres opening directly on Arnos Vale Bay. Today it operates somewhat like an Italian-style Club Med with a European tour clientele. Individual clients may have difficulty booking a room. A former English owner was a lover of nature, and he planted the place like a botanical garden, with frangipani and oleander predominating. In days of yore you might have run into one of the Beatles sneaking through the lush foliage, or perhaps a married movie star with a wife not his own. A Mediterranean aura prevails, but the bananaquits and mot-mots keep it definitely in the Caribbean. Its red-tile-roofed main house stands at the top of the hill. You can enjoy good drinks in the bar or on the al fresco patio, then go across to the dining room to be served one of the best meals on the island. Both an English fare and a Tobago cuisine are served, including such island dishes as callaloo soup, souse, and pelau. From this main house, you'll have a magnificent panorama out over a secluded crescent bay to the sea. Part of Arnos Vale's historical legacy can be seen in the dining room—an original grand piano built by Playel for the Paris Exhibition in 1851. The piano is completely hand-painted.

Rooms come in many different styles and shapes, ranging from the Jacamar just off the beach to the Coral Cottage with an aerial view of the bay. Most of the furniture is custom made of local cedar. With all meals included, the charge is $95 per person per night year-round. On the richly planted grounds is a freshwater swimming pool. Peace and tranquility are stressed, but occasionally native steel bands are brought in to play, and there are beach barbecues. In addition, you'll find a tennis court.

Crown Reef Hotel, P.O. Box 45, Storebay, Tobago, W.I. (tel. 809/639-8571), is handsomely modern, standing on landscaped grounds with much tropical greenery and flowers. It also opens onto its own coral reef and an excellent, uncrowded beach. Don't come here seeking local island color. However, if you want some of the finest contemporary facilities Tobago has to offer, then you're at the right place, and can select from among 115 well-furnished suites and bedrooms, each with a private balcony or patio. In winter, a single rents for $120 daily, and a double goes for $130 to $165 on the EP. *In off-season, EP terms in a single are $80 daily, going up to $90 in a double.* The dining room is approached from the lobby by a circular, open staircase, extending on rocks over water. The terrazzo lounge has deck chairs with pillows covered in flamboyant fabric. The menu has both Stateside and continental dishes, along with some Trinidadian specialties. Perched on a coral rock at water's edge is a thatched beach bar. Sometimes native dancers and steel bands are brought in. A freshwater swimming pool is set in the midst of the lush gardens. Most water sports are offered, including scuba-diving and snorkeling, and you can play tennis on the hotel's courts. The 18-hole golf course is nearby.

Turtle Beach, P.O. Box 201, Tobago, W.I. (tel. 809/639-2851), stands directly on one mile of sandy beach opening on Great Courtland Bay, on the leeward shore in the midst of a 600-acre coconut plantation. Housed in two-story units, all rooms are oceanfront and air-conditioned, with private baths containing both tub and shower, patio or balcony, and almost direct access to the beach. The location is just eight miles from the airport, from which taxi transfers are available. The inn is also five miles from Scarborough. The entrance loggia is the longest covered terrace on the island, where a slow pace sets the tempo of the relaxed, casual lifestyle of the hotel. While seated on sofas and in armchairs, you can enjoy tall fruit-and-rum drinks. Lunches are served around the garden pool or at the beach. Three times a week calypso music can be heard in the evening. Perhaps a steel band will be brought in. If you don't want the beach, you can swim in a freshwater pool. Bedroom accommodations lie in an interconnected series of white bungalows with V-shaped roofs, between beds of hibiscus and oleander. Units have individual air conditioning and smartly tailored furnishings. Rooms on the second floor have sloped open-beamed ceilings, with white walls and shuttered doors that can be pushed back to enlarge the living areas. EP rates are $120 in a single, $145 in a double in winter, *dropping to $70 in a single and $80 in a double in summer.* Fishing trips can be arranged, as can snorkeling at Buccoo Reef. A dive and watersports shop is on the hotel premises.

Kariwak Village, P.O. Box 27, Scarborough, Tobago, W.I. (tel. 809/639-8545), is a self-contained cluster of cottages that evoke the South Pacific in style. The location of this 18-room complex is about a six-minute walk from the beach and only ten minutes from the airport. The hotel's name was formed by combining Carib with Arawak, the original inhabitants of the Caribbean. The builders turned to the original elements of Tobago in their construction, making much use of palm fronds, raw teak, coral stone, and bamboo. EP singles in high season rent for $60 daily; couples pay $76. *In the low season, EP singles cost $36; doubles, $50.* Breakfast and dinner are about another $15 per person daily. Each well-furnished unit has air conditioning and a private bath. Live entertainment, at least in season, is provided on weekends. The food served in the main restaurant is among the best on the island, and you may want to come here for a meal even if you aren't staying here.

Sandy Point Beach Club, Crown Point, Tobago, W.I. (tel. 809/639-8533), is a winning miniature vacation village built in 1977 somewhat in the style of a Riviera condominium. Each apartment has a kitchenette, allowing guests to be independent. It's just a three-minute run from the airport, but its shoreside position makes it seem remote. The little village of peaked and gabled roofs is landscaped all the way down to the sandy beach, where there's a rustic Steak Hut which serves meals throughout the day and evening. The units, consisting of 20 suites and 22 studio apartments, are air-conditioned and fully equipped, each opening onto a patio, toward the sea, or onto a covered loggia. The rental units contain living and dining areas with pine trestle tables, plus satellite color TV. In some of the apartments is a rustic open stairway leading to a loft room with bunk beds, although there is a twin-bedded room on the lower level as well. *Double occupancy costs $42 to $50 daily in the off-season, EP,* and $70 to $80 daily in winter. Service and tax are extra. The hotel has a sauna, and you can emerge from its intense heat to the shade of a banyan tree beside a swimming pool. To avoid overcrowding, the hotel has added another swimming pool as well.

Richmond Great House, Belle Garden, Tobago, W.I. (tel. 809/639-4467), is one of the most charming accommodations on the island, an 18th-century Great House set on a 1,500-acre citrus-growing estate. In the vicinity of Richmond Beach, it is owned by Dr. Hollis R. Lynch, who is a professor of African history at Columbia. As befits his profession, he has decorated the mansion with African objects of art along with a collection of island antiques. Guests are free to explore the garden and grounds and later enjoy the pool and the barbecue. Accommodations are in five one-bedroom and one two-bedroom suites, each with an individualized decor. In winter, the single MAP rate is $60 nightly, going up to $105 in a double. *In summer, MAP is a real bargain at $50 nightly in a single or $80 in a double.* A taxi from the airport, a 45-minute drive away, costs $60 TT ($13.80).

Della Mira Guest House, Windward Rd., Scarborough, Tobago, W.I. (tel. 809/639-2531), is a simple West Indian guesthouse where the warm hospitality of Neville Miranda and his wife, Angela, is extended. The place is modest and intimate—in reality a small inn where there's an open living room area with pleasantly provincial furnishings. In an adjoining dining room Angela serves authentic island dishes. Tobagoans are fond of coming here, as it has a real atmosphere which most of the other hotels lack. The location is on a cool, airy site overlooking the sea, about half a mile from stores and churches and some 50 yards from the beach. You can also swim in a pool set in the lawn of the garden, around which a terrace has been built for sunning. The bedrooms overlook the garden and the pool, but some cheaper units look out onto the hills. The bedrooms, 14 in all, have a basic simplicity, nothing fancy, yet everything is clean and comfortable. All the rooms come with private bath, and about half of them are air-conditioned as well. In winter, rates are $20 to $28 daily in a single, $25 to $32 in a double. *In summer, prices are $18 to $22 daily in a single, $20 to $25 in a* *double.* Lunches or dinners range from $15. On the premises is one of Tobago's leading nightclubs, La Tropicale, plus a beauty salon. Mrs. Miranda, incidentally, is one of two licensed barbers on the island.

Man-o-War Bay Cottages, Charlotteville, Tobago, W.I. (tel. 809/660-4327). If you're seeking a Caribbean hideaway—that is, a cluster of beach cottages—then the Man-o-War might be for you. The cottages are a part of Charlotteville Estate, a 1,000-acre cocoa plantation. The entire estate is open to visitors, who may wander through at will. Pat and Charles Turpin rent out seven bungalows near a white sandy beach. Each unit comes complete with two bedrooms, a kitchen, a spacious living and dining room, a private bath, and a porch opening onto the sea. Year round you can rent a cottage at $70 daily or a large four-bedroom bungalow (big enough to sleep ten) for only $125 a day. A maid and or cook can be hired for very little extra. Near the colony is a coral reef that is an ideal ground for snorkelers. The couple will also arrange a boat rental if you want to explore Lovers' Beach. Many birdwatchers looking for rare species often book one of these bungalows. Scuba diving and guided nature tours are available. Man-o-War Cottages are 36 miles from the bustle of the airport. The ride follows a bumpy coastal road offering views over the sea and passing through many small villages en route.

Blue Waters Inn, Batteaux Bay, Speyside, Tobago, W.I. (tel. 809/660-4341), is a little inn run by Barbara and Fred Zollna. They are to be applauded for charging the same rates for foreign visitors as they do to local residents (unlike many, many places in the Caribbean which have two sets of tariffs). The remotely perched inn lies on the northeast coast of Tobago, about 24 miles from the airport and 20 miles from Scarborough. Figure either by private car or taxi that it's a 1½-hour drive along narrow, winding country roads. They rent out 17 rooms and cabañas, each unit with private shower and toilet. On the EP, rates in winter are $60 daily in a single, $65 in a double. *Summer prices are $34 in a single, $50 in a double.* The MAP supplement is $25. Meals are served in their casual restaurant, and there's also a bar dispensing tropical libations. This is an extremely informal place, so leave your fancy resortwear at home. Fishing, tennis, shuffleboard, scuba, and skindiving can be arranged, as well as boat trips to Little Tobago. The property is a veritable bird sanctuary, a boon for nature lovers and birdwatchers.

WHERE TO EAT: Most guests eat at their hotels, which seem to have a monopoly on the best chefs. However, there are more and more good independent restaurants.

Sugar Mill Restaurant, Mount Irvine Bay Hotel (tel. 809/639-8871). Its core is a 200-year-old sugar mill whose walls were fashioned from chiseled blocks of coral. Out of it radiate the spidery arms of a beamed ceiling, the shingles of which protect the dozens of tables from the direct sunlight. Open-air, breezy, and casually elegant, this is probably the best restaurant in Tobago. Nonresidents are welcome, but only if they phone for a reservation. Breakfast costs from $15 TT ($3.45) and is served from 7 to 10 a.m. Lunch, depending on how formal you want to be, goes for $20 TT ($4.60) to $60 TT ($13.80) and includes everything from salads and sandwiches to lamb chops provençale or sirloin steak. Dinner, from 7 to 10 p.m., includes a fixed-price menu at $80 TT ($18.40). On any given night the chef might prepare lobster bisque, a carbonade of beef, shrimp Newburg with rice pilaf, and filet of dolphin. Meals are usually accompanied by live music and entertainment, at least in season.

Turtle Beach Hotel Restaurant, Turtle Beach Hotel (tel. 809/639-2851). Informally casual, its tables sit on an outdoor veranda whose edges overlook a tropical garden and the sea. On certain nights, limbo dancers and Tobagoan musicians provide live entertainment. Lunch is served daily from 1 to 2:30 p.m.; dinner, from 8 to 9:30 p.m. Cuisine minceur is available as a calorie-conscious alternative to the other specialties. These include lobster thermidor, breast of chicken with paprika sauce, fish filet in cider, pan-fried kingfish, callaloo, and stuffed Plymouth crab back. Full dinners cost from $75 TT ($17.25), with less elaborate lunches going for $45 TT ($10.35). Reservations are suggested for nonresidents.

Old Donkey Cart House, Bacolet St., Scarborough (tel. 809/639-3551). An unusual and noteworthy restaurant, it occupies a green-and-white Edwardian house about half a mile south of Scarborough. Its entrepreneurial owner, Gloria Jones Schoen, capitalized on her exotic beauty by working as a fashion model in West Germany. She still makes occasional forays into the Teutonic world of couture, but most of her time is spent directing her polite staff. "Born, bred, and dragged up" in Tobago, she is today the island's leading authority on German wines, which she buys directly from well-established German vineyards and sells in her restaurant as appropriate complements to her Caribbean and Germanic cuisine. She's open from noon to 2 a.m. daily except Sunday when she opens at 6:30 p.m. Slide shows and sometimes performances of live music add to the Sunday-evening allure. When Gloria is away, her competent daughter, Samantha Mackey, replaces her. Full meals cost from $60 TT ($13.80). These might include stuffed crab back, shrimp and crabmeat cocktail, beef Stroganoff, omelets, and a succulent collection of shrimp, crabmeat, and fresh fish. When Ms. Schoen established her business in 1978, "sheep and goats scampered through the living room." Today you can dine behind a screen of bamboo and palmetto in the front garden or head for one of the plank-topped tables inside.

The Steak Hut, Sandy Point Beach Club, Crown Point (tel. 809/639-8533), serves the best meat on the island, specializing in U.S. sirloin, T-bone, porterhouse, and tenderloin. The location near the beach and swimming pool of this previously recommended hotel is ideal, especially in the evening. The seafront restaurant also features local fish steaks from shark, flying fish, grouper, dolphin, barracuda, and kingfish. A regular à la carte dinner costs $75 TT ($17.25). However, specials are staged many times. For example, every Friday night a three-course fish dinner costs $40 TT ($9.20), and a steak dinner goes for $50 TT ($11.50), with all the rum you can drink. A steel band plays most Friday nights. Every Wednesday a complete Indian curry dinner with a choice of curry shrimp or chicken or beef is available, costing $35 TT ($8.05). Daily hours are 7:30 a.m. to 10 a.m. if you want breakfast, noon to 3 p.m. for lunch, and 7 to 9 p.m. for dinner.

The Blue Crab, Robinson St., Scarborough (tel. 809/639-2737). One of my favorite restaurants in the capital, this family-run establishment occupies an Edwardian-era house with an oversize veranda. This is the domain of the Sardinha family, who returned to their native country after a sojourn in New York. Keeping their establishment together with "spit and love" after setting it up in 1984, they learned to make the most of local ingredients and local spices. Lunch is daily from 11 a.m. to 2:30 p.m., costing from $22 TT ($5.05). Dinners, however, require an advance reservation and might not always be available. When they are served, the menu will be dictated by whatever was available that day in the market place. The cost is likely to be from $35 TT ($8.05) unless lobster is served. If so, meals are about twice that much. Menu items include fresh seafood, shrimp, an array of Créole meat dishes grilled over coconut husks, flying fish in a mild curry-flavored batter, shrimp with garlic butter or cream, and a vegetable-laced rice dish of the day.

WHAT TO SEE: In Tobago's capital, **Scarborough,** you can enjoy a local market every morning except Sunday, listening to the sounds of a Créole patois.

The village-like place need claim your attention very little before you climb up the hill to **Fort King George,** about 430 feet above the town. Built by the English in 1779, it was later captured by the French. After that it jockeyed back and forth between various conquerors until nature decided to end it all in 1847, blowing off the roofs of its buildings. Sunset over Tobago is spectacular. The cannons still mounted had a three-mile range, and one is believed to have come from one of the ships of Sir Francis Drake (you can still see a replica of the *Tudor Rose*). One building used to house a powder magazine, and you can see the ruins of a military hospital. Artifacts are displayed in a gallery on the grounds.

From Scarborough you can drive northwest to **Plymouth,** Tobago's other town. In the graveyard of the little church is a tombstone dating from 1783 with a mysterious inscription: "She was a mother without knowing it, and a wife, without letting her husband know it, except by her kind indulgences to him."

Perched on a point at Plymouth is **Fort James,** which dates from 1768 when built by the British as a barracks. It is now mainly in ruins.

From Speyside you can make arrangements with some local fisherman to go to **Little Tobago,** an offshore 450-acre island where a bird sanctuary attracts ornithologists. Threatened with extinction in New Guinea, many birds, perhaps 50 species in all, were brought over to this little island in the early part of this century.

Off Pigeon Point lies **Buccoo Reef** (see the "Sporting Life" section) where sea gardens of coral and hundreds of colorful fish can be seen in waist-deep water. This is the natural aquarium of Tobago. Nearly all the major hotels arrange boat trips here to these acres of submarine gardens which offer the best scuba-diving and snorkeling. You can get right in among the various types of tropical fish and other marine creatures. Even nonswimmers can wade knee-deep in the crystal-clear waters. Remember to protect your head and body from the tropical heat and to guard your feet against the sharp coral. A broad-brimmed hat plus an old shirt are necessary, as are canvas shoes.

After about half an hour at the reef, passengers reboard their boats and go over to Nylon Pool, with its crystal-clear waters. There in this white sand bottom, about a mile offshore, you can enjoy water only three to four feet deep. After a swim, the boatman returns you to Buccoo Village jetty in time for a goat and crab race.

At the **Museum of Tobago History,** on the grounds of the Mount Irvine Bay Hotel (tel. 809/639-8871), you'll find artifacts, implements, and pottery of the Caribs and Arawaks who used to inhabit Tobago. Tobago's archeological and historic past comes alive. The museum is open from 5:30 to 8:30 p.m. on Tuesday and Thursday, from 4:30 to 7:30 p.m. on Sunday. Admission is $2 TT (46¢) for adults, 25¢ TT (6¢) for children.

SHOPPING: Scarborough's stores have a limited range of merchandise, more to tempt the browser than the serious shopper.

Stecher's, Main St. (tel. 809/639-2377), has a more famous and better branch in Trinidad. However, this store stocks a limited range of merchandise, including crystal, pipes from Scotland, Seiko watches, and gold jewelry.

Y. de Lima, Burnett St. (tel. 809/639-2464), has a small outlet in Scarborough (a much bigger supply is in Trinidad). Here there is a small range of merchandise, including jewelry and cameras. It's not duty free, however.

THE SPORTING LIFE: If beach-fringed Tobago wasn't in fact the alleged locale of Daniel Defoe's immortal story, the visitors who enjoy its superb beaches hardly seem to care. On Tobago sands you can still feel like Robinson Crusoe in a solitary cove, at least for most of the week before the Trinidadians fly over to sample the sands on a Saturday.

A good beach, **Back Bay,** is within an eight-minute walk of the Mount Irvine Bay Hotel. Along the way you'll pass a coconut plantation and an old cannon emplacement. Sometimes there can be dangerous currents here. But you can always enjoy exploring Rocky Point with its brilliantly colored parrot fish.

Try also **Man O'War Bay,** one of the finest natural harbors in the West Indies, at the opposite end of the island. Once there, you'll come to a long sandy beach, and you can also enjoy a picnic at a government-run rest house.

The finest for last, **Pigeon Point** on the island's northwest coast is the best-known bathing area with a long coral beach. Thatched shelters provide havens for changing into bathing attire, as well as tables and benches for picnics.

Golf

Tobago is the proud possessor of an 18-hole, 6,800-yard golf course at Mount Irvine. Called the **Tobago Golf Club** (tel. 809/639-8871), it covers 150 acres of breeze-swept courses and was featured in the "Wonderful World of Golf" TV series. The course—and even beginners agree—is considered "friendly" to golfers. As a guest of the Mount Irvine Bay Hotel you are granted temporary membership and use of the clubhouse and facilities. Resident hotel guests are entitled to discounts. All serious golfers should stay at the Mount Irvine. Greens fees are $55 TT ($12.65) per day.

Tennis

The Crown Reef (tel. 809/639-8571) and **Turtle Beach Hotels** (tel. 809/639-2851) have courts. The best courts, however, are at the **Mount Irvine Bay Hotel** (tel. 809/639-8871), where two good courts are available free to guests. There is a $3 surcharge for night games.

Scuba-Diving and Snorkeling

Unspoiled reefs off Tobago teem with a great variety of marine life. Colorful sponges and fish can be seen against a background of gorgonians and coral formations ranging from the tiniest spines to giant brain coral. Divers can swim through rocky canyons 60 to 130 feet deep, and underwater photographers can shoot pictures they won't find anywhere else. Snorkeling over the celebrated Buccoo Reef is one of the specialties of Tobago. Hotels arrange for their guests to visit this underwater wonderland.

The **Turtle Beach Hotel,** Great Courtland Bay (tel. 809/639-2851), is the best equipped for water sports. Scuba-diving is offered at prices covering equipment rental or for use of your own gear.

Dive Tobago Ltd., Pigeon Point, P.O. Box 53, Scarborough (tel. 809/639-3695), is the oldest and most established dive operation on Tobago, operated by Jimmy Young. It caters to the beginner as well as the experienced diver. A basic resort course, taking half a day and ending in a 30-foot dive, costs $50. Young is a certified PADI diver.

Tobago Scuba Ltd., Speyside (tel. 809/660-4066), offers scuba dives, snorkeling, and boat trips. The price for scuba dives is $30 to $35 each, depending on the number of plunges taken. All dives are guided, with a boat following. Exciting drift dives are available for experienced divers. Manta rays are frequently seen five minutes from the shore, and there is rich marine life with zonal compaction. Jane Boyle, owner-manager of the establishment, will rent you equipment for scuba-diving or snorkeling if you don't have your own.

Windsurfing

Instruction as well as rental of gear for experienced windsurfers, is offered at the **Turtle Beach Hotel,** Great Courtland Bay (tel. 809/639-2851).

Boating

The **Turtle Beach Hotel,** Great Courtland Bay (tel. 809/639-2851), also rents Sunfish for $50 TT ($11.50) per hour and paddleboats at $15 TT ($3.45) for half an hour or $25 TT ($5.75) per hour.

Deep-Sea Fishing

Stanley Dillon, Milford Bay (tel. 809/639-8765), takes anglers out on his 31-foot twin outboard with outriggers and fighting chairs. The boat holds a maximum of four persons. The price is to be negotiated with Captain Dillon.

Field Trips

Ten different field trips offer closeup views of Tobago's exotic and often rare tropical birds, as well as a range of other island wildlife. Two renowned naturalists of the Trinidad-Tobago area guide these excursions. They are David Rooks, four-time president of the Field Naturalist Club of Trinidad and Tobago, and Renson Jack, a game warden for the Forestry Division of the islands. The trips lead you to forest trails, coconut plantations, along rivers, and past waterfalls. Each trip lasts about two to three hours so you can take at least two per day if you like. One excursion goes to two nearby islands.

The price per trip is $15 per person. For details, get in touch with **Pat Turpin,** Man-O-War Bay Cottages, Charlotteville, Tobago (tel. 809/660-4327).

NIGHTLIFE: Hotels with nightlife, luring the well-heeled visitor, include **Mount Irvine Bay Hotel** (tel. 809/639-8871) and **Turtle Beach Hotel** (tel. 809/639-2851), both previously recommended. The Turtle Beach has a popular barbecue on Saturday night from 8 to 9:30, with poolside dancing to a steel band continuing until late.

CHAPTER XVI

THE DUTCH LEEWARDS

□ □ □

1. ARUBA
2. BONAIRE
3. CURAÇAO

As Dutch as a wooden shoe, the so-called ABC group of islands—Aruba, Bonaire, and Curaçao—lie just off the northern coast of Venezuela. The islands cover only 363 square miles, with a widely diversified population of some 225,000 people, many of whom speak Papiamento, a patois language, although Dutch is the official tongue.

Duty-free shopping and gambling are promoted by the governments in all three islands. Curaçao has the most Dutch atmosphere, with a number of 18th-century buildings. Curaçao, along with Aruba, also has the most developed tourist centers, with Bonaire attracting the most dedicated scuba-divers. Someone once said that there are more flamingos than people in Bonaire. Aruba has the best beaches and the most hotel accommodations.

These spotless islands still retain old-world charm and are clean and thriving.

The canny Dutch emerged from the European power struggle in the West Indies with these tiny specks of land, arid and for all appearances inconsequential. But they proceeded to turn these ugly-duckling properties into some of the most valuable real estate in the Caribbean.

On January 1, 1986, Aruba became a separate entity within the Kingdom of the Netherlands under a political arrangement called *Status Aparte*. Before that date, it was a member of the Netherlands Antilles, consisting of six Dutch Caribbean islands. With Aruba's new status, the Kingdom of the Netherlands has three separate components: the Netherlands, the Netherlands Antilles, and Aruba. The government of the Netherlands is responsible for the defense and foreign affairs of the kingdom, but other government tasks are carried out by each island country for itself.

In addition to Bonaire and Curaçao, the Netherlands Antilles encompasses Saba, St. Eustatius (Statia), and St. Maarten, already previewed in Chapter X, "Dutch Windwards in the Leewards."

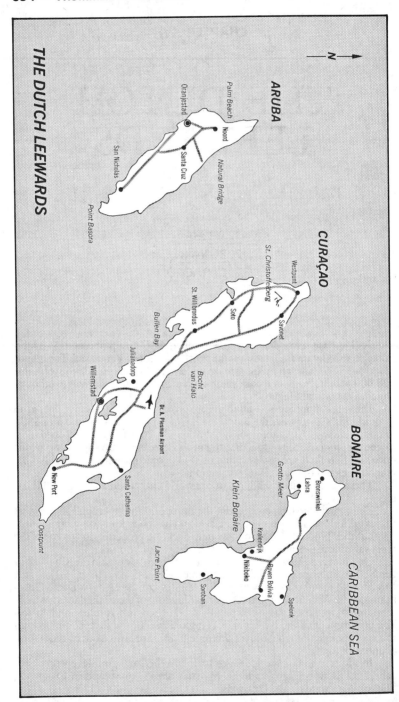

1. ARUBA

At first you'll think you're on a movie set for a Hollywood western, the terrain is so similar. But instead of cowboys you'll meet a friendly people, many of whom speak Papiamento, a mélange of Spanish, Portuguese, Dutch, and some Indian words.

Forget lush vegetation and palm-framed vistas in Aruba. That's impossible with only 17 inches of rainfall annually. Aruba is dry and sunny year round, its clean, exhilarating air desert-like. However, trade winds keep the island from becoming uncomfortably hot. At least you can be sure of the sun every day of your vacation in Aruba.

Cactus fences surround pastel-washed houses, divi-divi trees with their wind-blown look stud the barren countryside, free-form boulders are scattered about, and on occasion you'll come across an abandoned gold mine.

Aruba stands outside the hurricane path. Its coastline on the leeward side is smooth and serene, with sandy beaches; but on the eastern coast, the windward side, the look is rugged and wild, typical of the windswept Atlantic.

First inhabited by the Arawak Indians, Aruba was sighted by Spaniards in 1494. It was claimed for Spain in 1499 by Alonso de Ojeda, although Madrid never considered Aruba of any value. Near the culmination of the 80-year war between Spain and Holland, the Dutch took over in 1636. Pieter Stuyvesant was named governor of Aruba, a post he held for four years before going on to Nieuw Amsterdam. The English were in control between 1805 and 1816 during the Napoleonic Wars. When the English departed, the Dutch returned.

Gold was discovered in 1824 and was mined up until 1924 when the yield became so meager it ceased to be profitable. However, every now and then someone uncovers a big nugget and the excitement is generated all over again.

Aruba's rather bleak economic outlook changed in 1929 when Lago Oil and Transport Company, a subsidiary of Standard Oil of New Jersey, built a large refinery at the southeast tip of the island. Dating from those days, Aruba became one of the most prosperous islands in the West Indies. However, the refinery shut down in 1985, causing widespread unemployment.

Mainly in the 1970s Aruba entered the Caribbean resort sweepstakes when visitors discovered that it has one of the finest beaches in the West Indies stretching along its west coast. In addition to the sands, casinos in high-rise hotels draw the crowds today, as tourism has become Aruba's major industry.

Many visitors come to the island for the annual pre-Lenten **Carnaval,** a two-month-long festival with something going on day and night. Music, dancing, parades, costumes, "jump-ups," whatever—Carnaval is the highlight of Aruba's winter season.

GETTING THERE: Several major airlines service the route to and from Aruba, although the easiest connections for many areas of North America are on **American Airlines.** Aruba-bound passengers in the Northeast, including Boston and Philadelphia, can catch a daily flight leaving from New York's JFK Airport at 9:40 a.m. After about 4½ hours of flying time, the plane lands near the beaches of Aruba, giving passengers time for a brief sunbath before dinner. The return flight leaves Aruba every day at 4:15 p.m., touching down briefly at Curaçao before continuing on to JFK. Passengers departing from other parts of North America travel via San Juan. From San Juan, two nonstop flights depart daily for Aruba.

American's least expensive fare is included as part of a "land package," where prearranged and prepaid accommodations at selected hotels (reviewed in this guide) are booked at the same time as the air fare through American's tour department. The options available are too complicated for this brief overview, although an American Airlines phone reservations clerk, or a travel agent, will discuss them with you.

For clients who prefer to make their own hotel arrangements, American's cheapest high-season fare is a non-refundable super-saver ticket. Round-trip passage from New York to Aruba costs a low high-season price of $375 for weekday travel and $405 for weekend flights. (Weekday travel, for the purposes of this ticket, is defined as anything departing between noon Monday and noon Thursday.) Other restrictions require a 14-day advance purchase, payment in full within 24 hours after the reservation is made, and a stopover for one Saturday night in Aruba. Tickets of this type are not refundable if dates or destination are changed.

Passengers from Toronto or Montréal sometimes fly **Air Canada** to Miami in time to catch **Eastern's** nonstop flight from Miami to Aruba.

Air Aruba offers three daily round-trip flights between Aruba and Curaçao, a daily flight between Aruba and Caracas, and additional weekend service to Bonaire. The airline also has daily service to St. Maarten, Santo Domingo, and Valencia in Venezuela. Flight time between Aruba and Curaçao is 20 minutes.

GETTING AROUND: In Aruba, the **taxis** are unmetered, but rates are fixed, so it's necessary to tell the driver your destination and ask the fare before getting in. A ride from the airport to most of the hotels, including those at Palm Beach, costs $10 to $12 per car, and a maximum of four passengers are allowed to take the journey. Some of the local people don't tip, although it's good to give something extra, especially if the driver has helped you with a lot of luggage.

Buses

Aruba has a decent bus service. The fare is 90¢. Your hotel reception desk will know the approximate times the buses pass by where you're staying. There is regular service from 7:40 a.m. to 6:05 p.m.

Car Rentals

Unlike most Caribbean islands, Aruba makes it easy for the independent traveler to rent a car and explore on his or her own. The roads between the major tourist attractions are excellent, and a valid U.S. or Canadian driver's license is accepted by each of the major car-rental companies. Most of the big hotels have desks which will rent cars for you. Always ask them a day in advance and you'll stand a better chance of getting the car you specify.

Five of the nation's major car-rental companies maintain offices in Aruba, usually with both airport branches as well as outlets at some of the major hotels. High-season rates offered by most of the companies are fairly consistent: a peppy two- or four-door car with manual transmission and unlimited mileage costs a minimum of around $160 a week, although an occasional midwinter special might bring the weekly price on a no-frills car down to $130 per week with unlimited mileage. There's no tax imposed on car rentals in Aruba, and few hidden extras other than insurance.

Hertz, Avis, and **Budget Rent-a-Car** offer collision damage waivers to their clients. These policies, which, depending on the value of the car, cost about $10 a day at all three companies, reduce but do not always eliminate a driver's financial responsibility in the event of an accident. A close look at the fine print is needed.

The two contenders for the title of renter of the island's least expensive cars are Budget and Avis. For $153 to $160 per week, either company will rent a Toyota Corolla or a Toyota Starlet in high season, without air conditioning and with manual transmission. Many vacationers, however, avoid the blistering heat of Aruba by renting a car with air conditioning. In this more expensive category,

Hertz and Budget offer the least expensive cars, Toyota Corollas, priced at $216 and $225, respectively.

As a final note, under-age or over-age drivers might not be qualified for rentals at all three agencies. For insurance reasons, Budget requires that drivers in Aruba be between 23 and 65, Avis will rent only to qualified drivers between the ages of 23 and 70, and Hertz requires only that a qualified driver be older than 21.

For detailed information on rentals at the time of your trip, call the toll-free international departments of Budget (tel. 800/527-0700), Avis (tel. 800/331-2112), or Hertz (tel. 800/654-3131).

Scooters
New York Cycles & Scooters, Noord (tel. 011-297-8/33885), offers motorcycles and scooters at $18 to $30 per day. The shop is open from 8 a.m. to 6 p.m. Free pickup and delivery are provided. Minimum age for renters is 18, and gasoline is not included in the rates.

Sightseeing Taxi Tours
Taxis with English-speaking drivers are available as guides. Most of them seem well informed about their island and are eager to share it with you. A one-hour tour (and you don't need much more than that) is offered at a cost of $22 per hour for a maximum of five passengers.

Sightseeing Bus Tours
De Palm Tours, 142 L. G. Smith Blvd. in Oranjestad (tel. 011-297-8/2440), has offices at major hotels. Their most popular jaunt is a 3½-hour excursion leaving at 9:30 a.m. and costing $15 per person. The tour takes in the island's major attractions, including a haul across the windswept countryside with its divi-divi trees, continuing on to the north coast to see Aruba's Natural Bridge.

PRACTICAL FACTS: Aruba has a western-style democracy. The head of state is a governor appointed by the sovereign of the Kingdom of the Netherlands, with executive power being vested in the Council of Ministers, presided over by a prime minister. Legislative power lies with a parliament of 21 members, elected by popular vote. A Common Court of Justice of Aruba and the Netherlands Antilles and a Supreme Court of Justice in the Netherlands is the judicial branch of the government.

Banks: Hours are from 8 a.m. to noon and 1:30 to 3:45 p.m. Monday to Friday.

Currency: The currency is the Aruba florin, which is divided into 100 cents. Silver coins come in denominations of 5, 10, 25, and 50 cents and 1 and 2½ florins. The 50-cent piece, the square "yotin," is probably Aruba's best-known coin. The current exchange rate is $1 U.S. to 1.79 AFl. U.S. dollars are accepted throughout the island. *Note:* Unless otherwise stated, prices quoted in this chapter are in U.S. dollars.

Documents: To enter Aruba, U.S. and Canadian citizens may submit a valid passport or a birth certificate (or for U.S. citizens only, a voter registration card).

Electricity: The electrical current is 110 volts AC, 60 cycles, the same as in the U.S.

Emergencies: In an emergency, for the police, dial 100 or 011-297-8/24000. The fire department emergency number is 115.

Information: Go to the Aruba Tourist Authority, L. G. Smith Blvd. (tel. 011-297-8/23777), a two-story building opposite the Tamarijn Beach Hotel.

Language: The official language is Dutch, but nearly everybody also speaks English. The language of the street is often Papiamento or Spanish.

Medical care: To receive medical care, go to the **Horacio Oduber Hospital** (tel. 011-297-8/24300, also the number to call in case of a medical emergency), which opened in 1976. It is a modern building near Eagle Beach, with excellent medical facilities. Hotels also have medical doctors on call, and there are good dental facilities as well (appointments can be made through your hotel).

Taxes and service: The government of Aruba imposes a 5% room tax, as well as a $9.50 airport departure tax. At your hotel, you will have a 10% to 15% service charge added to charges for room, food, and beverages. Otherwise, tipping is up to you.

Telecommunications: Telegrams and Telexes can be sent by the **Government Telegraph and Radio Office** at the Post Office Building in Oranjestad or via your hotel. There is also an I.T.T. office at 33 Boecoetiweg (tel. 011-297-8/21458). Local and international telephone calls can be made also from the **Government Long Distance Telephone Office,** also in the Post Office Building, or through hotel operators. You can dial Aruba direct from mainland North America by using the international code number, 011, followed by Aruba's area code, 297-8, then the local five-digit number. Once in Aruba, you can call any number on the island by dialing only the last *five* digits of the numbers given in this section.

Time: This island is on Atlantic Standard Time year-round.

Water: The water, which comes from the world's second-largest desalinization plants, is pure.

Weather: Dry and sunny, Aruba has a median temperature of 83° Fahrenheit (trade winds, as mentioned, make it more bearable).

WHERE TO STAY: Most of Aruba's hotels are of the resort variety, bustling and self-contained. There's a tremendous dearth of family hotels or those of the budget variety. Guesthouses are few and tend to be booked up early in winter by faithful returning visitors. In season, it's imperative to make reservations way in advance. Don't ever arrive expecting to find a room on the spot. You must have an address to give Immigration when you arrive in Aruba.

The Resort Hotels

Aruba Concorde Hotel-Casino, 77 Lloyd G. Smith Blvd., Palm Beach, Aruba (tel. 011-297-8/24466), competes rather successfully for the title of "the biggest and the best" along the Palm Beach strip. The 18-story property is the quintessential Las Vegas–style hotel, set on the sands of Aruba. There are 500 ocean-view rooms, each with private balcony, closed-circuit color TV (movies shown from 11 a.m. to 3 a.m.), and radio with private channel music, and a vaguely continental decor. The designer was lavish in his colors, accented in vibrant walls, floors, and fabrics. Expensive suites are available, as you'd expect. Otherwise, single rooms range in price from $160 to $180 daily, with doubles going for $210 to $230, all winter tariffs. *In spring, summer, and fall, the prices are $130 to $175, single or double.*

The free-form swimming pool is Olympic size, and between the hotel and the sea is a tremendous playtime terrace with sunning areas and a multitude of lounge chairs. The beach offers probably the most crowded panorama of bodies of anywhere in the Caribbean. Professional tennis courts are lit for night games. Breakfast, lunch, and dinner are served in the Kadushi Restaurant, with its globe lighting and stylized tile cut-out murals on its pillars and walls. Perhaps the best experience is to descend the central cantilevered interior staircase to the lower level. It's a flow of various rooms, Japanese style, all open, with large planters and delicate screens setting off the various sections. White floors and walls of glass give a sense of space. In the evening guests dine at La Serre or any of the four other varied restaurants, later playing baccarat or roulette in the casino or enjoying nightclub entertainment in the Arubesque.

Aruba Palm Beach Hotel & Casino, L. G. Smith Boulevard, Palm Beach, Aruba (tel. 011-297-8/23900), is a white palacio with Moorish arches. At this sleek, stylish, high-rise total resort, built in 1968, you are given all the trimmings. The Dutch Arcade houses a shopping center behind colorfully painted reproductions of Holland-type storefronts. Staggered along its eight stories are 200 guest rooms, including pool-side lanais and oceanfront suites, all modern and first class. Every unit has quality and character, with many amenities, including air conditioning. Bedrooms overlook the swimming pool or the gardens, and all are ocean view. In winter, $145 daily is charged for a standard room, $225 daily for an oceanview cabaña, either single or double occupancy. For breakfast and dinner, add $37 per person. *Summer rates are $85 daily in a standard room, $145 daily in an oceanview cabaña, single or double.* For reservations in the U.S. and Canada, phone 800/345-2782 toll free.

This government-financed hotel spared little expense in developing a large sunning and sports area between the hotel and the sea. The Balashi Bar, informal and thatch-roofed, surrounds an overscale freshwater swimming pool, and there's a smaller pool for children. Surrounding gardens are well kept and planted with palms intermixed with more flamboyant varieties of shrubbery and trees. Scuba-diving, tennis, sailing, skindiving, even glassbottom-boat rides, can easily be arranged at the sports desk. For breakfast, choose from Arawak Coffeehouse, with a decorative theme of primitive hex signs and handsome Delft china, or the outdoor terrace buffet. Dine either in the elegant Rembrandt Room with walls of red velvet displaying many reproductions of the artist's finer works, where a dinner and floor show average $35, or at the outdoor Steak Pub, where the evening breeze carries the aromas of an open hearth cooking steaks, lobsters, and shrimp. For nightly divertissement, the disco Galactica, done in steel gray and red with chrome trim, offers good music. It's open seven days a week from 11 a.m. to 4 a.m. Disco action gets animated around 9 p.m. Of course, the prime nighttime target is the modernized Grand Casino.

Golden Tulip Aruba Caribbean, 81 L. G. Smith Boulevard, Aruba (tel. 011-297-8/33555, 212/832-2996 in New York City, or toll free 800/344-1212). Its original core was one of the first palace-style hotels in Aruba, and it reopened after massive renovations in 1986. Today it qualifies as one of the most stylish hotels on the island, boasting more than 400 accommodations. These are scattered among a quartet of different buildings sitting on a flat and sandy garden a few steps from one of the best beaches in Aruba. The main building's angular façade rises above a curved driveway whose centerpiece is a splashing fountain, huge weathered rocks, and a cluster of cactus. The lobby incorporates tones of blue and sea-green into many different themes, ranging from traditional to beach resort modern. Don't overlook the massive mural crafted from Delft tiles, depicting the world's first salute to the American flag in 1776. The hotel has a popular swimming pool shaped like a double-headed hatchet, a casino, four attractive restaurants and bars, four tennis courts, and an array of water-sports facilities, a health club, and a nightclub, along with a shopping arcade. Each of the accommodations has air conditioning, a satellite-reception color TV, a mini-bar, sunflooded windows, a private terrace or veranda, and a stylishly contemporary decor of semitropical motifs. Depending on the accommodation and its exposure, single or double rooms range from $175 to $230 daily in high season. *In low season, single or double rooms cost $100 to $165 daily.*

Americana Aruba Beach Resort & Casino, P.O. Box 218, Palm Beach,

Aruba (tel. 011-297-8/24500), is a high-rise resort with 419 king-size and double-bedded guestrooms and suites. Opened in 1975, the hotel underwent a $16 million renovation and expansion in 1989. The resort consists of twin eight-story towers. All units are air-conditioned and have ocean views from balconies, direct-dial phones, remote control TV, refrigerators, and hairdryers. *Off-season rates are $100 to $120 daily for two persons,* with winter prices going to $175 to $200 for two guests. The hotel on Palm Beach offers Aruba's first free-form pool complete with a built-in current, spas, and waterfalls that allow you to swim up to the bar Splash for your favorite tropical drink. Tradewinds offers lunch and dinner off the grill, and you can order breakfast or partake of a lavish buffet breakfast at The Veranda. Light lunch and dinner are also available. The Jardin Bresilien is a tropical café open from 6 p.m. to 2 a.m. It's a drink and ice cream emporium, serving such delights as raspberry daiquiri, Kahlua banana coladas, and a "Shark Bite." The Supper Club offers a full dinner menu with a show. The hotel has a casino and many shops as well as four tennis courts, a massage salon, a health club, and a sauna.

Holiday Inn Aruba Beach Resort, Palm Beach, Aruba (tel. 011-297-8/23600), with 602 rooms, is the most action-packed hostelry along the sands of Palm Beach. Private balconies frame vistas of white sands, and each air-conditioned bedroom comes with a TV offering in-house video movies, a private tile bath, and a phone. Bedrooms, built to Holiday Inn traditional standards, have color coordination and are well furnished, with wall-to-wall carpeting, two double beds, and large closets. In winter, singles cost $140 to $180 daily, while doubles go for $150 to $200. *In summer, terms are lowered to $75 to $105 daily in a single, $85 to $110 in a double.* For breakfast and dinner, add $33 per person daily. The Olympic-size swimming pool with distilled fresh water seems to have room for everybody, and it's surrounded by a sun terrace. There's a health spa with aerobics, sauna, and massage, plus six lit tennis courts, including one international court. Musicians serenade you as you dine in Le Salon, with its French gourmet cuisine, plus on Sunday an exotic buffet brunch and many other specialties. The Chinese restaurant, the Empress of China, features a Cantonese menu. Outside special events are Italian Night on Monday, King Neptune's Night on Wednesday, and Carnival Night on Friday. In addition, the hotel has the Grand Holiday Casino.

Divi-Divi Beach Hotel, Druif Bay Beach, Aruba (tel. 011-297-8/23300), stands near the largest beach on the island. A rambling, low-rise structure, it has Iberian architectural accents, offering some rooms in the bungalow style, others in two- or three-story buildings or lanais. In all, there are more than 200 units, all with private baths with tub and shower. Each has a private terrace or balcony and is fully air-conditioned. Casual and comfortable, the Divi-Divi is one of the island's friendliest oases. In winter, singles or doubles cost $200 to $220 daily. *In off-season, the charges are $100 to $150 daily in a single, $105 to $135 in a double.* For breakfast and dinner, add $40 per person to the daily tariffs. Meals are served on the casual Pelican Terrace or in the Red Parrot dining room. Sunday brunch is a popular occasion. On the grounds are two freshwater swimming pools and three Jacuzzis, and the hotel has a tennis court. All year, dancing and entertainment are offered nightly. The Alhambra Casino stands across the road from Divi-Divi.

Divi Tamarijn Beach Resort, Druif Bay Beach, Aruba (tel. 011-297-8/24150), the center of a trio of properties owned and well managed by the Divi Hotel chain, enjoys one of the longest beachfronts in Aruba. Built in a Dutch style of two-story units, it resembles a meandering assemblage of interconnected waterfront town houses. The narrow strip of sandy turf between the accommodations and the beach is planted with copses of almonds, palms, and sea grapes.

Facilities include a collection of hard-surface, lit tennis courts, and an array of water sports. At one end of the long and narrow property the open-air Bunker Bar is perched, as its name suggests, on stilts above a lopsided fortification remaining intact from World War II. On the premises are several drinking spots and a pair of tropical restaurants along with a rectangular swimming pool. There's also an armada of electric carts which will transport visitors to the Alhambra Casino and the Divi-Divi Beach Hotel. Each of the sun-flooded rooms contains air conditioning, a private bathroom, phone, radio, and big glass doors that slide open to accept the breezes from the beach. *In off-season, singles or doubles cost $95 daily,* that price going up to $200 daily in winter.

Talk of the Town Resort Hotel, 2 L. G. Smith Blvd., P.O. Box 564, Aruba (tel. 011-297-8/23380), was built as an eight-room structure in 1942. The 63 air-conditioned rooms surround a palm oasis courtyard, enormous pool, and Jacuzzi. Each unit has a ceiling fan, refrigerator, color cable TV, safe deposit box, and direct-dial phone. Most rooms have kitchenettes. In winter, singles cost $95 to $125 daily, and doubles go for $100 to $135. *In summer, doubles rent for $70 daily, with singles costing $65 to $75.* For breakfast and dinner, add $34 per person daily.

The hotel is well-known for its restaurant, one of the most famous in the Caribbean. In fact, the name of the restaurant, Talk of the Town, eventually replaced the name of the hotel, Coral Strand. The hotel and its beachside sister, the Manchebo, offer six different places to eat, including the Moorish-style Surfside, across from the Talk of the Town on the beach. At poolside in a sheltered dining room, meals are served every day from 6 a.m. to 2 a.m., and a latticed gazebo is the setting for cocktail parties. Musicians entertain every evening. The beach and sea are just a two-minute stroll across the road at Surfside Beach Club, offering a pool and two Jacuzzis. The nearest hotel to the town of Oranjestad, Talk of the Town is an easy 15-minute walk to shopping and sightseeing. The hotel is on the coastal road leading to the airport.

Manchebo Beach Resort Hotel, Manchebo Beach, Aruba (tel. 011-297-8/23444), offers spread-out beach-club facilities, in a setting across from the Alhambra Casino. Owned by the Cohens of Talk of the Town (guests have exchange privileges), the Manchebo consists of groups of two-story motel-like air-conditioned bedrooms, with balconies or patios overlooking the Caribbean. Its private-seeming 1,600 feet of beach strip is ideal for suntanning and water sports. Close to the surf line is a large freshwater swimming pool. On the grounds are facilities for volleyball, shuffleboard, and tennis. The 74 bedrooms all have private baths, TVs, refrigerators, and phones, and they are light and airy in feeling, with white walls. Many units have built-ins, and the baths are tile. In winter, singles pay from $130 daily for a room, and doubles cost $130 to $140. Add $34 for breakfast and dinner. *In summer, the single tariff is $70, and the double rate runs from $75.* The deluxe Manchebo Bucuti wing, recently added, contains 63 tropical rooms with balconies facing the sea, each with a microwave oven. Prices in this wing are $160 daily in winter, single or double, *$100 daily in summer, also single or double.* A relaxed, informal atmosphere prevails. On the grounds is the French Steak House (see my dining recommendations), plus a patio restaurant specializing in fish dishes. Addition of the Bucuti wing includes the Golden Galleon Pirates Nest restaurant, a full-size replica of a shipwrecked Dutch galleon, on the beach and poolside. Featured are international, Dutch, and seafood specialties, served from 9 a.m. to 11 p.m.

A Guesthouse

Many travelers prefer to visit Aruba on a much simpler basis than what we've been considering. There are some apartments and a handful of guesthouses overlooking the sea or within walking distance of a beach. Others are on a bus route, and still others require a car. My personal favorite follows:

The Edge's, 458 L. G. Smith Blvd., Malmok-by-the-Sea, Aruba (tel. 011-297-8/21072), favored by windsurfers, is a guesthouse complex of 11 units 50 yards across from the beach. It's less than a mile from the Holiday Inn Hotel and Casino going toward the lighthouse. A carpeted patio with chaise longues separates two rows of motel-style units, and each apartment has a private entrance and patio with furniture for outdoor dining. These are really efficiency units with kitchenette, refrigerator, dishes, toaster, coffee pot, and all utensils for cooking. All apartments are air-conditioned with large tile baths. Each unit has at least two beds and is pleasantly furnished and clean. There are two deluxe units and a luxury suite with king-size beds, sitting rooms, full kitchens, and private patios with a view of the ocean. In winter, double occupancy costs $56 to $100 per day, *the off-season charge being $35 to $50 for two persons per day.* An extra $10 is charged for each person over two per apartment. To the right of the entrance gate, you can watch sunsets from a whirlpool spa at no charge. The house lies only a short bus ride from Oranjestad.

Time-Share Properties

Time-sharing has become a major vacation investment in Aruba. Even if you're not interested for yourself, you may want to consider renting one temporarily as a one-time vacationer. The most recommendable ones are previewed below.

Divi Dutch Village, 93 L. G. Smith Blvd., Aruba (tel. 011-297-8/32300 or toll free 800/367-3484). Its high, angular sides evoke the chimneys of 17th-century Dutch buildings. Within a lush garden, the complex is not set directly on the beach, but the sands are only a short walk away. In the center of the compound, a re-creation of a tropical lagoon splashes water from an artificial grotto. Units contain satellite color TVs, air conditioning, complete kitchens, king-size beds, private Jacuzzis, and patios or verandas. Studios, one-bedroom apartments, and two-bedroom town houses are offered when they're not occupied by their investors. In high season, studios for one or two people rent for $280 daily, with one-bedroom apartments for two going for $330. *Low-season prices are $170 daily in a studio, $225 in a one-bedroom apartment.* The complex is owned and managed by the Divi Hotel chain.

Playa Linda Beach Resort, P.O. Box 235, Oranjestad, Aruba (tel. 011-297-8/31000). Designed in a ziggurat shape of receding balconies, the complex sits on a desirable stretch of white sandy beachfront sheathed in a façade of terracotta and cream. In winter, units with kitchens, private verandas, and air conditioning cost from $180 daily for double occupancy, going up to $450 for four guests. *In summer, two persons can stay here for $95 per day and four for $250.* Amenities and facilities at Playa Linda include a large free-form swimming pool, outdoor whirlpool baths, tennis courts, and a shopping arcade featuring a beauty parlor, perfumery, and souvenir and gift shop. The property is landscaped with tropical foliage and native Aruban flora.

Aruba Beach Club/Casa del Mar, P.O. Box 368, Oranjestad, Aruba (tel. 011-297-8/24595), were two properties built at different times, but now they're connected by a common wing and a shared reception desk. The older and more staid of the properties, the Aruba Beach Club, is a hotel of 133 rooms, dating from the late 1970s. Each of its pleasant units contains a kitchenette, air conditioning, cable-connected color TV, and a decor of tropical furniture. Its exterior embraces a rear courtyard, an expanse of seafront, and its own swimming pool. In winter, singles or doubles cost $165 daily. *In summer, these same units rent for $66 daily in singles, $70 in doubles.*

The newer time-share section, the Casa del Mar (tel. 011-297-8/23000), contains 32 tasteful, well-decorated apartments, with Jacuzzi tubs, well-equipped kitchens, verandas or patios, air conditioning, and sun-flooded views of the sea. In winter, a two-bedroom unit, suitable for one to six occupants, costs $275 daily, *the tariff dropping to $175 in summer.* Casa del Mar wraps itself around its own stretch of beachfront and a private courtyard fringed with palms and thatch-covered cabañas. In its center, a swimming pool, shaped like a pair of interconnected octagons, provides an alternative to the beach. Across from the Alhambra Casino, both resorts are encircled by urn-shaped balustrades. The establishments share the same tennis courts, bars, and an appealingly rustic restaurant, the Taverna.

ARUBA COOKERY: A few of Aruba's restaurants serve *rijsttafel,* the "Asian smörgåsbord," or *nasi goreng,* a "mini rijsttafel." In addition, a large number of Chinese restaurants operate in Oranjestad. Most of the major hotels have several dining options, ranging from fast food in coffeeshops to so-called gourmet restaurants. More and more Aruban specialties are beginning to appear on menus. French cuisine is the second major choice of most chefs. Sometimes, at least on off-season package deals, visitors on the MAP (breakfast and dinner) are allowed to dine around on an exchange plan with the other hotels.

Chez Mathilde, 23 Havenstraat (tel. 011-297-8/34968), is all the rage, the *restaurant français* of Oranjestad. It's expensive, with a dinner, served from 6 to 10 nightly, costing from $30 to $40, with wine, tax, and service included. But most satisfied customers agree that it is worth the price, especially those diners who order the chef's bouillabaisse, made with more than a dozen different sea creatures. Not only do you get distinguished food and service, including a haute cuisine preview of the classic French repertoire, but you can enjoy your repast in an elegant setting. The structure housing the restaurant was built in the 1800s, and it has been preserved more or less as it was originally. The intimate dining rooms contain beautifully set tables and a restrained but romantic decor. Over an apéritif, you'll have plenty of time to peruse the offerings of the evening, and the staff will be at hand to answer any questions about the comparatively large wine list.

La Dolce Vita, 164 Nassaustraat (tel. 011-297-8/25675). Once it was a private home, but since 1980 it has been the most acclaimed restaurant in Aruba, serving, as its name suggests, Italian specialties. It wasn't long before it was discovered by the food and wine critics of such prestigious Stateside magazines as *Gourmet.* Only dinner is served, costing from $25, seven days a week from 6 p.m. to midnight. Because of the popularity of "The Sweet Life," it's best to call and reserve a table, especially in high season, when it can quickly fill up. If you like pasta with salmon and cream (which became the rage in Italy in the 1980s), you'll find it served here. You might begin your repast, however, with a sampling of their antipasti, including fine Italian salami and cheese, along with artichokes and marinated squid. They also do a savory, perfectly flavored "kettle" of fruits de mer. Naturally you get some good veal, along with such familiar Italian standby dishes as baked clams and linguine. An espresso or perhaps some Italian ice cream will finish off your meal nicely.

Papagayo Restaurant, L. G. Smith Boulevard (tel. 011-297-8/24140), is one of the most delightful restaurants in Aruba. It's decorated like a forest, with live birds, trees, and plants. In addition to that, it opens onto a view of the harbor. It has steadily grown in popularity ever since it opened in 1983. Managed by Divi Resorts, it offers such tempting fare as linguine with lobster and seafood and chicken Papagayo (one of the chef's many specialties—stuffed breast of chicken). In addition to that, you get excellent prime steaks along with the superb fare of the northern Italian kitchen. Prices are moderate: a typical meal costs $20. Before dinner, you might want to have an apéritif in the lounge. It's open from noon to 2:30 p.m. and 5:45 to 10 p.m. daily. In addition, you may want to stop at **Tiki-Tiki Café** for tropical drinks and light lunches. Across the harbor, it's open from noon to 8 p.m.

Papiamento, 7 Wilhelminastraat (tel. 011-297-8/24544), considered one of the most desirable independent restaurants in Aruba, sits inside the thick stone walls of a 1930s West Indian house in the center of the capital. Transformed into a stylish and intimate hideaway by Arubian entrepreneur Eduardo Ellis, it boasts wide-plank floors, latticework ceilings, a changing exhibition of contemporary paintings (each of which is for sale), and such old-world touches as massive brass chandeliers. It's open daily for dinner from 7 p.m. to midnight. A distinguishing culinary feature is the way fresh meat or seafood is served raw on sizzling marble slabs so that your dinner is cooked in front of you the way you like it. Chicken or fish is cooked in an Aruba-made clay pot which is then broken open at your table. Full meals, costing from $40 each, might include fresh lobster, chicken breast, lamb chops, or mixed seafood cooked directly on the stone, selections from a salad bar, grilled veal cutlets, rack of lamb for two, lobster thermidor, and broiled porterhouse steak. Reservations are suggested, especially on weekends.

Bali Floating Restaurant, off L. G. Smith Blvd. (tel. 011-297-8/22131), is moored in Oranjestad's harbor. The restaurant is housed in an Oriental houseboat decorated with bamboo and Indonesian art. Diners are treated to the popular Indonesian rijsttafel (rice table), a complete meal of rice surrounded by 21 different dishes, served at your table in individual portions. The rijsttafel is not spicy, but the sambal (hot, hot) is served on the side for the more adventurous to try. A mini-version is served for lunch, as well as sandwiches and snacks. Expect to pay from $22 for a full rijsttafel, which may be ordered per person, but try to go with a group if possible, since it's a fun meal that everyone will enjoy. Besides the rijsttafel, the menu offers a fine selection of tenderloin steaks and fresh local fish dishes. Hours are noon to midnight daily.

Talk of the Town Restaurant, 2 L. G. Smith Blvd. (tel. 011-297-8/23380). When Ike Cohen was growing up in Rotterdam, he learned the meat business from his father. While still a boy he knew how to purchase meat for the family's wholesale butcher business. When he and his wife, Grete, founded the Talk of the Town Restaurant, Mr. Cohen applied that knowledge to his present business. Today his meat freezer is the best and most fully stocked on the island. A self-taught resort operator, Mr. Cohen now runs one of Aruba's best-known restaurants, lying between the airport and Palm Beach (see my hotel recommendation). From 5:30 to 10 p.m., candlelight dining is offered, backed up by a good wine list and live music. Mr. Cohen has always believed in feeding people well, and the portions here are large. The setting could easily be Miami, and there's no view—but people don't come here for that. They want to dine well. You can begin with escargots à la bourguignonne or perhaps vichyssoise. As mentioned, Mr. Cohen specializes in beef, such as the filet mignon Dutch style. He also offers a selection of seafood dishes, including king crab legs, Dover sole meunière, and the popular Caribbean snapper meunière. A complete meal could cost around $30 per person here. After 11 p.m., there's disco action.

Red Parrot, Divi-Divi Beach Hotel, Druif Bay Beach (tel. 011-297-8/23300), is one of the better hotel restaurants. You dine seated on sturdy Spanish armchairs, and the view is through arched windows framed with vines and plants, opening onto the sea. The Iberian decor is reflected by the rough stone walls and wood paneling, as well as the archways. The menu leads off with an unusual appetizer, tender scallops lightly cooked in saffron. Main-dish specialties include tropical-style chicken filled with kiwi and served with a lemon-butter sauce as well as a local favorite, keshi yena. In addition, the chef prepares good seafood daily. A dessert selection is made from the trolley. Expect to spend from $28 to $35 per person for a meal. On Tuesday night a buffet of local dishes is presented, everything enlivened by the Divi-Divi steel band, complete with a parade of award-winning carnival costumes and an island-wear fashion show and water ballet. Open from 6:45 to 10 p.m. daily.

De Olde Molen, Palm Beach (tel. 011-297-8/22060), is housed in a landmark, standing just across the street from the Concorde Hotel. It can be reached on foot from a number of Palm Beach hotels. Originally, the windmill in which the restaurant is housed was built in 1804 in Friesland, but it was torn down and shipped to Aruba where it was reconstructed piece by piece. Since 1960 it has been a tourist-focused destination for dinner, served nightly except Sunday from 6 p.m. to 11 p.m. Jackets are suggested for men. The chefs seem to change with some frequency here, but all of them know how to prepare an international cuisine with such classic offerings as pepper steak for two persons, veal Cordon Bleu, and shrimp provençale. Try also, if offered, the red snapper amandine. Some guests begin with a shrimp cocktail, although I prefer the thick Dutch split-pea soup. Many diners finish with Irish coffee. A meal can easily run around $22 to $35 per person. A 15% service charge is added to all bills.

Cattle Baron, 228 L. G. Smith Blvd. (tel. 011-297-8/22977). Its location amid a dry and dusty landscape beside the highway seems appropriate to its western theme. Amid a decor of ruffled gingham curtains, roughly textured planking, and wagon-wheel chandeliers, diners enjoy generous portions of aged U.S.-bred beef, as well as a scattering of seafood. Served by waiters whose costumes enhance the cattle baron theme, the specialties include Dutch steak, porterhouse steak, prime rib, barbecued ribs, and pepper steak. The seafood features red snapper San Francisco style (with crabmeat, mushrooms, and bordelaise sauce), broiled lobster, shrimp bisque, fish Oriental, and snapper arubiano (with Créole sauce, fried plantain, and funchi). Full meals cost from $20 and are served from noon to 3 p.m. every day except Sunday and from 6 to 11 p.m. nightly. Reservations are suggested.

Dragon-Phoenix, 31 Havenstraat (tel. 011-297-8/21928), in downtown Oranjestad, was launched by a kindly man who came from Canton province and brought his mild-flavored cuisine to Aruba with him. In these cool, comfortable surroundings, you can make selections from a large menu. If you're confused by such a big choice, I'd suggest a special Chinese rice table. Perhaps there will be four or five people in your party. Your party will receive the chef's special eggroll, sharkfin with chicken soup, chow kai kow with vegetables, shrimp in cashew nuts, lobster with oyster sauce, crabmeat with black-bean sauce, special fried rice, plus dessert. At least 18 Cantonese dishes are offered, including lobster chop suey. In addition, the chef has at least 22 other specialties. A complete meal is likely to cost about $22. It's open daily from 11:30 a.m. to 11 p.m.

Heidelberg, 136 L. G. Smith Blvd. (tel. 011-297-8/26888). About the last place you'd expect to find a restaurant with a name like Heidelberg is the desertlike island of Aruba. But here it is, serving dinner nightly, except Wednesday, from 6 to 11 p.m. Established in 1982, it became popular immediately. Arubans even come here to celebrate Christmas by ordering a fat, juicy Christmas goose. Here you get traditional German fare, including Wiener schnitzel, and goulash and noodles. In addition to goose, duck is well prepared. But before that, you may want to order the herring hausfrau style. Sauerbraten and good, rich-tasting soups are some of the other dishes served here. For dessert, select something from the trolley. Most diners, however, go for the strudel. Count on paying around $25 for a big, hearty, and altogether satisfying meal.

The **French Steak House,** Manchebo Beach Hotel, Manchebo Beach (tel.

011-297-8/23444), is a beachside bistro where the atmosphere is gracious and the food is good. Guests from the other hotels often come here for the romantic candlelit dining, and no one need worry about putting on a jacket or tie. It's easy to make a night of it if you dine here in these relaxed surroundings. The place is owned by Ike and Grete Cohen, who also run the previously recommended Talk of the Town. It's open from 6 to 11 p.m.; closed Monday. If you arrive between 6 and 7 p.m. you can order a five-course set dinner for $12. Or you can order à la carte, enjoying such chef's specialties as red snapper provençale or the classic veal Stroganoff flamed with vodka and madeira. You can also help yourself at a New York–style salad bar. Of course beef is featured, like chateaubriand or pepper steak for two people. If you order à la carte, chances are you'll end up paying from $30 per head.

Buccaneer, 11C Gasparito (tel. 011-297-8/26172), is a seafood restaurant with a saltwater aquarium. But you don't go here to watch the fish: you go to eat them. The atmosphere evokes (or means to) that of a ship's cabin. The location is near many of the major hotels, about two miles from Palm Beach (taxis are always waiting outside). The owners, Josef Munzenhofer and Peter Dorer, are also the chefs. For an opener, the pirate's hotpot is a seaworthy choice (a native fish soup that somehow manages to taste different every night). Among the "fruits of the sea," the lobster thermidor is everybody's favorite. I always ask the waiter for the catch of the day, which the kitchen will prepare with a Créole sauce. Meats are frozen of course, but well prepared, including tournedos in a number of ways. Every main dish is served with the vegetable of the day, along with a stuffed potato and salad on the side. Coup Melba or homemade cheesecake are favored to finish off your meal, which most likely will cost from $25. The service is excellent. Open from 5:30 to 10:30 p.m.; closed Sunday.

EXPLORING ARUBA: The capital of Aruba, **Oranjestad** attracts mainly shoppers instead of sightseers. The bustling city has a very Caribbean flavor, and it's part Spanish, part Dutch in architecture. Cutting in from the airport, the main thoroughfare, L. G. Smith Boulevard, goes along the waterfront and on to Palm Beach. But most visitors cross it heading for Nassaustraat or "Nassau Street." Here is where they find the best free-port shopping.

After a shopping trip, you might return to the harbor where fishing boats and schooners, many from Venezuela, are moored. Nearly all newcomers to Aruba like to take a picture of the **Schooner Harbor.** Not only does it have colorful boats docked along the quay, but boatmen display their wares in open stalls. The local patois predominates. A little farther along, at the fish market, fresh fish is sold directly from the boats. Also on the seaside of Oranjestad, **Wilhelmina Park** was named after Queen Wilhelmina of the Netherlands. A tropical garden has been planted along the water, and there's a sculpture of the Queen Mother.

Aside from shopping along Nassaustraat, the major attractions of Aruba are **Eagle Beach** and **Palm Beach,** considered among the finest in the Caribbean. Most of Aruba's hotels are stretched Las Vegas strip style along these pure-white sand stretches on the leeward coast.

Museums of Aruba

I know you didn't come to Aruba to look at museums, but just in case—

Museo Arubano, just off L. G. Smith Boulevard behind the government buildings, in the restored Fort Zoutman, contains material on the culture and history of Aruba, with artifacts dating from the earliest times of the island through colonial days and up to the present. The 18th-century fort, oldest building in Aruba, has at its entrance the King Willem III Tower, which served as a lighthouse for almost 100 years. Museum hours are 9 a.m. to 4 p.m. Monday to Friday, to noon on Saturday. Admission is 1 AFl (46¢). The place is also called the King Willem III Tower and Fort Zoutman Museum.

The **Archeology Museum,** 1 Zoutmanstraat (tel. 011-297-8/28979), is diagonally across the street from the police station. Its two rooms have displays of ancient Indian artifacts found mainly in Cer'i Noka near Santa Cruz. You'll see agricultural and home equipment, even skeletons of people who were buried in big earthenware urns. Open from 8 a.m. to noon and 1:30 to 4:30 p.m., the museum charges no admission.

A privately owned **shell collection** of the Adrian de Man family can be seen at 18 Morgenster (tel. 011-297-8/24246 for an appointment). The permanent collection, which includes a rare murex, is in a room at the rear of the de Mans' home. Shells from all over the world make up the display.

In the **Numismatic Museum,** 2-A Irausquin Plein (tel. 011-297-8/22185), in front of the post office and near St. Francis Catholic Church, you can see an outstanding collection of coins and paper currency. The museum, in the Ministry of Culture Building, is open from 7:30 a.m. to noon and 1 to 4:30 p.m. Monday to Friday. Admission is free, but donations are appreciated.

Out in the Country

If you can lift yourselves from the sands for one afternoon, you might like to drive into the **cunucu,** which in Papiamento means "the countryside." Here Arubans live in very modest but colorful pastel-washed houses. Of course, all visitors venturing into the center of Aruba want to see the strangely shaped divi-divi tree with its trade-wind-blown coiffure. Even though they live in a very dry climate where cactus thrives better than flowers, Arubans like to have bougainvillea, oleander, hibiscus, and other tropical plants around their homes. However, to grow them, they often use expensive desalinated water.

Rocks stud Aruba, and the most impressive ones are those found at **Ayo** and **Casibari,** to the northeast of Hooiberg. These stacks of diorite boulders are the size of buildings. The rocks, weighing several thousand tons, are a puzzle to geologists. On the rocks at Ayo are ancient Indian drawings. At Casibari, you can climb the boulder-strewn terrain to the top for a panoramic view of the island or wander around lower down looking at rocks Mother Nature has carved into seats and likenesses of prehistoric birds and animals. Casibari is open daily from 9 a.m. to 5 p.m. No admission is charged. There is a lodge at Casibari where you can buy souvenirs, snacks, soft drinks, and beer.

If the subject interests you, guides can also point out drawings on the walls and ceiling of the **Caves of Canashito,** south of Hooiberg. While there you may get to see the giant green parakeets.

Hooiberg is affectionately known as "The Haystack." It is Aruba's most outstanding landmark, and anybody with the stamina can take the steps all the way to the top of this 541-foot-high hill. One Aruban jogs up there every morning. From its precincts in the center of the island you can see Venezuela on a clear day.

On the jagged, windswept northern coast, the **Natural Bridge** has been carved out of the coral rock by the relentless surf. In a little café overlooking the coast you can order snacks. There you'll also find a souvenir shop with a large selection of trinkets, T-shirts, and wall hangings, all selling at reasonable prices.

You turn inland for the short trip to **Pirate's Castle** at Bushiribana, which stands on a cliff on the island's windward coast. This is actually a deserted gold mill from the island's now-defunct industry. Another gold mill is in the old ghost town on the west coast, **Balashi.**

You can continue to the village of Noord, known for its **St. Anne's Church** with a hand-carved Dutch altar dating from the 17th century.

East to San Nicolás

Driving along the highway more or less paralleling the south coast of Aruba toward the island's southernmost section, you may want to stop at the **Spanish Lagoon** (Spaans Lagoen), where legend says pirates used to hide out as they waited to plunder rich cargo ships in the Caribbean. Whatever the truth about that, today this is an ideal place for snorkeling, and you can picnic at tables under the mangrove trees.

On to the east, you'll pass an area called **Savaneta,** where some of the most ancient traces of human habitation have been unearthed. You'll see along here the first oil tanks marking the position of the Lago Oil & Transport Company Ltd., the Exxon subsidiary around which the town of San Nicolás developed, although it had been an industrial center since the days of phosphate mining in the late 19th century. A "company town" until the refinery was closed in 1985, San Nicolás, 12 miles from Oranjestad, is called the Aruba Sunrise Side, and tourism has become its main economic factor.

The town has a blend of cultures—customs, style, languages, color, and tastes. In the area are caves with Arawak Indian artwork on the walls and a modern innovation, a PGA-approved golf course with sand "greens" and cactus traps. **Boca Grandi,** on the windward side of the island, is a favorite windsurfing location; or if you prefer quieter waters, you'll find them at **Baby Beach** and **Rodgers Beach,** on Aruba's lee side.

Overlooking the latter two beaches is **Seroe Colorado** (Colorado Point), from which it's possible to see the coastline of Venezuela as well as the pounding surf on the windward side. You can climb down the cliffs, perhaps spotting an iguana here and there. Protected by law, the once-endangered saurians now proliferate in peace.

Other sights in the San Nicolás area are the **Guadarikiri Cave** and **Fontein Cave,** where you can see the Indian wall drawings, plus the **Huliba** and **Tunnel of Love** caves, with guides and refreshment stands. Guadarikiri Cave is a haven for wild parrots.

DINING AROUND THE ISLAND: Brisas del Mar, 222A Saveneta near the police station (tel. 011-297-8/47718), is like a place you might encounter in some outpost in Australia. Here in very simple surroundings, right at water's edge, Lucia Rasmijn opened this little hut with an air-conditioned bar in front at which the locals gather to drink the day away. The place is often jammed on weekends with many of the same local people, who come here to drink and dance. On Friday, Saturday, and Sunday, Mrs. Lucia Rasmijn offers entertainment, with home-grown talent playing everything from the guitar to the harp. In back the tables are open to the sea breezes, and nearby you can see a fisherman slicing the catch of the day, perhaps wahoo, selling it to local housewives. The cooks try to confine their menu to fish caught in the Caribbean. Perhaps you'll have the pan-broiled fish of the day, prepared Aruban style (with a Créole sauce), or breaded conch cutlet. Try also the baby shark steak with port wine. The breaded squid cutlet is yet another favorite. For an appetizer, perhaps you'll select the "fisherman's fish soup." Desserts are simple, including fresh fruit or ice cream. Expect to spend from $20 per person. The restaurant is open daily from noon to 3 p.m. and 6:30 to 10:30 p.m. It's always best to call first for a reservation to avoid making the trip there, only to find the place full. Even with a reservation, you still may have to wait more than an hour or so to get a seat if the place is really jumping. To reach the restaurant's location at Savaneta, turn off to the right from the main road leading from Oranjestad to San Nicolás between Anthony Sales and the police station. You'll need a car to get there or else you'll have to take a cab. By bus it's more than an hour's trip.

Marina Pirata, Pos Chiquito (tel. 011-297-8/47150), is probably the most authentically raffish seafood restaurant in Aruba. It lies a 15-minute drive east of Oranjestad, along an isolated section of the coastline known as Pos Chiquito. Its exterior boasts a series of false crenellations, giving it the appearance of a fortress. It was built over the water on the rusted hulk of a steel-sided barge, which in World War II was a hideout for Allied marines guarding the island's oil refineries. Every afternoon local fishermen deliver directly to the restaurant's pier whatever fresh fish they caught that day. Seafood is consumed in wind-cooled comfort amid a simple decor of exposed planking, picnic-style tables, and nautical lanterns. Full meals, costing from $20, are served every evening except Tuesday from 5 p.m. to 1 a.m. Lunch is served only on Sunday, when the restaurant remains open from noon to 11 p.m. in a continuous party which includes live music between 5 and 7 p.m.

Charlie's Bar, 56 B. v/d Veen Zeppenveldstraat, Mainstreet San Nicolás (tel. 011-297-8/45086), qualifies through its decor and history as the most interesting reason to visit San Nicolás. It's the most overly decorated bar in the West Indies, sporting an array of memorabilia and local souvenirs which, when assembled, create a Caribbean version of kitsch. Where roustabouts and roughnecks once brawled, you'll find tables filled with contented tourists admiring thousands of pennants, banners, and trophies dangling from the high ceiling. Two-fisted drinks are still served, but the menu has improved since the good old days when San Nicolás was one of the toughest towns in the Caribbean. Meals are offered from noon to 9:30 p.m. daily except Sunday and local holidays. The bar is open daily from 11 a.m. to midnight. Full meals cost 25 AFl ($14) and include grilled scampi, freshly made soups of the day, Créole-style squid, and churrasco.

SHOPPING: Aruba manages to compress six continents into the half-mile-long Nassaustraat, in what is called Mainstreet Shopping Center, in Oranjestad. Not technically a free port, the duty is so low (3.3%) that articles are attractively priced. Aruba also has no sales tax. You'll find the usual array of Swiss watches, German and Japanese cameras, jewelry, liquor, English bone china and porcelain, Dutch, Swedish, and Danish silver and pewter, French perfume, British woolens, Indonesian specialties, and Madeira embroidery. Delft blue pottery is an especially good buy. Some good buys include Holland cheese (Edam and Gouda), as well as Holland chocolate and English cigarettes in the airport departure area.

Store hours in general are Monday through Saturday from 8 a.m. to noon and 2 to 6 p.m. Many stores are also closed on Tuesday afternoon and some seem to keep irregular hours off-season, especially in the fall and spring.

The **Alhambra Shopping Bazaar** (tel. 011-297-8/35000), adjacent to the Alhambra Casino, is a blend of international shops, outdoor marketplaces, and cafés and restaurants. Merchandise ranges from fine jewelry, chocolates, and perfume to imported craft items, leather goods, clothing, and lingerie. Like the casino, the shopping bazaar is open seven days a week from early afternoon until early morning hours.

Seaport Village, the only enclosed mall in Aruba, contains more than 80 upscale shops and restaurants. The mall is decorated with tropical plants and rare birds from South America. It's open from 9 a.m. to 6 p.m. Monday to Saturday.

In the heart of Nassaustraat stands the legendary **Spritzer & Fuhrmann's** (tel. 011-297-8/24360), with its main building and the much-photographed carillon chiming "Bon Bini" (welcome). Gold and diamond jewelry and fine watches are sold here, not only for the discriminating taste of the connoisseur but also for the budget buyer seeking good jewelry. S&F also has a collection of fine china, crystal, and flatware, in most of the better-known brands. If you can't make it into town, you'll find branches of the store at the Holiday Inn and Divi-Divi.

Photo El Globo Aruba, 70 Nassaustraat (tel. 011-297-8/22900) fills your needs in photographic, hi-fi, and video equipment can be supplied in the world's best makes at good prices.

Little Switzerland Jewelers, 47 Nassaustraat (tel. 011-297-8/21192), is famous for its duty-free 14- and 18-karat gold jewelry and watches. They also carry a big variety of Swiss watches such as Rolex, Cartier, and Movado, and many more. Little Switzerland has many locations in Aruba, at most of the large hotels.

New Amsterdam Store, 10 Nassaustraat (tel. 011-297-8/21152), Aruba's leading department store, is best for linens, with its selection of napkins, placemats, and embroidered tablecloths with sources that range all the way from China. It has an extensive line of other merchandise as well, from Delft blue pottery to beachwear and boutique items, along with an exquisite gold collection, assorted gift items, porcelain figures by Lladró, watches, French and Italian women's wear, and leather bags and shoes.

Directly next door, the **Aruba Trading Company,** 14 Nassaustraat (tel. 011-297-8/22600), offers a complete range of attractive tourist items: perfumes, cosmetics, souvenirs, and gift items of porcelain, Delft, Hummel, and crystal ware, liquor, and cigarettes (the latter purchases can be delivered to your plane).

Casa del Mimbre, 76 Nassaustraat (tel. 011-297-8/27268), specializes in Colombian arts and crafts, including woolen ruanas, which are ponchos popularized by Avianca stewardesses. They also have souvenirs and gifts from Central America and other South American countries. Mayan napkins from Guatemala, woven wall hangings from Mexico, cowhide golf bags from Colombia—the collection is wide ranging and intriguing.

The **Artistic Boutique,** 25 Nassaustraat (tel. 011-297-8/23142), open from 9 a.m. to 6 p.m. with no siesta, stocks fine linens, hand-embroidered madeiras, orangies, and Irish linen articles, such as napkins, place mats, and guest towels. You may be able to find just what you want in the $2 corner. Crystal figurines, Oriental antiques, handmade rugs, paintings, jade and ivory artworks, silks, gold and silver jewelry, and hand-crafted articles of the islands and the Orient are among the treasures offered. There is a women's boutique on the second floor.

Gandelman Jewelers, at the beginning of Mainstreet and in the Alhambra Shopping Bazaar (tel. 011-297-8/29143), is the exclusive agent for the Gucci accessory collection, Baume & Mercier, Raymond Weil, and Tag-Heuer. A dazzling selection of precious stones, 14- and 18-karat gold jewelry, and famous watches has made them known throughout the Caribbean. The Gucci accessories include wallets, belts, handbags, and other items. Shops handling only the Gucci line are at the Americana Hotel, the Holiday Inn, and in the airport departure hall.

Penha, 11-13 Nassaustraat (tel. 011-297-8/24161), offers a selection of gifts, clothing, and perfumes, all in the top categories. For example, they are exclusive purveyors here of Giorgio, and they also have Estée Lauder, Lancôme, and Clinique cosmetics. Men's clothing includes that of designers such as Pierre Cardin, Papillon, Lanvin, and Givenchy, and women can choose garments from

Dior, Liz Claiborne, and Castoni. If you're shopping on a smaller scale, you'll find T-shirts and souvenirs here. Penha also has boutiques at the Tamarijn, Divi-Divi, Holiday Inn, and Americana hotels.

Boulevard Book and Drugstore (tel. 011-297-8/27358), in the Boulevard Shopping Mall, has a complete range of goods from books to cosmetics, candies, gifts, good quality T-shirts and sweatsuits, and unique souvenirs.

Tamarijn Hotel Giftshop and Minimarket, in the Tamarijn Beach Hotel (tel. 011-297-8/24150), offers a complete selection of gifts, souvenirs, and drugstore items, plus a full range of delicatessen offerings, liquor, and wines.

Divi-Divi Hotel Giftshop and Minimarket, in the Divi-Divi Beach Hotel (tel. 011-297-8/23300), is stocked like the Tamarijn shops, just previewed.

Philatelists interested in the wealth of colorful and artistic stamps issued in honor of the changed government status of Aruba can purchase a complete assortment, as well as other special issues, at the post office in Oranjestad.

THE SPORTING LIFE: Its western and southern shore, called the **Turquoise Coast,** is what attracts sun seekers to Aruba. Palm Beach and Eagle Beach (the latter closer to Oranjestad) are the best beaches. No hotel along the strip owns the beaches, all of which are open to the public. However, if you use any of the hotel's facilities, you'll be charged, of course. You can also spread your towel on Manchebo or Druif Bay Beach—in fact, anywhere along seven miles of uninterrupted sugar-white sands. In total contrast to the leeward side, the north or windward shore is rugged and wild.

Water Sports

Snorkeling, scuba-diving, windsurfing, waterskiing, and doing your own sailing are all part of the fun offered in the waters around Aruba. You can snorkel in rather shallow waters, and scuba-divers find stunning marine life with endless varieties of coral as well as tropical fish in infinite hues. At some points visibility is up to 90 feet. The goal of most divers is the German freighter *Antilia,* which was scuttled in the early years of World War II, lying off the northwest tip of Aruba, not too far from Palm Beach.

The best place to book water sports is from **De Palm Tours,** whose main office is at 142 L. G. Smith Blvd., Oranjestad (tel. 011-297-8/24400), although it also has offices at the major hotels as well. Here a certified teacher will give scuba-diving instruction at a cost of $50 per person. Subsequent dives can be arranged at $40 per person, as can scuba-diving trips for experienced divers. Snorkelers are often taken out on a boat ride to a site, with complete gear furnished, for $15 per person.

Pleasure Cruises

Visitors interested in combining a pleasant boat ride with a few hours of snorkeling can get in touch with **De Palm Tours.** This company maintains an office in seven of the island's hotels. Its main office is at 142 L. G. Smith Blvd. in Oranjestad (tel. 011-297-8/24400). For $28.50 per person they'll take you on a "fun cruise" aboard a catamaran. After a windswept sail of 1½ hours, passengers stop for three hours at their private De Palm island for snorkeling. Lunch and an open bar are included in the price. The tour, if participation warrants it, departs daily between 10 a.m. and 4 p.m.

Pelican Watersports, 10 Parrdenbaaistraat, Oranjestad (tel. 011-297-8/31228), has some attractive cruises in the daytime, at sunset, and by moonlight. You can sail aboard the pirate schooner *Topaz,* the 60-foot catamaran *Blue Melody,* or the 36-foot *Coconut,* or perhaps others of the company's fleet of boats. They offer day trips with lunch, sunset trips with open bar, and moonlights with buffet barbecue, and combinations of these voyages with snorkeling stops. Pelican also offers underwater expeditions, deep-sea fishing, and jetskiing.

Deep-Sea Fishing

In the deep waters off the coast of Aruba you can test your skill and wits against the big ones—wahoo, marlin, tuna, bonito, and sailfish. **De Palm Tours,** 142 L. G. Smith Blvd. in Oranjestad (tel. 011-297-8/24400), takes out a maximum of six people (four of whom can fish at the same time) on one of its four boats, which range in length from 27 to 34 feet. Half-day tours, with all equipment included, go for $135 to $160 for two persons, from $135 to $170 for four, and from $190 to $200 for six. The prices are doubled for full-day trips. Boats leave from the docks beside the Bali Floating Restaurant in Oranjestad. De Palm maintains seven branches, most of which lie within the precincts of Aruba's major hotels.

Windsurfing

In the past few years, windsurfing has become a popular pastime in Aruba, and the best center for this activity is **Windsurfing Aruba,** P.O. Box 256, Oranjestad (tel. 011-297-8/21036). The longest operating windsurfing center on the island, it offers packages that include not only equipment but a room as well. The operator is a longtime diver and fisherman whose expertise in Aruba's waters and currents is said to be the finest on the island. He also knows "the way of the winds."

Golf

Visitors can play at the **Aruba Golf Club,** 82 Golfweg (tel. 011-297-8/93485), near the oil refineries of San Nicolás at the eastern end of the island. Goats run across the course, and the oiled sand greens add zest to the game. This is actually an 11-hole course played in a variety of ways to make it an 18-hole game. Greens fees are $6 per person per day, with caddy fees priced at $5 per nine holes. The course is open daily except Monday from 8:30 a.m. to noon and 3 to 6 p.m. Fast-food items and sandwiches are available at the clubhouse and bar.

Tennis

Most of the island's beachfront hotels have tennis courts, often swept by trade winds, and some have top pros on hand to give instruction. Many of the courts can also be lit for night games (I don't advise playing in Aruba's noonday sun). Usually there's a $2 surcharge at night, although day games are free if you're a guest. Some hotels restrict their courts to use by guests.

Horseback Riding

Rancho El Paso, 44 Washington (tel. 011-297-8/23310), is run by Aruba's largest tour operator, De Palm. A stable of around 20 horses, the famous Paso Fino horses from South America, is maintained for the riding pleasure of visitors. Both beginners and advanced riders are accommodated. All tours are guided, and last one and two hours. Unless you're accustomed to the saddle you'd better opt for the one-hour tour. For the rugged, There's the two-hour tour, taking in both the countryside and beach rides.

AFTER DARK: The casinos of the big hotels along Palm Beach are the liveliest nighttime destinations. In plush gaming parlors, guests try their luck at roulette, craps, blackjack, and of course the one-armed bandits. **Americana Aruba** (tel.

011-297-8/24500) opens daily at 1 p.m. for slots, at 3 p.m. for blackjack and roulette and at 9 p.m. for all games. Early birds go to the **Aruba Concorde** (tel. 011-297-8/24466) at 10 a.m. for slots, 1 p.m. for games. The **Holiday Inn** (tel. 011-297-8/23600) wins the prize for all-around action. Its casino doors are open 22 hours a day, closing only for two hours to clean. The **Aruba Palm Beach** (tel. 011-297-8/23900) opens its gambling tables from 9 p.m. on. The **Golden Tulip Aruba Caribbean** (tel. 011-297-8/33555) has one of the newest casinos on the island.

The busiest casino in Aruba is the **Alhambra**, L. G. Smith Blvd. (tel. 011-297-8/35000). More than just a casino, it offers a collection of restaurants and boutiques, along with an inner courtyard designed like an 18th-century Dutch village. From the outside the complex looks Moorish, with serpentine mahogany columns and repeating arches rising to a pinnacle defined by a duet of sea-green domes. The desert setting of Aruba seems appropriate. A strapping "Moor" greets you at the door, shaking your hand to wish you luck.

Away from the gaming tables, cabaret shows are presented nightly except Sunday at 9 and 11 p.m. at the Aladdin Theater. Entrance to the show, whose stars and format change regularly, is $12 per person. No reservations are accepted, although tickets can be purchased in advance. Seating is on a first-come, first-served basis. The Alhambra has some 29 shops including boutiques selling perfume, souvenirs, T-shirts, swimwear, Delft Blue figurines, European high fashions, Gucci products, jewelry, leather goods, and local and South American crafts. There are also eating places, such as a 24-hour New York–style deli; Munchies for pizza, tacos, and snacks; Roseland with a buffet dinner nightly from 6 to 9 charging $9.95 for all you care to eat; and Lui's Place for tropical frozen cocktails. Roseland Disco is open daily except Sunday from 10:30 p.m. Owned and operated by Divi Resorts chain, the casino offers free transportation from its front door to each of the three Divi Resorts on the island. The casino and its satellites are open daily from 10 a.m. till very late at night.

Nongamblers or those who grow tired of the slots and tables can patronize the hotel's cocktail lounges and supper clubs. You don't have to be a guest of the hotel to visit to see the shows, but you should make a reservation. Tables at the big shows, especially in season, are likely to be booked early in the day. Usually you can go to one of the major hotel supper clubs and only order drinks. Expect to pay from $4 for most libations.

One of the best nightlife options on the island is **Stellaris Club,** Americana Aruba (tel. 011-297-8/24500). Dinner is served nightly except Monday from 6 to 10, with the show beginning at 10:30 p.m. In glamorous trappings, you can dine on an international cuisine, specializing in "new creations" of beef, seafood, veal, and poultry dishes. Dinner costs from $30. The show costs $10 per person, $5 with dinner.

Club Arabesque, Aruba Concorde (tel. 011-297-8/24466), inspired by Nevada, is a nightclub offering some of the grandest, glitziest, and most stylish acts in Aruba. For example, you're likely to see a bevy of dancers, the Copa Girls, presenting a music and dance extravaganza with artfully undressed costumes. Reservations are necessary, especially in high season, and the entrance price of $15 per person includes the first two drinks. Shows are presented nightly except Monday at 11.

On the disco circuit, **Club Scaramouche** (tel. 011-297-8/24954), in the penthouse of Seaport Village in Oranjestad, is clearly the leader. Island visitors may enjoy an evening for a charge of $5, or may obtain one of the VIP passes available in many of the leading hotels and some of the better restaurants. Jeans are not allowed, nor are tennis shoes or T-shirts. Hours are 9 p.m. to 5 a.m. Monday to Saturday, with a daily 4 to 7 p.m. cocktail hour. The Scaramouche is a posh and comfortable entertainment establishment, with an inlaid dance floor and Aruba's largest bar. Sumptuous leathers, spacious divans, and sparkling glassware form a backdrop for enjoyment of complimentary hors d'oeuvres and dancing to disco sound. However, there are intimate conversation nooks where the sound is controlled so that you can hear your companions talk.

Another leading disco is the **Contempo** at the Talk of the Town Restaurant (tel. 011-297-8/21990). After 10:30 p.m., there's dancing until 4 a.m. Music is by local groups or DJs. There are special nights, such as Ladies Night and a $1 night with drinks at a special low price. Dress is casual.

Surfside Beach Club (tel. 011-297-8/23380), across from the Talk of the Town hotel, is a tropical beach pavilion popular for its snacks served tapas style, for excellent dining, and for entertainment evenings with dancing. Tuesday and Friday, there's "Fire & Ice," with a flaming limbo show and audience participation, a frozen piña colada hour from 6 to 7 p.m., a big salad bar, and a hot buffet. You can eat and drink what you like from 6 to 10 p.m., all for a charge of $29. Then on Thursday night, they present the Bounty Beach BBQ, with a big steel band, dancing, games, a beach barbecue buffet, open bar from 6 to 7 p.m., and unlimited wine during the barbecue, plus a "pirate's seduction" cocktail. From 10 p.m. to 11 p.m., drinks are two for the price of one.

The **Bamboo Bar** (tel. 011-297-8/22131), on the Bali Pier (see my Bali Floating Restaurant recommendation under "Aruba Cookery"), is the home of Aruba's first piano bar. A "Happy Happy Hour" is featured from 6 to 8 p.m., while the sun sets over the harbor. Come in for drinks or open-air dining (same menu as the Bali Floating Restaurant) and enjoy the scene of boats and yachts bobbing at anchor. Romantic piano and guitar music sets the mood for a relaxing evening. The Bamboo Bar, open nightly, is one of Aruba's favorite meeting places.

2. BONAIRE

Unlike some islands, Bonaire isn't just surrounded by coral reefs. It *is* the reef! And its shores are thick with rainbow-hued fish. Five miles wide and 24 miles long, Bonaire is poised in the Caribbean, close to the Spanish Main. The island attracts those seeking that out-of-the-way spot, that uncrowded shore.

Bonaire is most often reached from its sister island of Curaçao, 30 miles to the west. Like Curaçao, it is desert-like, with a dry and brilliant atmosphere. Often it is visited by "day trippers," who rush through here in pursuit of the shy, elusive flamingo, the glamor bird of the Caribbean.

Boomerang-shaped Bonaire comprises about 112 square miles, making it the second largest of the ABC Dutch grouping. Its northern sector is hilly, tapering up to Brandaris Peak, all of 788 feet. However, the southern half, flat as a flapjack, is given over to bays, reefs, beaches, and a salt lake which attracts the flamingos. The island's population is approximately 10,000.

The island has powdery white beaches and turquoise waters, where underwater photographers find a visibility of 100 feet or more. Unspoiled Bonaire is one of the world's best scuba and snorkeling grounds, a beachcomber's retreat, and a birdwatcher's heaven, with 145 different species—not only the graceful flamingo, but the big-billed pelican, as well as bright-green parrots, snipes, terns, parakeets, herons, hummingbirds, and others. Bring a pair of binoculars.

Contrary to a popular misconception often published in travel guides, Bonaire doesn't mean "good air." Rather, it comes from an Indian language and signifies low country.

Bonaireans zealously want to protect their environment. Even though they eagerly seek tourism, they aren't interested in creating "another Aruba" with its high-rise hotel blocks. Spearfishing isn't allowed in their waters, nor is the taking or destruction of any coral or other living animal from the sea.

The island was sighted in 1499 by a party of explorers commanded by Amerigo Vespucci, who lent his name to the New World. Amerigo found some Indians living on the island in Stone Age conditions. After Spanish domination, Bonaire witnessed the arrival of the Dutch in 1634, perhaps seeking to protect Curaçao's flanks, an island they already occupied. Bonaire was assigned the duty of supplying livestock, corn, and salt.

Once the British occupied the island, eventually leasing it to a New York merchant for $2,400 annually, including the services of 300 "salt-mine" slaves.

The Dutch came back in 1816, setting up plantations to grow dyewood, cochenille, and aloes. At the abolition of slavery in 1863, the economy collapsed. Bonaire settled into a long, dreary depression. Relief came in the form of what was known as the "money order economy" era, when Bonaireans migrated to Curaçao and Aruba to work in the oil industry. Automation of that industry in the 1950s caused the loss of many jobs, and Bonaireans returned to their native island. Fortunately, instead of being plunged permanently back into depression, Bonaire was discovered, along with other Caribbean islands, by international tourism, and the economy began to look up. The first hotel opened in 1951. The salt pans were modified to use solar energy and became the most successful base of plants in the world. The island's power facilities were enlarged to ensure further development.

The big annual event is the **October Sailing Regatta,** a five-day festival of racing sponsored by the local tourist bureau. Now an international affair, the event attracts sailors and spectators from around the world, as a flotilla of sailboats and yachts anchor in Kralendijk Bay. If you're planning to visit during regatta days, make sure you have an iron-clad hotel reservation.

GETTING THERE: To facilitate the passage of Bonaire-bound passengers, **ALM Antillean Airlines** offers nonstop flights from New York's JFK Airport to Bonaire, an option many sun-lovers can work into their vacation schedules. Unfortunately, this flight goes to Bonaire only on Friday. If your schedule permits, ALM sells this ticket for $430 round trip, and you must pay for it one month in advance. To get that price, you must book from between 2 and 30 days at a Bonaire hotel in conjunction with the purchase of your ticket. ALM can explain how to do this if you call toll free at 800/327-7230.

Most passengers will fly to Bonaire via the Caribbean gateway of Miami. Several of these flights, I have found, connect efficiently with flights that ALM maintains to Curaçao, Aruba, and Bonaire.

The price of ALM's bargain basement flight from Miami to any of the ABC islands is $376 round trip (subject to change). To get that low price, passage must be paid a month in advance, and a hotel stopover must be booked in conjunction with the air ticket. This particular fare allows two free stopovers as a standard feature, making a visit to either Aruba or Curaçao (or both) an inexpensive addition to your visit to Bonaire. Depending on your day of transit, you can fly either nonstop from Miami (on Saturday and Sunday) or transfer through Curaçao. ALM flights from Curaçao reach Bonaire in 20 minutes.

GETTING AROUND: As per usual, **taxis** are unmetered, but the government has established rates. All licensed taxicabs carry a number plate with the letters "TX." Each driver should have a list of prices to be produced upon request. As many as four passengers can go along for the ride unless they have too much luggage. As examples of what rates to expect, a trip from the airport into town should cost $5. From 8 p.m. to midnight fares are increased by 25%, and from 11 p.m. until 6 a.m. they go up by 50%.

Car Rentals

It's easy to drive in Bonaire, and car rentals are reasonable. I recommend **Budget/Boncar** (tel. 011-588-7/8300, ext. 225 in town; tel. 011-588-7/8315 at the airport). This firm rents Suzuki Frontes, Suzuki Jeeps, Hondas, VW vans, Ford Econovans with 9 to 12 seats, and other vehicles starting at $23 per day with unlimited mileage. Your U.S. or Canadian driver's license, if valid, is acceptable for driving in Bonaire. One- and two-seater scooters are also available for rent. *Driving in Bonaire is on the right.*

Scooter Rentals

Happy Chappy Rentals, Kaya C. E. B. Hellmund (tel. 011-588-7/8761), can supply you with an 80-cc Suzuki on which two persons can ride for a cost of about $17 per day.

Sightseeing Tours

Bonaire Sightseeing Tours (tel. 011-588-7/8300, ext. 225) takes you on tours of the islands, both north and south, taking in the flamingos, slave huts, conch shells, Goto Lake, the Indian inscriptions, and other sights. The northern and the southern tours both last two hours, and each costs $10 per person. You can take a half-day City and Country Tour, lasting three hours and costing $15 per person, allowing you to see the entire northern section and the southern part as far as the slave huts. A special four-hour tour of Washington-Slagbaai National Park can be booked at a cost of $25 per person for a minimum of four. An all-day tour of the national park goes for $45 per person.

Most **taxi** drivers are informed about the sights of Bonaire and will take you on a tour. You must negotiate the price according to how long a trip you want and what you want to see.

PRACTICAL FACTS: Bonaire is part of the Netherlands Antilles (an autonomous part of the Netherlands), with its own legislative council, island council, and lieutenant governor.

Banks: Banking hours are usually from 8:30 a.m. to noon and 2 to 4 p.m. Monday to Friday.

Currency: Like the other islands of the Netherlands Antilles (Curaçao, St. Maarten, St. Eustatius, and Saba), Bonaire's coin of the realm is the Netherlands Antillean florin (NAf), sometimes called a guilder, equal to 56¢ in U.S. currency. However, U.S. dollars are also accepted.

Customs: There are no Customs requirements for Bonaire.

Documents: To enter Bonaire, all you need is proof of citizenship and a return or continuing ticket.

Electricity: The electric current is 127 volts AC, 50 cycles. Divers with precise equipment should provide their own converters.

Information: For tourist information in Bonaire, go to the **Tourist Office,** 23 Kaya Simón Bolívar, Kralendijk (tel. 011-588-7/8322). Hours are from 7:30 a.m. to noon and 1:30 to 5:30 p.m. Monday to Friday.

Language: English is widely spoken, but you'll hear Dutch, Spanish, and Papiamento.

Medical care: The island has a hospital, doctors, a dentist, an eye doctor, a visiting orthodontist, and a drugstore. A plane on standby at the airport takes seriously ill patients to Curaçao for treatment.

Taxes and service: The government requires a 5% room tax on all hotel rooms. Most hotels and guesthouses add a 10% service charge in lieu of tipping. Restaurants generally add a service charge of 15% to the bill. Upon leaving Bonaire, you'll be charged an airport departure tax of $10, so don't spend every penny. There is also an inter-island tax of $2.75.

Telecommunications: Service for telephone, Telex, telegraph, radio, and TV is available in English. To dial direct to Bonaire from the U.S., you must dial the area code, 011-588-8, and then the four-digit local number. To telephone within the island, you need only dial the four digits.

Time: Bonaire operates on Atlantic Standard Time year round.

Water: Drinking water is pure and safe. It comes from distilled seawater.

Weather: Bonaire is known for its climate, with temperatures hovering at 82° Fahrenheit. The water temperature averages 80°. It's warmest in August and September, coolest in January and February. The average rainfall is 22 inches, December through March being the rainiest months.

HOTELS: Hotels are low-key and unhassled, and all of them face the sea. There are no high-rises here, only low-lying, personally run operations where everybody gets to know everybody else rather fast. *A reminder:* Taxes and service charges are seldom included in the prices you will be quoted for your room. They will more likely be added to your bill, so don't be surprised when it is presented.

The Top Resorts

Divi Flamingo Beach Resort & Casino, Bonaire, N.A. (tel. 011-588-7/ 8285, 607/277-3484 in the U.S., or toll free 800/367-3484), is one of the most personalized and charming hotels in the ABC islands. This complete beachfront resort, with its watersports facilities and stylized bedrooms, is the product of the Wiggins family of Ithaca, New York. They discovered a neglected, gone-to-seed hotel with a cluster of flimsy wooden bungalows that had been used as an internment camp for German prisoners of World War II. With foresight and taste they turned it into a top-notch resort, offering both individual cottages and modern seafront rooms with private balconies resting on piers above the surf, so you can stand out and watch rainbow-hued tropical fish in the water below.

The resort's original 110 rooms were supplemented in 1986 with the addition of 40 stylish time-sharing units, forming Club Flamingo. Each of the units is rentable, when available, by the day or week. Accommodations in both sections are spacious, stylish, and sunny, with air conditioning, ceiling fans, private bathrooms, and a selection of Mexican accessories. The newer units are clustered into a green-and-white neo-Victorian pavilion facing its own curve-sided swimming pool. Each contains a stylish kitchenette with carved cupboards and cabinets of pickled hardwoods. Both sections benefit from the attentions of a pair of social hostesses and the proximity of a good dive operation and a beautiful beach. The most expensive period is from December 24 to January 1 and February 11 to February 24, when single or double occupancy is $105 to $180 daily, while studio apartments with kitchenettes rent for $200 daily. The rest of the winter (January 25 to February 10 and February 25 to April 7) single or double occupancy is priced at $90 to $150 daily, while apartments with kitchenettes cost $165. *In summer, singles are $55 to $85 daily, and doubles go for $60 to $90.* Units in the newer section rent for $175 daily for two people in high season, *dropping to $95 to $120 in low season.* On the premises, a pair of individually recommended restaurants include the Chibi-Chibi and the Calabas Terrace, providing a setting for relaxing and satisfying meals.

Bonaire Beach Hotel, P.O. Box 34, Bonaire, N.A. (tel. 011-588-7/8448,

212/840-6639 in the U.S., or toll free 800/223-9815), which was taken over by the government, lies about half a mile north of town on its own beach, Playa Leche (Milk Beach). With 142 rooms, it occupies 12 acres of land. Its headquarters is in a low-slung central building filled with plants. Long covered walkways lead across a sandy terrain through gardens to the comfortable air-conditioned accommodations. These lie in motel-like annexes scattered around a freshwater pool. High-season rates are $90 to $120 daily for double occupancy, *the rates dropping to $55 to $80 daily for two persons in summer.* From the accommodations, you are only a minute away from the beach and its bar restaurant. The hotel has diving facilities, a windsurfing school, two tennis courts (lit), and the beach bar and restaurant. The main building houses the reception desk, a boutique, and a conference room.

The Dive Resorts
Captain Don's Habitat, Bonaire, N.A. (tel. 011-588-7/8290, 212/535-9530 in New York, or toll free 800/223-5581), is a unique diving, snorkeling, and nature-oriented community with an air of congenial informality and a philosophy and lifestyle for those whose souls belong to the sea. The establishment is built on a coral bluff overlooking the sea and one of Bonaire's most popular dive sites. Habitat and its accompanying dive shop are the creation of Capt. Don Stewart, Caribbean pioneer and "caretaker of the reefs," a former Californian who sailed his schooner from San Francisco through the Panama Canal, arriving on a reef in Bonaire in 1962—and he's been here ever since. Called the "godfather of diving" on the island, Captain Don was instrumental in the formation of the Bonaire Marine Park, whereby the entire island became a protected reef. The captain still dives weekly, taking his guests to his favorite diving sites.

Habitat consists of eight oceanfront villas, nine spacious and airy two-bedroom cottages, four single economy rooms, and six double economy units. Each villa contains three doubles with air-conditioning and hot water. The villa suite has a full kitchen and seaside veranda. The cottages with kitchens, living rooms, and verandas may be the best value per person. All accommodations are within a minute's walk of the sea. Daily rates in high season, from December 17 to mid-April, are $25 daily in a single economy room, $48 double economy, $100 for one to two guests in a cottage, $120 for three in a cottage, and $132 for four guests. Villa doubles cost $125 to $150, and an entire villa rents for $300 for four occupants. *In off-season, mid-April to just before Christmas, daily rates are $18 for single economy, $34 for double economy, $78 for one to two people in a cottage, $96 for three in a cottage, and $108 in a similar accommodation for four. Doubles in a villa rent for $90 to $110 and entire villas for four guests cost $250.* Among the amenities are an on-site boutique, the Captain's Locker, and the recently renovated, open-air seaside Captain Don's Bar and Restaurant. Great attention has been put into the design of the adjoining terraced loggias and small terraces leading down to the water, providing an informal setting in which to relax, drink, eat, whatever. A meandering terracotta pathway is a seaside promenade linking the new villas with the Habitat Dive Shop and the rest of the Habitat community.

Sand Dollar Condominiums & Beach Club, Bonaire, N.A. (tel. 011-588-7/8738), with 56 units (so far), has the style, comfort, and convenience of a full-service hotel. On the beachfront a short distance north of Kralendijk, Sand Dollar offers studio apartments and one-, two-, and three-bedroom units. All are equipped with electric ranges, ovens, dishwashers, refrigerators, custom cabinets, and modern furnishings, and air conditioning, with decks or balconies facing the ocean. From mid-December to mid-April, studios for two persons rent for $125 daily, one-bedroom accommodations going for $155 for two persons, and two-bedroom units for four occupants costing $185. *Off-season, studios for* *two rent for $95 daily, one-bedroom apartments for two for $120, and two-bedroom units for four for $145.* The complex has a shopping center, tennis courts, restaurant and bar, casino, marina, and a swimming pool. In addition, the property is home to Bonaire's newest dive shop, Sand Dollar Dive and Photo (see "The Sporting Life" below). For more information on the property, contact Sylvia and Milton Weisberg, 50 Georgetown Rd., Bordentown, NJ 08505 (tel. 609/298-3844).

Carib Inn, P.O. Box 68, Bonaire, N.A. (tel. 011-588-7/8819). Set directly on the water, and containing only eight rooms, this hotel is occupied by dedicated scuba-divers who can purchase accommodations as part of a dive package. It was established by an American, Bruce Bowker. About half of the units ring an oval-shaped swimming pool; others are in separate cottages on the beach, facing the hotel's dock. Depending on the accommodation (six with kitchens and all with refrigerators), charges are $49 to $83 daily for two persons in winter. *In summer, they cost $39 to $79 for two guests.* Each room is air-conditioned with simple tropical furniture and few frills. A six-day dive package with a dozen boat dives, all the air you can use, welts, belt, and tank goes for $219. Unlimited beach diving over a six-day period, with air, tank, belt, and weights, costs $79.

DINING OUT: The food is generally acceptable. Nearly everything has to be imported, of course. Your best bet is fresh-caught fish and an occasional rijsttafel, the traditional Indonesian rice table, or try the local dishes. Popular foods are conch cutlet or stew, pickled conch, red snapper, tuna, wahoo, dolphin, fungi (a thick cornmeal pudding), rice, beans, saté (marinated meat with curried mayonnaise), goat stew, and Dutch cheeses.

Le Chic, Kaya C. E. B. Hellmund (tel. 011-588-7/8617), overlooking Kralendijk Harbor and the town pier, is an excellent French restaurant. The two-story building that houses it has been completely renovated, the interior decor being unmistakably French. Le Chic offers two menus: a small one consisting of finger foods and a large one featuring full-course dinners. The French kitchen specializes in fresh seafood, poultry, and beef dishes complemented with French sauces. Specialties include a variety of soups and bisques, homemade ice cream, and more than 40 cocktails. Dinner, the only meal served, costing from $25, can be ordered from 4:30 p.m. to midnight Monday to Saturday.

Chibi-Chibi, Divi Flamingo Beach Hotel & Casino (tel. 011-588-7/8285), is named after a yellow-breasted local bird. My favorite restaurant on the island, it is built on piers above the coral-encrusted sea bottom, rising in an imposing two-tier design of exposed planking and wooden balustrades. Schools of multi-colored tropical fish foam through the illuminated waters to perform their nightly water ballet. The chef prepares a continental menu with specialties such as seafood crêpe, Antillean onion soup, fettuccine flamingo, keshi yena (chicken, onions, raisins, and olives baked in Dutch gouda cheese), and of course, the freshest fish on the island. Full meals average $28. Dinner is served nightly from 6 to 10, and reservations are suggested.

Calabas Terrace, Flamingo Beach Resort & Casino (tel. 011-588-7/8285), with a veranda setting a few steps from the sea, is worth a visit. A pleasant staff works hard to guarantee a memorable dining experience. The chef draws an enthusiastic crowd by providing specialty theme buffets on no fewer than five nights weekly. In Sunday, it's roast beef and lamb buffet, followed by barbecue buffet Monday, Mexican buffet Tuesday, Italian buffet Wednesday, and seafood festival Thursday. On Friday and Saturday, the evening offering is local dishes seared over a mesquite grill. All dinners are served from 6 to 10 p.m., with buffets costing around $20 and à la carte dinners going for $30 and up. À la carte lunch is served from noon to 2:30 p.m., featuring hamburgers, salads, daily specials, and the famous South Philly cheese-steak sandwich. Lunches cost from $14. It is open daily.

Outside of the hotels, I prefer the **Beefeater,** 12 Kaya Grandi (tel. 011-588-7/8081), one of the island's oldest restaurants, in the heart of Kralendijk, opposite the tourist office. An Englishman, Richard Dove, a former inspector for the Michelin guides, created this handsome restaurant, decorating it with prints and pictures. It is found in an old town house. An apéritif is served in an intimate bar, and you're shown to your table where you'll enjoy excellent personal service in a dignified, somewhat elegant atmosphere. Steaks and seafood are the main feature. The chef prepares an excellent steak au poivre. Before your main course, try his pâté, crêpe, or conch. Expect to pay from 35 NAf ($19.60) to 50 NAf ($28) for a three-course meal. The restaurant is open Monday through Saturday for dinner only, from 6:30 to 11 p.m. In season, it's necessary to make a reservation.

Zeezicht, Kaya Corsow (tel. 011-588-7/8434), is the best place in the capital to go for a sundowner. You join the old salts or the people who live on boats to watch the sun go down, hoping to see the "green flash" that Hemingway wrote about. Pronounced *zay-zicht* and meaning "sea view," this place has long been popular with fishermen who like the excellent local cookery and the Chinese dishes. Rebuilt into a two-story operation, the restaurant offers an oyster soup that might be the best beginning. Perhaps you'll prefer a conch chop suey. A small rijsttafel is also offered. Fried fish is invariably featured, the catch coming from the nearby fish market. Lobster à la Zeezicht is occasionally offered, and there's always the Zeezicht steak. Count on parting with about $25. Zeezicht is open daily from 8:30 a.m. to 11 p.m.

China Garden, 47 Kaya Grandi (tel. 011-588-7/8480), is housed in a restored Bonairean mansion. Good-tasting Eastern dishes, with some Indonesian specialties, are served to West Indians and visitors. Portions are enormous, and prices are low, considering what you get. The chefs from Hong Kong also cook Chinese, American, and local dishes, and do so daily from 11:30 a.m. to 10 p.m. except Tuesday. A variety of curries ranges from beef to lobster. Seafood dishes, prepared in a variety of styles, including lobster in black-bean sauce, are served. Special culinary features include a Java rijsttafel and the nasi goreng special. The place is air-conditioned, seating 60 guests, and it offers courteous service. You can dine here for $22, but a lot of hungry scuba-divers spend a lot more, of course.

Restaurant Lisboa, Kaya Grandi (tel. 011-588-7/8286), in front of the Hotel Rochaline, lies beneath a vine-covered arbor. This restaurant is one of the best choices for a good meal outside the island's major hotels. Straw-covered bottles of wine dangle above your head as you enjoy a view of the nearby ocean and the little fish market. Breakfast is served daily from 7:30 to 11 a.m., lunch is from noon to 3 p.m., and dinner is on from 6:30 p.m. until the final diner finishes. The charge is $12 for lunch, from $20 for dinner. Specialties include fresh oysters, fresh fish with fried plaintain, octopus filet, several styles of pizza, grilled shrimp, deep-fried chicken legs, and fish soup.

Den Laman Aquarium Bar and Restaurant, Gouverneur Debrotweg (tel. 011-588-7/8955), next to the Hotel Bonaire, serves some of the best seafood on Bonaire. The restaurant has a huge, 9,000-gallon aquarium, covering two walls. Housed within are such creatures as sharks, along with beautiful and fascinating tropical fish. The fish are not just for viewing, as you'll soon agree after ordering a cocktail and an appetizer (shrimp, lobster, or mixed seafood). Another excellent beginning is the fish soup, the chef's special. The fresh fish of the day depends on what was caught, of course. Perhaps you'll order conch flamingo, a local favorite, or lobster thermidor. When it's featured, I always go for the red snapper

Créole. It's easy to spend $35 here, but also possible to dine for less. Dinner is served from 6 to 11 p.m. Closed Tuesday.

Bistro des Amis, 1 Kaya L. D. Gerharts (tel. 011-588-7/8003), is intimate, and it serves good food. In the heart of Kralendijk, the bistro is owned by a woman known only as "Lucille." She will tell you her specials of the day, which are likely to include the best onion soup on the island, escargots served piping hot in garlic butter, mousse of smoked eel, pepper steak in cream-cognac sauce, filet of duck in raspberry sauce, lamb cutlets, and scallops swimming in a velvety cream sauce. The wine selection is limited, but among the best on the island. Incidentally, you dine in air-conditioned comfort. Hours are 6:30 to 11 p.m. daily except Sunday, and there is often dancing so you can make a night of it. Count on a bill beginning at $22 for dinner. There's also a large bar if you'd like to drop in for a drink before dinner.

The Green Parrot, Sand Dollar Condominiums & Beach Club, P.O. Box 175 (tel. 011-599-7/8738), is set on a breeze-filled pier near a flat and sandy plot of lot, part of the complex of this previously recommended condo unit. It serves informal food, including burgers, pasta, sandwiches, and seafood dishes, with costs beginning at $15, going up. You can gaze at the waves, enjoy a tropical fruit drink, and find shelter from the searing sun. It is open daily from 8 a.m. to 10 p.m.

EXPLORING BONAIRE: The capital, **Kralendijk,** means "coral dike" and is pronounced *Kroll-en-dike,* although most denizens refer to it as *Playa,* Spanish for "beach." A dollhouse town of some 2,500 residents, it is small, neat, and pretty, also Dutch-clean, and its stucco buildings are painted in pastels of pink and orange, with an occasional lime green. The capital's jetty is lined with island sloops and fishing boats.

Kralendijk nestles in a bay on the west coast, opposite **Klein Bonaire,** or Little Bonaire, an uninhabited, low-lying islet a ten-minute swim from the capital.

The main street of town leads along the beachfront on the harbor. A Protestant church was built in 1834, and St. Bernard's Roman Catholic Church has some lovely stained-glass windows.

At Ford Oranje you'll see a lone cannon dating from the days of Napoleon. If possible, try to get up early to see the Fish Market on the waterfront, looking like a little gold Greek temple. Here you'll see a variety of strange and brilliantly colored fish.

Around town you'll probably see the official tourist guide and welcoming committee of one, Caicai Cecelia. In his sparkling white uniform and with his ever-present smile, he roams the streets, welcoming newcomers and offering advice and assistance. He's also a singer and has made records.

Bonaire Marine Park

To maintain the coral reef ecosystem off Bonaire and to ensure returns from scuba-diving, snorkeling, fishing, and other recreational activities, the Bonaire Marine Park was created, with the help of the International Union for Conservation of Nature and Natural Resources and of the World Wildlife Fund. The park incorporates the entire coastline of Bonaire and neighboring Klein Bonaire, defined as the "seabottom and the overlying waters from the high-water tidemark down to 200 feet." All park activities are controlled by island government legislation and a marine environment management program. The park is policed, and services and facilities are provided for visitors. These include a **Visitor Information Center** at the Karpata Ecological Center, park brochures, lectures, slide presentations, films, and permanent dive-site moorings.

Visitors are asked to respect the marine environment and to engage in no activities that may damage it, such as sitting on corals. All marine life is completely protected. This means no fishing or collecting of fish, shells, or corals, dead or alive. Spearfishing is forbidden. Anchoring is not permitted. All craft must use permanent moorings, except for emergency stops. Boats of less than 12 feet may use a stone anchor. Most recreation activity in the marine park takes place on the island's leeward side and among the reefs surrounding small, uninhabited Klein Bonaire.

The reefs are home to various coral formations that grow at different depths, ranging from the knobby brain coral at three feet to staghorn and elkhorn up to about ten feet deeper, and gorgonians, giant brain, and others all the way to 40 to 83 feet. Many species of fish inhabit the reefs, and the deep reef slope is home to a range of sponges, groupers, and moray eels.

The Tour North

After leaving Kralendijk, and passing the Bonaire Beach Hotel and the desalinization plant, you'll come to **Radio Nederland Wereld Omroep** (Dutch World Radio). It's a 13-tower, 300,000-watter. Opposite the transmitting station is a lovers' promenade, built by nature. It's an ideal spot for a picnic.

The road north is one of the most beautiful stretches in the Antilles, with turquoise waters on your left, coral cliffs on your right. You can stop at several points along this road where you'll find paved paths for strolling or bicycling.

Continuing, you'll pass the storage tanks of the Bonaire Petroleum Corporation, the road heading to **Gotomeer,** the island's loveliest inland sector, with a saltwater lake. Several flamingos prefer this spot to the salt flats in the south.

Down the hill the road leads to a section called **"Dos Pos"** or two wells, which has palm trees and vegetation in contrast to the rest of the island, where only the drought-resistant kibraacha and divi-divi trees, tilted before the constant wind, can grow, along with forests of cacti.

Bonaire's oldest village is **Rincon.** Slaves who used to work in the salt flats in the south once lived here. There are a couple of bars, including the Amstel and the Tropicana, where you can order beer before continuing on your journey. The Rincon Ice Cream Parlour makes homemade ice cream in a variety of interesting flavors. Above the bright roofs of the village is the crest of a hill called Para Mira or "stop and look."

A side path outside of Rincon leads to some Arawak Indian inscriptions supposedly 500 years old. The petroglyph designs are in pink-red dye. At nearby **Boca Onima,** you'll find grotesque grottoes of coral.

Before going back to the capital, you might take a short bypass to **Seroe Larguy,** which has a good view of Kralendijk and the sea. Lovers frequent the spot at night.

Washington/Slagbaai National Park

Just as the Bonaire Marine Park is aimed at the conservation of the underwater environment, so Washington/Slagbaai National Park is concerned with the conservation of the island's fauna, flora, and landscape. It is a changing vista highlighted by desert-like terrain, secluded beaches, caverns, and a bird sanctuary. Occupying 15,000 acres of Bonaire's northwesternmost territory, the park was once a plantation, producing divi-divi, aloe, charcoal, and goats. It was purchased by the Netherlands Antilles government, and since 1967 part of the land, formerly the Washington plantation, has been a wildlife sanctuary. The southern part of the park, the Slagbaai plantation, was added in 1978.

The park can be seen in a few hours, although it takes days to appreciate it fully. Touring the park is easy, with two routes: a 15-mile "short" route, marked by green arrows, and a 22-mile "long" route, marked by yellow arrows. The roads are well marked and safe, but somewhat rugged, although they are gradually being improved. Tickets cost $2 per person and can be purchased at the gate.

Whichever route you take, there are a few important stops you should make. Just past the gate is **Salina Mathijs,** a salt flat that is home to flamingos during the rainy season. Beyond the salt flat on the road to the right is **Boca Chikitu,** a white sand beach and bay. A few miles up the beach lies **Boca Cocolishi,** a two-part black sand beach. Its deep, rough seaward side is separated from the calm, shallow basin by a ridge of coralline algae. Hermit crabs walk the beach and shallow water.

The main road leads to **Boca Bartol,** a bay full of living and dead elkhorn coral, seafans, and reef fish. A popular watering hole good for birdwatching is **Poosdi Mangel. Wajaca** is a remote reef where many sea creatures live, including turtles, octopuses, and trigger-fish. Immediately inland towers 746-foot **Mount Brandaris,** Bonaire's highest peak, at whose foot is **Bronswinkel Well,** a watering spot for pigeons and parakeets. Some 130 species of birds live in the park, some with such exotic names as banana quilt and black-faced grassquit. Bonaire has few mammals, but you'll see goats and donkeys, perhaps even a wild bull.

Heading South

Leaving the capital again, you pass the **Trans World Radio** antennas, towering 500 feet in the air, transmitting with 810,000 watts. This is one of the hemisphere's most powerful medium-wave radio stations, the loudest voice in Christendom and the most powerful nongovernment broadcast station in the world. It beeps out interdenominational Gospel messages and hymns in 20 languages to countries as far away as Eastern Europe and the Middle East.

Later, you come on the salt flats where the brilliantly colored pink **flamingos** live. Bonaire shelters the largest accessible nesting and breeding grounds in the world. The flamingos build high mud mounds to hold their eggs. In the background, mounds of salt look like snow mountains, glistening in the sun. The birds are best viewed in spring when they're usually nesting and tending their young.

The salt flats were once worked by slaves, and the government has rebuilt some primitive stone huts, bare shelters little more than waist high. The slaves slept in these huts, returning to their homes in Rincon in the north on weekends. The centuries-old salt pans have been reactivated by the International Salt Company. Near the salt pans you'll see some 30-foot obelisks in white, blue, and orange. They were built in 1838 to help mariners locate their proper anchorages.

Farther down the coast is the island's oldest lighthouse, Willemstoren, built in 1837. Still farther along, Sorobon Beach and Boca Cai come into view. They're at landlocked **Lac Bay** which is ideal for swimming and snorkeling. Conch shells are stacked up on the beach. The water here is so vivid and clear you can see coral 65 to 120 feet down in the reef-protected waters.

SHOPPING: Kralendijk features an assortment of goods, including precious gemstone jewelry, wood, leather, sterling, ceramics, liquors, and tobacco at 25% to 50% less than in the U.S. and Canada. Prices are often quoted in U.S. dollars, and major credit cards and traveler's checks are usually accepted. Most shops are open from 8 a.m. to noon and 2 to 6 p.m. Walk along Kaya Grandi in Kralendijk to sample the merchandise.

Of course, the famous **Spritzer & Fuhrmann's** (tel. 011-588-7/8455) has a branch at 29 Kaya Grandi, selling elegant Swiss watches, clocks, and jewelry, the largest collection on Bonaire. You can also buy English china and French crystal here.

Fundashon Arte Industria Bonairiano, on J. A. Abraham Boulevard (no phone), is the best shop for handcrafts, including woodcarvings, goatskin leather articles, and jewelry.

Ki Bo Ke Pakus, Divi Flamingo Beach Hotel & Casino (tel. 011-588-7/8239), has some of the most imaginative merchandise on the island—Bonaire T-shirts, handbags, dashikis, locally made jewelry, batiks from Indonesia, Delft blue items, and khangas, the African material which can be worn a dozen ways.

Littman Jewelers, 35 Kaya Grandi (tel. 011-588-7/8160), is in an old Bonaire house which Steven D. and Esther Littman have restored to its original state. They sell Rolex and Chronosport watches, plus fine Orbit timepieces. The shop also carries many gift items. Next door, Mr. and Mrs. Littman have a shop called **Aries Cheez and Tee's,** selling T-shirts from standard to hand-painted, plus Dutch cheeses, chocolates, fine wines, imported crackers, and other food items.

Things Bonaire, on Kaya Grandi (tel. 011-588-7/8423), sells Jean Meiss hand-painted T-shirts and terry beachwear, as well as hand-painted pottery souvenirs. They also own the former Boutique Bonaire at the Bonaire Beach Hotel (tel. 011-588-7/8190), which they have expanded to many gift items, including Delft, pewter, black coral jewelry, locally made ceramics, sunglasses, and dresses from Greece and Ecuador, plus guayaberas, unisex shirts, men's and women's swim suits, shorts, T-shirts, and terry beachwear.

THE SPORTING LIFE: The true beauty on Bonaire is under the sea, where visibility is 100 feet 365 days of the year, and the water temperatures range from 78° to 82° Fahrenheit. Many dive sites can be reached directly from the beach, and sailing is another pastime. Birdwatching is among the best in the Caribbean, and for beachcombers there are acres and acres of driftwood, found along the shore from the salt flats to Lac.

Swimming

Bonaire has some of the whitest sand beaches in the West Indies. The major hotels have beaches, but you may want to wander down to the southeast coast for a swim at Sorobon and Boca Cai on Lac Bay. In the north, you may want to swim at Playa Foenchi, on the coastline of the Washington/Slagbaai National Park.

Snorkeling

In an unusual development for snorkelers, an easily accessible trail along Bonaire's shoreline has been identified and marked off in the Marine Park. Here a great many of the hundreds of fish and coral varieties to be found anywhere can be seen within a quarter-mile stretch of shallow water. The area attracts snorkelers from far and wide. While scuba enthusiasts come from all parts of the world to dive at Bonaire's 40-plus designated underwater scenic sites, snorkelers had not heretofore received special attention.

Scuba

One of the richest reef communities in the entire West Indies, Bonaire has plunging walls which descend to a sand bottom at 130 or so feet, abounding with hard corals, numerous seawhips, black coral trees, basket sponges, gorgonia, and swarms of rainbow-hued tropical fish. One magazine said Bonaire had "the lushest, most colorful coral reefs to be found anywhere." Most of the diving is done on the leeward side where the ocean is lake flat. There are more than 40 dive sites on sharply sloping reefs.

The waters off the coast of Bonaire received an additional attraction in 1984.

A rust-bottomed general cargo ship, 80 feet long, was confiscated by the police. Its contraband cargo, about 25,000 pounds of marijuana, was discovered hidden between a real and a false bulkhead. Its owners never came forward (obviously) to claim either the ship or cargo, so it remained in lonely disgrace, moored without purpose. Known as *Hilma Hooker* (familiarly dubbed "The Hooker" by everyone on the island), she sank without fanfare one calm day in 90 feet of water. Lying just off the southern shore near the capital, her wreck is now a popular dive site. Divers try to get a look at the massive propeller, whose brass is still visible if you scratch off a layer of the rapidly accumulating coral and algae.

Bonaire has a unique program for divers in that the major hotels offer personalized, closeup encounters with the island's fish and other marine life. That way, the diver can experience underwater contacts in different dimensions under the expertise of Bonaire's dive guides.

Dive I and **Dive II** (tel. 011-588-7/8285), at opposite ends of the beachfront of Divi Flamingo Beach Resort & Casino, are among the island's most complete scuba facilities. Demand was so great that several years ago, Scotland-born Peter Hughes, its Miami-based owner, split the well-known Bonaire branch in two, both operating out of well-stocked beachfront buildings and both charging the same prices and offering the same type of expeditions. At both Dive I and Dive II, diving equipment can be rented. A resort course for first-time divers costs $75, with full, open-water certification going for $300. An advanced, open-water course, incorporating five dives and teaching already registered divers such skills as underwater salvage, underwater navigation, deep dives, night dives, and drift dives, is offered for $180. There is also a one-day course specializing in the ecology of the coral reef. Alternate sessions concern themselves with vertebrates, another course with invertebrates. This course costs $75.

Captain Don's Habitat Dive Shop (tel. 011-588-7/8290) is a PADI five-star training facility. The open-air, full-service dive shop includes a classroom, photo/video lab, equipment repair, and compressor rooms around spacious seafront patios. Habitat's slogan is "Diving Freedom," and divers can take their tanks and dive anywhere any time of day or night, most often along "The Pike," half a mile of protected reef right in front of the shop and hotel. The highly qualified staff is there to assist and advise but not to police or dictate dive plans. Diving packages are based on six days and include unlimited air fills.

The **Bonaire Scuba Center** is on the 600-foot beach of the Bonaire Beach Hotel, where one of Bonaire's most spectacular reefs lies just 50 feet offshore. The center's equipment includes three flat-top boats, two Mako compressors, and diving equipment for 80 divers. The center caters to both novice and experienced divers. It offers resort and certification courses, guided boat and night dives, mini photo courses, and still- and movie-camera rentals. Boats are available to experienced groups for exploration trips. For reservations, get in touch with Bonaire Tours, Inc., P.O. Box 775, Morgan, NJ 08879 (tel. 201/566-8866).

A new facility, **Sand Dollar Dive and Photo,** at Sand Dollar Condominiums & Beach Club (tel. 011-588-7/8738), has been established by master instructor André Nahr, offering dive packages, PADI instruction, equipment rentals and repairs, and boat, land, and deep-dive trips. The photo shop offers underwater photo and video shoots, PADI specialty courses, E-6 processing, 48-hour print developing, equipment rental and repair, and a weekly slide and video presentation.

Dive-Inn Bonaire N.V., 27 Kaya C.E.B. Hellmund (tel. 011-588-7/8761), PADI Training Facility 1771, is a dive shop operated by Anton and Babs van der Heetkamp. Anton is the operator of the recompression chamber for Bonaire. Diving packages are available for certified divers, plus PADI scuba instruction and rental of scuba equipment. Dive-Inn Bonaire also offers snorkel trips, surfing, Sunfish sailing, and watertaxi rides, some to Klein Bonaire.

Deep-Sea Fishing

The island's offshore fishing grounds are virtually untouched, making for some of the best deep-sea fishing in the Caribbean. A good day's catch may include mackerel, tuna, wahoo, and swordfish, among the many species out there. If relaxation is what you have in mind, try a full- or half-day sailing charter.

Almost any hotel on the island can arrange this for you, usually through the well-recommended expert, **Chris Morkas.** You can reach him or his wife directly at his house at 69 Kaya Grandi (tel. 011-588-7/8774). A native Bonairean, he has been fishing almost since he was born. He offers two boats for half-day excursions. Prices are to be negotiated on the spot.

Boating

Every visitor to Bonaire wants to take a trip to uninhabited **Klein Bonaire.** The Flamingo Beach and Bonaire Beach hotels offer trips daily. You'll be left in the morning for a day of snorkeling, beachcombing, and picnicking, then picked up later that afternoon. Other hotels will also arrange a trip to the islet for you, perhaps including a barbecue.

For a sailing trip along the coast, **Dive-Inn Bonaire N.V.** (tel. 011-588-7/8761) takes passengers, anchoring near a beach where you can swim, skindive, or scuba-dive. A daily trip, lasting from 9:30 a.m. to 3:30 p.m., costs $35 per person, including sandwiches and soft drinks. A sunset trip is also offered, from 5 to 7 p.m. daily, for $15 per person, with rum punch included in the rates.

Most of the major hotels rent Sunfish or windsurfers for $10 per hour (they're free to guests of the Bonaire Beach Hotel). The Bonaire Beach Hotel also offers a sunset cruise to anyone who is interested, requiring a minimum of ten guests. It departs from the hotel every evening at 5 p.m., returning an hour later. You ride on a vessel that resembles a pontoon-supported floating barge. There's a cash bar, but snacks are free. The price is $8 per person, and it's best to reserve a seat 24 hours in advance.

Golf

This is not a serious sport here. There's only a miniature course at the Bonaire Beach Hotel.

Tennis

The **Bonaire Beach Hotel** (tel. 011-588-7/8448) has two good courts, which are illuminated for night play and covered with artificial grass. Use of the courts is free to guests of the hotel, but nonresidents pay $6 per half hour of play. A tennis pro is on the premises, and racquets and balls can be borrowed without charge.

NIGHTLIFE: Underwater slide shows provide entertainment for both divers and nondivers in the evening. **Capt. Don's Habitat** (tel. 011-588-7/8290) offers two shows weekly. On Monday at 8:45 p.m., Dee Scarr, dive guide, shows *Touch the Sea,* slides about the island's marine life and its interactions. Fish personalities are shown in their individual roles. On Wednesday at 8:45 p.m., Habitat's underwater photographer, André Nahr, shows his slides. For nondivers, Captain Don shows his *Above the Plimsoll Mark,* a view of Bonaire, at 9 p.m. Friday. The Bonaire Beach Hotel (tel. 011-588-7/8448) is the location for a slide show Wednesday at 9:30 p.m. presented by Bonaire Scuba Center. On Sunday at

9:30 p.m., an underwater video, *Discover the Caribbean,* is presented at the Flamingo Beach Hotel (tel. 011-588-7/8285). The shows are free.

Outside of the hotels, check out the action at **"E Wowo"** ("The Eye" in Papiamento), which lies right in the heart of town near the tourist office, at the corner of Kaya Grandi and L. D. Gerharts. It's distinguished by two flashing op art eyes. The club caters to members, but if you ask at your hotel desk you'll usually be granted an admission pass. Hours are Wednesday through Sunday from 9 p.m. until the early hours. The club (no phone) occupies the second floor of one of the oldest and most colorful Dutch colonial buildings on the island. It is the only nightclub in Bonaire. Admission costs 10 NAf ($5.60).

Upstairs over the already-recommended Zeezicht Bar and Restaurant, Kaya Corsow (tel. 011-588-7/8434), the same manager, Maddy Visser, also operates **Pirate House,** where you can eat and dance to disco music after 11 p.m. and occasionally see a show. Drinks cost around $3.

As part of Divi Flamingo Beach Hotel & Casino (tel. 011-588-7/8285), a **casino** opened in 1984 in a former residence adjoining the property. It is being promoted as "The World's First Barefoot Casino." Whatever the name, visitors are not allowed inside unless clad only in swimsuits. The casino is open daily except Monday from 8 p.m. to 4 a.m. Blackjack, roulette, poker, wheel of fortune, video games, and slot machines are available. Gambling on the island is under government regulations.

The **Black Coral Casino** at the Bonaire Beach Hotel (tel. 011-588-7/8448) was taken over by the government, and its policies and hours have fluctuated. Call the hotel before you arrive for a visit. One almost certain bet for a good time, however, is the hotel's Saturday-night buffet and folkloric show, beginning at 7:30 p.m. and lasting until 10:30. The cost is $15 per person. Entertainment usually begins at 9 p.m. Check with the hotel for whatever specialty night (if any) is being held on the night of your intended visit.

Karel's, the Waterfront (no phone). Almost Tahitian in its high-ceilinged, open-walled design, this popular bar is perched above the sea on stilts. You can sit at the long rectangular bar with many of the island's dive and boating professionals or else select a table near the balustrades overlooking the illuminated surf. Drinks cost from 4 NAf ($2.24) each, and are served every evening except Monday from 5 p.m. to 2 a.m.

3. CURAÇAO

Just 35 miles off the coast of Venezuela, Curaçao, the "C" of the Dutch ABC islands of the Caribbean, is the most populated in the Netherlands Antilles. It attracts visitors because of its people, who extend a big welcome, as well as its almost duty-free shopping, lively casinos, water sports, and international cuisine. Fleets of ocean-going tankers head out from its harbor to bring refined oil to all parts of the world.

Now a peaceful, self-governing part of the Netherlands, Curaçao was discovered not by Columbus, but by one of his lieutenants, Alonso de Ojeda, as well as Amerigo Vespucci, in 1499. The Spaniards exterminated all but 75 members of a branch of the peaceful Arawak Indians. However, they in turn were ousted by the Dutch in 1634, who also had to fight off French and English invasions.

The Dutch made the island a tropical Holland in miniature. Pieter Stuyvesant, stomping on his peg, ruled Curaçao in 1644.

The island was turned into a Dutch Gibraltar, bristling with forts. Thick ramparts guarded the harbor's narrow entrance, the hilltop forts (many now converted into restaurants) protected the coastal approaches.

Because of all that early Dutch building, what one finds today is more European flavor than anywhere else in the Caribbean. Curaçao is the most important island architecturally in the entire West Indies.

In this century, it remained sleepy until 1915 when the Royal Dutch/Shell Company built one of the world's largest oil refineries to process crude from Venezuela. Workers from some 50 countries poured into the island, turning Curaçao into a polyglot, cosmopolitan community.

Curaçao is only 37 miles long and 7 miles across at its widest point. After leaving the capital, Willemstad, you plunge into a strange, desert-like countryside that may remind you of the American Southwest. Three-pronged cactus studs the land, as do the spiny-leafed aloes and the weird divi-divi trees, with their coiffures bent by centuries of trade winds. The landscape is an amalgam of browns and russets.

Classic Dutch-style windmills are in and around Willemstad and in some parts of the countryside. These standard farm models pump water from wells to irrigate vegetation.

GETTING THERE: The air routes to Curaçao are strongly linked to those leading to and from Aruba, since several airlines combine flights from North America to both destinations.

Curacao's international airport, **Aeropuerto Internashonal Hato,** Plaza Margareth Abraham (tel. 011-599-9/82288), has an 11,155-foot runway, almost 200 feet wide, one of the largest in the Caribbean and with enough room to land a Boeing 747. The airport restaurant and other food and beverage facilities are open daily from 7 a.m. to 10:30 p.m.

American Airlines operates a daily flight to Curaçao which leaves from New York's JFK Airport at 9:30 a.m., in enough time to connect with incoming flights from many cities of the U.S. Northeast and Middle West. It stops in Aruba before continuing to Curaçao.

The return flight from Curaçao to JFK is nonstop, landing at the New York airport after 4½ hours of flight time. Round-trip air fare is cheaper when a passenger arranges prepaid hotel accommodations through American's tour desk simultaneously with air transport. However, clients who want to arrange their own transport can opt for American's Supersaver fare, which in midwinter requires a two-week advance booking, a Saturday night layover, with both departures on weekdays (with weekday defined as Monday to Thursday). Priced at $375 per round trip, the fare rises to $405 if you fly in either direction on a Friday, Saturday, or Sunday. For low-season passage, the fare is from $40 to $50 less. There is a 25% penalty for changes in itinerary.

Eastern Airlines services Curaçao from Miami, combining many of its frequent flights with touchdowns in Aruba. However, at presstime a strike has curtailed Eastern service, and the future of the airline is uncertain. Its toll-free number is 800/535-6660.

Likewise, **ALM** offers a daily afternoon flight to Curaçao from Miami, stopping at Haiti on the way. ALM also offers a daily flight to Curaçao from New York, and the route requires a stop at either Haiti or St. Maarten (depending on the day of the week) before continuing on to Curaçao. For connections to Curaçao from other islands (especially the ABC group), your best bet is usually ALM because of its frequent service in the Caribbean.

GETTING AROUND: Since **taxis** don't have meters, ask your driver to quote you the rate before getting in. Charges go up by 25% after 11 p.m. Drivers are supposed to carry an official tariff sheet which they'll produce upon request. Generally there is no need to tip, unless a driver helped you with your luggage. The cost from the airport to, say, the Las Palmas or Curaçao Caribbean is $9, and the charges can be split among four passengers. If a piece of luggage is so big the trunk lid won't close, you'll be assessed a surcharge of $1. In town, the best place to get a taxi is on the Otrabanda side of the floating bridge. To summon a cab, call 011-599-9/616711 (on the island, use only the last six digits).

Buses

Some of the hotels operate a free bus shuttle, taking you from the suburbs to the shopping district of Willemstad. A fleet of DAF yellow buses operate from Wilhelminapleim, near the shopping center, to most parts of Curaçao for an average fare of 40¢. Some limousines function as "C" buses. When you see one listing the destination you're heading for, you can hail it at any of the designated bus stops.

Sightseeing Taxi Tours

A tour by taxi costs about $15 per hour, and up to four passengers can go on the jaunt.

Sightseeing Tours

Taber Tours, Maduro Plaza, 19 Emancipatie Blvd. (tel. 011-599-9/ 79539), offers several tours, both day and night, to points of interest in and around Curaçao. The east part tour, costing $10 per person for adults, $5 for children under 12, takes you for a drive through Willemstad, to the Curaçao Liqueur distillery, through the residential area and the Bloempot shopping center, and to the Curaçao Museum (admission fee included in the tour price).

Gray Line Sightseeing, 22 Perseusweg (tel. 011-599-9/35799), also makes an interesting tour throughout the city and countryside.

Car Rentals

Since all points of tourist interest are easily accessible by paved roads, you may want to rent a car. U.S. and Canadian citizens can use their own licenses, if valid, and *traffic moves on the right*. International road signs are observed.

Several car-rental companies are represented in Curaçao, but **Budget Rent-a-Car,** the largest, offers one of the best high-season car-rental arrangements anywhere in the Caribbean. A four-passenger, two-door Toyota Starlet without air conditioning is rented for an unlimited-mileage rate of $186 per week. This rate requires a seven-day advance booking and a minimum rental of five days. Visitors who prefer a car with air conditioning can reserve a manual-transmission four-door Toyota Corolla for a weekly rate of $276.

Purchase of insurance in the form of a collision damage waiver is a good idea. This costs between $10 and $13 per day, depending on the value of the car, and lessens a driver's financial responsibility for collision damage in the event of an accident. If you decide to purchase this optional insurance, you'll pay up to the first $200 in the event of an accident. If you decide not to purchase this insurance, you'll pay up to the full value of damage in the event of an accident. Insurance benefits are roughly similar for all car-rental companies in Curaçao.

Budget maintains four locations at major hotels throughout the island, as well as a branch at the airport. A phone call from 7 a.m. to 11 p.m. to Budget's island headquarters, 517 F. D. Rooseveltweg (tel. 011-599-9/83466), can help to arrange transportation to the nearest outlet. Budget requires that drivers be between the ages of 23 and 65.

Visitors who don't meet these age requirements can try at **Avis** since its minimum age is 21 for drivers holding a credit card, 23 for drivers paying a cash deposit. Avis has no restrictions for drivers over 65. Avis operates air-conditioned fleets. A Toyota Starlet at Avis costs $233 per week and requires advance booking of at least two days.

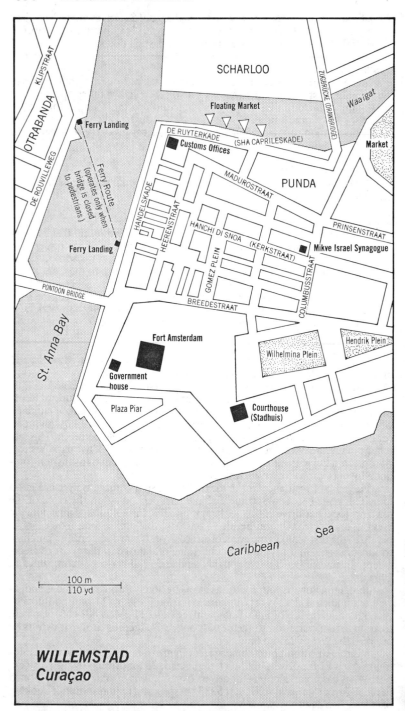

SCHARLOO

KLIPSTRAAT

OTRABANDA

ZUGBRÜCKE (DRAWBRIDGE)

Waaigat

Floating Market

Ferry Landing

DE RUYTERKADE

(SHA CAPRILESKADE)

DE ROUVILLEWEG

Customs Offices

Market

Ferry Route
(operates only when
bridge is closed
to pedestrians.)

MADUROSTRAAT

PUNDA

HANDELSKADE

HEERENSTRAAT

HANCHI DI SNOA

(KERKSTRAAT)

PRINSENSTRAAT

Ferry Landing

Mikve Israel Synagogue

GOMEZ PLEIN

COLUMBUSSTRAAT

PONTOON BRIDGE

BREEDESTRAAT

St. Anna Bay

Fort Amsterdam

Wilhelmina Plein

Hendrik Plein

Government
house

Plaza Piar

Courthouse
(Stadhuis)

Caribbean   Sea

100 m
110 yd

WILLEMSTAD
Curaçao

Hertz is also represented in Curaçao. The least expensive high-season rates, $233 for a week's rental of a Nissan with unlimited mileage, are about the same as the prices charged at Avis. Handling Hertz rentals in Curaçao is Ric Car Rental, 22 Perseusweg (tel. 011-599-9/613622).

All three companies maintain toll-free numbers for callers. For rates and information while still in the States, call Budget at 800/527-0700, Avis at 800/331-2112, or Hertz at 800/654-3131.

PRACTICAL FACTS: Curaçao, together with Bonaire, St. Maarten, St. Eustatius, and Saba, is in the Kingdom of the Netherlands as part of the Netherlands Antilles. Curaçao has its own governmental authority, relying on the Netherlands only for defense and foreign affairs.

Banks: Banking hours are from 8:30 a.m. to noon and 1:30 to 4:30 p.m. Monday to Friday. The only exceptions are the Banco Popular and the Bank of America, which remain open during the lunch hour, doing business from 9 a.m. to 3 p.m. Monday to Friday.

Consulate: For problems about passports or other matters, telephone the U.S. Consulate (tel. 011-599-9/613066).

Currency: While Canadian and U.S. dollars are accepted for purchases on the island, the official currency is the guilder (also called a florin), which is divided into 100 NA (Netherlands Antillean) cents. The exchange rate is $1 U.S. to 1.79 NAf. (Stated another way, 56¢ U.S. equals 1 NAf.) Shops, hotels, and restaurants usually accept most major U.S. and Canadian credit cards.

Documents: To enter Curaçao, proof of citizenship, such as a voter registration card or a passport, is required, along with a return or continuing airline ticket out of the country. No visa or vaccination is required.

Electricity: The electrical current is 110-130 volts AC, 50 cycles, the same as in North America, although many hotels will have adapters if your appliances happen to be European.

Information: For tourist information, go to the Curaçao Tourist Board, Plaza Piar (tel. 011-599-9/613397).

Language: Dutch, Spanish, and English are spoken in Curaçao, along with Papiamento, a language which combines the three major tongues with Indian and African dialects. The largest island in the Netherlands Antilles, Curaçao has 172,000 people representing more than 50 national groups.

Medical care: Medical facilities are well equipped, and the 820-bed St. Elisabeth Hospital, 193 Breedestraat (tel. 011-599-9/624900), near Otrabanda in Willemstad, is considered one of the most up-to-date facilities in the Caribbean.

Police: The police emergency number is 011-599-9/44444, but on the island you need dial only the 44444.

Post office: The post office is on Waaigat (tel. 011-599-9/61125).

Taxes and service: Curaçao levies a room tax of 5% on accommodations, and most hotels add 10% for room service. There is a departure tax of 17.70 NAf ($9.90) for international flights but only 10 NAf ($5.60) for domestic travel.

Telecommunications: For cable service, call 011-599-9/611433 for **All America Cables,** 011-599-9/613500 for **Landsradio.** For long distance telephone calls from the island, dial 021. Curaçao can be dialed direct from the U.S. mainland, using the international call code, 011, followed by the area code, 599-9, then the local number, of which the number of digits can vary. In Curaçao, of course, it is not necessary to use either the international call code or the area code.

Time: Curaçao is on Atlantic Standard Time, one hour ahead of Eastern Standard Time and the same as Eastern Daylight Saving Time.

Water: The drinking water comes from a modern desalinization plant and is safe to drink.

Weather: Curaçao has an average temperature of 81° Fahrenheit. Trade winds keep the island fairly cool, and it is flat and arid with an average rainfall of only 22 inches per year, hardly your idea of a lush, palm-studded tropical island.

A word of caution to swimmers: The sea water remains an almost-constant 76° Fahrenheit year round, with good underwater visibility, but beware of stepping on spines of the sea urchins which sometimes abound in these waters. To give temporary first aid for an embedded urchin's spine, try the local remedies of vinegar or lime juice, or as the natives advise, a burning match if you are tough. While the urchin spines are not fatal, they can cause several days of real discomfort.

WHERE TO STAY: Your hotel will be in Willemstad or in one of the suburbs, which lie only 10 to 15 minutes from the shopping center. The bigger hotels often have free shuttle buses running into town, and most of them have their own beaches and pools.

Remember that Curaçao is a bustling commercial center, and the downtown hotels often fill up fast with business travelers and visitors from neighboring countries on a shopping holiday. Therefore, reservations are always important.

Keep in mind, when making your travel plans, that the government room tax and service charge will probably be added to your final hotel bill.

The Upper Bracket

Curaçao Caribbean Hotel & Casino, P.O. Box 2133, Willemstad, Curaçao, N.A. (tel. 011-599-9/625000), is a distinguished, "honeycomb-on-stilts" high-rise resort on the outskirts of Willemstad, with a free bus service to take you shopping in town. It's a self-contained complex, with a charming little beach and cove set among rocky bluffs where a dive shop offers the best water-sports program on the island, including skindiving, sailing, deep-sea fishing, and sea Jeeps. You have a choice of two Grasstex tennis courts lit for night games. The structure is a block of rooms encased in a concrete façade, its arches not unlike Dutch lace. Most impressive to me is the wide, open lower lounge areas, giving everyone a trade-wind-swept view of Piscadera Bay. Furnished in wicker, the wall-less Pisca Terrace bar and restaurant opens onto an eight-pointed-star-shaped pool and the ruins of a fort two centuries old. You can order breakfast on this terrace. Glass-enclosed elevators built outside on the hotel offer a panoramic view as you're whisked to your room. The 200 refurbished bedrooms have much space, immaculate baths with big towels, air conditioning that really works, and traditional furnishings, plus breeze-cooled private balconies, and an ice machine on each floor. In winter, singles range in price from $125 to $165 daily, the difference based on the view. Doubles go for $130 to $170. *In summer, the single tariff is $85 to $105 daily, the price for twins being $90 to $110.* For breakfast and dinner, add another $32 per person daily. The Willemstad is an air-conditioned dining room offering meals from $25. The hotel also has a Spanish restaurant, Don Quijote. Mexican nights are popular, as are Antillean nights with folkloric shows. Of course, the casino is a major attraction. To the left as you enter the hotel is a well-stocked shopping complex, including a branch of Spritzer & Fuhrmann.

Golden Tulip Las Palmas Hotel and Vacation Village, Piscadera Bay, P.O. Box 2179, Willemstad, Curaçao, N.A. (tel. 011-599-9/625200), across from the Curaçao Caribbean, is ideal for those who seek a moderately priced resort, one of the stated goals of this guide. The atmosphere here is casual and convivial. The location is only two miles from Willemstad, on a breezy hillside a few hundred yards from the sea and its own little beach with water sports. The cacti that used to stud the hillside have now given way to a botanical garden. Accommodations are in a three-story, 100-room main building, or in one of the little casitas with Samoan-style roofs sprinkled through the hillside gardens. Think of a casita as your own self-contained summer house, the kind you might have at a beach resort. The main building has public rooms off the garden-style entry lounge. At its core is a courtyard, with a lily pond, bamboo, and flowering vines. Here you can start your day with a breakfast, later enjoying drinks and entertainment in the evening. Perhaps a family steel band will be brought in, or a fire-eating limbo dancer. Native-style buffet dinners are often hauled out of the kitchen.

Rooms in the main building have contemporary styling with bold colors, and each has a private bath and air conditioning. A single rents for $85 to $90 daily in high season, the tariff going up to $98 to $109 in a twin-bedded room. For breakfast and dinner on the MAP, expect to pay $32 per person in addition to the rates quoted. *Rates for off-season are $68 to $78 daily in a single, going up to $78 to $88 in a twin-bedded room.* The casitas, 94 in all, can accommodate four persons and possibly six (although that would be crowded). Each villa has two well-furnished bedrooms, a living room, a kitchenette, and a porch where you can set up breakfast you prepared yourself after shopping at the mini-market on the grounds. Even in the expensive winter months, these casitas cost $115 daily for two people, *that rate dropping to $110 in summer,* plus service and tax. The furnishings are in a rustic style, resting under beamed ceilings. The sliding doors enlarge the living room which can spill out onto the terrace. A fully equipped beach with a snackbar is less than 800 yards away from the entrance to the hotel. On the grounds is a tennis court lit for night games. Slot machines and croupiers are found inside the Las Palmas, although you can also go to the much bigger casino at the Curaçao Caribbean just across the way. Other sporting facilities include two swimming pools—one Olympic size for adults, plus a tiny wading pool for children. In the ocean-view restaurant, you can order Amstel beer, made with desalinated water, and good food, including some Antillean dishes. Every night there's dinner music, except on Saturday when a Caribbean night with a folklore show is presented.

Curaçao Plaza Hotel and Casino, P.O. Box 229, Plaza Piar, Curaçao, N.A. (tel. 011-599-9/612500), stands guard over the Punda side of St. Anna's Bay, as it's nestled in the ramparts of an 18th-century water fort on the eastern tip of the entrance to the harbor. It is in fact one of the harbor's two "lighthouses." Its designer saw fit to leave its ramparts intact, and now they serve as a promenade for guests. Of course, the hotel has to carry marine collision insurance, the only hostelry in the Caribbean with that distinction. The original part of the hotel followed the style of the arcaded fort. However, now there is a tower of rooms stacked 15 stories high. In winter, singles or doubles cost $90 to $135. *From mid-April until mid-December, the charge is lowered to anywhere from $70 to $105 daily in a single or double.* For breakfast and dinner, add another $30 per person daily to the rates quoted. Each of the 245 bedrooms—your own crow's nest—is attractively furnished with a private bath and phone, TV, air conditioning, and a small refrigerator.

The pool is placed inches away from the parapet of the fort. There's also a pool-side bar and suntanning area, with a lobby-level bar. Crowning the tower is a rooftop dining room that offers the most spectacular sunset views over Willemstad. It's the Penthouse Cocktail Lounge and Gourmet Room, open nightly from 7 to 11:30, and featuring not only dining but dancing. In the Waterfort Grill you can order New York–type sirloin steaks either at lunch or dinner. The Kini-Kini bar is an intimate oasis. The Waterfront offers buffet breakfasts and luncheons, and the Terrace Bar, with its view of the sea and the supertankers passing within a few feet, serves light lunches daily. The hotel also stages special events, including Caribbean nights and barbecue fiestas with dancing to local bands. It also has one of the most popular casinos on the island.

Holiday Beach Hotel & Casino, 31 Pater Eeuwensweg (P.O. Box 2178), Willemstad, Curaçao, N.A. (tel. 011-599-9/625400), built about a mile from the capital, opened in 1968 with 200 modern air-conditioned bedrooms. It has all the facilities of a complete resort hotel, erected along a sandy beach dotted with palm trees and a grassy land projection. The main part of the complex houses the Casino Royale, largest casino on the island, and the principal dining spot, the Green Terrace. The sleeping quarters are in two four-story wings, centering around a U-shaped garden with a large freshwater swimming pool. In size and amenities the bedrooms are well furnished, with two double beds in each unit, opening onto private balconies overlooking the water. Wall-to-wall carpeting, big tile baths, and lots of towels are just part of the comforts, along with phones and color TV. *In summer, singles cost $64 to $71 daily; doubles, $75 to $82.* In winter, rates go up to $80 to $90 daily in a single, $95 to $105 in a double, plus a daily energy surcharge per room. Rates are based on the EP. At the water-sports shop, Sun Dive, all water sports are arranged, and you can also play tennis on the regulation courts. Local entertainment is offered in the hotel's nightclub. After dinner, you can enjoy a drink in the Cocolishi Lounge before heading to the Casino Royale.

Princess Beach Hotel, Dr. Martin Luther King Blvd., Curaçao, N.A. (tel. 011-599-9/614944), is a two-story, lanai-style waterfront resort a short drive from the heart of the city, which is reached by frequent shuttle service. From a bird's-eye point of view, it's a huge chunk of sea-bordering property with its own docks for deep-sea fishing. All major water sports are featured, and a nine-hole golf course is nearby. On the grounds is a professional tennis court. A large, elevated saltwater swimming pool is centered between the building blocks housing 202 units, all air-conditioned with private baths. Remodeled in 1988, the rooms are done in subtle shades of green and pink, with plush carpeting and tropical furniture. The units look out over the beach and contain verandas or loggias attractively shielded by tropical plants. *In the off-season, singles range in price from $56 to $80 daily; doubles go for $72 to $90.* In winter, rates go up to $75 to $100 daily in a single, $90 to $130 in a double. For breakfast and dinner, add another $30 per person daily to the tariffs quoted. The best spot is the terrace where you can sun and drink. The pool bar is one of the most popular hangouts in Curaçao at happy hour. There is also an octagonal casino painted with vivid accents of magenta and turquoise, which is one of the busiest on the island. The main building housing the casino, supper club, cabaret, and other facilities is a reconstruction, following a fire that gutted the structure in the early 1980s. In one courtyard, a new generation of divi-divi trees is already being twisted by the constant winds, taking on eerie shapes. This hotel lies three miles east of Willemstad, between the seacoast road and a beach.

The Best Bargains

Avila Beach Hotel, 130-134 Penstraat, P.O. Box 791, Curaçao, N.A. (tel. 011-599-9/614377), is a beautifully restored 200-year-old mansion standing on the shore road leading eastward out of the city from the shopping center. It's the only beachfront hotel in Willemstad, set on its own small but lovely private beach. The mansion was built by the English governor of Curaçao during the occupation of the island by the British at the time of the Napoleonic Wars. Subsequent governors, including Dutch ones, have used the place as a retreat. Converted into a hotel in 1949, the mansion has added a modern bedroom wing opening toward the sea. It also has an open-air restaurant, Belle Terrace, with split-level dining and a bar area overlooking the beach (see my dining recommendations, below). While the Dutch architecture and colonial style have been preserved on the exterior, the interior of the mansion has been totally rebuilt with a spacious lobby, conference room, offices, and guest rooms. The 45 guest rooms and two suites are all air-conditioned and furnished with Scandinavian modern pieces. In all, it's a comfortable, family-style hotel. In winter, singles range from $90 to $102 daily and twins from $78 to $110. *Off-season, singles cost $60 to $80 daily, and twins go for $68 to $88.* MAP is an additional $35 per person. The hotel stands next door to the Octagon Museum, a building where Bolívar the Liberator used to visit his sisters.

Hotel Holland, 524 F. D. Rooseveltweg, Curaçao, N.A. (tel. 011-599-9/81120), is a few minutes' drive from the airport and contains a bar that is a popular gathering place. For a few brief minutes of every day, you can see airplanes landing from your perch at the edge of the poolside terrace, where well-prepared meals are served during good weather (see my dining recommendation). This property is the domain of ex-navy frogman Hans Vrolijk and his wife, Henne. Hans still retains his interest in scuba, arranging dive packages for his guests. He also directs the service at his Dutch-style restaurant, 'T Kokkeltje. The 20 accommodations have baths, air conditioning, TVs and videos, refrigerators, and balconies. Singles in winter range from $40 to $50 daily, with doubles costing $50 to $60. *In summer, the daily single rate is $40, rising to $50 in a double.*

Golden Tulip Coral Cliff Resort and Beach Club, Santa Marta Bay, P.O. Box 3782, Curaçao, N.A. (tel. 011-599-9/641610), is a group of bungalows with red roofs, surrounded by 18 acres of cliffs, mountains, and bays. The 35 apartments at the edge of the sea each has a kitchenette, climate control, and phone. Winter rates are $60 daily in a single, $70 in a double. *In summer, singles cost $45 daily, and doubles go for $55.* MAP is another $25 per person daily. Dining is in the Santa Marta Terrace Restaurant, an open-air social center, and you can relax at the Beach Bar or toast the sunset at the Cliffhanger Bar. The resort has 600 feet of private beach, an all-weather tennis court, and a number of water sports (see under "The Sporting Life," below). A shuttle bus makes regularly scheduled trips daily to Willemsted.

CURAÇAO COOKERY: The basic cuisine is Dutch, but there are many specialty items, particularly Latin American and Indonesian. The cuisine strikes many visitors as heavy for the tropics, and you may want to have a light lunch, ordering the more filling concoctions such as rijsttafel in the evening.

Erwtensoep, the well-known Dutch pea soup, is a popular dish, as is *keshi yena,* Edam cheese stuffed with meat, then baked. *Funchi,* a Caribbean tortilla, accompanies many local dishes. *Sopito,* fish soup often made with coconut water, is an especially good local dish, and conch is featured in curries and many other dishes.

Curaçao, the liqueur that made the island famous, is made from oranges.

The settings for dining are often dramatic, either in restored forts or haciendas, maybe al fresco.

De Taveerne, Landhuis Groot Develaar (tel. 011-599-9/370669), is a country manor house in a residential section. A red-brick octagonal cupola rises over the roof of the building, and inside where the cows used to be sheltered Holland-born Jerry Wielinga has created a tavern atmosphere with an antique decor. He and his wife, Anna, scoured Curaçao's old homes, finding furnishings for their charming restaurant, bar, and wine cellar. The setting is enhanced by burnished copper, white stucco walls, dark woods, and terracotta tiles. The chef has created a number of specialties, including a steak à escargots. To begin your meal, perhaps he'll have smoked Dutch eel, lobster soup, or snails bour-

guignonne. Other recommendable dishes include shrimp thermidor and sole
meunière. The chateaubriand Stroganoff for two persons is yet another specialty.
A complete meal will set you back $35. The restaurant is open for lunch from
noon to 2 p.m. and for dinner from 7 to 11 p.m. daily except Sunday. You should
definitely make a reservation.

Fort Nassau, near Point Juliana (tel. 011-599-9/613450), is a restored restaurant and bar built in the ruins of a formidably buttressed fort dating from
1792. From its Battery Terrace a 360-degree panorama unfolds of the sea, the
harbor, and Willemstad, just a five-minute drive away. You'll even see the Isla refinery. A signal tower on the cliff sends out beacons to approaching ships. The
inn has retained an 18th-century decor. Before you approach the restaurant, you
can enjoy an apéritif in a fashionably decorated bar. Many come up here just to
have a drink and watch the sunset. On cruise-ship days, the place overflows. The
restaurant serves both lunch and dinner. Smoked salmon with horseradish leads
off the list of appetizers, or you may prefer to begin with shrimp soup. From the
grill, you can order a 16-ounce T-bone steak, or perhaps you may want to try one
of the chef's specialties such as veal with fruit sauce. A limited selection of international desserts such as coffee mousse tops a most recommendable repast.
You'll spend from $20 to $30. You can dress casually and enjoy your meal in
air-conditioned comfort. Lunch is served from noon to 2 p.m. Monday to Friday. Dinner is nightly from 6:30 to 11. There's a cozy disco called Infinity in the
lower depths, open from 9 p.m. to 2 a.m. nightly. It has an intimate atmosphere,
a waterfall wall, and good music.

La Bistroëlle, Astroidenweg/Schottegatweg in the Promenade Shopping
Center (tel. 011-599-9/76929), is an elegant, family-run restaurant with an international cuisine and a good selection of wines, all served in a cozy, atmospheric place. The decor is one of high-backed chairs, brick accents, stucco, darkened
beams, and rustic chandeliers, like a French country inn. The location is in a residential area east of the harbor, a short drive from the center of Willemstad. The
continental cuisine is largely French, beginning with such selections as snails in
herb garlic butter. You might prefer instead mussels in a light whisky sauce. A rich
fish soup is served and a steaming French onion soup. Some of the chef's specialties include octopus in a vinaigrette sauce, sole Picasso, lobster thermidor, and
chicken saltimbocca. For dessert, you might prefer the crêpes suzette flavored
with Curaçao, for two people. A complete meal will run from 75 NAf ($42). The
place is open daily from noon to 2 p.m. and 7 to 11 p.m.

Rijsttafel Restaurant Indonesia and **Holland Club Bar,** 13 Mercuriusstraat
in Cerrito (tel. 011-599-9/612606), is the best place to go on the island to sample the Indonesian rijsttafel, the traditional rice table with all the zesty side
dishes. You're allowed to season your plate with peppers rated hot, very hot, and
palate-melting. You must ask a taxi to take you to this villa in the suburbs. The site
is near Salinja. The Holland Club bar is only for diners and their guests, who can
visit daily from noon to 2 p.m. and 6 to 9:30 p.m. except for lunch Sunday. At
lunchtime, the selection of dishes is more modest, but for dinner, Javanese cooks
prepare the specialty of the house, a rijsttafel consisting of 16, 20, or 25 dishes.
Warming trays are placed on your table and the service is buffet style. It's best to
go to this place with a party so that all of you can share in the fun and feast. A
dinner for two will cost $25 to $40. Before going you should call to make a reservation.

Bistro Le Clochard, on the Otrabanda side of the pontoon bridge (tel. 011-
599-9/625666), has been snugly fitted into the grim ramparts of Fort Rif at the
gateway to the harbor. Its entrance is marked with a brown canopy, which leads
into a series of rooms, each built under the stucco vaulting of the old Dutch fort.
Only one table has a view of the water, since the only window is the rectangular

opening that was formerly used to receive munitions from the adjacent stone quay. Overall, the colors are warm, reflecting copper utensils and exposed brick. A simulated grape arbor was installed above the bar of the pub area, Le Brick, where a piano sometimes provides live music. The place is well run, and the owners seem to anticipate the needs of their patrons. Cuisine is basically French, including a few dishes from the Alps such as raclette and two kinds of fondue. Dishes change every week, but the fare is likely to include roast hare flambéed in Calvados with a cream sauce, medallions of venison with a wild game sauce, guinea fowl with paprika, ham, garlic, and white wine, and wild boar chops in a mushroom-cream sauce. A full dinner will cost from $30. Lunches are less expensive. The restaurant is open from noon to 3 p.m. and 6:30 to 11 p.m. except Saturday at lunch and all day Sunday.

Wine Cellar, Ooststraat/Concordiastraat (tel. 011-599-9/612178), opposite the cathedral, is the domain of Leo and Renée Boogaard, who have one of the most extensive wine cartes on the island. They welcome you to air-conditioned comfort in their Victoriana dining room, as you slowly make your wine selection for the evening. Food isn't ignored either. The kitchen has good meat dishes, well prepared, and a limited selection of seafood. Count on spending from $25 for a meal, plus the cost of your wine. There are only eight tables, so reservations are essential. Hours are noon to 2 p.m. and 6 p.m. till "whenever." Only dinner is served Saturday and Sunday; closed Monday.

Le Recif (tel. 011-599-9/623824) is lodged under the arches of Fort Rif, near the shuttlebus stops for the Otrabanda hotels and the pontoon bridge. This place used to be a prison, but now it's one of the best places in town for Caribbean seafood. Its interior is festooned with fish nets and nautical implements hanging just below the vaulted ceilings. A terrace in front extends the darkly lit interior out into the sunshine. Full meals range from 60 NAf ($33.60) and might include shrimp Créole, Curaçao fish stew, red snapper Cordon Bleu, and conch soup. The ingredients for the seafood come either from neighboring waters, from Haiti, or from the Dominican Republic. Le Recif serves meals from noon to 2 p.m. and 6 to 11 p.m. Monday to Friday, with dinner the only meal offered on Saturday and Sunday.

Belle Terrace, Avila Beach Hotel, 130-134 Penstraat (tel. 011-599-9/614377), is an open-air restaurant in a 200-year-old mansion on the beachfront of Willemstad. In a relaxed and informal atmosphere, it offers split-level dining. The Schooner Bar, where you can enjoy a rum punch, is shaped like a weather-beaten ship's prow looking out to sea, with a thatch roof projecting from its mast. The restaurant, sheltered by an arbor of flamboyant branches, features Scandinavian and local cuisine with such special dishes as pickled herring, barracuda, and a Danish lunch platter. Local dishes, such as sopito (fish soup with coconut flavor) and keshi yena (Edam cheese stuffed with chicken, olives, raisins, and sweet peppers), are on the menu for both lunch and dinner. A special three-course meal is served every night except Saturday, in addition to a full à la carte menu. On Saturday night the chef has a beef tenderloin barbecue and a help-yourself salad bar. Fish is always fresh at Belle Terrace, and the chef prepares the catch of the day to perfection: grilled, poached, meunière, or amandine. Desserts include Danish pastry and cakes, as well as a cocoa sherbet served in a coconut shell. Expect to spend $10 to $18 for lunch, $22 to $28 for dinner. The special three-course dinner costs $22. It is open daily from noon to 2 p.m. and 7 to 9:30 p.m.

Bistro Larousse, 5 Penstraat (tel. 011-599-9/55418), built in 1742, is a typical little stone and plaster house with ornate edging on its roof. It is owned by Holland-born Nico Cornelisse, who installed a collection of 19th-century artifacts under the original beamed ceiling and extended the dining area onto an alcove-style second floor. Amid Colombian-made copper and iron chandeliers,

Victorian etched-globe lighting, and Oriental rugs, visitors are served on flow-ered china the foods they have chosen from well-prepared specialties. These in-clude cheese fondue for two people, red snapper Curaçao style, a soup made from fresh cherry tomatoes, beef Stroganoff, and several kinds of steaks. A dessert specialty is Dutch egg liqueur and fresh whipped cream laced with vanilla or chocolate fondue according to an old Swiss recipe. Full meals range from 85 NAf ($47.60). The establishment is open only for dinner from 6 p.m. to midnight daily.

Fort Waakzaamheid Tavern, Seru di Domi, Otrabanda (tel. 011-599-9/ 623633), was the old fort that Captain Bligh of *Bounty* fame captured in 1804. He laid seige to Willemstad for almost a month. In the fort a stone-and-hardwood tavern and restaurant have been installed, opening onto a view of the Otrabanda and the harbor entrance. The atmosphere is that of a country tavern. On the dinner menu, the fish soup will get you going, and you can follow with curried veal, Wiener schnitzel, or garlic shrimp. Lobster is the most expensive item on the menu, and you may settle instead for Curaçao snapper. Each day a fresh fried fish is offered, with a salad. Meals run from $20. The fort is open daily except Tuesday from 7 to 11 p.m. The bar remains open until 1 a.m. (even later on weekends).

Rodeo Ranch Saloon & Steakhouse, on Van Staverenweg in the suburban section of Cas Cora (tel. 011-599-9/615757), is a lot of fun. Stanley Gibbs and his Netherlands-born wife, Kathe, have created a touch of the Old West. There's a replica of a covered wagon set over the entrance, and an interior decor of rough-sawn planking, dark woods, and antique wagon wheels. So many guests of this popular place have attached their business cards to a bulletin board near the kitchen that it reads like a lesson in international geography. A "sheriff" (usually Stanley) greets visitors at the door in an outfit that includes a ten-gallon hat and a silver star. No one will mind if you just stop in for a drink at the dimly lit bar, but if you want one of the most generous dinners in town, you'll be presented with a cowhide-covered menu by a cowgirl/waitress. To the sounds of country and western music, you'll enjoy the specialties of steak, soup from the kettle, a chuck-wagon choice of potato specials, roast prime rib, and seafood. All steaks are U.S. prime beef, and are accompanied by as many visits as you want to make to the soup and salad bar. Don't dress up to go here. Casual is the keynote. You'll spend $25 for a full meal, which you can enjoy in air-conditioned comfort. Hot snacks are served at the happy hour from 5 to 7 p.m. Lunch is offered daily from noon to 2 p.m., with dinner from 5:30 to 11 p.m. The bar remains open till "whenever."

Bellevue Restaurant, Baai Macolaweg, Parera (tel. 011-599-9/54291), is in an edifice built in 1942 by the Americans as headquarters for the naval base protecting the island's oil refineries. In the late 1970s it was purchased by the Den Dulk family, whose culinary skills quickly made it one of the leading restaurants on the island. A trio of imitation palm trees decks the sunny interior, which sometimes hosts some of the biggest landowners on the island. It's run by Martin and Curaçao-born Johanna, with their son, Martin Jr. (winner of an island-wide contest to design the Curaçao national flag). They adhere strictly to local culinary lore in the preparation of their specialties. Your meal could begin with a bandera. Loaded with cream, "secret ingredients," and Curaçao rum, it is the first blue drink many visitors have ever tried, and its smooth, not-too-sweet flavor is delicious. This could be followed with oyster soup, cactus soup, stewed goat meat, a tasty okra soup, sauerkraut stew, papaya stew, shark meat, stewed cucumbers, or Edam cheese stuffed with meat and spices. Patrons looking for a cross-sampling of the local dishes might try the funchi table, which includes five local viands on one savory platter. The restaurant is open seven days a week, from noon to 2 p.m. and 7 to 10 p.m. Full meals range upward in price from around 55 NAf ($30.80).

Pisces Seafood, 476 Caracasbaaiweg (tel. 011-599-9/672181). This West Indian restaurant may be difficult to find, set as it is on a flat industrial coastline near a marina and an oil refinery, about 20 minutes from the capital. There's been a restaurant here since the 1930s, when sailors and workers from the oil refinery came for home-cooked meals. Today the simple frame building offers seating near the rough-hewn bar or in a breeze-swept inner room whose unglazed, open windows have hinged shutters to seal them off after closing. Pisces serves combinations of seafood that depend on the catch of the local fishermen. Main courses, served with rice, vegetables, and plantains, might include sopi, "seacat" (squid), mula (similar to kingfish), shark meat, red snapper, or any of these served, if you wish, in copious quantities for two or more persons in the Pisces platter. Shrimp and conch are each prepared three different ways: with garlic, with curry, or Créole style. Average meals cost from $20. The restaurant is open daily from noon to midnight.

Golden Star, 2 Socratesstraat (tel. 011-599-9/54795), is the best place to go on the island for "criollo" or local food. Inland from the coast road, leading southeast from St. Anna Bay, the air-conditioned restaurant is very simple, evoking a roadside diner. But it has a large menu of native dishes that are very tasty. Such Antillean dishes are featured as *carco stoba* (conch stew) and *bestia chiki* (goat-meat stew). Try also *bakijauw* (salted cod) and *concomber stoba* (stewed meat and marble-size spiny cucumbers). Other specialties include criollo shrimps (kiwa) and soppi carni. Everything is served with a side order of funchi, the cornmeal staple. Meals cost from 30 NAf ($16.80). The place is very friendly, and has a large local following with an occasional tourist dropping in. It's open daily from 11 a.m. till 1 a.m. The location is at the corner of Dr. Hugenholtzweg and Dr. Maalweg.

'T Kokkeltje, Hotel Holland, 524 F. D. Rooseveltweg (tel. 011-599-9/88044), is directed by Hans Vrolijk, an ex-frogman with the Dutch navy. This warmly decorated hideaway is especially popular around happy hour after most people finish daily work. You'll find the place on the scrub-bordered road leading to the airport, a few minutes away from the landing strips. If you want to follow your drinks with dinner, full meals cost from 55 NAf ($28) and include such specialties as nasi goreng, fresh fish in season, Dutch-style steak, Wiener schnitzel, Caribbean-style chicken, and split-pea soup. All dishes are accompanied by fresh vegetables and Dutch-style potatoes. Patrons enjoy their meals around the pool outside or in a paneled and intimately lit room near the bar. Hours are 7 a.m. to 11 p.m. daily.

Playa Forti, in the Westpunt area (tel. 011-599-9/640273), is a good address to know if you're touring the island. The restaurant is built on the foundation of a fortress dating from Bonaparte's day. Not only do you get good local food here, but one of the most spectacular sea views on the island. International dishes are presented, but it would be wiser to order some of the Antillean specialties, such as succulent goat stew which tastes a bit like veal. It's called *cabrito*. Try also keshi yena, a tasty mixture of beef and chicken, which has been pickled and cooked with tomatoes and onions, then wrapped in Edam cheese. *Ayaca* is a combination of chicken and beef, with olives, raisins, nuts, and spices wrapped in a soft corndough tortilla (it's packed and cooked in banana leaves). The fish soup makes a zesty opening. It's called *sopi di plata*. Or try the fried red snapper Curaçao style—that is, fried a golden brown, then covered in a sauce of tomatoes, onions, and green peppers. It's served with fried plantains and funchi, the local cornmeal preparation. Expect to pay from 35 NAf ($19.60) for a complete meal.

The waters of Westpunt are perfect for snorkeling and scuba-diving if you want to bring your own equipment. In the restaurant food is served from 10 a.m. to 6 p.m. except Monday. If you're touring, it's also possible to drop in for drinks in the afternoon.

EXPLORING CURAÇAO: Most cruise-ship passengers see only Willemstad —or, more accurately, the shops—but you may want to get out into the *cunucu,* or countryside, exploring the towering cacti and rolling hills topped by *landhuizen* (plantation houses) built more than three centuries ago. The 38-mile-long island can be seen in a day or so.

Willemstad

In Willemstad the Dutch found a vast natural harbor, a perfect hideaway along the Spanish Main. Not only is Willemstad the capital of Curaçao, it is also the seat of government for the Netherlands Antilles.

The city grew up on both sides of the canal. Today it is divided into the **Punda** and the **Otrabanda,** the latter literally meaning "the other side." Both sections are connected by the **Queen Emma Pontoon Bridge,** a pedestrian walkway.

Originally, ferryboats linked the two sections of town, since by the mid-19th century Willemstad had spread to both sides of St. Anna Harbor. In 1887 the American consul, Leonard B. Smith, convinced the city fathers that a bridge was a good idea. One year later the swinging pontoon bridge across the harbor opened, and the tolls made Smith a wealthy man. Powered by a diesel engine, it swings open many times every day to let ships from all over the globe pass in and out of the harbor.

The view from the bridge is of the old gabled houses in harmonized pastel shades such as lilac and aquamarine. The bright pastel colors, according to legend, are a holdover from the time when one of the island's early governors is said to have had eye trouble and flat white gave him headaches.

The colonial-style architecture, reflecting the Dutch influence, gives the town a "storybook" look, as is often said. Built three or four stories high, the houses are crowned by "step" gables and roofed with orange Spanish tiles. Hemmed in by the sea, a tiny canal, and an inlet, the streets are narrow, and they're crosshatched by still narrower alleyways. Except for the pastel colors, Willemstad may remind you of old Amsterdam. It has one of the most intriguing townscapes in the Caribbean.

Replacing the pontoon bridge, **Queen Juliana Bridge** opened to vehicular traffic in 1973. Spanning the harbor, it rises 195 feet, the highest bridge in the Caribbean and one of the tallest in the world.

The **Waterfront** originally guarded the mouth of the canal on the eastern or Punda side. Now it's been incorporated into the Curaçao Plaza Hotel.

The task of standing guard has been taken over by **Fort Amsterdam,** site of the Governor's Palace and the 1769 Dutch Reformed Church. The church still has a British cannonball embedded in it. The arches leading to the fort were tunneled under the official residence of the governor.

A corner of the fort stands at the intersection of Breedestraat and Handelskade, the starting point for a plunge into the island's major shopping district.

A few minutes' walk from the pontoon bridge, at the north end of Handelskade, is the **Floating Market,** where scores of schooners tie up alongside the canal, a few yards from the main shopping section. Docked boats arrive from Venezuela and Colombia, as well as other West Indian islands, to sell tropical fruits and vegetables, a little bit of everything in fact. The modern market under its vast cement cap has not replaced this unique shopping expedition which is fun to watch.

Between the I. H. (Sha) Capriles Kade and Fort Amsterdam stands the **Mikve Israel Emanuel Synagogue,** at the corner of Columbusstraat and Kerkstraat. Consecrated on the eve of the Passover in 1732, it antedates the first U.S. synagogue in Newport, Rhode Island, by 31 years. It houses the oldest Jewish congregation in the New World, dating from 1651. One of the oldest synagogue buildings in the western hemisphere, it is a fine example of Dutch colonial architecture, covering about a square block in the heart of Willemstad.

It was built around a Spanish-style walled courtyard, with four large portals. Sand covers the sanctuary floor following a Portuguese Sephardic custom, representing the desert where Israelis camped when the Jews passed from slavery to freedom. Early settlers, led by Samuel Coheno, were Sephardic refugees from a Portuguese pogrom. Four brass chandeliers hang from the arched ceiling.

The *theba* (pulpit) is in the center, and the congregation surrounds it. Highlight of the east wall is the Holy Ark, rising 17 feet, and a raised banca, canopied in mahogany, is on the north wall. The synagogue has services every Friday at 6:30 p.m. and Saturday at 10 a.m.; as well as similar holiday service times. Visitors are welcome to all services, with appropriate dress required.

Adjacent to the synagogue courtyard is the **Jewish Cultural Historical Museum,** housed in two buildings dating back to 1728. They were originally the rabbi's residence and the bathhouse. The 2½-centuries-old *mikvah,* or bath for religious purification purposes, was in constant use until around 1850 when this practice was discontinued and the buildings sold. They have been reacquired through the Foundation for the Preservation of Historic Monuments and turned into the present museum. On display are a great many ritual, ceremonial, and cultural objects, many of which are still in use by the congregation for holidays and life cycle events. The synagogue and museum are open to visitors Monday to Friday from 9 to 11:45 a.m. and 2:30 to 5 p.m. (on Sunday from 9 a.m. to noon if there is a cruise ship in port). There is a $2 entrance fee to the museum. The gift shop is in the synagogue office (tel. 011-599-9/611633).

A statue of Pedro Luís Brion dominates the square known as **Brionplein** right at the Otrabanda end of the pontoon bridge. Born in Curaçao in 1782, he became the island's favorite son and best-known war hero. Under Simón Bolívar, he was an admiral of the fleet and fought for the independence of Venezuela and Colombia.

West of Willemstad

The **Curaçao Museum,** Van Leeuwenhoekstraat (tel. 011-599-9/623777), can be walked to from the Queen Emma pontoon bridge. It was built in 1853 by the Royal Dutch Army Corps of Engineers as a military quarantine hospital for yellow fever victims and was carefully restored in 1946–1948 as a fine example of 19th-century Dutch architecture. Furnished with paintings, objets d'art, and antique furniture made in the 19th century by local cabinet-makers, it re-creates an atmosphere of an era gone by. A novelty is the polka-dot kitchen. The museum contains a large collection from the Caiquetio Indians, the early inhabitants described by Amerigo Vespucci as giants seven-feet tall. There is also a modest Children's Museum of Science in the basement with hands-on exhibits. Future plans call for the display of the fully restored cockpit of the Fokker F-XVIII trimoter which made the first commercial crossing of the southern Atlantic from the Netherlands to Curaçao in 1934. In the gardens are specimens of the island's trees and plants. There is also a reconstruction of a traditional music pavilion in the garden where Curaçao musicians give regular performances. Hours are from 9 a.m. to noon and 2 to 5 p.m. Tuesday to Saturday, 10 a.m. to 4 p.m. Sunday; closed Monday. Admission is 3 NAf ($1.70) for adults, 1.50 NAf (85¢) for children under 14.

The **Curaçao Seaquarium,** off Martin Luther King Boulevard at a site called Bapor Kibrá (tel. 011-599-9/616666), has more than 400 species of fish, crabs, anemones, and other invertebrates, sponges, and coral displayed and growing in a natural environment. This effect is achieved by pumping ocean water into the many pools and tanks so that the sea life indigenous to the area thrives. A rustic boardwalk connects the low-lying hexagonal buildings comprising the Seaquarium complex, erected on a point off which the ship, *Oranje Nassau,* broke up on the rocks and sank in 1903. The name of the site, Bapor Kibrá, means sunken ship. Besides the aquarium, there are two wild waterslides for teenagers and adults, plus a smaller one for small children. You can use the beach and water sports facilities or relax in the seaside bar and restaurant. Seaquarium is open daily from 10 a.m. to 10 p.m. Restaurant hours are 10 a.m. to 9 p.m., and the bar is open from 3 to 10 p.m. Monday to Friday, from 11 a.m. to 10 p.m. on Saturday and Sunday. Admission to the Seaquarium is $5.50 for adults, $2.75 for children under 15 years of age. It's a few minutes' walk along the rocky coast from the Princess Beach Hotel.

The **Curaçao Underwater Park,** established in 1983 with the financial aid of the World Wildlife Fund, stretches from the Princess Beach Hotel to the east point of the island, a strip of about 12½ miles of untouched coral reefs. There are 16 permanent mooring buoys in the park, where dive operators can safely tie up their boats without damage to the coral. Spearfishing, anchoring in the coral, and taking anything from the reefs except photographs are strictly prohibited. For information on snorkeling, scuba-diving, and trips in a glass-bottom boat to view the park, see "The Sporting Life," below.

Traveling northwest along the road, you reach the tip of the island. The **Landhuis Jan Kock,** on the road to Westpunt, is open to the public. Built in 1650, it is probably the oldest building on the island. The owner once stood on its adobe porch to watch slaves gather salt from huge flat fields flooded with sea water left to evaporate in the sun. The house, said to be haunted, was restored as a museum by the late Dr. Jan Diemont in 1960. Inside are many pieces from the 18th and early 19th centuries, including a hurdy-gurdy machine from this century. Daily tours are 9 to 10 a.m. Reserve in advance by phoning 011-599-9/88088).

Out toward the western tip of Curaçao, a high wire fence surrounds the entrance to the 4,500-acre **Christoffel National Park,** about a 45-minute drive from the capital. A macadam road gives way to dirt, surrounded on all sides by abundant cactus and in the higher regions by rare orchids. Rising from flat, arid countryside, 1,230-foot-high St. Christoffelberg is the highest point in the Dutch Leewards. Donkeys, wild goats, iguanas, the Curaçao deer, and many species of birds thrive in this preserve, and there are some Arawak Indian paintings on a coral cliff near the two caves. Piedra di Monton is nothing more than a rockheap accumulated by African slaves who worked on the former plantations. A folk legend passed down through the generations said that any worker would be able to climb to the top of the rockpile, jump off, and fly back home across the Atlantic. If, however, the slave had at any time in his life tasted a grain of salt, the magic would not work and he would crash to his death below. The park has 20 miles of one-way driving trails, with lots of flora and fauna along the way. The shortest trail is about 5 miles long, and because of the rough terrain, takes about 40 minutes to drive through. Various walking trails are available also. One of them will take you to the top of St. Christoffelberg in about 1½ hours. (Come early in the morning when it isn't so hot.) The park is open from 8 a.m. to 3 p.m. (open as early as 6 a.m. on Sunday). Admission is 2 NAf ($1.15). Also en route to

Westpunt, you'll come across a seaside cavern known as Boca Tabla, one of many such grottoes on this rugged, uninhabited north coast.

Playa Forti is a 45-minute ride from Punda in Willemstad. A stark region, it is characterized by soaring hills and towering cacti, along with 200-year-old Dutch land houses, the former mansions that housed the slaveowner plantation heads. For a dining suggestion, see my recommendation of the Playa Forti Restaurant.

North and East of Willemstad

Just northeast of the capital, **Fort Nassau** was completed in 1797 and christened by the Dutch as Fort Republic. It was built high on a hill, overlooking the harbor entrance to the south and St. Anna Bay to the north. It was fortified as a second line of defense in case Waterfort gave way. When the British invaded in 1807, they renamed it Fort George in honor of their own king. Later, when the Dutch regained control, they renamed it Orange Nassau in honor of the Dutch royal family. Today diners have replaced soldiers (see my restaurant recommendations).

Along the coast to the southeast of the town, the oddly shaped **Octagon House** (tel. 011-599-9/623777) on Penstraat was where the liberator, Bolívar, used to visit his two sisters during the wars for Venezuelan independence. Now a museum, it has been restored and furnished with antiques. It also contains some of the liberator's memorabilia. Hours are 8 a.m. to noon and 2 to 6 p.m., Monday through Saturday. No admission is charged.

From the house you can head north, going along the eastern side of the water, to the intersection of Rijkseenheid Boulevard and Fokkerweg. There you'll see the **Autonomy Monument,** a vibrant 20th-century sculpture representing the Dutch islands as birds feed from their nest.

In the area, the **Amstel Brewery** allows visitors to tour its plant where Curaçao beer is brewed from desalinated seawater. Hours are Tuesday from 10 a.m. to noon (telephone 011-599-9/612944 for more information).

In addition, the **Curaçao Liqueur Distillery,** P.O. Box 3353, offers free tours and tastes at Chobolobo, the 17th-century landhuis where the famous liqueur is made. Tours are Monday through Friday from 8 a.m. to noon and 1 to 5 p.m. (call 011-599-9/613526 for more information). The cordial, named after the region where it originated, is a distillate of dried peel of a particular strain of orange found only in Curaçao. Several herbs are added to give it an aromatic bouquet. It's made by a secret formula handed down through generations. One of the rewards of a visit here is a free snifter of the liqueur at the culmination of the tour.

On Schottegatweg West, lying northwest of Willemstad, past the oil refineries, lies the **Beth Haim Cemetery,** oldest Caucasian burial site still in use in the western hemisphere. Meaning "House of Life," the cemetery was consecrated before 1659. On about three acres are some 2,500 graves. The carving on some of the 17th- and 18th-century tombstones is exceptional.

Landhuis Brievengat (tel. 011-599-9/78344) gives visitors a chance to visit a Dutch version of an 18th-century West Indian plantation house. This stately building, set into a scrub-dotted landscape on the eastern side of the island, contains a few antiques, high ceilings, and a frontal gallery facing two entrance towers, said to have been used to imprison slaves and even for romantic trysts. The plantation was originally used for the cultivation of aloe and cattle, but an 1877 hurricane killed more than three-quarters of the livestock and the plantation operation ceased. The building was pulled down and the land purchased by Shell Oil. Around 1925 the remains of the structure were donated to the Society for the Preservation of Monuments, which rebuilt and restored it. Today it receives visitors for $1 daily from 9:30 a.m. to 12:30 p.m. and 3 to 6 p.m. Every Friday night, an exotic Indonesian dinner is served at the landhuis, for about $15. You can dance to local musical groups and experience an authentic island ambience. On the last Sunday of each month an open house is held, with folkloric dances and other activities. Local food specialties are served.

A SHOPPING EXPEDITION: The place is a shopper's paradise. Some 200 shops line the major shopping malls of such wooden-shoe-named streets as Heerenstraat and Breedestraat. Right in the heart of Willemstad, the **Punda** shopping area is a five-block district. Most stores are open Monday through Saturday from 8 a.m. to noon and 2 to 6 p.m. (some from 8 a.m. to 6 p.m.). When cruise ships are in port, stores are also open for a few hours on Sunday and holidays. To avoid the cruise-ship crowds, do your own shopping in the morning.

Look for good buys in French perfumes, Dutch Delft blue souvenirs, finely woven Italian silks, Japanese and German cameras, jewelry, silver, Swiss watches, linens, leather goods, liquor, and island-made rum and liqueurs, especially Curaçao.

Incidentally, Curaçao is not technically a free port, but its prices are low because of its low import duty.

I always head first to the legendary **Spritzer & Fuhrmann** (tel. 011-599-9/ 612600), on a corner of vehicle-free Gomezplein, the leading jewelers of the Netherlands Antilles. This name stands for great values, service, and integrity, whether you buy a $50,000 diamond ring or a $50 gold chain. The finest Swiss watches are found here. In addition to the main store, there are other S&F specialty stores in the heart of Curaçao, carrying fine china and crystal. You will find names like Waterford, Baccarat, Lalique, Hummel, and Lladró among their stock.

Penha & Sons, 1 Heerenstraat (tel. 011-599-9/612266), occupies the oldest building in town, built in 1708. Established in 1865, they're the distributor of such names as Chanel, Jean Patou, Yves Saint Laurent, and other perfumes, and cosmetics of Lancôme, Clinique, Clarins, and Estée Lauder, among others. The collection of merchandise at this prestigious store is quite varied—Hummel figurines and Delft blue souvenirs. Don't miss their men's and ladies' boutiques, where they feature travel- and sportswear. The firm has 14 other stores in Curaçao, Aruba, and St. Maarten.

Gandelman Jewelers, 35 Breedestraat (tel. 011-599-9/611854), has a large selection of fine jewelry set with diamonds, rubies, sapphires, emeralds, and other stones. Exclusive here is the Gucci line of handbags, wallets, belts, ties, scarves, and many other items. You will also find Swiss timepieces by Baume & Mercier, Raymond Weil, and Heuer, among others. Gandelman Jewelers has six stores in Aruba and Curaçao.

Boolchand's, 4B Heerenstraat, Punda (tel. 011-599-9/612798), features Seiko and Citizen watches and a complete line of cameras, photo, and audio-video equipment. A branch store, La Fortunata, has clothing for men, women, and children. Boolchand's has been in business since 1930.

On Gomezplein, you'll find the **New Amsterdam Store** (tel. 011-599-9/ 612437), on the corner of the popular plaza. On the ground floor they offer hand-embroidered wash-and-wear linens at 25% off. There's a wide selection of Swiss watches, including Oris and Seiko, gold and silver jewelry from Italy. In an upstairs sports boutique they stock a complete line of Adidas, Nike, and all kinds of sneakers as well as beachwear.

Kan Jewelers, 44 Breedestraat, Punda (tel. 011-599-9/612111), has been in the jewelry business for more than half a century. Its Willemstad store is in an

18th-century gabled building. They feature a superb collection of 14- and 18-karat gold jewelry, as well as famous brand Swiss watches, such as Rolex. They also carry an exclusive line of Rosenthal china, crystal, and flatware.

The **Yellow House (La Casa Amarilla),** on Breedestraat (tel. 011-599-9/613222), is housed in a 19th-century yellow-and-white building. It's been operating since 1887, selling an intriguing collection of perfume from all over the world, and is the exclusive distributor of such names as Christian Dior, Guerlain, and Van Cleef & Arpels.

Obra di Man, 57 Bargestraat (tel. 011-599-9/612413), is filled with authentic local handcraft items, including printed T-shirts, handmade dolls, hand-screened fabrics, carved driftwood, and filigree jewelry. They also have some merchandise from the Netherlands.

Boutique Gina, in the Curaçao Caribbean Shopping Gallery (tel. 011-599-9/625042), has some of the most sophisticated sportswear for women to be found on the island. They offer Triumph, Gottex, and Solar among their swimwear. Handbags, hats, T-shirts, costume jewelry, and batik clothing from Bangkok are also to be found here.

Bert Knubben Black Coral, at the Princess Beach Hotel, P.O. Box 2050 (tel. 011-599-9/614944), is a name synonymous with craftsmanship and quality. Although collection of black coral has been made illegal by the Curaçao government, an exception was made for Bert, a diver who has been harvesting corals from the sea and fashioning them into fine jewelry and objets d'art for more than 30 years.

THE SPORTING LIFE: Its beaches are not as good as Aruba's seven-mile strip of sand, but Curaçao does have some 38 beaches, ranging from hotel sands to secluded coves. Thirty minutes from town, in the Willibrordus area on the south side of Curaçao, **Daaibooi** is a good beach. It's free but there are no changing facilities. A good private beach on the eastern side of the island is **Santa Barbara Beach,** between the open sea and the island's primary water-sports and recreational area known as Spanish Water. It is on land owned by a mining company. On the same land are Table Mountain, a remarkable landmark, and an old phosphate mine. The natural beach has pure white sand and calm water. A buoy line protects swimmers against motor- and sailboats. Restrooms, changing rooms, a snackbar, and a terrace are among the amenities. You can rent water bicycles and small motorboats. The cost is 6NAf ($3.36) per carload of people. The beach, open daily from 8 a.m. to 6 p.m., has access to the Curaçao Underwater Park.

Water Sports

Most hotels offer their own programs of water sports. However, if your hotel isn't equipped, I suggest that you head for one of the most complete water-sports facilities in Curaçao, **Curaçao Seascape Dive and Watersports,** at the Curaçao Caribbean Hotel (tel. 011-599-9/625000, ext. 177). Specializing in snorkeling and scuba-diving trips to reefs and underwater wrecks, it operates from a hexagonal kiosk set on stilts above the water, just offshore from the hotel's beach.

Open from 9 a.m. to 4 p.m. seven days a week, the company offers snorkeling excursions for $15 per person, glassbottom-boat rides for $6, pedalboats for $10 per hour, powerful water scooters for $20 per half hour, waterskiing for $30 per half hour, and windsurfing at $20 per 1½ hours. A Sunfish rents for $20, and an introductory scuba lesson, conducted by a competent diver, goes for $30. Packages of four dives cost $90. Bottom fishing, with all equipment included, aboard a 22-foot Aquasport, is $100 for a half day, $180 for a full day. One trip enthusiastically endorsed by some readers departs from the hotel at 7 a.m., when participation warrants. The destination is Little Curaçao, midway between Curaçao and Bonaire. Clothes are optional once you get to the sugar-white sands of the island. Fishing, snorkeling, and the acquisition of an "overall tan" are highlights. The price is $40 per person, and the excursion lasts all day. Another possibility is a boat ride to one of Curaçao's more isolated beaches, Santa Barbara Beach. A full day's outing is $30 per person.

They can also arrange deep-sea fishing for $225 for a half-day tour carrying a maximum of six people, $425 for a full day. Drinks and equipment are included, but you'll have to get your hotel to pack your lunch.

Underwater Curaçao, adjacent to Curaçao Seaquarium and Curaçao Underwater Park (tel. 011-599-9/616666), has a complete underwater sports program. A fully stocked modern dive shop has retail and rental equipment. Peter Hughes designed the state-of-the-art dive boats used by the trained staff for instruction and scuba-diving. Individual dives and dive packages are offered, costing $25 for one dive, $120 for a six-dive package. A six-day unlimited package, including one night boat dive, is priced at $225. Complete vacation/dive packages are offered through cooperation of Curaçao's top resorts, including Holiday Beach Hotel, Golden Tulip Las Palmas, and the Princess Beach Hotel.

Scuba-divers and snorkelers can expect spectacular scenery in waters with visibility often exceeding 100 feet at the **underwater park** off the Princess Beach Hotel. There are steep walls, two shallow wrecks, lush gardens of soft corals, and more than 30 species of hard corals. Although access from shore is possible at Jan Thiel Bay and Santa Barbara Beach, most people visit the park by boat. For easy and safe mooring, the park has 16 mooring buoys, placed at the best dive and snorkel sites. A snorkel trail with underwater interpretive markers is laid out just east of the Princess Beach Hotel and is accessible from shore.

Santa Barbara Beach tours are also offered aboard the glassbottom boat, costing $15 per person and lasting four hours. A stop is made for snorkeling at *Towboat,* the wreck of a tug in shallow water, with snorkel equipment provided. Snacks and drinks are available at the beach. You can also take a one-hour trip into the Curaçao Underwater Park in the glassbottom boat for $5 per person.

Underwater Curaçao has a cabin cruiser available for half- or full-day deep-sea fishing trips. One to four people can make a half-day excursion for $150, the same number paying $250 for a full day. If you prefer bottom fishing, they'll take you to the best ocean spots, charging $125 for half a day for one to four people. Bait, lines, tackle, and soft drinks are provided.

A dive facility has been opened at **Golden Tulip Coral Cliff Resort and Beach Club,** Santa Marta Bay, P.O. Box 3782 (tel. 011-599-9/641610), with an extensive stock of equipment for rent or sale. PADI certified instruction in scuba diving is available for novices as well as expert divers. Swimming, snorkeling, windsurfing, sailing, and fishing are also offered.

Fishing

Chirino Sport Dòbel 6, 12 Orionweg, Zeelandia (tel. 011-599-9/613346), offers fishing trips aboard powerful boats, with sandwiches, refreshments, fresh fruits, and vegetables included in the prices. A four-hour trip costs $225 for three people, $12 for each additional person. Full-day (eight-hour) expeditions, are priced at $400 for three and an additional $20 for each extra person. Besides those voyages, Chirino has a combination of bottom fishing at from 6 to 10 p.m., plus trawling trips during the day. They do that at Klein Curaçao (Little Curaçao), the small island 15 miles southwest of the east point of Curaçao, right in the fishing grounds. Chirino has overnight facilities, and breakfast, lunch, dinner, refreshments, and fruit are included. The price for this overnight expedition is $650 for three people, $50 for each additional passenger.

Boating Tours
Taber Tours, Maduro Plaza, 19 Emancipatie Blvd. (tel. 011-599-9/ 76637), offers trips by sea as well as the sightseeing tours by bus recommended earlier. A combination sea excursion takes you to the Seaquarium, for a swim at Santa Barbara Beach, over the underwater park by glass-bottom boat, and snorkeling at a wreck (snorkeling equipment included). Soft drinks are served on board, and transportation to and from your hotel is provided. The cost is $27.50 per person for adults, $17.50 for children under 12. A sunset sailing trip, costing $25 for adults, $15 for children, includes two hours of sailing while you feast on cheese, French bread, and wine. A daytime trip, with lunch included, is the Coral sailing tour. You're picked up at your hotel, taken on a sailing trip to Santa Martha Bay, and served a light lunch at the Coral Cliff Hotel, where you can use all the hotel's facilities, including snorkeling gear. Beer and soft drinks are served during the sail. The cost is $35 for adults, $25 for children.

Tennis
There are courts at the Curaçao Caribbean, Golden Tulip Las Palmas, Princess Beach, and Holiday Beach Hotels. Las Palmas's court is open 24 hours a day.

Golf
Curaçao Golf and Squash Club in Emmastad is open to the general public by arrangement only. Telephone the day before you wish to play (tel. 011-599-9/62664). Greens fees are $10. Equipment can be rented at $3 for clubs, $2 for a pull cart, and $15 for an electric cart. The course is open on Monday from 8 a.m. to noon and 1 to 7 p.m. Other days, it's open from 8 a.m. to noon and 1 to 8 p.m., except that on Saturday and Sunday there's no lunch break.

A Fitness Center
Chirino, a sport and recreation center at 12 Orionweg, Zeelandia (tel. 011-599-9/613346), has fully equipped studios for bodybuilding, fitness training, jazz dancing, massage, and sauna. Programs for youngsters can be found in the kiddies' gym and *arte infantil,* where children learn to dance, act, sing, and play. Chirino is open from 7:30 to 10 a.m. and 4 to 9 p.m.

AFTER DARK: Most of the action spins around six **casinos** at the Curaçao Caribbean, the Holiday Beach, the Princess Beach, the Curaçao Plaza, and the Golden Tulip Las Palmas, all hotels previously recommended. These hotel gaming houses usually start their action at 2 p.m., and some of them remain open until 4 a.m. The Princess Beach serves complimentary drinks.

Sometimes a sailor in port heads for **Campo Alegre,** known as "the compound." Others refer to it as "happy valley." This is the most famous, or notorious, bordello in the Caribbean. In the vicinity of the airport, the bordello is privately run, but under strict government controls. Controls or not, business is way down because of the fear of AIDS.

The **Willemstad Room** at the Curaçao Caribbean (tel. 011-599-9/625000) books some of the best acts on the island. There are two dinner seatings, one at 7 p.m. and again at 9 p.m., with meals costing from $25. For current shows, check the bulletin board in the hotel's lobby or else call. Remember to make a reservation in season, as the room can fill up quickly with the hotel's own guests. Live entertainment is offered nightly except Wednesday, with show time at 11 p.m. The minimum consumption is about $10 per person.

Sabine's, Curaçao Plaza Hotel (tel. 011-599-9/612500). On the mezzanine level of Willemstad's most prominent hotel, this disco and nightclub has traditionally employed some of the best DJs on the island. Amid a blue-and-red decor dotted with artificial stars are three different bars and an animated crowd. Open seven nights a week from 10 p.m. to 3 a.m., the club asks $10 per person as a cover on Friday and Saturday. On other nights entrance is free. Live entertainment is sometimes offered between disco sessions.

La Fontaine Discothèque Night Club, 78 Cas Coraweg (tel. 011-599-9/ 73596), about a ten-minute taxi ride from the center of Willemstad, is one of the most sophisticated after-dark spots on the island. It has a modern design and an array of psychedelic lighting. This disco/nightclub occasionally has live shows. It's open from 10 p.m. to 4 p.m. Tuesday through Sunday, with drinks costing from $3. There's a $6 cover on weekends.

The **Holiday Beach Hotel and Casino,** 31 Pater Euwensweg (tel. 011-599-9/625400), presents some of the splashiest musical comedies and revues in Curaçao. You get the show and dinner for $28 per person. Dinner is served from 7 to 8:30 p.m., with show time at 9 p.m. A cocktail show, costing $15 and including two drinks, is at 11 p.m. On Friday and Saturday a Night Owl show, also costing $15 and including two drinks per person, is presented at 1 a.m. Reservations are required.

Studio Club, 2 Ontarioweg, Salinja (tel. 011-599-9/612272), is a place to come just for drinks if you wish, but you can also dance as much as you want to from 9 p.m. until 4 a.m., except on Monday, when it's closed, and on Friday and Saturday, when live shows feature local and international artists. On weekends, a cover charge of 15 NAf ($8.40) is levied, and reservations are advisable.

The **Temple Theater** (tel. 011-599-9/613410) is a restored landmark in the heart of Willemstad on the Wilhelminaplein by the Waterfort, built in 1867. A comfortable, air-conditioned, modern, multipurpose theater, it presents movies, plays, concerts, and stage shows.

Index

Maison de la Canne (near Trois-îlets), 442
Malecón (Santo Domingo), 220
Mandeville (Jamaica), 427–9
Maracas Beach (Trinidad), 640
Mariaco (Puerto Rico), 106
Marie-Galante (French West Indies), 488–90
Marigot (St. Martin), 490–1
  restaurants in and around, 497–500
  shopping, 502–4
Marigot Bay (St. Lucia), 547
  restaurants, 545–6
Marina Cay (British Virgin Islands), 188
Marley (Bob) Museum (Kingston), 376
Marriqua Valley (St. Vincent), 561
Marshall's Pen (Mandeville), 427, 429
Martha Brae (Montego Bay), 416
Martinique (French West Indies), 430–60
  Fort-de-France, 434–41; accommodations in and around, 435–6, 438; map of, 437; restaurants, 438–40; shopping, 440–1; sights and attractions, 434–5
  map of, 433
  nightlife and entertainment, 459–60
  north loop, 450–6; Basse-Pointe, 453–4; Grand Rivière, 454; Layritz, 452–3; Le Carbet, 450–1; Le François, 455–6; Le Prêcheur, 451–2; Le Robert, 455; Lorrain, 454; Montagne Pelée, 452; Sainte-Marie, 454; St-Pierre, 451; Trinité, 454–5
  Pointe du Bout, 442–3
  practical facts, 433–4
  shopping, 440–2
  sights and attractions; carnival, 434
  south loop, 446–50; Anse-à-Ane, 446–7; Anse d'Arlet, 447; Grande Anse, 447; Le Diamont, 447–8; Sainte-Anne, 448–50
  sports, 456–9
  transportation to and within, 431–3
  Trois-îlets, 442
Maskehorne Hill (Saba), 358
Mayagüez (Puerto Rico), 105–6
  accommodations, 93–4
Mayreau (The Grenadines), 572–3
Megaliths, Antigua, 269
Mercado Modelo (Santo Domingo), 222
Metric system, 35
Mico College (Kingston), 375
Mikve Israel Emanuel Synagogue (Willemstad), 701
Milk River Mineral Bath (near Kingston), 429

Miramar (San Juan, PR):
  accommodations, 68–9
  restaurants, 77–8
Misericordia, Puerta de la (Santo Domingo), 220
Miskito Cove (Montego Bay), 417
Mona Island (Puerto Rico), 106
Montagne Pelée (Martinique), 452
Montego Bay (Jamaica), 406–21
  accommodations, 406–12; first-class, 410–11; inclusive resorts, 408–10; less-expensive, 411–12; luxury, 406–8
  nightlife and entertainment, 420–1
  restaurants, 412–16
  shopping, 419–20
  sights and attractions, 416–19; Reggae Sunsplash Festival, 365–6
  sports, 366–8
Montserrat (British Leeward Islands), 249, 277–87
  accommodations, 279–81
  nightlife and entertainment, 286–7
  practical facts, 279
  restaurants, 281–4
  shopping, 285–6
  sights and attractions, 284–5
  sports, 286
  transportation to and within, 278–9
Montserrat Museum, 284–5
Morgan Lewis Mill (Barbados), 616
Morgan Lewis Sugar Windmill and Museum (Barbados), 618
Morne Lurin (St. Barthélemy), restaurants, 516–17
Morne Trois Pitons National Park (Dominica), 532
Mosquito Island (British Virgin Islands), 200–1
Moule-à-Chique (St. Lucia), 548
Musée Départmental de la Martinique (Fort-de-France), 435
Museo Arubano (Aruba), 666–7
Mustique (The Grenadines), 568–9

Nassau, Fort (Curaçao), 703
National Arena (Kingston), 375
National Heroes Park (Kingston), 375
National Library of Jamaica (Kingston), 375–6
National Museum and Art Gallery (Port-of-Spain), 638
National Palace (Santo Domingo), 220–1
National Pantheon (Santo Domingo), 219–20
National Stadium (Kingston), 375
National Zoological Park (Santo Domingo), 221
Navy Island (Jamaica), 388

NOW, SAVE MONEY ON ALL YOUR TRAVELS!
Join Frommer's™ Dollarwise® Travel Club

Saving money while traveling is never a simple matter, which is why, over 27 years ago, the **Dollarwise Travel Club** was formed. Actually, the idea came from readers of the Frommer publications who felt that such an organization could bring financial benefits, continuing travel information, and a sense of community to economy-minded travelers all over the world.

In keeping with the money-saving concept, the annual membership fee is low—$18 (U.S. residents) or $20 U.S. (Canadian, Mexican, and foreign residents)—and is immediately exceeded by the value of your benefits which include:

1. The latest edition of any TWO of the books listed on the following pages.

2. A copy of any Frommer City Guide.

3. An annual subscription to an 8-page quarterly newspaper *The Dollarwise Traveler* which keeps you up-to-date on fastbreaking developments in good-value travel in all parts of the world—bringing you the kind of information you'd have to pay over $35 a year to obtain elsewhere. This consumer-conscious publication also includes the following columns:

Hospitality Exchange—members all over the world who are willing to provide hospitality to other members as they pass through their home cities.

Share-a-Trip—requests from members for travel companions who can share costs and help avoid the burdensome single supplement.

Readers Ask . . . Readers Reply—travel questions from members to which other members reply with authentic firsthand information.

4. Your personal membership card which entitles you to purchase through the club all Frommer publications for a third to a half off their regular retail prices during the term of your membership.

So why not join this hardy band of international Dollarwise travelers now and participate in its exchange of information and hospitality? Simply send $18 (U.S. residents) or $20 U.S. (Canadian, Mexican, and other foreign residents) along with your name and address to: Frommer's Dollarwise Travel Club, Inc., Gulf + Western Building, One Gulf + Western Plaza, New York, NY 10023. Remember to specify which *two* of the books in section (1) and which *one* in section (2) above you wish to receive in your initial package of member's benefits. Or tear out the next page, check off your choices, and send the page to us with your membership fee.

FROMMER BOOKS
PRENTICE HALL TRAVEL
ONE GULF + WESTERN PLAZA
NEW YORK, NY 10023

Date_____

Friends:
Please send me the books checked below:

FROMMER™ GUIDES

(Guides to sightseeing and tourist accommodations and facilities from budget to deluxe, with emphasis on the medium-priced.)

☐ Alaska $13.95	☐ Japan & Hong Kong $13.95
☐ Australia...............$14.95	☐ Mid-Atlantic States. $13.95
☐ Austria & Hungary $14.95	☐ New England...............$14.95
☐ Belgium, Holland & Luxembourg...............$13.95	☐ New York State $13.95
☐ Bermuda & The Bahamas...............$14.95	☐ Northwest $14.95
☐ Brazil $14.95	☐ Portugal, Madeira & the Azores $13.95
☐ Canada...............$14.95	☐ Skiing Europe...............$14.95
☐ Caribbean...............$14.95	☐ Skiing USA—East. $13.95
☐ Cruises (incl. Alask, Carib, Mex, Hawaii, Panama, Canada & US) $14.95	☐ Skiing USA—West...............$13.95
	☐ South Pacific $13.95
☐ California & Las Vegas...............$14.95	☐ Southeast & New Orleans $14.95
☐ England & Scotland...............$14.95	☐ Southeast Asia...............$14.95
☐ Egypt...............$13.95	☐ Southwest...............$14.95
☐ Florida $14.95	☐ Switzerland & Liechtenstein $13.95
☐ France $14.95	☐ Texas $13.95
☐ Germany...............$14.95	☐ USA $15.95
☐ Italy $14.95	

FROMMER $-A-DAY® GUIDES

(In-depth guides to sightseeing and low-cost tourist accommodations and facilities.)

☐ Europe on $40 a Day...............$15.95	☐ New Zealand on $40 a Day $12.95
☐ Australia on $30 a Day $12.95	☐ New York on $50 a Day...............$13.95
☐ Eastern Europe on $25 a Day $13.95	☐ Scandinavia on $60 a Day $13.95
☐ England on $50 a Day...............$13.95	☐ Scotland & Wales on $40 a Day...............$12.95
☐ Greece on $30 a Day...............$12.95	☐ South America on $35 a Day $13.95
☐ Hawaii on $60 a Day...............$13.95	☐ Spain & Morocco on $40 a Day...............$13.95
☐ India on $25 a Day $12.95	☐ Turkey on $30 a Day...............$12.95
☐ Ireland on $35 a Day...............$13.95	☐ Washington, D.C., & Historic Va. on
☐ Israel on $35 a Day...............$13.95	$40 a Day...............$13.95
☐ Mexico on $25 a Day $13.95	

FROMMER TOURING GUIDES

(Color illustrated guides that include walking tours, cultural & historic sites, and other vital travel information.)

☐ Australia...............$9.95	☐ Paris...............$8.95
☐ Egypt...............$8.95	☐ Scotland...............$9.95
☐ Florence...............$8.95	☐ Thailand...............$9.95
☐ London...............$8.95	☐ Venice...............$8.95

TURN PAGE FOR ADDITONAL BOOKS AND ORDER FORM.

FROMMER CITY GUIDES

(Pocket-size guides to sightseeing and tourist accommodations and facilities in all price ranges.)

☐ Amsterdam/Holland $5.95
☐ Athens $5.95
☐ Atlantic City/Cape May $5.95
☐ Belgium $5.95
☐ Boston $5.95
☐ Cancún/Cozumel/Yucatán $5.95
☐ Chicago $5.95
☐ Dublin/Ireland. $5.95
☐ Hawaii $5.95
☐ Las Vegas $5.95
☐ Lisbon/Madrid/Costa del Sol $5.95
☐ London. $5.95
☐ Los Angeles. $5.95
☐ Mexico City/Acapulco $5.95

☐ Minneapolis/St. Paul $5.95
☐ Montréal/Québec City $5.95
☐ New Orleans $5.95
☐ New York $5.95
☐ Orlando/Disney World/EPCOT. $5.95
☐ Paris. $5.95
☐ Philadelphia $5.95
☐ Rio. $5.95
☐ Rome $5.95
☐ San Francisco. $5.95
☐ Santa Fe/Taos/Albuquerque. $5.95
☐ Sydney $5.95
☐ Washington, D.C.. . . . .$5.95

SPECIAL EDITIONS

☐ A Shopper's Guide to the Caribbean $12.95
☐ Beat the High Cost of Travel. $6.95
☐ Bed & Breakfast—N. America $11.95
☐ California with Kids $14.95
☐ Guide to Honeymoon Destinations
   (US, Canada, Mexico & Carib). $12.95
☐ Manhattan's Outdoor Sculpture $15.95

☐ Motorist's Phrase Book (Fr/Ger/Sp) $4.95
☐ Paris Rendez-Vous. $10.95
☐ Swap and Go (Home Exchanging) $10.95
☐ The Candy Apple (NY for Kids) $11.95
☐ Travel Diary and Record Book $5.95
☐ Where to Stay USA (Lodging from $3
   to $30 a night). $10.95

☐ Marilyn Wood's Wonderful Weekends (NY, Conn, Mass, RI, Vt, NH, NJ, Del,Pa) $11.95

☐ The New World of Travel (Annual sourcebook by Arthur Frommer previewing: new travel trends, new modes of travel, and the latest cost-cutting strategies for savvy travelers) (2nd edn.) $14.95

SERIOUS SHOPPER'S GUIDES

(Illustrated guides listing hundreds of stores, conveniently organized alphabetically by category)

☐ Italy $15.95
☐ London. $15.95

☐ Los Angeles. $14.95
☐ Paris. $15.95

GAULT MILLAU

(The only guides that distinguish the truly superlative from the merely overrated.)

☐ The Best of Chicago $15.95
☐ The Best of France $15.95
☐ The Best of Italy $15.95
☐ The Best of Los Angeles. $15.95

☐ The Best of New England. $15.95
☐ The Best of New York $15.95
☐ The Best of San Francisco. $15.95
☐ The Best of Washington, D.C.. . . . .$15.95

ORDER NOW!

In U.S. include $2 shipping UPS for 1st book; $1 ea. add'l book. Outside U.S. $3 and $1, respectively.

Allow four to six weeks for delivery in U.S., longer outside U.S.

Enclosed is my check or money order for $_____

NAME _____

ADDRESS _____

CITY _____ STATE _____ ZIP _____